Fodor's 2nd Edit

Southern Africa

The Guide for All Budgets, Completely Updated, with Maps and Travel Tips

Where to Stay, Eat,
and Explore

On and Off
the Beaten Path

When to Go,
What to Pack

Post-it® Flags,
Web Sites, and More

Fodor's Travel Publications • New York, Toronto, London, Sydney, Auckland
www.fodors.com

Fodor's Southern Africa

EDITOR: Melissa Klurman

Editorial Contributors: Sue Derwent, Myrna Robins, Jennifer Stern, Alice Thompson, Kate Turkington, Tara Turkington

Editorial Production: Tom Holton

Maps: David Lindroth, Ed Jacobus, *cartographers*; Rebecca Baer and Robert Blake, *map editors*

Design: Fabrizio La Rocca, *creative director*; Guido Caroti, *art director*; Jolie Novak, *senior picture editor*; Melanie Marin, *photo editor*

Cover Design: Pentagram

Production/Manufacturing: Colleen Ziemba

Cover Photograph: Peter Guttman

Copyright

Second Edition

ISBN 0–679–00919–1

ISSN 1528–4093

Important Tip

Although all prices, opening times, and other details in this book are based on information supplied to us at press time, changes occur all the time in the travel world, and Fodor's cannot accept responsibility for facts that become outdated or for inadvertent errors or omissions. So **always confirm information when it matters,** especially if you're making a detour to visit a specific place.

Special Sales

Fodor's Travel Publications are available at special discounts for bulk purchases for sales promotions or premiums. Special editions, including personalized covers, excerpts of existing guides, and corporate imprints, can be created in large quantities for special needs. For more information, contact your local bookseller or write to Special Markets, Fodor's Travel Publications, 280 Park Avenue, New York, NY 10017. Inquiries from Canada should be directed to your local Canadian bookseller or sent to Random House of Canada, Ltd., Marketing Department, 2775 Matheson Boulevard East, Mississauga, Ontario L4W 4P7. Inquiries from the United Kingdom should be sent to Fodor's Travel Publications, 20 Vauxhall Bridge Road, London SW1V 2SA, England.

PRINTED IN THE UNITED STATES OF AMERICA

10 9 8 7 6 5 4 3 2 1

CONTENTS

Maps

ON THE ROAD WITH FODOR'S

The more you know before you go, the better your trip will be. Southern Africa's most fascinating small museum or its most innovative fish house could be just around the corner from your hotel, but if you don't know it's there, it might as well be on the other side of the globe. That's where this book comes in. It's a great step toward making sure your next trip lives up to your expectations. As you plan, check out the Web as well. Whatever reference you consult, be savvy about what you read, and always consider the source. Images and language can be massaged to make places appear better than they are. And one traveler's quaint is another's grimy. Here at Fodor's, and at our on-line arm, Fodors.com, our focus is on providing you with information that's not only useful but accurate and on target. Every day Fodor's editors put enormous effort into getting things right, beginning with the search for the right contributors—people who have objective judgment, broad travel experience, and the writing ability to put their insights into words. There's no substitute for advice from a like-minded friend who has just come back from where you're going, but our writers, having seen all corners of southern Africa, are the next best thing. They're the kind of people you'd poll for tips yourself if you knew them.

Sue Derwent is a freelance journalist who has traveled extensively throughout southern Africa writing and researching for newspapers, magazines, radio, and television. She is the author of eight books, including *The Very Best of KwaZulu-Natal.* Her favorite city in South Africa is Durban, where she has been based, off and on, for the past 22 years.

Myrna Robins, who writes for various newspapers and magazines, is one of South Africa's most popular food writers. Author of several cookbooks, including *Cape Flavour—A Guide to Historic Restaurants of the Cape,* she divides her time between the Atlantic seaboard suburb of Blouberg and the exquisite hamlet of McGregor in the Riviersonderend mountains.

Jennifer Stern is the content manager of the official South African Tourism Web site, www.southafrica.net, and the author of *Southern Africa on a Budget* and *Guide to Adventure Travel in Southern Africa.* In the line of duty, she has braved strange wayside pubs, dived pristine reefs, paddled beautiful rivers, walked with wildlife, and ridden mountain bikes, horses, camels, and elephants all over the wilder parts of the subcontinent.

Kate Turkington is one of South Africa's best-known journalists and broadcasters. She is managing editor of *Marung, Flamingo,* and *Indwe,* the in-flight magazines for Air Botswana, Air Namibia, and SA Express Airways. She has waltzed at dawn in a Beijing square, fallen over Emperor penguins in Antarctica, lunched under a silken canopy with a rajah in Rajasthan, been winched over a raging river 9,000 ft up in the Andes, prayed with monks in Tibet's oldest monastery, and heard the stars sing in the Kalahari Desert.

Tara Turkington, a freelance journalist, lives in Kimberley in the Northern Cape, South Africa's biggest and most sparsely populated province, which she loves for its sense of desolation. She writes and photographs for a variety of South African magazines and newspapers, including the *Sowetan Sunday World,* and is particularly interested in South African heritage issues.

We'd like to thank South African Tourism (SATOUR), the Regional Tourism Organization of Southern Africa (RETOSA), South African Airways, Julian Harrison of Premier Tours, Wendy Toerien, and David Bristow for their help in preparing this edition.

Don't Forget to Write

Keeping a travel guide fresh and up-to-date is a big job. So we love your feedback—positive and negative—and follow up on all suggestions. Contact the Southern Africa editor at editors@fodors.com or c/o Fodor's, 280 Park Avenue, New York, NY 10017. And have a wonderful trip!

Karen Cure
Editorial Director

Southern Africa

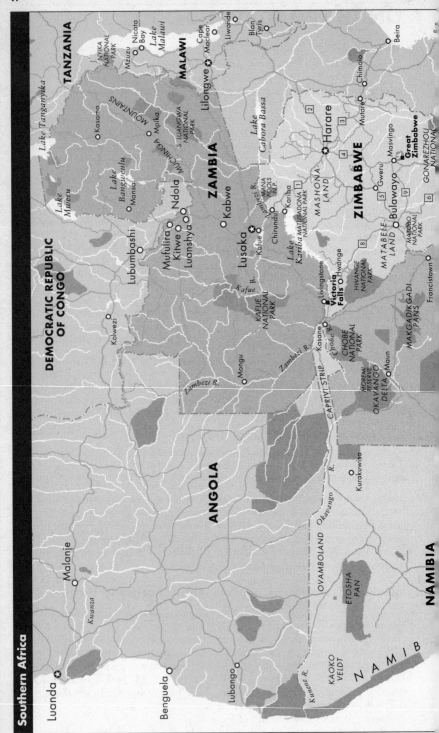

TANZANIA

Lake Tanganyika

NYIKA NATIONAL PARK

Mzuzu ○ Nicata ○ Bay

Lake Malawi

MALAWI

Cape Maclear ○

Liwonide ○

Blan Tyris ○

Beira ○

Kasana ○

MUCHINGA MOUNTAINS

Mpika ○ MUCHINGA 46

S. LUANGWA NATIONAL PARK

Lilongwe ✪

Chimoio ○

Lake Mweru

Lake Bangweulu

Mansa ○

Ndola ○

ZAMBIA

Kabwe ○

Lake Cabora Bassa

2

Harare ✪

Mutare ○

Masvingo ○

Great Zimbabwe ■

GONAREZHOU NATIONAL

Lubumbashi ○

DEMOCRATIC REPUBLIC OF CONGO

Mufulira ○ Kitwe ○ Luanshya ○

Lusaka ✪

Kafue ✪

Zambezi R.

Chirundu ○

MANA POOLS N.P.

Kariba ○

Lake Kariba

MASHONA-LAND

MATUSADONA NATIONAL PARK 1

4

ZIMBABWE

Gweru ○

5

Bulawayo ○

MATOBO NATIONAL PARK

3

9

6

Kolwezi ○

Kafue R.

KAFUE NATIONAL PARK

Livingstone ○

Victoria Falls ■ ○ Hwange

HWANGE NATIONAL PARK

MATABELE-LAND

8

MAKGADIKGADI PANS

Francistown ○

Mongu ○

Zambezi R.

Kasane ○

Chobe R.

CHOBE NATIONAL PARK

MOREMI RESERVE

OKAVANGO DELTA ○ Maun

Zambezi R.

CAPRIVI STRIP

ANGOLA

Malanje ○

Kuanza

Okavango R.

Kurakuwisa ○

OVAMBOLAND

ETOSHA PAN

NAMIBIA

Lubango ○

Benguela ○

Luanda ✪

KAOKO VELDT

Kunene R.

N A M I B

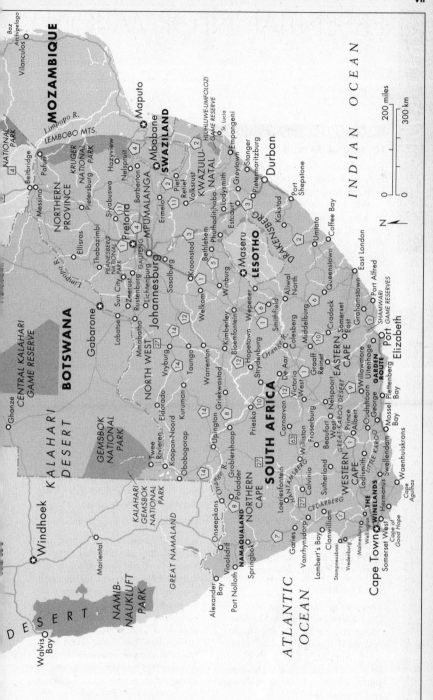

ESSENTIAL INFORMATION

AIR TRAVEL

TO SOUTH AFRICA

South African Airways (SAA) flies from New York (JFK) to Johannesburg and from Atlanta to Cape Town, sharing the route with Delta. When booking flights, check the routing carefully, as some are direct and some involve stopovers of an hour or two, which greatly increase the flying time. The options from Europe include SAA and most European national airlines. SAA, British Airways, and Virgin Atlantic fly between London and Johannesburg or Cape Town. Four major domestic airlines (two of which are subsidiaries of SAA) serve the country's nine principal airports for flights within South Africa.

TO ZIMBABWE

To get to Zimbabwe from the United States, you must connect through Johannesburg or through Europe or Australia. Zimbabwe's international gateways are Harare, Bulawayo, and Victoria Falls.

TO BOTSWANA

To get to Botswana, you'll have to connect through Johannesburg or Harare. The international gateways to Botswana are Gaborone (the capital), Maun (near the Okavango Delta), and Kasane (near Chobe National Park).

TO ZAMBIA

There are no direct flights from the United States to Zambia. The best option is to connect through Johannesburg or through London, from which you can fly British Airways to Lusaka. There are daily flights from Johannesburg to Livingstone on SAA and Nationwide.

TO NAMIBIA

To get to Namibia from the United States, you'll have to connect through Johannesburg, Cape Town, or Frankfurt. Air Namibia and Lufthansa fly to Windhoek from Frankfurt, and Air Namibia and South African Airways fly from Johannesburg and Cape Town.

TO SWAZILAND

There are no intercontinental direct flights to Swaziland, but Royal Swazi Air connects Mbabane with most southern African countries, and Swazi Express Airlines runs scheduled flights in a light plane from Durban. Your best bet for a connection is Johannesburg.

TO MOZAMBIQUE

SA Express and LAM (Mozambique Airlines) fly between Johannesburg and Maputo daily. TTA flies between Johannesburg and Vilanculos twice a week. LAM flies between Lisbon and Maputo once a week. and TAP (Air Portugal) flies between Lisbon and Johannesburg, via Maputo, twice a week.

TO LESOTHO

There are no direct intercontinental flights to Lesotho, but SA Airlink flies between Johannesburg and Moeshoeshoe I Airport three times a day Monday–Saturday and twice on Sunday.

TO MALAWI

South African Airways flies between Johannesburg and Lilongwe three times a week and between Johannesburg and Blantyre twice a week. Air Zimbabwe flies between Harare and Lilongwe twice a week. British Airways flies between London and Lilongwe once a week (Saturday). Ethiopian Airlines flies from Addis Ababa to Lilongwe three times a week. Kenya Airways flies between Nairobi and Lilongwe six times a week. Air Malawi flies between Lilongwe and most other major centers in the region.

BOOKING

When you book **look for nonstop flights** and **remember that "direct" flights stop at least once.** Try to avoid connecting flights, which require a change of plane. Two airlines may operate a connecting flight jointly, so ask if your airline operates every segment of the trip; you may find that the carrier you prefer flies you only part of the way. For more booking tips and to check prices and make on-line flight reservations, log on to www.fodors.com. Check out WEB www.kulula.com, which offers discount **Comair** flights.

CARRIERS

➤ MAJOR AIRLINES: **Delta** (☎ 800/ 221–2121). **South African Airways** (☎ 800/722–9675). **Virgin Atlantic** (☎ 01293/747–747).

➤ WITHIN SOUTH AFRICA: **British Airways** operating as Comair (☎ 011/921–0222). **South African Airways/SA Airlink/South African Express** (☎ 011/978–1111, WEB www.flysaa.com). **Nationwide** (☎ 011/ 390–1660).

➤ WITHIN BOTSWANA: **Air Botswana** (☎ 267/352–812).

➤ WITHIN MALAWI: **Air Malawi** (☎ 75–3181 or 75–0757).

➤ WITHIN MOZAMBIQUE: **Mozambique Airlines (LAM)** (☎ 01/42–600).

➤ WITHIN NAMIBIA: **Air Namibia** (☎ 061/298–1111).

➤ WITHIN ZAMBIA: **Zambian Airways** (☎ 290/1/22–5151) flies between Lusaka, Livingstone, Mfuwe, Ndole, and Kitwe.

➤ WITHIN ZIMBABWE: **Air Zimbabwe** (☎ 04/57–5111).

CHECK-IN & BOARDING

For domestic flights, arrive at the airport at least two hours before your scheduled departure time. For international flights, plan on arriving at the airport at least 2½ hours before departure, but be sure to ask your carrier whether it requires an earlier check-in.

Assuming that not everyone with a ticket will show up, airlines routinely overbook planes. When everyone does, airlines ask for volunteers to give up their seats. In return, these volunteers usually get a certificate for a free flight and are rebooked on the next flight out. If there are not enough volunteers, the airline must choose who will be denied boarding. The first to get bumped are passengers who checked in late and those flying on discounted tickets, so **get to the gate and check in as early as possible,** especially during peak periods.

Always **bring a government-issued photo I.D. to the airport;** even when it's not required, a passport is best.

CUTTING COSTS

The least expensive airfares to southern Africa are priced for round-trip travel and must usually be purchased in advance. Airlines generally allow you to change your return date for a fee; most low-fare tickets, however, are nonrefundable. It's smart to **call a number of airlines,** and when you are quoted a good price, **book it on the spot**—the same fare may not be available the next day. Always **check different routings** and look into using alternate airports. Also, price off-peak flights, which may be significantly less expensive than others. Travel agents, especially low-fare specialists (☞ Discounts & Deals, *below*), are helpful.

Consolidators are another good source. They buy tickets for scheduled international flights at reduced rates from the airlines, then sell them at prices that beat the best fare available directly from the airlines. Sometimes you can even get your money back if you need to return the ticket. Carefully read the fine print detailing penalties for changes and cancellations, purchase the ticket with a credit card, and **confirm your consolidator reservation with the airline.**

When you **fly as a courier,** you trade your checked-luggage space for a ticket deeply subsidized by a courier service. There are restrictions on when you can book and how long you can stay. Some courier companies list with membership organizations, such as the Air Courier Association and the International Association of Air Travel Couriers; these require you to become a member before you can book a flight.

Many airlines, singly or in collaboration, offer discount air passes that allow foreigners to travel economically in a particular country or region. These visitor passes usually must be reserved and purchased before you leave home. Information about passes can be difficult to track down on airline Web sites, which tend to be geared to travelers departing from a given carrier's country rather than to those intending to visit that country. Try typing the name of the pass into a search engine, or search for "pass" within the carrier's Web site.

A great way to find cheap tickets, if you can leave at the drop of a hat, is to check out www.lastminute.com or, within South Africa, www.kulula.com.

➤ CONSOLIDATORS: **Cheap Tickets** (☎ 800/377–1000 or 888/922–8849, WEB www.cheaptickets.com). **Discount Airline Ticket Service** (☎ 800/576–1600). **Unitravel** (☎ 800/325–2222, WEB www.unitravel.com). **Up & Away Travel** (☎ 212/889–2345). **World Travel Network** (☎ 800/409–6753).

➤ COURIER RESOURCES: **Air Courier Association** (☎ 800/282–1202, WEB www.aircourier.org). **International Association of Air Travel Couriers** (☎ 352/475–1584, WEB www.courier.org).

ENJOYING THE FLIGHT

State your seat preference when purchasing your ticket, and then repeat it when you confirm and when you check-in. For more legroom, you can request one of the few emergency-aisle seats at check-in, if you are capable of lifting at least 50 pounds—a Federal Aviation Administration requirement of passengers in these seats. Seats behind a bulkhead also offer more legroom, but they don't have under-seat storage. Don't sit in the row in front of the emergency aisle or in front of a bulkhead, where seats may not recline.

If you have dietary concerns, **ask for special meals when booking.** These can be vegetarian, low-cholesterol, or kosher, for example. It's a good idea to pack some healthy snacks and a small bottle (plastic) of water in your carry-on bag. On long flights, try to maintain a normal routine, to help fight jet lag. At night, **get some sleep.**

By day, **eat light meals, drink water** (not alcohol), and **move around the cabin** to stretch your legs. For additional jet-lag tips consult *Fodor's FYI: Travel Fit & Healthy* (available at bookstores everywhere).

Smoking policies vary from carrier to carrier. Many airlines prohibit smoking on all their international flights; others allow smoking only on certain routes or certain departures. Ask your carrier about its policy.

FLYING TIMES

When booking flights, **check the routing carefully.** Flights from New York to Johannesburg take approximately 15 hours direct or 17½ hours via Lagos. Atlanta to Cape Town is 15 hours direct or 18½ hours via Ilha do Sal, with a connection to Johannesburg. Atlanta to Johannesburg is 15½ hours direct, with a connection to Cape Town. The flying time between Johannesburg and Cape Town is two hours.

From London the flying time is about 11 hours to Johannesburg and 11½ hours to Cape Town direct. The return flights are about half an hour longer.

HOW TO COMPLAIN

If your baggage goes astray or your flight goes awry, complain right away. Most carriers require that you **file a claim immediately.** The Aviation Consumer Protection Division of the Department of Transportation publishes *Fly-Rights,* which discusses airlines and consumer issues and is available on-line. At PassengerRights.com, a Web site, you can compose a letter of complaint and distribute it electronically.

➤ AIRLINE COMPLAINTS: **Aviation Consumer Protection Division** (✉ U.S. Department of Transportation, Room 4107, C-75, Washington, DC 20590, ☎ 202/366–2220, WEB www.dot.gov/airconsumer). **Federal Aviation Administration Consumer Hotline** (☎ 800/322–7873).

RECONFIRMING

Check the status of your flight before you leave for the airport. You can do this on your carrier's Web site, by linking to a flight-status checker (many Web booking services offer these), or by calling your carrier or travel agent. Always confirm international flights at least 72 hours ahead of the scheduled departure time.

AIRPORTS

South Africa's major airports are Johannesburg, Cape Town, and, to a lesser extent, Durban. Johannesburg International Airport lies 19 km (12 mi) from the city. Most international flights arrive and depart at this airport. The airport has a tourist information desk, a VAT refund office, and a computerized accommodations service. Several international flights departing from Cape Town are also routed via Johannesburg.

Outside South Africa, southern Africa's major airports include Zimbabwe's Harare International Airport; Botswana's Sir Seretse Khama Airport, just north of Gaborone; Zambia's Lusaka International Airport; Namibia's Hosea Kutako International Airport east of Windhoek; Swaziland's Matsapha International Airport, just west of Manzini and about 40 km (25 mi) from the capital city of Mbabane; Mozambique's Maputo International Airport; Malawi's Lilongwe International Airport, and Lesotho's Moeshoeshoe I International Airport.

For listings of major airline numbers within South Africa, Swaziland, Zimbabwe, Botswana, Namibia, and Zambia, *see* the A to Z sections *in* the relevant chapters.

➤ AIRPORT INFORMATION: South Africa: **Johannesburg International Airport** (☎ 011/975–9963); **Durban International Airport** (☎ 031/451–6666); **Cape Town International Airport** (☎ 021/934–0407). Zimbabwe: **Harare International Airport** (☎ 014/57–5111 or 014/57–5188, 15 km [9 mi] south of city center). Botswana: **Sir Seretse Khama Airport** (☎ 267/35–1191, 15 km [9 mi] north of Gaborone). Zambia: **Lusaka International Airport** (☎ 01/27–1422, 4 km [2½ mi] northeast of Lusaka). Namibia: **Hosea Kutako International Airport** (☎ 062/54–0229, 40 km [25 mi] east of Windhoek). Swaziland: **Matsapha International Airport** (☎ 268/518–4455, 8 km [5 mi] west of Manzini and 40 km [25 mi] southeast of Mbabane). Lesotho: **Moeshoeshoe I International Airport** (☎ 266/35–0777, 20 km [12 mi] south of city). Mozambique: **Maputo International Airport** (☎ 01/46–5133 or 01/46–5074, 20 km [12 mi] north of city). Malawi: **Lilongwe International Airport** (☎ 265/70–0766, 28 km [17 mi] north of city).

BUSINESS HOURS

Business hours in major African cities are quite standard weekdays from about 9 to 5. Most banks close in midafternoon, but currency exchange offices usually stay open longer. In addition, post offices and banks are open on Saturday morning from about 9 to noon. Many shopping malls are open until 9 or 10 at night and are open on Sunday. In rural areas and small towns things are less rigid. Post offices often close for lunch, and, in very small towns and villages, banks may have very abbreviated hours.

BUS TRAVEL

Greyhound, Intercape Mainliner, and Translux Express operate extensive bus networks that serve all major cities in the region. The buses are comfortable, there are videos (sometimes), and tea and coffee are served on board. Distances are long; for example, Cape Town to Johannesburg takes 19 hours. Johannesburg to Durban is less stressful at about seven hours. The Garden Route is less intense if you take it in stages, but the whole trip from Cape Town to Port Elizabeth takes 12 hours.

For travelers with a sense of adventure, a bit of time, and not too much money, the Baz Bus runs a daily hop-on/hop-off door-to-door service between backpackers' hostels around South Africa and Swaziland, with inexpensive connections to Maputo in Mozambique. The Blue Arrow offers luxury transport between Harare, Bulawayo, and Victoria Falls in Zimbabwe. The Panthera Azul runs between Johannesburg, in South Africa, and Maputo, in Mozambique.

FARES

Approximate prices for Greyhound, Translux, and Intercape bus service: Cape Town to Pretoria, one-way R360–R400; Cape Town to Springbok, one-way R230–R260; Cape Town to Windhoek, one-way R360–R390; Cape Town to George, one-way R120–R150; Cape Town to Port Elizabeth, one-way R190–R210; Pretoria to Durban, one-way R170–

R190; Cape Town to Durban, one-way R400.

Baz Bus fares are higher but include intermediate stops: Cape Town to Durban costs R950 one-way, R1,300 round-trip.

➤ BUS INFORMATION: **Baz Bus** (☎ 021/439–2323, WEB www.bazbus.com). **Blue Arrow Luxury Coaches** (☎ 04/72–9514 or 04/72–9518 in Harare; 09/6–5548 in Bulawayo, WEB www.bluearrow.co.zw). **Greyhound** (☎ 011/249–8700 in Johannesburg; 012/323–1154 in Pretoria; 021/418–4310 in Cape Town; or book through **Computicket**, ☎ 083/909–0909, WEB www.greyhound.co.za). **Intercape Mainliner** (☎ 012/654–4114 in Pretoria; 021/386–4400 in Cape Town; or book through Computicket ☎ 083/909–0909, WEB www.intercape.co.za). **Panthera Azul** (☎ 011/337–7409 in Johannesburg; 01/49–8868 in Maputo, panthazul@netactive.co.za). **Translux** (☎ 011/774–3333 in Johannesburg; 021/449–3333 in Cape Town).

CAMERAS & PHOTOGRAPHY

There are camera shops and one-hour photo labs in even the smallest towns in South Africa and in most bigger towns in the countries farther north. For properly stored professional film and high-quality processing of transparency film, the best options are listed below.

➤ FILM & DEVELOPING: **ORMS Professional Photo Warehouse** (✉ Roeland Sq., Roeland St., Cape Town, ☎ 021/465–3574). **Kameraz** (✉ Rosebank Mews, Rosebank, Johannesburg, ☎ 27/11/880–2885).

➤ PHOTO HELP: **Kodak Information Center** (☎ 800/242–2424, WEB www.kodak.com).

EQUIPMENT PRECAUTIONS

Don't pack film and equipment in checked luggage, where it is much more susceptible to damage. X-ray machines used to view checked luggage are becoming much more powerful and therefore are much more likely to ruin your film. Try to **ask for hand inspection of film,** which becomes clouded after repeated exposure to airport X-ray machines, and **keep videotapes and computer disks**

away from metal detectors. Always **keep film, tape, and computer disks out of the sun.** Carry an extra supply of batteries, and **be prepared to turn on your camera, camcorder, or laptop** to prove to airport security personnel that the device is real.

The *Kodak Guide to Shooting Great Travel Pictures* (available at bookstores everywhere) is loaded with tips.

CAR RENTAL

Rates in southern Africa begin at R150 per day and 30¢ per kilometer (about 45¢ per mile) for an economy car. Economy cars have no air-conditioning and have manual transmissions. For an automatic-transmission car you'll pay about R250–R300 per day and up to R1 per kilometer, depending on the model. Check if insurance is included, and what it covers. You can rent four-wheel-drive vehicles or mobile homes from Maui Camper Hire.

➤ MAJOR AGENCIES: **Alamo** (☎ 800/522–9696, WEB www.alamo.com). **Avis** (☎ 800/331–1084; 800/879–2847 in Canada; 02/9353–9000 in Australia; 09/526–2847 in New Zealand; 0870/606–0100 in the U.K., WEB www.avis.com). **Budget** (☎ 800/527–0700; 0870/156–5656 in the U.K., WEB www.budget.com). **Dollar** (☎ 800/800–6000; 0124/622–0111 in the U.K., where it's affiliated with Sixt; 02/9223–1444 in Australia, WEB www.dollar.com). **Hertz** (☎ 800/654–3001; 800/263–0600 in Canada; 020/8897–2072 in the U.K.; 02/9669–2444 in Australia; 09/256–8690 in New Zealand, WEB www.hertz.com). **National Car Rental** (☎ 800/227–7368; 020/8680–4800 in the U.K., WEB www.nationalcar.com).

➤ LOCAL AGENCIES: In South Africa: **Felix Unite Vehicle Rental** (☎ 021/683–6433, FAX 021/683–6485). Throughout the region: **Maui Camper Hire** (☎ 27/11/396–1445 in Johannesburg, South Africa; 27/21/982–5107 in Cape Town, South Africa; 264/61/25–0654 in Windhoek, Namibia; 263/4/88–5550 in Harare, Zimbabwe; 263/13/3398 in Victoria Falls, Zimbabwe; 818/981–1270 in Los Angeles, WEB www.maui.co.za).

CUTTING COSTS

For a good deal, **book through a travel agent who will shop around.**

Do **look into wholesalers,** companies that do not own fleets but rent in bulk from those that do and often offer better rates than traditional car-rental operations. Prices are best during off-peak periods. Rentals booked through wholesalers often must be paid for before you leave home.

➤ WHOLESALER: **Auto Europe** (☎ 207/842–2000 or 800/223–5555, FAX 207/842–2222, WEB www.autoeurope. com).

INSURANCE

When driving a rented car you are generally responsible for any damage to or loss of the vehicle. You may also be liable for any property damage or personal injury that you may cause while driving. Before you rent, see what coverage you already have under the terms of your personal auto-insurance policy and credit cards.

REQUIREMENTS & RESTRICTIONS

To rent a car, you must be over 25 years old and have a minimum of five years' driving experience. In South Africa your own driver's license is acceptable. An International Driver's Permit is a good idea; it's available from the American or Canadian Automobile Association or, in the United Kingdom, from the Automobile Association or Royal Automobile Club.

SURCHARGES

Before you pick up a car in one city and leave it in another, **ask about drop-off charges or one-way service fees,** which can be substantial. Note, too, that some rental agencies charge extra if you return the car before the time specified in your contract.

CAR TRAVEL

South Africa, Namibia, and Botswana have a superb network of multilane roads and highways, some of which charge a toll. The speed limit on major highways is 120 kph (75 mph), but many drivers far exceed that. In fact, South Africans tend to be aggressive and reckless, thinking nothing of tailgating at high speeds and passing on blind rises. During national holidays the body count from highway collisions is staggering. The problem is compounded by widespread drunk driving, even though the legal blood-alcohol limit is 0.08. Local minibus taxis pose another threat, swerving in and out of traffic without warning to pick up customers. For obvious reasons the wearing of seat belts is required by law. It is dangerous to drive at night in rural areas, as roads are not always fenced and domestic or wild animals often stray onto the road. Although the roads are generally good, the distances are significant, and fatigue is also a major cause of accidents.

Mozambique has one long road going up the coast, and it is in fair condition, as are side roads to coastal resorts. Malawi's roads are either excellent (if they've been recently rebuilt) or potholed. Lesotho has an excellent tarred road along the western side of the country; most of the rest is four-wheel-drive territory. Zambia's roads are a tad worse for wear.

AUTO CLUBS

The Automobile Association of South Africa extends privileges to members of the American Automobile Association in the United States and the Automobile Association in Britain. Contact a local office in your home country for more information.

➤ IN SOUTH AFRICA: **Automobile Association of South Africa** (✉ Box 31017, Braamfontein, Johannesburg 2017, ☎ 011/799–1000 in Johannesburg; 021/419–6914 in Cape Town; 031/201–5244 in Durban; 080/001–0101 for 24-hr toll-free emergency).

GASOLINE

Huge 24-hour service stations are positioned at regular intervals along all major highways in South Africa, Botswana, and Namibia. Self-service stations do not exist, so an attendant will pump the gas, check the oil and water, and wash the windows. In return, tip him or her R2–R3. South Africa now has a choice of unleaded or leaded gasoline, and many vehicles operate on diesel—be sure you get the right fuel. Some South African–manufactured automobiles still need special engine modifications to enable them to run on unleaded fuel—check when booking a rental car as to what fuel to use. Gasoline is measured in liters, and expect to pay the equivalent of US$2–US$2.50 a gallon.

ROAD CONDITIONS

In very remote areas only the main road might be paved, while most secondary roads are of high-quality gravel. Traffic is often light in these areas, so be sure to **bring extra water, and carry a spare, a jack, and a tire iron** (your rental car should come with these).

In Zimbabwe and Botswana major highways typically have two lanes only. In the remote areas of Zimbabwe, you may still encounter "strip roads," which consist of two paved strips with wide dirt shoulders. When cars approach, drivers move the left side of their cars or trucks onto the dirt, each keeping the right (driver's) side on the pavement. In Namibia the paved roads are well maintained, as are the many dirt roads, but many are infrequently used, distances are enormous, and the weather is extreme. In some places you may see only one tiny town (with about 20 buildings) in 800 km (500 mi). Always take plenty of drinking water with you when traveling in Namibia. The roads in Zambia are generally pretty terrible. Lesotho has some pretty good tarred roads, but the majority of the country is considered four-by-four heaven. But you can get to most places you'd want to go in a small sedan. Roads in Mozambique are in a bit of a state, and driving is an adventure. **Never, under any circumstances, drive off the road in Mozambique,** unless it is a detour that has obviously been used by lots of other vehicles. There may still be land mines in the least likely places. Malawi's roads are also a bit of an adventure.

RULES OF THE ROAD

Southern Africans drive on the left. For pedestrians that means **look right before crossing the street.** South African roads have wide shoulders, separated from the main lanes by a yellow line. Slow traffic is expected to pull onto this shoulder to allow faster traffic to pass, but be sure that the shoulder ahead is not obstructed by cyclists, pedestrians, or a stopped vehicle. If a slower vehicle pulls onto the shoulder to allow you past, it's common courtesy to flash your hazard lights a couple of times in thanks. In

built-up areas road shoulders are occasionally marked by red lines. This is a strict "no-stopping" zone.

Many cities use mini–traffic circles in lieu of four-way stops. These are extremely dangerous because many drivers don't bother to stop. In theory, the first vehicle to the circle has right-of-way; otherwise, yield to the right. In practice, keep your wits about you at all times.

In South African parlance, traffic lights are known as "robots," and what people refer to as the "pavement" is actually the sidewalk. Paved roads are just called roads. And for Americans and Canadians, don't forget: **Drive left, and look right.**

CHILDREN IN SOUTHERN AFRICA

If you are renting a car, don't forget to **arrange for a car seat** when you reserve. For general advice about traveling with children, consult *Fodor's FYI: Travel with Your Baby* (available in bookstores everywhere).

FLYING

If your children are two or older, **ask about children's airfares.** As a general rule, infants under two not occupying a seat fly at greatly reduced fares or even for free. When booking, **confirm carry-on allowances** if you're traveling with infants. In general, for babies charged 10% of the adult fare you are allowed one carry-on bag and a collapsible stroller; if the flight is full, the stroller may have to be checked or you may be limited to less.

Experts agree that it's a good idea to use safety seats aloft for children weighing less than 40 pounds. Airlines set their own policies: U.S. carriers usually require that the child be ticketed, even if he or she is young enough to ride free, since the seats must be strapped into regular seats. Do **check your airline's policy about using safety seats during takeoff and landing.** Safety seats are not allowed everywhere in the plane, so get your seat assignments as early as possible.

When reserving, **request children's meals or a freestanding bassinet** (not available at all airlines) if you need them. But note that bulkhead seats, where you must sit to use the bassinet, may lack an overhead bin or storage space on the floor.

LODGING

Many of southern Africa's luxury lodges and private game reserves do not accept children under 10 or 12 without prior arrangement, and many other hotels require children to eat dinner at a separate, earlier seating. Some hotels and lodges allow children under a certain age to stay in their parents' room at no extra charge, but others charge for them as extra adults; be sure to **find out the cutoff age for children's discounts.**

Southern Sun, the giant hotel group that operates Southern Sun and Holiday Inn properties throughout the country, allows children under 18 to stay free if sharing with parents in select hotels. Pestana Hotels allows up to two children under 12 to stay free if sharing with parents. Extra children are charged a minimal amount.

➤ BEST CHOICES: **Pestana Hotels** (☎ 01/30–5000). **Southern Sun** (☎ 011/482–3500).

SIGHTS & ATTRACTIONS

Places that are especially appealing to children are indicated by a rubber-duckie icon (🦆) in the margin.

CONSUMER PROTECTION

Whether you're shopping for gifts or purchasing travel services, **pay with a major credit card** whenever possible, so you can cancel payment or get reimbursed if there's a problem (and you can provide documentation). If you're doing business with a particular company for the first time, **contact your local Better Business Bureau and the attorney general's offices** in your state and (for U.S. businesses) the company's home state as well. Have any complaints been filed? Finally, if you're buying a package or tour, always **consider travel insurance** that includes default coverage (☞ Insurance, *below*).

➤ BBB: **Council of Better Business Bureaus** (✉ 4200 Wilson Blvd., Suite 800, Arlington, VA 22203, ☎ 703/276–0100, FAX 703/525–8277, WEB www.bbb.org).

CUSTOMS & DUTIES

When shopping abroad, **keep receipts** for all purchases. Upon reentering the country, **be ready to show customs officials what you've bought.** If you feel a duty is incorrect, appeal the assessment. If you object to the way your clearance was handled, note the inspector's badge number. In either case, first ask to see a supervisor. If the problem isn't resolved, write to the appropriate authorities, beginning with the port director at your point of entry.

IN AUSTRALIA

Australian residents who are 18 or older may bring home A$400 worth of souvenirs and gifts (including jewelry), 250 cigarettes or 250 grams of tobacco, and 1,125 ml of alcohol (including wine, beer, and spirits). Residents under 18 may bring back A$200 worth of goods. Prohibited items include meat products. Seeds, plants, and fruits need to be declared upon arrival.

➤ INFORMATION: **Australian Customs Service** (Regional Director, ✉ Box 8, Sydney, NSW 2001, ☎ 02/9213–2000, FAX 02/9213–4000, WEB www.customs.gov.au).

IN CANADA

Canadian residents who have been out of Canada for at least seven days may bring in C$750 worth of goods duty-free. If you've been away fewer than seven days but more than 48 hours, the duty-free allowance drops to C$200; if your trip lasts 24 to 48 hours, the allowance is C$50. You may not pool allowances with family members. Goods claimed under the C$750 exemption may follow you by mail; those claimed under the lesser exemptions must accompany you. Alcohol and tobacco products may be included in the seven-day and 48-hour exemptions but not in the 24-hour exemption. If you meet the age requirements of the province or territory through which you reenter Canada, you may bring in, duty-free, 1.5 liters of wine *or* 1.14 liters (40 imperial ounces) of liquor *or* 24 12-ounce cans or bottles of beer or ale. If you are 19 or older you may bring in, duty-free, 200 cigarettes and 50 cigars. Check ahead of time with the Canada Customs and Revenue Agency or the Department of Agriculture for policies regarding meat products, seeds, plants, and fruits.

You may send an unlimited number of gifts (only one gift per recipient, however) worth up to C$60 each duty-free to Canada. Label the package UNSOLICITED GIFT—VALUE UNDER $60. Alcohol and tobacco are excluded.

➤ INFORMATION: **Canada Customs and Revenue Agency** (⌧ 2265 St. Laurent Blvd. S, Ottawa, Ontario K1G 4K3, ☎ 204/983–3500 or 506/636–5064; 800/461–9999, WEB www.ccra-adrc.gc.ca).

IN NEW ZEALAND

All homeward-bound residents may bring back NZ$700 worth of souvenirs and gifts; passengers may not pool their allowances, and children can claim only the concession on goods intended for their own use. For those 17 or older, the duty-free allowance also includes 4.5 liters of wine or beer; one 1,125-ml bottle of spirits; and either 200 cigarettes, 250 grams of tobacco, 50 cigars, *or* a combination of the three up to 250 grams. Meat products, seeds, plants, and fruits must be declared upon arrival to the Agricultural Services Department.

➤ INFORMATION: **New Zealand Customs** (⌧ Head Office, The Customhouse, 17-21 Whitmore St., Box 2218, Wellington, ☎ 09/300–5399, WEB www.customs.govt.nz).

IN SOUTHERN AFRICA

Visitors over 18 years of age may bring in duty-free gifts and souvenirs up to a total value of R1,250 (about $145), plus 400 cigarettes, 50 cigars, 250 grams of tobacco, 2 liters of wine, 1 liter of other alcoholic beverages, 50 ml of perfume, and 250 ml of toilet water into all the countries in the Southern Africa Common Customs Union (SACU). (An exception is that you may not take loose tobacco into Zimbabwe.) Botswana, Swaziland, Lesotho, Zimbabwe, Namibia, and Zambia are members of SACU. Any visitor entering these countries from or through South Africa is not liable for any customs duties. You will, however, need to complete a form listing items imported.

You may bring 200 cigarettes or 250 grams of tobacco in any form and 1 liter of spirits, beer, or wine into Malawi (perfume is not specifically addressed, but it's not likely to cause a problem). You are allowed to take US$100 worth of personal goods duty-free into Mozambique in addition to 5 liters (about a gallon) of wine, 1 liter of spirits, 400 cigarettes, 100 cigarillos, 50 cigars, 250 ml of toilet water, and 50 ml of perfume.

If you buy animal products to take home, including skins or legally culled ivory, make sure you get the requisite documentation from the seller.

IN THE U.K.

From countries outside the European Union, including South Africa, you may bring home, duty-free, 200 cigarettes or 50 cigars; 1 liter of spirits or 2 liters of fortified or sparkling wine or liqueurs; 2 liters of still table wine; 60 ml of perfume; 250 ml of toilet water; plus £145 worth of other goods, including gifts and souvenirs. Prohibited items include meat products, seeds, plants, and fruits.

➤ INFORMATION: **HM Customs and Excise** (⌧ Portcullis House, 21 Cowbridge Rd. E, Cardiff CF11 9SS, ☎ 029/2038–6423, WEB www.hmce.gov.uk).

IN THE U.S.

U.S. residents who have been out of the country for at least 48 hours (and who have not used the $400 allowance or any part of it in the past 30 days) may bring home $400 worth of foreign goods duty-free; the duty-free allowance drops to $200 for fewer than 48 hours.

U.S. residents 21 and older may bring back 1 liter of alcohol duty-free. In addition, regardless of your age, you are allowed 200 cigarettes and 100 non-Cuban cigars. Antiques, which the U.S. Customs Service defines as objects more than 100 years old, enter duty-free, as do original works of art done entirely by hand, including paintings, drawings, and sculptures. You may also send packages home duty-free, with a limit of one parcel per addressee per day (except alcohol or tobacco products or perfume worth more than $5). You can mail up to $200 worth of goods for personal use; label the package PERSONAL USE and attach a list of its contents and their retail value. If the package contains your used personal belongings, mark it PERSONAL GOODS RETURNED to avoid paying duties. You may send up to $100 worth of goods as a gift; mark the package UNSOLICITED GIFT. Mailed items do not affect your duty-free allowance on your return.

➤ INFORMATION: **U.S. Customs Service** (for inquiries, ✉ 1300 Pennsylvania Ave. NW, Washington, DC 20229, ☎ 202/354–1000, WEB www.customs.gov; for complaints, ✉ Customer Satisfaction Unit, 1300 Pennsylvania Ave. NW, Room 5.5A, Washington, DC 20229; for registration of equipment, ✉ Office of Passenger Programs, 1300 Pennsylvania Ave. NW, Room 5.4D, Washington, DC 20229, ☎ 202/927–0530).

DINING

The restaurants we list are the cream of the crop in each price category. Properties indicated by a ✕🏠 are lodging establishments whose restaurant warrants a special trip. Price categories below are given in rand and are for South Africa chapters 2–8. For other countries see the individual chapter Dining sections for price charts. Categories are as follows:

CATEGORY	COST*
$$$$	more than R65
$$$	R45–R65
$$	R25–R45
$	less than R25

Rates are for a main course.

Unless otherwise noted, the restaurants listed in this guide are open daily for lunch and dinner.

RESERVATIONS & DRESS

Dress in most restaurants tends to be casual, but draw the line at wearing shorts and a halter top to dinner at any restaurant away from the beach. Very expensive restaurants and old-fashioned hotel restaurants (where colonial traditions die hard) may require a jacket and tie. We mention dress only when men are required to wear a jacket or a jacket and tie.

Reservations are always a good idea; we mention them only when they're either essential or not accepted. Book as far ahead as you can, and reconfirm as soon as you arrive (large parties should always call ahead to check the reservations policy).

DISABILITIES & ACCESSIBILITY

South Africa is slowly adding facilities for travelers with disabilities, but standards vary widely from place to place. Many large chains now offer one or more rooms in their hotels specially adapted for travelers with disabilities. Zimbabwe, Botswana, Namibia, and Zambia have very few facilities for travelers with disabilities. Eco Access has information about accessible facilities, specifically for game lodges and outdoor activities, in southern Africa.

➤ ACCESSIBLE FACILITY INFORMATION: **Eco Access** (☎ 27/11/477–3676, WEB www.eco-access.org).

LODGING

When discussing accessibility with an operator or reservations agent, **ask hard questions.** Are there any stairs, inside *or* out? Are there grab bars next to the toilet *and* in the shower/tub? How wide is the doorway to the room? To the bathroom? For the most extensive facilities meeting the latest legal specifications, **opt for newer accommodations.** If you reserve through a toll-free number, consider also calling the hotel's local number to confirm the information from the central reservations office. Get confirmation in writing when you can.

TRANSPORTATION

➤ COMPLAINTS: **Aviation Consumer Protection Division** (☞ Air Travel, *above*) for airline-related problems. **Departmental Office of Civil Rights** (for general inquiries, ✉ U.S. Department of Transportation, S-30, 400 7th St. SW, Room 10215, Washington, DC 20590, ☎ 202/366–4648, FAX 202/366–3571, WEB www.dot.gov/ost/docr/index.htm). **Disability Rights Section** (✉ 950 Pennsylvania Ave. NW, Washington, DC 20530, ☎ 202/514–0301 or 800/514–0301, or 800/514–0383 TTY, for ADA inquiries; WEB www.usdoj.gov/crt/ada/adahom1.htm).

TRAVEL AGENCIES

In the United States, the Americans with Disabilities Act requires that travel firms serve the needs of all travelers. Some agencies specialize in working with people with disabilities.

In South Africa, travelers should contact Flamingo Tours.

➤ TRAVELERS WITH MOBILITY PROBLEMS: **Access Adventures** (✉ 206 Chestnut Ridge Rd., Scottsville, NY 14624, ☎ 716/889–9096, dltravel@ prodigy.net), run by a former physical-rehabilitation counselor. **CareVacations** (✉ No. 5, 5110–50 Ave., Leduc, Alberta T9E 6V4, Canada, ☎ 780/ 986–6404 or 877/478–7827, FAX 780/ 986–8332, WEB www.carevacations. com), for group tours and cruise vacations. **Flamingo Tours** (✉ Box 60554, Flamingo Sq., Cape Town 7441 South Africa, ☎ 27/21/557– 4496 or 27/82/420–2031, FAX 27/21/ 557–4496, info@flamingotours.co.za, WEB www.flamingotours.co.za). **Flying Wheels Travel** (✉ 143 W. Bridge St., Box 382, Owatonna, MN 55060, ☎ 507/451–5005 or 800/535–6790, FAX 507/451–1685, WEB www. flyingwheelstravel.com).

DISCOUNTS & DEALS

Be a smart shopper and **compare all your options** before making decisions. A plane ticket bought with a promotional coupon from travel clubs, coupon books, and direct-mail offers or on the Internet may not be cheaper than the least expensive fare from a discount ticket agency. And always keep in mind that what you get is just as important as what you save.

DISCOUNT RESERVATIONS

The prices quoted for accommodations are standard high-season prices. Some hotels have low-season prices, and many offer packages that bring the daily rate down. Some also offer flight and accommodation packages. Always inquire about specials.

There are some pretty good deals to be had on the Web—some of which require thinking ahead and some of which only work at the last minute. For cheap flights within South Africa, check out www.kulula.com—for which you'll need to plan ahead, as there are limited seats on each flight and they are booked up rather quickly.

Many tour companies (buses, airlines, accommodation establishments, and even adventures) find themselves with half-full trips or hotels. To take advantage of their offers, contact www.

lastminute.com. For discount accommodations try www.mtbeds.co.za.

Contact **discount reservation services** in your home state as well.

When shopping for the best deal on hotels and car rentals, **look for guaranteed exchange rates,** which protect you against a falling dollar. With your rate locked in, you won't pay more, even if the price goes up in the local currency.

➤ AIRLINE TICKETS: ☎ **800/AIR–4LESS.**

➤ HOTEL ROOMS: **Turbotrip.com** (☎ 800/473–7829, WEB www.turbotrip. com).

PACKAGE DEALS

Don't confuse packages and guided tours. When you buy a package, you travel on your own, just as though you had planned the trip yourself. Fly/drive packages, which combine airfare and car rental, are often a good deal.

ECOTOURISM

Southern Africa is a dry region, so water is a precious resource and should be used sparingly. Please take short showers and always turn taps off when not in use, especially when shaving or brushing teeth. When outdoors, don't litter or pick flowers. When hiking, don't take shortcuts on mountain slopes; this exacerbates erosion, already a major problem in many parts of the region. If you're camping, don't wash with soap or shampoo in streams, springs, or lakes. Also, avoid feeding wild animals—at best it can make them sick; at worst it may cause them to expect food from future visitors, who may be attacked. The animal will then be killed by wildlife authorities. Also use power sparingly, turning off lights when not in use. Electricity is a finite resource.

ELECTRICITY

To use electric-powered equipment purchased in the United States or Canada, **bring a converter and adapter.** The electrical current is 220 volts, 50 cycles alternating current (AC); wall outlets in most of the region take 15-amp plugs with three round prongs (the old British system), but some take the straight-edged three-prong plugs, also 15 amps.

If your appliances are dual-voltage, you'll need only an adapter. Don't use 110-volt outlets marked FOR SHAVERS ONLY for high-wattage appliances such as blow-dryers. Most laptops operate equally well on 110 and 220 volts and so require only an adapter. In remote areas (and even in some smart lodges) power may be solar or from a generator; this means that delivery is erratic both in voltage and supply. In even the remotest places, however, lodge staff will find a way to charge video and camera batteries, but you will receive little sympathy if you insist on using a hair dryer or electric razor.

EMBASSIES

➤ CANADA: **Canadian Embassy** (✉ 1103 Arcadia St., Hatfield, Pretoria, ☎ 012/422–3000).

➤ UNITED KINGDOM: **British High Commission** (✉ 255 Hill St., Arcadia, Pretoria, ☎ 012/483–1200, FAX 012/ 433–3207). **U.K. Consulate** (✉ 275 Jan Smuts Ave., Dunkeld West, Johannesburg, ☎ 011/327–0015, FAX 011/ 325–2131).

➤ UNITED STATES: **U.S. Embassy** (✉ 877 Pretorius St., Arcadia, Pretoria, ☎ 012/342–1048).

EMERGENCIES

Both Medical Rescue International (MRI), which is based in South Africa, and Medical Air Rescue Services (MARS), which is based in Zimbabwe, offer professional evacuation in the event of real emergency. Divers Alert Network (DAN) is operated locally through MRI and can be accessed either through their own emergency number or through MRI.

South Africa's national emergency number for the police is 10111; for an ambulance it is 10177. Consult the front page of the local telephone directories for other emergency numbers. You can call Medical Rescue International (**MRI;** ☎ 27/11/242– 0111; 0800/111–9990 for toll-free calls within South Africa only). From a mobile phone dial 112.

In **Zimbabwe** dial 994 (ambulance), 993 (fire), and 995 (police); also call Medical Air Rescue Services (MARS; 04/73–4513).

In **Botswana** dial 997 (ambulance), 998 (fire), and 999 (police), or if you are in a remote area, contact MRI in Johannesburg for emergency evacuation.

In **Namibia** dial 10111 (police) or 264/ 61/23–0505 for MRI. Other numbers are specific to cities, so check local directories.

In **Zambia** dial 999 for fire and ambulance, 991 for police, or MRI in Johannesburg or MARS in Zimbabwe (☞ *above* for both).

In **Swaziland** dial 5–2221 for general emergency, or contact MRI for medical emergency. From a mobile phone dial 112.

GAY & LESBIAN TRAVEL

The major cities of South Africa are very gay-friendly, particularly Cape Town, which has a very large gay population. Both Johannesburg and Cape Town have "pink routes," that highlight gay-friendly or gay-interest operators. The other countries in the region are somewhat more conservative, and gay people should be circumspect, especially in Zimbabwe and Namibia, both of which have very homophobic presidents and where homosexuality is, technically, illegal.

➤ GAY- & LESBIAN-FRIENDLY TRAVEL AGENCIES: **Africa Outing** (✉ 5 Alcyone Rd., Claremont, Cape Town, South Africa 7708, ☎ 27/21/671– 4028 or 27/83/361–1255, FAX 27/21/ 683–7377, afouting@iafrica.com, WEB www.afouting.com).

Different Roads Travel (✉ 8383 Wilshire Blvd., Suite 902, Beverly Hills, CA 90211, ☎ 323/651–5557 or 800/429–8747, FAX 323/651–3678, lgernert@tzell.com). **Kennedy Travel** (✉ 314 Jericho Turnpike, Floral Park, NY 11001, ☎ 516/352–4888 or 800/ 237–7433, FAX 516/354–8849, WEB www.kennedytravel.com). **Now Voyager** (✉ 4406 18th St., San Francisco, CA 94114, ☎ 415/626–1169 or 800/ 255–6951, FAX 415/626–8626, WEB www.nowvoyager.com). **Skylink Travel and Tour** (✉ 1006 Mendocino Ave., Santa Rosa, CA 95401, ☎ 707/ 546–9888 or 800/225–5759, FAX 707/ 546–9891, WEB www.skylinktravel. com), serving lesbian travelers.

HEALTH

The most serious health problem facing travelers in southern Africa is malaria, which occurs in the prime game-viewing areas of Mpumalanga and the Northern Province and in northern KwaZulu-Natal, in South Africa. The high-lying areas of Zimbabwe, Swaziland, and Zambia are malaria-free, but the low-lying river valleys are high-risk areas. Most of Namibia and Botswana are malaria-free; the exceptions are the Caprivi Strip of Namibia and the Okavango Delta of Botswana. All of Mozambique and most of Malawi (except the highlands) is high risk. Lesotho is absolutely malaria-free.

All travelers heading into malaria-endemic regions should **consult a health-care professional at least one month before departure** for advice. Unfortunately, the malarial agent *Plasmodium sp.,* seems to be able to develop a hardy resistance to new prophylactic drugs pretty quickly, so even if you are taking the newest miracle drug, **take great care to avoid being bitten by mosquitoes.** After sunset wear light-color, loose, long-sleeve shirts; long pants; and shoes and socks; and apply mosquito repellent. Always sleep in a mosquito-proof room or tent, and if possible, keep a fan going in your room. **If you are pregnant or trying to conceive, avoid malaria areas if at all possible.**

Many lakes and streams, particularly east of the watershed (i.e., in rivers flowing toward the Indian Ocean), are infected with *bilharzia* (schistosomiasis), a parasite carried by a small freshwater snail. The fluke enters through the skin of swimmers or waders, attaches itself to the intestines or bladder, and lays eggs. **Avoid wading in still waters** or in areas close to reeds. If you have been wading or swimming in doubtful water, dry yourself off vigorously with a towel immediately on exiting the water, as this will help to dislodge any flukes before they can burrow into the skin. Fast-moving water is considered safe. Have a checkup once you get home. Bilharzia is easily diagnosed, and it's also easily treated in the early stages.

During summer ticks may be found all over the region, even in open areas close to cities. If you intend to walk or hike anywhere, use a suitable insect repellent. After your walk examine your body and clothes for ticks, looking carefully for pepper ticks, which are tiny but just as virulent as their parents and can cause tick-bite fever. If you find a tick has bitten you, do not pull it off. If you do, you may pull the body off, and the head will remain embedded in your skin, causing an infection. Rather, smother the area with petroleum jelly, and the tick will eventually let go, as it will be unable to breathe; you can then scrape it off with a fingernail. If you are bitten, keep an eye on the bite. If the tick was infected, the bite will swell, itch, and develop a black necrotic center—this is a sure sign that you will develop tick-bite fever, which usually hits after about 8–12 days. Symptoms may be mild or severe, depending on the patient. This disease is not usually life threatening in healthy adults, but it is horribly unpleasant.

The low-lying areas of Zimbabwe, Botswana, and Zambia harbor tsetse flies, so **wear light-color clothing and insect repellent** in these areas (tsetse flies are attracted to dark colors, especially black, dark brown, and bright blue). Don't spend ages agonizing over whether you've been bitten by a tsetse fly. You'll know, as it is very painful. The risk of contracting sleeping sickness is not great, but the disease can be fatal, and it can move very fast, so be aware.

Southern Africa has no national health system, so **check your existing health plan to see whether you're covered while abroad** and supplement it if necessary. South African doctors are generally excellent. The equipment and training in private clinics rivals the best in the world, but public hospitals in all the countries covered tend to suffer from overcrowding and underfunding.

On returning home, if you experience any unusual symptoms, including fever, painful eyes, backache, diarrhea, severe headache, general lassitude, or blood in urine or stool, be sure to **tell your doctor where you have been.** These symptoms may indicate malaria, tick-bite fever, bilharzia, sleeping sickness (although the latter is unlikely), or some other tropical malady.

FOOD & DRINK

Unless signs indicate otherwise, you can drink the tap water and eat all fresh produce in South Africa, Swaziland, Lesotho, Botswana, and most of Namibia and Zimbabwe. Tap water in Zambia, Malawi, and Mozambique is suspect, especially in the rainy season, when water sources may easily become contaminated. Diseases that can be carried in contaminated water, food, or utensils include cholera and hepatitis A.

MEDICAL PLANS

No one plans to get sick while traveling, but it happens, so **consider signing up with a medical-assistance company.** Members get doctor referrals, emergency evacuation or repatriation, hot lines for medical consultation, cash for emergencies, and other assistance.

➤ MEDICAL-ASSISTANCE COMPANIES: **International SOS Assistance** (WEB www.internationalsos.com; ✉ 8 Neshaminy Interplex, Suite 207, Trevose, PA 19053, ☎ 215/245–4707 or 800/523–6586, FAX 215/244–9617; ✉ 12 Chemin Riantbosson, 1217 Meyrin 1, Geneva, Switzerland, ☎ 22/785–6464, FAX 22/785–6424; ✉ 331 N. Bridge Rd., 17-00, Odeon Towers, Singapore 188720, ☎ 338–7800, FAX 338–7611).

SHOTS & MEDICATIONS

Travelers entering South Africa within six days of leaving a country infected with yellow fever require a yellow-fever vaccination certificate. The South African travel clinics and the U.S.'s National Centers for Disease Control recommend that you be vaccinated against hepatitis A, and hepatitis B if you intend to travel to more isolated areas. Cholera injections are widely regarded to be useless, so don't let anyone talk you into having one, but the newer oral vaccine seems to be more effective. Depending on your destination, you may wish to take oral malaria prophylactic drugs. At time of writing Malarone is the preferred drug, with almost none of the possible side effects of once popular Lariam (mefloquine).

The U.S.'s Centers for Disease Control and Prevention (CDC) provides up-to-date information on health risks and recommended vaccinations and medications for travelers to southern Africa. In most urban or easily accessible areas you need not worry. However, if you plan to visit remote regions or stay for more than six weeks, check with the CDC's traveler's health line.

➤ HEALTH WARNINGS: **National Centers for Disease Control and Prevention** (CDC; National Center for Infectious Diseases, Division of Quarantine, Traveler's Health Section, ✉ 1600 Clifton Rd. NE, M/S E-03, Atlanta, GA 30333, ☎ 888/232–3228 general information; 877/394–8747 travelers' health line, FAX 888/232–3299; WEB www.cdc.gov).

INSURANCE

The most useful travel-insurance plan is a comprehensive policy that includes coverage for trip cancellation and interruption, default, trip delay, and medical expenses (with a waiver for preexisting conditions).

Without insurance you will lose all or most of your money if you cancel your trip, regardless of the reason. Default insurance covers you if your tour operator, airline, or cruise line goes out of business. Trip-delay covers expenses that arise because of bad weather or mechanical delays. Study the fine print when comparing policies.

If you're traveling internationally, a key component of travel insurance is coverage for medical bills incurred if you get sick on the road. Such expenses are not generally covered by Medicare or private policies. U.K. residents can buy a travel-insurance policy valid for most vacations taken during the year in which it's purchased (but check preexisting-condition coverage). British and Australian citizens need extra medical coverage when traveling overseas.

Always **buy travel policies directly from the insurance company;** if you buy them from a cruise line, airline, or tour operator that goes out of business you probably will not be covered for the agency or operator's default, a major risk. Before making any purchase, **review your existing health and**

home-owner's policies to find what they cover away from home.

➤ TRAVEL INSURERS: In the United States: **Access America** (✉ 6600 W. Broad St., Richmond, VA 23230, ☎ 800/284–8300, FAX 804/673–1491 or 800/346–9265, WEB www.accessamerica.com). **Travel Guard International** (✉ 1145 Clark St., Stevens Point, WI 54481, ☎ 800/826–1300; 715/345–0505 for international callers, FAX 800/955–8785, WEB www.travelguard.com).

➤ INSURANCE INFORMATION: In the United Kingdom: **Association of British Insurers** (✉ 51 Gresham St., London EC2V 7HQ, ☎ 020/7600–3333, FAX 020/7696–8999, WEB www.abi.org.uk). In Canada: **RBC Travel Insurance** (✉ 6880 Financial Dr., Mississauga, Ontario L5N 7Y5, ☎ 905/791–8700 or 800/668–4342, FAX 905/813–4704, WEB www.rbcinsurance.com). In Australia: **Insurance Council of Australia** (✉ Level 3, 56 Pitt St., Sydney NSW 2000, ☎ 02/9253–5100, FAX 02/9253–5111, WEB www.ica.com.au). In New Zealand: **Insurance Council of New Zealand** (✉ Level 7, 111–115 Customhouse Quay, Box 474, Wellington, ☎ 64/472–5230, FAX 64/473–3011, WEB www.icnz.org.nz).

LANGUAGE

South Africa has a mind-numbing 11 official languages: English, Afrikaans, Ndebele, North Sotho, South Sotho, Swati, Tsonga, Tswana, Venda, Xhosa, and Zulu. Happily for visitors, English is the widely spoken, unofficial lingua franca, although road signs and other important markers often alternate between English and Afrikaans (South African Dutch). Be warned that street names often alternate between the English and Afrikaans names, so, for example, "Wale Street" and "Waal Straat" are the same road.

South African English is heavily influenced by Afrikaans and, to a lesser extent, by some of the African languages. First-time visitors may have trouble understanding some regional South African accents. Listed below are some of the words you should know. For a list of culinary terms *see* Dining *in* Pleasures and Pastimes *in* Chapter 1.

Bakkie: pickup truck
Bonnet: hood (of a car)
Boot: trunk (of a car)
Bottle store: liquor store
Bra/bru/My Bra: Brother, term of affection or familiarity
Dagga/Zol: marijuana
Jol: a party or night on the town
Howzit?: literally, "How are you?" but used as a general greeting
Izit?: Really?
Just now: recently or any time in the near or distant future
Kraal: animal corral or traditional homestead.
Lekker: nice
Mushy: (in Zimbabwe only, pronounced *moo-*shy) nice, good, well done
Pavement: sidewalk
Petrol: gasoline
Robot: traffic light
Shame: "How cute" or "What a pity"
Shebeen: township bar
Sis: gross, disgusting
Sisi or Usisi: sister, term of affection or respect
Skollie/Skebenga/Tsotsi: thug, ruffian
Takkie: sneaker
Toyi-toyi: to dance in protest
Veld: open countryside
Yebo: yes or hello

Zimbabwe's official languages are Shona, Ndebele, and very widely spoken English. **Botswana**'s official languages are Setswana and English, which is widely spoken. The minority languages—Hambakushu, Kalanga, and the many San (Bushman) dialects, collectively referred to as *BaSarwa*—are not given much recognition. **Zambia** has more than 70 dialects, but there are only four main languages: Lozi, Bemba, Nyanja, and Tonga. English is widely spoken. **Namibia**'s official language is English, which is not that widely spoken, except in the cities and then often as a second language. Afrikaans is spoken by many residents of various races, and there is a large population of German-speaking people. The most widely spoken indigenous languages are Kwanyama (a dialect of Owambo), Herero, and a number of Nama (San) dialects, which are spoken by almost no one other than native speakers. Sesotho is the official language of **Lesotho,** and English is spoken in a limited fashion. **Mozambique** was a Portuguese colony, so that language is widely spoken. In the south the most widely spoken indigenous language is Shangaan, which is also spoken in Mpumalanga in South Africa. English is quite widely spoken in **Malawi,** but the official language is Chichewa, which is similar to the Nyanja spoken in Zambia.

LODGING

In the past there was a grading system for hotels in South Africa, so you would get a one-, two-, three-, four-, or five-star hotel. This system was done away with and replaced with a more subjective silver, bronze, and gold system that no one really understood. And then a crystal system was instigated. You will see remnants of all these systems, but none is officially in use. A new grading system is being formulated at time of writing—it's an ongoing thing.

Most hotel rooms come with private bathrooms that are often referred to as en suite, and you can usually choose between rooms with twin or double beds. A full English breakfast is often included in the rate, particularly in more traditional hotels. In most luxury lodges the rate usually covers the cost of dinner, bed, and breakfast, while in game lodges the rate includes everything but alcohol. A self-catering room is one with kitchen facilities.

Be warned, though, that in southern Africa words do not necessarily mean what you think they do. The term *lodge* is a particularly tricky one. A guest lodge or a game lodge is almost always an upmarket, full-service facility with loads of extra attractions. But the term *lodge* when applied to city hotels often indicates a minimum-service hotel. These are usually very well appointed and comfortable, but have no bar, restaurant, or room service and thus offer very good-value bed-and-breakfast accommodations. Examples are the Protea Lodges (as opposed to Protea Hotels), City and Town Lodges, and Holiday Inn Garden Courts.

The lodgings we list are the cream of the crop in each price category. We always list the facilities that are available—but we don't specify whether they cost extra: when pricing accommodations, always ask what's included and what costs extra. Price categories

are based on a property's least expensive standard double room at high season (excluding holidays). Properties indicated by a ✕⊞ are lodging establishments whose restaurant warrants a special trip. Mailing addresses, if different from the street address, are given in parentheses in the service information at the end of the review.

Price categories below are given in rands and are for South Africa, Chapters 2–8. For other countries see the individual chapter Lodging sections for price charts. Categories are as follows:

CATEGORY	REGULAR LODGING*	SAFARI LODGES*
$$$$	more than R750	more than R2,500
$$$	R500–R750	R1,750–R2,500
$$	R250–R500	R1,000–R1,750
$	less than R250	less than R1,000

Rates are for a double room, including VAT. The cost for safari lodges includes all meals and activities and may include drinks.

Assume that hotels operate on the European Plan (EP, with no meals) unless we specify that they use the Continental Plan (CP, with a Continental breakfast daily), Breakfast Plan (BP, with a full breakfast daily), Modified American Plan (MAP, with breakfast and dinner daily), or Full American Plan (FAP, including all meals). Some properties are fully Inclusive, with the price including most activities. Most game lodges use the fully inclusive plan.

B&BS

There are thousands of B&B's scattered all over the region. As in most other parts of the world, many are very small and personalized, giving the visitor an insight into the lives of locals. For more info contact BABASA (Bed and Breakfast Association of South Africa). Portfolio of Places publishes a respected list of South Africa's best bed-and-breakfasts that may also be useful. It also offers a similar guide to small hotels and lodges.

➤ RESERVATION SERVICES: **BABASA (Bed and Breakfast Association of**

South Africa; ⊠ Box 2005, Groen-kloof 0027, ☎ FAX 012/480–2041, babasa@babasa.co.za, WEB www.babasa.co.za). **Portfolio of Places** (☎ 011/880–3414 in Johannesburg, FAX 011/788–4802).

FARM STAYS

Jacana Marketing and Reservations offers a range of farms, coastal, and country cottages, as well as privately operated hiking, biking, and horse trails in country areas.

➤ CONTACT: **Jacana Marketing and Reservations** (⊠ Box 95212, Waterk-loof 0145, South Africa, ☎ 012/346–3550, –3551, or –3552, FAX 012/346–2499, info@jacanacollection.co.za, WEB www.jacanacollection.co.za).

GAME LODGES

Safariplan/Wild African Ventures and Classic Safari Camps of Africa repre-sents a number of the best and most exclusive game lodges in southern and East Africa.

➤ CONTACTS: **Classic Safari Camps of Africa** (⊠ Box 2441, Northriding 2162, South Africa, ☎ 011/465–6427, FAX 011/465–9309, classics@classicsafaricamps.com, WEB www.classicsafaricamps.com). **Portfolio of Places** (☎ 011/880–3414 in Johannes-burg, FAX 011/788–4802). **Safariplan/Wild African Ventures** (⊠ 673 E. Cali-fornia Blvd., Pasadena, CA 91106, ☎ 800/358–8530).

HOME EXCHANGES

If you would like to exchange your home for someone else's, **join a home-exchange organization,** which will send you its updated listings of avail-able exchanges for a year and will include your own listing in at least one of them. It's up to you to make specific arrangements.

➤ EXCHANGE CLUBS: **HomeLink International** (⊠ Box 47747, Tampa, FL 33647, ☎ 813/975–9825 or 800/638–3841, FAX 813/910–8144, WEB www.homelink.org; $106 per year). **Intervac U.S.** (⊠ Box 590504, San Francisco, CA 94159, ☎ 800/756–4663, FAX 415/435–7440, WEB www.in-tervacus.com; $93 yearly fee includes one catalogue and on-line access).

HOSTELS

No matter what your age, you can **save on lodging costs by staying at hostels.** In some 4,500 locations in more than 70 countries around the world, Hostelling International (HI), the umbrella group for a number of national youth-hostel associations, offers single-sex, dorm-style beds and, at many hostels, rooms for couples and family accommodations. Member-ship in any HI national hostel asso-ciation, open to travelers of all ages, allows you to stay in HI-affiliated hostels at member rates; one-year membership is about $25 for adults (C$35 for a two-year minimum mem-bership in Canada, £12.50 in the U.K., A$52 in Australia, and NZ$40 in New Zealand); hostels run about $10–$25 per night. Members have priority if the hostel is full; they're also eligible for discounts around the world, even on rail and bus travel in some countries.

➤ ORGANIZATIONS: **Backpacker Tourism South Africa–BTSA** (WEB www.btsa.co.za). **Hostelling Interna-tional—American Youth Hostels** (⊠ 733 15th St. NW, Suite 840, Washing-ton, DC 20005, ☎ 202/783–6161, FAX 202/783–6171, WEB www.hiayh.org). **Hostelling International—Can-ada** (⊠ 400–205 Catherine St., Otta-wa, Ontario K2P 1C3, ☎ 613/237–7884; 800/663–5777 in Canada, FAX 613/237–7868, WEB www.hihostels.ca). **Youth Hostel Association Australia** (⊠ 10 Mallett St., Camperdown, NSW 2050, ☎ 02/9565–1699, FAX 02/9565–1325, WEB www.yha.com.au). **Youth Hostel Association of England and Wales** (⊠ Trevelyan House, 8 St. Ste-phen's Hill, St. Albans, Hertfordshire AL1 2DY, U.K., ☎ 0870/870–8808, FAX 01727/844126, WEB www.yha.org.uk). **Youth Hostels Association of New Zealand** (⊠ Level 3, 193 Cashel St., Box 436, Christchurch, ☎ 03/379–9970, FAX 03/365–4476, WEB www.yha.org.nz).

HOTELS

International hotel groups, such as Hyatt International and Sheraton, are moderately well represented around the region. Major South African con-glomerates include Protea and the Southern Sun Group, which runs Southern Sun Hotels and Holiday Inn Hotels. Southern Sun Group manages the budget French hotel chain For-mule 1 and the South African Inter-Continental Hotels.

There are a number of marketing associations that represent a collection of similar establishments. The Mantis Collection consists of a number of beautiful lodges in some of the most scenic parts of South Africa, Zimbabwe, and Mozambique. The Unique Cape Route markets a number of lovely guest houses between Cape Town and Port Elizabeth.

➤ CENTRAL RESERVATION NUMBERS: **Formule 1** (☎ 011/807–0750, WEB www.hotelformule1.co.za). **Hyatt International** (☎ 800/228–9000 in the U.S.). **Inter-Continental** (☎ 011/802–6876 in southern Africa; 800/327–0200 in the U.S., WEB www.interconti.com). **Protea** (☎ 021/419–8800; 0800/11–9000 toll-free, WEB www.proteahotels.com). **Sheraton** (☎ 800/325–3535 in the U.S., WEB www.sheraton.com). **Southern Sun** (☎ 011/482–3500, WEB www.southernsun.com).

➤ HOTEL ASSOCIATIONS: **Mantis Collection** (✉ Box 10802, Steenberg Estate, Cape Town 7945, South Africa, ☎ 27/21/713–2222, FAX 27/21/713–2251, info@mantiscollection.com, WEB www.mantiscollection.com). **Unique Cape Route** (✉ 41 Whittler's Way, Hout Bay, Cape Town 7806, South Africa, ☎ 27/21/790–8766, FAX 27/21/790–3959, reservations@caperoute.com, WEB www.caperoute.com).

➤ PUBLICATION: **Portfolio of Places** (☎ 011/880–3414 in Johannesburg, FAX 011/788–4802).

MAIL & SHIPPING

The mail service in southern Africa is not spectacularly reliable. Mail can take weeks to arrive, and money and other valuables are frequently stolen from letters and packages. You can buy stamps only at post offices, open weekdays 8:30–4:30 and Saturday 8–noon. In South Africa stamps for local use only, marked STANDARDISED POST, may be purchased from newsagents in booklets of 10 stamps. Federal Express and several other express-mail companies offer more reliable service, as does the new Fast Mail and Speed Courier services.

Except in South Africa and Lesotho, postal codes are not used because of the relatively small populations of southern African countries.

RECEIVING MAIL

The central post office in each city has a poste restante desk that will hold mail for you. Be sure the post office's mail code and your name are prominently displayed on all letters. Most hotels also accept faxes and express-mail deliveries addressed to their guests. If you have trouble retrieving your mail, ask the clerk to check under the initial of your first name (and any other). So, for example, check under J, R, and S if your name is John Robert Smith.

A better place to receive mail is at American Express offices; for a list of offices worldwide, write for AE's "Traveler's Companion."

➤ MAIL SERVICE: **American Express** (✉ Box 678, Canal Street Station, New York, NY 10013).

MONEY MATTERS

Because of inflation and currency fluctuations it's difficult to give exact exchange rates. It's safe to say, though, that the region is an extremely cheap destination for foreign visitors. With the weakness of southern African currencies against major foreign currencies, visitors will find the cost of meals, hotels, and entertainment considerably lower than at home. Botswana, with its stable economy and currency, is probably the most expensive destination in the region.

A fabulous bottle of South African wine costs about $6 (double or triple in a restaurant), and a meal at a prestigious restaurant won't set you back more than $30 per person. Double rooms in the country's finest hotels may cost $200 a night, but $75 is more than enough to secure high-quality lodging in most cities. Hotel rates are at their highest during peak season, November through March, when you can expect to pay anywhere from 50% to 90% more than in the off-season.

Not everything in South Africa is cheap. Expect to pay international rates and more to stay in one of the exclusive private game lodges in Mpumalanga, the Northern Province, or KwaZulu-Natal. Mala Mala, one of the best-known lodges in the country, charges about $1,000 per couple per night. Flights to South

Africa and within the country itself are also extremely expensive.

The following were sample costs in **South Africa** in U.S. dollars at time of writing: cup of coffee, $1; bottle of beer in a bar, $1; quarter roasted chicken with salad and drink at a fast-food restaurant, $4–$5; room-service sandwich in a hotel, $4–$7; 2-km (1-mi) taxi ride, $6–$8.

The following were sample costs in **Zimbabwe** in U.S. dollars at time of writing: cup of coffee, $1; bottle of beer in a bar, 75¢; average cost of lunch in cities, $4–$8; room-service sandwich in a hotel, $5; 2-km (1-mi) taxi ride, $3.

The following were sample costs in **Botswana** in U.S. dollars at time of writing: cup of coffee, $1.50; bottle of beer in a bar, $1.50; average cost of lunch in cities, $8–$10; room-service sandwich in a hotel, $8; 2-km (1-mi) taxi ride, $5.50.

The following were sample costs in **Namibia** in U.S. dollars at time of writing: cup of coffee, 75¢–$1.50; bottle of beer in a bar, $1; average cost of lunch in cities, $3–$5; room-service sandwich in a hotel, $4–$7; 2-km (1-mi) taxi ride, $4–$5.

The following were sample costs **Zambia** in U.S. dollars at time of writing: cup of coffee, $1; bottle of beer in a bar, 75¢; average cost of lunch in cities, $3.50; room-service sandwich in a hotel, $5; a 2-km (1-mi) taxi ride, $1.

The following were sample costs in **Swaziland** in U.S. dollars at time of writing: cup of coffee, 75¢–$1; bottle of beer in a bar, 80¢–$1.50; average cost of lunch in cities, $3–$6; room-service sandwich in a hotel, $3.50; a 2-km (1-mi) taxi ride, $4–$6.

The following were sample costs in **Mozambique** in U.S. dollars at time of writing: cup of coffee, $2; bottle of beer in a bar, $1.50–$2.50; average cost of lunch in cities, $10–$15; room-service sandwich in a hotel, $10; 2-km (1-mi) taxi ride, $6–$8.

The following were sample costs in **Malawi** in U.S. dollars at time of writing: cup of coffee, 75¢–$2; bottle of beer in a bar, $1–$1.50; average cost of lunch in cities, $6–$10; room-service sandwich in a hotel, $10; 2-km (1-mi) taxi ride, $4–$6.

The following were sample costs in **Lesotho** in U.S. dollars at time of writing: cup of coffee, 75¢; bottle of beer in a bar, 80¢–$1.50; average cost of lunch in cities, $3–$6; room-service sandwich in a hotel, $5; 2-km (1-mi) taxi ride, $4–$6.

Prices quoted throughout the book are in local currency where possible. Most operators in Zambia, Malawi, Zimbabwe, and Mozambique will only accept foreign currency, as the local money is rather volatile. Almost all the tourist destinations in Botswana are priced in dollars, as are some in South Africa and Namibia. Prices throughout this guide are given for adults. Substantially reduced fees are almost always available for children and students with valid international student cards.

For information on taxes *see* Taxes, *below.*

ATMS

Before leaving home, **make sure that your credit cards have been pro-grammed for ATM use in South Africa** (most South African ATMs take five-digit PIN numbers). Note that Discover is accepted mostly in the United States. Local bank cards often do not work overseas or may access only your checking account; **ask your bank about a MasterCard/Cirrus or Visa debit card,** which works like a bank card but can be used at any ATM displaying a MasterCard/Cirrus or Visa logo. These cards, too, may tap only your checking account; check with your bank about their policy.

CREDIT CARDS

In both Namibia and Zambia Master-Card and Visa are preferred by business owners to American Express because of substantial charges levied by Amex to proprietors. Even with MasterCard and Visa, business owners in Zambia often prefer cash (or traveler's checks) to credit cards, and some smaller hotels levy a fee up to 10% to use credit. In some remote areas it is difficult for proprietors to obtain authorization for credit-card transactions, so it's a good idea to carry cash or traveler's checks.

Throughout this guide, the following abbreviations are used: **AE**, American Express; **DC**, Diners Club; **MC**, MasterCard; and **V**, Visa.

➤ REPORTING LOST CARDS: **Amex** (☎ 011/710–4747), **Diners Club** (☎ 021/686–1990 or 011/482–2203), **MasterCard** (☎ 080/099–0418 toll free), **Visa** (☎ 080/099–0475 toll free).

CURRENCY

The unit of currency in **South Africa** is the rand (R), with 100 cents (¢) equaling R1. Bills come in R10, R20, R50, R100, and R200 denominations, which are differentiated by color. Coins are minted in R5, R2, R1, 50¢, 20¢, 10¢, 5¢, 2¢, and 1¢ denominations.

Namibia's currency is the Namibian dollar, which is linked to the South African rand, as is **Swaziland**'s lilangeni (plural emalangeni) and **Lesotho**'s loti (plural maloti). In both these countries you can use rand quite freely, but Namibia's currency is not usable in South Africa, except unofficially at border towns.

Zimbabwe's currency is the Zimbabwe dollar. There are Z$2, Z$5, Z$10, Z$20, and Z$50 bills; coins come in 1¢, 5¢, 10¢, 20¢, 50¢, and Z$1 denominations. At time of writing, this currency was particularly volatile.

Botswana's pula is the strongest and most stable currency is southern Africa and is broken down into 100 thebes. There are P1, P2, P5, P10, P20, and P50 bills, and 1t, 2t, 5t, 10t, 25, 50t, and P1 coins.

Zambia's currency is the Zambian kwacha, which comes in denominations of ZK5, ZK10, ZK50, ZK100, ZK500, ZK1,000, ZK5,000, and ZK10,000 bills, necessitating the carrying of huge wads of notes. The kwacha is theoretically divided into 100 ngwees but, as you can buy nothing for one kwacha, an ngwee is as useless as it is difficult to pronounce.

Malawi's Malawian kwacha is broken down into 100 tambalas—which are also pretty worthless, but the Malawian kwacha is worth much more than the Zambian one, so be careful. Coins come in denominations of 1, 2, 5, 10, 20, and 50 tambalas and 1 kwacha. Notes are in denominations of 5, 10, 20, 50, 100, and 200 kwachas.

Mozambique's currency has been seriously devalued over the last few years. Theoretically, the unit of currency is the meticais, but it is actually 1,000 meticais, colloquially known as a "mil," with 100-meticais notes used for buying such items as a box of matches or single candies. You will need to pay for hotel accommodations with foreign currency.

CURRENCY EXCHANGE

At time of writing conversion rates (to the US$) for southern Africa were as follows: **South Africa**, R11.50 (Namibian dollar, Lesotho loti, and Swaziland lilangeni the same); **Botswana**, P7; **Zambia**, ZK3,850; **Malawi**, MK77; and **Mozambique**, 22,850 mil. Because of **Zimbabwe**'s foreign currency crisis, the government has artificially frozen the "official" bank rate at around Z$55–Z$60. The true value of the Zimbabwean dollar, though, is far less; there is a parallel rate (not quite the same as the black market), which is the rate you will get from official bureaux de change. The parallel rate had risen from about Z$200 to Z$300 at time of writing.

For the most favorable rates in southern Africa, **change money through banks.** Although ATM transaction fees may be higher abroad than at home, ATM rates are excellent because they are based on wholesale rates offered only by major banks. You won't do as well at exchange booths in airports or rail and bus stations, in hotels, in restaurants, or in stores. In Zimbabwe pay in foreign currency and change money at bureaux de change rather than banks or hotels. To avoid lines at airport exchange booths, **get a few rands before you leave home**—they can be used in every country in the region, except Botswana, where you can use U.S. dollars anywhere.

In Zambia, Zimbabwe, and Mozambique, you may be invited to do a little informal foreign exchange by persuasive street financiers, who will offer you excellent rates. Resist the temptation—it's not worth the risk of being ripped off or caught and arrested.

To avoid administrative hassles, keep all foreign-exchange receipts until you leave southern Africa, as you may need them as proof when changing any unspent local currency back into your own currency. You may not take more than R5,000 in cash out of South Africa. For more information you can contact the **South African Reserve Bank** (✉ Box 427, Pretoria 0001, ☎ 012/313–3911).

➤ EXCHANGE SERVICES: **International Currency Express** (☎ 888/278–6628 for orders). **Thomas Cook Currency Services** (☎ 800/287–7362 for telephone orders and retail locations, WEB www.us.thomascook.com).

TRAVELER'S CHECKS

Do you need traveler's checks? It depends on where you're headed. If you're going to rural areas and small towns, go with cash; traveler's checks are best used in cities. Lost or stolen checks can usually be replaced within 24 hours. To ensure a speedy refund, buy your own traveler's checks—don't let someone else pay for them: irregularities like this can cause delays. The person who bought the checks should make the call to request a refund.

PACKING

In southern Africa it's possible to experience muggy heat, bone-chilling cold, torrential thunderstorms, and scorching African sun all within a couple of days. The secret is to pack lightweight clothes that you can wear in layers, and at least one sweater. **Take along a warm jacket, too,** especially if you're going to a private game lodge. It can get mighty cold sitting in an open Land Rover at night. It really and truly does get very cold in almost every part of southern Africa, so don't fall into the it's-Africa-so-it-must-always-be-hot trap.

Southern Africans tend to dress casually, donning shorts and T-shirts as soon as the weather turns pleasant. Businessmen still wear suits all over the region, but, especially in South Africa, dress standards have become less rigid and more interesting since ex-president Nelson Mandela redefined the concept of sartorial elegance with his Madiba shirts. You can go almost anywhere in neat, clean, casual clothes, but you can still get dolled up to go to the theater or opera, if you wish. Dinner on the *Blue Train* and in some of the smarter hotels is formal. An interesting development since 1994 is that invitations to social and official events prescribe dress code as "formal or traditional," so it really is quite acceptable for men to appear at the opera or the opening of Parliament in skirts made of monkey tails. (But don't try it as a foreigner, although you may wear a kilt or Native American feathered headdress if it is culturally appropriate for you.)

In summer lightweight cottons are ideal, but highveld (the high interior plateau of South Africa, Zimbabwe, and Zambia) evenings can be decidedly cool, and the desert nights in Botswana and Namibia are downright freezing. Despite the chilly nights and mornings, daytime temperatures in these regions can get pretty high—easily over 21°C (70°F) in winter and over 37°C (100°F) in summer. In the low-lying areas of the northern part of the region, the summer temperatures often go over 37°C (100°F), with accompanying high humidity. Lesotho can get extremely cold—freezing-to-death cold—so do take warm clothes.

It's easy to get fried in the strong African sun, especially in mile-high Johannesburg, where the temperature can be deceptively cool. Pack plenty of sunscreen, sunglasses, and a hat. An umbrella comes in handy during those late-afternoon thunderstorms but is almost useless in Cape Town in the winter as it will get blown inside out. But do take a waterproof coat.

If you're heading into the bush, consider packing binoculars, a strong insect repellent like 100% DEET, and sturdy pants (preferably cotton) that can stand up to the wicked thorns that protect much of the foliage. Avoid black, white, and garish clothing, which will make you more visible to animals (and insects, which tend to mistake you for a buffalo if you wear black); medium tones will make you blend in most, but you don't have to look like an extra on the set of *Out of Africa*, so don't rush out and buy a suitcase of designer khaki—you'll just look like a tourist. And leave behind perfumes, which mask the smell of the bush and also attract insects. Lightweight hiking boots are a good idea if you plan to set out on any of South Africa's great trails; otherwise, a sturdy pair of walking shoes should suffice.

Make copies of all your important documents and leave them with someone at home who can courier them to you if you should be unlucky enough to lose them all.

In your carry-on luggage, **pack an extra pair of eyeglasses or contact lenses and enough of any medication** you take to last the entire trip. You may also ask your doctor to write a spare prescription using the drug's generic name, since brand names may vary from country to country. In luggage to be checked, **never pack prescription drugs or valuables.** And don't forget to carry with you the addresses of offices that handle refunds of lost traveler's checks. Check *Fodor's How to Pack* (available in bookstores everywhere) for more tips.

To avoid customs and security delays, carry medications in their original packaging; don't pack any sharp objects, including knives of any size or material, scissors, manicure tools, and corkscrews, or anything else that might arouse suspicion. If you need such objects on your trip, consider shipping them to your destination or buying them there.

CHECKING LUGGAGE

How many carry-on bags you can bring with you is up to the airline. Most allow two, but not always, so make sure that everything you carry aboard will fit under your seat or in the overhead bin. Get to the gate early, so you can board as soon as possible. Note that if you have a seat at the back of the plane, you'll probably board first, while the overhead bins are still empty.

If you are flying internationally, note that baggage allowances may be determined not by piece but by weight—generally 88 pounds (40 kilograms) in first class, 66 pounds (30 kilograms) in business class, and 44 pounds (20 kilograms) in economy.

Airline liability for baggage is limited to $2,500 per person on flights within the United States. On international flights it amounts to $9.07 per pound or $20 per kilogram for checked baggage (roughly $640 per 70-pound bag) and $400 per passenger for unchecked baggage. You can buy additional coverage at check-in for about $10 per $1,000 of coverage, but it excludes a rather extensive list of items, shown on your airline ticket.

Before departure, **itemize your bags' contents** and their worth, and label the bags with your name, address, and phone number. (If you use your home address, cover it so potential thieves can't see it readily.) Inside each bag, **pack a copy of your itinerary.** At check-in, **make sure that each bag is correctly tagged** with the destination airport's three-letter code. If your bags arrive damaged or fail to arrive at all, file a written report with the airline before leaving the airport.

CHECKING LUGGAGE ON BUSH FLIGHTS

If you are visiting a game lodge deep in the bush, you will be arriving by light plane—and you really will be restricted to 10 kilograms (22 pounds) of luggage in a soft bag. Excess luggage can usually be stored with the operator till your return. Don't just gloss over this: charter operators take weight very seriously, and some will charge you for an extra ticket if you insist on bringing excess baggage. The transfers to the Bazaruto Archipelago are by light plane, too, so try to limit your baggage. You don't need many clothes, anyhow. And don't worry—they'll always make space for dive gear (less cylinders and weights, of course).

PASSPORTS & VISAS

When traveling internationally, **carry your passport** even if you don't need one (it's always the best form of I.D.) and **make two photocopies of the data page** (one for someone at home and another for you, carried separately from your passport). If you lose your passport, promptly call the nearest embassy or consulate and the local police.

When traveling across borders within southern Africa, remember that you may need a reentry visa to get back into the country you just left.

U.S. passport applications for children under age 14 require consent from both parents or legal guardians; both parents must appear together to sign the application. If only one parent appears, he or she must submit a written statement from the other parent authorizing passport issuance for the child. A parent with sole authority must present evidence of it when applying; acceptable documentation includes the child's certified birth certificate listing only the applying parent, a court order specifically permitting this parent's travel with the child, or a death certificate for the nonapplying parent. Application forms and instructions are available on the Web site of the U.S. State Department's Bureau of Consular Affairs (www.travel.state.gov).

U.S. CITIZENS

All U.S. citizens, even infants, need only a valid passport to enter South Africa, Swaziland, Botswana, Lesotho, Malawi, and Namibia for visits of up to 90 days. Business visitors to Namibia need visas. Mozambican visas must be obtained prior to entry and cost between R125 and R200 for a single-entry visa. You can buy double-entry visas at twice the price. You can buy visas at point of entry into Zimbabwe for US$30 for a single entry or US$45 for a double entry. If you leave Zimbabwe for more than 24 hours, you will need to buy another (unless you splurged on a multiple entry), so think before you save that US$15. There are fun things just over the border. You need a visa for Zambia, which you can buy at the border. The prices are US$25 for a single entry or transit visa, US$40 for a double, and US$80 for a multiple entry. A day visa costs US$10. But take note that the visa requirement is waived if you have prebooked with a bona fide Zambian-registered tour operator.

CANADIANS

You need only a valid passport to enter South Africa, Swaziland, Namibia, Zimbabwe, Lesotho, Malawi, and Zambia for stays of up to 90 days. Mozambican visas must be obtained prior to entry and cost between R125 and R200 for a single-entry visa. You can buy double-entry visas at twice the price. You need a visa for Zambia, which you can buy at the border. The prices are US$25 for a single entry or transit visa, US$40 for a double, and US$80 for a multiple entry. A day visa costs US$10. But take note that the visa requirement is waived if you have

prebooked with a bona fide Zambian-registered tour operator.

U.K. CITIZENS

Citizens of the United Kingdom need only a valid passport to enter South Africa, Swaziland, Namibia, Lesotho, Malawi, and Zimbabwe for stays of up to 90 days. Zambian visas cost US$33 for a single-entry or US$45 for a multiple-entry visa. Mozambican visas must be obtained prior to entry and cost between R125 and R200 for a single-entry visa. You can buy double-entry visas at twice the price. You need a visa for Zambia, which you can buy at the border. The prices are £35 for a single-entry or transit visa and £45 for a double- or multiple-entry visa. A day visa costs US$10. But take note that the visa requirement is waived if you have prebooked with a bona fide Zambian-registered tour operator.

PASSPORT OFFICES

The best time to apply for a passport or to renew is in fall and winter. Before any trip, check your passport's expiration date, and, if necessary, renew it as soon as possible.

➤ AUSTRALIAN CITIZENS: **Australian State Passport Office** (☎ 131–232, WEB www.dfat.gov.au/passports).

➤ CANADIAN CITIZENS: **Passport Office** (☎ 819/994–3500; 800/567–6868 in Canada, WEB www.dfait-maeci.gc.ca/passport).

➤ NEW ZEALAND CITIZENS: **New Zealand Passport Office** (☎ 04/494–0700 or 04/474–8100 for application procedures, WEB www.passports.govt.nz).

➤ U.K. CITIZENS: **London Passport Office** (☎ 0870/521–0410, WEB www.ukpa.gov.uk) for application procedures and to request an emergency passport.

➤ U.S. CITIZENS: **National Passport Information Center** (☎ 900/225–5674; calls are 35¢ per minute for automated service, $1.05 per minute for operator service; WEB www.travel.state.gov). **Office of Passport Services** (☎ 202/647–0518).

SAFETY

Crime is a major problem in the whole region, particularly in large cities, and all visitors should take precautions to protect themselves. **Do not walk alone at night,** and exercise caution even during the day. Avoid wearing flashy jewelry (even costume jewelry), and don't invite attention by wearing an expensive camera around your neck. If you are toting a handbag, wear the strap across your body; even better, wear a money belt, preferably hidden from view under your clothing. When sitting at airports or at restaurants, especially outdoor cafés, make sure to keep you bag on your lap or between your legs—otherwise it may just quietly "walk off" when you're not looking.

Carjacking is another problem, with armed bandits often forcing drivers out of their vehicles at traffic lights, in driveways, or during a fake accident. Keep your car doors locked at all times, and leave enough space between you and the vehicle in front so you can pull into another lane if necessary. If you are confronted by an armed assailant, do not resist. Because of the number of sophisticated antihijacking and vehicle-tracking devices being used, carjackers may try to force you off the road, so as to steal the car while the engine is running. Another possibility is being forced to accompany carjackers for some time, showing them where the hidden emergency switches are. If this happens, don't panic, scream, or otherwise draw attention to yourself. Follow their instructions very carefully, and do not attempt to try to remove your valuables or other items from the car—you'll have a far better chance of emerging from the experience unscathed.

Make sure you know exactly where you're going. Purchase a good map and obtain comprehensive directions. Taking the wrong exit off a highway into a township could lead you straight to disaster. Many cities are ringed by "no-go" areas. Learn from your hotel or the locals which areas to avoid.

Never, ever visit a township or squatter camp on your own. Unemployment is rife, and obviously affluent foreigners are easy pickings. If you wish to see a township, check with reputable companies, which run excellent tours and know which areas to avoid. Book yourself on one of these instead.

The countryside is less intense and crime is not as common, but **always remain alert,** and **don't let a false sense of security lead you into behaving foolishly.** Avoid wandering alone in deserted areas, unless you know where you are. Most hiking trails and tourist areas are reasonably safe, but crime can and does happen anywhere.

Before your trip check with the U.S. State Department (☎ 202/647–5225, travel.state.gov) to see if there are any current advisories about the country you are planning to visit.

But before you rush to cancel a trip, remember southern Africa is a very big place. Something happening in Zimbabwe will have no effect whatsoever on tourists in Cape Town, Kruger National Park, Zambia, or Mozambique—and even in parts of Zimbabwe. It really is worth your while to get good, up-to-date information from locals. Be assured, most tour operators would rather cancel a trip than risk a nasty incident, and they are usually in a good position to ascertain the real risks.

SENIOR-CITIZEN TRAVEL

Senior citizens in South Africa often receive discounts on admission prices and tickets if they can show valid pensioner's cards, which prove they they are on a fixed income, as age itself is no indication of financial status. As a foreigner, though, you are unlikely to get a discount.

When traveling in deep rural areas where people have not been urbanized, you will find that local youths, children, and even younger adults treat senior citizens with a great deal of respect, as age is revered in Africa.

➤ EDUCATIONAL PROGRAM: Elderhostel (✉ 11 Ave. de Lafayette, Boston, MA 02111-1746, ☎ 877/426–8056, FAX 877/426–2166, WEB www.elderhostel. org).

SHOPPING

Southern Africa is not the sort of place to shop for high-tech consumer goods, as they are quite expensive and import duties are so high you will almost certainly get a better deal on any nonlocal goods at home.

By and large, you'll find that South Africa has more Pan-African crafts and artifacts than you will find in Zimbabwe or Botswana. If you see a handpainted Ghanese barbershop sign that you like in Cape Town or Johannesburg, for example, don't expect to find any others in Harare or Gaborone.

If you look around, you can find some excellent clothing buys, ranging from traditional "African chic" outfits to haute couture and including, of course, some very well made and reasonably priced outdoor goods.

SMART SOUVENIRS

Traditional arts and crafts—whether they're made in South Africa or other African countries—are very good buys. Keep an eye out for Zulu baskets, Ndebele beaded aprons, Zimbabwean printed fabrics, Kuba cloth from Zaire, fetishes and masks from West Africa, and Mali mud cloth and wedding blankets.

WATCH OUT

Be wary of cheap imitations: "ebony" carvings often achieve their black luster through the use of shoe polish. Real ebony is heavy, and you can't scratch the black off—although think hard before buying it, anyway, as wood carving is contributing to the deforestation of Africa. Be aware that ivory is freely sold in southern Africa but only to local residents, so don't be tempted to buy any, as you won't be able to get it home. You will also find (especially in Victoria Falls) many small carvings from hippo teeth; if you buy these, you may need to do some smart talking to get them across borders, as to the untrained eye it is almost indistinguishable from ivory.

WINE

Many wineries will mail your wine purchases to your home, as will the major wine shops. You are allowed a maximum of 24 bottles per person, at a cost of US$10 a bottle. Shipping takes about two weeks.

➤ SHIPPERS: Steven Rom (⊠ Checkers Galleria Centre, 76 Regent Rd., Sea Point, South Africa, ☎ 021/439–6043, FAX 021/434–0401, rom@iafrica.com, WEB www.wineseller.co.za). Vaughan Johnson's Wine Shop (⊠ Pier Head, Dock Rd., Box 50012, Waterfront, Cape Town, 8002 South Africa, ☎ 021/419–2121, FAX 021/419–0040,

vjohnson@mweb.co.za, WEB www.vaughanjohnson.com).

➤ IMPORTERS: If you don't want to take the risk, contact one of the companies in the United States and Canada that import a wide range of Cape wines: Cape Venture Co. (☎ 203/329–6663), South African Wine Club (☎ 800/504–9463), or Maisons Marques & Domaines U.S.A. (☎ 510/286–2010); and in Canada, Remy Canada, Inc. (☎ 416/485–3633), or Peter Mielzynski Agencies, Ltd. (☎ 905/820–8180).

STUDENTS IN SOUTH AFRICA

To save money, **look into deals available through student-oriented travel agencies.** To qualify, you'll need a bona fide student ID card. Members of international student groups are also eligible.

➤ IDs & SERVICES: Council Travel (⊠ 205 E. 42nd St., 15th floor, New York, NY 10017, ☎ 212/822–2700 or 888/226–8624, FAX 212/822–2719, WEB www.counciltravel.com). Travel Cuts (⊠ 187 College St., Toronto, Ontario M5T 1P7, Canada, ☎ 416/979–2406; 888/838–2887, FAX 416/979–8167, WEB www.travelcuts.com).

STA Travel (⊠ 31 Riebeeck St., Cape Town 8001, ☎ 021/418–6570, FAX 021/418–4689, WEB www.statravel.co.za) specializes in youth and student travel.

GREAT OPTIONS

One of the best ways of getting around southern Africa is on the Baz Bus, a budget door-to-door bus catering especially to the needs of backpackers and going around the whole of South Africa and Swaziland, as well as to Victoria Falls and Bulawayo. You don't have to be young, but a cool attitude helps. Another exciting (although pricier) option is to go with rock-ant, an operator that does escorted adventure tours around South Africa and Lesotho. Prices range from US$4,500 for a 30-day trip to US$5,500 for a 40-day one. Prices include all transfers; transport; meals; activities such as bungee jumping, horseback trail riding, diving, surfing (with instruction), and rafting; and all equipment.

➤ OPERATORS: **Baz Bus** (✉ 8 Rosedene Rd., Sea Point, Cape Town 8005, ☎ 021/439–2323, FAX 021/439–2343, info@buzbus.co.za, WEB www.bazbus.co.za). **rock-ant** (✉ 26 Ronalds Rd., Kloof 3610, ☎ 082/807–0593 or 082/802–7091, WEB www.rock-ant.co.za).

TAXES

HOTEL

Most countries in southern Africa levy a bed tax on hotels. It is usually included in the price quoted and is included in all prices listed in this book.

VALUE-ADDED TAX

In South Africa the value-added tax (VAT), currently a whopping 14%, is included in the price of most goods and services, including hotel accommodations and food. To get a VAT refund, foreign visitors must present their receipts (minimum of R250) at the airport and be carrying any purchased items with them or in their luggage. You must fill out Form VAT 255, available at the airport VAT refund office. Whatever you buy, **make sure that your receipt is an original tax invoice, containing the vendor's name and address, VAT registration number, and the words *tax invoice*.** Refunds are paid by check, which can be cashed immediately at an airport bank. If you have packed your purchases in luggage you intend to check, be sure you visit the VAT refund desk before you go through check-in procedures. For items in your carry-on baggage, visit the refund desk in the departures hall.

TELEPHONES

The phone system in the region is pretty good, with Botswana's probably the most reliable, but there are problems. A major difficulty is the high cost of scrap copper, so it's not unknown for a couple of miles of telephone cable to go missing overnight, leaving large areas incommunicado—even in Johannesburg. Cell phones are ubiquitous and, especially in South Africa, have quite extensive coverage. Your best, cheapest, and least complicated way of making and receiving phone calls is to **obtain international roaming service from your cell phone service provider before you leave home.** Cell phones can also be rented by the day, week, or longer from the airport on your arrival.

➤ CELLULAR PHONE RENTAL: **GSM** (☎ 021/934–4951 in Cape Town; 011/394–8834 in Johannesburg; 031/469–2796 in Durban; 041/507–7370 in Port Elizabeth; 043/706–0353 in East London; 044/876–0000 in George).

AREA & COUNTRY CODES

The country code for South Africa is 27; for Swaziland, 268; for Zimbabwe, 263; for Botswana, 267; for Namibia, 264; for Lesotho, 266; for Malawi, 265; for Mozambique, 258; and for Zambia, 260. When dialing from abroad, drop the initial 0 from local South African, Namibian, Zambian, Mozambican, and Zimbabwean area codes. Swaziland, Lesotho, Malawi, and Botswana have no area codes.

The country code is 1 for the United States and Canada, 61 for Australia, 64 for New Zealand, and 44 for the United Kingdom.

CALLING FOR RESERVATIONS

Many lodges and operators are in very remote locations, so their booking offices can be quite far away—even in another country. For example, a lodge in Zambia may have booking offices in Zimbabwe and South Africa. Many Mozambican and Lesotho lodges have booking offices in South Africa. This does create confusion, but telephone numbers are listed as they should be dialed if you were in the country the chapter is about, so for booking you will drop the access code (which is usually 00) and add your own access code and then dial the international and local code (the initial zero of the area code will already have been dropped).

DIRECTORY & OPERATOR ASSISTANCE

In South Africa for directory assistance call ☎ 1023 for local calls or ☎ 1025 for national long-distance calls. For international operator assistance dial ☎ 0903.

LOCAL CALLS

Local calls are very cheap, although all calls from hotels attract a hefty premium. Remember, calls from Zimbabwe to Zambia, for example, are international calls—even if you can virtually see the caller on the other side of the river. Cell phones do have an advantage, as near borders you can use them as if you were in the other country. So South African cell phones work in parts of Lesotho, Swaziland, and Mozambique, and Zimbabwean cell phones work in parts of Zambia.

LONG-DISTANCE SERVICES

AT&T, MCI, and Sprint access codes make calling long distance relatively convenient, but you may find the local access number blocked in many hotel rooms. First ask the hotel operator to connect you. If the hotel operator balks, ask for an international operator, or dial the international operator yourself. One way to improve your odds of getting connected to your long-distance carrier is to travel with more than one company's calling card (a hotel may block Sprint, for example, but not MCI). If all else fails, call from a pay phone.

In Botswana and Swaziland, there are no access agreements to allow you to use U.S. long-distance services. Thus, you will not be able to make calls using your U.S. calling card from Botswana or Swaziland.

➤ ACCESS CODES: **AT&T Direct** (☎ 0800/99–0123 from South Africa; 0800/110–899 from Zimbabwe). **MCI WorldPhone** (☎ 0800/990–011 from South Africa). **Sprint International Access** (☎ 0800/990–001 from South Africa; 0800/180–280 from Botswana).

PUBLIC PHONES & PHONE CARDS

South Africa, Swaziland, Zimbabwe, Namibia, and Botswana have two types of pay phones: coin-operated phones that accept a variety of coins and card-operated phones. Phone cards are available in several denominations and are useful as they free you from the hassle of juggling handfuls of coins. In addition, a digital readout tells you how much credit remains while you're talking. Telephone cards are available at newsagents, convenience stores, and telephone company offices.

TIME

The whole of southern Africa operates on CAST (Central African Standard Time), which is two hours ahead of Greenwich mean time. That makes it seven hours ahead of North American eastern standard time (six hours ahead during eastern daylight savings time). The only exception is Namibia, which operates on Winter Time (one hour behind CAST) from 2 AM on the first Sunday of April till 2 AM on the first Sunday of September.

TIPPING

Tipping is an integral part of South African life, and tips are expected for services that you might take for granted at home. Most notable among these is when you fill up with gas; there are no self-service stations, and you should tip the attendant R2–R3 if he or she offers to clean your windshield, check your oil and water, and is generally helpful. In restaurants the size of the tip should depend on the quality of service, but 10% is standard, unless, of course, a service charge has already been added to the bill. Give the same percentage to bartenders, taxi drivers, and tour guides. Hotel porters should receive R1.50–R2 per bag. Informal parking attendants operate in the major cities in South Africa and even in some tourist areas. Although they often look a bit seedy, they do provide a good service, so tip them a couple of rand if your car is still in one piece when you return to it.

Tipping is less common in other southern African countries, but it is always appreciated. Loose change or 10% is appropriate.

At the end of your stay at a private game lodge, you're expected to tip both the ranger and the tracker. Tipping guidelines vary from lodge to lodge, but plan to give the local equivalents of about US$10 per person per day to the ranger and not much less to the tracker; an additional tip of US$25 for the general staff would be sufficient for a couple staying two days.

TOURS & PACKAGES

Because everything is prearranged on a prepackaged tour or independent vacation, you spend less time planning—and often get it all at a good price.

BOOKING WITH AN AGENT

Travel agents are excellent resources. But it's a good idea to collect brochures from several agencies as some agents' suggestions may be influenced by relationships with tour and package firms that reward them for volume sales. If you have a special interest, **find an agent with expertise in that area**; the American Society of Travel Agents (ASTA; ☞ Travel Agencies, *below*) has a database of specialists worldwide.

Make sure your travel agent knows the accommodations and other services of the place being recommended. Ask about the hotel's location, room size, beds, and whether it has a pool, room service, or programs for children, if you care about these. Has your agent been there in person or sent others whom you can contact?

Do some homework on your own, too: local tourism boards can provide information about lesser-known and small-niche operators, some of which may sell only direct.

BUYER BEWARE

Each year consumers are stranded or lose their money when tour operators—even large ones with excellent reputations—go out of business. So **check out the operator.** Ask several travel agents about its reputation, and try to **book with a company that has a consumer-protection program.** (Look for information in the company's brochure.) In the United States, members of the National Tour Association and the United States Tour Operators Association are required to set aside funds to cover your payments and travel arrangements in the event that the company defaults. It's also a good idea to choose a company that participates in the American Society of Travel Agents' Tour Operator Program (TOP); ASTA will act as mediator in any disputes between you and your tour operator.

Remember that the more your package or tour includes the better you can predict the ultimate cost of your vacation. Make sure you know exactly what is covered, and **beware of hidden costs.** Are taxes, tips, and transfers included? Entertainment and excursions? These can add up.

➤ TOUR-OPERATOR ASSOCIATIONS: **American Society of Travel Agents** (☞ Travel Agencies, *below*). **National Tour Association** (NTA; ✉ 546 E. Main St., Lexington, KY 40508, ☎

859/226–4444 or 800/682–8886, WEB www.ntaonline.com). **United States Tour Operators Association** (USTOA; ✉ 275 Madison Ave., Suite 2014, New York, NY 10016, ☎ 212/599–6599 or 800/468–7862, FAX 212/599–6744, WEB www.ustoa.com).

SPECIALTY TOUR OPERATORS

The advantages of dealing with a tour operator that specializes in the area you are planning to visit include better access to special deals, specialized local knowledge, and understanding of seasonal peculiarities. For example, a local operator won't send you on a Delta trip at the wrong time of year.

➤ LOCAL CONTACTS: **Big Five** (✉ 1551 SE Palm Ct.,Stuart, Florida 34994, ☎ 800/244–3483, WEB www.bigfive.com). **Bushwillow Consulting** (☎ 27/011/672–3554 or 27/082/854–4281, bwillow@global.co.za). **CC Africa** (✉ PO Box 16336, Vlaeberg 8018, Cape Town, South Africa, ☎ 27/021/425–0222, WEB www.ccafrica.com). **Fairfield Tours** (☎ 27/021/930–3534, FAX 27/021/930–1850, WEB www.fairfieldtours.com). **Felix Unite Tourism Group** (☎ 27/021/683–6433, FAX 27/021/683–6486, bookings@felix.co.za, WEB www.felixunite.co.za). **Premier Tours** (✉ 217 S. 20th St., Philadelphia, PA 19103, ☎ 215/893–9966 or 800/545–1910 or 800/545–1910), WEB premiertours.com). **Thompson's South Africa** (☎ 27/031/250–3100, FAX 27/031/201–3202, info@thompsonssa.com, WEB www.thompsonssa.com). **United Touring Company (UTc;** ☎ 27/021/419–8301 or 27/083/268–0383, FAX 27/021/419–2422, utc@utcza.co.za, WEB www.utc.co.za). **Wild Frontiers** (☎ 27/011/702–2035, FAX 27/011/468–1655, wildfront@icon.co.za).**Wilderness Safaris** (☎ 27/011/807–1800, FAX 27/011/807–2110, WEB www.wilderness-safaris.com, enquiry@wilderness.co.za). **ZTC** (☎ 27/011/880–4890, FAX 27/011/880–0119, info@ztc.co.za, WEB www.ztc.co.za).

TRAIN TRAVEL

Mainline Passenger Services, part of the South African rail network known as Spoornet, operates an extensive system of passenger trains connecting most major cities. Departures are usually limited to one per day, although trains covering minor routes leave less frequently. Distances are vast, so many journeys require overnight travel. The service is good and the trains safe and well maintained, but this is far from a luxury option. Traveling first class doesn't cost much more than second class but also doesn't offer much more. Basically, you'll be sharing your compartment with a maximum of three others; in second-class there is a maximum of five. In practice, the second-class compartments are rarely full (except in peak season); in either case, you will be using a communal toilet and shower (if you dare). The compartments have a washbasin. Bedding can be rented. The dining car serves pretty ordinary food, but it's reasonably well cooked and inexpensive. Third class is an adventure! Spoornet has recently started a new service with much better food and slightly better service, but you still have to deal with that communal bathroom. You must reserve tickets in advance for first- and second-class accommodations, whereas third-class tickets require no advance booking. You can book up to three months in advance with travel agents, reservations offices in major cities, and at railway stations.

Namibian train travel meets about the same standard as its South African counterpart. Train travel in Zimbabwe is cheap and, much like Spoornet, not bad, although the communal toilets seem to get into a worse state by the end of the trip. Train travel in Botswana is also not bad, but the distances don't warrant overnight travel. **Zambian railways are best avoided,** especially between Livingstone and Lusaka, as track maintenance is somewhat erratic. Swaziland is so tiny there's not much point in catching a train. You can take a train from Johannesburg to the Mozambique border. All the above options are in the budget range.

➤ CONTACT: **Mainline Passenger Services** (✉ Box 2671, Joubert Park 2044, ☎ 011/773–2944).

LUXURY TRAIN TRIPS

A trip aboard the famous *Blue Train* has long been one of the highlights of any trip to South Africa. Compartments are individually air-conditioned and have remote-operated blinds and curtains, TV, and a personal mobile phone for contacting your butler/valet or making outgoing calls. The comfortably furnished lounge car offers refreshments and drinks throughout the day and is a good place to meet fellow travelers. There are two trains: the classic and the African theme, which, while maintaining the same very high standard, is decorated with African touches such as faux animal-skin furniture and somewhat more exotic uniforms for the staff. In the well-appointed dining car, men are required to wear jacket and tie to dinner. On the Pretoria–Cape Town route, guests are treated to champagne when the train stops in Kimberley and taken by coach on a tour of the historic diamond-mining town.

In addition to its regular run between Cape Town and Pretoria, the *Blue Train* does monthly trips between Pretoria and Hoedspruit, in the Northern Province, where you can spend some time viewing game; Victoria Falls, in Zimbabwe; and also between Cape Town and Port Elizabeth via the Garden Route. All meals and alcohol are included in the ticket price, which ranges from R5,400 for a double in low season between Hoedspruit and Pretoria to R17,400 for a deluxe double in high season between Vic Falls and Pretoria, both one-way.

Another luxury option is **Rovos Rail.** Sixty beautifully restored Edwardian-era carriages make up three trains, which are drawn by a steam engine on certain sections. This opulent train carries a maximum of 72 passengers, attended by up to 21 staff members, including two gourmet chefs. Regular weekly trips are run between Pretoria and Cape Town and Pretoria and Victoria Falls (both two nights). Biweekly overnight trips are run between Cape Town and George and between Pretoria and Komatipoort, on the Mozambique Border, through Mpumalanga and the Northern Province, in season. Every May a seven-day trip from Cape Town to Swakopmund (and back) is run, and in July there is a 13-day epic from Cape Town to Dar es Salaam (and, of course, back again). Prices per person sharing range from R3,995 for a deluxe suite on the Pretoria–Malelane run, to R26,390 for the Royal Suite on the *African Collage,* which is a seven-night, eight-day trip from Pretoria to Cape Town the long way round. The single-occupancy supplement is 50%. The cost of the Cape Town–Dar es Salaam trip ranges from US$7,600 to US$9,950 one-way, with a single supplement of US$3,000. The ticket covers everything, including alcohol, meals, and scheduled excursions.

If you're more interested in authenticity than luxury, the **Union Limited Steam Rail Tours** will transport you straight back to the great days of rail—from the 1920s to 1940s. The Transnet Heritage Foundation is dedicated to keeping old railway stock rolling in as close to original condition as possible. So, be warned—these are pretty authentic, and that means communal ablutions, although they have made some concessions like gas water heaters instead of coal. The coaches have not been modernized, and the original four-sleeper takes two people, while the two-sleeper coupe is only used as a single. If this sounds far too primitive, there are six suites with en-suite showers—another small concession to contemporary standards. The dinners are formal silver-service affairs, with stewards in period uniform, and the menus are the old, traditional Spoornet fare—soup, fish, main course with lots of meat, and dessert. Small concessions have been made to modern tastes, like the addition of fresh salads and fruit (unheard of in the days of limited refrigeration), and the stoves are also now gas instead of coal.

The trip leaves Cape Town on Tuesday, spending five nights and six days meandering around the Garden Route and doing the odd day tour. The standard fare is R2,600 per person, sharing or single, or R22,400 per suite, which sleeps two people in luxury. The fare includes all meals, side trips, and activities but does not include drinks.

➤ CONTACTS: **Blue Train** (✉ Box 2671, Joubert Park 2044, ☎ 011/773–7631, 𝖥𝖠𝖷 011/773–7643). **Rovos Rail** (✉ Box 2837, Pretoria 0001, ☎ 012/323–6052, 𝖥𝖠𝖷 012/323–0843). **Union Limited Steam Rail Tours** (☎ 021/449–4391, 𝖶𝖤𝖡 www.steamsa.co.za).

TRAVEL AGENCIES

A good travel agent puts your needs first. Look for an agency that has been in business at least five years, emphasizes customer service, and has someone on staff who specializes in your destination. In addition, **make sure the agency belongs to a professional trade organization.** The American Society of Travel Agents (ASTA)—the largest and most influential in the field with more than 26,000 members in some 170 countries—maintains and enforces a strict code of ethics and will step in to help mediate any agent-client disputes involving ASTA members if necessary. ASTA (whose motto is "Without a travel agent, you're on your own") also maintains a Web site that includes a directory of agents. (If a travel agency is also acting as your tour operator, *see* Buyer Beware *in* Tours & Packages, *above.*)

➤ LOCAL AGENT REFERRALS: **American Society of Travel Agents** (ASTA; ✉ 1101 King St., Suite 200, Alexandria, VA 22314 ☎ 800/965–2782 24-hr hot line, 𝖥𝖠𝖷 703/739–7642, 𝖶𝖤𝖡 www.astanet.com). **Association of British Travel Agents** (✉ 68–71 Newman St., London W1T 3AH, U.K., ☎ 020/7637–2444, 𝖥𝖠𝖷 020/7637–0713, 𝖶𝖤𝖡 www.abtanet.com). **Association of Canadian Travel Agents** (✉ 130 Albert St., Suite 1705, Ottawa, Ontario K1P 5G4, Canada, ☎ 613/237–3657, 𝖥𝖠𝖷 613/237–7052, 𝖶𝖤𝖡 www.acta.net). **Australian Federation of Travel Agents** (✉ Level 3, 309 Pitt St., Sydney NSW 2000, Australia, ☎ 02/9264–3299, 𝖥𝖠𝖷 02/9264–1085, 𝖶𝖤𝖡 www.afta.com.au). **Travel Agents' Association of New Zealand** (✉ Level 5, Tourism and Travel House, 79 Boulcott St., Box 1888, Wellington 10033, New Zealand, ☎ 04/499–0104, 𝖥𝖠𝖷 04/499–0827, 𝖶𝖤𝖡 www.taanz.org.nz).

VISITOR INFORMATION

All the countries listed below are members of RETOSA (Regional Tourism Organization of Southern Africa), based in Johannesburg.

➤ REGIONAL INFORMATION: **RETOSA** (Regional Tourism Organization of Southern Africa; ✉ Box 7381, Halfway House, Johannesburg 1685, South Africa, ☎ 011/315–2420, 𝖥𝖠𝖷 011/315–2422).

SOUTH AFRICA

For information about traveling to and within South Africa before you go, contact the nearest office of **South African Tourism.**

➤ SOUTH AFRICAN GOVERNMENT TOURIST OFFICES: **U.S.** (⊠ 500 5th Ave., Suite 2040, New York, NY 10110, ☎ 800/822–5368, FAX 212/764–1980; ⊠ 9841 Airport Blvd., Suite 1524, Los Angeles, CA 90045, ☎ 800/782–9772, FAX 310/641–5812). **Canada** (⊠ 4117 Lawrence Ave. E, Suite 2, Scarborough, Ontario M1E 2S2, ☎ 416/283–0563, FAX 416/283–5465). **South Africa** (⊠ Private Bag X164, Pretoria 0001, ☎ 012/347–0600, FAX 012/347–6199). **U.K.** (⊠ 5–6 Alt Grove, Wimbledon SW19 4DZ, ☎ 0181/944–8080, FAX 0181/944–6705).

ZIMBABWE

➤ ZIMBABWE TOURIST OFFICE: **U.S.** (⊠ 1270 Ave. of the Americas, Suite 2315, New York, NY 10020, ☎ 212/332–1090). **Canada** (⊠ Zimbabwe High Commission, 332 Somerset St., West Ottawa, Ontario K2P 0J9, ☎ 613/237–4388). **U.K.** (⊠ Zimbabwe Tourism Office, 429 Strand, London WC2R 05A, ☎ 171/240–6169, FAX 171/379–1167). **Zimbabwe** (⊠ Zimbabwe Tourist Authority, Box CY286 Harare, ☎ 04/75–8730 through 04/75–8734, FAX 04/75–8712, –8713, or –8714).

BOTSWANA

➤ DEPARTMENT OF TOURISM, MINISTRY OF COMMERCE AND INDUSTRY: **Botswana** (⊠ Private Bag 0047, Gaborone, ☎ 267/35–3024 or 267/31–3314, FAX 267/30–8675). **U.S. and Canada** (⊠ 3400 International Dr. NW, Suite 7M, Washington, DC 20008, ☎ 202/244–4990). **U.K.** (⊠ 6 Stratford Pl., London W1N 9AE, ☎ 171/499–0031).

NAMIBIA

➤ NAMIBIAN EMBASSY: **U.S. and Canada** (⊠ 1605 New Hampshire Ave. NW, Washington, DC 20009, ☎ 202/986–0540, FAX 202/986–0443). **U.K.** (⊠ 6 Chandos St., London W1MOLQ, ☎ 171/636–6244, FAX 171/636–7594). **Namibia** (Ministry of Environment and Tourism; ⊠ Private Bag 13346, Windhoek, ☎ 061/284–2366, FAX 061/22–1930).

ZAMBIA

➤ ZAMBIAN NATIONAL TOURIST BOARD: **U.S. and Canada** (⊠ 237 E. 52nd St., New York, NY 10022, ☎ 212/308–2155), FAX 212–758–1319). **U.K.** (⊠ 2 Palace Gate, Kensington, London W85NG, ☎ 171/589–6343, FAX 171/581–1353).

SWAZILAND

➤ SWAZILAND HIGH COMMISSION: **U.S. and Canada** (⊠ 3400 International Dr. NW, Suite 3M, Washington, DC 20008, ☎ 202/362–6683).

U.S. GOVERNMENT ADVISORIES

➤ CONTACT: **U.S. Department of State** (⊠ Overseas Citizens Services Office, Room 4811, 2201 C St. NW, Washington, DC 20520, ☎ 202/647–5225 for interactive hot line, WEB www.travel.state.gov); enclose a business-size SASE.

WEB SITES

Do check out the World Wide Web when planning your trip. You'll find everything from weather forecasts to virtual tours of famous cities. Be sure to **visit Fodors.com** (www.fodors.com), a complete travel-planning site. You can research prices and book plane tickets, hotel rooms, rental cars, vacation packages, and more. In addition, you can post your pressing questions in the Travel Talk section. Other planning tools include a currency converter and weather reports, and there are loads of links to travel resources.

Check out www.wildnetafrica.net for information on safaris; or www.getawaytoafrica.com and www.outthere.co.za for travel and adventures in southern Africa generally. For more information specifically on South Africa, visit: www.southafrica.net; on Botswana, www.gov.bw; on Swaziland, www.mintour.gov.sz; on Namibia, www.iwwn.com.na/namtour/namtour.html; on Zambia, www.africa-insites.com/zambia. Zimbabwe doesn't have a good official Web site, but you can check out the Web sites of the major tour companies—try www.utc.co.zw or www.landela.co.zw.

WHEN TO GO

As southern Africa is in the southern hemisphere, its seasons are opposite to those in the northern hemisphere—

it's summer there during the North American and European winter.

Peak tourist season is from November through March, when hotel prices rise dramatically and making a reservation can be difficult. The situation is exacerbated during major school holidays—especially December 1–January 15, the South African summer vacation—when South African families take to the roads in droves. Schools also have two weeks' vacation around Easter and a month in July or August, when the warmer parts of the region, especially Kariba, Victoria Falls, Mozambique, and KwaZulu-Natal, are particularly popular. Zimbabwean winter holidays are in August.

The most popular time to visit Cape Town is from November through January, although February and March offer the best weather. Keep in mind, however, that the shoulder months of October and April can be fabulous and uncrowded. Cape winters (May–August) are notorious for cold, windy, rainy weather, but in reality these are miserable days interspersed with glorious sunny days that rival the best summer days in Britain. This season is known as the "secret season," during which really good deals can be had. As long as you stay for a week or more, you're bound to have at least a few days of gorgeous weather.

Much of the rest of the region receives its rain in the hot summer months, which is the worst time for watching game, as the abundant standing water enables the animals to spread out over a large area and the luxuriant new growth makes it difficult to see anything. The rains usually end in about March or April, from which point the standing water starts to dry up and the vegetation to be eaten, so game viewing improves throughout the dry season. By October there is usually very little standing water and vegetation cover, making game viewing excellent, although the hot, humid conditions may be a bit uncomfortable. Once the rains start, usually in November, game viewing takes a second place to bird-watching as the summer migrants arrive.

Johannesburg and the highveld enjoy glorious summers, with hot, sunny days broken by afternoon thunderstorms. Winter nights are frosty; days are generally mild and sunny but can be decidedly chilly, with rain, sleet, and even a little snow. Lesotho and the high-lying areas of South Africa can get snow at any time of year, although it is pretty rare. Even Swaziland gets snow in the highlands, sometimes.

The coastal areas of KwaZulu-Natal are warm year-round, but summers are steamy and hot, and August sees high winds buffet the coastline. The water along the KwaZulu-Natal coast is warmest in February, but it seldom dips below 17°C (65°F) at any time of year. The Drakensberg Mountains can be bitterly cold in winter, often with snow, and are dry and brown. In summer the mountains are a bright green with new grass, and is warm but spectacular thunderstorms pose a real threat to hikers in that high altitude.

Southern Africa, like the rest of the world, has been experiencing erratic climate recently, so pack good rain gear wherever you go; remember to bring layers for the colder days; and always bring shorts, T-shirts, sandals, a sun hat, and a swimsuit.

CLIMATE

The following are average daily maximum and minimum temperatures for some major cities in southern Africa. For additional information on seasonal temperatures in the various countries covered, *see* the When to Tour sections at the beginning of the relevant chapters.

CAPE TOWN

Jan.	79F	26C	May	68F	20C	Sept.	66F	19C
	61	16		48	9		48	9
Feb.	81F	27C	June	64F	18C	Oct.	70F	21C
	61	16		46	8		52	11
Mar.	77F	25C	July	64F	18C	Nov.	75F	24C
	57	14		45	7		55	13
Apr.	73F	23C	Aug.	64F	18C	Dec.	77F	25C
	54	12		46	8		59	15

DURBAN

Jan.	82F	28C	May	77F	25C	Sept.	73F	23C
	70	21		57	14		59	15
Feb.	82F	28C	June	73F	23C	Oct.	75F	24C
	70	21		52	11		63	17
Mar.	82F	28C	July	73F	23C	Nov.	77F	25C
	68	20		52	11		64	18
Apr.	79F	26C	Aug.	73F	23C	Dec.	81F	27C
	63	17		55	13		68	20

JOHANNESBURG

Jan.	79F	26C	May	66F	19C	Sept.	73F	23C
	59	15		45	7		50	10
Feb.	77F	25C	June	61	16C	Oct.	75F	24C
	57	14		39	4		52	11
Mar.	75F	24C	July	63F	17C	Nov.	75F	24C
	55	13		39	4		55	13
Apr.	70F	21C	Aug.	66F	19C	Dec.	77F	25C
	50	10		43	6		57	14

SKUKUZA (KRUGER NATIONAL PARK)

Jan.	91F	33C	May	82F	28C	Sept.	84F	29C
	70	21		50	10		55	13
Feb.	90F	32C	June	79F	26C	Oct.	86F	30C
	68	20		43	6		61	16
Mar.	88F	31C	July	79F	26C	Nov.	88F	31C
	66	19		43	6		64	18
Apr.	84F	29C	Aug.	81F	27C	Dec.	90F	32C
	59	15		48	9		68	20

LUSAKA, ZAMBIA

Jan.	79F	26C	May	77F	25C	Sept.	84F	29C
	62	17		53	11		58	14
Feb.	79F	26C	June	73F	23C	Oct.	89F	31C
	62	17		48	9		63	17
Mar.	79F	26C	July	73F	23C	Nov.	85F	29C
	61	16		48	9		63	17
Apr.	80F	26C	Aug.	77F	25C	Dec.	80F	27C
	58	14		51	10		62	17

GABORONE, BOTSWANA

Jan.	90F	32C	May	76F	24C	Sept.	84F	29C
	64	18		42	5		48	9
Feb.	88F	31C	June	72F	22C	Oct.	88F	31C
	64	17		35	2		57	14
Mar.	85F	29C	July	72F	22C	Nov.	89F	32C
	59	15		34	1		61	16
Apr.	82F	28C	Aug.	76F	24C	Dec.	90F	32C
	51	11		39	4		63	17

➤ FORECASTS: **Weather Channel Connection** (☎ 900/932–8437), 95¢ per minute from a Touch-Tone phone.

FESTIVALS AND SEASONAL EVENTS

There is so much going on during the year, what follows is just a sample. Contact the tourism authorities or check the Web for further information.

➤ NOV.: The **94.7 Challenge** is Johannesburg's biggest cycle race. It's—surprise—94.7 km (just under 60 mi), which is not that far, but it's pretty hilly.

➤ NOV.: **Nedbank Golf Challenge**, held at Sun City, is the richest golf tournament in the world.

➤ MID DEC.: The **Mother City Queer Project** is the highlight of the social calendar for the less conservative of Cape Town's residents. With a different theme every year, this costume party is attended by both straight and gay people, but it really is about as camp as a row of pink tents.

➤ DEC./JAN.: The **Ncwala, or First Fruits Ceremony,** is common to many African tribes of Nguni origin and takes place in KwaZulu-Natal, Swaziland, and Zambia. The king blesses the harvest by ritually tasting the first fruits.

➤ DEC./JAN./FEB.: The **Spier Summer Season** is an extravaganza of music and theater performances at the Spier Estate, in Stellenbosch.

➤ EARLY JAN.: The 17-day **Cape Coon Carnival** celebrates the New Year in grand style, as thousands of coloreds (the South African term for people of mixed Khoi-San, Malay, black, and/or European descent) dressed in bright costumes take to the streets of Cape Town to sing and dance.

➤ JAN. 2003: **Cape to Rio Yacht Race.** The fun fleet leaves on January 4, with the serious sailors setting off a week later, on January 11. Even if you don't follow the whole race, the start is a fantastic spectacle, either from a boat, Robben Island, or the top of Table Mountain.

➤ JAN/FEB.: In summer, when the water level is high, the tough three-day, 120-km (about 70-mi) kayak **Dusi Marathon** takes place on the Msinnduzi River which runs from Pietermaritzburg to Durban.

➤ FEB.: The **Midmar Mile** is a rather tough swimming race in the freezing cold Midmar Dam, between Durban and Pietermaritzburg in the KZN Midlands.

➤ FEB.: The **FNB Vita Dance Umbrella** is a three-week-long showcase of local dance at the University of the Witwatersrand, Johannesburg.

➤ EARLY MAR.: The **Argus Cycle Tour** is the largest individually timed race in the world, with about 40,000 competitors riding a scenic 115-km (about 70-mi) course.

➤ LATE MAR.: The **North Sea Jazz Festival,** a showcase of international jazz, is held at Cape Town's Good Hope Centre.

➤ MAR. OR APR.: The annual **Nederburg Auction** is *the* event on the wine calendar. It's the place to be seen, even if you don't bid, as South Africa's finest old and new wines go under the hammer.

➤ MAR./APR.: The **Klein Karoo Kunstefees** takes place in Oudtshoorn and is a celebration of Afrikaans culture, although there are performances in English as well.

➤ MAR./APR.: The **Ko-umbuka Ceremony,** in Western Zambia, takes place at a different time each year, depending on the river level. When the time is right, the whole village, led by the king in a ceremonial barge, moves to high ground.

➤ APR.: The **Two Oceans Marathon** draws 8,000 runners for perhaps the most scenic race in the world, a grueling 56-km (35-mi) course that circumnavigates part of the Cape Peninsula.

➤ APR.: **Splashy Fenn,** in KwaZulu-Natal, is one of the most popular music festivals in South Africa. Originally concentrating on folk music, it is rapidly becoming more contemporary.

➤ LATE APR.: The 100-km (60-mi) **Tour d' Urban** cycle race is held on the last Sunday of April.

➤ MAY: The **Pink Loerie Festival,** in the pretty coastal town of Knysna, is a celebration of gay pride and culture.

➤ JUNE: The **Comrades Marathon** is an agonizing 80-km (50-mi) double marathon and South Africa's most famous sporting event. The race, run between Pietermaritzburg and Durban, wends through the glorious scenery of the Valley of a Thousand Hills.

➤ JUNE–JULY: The **ragged tooth sharks** are in residence on the reefs of southern KwaZulu-Natal for their annual breeding season. Divers may visit them on escorted dives.

➤ JUNE–SEPT.: Yes, it's the **skiing season.** Not that it means a lot. Tiffindel, in the Eastern Cape, is South Africa's only ski resort. The skiing is far from the best in the world, but it's dependable, with snow guaranteed for three months.

➤ JULY: The **Durban July** is one of the country's biggest horse races and a definite fashion love fest, where race goers compete to wear the most outrageous, glamorous attire.

➤ JULY: The **Gunston 500 Surfing Championships,** which takes place in a number of centers along the coast, usually ending in Durban, draws the world's best to compete in the South African leg of the international surfing circuit.

➤ JULY: The **National Arts Festival** in Grahamstown is South Africa's most famous celebration of the arts, a wild and wacky 10-day extravaganza showcasing the best of South African theater, film, dance, music, and art.

➤ JULY: The **Knysna Oyster Festival** is about much more than oysters. The whole town puts on its finery. There are road races, mountain-bike races, cookouts and—of course—oysters, oysters, and oysters.

➤ AUG.: In early August the hills around Pretoria ring with music, as some of South Africa's best bands, and best partyers, assemble for the annual **Oppikoppi Music Festival.**

➤ AUG.: **Imana Wild Coast Challenge.** This mountain-bike ride of about 195 km (140 mi) traverses some of the most spectacular scenery in South Africa, skirting the beaches and cliffs of the Wild Coast and occasionally heading inland.

➤ AUG.–SEPT.: The **wildflowers of Namaqualand and the West Coast** are one

of nature's great spectacles, with bright spring blooms emerging in their millions from the seemingly barren semidesert. Several of the region's towns hold major flower festivals.

➤ AUG.–SEPT.: The **Umhlanga Ceremony** takes place every spring in Swaziland, when marriageable girls pay homage to the mother of the king by bringing her reeds to renew the enclosure around her house. Legend has it that if the girl is not a virgin, the reeds will wilt before delivery and be useless.

➤ AUG.–NOV.: The annual **whale migration** of southern right whales takes place along the coast from Port Elizabeth to Cape Town and beyond along the West Coast. In Cape Town and the Overberg they come very close to shore, giving even landlubbers a great view of these graceful leviathans.

➤ SEPT.: The **Natal Witness Hilton Arts Festival** showcases the pick of South African theater at Hilton College in the KwaZulu-Natal Midlands.

➤ SEPT.: It's really just a time of partying and a bit of hectic consumerism with a whale motif, but the **Hermanus Whale Festival** is fun nevertheless.

➤ SEPT.: The **Plett Eco Festival** is held the last week of the month in Plettenburg. Look for art exhibitions, sporting and environmental events, and a whale and dolphin symposium.

➤ OCT.: Purple **jacaranda blossoms** blanket both South Africa's and Zimbabwe's capital cities, Pretoria and Harare, respectively.

1 DESTINATION: SOUTHERN AFRICA

Ubuntu (It's About Being Human)

What's Where

Pleasures and Pastimes

Southern African Politics

Fodor's Choice

UBUNTU (IT'S ABOUT BEING HUMAN)

I WAS BORN IN THE SHADOW of Table Mountain and have lived close to its protective embrace ever since. I gazed at its eastern face, lighted by the rising sun, every morning on my way to school. It was my playground and my point of reference. I unconsciously absorbed something of this elemental rock and oriented my days around it. And then, as I got older, slowly I started moving farther afield—from the very tip of Africa north. As a student I had great dreams of traveling the world, but my budget limited me initially to long hikes in the Cedarberg, visits to the game reserves of KwaZulu-Natal, and, later, quick sorties to Zimbabwe, Namibia, or Botswana. Although I still hankered after exotic locations, I was starting to get hooked on what was on offer in my own backyard. I had fallen in love with the rocks and flowers of the Cedarberg, developed a strange longing for the smell of the bush, and started a lifelong fascination with the space, silence, surprisingly diverse life, and unbelievable stars of the Kalahari.

Although the scenery and game of southern Africa are always fantastic, some of my most wonderful memories have involved chance encounters with people. For instance, I once spent a few hours sitting in the sun waiting for a bus in Mozambique, and by the time it arrived and I clambered on, I was all hot and sweaty. A few miles farther on the bus conductor leaned out the door and bought two green coconuts. He kept one and handed me the other, seeing by my pink-flushed face that I was in need of cool sustenance. On another occasion, I'd been trekking through the Transkei, and (yes, I know) I wanted to check my voice mail. I wandered around, cell phone in hand looking for a signal, when I noticed someone waving from a nearby hut. I approached and saw an elderly woman, bent over almost double and wearing a traditional headdress. She pointed in the opposite direction to the one I'd been heading and, speaking no English, repeated the one word *phezulu,* which means "on top." I followed her advice and headed to the lowish hill she had pointed out instead of the more distant one I had

decided on and, sure enough, got excellent reception. Africa always has some surprise up its sleeve.

The first time I saw a caracal was not in a game park—but on the side of the national road at 4 in the morning as I drove to a distant destination. On a boat transfer to the airport in Mozambique, I saw a dugong, slowly turning to look at me before diving back to the turtle grass. A humpback whale surfaced mere yards from my kayak while I was paddling in Plett. I remember the first time I rode an elephant—the texture of its rough skin under my hands. Once I galloped with a herd of zebra, their striped rumps all around me in the dust-filtered light of a delta sunset while my sturdy, dependable mount kept pace.

The sense of wonder I have for the southern part of Africa never fades but grows stronger and stronger the more I see. I can be transported to another realm by gazing at rock paintings, trying to imagine the inspiration for these glowing artworks. And Africa is probably the best place to ponder the mysteries of our existence and our origins, as it seems that this is where we became human. It was here we first learned to walk on our own two, rather unusually shaped, feet. Here we explored the possibilities afforded us by our wondrous thumbs, and it's probably here we learned to speak and to harness the power of the sun and lightning—confining it to temporary hearths—using it to define our existence, to set us apart.

And we continue to experiment with new ways of living, new ways of interacting. Sometimes a seemingly good idea can go horribly wrong, as is happening with the political unrest in Zimbabwe as I write this, and sometimes we seem to get it right. South Africa is the newest democracy in the world. It's a place where we are actively and consciously trying to change the way we relate to other people. Our democracy is built on a fledgling culture of forgiveness, a culture of understanding. It's not actually anything new. It's just a new take on the old African concept of *ubuntu*—the principle that we exist solely because others exist. We are defined by our interaction with other people.

Come and see for yourself. Come and play in our forests, frolic in our oceans and rivers, inhale the heady perfume of our flowers and veld. Marvel at our wildlife, sit down around a fire under the star-studded sky, and share with us. Share our memories and our dreams, our concerns and our hopes, as we explore our history to forge a future.

Pliny the Elder had it right way back in AD 77 when he said, "*Ex Africa semper aliquid novi*"—Out of Africa, always something new.

— By Jennifer Stern

WHAT'S WHERE

Johannesburg and Surroundings
A mile high, South Africa's largest city sprawls across the highveld plateau, its soaring skyscrapers giving way to endless suburbs. Johannesburg was built—literally and figuratively—on gold, and the relentless pursuit of wealth has imbued it with a pulsing energy. Much of the antiapartheid struggle was played out in the dusty black townships ringing the city, and a tour of Soweto and the city center will give you a feel for the new South Africa.

Mpumalanga, Northern Province, and Kruger National Park
Classic Africa—the Africa of heat, thorn trees, and big game—unfolds before you in Mpumalanga and the Northern Province, on the Mozambique border. The great allure here is game watching, either in famed Kruger National Park or in an exclusive private reserve. But the area has much more to offer than animals. The Drakensberg (Afrikaans for "Dragon Mountains" divides the subtropical lowveld from the high interior plateau. Tucked away in these mountains of mists, forests, waterfalls, and panoramic views lie some of South Africa's most luxurious hotels and lodges, as well as beautiful hikes, river trips, horse trails, and historic gold-rush towns. In the far northeast the mysterious Venda region is a land of strange forests, of myth and legend.

Cape Town and the Peninsula
Capetonians tend to look with pity on those who don't have the good fortune to live in their Eden. Their attitude is understandable—Cape Town is indeed one of the world's fairest cities. Backed by Table Mountain, the city presides over a coastline of unsurpassed beauty: of mountains cascading into the sea, miles of beaches, and 17th-century wineries snoozing under giant oaks. Modern South Africa was born here, and the city is filled with historic reminders of its three centuries as the sea link between Europe and the East.

The Western Cape
This diverse region serves as the weekend playground for Capetonians. The jewel of the province is the Winelands, a stunning collection of jagged mountains, vine-covered slopes, and centuries-old Cape Dutch estates that produce some of the world's finest wine. Farther afield, the Overberg is a quiet region of farms and beach resorts that ends at Cape Agulhas, the southernmost tip of Africa. The long, lonely coastline is a marvel of nature—rocky mountains dropping sheer to the sea, pristine beaches, and towering dunes. The west coast and Namaqualand is a desolate landscape dotted with tiny fishing villages and isolated diamond mines. Every spring the semidesert region's wildflower explosion is a nonpareil sight. Inland, the Cedarberg Mountains offer fantastic scenery and hiking.

The Northern Cape
A rugged, lonely land, much of it with vistas of desert and semidesert, the Northern Cape reaches across a third of South Africa and incorporates some of the country's most unforgettable travel destinations. Along the country's northwestern seaboard lies Namaqualand, which each year produces a springtime paradise of wildflowers famous the world over. In the central north is the Kalahari, a harsh landscape of dunes and scrub that, surprisingly, offers superb game viewing. On the province's eastern border and in the country's geographical center lies the historic city of Kimberley, where diamonds have been mined for 130 years.

The Garden Route and Little Karoo

The Garden Route is a beautiful 208-km (130-mi) stretch of coast that takes its name from the region's year-round riot of vegetation. Here you'll find some of South Africa's most inspiring scenery: forest-cloaked mountains, myriad rivers and streams, and golden beaches backed by thick, indigenous bush. You'll also find Plettenberg Bay, South Africa's glitziest beach resort, and Knysna, a charming town built around an oyster-rich lagoon. The Little Karoo, separated from the coast by the Outeniqua Mountains, is a semiarid region famous for its ostrich farms, turn-of-the-20th-century "feather palaces," and the Cango Caves, one of the world's most impressive networks of underground caverns.

Eastern Cape

The Eastern Cape is South Africa's most diverse province: small, sleepy cities; long deserted beaches; fabulous mountain wildernesses; huge game reserves; fascinating villages; and myriad wonderful cultural attractions. The Eastern Cape probably has the most interesting cultural heritage of any South African province, with a long history of resistance to colonialism and apartheid. It was here that South Africans of various hues and political persuasions first met. The British colonialists, the Boer settlers, the Xhosa tribespeople, the Khoi herders, and the San hunters all had intense clashes in this historically rich region.

Durban and KwaZulu-Natal

Steamy heat, the heady aroma of spices, and a polyglot of English, Hindi, and Zulu give the bustling port city of Durban a tropical feel. Some of the country's most popular bathing beaches extend north and south of the city; inland you can tour the battlefields where Boer, Briton, and Zulu struggled for control of the country. The Drakensberg is a breathtaking sanctuary of soaring beauty, crisp air, and some of the country's best hiking. In the far north Hluhluwe-Umfolozi and several private reserves have wildlife rivaling that of Mpumalanga.

Swaziland

From rolling hills in the northwest to the purple Lubombo Mountains in the east, Swaziland has the look of an African paradise, where you can explore crafts markets, ride horses through the Ezulwini Valley, and raft the mighty Usutu River. There is fantastic hiking in the Malalotja Nature Reserve, in the north, and game viewing in Hlane, Mkhaya, and Mlawula, in the southern part of the country.

Zimbabwe

Zimbabwe has wonderful game reserves, luxury lodging, fantastic scenery, hair-raising white-water rafting, and wonderfully friendly people. Unfortunately, recent political developments have had disastrous effects on its infrastructure, particularly its fuel supply. This is not a good choice for a self-drive vacation. However, many tourist destinations—such as Victoria Falls—have been virtually unaffected, and you can still fly in as part of a travel package.

Botswana

Botswana is a natural wonder. Its variety of terrains, from vast salt pans to the waterways of the Okavango Delta to the Kalahari Desert, have a diversity seldom found in such a small area. And with so little industry blotting the sky, the stars may seem brighter than you have ever seen them. The Kalahari Bushmen say that you can hear the stars sing—listen.

Namibia

Although all the countries in southern Africa are beautiful, perhaps there's none quite as spectacularly unique as Namibia. Huge canyons, eerie desertscapes, dramatic coastlines, and Etosha National Park all vie for your attention. Hand in hand with some of Africa's most awesome wilderness goes a first-world infrastructure and German efficiency—the legacy of more than 100 years of colonial rule. You'll also encounter a strong sense of quiet here, as Namibia has fewer people per square mile than almost anywhere else in Africa.

Lesotho

Lesotho is a tiny country entirely within South Africa's borders. With its lowest point about 5,000 ft above sea level, it is one of the most mountainous regions in southern Africa. Although newish tarred roads allow easy access to some of the major attractions, the country's infrastructure is rather rudimentary. The main attractions are hiking, pony trails, and four-wheel-drive excursions—on what passes for roads in some parts.

Mozambique

Once the most fashionable destination in southern Africa, Mozambique has had a series of disasters—political as well as natural. Hit by cyclones and devastating floods shortly after years of horrific war, this lovely country nevertheless retains its allure. Azure seas, snowy beaches, crystalline waters, waving palms, smiling people, abundant seafood, and a languid tropical climate attract more than just the scuba divers and anglers who flock to the coastal resorts in droves.

Zambia

Zambia is one of the finest safari destinations in Africa. The parks are huge, isolated, and surprisingly unspoiled. There are simple campsites near or in all major reserves for those on a budget, but the more upmarket game lodges will not disappoint. Walking safaris in Kafue or Luangwa and canoeing safaris along the Zambezi are some of the finest wildlife experiences in the world. And for the truly wild at heart, there's rafting below Victoria Falls in awesome Batoka Gorge.

Malawi

Malawi is a long, thin country whose borders are defined by the incredibly beautiful Lake Malawi. It markets itself as the warm heart of Africa, and it's not far off. The people are friendly, and the weather is warm. The main attraction is the lake— for paddling on, lounging next to, and swimming in. Diving and snorkeling are also excellent, with hundreds of species of colorful freshwater tropical fish. It's not as good a game destination as some other southern African countries—Zimbabwe, Zambia, Botswana, and South Africa— but Liwonde National Park has large herds of elephants, lions, and other animals, and the high-altitude Nyika National Park has montane grassland and unique faunal and floral assemblage.

PLEASURES AND PASTIMES

Air Sports and Aviation

Southern Africa has some fantastic paragliding and hang-gliding venues. Cape Town, the Garden Route, and the Drakensberg are favorite spots, while the hot Northern Cape is very popular for cross-country winch-launched flights. Namibia has one of the best gliding venues in the world. Going hot-air ballooning is a popular getaway from the city in the areas near Johannesburg. You can take an aerobatic flight near Cape Town or on the Garden Route, fly over Victoria Falls in a microlight, or do an aerial city tour of Johannesburg in a vintage plane. The sky's the limit.

Beaches

South Africa has some of the finest beaches on earth—hundreds of miles of white, soft, sandy beaches, often without a soul on them. The surf is big, and dangerous undertows and side washes are common, although there are also some wonderful, safe swimming beaches. Beaches in major cities have lifeguards, and helicopters periodically patrol the coastline. Cape Town and the entire Western Cape have glorious beaches, but the water is extremely cold year-round, and wind can be a problem. The water is warmer along the Garden Route, with the best swimming at Plettenberg Bay. Around Durban and the resorts of KwaZulu-Natal, the water is ideal for swimming. All major resort beaches in KwaZulu-Natal are protected by shark nets. For truly deserted beaches and warm water, head to Rocktail Bay Lodge, in the far north of KwaZulu-Natal. For great snorkeling and diving and fantastic warm-water swimming, you can't do better than one of the many resorts in Mozambique. And don't disregard the lovely golden-sand beaches on the shores of Lake Malawi.

Big-Game Adventures

Southern Africa may not have the vast herds of East Africa, but it has far more species of animals. In fact, nowhere else on the continent do wild animals enjoy better protection than in southern Africa, and nowhere do you have a better chance of seeing Africa's big game. South Africa, Namibia, Zimbabwe, Zambia, and Swaziland all offer reasonably priced national parks, while Botswana deliberately keeps park entry fees high to minimize tourist damage. In almost every part of the region, though, you can find some exclusive paradise where you will be pampered in a luxury lodge.

Bird-Watching

South Africa ranks as one of the finest bird-watching destinations on the planet. Kruger National Park alone has recorded more than 500 bird species, many of breathtaking beauty. Birds in Zimbabwe, Botswana, and Namibia are spectacular as well. Look for sacred ibis, a variety of eagles and falcons and vultures, red- and yellow-billed hornbills, numerous egrets and storks, and the spectacularly beautiful lilac-breasted roller, to name a few. The best time for bird-watching is October–April, when migrants are in residence.

Canoeing and White-Water Rafting

From gentle scenic floats and short sea-kayak trips to hectic white-water or epic expeditions, southern Africa offers some of the best paddling around. Try the Orange River, on the border of South Africa and Namibia, for scenery and gentle rapids; the Kunene, on the border of Angola and Namibia, for white water, remoteness, and scenery; and the Tugela, in KwaZulu-Natal, the Usutu, in Swaziland, or the mighty Zambezi, on the border of Zimbabwe and Zambia, for white water.

Climbing

Southern Africa has some of the best rock climbing in the world—a fact hidden from the international climbing fraternity during the many years of political and sports isolation during the apartheid era. There are excellent venues all over the region, but Cape Town does stand out. With literally hundreds of bolted and natural climbing routes on good-quality sandstone and granite right within the city limits, this is surely one of the most climber-friendly cities in the world.

Cricket

White South Africans are crazy about cricket—during international matches you'll often find crowds gathered in pubs around large-screen televisions. A major push is under way to introduce cricket into black communities, but it remains essentially a white sport.

Cycling

You can do a gentle cycle through the Winelands of the Cape or to the scenic Cape Point or across the bridge at Victoria Falls. There are great mountain biking trails all over South Africa, and the whole of Lesotho is mountain biking heaven. You can even do a big game safari by bike in Swaziland or Botswana. If you're a keen cyclist, the Argus Cycle Tour, in Cape Town in March, is the biggest individually timed event in the world. It's 115 km (about 70 mi) long, and contestants number more than 30,000.

Dining

Southern Africa won't unseat France anytime soon from its culinary throne. But there are four bright spots that you should keep in mind. The first is the abundance of fresh seafood, from plump Knysna oysters to enormous Mozambican prawns to the local lobsters, known as crayfish. The second is the country's love affair with Indian cuisine, first brought to South Africa by indentured laborers in the 19th century. Samosas and curries appear on almost every menu. The third is South Africa's own Cape Malay cuisine, a centuries-old blend of recipes brought by early Dutch settlers and slaves transported from the Dutch East Indies. Most evident in the Cape, the cuisine is characterized by mild, fruity curries and the use of aromatic spices. And last is the ubiquitous *braai*. This is a South African institution of note—and it really is so much more than the average barbecue. As well as meat of all kinds, including the essential *boerewors* (sausages), there is also fish, crayfish tails, spicy *sosaties* (kebabs), *pap en sous* (cornmeal), and the inevitable *potjiekos* (stew). And, of course, no braai is complete without beer.

A brief glossary of cooking terms:

Biltong. An integral part of South African life, biltong is air-dried meat, made of everything from beef to kudu. Unlike jerky, it's not smoked. Strips of meat are dipped in vinegar, rolled in salt and spices, and hung up to dry. You can buy it in strips, ready-cut into bite-size chunks, or grated—which is often served on bread and butter.

Bobotie. A classic Cape Malay dish consisting of delicately spiced ground beef or lamb topped with a savory custard.

Boerewors. Afrikaans for farmer's sausage (pronounced "*boo*-rah-vorse"), this coarse, flavorful sausage has a distinctive spiciness. It's a standard feature at *braai*s.

Bredie. Bredie is a slow-cooked stew, usually made with lamb and green beans, tomatoes, or *waterblommetjies*—indigenous water flowers.

Bunny chow. It's not a fancy name for salad. This Durban dish is a half loaf of bread hollowed out and filled with meat or vegetable curry.

Gatsby. Often eaten on the streets of Cape Town (and only in Cape Town), this is a whole loaf of bread cut in half lengthwise and filled with fish or meat with lettuce, tomato, and french fries.

Line fish. This is the generic restaurant term for fish caught on a line, as opposed to a net, and the assumption is that quality is better as a result. Kingklip is one very common and tasty line fish. If you ever see *galjoen* on the menu, order it (don't even try to pronounce it—just point). It's South Africa's national fish—endemic, not very common, and quite distinctive in taste and texture, with lightly marbled flesh.

Pap. Also known as *putu, sadza* in Zimbabwe, and *nshima* in Zambia, pap (pronounced "pup") is a maize-meal porridge that is a staple for many black South Africans. At braais you may find it served as an accompaniment to boerewors, topped with stewed tomato and onion—and referred to as *pap en sous* (pronounced "*sew*-ss").

Peppadews. This is a pretty weird but wonderfully tasty delicacy. It's a patented vegetable, so you may see it under different names, usually with the word *dew* in them. It's a sort of a cross between a sweet pepper and a chili and is usually sold pickled. It's delicious in everything from salads to pizza to pasta.

Peri-Peri. Based on the searing hot *piri-piri* chili, peri-peri sauce was introduced by Portuguese immigrants from neighboring Mozambique. There are as many recipes as there are uses for this tasty condiment and marinade. Some recipes are tomato-based, while others use garlic, olive oil, and brandy.

Potjie. Sometimes called potjiekos, this is another type of stew (pronounced "*poy*-key"), simmered in a three-legged wrought-iron cooking pot (the potjie itself). Visitors to private game lodges are likely to sample venison potjiekos at least once during their stay.

Sosaties. In this South African version of a kebab, chunks of meat are marinated in Cape Malay spices and grilled.

Fishing

South Africans are among the most avid anglers in the world. During peak holidays the long coastline is lined with surf casters trying for everything from cob to stump nose, rock cod, shad, and blacktail. Fly-fishing is a major draw. There are numerous trout dams and streams in all the high-lying areas, but the indigenous yellow fish is considered a greater challenge. In the Okavango Delta and all along the Zambezi River you can try to bag an aptly named tiger fish—an incredibly strong fighter, with jaws like a bear trap. It makes a bass look like a bluegill.

Flora

South Africa's floral wealth is astounding. Many small parks in South Africa support more plant species than the entire North American continent. Nowhere is this blessing of nature more evident than in the Cape, home to the smallest and richest of the world's six floral kingdoms. More than 8,500 species of plants grow in the province, of which 5,000 are endemic. Much of the Cape vegetation consists of *fynbos* (pronounced "*feign*-boss"), hardy, thin-leaved plants ideally suited to the Cape environment. Proteas, including the magnificent king protea, are examples of fynbos. In the northern Cape's Namaqualand, on the country's west coast, an annual show of spring flowers—including billions of orange Namaqualand daisies—is a spectacular wonder unrivaled anywhere else on earth.

Golf

The success of local heroes like Gary Player, David Frost, and Ernie Els confirms that golf in South Africa has a fervent following. The country has dozens of championship-quality courses, many designed by Gary Player himself. The stretch of coastline extending south from Durban has gone as far as to christen itself the Gold Coast, but it has serious competition from the Garden Route. You can play on almost any course in the country, and greens fees are low compared with those in the United States.

Hiking

Hiking is a major activity in South Africa, and you'll find trails almost everywhere you go. Perhaps the most exciting hikes are the wilderness trails conducted by rangers in Kruger National Park and Hluhluwe-Umfolozi, where you sleep out in the bush and spend the day tracking animals, learning about the ecology, and becoming familiar with the ways of the wild. The country's most popular route is the Otter Trail, a five-day hike that runs along the coast of the Garden Route. Other hikes, ranging in length from a couple of hours to a week, wend through the scenic splendors of the Drakensberg, the Cedarberg, in the Cape, and the Mpumalanga and Northern Province escarpment and forests.

Lesotho has fantastic but rather hardcore hiking through its endless highlands, and the Malalotja Nature Reserve, in Swaziland, has wonderful montane grassland hiking trails. In most other southern African countries hiking is limited to escorted walking safaris, although Zimbabwe's Eastern Highlands are also a favorite destination. Hiking is not recommended in Mozambique because of the possibility of stepping on a land mine in remote areas. Malawi has lovely high-altitude hiking in the flower-, bird-, and game-rich Nyika Plateau National Park.

Horse Trails

There are fantastic horse trails, ranging from a gentle stroll through the vineyards of the Cape or a quick canter on the beach to a hectic expedition through big-game country in Zimbabwe or Botswana. Most of the latter are only for experienced riders, as you ride among big game such as elephants, lions, or buffalo. There is a very strenuous trail through the Namib Desert and a lovely ride through Malawi's Nyika Plateau.

Rugby

Although long associated with white Afrikaners, rugby became a unifying force in South Africa during the 1995 Rugby World Cup, when South Africa's Springboks beat the New Zealand All Blacks in the final, sparking a nationwide celebration among all races. The audience is still mostly white, but it is changing. The national side, too, is slowly losing its pale complexion—first with the legendary stalwart, Chester Williams, and then the brilliant and diminutive Breyton Paulse, who was shortly followed by fullback Conrad Jantjies. Rugby is taken very, very seriously in South Africa and inspires a devotion bordering on religion. In addition to a series of international matches staged each year, the rugby calendar is notable for the Currie Cup, played to decide the best provincial team in the country.

Scuba Diving

Diving in southern Africa ranges from the icy kelp forests off Cape Town to the warm, tropical coral reefs of Mozambique or northern Maputaland, in KwaZulu-Natal. There are dive shops, schools, and resorts all along the coast and in Gauteng. There are also some good diving and dedicated dive centers in Malawi, where the water is warm, clear, and fresh and filled with colorful little tropical fish.

Soccer

If rugby is what gets white South African men out of bed on a weekend, soccer does the same for their black counterparts. Sure, there is an increasing overlap, but each game is still quite culture specific. And soccer is taken every bit as seriously as rugby.

Surfing

In the cult movie *Endless Summer,* globe-trotting surfers discovered the perfect wave at Cape St. Francis, near Port Elizabeth. South Africa *is* one of the major surfing countries in the world, with South Africans figuring prominently on the professional circuit. Durban is probably the center of wave mania, hosting a series of international competitions each year; other great surfing spots include Jeffrey's Bay and East London. The beaches around Cape Town and up the West Coast (Elands Bay, in particular) are popular, too, although you need a good wet suit to survive the cold water. The Wild Coast has some fantastic surf, but the best beaches are pretty remote. There's also some excellent surf in Mozambique, particularly Ponta do Ouro, Ponta Malongane, and Tofu, near Inhambane. The water off the Namibian coast is freezing, but there are some spectacularly long breaks (of more than half a mile—no kidding).

Wine

Forgotten during the years of international sanctions, South African wines are only now getting the recognition they deserve. Visitors will be delighted by the quality and range of wines available, including pinotage, a uniquely South African blend of pinot noir and cinsault (or cinsaut) grapes (cinsault is known in South Africa as Hermitage). Equally appealing are the low, low prices: Expect to pay no more than $10 for a fantastic bottle of wine and $20 for a superb one. Unfortunately, wine prices are almost doubled in restaurants but are still pretty reasonable. Zimbabwe, too, has a fledgling wine industry, but the results, while drinkable, are more of a curiosity than anything.

SOUTHERN AFRICAN POLITICS

Politics is about power and access to resources, and perhaps that's what makes southern African politics so confusing. In the tribal system, which is basically a benevolent dictatorship, everything was owned by the community, or the chief, which amounted to the same thing. And the chief would decide on the use of this communal property, although he would be guided by a council. Botswana is one place where this time-honored practice is still seen. Each person owns his or her own *kgotla* chair—a light but sturdy folding chair that is easy to carry, so it can be taken into the central *kgotla*, or meeting place. And though elements of the tribal system remain in deep rural areas, in general, African politics has changed to fit the European mold.

The parliaments of most southern African countries are headed by the party that grew out of that country's liberation movement—South Africa's ANC (African National Congress), Namibia's SWAPO (South West Africa People's Organization), Zimbabwe's ZANU-PF (Zimbabwe African National Union–Patriotic Front), and Mozambique's FRELIMO (Frente de Liberta Vão de Mozambique). And in many cases this postcolonial government created a one-party state, either by design or default.

Malawi was a one-party dictatorship under Hastings Banda's Malawi Congress Party until 1993, when alternative political parties were allowed. The United Democratic Front, led by Bakili Muluzi, won the first multiparty election in 1994 and has been in power ever since. Zambia was a one-party state, under the leadership of Kenneth Kaunda, from 1972 until 1991. Kaunda's well-meaning assistance to the liberation struggles of other southern African countries, not least of which was the one in South Africa; the consistently falling price of copper; and his well-intentioned attempt to institute a form of African socialism resulted in serious economic woes. In the first multiparty elections he was ousted by Frederick Chiluba, who is still Zambia's president. Although Namibia is in name a multiparty democracy, SWAPO is pretty unassailable. South Africa is also a multiparty democracy, but the ANC holds more than 50% of the seats in parliament, and there is no real opposition, despite some rather strange alliances that have come and gone. Botswana is a multiparty democracy, although the Botswana Democratic Party (BDP) holds an enormous majority. In 1999 Festus Mogae became the third president since independence, in 1966.

Two rather unusual exceptions to this democratic model are Swaziland and Lesotho, both of which are constitutional monarchies. In both cases the king has very real power but is guided by parliament. In Swaziland, in particular, the king's authority has been challenged by trade unions and other progressive forces.

Zimbabwe is a sad and interesting case. On independence, in 1980, many held out great hope for this wonderful country—so much so that a blind eye was turned to the systematic destruction of all opposition Robert Mugabe's ZANU (later ZANU-PF) party. Zimbabwe has two major tribal groupings—the Shona and the Ndebele. Mugabe's party is mainly Shona, and the Ndebele, who live in the southeastern part of the country, are—to put it in Orwellian terms—less equal. Since independence all public facilities in Matabeleland have been neglected in favor of the areas in which Mugabe has a loyal following. In 1992 the first land expropriations took place—relatively peacefully. Productive farms, mostly owned by whites, were taken—to be given to the landless, who are mostly black—but were instead given to cabinet ministers and other political favorites. This continued quietly until, in 2000, the system became even more ominous, with farms given to groups of "war veterans," many of whom were born a few years after the end of the war of liberation. Although there is a parliament in Zimbabwe, Mugabe has mostly ignored its authority. A presidential election took place in early 2002, but Mugabe denied access to foreign election monitors and threatened foreign journalists reporting on the election with trial by military tribunal. The very popular Movement for Democratic Change (MDC), led by Morgan Tsvangirai, has been subject to intense intimidation, and many observers fear for Tsvangirai's life. Time will tell.

FODOR'S CHOICE

Special Moments

South Africa

A sunset picnic atop Table Mountain, Cape Town. Pack a bottle of chilled Cape wine and good bread and cheese, and take the cable car to the summit, where views stretch forever and sunset never quits. Warning: This is *extremely* romantic.

Walking in wildflowers in spring, Namaqualand. The "garden of the gods" is an apt epithet for the annual wildflower spectacle, when the drab desert hillsides explode in a rainbow of colors.

Watching whales on the Cape Coast. From July to November southern right whales make their annual procession up the coast of South Africa. From the cliff-top walkways of Hermanus you look straight down on these graceful behemoths, or get a closer view from a boat in Plettenberg Bay.

Hiking at Cathedral Peak, Drakensberg. The awe-inspiring beauty of the mountains around Cathedral Peak makes it a hiker's dream, with dozens of walks and trails that tackle the surrounding peaks or disappear into hidden gorges and valleys. Take a cooling dip in a mountain stream, search for ancient Bushman paintings, or just drink in the unbelievable views.

A game drive in the bushveld. Few things in life are more thrilling than trailing a pride of lions through the bush in an open Land Rover.

Zimbabwe

Soaking in the peace of Matobo. The silence, the space, and the sheer volume of solid rock under you gives you a sense of the immense power of the earth. It is a truly spectacular place and one that is considered holy by residents of many cultural heritages and religions.

Botswana

Messing about in a *mokoro*. Glide silently with your solitary, skillful poler through the crystal-clear waters of the Okavango Delta. It will be a moment of peace that will return to you long after you've left the delta and Africa behind.

Stargazing in the Kalahari. Nowhere on earth will you see stars brighter than in the Kalahari, where the glittering sky curves down to the horizon on every side of you.

Namibia

Etosha National Park. After supper take a blanket and a flask of coffee and await the nightly performance as a huge variety of animals come to drink at the floodlighted water hole on the edge of the camp.

The Skeleton Coast. Experience the rugged, untamed beauty of this dangerous coast, with its shipwrecks, rolling fogs, and array of unique flora and fauna, one of the last true wilderness areas of the world.

Sossusvlei. Watch the sun rise or begin to set over the highest and possibly most beautiful sand dunes in the world. To watch the colors change from pale honey to amber, rose, russet, and deep pink is a memorable—and spiritual—experience.

Zambia

White-water rafting on the Zambezi River, below Victoria Falls. A white-water trip down one of Africa's great rivers is a nonstop roller-coaster ride of thrills and spills, with the added grandeur and drama of the surrounding landscape.

Walking safari in South Luangwa National Park. Deep into the bush, far from any semblance of civilization, these walking trails are considered by many to be the ultimate wildlife experience.

Picnic on the edge of the abyss. Organize a picnic brunch, lunch, or high tea on Livingstone Island, on the very edge of Victoria Falls, to give new meaning to a "view" with your meal.

Lesotho, Mozambique, Malawi

Ride a pony across the Roof of Africa, Lesotho. Time stands still as you ride like the locals do across this high, remote mountain kingdom.

Eat prawns by the bucketful, Mozambique. Relax on a shady veranda overlooking the sea and munch away on Mozambique's famed seafood to your heart's content.

Diving the Indian Ocean coral reefs, Mozambique. Glide gently through crystal-clear warm water surrounded by flittering schools of colorful tropical fish, or hang suspended in awe as a whale shark or manta ray swims past.

Paddle the Lake of Stars, Malawi. Lake Malawi shimmers in the sunlight, reflecting light in myriad star points. The water is warm and calm, and you can paddle between beautiful deserted islands where you stay in comfortable tented camps.

Dining

South Africa

Bosman's, Paarl. Superb Continental cuisine and peerless service make dinner at this elegant Winelands restaurant in the famous Grand Roche Hotel an affair to remember. $$$$

Buitenverwachting, Cape Town. A gorgeous, historical winery provides the backdrop for the best food in the Cape, a mouthwatering blend of Continental savoir faire and the freshest Cape ingredients. Simply not to be missed. $$$$

Linger Longer, Johannesburg. When goose-liver pâté sets you on cloud nine before you even reach main courses of crisped duckling or boned loin of lamb with garlic and mustard, you'll know that, without a doubt, this is Johannesburg's finest. $$$$

Royal Grill, Durban. This lovely restaurant is a standard-bearer of culture in Durban, a reminder of a grander, more gracious age. Delicate Continental cuisine complements its turn-of-the-20th-century elegance. $$$$

Cybele Forest Lodge, Kiepersol. Traditional five-course dinners, prepared with flair and skill, make a trip to this cozy sanctuary in the hills well worthwhile. $$$–$$$$

Jemima's Restaurant, Oudtshoorn. Enjoy the best of the fruits of Cape farming in this family-run restaurant where the majority of the raw ingredients come from the farm back home. Charm, friendly service, great food local wines, olive oils, and preserves make this a winner. $$–$$$

Muisbosskerm, Lambert's Bay. Traditional Afrikaner food and alfresco dining on the beach are the draws of this west-coast favorite, where you watch seafood being cooked on open fires and in huge black pots. It's rustic, beautiful, and a lot of fun. $$

Lodging

South Africa

Cape Grace, Cape Town. On the V&A Waterfront, this hotel combines majestic views with attentive service and a sophisticated atmosphere. $$$$

Cleopatra Mountain Farmhouse. An enchanting hideaway tucked away at the foot of the Drakensberg Mountain Range. $$$$

Mount Nelson, Cape Town. The grand old dame of Cape Town, this historic hotel has been the place to see and be seen in Cape Town for nearly a century. $$$$

Saxon, Johannesburg. The beautiful grounds, impeccable service, and luxurious rooms here will make you feel that you've found an enchanted oasis. $$$$

Assegai Lodge, Grahamstown. Host Savvas and resident butler Sean will ensure that your stay at the eastern Cape's oldest surviving building will be memorable. Yard-thick walls with rifle slots echo a long and documented history. $$$

Bitou River Lodge, Plettenberg Bay. This is one of the most soothing locations in South Africa. Restful rooms overlook a tranquil garden and quiet, bird-filled river. And at the reasonable B&B rates, you can afford to spend a week or two here just chilling. But the hub of Plettenberg Bay is a mere 10 minute's drive. $$$

Victoria Junction, Cape Town. This loft-style minimalist hotel is a refreshing change from the usual city lodging choices. The staff is young, funky, and superefficient. $$–$$$

Zimbabwe

Victoria Falls Hotel, Victoria Falls. The very walls of this lovely old hotel seem aware of their history, and the dedicated staff works diligently to live up to it. The views are great, and the food is excellent. *$$$*

Zambia

The River Club, Livingstone. The center of this lovely lodge is an old farmhouse redolent with history. Rowing races were held in front of the sweeping lawns, among the hippos and crocs, as the many photographs on the walls attest. The colonial feel continues with late-night croquet games. *$$$$*

Tongabezi, Livingstone. Colonial finesse meets arcadian Africa on the bank of the mighty Zambezi River. Choose the Tree House, Bird House, or Honeymoon Suite for the most romantic and breathtaking bush accommodations in Africa. Then enjoy a game of tennis followed by gin and tonics and champagne. *$$$$*

Lesotho and Mozambique

Hotel Polana, Maputo, Mozambique. Timeless elegance, attentive service, and wonderful views over the bay of Maputo make this one of the great hotels of Africa. *$$*

Malealea Lodge, Lesotho. This lovely, friendly lodge is pretty basic but very comfortable. Centered around a country trading post, it's been in the same family for generations and is the best place to base yourself for hiking, mountain biking, or pony trekking. *$*

Private Game Lodges

South Africa

Earth Lodge, Sabi Sabi. Less is certainly more at the daringly different Earth Lodge, a cross between a Hopi cave dwelling and a medieval keep, and like no other lodge in southern Africa. *$$$$*

Londolozi Tree Camp, Sabi Sands. This small lodge does almost everything right, from having rooms of unmatched elegance to providing superb cuisine and game viewing. It's a class act all the way. *$$$$*

Phinda Forest Lodge, Zululand. Hidden in the green world of a sand forest, this elegant lodge uses glass instead of walls to make you feel like you're living outside. The effect is startling and magnificent, as are the animal watching and range of activities. *$$$$*

Tanda Tula, Timbavati. You sleep under canvas, but luxury is the name of the game at this super bush camp. Enjoy private bathrooms, comfy beds, and tasteful furnishings while listening to lions roar outside your tent. *$$$$*

Tswalu Kalahari Reserve, Northern Cape. The location, in the southern Kalahari, gives this lodge an otherworldly feel and appeal. The luxurious accommodations set amid red dunes and beneath a blue sky make Tswalu unique in Africa. *$$$$*

Rocktail Bay Lodge, Maputaland. With miles of empty beaches, giant turtles, dune forests—nothing but nature as far as the eye can see—this tiny lodge is one of the most special places in the country. *$$$*

Zimbabwe

Matusadona Water Wilderness, Kariba. All afloat in a tiny cove on a wide, wide dam. Wooden chalets built on huge pontoons are tethered to semisubmerged trees. Elephants come to drink mere yards from your doorstep, and birds perch on your railings. *$$$$*

Ruckomechi Camp, Mana Pools. The Zambezi River coursing by on one side, fertile terraces reaching back to thick woodlands, and the country's finest wildlife make time spent at Ruckomechi an African idyll. *$$$$*

Botswana

Duba Plains, Okavango Delta. This intimate, tented safari camp tucked into the delta's farthest reaches is surrounded by an abundance of game. The private island setting only adds to its unique quality. *$$$$*

Jack's Camp, Makgadikgadi Pans. At the only desert camp in the harshly mesmerizing Kalahari, venture into the impenetrable Makgadikgadi salt pans on four-wheel-drive quad bikes, search for Stone Age implements where no one may have set foot for eons, and sleep out under the desert stars. *$$$$*

Kwando Reserve, Chobe area. The Kwando wildlife experience captures the essence of Botswana—ancient, immense, and unspoiled. With only two camps of six tents apiece, you are guaranteed exclusivity and privacy as you watch wall-to-wall big game in a half-million acres of uncharted wilderness. *$$$$*

Xigera, Moremi Game Reserve. Overlooking the floodplain, this camp offers mokoro and boat safaris and has access to water year-round. Old-fashioned elegance and comfort await you when you return to the lovely camp. *$$$$*

Namibia

Ongava Lodge, Etosha National Park. Set on the southern boundary of Etosha, this luxurious and beautifully sited lodge has its own surrounding game reserve as well as its own entrance into Etosha. *$$$$*

Sossusvlei Mountain Lodge, Sossusvlei. Desert villas at the foot of ancient mountains are built of natural rock here and look out over a plain ringed by peaks. It would be difficult to match their luxury anywhere else in Namibia. *$$$$*

Wilderness Damaraland Camp, Damaraland. From your comfortable walk-in tent look out over a landscape of awesome craggy beauty formed by millions of years of unending geological movement. *$$$$*

Skeleton Coast Camp, Skeleton Coast Park. If you long for one of the most remote wilderness areas on earth, you won't find a more desolate and unique spot than this camp, in the 660,000 acres of the Skeleton Coast National Park. *$$$$*

2 JOHANNESBURG AND ENVIRONS

Vast in size and in human ambition, Johannesburg is built on gold, and the relentless pursuit of wealth has imbued it with a pulsing energy. Much of the country's antiapartheid struggle was played out in the dusty black townships ringing the city, and a tour of Soweto will give you a feel for the new South Africa. Arrange a trip down a gold mine, and then take yourself north to Pretoria, the genteel capital of South Africa, to the Cradle of Humankind, or to the Magaliesberg.

By Andrew
Barbour

Updated by
Jennifer Stern

THE LARGEST CITY IN SUB-SAHARAN AFRICA, Johannesburg is a modern, bustling metropolis that powers the country's economy. It is the center of a vast urban industrial complex that covers most of the province of Gauteng (roughly pronounced *how*-teng, Sotho for "place where the gold is"). Home to more than 6 million people, it sprawls across the featureless plains of the mile-high highveld, spawning endless suburbs that threaten even Pretoria, more than 50 km (30 mi) distant. It feels like Los Angeles in the veld, and most visitors leave almost as quickly as they arrive.

Jo'burg, as it is known, owes its existence to vast underground riches. Although substantial deposits were recorded as early as 1881, gold was officially discovered here in 1886 by an Australian, George Harrison, who stumbled on a surface deposit while prospecting on the Witwatersrand (White-Water Ridge). Unknown to him, he was standing atop the world's richest gold reef, and his discovery sparked a gold rush unrivaled in history. Gold remains the lifeblood of Johannesburg, and ringing the city are the mines, now descending more than 3 km (2 mi) into the earth, from which the precious yellow metal is extracted.

It's difficult to overstate the impact of these goldfields on the development of Johannesburg and modern South Africa. In 1899 Britain engineered a war with the Boer republic just to get its hands on them, and the entire cultural and political fabric of black South Africa has been colored by gold. Over the last century British and Irish fortune hunters, many of whom became wealthy mining magnates and settled in today's Parktown suburb, together with millions of blacks from South Africa, Mozambique, Zimbabwe, and Botswana, made the long journey to eGoli (a Zulu name meaning "the place of gold") to work in the mines. Forced to live in all-male hostels far from their families, the black mine workers developed a distinct mine culture that they took with them when they returned to their villages. Go to a wedding in a remote corner of Zululand, and you'll notice that traditional dancers keep their arms and legs close to their bodies, a dance style that developed from necessity in the mining hostels' narrow, overcrowded corridors. Today this dance has evolved into the stamping, rhythmic style called "gumboot dancing."

To understand Johannesburg, you have to think in four dimensions—the first three are height, depth, and width. It's one of the highest cities in the world, built on the deepest mines in the world, and it spreads out in every direction, devouring open land at an alarming pace, with subterranean connections that link it to its water supplies in faraway KwaZulu-Natal and even neighboring countries. The fourth dimension is time. It's a dynamic place that changes at a rate most visitors can't quite seem to understand, and the inhabitants of this frenetic city are constantly on the move.

Ever since the discovery of gold at the end of the 19th century, people have moved to, in, and around Johannesburg driven by need, greed, or just plain unbridled ambition. The miners' shacks gave way to the skyscrapers of downtown, and the rude dwellings of upwardly mobile adventurers became the opulent mansions of Parktown and Houghton. Black mine workers, whose presence was deemed undesirable in the midst of the nouveau riche, were moved away to the southwest fringes of the rapidly expanding city to what is now Soweto, an acronym for South Western Townships. The city grew up and out as the wealth poured in, and Hillbrow, near the city center, became the most happening place in South Africa from the 1950s through the 1980s. As the wealth congregated in one place, those who coveted that wealth homed in on it. In the 1980s and 1990s the affluent moved north to the northern suburbs to escape the crowding. Then the industries were slowly edged out of the city center, and the trend followers were edged out of Hillbrow, as the somewhat less legal aspect of the pursuit of wealth followed them. As businesses moved out to the north, Hillbrow became the de facto new central business district, and as the nightlife moved out to Yeoville, it became the new in spot. And sure enough, the crime followed to where the people and businesses had relocated.

Johannesburg is caught in this endless dance, as people pour in from all over the country and the continent following the lure of lucre. At the time of writing, Yeoville still is a place where only the desperate, brave, or adventurous venture at night, and Hillbrow has become a true African city, with a wild and wacky nightlife and a vibrant street culture. It's a place where you need to watch yourself and keep your wits about you, but carry very little else. The safe nightlife is now centered around the northern suburbs and Melville, in the east, or the sanitized indoor playgrounds of Gold Reef Casino or Montecasino. But Jo'burg has a few aces up its sleeve. Although most residents of the northern suburbs consider the city center a no-go area, it is poised on the brink of an economic and social revival. Watch this space.

Less than an hour north of Johannesburg lies Pretoria, the country's pleasant capital. Though it was once a bastion of hard-line Afrikanerdom, the town now has a refreshing cosmopolitan breeze blowing through the streets. In addition to its several historic buildings, Pretoria is renowned for its jacaranda trees, whose purple blossoms blanket the city in September and October. Like Johannesburg, Pretoria lies in the tiny province of Gauteng, a conurbation on the highveld, 6,000 ft above sea level. You have to travel 90 minutes beyond the borders of Gauteng to reach Sun City, an entertainment and gambling resort set amid the arid beauty of North West Province. You'll find Las Vegas–style hotels, championship golf courses, and water rides, as well as Pilanesberg, a pocket-size game reserve covering an ancient volcanic caldera.

Just on the outskirts of Johannesburg and Pretoria is the Cradle of Humankind and the Magaliesberg. The Cradle is a World Heritage Site with a spectacularly rich fossil record. It is there that the remains of the first hominid, *Australopithecus,* were found, as well as records of the earliest known use of fire. For the wild at heart who want to escape the city limits, the Magaliesberg area offers a restful break, with lovely mountain scenery, farmlands, and quiet country roads. You can take a hike; go hot-air ballooning, horseback riding, or mountain-bike riding; visit delightful roadside stalls; admire the scenic vistas across Hartbeespoort Dam; or explore country pubs or tea gardens.

Pleasures and Pastimes

Arts and Crafts
There is a plethora of art galleries and crafts outlets in the city. As well as indigenous crafts, Jo'burg is a good place to buy artifacts from the rest of Africa. Or head into the countryside on Johannesburg's northwestern side, where the region's creative talent hosts the wonderful Crocodile River Ramble. Drive down farm roads to visit the galleries and studios of artists, sculptors, potters, woodworkers, and others. You can do a specialized art trip to Soweto if you arrange one with a tour operator. The Magaliesberg is also an increasingly good spot to shop for art, as artists who want to leave the urban hustle often take refuge here.

Culture and History

If you are remotely interested in the adventure of being human, or in the history of South Africa, this is the place for you. The Cradle of Humankind is an absolute must-see if you are curious about your origins. A visit to Soweto or Alexandra is a window onto a totally new world for many people, and there are a number of museums and historical buildings that may give you an insight into the South African psyche.

Hiking

The Melville Koppies, near the suburb of Northcliff, have good places to walk—which are enhanced by the company of a member of the botanical society on the first, second, and third Sunday of every month. Hikers and climbers revel in the Magaliesberg region, a magnificent geologic fault that runs northwest of Johannesburg between Rustenburg and Pretoria.

Lodging

When you are choosing a hotel in Johannesburg, your most important consideration should be location. Almost all the main hotels in the the central business district (CBD) have closed down and been replaced by new ones in the northern suburbs. The smaller places, like Magaliesberg and the Cradle, have some delightful guest houses and B&Bs.

Outdoor Adventures

Although Johannesburg and its environs are decidedly urban, there are plenty of adventure opportunities. You can sand-board down a mine dump, go horseback riding through a small game reserve, do a tandem skydive, go hot-air ballooning, or fly in a vintage plane—all within an hour or two of the city.

Exploring Johannesburg and Environs

The city is growing rapidly, and the whole area from south of the city to Pretoria is one huge urban sprawl, with the northern suburbs, in effect, the new city center. Most visitors seem to be more comfortable in this glitzy First-World part of the city, and unless you are particularly interested in inner-city environments, you'll probably want to give the older city center a miss. However, at the time of writing, the city center is undergoing a face-lift, and more and more areas are slowly becoming accessible. If you are interested in visiting, it's a good idea to go with a guide or a group. Soweto is well worth a visit, although it's a good idea to take a guided tour here as well, for two reasons. First, it's a sprawling city that can seem rather boring if you don't know what to look for, where to go, and how to interpret what you're seeing. Second, also because it is a huge, sprawling, monotonous city—you're almost certain to get lost.

Though Johannesburg is rarely associated with the great outdoors, it has its share of pleasant parks and nature reserves hugging the outskirts of the city. In the outer areas it's possible to envision how the inland plateau must have appeared to the first settlers in the region. Beyond this lies the largely unspoiled Magaliesberg region, which is a haven from the busy city for many. Also close by is the fascinating Cradle of Humankind. A little farther afield is the lovely Pilanesberg Game Reserve and its rather brash neighbor, Sun City—a rather crass casino resort in the bush.

Pretoria, the Jacaranda City, is generally warmer and more wholesome than its up-country cousin. Leafy avenues crisscross peaceful suburbs, and much of its cultural heritage remains intact, preserved in museums and national monuments. It's altogether quieter, gentler, and more gracious than Johannesburg.

It is virtually impossible to see anything of Johannesburg and its surrounds without a car. Your best bet is to rent one, decide what you want to see, get a good road map, and work from there. However, it's not advisable to drive yourself into downtown or Soweto. If you're only staying a day or two, you could also just stick to escorted trips.

Great Itineraries

Few people plan to spend long in the Gauteng area—usually it's a necessary stopover between flights. However, it really doesn't deserve the epithet *boring* that it seems to have picked up, and spending a few days here is not the life sentence Capetonians, for example, consider it to be.

IF YOU HAVE 1 OR 2 DAYS

If you have only one day in Jo'burg, take a tour of **Soweto** ⑮ or **Alexandra** ⑩, go shopping, and then head out to Muldersdrift for a wild and wacky African dinner at the Carnivore restaurant. If you have a second day, focus on what interests you most: perhaps a day trip to the **Cradle of Humankind,** where you'll explore the sites of some of the latest and most significant paleontological discoveries in the world, or take a jaunt to **Sun City.** You could start the day off with a balloon ride before sunset and then amble through the **Magaliesberg** area, wandering from coffee shop to art studio. Other options include a tour of the **Premier Mine at Cullinan,** near Pretoria, or a visit to **Gold Reef City** ⑯ and the Apartheid Museum. Each of these options could take up a half or full day.

IF YOU HAVE 3 OR 4 DAYS

Spend the first two days as described above, overnighting, perhaps, at ⊞ **Misty Hills.** En route back to Johannesburg on day three, visit **Cullinan Mine** and do a short walking tour of **Pretoria.** On day four do some shopping in the morning, visiting the **Bruma Flea Market** or the curio sellers outside **Rosebank Mall.** If you're feeling energetic or you just need some peace and quiet, you can stay in a chalet at ⊞ **Mountain Sanctuary Park,** in the Magaliesberg, for a night or two, and go for long walks every day.

IF YOU HAVE 5 OR MORE DAYS

Very few people spend this long *in* Johannesburg. If you are planning to, you probably know what you're after. It's more likely, though, that you'll be spending at least some of the time away from the major urban centers. Both the Magaliesberg and Cradle areas can keep you happy for three or four days each. Spend one day visiting crafts centers, spend at least one day either visiting Sterkfontein Caves or doing an interpretive tour of the Cradle. A tour of the Premier Diamond Mine is also a good idea. Then decide between culture and wildlife. You can spend two nights in ⊞ **Pretoria,** visiting the many museums there, or go to ⊞ **Pilanesberg** to see some game and, perhaps, to pop next door to the **Sun City** complex to see the **Lost City** and maybe play a round of golf on the excellent Gary Player–designed course.

Sights to See

Numbers in the text correspond to numbers in the margin and on the Johannesburg map.

❹ **Gertrude Posel Gallery.** Don't let the mediocre exhibitions of contemporary art upstairs put you off—go downstairs to see the first-rate Standard Bank Collection of African Art. Much of the work, particularly the beadwork, comes from southern Africa. There are also masks,

Johannesburg

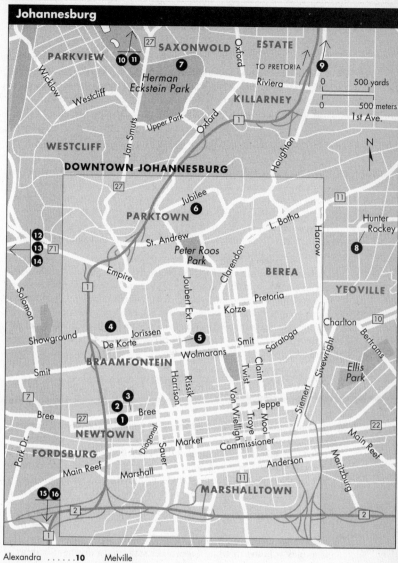

headrests, pots, drums, and initiation statues from West Africa, as well as Kuba cloth from Zaire. ⊠ *Campus level, Senate House, University of Witwatersrand, Jorissen St.,* ☎ *011/717–1360.* ☑ *Free.* ☉ *Tues.– Fri. 10–4.*

⑤ Gold Mining Statue. One of the most famous symbols of the city, this 1960 statue depicts three men—two black and one white—drilling a rock face. It's a beautifully balanced sculpture that captures the physical effort of mining for gold deep under the ground. The bronze statue, by sculptor David McGregor, was a gift from the Transvaal and Orange Free State Chambers of Mines. ⊠ *Rissik and De Korte Sts., Braamfontein.*

⑯ Gold Reef City. Fifteen kilometers (9 miles) south of downtown is the most popular visitor attraction in the city. If you like theme parks, this is the one to visit. Although it has all the usual rides and kitsch amusements, it *is* based on the real history of Johannesburg. Highlights are descending into an old gold mine (additional fee), seeing molten gold being poured, and watching a gumboot dance, a riveting hostel dance developed by black miners.

At time of writing, an **Apartheid Museum** was set to open on a 7-acre area next to Gold Reef City. It's no secret that the apartheid system was an unjust and inequitable system, but it's impossible for most of us to imagine what it was really like. So, following the example of the Holocaust Museum in Washington, D.C., the Apartheid Museum will randomly classify you into a race category, issue you papers and passes, and give you an opportunity to experience, if only for a second, some of the injustices that made up the apartheid system. ⊠ *Northern Pkwy., off N1, Ormonde,* ☎ *011/248–6800,* WEB *www.goldreefcity.co.za.* ☑ *R32.* ☉ *Tues.–Sun. 10–4:40. Dancing at 11:30 and 3; mine tours every 30 mins 10–5.*

☾ ⑭ Johannesburg Botanical Gardens and Emmarentia Dam. This gigantic parkland is a wonderful haven amid the bustle of a big city and a fine place to walk. You can relax on benches beneath weeping willows surrounding the dammed pond or wander across to the rose and herb gardens, filled with arbors, statues, fountains, and ponds. Boating is available on the dam. If you're here on a Saturday or Sunday, expect to bump into several bridal parties. ⊠ *Olifants Rd., Emmarentia,* ☎ *011/782–7064.* ☑ *Free.* ☉ *Daily sunrise–sunset.*

⑨ Lippizaner Centre. Midway between Johannesburg and Pretoria, this complex is home to white Lippizaner stallions, a distinguished breed of horses with a centuries-old lineage. The horses are trained in the classic Spanish riding style and during their weekly shows perform a complex ballet of exercises to the strains of Verdi, Mozart, and Handel. ⊠ *Dahlia Rd., Kyalami,* ☎ *011/702–2103 or 011/468–2719.* ☑ *R50.* ☉ *Performances Sun. at 11 AM.*

❸ Market Theatre Complex. For two decades this theater complex (the city's original fruit market) has kept the flag of quality and experimental theater alive on the highveld. You'll also find an interesting collection of alternative shops, galleries, bars, and coffeehouses here. ⊠ *Bree and Wolhuter Sts., Newtown,* ☎ *011/832–1641,* WEB *www.markettheatre. co.za.*

⑫ Melville. The trendy suburb of Melville essentially grew around the South African Broadcasting Company (SABC) in nearby Auckland Park. It was once an average middle-class enclave until several well-known South African television and radio personalities migrated to the area, turning it into one of the hippest places in Johannesburg. Seventh Street has a number of pleasant shops and coffeehouses with sidewalk seating. Although you may not find anything uniquely African here, you'll see how suburban South Africa entertains itself, particularly on the weekend, when coffeehouses are filled and shop and boutique owners do a brisk trade.

⑬ **Melville Koppies.** This small nature reserve is across Judith Road on the southern side of the Johannesburg Botanical Gardens. You can take guided ecology walks with volunteer guides, many of whom are members of the local botanical society; they'll introduce you to the rich diversity of highveld flora found here. There is also an archaeological site dating to the Iron Age. Bird-watching is excellent here; expect to see many varieties of grassland and highveld birds as well as species found in the area's suburban gardens. The reserve is managed entirely by volunteers, hence the strange opening times. You can book a special tour outside these times by calling ☎ 011/888–4831. ⊠ *Judith Rd. and DF Malan Dr., Melville,* ☎ *011/788-7571.* ☞ *Free.* ☉ *1st and 3rd Sun. of each month 3–6; 2nd Sun. of each month 8:30–11:30.*

❷ **Museum Afrika.** This is the first major museum to attempt to give credit to the contributions of blacks to the development of the city. An excellent exhibit traces the impact of gold on the lives of the black population, from the miners forced to live in male-only hostels to the residents of the burgeoning townships with their squatter camps, *shebeens* (bars), and vibrant jazz. Another exhibit covers the fight for democracy and the events leading to the elections that gave Nelson Mandela the presidency. The museum also has first-rate displays of ancient San (Bushmen) rock art, Gandhi's sojourn in Johannesburg, and the Boer pioneer history. Upstairs, the Bensusan Museum examines the art and technology of cameras with fun hands-on exhibits. ⊠ *121 Bree St., Newtown,* ☎ *011/833-5624.* ☞ *R5.* ☉ *Tues.–Sun. 9–5.*

❶ **SA Centenary Centre Breweries Museum.** This unique museum is dedicated to a great South African favorite—beer! (And South African Breweries is the country's—and now Africa's—largest brewery.) You'll find out all about the history of beer brewing in South Africa and the process of beer making. Afterward, enjoy a complimentary beer in a delightful country-style pub. ⊠ *President and Bezuidenhout Sts. (entrance on Becker St.), Newtown,* ☎ *011/836-4900,* WEB *www.sabcentenary. co.za.* ☞ *R10.* ☉ *Tues.–Sat. 10–6.*

❼ **South African National Museum of Military History.** Set in a park, the two exhibition halls and rambling outdoor display here focus on South Africa's role in the major wars of the 20th century, with an emphasis on World War II. The Anglo-Boer War memorial is the most striking landmark of the northern suburbs. On display are Spitfire and Messerschmidt fighters (including what is claimed to be the only remaining ME110 jet night fighter), various tanks of English and American manufacture, and a wide array of artillery. Among the most interesting exhibits are the modern armaments South Africa used in its war against the Cuban-backed Angolan army during the 1980s, including highly advanced artillery, French-built Mirage fighters, and Russian tanks stolen by the South Africans from a ship en route to Angola. More recent exhibits include the national military art collection, memorabilia from the Anti-Conscription Campaign, and an exhibit on the history of Umkhonto-we-Sizwe (Spear of the Nation), or MK (the African National Congress's military arm), from inception until its incorporation into the South African National Defence Force. ⊠ *20 Erlswold Way,* ☎ *011/646-5513,* WEB *www.militarymuseum.co.za.* ☞ *R5.* ☉ *Daily 9–4:30.*

Neighborhoods

⑩ Alexandra. Less well known than Soweto, Alexandra is a small crowded suburb right on Sandton's doorstep where black people have been able to buy freehold land for decades. It has developed into a vibrant community and seems to have less emotional baggage than "planned" locations, which were usually forced on unwilling residents. It was here that Nelson Mandela had his first home in Johannesburg. Although you're not likely to get lost here, as in Soweto, it's still worth taking a guide as, without interpretation, it looks just like any other area of low-income housing. **Fannie Maringa** (☎ 082/693–6240), part of the Alexandra Tourism Association, is the best person to contact to organize tours.

⑥ Parktown. A superb way to introduce yourself to the colonial history of early Johannesburg is to stroll through this suburb perched on the Braamfontein Ridge. The city's early mining magnates, such as the Oppenheimers and the Cullinans, settled here and commissioned renowned architects—most notably, Sir Herbert Baker—to build their magnificent houses, many of which are national monuments. In many cases interiors have been converted to modern uses, but exteriors remain authentic. The Parktown–Westcliff Heritage Trust fought to preserve these old mansions, many of which were almost demolished to make way for the ubiquitous office blocks that cover much of southern Parktown.

Perhaps the cream of the suburb's architectural treasures is **Northwards,** on Rockdale Avenue, designed by Sir Herbert Baker, one of South Africa's premier architects during the late 1800s and early 1900s. For many years it was the home of socialite Jose Dale Lace, whose ghost is said to still grace Northwards's Mistral's Gallery. What is now Wits Business School, on St. David's Place, is the mansion **Outeniqua,** built in 1906 for the managing director of Ohlssons Breweries. Across the road is a house known as **Eikenlaan,** built in 1903 for James Goch, a professional photographer and the first to use flash photography in South Africa. In June 1985 the home was turned into a rather garish franchise of the Mike's Kitchen steak-house chain.

Contact the **Parktown–Westcliff Heritage Trust** (☎ 011/482–3349, mornings only) to arrange a guided tour of the area. During September the trust hosts a Heritage Weekend, with bus and walking tours accompanied by informative guides. The trust also has a guided "Johannesburg Gold" tour on the third weekend of every month for R70. You can book through Computicket (☎ 083/909–0909).

⑧ Rockey Street. This street is a slice of New York's East Village in Africa. However, it is fast degenerating into a slum. Hard-rock clubs and ethnic eateries rub shoulders with tattoo parlors, secondhand bookshops, lingerie and leather stores, and boutiques selling African beads. Out on the street, white youths with pink mohawks and nose rings hang out with blacks dressed in the latest fashions.

⑪ Rosebank. This suburb linking Parktown and Sandton is attractive, but it lacks the old-world charm of places such as Melville. Street vendors clutter the sidewalks selling curios including large wooden African animals, malachite jewelry, and colorful printed fabrics. The large shopping malls here have lots of chrome and glass; shops are interspersed with several restaurants. Rosebank Mall is home to a large movie complex specializing in art-house films from around the world. You can, however, find quiet squares away from the constant hive of activity. On sunny highveld days (of which there are many), you can dine alfresco at one of Rosebank's numerous sidewalk cafés.

★ ⓯ **Soweto.** A strange place indeed, the South Western Township (Soweto), as it was dubbed by Johannesburg's white counselors, who established it between the two world wars as a dormitory enclave to serve the city's growing industrial needs, is home to between 2 and 3 million people. What it lacks in infrastructure, it more than makes up for in soul; the still largely working-class population here knows how to live for today, which accounts for the high energy level of this place, which seethes with music, jive, and humor. Everywhere you turn it seems a party is breaking out. And what other place on earth can boast of having had two Nobel laureates living within a block of each other: For most of his adult life Anglican archbishop Desmond Tutu lived on Vilakazi Street, in Orlando West, otherwise known as Phefeni. And for most of that time his close neighbor would have been an attorney named Nelson Rolihlala Mandela, except that the latter spent most of *his* adult life incarcerated on Robben Island. (South Africa has two other Nobel Peace Prize winners—the first was ANC founder Albert Luthuli, and the fourth is ex-president F. W. De Klerk.)

Soweto is a chaotic, virtually homogenous sprawl that, even if you found your way in, you'd probably struggle to find your way out of again— let alone around. Your only opportunity to see the place, therefore, is to take a guided tour. There are bus tours offered by various companies, but it is preferable to hire a private guide or join a smaller group tour. You can ask for a special-interest tour, such as art, traditional medicine, restaurants, nightlife, or memorials. The standard tours usually includes some or all of the following:

Freedom Square, in Kliptown, is an important piece of South African iconography, for it was on an open piece of ground here that South Africa's first genuinely democratic forum was formed, under the banner of the African National Congress (ANC), on June 25, 1955. During this three-day meeting the Freedom Charter was drawn up and adopted as the blueprint of the liberation struggle. It has the same significance in South Africa as the drawing up of the U.S. Declaration of Independence and Bill of Rights has to Americans.

The **Tutu and Mandela houses** are close together and close to the **Holy Cross Church,** the home parish of Bishop Tutu. Even more central to the liberation struggle was the Catholic **Regina Mundi Church,** which throughout the harshest years of repression, from 1976 to 1990, was a refuge of peace, sanity, and steadfast moral focus for the people of Soweto. A tour here will include the stories behind every bullet hole and should be a must-visit part of any Soweto tour.

On a previously open plot opposite Holy Cross, a stone's throw (in those days literally) from the Tutu and Mandela homes, is the **Hector Peterson Memorial,** not much to look at, perhaps, but a crucial landmark for the city. Peterson, a student, was the first victim of police fire on fateful June 16, 1976, when schoolchildren rose up virtually as one to protest their second-rate "Bantu" education system.

On a small hill overlooking Orlando West is the empty fortress-home of **Winnie Mandela,** and beyond that is old-town **Diepkloof,** side by side with the new **Diepkloof Extension,** dating to the mid-1970s, when bank loans first became available to black property owners. The difference in the two is quite startling: the dreary prefabricated "box" houses of Diepkloof next to what looks like a lower-middle-class suburb anywhere.

Orlando proper (named after the Johannesburg counselor Edwin Orlando, who persuaded his council to build simple but sturdy homes for

HECTOR PETERSON AND THE FREEDOM MOVEMENT

O**N JUNE 16, 1976,** a group of schoolchildren in Soweto marched to protest the use of Afrikaans as the primary language of education in Bantu (or black) schools. This was a far more political issue than just classroom language. Not only was Dutch-based Afrikaans considered the "language of the oppressor" by blacks, it also made it more difficult for students to learn, as most spoke an African language and, as a second language, English.

The march turned nasty quickly. The protesters, mostly young students, got somewhat overexuberant, and so, too, did the police. The police started firing into the youthful crowd. The first person of many to die, in what was only the beginning of a long and contracted struggle, was Hector Peterson. A picture of Peterson in the arms of a crying friend was flashed around the globe and brought the face of apartheid home to many parts of the world.

The memorial is nothing grand. And Hector Peterson was just a schoolboy, just someone trying to ensure a better life for himself and his friends, family, and community. But his name lives on and it's thanks to him, and the many others who also gave their lives in the cause of freedom, that South Africa has become the place it is today.

— Jen Stern

the squatters here back in 1932) is home to the fantastically popular Orlando Pirates soccer team. Nearby **Dube** is where many of the evicted residents of **Sophiatown**—a melting pot of music, bohemianism, crime, and multiracialism that insulted Afrikaner Calvanism and nationalism— were resettled in 1959. At the time they brought an exciting vibe to the dreary, homogenous dormitory town, and this can still be seen in the relative variety of houses here.

Oppenheimer Park is the only official green space in Soweto (as opposed to stream courses and wetlands). Here you can see the ruins of **Kekhayalendaba,** the center built by South Africa's best-known traditional healer, artist, and oral historian, Credo Mutwa. It is a fascinating place, treated with both reverence and dread by all Soweto residents.

It's worth asking to see a *sangoma,* or traditional healer, and a visit to **Wandie's Place** is almost de rigueur. Both Michael Jackson and Bill Clinton returned here after their first visit.

DINING

There is no way to do justice to the sheer scope and variety of Johannesburg's restaurants in a few pages. What follows is a (of necessity subjective) list of some of the best. Try asking locals what they recommend; eating out is the most popular form of entertainment in Johannesburg, and everyone has a list of their favorite spots.

Downtown Johannesburg Dining and Lodging

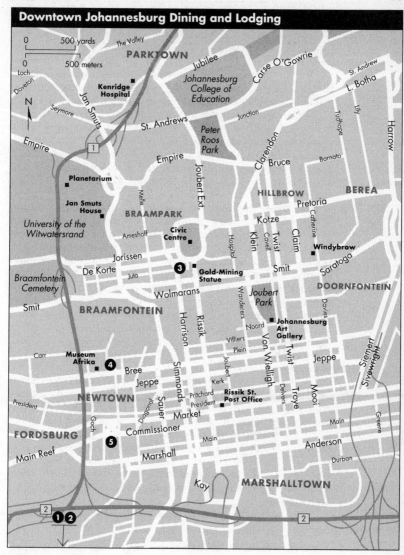

Dining

Chon Hing **5**

Gramadoelas
at the Market
Theatre **4**

Three Ships **1**

Wandie's Place . . . **2**

Lodging

Gold Reef City
Hotel **1**

Protea
Parktonian **3**

Downtown

$$$–$$$$ ✕ **Gramadoelas at the Market Theatre.** This interesting restaurant
specializes in the food of ordinary South Africans but also has a few
dishes from farther north in the continent. Try *umngqusho*—beans and
whole corn—or, if you're feeling adventurous, *mogodu*, unbleached ox
tripe, or *moroho*, mopane worms. Cape Malay food, however, is the
mainstay here, such as rich *bredie* (lamb casserole in a tomato sauce),
sosaties (grilled kebabs made with meat, dried apricots, green peppers,
mushrooms, and onions), and *bobotie* (a casserole of minced lamb).
There's also Moroccan couscous or Zanzibar duck, braised with gin-
ger and cloves. Meat lovers will like the selection of game meats such
as the kudu panfried with dried fruit and spices. ⊠ *Market Theatre,
Wolhuter St., Newtown,* ☎ *011/838–6960. AE, DC, MC, V. Closed
Sun. No lunch Mon.*

$$$–$$$$ ✕ **Three Ships.** This restaurant was *the* place to dine in the '70s and
'80s, when it was in the then-ultrasmart Carlton Hotel, in the center
of the city. The hotel has been mothballed, and every piece of furni-
ture, paneling, and crockery in the restaurant has been moved to the
Gold Reef City Casino, where it reopened in April 2000. The menu
has some old favorites, like chateaubriand with sauce béarnaise, and
some new innovations such as cream cheese and rosemary polenta. For
starters try the crisp potato pancake with salmon caviar and crème
fraîche, or the assorted wild mushrooms in pastry with a cognac cream
and sauce *vierge* (tomato, olive oil, and lemon juice). ⊠ *Gold Reef City
Casino, Northern Parkway, Ormonde,* ☎ *011/248–5333. AE, DC, MC,
V. No lunch.*

$$–$$$ ✕ **Chon Hing.** Tucked away in a side street and looking a little world-
weary, this Chinese restaurant is still one of the best-kept secrets of
the cognoscenti. No cloths mask the Formica tabletops, and the chairs
are upholstered in red plastic, but in a place like this it's the food that
keeps people coming back. You can order one of the set menus, but
you're better off selecting dishes from the two pages at the back of
the menu. Good choices are beef flank served with noodles or rice,
prawns stuffed with minced chicken, and calamari in black bean
sauce. For a real treat order the steamed rock cod. ⊠ *26 Alexander
St., at John Vorster Sq., Ferreirastown,* ☎ *011/834–3206. AE, DC,
MC, V. BYOB.*

Soweto

$ ✕ **Wandie's Place.** Wandie's isn't the only good township restaurant,
★   but it is the best known and one of the most popular spots in Jo'burg.
The decor is eclectic township (i.e., a bit makeshift), the waiters are
smartly dressed in bow ties, and the food is truly African. Meat stews,
imifino—a wild-spinach dish—sweet potatoes, beans, maize porridge,
traditionally cooked pumpkin, chicken, even some tripe are laid out
in a buffet in a motley selection of pots and containers. A selection of
salads is the only concession to Western tastes. The food is hot, the
drinks are cold, the conversation flows. You may be unlucky and end
up here with a tour bus, but it's big enough to cope. It's not that dif-
ficult to find, and parking is safe, but it's probably better to organize
a visit here on a guided trip. ⊠ *618 Makhalamele St., Dube Village,
Soweto,* ☎ *011/982–2796. AE, DC, MC, V.*

Northern Suburbs

$$$$ ✕ **Linger Longer.** Ever since the annual Top Ten restaurant awards were
★   initiated by *Wine* magazine a decade ago, this restaurant has stood
among the top three. Set in the spacious grounds of a former home

Northern Suburbs Dining and Lodging

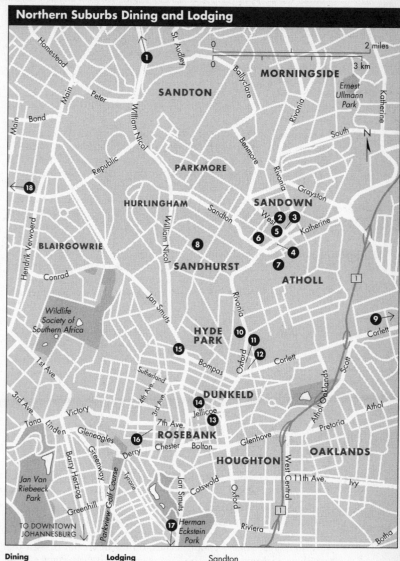

Dining

Butcher Shop and
Grill **4**
Cranks **14**
Graasroots **3**
Linger Longer **7**
Mastrantonio **10**
Plaka Taverna **12**
The Ritz **16**
Singing Fig **9**
Yamoto **11**

Lodging

Balalaika
Protea and
Crown Court **2**
Mercure Inn **18**
The
Michelangelo **5**
Palazzo at
Montecasino **1**
Park Hyatt
Hotel **13**

Sandton
Sun & Towers
Inter-Continental . . .**6**
Saxon **8**
Ten Bompas **15**
Westcliff **17**

in Wierda Valley, it has an air of gracious elegance. Some rooms have a Wedgwood-like quality—deep green walls with pale trim and striped curtains—whereas others glow in salmon pink. A goose-liver pâté appetizer is one of the dishes that made Linger Longer famous. Excellent main courses include crisp duckling in ginger sauce. Among the imaginative desserts, crepes filled with warm cream cheese, vanilla, and brandied raisins are particularly good. ⊠ *58 Wierda Rd. E, Wierda Valley,* ☎ *011/884–0465. AE, DC, MC, V. Closed Sun. No lunch Sat.*

$$$$ ✕ **Yamoto.** If you can judge an ethnic restaurant by who eats there, this has got to be the best Japanese restaurant in town, as less than half the tables are occupied by non-Japanese on any given night. The menu has three focuses: the sushi bar, which is well loved and patronized by the northern suburbs set; the *tepanyaki* menu, with a variety of grilled seafood and meats; and a good noodle bar with an extensive variety of both rice and wheat noodles. ⊠ *Oxford Manor, corner of Oxford and Chaplin Sts., Illovo,* ☎ *011/880–9781. Reservations essential. AE, DC, MC, V. Closed Mon. No lunch Sat.*

$$$–$$$$ ✕ **Butcher Shop and Grill.** This is the best place in town for serious carnivores, with prime South African meat aged to perfection by Alan Pick, the butcher/owner. Game—such as kudu, springbok, and ostrich—appears regularly on the list of specials, and for lighter appetites there's chicken and line fish. ⊠ *Sandton Sq., Sandton,* ☎ *011/ 784–8676. AE, DC, MC, V.*

$$$–$$$$ ✕ **The Ritz.** A quaint old house in Parktown North where you can sit inside under the lovely pressed-tin ceiling or opt for the adjoining conservatory, with hanging plants and a large skylight. For starters try the delectable duck livers sautéed in chili and mango and served with a light coconut-coriander sauce and nan bread. Stay with the duck for your main course, glazed with a fresh-fruit compote and served with gooseberry and orange sauce. Try the chocolate mousse gâteau—layers of light and dark chocolate mousse, on a chocolate sponge, floated on a chocolate coulis—for a decadent ending to your meal. ⊠ *17 3rd St., Parktown North,* ☎ *011/880–2470. AE, DC, MC, V. Closed Sun. No lunch Sat.*

$$–$$$$ ✕ **Mastrantonio.** This is the original (and still the best) of the chain of Mastrantonios in Jo'burg. Although it's always packed, the service is surprisingly quick and the food superb. This is *the* place to go for great pasta and totally superb, unbelievably light melt-in-your-mouth gnocchi—considered by some locals to be the best in town. Try it with the *forestier* sauce, finely chopped mushrooms in cream, or—an old standby—sage and butter. The Muscovite sauce is rather unusual but well loved by some—a basic tomato sauce with the addition of vodka and peas. ⊠ *5c Illovo Centre, Rivonia Rd., Illovo,* ☎ *011/268–0901. AE, DC, MC, V. No dinner Sun.–Mon.*

$$–$$$ ✕ **Singing Fig.** The decor at this extremely popular neighborhood restaurant can only be described as Karoo meets Tuscany, with apricot walls, white tablecloths, and beautiful old globe chairs. The menu, scribbled on a blackboard, changes daily. For starters try the mussels steamed in white wine and flavored with orange and fennel. The duck à l'orange and oxtail are two classics that have regulars coming back time and again. But for something a little different, try the Norwegian salmon, skewered with pickled ginger, crusted with lime and wasabi, and grilled. For dessert, indulge in the signature homemade fig-and-vanilla ice cream, made with dried figs cooked in port. ⊠ *44 The Avenue, Norwood,* ☎ *011/728–2434. Reservations essential. AE, DC, MC, V. Closed Mon. No dinner Sun.*

$–$$$ ✕ **Plaka Taverna.** Greek music floats above the buzz of conversation, a souvlaki spit turns slowly near the door, and a refrigerated case displays an array of meze (small appetizers) at this quaint Greek taverna. Most people sit on the roofed terrace or at the few street-side tables; the surprisingly spacious inside dining area has a slightly more formal feel. Start with a couple of glasses of ouzo (an anise-flavor liqueur) and share a platter of souvlaki, feta, olives, cucumber, and tomato. Follow that with a platter of meze, a Greek salad, and a carafe of wine, and your bill will still be about R50 per person. On weekend evenings belly dancers mingle between the tables, and Greek dancers do the Zorba to a backdrop of ouzo and "controlled" plate breaking. ⊠ *3 Corlett Dr., Illovo,* ☎ *011/788–8777. AE, DC, MC, V.*

$$ ✕ **Cranks.** This funky Thai/Vietnamese restaurant has been a Jo'burg
★ favorite for more than 16 years. Brightly colored cloths cover tables that spill out onto the square, and the eclectic decor usually raises an eyebrow or two by passersby. Green curries are a classic, but a more interesting choice is the mussels in spicy tamarind sauce. There are also good vegetarian options such as K-B-2, crispy fried baby potatoes with cashews and chili. There's live music on Friday and Saturday nights. ⊠ *Rosebank Mall, Rosebank,* ☎ *011/880–3442. AE, DC, MC, V.*

$$ ✕ **Graasroots.** Fresh, innovative meatless fare is the order of the day
★ here. The layered potato pancake with grilled vegetables and pesto is a winner. There's a large variety of freshly squeezed juices, try the carrot, orange, and ginger. It's not just for the lettuce-leaf-and-sprouts brigade, though, as shown by the rich chocolate cake and creamy lattes and cappuccinos. ⊠ *Village Walk, Maude St., Sandton,* ☎ *011/883–6020. AE, DC, MC, V.*

LODGING

Downtown

$$ 🏨 **Gold Reef City Hotel.** Small buildings with Victorian-style wrought-iron trim make up this hotel spread over a large part of the Gold Reef City theme park. All rooms are furnished in Victorian period style, with claw-foot baths and reproduction furniture. As the entire hotel is within the theme park, it's safe to walk around at night—even across the highway on the pedestrian bridge to the nearby casino. The restaurant, Barney's, specializes in a range of South African food, from Cape Malay bobotie and Durban curry to the inevitable ostrich meat. ⊠ *Shaft 14, Northern Pkwy. (mailing address: Box 25, Gold Reef City 2159),* ☎ *011/248–5700,* ℻ *011/248–5791,* 🕸 *www.threecities.co.za. 73 rooms. Restaurant, bar, pool. AE, DC, MC, V. BP.*

$$ 🏨 **Protea Parktonian.** Close to the Rotunda transport center, the major theaters, and just a three-minute drive from the central business district, this Braamfontein property offers the best value in the city—even if its neighborhood isn't safe to walk in at night. The guest rooms are all suites, by far the largest of any city hotel. All have a separate living room and bedroom, minibar, cable TV, and veranda. You can enter the hotel directly from a secure parking garage, and there's a free shuttle to Gold Reef City, Rosebank, and the northern suburbs. ⊠ *120 De Korte St., Braamfontein (mailing address: Box 32278, Braamfontein 2017),* ☎ *011/403–5740,* ℻ *011/403–2401. 294 rooms. 2 restaurants, bar, room service, pool, health club. AE, DC, MC, V. BP.*

Northern Suburbs

$$$$ 🏨 **The Michelangelo.** As though taken from a street in Florence, this hotel forms the northern facade of much-touted piazza-inspired Sandton Square. But whereas the hotel is unusually tasteful, even grand, the square—to quote a local architect—is to an Italian piazza what Donald Duck is to Swan Lake. A member of the Leading Hotels of the World group, the hotel has all the class, comforts, and facilities you'd expect from a top establishment. The atrium-style pool area is a feature to note. ⊠ *West St., Sandton Square (mailing address: Box 784682, Sandton 2146),* ☎ *011/282–7000,* FAX *011/282–7171. 242 rooms. Restaurant, 2 bars, room service, pool, sauna, health club. AE, DC, MC, V.*

$$$$ 🏨 **Palazzo at Montecasino.** Built in the style of a Tuscan Villa, the hotel
★ is set among formal herb gardens. Public rooms are on a grand scale, and the whole is decorated in gilt, marble, and terra-cotta, with small touches of trompe l'oeil. The rooms are spacious, with rich tapestry-style draperies, a canopied bed, gilt-framed mirrors and prints, and dark wooden furniture. Large picture windows and light terra-cotta tiles lighten the effect. The hotel is done with so much more style, attention to detail, and class than the adjacent casino and mall that it's almost impossible to believe they're connected. This is a good choice for a business stay. The service is impeccable. ⊠ *Montecasino Blvd., Fourways 2055 (mailing address: Private Bag X125, Bryanston 2021),* ☎ *011/510–3000,* FAX *011/510–4000,* WEB *www.interconti.com. 215 rooms, 31 suites. Restaurant, bar, in-room data ports, in-room fax, pool, gym, casino, business center, meeting rooms. AE, DC, MC, V.*

$$$$ 🏨 **Park Hyatt Hotel.** If you like lots of black, gold, and glass decor, this one's for you. Enormous picture windows have stunning views over the northern suburbs. The black-and-gold theme extends to the rooms, which are elegant and luxurious. Should you book one of the Regency Club suites, you'll have complimentary cocktails and even more glorious views. Local art lines the walls in discreetly lighted passageways, and there's an ultramodern restaurant, a wine bar, and a solar-heated pool on the roof. The hotel has an airport greeting service and can make arrangements for baby-sitting and car rental. Sunday brunch is a favorite with guests and local families alike. ⊠ *Oxford Rd. and Biermann Ave., Rosebank (mailing address: Box 1536, Saxonwold 2132),* ☎ *011/280–1234,* FAX *011/280–1238,* WEB *www.hyatt.co.za. 244 rooms. 2 restaurants, bar, in-room data ports, room service, pool, health club, laundry service. AE, DC, MC, V.*

$$$$ 🏨 **Sandton Sun & Towers Inter-Continental.** Adjoining one of the largest malls in the country, the Sun and Sun Towers are two nominally separate hotels, linked by a walkway and sharing facilities. Both occupy high-rises with commanding views of the northern suburbs and the highveld. The focal point of each hotel is a central atrium soaring the height of the building. Guest rooms are small but superbly laid out, with understated lighting and elegant decorative touches. There is little to recommend one hotel over the other, although the towers are smaller and farther removed from the bustle of Sandton Mall. The towers also have two full floors of executive suites, with their own bar, breakfast room, and full-time staff. ⊠ *5th and Alice Sts., Sandton 2146,* ☎ *011/780–5000,* FAX *011/780–5002,* WEB *www.southernsun.com. 525 rooms, 39 suites. 4 restaurants, bar, coffee shop, room service, hair salon, sauna, health club, laundry service, concierge floor, business services. AE, DC, MC, V.*

$$$$ ⊞ **Saxon.** From the moment you drive through the private gate and
★ up the landscaped driveway, you know you've arrived someplace special. This sophisticated and exclusive-feeling hotel blends African decor
with a light and airy design to create the sense of a private oasis. Every
spacious and elegant suite has an open floor plan and private outdoor
access into some part of the 6 acres of lushly manicured grounds.
Rooms have every imaginable luxury, from deep soaking tubs to DVD
players. The staff of butlers assures you personalized and attentive service. ⊠ *36 Saxon Rd., Sandhurst 2132,* ☏ *011/292–6000,* FAX *011/292–
6001,* WEB *www.thesaxon.com. 26 suites. Restaurant, lounge, in-room
data ports, in-room fax, minibars, 2 pools, gym, library, concierge, meeting rooms. AE, DC, MC, V. BP.*

$$$$ ⊞ **Westcliff.** This fantastic hotel has breathtaking views of the wooded
★ northern suburbs, which are best appreciated from the secluded swimming pool terrace. Bedrooms are in multistoried villas, each with its
own balcony: some face twisting lanes and others the highveld beyond.
The feel is cozy Mediterranean, with soft pink structures blending
with the sandstone foundations. The enormous bathrooms have marble vanities and huge soaking tubs. The cuisine, service, and facilities
are all world class. ⊠ *67 Jan Smuts Ave., Westcliff 2193,* ☏ *011/646–
2400,* FAX *011/646–3500,* WEB *www.westcliffhotel.orient-express.com.
104 rooms, 14 suites. 2 restaurants, bar, in-room data ports, in-room
fax, room service, pool, hair salon, tennis court, gym, business services.
AE, DC, MC, V. EP.*

$$$–$$$$ ✕⊞ **Ten Bompas.** There are a number of small boutique hotels and guest
houses in the northern suburbs, but none quite match the élan of this
eclectic hotel-cum-restaurant and art gallery. Each suite has been in-
dividually created by a different interior designer, and decor ranges from
art deco–African to muted romantic. The restaurant matches the hotel's
fashionable decor, and the service and food are some of the best in the
city. Some of the thoughtful extras included in the room price are a
stocked minibar and laundry. ⊠ *10 Bompas Rd., Dunkeld West (mail-
ing address: Box 786064, Sandton 2146),* ☏ *011/325–2442,* FAX *011/
341–0281,* WEB *www.tenbompas.com. 10 suites. Restaurant, bar, in-room
fax, pool, meeting rooms. AE, DC, MC, V. BP.*

$$ ⊞ **Balalaika Protea and Crown Court.** The large garden here—a definite rarity in Jo'burg—sets this hotel apart from other similar north-
ern suburb properties. It's conveniently located in the middle of
Sandton and connected to the Village Walk shopping mall by a pedestrian walkway. It is actually two hotels run as one, each with its own
character. The Crown Court is somewhat smarter, with bigger rooms,
separate showers in all the bathrooms, and in-room dedicated modem
lines. All rooms have TVs, tea and coffee stations, minibars, and
phones. The suites in the Crown Court are spacious and have spa baths.
⊠ *Maude St., Sandton (mailing address: Box 783372, Sandton 2146),*
☏ *011/322–5000,* FAX *011/322–5023,* WEB *www.proteahotels.com.
301 rooms, 24 suites. 2 restaurants, bar, 2 pools, meeting rooms. AE,
DC, MC, V.*

$ ⊞ **Mercure Inn.** Conveniently located in Randburg near the waterfront
and the commercial center, this minimum-service hotel is a good
choice if you're looking for clean, comfortable, no-frills accommodation
at a good price. The rooms are smallish but have TVs, tea and coffee
stations, and telephones. Room service is from the nearby MacRib fast-
food restaurant. ⊠ *Republic Rd. at Randburg Waterfront, Randburg,* ☏ *011/326–3300,* FAX *011/789–4175. 104 rooms. Bar. AE, DC,
MC, V.*

NIGHTLIFE AND THE ARTS

The best place to find out what's going on in Johannesburg is in the "Tonight" section of the *Star,* Johannesburg's major daily. Another great source of information is the "Friday" supplement of the weekly *Mail & Guardian,* which is published on Friday. Almost all performances can be booked through **Computicket** (☎ 083/909–0909).

The Arts

Classical Music

The Johannesburg Philharmonic Orchestra and the Chamber Orchestra of South Africa both give performances, irregularly, at **City Hall** (⌧ President and Simmonds Sts., Johannesburg Central). Unfortunately, the future of classical music is uncertain in Jo'burg; check the papers or contact Gauteng Tourism for performance information.

Theater

The **Civic Theatre** (⌧ Loveday St., Braamfontein, ☎ 011/403–3408 for information; 083/909–0909 Computicket) is Johannesburg's principal cultural venue. Housed in a slick, modern complex, the Civic has one enormous theater and three smaller stages. Many productions have a South African focus, such as works by local talents Pieter-Dirk Uys and Paul Slabolepszy.

The **Market Theatre** (⌧ Bree and Wolhuter Sts., ☎ 011/832–1641) occupies an old produce market that dates to the early 1900s. Now completely refurbished, the three-theater complex has a wealth of character and includes a great bar and restaurant and an art gallery with changing exhibits. Theater productions encompass everything from plays by Athol Fugard to to comedies imported from London's West End. The theater occasionally features ethnic African music. Experimental plays get the litmus test of audience approval at the Market Theatre Laboratory, across Bree Street.

Nightlife

Multiracial Hillbrow used to be the city's nightlife center, but the neighborhood has become a crime-ridden, no-go zone full of hookers, massage parlors, and porno houses. The in crowd then moved to **Rockey Street** in Yeoville, which still has quite a happening nightlife scene with clubs and bars offering everything from jazz to grunge. Unfortunately, the crime element followed its main source of income, and now the area is also a popular hangout for drug dealers, addicts, and the odd mugger. In its place, **Rosebank** has emerged as the hot new spot, and you'll find clubs, bars, and coffee shops scattered through the neighborhood, particularly along Oxford Road. Many residents of the northern suburbs, concerned about personal safety, head to the modern **Randburg Waterfront** (⌧ Republic Rd., Randburg), a bland, gimmicky, mall-like development of almost 100 restaurants, bars, and clubs clustered around an artificial lake. Those in the know, though, head off to **Melville,** which has been popular for decades, hasn't deteriorated into a slum, is moderately safe to wander around, and just seems to stay the same.

Bars and Pubs

Radium Beer Hall (⌧ 282 Louis Botha Ave., Orange Grove, ☎ 011/728–3866), opened in 1929, is the oldest pub still operating in the city. The 19-piece jazz band Fat Sound plays on the first Sunday of every month, and there is live music late on every Wednesday, Friday, and

Saturday. Known for its hearty Portuguese food (*prego* rolls, *peri-peri* chicken), it is casual verging on the rough. Don't go here at night except in a group or with locals. The cover charge ranges from R10 to R35 (the latter for the big band), depending on performers.

Live Music and Nightclubs

Back of the Moon (✉ Gold Reef City Casino, Ormonde, ☎ 011/496–1423) is a rather sophisticated re-creation of a '50s-style nightclub presided over by its owner, Felicia Mabuza-Suttle, SA's own Oprah Winfrey wanna-be. There's good live jazz. It's closed Monday.

The **Bass Line** (✉ 7 7th St., Melville, ☎ 011/482–6915) is the trendiest young hangout in town, playing mostly jazz and world music—an origin-sensitive combination of rock and roll, rap, and Afro-rock. It's closed on Monday.

Kippies (✉ Market Theatre complex, off Bree St., Newtown, ☎ 011/838–1271) is the city's premier jazz venue, with traditional and township South African jazz. It also serves light meals from Kofifi's kitchen next door.

The **Roxy Rhythm Bar** (✉ 20 Main Rd., Melville, ☎ 011/726–6019) has been going for over a decade and is still a hot favorite playing jazz, rock, and local music. It's closed on Sunday.

OUTDOOR ACTIVITIES AND SPORTS

Participant Sports

Golf

Johannesburg's finest golf courses are open to foreign visitors, although weekend play tends to be restricted to members only. Expect to pay R300–R400 for a round. You can rent clubs for about R150 from **Allan Henning Golf Shop** (☎ FAX 011/485–4899) at the Royal Johannesburg.

The century-old **Royal Johannesburg and Kensington Golf Club** (✉ Fairway Ave., Linksfield North, ☎ 011/640–3021) has two courses: the East Course is the more popular of the two and has hosted the South African Open seven times. The **Wanderers Golf Club** (✉ Rudd Rd., Illovo, ☎ 011/447–3311) has had its bunkers reshaped and its tees rebuilt. **Glendower Club** (✉ Marais Rd., Bedfordview, ☎ 011/453–1013) lies in a bird sanctuary. The numerous water hazards and extra length make this one of the most challenging courses in the country.

Hang Gliding, Skydiving, and Flying

There is better paragliding and hang gliding than you would think close to the city. One of the most popular launch sites is at Hartbeespoort Dam—controlled by **1st Paragliding Club** (☎ 082/851–5775, 082/579–2132, or 083/452–0437). **Icarus Skydiving School** (☎ 011/452–8858) has first-jump courses and tandem jumps for beginners and regular jumps for experienced skydivers (log book essential). **Air Routes** (☎ 082/467–4180, 082/678–8221, or 082/414–5275) offers a scenic flight in a vintage DC-3 or a Dakota, aircraft over Johannesburg and the Hartbeespoort Dam followed by a buffet breakfast at Wings, the restaurant at Lanseria Airport. Sparkling wine and orange juice are served during the flight. The cost is R395.

Horseback Riding

Horseback Africa (☎ 012/734–1300 or 082/789–9002) has well-organized rides in a game reserve near Cullinan, about 90 km (55 mi) from Jo'burg. Trips are about R575 for a full day, including transportation from Jo'burg and a light picnic lunch. They're particularly well suited for beginners or nervous people, but experienced riders can have a fun canter, too.

Outdoor Adventures

Pure Rush Industries (☎ 082/605–1150) will take you sand boarding down a mine dump, or rappeling off a building.

River Tours and Safaris (☎ 011/803–9775) offers short paddling trips through some small rapids on the Vaal River near Johannesburg.

SA Fly Fishing Safaris (☎ 082/885–0589) can show you where and how to catch an indigenous yellow fish or, if you prefer, a less challenging trout.

Sunwa Ventures (☎ 056/817–7107) is based at Parys, on the Vaal River about an hour's drive from Johannesburg, where it offers short, easy white-water trips.

Spectator Sports

Cricket

The **Wanderers' Club** (✉ 21 North St., Illovo) is the country's premier cricket ground and the site of many of the international contests between South Africa and touring sides from England and its former colonies. All matches are administered by the **Gauteng Cricket Union** (☎ 011/788–1008).

Rugby

South Africa's showcase rugby stadium is **Ellis Park** (✉ Staib St., Doornfontein, ☎ 011/402–8644), where the Springboks beat New Zealand's All Blacks to win the 1995 World Cup, a crowning moment in South African rugby history. It's a magnificent stadium, capable of seating nearly 65,000 people.

Soccer

Soccer has a far bigger following than either rugby or cricket in South Africa. Games are played all over the city, but the biggest bouts are at **Ellis Park** (☞ Rugby, *above*). The most popular teams in the whole of South Africa are the legendary Johannesburg rivals—the Orlando Pirates and the Kaiser Chiefs.

SHOPPING

Johannesburg is the best place in the country to buy quality African art, whether it's tribal fetishes from central Africa or oil paintings by early settlers. Dozens of galleries and curio shops are scattered throughout the city, often selling the same goods at widely different prices. Newtown Market Africa, which you should consider seeing before making purchases elsewhere, has the best prices.

And if you thought America had a thing for malls, wait until you see Jo'burg's northern suburbs. Blink and another mall has gone up. Even more astonishing is how exclusive they are, lined with chichi shops selling the latest from Italy, France, and the States—at twice the price you would pay at home. Most malls also have department stores like Edgars and Woolworth's (the South African branch of Britain's Marks & Spencer), as well as movie theaters and restaurants.

Malls

The major mall in Johannesburg is **Sandton City** (✉ Sandton Dr. and Rivonia Rd.), with hundreds of stores and a confusing layout that almost guarantees you'll get lost. The wing of shops leading from the mall to the Sandton Sun Hotel has some worthwhile African art galleries. Adjoining Sandton City is **Sandton Square** (✉ 5th St.), built to resemble an Italian piazza (but a bland facsimile), complete with expensive Italian shops, including an ice cream parlor, bakeries, and restaurants. Closer to the city, **Hyde Park Corner** (✉ Jan Smuts Ave., Hyde Park) is the city's most upscale shopping center, where fashion victims come to sip cappuccino and browse in Exclusive Books, a branch of the country's best chain of bookstores. Rosebank is a happening suburb focused on a conglomeration of shopping centers, of which the most notable are **The Zone, Rosebank Mall,** and **The Firs** in the block defined by Biermann Avenue, Baker Street, Oxford Road, and Bath Street. It's a safe environment, where you can actually walk and sit outside—something of a novelty in security-conscious Johannesburg. This is the place to come for casual alfresco lunches at one of the area's many cafés and restaurants. There is a covered crafts market at the entrance to Rosebank Mall and, on Sunday, a rooftop flea market. The **Monte Casino** (✉ William Nicol Dr., Fourways) is a reconstructed Tuscan village built under a fake sky set on perpetual twilight. Plastic ducks swim in a tinkling waterway that threads its way past the restaurants and casino. Local teenagers love this place.

Markets

If you believe that bigger is better, **Bruma Market World** is for you. It's the biggest flea market in South Africa, and you will find anything you can imagine there—and probably a whole lot you can't. If you know what you want, you'll have to search for it between the West African curios, South American clothing, wire sculptures, cheap plastic geegaws, and handmade "designer" clothes created in someone's living room. ✉ *Bruma,* ☎ *011/622–9647.* ☉ *Tues.–Sun. 9–5.*

Newtown Market Africa, a flea market held every Saturday in front of the Market Theatre, is the best place in town for African art and curios at low prices. Vendors from Cameroon, Nigeria, and Zaire come here to sell masks, fetishes, traditional wooden pillows, Kuba raffia cloth, and Mali blankets. Bargain hard, and you should be able to get vendors to knock a third off the price. ✉ *Wolhuter St., between Bree and Jeppe Sts.* ☉ *Sat. 9–4.*

Rosebank's Rooftop Fleamarket has locally made crafts, kitsch, bread, cheese, biltong, and mass-produced African curios, like the dark-wood Malawian wood carvings. Frequently, African musicians, dancers, and buskers entertain the roving Sunday crowds. Flea markets both here and in Cape Town have become the best place on the continent to find genuine and often very valuable curios from far and wide, particularly the Congo and West Africa—snap up any Benin bronzes you come across, for they are the bargain of the millennium. ✉ *Rosebank Mall, 50 Bath Ave., Rosebank.* ☉ *Sun. 9:30–5.*

Specialty Stores

African Art

Everard Read Gallery is one of the largest privately owned galleries in the world. It acts as agent for several important South African artists, as well as a number of international contemporary artists. The gallery specializes in wildlife paintings and sculpture. ✉ *6 Jellicoe Ave., Rosebank,* ☎ *011/788–4805.* ☉ *Mon.–Sat. 9–6.*

Kim Sacks Gallery, in a lovely old home, has one of the finest collections of authentic African art in Johannesburg. Displayed throughout its sunny rooms are Zairian raffia cloth, Mali mud cloth, Zulu telephone-wire baskets, and an excellent collection of original masks and carvings from across the continent. Prices are high. ⊠ *153 Jan Smuts Ave., Parkwood,* ☎ *011/447–5804.* ⊙ *Weekdays 9:15–5, Sat. 10–5, some Sun. 10–1.*

Rural Craft has a good collection of Xhosa and Ndebele beadwork, including wedding aprons and jewelry. The shop also sells fabrics made by rural Ndebele, Xhosa, and Zulu women. ⊠ *Shop 42E, Mutual Gardens, 31 Tyrwhitt Ave., Rosebank,* ☎ *011/880–9651.* ⊙ *Weekdays 8:30–4:30, Sat. 9–2:30.*

Totem Gallery specializes in artifacts from West and central Africa, including Kuba cloth from Zaire, Dogon doors from Mali, glass beads, masks from Burkina Faso, and hand-painted barbershop signs. Some pieces come with detailed descriptions of their history. Prices are high. ⊠ *U17 Sandton City,* ☎ *011/884–6300.* ⊙ *Weekdays 9–6, Sat. 9–5.* ⊠ *The Firs, Rosebank,* ☎ *011/447–1409.* ⊙ *Weekdays 9–5, Sat. 9–2.*

Books

Exclusive Books is the best chain of bookstores in the country, with a great selection of African literature, history, travel, and culture. You can select a book, order a designer coffee from the integrated Seattle Coffee Company, and then read in comfort all day. ⊠ *Sandton City,* ☎ *011/883–1010;* ⊠ *Hyde Park Corner,* ☎ *011/325–4298;* ⊠ *The Zone, Rosebank,* ☎ *011/327–5736;* ⊠ *Rosebank Mall Rosebank,* ☎ *011/784–5419.*

Gold and Diamonds

Kruggerrands, with images of President Kruger and a springbok on either side, are among the most famous gold coins minted today. They lost some of their luster during the apartheid years, when they were banned internationally. Kruggerrands are sold individually or in sets containing coins of 1 ounce, ½ ounce, ¼ ounce, and ⅟₁₀ ounce of pure gold. You can buy Kruggerrands through most city banks, but several branches of First National Bank sell them over the counter. The most convenient branches are in Sandton City and Rosebank.

Schwartz Jewellers (⊠ Sandton City, ☎ 011/783–1717) is a diamond wholesaler and manufacturing jeweler offering a large range of classical and ethnic African pieces as well as offering a custom design service.

Pretoria

Pretoria is overshadowed by Johannesburg, 48 km (30 mi) to the south, and few people outside South Africa know it as the country's capital. It's a pleasant city, with historic buildings and a city center that is easily explored on foot. Pretoria is famous for its jacaranda trees, which are seen at their best in spring (September–October), when the city is blanketed with their purple blossoms. Founded in 1855, the city was named after Andries Pretorius, the hero of the Battle of Blood River, and for many years it remained a bastion of Afrikaner culture. With the triumph of the Nationalist Party in 1948, it also became the seat of the apartheid government, and the city developed a reputation for hard-line insularity. Much of that has changed in recent years, and President Thabo Mbeki now occupies the lovely Union buildings overlooking the city. International acceptance of the new South Africa has also seen an influx of foreign embassies and personnel, bringing a refreshing cosmopolitanism to Pretoria. As a result, many of the country's finest restaurants are here.

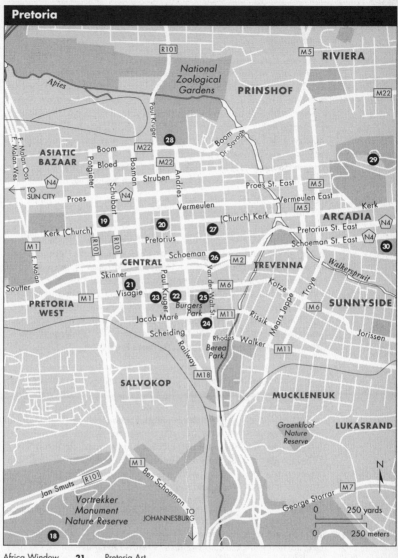

Pretoria

A Good Tour

Numbers in the text correspond to numbers in the margin and on the Pretoria map.

If you're coming from Johannesburg, your first stop should be the **Voortrekker Monument and Museum** ⑱. To get there, take the Eufees Road exit from the R28. At the traffic lights at the bottom of the exit, turn left. Turn right at the next set of traffic lights. The entrance gates to the monument are on the right-hand side of the road, shortly after the traffic lights. Return to the highway (R28), and drive north into the city. The R28 becomes Potgieter Street going into Pretoria central (this is a one-way street going north). Turn right on Kerk Street. The **Kruger House Museum** ⑲ is on your left. Street parking is available. Walk four blocks east down Kerk to **Church Square** ⑳.

Head back to Kerk Street and collect your car. Drive one block east and turn right onto Schubart Street (a one-way street going south). Drive four blocks south until you reach Visagie Street. Turn left on Visagie Street and park in the grounds of the **Africa Window** ㉑, the cultural history museum. From there walk two blocks and turn right into Paul Kruger. On your left will be the **Transvaal Museum** ㉒, the best natural science museum in the country. Across the road from the museum stands **City Hall** ㉓. Walk south down Paul Kruger Street and turn left on Jacob Maré Street. On your left you'll pass the attractive Barton Kip House, which is not open to the public. Continue until you reach the high-Victorian landmark and national monument **Melrose House** ㉔. Cross the street to view beautiful **Burgers Park** ㉕.

You can then backtrack to your car and do the following as a drive, or if you're feeling energetic, you can continue down Jacob Maré Street and turn left on Van der Walt Street at the corner. Walk three blocks to Skinner Street. At the corner Skinner and Van der Walt streets you'll pass the brick **Staats Model School** ㉖, the first school in this pioneer town—unfortunately not open to the public. Continue north along Van der Walt Street for two blocks until you reach Pretorius Street. On your right is **J. G. Strijdom Square** ㉗ and the awe-inspiring State Theatre and Opera House. Walk west on Pretorius Street past Church Square, left into Bosman, and right into Visage to get back to the Africa Window, where you will have parked your car.

As you exit onto Visagie Street, turn left and then right into Potgieter and right again into Schoeman. Continue for about 10 blocks and turn right into Wessels. Park and visit the **Pretoria Art Museum** ㉚. Go back into Wessels, across Schoeman and straight until you hit Kerk Street. Turn right, and the **Union Buildings** ㉙ will be on your left. Take the first available road right and then left again into Schoeman. Continue out of town and take the N1 to Johannesburg. Follow the official brown tourist signs indicating **Smuts House.** Retrace your steps back to the N1 and head back to Johannesburg.

It will take about 30 minutes to travel from Johannesburg to Pretoria on the N1. As you near Pretoria, the N1 branches. Take the R28 to enter the city center. If you want to see everything, schedule an entire day in Pretoria. The walk alone will probably take a morning. A trip to Cullinan will take at least half a day.

Sights to See

★ ㉑ **Africa Window.** This National Museum of Cultural History has permanent interpretive exhibitions of San art, people's relations to the stars, and others as well as a range of temporary exhibitions and movies. Don't miss the Ndebele mural along the wall at the entrance. ✉ *Visagie Street, between Bosman and Schubart,* ☎ *012/324–6082,* WEB *home.global. co.za/~nchm.* 🖾 *R10.* ☉ *Daily 8–4.*

㉕ Burgers Park. This lovely parkland lies across the road from Melrose House. Note the gates, which are all that remain of yet another Victorian mansion that lost out to the developers. Heady scents will lead you to fragrant rose gardens and flower beds filled with indigenous plants. At the center of the park, a converted Victorian house now contains a delightful restaurant. ✉ *Jacob Maré St. between Van der Walt and Andries Sts.* 🖾 *Free.*

⑳ Church Square. A statue of President Kruger by Anton van Wouw dominates the pleasant square, which is flanked by some of Pretoria's most historic buildings: the Old Raadsaal (Town Hall), built in early Italian Renaissance style; the Palace of Justice, which was used as a military hospital during the Boer War; and the modern Provincial Administration Building. President Kruger arranged for the construction of many of these buildings. ✉ *Bordered by Paul Kruger St. and Church St.*

NEED A
BREAK?

Cafe Riche (☎ 012/328–3173), on Church Square, is one of the better coffee shops in the center of town. As well as a good à la carte menu, it serves the excellent coffees, *tremazzini* (small toasted sandwiches), sandwiches, and salads. You can sit outside and watch the informal parking attendants–cum–itinerant car washers waving their trademark white(ish) cloths in a circle in the air to attract clients.

㉓ City Hall. An imposing structure that borrows freely from classical architecture, the building has a tympanum on the front by Coert Steynberg, one of South Africa's most famous sculptors—it symbolizes the growth and development of Pretoria. Statues of Andries Pretorius, the hero of the Battle of Blood River, and his son Marthinus, the city's founder, stand in the square fronting City Hall. ✉ *Paul Kruger St. (opposite Transvaal Museum, at end of gardens),* ☎ *012/326–5012.* ☉ *Weekdays 8–3.*

OFF THE
BEATEN PATH

CULLINAN DIAMOND MINE – If you head north on the N1, you'll find this site about 48 km (30 mi) from the city. This fully operational mine is three times the size of the famous hole at Kimberley. The 3,106-carat Cullinan diamond was unearthed here in 1905, a giant crystal that was later cut into several smaller stones including the Star of Africa. Machinery extracts 12 tons of kimberlite and 6,000 carats of diamonds each day. About 80% of these are for industrial use, but the rest are high-grade gems. On the mine's tour you'll see the big hole, watch a 12-minute video, pass through a typical mine security check, view replicas of the most famous diamonds, and travel through a mock-up of an underground tunnel. You can buy diamonds and custom-made pieces from the resident jeweler. You must reserve in advance for tours; no children under 10 are permitted. There's an underground tour on the second Friday of every month for R75. ✉ *Premier Diamond Tours, 95 Oak Ave., Cullinan,* ☎ *012/734–0260.* 🖾 *R22.* ☉ *Tours weekdays at 10 and 2:30, weekends at 10.*

If you really want to do Cullinan in style, **Schwartz Jewellers,** in Johannesburg (☎ 011/783–1717), has chauffeur-driven excursions at R600 per person for a minimum of eight people. The trip includes transportation, lunch, snacks, all tours, and a chance to browse the on-site jewelry store.

The delightful old Victorian mine director's house has been turned into a guest house and tea garden, **Oak House** (☎ 012/305–2364), and has breakfast, light lunches, and teas on weekends only, from 8 to 4.

㉗ J. G. Strijdom Square. Despite the fervid anticommunist stance of the old Nationalist government, the square's monumental architecture bears a striking resemblance to that of former Soviet states. It had been dominated by a huge bust of former prime minister Strijdom, which looked disturbingly like that of Lenin. Interestingly, on May 31, 2001—exactly 40 years to the day after the Nationalist government declared South Africa a republic—the supporting structure of the whole edifice crumbled, and Strijdom fell unceremoniously onto the pavement. At time of writing, funding has been set aside to repair the damage to the actual square, but poor old Strijdom is not going to be put back on his pedestal. ✉ *Church and Van der Walt Sts., next to State Theatre.*

⑲ Kruger House Museum. This was once the residence of Paul Kruger, president of the South African republic between 1883 and 1902 and one of the most revered figures in South African history. The home, still fully furnished, is humble and somber, befitting this deeply religious leader who loved to sit on the front *stoep* (veranda) and watch the world go by. Exhibits in the adjoining museum trace Kruger's career, culminating in his exile by the British and eventual death in Switzerland in 1904. Of particular interest are the expressions of support that Kruger received from all over the world, including the United States, when Britain instigated the Boer War (1899–1902). Across the road is the Dutch Reformed Church (now a national monument), where Mrs. Kruger is buried. ✉ *Kerk St. at Potgieter St.,* ☎ *012/326–9172.* ▣ *R10.* ☉ *Weekdays 8:30–4, weekends 9–4.*

㉔ Melrose House. Built in 1886, this opulent structure is one of the most beautiful Victorian homes in the country, with marble columns, mosaic floors, and lovely stained-glass windows. The house is furnished in period style. Its dining room is where the 1902 Treaty of Vereeniging was signed, ending the Boer War. ✉ *275 Jacob Maré St.,* ☎ *012/322–2805.* ▣ *R3.* ☉ *Tues.–Sun. 10–5.*

㉘ National Zoological Gardens. Pretoria's zoo is considered one of the world's best, with an enormous collection of animals from almost every continent. The animal enclosures here are much larger than those of most zoos, but a cage is still a cage. However, like any modern zoo worth its name, this is just the public facade for a much larger organization that specializes in the research and breeding of endangered species. A cable car (R8) transports visitors high above the zoo to a hilltop lookout. ✉ *Boom St.,* ☎ *012/328–3265,* [WEB] *www.pretoria-zoo.co.za.* ▣ *R20.* ☉ *Daily 8–5:30.*

㉚ Pretoria Art Museum. This unimpressive gallery space houses a very impressive collection of South African art in a constantly changing series of exhibitions. ✉ *Schoeman and Wessels Sts.,* ☎ *012/344–1807 or 012/344–1808.* ▣ *R3.* ☉ *Tues.–Sat. 10–5, Wed. 10–8, Sun. noon–5.*

Smuts House. This simple country house was the residence of Jan Christian Smuts, who played active roles in the South African War as well as the First and Second World Wars and was instrumental in setting up the League of Nations (forerunner of the United Nations). Despite his military background, he was committed to working for peace and remains one of South Africa's most interesting historical characters. His home illustrates the simple manner in which he lived until his death in 1950. There is a tea garden on the large grounds and an adjacent campsite. There is a village market on the grounds on the second and last Saturdays of each month. ⊠ *Jan Smuts Ave., Irene,* ☎ *012/667–1176.* 🎟 *R5.* ☉ *Weekdays 9:30–4:30, weekends 9:30–5.*

❷❻ **Staats Model School.** The building is a fine example of a late-19th-century Transvaal Republic school. During the Boer War it served as a prison for British officers. It was from here that Winston Churchill made his famous escape after Boers captured him near Ladysmith. Appropriately, the school now houses an education department. It is not open to the public. ⊠ *Skinner and Van der Walt Sts.*

🐾 ❷❷ **Transvaal Museum.** The extensive collection of land and marine animals from around the world at this natural history museum, with an emphasis on African wildlife, is worth a visit. The museum also contains the Austin Roberts Bird Collection, the most comprehensive display of African birds in southern Africa. Much of the museum is laid out with students in mind, and exhibit descriptions are exceptionally informative. Of particular interest are the Genesis exhibits, tracing the evolution of life on earth, and the geology section, with displays of weird and wonderful rocks and minerals. Mrs. Ples, the famous australopithecine fossil found at Sterkfontein (in the Cradle of Humankind) resides here. ⊠ *Paul Kruger St., across from City Hall,* ☎ *012/322–7632,* WEB *www.nfi.org.za.* 🎟 *R8.* ☉ *Mon.–Sat. 9–5, Sun. 11–5.*

❷❾ **Union Buildings.** Designed by Sir Herbert Baker, one of South Africa's most revered architects, this impressive cream-sandstone complex is his masterpiece and home to the administrative branch of government, which now serves as the headquarters of President Thabo Mbeki. The complex incorporates a hodgepodge of styles—an Italian-tile roof, wooden shutters inspired by Cape Dutch architecture, and Renaissance columns—that somehow work beautifully. Formal gardens step down the hillside in terraces, dotted with war memorials and statues of former prime ministers. There is no public access.

❶❽ **Voortrekker Monument and Museum.** It is indicative of the tolerance of the (admittedly not perfect) new South African government that this unabashed tribute to the ideals at the heart of apartheid remains. Completed in 1949, the monument honors the Voortrekkers, Boer families who rejected British rule in the Cape and in 1835–38 trekked into the hinterland to found their own nation. The Hall of Heroes traces in its frieze the momentous events of their Great Trek, culminating in the Battle of Blood River (December 16, 1838), when a small force of Boers defeated the Zulu army without losing a single life (☞ Chapter 7). The Voortrekkers considered this victory a confirmation of their special relationship with God. An adjoining museum displays scenes and artifacts of daily Voortrekker life, as well as the Voortrekker Tapestries, 15 pictorial weavings that trace the historical high points of the Great Trek. ⊠ *Off R28,* ☎ *012/323–0682.* 🎟 *Monument R10, museum R5.* ☉ *Daily 9–4:45 (last entry at 4:30).*

Dining

$$$$ ✕ **La Madeleine.** Noted for its classic and creative French cuisine, this
★ restaurant ranks among the country's top 10 on most critics' lists. The wine list, too, is exceptional. The menu changes daily, depending on what's available at the market. For starters expect calamari tubes stuffed with ratatouille or oysters and mussels in a curry cream sauce. For a main dish try to select among rack of lamb with fresh vegetables and olives, line fish in champagne sauce, ostrich fillet with cranberry sauce, and veal in muscat sauce. In season try the strawberries in black pepper and balsamic vinegar with mascarpone ice cream. ⊠ *122 Priory Rd., Lynnwood,* ☎ *012/361–3667. Reservations essential. AE, DC, MC, V. Closed Sun.–Mon. No lunch Sat.*

$$$–$$$$ ✕ **Cynthia's.** This bistro-style restaurant is a good place to try some local game or seafood. Locals flock here for the line fish cooked on an open grill. Another favorite is the trio of game fillets with three sauces, usually mustard, wine and mushroom, and béarnaise. ⊠ *Maroelana Centre, Maroelana St.,* ☎ *012/460–3229. Reservations essential. AE, DC, MC, V.*

$$$–$$$$ ✕ **O'Galito's.** You'll find it hard to believe you're nearly 500 km (300 mi) inland at this restaurant dedicated to seafood. Of course, there's no sea view, but if you have an enormous imagination, the big airy spaces and white tables bring to mind the beach. The Galito platter is the most expensive and most popular dish on the menu, with langoustines, king prawns, small crayfish (lobster), mussels, grilled calamari, baked oysters, and french fries and rice. There is a limited vegetarian menu and old favorites such as peri-peri chicken for the less adventurous. ⊠ *367 Hilda St., Hatfield,* ☎ *012/342–6610. AE, DC, MC, V.*

$$–$$$$ ✕ **Casa José.** Prawns, fish, and chicken prepared in a spicy peri-peri style are some of the popular Mozambican specialties that are prepared to perfection here. Occasionally Tex, the owner, finds some rabbit, which he does in the Portuguese way, and for the real traditionalists, there's *bacalhau* (salt cod) grilled with olive oil and garlic. Expect to sit among tables filled to capacity with Mozambican expats chatting loudly in Portuguese. ⊠ *Waterkloof Centre, corner Crown and Main Sts., Waterkloof,* ☎ *012/460–8068. AE, DC, MC, V.*

Lodging

$$$$ ⊡ **Illyria House.** Although there are more grand hotels in town, sheikhs
★   and presidents have been known to request to be moved to this small but very special suburban guest house on Muckleneuk Hill overlooking the city bowl. The house takes its name from the mythical place where Shakespeare set his romantic *Twelfth Night* comedy, and the house and gardens feel as though they're part of an elaborate stage set for the play. Presiding over the array of French antiques and over-the-top Venetian light fittings is vivacious owner and host Marietjie van der Walt. There is a dining room but no set menu—the butler and chef will discuss options with you each day and then shop just for you. Nothing is too much, which explains something of the lodge's appeal. If it's available, ask for the Katarina Suite, with its view of the Union Buildings. ⊠ *327 Bourke St., Muckleneuk, Pretoria,* ☎ *012/344–5193 or 012/344–4641,* ⅎ*ᴬˣ* *012/344–3978,* ⍵ᴱᴮ *www.illyria.co.za. 7 suites. AE, DC, MC, V. BP.*

$$$–$$$$ ⊡ **Sheraton Pretoria.** The first five floors here consist of standard or classic rooms, all decorated in shades of cream with Italian marble tiles. The top two floors comprise the Towers: 36 executive rooms and seven suites, each with a personal computer, decorated in subtle African theme with shades of green, brown, and ocher. The Royal Suite has, of all things, bulletproof glass. Ask for a room overlooking the Union Building Gardens. Sunday brunches are long, leisurely affairs with live jazz on the terrace. ⊠ *643 Church St., at Wessels,* ☎ *012/429–9999,* ⅎᴬˣ *012/429–9300,* ⍵ᴱᴮ *www.sheraton.com. 168 rooms, 7 suites. 3 restaurants, 2 bars, pool, massage, sauna, health club. AE, DC, MC, V.*

$$$ ⊡ **Irene Country Lodge.** This tranquil village and its adjacent meadows are where soldier, philosopher, and statesman Jan Christiaan Smuts chose to make his home when he craved nature during his political career—a sort of Walden Pond. Majestic old oak trees add to the sense of country, but it's just a stone's throw from Pretoria and close to both Johannesburg and its airport. Rooms are spacious and decorated in a variety of themes ranging from light florals to a dark blue wild duck motif. The Oak Tree restaurant is justification for not hav-

ing to venture farther for your needs. ⊠ *Irene Village, Nellmapius Dr., Irene,* ☏ *012/667–6464,* 𝔽𝔸𝕏 *012/667–6476. 47 rooms, 2 suites. Restaurant, bar, coffee shop, room service, pool. AE, DC, MC, V. BP*

The Arts

Pretoria is a quiet city, but **Hatfield Square** is pretty much *the* place to go at night. In the area defined by Burnett, Hilda, and Festival streets and just off Duncan Street, it's a hodgepodge of bars, coffeehouses, and restaurants. It's safe to walk there at night, and you'll find an interesting mix of slightly rowdy students, young professionals, diplomats, politicians, and a few creative types.

THEATER

The **Renaissance State Theatre Pretoria** (⊠ Church St., ☏ 012/322–1665) is the largest theater in Africa, but it may close down. At the time of writing, it was uncertain what its future held, but there are serious attempts to salvage this icon of the arts. In all probability, when you read this, there will be wonderful performances—phone and find out.

Shopping

Ntlhoro Muti and Curio Shop. As well as a few kitsch souvenirs, you'll find a range of authentic *muti* (traditional herbal medicines) in this interesting little store. ⊠ *Corner Paul Kruger and Minnaar Sts.,* ☏ *012/ 320–6404.* ⊙ *Weekdays 8–5, Sat. 8–1.*

Cradle of Humankind

Declared a World Heritage Site in December 1999, the Cradle of Humankind is an area of about 100,000 acres and contains some of the richest fossil sites in the world. As well as the immense treasure of hominid remains, there are also artifacts and fossils dating to Stone Age and Iron Age times. There are 12 explored sites, although only Sterkfontein Caves is open regularly to the public. To see any of the others, you will need to arrange an escorted tour. Even before the World Heritage status, many local landowners created the Kromdraai Conservancy to preserve the area, and there are many other attractions, including small game reserves. For general inquiries about the Cradle area, contact **Conserv Tours** (☏ 011/957–0034). **Palaeotours** has escorted trips to many of the palaeololgicalsites along with an informed, user-friendly interpretation. (☏ 011/837–6660).

★ **Sterkfontein Cave** is the most well known of the area's sites. It was here, in 1936, that Dr. Raymond Dart discovered his now famous Mrs. Ples, as she is popularly known, or *Australopithecus africanus,* the first identified "missing link" providing evolutionary evidence of the connection between humans and apes. Guided tours take about one hour. Unfortunately, the limestone formations were almost totally stripped for making cement by early miners. Tours last an hour and leave on the half hour. ⊠ *Sterkfontein Caves Rd., Kromdraai,* ☏ *011/956–6342.* 🎫 *R12.* ⊙ *Tues.–Sun. 9:30–3:30.*

For some far more recent history, you can tour the **Old Kromdraai Gold Mine,** one of the oldest gold mines in the country. It's a little spooky as you don a miner's helmet and wander into its murky depths. ☏ *011/ 957–0205.* 🎫 *R25.* ⊙ *Weekends 9–5.*

You can spot most of the Big Five at nearby **Rhino and Lion Park,** where ostriches peck at your windows in the vain hope of being fed, herds of wildebeest and antelope dot the plains, and rhinos slumber in thorn tree thickets. Don't miss the lion, wild dog, and cheetah enclosures and the vulture hide and "restaurant" (feeding area), but be warned—the animals tend to be very frisky. Feeding times vary between species and age groups, so phone to check. As well as a self-drive tour, you can do an escorted game drive, mountain-bike ride, or horse trail (fee). ✉ *Kromdraai Rd., Kromdraai,* ☎ *011/957–0109.* 🎟 *R30.* ☉ *Daily 8–5.*

Wonder Cave is a huge single-chamber cave with a number of intact stalagmites and stalactites. It's easy to get into, with an elevator taking you all the way down, or if you're feeling adventurous, you can rappel in (fee). ✉ *Kromdraai Rd., Kromdraai,* ☎ *011/957–0034 or 011/957–0106.* 🎟 *R25.* ☉ *Daily 8–5.*

Dining and Lodging

$$$$ ✕ **The Gorge Restaurant.** This restaurant is really all about the view. In the daytime you can gaze out over a dramatic river gorge with a pleasant-sounding little waterfall, and at night you can see, literally, to the ends of the universe—the restaurant has a 16-inch Cassegrain telescope with an Apogee 7 camera that enables the resident astronomer to project the real-time night sky onto a screen in the dining room (if it's cloudy, they use images from sometime during the previous week). An informative talk is followed by a session of comet or supernova hunting—you may even get to name one. The food is good although not particularly imaginative—consisting of a buffet of braais, stir-fries, carved meats, salads, and other old favorites. But let's face it, when diners spend ages staring into outer space with their jaws hanging open, forgetting to eat, the food has to be robust—and the chef nontemperamental. ✉ *At Aloe Ridge Hotel, off M5 (mailing address: Muldersdrift 1747),* ☎ *011/957–2070. AE, DC, MC, V.*

$$–$$$$ ✕ **Cornutti the Cradle.** After you park your car a few hundred yards from the restaurant, a driver in a golf cart will chauffeur you down the steep hill to your destination. Here tables are lined up on a huge veranda overlooking a 6,600-acre game reserve. The overall impression is one of light, space, and silence—except on Friday night, when live jazz is offered. But it's not just about the setting—the menu is pretty impressive, too. The menu changes frequently but offers mostly Italian dishes. Choices may include beef carpaccio with avocado and Parmesan, baked polenta with Gorgonzola and tomato, or braised lamb shank with red wine and balsamic vinegar. Baked quince with ice cream is a dessert favorite. There's also an impressive wine list with many local specialties. ✉ *The Cradle of Humankind, Gauteng,* ☎ *011/659–1622. AE, DC, MC, V. Closed Mon.–Tues. No dinner Sun.*

$$–$$$ ✕ **The Carnivore.** A meal here is a must if you're in the area—although
★ it's not the place for a quiet romantic dinner because the huge space lends itself to a loud and rather frenetic scene. Game meat—such as warthog, impala, crocodile, and others—vies for space around an enormous open fire with tamer fare like pork and mutton. Great hunks of the meat are brought around to your table on Masai spears and carved directly onto your plate until you (literally) surrender by lowering the flag on your table. It's an eat-as-much-as-you-can set menu for R120. Surprisingly, there's also an excellent vegetarian à la carte menu with African delicacies such as *aviyal*—a spicy mixed vegetable dish cooked in coconut milk—and *kumbi baji*—mushrooms and peas cooked in a spicy yogurt sauce. ✉ *Misty Hills,* ☎ *011/957–2099. AE, DC, MC, V.*

$$–$$$ 🏨 **Toadbury Hall.** This small country hotel is peaceful and pretty, set in lovely spacious grounds. The rooms are predominantly white enlivened with bold, framed botanical prints. All rooms have underfloor heating, and bathrooms have separate showers and two hand basins. It's a great place to escape the city. ⊠ *On the M5 (mailing address: Box 746, Muldersdrift 1747),* ☎ *011/659–0335,* FAX *011/659–0058,* WEB *www.toadburyhall.co.za. 6 rooms, 1 suite. Restaurant, bar, pool, 2 tennis courts, meeting rooms. AE, DC, MC, V. BP. No children under 12.*

$$ 🏠 **Glenburn Lodge.** Hot-air balloon launches originate here, making this is a good spot stay if this early-morning activity is on your agenda. Although it's a well-run establishment, it lacks sparkle. Comfortable chalets are built in something approaching a suburban subdivision style, but the rooms are bright and cheerful, decorated in stripes, geometrics, and, befitting the Scottish theme, tartans. ⊠ *Off DF Malan Dr., follow signs to Kromdraai and turn off onto gravel drive for 2 km (1 mi) (mailing address: Box 492, Muldersdrift 1747),* ☎ *011/957–2691,* FAX *011/957–2697,* WEB *www.glenburn.co.za. 45 rooms, 3 suites, 32 chalets. Restaurant, bar, 2 pools, tennis court, gym, volleyball, fishing, meeting rooms. AE, DC, MC, V.*

$$ 🏠 **Misty Hills Country Hotel.** This attractive hotel is spread over a huge
★ expanse of landscaped gardens with tinkling waters, banks of white roses, and authentic African sculptures. The rooms are predominantly white with African artwork. Suites have outside showers in an enclosed garden and, in the case of the royal suites, a plunge pool. There is an excellent spa on site offering the whole range of massage, beauty, and health therapy treatments. The Carnivore restaurant is worth a visit even if you're not staying here. ⊠ *Drift Blvd., off M5, about 10 km (6 mi) from Krugersdorp and 40 km (24 mi) from Pretoria on the R28 (mailing address: Private Bag 1, Muldersdrift 1747),* ☎ *011/957–2099,* FAX *011/957–3212,* WEB *www.mistyhill.co.za. 94 rooms, 8 suites. 2 restaurants, bar, 3 pools, sauna, spa, tennis, gym, volleyball, recreation room, meeting rooms. AE, DC, MC, V. BP.*

Shopping

On the edge of the Cradle, as it's called, is the **Crocodile River Arts & Crafts Ramble** (☎ 011/662–2810), a route set up by local artists, potters, sculptors, and other craftspeople.

Outdoor Activities

Hot-air ballooning trips are offered very early every morning, weather permitting, by **Air Track Adventures** (☎ 011/957–2322, FAX 011/957–2360). The flight costs R1,150 and includes breakfast and sparkling wine.

The Magaliesberg

The Magaliesberg is a range of hills stretching 120 km (74 mi) between Pretoria and the town of Rustenburg, about a 90-minute drive northwest of Johannesburg. The Boer War once raged here, and the remains of British blockhouses can still be seen. However, the region is most remarkable for its natural beauty. Grassy slopes cleft by ocher buttresses, streams adorned with ferns, waterfalls plunging into pools, and superb rock formations contribute to the Magaliesberg's unique beauty. Activities in the area focus on the outdoors—you can go hiking, mountain biking, horseback riding, swimming in crystal streams, take a picnic lunch to one of the natural hideaways, or take a dawn balloon flight over the area followed by champagne breakfast.

The Magaliesberg Mountains and the town of Magaliesburg (note the spelling difference) are both very popular with locals, and the main areas and attractions get extremely crowded on weekends.

NEED A
BREAK?
Pop into **Rosemary Cottage** (☎ 014/577–1600, ☼ Thurs.–Mon. 9–
4:30) at Magalies Trading Centre. Choose between coffee, herbal tea,
a salad, or a delicious sandwich like salmon and dill with homemade
macadamia mayonnaise. If possible, try to resist the handmade choco-
lates for sale in the adjacent minideli, which also sells fresh herbs and
herbal candles.

If all this sounds too passive and you want to hike, the best bet is to
set off from **Mountain Sanctuary Park.**

Dining and Lodging

$$$–$$$$ ✕⌹ **De Hoek Country House.** In France this would be called an auberge,
or country inn, and it wouldn't be out of place in Provence with its dressed
stone and heavy timber-beam construction. De Hoek is very exclusive
and set in semi-indigenous gardens in the exquisite Magalies River val-
ley. Rooms are in a double-storied stone building along the river and are
quiet and classical, with deep golden-yellow walls and dark mahogany
furniture. Superior suites have fireplaces, and all rooms have under-floor
heating. However, the food is what brings most people here. Classic French
techniques applied to contemporary ingredients result in an eclectic
menu. Try the prawn-and-vegetable spring rolls served with glass noo-
dles or poached beef fillet with truffle-infused mashed potatoes. ⊠ *Sign-
posted off the R24 just north of Magaliesburg (mailing address: Box 117,
Magaliesburg, 2805),* ☎ *014/577–1198,* FAX *014/577–4530,* WEB *www.
dehoekcountryhouse.com. 4 rooms, 16 suites. Pool, archery, croquet, hik-
ing, fishing, library. AE, DC, MC, V. BP.*

$$$–$$$$ ⌹ **Mount Grace Country House Hotel.** This peaceful, village-style coun-
try hotel near the town of Magaliesburg has accommodations in de-
lightful buildings of differing heights, which have glorious views of the
mountains, valley, and landscaped gardens. The Mountain Village is
the most luxurious lodging, with sunken baths, heated towel rails, a
minibar, and endless views of the area. If you're looking for more pri-
vacy, you might prefer to stay at Grace Village, which is a little more
secluded and farther down the mountain. The most reasonable lodg-
ing is the Thatchstone Village. Country-style decor—thatch, wood, and
wicker—creates a delightful ambience in the hotel, and the food is whole-
some country fare. ⊠ *On the R24 to Hekpoort, near town of Maga-
liesburg (mailing address: Private Bag 5004, Magaliesburg 1791),* ☎
014/577–1350, FAX *014/577–1202,* WEB *www.grace.co.za. 90 rooms. 2
restaurants, bar, 3 pools, tennis court, bowling, croquet, hiking, fish-
ing, billiards, library. AE, DC, MC, V. BP.*

$$–$$$ ⌹ **Valley Lodge.** Although it's a bit too big to be called a hideaway,
there's a great country feel here attributable to the elegantly furnished
rooms, the bird sanctuary, the 240-acre nature reserve, and the tinkling
stream that runs through it. It is very popular with corporate groups,
but it's big enough to find a quiet spot away from it all. Rooms have
small sitting areas and are decorated with country accents some have
four-poster beds and fireplaces. ⊠ *Jennings St. (mailing address: Box
13, Magaliesburg 1791),* ☎ *014/577–1301 or 014/577–1305,* FAX *014/
577–1306,* WEB *www.valleylodge.co.za. 64 rooms. Restaurant, bar, in-
room data ports, pool, putting green, 3 tennis courts, gym, volleyball,
hiking, horseback riding, fishing. AE, DC, MC, V. BP.*

$$ ⌹ **Green Hills.** A lovely, peaceful, romantic B&B, this place is just right
★   for a break from the hustle and bustle of the city. Rooms are in three
separate cottages in a lovely garden. Attractive ceramic fireplaces are aglow
on cold winter nights. The bathrooms are spacious, with large showers
and separate baths. Nothing is too much trouble for hosts Peter and Etaine,
who will make dinner, picnic hampers, or braais by arrangement. Rooms

have tea and coffee stations and (befitting its romantic image) no TVs. ✉ *11 km (7 mi) from Magaliesburg, on the T1, near Bekker School (mailing address: Box 286, Magaliesburg 1791),* ☎ *014/577–2063. 3 rooms. Hiking, fishing. No credit cards. BP.*

$$ 🏠 **Jameson Country Cottages.** These pretty, well-appointed self-catering cottages can sleep four or six people and have stoves, fridges, TVs, and a good selection of culinary appliances. Set in an attractive garden around a pool and adjacent to a cane furniture factory and shop, they offer excellent value for the money. ✉ *On the R509, 10 km (6 mi) from Magaliesburg (mailing address: Box 96, Magaliesburg 1791),* ☎ *014/ 577–1361 or 083/301–5791,* ℻ *014/577–4621,* 🌐 *www.westcane.co.za. 6 cottages. Pool, driving range, gift shop. AE, DC, MC, V.*

$ 🏠 **Mountain Sanctuary Park.** Don't let the rather terse list of rules at
★ the entrance put you off this place, but do heed it as a warning the owners are fiercely protective of their little piece of paradise—and justly so. This is a simple campsite, with spotless ablutions, on-site caravans, and some basic but clean and comfortable self-catering cottages with electricity, hot water, and cooking facilities. The emphasis here is on the surrounding 2,200 acres of mountains, pools, waterfalls, and streams, where you can hike a different route every day—each more beautiful than the last. Pets and radios are forbidden, but the sound of children's laughter is welcome. ✉ *40 km (25 mi) from Magaliesburg on a dirt road, or 15 km (9 mi) from the N4,* ☎ *014/534–0114 or 082/371–6146,* ℻ *014/534–0568,* 🌐 *www.mountain-sanctuary. co.za. 30 campsites, 3 chalets, 3 caravans. Pool. No credit cards.*

Shopping

Most visitors just amble around the area exploring the many crafts shops and studios and nibbling away in coffee shops. If you want to do some fun shopping, try browsing through the **Magalies Trading Centre,** on the R24. You'll find information on accommodations and general attractions in the area at **Magalies Reservations** (☎ 014/577–1733). **Crystal Feeling** (☎ 014/577–2182) has many fascinating decorative and healing crystals. Check out the fantastic handmade furniture at **Delcardo** (☎ 014/577–3509). About 10 km (6 mi) out of town on the R509 is **Western Cane Trading** (☎ 014/577–1361), where you can browse through a huge warehouse of cane, wood, and iron furniture. There's a good coffee shop here, and they also sell gourmet items.

Outdoor Activities

You could do a horse ride with **Roberts Farm Horse Trails** (☎ 014/ 577–3332). This is a working farm that offers trails as an addition to the more serious business of growing crops and raising cattle. They do slow rides for beginners during the week and on Saturday, farming schedules permitting, and longer rides on Sunday. Be warned, though: the Sunday-morning rides are fast and furious, so don't join one if you're not sure you can take the pace. A fun and fascinating way to start the day is with an early-morning balloon ride. **Bill Harrops Original Balloon Safaris** (☎ 011/705–3201) flies daily, weather permitting. A flight costs R1,420, including breakfast and sparkling wine.

Pilanesberg and Sun City

The 150,000-acre **Pilanesberg National Park** is centered on the caldera of an extinct volcano dating back some 100 million years. Rings of concentric mountains converge on a central lake filled with crocodiles and hippos. Open grassland, rocky crags, and densely forested gorges provide ideal habitats for a wide range of plains and woodland game, including rare brown hyenas, sables, and gemsboks.

Since the introduction of lions in 1993, Pilanesberg can boast the Big Five. Today it's hard to believe the park, reclaimed from farmland, was ever anything but wild. It is a bird-watcher's paradise, with a vast range of grassland species, waterbirds, and birds of prey.

It's a particularly accessible park in every sense. It's close to Johannesburg, inexpensive, and, best of all, malaria free.

You can drive around the park in your own vehicle or join an escorted safari with **Pilanesberg Safaris** (☎ 014/555–5469). For a different perspective try a balloon safari with **Air Track Adventures** (☎ 011/957–2322, FAX 011/957–2360). A one-hour flight costs R1,550 per person, which includes game drives, sparkling wine, and full breakfast at Bakubung or Kwa-Maritane.

Sun City is a huge entertainment-and-resort complex in the middle of dry bushveld, 177 km (110 mi) northwest of Johannesburg. It's the dream child of Sol Kerzner, the South African entrepreneur who first saw the possibilities of a casino in the rocky wilds of the Pilanesberg Mountains (that, being in the homeland of Bophuthatswana, were exempt from South Africa's then-strict antigambling laws). Now, nearly two decades later, Sun City comprises four hotels, two casinos, major amphitheaters, and a host of outdoor attractions. The complex is split into two parts: the original Sun City and the Lost City, a project anchored by the magnificent Palace Hotel.

Comparisons with Las Vegas are inappropriate. Sun City is a resort, not a city, although it does rely on the same kinds of entertainment: gambling, slot machines, topless revues, and big-time extravaganzas. Sun City stages enormous rock concerts, major boxing bouts, the annual Sun City Golf Challenge, and the occasional Miss World Pageant. It also displays that familiar Vegas sense (or lack) of taste—with the Palace a notable exception—doling out the kind of ersatz glitter and glare that appeals to a shiny polyester crowd. Whatever your feelings about the complex, you have to admire Kerzner's creativity when you see the Lost City, where painted wild animals march across the ceilings, imitation star-spangled skies glitter even by day, lush jungles decorate the halls, and stone lions and elephants keep watch over it all.

The resort burst onto the international scene in the apartheid era, when a few American and British music stars broke the cultural boycott to play Sun City. Back then it was part of Bophuthatswana, one of the nominally independent homelands designed to give blacks a semblance of self-government (although no one was ever given the choice to become a member of a homeland, and once you did become part of one you no longer had even basic rights as a South African citizen). Today Bophuthatswana has been reabsorbed into South Africa as part of the North West Province.

Sun City's genuine appeal lies not in the slots but in nearby Pilanesberg National Park and a full round of outdoor sports and activities, including two Gary Player–designed golf courses and an artificial lake where visitors can water-ski, parasail, sailboard, or surf in the Valley of the Waves, a giant pool that creates perfect waves for bodysurfing.

Lodging

Accommodations in Sun City are very expensive, and only the Palace can justify its rates. You may opt to stay instead in the nearby rest camps and private lodges of the Pilanesberg Game Reserve.

$$$$ 🏨 **Bakubung.** Abutting the national park, this lodge sits at the head of a long valley with terrific views of a hippo pool that forms the lodge's central attraction—it's not unusual to have hippos grazing 100 ft from the terrace restaurant. Despite this, the lodge never really succeeds in creating a bush feel, perhaps because it's such a big convention and family destination. Its brick buildings also feel vaguely institutional. Nevertheless, the guest rooms, particularly the executive studios, are very pleasant, thanks to light pine furniture, colorful African bedspreads, and super views of the valley. The lodge conducts game drives (fee) in open-air vehicles, as well as ranger-guided walks. A shuttle bus (R50 round-trip) runs to Sun City, 10 km (6 mi) away. ⊠ *Pilanesberg National Park (mailing address: Box 294, Sun City 0316),* ☎ *014/552–6000; 011/806–6888 for reservations,* ℻ *014/552–6300,* WEB *www.legacyhotels.co.za. 76 rooms, 66 chalets. Restaurant, bar, café, pool, tennis court. AE, DC, MC, V.*

$$$$ 🏨 **The Cascades.** The lavish use of mirrors, brass, and black marble in the lobby sets the tone for this rather overpriced hotel only yards from Sun City's massive entertainment center. Rooms are decorated in soothing rust colors highlighted with bold blues and yellows. All overlook the Gary Player golf course, the gardens, and an artificial waterfall. For the best views request a room on an upper floor. ⊠ *Box 7, Sun City,* ☎ *014/557–1020 or 011/780–7800 for central reservations,* ℻ *014/557–3442. 243 rooms. 2 restaurants, 2 bars, room service, pool. AE, DC, MC, V. BP.*

$$$$ 🏨 **Kwa Maritane.** Unfortunately, this hotel fails to take advantage of its setting in a bowl of rocky hills on the edge of the national park—definitely its greatest asset. Many hotel buildings look inward onto swimming pools and lawns. And, as at Bakubung, the bustle of convention goers and children tends to drown out the mesmerizing sound of the bush. The big exception is the resort's terrific blind, overlooking a water hole and connected to the lodge via a tunnel. Guest rooms, with high thatched ceilings and large glass doors that open onto a veranda, are comfortable. Guests can pay to go on day or night game drives in open-air vehicles or to go on guided walks with an armed ranger. ⊠ *Pilanesberg National Park (mailing address: Box 39, Sun City, 0316),* ☎ *014/552–5100 or 011/806–6888 for reservations,* ℻ *014/552–5333,* WEB *www. legacyhotels.co.za. 155 rooms. Restaurant, bar, 2 pools, sauna, miniature golf, tennis court. AE, DC, MC, V.*

$$$$ 🏨 **Palace of the Lost City.** Given the tackiness of Sun City, you would
★ think any hotel based on the concept of a lost African palace would suffer from theme-park syndrome, but happily that's not the case here. Sculpted cranes and leaping kudu appear to take flight from the hotel towers, elephants guard triumphal stairways and bridges, and graceful reminders of ersatz Africa strike you at every turn. No expense has been spared, and the attention to detail is mind-boggling. All rooms have hand-carved doors and furnishings; the jungle paintings on the ceiling of the lobby's rotunda took 5,000 hours to complete; and the hand-laid mosaic floor is made up of 300,000 separate tiles. Guest rooms, done in rich earth tones, blend African motifs with delicate Eastern touches. The opulence and theme of the place haven't helped to ameliorate the long-term dissatisfaction of the staff at the whole Sun City complex, and not-so-occasional strikes do result in erratic service. ⊠ *Box 308, Sun City 0316,* ☎ *014/557–3131 or 011/780–7800 for central reservations,* ℻ *014/557–4302. 338 rooms. 2 restaurants, 2 bars, room service, pool, meeting rooms. AE, DC, MC, V. EP.*

$$$$ 🏨 **Sun City Hotel and Casino.** This is the original Sun City property, and it still houses the gaming casino, banks of slot machines, and a topless extravaganza. If gambling and nonstop action are your scene, this will appeal to you, but most people find its tackiness overwhelming. The main room is decked out like a Tarzan jungle, with palms and

artificial waterfalls, rope walkways, and rain forest and bamboo murals. The sound of rushing water drowns out the jangle of the slots somewhat, but nothing can conceal the jarring glitter of this lurid spectacle. Thankfully, rooms—in cream and white with old Cape-style furnishings—are more sedate. ⊠ *Box 2, Sun City,* ☎ *014/552–1001; 011/780–7800 for central reservations,* ℻ *014/557–4210. 340 rooms. 4 restaurants, 2 bars, room service, pool, casino. AE, DC, MC, V. BP.*

$$$$ ⊞ **Tshukudu Game Lodge.** By far the most stylish option in the area,
★ Tshukudu is built into the side of a steep, rocky hill and overlooks open grassland and a large water hole where elephants come to bathe. If you watch long enough, you'll probably see most of the Big Five from your veranda. Winding stone stairways lead up the hill to lovely, thoughtfully set thatched chalets with private balconies, wicker furniture, bold African materials, and black-slate floors. Fireplaces, minibars, and mosquito nets are standard, and sunken bathtubs have spectacular views of the water hole. It's a long, 132-step climb to the main lodge on the summit, making this an impractical choice for those with mobility problems. At night you can use a spotlight to illuminate game at the water hole below. ⊠ *Pilanesberg National Park,* ☎ *014/552–6255; 011/806–6888 for reservations,* ℻ *014/522–6266,* 🕸 *www.legacyhotels.co.za. 6 chalets. Pool. AE, DC, MC, V. FAP.*

$$$–$$$$ ⊞ **Manyane.** The cheapest lodging in the Sun City area, the park's main rest camp lies in a thinly wooded savanna east of the Pilanesberg's volcanic ridges. Modeled after Kruger's modern rest camps, Manyane is short on charm but long on functional efficiency and cleanliness. Thatched roofing helps soften the harsh lines of bare tile floors and brick. Guests can choose either a two-, four-, or six-bed chalet, all with fully equipped kitchens and bathrooms. Short self-guided nature trails from the chalets are available, giving interesting background to the geology and flora of the park. ⊠ *Pilanesberg National Park,* ☎ *014/555–6135,* 🕸 *www.goldenleopard.co.za. 60 chalets. Restaurant, bar, pool, miniature golf, playground. AE, DC, MC, V.*

JOHANNESBURG A TO Z

To research prices, get advice from other travelers, and book travel arrangements, visit www.fodors.com.

AIR TRAVEL
CARRIERS
Major airlines serving Johannesburg include Air Namibia, British Airways, KLM Royal Dutch Airlines, Qantas, Singapore Airlines, South African Airways, and Virgin Atlantic Airways. In addition to South African Airways, the major domestic carriers serving Johannesburg are British Airways, operated by Comair, and S.A. Airlink.

➤ AIRLINES AND CONTACTS: **Air Namibia** (☎ 011/390–2876). **British Airways** (☎ 011/441–8600). **Comair** (☎ 011/921–0222). **KLM Royal Dutch Airlines** (☎ 011/881–9696). **Qantas** (☎ 011/441–8600). **Singapore Airlines** (☎ 011/880–8566). **South African Airways** and **S.A. Airlink** (☎ 011/978–1111). **Virgin Atlantic Airlines** (☎ 011/340–3400).

AIRPORTS AND TRANSFERS
Johannesburg International Airport lies 19 km (12 mi) from the city. Most international flights depart from this airport. The airport has a tourist information desk, a VAT refund office, and a computerized accommodation service.

Magic Bus operates a minibus airport service every half hour that stops at the Holiday Inn Crowne Plaza (Sandton), the Balalaika, and the Sandton Sun & Towers. The trip costs R75 and takes 35–50 minutes. Magic Bus also offers door-to-door pickup anywhere in the city starting at about R180 for the first two passengers.

Observer Tours is one of the best companies in Johannesburg for chauffeur-driven cars and will do transfers anywhere in the Gauteng area and even a bit farther afield. Expect to pay about R200–R250 for a transfer between the airport and the northern suburbs.

The Rotunda, outside the Johannesburg train station, at Leyds and Loveday Streets in Braamfontein, is the main terminal for airport shuttles if you're transferring directly between a train or an intercity bus and the airport. Phala Tours provides shuttles from here to the airport for about R60–R70.

There are scores of licensed taxis hanging around outside the airport terminal. They must legally have a working meter. Expect to pay about R200–R250 for a trip to Sandton.

➤ AIRPORTS AND TRANSFERS: **Johannesburg International Airport** (☎ 011/975–9963). **Magic Bus** (☎ 011/608–1662; 011/394–6902 airport office). **Observer Tours** (☎ 011/616–3790 or 082/410–0209). **Phala Tours** (☎ 011/975–0510).

BUS TRAVEL
All intercity buses depart from the Rotunda, the city's principal transport hub. Greyhound and Translux operate extensive routes around the country. Intercape Mainliner runs to Cape Town. Panthera Azul runs between Johannesburg and Maputo. The Baz Bus does not depart from the Rotunda but operates a hop-on, hop-off door-to-door service stopping at backpackers' hostels between Johannesburg and Durban on two routes—via the Drakensberg; or via Mpumalanga, Swaziland and Zululand—and then on to Cape Town.

➤ BUS INFORMATION: **Baz Bus** (☎ 021/439–2323, WEB www.bazbus.com). **Greyhound** (☎ 011/249–8700, or book through Computicket 083/909–0909; 012/323–1154 Pretoria booking office, WEB www.greyhound.co.za). **Intercape Mainliner** (☎ 012/654–4114, or book through Computicket 083/909–0909, WEB www.intercape.co.za). **Panthera Azul** (☎ 011/337–7409 or 011/337–4209). **Translux** (☎ 011/774–3333).

CAR RENTAL
Major rental agencies have offices in the northern suburbs and at the airport.

➤ LOCAL AGENCIES: **Avis** (✉ 167A Rivonia Rd., Sandton, ☎ 011/884–2221; Johannesburg International Airport, ☎ 011/394–5433, WEB www.avis.co.za). **Budget** (✉ Holiday Inn Crowne Plaza, at Rivonia Rd. and Grayston Dr., Sandton, ☎ 011/883–5730; Johannesburg International Airport, ☎ 011/394–2905, WEB www.budget.co.za). **Europcar** (✉ Oxford Manor, corner Chaplin Oxford and Chaplin Sts., Illovo, ☎ 011/447–6573; Johannesburg International Airport, ☎ 011/394–8832, WEB www.europcar.ca.za). **Hertz** (✉ 196 Oxford Rd., at Chaplin St., Illovo, ☎ 011/327–6589; Johannesburg International Airport, ☎ 011/390–2066, WEB www.hertz.co.za). **Imperial** (✉ Sandton Sun Hotel, at 5th and Alice Sts., Sandhurst, ☎ 011/883–4352; Johannesburg International Airport, ☎ 011/394–4020, WEB www.imperial.ih.co.za). **Tempest Car Hire** (✉ Sandton, ☎ 011/784–3343; Johanneburg International Airport, ☎ 011/394–8626, WEB www.tempestcarhire.co.za).

EMBASSIES AND CONSULATES
Pretoria is the capital of South Africa, and most embassies are there; however, some countries also maintain consulates in Johannesburg.

➤ AUSTRALIA: **Australian High Commission** (✉ 292 Orient St., Arcadia, Pretoria, ☎ 012/342–3740).

➤ CANADA: **Canadian Embassy** (✉ 1103 Arcadia St., Hatfield, Pretoria, ☎ 012/422–3000).

➤ UNITED KINGDOM: **British High Commission** (✉ 255 Hill St., Arcadia, Pretoria, ☎ 012/483–1200, FAX 012/433–3207. **U.K. Consulate** ✉ 275 Jan Smuts Ave., Dunkeld West, ☎ 011/327–0015, FAX 011/325–2131.

➤ UNITED STATES: **U.S. Embassy** (✉ 877 Pretorius St., Arcadia, Pretoria, ☎ 012/342–1048).

EMERGENCIES

In the event of a medical emergency, you're advised to seek help at one of the city's private hospitals. Among the most reputable are Milpark Hospital and Sandton Medi-Clinic.

➤ EMERGENCY SERVICES: **Ambulance** (☎ 999). **Emergencies** (☎ 10111 landline; 112 mobile line). **Police** (☎ 10111).

➤ HOSPITALS: **Milpark Hospital** (✉ 9 Guild Rd., off Empire Rd., Parktown, ☎ 011/480–5600). **Sandton Medi-Clinic** (✉ Main St. and Peter Pl., off William Nicol, Lyme Park, ☎ 011/709–2000).

TAXIS

Don't expect to rush out into the street and hail a taxi. There are taxi ranks at the airport, the train station, and the Rotunda, but as a rule you must phone for a cab. Taxis should be licensed and have a working meter. Ask the taxi company how long it will take the taxi to get to you—many taxis are radioed while on call, and the time to get to your area may vary considerably, depending on whether there is a taxi in the vicinity already. The meter starts at R2 and clicks over at a rate of R5 per kilometer. Expect to pay about R180–R250 to the airport from town or Sandton and about R100 to the city center from Sandton. The charge for waiting time is about R40–R50 per hour.

➤ TAXI COMPANIES: **Maxi Taxi** (☎ 011/648–1212). **Rose Taxis** (☎ 011/403–9625).

TOURS

For city tours call Springbok Atlas or Gold Reef City Tours. They both have two- to three-hour tours of the city that may include visits to the city center, the diamond-cutting works, and some of the city's more interesting parks and suburbs. Other tours explore Pretoria; Cullinan, a working diamond mine; Sun City; and the Pilanesberg National Park. The Adventure Bus is an excellent way of seeing Johannesburg in a short time. Observer Tours will do tailor-made, chauffeur-driven tours for one or two people or small groups. JMT Tours and Safaris can arrange a trip to Soweto.

➤ TOUR-OPERATOR RECOMMENDATIONS: **Adventure Bus** (☎ 011/975–9338, 011/975–2253 or 082/413–9192). **Gold Reef City Tours** (☎ 011/496–1400). **JMT Tours and Safaris** (☎ 083/307–6038, ☎ FAX 011/980–6038). **Observer Tours** (☎ 011/616–3790 or 082/410–0209). **Springbok Atlas** (☎ 011/396–1053, WEB www.springbokatlas.com).

DIAMOND AND GOLD TOURS

Mynhardts conducts 45-minute tours of its diamond-cutting operation. You can also purchase diamonds if you wish. (For information on a tour of a working diamond mine, *see* Cullinan Diamond Mine, *above*.). ✉ *240 Commissioner St., Johannesburg Central,* ☎ *011/334–8897 or 011/334–2693,* WEB *mynhardt@iafrica.com.* 🎫 *Free.* ☉ *Weekdays 8:30–4:30, by appointment only.***Schwartz Jewellers** has tours of its workshops in Sandton, where you can see stone grading and gold pouring and, of course, buy the finished product. Tours are by appointment only and include a delicious tea. ☏ *011/783–1717.* ☒ *R30.* ⏲ *By appointment only.*

TOWNSHIP TOURS

Contact the **Alex Tourism Forum** for information about tours to and in Alexandra. For tours of Soweto and/or Alex contact Gold Reef City Tours (☞ Tours, *above*). **JMT Tours and Safaris** conducts tours of Soweto.

➤ TOUR INFORMATION: **Alex Tourism Forum** (☏ 011/882–3899). **JMT Tours and Safaris** (☏ 083/307–6038).

WALKING TOURS

Walk Tours has a range of walking tours of the city center, the northern suburbs, and Alexandra in addition to specialized tours such as art, sport, or other special interests.

➤ TOUR INFORMATION: **Walk Tours** (☏ 011/444–1639).

TRAIN TRAVEL

Johannesburg's train station is opposite the Rotunda in Braamfontein. The famous, luxurious *Blue Train,* which makes regular runs to Cape Town as well as the Lowveld and Victoria Falls (☞ Rail Travel *in* Smart Travel Tips A to Z), departs from here, as do Mainline Passenger Services trains to cities around the country. Trains to other major cities include the *TransKaroo* to Cape Town, the *Komati* to Nelspruit in Mpumalanga, and the *TransNatal* to Durban. Many of these national services have overnight trips and are acceptable but not terribly comfortable, offering good value for the money.

➤ TRAIN INFORMATION: **Mainline Passenger Services** (☏ 011/773–2944.). **Train station** (✉ Leyds and Loveday Sts.).

TRANSPORTATION AROUND JOHANNESBURG

Most visitors need concern themselves only with the city center and the northern suburbs. The city center is laid out in a grid, making it easy to get around, but it's not advisable to tour the area on foot except in groups or with a local guide. Jan Smuts Avenue runs north from the city center right through the major suburbs of Parktown, Rosebank, Dunkeld, Hyde Park, Craighall, and Randburg. The William Nicol Highway splits off this avenue and runs toward Sandton, the emerging new city center. An easier way to get from the city center to Sandton is up the M1, which splits to become the N1 South, leading toward Roodepoort and the southern suburbs, or the N1 North, leading toward Pretoria, where it splits into the R28, going to Pretoria in the east and Krugersdorp, Magaliesburg, and the Cradle of Humankind in the west. The N1 continues north to Pietersburg, Zimbabwe, and, ultimately, Cairo. If you plan to drive yourself around, get a *good* map.

One of the best ways to explore Johannesburg is on the Adventure Bus. Buses leave the Sandton Towers at 9, 10, 11, 12:30, 1:30, and 2:30 and follow a route around the city center, Gold Reef City, and the northern suburbs. You may jump on and off as many times as you like, and your ticket (R60) is valid for 24 hours. Stops include the major malls, Bruma Flea Market, Gold Reef City, the main museums and galleries, and the zoo. There is a tour guide on the bus who gives a running commentary and can advise on stops. There are no tours on Monday.

➤ TRANSPORTATION INFORMATION: **Adventure Bus** (☏ 011/975–9383 or 082/413–9192).

VISITOR INFORMATION

Gauteng Tourism is responsible in theory for information on the whole province, but you usually get better service from smaller information bureaus. Magalies Reservations and Conserve Tours are private information and booking centers operating in the Magaliesberg and Cradle of Humankind areas, respectively, and are a bit more organized than the "official" offices.

➤ TOURIST INFORMATION: **Conserve Tours** (☎ 011/957–0034). **Gauteng Tourism Centre** (✉ Rosebank Mall, ☎ 011/327–2000). **Magalies Reservations** (☎ 014/577–1733).

3 MPUMALANGA AND KRUGER NATIONAL PARK

Archetypal Africa—open country full of big game and primal wilderness—unfolds before you in Mpumalanga. Its most obvious allure is game-watching in and around Kruger National Park. But don't miss out on the majestic Drakensberg—mountains of mists, forests, waterfalls, and panoramic views around which you'll find some of South Africa's most luxurious hotels and lodges, as well as historic gold-rush towns and fantastic hiking and fishing.

Updated by
Kate Turkington

Mpumalanga spreads east from Gauteng to the border of Mozambique. In many ways it's South Africa's wildest and most exciting province. The 1,120-km (700-mi) Drakensberg Range—which originates in KwaZulu-Natal—divides the high, interior plateau from a low-lying subtropical belt that stretches to Mozambique and the Indian Ocean. The Lowveld—where Kruger National Park alone covers a 320-km (200-mi) swathe of wilderness—is classic Africa, with as much heat, dust, untamed bush, and big game as you can take in.

Larger than Israel and approximately the same size as Wales, Kruger National Park encompasses diverse terrain ranging from rivers filled with crocodiles and hippos to rocky outcrops and thick thorn scrub. Roaming this classic slice of Africa are animals in numbers large enough to make a conservationist squeal with delight: 1,500 lions, 7,500 elephants, 1,300 white rhinos, and 30,000 buffalo—although you'll usually see them in far smaller herds of several dozen at a time. With credentials like these, it's not a surprise that Kruger and the private game reserves abutting its western borders provide the country's best and most fulfilling game experience; in fact, it's highly likely you will see all of the Big Five—buffalo, leopard, lion, elephant, and rhino—in an average two- to three-day stay at one of the private game reserves.

The Drakensberg Escarpment rises to the west of Kruger and provides a marked contrast to the Lowveld: it's a mountainous area of trout streams and waterfalls, endless views, and giant plantations of pine and eucalyptus. Lower down, the forests give way to banana, mango, and papaya groves. People come to the escarpment to hike, unwind, soak up its beauty, and get away from the heat of the Lowveld. Touring the area by car is easy and rewarding, and you can reach many of the best lookouts without stepping far from your car.

Some of South Africa's most interesting historic events took place here. In the settlement's early days, there were frequent conflicts between the local Pedi people and European settlers. This subsequently gave way to eruptions between Boer and Brit, both seeking control of what was turning out to be a rich land. Then there was the Pilgrim's Rest gold strike of 1873, creating the very substance of bush lore and adding to Mpumalanga's appeal.

The gold rush here was every bit as raucous and wild as those in California and the Klondike, and legend has it that you can still find a few old-time prospectors panning for gold in the area. Fortune seekers from all over the world descended on these mountains to try their luck in the many rivers and streams. Although the safest route to the goldfields was the 800-km (500-mi) road from Port Natal (now Durban), many opted for a 270-km (170-mi) shortcut from Lourenço Marques (now Maputo), in Mozambique, through the wilds of the Lowveld, where malaria, yellow fever, lions, and crocodiles exacted a dreadful toll. Part of that route still survives (albeit in a more refined version) in the form of Robber's Pass, a scenic route winding down from Lydenburg to Pilgrim's Rest.

Those early gold-mining days have been immortalized in *Jock of the Bushveld*, a classic of South African literature. Jock was a Staffordshire terrier whose master, Sir Percy Fitzpatrick, worked as a transport rider during the gold rush. After a stint at the Barberton *Herald* (now Nelspruit's *Lowvelder*) as a staff reporter, Sir Percy entertained his children with tales of Jock's exploits as they logged their miles in Mpumalanga, braving leopards, baboons, and all manner of dangers.

Rudyard Kipling, who wandered this wilderness as a reporter covering the First Anglo-Boer War, in the early 1880s, encouraged Fitzpatrick to write down the stories. One hundred years later Jock is still a household name in South Africa. You'll see dozens of Jock-of-the-Bushveld markers all over Mpumalanga, seemingly wherever he cocked a leg.

Although some of the "*bundu*-bashing" (bushwhacking) and gold-rush atmosphere still exists here, depending on where you go, the rough-and-ready days of the pioneering Lowveld are almost gone. If you dig deep, you can still find traces of the last of the big-game hunters and pioneers of the Lowveld—which can make for entertaining conversation at the tap. More and more, however, luxury guest lodges prove to be the modern-day gold rush. People from around the globe come to indulge in the lodges' elegant dinners and huge English breakfasts in a variety of stunning locales.

Warning: The Lowveld area, which stretches from Malelane (east of Nelspruit) to Komatipoort, on the Mozambique border, and up throughout Kruger National Park, is a malarial zone, and you should take antimalarial drugs before and during your visit.

Pleasures and Pastimes

Big-Game Adventures

There is nothing quite like tracking rhinos on foot—with an armed ranger leading the way, of course—or having an elephant mock-charge to within yards of your Land Rover. The slow-motion gallop of a giraffe, the cocky trot of a hyena, and the interactions of the smaller creatures of the bush—such as the dwarf mongoose or the bush baby—are all Mpumalanga musts. If you don't stay in one of the area's private game lodges, be sure to go out with a park ranger on one of the wilderness trails to get your feet on the ground in the wilds of South Africa.

Dining

As Mpumalanga continues to get more tourist traffic, the region's culinary scene keeps getting better—both in higher-end restaurants and attractive cafés. A number of private game lodges on the fringe of Kruger National Park serve fairly sophisticated fare, which can add romance to a couple of nights in the bush.

Lodging

The quality of service and accommodations in Mpumalanga and Kruger is very high by most international standards. Accommodations vary from the ultimate in luxury in some of the private camps to fairly basic in the Kruger Park huts. The advantage of a private lodge is that everything is included—accommodations, meals, beverages, game drives, and activities—and you'll be treated like royalty. If you prefer to do your own thing, then opt for self-service bungalows and huts, arm yourself with field guides, and take to the open road yourself. It's essential to book well in advance for self-service accommodations, and if you can, avoid the months of July and December, which are South African school holidays.

You can also choose from several other options, including regular hotels. If you're watching your pennies, consider staying at a self-service cottage and driving to one of the lodges for dinner—usually a good value.

At most guest lodges on the escarpment, prices include a dinner consisting of from three to five courses and a full English breakfast. Vegetarians should call ahead to make special arrangements. Some lodges and hotels have special rates, particularly midweek or during the win-

---

Close-Up

BIG GAME AND HOW TO SEE IT

WATCHING GAME IN THE BUSH is very different from sitting in front of your TV set. It demands energy, concentration, and luck. Happily, though, Mpumalanga has it all, including the Big Five—elephant, lion, leopard, buffalo, and rhino. The easy option is a private game reserve where knowledgeable rangers take you out in an open vehicle or on foot and find the game for you. Ask questions—however dumb they may sound—and find out as much as possible about what you see. If you've had a particular animal or bird on your lifetime wish list, then ask your ranger to do his best to find it. If you're self-driving, arm yourself with a couple of good field guides on animals and birds and a "Find It" guidebook on the Kruger Park (available at the entrance gates and camp shops). Drive slowly, stop and take time at water holes, and keep your ears and eyes open. Do not leave your vehicle unless permitted. Talk to other visitors, read the camp "game sighting" notice board and the visitors' book daily. If you see vehicles stopped in the road, approach slowly and find out what's being looked at. But don't forget also to absorb the total bush experience—big and little creatures of all kinds, trees, plants, sounds, colors, shapes, forms, and smells. Look for the Little Five too—the elephant shrew, the lion ant, the leopard tortoise, the buffalo weaver, and the rhinoceros beetle.

— Kate Turkington

---

ter low season. Many do not accommodate children under 12 or 14—inquire when you make reservations.

In the Kruger National Park region the decision you'll need to make is whether to stay in a national-park rest camp or in a private game lodge, a choice that might have everything to do with your budget: the cost of rest-camp accommodations begins at R350 per night for a couple (lodging only), and private lodges cost between R750 and R6,000 per person, per night (room, board, and activities included). That said, for the price, the intimacy and expertise of private lodges and their staff often make for the experience of a lifetime.

Exploring Mpumalanga and Kruger National Park

Great Itineraries

Mpumalanga has a wealth of activities, from poking around cultural villages to hiking on mountain trails, looking into local history, taking in panoramic views, and driving and tramping around game reserves. If you have only a couple of days in the area, split them between the mountain scenery of the escarpment and wildlife viewing in the Lowveld. If you have more time, you could complete a tour of the Drakensberg Escarpment area in two days, but you're better off budgeting three or more if you plan to linger anywhere. To take in parts of Kruger National Park or one of the private game lodges—which is simply a must—add another three days or more. The best way to get around Mpumalanga is by car, either from Johannesburg or after flying into Nelspruit, Hoedspruit, or Skukuza. Don't forget that Swaziland (☞ Chapter 9) is less than two hours southeast of Nelspruit. If you plan to go to Swaziland, the town of Barberton makes a pleasant stopover on the way south.

Numbers in the text correspond to numbers in the margin and on the Mpumalanga map.

IF YOU HAVE 3 DAYS

Fly into the regional capital of Nelspruit; then rent a car and drive to ⊞ **Pilgrim's Rest** ⑧ or ⊞ **Graskop** ⑨ for lunch, followed by an afternoon of taking in views of the escarpment's edge at the **Pinnacle** ⑩, **God's Window** ⑪, and one of the spectacular local waterfalls. If you feel like going on a longer-range afternoon drive, head up to spectacular **Blyde River Canyon Nature Reserve** for a look at the **Three Rondawels** ⑮ rock formations. Stay overnight in Graskop, Pilgrim's Rest, or Sabie. The next morning make your way down to the Lowveld to Kruger National Park or one of the private lodges listed at the end of this chapter. Whether you opt for the national park or a private reserve, be sure to get in a day or night bush drive *and* a bush walk with an armed ranger. These complementary activities will give you the broadest experience of wildlife. If animals are actually your prime reason to come to Mpumalanga, you could decide to spend all three days in the park or at a private reserve. If you plan to spend the rest of your vacation in civilization, a minimum of three days in the bush is advisable.

IF YOU HAVE 5 DAYS

With five days your biggest decision will be how much time to spend wildlife-watching and how much to spend exploring the escarpment and its historic towns. If you are planning to see game in Zimbabwe or Botswana, take three days around the mountains and two in and around Kruger National Park. Start off on a drive from Johannesburg to ⊞ **Dullstroom** ①, which is known for its restaurants and lodges and for superb trout fishing. If you don't spend the night, have lunch and continue through **Lydenburg** ②. Beautiful **Long Tom Pass** ③ will take you toward ⊞ **Sabie** ⑤, which is a good town in which to overnight. The next day, head to ⊞ **Pilgrim's Rest** ⑧ to take in a little local history at the town's museums or through **Graskop** ⑨ to see some of the escarpment's most scenic vistas. If you are going to spend three days in the bush, head down to Kruger or to a private lodge to make it there in time for dinner and a night game drive. Otherwise, spend the night in Pilgrim's Rest or Graskop and start out early the next morning for **Blyde River Canyon Nature Reserve** with its hiking trails and escarpment scenery.

An alternative route out of Johannesburg would take you straight to the **Lowveld National Botanical Gardens** ⑳, outside Nelspruit. From there continue to ⊞ **White River** ⑲, perhaps taking a day trip to **Barberton** ㉑, an early gold-rush town with interesting period houses and nearby outdoor activities. You could then approach Kruger National Park from the south.

IF YOU HAVE 7 TO 10 DAYS

The best way to structure a longer stay in Mpumalanga is to set aside four or more days in the bush—half at Kruger and half in a private lodge, perhaps. Then split the rest of your time between the escarpment and the Lowveld. If you're planning to continue to Swaziland, note that it's an extremely rough dirt road to Swaziland from Barberton, although the town is a mere 35 km (21 mi) to the border post at Josefsdal–Bulembu. It's a much better option to travel to Malelane on the N4 and then take the road to the border at Matsamo–Jeppe's Reef. That road is paved all the way and affords spectacular views as it winds through the hills.

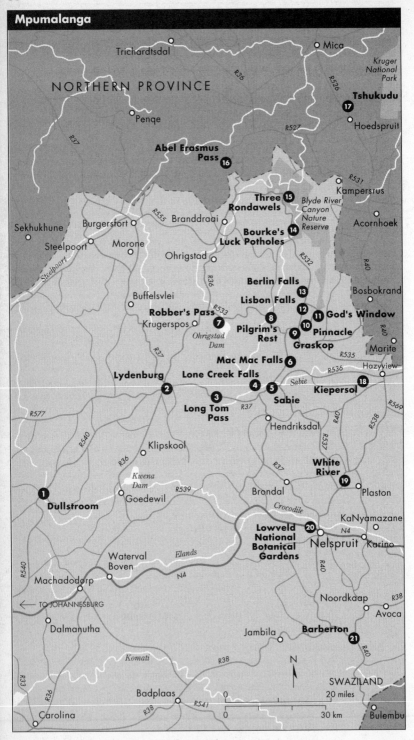

Mpumalanga

NORTHERN PROVINCE

Trichardtsdal

Mica

Kruger National Park

R26

R526

Penqe

Tshukudu ⑰

Hoedspruit

R37

R527

Abel Erasmus Pass ⑯

R531

Kampersrus

Three Rondawels ⑮

Blyde River Canyon Nature Reserve

Acornhoek

Branddraai

R555

Sekhukhune

Burgersfort

Bourke's Luck Potholes ⑭

R40

Steelpoort

Morone

Ohrigstad

R532

Bosbokrand

Steelpoort

Buffelsvlei

Berlin Falls ⑬

R533

Lisbon Falls ⑫

R36

God's Window ⑪

Robber's Pass ⑦

⑧

Krugerspos

Ohrigstad Dam

Pilgrim's Rest

⑨ ⑩ Pinnacle

Graskop

R40

R37

Marite

R535

Mac Mac Falls ⑥

Hazyview

Lone Creek Falls ④ ⑤

Sabie

Kiepersol ⑱

Lydenburg ②

③

Sabie

R536

Long Tom Pass

R37

Hendriksdal

R538

R569

Klipskool

R537

White River ⑲

R577

R540

R36

Plaston

Kwena Dam

R539

Brondal

KaNyamazane

① Dullstroom

Goedewil

Crocodile

Lowveld National Botanical Gardens ⑳

Nelspruit

Karino

R40

Waterval Boven

Elands

N4

← TO JOHANNESBURG

Machadodorp

Noordkaap

R38

R540

Avoca

Dalmanutha

Jambila

Barberton

R40

Komati

R38

R33

R36

⑳₁

N

SWAZILAND

Badplaas

R541

0   20 miles

0   30 km

Carolina

R38

Bulembu

When to Tour Mpumalanga and Kruger National Park

Where you stay on the escarpment may well dictate the kind of weather you get. High up, around Pilgrim's Rest, Graskop, and Sabie, the weather can be chilly, even in summer. At these elevations fog and mist can also be a hazard, especially while driving. On the other hand, summer in the Lowveld is downright sultry.

Kruger National Park is hellishly hot in midsummer (December–March), with afternoon rain a good possibility. The bush is green, the animals sleek and glossy, and the bird life prolific, but you won't see as many animals. Dense foliage makes finding them harder, and they don't need watering holes and rivers, which make them easy to spot as they come to drink. Winter is great for game viewing, on the other hand, as trees are bare and animals congregate around the few available water sources. With cooler weather you might even see lions and leopards hunting by day. Lodges drop their rates as much as 30%–40% off peak season highs. The drawbacks are cold (but sunny) weather, bare trees and bush, and animals that can look thin and out of condition.

Shoulder seasons are a happy compromise. October and November weather is pleasant, with trees are blossoming and migrant birds arriving. Even better, antelope herds begin to drop their young. April temperatures are also fine, with many migrant birds still around, and the annual rutting season will have begun, when males compete for the right to mate with females and are much more active and visible.

There are various annual festivals worth seeing as well. Komatipoort hosts an agricultural and prawn festival in April in which you can take part in a *bok-drol-spoeg*—literally Afrikaans for "buck-dropping-spit"—competition, in which local lads see who can spit antelope pellets the farthest. Sabie has its annual Forest Festival in April, where you can see lumberjacks cutting up logs in a matter of seconds. In Northern Province, Hoedspruit hosts an annual Wild Festival on a mid-April weekend, when you can taste all kinds of game meat and *biltong* (the much-loved local jerky).

Nelspruit hosts the Lowveld Agricultural Show in August, if you're interested in a look at South African farm life. In September there is a fly-fishing competition in whichever town hosts it for the year, which might be Dullstroom, Lydenburg, or Machadodorp. Dates for these festivals vary from year to year; SATOUR and local publicity associations will have specific dates.

MPUMALANGA

Next to Cape Town and the Winelands, Mpumalanga should be high on your South African itinerary. Nowhere else in the country can you spend one day seeing spectacular wildlife, the next climbing or gazing over the escarpment, and a third poking around some of the country's most historic towns—spending a minimum amount of time in the car getting from place to place.

Dullstroom

❶ *2½ hrs east of Johannesburg on the N4 turn off for Belfast and follow the R540 out of town for 35 km (21 mi).*

The tiny hamlet of Dullstroom sits amid rolling, grass-covered mountains and sparkling streams. At 6,600 ft, it's one of the coldest towns in South Africa, and sweaters and roaring fires are common comforts even in midsummer. Dullstroom is the trout-fishing capital of

Mpumalanga. The fish were introduced into the streams of the Mpumalanga Drakensberg at the turn of the 20th century, and trout fishing is now the third-largest moneymaker in the region, after timber and tourism. There are very good dining and lodging in town.

Just off the R540, approximately 9 km (6 mi) from Dullstroom as you drive toward Lydenburg, the **Dullstroom Bird of Prey Center** is home to several species of South African birds of prey that have been injured and rehabilitated and are now semitame. Birds can be viewed in aviaries, but time your visit to arrive at 10:30 AM or 2:30 PM, when the staff flies the birds and gives talks on their hunting and survival techniques. Enjoy the antics of the lesser spotted owl, see lanner falcons hunting a lure, and watch the falconer "call in" booted or tawny eagles. The session takes about an hour and is well worth the stop. While you're visiting the center, stop in at the **Owl and Oak Trading Post,** a three-shop complex that sells a variety of country and home-decor gifts complete with a small restaurant where you can have a cup of tea or a full meal. ☒ *R540,* ☎ *013/254–0777.* ☜ *R20.* ☉ *Daily 9–4:30.*

Dining and Lodging

$$–$$$$ ✕ **Die Tonteldoos Bistro and Deli.** This small bistro is a popular stop for breakfast, lunch, or weekend dinner on your way to or from the Lowveld. Owner Brian Whitehorn's menu is heavily influenced by French cuisine, with many sauces based on rich reductions. Try grilled duck breast with raspberry vinegar sauce as well as any of the game pies. Then treat yourself to apple mousse with cream or brandy sponge pudding. Garden salads and open sandwiches on chunky whole-wheat bread are popular snacks. Reservations are essential on weekends. The bistro closes at 5 on weekdays. ☒ *On R540, Dullstroom,* ☎ *013/ 254–0115. AE, DC, MC, V.*

$$$$ ✕▥ **Walkersons.** Set on a 1,500-acre farm of grass-covered hills laced with trout streams, the main lodge, built of stone and thatch, overlooks a small dam and is decorated with a wealth of antiques and works of art including Persian rugs, French tapestries, and 19th-century English oils. All rooms face the lake and have sponge-painted walls, mosquito nets, and fireplaces. Two-thirds of the farm has been made into a nature reserve populated with wildlife like wildebeest, springbok, blesbok, and zebra. There are several walking trails to follow through the reserve, or you can take a two-hour game drive in an open Land Rover. The lodge's five-course dinner (R90) is flawlessly presented. A meal might begin with Roquefort mousse with figs or smoked trout in phyllo baskets. Following a soup of brandied butternut squash and nutmeg, expect a main course such as ostrich kebabs or beef fillet with green-pepper sauce. ☒ *Off R540, 13 km (8 mi) north of Dullstroom (mailing address: Box 185, Dullstroom 1110),* ☎ *013/254–0246,* 𝖥𝖠𝖷 *013/254–0260,* 𝖶𝖤𝖡 *www.walkersons.co.za. 18 rooms, 2 suites. Restaurant, bar, pool, hot tub, fishing, hiking, horseback riding. AE, DC, MC, V. MAP.*

$$$ ✕▥ **Critchley Hackle Lodge.** Foreign travelers often use this country lodge midway between Johannesburg and Kruger Park as a one-night stopover on their way to the Lowveld, but for South Africans it's more of a weekend getaway, with its lovely antiques and crackling fireplaces. The atmosphere is very relaxed and the staff quite friendly. Rooms in stone-and-brick cottages arranged around a trout dam all have their own fireplaces. Wooden chests, floral curtains, and rough brick walls contribute to the atmosphere of warm rusticity. The lodge has a large, informal dining room overlooking the dam—a perfect location to savor the delicious four-course dinners that could start with baked trout (almost certainly caught that morning) and finish with malva pudding or homemade cheesecake. ☒ *On R540 (mailing address: Box 141, Dullstroom 1110),*

☎ *013/254–0145,* FAX *013/254–0262,* WEB *www.critchleyhackle.co.za.*
23 rooms. Restaurant, bar, pool, tennis, fishing. AE, DC, MC, V. MAP.

$ ✕🏨 **Dullstroom Inn.** In an old trading store that dates from 1910, the inn has rooms that are small but attractively decorated in colonial style, with floral patterns and old-fashioned iron bedsteads. Rooms do not have a phone or television. If you're not staying at the inn, it's still worth stopping at the wood-paneled pub, with its roaring fire and excellent selection of draft lagers and bitters. The extensive menu has such staples as steak-and-kidney pie, ploughman's lunch, and oxtail. Try the trout specialties and the sticky toffee pudding. ✉ *Teding van Berkhout and Oranje Nassau Sts. (mailing address: Box 44, Dullstroom 1110),* ☎ *013/254–0071,* FAX *013/254–0278,* WEB *www.dullstroom.co.za. 11 rooms. Restaurant, pub. AE, DC, MC, V. CP.*

Lydenburg

❷ *58 km (36 mi) northeast of Dullstroom on the R540.*

In an open plain between the Drakensberg and Steenkampsberg mountains, Lydenburg was founded in 1849 after the early Boer settlers (Voortrekkers) were forced to abandon their original homestead at Andries-Ohrigstad, where many of them died from malaria. Shaken by those years of death and misery, the survivors gave the new town the name Lydenburg, which means "town of suffering." Ironically, Lydenburg prospered so well that in 1857 its citizens seceded from the Transvaal during the incessant bickering that marked relations among Voortrekker factions. "De Republiek Lydenburg en Zuid-Afrika," as the new country was known, remained independent for three years before rejoining the Transvaal.

❸ Spectacular as **Long Tom Pass** is, this mountain pass is more famous for its historical associations than its scenic beauty. For it was here, from September 8 to 11, 1900, that one of the last pitched battles of the Second Anglo-Boer War (1899–1902) was fought. Lydenburg had fallen easily to the British on September 7, but the retreating Boers reformed on the heights above town and began shelling the British with their two remaining Creusot siege guns. Known as long toms because of their long barrels and range, these guns could hurl a 90-pound shell a distance of nearly 9½ km (6 mi). The guns were a tremendous headache for the British, who could not match their range. The Boers, struggling to get these monsters up the pass, can hardly have felt any more kindly toward them—at least 16 oxen were required to pull each gun. It took the British two days to push the Boers out of their positions on the pass and drive them over the steep wall of the escarpment. Even then, the Boers managed to set up a gun position on the other side of the valley to shell the British as they maneuvered down the Staircase, a series of switchbacks zigzagging down the pass. You can still see shell holes in the Staircase. From town follow the R37 toward Sabie as it begins its winding ascent to the pass.

❼ If you're bypassing Sabie and want to go straight to Pilgrim's Rest from Lydenburg, try **Robber's Pass,** another spectacular mountain drive. The pass was originally the road linking Lydenburg with Pilgrim's Rest and Delgoa Bay (now Maputo) and was called the Berg Road. During the gold rush the region attracted its share of thieves and desperate men, and highway robberies became common; in fact, so many stagecoaches were held up by highwaymen that the Berg Road was dubbed "Robber's Pass"—a name it bears to this day. The scenic pass affords panoramic vistas of high, rolling hills and deep, green valleys. Small farms abound, and eucalyptus and wattle plantations alternate with open grassland. A number of view sites enable you to take your fill of the picturesque scenery. Shortly after entering the pass, you'll see the turnoff to **Origstad Dam** on your right. The dam is a favorite with bird-watchers, with a wide variety of grassland and mountain species having been recorded. To reach Robber's Pass, take the R36 from Lydenburg toward Origstad; approximately 29 km (18 mi) from town, turn right on the R533 toward Pilgrim's Rest. The road winds some 27 km (17 mi) down to its final destination.

Sabie

❺ *30 km (19 mi) east of Lydenburg.*

As you descend Long Tom Pass, the town of Sabie comes into view far below, in a bowl formed by the surrounding mountains. It is by far the most pleasant and enjoyable town in the region, with plenty of restaurants, shops, and bars. It makes a great base for exploring.

Gold was first discovered in appreciable amounts in Mpumalanga in the area around present-day Sabie. On November 6, 1872, a prospector named Tom McLachlan located deposits of gold in a creek on the farm known as Hendriksdal, now a small hamlet about 16 km (10 mi) from Sabie. Sabie itself owes its origins to an altogether luckier strike. In 1895 Henry Glynn, a local farmer, hosted a picnic at the Klein Sabie Falls. Loosened up by a few drinks, his guests started taking potshots at empty bottles arrayed on a rock ledge. The flying bullets chipped shards of rock off the cliff face, revealing traces of gold beneath. Fifty-five years later, when mining operations closed down, more than 1 million ounces of gold had been taken from the Klein Sabie Falls.

Today timber has replaced gold as the community's livelihood. The town sits in the heart of the world's largest man-made forest—more than 1.1 million acres of exotic pine and eucalyptus. The first forests were planted in 1876 to provide the area's mines with posts and supports. Today much of the timber is still used to prop up shafts in the Gauteng gold mines.

As its name suggests, the town's **Market Square** was the commercial hub of Sabie in its early days. On the square pleasant gardens surround **St. Peter's Anglican Church.** The solid stone building was designed by famed architect Sir Herbert Baker and built by Italians in 1913. Just outside the First National Bank you can still see the old **hitching rail** (1911), where travelers would tether their horses. Also in the square is a **Jock of the Bushveld marker,** said to commemorate Jock and Sir Percy Fitzpatrick's arrival in Sabie in 1885.

❹ **Lone Creek Falls** is the prettiest and most peaceful of three local waterfalls. An easy paved walkway leads to the falls, which plunge 225 ft from the center of a high, broad rock face framed by vines and creepers. The path crosses the river on a wooden bridge and loops through the forest back to the parking lot. If you're feeling energetic, follow the steep steps leading up to the top of the falls. Leave town on Main Road and turn left onto Old Lydenburg Road. This 6½-km (4-mi) dead-end road leads to three of the region's principal waterfalls—Bridal Veil Falls, Horseshoe Falls, and, the last stop along the road, Lone Creek Falls, which is the most accessible of the three to the elderly and those with disabilities.

❻ **Mac Mac Falls,** another local waterfall, is arguably the most famous of all in Mpumalanga. Set in an amphitheater of towering cliffs, the water plunges 215 ft into a pool, and rainbows play in the billowing spray. The falls owe their interesting name to President Thomas Burger, who, while visiting the nearby gold diggings at Geelhoutboom in 1873, noticed that many miners' names began with "Mac," revealing their Scottish background. He promptly dubbed the area Mac Mac.

Unfortunately, you can view the falls only from an observation point surrounded by thick wire fencing, which destroys much of the atmosphere. On top of that, the fence is in poor condition, and the litter lying around it is dismaying. But if you are passing here on the way from Sabie to Graskop or Pilgrim's Rest, you might want to stop nonetheless. There are also a number of curio peddlers here; they are among the cheapest in the area.

Dining and Lodging

$$ ✕ **Loggerhead Restaurant.** An attractive eatery with a central location, the Loggerhead, as you might expect from the name, is dominated by heavy wooden furniture; however, colorful napkins and sparkling glass and tableware brighten the room. Lounge furniture arranged around the fireplace and a small bar make pleasant nooks to gather for a predinner drink. As with many establishments on the escarpment, trout features on the menu, along with a wide range of standard dishes such as grilled steaks, schnitzels, fresh line fish, and desserts like ice cream with chocolate sauce and apple pie. ⊠ *Old Lydenburg Rd. and Main St. 1260 (mailing address: Box 334, Sabie 1260),* ☎ *013/764–3341,* FAX *013/764–3089. AE, DC, MC, V. Closed Mon.*

$$–$$$ 🏠 **Sabie Town House.** A beautifully appointed bed-and-breakfast with sweeping views of the hill country around Sabie, the main house has local Sabie River stone and lush gardens: on entering the driveway, you could be forgiven for thinking you had wandered into an atrium. The spacious rooms are individually decorated, and four have their own entrances. There's a *boma* (outdoor eating area) overlooking the gorge, and inside, the public rooms are light and airy and include a large swimming pool area where breakfast is sometimes served. A three-course dinner of a traditional *potjiekos* (stew) is available for guests only. ⊠ *1 Power St., Sabie 1260 (mailing address: Box 134, Sabie 1260),* ☎ *013/764–2292,* FAX *013/764–1988,* WEB *www.sabietownhouse.8k.com. 4 rooms, 2 suites. Lounge, minibars, pool. MC, V. BP.*

Pilgrim's Rest

❽ *16 km (10 mi) north of Sabie on R533.*

Pilgrim's Rest is a delightful, albeit touristy, reminder of gold-rush days. It was the first proper gold-mining town in South Africa, centered on the richest gold strike in Mpumalanga. Alec "Wheelbarrow" Patterson, a taciturn Scot who had struck out on his own to escape the hordes of new miners at Mac Mac, discovered gold here in September 1873. Mining operations ceased only in 1972, and since then the entire town has been declared a national monument. Many of the old corrugated-iron houses have been beautifully restored and now serve as museums, hotels, gift shops, and restaurants. It's definitely worth a visit, even for just a few hours.

Those corrugated-iron houses that you see today date from the more staid years after 1900 when Pilgrim's Rest had become a company town. During the mad years of 1873–75, when most of the alluvial gold was panned by individual prospectors, Pilgrim's Rest consisted of nothing more than a collection of tents and mud huts. Rumors about the richness of the strike quickly carried around the world, and miners drifted in from California, Australia, and Europe. By January 1874 more than 1,500 diggers were working Pilgrim's Creek. Only a few struck it rich; the rest spent their earnings in local hostelries until their claims played out and they drifted off.

Your first stop should be the **Pilgrim's Rest Information Centre** in the middle of town, where you can buy tickets to the various museums. A R5 combined ticket is good for the Dredzen Shop and House Museum, the House Museum, and Pilgrim's and Sabie News Printing Museum. ⊠ *Main St.,* ☎ *013/768–1060,* FAX *013/768–1113.* ⊙ *Daily 9–12:45 and 1:15–4:30 (will stay open until later if you phone ahead).*

Start your walking tour at the top end of town, at **St. Mary's Anglican Church.** Built in 1884, the iron-roof stone building replaced the original makeshift wattle-and-daub structure. It really must have been an uphill battle for the early ministers to lure miners from the town's 18 canteens. After a backbreaking week spent on the sluices, Holy Communion just didn't pack the punch of a belt of Cape brandy or Squareface gin. ⊠ *Main St.*

The tiny **Pilgrim's and Sabie News Printing Museum** is full of displays of antique printing presses and old photos. The building, constructed in the late 19th century as a residence, later served as the offices of the weekly *Pilgrim's and Sabie News.* The first newspaper in Pilgrim's Rest was the *Gold News,* published in 1874 and notable for its libelous gossip. The editor, an Irishman by the name of Phelan, felt obliged to keep a pair of loaded pistols on his desk. The printing museum is up Main Street from St. Mary's church. ⊠ *Main St., Uptown,* ☎ *no phone.* ⊙ *Daily 9–1 and 1:30–4.*

NEED A BREAK?   If you do nothing else in Pilgrim's Rest, stop for a drink at the **Royal Hotel bar** (⊠ Main St., Uptown, ☎ 013/768–1100). The building first served as a chapel at a girls' school in Cape Town. It was dismantled in 1870, shipped to Lourenço Marques (now Maputo), then carried by ox wagon to Pilgrim's Rest, where it ministered a different kind of spirit to thirsty miners. The bar retains much of its gold-rush atmosphere, with wood-panel walls, an antique cash register, and a wonderful old bar counter. If you're hungry, you can order fish-and-chips or a hamburger.

The **House Museum,** across and up the street from the Royal Hotel, re-creates the way of life of a middle-class family in the early part of the 20th century. The house was built in 1913 of corrugated iron and wood and is typical of buildings erected at the time throughout the area. ⊠ *Main St., Uptown,* ☎ *no phone.* ⊙ *Daily 9–12:45 and 1:15–4:30.*

The **Pilgrim's Rest Cemetery** sits high on the hill above Main Street. The fascinating inscriptions on the tombstones evoke the dangers and hardship of life in Mpumalanga a century ago. That of Fred Sanders, for example, tells how he was "shot in a skirmish on the 27th August, 1878, aged 24." Tellingly, most of the dead were in their twenties and thirties and hailed from Wales, Scotland, and England. The cemetery owes its improbable setting to the Robber's Grave, the only grave that lies in a north–south direction. It contains the body of a thief who was banished from Pilgrim's Rest for stealing gold from a tent, after which he was tarred and feathered and chased out of town; the man foolishly returned and was shot dead. He was buried where he fell, and the area around his grave became the town's unofficial cemetery. To get here, follow the steep path that starts next to the picnic area, near the post office.

In 1930, 16 general dealers lined the streets of Pilgrim's Rest. By 1950 mine production had taken a nosedive, and most of the businesses had shut down. The **Dredzen Shop and House Museum** re-creates the look of a general dealer during those lean years. The attached residence focuses on life in Pilgrim's Rest in the years immediately following World

War II. After you come down the hill from the cemetery, turn left on Main Street to get to the museum. ⊠ *Main St., Uptown,* ☎ *no phone.* ⊙ *Daily 9–1 and 1:30–4.*

Guided tours are offered of **Alanglade,** the beautiful home of the Transvaal Gold Mining Estates' (TGME) mine manager, set in a forested grove 2 km (1 mi) north of town. The huge house was built in 1916 for Richard Barry and his family and is furnished with pieces dating from 1900 to 1930. Look carefully at the largest pieces—you will see that they are segmented, which was done so they could be taken apart and carried on ox wagons. ⊠ *Vaalhoek Rd., off R533,* ☎ *no phone.* ⊠ *R20 for a guided tour (including refreshments). Tickets available at information center.* ⊙ *Tours Mon.–Sat. at 11 and 2, reserve 30 mins in advance.*

At the **Diggings Museum,** in the creek where the alluvial gold was originally panned, you'll find displays of a water-driven stamp battery and some of the tents and wattle-and-daub huts typical of the early gold-rush years. The tour lasts about an hour and is more of an enjoyable experience than an informative one. The retired prospector who conducts the tours enlivens the proceedings with yarns about the old days. You'll also see a display of gold panning and get to poke around in some of the old diggings. The museum is about 2 km (1 mi) south of Pilgrim's Rest on R533. ⊠ *R533,* ☎ *no phone.* ⊠ *R5. Tickets available at information center.* ⊙ *Tours daily at 10, 11, noon, 2, and 3.*

Dining and Lodging

$ ✕ **Scott's Café.** Visit this delightful restaurant to try one of its dozens of varieties of specialty pancakes (crepes). Both savory (stir-fried chicken) and sweet (fried nuts and cinnamon with chocolate sauce) are on the menu, as well as sandwiches and salads. Meals can be eaten outside on the pleasant wide veranda. There's also an interesting little arts-and-crafts shop. It's open from 9 to 6. ⊠ *Main St.,* ☎ *013/768–1061. DC, MC, V.*

$ ✕ **Vine Restaurant and Pub.** In a former trading store dating from 1910, the Vine uses antique sideboards, sepia photos, and country-style wooden furniture to capture a gold rush–era feeling. The food is straightforward and hearty. Try traditional South African *bobotie* (curried ground-mutton pie), *potjiekos* (stew), digger's stew served in a digger's gold-prospecting pan, or *samp* (corn porridge). The pub in back is a good place to meet the locals and is also the only place in town offering regular sports coverage on television. ⊠ *Main St., Downtown,* ☎ *013/768–1080. DC, MC, V.*

$$$$ ▥ **Royal Hotel.** Established in 1873, this hotel dates to the very beginning of the gold rush in Pilgrim's Rest—you'll see its corrugated-iron facade in sepia photos displayed around town. The hotel is spread out over 10 quaint wood-and-tin buildings, and rooms are decorated with reproduction four-poster beds, wood ceiling fans, sumptuous deep baths, and marble-and-oak washstands. Activities arranged by the hotel include horseback riding, gold panning, hiking, golf, museum visits, and trout fishing. ⊠ *Main St., Uptown (mailing address: Box 59, Pilgrim's Rest 1290),* ☎ *013/768–1100,* FAX *013/768–1188,* WEB *www.royal-hotel.co.za. 50 rooms. Restaurant, bar. AE, DC, MC, V. BP.*

$ ▥ **District 6 Miners' Cottages.** On a hill above Pilgrim's Rest, these self-★ catering cottages are the best value in town. The cottages are all miners' homes dating to 1920, and they're delightful. From their verandas are spectacular views of the town and surrounding mountains. The interiors are furnished with period reproductions, complete with wooden floors, brass bedsteads, and claw-foot tubs. Each cottage consists of a small living room, two double bedrooms, a fully equipped kitchen and pantry, and a bathroom. You can walk to the two restaurants in town in five minutes. If you arrive after hours, pick up keys from Royal Hotel. ⊠ *District 6, Pilgrim's Rest (mailing address: Private Bag X516, Pilgrim's Rest 1290)*, ☎ *013/768–1211. 7 cottages. No credit cards.*

Hiking

The **Golden Trail,** a self-guided hiking trail, takes from two to three hours to complete and guides you through historical areas around town and on part of the Prospector's Hiking Trail, which requires an overnight excursion on its own. The walk begins at the Pilgrim's Rest Cemetery and ends at the Diggings Museum and takes in proteas, rolling grassland, indigenous forest, and the remains of Pilgrim's Rest's mining sights, such as the Jubilee Orebin, the Reduction Works, and the old Cocopan railway line. There are beautiful views over the town and of Black Hill, the region's highest point. *Book reservations and obtain maps at the information center. Guided walks available for groups of 6 people or more—book in advance at the information center.* ☞ *R15.*

The 1,225-acre **Mount Sheba Nature Reserve** contains one of the last stands of indigenous forest in the Transvaal Drakensberg. Fourteen trails of varying difficulty run through the reserve, each taking from 1½ to 2½ hours to complete. Some walks lead to waterfalls hidden in the bush or to pools where you can swim. A map is available from the reception desk at Mount Sheba Hotel. A word of warning: the dirt access road to Mount Sheba is not in very good condition. ⊠ *Follow brown signs to Mount Sheba from Robber's Pass—the R533 to Lydenburg.*

Graskop

🟢 *20 km (13 mi) southeast of Pilgrim's Rest.*

In the 1850s the farm Graskop—so named because of the vast tracts of grassveld and singular lack of trees in the area—was owned by Abel Erasmus, who later became the local magistrate. The little town was declared a township in 1914, and in 1918 the first school was built. Graskop considers itself the "Window on the Lowveld," and several nearby lookouts do have stunning views over the edge of the escarpment. Even if the town itself is largely forgettable, it does make a good base for exploring. It's also where you'll find amenities such as a post office, public telephones, a selection of shops and eateries, and a garage. The nearby Blyde River canyon is spectacular; farther afield you can get in a day of game viewing beyond Abel Erasmus Pass at Tshukudu.

🔟 The **Pinnacle** is a 100-ft-high quartzite "needle" that rose dramatically out of the surrounding fern-clad ravine countless millennia ago. Beneath and to the right of the viewing platform, there is a plateau that you can see only from the topmost of eight waterfalls: the watercourse drops down some 1,475 ft in a series of alternating falls and cascades. From Graskop take the R532 north and turn right after 2½ km (1½ mi) onto the R534, marked "God's Window." Continue 1½ km (1 mi) and look for a brown sign to THE PINNACLE, indicating the parking area on the right.

⑫ Set in a bowl between hills, **Lisbon Falls** cascade 120 ft onto rocks below, throwing spray over a deep pool. You can hike down to the pool on a path from the parking area. From God's Window turn right onto the R534 and continue 6 km (4 mi). At the T junction with R532, turn left (toward Graskop); after 1 km (½ mi) turn right onto the road marked Lisbon Falls.

A small stream, Waterfall Spruit, runs through a broad expanse of grass- land to **Berlin Falls.** The cascade itself is a thin stream that drops 150 ft into a deep-green pool surrounded by tall pines. Berlin Falls is a lit- tle over 2 km (1 mi) north of Lisbon Falls off the R532.

Leaving Graskop, traveling toward Hazyview, you'll enter the lovely **Koewyns Pass.** Unfortunately, there are few vista viewing points, but you'll still get sweeping views of Graskop Gorge. Look for the turnoff to **Graskopkloof,** on your left as you leave town, and stop to get a closer view into this deep, surprisingly spectacular gorge. In the rainy season two waterfalls plunge to the river below.

Dining and Lodging

$ ✕ **Harrie's Pancake Bar.** Harrie's was the original pancake bar in the area, and it's still the best. (Tour groups know this, too, so you might have to stand in line on weekends and during high season.) If the weather's fine, take a seat on the veranda overlooking the street. Other- wise, warm yourself by the fire inside and listen to classical music while mulling over the selection of pancakes and infusion coffees. Pancakes in South Africa are a thicker version of crepes, stuffed with either dessert fillings or savories like ground beef, Dutch bacon, ratatouille, or spinach and feta. Harrie's is open daily 8–5, although the restaurant stays open longer during peak season. ⊠ *Louis Trichardt Ave. and Kerk St.,* ☎ *013/767–1273. MC, V.*

$$ ⊞ **Lisbon Hideaway.** In a peaceful meadow overlooking a small stream, ★ this self-service establishment makes a great base from which to ex- plore the escarpment. Graskop, several waterfalls, and the magnificent viewpoints of God's Window are minutes away. Accommodations are in modern, comfortable wood cabins, done in wicker and floral pat- terns. Each cabin sleeps a maximum of six, with two bedrooms, a liv- ing–dining room, and a fully equipped kitchen. Don't let doing your own cooking put you off. Talkative owner Phillip Flischman runs the Spar supermarket in Sabie and will stock the kitchen for you on re- quest. ⊠ *Lisbon Falls Rd. off R532, 10 km (6 mi) from Graskop (mail- ing address: Box 43, Graskop 1270),* ☎ *013/767–1851 or 083/271– 3183. 3 log cabins. MC, V.*

$$ ⊞ **West Lodge.** If you're looking for an upmarket accommodation close to town and easily accessible to the R532 (which takes you to the scenic delights around Graskop), this attractive B&B has it all. West Lodge's rooms are decorated with pastels and crisp, white linens that give the rooms a light, airy feel. Two rooms are in the main house and face an area known as the Fairyland, which exists as a communal farm area. It was here that Sir Percy Fitzpatrick set up camp on his way to Lydenburg. The two other rooms are in a spacious annex. Formal En- glish country gardens, public areas filled with interesting objects, and warm hospitality make this a comfortable place to stop for the night. ⊠ *12–14 Huguenot St., Graskop 1270 (mailing address: Box 2, Graskop 1270),* ☎ *013/767–1390. 4 rooms. Library. No credit cards. BP.*

$ ⊞ **Graskop Hotel.** This attractive hotel's public areas are decorated with an interesting collection of African art. Zulu baskets brighten long cor- ridors, avant-garde metal ostriches flank the foyer, and Swazi pots and sculpture dot the lounge. Rooms are light and airy, with white walls, green wicker furniture, and lots of blond wood. Unfortunately, the walls are too thin to keep out noise from neighboring rooms. If you want something quieter, ask for one of the garden rooms. ⊠ *Main St. (mail- ing address: Box 568, Graskop 1270),* ☎ FAX *013/767–1244. 24 rooms, 18 with bath; 5 family cottages; 10 garden rooms. Bar, coffee shop, pool. AE, DC, MC, V. BP.*

Blyde River Canyon Nature Reserve

60 km (40 mi) northeast of Graskop.

As you head north from Graskop, after passing Lisbon and Berlin Falls, the dense plantations of gum and pine fall behind, and the road runs through magnificent grass-covered peaks. Once inside the nature reserve, turn off to **Bourke's Luck Potholes.** Named after a gold prospector, the potholes are holes carved into the rock in the gorge where the Treur and Blyde rivers converge. The holes were created over eons by the abrasion of pebbles suspended in the swirling water. How these two rivers came to be named is part of Mpumalanga lore: Pioneer (Voortrekker) leader Hendrik Potgieter led an expedition to Lourenço Marques (now Maputo) in 1840, leaving the womenfolk behind near Graskop. The men took so long to return that the women gave them up for dead, named the river beside which they camped the Treur (sorrow), and set off for home. En route they were met by the returning men as they were about to wade across a river, and so overjoyed were they that they named the river the Blyde (joy).Here, too, is the headquarters for the **Blyde River Canyon Nature Reserve,** one of South Africa's scenic highlights. The canyon begins here and winds northward for nearly 30 km (20 mi). Several long canyon trails start from here (☞ Hiking, *below*), and an interesting nature center explains the geology and ecology of the canyon. The canyon proper begins some 27 km (19 mi) north of Berlin Falls. ✉ *15 km (9 mi) northeast from Graskop on the R532,* ☏ *013/769–6019.* 🎫 *R10.* ⊙ *Reserve daily 7–5, visitor center daily 7:30–4.*

Part of the Blyde River Canyon Nature Reserve, **God's Window** is the most famous of the Lowveld lookouts. As such it is geared for tourists, with toilet facilities, paved parking areas, curio vendors, and marked walking trails. The altitude here is 5,700 ft, just a little lower than Johannesburg. But you still feel as though you're standing on top of the world because the escarpment drops away almost vertically to the Lowveld. Paved walking trails lead to various lookouts. The God's Window lookout has a view back along the escarpment framed between towering cliffs. For a broader panorama follow the paved track up through the rain forest to a small, unfenced area that offers sweeping views of the entire Lowveld. On sunny days carry water—it's a 10-minute climb. From the Pinnacle turn right onto R534, pass two overlooks, and after 4½ km (2¾ mi) turn into the parking area on the right.

Continuing north from Bourke's Luck Potholes, you get occasional glimpses of the magnificent canyon and the distant cliffs of the escarpment. Nowhere, however, is the view better than from the **Three Rondawels** (Drie Rondawels), 14 km (9 mi) from the Potholes. This is one of the most spectacular vistas in South Africa—you'll find it in almost every travel brochure. The Blyde River, hemmed in by towering buttresses of red rock, snakes through the bottom of the canyon. The Three Rondawels are rock formations that bear a vague similarity to the round, thatched African dwellings known as *rondawels.*

Before Europeans moved into the area, the indigenous local people named the Three Rondawels the "Chief and His Three Wives." The flat-top peak to the right is *Mapjaneng* (the Chief), named in honor of a Mapulana chief, Maripe Mashile, who routed invading Swazi at the battle of *Moholoholo* (the very great one). The three wives, in descending order from right to left, are Maseroto, Mogoladikwe, and Magabolle.

The descent down the escarpment through **Abel Erasmus Pass** is breathtaking. (From the Three Rondawels, take the R532 to a T junction and turn right onto the R36.) Be careful as you drive this pass—the local

African population has taken to grazing cattle and goats on the verges, and you may be surprised by animals on the tarmac as you round a bend. The **J. G. Strijdom Tunnel,** burrowing through the mountainside, serves as the gateway to the Lowveld. At the mouth of the tunnel are curio and fruit stalls where you can buy clay pots, African masks, wooden giraffes, and subtropical fruit. As you emerge from the dark mouth of the tunnel, the Lowveld spreads out below, and the views of both it and the mountains are stunning. On the left, the Olifants River snakes through the bushveld, lined to some extent by African subsistence farms.

Once on the flat plains of the Lowveld, the road cuts east through bushveld scrub, alternating with plantations of mango and citrus. Keep an eye out for a lovely example of a baobab tree, on the right-hand side next to a fruit stand. These weird and wonderful trees don't grow much farther south than this.

Lodging

$$$ ⌂ **Belvedere Guest House.** A good place for overnighting in the canyon is this self-catering guest house within the spectacular Blyde River canyon. Completed in 1915, this grand old house originally served as quarters for the workers of the now-inoperative Belvedere power station. You can relax in the spacious lounge with a fireplace and prepare your meals in the roomy farmhouse-style kitchen. Three of the bedrooms, as well as the lounge and kitchen, open onto a broad veranda that sweeps along all four sides of the house and has breathtaking views dominated by the awesome walls of the Blyde River canyon. There are some short but fascinating walks from the house into the vicinity don't miss out on the marked trail to the awesome Dientjie Falls. ✉ *Mpumalanga Parks Board, Central Reservations, Box 1990, Nelspruit 1200,* ☎ *013/759–5432,* ℻ *013/755–3928. 1 house that sleeps 9. MC, V.*

Hiking

The **Blyde River Canyon Trail** is a 29-km (18-mi) three-day hike that runs from God's Window right along the edge of the escarpment to the Sybrand van Niekerk Resort. The mountain scenery is spectacular, making it one of the most popular trails in the country. Several shorter trails explore the canyon from trailheads at Bourke's Luck Potholes. The number of hikers on these trails is controlled, so it's essential to reserve far in advance. To do so, contact the **Blyde River Canyon Nature Reserve office** (☎ 013/769–6019).

Hoedspruit

63 km (39 mi) northeast of Graskop.

Hoedspruit itself is a nondescript place, little more than a supply depot for the surrounding farms.

From Hoedspruit turn left onto R40 and drive 4 km (2½ mi) to ⑰ **Tshukudu.** This 12,350-acre game farm bills itself as a safari lodge, but it's more like an animal park. Go somewhere else for a two- or three-night big-game adventure, but stop here for a day visit where you can do a bush walk (R60) followed by breakfast, or a morning game drive (R80) and then stay for lunch (R75). The highlight of the day is the chance to meet some of the farm's orphaned animals, many of them completely tame. Don't be surprised if you're ambushed by a tame, gentle lion; nudged by a wildebeest; or accompanied by two young elephants on your bush walk. Advance reservations are essential. ✉ *On R40, north of Hoedspruit,* ☎ *015/793–2476 or 015/793–1886,* ℻ *015/793–2078.* ☉ *By appointment only.*

Lodging

$$$$ ⊡ **Mohlabetsi Safari Lodge.** In Balule (an area adjoining Kruger National Park), this small, relaxed game lodge offers a true hands-on bush experience. It's unlikely you'll see all the Big Five—although elephants, lions, and buffalo have been known to wander through camp—but you *will* experience true Africa. Game drives and long bush walks, all accompanied by experienced game rangers, are the main feature of the lodge. The public areas of the lodge have informal cane furniture and a bar area on a wide, thatched veranda, where you can relax and look out over surprisingly green lawns to a water hole. Spacious, thatched *rondawels* (round lodging huts modeled after traditional African dwellings) have a decor that echoes the colors and themes of the bushveld. Delicious cuisine is served in a tranquil *boma* (outdoor eating area). Although informal, the lodge is extremely personal: rangers and staff are always on hand to offer you a drink or identify a bird you've seen. ⊠ *On R40, north of Hoedspruit (mailing address: Box 862, Hoedspruit 1380),* ☎ *015/793–2166,* WEB *www.mohlabetsi.co.za. 7 rondawels. 2 bars, 2 lounges, pool. AE, DC, MC, V. FAP.*

Hazyview

93 km (57 mi) south of Hoedspruit.

The town itself is nothing to write home about—it's the main commercial center for the local African population and has a tendency to be crowded and littered. However, you'll pass through en route to the Numbi and Paul Kruger gates to the Kruger National Park or to reach the Sabi Sand Private Reserve gate. Despite the less-than-idyllic downtown, there are some attractive places to stay in the area, particularly if you'll be arriving too late to reach reserve gates by closing time.

Dining and Lodging

$$$ ✕⊡ **Umbhaba Lodge and Restaurant.** This exquisite establishment is accessed from the R40, just past the main shopping area of Hazyview. Lush, beautifully landscaped gardens are a big feature of Umbhaba, starting with a man-made waterfall cascading off the roof of the reception area into a lily pond. There are panoramic views from most public areas, which are sumptuously and strikingly decorated. You'll stay in one of the thatched, whitewashed chalets, arranged in a horseshoe around the gardens, where waterfalls, pools, and lush, green vegetation predominate. Enormous windows let in lots of light, and white walls and tile floors set off rich velvet drapes and luxurious silk brocade and leather furniture. The restaurant has sliding glass doors that highlight the beautiful view, and when the weather is warm, you can enjoy your breakfast or lunch alfresco on the terrace. The cuisine is Pan-African, and your dinner could include specialties such as fish potjie (stew); panfried sole served with mushroom quenelles and shrimp velouté; and warthog pie. Umbhaba can arrange activities into the Kruger National Park and surrounding areas. ⊠ *On R40, east of Hazyview (mailing address: Box 1677, Hazyview 1242),* ☎ *013/737–7636,* FAX *013/737–7629. 22 suites. Restaurant, bar, pool. AE, DC, MC, V. BP.*

$ ⊡ **Chilli Pepper Lodge.** Set among rolling hills with emerald-green views, this attractive B&B is a lovely place to stop if you're headed from Sabie to the Kruger National Park or the Sabi Sand Private Reserve. Green lawns slope down to a man-made dam and swimming pool where ornamental birds and animals watch you from the water's edge. Accommodation are in fantastically furnished suites, each with a different theme and unique features—a crocodile light fitting over the bed in the African Suite, a huge iron bedstead in the Victorian Room, red poppies romping across the bedspreads in the Cottage Room. No children under 14. ⊠ *On the R536, between Sabie and Hazyview (mailing address: Box 193, Kiepersol 1241),* ☎ *013/737–8373,* FAX *013/737–8258,* WEB *www.chillipepperlodge.co.za. 5 suites. Pool, kitchenettes. MC, V. BP.*

Kiepersol

⑱ *28 km (17½ mi) east of Sabie.*

This one-road town used to be a trading station. Bananas were grown nearby. There's little here beyond its church and hotel.

Dining and Lodging

$$$$ ✕🖻 **Blue Mountain Lodge.** A member of Small Luxury Hotels of the World, this exclusive retreat focuses on creating a fantasy getaway for jaded city dwellers. The owners, Valma and Kobus Botha, both worked in the film industry, and their lodge has a setlike quality. Artificial moss adds instant age to stonework, and sponge painting creates an illusion of fading murals on palace walls. The Victorian suites are huge, impeccably maintained, and of better value than those in other similar establishments. Each room follows a theme, ranging from English country to American Colonial, and all have fireplaces, verandas, and minibars but no TVs. The best is the *Out of Africa* suite, done all in white, with billowing mosquito netting, white bedspreads, lots of wood, and a claw-foot bathtub in the center of the room. Avoid the less expensive Quadrant suites, however. Set in a cobbled courtyard reminiscent of Old Europe, they feel too sharp and angular, a flaw not helped by gaudy stripes painted on the walls. Meals are a refreshing departure from the traditional offerings of other lodges. The set price dinner, R120, has an international flavor—try roasted fillet of beef with stir-fried greens served with tapenade hollandaise or *cabeljou* (a local sea fish) with litchi sauce. Presentation and service are superb. ⊠ *Off R536, 10 km (6 mi) east from Kiepersol (mailing address: Box 101, Kiepersol 1241),* ☎ FAX *013/737–8446. 13 rooms. Restaurant, bar, pool, fishing. AE, DC, MC, V. MAP.*

$$$–$$$$ ✕🖻 **Cybele Forest Lodge.** Cybele started the whole concept of the
★ country lodge in Mpumalanga, and to a large extent it still sets the pace, as its awards suggest. Cybele's service is what separates it from its competitors, and that's essentially what you pay for. The staff members have achieved a fine mix of professionalism and friendliness, and they go out of their way to make you feel special. The English-country decor of the main lodge complements the service. Guest rooms are separate from the public areas—which makes for privacy but less intimacy. The cottage and studio rooms are small and undistinguished. The larger Garden and Courtyard suites are more comfortable. The magnificent Paddock suites, with thatch roofs and spectacular views over the forested hills, have their own garden and swimming pool and a private outdoor shower hidden in the foliage—sort of a Blue Lagoon scene for the over-40 crowd. Cybele built much of its reputation on the quality of its food, and it certainly keeps customers coming back. The traditional dinner melds classic French and traditional English country cooking. A light mushroom broth might be followed by risotto with ratatouille, then a choice of rack of lamb or trout fillets with a light lemon-cream sauce. For dessert a rich gâteau with chocolate sauce is typical. To rid yourself of some of those calories, take a leisurely walk, do some bird-watching, try your hand at rainbow trout fishing, or go horseback riding. ⊠ *Off R40 between Hazyview and White River (mailing address: Box 346, White River 1240),* ☎ *013/764–1823,* FAX *013/764–1810,* WEB *www.cybele.co.za. 12 rooms. Restaurant, bar, pool, horseback riding, fishing. AE, DC, MC, V. MAP.*

White River

⓳ *35 km (22 mi) southeast of Sabie.*

The R40 runs south through Lowveld thorn-scrub, with the distant barrier of the escarpment visible on the right. It passes through the service town of Hazyview before continuing on to White River, a pleasant farm town with several interesting arts-and-crafts shops.

Dining and Lodging

$$$$ ✕🏨 **Highgrove House.** On a hillside overlooking avocado and banana
★   orchards, this former farmhouse is considered one of the very best lodges in the country, with numerous awards to its credit. Rooms are in white cottages scattered about lovely gardens, and each has a veranda, sitting area, and fireplace. The decor has colonial overtones, with plenty of gathered curtains and floral upholstery. The atmosphere here tends to be rather formal but pays dividends, as the lodge is immaculate. Highgrove serves an excellent Anglo-French dinner. A typical meal might be a melange of Knysna oysters, quail eggs, and caviar with a sour-cream dressing followed by slivers of guinea fowl and foie gras with a port and cranberry sauce. One heavenly dessert is tartlets of fresh figs and almonds. Weather permitting, lunch and breakfast are served in the gazebo by the pool. Nonguests must reserve ahead for meals. ⊠ *R40 between Hazyview and White River (mailing address: Box 46, Kiepersol 1241),* ☎ *013/764–1844,* 𝖥𝖠𝖷 *013/764–1855,* 𝖶𝖤𝖡 *www.highgrove.co.za. 8 suites. Restaurant, bar, pool. MC, V. MAP.*

$$ ✕🏨 **Huala Lakeside Lodge.** This attractive lodge sits on a forested promontory, surrounded on three sides by a large dam. All rooms have water views, and the majority of activities involve swimming or boating on the lake. Guest rooms, in sandy yellow cottages, have a warm, comfortable feel thanks to overhead beams, ivory stucco walls, and matching bedspreads and curtains. If you can, book the Malachite Suite, in a lovely cottage set apart from the main buildings, with a four-poster bed and its own swimming pool. The lodge's five-course dinner is served in an elegant, candlelighted room and is a delicious affair; start with an appetizer of chicken liver parfait served with homemade apricot and orange chutney on brioche toast or a delicate soup of carrot with lime, coriander, coconut, and spinach; then move on to a main course like a hot Mediterranean vegetable gâteau, served with basil pesto. A changing array of delectable desserts may include homemade pecan pie with fresh cream or a South African specialty—milk tart. Breakfast and light lunches are served on the veranda under large umbrellas overlooking the pool and lake. ⊠ *Off R40 between Hazyview and White River (mailing address: Box 1382, White River 1240),* ☎ *013/764–1893,* 𝖥𝖠𝖷 *013/ 764–1864,* 𝖶𝖤𝖡 *www.huala.co.za. 221 rooms. Restaurant, bar, room service, pool, hiking, fishing. AE, DC, MC, V. MAP.*

$$ ✕🏨 **Kirby Country Lodge.** This is one of those relaxed places where you can kick back and not worry about appearances. If the rooms aren't as fancy as those at some other lodges, they're not as expensive either. That 70% of its guests are repeat or referral visitors is an indication this lodge is doing something right. Owners John and Jennifer Ilsley personally welcome you to their thatched, white-brick farmhouse set in pleasant gardens shaded by enormous trees. Spacious, comfortable rooms have phones and fans but no air-conditioning. A seasonal table d'hôte menu is served for dinner. The four-course meal focuses on the creative use of homegrown produce and a vegetarian menu is available on request. Choose South African wines to complement the meal from the lodge's extensive wine list. Lunch is for residents only, and nonguests must book for dinner. ✉ *Off R538 between White River and Plaston (mailing address: Box 3411, White River 1240),* ☎ *013/ 751–2645. 9 rooms. Restaurant, bar, pool. AE, DC, MC, V. MAP.*

Nelspruit

19 km (12 mi) southwest of White River on the R40.

❷⓿ Although it is the capital of Mpumalanga, Nelspruit has little to offer other than the **Lowveld National Botanical Gardens.** Set on the banks of the Crocodile River, these gardens display more than 500 plant species indigenous to the valley, including a spectacular collection of cycads and ferns. Several trails wind through the gardens, one leading to a pleasant waterfall. ✉ *3 km (2 mi) outside Nelspruit on White River Rd.,* ☎ *013/752–5531.* 🎫 *R7.* ☉ *Oct.–Apr., daily 8–6; May–Sept., daily 8–5:15.*

Barberton

❷❶ *50 km (31 mi) south of Nelspruit on the R40.*

The history of the southern Lowveld and Middleveld—between the southern boundary of Kruger National Park, the Swaziland border, and the village of Badplaas, to the west—begins in the hills and valleys of the region, where Bushman rock paintings, archaeological ruins, wagon trails, and early gold diggings are all easily accessible. Routes to the Lowveld via Badplaas and Barberton pass through beautiful mountain scenery on quiet country roads.

The Barber family, which made significant gold discoveries in the 1880s, named this historical town, among the oldest in the area. It was the seat of South Africa's first gold stock exchange. Yet two years after gold was discovered, Barberton was all but deserted by prospectors, who moved to the Witwatersrand, where Johannesburg's mining continues to this day. Barberton is now a thriving agricultural center and a tourist haven with a number of memorials linked to its pioneering days. The town has several hiking trails following the paths of early miners. The requisite statue of Jock of the Bushveld stands proudly in the center of town, along with a statuesque town hall. Here you'll also find the Garden of Remembrance, marking the fallen soldiers of both the Anglo–Boer War and World War II.

Barberton makes for an easy day trip from Sabie or Nelspruit. When you get into town, look for the **Market Square**'s information bureau and the **Victorian Tea Garden** for a cup of tea. Activities can be arranged through the **Barberton Information Bureau** (✉ Market Square, ☎ 013/712–2121).

The **Barberton Museum**'s best exhibits cover gold-mine culture and history. Some of that culture has to do with colorful gold-rush characters like the infamous Cockney Liz, a hotel barmaid and prostitute. ✉ *Bias Bldg., Pilgrim St.,* ☎ *013/712–4281.* 🎫 *Free.* ☉ *Daily 9–4.*

For a look at the lifestyle of a turn-of-the-20th-century upper-middle-class Barberton family, visit the 1904 **Belhaven House Museum,** whose late-Victorian–early-Edwardian furnishings seem a world apart from the rowdy gold-rush side of town. ✉ *Town Square, Lee St.* 🎫 *R4 (includes Stopforth House).* ☉ *Guided tours only, weekdays at 10, 11, noon, 2, and 3.*

Baker and general dealer James Stopforth built the original wood-and-iron house and outbuildings (stable, woodwork shed, and outside bedroom) of **Stopforth House** in 1886. It was rebuilt in 1892, and the Stopforth family occupied it until 1983. ✉ *18 Bowness St.* 🕮 *R4 (includes Belhaven House).* ⊙ *Guided tours only, Mon.–Sat. at 10, 11, noon, 2, and 3.*

For a brief period in the 1880s and '90s, Barberton's **De Kaap Stock Exchange** was a mainstay of the region's economy. It served as the country's first gold exchange. The region's gold mines still operate—and all are more than 100 years old. The exchange's facade has been preserved as a National Monument since 1965. ✉ *Pilgrim St..* 🕮 *Free.*

The **Fortuna Mine Hiking Trail,** in the southern part of Barberton, is nestled in the foothills of Lone Tree Hill, one of the better-known peaks of the Makonja range. The 2-km (1½-mi) trail passes through an area populated by some 80 tree species. After a little more than ¼ km (¹⁄₁₀ mi), the trail reaches an old mining tunnel, which was driven through the rocky hillside in the early 1900s for the transport of gold-bearing ore to the Fortuna Mine. Insufficient quantities of gold were found for the mining operation, but the rock formations here are estimated to be 400 million years old, which makes them the oldest sedimentary rock formations yet found on earth. Allow 1½ hours for the hike.

A visit to **De Brug Ostrich Farm** will show you how ostriches are bred and how these flightless birds live. There is an interesting gift shop on the premises selling a variety of decorated ostrich eggs and items made from them. ✉ *Off R40 (from Nelspruit) on the Kaapsehoop road,* ☎ *013/712–5265.* 🕮 *R20.* ⊙ *Tues.–Sun., entry at 10 and 3 only.*

Gold Panning Expeditions leave from the Diggers Retreat Hotel, outside Barberton on the Kaapmuiden road. The tours explore one of the area's rivers—Louws Creek, Honeybird Creek, Revolver Creek, or Kaap River—where alluvial gold was once panned. Watch gold-panning demonstrations, try panning yourself, or learn about the region's gold-mining history from an informative guide. ✉ *Off R40 (from Nelspruit) on the Kaapsehoop road,* ☎ *083/482–1803.* 🕮 *R50.* ⊙ *Daily 10–2.*

Mpumalanga A to Z

To research prices, get advice from other travelers, and book travel arrangements, visit www.fodors.com.

AIR TRAVEL

Nelspruit Airport is a one-hour hop from Johannesburg, about half that from other points in Mpumalanga.

➤ AIR TRAVEL INFORMATION: **S.A. Airlink** (☎ 013/741–3557 or 013/ 741–3558).

BUS TRAVEL

Greyhound runs daily between Johannesburg and Nelspruit (Panorama Hotel, opposite Joshua Doore Centre). The trip takes five or six hours.

Public bus service is limited or nonexistent in Mpumalanga. If you don't have your own car, you're dependent on one of the tour companies to get around the escarpment and into the game reserves. Many of these companies also operate shuttle services that transfer guests between the various lodges and to the airport. It's usually possible to hire these chauffeured minibuses on an hourly or daily rate.

➤ BUS INFORMATION: **Greyhound** (☎ 013/753–2100).

CAR RENTAL

Avis, Budget, and Imperial all have offices at Nelspruit Airport. Avis also has a desk at Skukuza Airport, in Kruger National Park. Imperial's Nelspruit office will deliver cars to Skukuza for clients.

➤ LOCAL AGENCIES: **Avis** (☎ 013/741–1087 or 013/741–1088; 013/735–5651 for Skukuza Airport). **Budget** (☎ 013/741–3871). **Imperial** (☎ 013/741–3210; 013/741–3210 for Nelspruit office).

CAR TRAVEL

Renting a car is the only option if you really want to explore Mpumalanga. It takes approximately four hours to drive the 350 km (220 mi) from Johannesburg to Nelspruit, capital of Mpumalanga and a major gateway to the region. The best route is north from Johannesburg on the N1 to Pretoria East, then east on the N4, passing the towns of Witbank and Middelberg.

Note: The N4 is an expensive toll road—and there is no real alternative route, so it's difficult to avoid paying the high fees. Expect to pay at least R150 on a one-way trip from Johannesburg to Nelspruit or Malelane. Cash or credit cards are accepted: you will be charged between R20 and R30 per toll.

EMERGENCIES

In case of an emergency contact the police. In the event of a serious medical emergency, contact MRI, which offers emergency helicopter services.

The best-equipped hospitals in the Lowveld are in Nelspruit: Nelspruit Private Hospital and Rob Ferreira Hospital.

➤ CONTACTS: **Police** (☎ 10111). **MRI** (☎ 080/011–8811). **Nelspruit Private Hospital** (☎ 013/744–7150). **Rob Ferreira Hospital** (☎ 013/741–3031).

TOURS

All tour operators offer a package of trips that cover the major sights of the escarpment, as well as game-viewing trips into Kruger National Park and private reserves. The most reputable operators in the area are Dragonfly Safaris and Welcome Tours.

National Airways Corporation offers all types of helicopter charters, including lodge hopping. Deserving special mention is the "Misty Mountain" experience, during which a guest is taken on a helicopter journey from one waterfall and site to another, stopping off at the Pinnacle, near Graskop, for a picnic breakfast.

➤ TOUR-OPERATOR RECOMMENDATIONS: **Dragonfly Safaris** (⊠ Box 346, White River 1240, ☎ 013/764–1823, FAX 013/764–1810). **National Airways Corporation** (☎ 013/741–4651). **Welcome Tours** (⊠ Box 2191, Parklands 2121, ☎ 011/328–8050, FAX 011/625–6633).

TRAIN TRAVEL

Spoornet's *Komati* train travels between Johannesburg and Nelspruit via Pretoria daily. The trip takes about 12 hours. The luxury *Blue Train* (☞ Rail Travel *in* Smart Travel Tips A to Z) also makes occasional runs from Pretoria to Nelspruit; Rovos Rail (☞ Train Travel *in* Smart Travel Tips A to Z), the Edwardian-era competitor of the *Blue Train*, travels from Pretoria to Komatipoort, just outside Kruger National Park. Most passengers combine a journey on Rovos Rail with a package trip to a game reserve or one of the exclusive lodges on the escarpment.

➤ TRAIN INFORMATION: **Komati train** (☎ 011/773–2944).

VISITOR INFORMATION

The Barberton Information Bureau is open weekdays 8–4:30 and Saturday 8:30–noon. Graskop Information and Reservations is open weekdays 8–4:30 and Saturday 9–1. Pilgrim's Rest Information Centre is open daily 9–12:45 and 1:15–4:30. Sondelani Travel & Info, the SATOUR office in Sabie, provides information on the area and hires out mountain bikes. It is open daily 8–5.

➤ TOURIST INFORMATION: **Barberton Information Bureau** (✉ Market Sq., ☎ 013/712–2121, FAX 013/712–5120). **Graskop Information and Reservations** (✉ Spar Center, Pilgrim's Rd., ☎ 013/767–1833, FAX 013/767–1855). **Pilgrim's Rest Information Centre** (✉ Main St., ☎ 013/768–1060). **Sondelani Travel & Info** (✉ Woodsman Center, Main St., Sabie, ☎ 013/764–3492).

KRUGER NATIONAL PARK

Kruger lies in the hot Lowveld, a subtropical section of Mpumalanga and Northern Province that abuts Mozambique. The park cuts a swathe 80 km (50 mi) wide and 320 km (200 mi) long from Zimbabwe and the Limpopo River, in the north, to the Crocodile River, in the south. Along the way it crosses 14 different ecozones, each supporting a great variety of plants, birds, and animals.

The southern and central sections of the park are where you will probably see the most game. Riverine forests, thorny thickets, and large, grassy plains studded with knobthorn and *marula* trees are typical of this region and make ideal habitats for a variety of animals, including black and white rhinos (once on the verge of extinction), leopards, and giraffes. The most consistently rewarding drive in the park is along the road paralleling the Sabie River from Skukuza to Lower Sabie.

As you head north to Olifants and Letaba, you enter major elephant country, although you're likely to spot any number of other animals as well, including lions and cheetahs. North of Letaba, however, the landscape becomes a monotonous blur of *mopane*, nutrient-poor land that supports a smaller numbers of animals. Some species, most notably *tsessebe* and roan antelope, thrive up here nevertheless. Elephants are partial to mopane, and there's a good chance of seeing these huge beasts here, too. If you have a week in Kruger, it's worth driving north to check it out—there are also fewer people up there if you want to avoid the crowds during the busy seasons. With less time than that, you should stick to the southern and central sections of the park.

Summer in Kruger can be uncomfortably hot—temperatures of 100°F are common from November to March—and many northern European visitors become simpering puddles of discontent. If you feel the heat, come at another time or stay in the cool uplands of the Mpumalanga Drakensberg and visit Kruger just for game drives. Whatever you do, *avoid the park during school vacations*. During the July and Christmas holidays, Kruger looks more like summer camp than a game reserve. Reservations are hard to obtain (book a year in advance), and hour-long traffic jams at game sightings are not uncommon.

Park entrance fees in recent years have fluctuated dramatically—increases of up to 15% per annum per year have suddenly become the norm. You will need to pay admission per person and per car. Service standards have deteriorated somewhat, unfortunately, despite the price increases. Enormous staff turnovers and cuts in government spending have taken their toll. Don't expect wonders, and tell the national parks or the camp manager if you experience problems. At time of writing, admission was R30 per person and R24 per car.

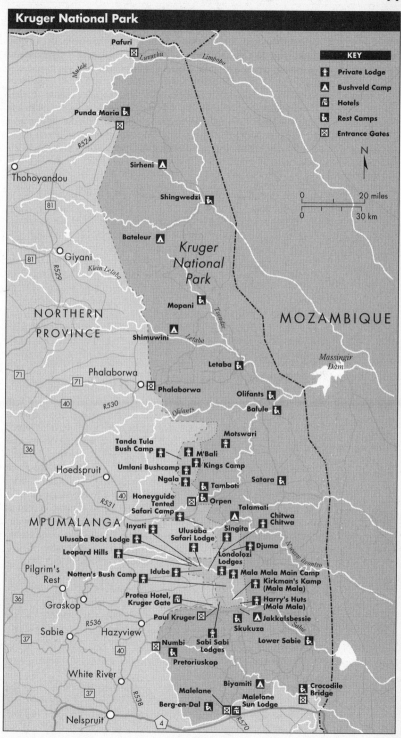

Kruger National Park

KEY

- 🏠 Private Lodge
- ⛺ Bushveld Camp
- 🏨 Hotels
- 🏕 Rest Camps
- ⊠ Entrance Gates

N

| 0 | 20 miles |
| 0 | 30 km |

Pafuri ⊠

Luvuvhu

Limpopo

Mutale

Punda Maria 🏠
⊠

R524

Sirheni ⛺

Shingwedzi 🏕

Thohoyandou ○

R81

Bateleur ⛺

Kruger National Park

MOZAMBIQUE

R81

Giyani ○

R529

Klein Letaba

Mopani 🏕

NORTHERN PROVINCE

Shimuwini ⛺

Letaba

Tsende

R71

Phalaborwa

R71

Phalaborwa ⊠ ○

R530

Letaba 🏕

Massingir Dam

R40

Olifants 🏕

Olifants

Balule 🏕

R36

Motswari 🏠

Tanda Tula Bush Camp 🏠

M'Bali 🏠

Umlani Bushcamp 🏠

Kings Camp 🏠

Hoedspruit ○

Ngala 🏠

Tamboti 🏕

Satara 🏕

Honeyguide Tented Safari Camp 🏠

Orpen 🏕 ⊠

R531

R40

Talamati ⛺

Chitwa Chitwa 🏠

MPUMALANGA

Inyati 🏠

Singita 🏠

Ulusaba Safari Lodge 🏠

Djuma 🏠

Ulusaba Rock Lodge 🏠

Leopard Hills 🏠

Londolozi Lodges

Nwaswitsontso

Notten's Bush Camp 🏠

Idube 🏠

Mala Mala Main Camp 🏠

Pilgrim's Rest

Kirkman's Kamp (Mala Mala) 🏠

R36

Graskop ○

Profea Hotel, Kruger Gate 🏨

Harry's Huts (Mala Mala) 🏠

Paul Kruger ⊠

Jakkalsbessie ⛺

Skukuza

Sabie

R37

Sabie ○

R536

Hazyview

Numbi ⊠

Sabi Sabi Lodges 🏠

Lower Sabie 🏕

Pretoriuskop 🏕

White River ○

R538

Biyamiti

Crocodile Bridge ⊠

R37

Malelane

Malelane Sun Lodge 🏨

Berg-en-Dal ⛺

⊠

Nelspruit ○

R4

R570

Bush Drives

First-time visitors sometimes feel a little lost driving themselves through the park: they don't know what to look for, and they can't identify the animals they do find. An affordable solution is to hire a game ranger to show you the park and its animal inhabitants. All the major rest camps offer ranger-led bush drives in open-air Land Rovers (minimum of two people). Not only can rangers explain the finer points of what you're seeing, but they can also take you into areas off-limits to the public. They may even take you on short walks through the bush, something else you can't do on your own. Day excursions cost about R150 per person, less than renting a car for a day. Book drives at least a week in advance.

Night Drives

★ Even if you tour the park by yourself during the day, be sure to go on a ranger-led night drive, when the park is closed to regular visitors. Passengers sit in large open-air vehicles, and rangers use powerful spotlights to pick out animals, including nocturnal creatures that you would never see otherwise, such as bush babies, servals, civets, and, if you're really lucky, aardvarks. Night is also the time when hyenas, lions, and leopards hunt. These opportunities alone make a night drive an unmissable experience. These drives are offered at all the main rest camps and bushveld camps. The three- to four-hour trip leaves the rest camps half an hour before the gates close. Night drives cost about R75 per person (no children under 6), and it's advisable to reserve in advance. Don't forget your binoculars and cameras and take a warm jacket whatever the season.

Wilderness Trails

★ Spend a few days hiking through the wilds of Africa, and you'll probably never be satisfied driving around a game reserve again. On foot you gain an affinity for the animals and the bush that's impossible in the confines of a car. Kruger has seven wilderness trails, each of which can accommodate eight people. Led by an armed ranger, you'll spend the day walking through the bush, returning each day to the same trail camp. These trails are not get-fit hikes but slow meanders, the point being to learn about your surroundings: the medicinal purposes of trees, the role of dung beetles in the ecology, even how to recognize animals by their spoor. In general, you can't get as close to animals on foot as you can in a vehicle. You *will* see animals, though, and many hikers can recount face-to-face encounters with everything from rhino to elephant and lion. It's a heart-pumping thrill you won't soon forget. Hikes last three nights and two days (starting on Sunday and Wednesday), and you should be prepared to walk as much as 19 km (12 mi) a day. No one under 12 or over 60 is allowed. Hikers sleep in rustic two-bed huts and share a reed-wall bathroom with flush toilets and showers. Meals are simple bush fare, including stews and barbecues; you must provide your own booze and soft drinks. These trails are incredibly popular—try to reserve 13 months in advance, when bookings open. The cost is approximately R1,300 per person per trail.

Bushman Trail. In the southwestern corner of the park, this trail takes its name from the San rock paintings and sites found in the area. The trail camp lies in a secluded valley dominated by granite hills and cliffs. Game sightings frequently include white rhino, elephant, and buffalo. Check in at Berg-en-Dal.

Metsimetsi Trail. The permanent water of the nearby N'waswitsontso River makes this one of the best trails for winter game viewing. Midway between Skukuza and Satara, the trail camp hunkers in the lee of a mountain in an area of gorges, cliffs, and rolling savanna. Check in at Skukuza.

Napi Trail. Sightings of white rhino are common on this trail, which runs through mixed bushveld between Pretoriuskop and Skukuza. Other frequent sightings include black rhino, cheetah, leopard, and elephant. If you're lucky, you may also see nomadic wild dogs. The trail camp hides in dense riverine forest at the confluence of the Napi and Biyamiti rivers. Check in at Pretoriuskop.

Nyalaland Trail. They don't come much more remote than this trail camp, in pristine wilderness in the far north of the park. Bird-watching is the big thrill in this land of huge baobabs and fever trees. The camp lies on the bank of the Madzaringwe Spruit, near the Luvuvhu River. You're almost sure to see hippo, crocodiles, nyala, and elephant. Check in at Punda Maria.

Olifants Trail. East of the Olifants rest camp, this trail camp commands a great view of the Olifants River and affords regular sightings of elephant, lion, buffalo, and hippo. The landscape varies from riverine forest to the rocky foothills of the Lebombo Mountains. Check in at Letaba.

Sweni Trail. East of Satara, this trail camp overlooks the Sweni Spruit and savanna dotted with marula and knobthorn trees. The area attracts large herds of zebra, wildebeest, and buffalo—with their attendant predators, lion and spotted hyena. Check in at Satara.

Wolhuter Trail. If you want to come face to face with a white rhino, choose this trail midway between Berg-en-Dal and Pretoriuskop. The undulating bushveld, interspersed with rocky *kopjes* (hills), is ideal habitat for these tremendous prehistoric beasts, but you're also likely to see elephant, buffalo, and lion. Check in at Berg-en-Dal.

National Parks Lodging

It's necessary to book a year in advance if you want a room during peak seasons (December–January and July). Reservations must be made directly with the National Parks Board.

Rest Camps

A couple staying in a rondawel with a private bath can expect to pay around R350 per night. Costs increase for additional beds. Sometimes camps describe their accommodations as cottages, bungalows, or huts. As a rule of thumb, here's what's meant (however, keep in mind that each camp is different): huts are very basic with no modern conveniences; cottages are a bit bigger; bungalows are the largest and have more facilities. A site to pitch your own tent costs R70 for up to two people throughout the park. All camps except Balule and Tamboti have gas stations and stores on-site. ⊠ National Parks Board: Box 787, Pretoria 0001, ☎ 012/343–1991, ⨳ 012/343–0905, MC, V.

$–$$ 🛏 **Balule.** On the bank of the Olifants River, this rustic camp differs radically from the others and will appeal to those who want to experience the true feel of the bush. There are no shops or restaurants, and there's no electricity, either—only lanterns. Accommodations are in basic three-bed huts with no windows (vents only) and shared bathroom facilities. Cooking is done in a communal kitchen. You must check in at Olifants, 11 km (7 mi) away. *6 huts, 15 camping sites.*

$–$$ 🛏 **Berg-en-Dal.** This rest camp lies at the southern tip of the park, in a basin surrounded by rocky hills. Berg-en-Dal is known for its white rhino, leopard, and wild dog, but it lacks the tremendous game density of some of the camps farther north. A small dam runs by one side of the perimeter fence, offering good game viewing, including a close look at cruising crocodiles. Berg-en-Dal itself is one of the more attractive camps, drawing great benefit from its thoughtful landscaping, which has left much of the indigenous vegetation intact. The strategic positioning of accommodations among bushes and trees affords more seclusion than older camps. There are three-bed chalets and family cottages that sleep six in two bedrooms. All huts come with fully equipped kitchens, including pots, pans, and cutlery. *63 chalets, 23 family cottages, 2 guest houses. Restaurant, cafeteria, pool, coin laundry.*

$–$$ 🖼 **Crocodile Bridge.** In the southeastern corner of the park, this small rest camp doubles as an entrance gate and makes a convenient stopover if you arrive too late to reach another camp. Although the Crocodile River provides the scenic backdrop for the camp, any sense of being in the wild is quickly shattered by views of power lines and farms on its south side. The road leading from the camp to Lower Sabie is well known for its sightings of general game as well as buffalo, rhino, cheetah, and lion. A hippo pool lies just 5 km (3 mi) away. Accommodations are in two- or three-bed huts with fully equipped kitchenettes and private bathrooms en suite. The East African safari tents, which sleep one or two people, are very popular. *199 huts, 20 tents. Coin laundry.*

$–$$ 🖼 **Letaba.** Overlooking the frequently dry Letaba River, this lovely camp sits in the middle of elephant country in the central section of the park. Excellent game-viewing sites in the area are the Engelhardt and Mingerhout dams. The camp itself has a real bush feel: all the huts are thatched, and the grounds are overgrown with apple leaf trees, acacias, mopane, and lala palms. The restaurant and snack bar, with attractive outdoor seating, look out over the broad, sandy riverbed. Even if you aren't staying at Letaba, stop in for the superb exhibit on elephants at the Environmental Education Centre. Accommodations are in large cottages and two-, three-, and four-bed rondawels, some without bathrooms and kitchenettes. Cooking utensils are not provided. Unfortunately, dense local foliage means that few rooms have views. Attractive alternatives are the large, East African–style safari tents furnished with four beds, tables and chairs, a refrigerator, and a fan. The campground, on the fence perimeter, offers lots of shade. *93 bungalows, 5 huts, 20 safari tents, 10 cottages, 1 guest house. Restaurant, cafeteria, coin laundry.*

$–$$ 🖼 **Lower Sabie.** This is one of the most popular camps in Kruger for good reason: it has tremendous views over a broad sweep of the Sabie River and sits in one of the best game-viewing areas of the park (along with Skukuza and Satara). The camp is well known for white rhino, lion, and cheetah, and elephant and buffalo frequently come down to the river to drink. The vegetation around the camp consists mainly of grassland savanna interspersed with marula trees and knobthorn, and there are plenty of watering holes within a few minutes' drive. Lower Sabie is small compared with minitowns like Skukuza, and you get a pretty good feel for the surrounding bush. Accommodations are in five-bed cottages and one-, two-, three-, and five-bed huts, some of which lack kitchens and bathrooms. Cooking utensils are also not provided. At time of writing, Lower Sabie was being rebuilt after serious flooding. Call ahead to confirm that it's operational. *20 huts, 63 cottages, 1 guest cottage (sleeps 5), 1 guest house (sleeps 7). Restaurant, cafeteria, coin laundry.*

$–$$ 🖼 **Mopani.** Built in the lee of a rocky kopje overlooking a dam, this is one of Kruger's biggest camps. The dam and the camp are an oasis for both animals and people amid the numbing monotony of the mopane shrubveld in the northern section of the park. You will probably see more game from the rest camp than you will in hours of sweaty driving through the surrounding country. Constructed of rough stone, wood, and thatch, the camp merges well into the thick vegetation. Shaded wood walkways connect the public areas, all of which overlook the dam—the view from the open-air bar is outstanding. The restaurant is à la carte (you must reserve before 6) and the food far superior to the buffet-style fare served at other rest camps. The cottages, too, are better equipped and much larger than their counterparts elsewhere in Kruger. Units with kitchenettes come with a full complement of crockery, cutlery, and cooking utensils, and six-bed family cottages are nothing less than fully furnished houses. *45 bungalows, 57 cottages, 2 guest houses (each sleep 8). Restaurant, bar, cafeteria, pool, coin laundry.*

$-$$ **Olifants.** In the central section of the park, Olifants has the best setting of all the Kruger camps, high atop cliffs on a rocky ridge with panoramic views over the distant hills and the Olifants River below. A lovely thatch-sheltered terrace allows you to sit for hours with a pair of binoculars and pick out the animals below. Lions often make kills in the river valley, and elephant, buffalo, giraffe, kudu, and other game come down to drink and bathe. Do whatever it takes to secure one of the thatched rondawels overlooking the valley. It's worth reserving these rondawels for at least two nights (book a year in advance) so you can hang out on the veranda and watch Africa unfold below. Olifants offers a lot more than a good view, however. It's a charming old camp, graced with wonderful indigenous trees like sycamores and knobbly figs, mopane, and sausage trees. Accommodations are in two- and three-bed thatched rondawels, some with fully equipped kitchens. The camp has a big drawback in not having a swimming pool—a must during summer, when temperatures soar. *109 rondawels, 3 cottages, 2 guest houses. Restaurant, cafeteria, coin laundry.*

$-$$ **Orpen.** Little needs to be said about this tiny rest camp, which lies just yards from Orpen Gate, in the central section of the park. The only reason to stay here is if you arrive at the gate too late to make it to another camp before the roads are closed, although there is good game in the vicinity. None of the two-bedroom units have bathrooms or cooking facilities. The rooms, arranged in a rough semicircle around a large lawn, look out toward the perimeter fence, about 150 ft away. There are also three comfortable family cottages with cooking facilities. *12 huts, 3 guest cottages.*

$-$$ **Pretoriuskop.** This large rest camp, conveniently close to the Numbi Gate in the southwest corner of the park, makes a good overnight stop for new arrivals. The landscape here consists of rocky kopjes and steep ridges that provide an ideal habitat for mountain reedbuck and klipspringers. The area's sourveld vegetation also attracts browsers like giraffe and kudu, as well as white rhino, lion, and wild dog. Like several other Kruger camps, Pretoriuskop is laid out so guests see less of the surrounding bush than of their neighbors grilling *boerewors* (farm-style sausages) and chops. Accommodations are in typical thatched rondawels and cottages, some of which lack bathrooms and kitchens. The campground enjoys some shade, but sites lack privacy. *82 rondawels, 52 bungalows, 6 cottages. Restaurant, cafeteria, pool, coin laundry.*

$-$$ **Punda Maria.** Few foreign visitors make it to this camp in the far northern end of the park, near Zimbabwe. This is a shame, for in many ways it offers the best bush experience of any of the major rest camps. It's a small enclave, with whitewashed, thatched cottages arranged in terraces on a hill. The camp lies in the sandveld, a botanically rich area notable for its unique plant life and birds. An interesting nature trail winds through the rest camp. Be sure to visit Pafuri picnic site, 46 km (28½ mi) north of Punda, to experience the full richness of the northern Kruger, where the bird life and varied vegetation types are exceptional. You'll find *braii* (barbecuing) facilities and a constantly boiling kettle here, and you'll picnic under massive thorn trees, leadwoods, and jackalberry trees on the banks of the Luvuvhu River—the haunt of the beautifully plumed *Narina trogon* bird and fishing owls. Two-bed huts all come with private bathrooms en suite, and many have fully equipped kitchenettes. There are also delightful secluded six-bed cottages up on a hill above the rest of the camp. *22 huts, 2 cottages. Restaurant.*

$–$$ 🏨 **Satara.** Second in size only to Skukuza, this camp sits in the middle of the hot plains between Olifants and Lower Sabie, in the central section of Kruger. The knobthorn veld surrounding the camp provides the best grazing in the park and attracts large concentrations of game, which in turn attract plenty of lion. Just standing at the perimeter fence, you often see giraffe, zebra, and waterbuck and other antelope. Despite its size, Satara has far more appeal than Skukuza, possibly because of the privacy it offers—the huts aren't all piled on top of one another—and possibly because of the tremendous bird life that flies in from the bush. The restaurant and snack bar are very pleasant, with shady seating overlooking the lawns and the bush beyond. Accommodations are in large cottages and two- or three-bed thatched rondawels, some with kitchenettes (no cooking utensils). The rondawels, arranged in large circles, face inward onto a central, parklike space. Campsites are secluded, with an excellent view of the bush, although none of the sites enjoy much shade. *153 bungalows, 10 cottages, 3 guest houses. Restaurant, cafeteria, coin laundry.*

$–$$ 🏨 **Shingwedzi.** This camp lies in the northern section of the park, amid the blistering plains of mopane shrubveld. The camp benefits enormously from the riverine growth associated with the Shingwedzi River and Kanniedood Dam. As a result, you will probably find more game right around the camp than anywhere else in the region. Don't miss out on the river drive, which offers some of the best game-viewing in the park. Among the species that thrive in the harsh mopane environment are elephant, roan antelope, Sharpe's *grysbok,* and *tsessebe.* The use of thatch and unworked tree trunks as roof supports gives the camp a rugged, pioneer feel. Both the restaurant (à la carte) and outdoor cafeteria have views over the Shingwedzi River. Accommodations are of two types, A and B. Choose A. These whitewashed units have steeply pitched thatched roofs that accommodate an additional two-bed loft; some also have fully equipped kitchenettes. The B units, painted a dull beige, are built of brick and roofed with unsightly tile; although most have bathrooms, none has kitchenettes. It's anyone's guess why all the huts face each other across a mopane grove, ignoring the lovely views of the bush beyond the perimeter fence. The campground is large but barren (except in early spring when the gorgeous bright pink impala lilies are in bloom), with almost no shade. *25 huts, 54 bungalows, 1 cottage, 1 guest house. Restaurant, cafeteria, pool, coin laundry.*

$–$$ 🏨 **Skukuza.** By far the largest camp in Kruger, it Skukuza serves as the park's headquarters. It's large and crowded enough to pass for a small town—with a gas station, police station, post office, car rental, grocery store, and library—and as a result, it has completely lost all bush feel. At times you wonder if you're in a game reserve at all. Skukuza is popular for good reason, though. It's easily accessible by both air and road, and it lies in a region of thorn thicket that supports a high density of game, including lion, cheetah, and hyena. The camp itself sits on a bank of the crocodile-infested Sabie River, with good views of thick reeds, dozing hippos, and grazing waterbuck. A museum and education center offers an interesting look at the history and ecology of the park. There are both bush drives and night drives to see game. Accommodations are in two- or three-bed rondawels and four-bed cottages, as well as four- and six-bed family cottages. Most units are equipped with cooking utensils and kitchen facilities. Some rondawels lack kitchens, but all have refrigerators. Guests also have the option of staying in permanent tents of the sort used on luxury East African safaris. Sited on a concrete platform, each tent comes with two or four beds, a cupboard, a refrigerator, and a fan. *199 bungalows, 16 cottages, 4 guest houses, 20 safari tents. Restaurant, cafeteria.*

$–$$ 🏕 **Tamboti.** Kruger's first tented camp has a name with the romantic ring of a traditional East African safari, but communal facilities can make it a bit like an upmarket campsite. Nevertheless, it is one of Kruger's most popular camps, boasting an average annual occupancy rate of around 90%. Its position on the banks of the frequently dry Timbavati River is superb, among apple leaf trees, sycamore figs, and jackalberries. From your tent it isn't uncommon to see elephants just beyond the barely visible electrified fence digging in the riverbed for moisture, which is why you need to book well ahead to get a place. Each of the walk-in tents has its own deck overlooking the river, but the ones to make a beeline for are those that enjoy the deep shade of large riverine trees—something to value highly in the midsummer sweat. All kitchen, washing, and toilet facilities are in two shared central blocks, and you have to bring all your own cooking and eating utensils. *30 safari tents.*

Bushveld Camps

If you're prepared to cook for yourself, Kruger's bushveld camps are infinitely more attractive than the major rest camps. They're small and intimate—you can't get lost the way you can at Skukuza—and access is restricted to residents only. As a result, you experience more of the bush and less of fellow travelers. These camps do not have restaurants, gas pumps, or grocery stores, but all huts have fully equipped kitchens. The only drawback is that most cottages are intended for four or more people. Because of the four-bed minimum requirement, most bushveld camps cost R600 per night. The handful of one-bedroom cottages at Biyamiti, Shimuwini, Sirheni, and Talamati go for R500 per night.

$$$ 🏠 **Bateleur.** Hidden in the northern reaches of the park, this camp, the oldest of the bushveld camps, is one of the most remote destinations in Kruger. Shaded by tall trees, the camp overlooks the dry watercourse of the Mashokwe Spruit. A raised platform provides an excellent vantage point from which to view game coming to drink from rainy-season pools, and two nearby dams draw a variety of animals. The camp accommodates a total of 34 people in seven family cottages. Each thatched cottage has two bathrooms, a fully equipped kitchenette, and veranda. There are bush drives and night drives. *7 cottages.*

$$–$$$ 🏠 **Biyamiti.** Close to the park gate at Crocodile Bridge, this large camp overlooks the normally dry sands of the Biyamiti River. The vegetation is mixed combretum woodland, which attracts healthy populations of kudu, impala, and elephant, as well as lion and black and white rhino. The camp consists of 15 thatched cottages, which can accommodate 70 people. All cottages have large verandas and fully equipped kitchens. *15 cottages.*

$$–$$$ 🏠 **Shimuwini.** Bird-lovers descend in droves on this isolated camp, set on a lovely dam on the Letaba River. Towering jackalberry and sycamore fig trees offer welcome shade, as well as refuge to a host of local and migratory birds. Away from the river, the riverine forest quickly gives way to mopane—bush-willow woodland, not typically known for supporting large amounts of game. Even so, roan and sable move through the area, and in the peak of summer elephants arrive to browse on the mopane. The camp can house 71 guests in one-, two-, and three-bedroom cottages, all with verandas and kitchens. There are bush drives and night drives. *16 cottages.*

$$-$$$ ⊞ **Sirheni.** Another major bird-watching camp, Sirheni sits on the edge of Sirheni Dam, in the far north of the park. A rewarding drive for birders and game spotters alike runs along the Mphongolo River, the area can't rival the game density of the Sabie and Crocodile river basins farther south, although there's a water hole at the camp that attracts plenty of game particularly in the dry winter months including leopard, lion, and rhino. A maximum of 80 guests can stay in the camp's one- and two-bedroom cottages, all with their own verandas and fully equipped kitchens. *15 cottages.*

$$-$$$ ⊞ **Talamati.** On the banks of the normally dry N'waswitsontso River in Kruger's central section, this tranquil camp offers one of the best game-viewing experiences in the park. Grassy plains and mixed woodlands provide an ideal habitat for herds of impala, zebra, and wildebeest, as well as lion, cheetah, and elephant. Two hides (blinds) give guests a chance to watch birds and game from the camp itself. The camp can house 80 people in four- and six-bed cottages, all fully equipped. *15 cottages.*

Near Kruger National Park

$$$$ ⊞ **Malelane Sun Lodge.** This pleasant hotel offers a level of luxury that cannot be matched by rest camps inside the park. If you're prepared to pay the entrance fee to Kruger Park every day, you can have the best of Kruger and a comfortable base, too. The hotel sits just yards from the park's Malelane Gate, overlooking the Crocodile River. The focal point is a creatively sculpted swimming pool, edged with manicured lawns and served by a thatched bar area. Rooms are done in subtle greens and lighted by faux miners' lanterns but lack a bush feel. The lodge is in close proximity to Swaziland and the casino there. ✉ *Off N4 toward Malelane Gate (mailing address: Box 392, Malelane 1320),* ☎ *013/790–3304,* FAX *013/790–3303. 102 rooms. Restaurant, bar, room service, pool, 9-hole golf course. AE, DC, MC, V. CP.*

$$$$ ⊞ **Protea Hotel Kruger Gate.** Next to the Paul Kruger Gate, this at-
★ tractive hotel gives you a luxury alternative to the bare-bones accommodations of Kruger's rest camps. The hotel has two major advantages: quick access to the south-central portion of the park, where game viewing is best; and it *feels* likes it's in the wilds of Africa. Dinner is served in a *boma*, a traditional reed enclosure around a blazing campfire; rangers lead guided walks through the surrounding bush; and guests can even sleep overnight in a tree house. The rooms are connected by a raised wood walkway that passes through thick indigenous forest. Rooms have Spanish-tile floors and standard hotel furniture, as well as air-conditioning, cable TVs, and minibars. ✉ *R536, next to Paul Kruger Gate (mailing address: Box 54, Skukuza 1350),* ☎ *013/735–5671,* FAX *013/ 735–5676. 96 rooms. 2 restaurants, 4 bars, room service, pool, tennis court. AE, DC, MC, V. MAP.*

PRIVATE GAME RESERVES AND LODGES

CATEGORY	COST*
$$$$	over R2,500
$$$	R1,750–R2,500
$$	R1,000–R1,750
$	under R1,000

All prices are per person sharing a double room, including all meals, bush walks, and game drives.

Mpumalanga is the heart of South Africa's big-game country, where you'll find the country's most famous private lodges and some of the best wildlife viewing in the world. All lodges reviewed below lie in game reserves adjoining immense Kruger National Park. In the last few years most of the veterinary fences separating Kruger from these reserves have been dismantled, allowing game to roam freely back and forth.

The most famous and exclusive of these parks is the **Sabi Sand Game Reserve.** Collectively owned and managed, the 153,000-acre reserve is home to dozens of private lodges, including Mala Mala and Londolozi. The Sabi Sand fully deserves its exalted reputation, boasting perhaps the highest game density of any private reserve in southern Africa. North of the Sabi Sand lies the 59,000-acre **Manyeleti Game Reserve.** During the apartheid era this park was reserved for blacks, who were not allowed into the country's major national reserves. It remains a public park today, although a couple of lodges have won private concessions. The **Timbavati Game Reserve,** also collectively owned and managed, lies north of the Manyeleti. The 185,000-acre Timbavati is renowned for its rare white lions, the product of a recessive gene that surfaces occasionally. Generally speaking, the Timbavati has plenty of lions and more elephant breeding herds than Sabi Sand, but it lacks a large rhino population—rumor has it that the rhinos keep crossing back into the Kruger National Park.

All lodges will arrange pickups from the airports at Skukuza, Nelspruit, Phalaborwa, or Hoedspruit. Some have their own private airstrips and can arrange for you to fly in by light aircraft.

Lodges covered below are marked on the Kruger National Park map.

Sabi Sand Game Reserve

Although not all lodges own vast tracts of land, most have traversing rights over anything from about 15,000 acres to around 45,000 acres of Sabi Sand land. With an average of 14–20 vehicles out looking for game and communicating via radio to ensure that guests see all the animals they want, the chances are very good you will see the Big Five in an average two- to three-day stay in the region. Expect to see large herds of elephant, particularly in the fall, when they migrate from Kruger in search of water and better grazing. The Sabi Sand is also the best area for leopard sightings: game rangers have written books about these beautiful, elusive felines after a spell in the Sabi Sand. There are several lion prides, and, occasionally, the increasingly rare wild dogs will migrate from Kruger to a den in the Sabi Sand. Privileged indeed is the lodge that is graced by a visit from these nomadic animals. White rhino may also be seen, along with giraffe, Cape buffalo, most antelope species, wildebeest, and zebra. It's also an excellent area for bird-watchers, and most game rangers will oblige you in your search for lilac-breasted rollers, francolins, guinea fowl, robins, or whatever else you fancy. (Try to go in a group or link up with other bird-watchers if you can—this seems to best way to spot the most birds.)

The program at almost every lodge rarely deviates from an accepted pattern: an early-morning game drive, during which refreshments may be served, usually followed by a full English breakfast or brunch. After that there's an optional bush walk with a ranger, where you can see the small creatures of the bush, although you could also happen on giraffe, antelope, or even one of the Big Five. The rest of the day is spent at leisure, so don't forget to pack a good book or two. If it's hot, most establishments have at least a splash pool. One thing you won't do at these lodges is go hungry—some give you a full luncheon, while others serve a substantial tea before taking off for an afternoon game drive. "Sundowners" (cocktails) are then served in the bush, either as the sun goes down or at dusk (or later, if you're tracking down something interesting in the African bushveld). Then it's time to see nocturnal animals: trackers and rangers use handheld spotlights for the purpose. On a good night you may see creatures such as leopards, lions (which hunt at night), hyenas, jackals, porcupines, pangolins, and serval or genet cats. On your return to the lodge, it's time for predinner drinks, followed by a three- or five-course dinner. These are usually served in a boma around a crackling log fire.

Mala Mala is the only lodge in the Sabi Sand that appears to deviate from the theme. In winter it's possible to go out looking for game for most of the day, pausing only briefly for lunch and a siesta.

The following two lodges are in the northern reaches of the Sabi Sand Reserve and are not accessed via the paved road in the south. Access is via a very bumpy dirt road, signposted from the town of Acornhoek on the R40, north of Hazyview. There are 64 km (25 mi) of potholes, corrugations, and washed-away road. The road is seldom graded and deteriorates quickly during the rainy season. Follow the signs carefully and don't go off onto side roads, which are worse. Check with the lodge about access if you're driving, but you may prefer to fly in instead.

Chitwa Chitwa

Chitwa Chitwa is a small camp in the isolated northern reaches of Sabi Sand Game Reserve. Run by a married couple, Charl and Maria Brink, this camp has a youthful spirit and places much emphasis on style. ✉ *Reservations: Box 781854, Sandton 2146,* ☎ *013/735–5357 for lodge; 011/883–1354 or 011/784–8131 for head office,* 𝖥𝖠𝖷 *011/783–1858,* 𝖶𝖤𝖡 *www.chitwa.co.za. FAP. AE, DC, MC, V.*

$$$ ✕🛏 **Chitwa Chitwa Game Lodge.** This is the main camp for Chitwa Chitwa and is on one of the largest lakes in the Sabi Sand. The spacious bar and lounge area has a high thatched roof and through picture windows fabulous views across the lake. There's lots of wood, and the neutral color schemes are relaxed and informal. Accommodations are in stylish, individually decorated chalets, each of which has uninterrupted views of the surrounding bushveld. Minimalist decor combines contemporary and African elements. The delicious African/Mediterranean food (try the venison) is served in a traditional boma or at the indoor restaurant. *6 chalets, 3 suites (18 guests). Bar, air-conditioning, pool, private airstrip.*

$$$ ✕🛏 **Chitwa Chitwa Safari Lodge.** More relaxed and comfortable than the main camp, this lodge is also slightly smaller, accommodating a maximum of 10 guests. In a forest of knobthorn trees beside an enormous lake, Safari Lodge also boasts fantastic waterside views. The thatched roof of the lounge–bar area is supported on old tree trunks; meals are often served on a wooden deck that overlooks the dam. Spacious chalets are decorated in colonial style, with creamy colors, lots of wood, and billowing mosquito nets. As at the Game Lodge, the cuisine is superb. *5 chalets (10 guests). Bar, air-conditioning, pool, private airstrip.*

Djuma

Djuma (Shangaan for "roar of the lion") abuts Chitwa Chitwa in the northeast corner of the Sabi Sand Game Reserve and uses the same entrance gate as its neighbor. Djuma was the first game reserve in Africa to place permanent cameras at water holes and on a mobile vehicle so that Web surfers (www.africam.com) can watch the goings on in the

African bush 24/7. Your hosts are husband-and-wife team Jurie and Pippa Moolman, who are passionate about their work (Jurie has a B.S. in ecology). Although there's a very good chance of seeing the Big Five during the bush walk after breakfast and the two game drives per day, Djuma also caters to those with special bushveld interests, such as bird-watching or tree identification. Djuma's rangers and trackers are also adept at finding seldom-seen animals such as Cape wild dogs, spotted hyenas, and genet cats. You'll find none of the formality that prevails at larger lodges, and the members of the staff eat all their meals with you and join you around the fire. In fact, Djuma prides itself on its personal service and feeling of intimacy. There are three camps to choose from. ✉ *Reservations: Box 338, Hluvukani 1363,* ☏ *013/735–5118,* 𝖥𝖠𝖷 *013/735–5070,* 𝖶𝖤𝖡 *www.djuma.co.za. Private airstrip. FAP. AE, DC, MC, V.*

$$$$ ✕⊞ **Vuyatela.** The most upmarket camp at Djuma, it was created with a contemporary rather than a classic colonial feel. Bright colors, vibey designs, hand-painted napkins, and candy-wrapper place mats combine with traditional leather chairs, thatch, and hand-painted mud walls. Look out for some great contemporary African township art, both classic and "naif" artifacts, and especially for the chandelier made with old Coca-Cola bottles above the dining table. The camp is unfenced, and it's quite usual to see kudu nibbling the lawns and flower beds or giraffes towering above the rooftops. Accommodations are in comfortable and beautifully decorated thatched chalets with private plunge pools. *8 suites (16 guests). Bar, air-conditioning.*

$$$ ✕⊞ **Bush Lodge.** The lodge is nestled in a grove of Tamboti trees and overlooks two water holes. It's a comfortable, more homely safari camp with thatched chalets. *8 chalets (16 guests). Bar, air-conditioning, pool.*

$ ✕⊞ **Galago Camp.** Galago means "lesser bush baby" in Shangaan, and the camp is a delightful little spot with cooking facilities and great views over an open plain. *5 suites (10 guests). Pool.*

The following lodges are in the southern sector of the Sabi Sand Game Reserve and are accessed from the Kruger Gate road, via Hazyview.

Idube

$$$ ✕⊞ Tucked away in the Sabi Sand Game Reserve, this small lodge sits in a grassy clearing overlooking a dam. Idube prides itself on its personal attention and relaxed atmosphere, and it gets a lot of repeat business as a result. Guests eat together at long tables, on a wooden deck, or round the fire in the boma, and the informal atmosphere generated by the staff makes this potentially awkward experience easy and fun. Dinners in the bush are also arranged on occasion. The public rooms make effective use of thatch, wood, and African art to create a bush ambience. The guest rooms, however, are a disappointment, built of institutional brick with tile roofs and floors. They're very large, though, and huge sliding doors give guests a good view of the surrounding bush. ✉ *Box 2617, Northcliff 2115,* ☏ *011/888–3713,* 𝖥𝖠𝖷 *011/888–2181,* 𝖶𝖤𝖡 *www.idube.com. 9 rooms (18 guests). Bar, pool, private airstrip. AE, DC, MC, V. FAP.*

Inyati

$$$$ ✕⊞ Set on a hillside in Sabi Sand, this lovely lodge presides over a broad sweep of lawns running down to the Sand River and a hippo pool. Life here unfolds on the thatched veranda, where guests use binoculars to scan the bush-covered hills for lion and other game. A wooden viewing deck, set under large trees by the river, offers an even better vantage point from which to see animals coming to drink. Inyati delivers the animals and much, much more. The service is among the best of all the lodges, a welcome mix of professionalism and friendliness. A glass of champagne might materialize after a game drive, or a bottle of sherry may accompany sautéed mushrooms at lunch. The food at Inyati is excellent, head and shoulders above that at comparably priced lodges. You'll stay in a simple thatched cottage with rustic log furniture and African-inspired materials and curios. ⊠ *Box 38838, Booysens 2016,* ☎ *011/880–5950,* FAX *011/788–2406,* WEB *www.inyati.co.za. 10 rooms (20 guests). Bar, air-conditioning, pool, health club, private airstrip. AE, DC, MC, V. FAP.*

Leopard Hills

$$$$ ⚹ ✕⛺ Set on the edge of a rocky outcrop, this gorgeous lodge has an impressive view of the surrounding bushveld (although not to quite the same extraordinary extent as Ulusaba). Leopard Hills' colonial-style decor is among the most impressive of all the lodges in the region: public areas are furnished in dark woods, and rich, deep colors predominate. The rooms themselves are decorated in natural shades of brown, cream, and honey, with lots of crisp white linen and billowing mosquito nets, while bathrooms have the ultimate luxury of his-and-hers showers. The attention to detail is amazing, from the hand-carved wood inlays of leopards in the reception area to the ceramic chameleon running around the dressing table. You can look out over the surrounding savanna from your romantic glass-fronted bathroom. The lodge is designed to take full advantage of the bushveld panorama, whether you're relaxing in the public rooms, lazing by the pool, or enjoying a meal on the small deck. ⊠ *Box 3619, White River 1240,* ☎ *013/735–5141,* FAX *013/735–5134,* WEB *www.leopardhills.com. 8 rooms (16 guests). Bar, air-conditioning, in-room safes, minibars, pool, private airstrip. AE, DC, V. FAP.*

Londolozi

Londolozi is the youngest of the leading lodges in the Sabi Sand, having only started its operations in 1974, when the Varty family, the owners of the property, were obliged to pay death duties when the family patriarch passed away. They decided their best option was to start a lodge on the property—and so Londolozi was born. The lodge concept proved extremely successful, and Londolozi gradually evolved into the popular upscale place you see today. Its popularity has been greatly assisted by the massive publicity campaign by John Varty, who has filmed a series of popular wildlife videos here featuring stories of the animals in the Sabi Sand, Londolozi, and his family.

In the heart of Sabi Sand Game Reserve, Londolozi offers outstanding service and superior accommodations and food. Londolozi is part of CC Africa, one of the most highly regarded wildlife companies on the continent. All waste is recycled or composted, and rangers show enormous respect for the land. Acting as a focal point from all Londolozi's camps, and adding to the game-viewing experience are the 19 km (12 mi) of Sand River that meander through the property. Londolozi comprises three camps, all within a few hundred yards of each other on a bank of the Sand River. Founders Camp and Pioneer Camp—two tiny, intimate camps, set deep in a forest of ebony and boerbean wood—were formerly known as Londolozi Bush Lodge. Regular bush dinners and breakfasts make an interesting change from dining out on the wooden deck or in the boma. In keeping with its conservation-for-the-people approach, Londolozi has developed a crafts village where items are produced by members of the local Shangaan community that borders the Sabie Sand Game Reserve, and proceeds go toward providing services and building roads, schools, and hospitals. ⊠ *Private*

Bag X27, Benmore 2010, ☎ *013/735–5653 or 011/809–4300,* FAX *011/809–4400,* WEB *www.ccafrica.com. AE, DC, MC, V. FAP.*

$$$$ ✕🖼 **Bateleur Camp.** The largest of Londolozi's camps, Bateleur has both chalets and suites. (The Bateleur eagle is one of southern Africa's most spectacular and endangered birds.) The lodge is an enormous thatched A-frame that extends out onto a broad wooden deck above the riverbank. Fireplaces, comfy armchairs, and bookcases filled with wildlife literature give a warm, lived-in feel. Rising from below the deck, an enormous jackalberry tree provides cooling shade. Behind the deck is a group of thatched rondawels that was the original hunting camp owned by the Varty family. They now do duty as a reading room, a wine cellar, and an interpretive center where history talks, carving demonstrations, and other events are held. Chalet rooms are smaller than in the satellite camps, but all have air-conditioning, minibars, and safes. Room decor is rather tired and dull, featuring lots of black, beige, and brown, but a refurbishment program is under way. On the plus side, there are beautiful views from every room, each with its own veranda and plunge pool, and bathrooms have both indoor and outdoor showers. Private dinners may be arranged on request. *8 chalets, 4 suites (20 guests). Bar, pool, private airstrip.*

$$$$ ✕🖼 **Founders Camp.** Here you'll stay in stone-and-thatch chalets, warmly furnished and decorated in cream, brown, and neutral shades with fascinating African artifacts and linked by a series of meandering pathways. Relax on the thatched split-level dining and viewing decks that jut out over a quiet by-water of the Sand river and watch the animal and bird worlds go by. After your game drive or walk, cool off in the tree-shaded swimming pool, which also overlooks the river. *5 chalets, 1 suite (12 guests). Bar, air-conditioning, pool, private airstrip.*

$$$$ ✕🖼 **Pioneer Camp.** This is a loving tribute to the early days and legendary characters of Sparta, the original name of the Londolozi property. Return to a past world of faded sepia photographs, old hunting prints, horse-drawn carts, and scuffed safari treasures. This really is an *Out of Africa* scenario. In winter sink deeply into your leather armchair in front of your own blazing fireplace as you relive the events of the day, or in summer sit outside in your own outdoor dining room and listen to Africa's night noises as you dine on scrumptious food. *3 chalets, 3 suites (12 guests). Bar, pool, private airstrip.*

$$$$ ✕🖼 **Safari Lodge.** If you're looking for that perfect, private place for a family gathering or small team getaway, then look no farther than this lodge, tucked away in its own private corner of the Londolozi property in thick riverine bush. Intimate twin-bedded chalets with private baths nestle in dense riverine vegetation. Each has a wooden deck, personal bar, overhead fan, and an indoor/outdoor shower. The main area has a comfortable and stylish lounge, an outdoor deck for bird- and game-spotting, and a boma where you dine on delicious dinners under the stars. Although the camp is tiny, it still offers the spectacular wildlife and personal attention that has made Londolozi world famous. *6 rooms (12 guests). Bar, air-conditioning, pool.*

$$$$ ✕🖼 **Tree Camp.** Shaded by thick riverine forest, this magnificent lodge
★ is Londolozi's top-of-the-line camp. The lodge is built into the riverbank and makes clever use of the natural rock and indigenous forest. The main living area consists of a huge, thatched A-frame with a wooden deck on stilts jutting out over the river. Guest rooms, in thatched chalets, are an exquisite blend of modern luxury and *Out of Africa* chic: track lighting captures the glow of burnished Rhodesian teak; mosquito nets drape languidly over snow-white beds; and old railway sleepers, skillfully crafted into furniture and window frames, add

to the rich textures of the room. All rooms also have their own plunge pools, and if you simply can't tear yourself away, private dinners may be arranged on request. From the central wraparound deck, you look out onto a world of cool green forest dominated by an ancient African ebony tree. *6 suites (12 guests). Bar, pool, private airstrip.*

Mala Mala

Mala Mala started the whole frenzy about the Big Five, and it still places a huge emphasis on delivering what was once the ultimate hunters' prize—buffalo, leopard, lion, elephant, and rhino. It has been operating for 30 years as a photo safari lodge, and much of the game is now completely habituated to the presence of the lodge's Land Rovers, allowing them to come extremely close. The biggest advantage Mala Mala has over its competition, however, is its size: 54,300 private acres, a full third of the Sabi Sand Game Reserve, including a 32-km (20-mi) boundary with Kruger National Park. Another major bonus is the lodge's 53 km (33 mi) of river frontage, which attracts animals to the sweet grasses that grow on the banks. The dense riverine forest is an ideal habitat for leopards and birds.

Mala Mala enjoys a reputation as the best safari lodge in Africa. Its name carries a real cachet in jet-set circles, and international celebrities, politicians, and industry tycoons flock here. Without question, Mala Mala does offer a superb game experience, but after many years the competition has caught up and surpassed them style wise. Today Mala Mala's guest rooms can't hold a candle to the glorious mix of bush and luxury offered by Londolozi's Tree Camp, Singita, Ulusaba, or Sabi Sabi's Earth Lodge, and its food is no better than that of a half dozen other lodges in Mpumalanga. Mala Mala's rangers are more than your guides to the game—they are your hosts and valets for your entire stay, hovering by your elbow to fetch you drinks and pool towels. They usually eat meals with you, and it almost comes as a surprise when they don't follow you into the bedroom at the end of the day. Some visitors may find the constant attention irritating. Mala Mala operates three camps, ranging from the ultraexpensive Main Camp to the budget Harry's Camp. ⊠ *Box 2575, Randburg 2125,* ☎ *031/765–2900,* FAX *031/765–3365,* WEB *www.malamala.com. AE, DC, MC, V. FAP.*

$$$$ ✕⊞ **Main Camp.** For first-time visitors to Africa, this large camp overlooking the Sand River offers a very gentle introduction to the bush. However, it won't give you much of true safari lodge feel: the hotel could conceivably be transported to a Johannesburg suburb without feeling out of place. The guest rooms, a mix of rondawels and larger suites, could be in any luxury hotel in the world. Each room has two bathrooms to make it easier for couples to prepare for early-morning game drives. Beige wall-to-wall carpet adds to its generic hotel feel. Fortunately, the main public area is steeped in African lore. Drawing on the camp's history as a hunting lodge, the lounge displays a host of animal skins and heads, old hunting spears, and antique rifles. Massive elephant tusks frame a huge fireplace, and African sculptures and reference books dot the tables. *25 rooms (50 guests). Bar, pool, private airstrip.*

$$$ ✕⊞ **Harry's Camp.** The huge advantage of staying here is that you get the Mala Mala game experience but at nearly half the cost of Main Camp, which explains why it's almost always full. Rooms and common areas are decorated in an Ndebele tribal decor theme and look out over the banks of the perennial Sand River. The camp's small size allows you an intimate slice of Africa, and because of the closely set rooms and low prices, there's a fun, young vibe here, too. *12 rooms (24 guests). Bar, pool, private airstrip.*

$$$
★ ✕🏠 **Kirkman's Kamp.** This lodge is an absolute delight, with far more charm—at a much lower price—than Main Camp. The atmosphere is also far more relaxed and friendly. At its core stands a 1920s farmstead, a relic of the days when this area was a cattle ranch. With its corrugated-iron roof and deep verandas, it has a strong colonial feel that will appeal to Britons and those who've watched *Out of Africa* more than twice. The camp is a tribute to Harry Kirkman, the manager of the cattle farm and one of the first game rangers at Kruger National Park. The main room, once the homestead, with high wood ceilings and creaking overhead fans, is lined with trophy heads, old maps of the Transvaal, sepia photos of Kirkman's hunting experiences, and antique rifles. It all spirits you back to another age, and the atmosphere is magical. The homestead and guest rooms overlook a broad sweep of lawn leading down to the Sand River. The rooms, constructed in recent years, continue the colonial theme, with claw-foot tubs in the bathrooms, white wood-slat ceilings, old photos, and French doors opening onto small verandas. *18 guest cottages (36 guests). Bar, pool, private airstrip.*

Notten's Bush Camp

Unlike many other lodges, Notten's has only one Land Rover, so you'll enjoy a high degree of privacy on your game drives. Your knowledgeable, friendly rangers will not only tell you about the animals but will also impart a wealth of information about everything from trees to insects and birds.

$$$
✕🏠 You may or may not see the Big Five at this delightful little camp, but if you do, you could have the bush experience of your life. Nestled between Mala Mala, Londolozi, and Sabi Sabi, Notten's family-run operation is the antithesis of the animal treasure hunts conducted by its more famous neighbors. Owners Gilly and Bambi Notten personally tend to their guests, and a stay at their camp is like a visit with good friends who happen to live in the bush. It's a measure of the Nottens' success that 70% of their guests are return visitors. The lodge has simple cottages lighted only by paraffin lamps and candles. At night flickering torches line the walkways, and a hurricane lantern on your veranda guides you back to your room. The camp is rustic, with no electricity, but inside, the cottages are comfortable and welcoming. After the evening game drive, guests meet for drinks in the boma and then dine together under the stars. Breakfast and tea are served in an open-sided shelter overlooking a grassy plain and a pan where animals come to drink. A lounge area is furnished with comfy chairs, bookshelves filled with wildlife literature, and a refrigerator where guests help themselves to drinks. For weekends and major holidays you need to make reservations about six months in advance; at other times two months is usually sufficient. ✉ *Box 622, Hazyview 1242,* ☏ *013/735–5105,* FAX *013/735–5970,* WEB *www.nottens.com. 5 rooms (10 guests). Bar, pool. No credit cards. FAP.*

Sabi Sabi

At the southern end of Sabi Sand Game Reserve, Sabi Sabi is one of the best and the largest private safari operation in Mpumalanga, and is also among the most expensive. It was also one of the first lodges, along with Londolozi, to offer photo safaris, and to link ecotourism, conservation, and community. Bush Lodge, the largest camp, overlooks a busy water hole, while the exclusive Selati Lodge has an intimate, old-Africa atmosphere. And setting a new standard for African game lodges is the magnificent, innovative, eco-friendly Earth Lodge. But it's not only the superb accommodations that draw guests to Sabi Sabi in such large numbers, it's also the sheer density of game supported by its highly varied habitats. That's not to say Sabi Sabi is simply about bagging the Big Five. Although you do stand an excellent chance of seeing them, there's a strong emphasis here on ecology; guests are encouraged to broaden their experience to become aware of the birds, smaller animals, and myriad sounds and smells of the bush. ✉ *Box 52665, Saxonwold 2132,* ☎ *011/483–3939,* FAX *011/483–3799,* WEB *www.sabisabi.com. AE, DC, MC, V. FAP.*

$$$$ ✕☷ **Bush Lodge.** This large lodge overlooks a water hole and the dry course of the Msuthlu River. The reception area leads back through attractive open courtyards to a thatched and open-sided dining area, an airy bar, and a lounge where residents can watch nature videos. Public rooms are tastefully decorated with African art and artifacts, animal skulls, and African prints. An observation deck has magnificent views of game at the water hole, as does the pool. Chalets, all thatched, are connected by walkways that wend through manicured lawns and beneath enormous shade trees. The five thatched suites are lovely, decorated with wicker and pretty African-print bedspreads and upholstery. Each suite has a deck overlooking the dry river course, an outside as well as an inside shower, and air-conditioning. Chalets are older and somewhat smaller (some say more intimate) but still roomy and beautifully decorated in ethnic design and with personal wooden decks. *21 chalets, 5 suites (54 guests). Bar, pool.*

$$$$ ✕☷ **Earth Lodge.** Don't expect designer ethnic chic here, there's not
★ a knickknack or bit of clutter anywhere in this avant-garde lodge. Less is certainly more at the daringly different Earth Lodge, a cross between a Hopi cave dwelling and a medieval keep, and like no other lodge in southern Africa. When you arrive, there's nothing to be seen but bush and high grass-covered hummocks until you descend a hidden stone pathway leading into and under the hills and opening out into a breathtakingly beautiful landscape of boulders, streams, cascading water, and far horizons. The lodge is built of rough-textured dark brown walls encrusted with wisps of indigenous grasses. Vases of bright orange crane flowers complement surfaces sculpted from fallen ancient trees, while the chairs and tables are daringly modern—an orange chamois leather chair looks 1950s 5th Avenue from the front, but from behind its legs are silver horns. Walk along a sandy path between grassy knolls and bush down steps to your suite, hidden from view except for its mud-domed roof. Inside it's huge, with a sitting area, megabathroom, and sleeping area, and then there's the veranda with plunge pool and an outdoor shower. You'll also have your own unobtrusive butler to satisfy your every whim. The boma, sculpted from roots and branches and lighted by dozens of burning lanterns, is the stuff of fairy tales. *13 suites (26 guests). Bar, pool, spa, library.*

$$$$ ✕☷ **Selati Lodge.** Formerly a private hunting lodge, Selati is one of the most intimate and stylish old colonial-style of the Sabi Sabi accommodations. A turn-of-the-20th-century atmosphere is created by the use of train memorabilia that recalls the now-defunct Selati railroad that once passed this way. There's no electricity, and the lodge flickers at night under the light of the original shunters' oil lamps; in one thatched chalet old leather suitcases serve as a table, while in another an antique sewing machine has a new lease on life as a vanity table. Deep-color wood, cream fabrics, and mosquito nets draped over large double beds hark back to the traditional East African safari. As you'd expect with this level of luxury, each cottage has a private bath, but each also has the added bonus of its own outdoor shower. *8 chalets (16 guests). Bar, pool.*

Singita

★ This is undoubtedly one of the most luxurious lodges in Sabi Sand Game Reserve. For unfettered extravagance Singita (Shangaan for "the miracle") leaves lodges like Londolozi and Mala Mala far behind. Singita has two camps, each with its own distinct character and charm. Ebony Lodge is inspired by African colonial style and Boulders Lodge is traditional African ethnic. Although Singita offers much the same bush experience as the other lodges, its public areas and dining options help set it apart. Enjoy a riverside breakfast, a picnic lunch, or a starlighted supper in the bush—all very popular options—or stay in camp and browse in the reading rooms and wine cellars, or just sit back and feast your eyes on the beautiful views over the bushveld. ⊠ *Box 650881, Benmore 2010,* ☎ *011/234–0990,* ℻ *011/234–0535,* WEB *www.singita.co.za. Private airstrip. AE, DC, MC, V. FAP.*

$$$$ ╳⌷ **Boulders Lodge.** If you've been to Great Zimbabwe, you'll immediately recognize Boulders as an exact replica of the exterior of the monument. Large ponds guard the entrance to the public areas, where decor combines the modern with the bushveld, although coffee tables mounted on imitation gemsbok horns can be a little kitschy. In the dining room the impossibly high walls and a minimum of windows make the place dark during the day. Visit the incredible wine cellar—which stocks vintages you probably won't find anywhere else in the country—both to choose your wine for dinner and to do some wine tasting. Suites here are elegant and sumptuous without being over the top: four-poster beds festooned in yards of white mosquito netting and bathrooms with claw-foot baths and indoor and outdoor showers are just a few of the details. All units have private plunge pools, and you can even enjoy a health or beauty treatment on your own private veranda as you gaze out at the African bush. Picture windows in all units look out over the Sand River and the African bush, as does the enormous wooden deck beneath the trees where meals are served. *9 suites (18 guests). Bar, pool.*

$$$$ ╳⌷ **Ebony Lodge.** Each cottage or suite here has a double-sided fireplace, separate living room, enormous veranda—even an outside shower in case your inner Tarzan feels confined in the cavernous one in the bathroom. Furnishings are reminiscent of a country house, although a quick glance through enormous picture windows will remind you that you are in fact in the African bush. Mosquito nets, railway-sleeper furniture, masks, beads, and animal skulls round out the African decor. Suites are fronted by walls of glass opening onto an expansive teak deck with a private plunge pool that has magnificent views of the Sand River. Rooms are lavishly furnished with a combination of antique and contemporary African pieces. The main lodge consists of a giant, thatched A-frame and a large deck raised on stilts overlooking the river. An enormous fireplace topped by a stuffed buffalo head dominates the room, and zebra skins, skulls, and trophy horns complete the safari theme. At dinner fine glass and china foster a colonial formality that works surprisingly well. *9 suites (18 guests). Bar, air-conditioning, pool.*

Ulusaba Private Game Reserve

Ulusaba is owned by Limited Edition Virgin Hotels, a Richard Branson enterprise that's supposed to reflect his personal attitude toward accommodations: super-luxurious surroundings, exceptional food, a spectacular setting, and an atmosphere comfortable and convivial enough that you can go barefoot to dinner (although that's not really recommended in the bush). The atmosphere is congenial and informal: it's the kind of place where your ranger will happily sit up until late in the bar gabbing, if that's what you want. Ulusaba employs a very young, very enthusiastic, and very attractive staff. And because the staff is youthful, so, too, is the clientele, especially at Safari Lodge. That said, you'd be hard-pressed to find a more enthusiastic or knowledgeable crew in the Sabi Sands. ⊠ *Box 71, Skukuza 1350,* ☎ *013/735–5460,* FAX *013/735–5171,* WEB *www.ulusaba.com. Private airstrip. AE, DC, MC, V. FAP.*

$$$$ ✕⊡ **Rock Lodge.** Perched atop a rocky hill in Sabi Sand Game Reserve, this magnificent aerie has all the makings of the finest game lodge on the continent. The lodge is built into the side of a cliff, 850 ft above a water hole and the bushveld plains. The road leading up to the lodge is so steep that guests must be driven up in four-wheel-drive vehicles, and the view from the top is mind-blowing. A maze of stone walkways and steps gives the lodge a fortresslike feel; and in the inky blackness of an African night, Ulusaba seems to hover over the veld like a space-craft. The view from the enormous wooden deck off the lounge is incredible: you'll feel like the lord of all you survey. The rooms provide some of the finest accommodations you will find in a game lodge. Huge windows have panoramic views of the bush, and high thatched ceilings and white stucco walls create a light, airy effect. The three public areas—the pool deck, restaurant, and bar—are ingeniously built into a cliff face. *11 rooms (22 guests). Bar, pool, private airstrip.*

$$$$ ✕⊡ **Safari Lodge.** If you're lucky, while you're traversing the swinging rope walkways that connect the private, thatched-roof rondawels and airy, bush-elegant public areas at this beautiful camp, an elephant may walk right under your feet. The grounds here have been designed with plenty of room for a jumbo or two to meander out of harm's way straight through the middle of camp. When you reach your rondawel, you'll find thoughtful modern touches such as automatic citronella room misters alongside romantic African decor such as four-poster hewn-log beds draped with mosquito netting. Private decks and bathrooms with expansive views over the Sabi Sands let you keep an eye on the bush at all times. Safari guides here are young, enthusiastic, and knowledgeable. The food is gourmet quality and the service seemingly relaxed but always attentive. Both the clientele and staff here are on the young side, but don't let that deter you from one of the best experiences in the bush. *10 rooms (20 guests). Bar, air-conditioning, pool.*

Manyeleti Game Reserve

The Manyeleti Game Reserve is a public park covering 59,280 acres and adjoining Kruger National Park, but it's amazingly underused, and you will see very few other vehicles while you're here. The park's grassy plains and mixed woodland attract good-size herds of general game and their attendant predators. You have a strong chance of seeing the Big Five here, but Manyeleti lodges tend to focus more on providing an overall bush experience than simply rushing after big game for its own sake. You'll learn about trees, birds, and the bushveld ecosystems and will very often get the chance to walk in the bush. In fact, it's not unusual to be following a rhino on a game drive when your ranger stops and suggests that you follow it on foot as far as you can. Let your ranger know if there's any animal you *really* want to see and he'll endeavor to find it for you. Most rangers and lodges work together and are in contact with one another via radio, so if one vehicle sees something special, there's a good chance that you will, too. It's common policy to have no more than three or four vehicles on a sighting at any one time, so you may have to wait your turn—but it's generally worth it.

Honeyguide Tented Safari Camp

This tented camp offers the best value of all the Mpumalanga lodges, especially if you stay at its budget Trails Camp, which specializes in highly regarded foot safaris. The camp brilliantly achieves the delicate balance of combining professional service with a casual atmosphere—a welcome relief if the stuffy over-attentiveness of some of the more upscale lodges isn't to your taste. ✉ *Box 781959, Sandton 2146,* ☎ *011/880–3912,* 𝖥𝖠𝖷 *011/447–4326,* 𝖶𝖤𝖡 *www.honeyguidecamp.com. AE, DC, MC, V. FAP.*

$$ ◬ **Honeyguide Tented Safari Camp.** Honeyguide was one of the first
★ lodges to use the luxury East African–style safari tents that have since become so popular. But to call these comfortable canvas homes "tents" is really an insult because they have everything a more conventional room does while giving you the true feel of camping in the wild. Each one is large enough to accommodate two beds, a cupboard, clothing shelves, and battery-operated lights. A private bathroom, accessed through the back zip of the tent, provides complete privacy, as well as hot showers. Four of the 12 tents are larger and a little more expensive than the others and have baths as well. A shaded wooden deck extends from the front of the tent and overlooks a dry riverbed and thick riverine forest. Despite its economy price tag, the camp has some true luxury touches: tea or coffee served in your tent at dawn and a fully stocked bar on each vehicle for sundowner cocktails. Meals are served in a big safari tent around a long wooden table where you can swap animal war stories with your fellow guests in an intimate relaxed atmosphere. *12 tents (24 guests). Bar, pool, private airstrip.*

$ ◬ **Trails Camp.** Representing a growing trend among the Mpumalanga private game reserves, this intimate and thoroughly rustic camp is light-years from the large, formal lodges of Sabi Sand. Don't expect smartly decked-out waiters, ethnic-chic decor, or pampering. But for a raw experience of the bush, you'll find this camp and its rock-bottom price tag hard to beat. Two-bed tents have private bathrooms that are open to the African sky, and meals are cooked by a chef over an open fire. If you've switched off your cell phone and want to leave civilization behind, the real joy here is that there are no vehicles. Most of your game outings are done on foot (there's a short game drive each evening), and you can experience the thrill of sneaking around rhinos or lions, being charged by buffalo, or holding dung beetles in your hand. Rangers also teach guests about other, smaller aspects of the bushveld, including the habits and behavior of various animals, the medicinal (and other) uses of plants and trees, and some tips about animal tracking. *4 tents (8 guests). Bar, private airstrip.*

Timbavati Game Reserve

The Timbavati is the northernmost of the private reserves that are open to tourists. If you desperately want to see rhinos, there's a good chance that you might miss them, as they are scarce in this region. However, the Timbavati has a relatively large lion population, and it's likely that you will also see leopards, buffaloes, and spotted hyenas. Lodges here tend to have fewer vehicles in the field on average than in the Sabi Sand, although rangers work together to ensure that you see all you want. The animals are relaxed in the presence of vehicles, and you may be able to follow a particular lion pride or leopard with cubs for a day or two. If you're lucky, you might see wild dogs, as these migrate irregularly to this region from Kruger. Rangers and staff are wildlife enthusiasts, and several will regale you with tales of the bush.

King's Camp

One of the most comfortable and popular lodges in the Timbavati, the camp itself is unfenced, and it's quite usual to have warthogs and antelope grazing on the lawn; there's also a water hole close enough that you can view elephants coming to drink while you laze by the pool. A spotlight on the water after dark means you can enjoy nocturnal sightings, too.

$$$ ✕⌨ **King's Camp.** Although luxurious, the lodge maintains a relaxed, informal air that soon has strangers chatting away like long-lost friends. You'll stay in thatched rondavels decorated with white linen, billowing mosquito nets, wooden furniture, and sepia photographs. The bathrooms are enormous and contain both bath and shower. There's a glass-enclosed lounge and bar where you can relax on huge sofas and a dining area that extends outside onto a raised platform to allow for alfresco lunch and dinner. ✉ *Box 427, Nelspruit 1200,* ☎ *013/753–2028,* ℻ *013/753–3377,* 🕸 *www.kingscamp.com. 8 rooms, 3 suites (24 guests). Bar, pool. AE, DC, MC, V.*

Motswari

In a remote corner of the Timbavati, bordering the unfenced Kruger National Park is the Motswari Game Reserve. Family owned and established more than 50 years ago, with an ongoing commitment to conservation, the reserve is home to an exceptionally attractive camp —Motswari. At Motswari there is a stronger emphasis on walking and enjoying the bush experience than at most lodges, and guests are encouraged to do a long walk instead of a game drive at least once during their stay. In winter guests encounter elephant almost every day on these walks. The rangers are all highly qualified and knowledgeable about the animals and the area's ecosystem. ✉ *Box 67865, Bryanston 2021,* ☎ *011/463–1990,* ℻ *011/463–1992,* 🕸 *www.motswari.co.za. Private airstrip. AE, DC, MC, V.*

$$$ ✕⌨ **Motswari.** At Motswari you'll stay in a traditional thatch rondawel with private bath made cozily inviting with warm earth-tone fabrics that blend in beautifully with the natural thatch reeds above your head and the cane furniture. You can shower under the stars in your own outside shower (or inside, if you prefer) or sit out on the large, shady veranda that looks down on the water hole—you'll almost certainly see buffalo and elephant coming down to drink. *11 chalets, 4 suites (30 guests). Bar, pool, private airstrip.*

Ngala

Ngala means "the place of the lion" and certainly lives up to its name. There's wall-to-wall game, and you'll almost certainly see more than one of the King of the Beasts as well as leopard, rhino, elephant, and buffalo, among others. This exclusive lodge is the only private game reserve to be included in the Kruger National Park, and the first three-way partnership between private sector, state, and nongovernmental organization. It lies in mopane shrubveld in the Timbavati Game Reserve and is part of CC Africa, previously the Conservation Corporation. Ngala's main advantage over Sabi Sand is its proximity to four major ecozones—mopane shrubveld, marula combretum, acacia scrub, and riverine forest—which provide habitats for a wide range of animals. As this camp is in the Kruger National Park and unfenced, be sure to always walk with a guide after dark, and don't bump into one of the huge grazing hippos.

Most luxury safari lodges and camps don't allow children under 12, but Ngala not only welcomes kids, it also puts on a range of activities for them. Ngala rangers, trackers, and general staff are specially trained to look after children and their needs, and what's more they seem to generally delight in their company. After the morning game drive, the kids are whisked away to go on a bug hunt, visit a local village, go fishing or frogging, and lots of other exciting kid-friendly activities. For more details contact CC Africa. ✉ *Private Bag X27, Benmore 2010,* ☎ *015/793–1453,* FAX *015/793–1555,* WEB *www.ccafrica.com. AE, DC, MC, V.*

$$$$ ✕🔲 **Main Camp.** The main lodge has a Mediterranean style and sophistication that are refreshing after the hunting-lodge decor espoused by so many lodges. Track lighting and dark-slate flooring and tables provide an elegant counterpoint to high thatched ceilings and African art. A massive, double-sided fireplace dominates the lodge, opening on one side onto a lounge filled with comfy sofas and chairs and on the other a dining room. Dinner at Ngala is more formal than at most lodges, served in a reed-enclosed boma or in a tree-filled courtyard lighted by lanterns with crystal glasses and silver place settings. Guest cottages, set in mopane shrubveld with no views, contain two rooms, each with its own thatched veranda. Rooms make extensive use of hemp carpeting, thatch, and dark beams to create an appealing warmth. *20 rooms, 1 suite (22 guests). Pool, meeting room.*

$$$$ ⚠ **Ngala Tented Safari Camp.** It seems that the marula seeds softly
★ falling on the tents are applauding this gorgeous little tented camp shaded by a canopy of giant trees. You'll feel like a sultan as you lie beneath your billowing, honey-color canvas roof that acts as a canopy for your basket-weave handmade bed and headboard. Polished wooden floors, gauze-screened floor-to-ceiling windows, green-and-cream curtains that fall from ceiling-high rods along with a dressing area with his-and-her stone washbasins and a gleaming old-fashioned style bath—all are so roomy, elegant, and luxurious it's almost impossible to believe you're in a tent. The camp's dining area and lounge have an almost nautical feel. Huge wooden decks are tethered by guy ropes and stout poles on the very edge of the Timbavati River. It seems as if at any moment you could be gently blown into the sky over the surrounding bushveld. *6 tent (12 guests). Pool.*

Tanda Tula Bush Camp

At this luxury tented camp in the Timbavati you'll be closer to the bush than at almost any other lodge. When lions roar nearby, the noise sounds like it's coming from under the bed. The reason is simple: guests sleep in East African safari-style tents with huge window flaps that roll up, leaving you staring at the bush largely through mosquito netting. The effect is magical and much more rewarding than sleeping in a conventional room.

$$$$ ⚠ **Tanda Tula Bush Camp.** Of the tented camps in Mpumalanga,
★ Tanda Tula is by far the most luxurious. Each tent is beautifully decorated with wicker chairs, bedspreads made from colorful African materials, and elegant side tables, a cupboard, and dresser. An oscillating fan and electric lights add a convenient modern touch. Bathrooms are private and wooden decks overlook the dry bed of the Nhlaralumi River. A large, open-sided thatched shelter serves as the main lounge, where breakfast and lunch are served. Of particular note are Tanda Tula's bush *braais,* held in the dry bed of the Nhlaralumi River with the moon reflecting off the bright sand. It's worth noting that although the lodge can accommodate a maximum of 24 guests, it usually keeps numbers down to 16, a device that makes it easy to mix with people. ✉ *Box 151, Hoedspruit 1380,* ☎ FAX *015/793–3191 (For reservations: Constantia Uitsig, Box 32, Constantia 7848, Western Cape),* ☎

021/794–6500, FAX *021/794–7605,* WEB *www.tandatula.co.za. 12 tents (24 guests). Bar, pool, private airstrip. AE, DC, MC, V.*

Umlani Bushcamp

Umlani places a stronger emphasis on bush walks than other lodges, and an armed ranger usually hops off the vehicle and leads you in search of rhino or other game as often as he can during the morning game drive. Animals run from humans who are on foot, so don't expect to get up close and personal with an elephant. However, the visceral thrill of seeing big game while on foot, even from 150 ft away, more than compensates—plus you learn a tremendous amount about bushveld ecology. In the evening a ranger takes guests on a conventional game drive.

$$ ⊞ **Umlani Bushcamp.** Snoozing under enormous shade trees in the Timbavati, this superb bush camp offers you a very different experience from the other lodges. The focus here is on a bush experience, as opposed to the search for big game, and accommodations are accordingly rustic. Guests sleep in rondawels made from reeds and thatch, the bed is protected by a mosquito net, and private bathrooms are exhilaratingly open to the sky and fenced in with bamboo. Communal facilities include a thatched covered boma facing a dry riverbed and a large boma and reed-wall dining area. There's no electricity here, but the kerosene lanterns and candles add to the bush ambience. Despite this, there are facilities where you can charge your video-camera battery. It's not everyone's cup of tea, but you really feel like you're out in the African wilds, and the atmosphere is fun and relaxed. ⊠ *Box 26350, Arcadia, Pretoria 0007,* ☎ *012/803–4000,* FAX *012/803–6313,* WEB *www.umlani. com. 8 rondawels, 1 four-bed family unit (16 guests). Bar, pool. AE, DC, MC, V.*

Kruger National Park A to Z

To research prices, get advice from other travelers, and book travel arrangements, visit www.fodors.com.

AIR TRAVEL

For information about bus, train, and plane transport to Nelspruit, 50 km (31 mi) from Kruger's Numbi Gate and 64 km (40 mi) from Marlene Gate, *see* Mpumalanga A to Z, *above.*

Two airlines fly into the park or to nearby airports. S.A. Express has daily flights between Johannesburg and Skukuza, which is the park headquarters and the largest rest camp in the park. One of these goes via Hoedspruit, a small service town close to Kruger's Orpen Gate that is also convenient for some of the private game lodges on the west side of the national park. All passengers landing at Skukuza must pay an R30 entrance fee to the park; if, however, you are not going to stay in the park, the charge is R80. S.A. Airlink sends at least one flight a day from Johannesburg to Phalaborwa, a mining town on the edge of the park's central section.

➤ AIRLINES AND CONTACTS: **S.A. Airlink** (☎ 015/781–5823 or 015/781–5833). **S.A. Express** (☎ 011/978–5390).

BUS TRAVEL

For information about bus, train, and plane transport to Nelspruit, 50 km (31 mi) from Kruger's Numbi Gate and 64 km (40 mi) from Malelane Gate, *see* Mpumalanga A to Z, *above.*

CAR RENTAL

Avis is the only car-rental agency with an office at Skukuza, inside the park. The Nelspruit branch of Imperial will deliver a car to Skukuza for you. If you have five or more people in your group, consider hiring a minibus. Not only do you get your own window, but you also sit much higher than in a regular car—a big plus when you're searching for game hidden in dense bush. Avis, Budget, and Imperial have rental desks at Phalaborwa airport.

➤ LOCAL AGENCIES: **Avis** (☎ 013/735–5651; Phalaborwa Airport, ☎ 015/781–3169). **Budget** (Phalaborwa Airport, ☎ 015/781–5823). **Imperial** (☎ 013/741–3210; Phalaborwa Airport, ☎ 015/781–5404).

CAR TRAVEL

From Johannesburg drive north on the N1 to Pretoria East and then head east on the N4 to Nelspruit, where you can choose which of the park's entrances to use. The Malelane and Numbi gates, closest to Nelspruit, are between about four and five hours from Johannesburg.

Note: The N4 is an expensive toll road—and there is no real alternative route, so it's difficult to avoid paying the high fees. Expect to pay at least R150 on a one-way trip from Johannesburg to Nelspruit or Malelane. You can pay with cash or plastic for the purpose: you will be charged around R20–R30 per toll.

Depending on the month, rest-camp gates close between 5:30 and 6:30 at night and open again between 4:30 and 6:30 in the morning. The driver of any vehicle caught on the roads between these hours is liable to a fine or prosecution. Admission to the park is R24 per vehicle, plus R30 for each visitor, whether you're staying overnight or longer.

CHILDREN ON SAFARI

If you'd like to ignite in your kids a passion for and commitment to the environment and wildlife, then send them to Bushschools while you're doing your own safari. Run by Shan Varty (of Londolozi fame) and Kate Groch, these programs are for children of all ages and take place at CC Africa's well-known and highly respected lodges: Londolozi, Bongani Mountain Reserve, and Ngala, in Mpumalanga; and Phinda, in KwaZulu-Natal. Your kids will be given the opportunity in a safe but exciting environment to learn by discovery. Their days will be spent tracking the Big Five, discovering traditional uses of plants, exploring mountain streams, playing camouflage games, hiking, and experiencing and exploring the local cultures. Children stay with their parents in the same chalets or in their own chalets next to their parents (optional) and will have planned activities during the length of their parents' stay. The cost is US$120 per day, which includes accommodations, food, drink, activities, and Bushschools activity packs.

➤ CHILDREN PROGRAM INFORMATION: **Bushschools** (☎ 083/308–0757 or 27/11/784–9376, ℻ 011/883–6472). **CC Africa** (✉ Private Bag X27, Benmore 2010, ☎ 013/735–5653 or 011/809–4300, ℻ 011/809–4400, WEB www.ccafrica.com).

TOURS

S.A. Express is the biggest safari company in Kruger and the only commercial flight operator in the region. You can choose from a variety of tour packages ranging from quickie overnight jaunts to five-day extravaganzas that also take in the scenic splendors of the Mpumalanga Escarpment. You'll fly into Skukuza on one of S.A. Express's regularly scheduled flights, tour the park in minibuses, and sleep in rest camps, usually Skukuza. Tour leaders are knowledgeable about the park's ecosystems and usually know where to find animals you would probably miss on your own. Other operators offering minibus tours of Kruger Park are Game Encounter, Springbok Atlas, and Welcome Tours.

Reservations for all accommodations, bush drives, wilderness trails, and other park activities for self-organized tours must be made through the National Parks Board.

► Tour-Operator Recommendations: **Game Encounter** (⊠ Box 48737, Roosevelt Park 2129, ☎ FAX 011/888–2100). **National Parks Board** (Box 787, Pretoria 0001, ☎ 012/343–1991, FAX 012/343–0905, WEB www.parks-sa.co.za). **S.A. Express** (⊠ Box 101, Johannesburg International Airport, Johannesburg 1627, ☎ 011/978–5390, FAX 011/978–6384). **Springbok Atlas** (⊠ Box 14884, Bredell 1623, ☎ 011/396–1053, FAX 011/396–1069). **Welcome Tours** (⊠ Box 2191, Parklands 2121, ☎ 011/328–8050, FAX 011/442–8865, WEB www.welcome.co.za).

TRAIN TRAVEL

For information about bus, train, and plane transport to Nelspruit, 50 km (31 mi) from Kruger's Numbi Gate and 64 km (40 mi) from Malelane Gate, *see* Mpumalanga A to Z, *above*.

4 CAPE TOWN AND THE PENINSULA

Backed by the familiar shape of Table Mountain, Cape Town presides over a coastline of unsurpassed beauty: of mountains edging the sea, miles of beaches, and 18th-century wineries napping under giant oaks. Modern South Africa was born here, and the city is filled with reminders of its historic role in overseas trade between Europe and the East. Today Cape Town is home to the country's best museums, restaurants, and hotels.

Updated by
Jennifer Stern

F YOU VISIT ONLY ONE PLACE in South Africa, make it Cape Town. Sheltered beneath the familiar shape of Table Mountain, this historic city is instantly recognizable, and few cities in the world possess its beauty and style.

A stroll through the lovely city center reveals Cape Town's three centuries as the sea link between Europe and the East. Elegant Cape Dutch buildings with their whitewashed gables abut imposing monuments to Britain's imperial legacy. In the Bo-Kaap neighborhood the call to prayer echoes from minarets while the sweet tang of Malay curry wafts through the cobbled streets. And everywhere, whether you're eating outdoors at one of the country's best restaurants or sipping wine atop Table Mountain, you sense—correctly—that this is South Africa's most urbane, civilized city.

As impressive as all this is, though, what you will ultimately recall about Cape Town is the sheer grandeur of its setting—Table Mountain rising above the city, the sweep of the bay, and mountains cascading into the sea. You will likely spend more time marveling at the views than anything else.

The city lies at the northern end of the Cape Peninsula, a 75-km (44-mi) tail of mountains that hangs down from the tip of Africa, ending at the Cape of Good Hope. Drive 15 minutes in any direction, and you may lose yourself in a stunning landscape of 18th-century Cape Dutch manors, historic wineries, and white-sand beaches backed by sheer mountains. Francis Drake wasn't exaggerating when he said this was "the fairest Cape we saw in the whole circumference of the earth," and he would have little cause to change his opinion today. You could spend a week exploring just the city and peninsula—and a lifetime discovering the nearby wonders of the Western Cape, including the Winelands, one of the great highlights of a trip to South Africa.

Capetonians know they have it good and look with condescending sympathy on those with the misfortune of living elsewhere. On weekends they hike, sail, and bike in their African Eden. At night they congregate at the city's fine restaurants, fortified with the Cape wine that plays such an integral role in the city's life. Laid-back Cape Town has none of the frenetic energy of hard-nosed Johannesburg. Maybe that's because Cape Town doesn't need to unearth its treasures—the beauty of the place is right in front of you as soon as you roll out of bed.

In this respect the city is often likened to San Francisco, but Cape Town has what San Francisco can never have—history and the mountain. Table Mountain is key to Cape Town's identity. It dominates the city in a way that's difficult to comprehend until you visit. In the afternoon, when creeping fingers of clouds spill over the mountain and reach toward the city, the whole town seems to shiver and hold its breath. Depending on which side of the mountain you live, it even dictates when the sun will rise and set.

Indeed, the city owes its very existence to the mountain. The freshwater streams running off its slopes were what first prompted early explorers to anchor here. In 1652 Jan van Riebeeck and 90 Dutch settlers established a revictualing station for ships of the Dutch East India Company (VOC) on the long voyage east. The settlement represented the first European toehold in South Africa, and Cape Town is still sometimes called the Mother City.

Those first Dutch settlers soon ventured into the interior to establish their own farms, and 140 years later the settlement supported a population of 20,000 whites as well as 25,000 slaves brought from distant lands like Java, Madagascar, and Guinea. Its position on the strategic cusp of Africa, however, meant the colony never enjoyed any real stability. The British, entangled in a global dogfight with Napoléon, occupied the Cape twice, first in 1795 and then more permanently in 1806. With them they brought additional slaves from Ceylon, India, and the Philippines. Destroyed or assimilated in this colonial expansion were the indigenous Khoikhoi (Hottentots), who once herded their cattle here and foraged along the coast.

For visitors used to hearing about South Africa's problems in black and white, Cape Town will come as a surprise—the city is black, white, and colored. Today more than 1 million coloreds—the term used to describe people of mixed race, Malay, Indian, or of Khoikhoi or slave descent—live in the city and give it a distinct spice.

Perhaps the greatest celebration of this colored culture is the annual Coon Carnival, when thousands of wild celebrants take to the streets in vibrant costumes to sing *moppies* (vaudeville-style songs), accompanied by banjos, drums, and whistles. The carnival is the most visible reminder of a way of life that saw its finest flowering in District Six, a predominantly colored but truly multiracial neighborhood on the fringes of the city center whose destruction was a tragic result of apartheid in Cape Town. District Six was a living festival of music and soul, a vibrant community bound by poverty, hope, and sheer joie de vivre. In 1966 the Nationalist government invoked the Group Areas Act, rezoned District Six a whites-only area, and razed it. The scars of that event still run deep. A new museum seeks to recapture the mood of the lost community, and a move is afoot to build low-cost housing in the area, although it has been suggested that it be turned into some kind of living monument, instead.

Other legacies of apartheid fester. Each year for decades, thousands of blacks have streamed to the Cape in search of work, food, and a better life. They end up in the squatter camps of Crossroads and Khayelitsha, names that once flickered across TV screens around the globe. Many visitors never see this side of South Africa, but as you drive into town along the N2 from the airport, you can't miss the pitiful shacks built on shifting dunes as far as the eye can see—a sobering contrast to the first-world luxury of the city center. A tour of these areas offers a glimpse of the old South Africa—and the enormous challenges facing the new one.

Pleasures and Pastimes

Beaches
The Cape's beaches on both the Atlantic and False Bay sides are truly legendary. They stretch endlessly, and you can walk for miles without seeing a fast-food outlet or cool-drink stand. But you will see seagulls, dolphins, penguins, and whales (in season). Forget swimming in the Atlantic—even a dip will freeze your toes. The heat plus the scent of coconut-oiled beauties make for a heady atmosphere. The "in" crowd flocks to Clifton, a must for sunbathers. Although Camps Bay, Llandudno, and Sandy Bay have their attractions, if it's swimming you're into, take yourself to the warmer waters of St. James, Kalk Bay, Fish Hoek, and Simonstown, all on the False Bay side. Windsurfers congregate at Blouberg, where several competitions are held. Don't miss Boulders or Seaforth for snorkeling among great rocks in secluded coves and pools.

History

Wherever you are, there's history in the air. Take a cultural tour of the townships and Bo-Kaap to see communities still struggling to emerge from the yoke of apartheid. Take a tour of Robben Island, where Nelson Mandela and thousands of other political prisoners were imprisoned for so many long years. Cape Town's small, so walking tours are easy, and you can pack in a lot in just a few hours.

Markets

Cape Town has the best markets in the country—informal, creative, artistic, with a good selection of the usual tatty or really splendid African curios. The Waterfront markets are tremendous, and serious goody hunters might strike gold at the Greenpoint open-air market on a Sunday. Greenmarket Square's terrific: Look out for the special rubber-tire sandals. The Rondebosch Park Craft Market, on the first Saturday of the month, has unusual items, as does the Constantia Market, held on summer weekends. Read the papers for up-to-date listings on these and other ephemeral markets, such as the Observatory Holistic Lifestyle Fair, held on the first Sunday of the month.

Outdoor Activities

Cape Town is the adventure capital of South Africa, with great surfing, wonderful diving, world-class climbing, excellent paragliding and hang gliding, horseback riding along lonely beaches or bright green vineyards, and hectic single-track mountain biking as well as some fun and easy biking trails, sailing, kite flying, and, of course, hiking and walking along the slopes of Table Mountain or the edge of the sea. Or for something totally different, hurtle earthward in a tandem sky dive with Table Mountain as a backdrop, or fly upside down in an aerobatic plane. You'll be spoiled by all the choices.

Picnics

Cape Town is the ultimate picnic land. Pack a basket and head off to Rondevlei to bird-watch or to the top of Table Mountain to enjoy gorgeous views. Capetonians love evening beach picnics at the end of long summer days. Choose Bakoven, Clifton, or Llandudno and watch the pink sun turn crimson before it slips below the horizon.

EXPLORING CAPE TOWN

Cape Town is surprisingly small. The area between Table Mountain and Table Bay, including the city center and the nearby suburbs, is known as the City Bowl. In the city center an orderly street grid and the constant view of Table Mountain make it almost impossible to get lost. Major arteries running toward the mountain from the sea are Adderley, Loop, and Long streets; among the major cross streets are Strand, Longmarket, and Wale, which, be warned, is alternately written as WALE ST. and WAALST, on signs. The heart of the historic city—where you'll find many of the museums and major buildings—is Government Avenue, a pedestrian mall at the top of Adderley Street. St. George's Mall, another major pedestrian thoroughfare, runs the length of commercial Cape Town.

Cape Town has grown as a city in a way that few others in the world have. Take a good look at the street names. Strand and Waterkant (meaning "waterside") streets are now far from the sea. However, when they were named, they were right on the beach. An enormous program of dumping rubble into the ocean extended the city by a good few square miles (this can, no doubt, be attributed to the Dutch obsession with reclaiming land from the sea). Almost all the city on the seaward side of Strand and Waterkant is part of the reclaimed area of the city known as the Foreshore.

Once you leave the city center, orienting yourself becomes trickier. As you face Table Mountain from the city, the distinctive mountain on your left is Devil's Peak; on the right are Signal Hill and Lion's Head. Signal Hill takes its name from a gun fired there every day at noon. If you look carefully, you will see that Signal Hill forms the rump of a reclining lion, while the maned Lion's Head looks south past Table Mountain (this is best seen from the N1 driving in to town). On the other side of Signal Hill and Lion's Head lie the Atlantic communities of Sea Point, Clifton, and Camps Bay. Heading the other way, around Devil's Peak, you come to Cape Town's exclusive southern suburbs—Rondebosch, Newlands, Claremont, and Constantia. The happening Waterfront lies north of the City Bowl on the other side of the horrendous freeways that separate the docks from downtown.

The Cape Peninsula, much of which is included in the newly proclaimed Cape Peninsula National Park (CPNP), extends 40 km (25 mi) below the city. The park comprises Table Mountain, most of the high-lying land on the Peninsula Mountain chain that runs down the center of the peninsula, what used to be known as the Cape Point Nature Reserve, and Boulders Beach. The steep mountain slopes leave little room for settlement in the narrow shelf next to the sea. The east side of the peninsula is washed by the waters of False Bay. Here, connected by a coastal road and railway line, lie the suburbs of Muizenberg, St. James, Kalk Bay, and Fish Hoek, as well as the naval base at historic Simonstown. The western shores of the peninsula are wilder and emptier, pounded by huge Atlantic swells. In addition to the tiny hamlets of Scarborough, Kommetjie, Noordhoek, and Llandudno, you'll find the fishing port of Hout Bay.

Great Itineraries

IF YOU HAVE 2 DAYS

On your first day take an early morning city walk to see the sights or take a half-day city tour. You will see the **Company's Gardens,** the **Castle of Good Hope, City Hall,** the **Bo-Kaap,** and other historical highlights.

For lunch go to the **V&A Waterfront** and eat at one of the outside restaurants if the weather's good, inside if it's not. Visit the various waterfront attractions, including the **Aquarium** (a must) and the **SAS Somerset.** If you don't dine at the Green Dolphin and listen to terrific jazz, then move away from the waterfront and go uptown.

Perhaps have dinner in one of the city's many excellent restaurants and then go to the theater, ballet, or opera at the **Artscape Theatre Complex** or at the **Baxter Theatre.** For a real taste of contemporary African–New Age Cape Town fusion, go to the Drum Cafe, on Glynn Street, to watch a performance and maybe join in a drum circle.

The next morning take a **Robben Island** tour, which takes 3½ hours. On your return go straight to the **Lower Cableway** and ride to the summit of **Table Mountain.** Have lunch in the restaurant and hike one of the trails—walks can last from a few minutes to a few hours.

When you come down from the mountain, drive to **Camps Bay** and dine at a beach-view restaurant. Then kick off your shoes and walk on the beach. To round out the evening, you might want to take in a show at the Playhouse Theatre in Camps Bay.

IF YOU HAVE 5 OR MORE DAYS

Spend the first day or two exploring Cape Town. There's a lot to see. Pop into museums and galleries, visit **Bo-Kaap,** and wander around this old Cape Malay area with its cobblestone streets and quaint buildings. On the afternoon of the second day browse along the waterfront.

On the morning of Day 3 explore **Robben Island** and, on your return, lunch at the waterfront. In the afternoon you might visit the castle or have high tea at the **Mount Nelson hotel.** In the evening head out to the vibey suburb of Observatory for dinner, and then wander down Lower Main Road, perhaps popping in for a drink or late-night coffee at a café.

On Day 4 drive out to **Constantia Winelands.** Visit the estates, enjoy the countryside, do a little wine tasting, have lunch, and then in the afternoon drive over Constantia Nek to Hout Bay. Go to the harbor and take an early afternoon cruise to Seal Island. For a more adventurous activity, maybe admire the sunset from the back of a horse on Noordhoek or Hout Bay Beach or from a kayak out at sea. If the conditions are right, you could do a tandem paraglider flight off Lion's Head, landing at the popular La Med just in time for cocktails overlooking the beach. Even if you don't paraglide in here, have dinner on this side of the mountain, at Greenpoint, Sea Point, or Camps Bay.

Day 5 is penguin day. You simply have to take the trek—it's a fairly long drive—and wend your way along the False Bay coast to Boulders Beach, in Cape Peninsula National Park, where you'll find Cape penguins in profusion. This is one of the few mainland sites in the world where these comical little creatures live and breed. Then go on a little farther for a seafood lunch at Millers Point. In the afternoon grab your map and follow the road to the Cape of Good Hope, part of the national park (there's a separate admission fee), and, of course, Cape Point. You can take the steep walk to the point, or take the funicular. It looks as if this is where the Indian and Atlantic oceans meet—sometimes there is even a line of foam stretching out to sea—but of course it's not. No matter, it's a dramatic spot.

Table Mountain

Along with Victoria Falls on the border of Zimbabwe and Zambia, Table Mountain is one of southern Africa's most beautiful and impressive natural wonders. The views from its summit can reduce you to speechless awe. The mountain rises more than 3,500 ft above the city, its flat top visible to sailors 65 km (40 mi) out to sea. In summer, when the southeaster blows, moist air from False Bay funnels over the mountain, condensing in the colder, higher air to form a tablecloth of cloud. Legend attributes this low-lying cloud to a pipe-smoking contest between the devil and Jan van Hunks, a pirate who settled on Devil's Peak. The devil lost, and the cloud serves to remind him of his defeat.

The first recorded ascent of Table Mountain was made in 1503 by Portuguese admiral Antonio de Saldanha, who wanted to get a better sense of the topography of the Cape Peninsula. He couldn't have asked for a better view. In one direction you look down on today's city, cradled between Lion's Head and Devil's Peak. In another you see the crescent of sand at Camps Bay, sandwiched between the sea and the granite faces of the Twelve Apostles. Farther south the peninsula trails off toward the Cape of Good Hope, its mountains forming a ragged spine between False Bay and the empty vastness of the Atlantic. No matter where you look, you just can't get over how high you feel.

Despite being virtually surrounded by the city, Table Mountain is a remarkably unspoiled wilderness. Most of the Cape Peninsula's 2,200 species of flora are found on the mountain—there are about as many plant species in the Cape Peninsula as there are in the whole of North America and Europe combined—including magnificent examples of Cape Town's wild indigenous flowers, known as *fynbos*. The best time to see the mountain in bloom is between September and March, although you can be sure to find some flowers whatever the time of year. Long gone are the days when Cape lions, zebras, and hyenas roamed the mountain, but you can still glimpse *grysboks* (small antelopes) or baboons, and cute, rabbitlike *dassies* (rock hyraxes) congregate in large numbers near the Upper Cable Station.

Atop the mountain, well-marked trails offering 10- to 40-minute jaunts crisscross the western Table near the Cableway. Many other trails lead to the other side of Platteklip Gorge and into the mountain's catchment area, where you'll find reservoirs, hidden streams, and more incredible views. Be aware, though, that weather on the mountain can change quickly. Even if you're making only a short visit, take a sweater. If you're planning an extended hike, carry water, plenty of warm clothing, and a mobile phone.

During the warm summer months Capetonians are fond of taking picnic baskets up the mountain. The best time to do this is after 5: some say sipping a glass of chilled Cape wine while watching the sun set from Table Mountain is one of life's great joys. Otherwise, you can eat at the large self-service restaurant, which offers an eclectic buffet, including some South African–style food, such as Malay curry, and a range of Mediterranean mezes (appetizers). The hot breakfasts are great. The smaller bistro serves cocktails and a range of coffees and pastries. The restaurant is open from 8:30 to 3:30 and the bistro from 10 until the last cable car. As you might expect, both restaurants offer a good wine list with local wines predominating. For noshers, there's a convenient fast-food kiosk.

If you're feeling adventurous, try a rappel from the top—it's only 370 ft, but you're hanging out over 3,300 ft of air. You have only two ways of reaching the top of the mountain: Walk, or take the Cableway.

Riding the Cableway

Cable cars take from three to five minutes to reach the summit. There used to be terrible congestion at the Lower Cable Station, but the building of the new **Cableway,** with two large, wheelchair-friendly revolving cars that give a 180-degree view, has eased things somewhat. You can't prebook for the cable car, but the longest you'll have to wait is about an hour, and then only in peak season (December 15–January 15). Several tour operators include a trip up the mountain in their schedules. ⊠ *Tafelberg Rd.,* ☎ *021/424–8181,* WEB *www.tablemountain.co.za.* ▨ *R85 round-trip, R45 one-way (depending on season).* ☉ *Dec.–May, daily 8:30 AM–9 PM; June–Aug., daily 8:30–6; Sept.–Nov., daily 8–7:30.*

The Lower Cableway lies on the slopes of Table Mountain near its western end. It's a long way from the city on foot, and you're better off traveling by car, taxi, or *riki* (a slow, low-tech minibus). To get there from the City Bowl, take Buitengracht Street toward the mountain. Once you cross Camp Street, Buitengracht becomes Kloof Nek Road. Follow Kloof Nek Road through the residential neighborhood of Gardens to a traffic circle; turn left on Tafelberg Road and follow signs to the Lower Cableway.

A taxi from the city center to the Lower Cableway (one-way) costs about R70–R90, and a riki costs R15–R20 per person, but they are only available during the week.

Walking Up the Mountain

More than 300 walking trails wend their way up the mountain, but the only easy route up the front section is via Platteklip Gorge. You can start at the Lower Cable Station, but remember that you need to walk about 3–4 km (2–2½ mi) to the left (east) before heading up. It is easier but slightly less scenic to walk along Tafelberg Road until the PLATTEKLOOF GORGE sign and then head up. Once on the right path you shouldn't get lost. There is no water in Platteklip Gorge; you *must* take at least 2 liters (½ gallon) of water per person. Table Mountain can be dangerous if you're not familiar with the terrain. Many paths that look like good routes off the mountain end in treacherous cliffs. Do not underestimate this mountain. It may be in the middle of a city, but it is not a genteel town park. Always take warm clothes and a mobile phone, and let someone know of your plan. The mountain is quite safe if you stick to known paths. If you are on the mountain and the weather changes dramatically (heavy rain, mist) and you can't tell where you are, just sit tight—you will be rescued as soon as the weather permits. Walking around in the mist is quite dangerous. There are several routes from Kirstenbosch National Botanic Gardens that are wonderful, easy, and scenic but that take you to a section of the mountain that is far from the front table and the cable station. Of course, if you're prepared to go the distance, you can do the quite long and very scenic, but challenging, walk from the top of the Kirstenbosch routes to the front table.

If you don't feel comfortable tackling the mountain alone, contact **Cape Eco Trails** (☎ 021/785–5511, 🌐 www.capetrails.com), which offers guided walks to the top and all over the mountain. Or, you can contact one of the climbing schools listed in Outdoor Activities and Sports, which will escort hikes but not too eagerly, as they tend to concentrate more on climbing. Expect to pay R200–R600 per person, depending on group size, which may include a one-way cable-car ride.

The City Center

Numbers in the text correspond to numbers in the margin and on the Cape Town map.

A Good Walk

Begin your walk at **Cape Town Tourism's Information Office** ①, on the corner of Burg and Castle streets (one block up from Strand Street). At no time during the walk will you be more than 15 minutes from this starting point. Head down Castle and turn right onto **Adderley Street** ②, directly opposite the **Golden Acre** ③ shopping center. Turn left on Darling Street and head toward the **Castle of Good Hope** ④ and the **Grand Parade** ⑤. Just across the way is the beautiful **City Hall** ⑥. Retrace your steps toward Adderley Street, turning left one block before you get there onto Parliament Street to reach the austere **Groote Kerk** ⑦. The Groote Kerk faces Church Square, now a parking lot, where churchgoers used to unharness their oxen. On the skinny traffic island in the middle of Spin Street is a concrete plaque marking the **Slave Tree** ⑧. A brass plaque commemorating the slave tree and a cross section of the tree itself are on display in the **South African Cultural History Museum** ⑨, next door on Adderley Street. Here Adderley swings to the right to become Wale Street (Waalstraat), but if you continue straight on, you'll be walking up Government Avenue, a wide and attractive squirrel-filled, tree-lined walkway that leads past many of the country's most important institutions and museums. On your right is the **South African Library** ⑩, the oldest in the country, and **Company's Gar-**

dens ⑪. This is a great place to sit and watch the world go by. Buy a bag of peanuts from a vendor and feed the pigeons and squirrels. Continue along Government Avenue, and walk past Parliament to the **Tuynhuys** ⑫. The **South African National Gallery** ⑬ stands farther up Government Avenue, on your left, and opposite it on your right are the **South African Museum** ⑭ and the Planetarium. The temple in front of the South African Museum is the **Delville Wood Monument** ⑮. Walk through the alleyway on the left of the gallery onto Hatfield Street to reach the **South African Jewish Museum** ⑯, the Cape Town Holocaust Center, and the imposing **Great Synagogue** ⑰, South Africa's mother synagogue. Carry on up Hatfield toward the mountain and take the first small tree-lined lane to the right; this will lead you back to Government Avenue. Turn left to go to **Bertram House** ⑱, at the top of the avenue, and then backtrack and turn left to cut across the front of the South African Museum to Queen Victoria Street. For something completely different, head down Bloem to **Long Street** ⑲. Turn left on Wale Street and walk four blocks to the **Bo-Kaap** ⑳. Near the corner of Wale and Rose streets stands the **Bo-Kaap Museum** ㉑. Retrace your steps down Wale Street to **St. George's Cathedral** ㉒. Across Wale is the entrance to **St. George's Mall** ㉓. From there turn left onto **Church Street** ㉔, where you'll find art galleries, African curio shops, a flea market, and a great coffee shop (Mozart's) in the short section between Burg and Long. It's worth turning left onto Long to see the attractive old buildings, but if you're short on time or energy, turn right (away from the mountain) onto Longmarket and then amble around **Greenmarket Square** ㉕, the center of the city since 1710. The **Old Town House** ㉖ faces the square on the mountain side. Work your way back to Long Street and walk away from the mountain. When you reach Strand Street, turn right to reach the **Koopmans–De Wet House** ㉗. Turn right again onto Burg, and you'll be back at Cape Town Tourism.

TIMING

To get the most from this tour, you'll need to set aside a whole day. Start at about 9, when most workers have finished their commute, and then stop for a long, leisurely lunch during the hottest part of the day, finishing the tour at about 4. Make sure to finish the tour before 5, when rush hour congestion takes over the streets.

Sights to See

❷ **Adderley Street.** Originally named Heerengracht after a canal that ran the length of the avenue, this street has always been Cape Town's principal thoroughfare. It was once the favored address of the city's leading families, and its oak-shaded sidewalks served as a promenade for those who wanted to see and be seen. By the mid-19th century the oaks had all been chopped down and the canal covered as Adderley Street became the main commercial street. By 1908 it had become such a busy thoroughfare that the city fathers paved it with wooden blocks in an attempt to dampen the noise of countless wagons, carts, and hooves.

⑱ **Bertram House.** Built around 1840, this is the only surviving Georgian brick town house in Cape Town. Once a common sight in the city, these boxlike two-story houses were a response by the English community to Cape Dutch architecture. The projecting front porch was intended to shield the house from the worst effects of the frequent southeasters. The collection of furniture, silver, jewelry, and porcelain recaptures the look and feel of an early 19th-century home. The catalog available at the entrance describes the entire collection. ⊠ *Government Ave. and Orange St.,* ☎ *021/424–9381.* ☞ *R5.* ☉ *Tues.–Sat. 9:30–4:30.*

Cape Town

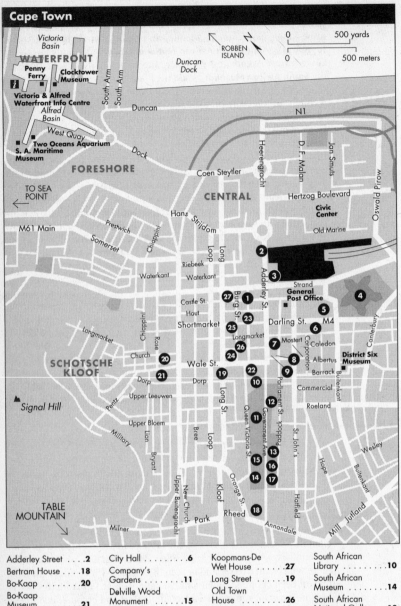

Victoria Basin

WATERFRONT

Penny Ferry

Clocktower Museum

Victoria & Alfred Waterfront Info Centre

Alfred Basin

West Quay

Two Oceans Aquarium

S. A. Maritime Museum

FORESHORE

ROBBEN ISLAND

Duncan Dock

0   500 yards

0   500 meters

Duncan

N1

Coen Steytler

CENTRAL

Hertzog Boulevard

Civic Center

Old Marine

TO SEA POINT

Hans Strijdom

Heerengracht

D. F. Malan

Jan Smuts

Oswald Pirow

M61 Main

Prestwich

Somerset

Chiappini

Long

Loop

Riebeek

Waterkant

Waterkant

Adderley St.

Burg St.

Strand

General Post Office

Canterbury

Castle St.

Hout

Shortmarket

Darling St.

M4

Corporation

Mostert

Caledon

District Six Museum

Albertus

Barrack

Longmarket

Church

Rose

Chiappini

Longmarket

Wale St.

Commercial

Roeland

SCHOTSCHE KLOOF

Dorp

Dorp

Buitenkant

Signal Hill

Upper Leeuwen

Pentz

Long St.

Parliament St.

Government Ave.

St. John's

Wesley

Lion

Upper Bloem

Queen Victoria St.

Hope

Military

Bryant

Bree

Loop

Hatfield

Buitenkant

TABLE MOUNTAIN

New Church

Upper Buitengracht

Park

Kloof

Orange St.

Rheede

Annandale

Mill

Jutland

Milner

Index

Government Avenue ends opposite the impressive gateway to the **Mount Nelson** hotel (⌧ 76 Orange St., ☎ 021/423–1000), complete with two pith-helmeted gatekeepers, which was erected in 1899 to welcome the Prince of Wales on his visit to the Cape. The Nellie, as it's known, remains Cape Town's most fashionable and genteel social venue. More important, it serves the city's best high tea, although the Table Bay Hotel at the V&A Waterfront also provides a memorable version. Both hotels provide a pastry selection to tempt even the most jaded palate.

★ ⓴ **Bo-Kaap.** In the late 17th and early 18th centuries this district was the historic home of the city's Muslim population brought from the East as slaves. Today the area remains strongly Muslim, and it's fascinating to wander the narrow cobbled lanes past mosques and colorful flat-roof houses. Many homes combine elements of Cape Dutch and British architecture, and altogether they represent the largest collection of pre-1840 architecture in South Africa. The Bo-Kaap is also known as the Malay quarter, despite that its inhabitants originated from all over, including the Indonesian archipelago, India, Turkey, and Madagascar.

㉑ **Bo-Kaap Museum.** Built in the 18th century, this museum was originally the home of Abu Bakr Effendi, a well-known member of the Muslim community. The house has been furnished to re-create the lifestyle of a typical Malay family in the 19th century. Since the exhibits aren't labeled, you might do better to visit the museum as part of a guided tour of the Malay quarter. ⌧ *71 Wale St.,* ☎ *021/424–3846,* WEB *www. museums.org.za.* ⌧ *R5.* ⌚ *Mon.–Sat. 9:30–4:30.*

❶ **Cape Town Tourism Information Office.** This is one of the best information offices in South Africa. It's light and bright and breezy and filled with really helpful people. There is a *bureau de change,* a wine shop, with tasting, an Internet café, coffee shop, and loads of information, including a National Parks desk, and an accommodations desk. ⌧ *The Pinnacle at Burg and Castle Sts (Box 1403), 8000,* ☎ *021/426–4260,* FAX *021/426–4263,* WEB *www.cape-town.org.* ⌚ *Weekdays 9–6, Sat. 8:30–2, Sun. 9–1.*

★ ❹ **Castle of Good Hope.** Despite its name the castle isn't one of those fairy-tale fantasies you find perched on a cliff above the Rhine. It's a squat fortress that hunkers into the ground as if to avoid shell fire. Built between 1665 and 1676 by the Dutch East India Company (VOC) to replace an earthen fort constructed by Jan van Riebeeck in 1652, it's the oldest building in the country. Its pentagonal plan, with a diamond-shape bastion at each corner, is typical of the Old Netherlands defense system adopted in the early 17th century. The design was intended to allow covering fire to be provided for every portion of the castle. As added protection, the whole fortification was surrounded by a moat, with the sea nearly washing up against its walls. The castle served as both the VOC headquarters and the official governor's residence and still houses the regional headquarters of the National Defence Force. Despite it bellicose origins, no shot has ever been fired from its ramparts, except ceremonially.

You can wander around on your own or join one of the guided tours that leave at 11, noon, or 2, at no extra cost. Also worth seeing is the excellent William Fehr Collection, housed in the governor's residence. The collection consists of antiques, artifacts, and paintings of early Cape Town and South African history. Conservationists should go upstairs to see John Thomas Baine's *The Greatest Hunt in Africa,* celebrating a "hunt" in honor of Prince Alfred, when nearly 30,000 animals were driven together and slaughtered. ⌧ *Buitenkant St.,* ☎ *021/469–1249.*

 R15. *Mid-Jan.–mid-Dec., Mon.–Sun. 9–4:30; mid-Dec.–mid-Jan., daily 9–4.*

De Goewerneur Restaurant (Buitekant St., 021/469–1202) is in the central courtyard of the Castle of Good Hope and, from the veranda, offers a pleasing view of the lawn and the buildings beyond. It is open Mon.–Sat. 9–4 for light meals and teas.

㉔ Church Street. The center of Cape Town's art and antiques business, the section between Burg and Long streets is a pedestrian mall, filled with art galleries, antiques dealers, and small cafés. This is the site of a daily antiques and flea market.

❻ City Hall. The old seat of local administration is home to the Cape Town Philharmonic Orchestra (which also holds performances at the Artscape Theatre Complex) and the City Library. It was from a balcony here, overlooking Darling Street, that Nelson Mandela gave his historic speech on his release from prison.

★ ⓫ Company's Gardens. These are all that remains of a 43-acre garden laid out by Jan van Riebeeck in April 1652 to supply fresh vegetables to ships on their way to the Dutch East Indies. By 1700 free burghers were cultivating plenty of crops on their own land, and in time the VOC vegetable patch was transformed into a botanic garden. It remains a delightful haven in the city center, graced by fountains, exotic trees, rose gardens, aviaries, and a pleasant outdoor café. At the bottom of the gardens, close to Government Avenue, look for an **old well** that used to provide water for the town's residents and the garden. The old water pump, engraved with the maker's name and the date 1842, has been overtaken by an oak tree and now juts out of the tree's trunk some 6 ft above the ground. A huge **statue of Cecil Rhodes** looms over the path that runs through the center of the gardens. He points to the north, and an inscription reads, YOUR HINTERLAND IS THERE, a reference to Rhodes's dream of extending the British Empire from the Cape to Cairo. *Rhodes Dr., just past the university.* *Daily sunrise–sunset.*

⓯ Delville Wood Monument. The monument honors South Africans who died in the fight for Delville Wood during the great Somme offensive of 1916. Of the 121 officers and 3,032 soldiers who participated in the three-day battle, only five officers and 750 soldiers survived unhurt. Facing the memorial is a **statue of Brigadier-General Lukin,** who commanded the South African infantry brigade during World War I.

❸ Golden Acre. Until earlier in the century this part of the city was all at sea—literally. The land was reclaimed as part of a program to expand the docks. If you look at old paintings of the city, you will see that originally waves lapped at the very walls of the castle, now more than half a mile from the ocean. At the bottom of the escalator leading from the railway station into the Golden Acre is a thin black line that marks the approximate position of the shoreline in 1693. A bit farther on, enclosed in glass, are the remains of Cape Town's first reservoir, which was uncovered when the foundations of the Golden Acre were being dug.

❺ Grand Parade. Once a military parade ground, this is now just a bleak parking lot. A statue of Edward VII serves as a parking attendant. It was here, on his release on February 11, 1990, after 27 years in prison, that Nelson Mandela addressed an adoring crowd of more than 100,000 supporters. Today this is the site of South Africa's oldest flea market, which has been held on Wednesday and Saturday mornings for decades. It's not particularly tourist oriented, but it is the best place to see some of the "real" Cape Town, as it's here that many locals in the know get all manner of goods at bargain prices. Also, pop into one of the rather kitschy food stalls and try a *gatsby* (a sandwich on a long roll filled with french fries, lettuce, tomato, and a choice of fresh or pickled fish, curry, or steak), a *salomie* (roti, a soft round bread, wrapped around a curry filling), or a few *samosas* (fried, filled dough triangles) for a cheap lunch and a genuine cultural experience. And finish off with some *koeksusters* (sweet, braided, lightly spiced, deep-fried pastries) for dessert.

⑰ Great Synagogue. Built in 1903 in the baroque style, this synagogue has notable twin towers and a dome. This forms the center of a Jewish complex, which includes the South African Jewish Museum, the Jacob Gitlin Library, and the Cape Town Holocaust Centre, which is housed in the Albow Centre, next door. ⊠ *88 Hatfield St.,* ☎ *021/465–1405.* ⊙ *Mon. 11–5, Tues. and Sun. 10–4, Wed. 11–3, Thurs. 10–3.*

★ ㉕ Greenmarket Square. For more than a century this cobbled square served as a forum for public announcements, including the 1834 declaration abolishing slavery. In the 19th century the square became a vegetable market as well as a popular watering hole—the city's hardest boozers used to drink themselves comatose at the nearby Old Thatched Tavern and London Hotel. Today the square is a fun open-air market, with vendors selling a wide selection of clothing and sandals, as well as African jewelry, art, and fabrics. For gift buying it's virtually unbeatable.

❼ Groote Kerk (Great Church). One of the most famous churches in South Africa, Groote Kerk was built in 1841 on the site of an earlier Dutch Reformed church dating from 1704. The adjoining clock tower is all that remains of that earlier building. Among the building's interesting features are the enclosed pews, each with its own door. Prominent families would buy their own pews—and lock the doors—so they wouldn't have to pray with the great unwashed. The enormous pulpit is the joint work of famous sculptor Anton Anreith and carpenter Jan Jacob Graaff. The lions supporting it are carved from local stinkwood; the upper portion is Burmese teak. The organ, with nearly 6,000 pipes, is the largest in the southern hemisphere. Approximately 200 people are buried beneath the Batavian soapstone floor, including eight governors. There are free guided tours on request. ⊠ *43 Adderley St. (enter on Church Sq.),* ☎ *021/461–7044.* ⊠ *Free.* ⊙ *Weekdays 10–2; services Sun. at 10 AM and 7 PM.*

㉗ Koopmans–De Wet House. Now a museum, this lovely 18th-century home is a haven of peace in the city center. The structure you see today dates largely from the period 1771–93. It is notable for its neoclassic facade, which has been variously attributed to Anton Anreith and Louis Thibault. The house enjoyed its heyday under Maria de Wet (1834–1906), a Cape Town socialite who entertained most of the major figures in Cape society, including Boer presidents and British governors. The furnishings date to the early 19th century, when the house belonged to Maria's grandmother. The collection includes a stunning selection of antiques, carpets, paintings, and porcelain. It's worth buying the excellent guide to the museum, which describes every item in the collection. ⊠ *35 Strand St.,* ☎ *021/424–2473.* ⊠ *R5.* ⊙ *Tues.–Sat. 9:30–4:30.*

⑲ Long Street. The section of Long between Orange and Wale streets is lined with magnificently restored Georgian and Victorian buildings. Wrought-iron balconies and fancy curlicues on these colorful houses create an impression reminiscent of the French Quarter in New Orleans. During the 1960s Long Street did a good imitation of the Big Easy, including having a host of bars, prostitutes, and sleazy hotels. Today antiques dealers, secondhand bookstores (Clarke's is a must), pawnshops, the Pan-African Market, and funky and vintage clothing outlets make it the best browsing street in the city. There's also a good selection of backpackers' lodges. At the mountain end is Long Street Baths, an indoor swimming pool and old Turkish hammam.

26 Old Town House. For 150 years this was the most important civic building in Cape Town. Built in 1755 as a guardhouse, it also saw duty as a meeting place for the burgher senate, a police station, and from 1840 to 1905 as Cape Town's city hall. The building is a beautiful example of urban Cape Dutch architecture, with thick whitewashed walls, green-and-white shutters, and small-paned windows. Today the former city hall is home to the Michaelis Collection, an extensive selection of 17th-century Dutch paintings, as well as changing exhibits. ⊠ *Greenmarket Sq.,* ☎ *021/424–6367,* WEB *www.museumsonline.co.za.* ☑ *Free.* ☉ *Weekdays 10–5, Sat. 10–4.*

NEED A BREAK?   The **Ivy Garden** (⊠ Greenmarket Sq., ☎ 021/424–6367), in the courtyard of the Old Town House, serves light lunches and teas in a leafy, green setting. Seating on the veranda overlooks the hustle and bustle of Greenmarket Square.

8 Slave Tree. Slaves were auctioned under the tree that once stood here. A cross section of the enormous Canadian pine is displayed at the South African Cultural History Museum. Slavery began in the Cape Colony in 1658, when free burghers petitioned the government for farmhands. The first group of 400 slaves arrived from Guinea, Angola, Batavia (modern Java), and Madagascar. During the first British occupation of the Cape (1795–1803), 17,000 slaves were brought from India, Ceylon, and the Philippines, swelling the total slave population to 30,000. Slavery was abolished by the British in 1834, an act that served as the final impetus for one of South Africa's great historical events, the Great Trek, when thousands of outraged Afrikaners set off in their covered wagons to establish a new state in the hinterland where they would be free from British taxation and laws.

★ 9 South African Cultural History Museum (also known as the Slave Lodge). Built in 1679 by the Dutch East India Company to house slaves, this building, although beautiful, has a rather nasty history. Currently, the museum offers an excellent overview of South Africa's early settler history. Displays detailing the settlement and colonization of the Cape are superb; letters, coins, paintings, clothes, and furniture bring the period almost palpably to life. The museum also has minor collections of Roman, Greek, Egyptian, and Asian antiquities, as well as displays of antique silver, musical instruments, glass, ceramics, weapons, and coins. From 1815 to 1914 the building housed the supreme court. At the time of writing, the future of the museum was under debate, and it may soon be turned into a slavery museum. ⊠ *Adderley and Wale Sts.,* ☎ *021/461–8280,* WEB *www.museums.org.za.* ☑ *R7.* ☉ *Mon.– Sat. 9:30–4:30.*

16 South African Jewish Museum. The museum captures the story of South African Jewry from its early beginnings, spanning 150 years. The "Themes of Memories" (immigrant experiences), "Reality" (integration into South Africa), and "Dreams" (visions) exhibits are dynamically portrayed, represented by high-tech multimedia and interactive displays, reconstructed sets, models, and Judaica artifacts. There is also a computerized Discovery Center with a roots bank, a temporary gallery for changing exhibits, a museum restaurant and shop, and an auditorium. ⊠ *88 Hatfield St.,* ☎ *021/465–1546,* WEB *www.sajewishmuseum.co.za.* ☑ *R25–R30.* ☉ *Sun.–Thurs. 10–5, Fri. 10–2.*

⑩ South African Library. The National Reference Library, as it is also known, owes its existence to Lord Charles Somerset, governor of the Cape Colony, who in 1818 imposed a wine tax to fund the creation of a library that would "place the means of knowledge within the reach of the youth of this remote corner of the Globe." In 1860 the library moved into its current home, a neoclassic building modeled after the Fitzwilliam Museum in Cambridge, England. The library has an extensive collection of Africana, including the works of many 18th- and 19th-century explorers. ✉ *Botanical Gardens,* ☎ *021/424–6320.* ⎙ *Free.* ☉ *Weekdays 9–5.*

⑭ South African Museum. This is a natural history museum with some interesting cultural hangovers. Probably the strangest is the section on ethnography and archaeology, which, many argue, should be in the Cultural History Museum. Far more interesting is the section on the fossil remains of prehistoric reptiles and other animals, and the quite spectacular Whale Well—where musical recitals are often held, under suspended life-size casts of enormous marine mammals. The adjoining planetarium stages a variety of shows throughout the week. ✉ *25 Queen Victoria St.,* ☎ *021/424–3330,* FAX *021/424–6716,* WEB *www.museums.org.za.* ⎙ *Museum R8, planetarium R10.* ☉ *Museum daily 10–5; planetarium shows Tues.–Fri. at 1, weekends at noon, 1, and 2:30.*

★ ⑬ South African National Gallery. Don't miss this art gallery. The museum houses a good collection of 19th- and 20th-century European and British works, but it's most interesting for its South African works, many of which reflect the country's traumatic history. The director is known for innovative, brave, and sometimes controversial exhibitions. The museum café serves salads, sandwiches, pastas, and cakes. Free guided tours are given on Wednesday at 1 and Saturday at 3. ✉ *Government Ave., Gardens,* ☎ *021/465–1628,* WEB *www.museums.org.za.* ⎙ *R5.* ☉ *Tues.–Sun. 10–5.*

㉒ St. George's Cathedral. The cathedral was once the religious seat of one of the most recognizable faces—and voices—in the fight against apartheid, Archbishop Desmond Tutu. In his position as the first black archbishop of Cape Town, he vociferously denounced apartheid and relentlessly pressed for a democratic government. The present Anglican cathedral was designed by Sir Herbert Baker in the Gothic Revival style; construction began in 1901, using sandstone from Table Mountain. The structure contains the largest stained-glass window in the country, some beautiful examples of late-Victorian stained glass, and a 1,000-year-old Coptic cross. If you want to hear the magnificent organ, go to the choral evensong at 5:30 on Wednesday evening, the 9:15 AM or 7 PM mass on Sunday, or the 11 AM mass on the last Sunday of every month. ✉ *Wale St.,* ☎ *021/424–7360.* ⎙ *Free.* ☉ *Daily 8–5. Services weekdays at 7:15 and 1:15; Tues. and Fri. also at 5:30 PM; Sat. at 8 AM; Sun. at 7 AM, 8 AM, 9:15 AM, and 7 PM.*

㉓ St. George's Mall. This promenade stretches almost all the way to the Foreshore. Shops and cafés line the mall, and street vendors hawk everything from T-shirts to African arts and crafts. Buskers and dancers gather daily to entertain the crowds.

⑫ Tuynhuys (Town House). Parts of the Tuynhuys date to the late 17th and early 18th centuries. The building contains the offices of the state president and is not open to the public.

The Victoria & Alfred Waterfront

The Victoria & Alfred Waterfront is the culmination of a long-term project undertaken to breathe new life into the historical dockland of the city. It is one of Cape Town's most vibrant and exciting attractions and is the focus of the city's nightlife and entertainment scene. Hundreds of shops, movie theaters, restaurants, and bars share quarters in restored warehouses and dock buildings, all connected by pedestrian plazas and promenades. It's clean, it's safe, and it's car free.

A Good Walk

It makes sense to begin your walk at the **Victoria & Alfred Waterfront Information Centre** (which you should visit before you do anything else to get the latest news on this constantly changing part of the city). Leave the Information Centre on the Dock Road side (away from the sea), turn right, and walk down Dock Road to the long, narrow stone shed that once housed the **Rocket Life-Saving Apparatus.** Next door is **Mitchell's Waterfront Brewery.** The heady smell of malt emanating from Mitchell's will be enough to send anyone with a thirst into the adjoining **Ferryman's Tavern.** Facing Ferryman's Tavern is the **AGFA Amphitheatre.** From the amphitheater walk over to Quay 5 (in front of Tequila Cantina) and the **Victoria Basin,** where you can see the historic, but not particularly aesthetic, Robben Island embarkation point, where prisoners were shipped to the prison and relatives boarded the ferry to visit their loved ones. Walk back past the red Fisherman's Choice restaurant to Market Square and the mustard-color **Union-Castle House.** Walk past the National Sea Rescue Institute (NSRI) shed and around the bottom of Alfred Mall, between the Green Dolphin and the Hildebrand and over the Swing Bridge to what used to be called Berties Landing (and still is by most Capetonians). You can't miss it—head for the bright orange clock tower. Here you may see seals resting on a platform just near the embarkation point for the Robben Island Ferries. Also here is the ticket office for Robben Island and a small shop selling island memorabilia. From here you can backtrack over the swing bridge, but it's much more interesting to walk past the Fish Quay and turn right along the rather tacky-looking road, where you are bound to see a few boats in dry dock being painted or serviced. This is the unprettified section of the harbor, but it is quite safe. Follow the road up to the traffic circle and then turn right and head toward the Cape Grace Hotel, in front of which is the **SAS Somerset.** The ship is part of the **South African Maritime Museum.** Head back toward the Alfred Mall, looking left as you cross the second bridge, to see if there is a ship in drydock. Slip to the left of the mall and visit the SA Maritime Museum. Then amble around the Waterfront Trading Company, which is designed to spit you out the other end, right in front of the **Two Oceans Aquarium.** Then head back toward the information center, taking the stairs on the left up to Portswood Ridge, where there are several late-19th-century buildings once used by the harbor administration. At the top of the stairs stand the brick Time Ball Tower, the **Harbour Master's Residence,** and the Dragon Tree. Take the stairs back down and cross Dock Road to return to your starting point.

TIMING

You could complete this tour in half a day, but that won't give you much time for shopping, coffee stops, or lunch. A more leisurely approach would be to set aside a whole day.

Sights to See

AGFA Amphitheatre. This popular outdoor performance space mounts shows almost daily, ranging from concerts by the Cape Town Philharmonic Orchestra to gigs by jazz and rock bands. Check with the Victoria and Albert Information Centre for the schedule of events. The amphitheater stands on the site where, in 1860, teenage Prince Alfred inaugurated the construction of a breakwater to protect shipping in the harbor. Table Bay was never an ideal natural harbor. In winter devastating northwesterly winds pounded ships caught in the exposed waters. Between 1647 and 1870 more than 190 ships went down in Table Bay. Since the breakwater was built, only 40 ships have foundered here.

Ferryman's Tavern. With the heady smell of malt emanating from Mitchell's Brewery adjoining the pub, you won't have to wait long for a nice cool one. Constructed in 1877 of bluestone and Table Mountain sandstone, this is one of the oldest buildings in the harbor. Before 1912 the temperance movement in Cape Town had managed to force a ban on the sale of alcohol within the docks. As a result, a host of pubs sprang up just outside the dock gates, particularly along Dock Road. ⊠ *Market Plaza,* ☎ *021/419-7748.*

Harbour Master's Residence. Built in 1860, this edifice has a beautiful, century-old dragon tree, a native of the Canary Islands, in front. The resin of this tree species, called dragon's blood, was used in Europe to treat dysentery and is still used in all manner of Asian medicines.

Mitchell's Waterfront Brewery. This is one of a handful of microbreweries in South Africa. The brewery produces four beers: Foresters Draught Lager, Bosuns Bitter, Ravenstout, and Ferryman's Ale. Tours, for which reservations are essential, include beer tasting and a look at the fermentation tanks. ⊠ *Dock Rd.,* ☎ *021/418-2461.* 💳 *R10.* ☉ *Weekdays 11–3.*

★ **Robben Island.** Made famous by its most illustrious inhabitant, Nelson Rolihlahla Mandela, this island, whose name is Dutch for "seals," has a long and mostly sad history. At various times a prison, a leper colony, mental institution, and military base, it is finally filling a positive, enlightening, and empowering role in its new incarnation as a museum. As well as Mandela, Robert Sobukwe, and Walter Sisulu, there have been some fascinating (reluctant) inhabitants of this at once formidable and beautiful place. One of the first prisoners was Autshumato, known to the early Dutch settlers as "Harry the Hottentot." He was one of the main interpreters for Jan van Riebeeck in the mid-17th century, as was his niece, Krotoa, who was also imprisoned on the island when she fell into disfavor. In 1820 the British thought they could solve some of the problems they were having on the Eastern Cape frontier by banishing Xhosa leader Makhanda to the island. Both Autshumato and Makhanda (also spelled Makana) escaped by rowboat, but Makhanda didn't make it. Notice when you go to the island that the two sleek high-speed ferries are called *Autshumato* and *Makana.*

Tours of the island are organized by the Robben Island Museum, and visitors are taken around the island and the prison by guides who were themselves political prisoners (mostly.) Tours leave from the jetty near the Fish Quay ("Berties") on the hour every hour between 9 and 3, except 1. The boat crossing takes 30 minutes. The island tour itself lasts 2½ hours, during which time you walk through the prison and see the cell in which Mandela was imprisoned, as well as the stark quarry where the former president pounded rocks for so many years. During peak season (mid-December–mid-January) it may get pretty crowded, so reserve in advance.

The tour offered by the **Robben Island Museum** (☎ 021/419–1300) is the only one that actually visits the island; several operators advertise Robben Island tours and just take visitors on a boat trip *around* the island. ☎ *021/419–1300,* 🌐 *www.robbenisland.org.za.* 💳 *R100.* ☉ *Daily 9–3 (last ferry leaves island at 6).*

South African Maritime Museum. The museum provides a look at ships and the history of Table Bay, including a model of Cape Town Harbor as it appeared in 1886. In the model workshop you can watch modelers build scale replicas of famous ships.

Also here is the **SAS** *Somerset,* the only surviving boom-defense vessel in the world. During World War II harbors were protected against enemy submarines and divers by booms, essentially metal mesh curtains drawn across the harbor entrance. The *Somerset* (then named the HMS *Barcross*) controlled the boom across Saldanha Bay, north of Cape Town. You can explore the entire ship, including the bridge and the engine room. ⊠ *Dock Rd.,* ☎ *021/419–2505.* 🖃 *R10, SAS Somerset R5.* ☉ *Daily 10–5.*

Time Ball Tower. The tower was built in 1894, before the advent of modern navigational equipment, when ships' crews needed to know the exact time to help them calculate longitude. Navigators set their clocks by the time ball, which fell every day at 1 PM, much like the ball that marks the stroke of midnight in New York's Times Square on New Year's Eve.

★ ☉ **Two Oceans Aquarium.** The aquarium is thought to be one of the finest in the world. Stunning displays show the marine life of the warm Indian Ocean and the cold Atlantic Ocean. It's a hands-on place, with a touch pool for children and opportunities for certified divers to explore the vast, five-story kelp forest or the predator tank, where you share the water with a couple of large ragged-tooth sharks (*Carcharias taurus*). And for something completely different, you can do a copper helmet dive with antique dive equipment in the predator tank. The aquarium also runs "the most fun baby-sitting service in the world." Drop your children (ages 7–12) off anytime after 6:30 with a sleeping bag, and head off to the waterfront to party (R85 per child). They will be fed, given a gift pack, taken on a tour, shown a video, led in games, and, after all the excitement, given a chance to "sleep with the fish." There is full-time supervision, and security is tight. If you like, you may pick them up after midnight, but they probably won't want to leave. ⊠ *Dock Rd., Waterfront,* ☎ *021/418–3823,* WEB *www.aquarium.co.za.* 🖃 *R45–R55, R350 for dives (R275 with own gear); R950 for copper-helmet dive.* ☉ *Daily 9:30–6.*

Union-Castle House. Designed in 1919 by Sir Herbert Baker, the house was headquarters for the famous Union-Castle shipping line. Before World War II many English-speaking South Africans looked upon England as home, even if they had never been there. The emotional link between the two countries was symbolized most strongly by the mail steamers, carrying both mail and passengers, that sailed weekly between South Africa and England. In 1977, amid much pomp and ceremony, the last Union-Castle mail ship, the *Windsor Castle,* made its final passage to England. Even today older South Africans like to wax lyrical about the joys of a voyage on one of those steamers. Union-Castle House is now home to several banks and small businesses. Inside Standard Bank you can still see the iron rings in the ceiling from which mailbags were hung. ⊠ *Quay 4.*

Victoria & Alfred Waterfront Information Centre. The center, opposite the V&A Hotel, has the lowdown on everything happening in the area, including upcoming events and shows. Here you can arrange walking tours of the waterfront, book accommodations, and get information about the whole Western Cape. A scale model shows what the waterfront will look like when it's finished. ⊠ *Pierhead,* ☎ *021/408–7600,* FAX *021/408–7605,* WEB *www.waterfront.com.* ☉ *Oct.–Apr., daily 9–6; May–Sept., daily 8–5.*

Victoria Basin. The basin was constructed between 1870 and 1905 to accommodate the huge increase in shipping following the discovery of diamonds at Kimberley and gold on the Witwatersrand. Across the basin is the South Arm, used as a debarkation point for British troops, horses, and material during the Boer War (1899–1902). Much of the fodder for the British horses was shipped in from Argentina and was catastrophically infested with rats and fleas. As a result, bubonic plague broke out in Cape Town in February 1901, creating wholesale panic in the city. African dockworkers, suspected of harboring the disease, were forbidden to leave the city and ultimately confined to specific quarters. During the epidemic 766 people contracted the plague; 371 died.

The Peninsula

This driving tour takes you south from Cape Town on a loop of the peninsula, heading through the scenic southern suburbs before running down the False Bay coast to Cape Point. It's a magnificent drive back to the city along the wild Atlantic coast. Plan a full day to travel the entire loop, more if you want to stop along the way.

Numbers in the text correspond to numbers in the margin and on the Cape Peninsula map.

A Good Drive

Take the N2 or De Waal Drive (M3) out of the city center. The two highways merge near Groote Schuur Hospital and split again soon after. Bear right, taking the M3 (signposted SOUTHERN SUBURBS/MUIZENBERG), and look up at the mountain—you will see zebras, gnu, and eland grazing peacefully. After 1 km (½ mi) you'll pass **Mostert's Mill** ㉙ on your left, one of two remaining windmills in the Cape, and on your right you'll see the beautifully situated campus of the University of Cape Town, nestled against the slopes of Devil's Peak. Continue on the M3 for another 1 km (½ mi) to the exit marked with a sign to the **Rhodes Memorial** ㉚. Return to the M3 and head south toward Muizenberg. After 1½ km (1 mi) exit right onto Rhodes Avenue (M63). This leafy road winds through large trees to the **Kirstenbosch National Botanic Gardens** ㉛, one of the most beautiful spots in the Cape. Turn right as you leave the botanic gardens. When you reach a T junction, turn right again and begin the winding climb to the pass at Constantia Nek. From the traffic circle at the top you can either cut over the mountains and down into Hout Bay or turn left onto the M41 (the sign reads WYNBERG AND GROOT CONSTANTIA) and begin the snaking descent into Constantia and **Groot Constantia** ㉜. Leaving Groot Constantia, turn right on Main Road and then right again onto Ladies Mile Extension (a sign points you to Muizenberg and Bergvliet). Another right at the first traffic light puts you on Spaanschemat River Road, and a farther right turn funnels you onto Klein Constantia Road. Follow this to **Buitenverwachting** ㉝. Turn left out of Buitenverwachting and continue for ½ km (¼ mi) to **Klein Constantia** ㉞. Head back down Klein Constantia Road, and turn right into Spaanschemat River Road. After about 3 km (2 mi) turn left onto Tokai Road and right again at the PORTER SCHOOL sign and drive 1 km (½ mi) to **Tokai Manor** ㉟. Return to the junction and continue straight on Tokai Road, through the traffic circle, and to Steenberg Country Hotel, Golf Estate, and Vineyards on your right. On the left is Pollsmoor Prison, where Nelson Mandela stayed after he was moved from Robben Island. Turn left at the T junction and continue to the Main Road (M4) and turn right again. After ½ km (¼ mi) Boyes Drive leads off the M4. The M4, or Main Road, on the other hand, takes you through **Muizenberg** ㊱, where the Main Road runs parallel to the sea. Watch on your right for a De Post Huys, a small thatched building with rough whitewashed walls, and the imposing facade of the Natale Labia Museum. Continue to Rhodes Cottage Museum. From Muizenberg Main Road heads down the peninsula, hugging the shore of False Bay. Strung along this coastline are a collection of small villages that long ago merged to form a thin suburban belt between the ocean and the mountains. **Kalk Bay** ㊲, **Fish Hoek** ㊳, and **Simonstown** ㊴ are all on this stretch. Simonstown is the last community of any size before you reach Cape Point. From here the road traverses a wild, windswept landscape as beautiful as it is desolate. You can stop at tiny **Boulders Beach** ㊵ to look at the colony of African penguins. The mountains, covered with rugged fynbos, descend almost straight into the sea. Don't be surprised to see troops of baboons lounging beside the road as you approach the **Cape of Good Hope** ㊶ section of Cape Peninsula National Park. Close the windows of your car and don't attempt to feed the baboons. They are dangerous. Before you reach the Cape Point gate, look left, and you will see the almost outrageously beautiful settlement of Smitswinkel Bay—accessible only on foot via a steep and narrow path. Turn left out of the Cape Point gate onto the M65 to **Scarborough** ㊷ and **Kommetjie** ㊸. From Kommetjie the M65 leads to a major intersection. Turn left onto the M6 (Hout Bay), go through one set of lights, and then turn left again, following the signs to Hout Bay. The road passes through the small community of **Noordhoek** ㊹ before beginning its treacherous climb around **Chapman's Peak Drive** ㊺, which has been closed indefinitely because of dangerous rock falls. So go and have a look at Noordhoek, and then retrace your route to the beginning of **Ou Kaapse Weg** ㊻, Old Cape Road. Head over the mountain through the Silvermine section of the CPNP, and turn left at the T junction. Continue past Steenberg and Pollsmoor, and then turn left into Klein Constantia Road as if you were returning to Buitenverwachting, but turn immediately right. Continue till the end, turn right into Pagasvlei Road, follow the curve, and then turn left into Constantia Main Road. You'll go past Groot Constantia on your left. Stay left at the traffic circle at Constantia Nek and drive down into **Hout Bay** ㊼. Turn right onto the M6 (a sign reads CITY AND LLANDUDNO). After less than than 1 km (½ mi), turn right on Valley Road to the **World of Birds** ㊽. From Hout Bay the M6 climbs past the exclusive community of Llandudno and then runs along the coast to **Camps Bay** ㊾. Follow Victoria Road (M6) out of Camps Bay and turn right at the sign reading KLOOF NEK ROUND HOUSE. This road snakes up the mountain until it reaches a five-way intersection at Kloof Nek. Make a sharp left onto the road leading to **Signal Hill** ㊿. For more great views of the city, return to the Kloof Nek intersection and take **Tafelberg Road** (51).

TIMING

You really could spend three days on this tour, either moving slowly around the peninsula, staying in a different guest house each night, or scuttling back to a central spot at the end of the day. The distances are not that great, and you could easily base yourself in the southern suburbs and head out in a different direction on each of two or three days. Or pick a few things that interest you most and spend a single day just visiting those spots.

Sights to See

★ ㊵ **Boulders Beach.** This series of small coves lies on the outskirts of Simonstown among giant boulders. Part of the Cape Peninsula National Park, the beach is best known for its resident colony of African penguins. You must stay out of the fenced-off breeding beach, but the birds will probably come waddling up to you to take a look. WEB *www.cpnp.co.za.* *R10.* *Daily 9–6.*

123

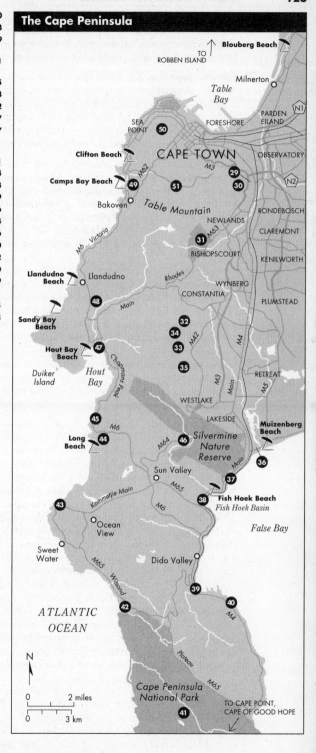

The Cape Peninsula

Boyes Drive. If you prefer scenic views to historical sites, Boyes Drive is probably a better option than the main highway. The drive runs high along the mountains, offering panoramic views of False Bay and the Hottentots Holland Mountains before rejoining the M4 at Kalk Bay.

㉝ Buitenverwachting. A gorgeous winery that was also once part of Van der Stel's original Constantia farm, Buitenverwachting means "beyond expectation," and its setting certainly surpasses anything you might have imagined: An oak-lined avenue leads past the Cape Dutch homestead to the thatched modern cellar. Acres of vines spread up hillsides flanked by more towering oaks and the rocky crags of the Constantiaberg.

Buitenverwachting's wine is just as superb as its setting. The largest seller is the slightly dry buiten blanc, an easy-drinking blend of a few varieties. The best red is Christine, which until the 1991 vintage was known as Grand Vin; it's a blend of mostly cabernet sauvignon and 30% merlot. The winery's restaurant is probably the finest in the Cape. ⊠ *Off Klein Constantia Rd.,* ☎ *021/794–5190,* FAX *021/794–1351.* ☞ *Tastings free.* ⊙ *Weekdays 9–5, Sat. 9–1.*

NEED A BREAK?

Buitenverwachting serves great picnic lunches under the oaks on the estate's lawns. It's an idyllic setting and a most civilized way to cap a morning of wine tasting. Each picnic basket is packed with a selection of breads, meat, chicken, pâtés, and cheeses. You can buy a bottle of estate wine as an accompaniment to the meal. The **picnic** costs R55 per person, and reservations are essential. ☎ *021/794–1012. Closed Sun.*

㊾ Camps Bay. This is a popular holiday resort with a long beach and plenty of restaurants and bars. The craggy faces of the Twelve Apostles, huge granite buttresses reaching down to the sea from the mountains behind, loom over the town.

★ **㊶ Cape of Good Hope.** Once a nature reserve on its own, this now forms part of Cape Peninsula National Park. This section covers some 19,100 acres, including Cape Point and the Cape of Good Hope. Much of the park consists of rolling hills covered with fynbos and laced with miles of walking trails, for which maps are available at the park entrance. It also has beautiful deserted beaches. Eland, baboon, ostrich, and bontebok are among the animals that roam the park. A tarred road runs 14 km (8 mi) to the tip of the peninsula. A turnoff leads to the Cape of Good Hope, a rocky cape on the southwesternmost point of the continent. A plaque marks the spot—otherwise you would never know you're standing on a site of such significance. The opposite is true of Cape Point, a dramatic knife's edge of rock that slices into the Atlantic. Looking out to sea from the viewing platform, you feel you're at the tip of Africa, even though that honor officially belongs to Cape Agulhas, about 160 km (100 mi) to the southeast. From Cape Point the views of False Bay and the Hottentots Holland Mountains are breathtaking. The walk up to the viewing platform and the old lighthouse is very steep; a funicular (R22 round-trip, R15 one-way) makes the run every three or four minutes. Take an anorak or sweater—the wind can take your breath away. A large sit-down restaurant has better views than food (but that is saying a lot), and a kiosk sells snacks. A gift shop completes the picture. During peak season visit Cape Point as early in the day as you can; otherwise you'll be swamped by horrendous numbers of tourist buses and their occupants. Fun alternatives include an escorted bike trip to the point and an overnight hike with comfortable basic accommodations and incredible views, which is booked through the parks board. Be wary of baboons in the parking lot that have been known to steal food. They can be dangerous if provoked. ⊠ *Off the*

M65, ☎ *021/780–9526 or 021/780–9204,* WEB *www.cpnp.co.za.* ✉ *R20.* ⊙ *Oct.–Mar., daily 7–6; Apr.–Sept., daily 7–5.*

45 **Chapman's Peak Drive.** This fantastically scenic drive has been indefinitely closed due to deterioration and rock falls. However, you may drive onto the first section from Hout Bay just to get an idea of what it was like. With any luck it may be reopened in the future.

Constantia. Backed by the rugged mountains of the Constantiaberg and overlooking the Cape Flats and False Bay, Constantia is an idyllic spot to while away a day—or a week. Vineyards carpet the lower slopes, while plantations of pine predominate higher up. This is very much the domain of the suburban gentry. If you don't have time to visit the Winelands, Constantia is a must. Here you'll find five excellent estates—Buitenverwachting, Groot Constantia, Klein Constantia, Constantia Uitsig, and the relatively new Steenberg.

De Post Huys. One of the oldest buildings in the country, De Post Huys was constructed in 1673 as a lookout post and signal station. It now houses the **SA Police Historical Museum**, with exhibits ranging from drug-related paraphernalia to the role of the police in the freedom struggle. ⊠ *Main Rd.,* ☎ *021/788–7035 or 021/788–7031.* ✉ *Free.* ⊙ *Weekdays 8–3:30.*

38 **Fish Hoek.** This is one of the most popular resort towns on the False Bay coast, with a smooth, sandy beach that is protected on the south side from the summer southeasters by Elsies Peak. It's one of the best places to see whales during calving season—from approximately August to November—though there have been whale sightings as early as June and as late as January. Until recently, Fish Hoek was the only teetotaling town in the country. In 1810 Lord Charles Somerset issued the first grant of British crown land in Fish Hoek on condition that no wine house should ever exist on the property. Somerset was evidently alarmed by the excesses associated with a wine house near Kommetjie, where wagon drivers would become too drunk to deliver their supplies to the Royal Navy at Simonstown. Jagers Walk, from the south side of Fish Hoek Beach to Sunny Cove, is a pleasant, scenic, wheelchair-friendly pathway that meanders through the rocks, giving access to some sheltered natural rock pools that are just great for swimming. The snorkeling is good, too.

★ **32** **Groot Constantia.** Constantia takes its name from the wine estate founded here in 1685 by Simon van der Stel, one of the first Dutch governors of the Cape. After his death in 1712 the land was subdivided, with the heart of the estate preserved at Groot Constantia. The enormous complex enjoys the status of a national monument and is by far the most commercial and touristy of the wineries. Van der Stel's magnificent homestead, the oldest in the Cape, lies at the center of Groot Constantia. It's built in traditional Cape Dutch style, with thick whitewashed walls, a thatched roof, small-pane windows, and ornate gables. The house is a museum furnished with exquisite period pieces. The old wine cellar sits behind the manor house. Built in 1791, it is most famous for its own ornate gable, designed by sculptor Anton Anreith. The cellar houses a wine museum, with displays of wine-drinking and storage vessels dating to antiquity.

In the 19th century the sweet wines of Groot Constantia were highly regarded in Europe and especially favored by King Louis Philippe and Bismarck. Today Groot Constantia is known for its splendid red wines. The best is the excellent Gouverneurs Reserve, made mostly from cabernet sauvignon grapes with smaller amounts of merlot and cabernet franc. Full of tannin and fruit, this big, robust wine is a Bordeaux style. The pinotage is consistently good, too, reaching its velvety prime in about five years. The estate operates two restaurants: the elegant Jonkershuis and the Tavern, which serves light meals at picnic tables on the lawn. You can also bring your own picnic and relax on the lawns behind the wine cellar. ⊠ *Off Main Rd.,* ☎ *021/794–5128 for winery; 021/794–5067 for museum.* ⊡ *Museum R8, wine tasting R12, cellar tour R11.* ☉ *Museum: daily 10–5; winery: Dec.–Apr., daily 9:30–6; May–Nov., daily 10–5.*

Groote Schuur Hospital. Dr. Christian Barnard performed the world's first heart transplant here in 1967. Just off Main Road you'll see this visible landmark on the slopes of Table Mountain below the scenic De Waal Drive. The Transplant Museum and Educational Center is worth a visit if you're interested in medical history or techniques. ☎ *021/404–5232.* ⊡ *R5.* ☉ *Weekdays 9–2.*

④⑦ Hout Bay. Cradled in a lovely bay and guarded by a 1,000-ft peak known as the Sentinel, Hout Bay is the center of Cape Town's crayfishing industry, and the town operates several fish-processing plants. Mariner's Wharf is Hout Bay's salty answer to the waterfront in Cape Town, a collection of bars and restaurants on the quayside. You can buy fresh fish at a seafood market and take it outside to be grilled. You should also try *snoek*—a barracuda-like fish that is traditionally eaten smoked. Cruise boats depart from Hout Bay's harbor to view the **seal colony** on Duiker Island.

Irma Stern Museum. This museum is dedicated to the works and art collection of Stern (1894–1966), one of South Africa's greatest painters. The museum is administered by the University of Cape Town and occupies the Firs, the artist's home for 38 years. She is best known for African studies, particularly her paintings of indigenous people inspired by trips to the Congo and Zanzibar. Her collection of African artifacts, including priceless Congolese stools and carvings, is superb. ⊠ *Cecil Rd., Rosebank,* ☎ *021/685–5686,* WEB *www.museums.org.za/irma.* ⊡ *R7.* ☉ *Tues.–Sat. 10–5.*

★ ③⑦ Kalk Bay. The name of Kalk Bay recalls that seashells were once baked in large kilns near the shore to produce lime (*kalk*). This is one of the most fascinating destinations on the peninsula. A small harbor, where you can buy fish so fresh it wriggles, shelters a weathered fishing fleet, and tiny cottages crowd the narrow cobbled streets, clinging to the mountain. Funky crafts shops, galleries, antiques shops, and cozy bistros can fill a whole day of rambling. Gnarled fishingfolk rub shoulders with Rastafarians, surfers, yuppies, New Age trendies, and genteel ladies with blue hair rinses. The Brass Bell is a great place to down a few beers in the sun while local surfers strut their stuff on Kalk Bay Reef—a nice hollow left—barely yards from your comfortable table. You can walk up one of the many steep stairways to Boyes Drive and from there up the mountain.

★ ③① Kirstenbosch National Botanic Gardens. The gardens extend up the eastern slopes of Table Mountain, overlooking the Cape Flats and distant Hottentots Holland Mountains. Walking trails meander through the gardens, and grassy banks are ideal for a picnic or afternoon nap. The plantings are limited to species native to southern Africa, including fynbos—hardy, thin-leaved plants that proliferate in the Cape. Among these are proteas, including silver trees and king proteas, ericas, and *restios* (reeds). Highlights include a large cycad garden, the Bird Bath (a beautiful stone pool built around a crystal-clear spring), and the fragrance garden, which is wheelchair friendly and has a tapping rail and braille interpretive boards. Those who have difficulty walking can take a comprehensive tour lasting between 45 minutes and an hour (R12) by six-person cart. There is also a wheelchair trail that goes off the main paths into the wilder section of the park and gets close to the feel of the mountain walks. Concerts are held here on summer Sundays starting an hour before sunset. With Table Mountain as a magnificent backdrop and the gardens all around, you can catch the best of South Africa's entertainment with everything from classical music to township jazz to rock and roll. A visitor center leads into the conservatory and houses a restaurant, bookstore, and coffee shop. ⊠ *Rhodes Ave., Newlands,* ☎ *021/799–8800,* WEB *www.nbi.ac.za.* ⊠ *R15.* ☉ *Apr.–Aug., daily 8–6; Sept.–Mar., daily 8–7.*

34 **Klein Constantia.** Klein (rhymes with "stain") means "small" in Afrikaans and indicates the relative size of this portion of van der Stel's original Constantia estate. The winery has an impressive modern cellar, deliberately unobtrusive so as not to detract from the vine-covered mountain slopes. Its Cape Dutch homestead, visible as you drive in, was built in the late 18th century. This estate produces wines of superb quality, as awards displayed in the tasting area attest. The excellent sauvignon blanc is used as a point of reference by many South African connoisseurs and vintners. Whereas early vintages were particularly opulent, more recent ones have been a little racy on first release. The closest you'll come to the famous Constantia wine of the 18th century is the Vin de Constance, a sweet wine made from predominantly Muscat de Frontignan grapes. The cabernet sauvignon is one of the best produced in the Cape—a collector's wine that will develop wonderfully over time. ⊠ *Klein Constantia Rd., Constantia,* ☎ *021/794–5188,* FAX *021/794–2464,* WEB *www.kleinconstantia.com.* ⊠ *Free.* ☉ *Weekdays 9–5, Sat. 9–1. Cellar tours by appointment. No tours on Sat.*

43 **Kommetjie.** A pleasant, somewhat isolated suburb, Kommetjie has a scenic 45-minute walk down Long Beach that leads to the wreck of the *Kakapo,* a steamship that ran aground on her maiden voyage in 1900. This is a surfer's paradise, with some really big wave spots and a few gentler breaks. The nearby Imhoffs Gift complex is a must, especially if you have children. There are a nature park, with loads of birds, a snake park, camel rides, horse rides, a petting farm, crafts shops and, of course, a coffee shop.

29 **Mostert's Mill.** Built in 1796, this thatched wheat mill consists of a tower with a rotating cap to which sails were attached. Mills like this were once common in the area. Inside is the original mechanism, but it's not necessarily worth pulling off the highway to see. ⊠ *Rhodes Dr., Mowbray,* ☎ *no phone.* ☉ *Daily 9–5.*

36 **Muizenberg.** At the turn of the 20th century this was the premier bathing resort in South Africa, attracting many of the country's wealthy mining magnates, as the many mansions along Baden Powell Drive attest. Long gone, though, are the days when anyone thought of Muizenberg as chic. A drab complex of shops and fast-food outlets, complete with kiddie pools and miniature golf, blights the beachfront, and the views of mountains and sea cannot make up for it. The whole area is in a state of not-so-genteel decay, and many beautiful art deco beachfront buildings have become slums. That doesn't stop beginner surfers and keen dog walkers from utilizing the still-wonderful beach, but, quite honestly, they give the area on the sea side of the railway line a miss.

44 **Noordhoek.** Noordhoek is a popular beach community with stunning white sands that stretch forever. The bordering village has become a retreat for the arts-and-crafts community, and there are lots of galleries and boutiques selling unusual items. You can walk all the way between

Kommetjie and Noordhoek on the aptly named Long Beach. It's also very popular with horseback riders and surfers.

★ ㊻ **Ou Kaapse Weg.** This is the shortest (and most scenic) route between Noordhoek and Constantia since the closure of Chapman's Peak. It's spectacular in its own right, with lovely flowers and distant vistas of False Bay, in the east, and the Atlantic, in the west.

Rhodes Cottage Museum. Considering the great power wielded by Cecil John Rhodes (1853–1902), one of Britain's great empire builders, his seaside cottage was surprisingly humble and spare. Yet this is where the man who was instrumental in the development of present-day South Africa chose to spend his last days in 1902, preferring the cool sea air of Muizenberg to the stifling opulence of his home at Groote Schuur. The cottage, including the bedroom where he died, has been completely restored. Other rooms display photos documenting Rhodes's life. His remains are buried in the Matopos Hills, in Zimbabwe. ⊠ *246 Main Rd., Muizenberg,* ☎ *021/788–1816.* 🎫 *Free.* ☉ *Tues.–Sun. 10–1 and 2–5.*

★ ㉚ **Rhodes Memorial.** Rhodes served as prime minister of the Cape from 1890 to 1896. He made his fortune in the diamond rush at Kimberley, but his greatest dream was to forge a Cape–Cairo railway, a tangible symbol of British dominion in Africa. The classical-style granite memorial sits high on the slopes of Devil's Peak, on part of Rhodes's old estate, Groote Schuur. A mounted rider symbolizing energy faces north toward the continent for which Rhodes felt such passion. A bust of Rhodes dominates the temple—ironically, he's leaning on one hand as if he's about to nod off. ⊠ *Off Rhodes Dr., Rondebosch.* 🎫 *Free.*

NEED A BREAK? The **Rhodes Memorial Tea Garden** (☎ 021/689–9151), tucked under towering pines behind the memorial, is a pleasant spot that serves tea or a light lunch.

㊷ **Scarborough.** The town is a tiny holiday community with one of the best beaches on the peninsula. Scarborough is becoming popular with artists and craftspeople, and you'll find their offerings exhibited at informal galleries. From Scarborough to Kommetjie the road hugs the shoreline, snaking between the mountains and the crashing surf. This part of the shore is considered unsafe for swimming, but experienced surfers and boardsailers revel in the wind and waves.

㊿ **Signal Hill.** Here the road swings around the shoulder of Lion's Head, then runs along the flank of Signal Hill. The views of the city below and Table Mountain are superb. The road ends at a parking lot overlooking Sea Point and all of Table Bay. Be careful around here, especially if it's deserted. There have been incidents of violent crime.

★ ㊴ **Simonstown.** Because Simonstown is a naval base, and has been for many years, a large part of the seafront is out of bounds. Even worse, defense force personnel knock off at 4 during the week, when the single-lane road going out of Simonstown is stop–start traffic (as it is in the morning). Despite this it's an attractive town with many lovely old buildings and is close to what are possibly the peninsula's best swimming beaches, Seaforth and Boulders. Simonstown has had a long association with the Royal Navy. It was here in 1795 that British troops landed before defeating the Dutch at the Battle of Muizenberg, and the town served as a base for the Royal Navy from 1814 to 1957, when the naval base was handed over to the South African navy.

Jubilee Square, a dockside plaza that serves as the de facto town center, is just off the main road (St. George's Road). Next to the dock wall stands a sculpture of **Just Nuisance**, a Great Dane adopted as a mascot by the Royal Navy during World War II. Just Nuisance apparently liked his pint of beer and would accompany sailors on the train into Cape Town. He had the endearing habit of leading drunken sailors— and only sailors—that he found in the city back to the station in time to catch the last train. The navy went so far as to induct him into the service as an able seaman attached to the HMS *Afrikander*. He died at the age of seven in April 1944 and was given a military funeral. Just below Jubilee Square is the newly built Simonstown Waterfront Centre, with numerous artsy shops, including a Just Nuisance store, where you can buy a present for your pooch back home.

NEED A
BREAK?

Berthas Restaurant (⊠ Wharf's Rd., Simonstown, ☎ 021/786–2138) serves excellent meals overlooking the jetty, where charter boats take off for whale-watching (in season) and trips to Cape Point. The attached coffee shop has just as good a view and serves light lunches and teas.

Penguin Point Cafe (⊠ Boulders Beach parking lot, ☎ 021/786–1758) has a huge veranda with views over False Bay. It serves hearty breakfasts, light lunches, teas, and dinner. There's a full bar, and it's a great place to watch the sun set—if you're sharp, you'll remember that you're facing east, not west, but don't let that deter you. False Bay sunsets are spectacular. Consisting mostly of reflected light, they are pastel pink, pale blue, lavender, and gold, unlike the more common red and orange variety.

⑤ Tafelberg Road. The road crosses the northern side of Table Mountain before ending at Devil's Peak. From the Kloof Nek intersection you can descend to Cape Town directly or return to Camps Bay and follow the coastal road back to the city. This route takes you through the beautiful seaside communities of Clifton and Bantry Bay and then along the seaside promenade in Sea Point.

㉟ Tokai Manor. Built in 1795, this is one of the finest Cape Dutch homes in the country. Famed architect Louis Michel Thibault designed its facade. The homestead is reputedly haunted by a horseman who died when he tried to ride his horse down the curving front steps during a drunken revel. You can stop for a look, but the house is not open to the public.

㊽ World of Birds. Here you can walk through aviaries housing 450 species of indigenous and exotic birds, including eagles, vultures, penguins, and flamingos. No cages separate you from most of the birds, so you can get some pretty good photographs; however, the big raptors are kept behind fences. ⊠ *Valley Rd., Hout Bay,* ☎ *021/790–2730,* WEB *www.worldofbirds.org.za.* ☞ *R28.* ☉ *Daily 9–6.*

OFF THE
BEATEN PATH

DISTRICT SIX MUSEUM – Housed in the Buitenkant Methodist Church, this museum preserves the memory of one of Cape Town's most vibrant multicultural neighborhoods and of the district's destruction in one of the cruelest acts of the apartheid Nationalist government. District Six was proclaimed a white area in 1966, and existing residents were evicted from their homes, which were razed to make way for a white suburb. The people were forced to resettle in bleak outlying areas on the Cape Flats, and by the 1970s all the buildings, except churches and mosques, had been demolished. Huge controversy accompanied the proposed redevelopment of the area, and only a small housing component, Zonnebloem, and the campus of the Cape Technicon have been built, leaving much of the ground still bare—a grim reminder of the past. There are plans to bring former residents back into the area and reestablish the suburb; however, the old swinging District Six can never be re-created. The museum consists of street signs, photographs, life stories of the people who lived there, and a huge floor plan, where former residents can identify the site of their homes. ⊠ *25A Buitenkant St.,* ☎ *021/461–4735 or 021/465–8009,* WEB *www.districtsix.co.za.* ✉ *Free.* ⊗ *Mon.–Sat. 9–4.*

BEACHES

With panoramic views of mountains tumbling to the ocean, the sandy beaches of the Cape Peninsula are stunning and are a major draw for Capetonians and visitors alike. Beautiful as the beaches may be, don't expect to spend hours splashing in the surf. The water around Cape Town is very, very cold, but you get used to it. Beaches on the Atlantic are washed by the Benguela Current flowing up from the Antarctic, and in midsummer the water hovers around 10°C–15°C (50°F–60°F). The water on the False Bay side is usually 5°C (9°F) warmer. Cape beaches are renowned for their clean, snow-white powdery sand. Beachcombers will find every kind of beach to suit them, from intimate coves to sheltered bays and wild, wide beaches stretching forever. If you are looking for more tropical water temperatures, head for the warm Indian Ocean waters of KwaZulu–Natal or the Garden Route.

The major factor that affects any day at a Cape beach is wind. In summer howling southeasters, known as the Cape Doctor, are all too common and can ruin a trip to the beach; during these gales you're better off at Clifton or Llandudno, on the Atlantic side, or the sheltered but very small St. James Beach, on the False Bay side, and maybe even the southern corner of Fish Hoek Beach or one of the pools along Jagers Walk. Boulders and Seaforth are also often sheltered from the southeaster.

Every False Bay community has its own beach, but most are not reviewed here. In comparison with Atlantic beaches, most of them are rather small and often crowded, sandwiched between the sea and the commuter rail line, with Fish Hoek a major exception. South of Simonstown, the beaches tend to be more wild and less developed, except for the very popular Seaforth and Millers Point beaches. At many beaches there may be powerful waves, strong undertow, and dangerous riptides. Lifeguards work the main beaches, but only on weekends and during school breaks. Other beaches are unpatrolled. Although it is nice to stroll along a lonely beach, remember it's risky to wander off on your own in a deserted area.

Atlantic Coast

The beaches below are listed from north to south and are marked on the Cape Peninsula map in the Exploring section.

Blouberg. Make the 25-km (16-mi) trip north from the city to the other side of Table Bay, and you'll be rewarded with an exceptional (and the most famous) view of Cape Town and Table Mountain. It's divided into two parts: Big Bay, which hosts surfing and sailboarding contests; and Little Bay, better suited to sunbathers and families. It's frequently windy here, which is fine if you want to fly a kite but a nuisance otherwise. (Buy a brightly colored high-tech number at the Kite Shop in Victoria Wharf at the waterfront and relive your childhood.) Swim in front of the lifeguard club. The lawns of the Blue Peter Hotel are a favorite sunset cocktail spot, especially with tired windsurfers. ⊠ *Follow N1 north toward Paarl and then R27 to Milnerton and Bloubergstrand.*

Clifton. This is where the "in" crowd comes to see and be seen. Some of the Cape's most desirable houses cling to the slopes above the beach, and elegant yachts often anchor in the calm water beyond the breakers. Granite outcroppings divide the beach into four segments, imaginatively known as First, Second, Third, and Fourth beaches. Fourth Beach is popular with families, while the others support a strong social and singles scene. Swimming is reasonably safe here, although the undertow is strong and the water, again, freezing. Lifeguards are on duty. On weekends and in peak season Clifton can be a madhouse, and your chances of finding parking at these times are nil. If you plan to visit the beaches in midsummer, consider renting a scooter or motorcycle instead of a car or taking a shuttle from your hotel. ⊠ *Off Victoria Rd., Clifton. Hout Bay bus from OK Bazaars on Adderley St.*

Camps Bay. The spectacular western edge of Table Mountain, known as the Twelve Apostles, provides the backdrop for this long, sandy beach that slopes gently to the water from a grassy verge. The surf is powerful, and there are no lifeguards, but sunbathers can cool off in a tidal pool or under cool outdoor showers. The popular bars and restaurants of Camps Bay lie only yards away across Victoria Road. One drawback is the wind, which can blow hard here. ⊠ *Victoria Rd. Hout Bay bus from OK Bazaars on Adderley St.*

Llandudno. Die-hard fans return to this beach again and again, and who can blame them? Its setting, among giant boulders at the base of a mountain, is glorious, and sunsets here attract their own aficionados. The surf can be very powerful on the northern side of the beach (where you'll find all the surfers, of course), but the southern side is fine for a quick dip—and in this water that's all you'll want. Lifeguards are on duty on weekends and in season. If you come by bus, brace yourself for a long walk down (and back up) the mountain from the bus stop on the M6. Parking is a nightmare, but most hotels run shuttles during summer. ⊠ *Llandudno exit off M6 and follow signs. Hout Bay bus from OK Bazaars on Adderley St.*

Sandy Bay. Backed by wild dunes, Cape Town's unofficial nudist beach is also one of its prettiest. Sunbathers can hide among rocky coves or frolic on a long stretch of sandy beach. Shy nudists will appreciate its isolation, 20 minutes on foot from the nearest parking area in Llandudno. Wind, however, can be a problem: If you're caught in the buff when the southeaster starts to blow, you're in for a painful sandblasting. Getting here by bus means a very long walk going down and up the mountain; parking is very difficult. ⊠ *Llandudno exit off M6 and follow signs to Sandy Bay. Hout Bay bus from OK Bazaars on Adderley St.*

Hout Bay. This beach appears to have it all: a knockout view of the mountains, gentle surf, and easy access to the restaurants and bars of Mariner's Wharf. The reality is not quite so stunning, with the town's industrial fishing harbor and its mini–oil slicks and other waste products nearby. ⊠ *Off the M6, Hout Bay. Hout Bay bus from OK Bazaars on Adderley St.*

Long Beach. This may be the most impressive beach on the peninsula, a vast expanse of white sand stretching 6½ km (4 mi) from the base of Chapman's Peak to Kommetjie. It's also one of the wildest and least populated, backed by a lagoon and private nature reserve. Because of the wind, it attracts horseback riders and walkers rather than sunbathers, and the surfing is excellent. There is no bus service. ⊠ *Off M6, Noordhoek.*

False Bay

Muizenberg. Once the fashionable resort of South African high society, this long, sandy beach has lost much of its glamour and now appeals to families and beginner surfers. A tacky pavilion houses a swimming pool, water slides, toilets, changing rooms, and snack shops. The beach is lined with colorful bathing boxes of the type once popular at British resorts. Lifeguards are on duty, and the sea is shallow and reasonably safe. ⊠ *Off the M4.*

Fish Hoek. With the southern corner protected from the southeaster by Elsies Peak, this sandy beach attracts retirees, who appreciate the calm, clear water—it may be the safest bathing beach in the Cape. The middle and northern end of the beach is also popular with catamaran sailors and sailboarders, who often stage regattas offshore. Jager Walk, a pathway that runs along the rocky coastline, begins at the beach's southern end.

DINING

By Myrna Robins

Cape Town is the culinary capital of South Africa. Nowhere else in the country is the populace so discerning about food, and nowhere else is there such a wide selection of restaurants. Western culinary history here dates back more than 300 years—Cape Town was founded specifically to grow food—and that heritage is reflected in the city's cuisine. A number of restaurants operate in historic town houses and 18th-century wine estates.

Many restaurants are crowded in high season, so it's best to book in advance whenever possible. With the exception of the fancier restaurants in hotels—where a jacket is required—the dress code in Cape Town is casual (but no shorts). For a description of South African culinary terms, *see* Pleasures and Pastimes *in* Chapter 1. For price ranges *see* Dining *in* Smart Travel Tips A to Z.

City Bowl

$$$$ ✕ **Atlantic Grill Room.** The flagship restaurant at the luxurious Table Bay Hotel holds a prime position at the city's waterfront development. The room is decorated with updated colonial elegance, and seating on the terrace has stunning views of working docks against a mountain backdrop. Sophisticated menus combine elements from Asia and Europe, along with local ingredients like crayfish and venison. First courses include a terrine of baby leeks and langoustines with a pepperoni-almond dressing and a goat-cheese savarin dressed with a lavender vinaigrette. For a main course tournedos of eland (venison) are partnered by wild-mushroom duxelles, juniper-berry sauce, and tempura vegetables. A selection of salads and pastas provides conservative alternatives. Artistically plated desserts offer fruity creations with an Asian slant. The extensive wine list presents a vast choice of the best of the Cape. ⊠ *Table Bay Hotel, Quay 6, V&A Waterfront,* ☎ *021/ 406–5688. AE, DC, MC, V. Closed Mon.*

$$$$ ✕ **Blue Danube.** Updated classics from Western and central Europe dominate the menu at this restaurant in a former home on the city perimeter. Tasting talented chef Thomas Sinn's fare has become an essential item on the itineraries of many European and upcountry visitors. Complimentary appetizers precede starters like duck spring rolls on curried lentils and Viennese beef consommé with dumplings. Robust main courses include *crepinettes* (meat wrapped in caul fat) of springbok (venison) with shallot sauce and roast rack of Karoo lamb teamed with a potato gratin. Desserts are worth every delicious calorie—contemplate date-and-cashew-nut crepes with a hazelnut-praline ice cream or indulge in Kaiserschmarrn (a type of Austrian pancake torn into pieces and fried with sugar) with ice cream. Unhurried, professional service and a carefully selected wine list are hallmarks here. ⊠ *102 New*

Cape Town Dining and Lodging

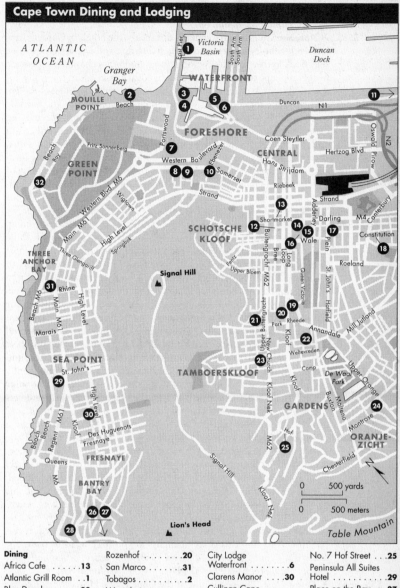

Dining

Africa Cafe **13**
Atlantic Grill Room . .**1**
Blue Danube **23**
Bukhara **15**
Cafe Mozart **16**
Cape Colony
Restaurant **22**
Ocean Basket **19**
Panama Jack's **11**
Quay West **3**
The Restaurant **9**
Rozenhof **20**
San Marco **31**
Tobagos **2**
Wangthai **8**

Lodging

Best Western Cape
Suites Hotel **18**
Breakwater Lodge . .**7**
Cape Grace Hotel . .**3**
Cape Heritage
Hotel **12**
Cape Milner
Hotel **21**
City Lodge
Waterfront **6**
Clarens Manor **30**
Cullinan Cape
Town Waterfront **5**
Ellerman House **28**
Holiday Inn
Garden Court–
Greenmarket
Square **14**
La Splendida **32**
Monkey Valley **26**
Mount Nelson **22**
No. 7 Hof Street . . .**25**
Peninsula All Suites
Hotel **29**
Place on the Bay . . .**27**
Protea Victoria
Junction **10**
Table Bay Hotel **1**
Townhouse Hotel . . .**17**
Victoria & Alfred
Hotel **4**
Villa Belmonte **24**

Church St., Tamboerskloof, ☎ *021/423–3624. AE, DC, MC, V. Closed Sun. No lunch Mon. and Sat.*

$$$$ ✕ **Rozenhof.** Within easy walking distance of the hotels in Gardens, this late-18th-century town house offers stylish fare and one of the best wine selections in town. Yellowwood ceilings and brass chandeliers provide historical Cape touches, and works by local artists adorn the walls. Inspiration from Asia and the Mediterranean is detectable, but cuisine here is noted more for consistently good quality served in cozy and friendly surroundings. Management has learned not to even think of removing classic first courses like the cheese soufflé sauced with mustard cream and the quartet of innovative summer salads. Crispy roast duck with a choice of fruity sauces is also a time-honored favorite. Layers of local Gorgonzola and mascarpone paired with preserved figs and a glass of port make a savory-sweet alternative to finales such as ginger-and-lemongrass ice cream encased in coconut-and-lime biscuits. ⊠ *18 Kloof St.,* ☎ *021/424–1968. AE, DC, MC, V. Closed Sun. No lunch Sat.*

$$$–$$$$ ✕ **Cape Colony Restaurant.** Tall bay windows, a high domed ceiling, and a giant trompe l'oeil mural—an inventive evocation of Table Mountain in the days of yore—are a befitting setting for the city's most historic and unashamedly colonial hotel. Renowned executive chef Garth Stroebel presents stylish fare based on a wide spectrum of southern African ingredients. Most are given voguish treatment—Mediterranean and Asian techniques dominate—while some dishes reflect the unique flavors of the region's indigenous Cape Malay heritage. The best seafood choices come as first courses, including crayfish bisque served with shrimp *bruschetta* or rice-battered Natal prawns perched on a beet and daikon salad. Smoked crocodile, carpaccio of spiced ostrich, and a warm guinea-fowl Waldorf salad are starters that star the continent's exotic items. Karoo loin of lamb with Moroccan spices is a popular entrée. An authoritative wine list offers the best South African vintages supplemented by French champagnes. ⊠ *Orange St., Gardens,* ☎ *021/483–1000. Reservations essential. AE, DC, MC, V. No lunch.*

$$$–$$$$ ✕ **Panama Jack's.** In this raw-timber structure in the heart of the docks, the music is loud, the tables are crowded, and the decor is nonexistent, but nowhere in town will you find bigger crayfish. Your choice, made from large open tanks, is weighed before being grilled or steamed. Expect to pay about R30 per 100 grams (R300 a kilogram) for this delicacy and a similar price for extra-large black tiger prawns. There is plenty of less expensive seafood on offer as well, and daily specials such as baby squid and local line fish are competitively priced. It can be difficult to find this place at night, so you may want to come for lunch if it's your first visit. ⊠ *Royal Yacht Club basin, off Goliath Rd., Docks,* ☎ *021/447–3992. AE, DC, MC, V. No lunch Sat.*

$$$–$$$$ ✕ **Quay West.** The restaurant at the Cape Grace Hotel overlooks the bascule bridge gateway to the international yacht basin at the waterfront. The decor is cool, uncluttered, and inviting, with comfortable wicker chairs and crisp table settings. Menus are as appetizing as the maritime view and as elegant as the interior. A delectable selection of starters—many of which could double as a light supper—includes African compositions such as smoked venison salad, a biltong (similar to jerky) and feta soufflé, and a warm crocodile salad. For main courses try a free-range roast chicken paired with grilled polenta and Mediterranean vegetables or grilled Norwegian salmon sauced with a coconut-and-lobster reduction. A short dessert list includes Cape brandy pudding teamed with marmalade ice cream. The carefully compiled wine list is well annotated, and the popular Bascule bar stocks more than 300 varieties of whiskey. The lunch menu varies significantly from dinner; the breakfast buffet is a firm favorite with locals. ⊠

Cape Grace Hotel, West Quay, V&A Waterfront, ☎ *021/418–0520. AE, DC, MC, V.*

$$$–$$$$ ✗ **Tobagos.** The restaurant is a series of intimate areas, and the terrace extends into a vast deck for cocktails and alfresco meals. Executive chef Jeffrie Siew, who has launched several top South African hotel restaurants, moves effortlessly from Asian to Western cuisines. Among the stars on the starter menu is chicken *satay* with peanut sauce, while the Cape's star ingredient, crayfish, is given Italian treatment, served grilled with pesto and a white-wine risotto. A small but trendy dessert list includes *panna cotta* (a light and smooth custard) and a dark chocolate mousse set into an envelope of cacao and teamed with pistachio ice cream. ⊠ *Radisson Hotel Waterfront, Beach Rd., Granger Bay,* ☎ *021/418–5729. AE, DC, MC, V.*

$$–$$$$ ✗ **Bukhara.** Set above a pedestrian mall lined with antiques shops and stalls, this hugely popular restaurant has delectable and authentic northern Indian fare. Even red walls and dark furniture do little to minimize the cavernous interior, which also showcases an open kitchen. Delicious garlic nan bread starts proceedings, which could include a selection from the tandoor oven, along with a choice of curries. Lamb marinated with yogurt and spices will please sensitive palates, while prawns come in several guises: the spicy coconut curry with tamarind is a firm favorite. Vegetarians have a delicious and inexpensive selection to contemplate, such as *tandoori* homemade cheese and vegetables. ⊠ *33 Church St.,* ☎ *021/424–0000. Reservations essential. AE, DC, MC, V. No lunch Sun.*

$$$ ✗ **Africa Cafe.** Its relocation from suburban house to a well-restored 18th century city square was a happy occasion for both diners and staff. Visitors now have a choice of air-conditioned rooms, including the Zulu Room with its adjoining roof deck that has spectacular sunset views. Multicolored cloths and stunning hand-glazed crockery complement an equally vibrant cuisine. Fresh fruit cocktails accompany a communal feast, with dishes originating from Ethiopia to Zambia, from Kenya to Angola. There are no starters or entrées, but rather a tasty series of patties, dips, puffs, and pastries accompanied by addictive dips, along with dishes like Moroccan lamb and date stew and Cape Malay chicken *biryani.* Vegetarian dishes are profuse, with the Soweto *chakalaka* a fiery example of a cooked vegetable relish. The cost of this colorful culinary abundance is R95 a person. Wines from Cape estates are available, but ask for *umqomboti* beer for an authentic accompaniment. ⊠ *108 Shortmarket St.,* ☎ *021/422–0221. AE, DC, MC, V. Closed Sun. No lunch.*

$$–$$$ ✗ **Wangthai.** Although some Thai restaurants have fallen by the wayside as the trend for this cuisine passes its peak, good and authentic outlets like this one continue to flourish. Top starters include *tom yum goong,* spicy prawns swimming in a broth scented with lemongrass, and a beautifully spiced dish of eggplant with basil and chili. Colorful stir-fries of beef, pork, and chicken vie with deep-fried fish served with sweet-and-sour, hot, and mild sauces or pungent red and green curries, tempered by coconut milk and mounds of sticky rice. The restaurant has an open kitchen and attractive Asian decor, and it occupies a prime spot on a trendy late-night strip between the city and the Atlantic seaboard. ⊠ *105 Paramount Pl., Main Rd., Green Point,* ☎ *021/ 439–6164. AE, DC, MC, V. No lunch Sat.*

$–$$ ✗ **Cafe Mozart.** This continental-style café and coffee shop is a 30-year-old institution, housed in a tall narrow building between antiques shops and art galleries. Its lemon-color walls are lined with mirrors and music-themed posters, and its tables are dressed with lace cloths. Regulars head inside, while the passing trade sits under umbrellas at pavement tables. Appetizing breakfast selections can be enjoyed all day, and the menu has a good selection of sandwiches and salads. But it's the daily specials—and the soups in particular—that most diners choose. Featherlight quiches, such as smoked salmon and Brie, come with fresh salad on parsley-dusted plates. Decadent desserts, made daily, are usually sold out by 2. Its version of lemon meringue gives new meaning to this familiar favorite. ✉ *37 Church St.,* ☎ Ⅲ *021/424–3774. Reservations essential. AE, DC, MC, V. Closed Sun. No dinner. BYOB.*

$–$$ ✕ **Ocean Basket.** On Restaurant Mile along the city fringe, this informal venue has few competitors in the field of bargain-price, ocean-fresh, well-cooked seafood. You can sit facing the street or find a table in the courtyard at the back. Calamari—stewed, curried, pickled, or in a salad—features prominently among the starters. The catch of the day is listed on the many blackboards lining the mustard-yellow walls, but delicately flavored hake-and-chips is the budget draw card. Standard entrées range from excellent Cajun-style grilled calamari to a huge seafood platter for two. Tartar, chili, and garlic sauces come on the side, and Greek salads are authentic. Desserts are average. ✉ *75 Kloof St.,* ☎ *021/422–0322. Reservations not accepted. AE, DC, MC, V.*

Atlantic Coast

$$$$ ✕ **The Restaurant.** Although neither the name nor the decor would win prizes for originality, the same cannot be said for patron-chef Graeme Shapiro's brilliant cutting-edge cuisine. Loyal fans know they will find neither chicken nor beef on the menu, but could start their meal with seared oysters and foie gras on brioche, sauced with Cape brandy cream or, for half the price, an equally delectable appetizer of goat's cheese baklava studded with walnuts and accented with a roasted red bell pepper relish. Line fish, sauced with passion fruit and served with hot buttered cucumbers, and grilled venison served with red cabbage, a celeriac *rosti,* and wild tea and red-currant sauce, are both worth trying. Gourmets also rave about the red China pork and prawns braised with rock candy and shiitake mushrooms. The raspberry-filled version of sago pudding (akin to tapioca), partnered by cinnamon ice cream, sets new standards in the comfort dessert genre. ✉ *51a Somerset Rd., Green Point,* ☎ *021/419–2921. Reservations essential. AE, DC, MC, V. Closed Sun. No lunch.*

$$$–$$$$ ✕ **San Marco.** Restaurants open and close in Cape Town with alarming speed, but this Italian institution in Sea Point is a happy exception, a meeting place for generations of diners since it first opened its doors as a gelateria. Come here not for the decor but for the consistency and authenticity of dishes that are all cooked to order. Although it's been taken over by a second Italian family, the original chef has stayed on, continuing to conjure up superb grilled calamari and tossing homemade pasta with simple, flavorful sauces. Luxurious langoustines are well priced here. As always the veal dishes—particularly *escalopes* cooked with sage and white wine—are especially good. If one of the less common Cape line fish such as elf (shad) is offered, don't miss it. Finish with a selection of the house's renowned ice creams and sorbets, which are dressed with a splash of liqueur. ✉ *92 Main Rd., Sea Point,* ☎ *021/439–2758. Reservations essential. AE, DC, MC, V. Closed Tues. No lunch Mon.–Sat.*

$$–$$$$ ✕ **Blues.** Doors open to frame an inviting vista of palms, sand, and azure sea from the balcony of this popular restaurant in Camps Bay. Although the mood and menu are largely Californian, appetizers such as smoked springbok (venison) add African flair. The pasta is deservedly popular, and spaghettini with saffron cream, black mussels, and baby fennel is not only delicious, but also the most affordable entrée on the menu. Others settle for lamb chops with an eggplant, caper,

Cape Peninsula Dining and Lodging

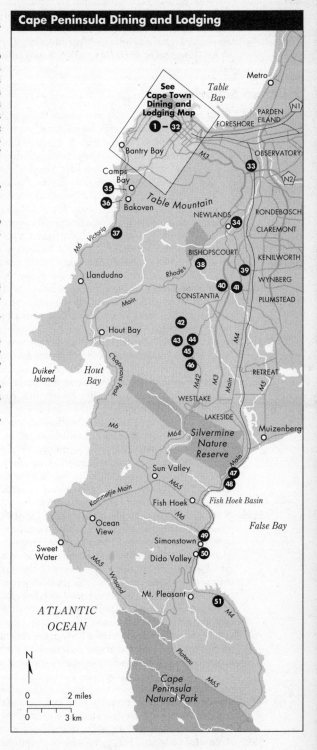

and olive relish or splurge on the luxurious but pricey seafood platter. Popular desserts include the chocolate pecan brownie topped with vanilla ice cream and hot chocolate sauce. ⊠ *The Promenade, Victoria Rd., Camps Bay,* ☎ *021/438–2040. Reservations essential. AE, DC, MC, V.*

Southern Suburbs

$$$$ ✕ **Au Jardin.** Tucked away in a corner of the historic Vineyard hotel in Newlands, complete with fountain and views of Table Mountain, the restaurant serves classic French cuisine imbued with subtle Cape and Mediterranean accents. Appetizers might include smoked kudu (venison) and garlic terrine with a rocket (arugula) salad or mille-feuille of eggplant and tomato with a mushroom sauce. Panfried beef fillet is paired with a Savoy cabbage parcel and lyonnaise potatoes. Along with classic finales like Grand Marnier soufflé, you'll find innovative combinations such as guava-and-coconut sabayon with rum-raisin ice cream. There's a menu dégustation, and the lighter à la carte menu at lunch is a good value. The wine list presents the best of the Cape, but there are French labels as well. ⊠ *Vineyard Hotel, Colinton Rd., Claremont,* ☎ *021/683–1520. AE, DC, MC, V. Closed Sun. No lunch Sat. and Mon.*

$$$$ ✕ **Buitenverwachting.** On a historic wine estate in Constantia, this su-
  ★   perb restaurant is consistently rated among the country's best. Window-side tables have views of the vineyards sloping up toward the mountains. Menus change daily but always consist of meticulously prepared dishes plated with artistic flair. Imaginative starters include *ballotine* of leek, green onion, and pepper mousse with crayfish *crostini* and a duo of tapenades, while a timbale of wild and cultivated mushrooms comes with a trio of rabbit on a balsamic honey and thyme jus. Creations like guinea fowl with a creamy leek-and-shiitake tagliatelle teamed with a beetroot-and-apple salad compete with venison in the form of loin of springbok in a truffle-and-mushroom sauce. Local fruits star in imaginative works of dessert art, as in the passion-fruit mousse and grapefruit granita partnered by a pawpaw-and-guava salad. Gourmet vegetarians will relish a separate five-course menu, and there is also a three-course lunch menu. ⊠ *Klein Constantia Rd., Constantia,* ☎ *021/794–3522. Reservations essential. AE, DC, MC, V. Closed Sun.–Mon. and July. No lunch Sat.*

$$$$ ✕ **The Cellars.** Classic table settings and highly professional service complement artfully presented fare at this restaurant in the historic Cellars-Hohenort Hotel in Constantia. Since renowned British chef Phil Alcock took over the kitchens, menu items have become more understated in their description. This may belie the quality, which is better than ever, with increased emphasis on freshness and maximum use of seasonal ingredients. Green peas team with foie gras in an unusual soup, while another appetizer combines poached salmon with cauliflower, sauced with horseradish cream. For a main course try the slow-roasted cannon of lamb teamed with a herb puree and ratatouille or sample the gastronomic leapfrog across continents in the form of char-grilled fillet of ostrich with bubble and squeak (cabbage and potatoes) and a green bell pepper and corn jus. For dessert fans there's tart Tatin teamed with five-spice ice cream and vanilla soufflé paired with chocolate bread-and-butter pudding. The extensive wine list has won several awards. ⊠ *15 Hohenort Ave., Constantia,* ☎ *021/794–2137. Reservations essential. AE, DC, MC, V.*

$$$$ ✕ **Constantia Uitsig.** This restaurant in a restored farmstead attracts a large, loyal following. Reserve a table on the enclosed veranda for tremendous views of the mountains. The menu is a pricey and harmonious blend of northern Italian and Provençal cuisines. Carpaccio

comes in two guises—a fish version is dressed with soy, vinegar, sesame oil, ginger, and seaweed, while the beef comes with rocket (arugula), Parmesan, and a classic vinaigrette. Many diners start with home-made pasta before going on to main courses that include line fish served with crisp cabbage and a spicy sauce and an uncommon treat of sweetbreads sautéed with bacon, peas, mushrooms and marsala wine. Desserts include iced berries with a hot white chocolate sauce. ⊠ *Spaanschemat River Rd., Constantia,* ☏ *021/794–4480. Reservations essential. AE, DC, MC, V. No lunch Mon.*

$$$$ ✗ **Parks.** This restored Victorian villa in Constantia has been jam-packed since it opened more than five years ago. The reasons are twofold: The elegant decor is convivial not intimidating, and Michael Olivier's zesty contemporary cuisine strikes the right chord with patrons. Several dishes can be ordered in starter or main portions, and there's a good choice of wines by the glass. Local Camembert is baked with tomato and eggplant in phyllo, while gravlax made of Cape salmon trout is seared and teamed with new potatoes and a beetroot salsa. Try the peren-nially popular blackened Cajun-style fish with herbed crème fraîche or, in an inventive turn on a British classic, ostrich fillet Wellington with bush-tea-flavored polenta and juniper-berry sauce. Desserts are obli-gatory here, with choices such as crème brûlée garnished with poached dried apricots and panna cotta served with caramelized blood orange. ⊠ *114 Constantia Rd., Constantia,* ☏ *021/797–8202. Reservations essential. AE, DC, MC, V. Closed Sun. No lunch Sat.*

$$$–$$$$ ✗ **La Colombe.** The Uitsig farm is also home to a Provençal restaurant
★ that is collecting accolades from gourmets around the globe along with devotees of southern French fare. The walls and woodwork of this small restaurant are painted sunshine yellow and sky blue, and French doors in the dining room open onto a courtyard. Chef Franck Dan-gereux transforms local produce into a menu that sings of his native French province: Expect flavorful renderings of *pan bagna* (salad *niçoise* sandwiched into French bread), or start with carpaccio of tuna with a sweet tomato sauce. Entrées include a satisfying peasant dish of grilled sausage and soybeans with a baby marrow puree or go·up-market with grilled noisettes of springbok (venison) in honey jus with Cape Malay spice. Desserts range from fruity sorbets to a wicked ter-rine of dark chocolate, further enriched with caramel sauce. ⊠ *Uitsig Farm, Spaanschemat River Rd., Constantia,* ☏ *021/794–2390. Reser-vations essential. AE, DC, MC, V. Closed Tues. No dinner Sun.*

$$$–$$$$ ✗ **Steenberg.** The original winery on this historic estate makes a lux-uriously dressed home for the restaurant, which also serves the bou-tique hotel in the 18th-century manor house across the court. Coziness is guaranteed at tables set in alcoves created from the original vats. Ex-ecutive chef Garth Almazan keeps his prices reasonable while not compromising on quality. Among the first courses are a seafood *laksa* (rice noodles with spicy coconut milk sauce), and a warm Asian os-trich salad with glass noodles and Japanese ginger. Winter specials of oxtail casserole and slow-braised lamb shank are always in demand. A chocolate trio and a spiked crème brûlée are among the most pop-ular finales. Diners who enjoy food and wine pairing will appreciate the excellent selection of estate wines by the glass. ⊠ *Steenberg Hotel, Steenberg Rd., Tokai,* ☏ *021/713–2222. AE, DC, MC, V.*

$$$ ✗ **Jonkershuis.** This establishment offers classic Cape hospitality in a 19th-century building adjoining the gracious manor house at Groot Constantia, the Cape's oldest wine estate. Fresh line fish and roast loin of lamb keep company on the menu with classic *bobotie*—spiced minced beef studded with dried fruit and nut slivers and topped with a savory baked custard—and *smoorsnoek,* a popular Cape fish braised with onion, potato, and chili and served with baked sweet potatoes in

a fresh orange sauce. The traditional chicken pie is made from a recipe handed down through generations of Dutch settlers. To taste all these dishes, ask for a Cape sampler. Jonkershuis also serves hearty breakfasts and light refreshments. ⊠ *Groot Constantia Estate, Main Rd., Constantia,* ☎ *021/794–6255. Reservations essential. AE, DC, MC. No dinner Sun.–Mon.*

False Bay

$$–$$$$ ✕ **Bertha's Restaurant and Coffeehouse.** Alfresco dining at this well-positioned waterfront venue offers a feast for both palate and eye. Boating activities from the naval dockyard on one side and yacht club on the other enliven vistas of sparkling water against a mountain backdrop. The contemporary menu makes good use of local produce, such as Atlantic black mussels, which are poached in chili-sparked, thyme-scented white wine. Although standard fare of pizzas, steak, and ribs is popular, seafood, pasta, and chicken satays make tempting alternatives. In demand is the inexpensive fried hake in beer batter with chips (french fries). From a small dessert list the double chocolate tart with mascarpone cream cheese gets rave reviews. Lunch here is popular, so it's a good idea to reserve in advance. ⊠ *1 Wharf Rd., Simonstown,* ☎ *021/786–2138. AE, DC, MC, V.*

$$ ✕ **Brass Bell.** Whether diners choose to eat in the main restaurant, in the cabin, on the terrace, or in the gazebo, they enjoy views of False Bay, frolicking surfers, and fishing boats heading for the harbor. This cheerful, informal place can get crowded and noisy. There's a choice of four menus: the main restaurant presents more formal fare, the other areas keep to lighter, more casual meals—all of which offer good value for the money. The emphasis is on fish and seafood, but vegetarians and carnivores alike will find sufficient items to please them. The fare is mostly straightforward, enlivened by a few traditional Cape and Mediterranean dishes. ⊠ *Waterfront, Kalk Bay,* ☎ *021/788–5456. AE, DC, MC, V.*

$$ ✕ **Olympia Cafe.** Opposite the fishing harbor, between antiques shops and old-fashioned bric-a-brac stores, is the unprepossessing entrance to this tiny eatery, furnished with 10 mismatched tables and a counter along the shop window. It's long been a best-kept secret among locals and regular visitors, who don't mind waiting for a table. The quality of the mostly Mediterranean fare is consistently high and the prices astonishingly low. A delectable dish of a duo of eggplant rolls, one filled with butternut squash and ricotta, the other sweet potato and ricotta, sauced with piquant tomato and served with grilled polenta is a perennial favorite. Rare tuna steak with mashed potatoes and ratatouille is delectable. The chef also serves more than 12,000 delicious omelets each year, accompanied by excellent croissants and crusty loaves from the cafe's bakery up the road. ⊠ *134 Main Rd., Kalk Bay,* ☎ *021/788–6396. Reservations not accepted. No credit cards. Closed Mon. No dinner Tues.–Wed. and Sun.*

LODGING

Finding lodging in Cape Town can be a nightmare during high season (December–January), as many of the more reasonable accommodations are booked up. It is worth traveling between April and August, if you can, to take advantage of the "secret season" discounts. If you arrive in Cape Town without a reservation, head for Cape Town Tourism's Information Centre, which has a helpful accommodations desk.

Hotels in the city center are a good option if you're here on business. During the day the historic city center is a vibrant place. At night, though, it's shut up tight; night owls may prefer a hotel amid the nonstop action of the redeveloped waterfront. Hotels and B&Bs in the southern suburbs, especially Constantia, offer unrivaled beauty and tranquillity and make an ideal base if you're exploring the peninsula. You'll need a car, though, and should plan on 15–30 minutes to get into town. Atlantic Coast hotels provide the closest thing in Cape Town to a beach-vacation atmosphere despite the cold ocean waters.

Keep in mind that international flights from the United States and Europe arrive in the morning and return flights depart in the evening. Because most hotels have an 11 AM checkout, you may have to wait for a room if you've just arrived; if you're leaving, you will be hauled kicking and screaming out of your room hours before your flight. Most hotels will try to accommodate you, but they often have no choice in peak season. Some of the larger hotels have residents-only lounges where you can spend the hours awaiting your flight. Note that many small luxury accommodations either do not permit children or have minimum age restrictions. It's a good idea to inquire in advance if this will be an issue.

Cape Town is regarded as one of the top backpackers' destinations in the world, with more than 50 hostels. Contact **Backpacker Tourism, South Africa** (BTSA; ☎ 021/462–5888) for information.

The most reliable source of good B&B establishments is the **Bed & Breakfast Bureau** (☎ 021/794–0030, FAX 021/794–0031, WEB www.bookabed. co.za). Or try the **Portfolio of Places** (☎ 011/880–3414, FAX 011/788–4802, WEB www.portfoliocollection.com) brochure. If you don't like tiptoeing around someone's house, or you want to save money, consider renting a fully furnished apartment, especially if you're staying two or more weeks. Contact **Holiday Booking Services** (✉ Box 27269, Rhine Rd., 8050, ☎ 021/434–8222, WEB www.capeholiday.com), with more than 500 high-quality, furnished, fully stocked apartments on its books.

The **de Waterkant Village** is Cape Town's first and only guest street, an entire little community of houses to rent. There are 30 beautifully restored, small, self-catering houses with daily housekeeping services that are unusual, trendy, classy, and quite charming. The high-season double-occupancy rate is about R850 per night. All are near the harbor, as the name implies. ✉ *1 Loader St., 8000,* ☎ *021/422–2721,* FAX *021/418–6082,* WEB *www.dewaterkant.com. AE, DC, MC, V.*

City Bowl

$$$$ 🏨 **Cape Milner Hotel.** Previously the Mijlhof Manor, this attractive, well-positioned hotel has been extensively refurbished and extended. The new look is clean, classical, and contemporary, with rooms decorated in restful shades of gray, white, and black. The terrace has wonderful views of Table Mountain. ✉ *2 Milner Rd., Tamboerskloof, 8001,* ☎ *021/426–1101,* FAX *021/426–1109,* WEB *www.threecities.co.za. 55 rooms, 2 suites. 2 bars, 2 lounges, restaurant, air-conditioning, pool, meeting rooms, parking (fee). AE, DC, MC, V. BP.*

$$$$ 🏨 **Mount Nelson.** This distinctive pink landmark is the grande dame
★ of Cape Town. Since it opened its doors in 1899 to accommodate passengers of the Union-Castle steamships, it has been the focal point of Cape social life. It retains an old-fashioned charm and gentility that other luxury hotels often lack: high tea is served in the lounge to piano accompaniment; the Grill Room offers a nightly dinner dance; and the staff almost outnumbers the guests. The hotel stands at the top of Government Avenue, but, surrounded as it is by 7 acres of manicured gardens, it might as well be in the country. For peak season, December–

March, it's advisable to book a year in advance. ✉ *76 Orange St., 8001,* ☎ *021/423–1000,* FAX *021/424–7472,* WEB *www.mountnelsonhotel. orient-express.com. 145 rooms, 56 suites. 3 restaurants, bar, 2 pools, gym, 2 tennis courts, squash. AE, DC, MC, V. BP.*

$$$ 🏨 **Best Western Cape Suites Hotel.** This is a village-style hotel, with low buildings and adjoining individual units, five minutes from the center of Cape Town, near Parliament, and a 15-minute walk from the waterfront. Rooms are spacious and pleasantly furnished, and all come with a fully equipped kitchen. Some rooms have mountain views; others look into the city. Although it's on a corner site, the hotel is well insulated, so traffic noise is not a major problem; inner rooms tend to be quieter. If you have a car, you can park it virtually outside your room. A free shuttle takes guests to popular sights within about 13 km (8 mi) of the hotel. ✉ *Constitution and de Villiers Sts. (Box 51085, Waterfront), 8002,* ☎ *021/461–0727,* FAX *021/462–4389,* WEB *www.capesuites.co.za. 126 suites. 2 restaurants, bar, 2 pools, gym, recreation room, free parking. AE, DC, MC, V. EP.*

$$–$$$ 🏨 **Villa Belmonte.** In a quiet residential neighborhood on the slopes above the city, this small guest house offers privacy and luxury in an attractive Dutch Revival residence. The owners have sought to create the feeling of an Italian villa through the use of marbling, molded ceilings, and natural wood floors. Wide verandas have superb views of the city, Table Mountain, and Devil's Peak. Rooms have colorful draperies, wicker furniture, and small-pane windows. It's a 20-minute walk to the city center. ✉ *33 Belmont Ave., Oranjezicht 8001,* ☎ *021/ 462–1576,* FAX *021/462–1579. 14 rooms. Restaurant, bar, room service, pool. AE, DC, MC, V. BP.*

$$ 🏨 **Cape Heritage Hotel.** This friendly, attractive, well-run hotel is part
★ of the Heritage Square development and as such has direct access to a host of restaurants, shops, and art galleries. Originally built as a private home in 1771, it is now the only black-owned and -managed major hotel in Cape Town. Teak beamed ceilings and foot-wide yellowwood floorboards echo the building's gracious past, and the spacious rooms are individually decorated. Some have four-poster beds, others exposed brickwork, but each has its own special charm. Rooms overlooking the attractive courtyard—filled with tables sheltering under what is claimed to be the oldest grapevine in South Africa—may be a little noisy, but the revelry stops at midnight sharp. Do take the time to look at the many photographs depicting the building before, during, and after renovation. Parking is across the street in a section of a public parking lot with good security, and the hotel is centrally located, close to parliament and the business district. ✉ *90 Bree St., 8001,* ☎ *021/424–4646,* FAX *021/424–4949,* WEB *www.capeheritage.co.za. 14 rooms. Bar, 5 restaurants, breakfast room, 2 lounges, hair salon, shops. AE, DC, MC, V.*

$$ 🏨 **Holiday Inn Garden Court–Greenmarket Square.** Facing historic Greenmarket Square, this minimum-service hotel has one of the best locations in the city, especially for those who don't have a car. Mountain-facing rooms overlooking the square are pleasant, but the dawn chorus of vendors setting up their stalls may drive you to distraction. The outdoor section of the restaurant, Cycles on the Square, is a popular choice with great views of the market. Parking is a major headache in this part of town. ✉ *10 Greenmarket Sq. (Box 3775), 8000,* ☎ *021/ 423–2040,* FAX *021/423–3664. 170 rooms. Restaurant, bar. AE, DC, MC, V. EP.*

$$ 🏨 **Townhouse Hotel.** Its proximity to government buildings and its easygoing atmosphere (not to mention extremely competitive rates) make the Townhouse a popular choice. Rooms are decorated in gentle pastels with soft, warm curtains. Request a view of the mountain. ✉ *60 Corporation St. (Box 5053), 8000,* ☎ *021/465–7050,* FAX *021/465–3891,*

WEB *www.townhouse.co.za. 104 rooms. Restaurant, bar, room service, health club, airport shuttle. AE, DC, MC, V.*

$ 📷 **No. 7 Hof Street.** It's if you're staying for a while and have better things to spend your money on than accommodations, this lovely B&B offers excellent value for the money. It's close to everything and within walking distance of the Gardens. The rooms are outside with a separate entrance, and the whole place has a welcoming, homey feel. The rooms are unpretentious, pleasant, clean, and comfortable. One room has a shower and bath, and the other only a bath. ✉ *7 Hof St., Gardens 8001,* ☎ *082/808–3854,* ☎ FAX *021/424–4984. 2 rooms. Breakfast room, pool. No credit cards. CP.*

Waterfront

$$$$ 📷 **Cape Grace Hotel.** It's not a surprise that this well-appointed, ex-
★ clusive hotel at the V&A Waterfront became an instant success. Built on a spit of land jutting into a working harbor, the Cape Grace offers views of seals frolicking in the surrounding waters and seagulls soaring above. The large guest rooms have harbor or mountain views. Elegant and understated with both French period decor and a wonderful modern design, it's owned and run by one of the country's leading hotelier families, the Brands. The attention to detail throughout is outstanding, from the antique pieces to the fresh flowers in the rooms. There's a wonderful well-stocked library for browsing and a superb restaurant, Quay West, which serves local and international cuisine. Guests have free use of the nearby health club and the hotel's courtesy car for service into the city. Booking well in advance is essential. ✉ *West Quay, V&A Waterfront, 8002,* ☎ *021/410–7100,* FAX *021/419–7622,* WEB *www.capegrace.com. 122 rooms. Restaurant, bar, pool, library. AE, DC, MC, V. EP.*

$$$$ 📷 **Cullinan Cape Town Waterfront.** Just opposite the entrance to the waterfront, this sparklingly white hotel has a spacious marble-tile lobby and huge picture windows draped in rose and gold that lead out to the pool. An enormous double-curving gilt staircase completes the picture. The rooms are quite restrained, with muted green carpets and floral notes; bathrooms are well laid out with separate showers and are quiet and understated in white tile and gray marble. ✉ *1 Cullinan St., V&A Waterfront, 8001,* ☎ *021/418–6920,* FAX *021/418–3559,* WEB *www.southernsun.com. 416 rooms. Restaurant, bar, room service, pool, health club. AE, DC, MC, V. EP.*

$$$$ 📷 **Protea Victoria Junction.** With its spot on Main Road, Greenpoint, adjacent to the waterfront, and its distinctly funky and art deco–style decor, the hotel is popular with those looking for something different. The spacious loft rooms have high ceilings and beds on special platforms, but be warned: You have to be nimble to climb to your large double bed in the upstairs section of the room. You'll be pleased to hear the standard rooms have ordinary knee-level beds but are still quite funky and chic. The Set is a trendy restaurant for business lunches and has a great range of salads and quite innovative fare, and the bar always jumps at happy hour. ✉ *Somerset and Ebenezer Rds., Greenpoint (Box 51234, Waterfront), 8002,* ☎ *021/418–1234,* FAX *021/418–5678,* WEB *www.proteahotels.com. 172 rooms. Restaurant, coffee shop, bar, pool. AE, DC, MC, V.*

$$$$ 📷 **Table Bay Hotel.** This glitzy hotel is a prime spot at the tip of the V&A Waterfront. The decor is sunny and eclectic, with picture windows, marble mosaic and parquet floors, and lots of plants, including the hotel's trademark orchid arrangements, containing more than 1,000 blooms. In the lounge you can browse through the selection of international newspapers as you sit by the fireside, relaxing to live cham-

ber music. The rooms, although understated, are colorful and bright, with marble-and-tile bathrooms with roomy showers. Service can be a frustratingly inattentive at times. The hotel has direct access to the large Waterfront mall. ⊠ *Quay 6, V&A Waterfront, 8002,* ☎ *021/ 406–5000,* 𝔽𝔸𝕏 *021/406–5767,* 𝚆𝙴𝙱 *www.suninternational.com. 239 rooms, 15 suites. 3 restaurants, 2 bars, lobby lounge, pool, hair salon, spa, health club, business services, meeting room. AE, DC, MC, V. BP.*

$$$$ 🏨 **Victoria & Alfred Hotel.** You couldn't find a better location for this upmarket hotel, in a converted warehouse smack in the middle of the waterfront surrounded by shops, bars, and restaurants. Rooms are huge, furnished in neo–Cape Dutch style, and decorated in muted tones of rust and sea green. Views from the costlier mountain-facing rooms are spectacular, encompassing not only Table Mountain but the city and docks as well. Waterfront buses leave regularly for the city center, a five-minute ride. ⊠ *Pierhead (Box 50050), Waterfront, 8002,* ☎ *021/ 419–6677,* 𝔽𝔸𝕏 *021/419–8955,* 𝚆𝙴𝙱 *www.v-and-a.co.za. 68 rooms. Restaurant, bar, room service. AE, DC, MC, V.*

$$$ 🏨 **City Lodge Waterfront.** Location is everything at this no-frills chain hotel, a five-minute walk from the waterfront and 10 minutes from the city center. Rooms are standard, decorated with ship prints and blond-wood furniture, and all have TVs and tea/coffeemakers. ⊠ *Dock and Alfred Drs., Waterfront (Box 6025, Roggebaai), 8012,* ☎ *021/419– 9450,* 𝔽𝔸𝕏 *021/419–0460,* 𝚆𝙴𝙱 *www.citylodge.co.za. 164 rooms. Bar, breakfast room, pool. AE, DC, MC, V. BP.*

$$ 🏨 **Breakwater Lodge.** You won't find another hotel this close to the waterfront offering rates so low. Built in a converted 19th-century prison on Portswood Ridge, the Breakwater certainly won't win any awards for charm or coziness. Its history is quite evident in the long, narrow corridors, which lead to tiny, sparsely furnished cells (sorry, rooms). Nevertheless, the rooms are clean and have TVs, phones, and tea- and coffeemakers. Ask for a room with a view of Table Mountain. ⊠ *Portswood Rd., Waterfront, 8001,* ☎ *021/406–1911,* 𝔽𝔸𝕏 *021/406–1070,* 𝚆𝙴𝙱 *www.breakwaterlodge.co.za. 327 rooms, 110 family units without bath. 2 restaurants, bar. AE, DC, MC, V.*

Atlantic Coast

$$$$ 🏨 **Bay Hotel.** Of the luxury hotels in and around Cape Town, this beach hotel in Camps Bay is the most relaxed and unpretentious. The three-story structure is across the road from a white-sand beach and is backed by the towering cliffs of the Twelve Apostles. From the raised pool deck guests look out over sea and sand, far from the hurly-burly of Cape Town. Cane furniture, colorful paintings, and attractive peach and sea tones make the rooms bright. Service is excellent, with an emphasis on privacy. Ask for a premier room if you want a sea view. ⊠ *Victoria Rd. (Box 32021), Camps Bay 8040,* ☎ *021/438–4444,* 𝔽𝔸𝕏 *021/ 438–4455,* 𝚆𝙴𝙱 *www.halcyonhotels.co.za. 76 rooms. Restaurant, bar, room service, pool. AE, DC, MC, V. EP. No children under 12.*

$$$$ 🏨 **De Oudekraal Hotel.** This luxurious hotel has the most fantastic location—which has turned out to be a mixed blessing. Built amid great controversy, it's the only building between Camps Bay and Llandudno, bordering on the Cape Peninsula National Park (it was built just before the park's status was proclaimed) and is uncomfortably close to a historical Muslim *kramat* (holy burial site). Despite the vociferous objections of the Muslim community and conservationists, here it stands. And it is a really nice hotel. All the rooms are comfortably and stylishly decorated in shades of blue, for the sea-facing ones, and brown and green for those facing the mountains. Built high up, it has a spectacular sea view, and the busy Victoria Road is totally out of sight beneath you. ✉ *Victoria Rd. (Box 32117), Camps Bay 8040,* ☎ *021/ 437–9000,* FAX *021/437–9001,* WEB *www.deoudekraal.co.za. 48 rooms, 22 suites. Restaurant, bar, pool, meeting room, travel services. AE, DC, MC, V. EP.*

$$$$ ★ 🛏 **Ellerman House.** Without a doubt, this is one of the finest (and most expensive) hotels in South Africa. Built in 1912 for shipping magnate Sir John Ellerman, the hotel sits high on a hill in Bantry Bay and has stupendous views of the sea. Broad, terraced lawns fronted by elegant balustrades step down the hillside to a sparkling pool. The drawing and living rooms, decorated in Regency style, are elegant yet not forbiddingly formal. Guest rooms have enormous picture windows, high ceilings, and spacious tile bathrooms. The hotel accommodates only 22 guests, and a highly trained staff caters to their every whim. In the kitchen four chefs prepare whatever guests request—whether it's on the menu or not. All drinks except wine and champagne are included in the rates. ✉ *180 Kloof Rd., Bantry Bay 8001 (Box 515, Sea Point 8060),* ☎ *021/439–9182,* FAX *021/434–7257,* WEB *www.ellerman.co.za. 11 rooms. Restaurant, bar, room service, pool, sauna, gym. AE, DC, MC, V. CP.*

$$$$ 🛏 **Peninsula All Suites Hotel.** In an 11-story building just across the road from the ocean, this exclusive establishment whose accommodations have fully equipped kitchens is ideal for families or groups of friends. Guests can choose from a variety of suites that sleep from four to eight people and have incredible views of the sea. The larger suites are the most attractive, full of light and air, thanks to picture windows, sliding doors, wide balconies, and white-tile floors. Small studio suites look more like conventional hotel rooms. Each suite has a fully equipped kitchen with microwave oven. The hotel is a time-share property, so booking during the busy December holiday could be a problem. ✉ *313 Beach Rd., Sea Point 8001 (Box 768, Sea Point 8060),* ☎ *021/439– 8888,* FAX *021/439–8886,* WEB *www.peninsula.co.za. 110 suites. Restaurant, bar, room service, 2 pools, sauna, gym. AE, DC, MC, V.*

$$$$ 🛏 **Place on the Bay.** These luxury self-catering apartments are on the beachfront in Camps Bay, within easy walking distance of a host of restaurants and bars. Apartments are tasteful, modern affairs that make extensive use of glass. Many units have good sea views from their balconies. If you really want to have it all, take the magnificent penthouse, which occupies the entire top floor and comes with its own swimming pool, for about R15,000 per day. All units have daily housekeeping service. ✉ *Fairways and Victoria Rds., Camps Bay 8001,* ☎ *021/438– 7060,* FAX *021/438–2692,* WEB *www.theplaceonthebay.co.za. 21 apartments. Restaurant, bar, pool. AE, DC, MC, V.*

$$$ 🛏 **Clarens Manor.** This beautiful guest house is at once invigorating and extremely restful. Original art, antique furniture, and a few African artifacts stand out against the soft sunshine-yellow walls. Upstairs rooms are grand in size and decor, and the downstairs lounges and dining room are warm and comfortable. Forget the sea view—it's nothing compared to the magnificent spectacle of Lion's Head looming over you as you gaze from the mountain-facing rooms. Lovingly prepared meals are served around one huge table and resemble private dinner parties. Sherry and port, laundry service, and airport shuttle are included in the price. There's a two-night minimum on weekends. If driving, enter Clarens Road from High Level Road, not Regent Street, as it is one-way. ✉ *35 Clarens Rd., Sea Point, 8060,* ☎ *021/434–6801,* FAX *021/ 434–6845. 7 rooms. Dining room, 2 lounges, pool, laundry service. AE, DC, MC, V. BP.*

$$$ 🛏 **La Splendida.** Designed to look like a Miami South Beach art deco hotel, this trendy all-suites addition to the Cape Town scene has a great location on Beach Road, Mouille Point. Ask for a sea- or mountain-

facing room, either of which has great views. Well-proportioned rooms are zanily decorated with bright colors and natural fabrics, and the overall feeling is light and airy. Cafe Faro, the outstanding hotel restaurant with interesting eclectic cuisine, is a favorite with local yuppies. The V&A Waterfront is a seven-minute walk. You have a choice of executive or penthouse suites (slightly larger and a bit more expensive), but whichever you choose, you'll be very comfortable. ⊠ *121 Beach Rd., Mouille Point, 8001,* ☎ *021/439–5119,* FAX *021/439–5112,* WEB *www. lasplendida.co.za. 22 suites. Restaurant, lap pool. AE, DC, MC, V.*

$$$ 🏨 **Monkey Valley.** This secluded resort is one of the best places on the
★ peninsula for families and is very popular for small conferences. Built on stilts, each of the self-catering thatched log cottages lies in an indigenous milk-wood forest overlooking a nature reserve and the white sands of Noordhoek Beach. Cottages have two or three bedrooms, fully equipped kitchens, and large balconies. The wood interiors are attractive and rustic, brightened by floral fabrics, cottage-style furniture, and fireplaces. Rooms are similarly decorated, and some have pretty Victorian bathrooms. The resort has its own restaurant, and there is a large grocery store 5 km (3 mi) away. Owner Judy Sole runs an outstanding establishment and is a character in her own right. ⊠ *Mountain Rd. (Box 114), Noordhoek 7985,* ☎ *021/789–1391,* FAX *021/789–1143. 34 rooms, 17 cottages. Restaurant, bar, pool, playground, convention center. AE, DC, MC, V. BP.*

$$ 🏨 **Whale Cottage, Bakoven.** This light and airy B&B is fantastically positioned about 200 yards from Bakoven Beach and an easy half-mile walk from Camps Bay Beach. The light, bright, breezy rooms are decorated in a marine or nautical theme and have wonderful sea views. If you want privacy, opt for a downstairs room, as all the upstairs ones open on to the same balcony. ⊠ *50 Victoria Rd., Bakoven, 8005,* ☎ *021/438–3840,* FAX *021/438–4388. 6 rooms. Breakfast room, pool. AE, DC, MC, V. CP.*

Southern Suburbs

$$$$ 🏨 **Cellars-Hohenort Country House Hotel.** It's easy to forget the out-
★ side world at this idyllic getaway in Constantia. Set on 9 acres of gardens on the slopes of Constantiaberg, this luxury hotel commands spectacular views across Constantia Valley to False Bay. The 18th-century cellars of the Klaasenbosch wine estate and the Hohenort manor house form the heart of the hotel. Guest rooms are large and elegant, furnished in English-country style with brass beds, flowery valances, and reproduction antiques. Rooms in the manor house have the best views of the valley. Although the hotel lacks the historical significance of the Alphen, it offers a level of luxury and tranquillity that its more famous competitor cannot match. The Presidential Suite sleeps a family of six. ⊠ *93 Brommersvlei Rd. (Box 270), Constantia 7800,* ☎ *021/ 794–2137,* FAX *021/794–2149,* WEB *www.cellarshohenort.com. 55 rooms, 1 suite. 2 restaurants, 2 bars, room service, 2 pools, hair salon, tennis court. AE, DC, MC, V. BP.*

$$$$ 🏨 **Constantia Uitsig Country Hotel.** This 200-acre winery has an envi-
★ able setting, backed by the magnificent mountains of the Constantiaberg and overlooking the vineyards of Constantia Valley. Rooms, in whitewashed farm cottages set amid manicured lawns and gardens, are comfortable and inviting. Wicker headboards, timber ceilings, and bright floral patterns add a rustic feeling. The restaurant in the original farmhouse draws diners from all over the Cape. If you value peace and quiet, this is a great place to stay. ⊠ *Spaanschemat River Rd. (Box 32), Constantia 7848,* ☎ *021/794–6500,* FAX *021/794–7605,* WEB *www.*

constantiauitsig.co.za. 16 rooms. Restaurant, room service, 2 pools. AE, DC, MC, V.

$$$$ 🏠 **Steenberg Country Hotel.** One of the oldest estates in the area, the original farm, called Swaaneweide aan den Steenberg, was granted to the four-time widow Catherina Ustings by her lover, Simon van der Stel, the governor of the Cape, in the late 17th century, and so she became the first woman to own land in South Africa. The original buildings have been painstakingly restored, the gardens manicured to perfection, and the vineyards replanted higher up on the mountain. The original vineyards have been converted to a championship 18-hole golf course. The buildings are spectacular and are all furnished in antiques, as are guest rooms, that are done in a Provençal style, with yellow-painted wood and salvaged barn floorboards. ⊠ *Steenberg and Tokai Rds., Tokai 7945,* ☎ *021/713–2222,* FAX *021/713–2221,* WEB *www.steenberg.com. 23 rooms, 1 suite. Restaurant, bar, 2 pools, hair salon, 18-hole golf course. AE, DC, MC, V. BP.*

$$$$ ✕🏠 **The Vineyard.** Set in 6 acres of rolling gardens overlooking the Lies-
★ beek River in residential Newlands, this comfortable hotel was built around the 18th-century weekend home of Lady Anne Barnard. The lobby is paved in worn terra-cotta tiles and revolves around the leafy breakfast room. The views of the back of Table Mountain are spectacular, but at a better rate, a courtyard-facing room offers views of a veritable rain forest growing amid gurgling waters. The hotel is 10 minutes by car from the city but within walking distance of the Newlands sports arenas and the shops of Cavendish Square. Au Jardin, the classic French restaurant, is very well regarded. ⊠ *Colinton Rd. (Box 151), Newlands 7725,* ☎ *021/683–3044,* FAX *021/683–3365,* WEB *www.vineyard.co.za. 160 rooms. 2 restaurants, bar, room service, pool, gym. AE, DC, MC, V.*

$$$–$$$$ 🏠 **Alphen Hotel.** Built sometime between 1750 and 1770 in Cape Dutch style, the former manor house is now a national monument and one of the Cape's historic treasures. The owners are descendants of the distinguished Cloete family, which has farmed the land around Constantia since 1750. Cloete paintings and antiques, each with a story to tell, adorn the public rooms. Rooms range in size from compact to rather large. A small drawback is the slight traffic noise from the nearby highway in rush hour. Only luxury rooms have air-conditioning. ⊠ *Alphen Dr. (Box 35), Constantia 7848,* ☎ *021/794–5011,* FAX *021/794–5710,* WEB *www.alphen.co.za. 34 rooms. Restaurant, bar, room service, pool. AE, DC, MC, V. BP.*

$$ 🏠 **Koornhoop Manor Guest House.** This is one of the best values in Cape Town. A lovely Victorian house set in a pretty garden, Koornhoop is best described as extremely nice and totally unpretentious. The rooms, which vary in size, are simply decorated in pretty florals, and all have private bath and tea and coffee stations. The hotel is very central and is within safe walking distance of a huge range of restaurants in the vibey young suburb of Observatory, five minutes' drive from the city and convenient to the railway station. A communal TV room with an honor bar is a convivial meeting place. You need to book quite far in advance to take advantage of this little gem. ⊠ *Wrench and Nuttal Rds., Observatory 7925,* ☎ FAX *021/448–0595,* WEB *www.geocities.com/ koornhoop. 8 rooms, 1 three-bedroom apartment. No credit cards. BP.*

$$ 🏠 **Palm House.** Towering palms dominate the manicured lawns of this peaceful guest house straddling the border of Kenilworth and Wynberg, a 15-minute drive from the city. The house is an enormous, stolid affair, built in the early 1920s by a protégé of Sir Herbert Baker and filled with dark-wood paneling, wood staircases, and fireplaces. Guest rooms are large and decorated with bold floral fabrics and reproduction antiques. Upstairs rooms benefit from more air and light. Guests often meet for evening drinks in the drawing room. ⊠ *10 Oxford St., Wynberg*

7800, ☎ 021/761–5009, FAX 021/761–8776, WEB *www.thepalmhouse. co.za. 10 rooms. Bar, pool. AE, DC, MC, V. BP.*

False Bay

$$$ 🏨 **Quayside Lodge.** This limited-service hotel has wonderful views over Simon's Bay, the harbor, and the yacht club. On Jubilee Square, part of the newly built Simonstown Waterfront, it's right in the action. Only five rooms are not sea facing, and all are light and airy, combining lime-washed wood with white walls and pale blue finishes. "Room service" can be arranged from the adjacent Bertha's restaurant or coffee shop. ⊠ *Jubilee Sq., Main Rd., Simonstown,* ☎ 021/786–3838, FAX 021/786–2241, WEB *www.quayside.co.za. 25 rooms, 3 suites. AE, DC, MC, V. BP.*

$–$$ 🏨 **Boulders Beach Guesthouse.** Positioned just a few steps from the beautiful Boulders Beach—the best swimming beach in Cape Town— this comfortable guest house is a winner. The understated rooms are decorated with elegant black wrought-iron furniture and snow-white linens, creating a restful, minimalist feel. The adjacent restaurant and pub are a bit more boisterous. ⊠ *4 Boulders Pl., Boulders, Simonstown 7975,* ☎ 021/786–1758, FAX 021/786–1826, WEB *www.bouldersbeach. co.za. 13 rooms. Restaurant, bar. AE, DC, MC, V. BP.*

NIGHTLIFE AND THE ARTS

Although *SA City Life* also lists events in Durban and Johannesburg, along with *Cape Review,* it's the best monthly roundup of entertainment in Cape Town. For weekly updates try "Friday," the entertainment supplement of the *Mail & Guardian,* or the "Top of the Times" in Friday's *Cape Times.* Both are informed, opinionated, and up-to-date. The *Argus* newspaper's "Tonight" section gives you a complete daily listing of what's on, plus contact numbers. Tickets for almost every cultural and sporting event in the country (including movies) can be purchased through **Computicket** (☎ 083/909–0909). Cape Town is a very gay-friendly city. For information on the gay scene, contact **Africa Outing** (☎ 021/671–4028 or 083/273–8422, WEB www.afouting.com).

The Arts

The **Artscape** (⊠ D. F. Malan St., Foreshore, ☎ 021/421–7839 for inquiries; 021/421–7695 for bookings; 083/909–0909 for Computicket, WEB www.artscape.co.za), a huge and unattractive theater complex, is the hub for performing arts and other cultural activities. Cape Town City Ballet and the Cape Town Philharmonic Orchestra, as well as the city's theater and opera companies, make their homes in the center's three theaters. Since 1994 there's been a conscious effort throughout the country to make the performing arts more representative and multicultural. The formerly Eurocentric emphasis has subsided, and today there's a palpable African-arts excitement in the air. Classics are still well represented, as are the latest contemporary worldwide trends. During summer, when the weather's good, Cape Town has its own version of New York City's Central Park's Shakespeare in the Park at the excellent **Maynardville Open-Air Theatre,** in Wynberg. Booking is through Computicket (☎ 083/909–0909). Theatergoers often bring a picnic supper to enjoy before the show.

Classical Music

The **Cape Town Philharmonic Orchestra,** alternates performing at city hall and at the Artscape Theatre Center. The **Spier Summer Festival** held at the Spier Winery and Hotel in the Winelands takes place between November and February, has a varied program, and performances are held under the stars in an amphitheater at the Spier Wine Estate. You can take Spier's own vintage steam train out to the estate, wine and dine at one of the three restaurants or have a picnic dinner prepared by the estate, then enjoy the show, and return to Cape Town on the train. And in October the attractive village of Franschhoek in the Winelands hosts the Fête de la Musique, featuring many visiting artists, most of them from France. As part of its program to introduce classical music to the general public, the Philharmonic Orchestra also stages a series of lunchtime concerts in the foyer of the Nico complex. Far more exciting, though, would be to watch the orchestra at one of its two appearances at the Kirstenbosch Gardens open-air concerts. They usually do the first and last concerts of the season. The orchestra has hosted several guest conductors from Europe and the United States and has an active program, which includes a summer program of free concerts at the outdoor AGFA Amphitheatre, at the waterfront.

Film

Ster-Kinekor and Nu Metro screen mainstream movies at cinema complexes all over the city. The waterfront alone has two movie houses with 16 screens altogether, which gives you a huge choice. Check newspaper listings for what's playing. At Cavendish Square and the waterfront, the Cinema Nouveau concentrates on showing foreign and art films.

IMAX Cinema (⊠ BMW Pavilion, Waterfront, ☎ 021/419–7365, WEB www.imax.co.za), with a giant, nearly hemispherical, five-story screen and six-channel wraparound sound, makes viewers feel as if they're participating in the filmed event. Movies usually concentrate more on visuals than story line, such as wildlife, extreme sports, underwater marine life, or even rock concerts.

The **Labia** (⊠ 68 Orange St., Gardens, ☎ 021/424–5927, WEB www.labia.co.za) is an independent art house that screens quality mainstream and alternative films, including the works of some of the best European filmmakers. There are four screens. A small coffee bar serves snacks.

Theater

The **Baxter Theatre Complex** (⊠ Main Rd., Rondebosch, ☎ 021/685–7880, WEB www.baxter.co.za) is part of the University of Cape Town and has a reputation for producing serious drama and wacky comedies, as well as some rather experimental stuff. The complex features a 657-seat theater, a concert hall, a smaller studio, and a restaurant and bar.

Nightlife

The city's nightlife is concentrated in the revitalized harbor. You can always find something to do at the front, given that there's more than a dozen cinema screens, 40 restaurants, and 10 bars from which to choose. The rest of the city center, except for isolated restaurants and bars, empties out after business hours, and lone couples may not feel safe walking these deserted streets at night. The big exception is the few square blocks around the intersection of Long and Orange streets, which have become a cauldron of youth-oriented nightclubs, bars, and restaurants. Even here, though, exercise caution late at night. Sea Point, once a major after-dark scene, has lost much of its business to the waterfront. Depending on your outlook, however, you might relish the opportunity to visit here and see a bit of contemporary black South African culture and partake in some good music and nightlife.

Bars and Pubs

The **Perseverance Tavern** (✉ 83 Buitenkant St., Gardens, ☎ 021/461–2440), which dates to 1836, claims to be the oldest tavern in the city. The facade has been beautifully restored, but you may feel claustrophobic in the small, interconnected rooms; the clientele here is pretty rowdy. The popular **Obz Cafe** (✉ 115 Lower Main Rd., Observatory, ☎ 021/448–5555) is a big and funky bar/café with excellent coffee, good food, and cocktails. **Long Street Cafe** (✉ 259 Long St., ☎ 021/424–2464) is a favorite with locals, serving up light tasty dishes, coffee, and, of course, cocktails.

The **Sports Café** (✉ Victoria Wharf, Waterfront, ☎ 021/419–5558) is a huge place with large-screen TVs. The bar gets into the spirit of major foreign sporting events like the Super Bowl and the FA Cup Final (England's soccer championship) and is undoubtedly the best place to watch sports in the city. **Quay Four** (✉ Quay 4, ☎ 021/419–2008), also at the waterfront, is big with the after-work suit-and-tie brigade, which clogs picnic tables on the wooden deck overlooking the harbor. **Ferryman's** (✉ Dock Rd., V&A Waterfront, ☎ 021/419–7748) has a roaring fire inside on winter nights in addition to an outdoor deck area and a suit-and-tie crowd. The restrained but fairly funky crowd leans toward **Cafe Erte** (✉ 265 Main Rd., Three Anchor Bay, ☎ 021/434–6624), which is very gay-friendly.

Clubs

Nightclubs in Cape Town change faster than the weather. The area bounded by Loop, Long, Wale, and Orange streets is the best place to get a feeling for what's going on in town. An old diehard is **Corner House** (✉ Glynn and Canterbury Sts., ☎ no phone), which plays music from the 1980s onward.

For clubs with live music your best bet is **Mama Africa** (✉ Long St., ☎ 021/424–8634), with live music Monday through Saturday and usually a marimba band on Wednesday night and authentic African food, authentic African music, and authentic African pulse. Probably the best spot in town is the **Drum Cafe** (✉ Glynn St., ☎ 021/461–1305), which has live performances by percussionists from all over Africa. On Wednesday there is a drum circle and on Monday a women's drum circle (men are welcome but may not drum).

Jazz

Many of the mainstream jazz clubs in the city double as restaurants. Cover charges range from R15 to R30. The **Green Dolphin Jazz Restaurant** (✉ Waterfront, ☎ 021/421–7471) attracts some of the best mainstream musicians in the country as well as a few from overseas. The cover charge is R15–R20. **Winchester Mansions Hotel** (✉ Beach Rd., Sea Point, ☎ 021/434–2351) does a mellow Sunday brunch in the courtyard for about R110 with some of the city's best jazz musicians livening the scene. Other than the above, the hot venues change so quickly, it's best to get info when you're here. Cape Town Tourism has a list of good jazz venues and attempts to keep up with the frequent changes.

OUTDOOR ACTIVITIES AND SPORTS

Cape Town is the adventure capital of the universe. Whatever you want to do—dive, paddle, fly, jump, run, slide, fin, walk, or clamber—this is the city to do it in. **Adventure Village** (☎ 021/424–1580, WEB www.adventure-village.co.za) books a range of activities from its offices at the top of Long Street, which it shares with Abseil Africa. **African Adventure Travel Centre** (☎ 021/424–1037, WEB www.abisa.co.za) is a multiactivity center in Long Street that offers general travel advice, a bureau de change, Internet café, and adventure booking.

Participant Sports

Abseiling (Rappelling)

Abseil Africa (☎ 021/424–1580, WEB www.adventure-village.co.za) offers a 350-ft abseil off the top of Table Mountain for about R200, not including cable car, and over a waterfall in the mountains about an hour's drive away for about R400–R450, including transportation and lunch.

Aerobatic Flight

To fly upside down in an aerobatic plane, contact **Air Combat Cape Town** (☎ 083/462–0570). Costs range from about R800 to R1,000.

Climbing

Cape Town has hundreds of bolted sport routes around the city and peninsula, ranging from an easy 10 to a hectic 30. Both Table Mountain Sandstone and Cape Granite are excellent hard rocks. There are route guides to all the major climbs and a number of climbing schools in Cape Town. **Cape Town School of Mountaineering** (☎ 021/671–9604) operate from Orca Industries, a diving and climbing shop in Claremont. The **Leading Edge** (☎ 021/715–3999 or 083/309–1554) offers climbing and hiking training and escorted trips in both disciplines. **High Adventure** (☎ 021/447–8036) specializes in climbing in the Cape Town area.

Diving

The diving around the Cape is excellent, with kelp forests, cold-water corals, very brightly colored reef life, and numerous wrecks. An unusual experience is a dive in the Two Oceans Aquarium. CMAS, NAUI, and PADI dive courses are offered by local operators, beginning at about R1,500. **Iain's Scuba School** (☎ 021/439–9322 or 082/894–6054) is a good choice for a dive course. **Underwater World** (☎ 021/461–8290) is a dive shop in the city that also offers courses. **Orca Industries** (☎ 021/671–9673) is based in Claremont and offers dive courses and charters. **Farside Adventures** (☎ 021/786–2599), in Simonstown, is conveniently based for False Bay Diving.

Fly-Fishing

You will find no captive-bred, corn-fed trout lurking in sluggish dams near Cape Town. But in the mountains, just an hour or so away, you'll encounter wild and wily fish in wild and wonderful rivers. The season runs from September 1 to May 31. **Ultimate Angling** (☎ 083/626–0467 or 021/686–6877) offers escorted tours, all the equipment you'll need, and advice.

Golf

Most golf clubs in the Cape accept visitors, but prior booking is essential. Expect to pay R250–R350 for 18 holes and between R120 and R250 per game to rent golf clubs. Most clubs offer equipment rental. The Winelands in particular have some spectacular courses. **Clovelly Country Club** (⊠ Clovelly Rd., Clovelly, ☎ 021/782–6410), near Fish Hoek, is a tight course that requires masterful shot placement from tee to green. **Milnerton Golf Club** (⊠ Bridge Rd., Milnerton, ☎ 021/552–1047), sandwiched between the sea and a lagoon, is the Western Cape's only links course and can be difficult when the wind blows. **Mowbray Golf Club** (⊠ Raapenberg Rd., Mowbray, ☎ 021/685–3018), with its great views of Devil's Peak, is a magnificent parkland course that has hosted several major tournaments; there are a number of interesting water holes. Unfortunately, noise from the highway can spoil the atmosphere. Founded in 1885, **Royal Cape Golf Club** (⊠ Ottery Rd., Wyn-

berg, ☏ 021/761–6551) is the oldest course in Africa and has hosted
the South African Open many times. Its beautiful setting and immaculate fairways and greens make a round here a must for visitors. The
club does not rent equipment. The challenging and scenic **Steenberg
Golf Estate** (✉ Steenberg and Tokai Rds., Tokai, ☏ 021/713–1632) is
the most exclusive and expensive course on the peninsula. A game costs
more than R400 per person unless you're staying in the hotel. Dress
codes are strictly enforced here.

Hiking and Kloofing (Canyoning)

Cape Town and the surrounding areas offer some of the finest hiking
in the world, mostly through the spectacularly beautiful mountains. Kloofing, known as canyoning in the United States, is the practice of following
a mountain stream through its gorge, canyon, or kloof by swimming,
rock hopping, and jumping over waterfalls or cliffs into deep pools. There
are some exceptional kloofing venues in the Cape. **Abseil Africa** (☏ 021/
424–1580, WEB www.adventure-village.co.za) runs a kloofing and abseiling trip on the Steenbras River, better known as Kamakaze Kanyon.
Cape Eco Trails (☏ 021/785–5511, WEB www.capetrails.com) has various escorted hikes. There is a fantastic overnight hiking trail in the Cape
Point section of **Cape Peninsula National Park** (☏ 011/780–9526), but
you need to book ahead. You can do a sort of pseudo-overnight hike
on Table Mountain. **Silvermist Mountain Lodge** (☏ 021/794–7601, WEB
www.SilvermistMountainLodge.com) can arrange to shuttle you between
the Lower Cable Station and the lodge in Constantia—about four–six
hours' walk from the Upper Cable Station. You could then spend a comfortable night in one of the cottages with full kitchens at the lodge and
walk farther the next day if you like.

Horseback Riding

Sleepy Hollow Horse Riding (☏ FAX 021/789–2341) offers 1½- and two-
hour rides down Long Beach, a 6-km (4-mi) expanse of sand that
stretches from Noordhoek Beach to Kommetjie.

Sea Kayaking

Coastal Kayak Trails (☏ 021/439–1134, WEB www.kayak.co.za) has regular sunset and sunrise paddles off Sea Point. **Sea Kayaking Unlimited**
(☏ 021/424–8114, WEB www.faceadrenalin.com) offers regular scenic
paddles off Hout Bay to Seal Island and below Chapman's Peak.

Skydiving

You can do a tandem sky dive (no experience necessary) and have your
photograph taken hurtling earthward with Table Mountain in the
background with **Cape Parachute Club** (☏ 082/800–6290).

Spectator Sports

It's easy to get tickets for ordinary club matches and for interprovin-
cial games. Getting tickets to an international test match is more of a
challenge; however, there's always somebody selling tickets—at a price,
of course.

Cricket and Rugby

The huge sporting complex off Boundary Road in Newlands is the home
of the **Western Province Cricket Union** (☏ 021/683–6420). The **Western Province Rugby Football Union** (✉ Newlands, ☏ 021/689–4921)
also has its headquarters at Newlands. Next door to the Newlands sporting complex, in the South African Sports Science Institute, is the **SA
Rugby Museum** (☏ 021/685–3038), open weekdays 9–4.

Soccer

Soccer in South Africa is much more grassroots than cricket or rugby
and is very big in the townships. Amateur games are played from

March to September at many venues all over the peninsula. Professional games are played from October to April at Greenpoint Stadium, Athlone Stadium, and Newlands. Watch the press for details.

SHOPPING

A number of stores in Cape Town sell African art and crafts, much of which comes from Zululand or neighboring countries. Street vendors, particularly on St. George's Mall and Greenmarket Square, often sell the same curios for half the price.

Markets

Greenmarket Square. You can get good buys on clothing, T-shirts, hand-crafted silver jewelry, and locally made leather shoes and sandals. It's lively and fun whether or not you buy anything. ⊙ *Mon.–Sat. 9–4:30.*

Waterfront Trading Company. In this indoor market more than 140 artists show their work, an assortment of handcrafted jewelry, rugs, glass, pottery, and leather shoes and sandals. ⊠ *Waterfront,* ☎ *021/408–7842.* ⊙ *Daily 9:30–6.*

Specialty Stores

AFRICAN ART

African Image. Look here for traditional and contemporary African art and curios, colorful cloth from Nigeria and Ghana, plus West African masks, Malian blankets, and beaded designs from southern African tribes. A variety of Zulu baskets are also available at moderate prices. ⊠ *Burg and Church Sts.,* ☎ FAX *021/423–8385.* ⊙ *Weekdays 8:45–5, Sat. 9–1:30.*

The Pan-African Market. The market extends over two floors of a huge building and is a jumble of tiny stalls, traditional African hairdressers and tailors, potters, artists, musicians, and drummers. There is also a small, very African restaurant. If you're not going to visit countries to the north, go here. You'll get an idea of what you're missing. ⊠ *76 Long St.,* ☎ *021/426–4478.* ⊙ *Weekdays 9–5, Sat. 9–3.*

AFRICAN CLOTHING AND FABRICS

Mnandi Textiles. Here you'll find a range of African fabrics, including traditional West African prints and Dutch wax prints. The store sells ready-made African clothing for adults and children. You can also have items made to order. ⊠ *90 Station Rd.,* ☎ *021/447–6814,* FAX *021/447–7937.* ⊙ *Weekdays 9–5, Sat. 9–1.*

N.C.M. Fashions–African Pride. This is the place to go for traditional clothing from all over Africa. One of the most striking outfits is the brightly colored *bubu,* a loose-fitting garment with a matching head wrap, or try a traditional Xhosa outfit, complete with braiding, beads, and a multilayer wraparound skirt. You can buy off the rack or order a custom outfit from a wide selection of fabrics. ⊠ *173 Main Rd., Claremont,* ☎ *021/683–1022.* ⊙ *Weekdays 9–5:30, Sat. 9–1:30.*

BOOKS

Clarke's Bookshop. A local favorite, you'll find a fantastic collection of Africana books here as well as a good selection of antiquarian titles and some esoterica. ⊠ *211 Long St.,* ☎ *021/423–5739.* ⊙ *Weekdays 9–5, Sat. 9–1.*

Exclusive Books. This is one of the best all-around bookshops in the country. The chain carries a wide selection of local and international periodicals and coffee-table books on Africa. An integrated coffee bar allows you to browse at a comfortable table with an espresso or cappuccino. Be prepared, though, to pay at least twice as much for books here as you would in the United States or Britain. ⊠ *Shop 225, Victoria Wharf, Waterfront,* ☎ *021/419–0905.* ☉ *Mon.–Thurs. 9 AM–10:30 PM, Fri.–Sat. 9 AM–11 PM, Sun. 10–9.* ⊠ *Lower Mall, Cavendish Sq., Claremont,* ☎ *021/674–3030.* ☉ *Mon.–Thurs. 9–9, Fri.–Sat. 9 AM– 11 PM, Sun. 10–9.*

CAPE TOWN A TO Z

To research prices, get advice from other travelers, and book travel arrangements, visit www.fodors.com.

AIR TRAVEL

Cape Town International Airport, lies 22½ km (14 mi) southeast of the city in the Cape Flats. The airport is tiny: the domestic and international terminals are no more than 200 yards apart. In addition to a VAT refund office, there is a Western Cape Tourism Board booth with an accommodations hot line, open daily 7–5, that provides information on guest houses around the city. Trust Bank exchanges money weekdays 9–3:30 and Saturday 8:30–10:30; it stays open later for international arrivals and departures.

International carriers flying into Cape Town include Air Namibia, British Airways, Lufthansa, and South African Airways. The major domestic carriers serving Cape Town are British Airways/Comair, Sabena/Nationwide, and South African Airways, SA Airlink, and SA Express.
➤ AIRLINES AND CONTACTS: **Cape Town International Airport** (☎ 021/ 934–0407). **Air Namibia** (☎ 021/936–2755). **British Airways** (☎ 086/ 001–1747). **British Airways/Comair** (☎ 086/001–1747). **Lufthansa** (☎ 086/057–2573, WEB www.lufthansa.com). **Sabena/Nationwide** (☎ 021/ 936–2050, WEB www.flynationwide.com). **South African Airways, SA Airlink,** and **SA Express** (☎ 021/936–1111, WEB www.flysaa.com).

AIRPORT TRANSFERS

You'll need to call a shuttle from the airport if you'd like one, as there are no scheduled shuttles from Cape Town Airport. A trip between the airport and the city center costs between R60 and R150, depending on direction and number of passengers. Or travel in comfort in a stretch limo from Cape Limo Services for about R700 per hour, with a minimum of an hour and a half, or R350–R400 per hour for longer trips.
➤ TAXIS AND SHUTTLES: **Cape Limo Services** (☎ 021/785–3100). **Gary's Shuttles** (☎ 021/426–1641). **Magic Bus** (☎ 021/510–6001).

BUS TRAVEL

Greyhound offers daily overnight service to Johannesburg and Pretoria. Intercape Mainliner operates a far more extensive network of routes in the Western Cape than does Greyhound, with daily service up the N7 to Springbok and Windhoek, along the Garden Route to George and Port Elizabeth; a bus also travels daily to Johannesburg. Both Intercape and Greyhound can be booked through Computicket. The Baz Bus offers a service aimed mostly at backpackers who don't want to travel vast distances in one day and don't have transportation to get to train or bus stations. It's a hop-on/hop-off service that is more expensive than the straight bus but so much more convenient—especially if you're planning a long trip in short stages.

Overnight service one-way to Johannesburg and Pretoria is about R375–R450. Cape Town to Springbok is about R240–R280 and Cape Town to Windhoek about R380–R450. It's about R120–R160 to

George and R400–R450 to Durban. The Baz Bus hop-on/hop-off trip to Durban is about R930–R1,000 and is valid for about a year.

➤ BUS INFORMATION: **Baz Bus** (☎ 021/439–2323, FAX 021/439–2343, WEB www.bazbus.co.za). **Greyhound** (✉ 1 Adderley St., ☎ 021/418–4310; 083/909–0909 for Computicket, WEB www.greyhound.co.za). **Intercape Mainliner** (✉ 1 Adderley St., ☎ 021/386–4400; 083/909–0909 for Computicket, WEB www.intercape.co.za). **Translux Express Bus** (✉ 1 Adderley St., ☎ 021/449–3333).

BUS TRAVEL WITHIN CAPE TOWN

The only bus that visitors are likely to use is the waterfront shuttle, as all the others are very slow and infrequent. It runs about every 10 minutes and costs about R4. You will also see local minibus taxis tearing around town at high speed, stuffed to capacity with hapless commuters. These buses ply routes all over the city and suburbs, but you can flag them down anywhere along the way. The depot is above the train station. For the modest fare of R5–R10 you'll have an opportunity to experience some local atmosphere and incidentally get to where you're going quite efficiently—although far from elegantly.

CAR RENTAL

Most large car-rental agencies have offices in the city and at the airport and offer similar rates; expect to pay through the nose if you rent by the day. A Nissan Sentra or Toyota Corolla with a radio and tape player, automatic transmission, and air-conditioning costs about R220–R350 per day including 200 km (120 mi), plus R2.50–R3.00 for each additional kilometer. A no-frills Volkswagen Golf or Opel Corsa will cost you about R150–R200 per day, also including 200 km (120 mi), plus R1.05–R2.00 for each additional kilometer—these cars have manual transmission, so you'll have to be happy shifting gears. If you rent for five days or more, you could get unlimited kilometers. The quoted prices include insurance that covers 75%–90% of liability costs, but you can pay extra for 100% coverage. Among the major rental agencies in Cape Town proper are Avis, Budget, Europcar, and Hertz.

➤ MAJOR AGENCIES: **Avis** (✉ 123 Strand St., ☎ 021/424–1177; 021/934–0808 at the airport; 0800/002–1111 toll-free, WEB www.avis.co.za). **Budget** (✉ 120 Strand St., ☎ 021/418–5232; 021/934–0216 at the airport, WEB www.budget.co.za). **Europcar** (☎ 021/418–0670, WEB www.europcar.co.za). **Hertz** (✉ 40 Loop St., ☎ 021/425–8251, WEB www.hertz.co.za).

CAR TRAVEL

Parking in the city center can be a hassle. Parking spaces are so scarce that most hotels charge extra for the service, and even then you won't be guaranteed a space. You can usually find parking out on the Pay and Display lots on Buitengracht Street or on the Grand Parade. Wherever you park, you will be accosted by an informal (or semiformal) parking attendant. It's a good idea to pay him a rand in advance and then another rand or two if you return to find your car safe. The Sanlam Golden Acre Parking Garage, on Adderley Street, offers covered parking, as does the Parkade, on Strand Street.

The main arteries leading out of the city are the N1, which runs to Paarl and, ultimately, Johannesburg; and the N2, which heads to the Overberg, the Garden Route, Eastern Cape, and, ultimately, Durban. The N7 goes up to Namibia and leads off the N1. The M3 (colloquially and rather loosely referred to as the Top Highway, the Top Freeway, or the Blue Route) leads to Constantia, Muizenberg, and the small towns of the peninsula; it splits from the N2 just after Groote Schuur Hospital, in the shadow of Devil's Peak.

EMBASSIES AND CONSULATES

➤ AUSTRALIA: **Australian High Commission** (✉ Thibault Sq., BP Centre, 14th floor, ☎ 021/419–5425, FAX 021/419–7345).

➤ CANADA: **Canadian High Commission** (✉ Reserve Bank Bldg., 19th floor, St. George's Mall, ☎ 021/423–5240, FAX 021/423–4893).

➤ UNITED KINGDOM: **British Consulate** (✉ 8 Riebeeck St., ☎ 021/405–2400).

➤ UNITED STATES: **U.S. Consulate** (✉ Broadway Bldg., Heerengracht [bottom of Adderley St.], ☎ 021/421–4280, FAX 021/425–4151, WEB www.usembassy.state.gov/southafrica).

EMERGENCIES

The police operate a Tourist Assistance Unit for foreign visitors who are robbed or experience other trouble. The unit can provide translators and will help you contact your embassy or consulate if need be.

Although public hospital emergency rooms do offer good service, they are hopelessly understaffed and underfunded and have to deal with a huge number of local people, most of whom cannot afford any alternative. As a visitor you should contact one of the private clinics; make sure that you have overseas medical insurance that's good in southern Africa before you leave home.

➤ EMERGENCY SERVICES: **Ambulance** (☎ 10177). **Police** (☎ 10111). **Tourist Assistance Unit** (✉ Tulbagh Sq., ☎ 021/421–5115).

➤ HOSPITALS: **City Park Hospital** (✉ 181 Longmarket St., ☎ 021/480–6111). **Claremont Hospital;** ✉ Harfield and Main Rds., Claremont, ☎ 021/670–4300). **Constantiaberg Medi-clinic** (✉ Boundary Rd., Diep River, ☎ 021/799–2911). **Newlands Surgical Clinic** (✉ Pick and Pay Center, corner Main Rd. and Keurboom Rd., Claremont, ☎ 021/683–1220). **Panorama Medi-clinic** (✉ Rothchild Blvd., Panorama, ☎ 021/938–2111).

MONEY MATTERS

CURRENCY EXCHANGE

Don't even think about changing money at your hotel. The rates at most hotels are outrageous, and the city center is swamped with banks and bureaux de change that give much better rates. American Express's downtown office is open weekdays 8:30–5 and Saturday 9–noon; at the waterfront, weekdays 9–7 and weekends 9–5. Rennies Travel's downtown office is open weekdays 8:30–5 and Saturday 9–noon. The waterfront location is open until 9 daily.

➤ EXCHANGE SERVICES: **American Express** (✉ Thibault Sq., ☎ 021/408–9700; ✉ Shop 11A, Alfred Mall, ☎ 021/419–3917, WEB www.amex.co.za). **Rennies Travel**'s (✉ 2 St. George's Mall, ☎ 021/418–1206; ✉ Upper Level, Victoria Wharf, Waterfront, ☎ 021/418–3744).

TAXIS

Taxis are metered and reasonably priced and offer an easy, quick way to get around a city where parking is such trouble. Don't expect to see the throngs of cabs you find in London or New York. You may be lucky enough to hail one on the street, but your best bet is to summon one by phone or head to a major taxi stand—Greenmarket Square and the top and bottom (opposite the station) of Adderley Street. Sea Point Taxis, probably the most reliable of the companies, starts the meter at R2 and charges R7 per kilometer. Waiting time is charged at about R50 an hour. Another reputable company is Marine Taxis. Expect to pay R40–R60 for a trip from the city center to the waterfront.

➤ TAXI COMPANIES: **Marine Taxis** (☎ 021/434–0434). Another reputable company is **Sea Point Taxis** (☎ 021/434–4444).

TOURS

A host of companies offer guided tours of the city, the peninsula, the Winelands, and anyplace else in the Cape you might wish to visit. Hylton Ross, Classic Cape Tours, Mother City Tours, Welcome Tours and Safaris, and Springbok Atlas offer bus tours of all the major attractions in the Cape Town area. Prices range from about R180–R200 for a half-day trip to about R300–R350 for a full-day tour. If you're a little more adventurous, you may prefer an outing with Ferdinand's Tours—somewhat less staid than the run-of-the-mill tour. It does an excellent wine route trip that includes a visit to a shebeen (an unlicensed drinking establishment) as a contrast. An even more adventurous tour would be a bike/bus tour with the Baz Bus—it does the usual peninsula route with a trailer of bikes—you cycle the fun parts and sit in the bus for the in-between bits. If you're tired, you can just opt out of the cycling. It costs about R200.

Muse-Art Journeys conducts fascinating tours covering the cultural life of Cape Town, including art, music, crafts, and architecture. The graffiti tour is a real eye-opener and includes an introduction to hip-hop art and music. The cost is about R160.

➤ CONTACTS: **Baz Bus** (☎ 021/439–2323, FAX 021/439–2343, WEB www.bazbus.com). **Classic Cape Tours** (☎ 021/686–6310, FAX 021/686–9216, WEB www.classiccape.co.za). **Ferdinand's Tours** (☎ 021/465–8550 or 083/462–0425, FAX 021/448–0003, WEB www.ferdinandstours.co.za). **Hylton Ross Tours** (☎ 021/511–1784, FAX 021/511–2401, WEB www.hyltonross.co.za). **Mother City Tours** (☎ 021/448–3817, FAX 021/448–3844, WEB www.mctours.co.za). **Muse-Art Journeys** (☎ 021/919–9168). **Springbok Atlas** (☎ 021/460–4700, WEB www.springbokatlas.com). **Welcome Tours & Safaris** (☎ 021/510–6001, FAX 021/510–6023, WEB www.welcome.co.za).

BOAT TOURS

Until the middle of the 20th century most travelers' first glimpse of Cape Town was from the sea, and that's still the best way to get a feeling for the city, with its famous mountain as a backdrop. Waterfront Charters offers a range of boats, ranging from sailing boats to large motor boats, and operates out of the Waterfront. A sunset cruise costs about R100. Drumbeat Charters does regular Seal Island trips that last about 40 minutes and cost about R35–R50. Tigger Too concentrates on more comfortable trips for smaller groups out of Hout Bay. It offers a lunch cruise (four hours, including three-course meal) for R370–R400 and a sunset cruise with snacks and sparkling wine for R155–R170.

Boat trips to Robben Island don't actually land on the famous island. If you want to tour the island where Nelson Mandela spent a good chunk of his life, you need to organize a tour through the Robben Island Museum.

➤ FEES AND SCHEDULES: **Drum Beat Charters** (☎ 021/438–9208). *Tigger Too* **Charters** (☎ 021/790–5256, WEB www.tiggertoo.co.za). **Waterfront Charters** (☎ 021/418–0134, WEB www.waterfrontcharters.co.za).

HELICOPTER TOURS

Court Helicopters and Civair Helicopters offer tours of the city and surrounding area ranging in length from 20 minutes to several hours. Custom tours can be arranged.

➤ FEES AND SCHEDULES: **CHC Helicopters (Africa)** (✉ Waterfront, ☎ 021/425–2966). **Civair Helicopters** (✉ Waterfront, ☎ 021/419–5182, WEB www.civair.co.za).

WALKING TOURS

Legend Tours offers Walk to Freedom tours that cover District Six, Bo-Kaap, the townships, and Robben Island. The well-informed guides lead the tours, casting a strong historical and political emphasis.

➤ FEES AND SCHEDULES: **Legend Tours** (☎ 021/697–4056, ℻ 021/697–4090, 🕸 www.legendtourism.co.za).

TRAIN TRAVEL

Cape Town's train station is in the heart of the city, and there are a number of trains that operate from the station, including the *Trans-Karoo, Southern Cross* (which is a night ride, so forget about seeing the splendors of the Garden Route), the *Union Limited Steam Train,* the luxury *Blue Train,* and the luxurious *Rovos Rail Pride of Africa,* which also travels from Cape Town to Johannesburg and up the Garden Route.

Cape Metro is Cape Town's commuter line and offers regular but infrequent service to the southern suburbs and the towns on the False Bay side of the peninsula, including Muizenberg, St. James, Kalk Bay, Fish Hoek, and Simonstown.

All trains depart from Cape Town station on Adderley Street. Cape Metro also serves Paarl, Stellenbosch, and Somerset West, in the Winelands.

If you travel on the Metro train during off-peak periods, choose as crowded a compartment as you can, and be alert to your surroundings when the train is stopped at a station, as agile young bag-snatchers can slip in and out pretty quickly and target "dreamy" passengers or those engrossed in a book. Strange as it sounds, you may be safer standing in a cramped third-class carriage than sitting comfortably in splendid isolation in an empty first-class one.

FARES AND SCHEDULES

Mainline Passenger Services' *Trans-Karoo* runs daily between Cape Town and Johannesburg; the trip takes about 25 hours and costs about R400 first-class. The *Southern Cross* makes the 24-hour trip to Port Elizabeth on Friday and back on Sunday (R235 first-class). The *Blue Train* (☞ Train Travel *in* Smart Travel Tips A to Z) makes the Cape Town–Johannesburg run three times per week and the Cape Town–Port Elizabeth run once a month. Depending on the compartment, time of year, and route, the trip can cost anywhere between R4,000 and R20,000. The Rovos Rail trip from Cape Town to Pretoria costs between R7,500 and R1,000. The Cape Metro trip to False Bay takes 45–60 minutes and costs about R20 for a one-way first-class ticket. The trains do not run after 7 PM during the week or after about 2 PM on Saturday. There is one train an hour between about 7:30 and 11 and between 3:30 and 7:30 on Sunday.

➤ TRAIN INFORMATION: *Blue Train* (☎ 021/449–2672, 🕸 www.bluetrain.co.za). **Cape Metro** (☎ 080/065–6463). **Cape Town train station** (✉ Cape Town station, Adderley St., ☎ 021/449–3871). *Rovos Rail Pride of Africa* (☎ 021/421–4020, 🕸 www.rovos.co.za).

RESERVATIONS

The reservations office at the Cape Town station is open Monday–Thursday 8–4:30, Friday 8–4, and Saturday 8–noon.

TRANSPORTATION AROUND CAPE TOWN

If you confine yourself to the city center, you won't need a car—in fact, the shortage of parking spaces makes having a car in the city a nightmare. A rental car is your only feasible option, however, if you want to explore the peninsula or the Winelands and are not on a guided tour. Another fun and practical option is to rent a scooter (which eliminates parking problems) from African Buzz, on Long Street, for R160–R200 per day for unlimited kilometers, or a motorcycle from Mitaka, in Sea

Point, for R350–R450 per day, which includes 300 km (180 mi) (thereafter, about R1 per kilometer).

➤ MOTORCYCLE/SCOOTER RENTAL: **African Buzz** (☎ 021/423–0052, FAX 021/423–0056). **Mitaka** (☎ 021/439–6036, WEB www.mitaka.co.za).

VISITOR INFORMATION

Cape Town Tourism is the city's official tourist body and offers information on tours, hotels, restaurants, rental cars, and shops. It also has a coffee shop, wine shop, and Internet café. The staff also makes hotel, tour, travel, and walking-tour reservations. It is open weekdays 9–6, Saturday 8:30–2, and Sunday 9–1.

➤ TOURIST INFORMATION: **Cape Town Tourism** (✉ The Pinnacle at Burg and Castle Sts. [Box 1403], 8000, ☎ 021/426–4260, FAX 021/426–4263, WEB www.cape-town.org).

5 THE WESTERN CAPE

The wonders of the Western Cape are nearly endless. The jagged mountains, elegant estates, and delicious vintages of the Winelands; the pristine, mountain-edged beaches and historic towns of the Overberg; and the glorious wildflowers, old fishing villages, and interior ranges of the West Coast provide some of South Africa's most memorable experiences.

By Andrew
Barbour

Updated by
Jennifer Stern
and Myrna
Robbins

ANCHORED BY CAPE TOWN in the southwest, the Western Cape is South Africa's most delightful province, a sweep of endless mountain ranges, empty beaches, and European history dating back more than three centuries. In less than two hours from Cape Town you can reach most of the province's highlights, making the city an ideal regional base.

The historic Winelands, in the city's backyard, produce fine wine amid the exquisite beauty of rocky mountains, serried vines, and elegant Cape Dutch estates. By South African standards this southwestern region of the Cape is a settled land, with a sense of tradition and continuity lacking in much of the rest of the country. Here farms have been handed down from one generation to another for centuries, and old-name families like the Cloetes have become part of the fabric of the region.

Even first-time visitors may notice subtle differences between these Cape Afrikaners and their more conservative cousins in the hinterland. For the most part they are descendants of the landed gentry and educated classes who stayed in the Cape after the British takeover in 1806 and the emancipation of the slaves in 1834. Not for them the hard uncertainties of the Great Trek, when ruddy-faced Boer (South Africans of Dutch or Huguenot descent) farmers, outraged at British intervention, loaded their families into ox wagons and set off into the unknown, a rifle in one hand and a Bible in the other.

The genteel atmosphere of the southwestern Cape fades quickly the farther from Cape Town you go. The Overberg, separated from the city by the Hottentots Holland Mountains, presides over the rocky headland of Cape Agulhas, where the Indian and Atlantic oceans meet (officially) at the southernmost tip of the continent. Unspoiled beaches and coastal mountains are the lure of this remote area. North of Cape Town on the West Coast, civilization drops away altogether, bar a few lonely fishing villages and mining towns. Each spring, though, the entire region, stretching up into Namaqualand in the Northern Cape Province, explodes in a spectacular wildflower display that slowly spreads inland to the desiccated Namaqualand and the Cedarberg (Cedar Mountains).

Wildflowers are one extraordinary element of a region truly blessed by nature. The Western Cape is famous for its *fynbos* (pronounced "*feign*-boss"), the hardy, thin-leaf vegetation that gives much of the province its distinctive look. Fynbos composes a major part of the Cape floral kingdom, the smallest and richest of the world's six floral kingdoms. More than 8,500 plant species are found in the province, of which 5,000 grow nowhere else on earth. The region is dotted with nature reserves where you can hike through this profusion of flora, admiring the majesty of the king protea or the shimmering leaves of the silver tree. When the wind blows and mist trails across the mountainsides, the fynbos-covered landscape takes on the look of a Scottish heath.

Not surprisingly, people have taken full advantage of the Cape's natural bonanza. In the Overberg and along the West Coast, rolling wheat fields extend to the horizon, while farther inland jagged mountain ranges hide fertile valleys of apple orchards, orange groves, and vineyards. At sea hardy fishermen battle icy swells to harvest succulent crayfish (Cape lobsters), delicate *perlemoen* (a type of abalone), and a variety of line fish, such as the delicious *kabeljou*.

For untold centuries this fertile region supported the Khoikhoi and San (Bushmen), indigenous peoples who lived off the land as pastoralists and hunter-gatherers. With the arrival of European settlers, however, they

The Western Cape

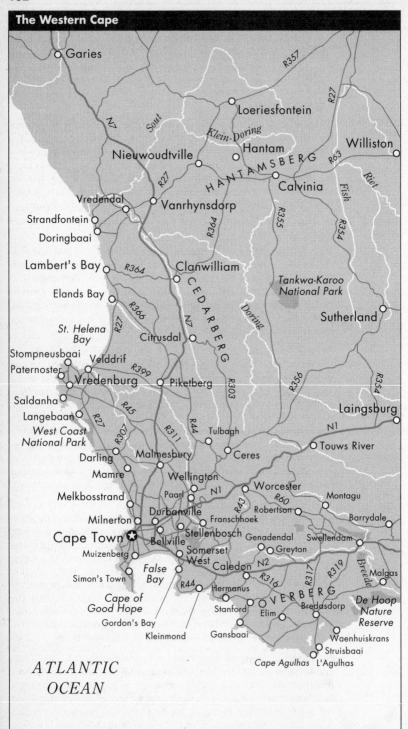

Garies

Loeriesfontein

R357

R27

Williston

N7

Sout

Klein-Doring

Hantam

Nieuwoudtville

R63

R27

H A N T A M S B E R G

Calvinia

Vredendal

Vanrhynsdorp

Fish

Riet

R364

R355

R354

Strandfontein

Doringbaai

Lambert's Bay

R364

Clanwilliam

C E D A R B E R G

Tankwa-Karoo
National Park

Elands Bay

R366

R27

Doring

Sutherland

St. Helena
Bay

N7

Citrusdal

Stompneusbaai

Velddrif

R399

Paternoster

Vredenburg

Piketberg

R356

R354

Saldanha

R303

Laingsburg

Langebaan

West Coast
National Park

R27

R45

R307

R311

R44

Tulbagh

N1

Darling

Ceres

Touws River

Mamre

Malmesbury

Wellington

Worcester

Montagu

Melkbosstrand

Paarl

N1

R43

R60

Robertson

Barrydale

Milnerton

Durbanville

Franschhoek

Cape Town ☆

Bellville

Stellenbosch

Genadendal

Swellendam

Muizenberg

Somerset
West

Greyton

R317

R319

Breede

Malgas

Simon's Town

False
Bay

Caledon

N2

R316

O V E R B E R G

De Hoop
Nature
Reserve

Cape of
Good Hope

R44

Hermanus

Elim

Bredasdorp

Gordon's Bay

Stanford

Kleinmond

Gansbaai

Waenhuiskrans

Struisbaai

Cape Agulhas

L'Agulhas

ATLANTIC
OCEAN

were chased off, killed, or enslaved. In the remote recesses of the Cedarberg and along the West Coast, you can still see the fading rock paintings left by the San, whose few remaining clans have long since retreated into the Kalahari Desert. The population of the Western Cape today is largely "colored," a catchall term to describe South Africans of mixed race and descendants of imported slaves, the San, and the Khoikhoi.

Pleasures and Pastimes

Architecture

The most visible emblem of local culture is Cape Dutch architecture. As you travel from estate to estate, you will see a number of 18th- and 19th-century manor houses that share certain characteristics: thick white-washed walls, thatched roofs curving around elegant gables, and small-pane windows framed by wooden shutters. It's a classic look—a uniquely Cape look—ideally suited to a land that is hot in summer and cold in winter. The Cape Dutch style developed in the 18th century from traditional long houses: simple rectangular sheds capped by thatch. As farmers became more prosperous, they added the ornate gables and other features. Several estates, most notably Vergelegen and Boschendal, have opened their manor houses as museums.

Art and Crafts

The well-respected galleries throughout this region could surprise you with anything from protest paintings from the apartheid era to high-quality ceramics and pewter work. Also keep an eye open for smaller local crafts shops, which can provide you with unique souvenirs.

Dining

South African cuisine at its finest can be found in the Western Cape. If silver service is not your cup of tea, however, the local laid-back country-style cooking can be just as satisfying. The area is home to some of the country's best Cape Malay cuisine, characterized by mild, slightly sweet curries and the use of aromatic spices. Be prepared for fluctuations in the level of service. Generally, South Africans are still trying to get this right, but there are some remarkable exceptions to what appears to be a general go-slow rule of thumb. For a description of South African culinary terms, *see* Pleasures and Pastimes *in* Chapter 1. For price ranges *see* Dining *in* Smart Travel Tips A to Z.

Golf

Fourteen golf courses lie within a 45-minute drive of the center of the Winelands, and four are situated within the Winelands themselves. All accept foreign visitors and most rent clubs. Greens fees for 18 holes range from R140 to R360. You shouldn't have a problem finding a course to your liking, with one of the best being the Gary Player–designed Erinvale, in Somerset West.

Lodging

The Winelands and Overberg are sufficiently compact that you can make one hotel your touring base for your entire stay. Stellenbosch and Paarl offer the most flexibility, situated close to dozens of wineries and restaurants, as well as the major highways to Cape Town. Tourist offices have extensive information on bed-and-breakfasts and self-catering (self-service) options, many of which are less expensive than hotels and often give you a more personal taste of life in the Winelands. Franschhoek is comparatively isolated, which many visitors consider a blessing. The West Coast and Cedarberg are a bit more spread out, so you'll want to stay in one place for a day or two and then move on.

Scenery

Few places in the world can match the drama of the Winelands, where African mountains rise sheer above vine-covered valleys and 300-year-old homesteads snooze in the shade of giant oaks. It's a place of such enviable beauty that you might catch yourself glancing through the local real-estate pages. Less obviously pretty, the West Coast has a minimalist aesthetic that tends to grow on you, and the Cedarberg Mountains are so spectacularly rugged, they leave most visitors breathless in admiration.

Wine

Buried for years by sanctions, South African wines were largely unknown on the international scene. With the demise of the apartheid era, South African wine exports soared. No one could have expected such interest; as a result, the best are now in short supply in their country of origin, and South African wine lovers are peeved at the price they have to pay for a bottle of good local vino. Armed with foreign currency and a favorable rate of exchange, you will, however, still be able to get a good value for your money. Although the quantity of South African red wines remains a problem until the extensive new vine plantings come of age and the supply increases, the quality is improving with each vintage. Cape reds have recently won a slew of international awards. You must taste pinotage, South Africa's own grape variety, a hybrid of pinot noir and cinsaut (or hermitage, as it was once called in the Cape). If you're really serious about wine, arm yourself with *John Platter's Wine Guide,* an annual pocket guide, or buy a copy of *WINE* magazine, a monthly publication that specializes in detailed features on local wineries. For a really in-depth read—and, incidentally, some fantastic photos—you can't beat the beautiful coffee-table *Wines and Vineyards of South Africa,* by Wendy Toerien.

Keep in mind that many wineries close for lunch during the week, shut up shop at midday on Saturday, and don't open at all on Sunday.

Exploring the Western Cape

North of Cape Town, the West Coast and the neighboring interior are renowned for seafood and wildflowers, respectively. To the south are the important wine-producing centers of Paarl, Stellenbosch, and Franschhoek and to the east the historically significant and scenic Swellendam area. The southern tip of Africa, Cape Agulhas, can be reached by leaving the inland region and traveling south to the coast. The southern coastal area incorporates the small towns or villages of Gansbaai, Hermanus, Kleinmond, and Gordon's Bay.

Great Itineraries

Many people spend their entire vacations in the Western Cape after getting a big-game fix in Mpumalanga. Although it's possible to explore Cape Town and the Winelands in three or four days—the area is compact enough to allow it—you need six or seven to do it justice. You can get a good sense of either the Overberg or the West Coast on a three- or four-day jaunt, but set aside a week if you plan to tackle more than one or two of the regions in this chapter. The most practical and enjoyable way to explore the region is by car.

Numbers in the text correspond to numbers in the margin and on the Winelands map.

IF YOU HAVE 3 DAYS

From Cape Town take the N2 to **Stellenbosch** ⑤ and have a look around the town. In the afternoon head off along the R304 toward **Simonsig** ⑭ and **Villiera** ⑮ for some wine tasting and continue to 🏛 **Grande Roche** in **Paarl** ㉜. The next day, head to **Franschhoek** ㉓, and then visit **Fairview** ㉘ where you can taste some goat cheese with your wine. Pop into **Backsberg** ㉖ and then head off to **Rhebokskloof** ㉚ for some wine tasting and perhaps lunch. After lunch go for a short horse ride or a wagon ride. Return to Paarl via **Nelson's Creek** ㉛ and sample some of the New Beginnings wines. On your third day head back to Cape Town, taking a long scenic route if you have the time. One of the best would be to leave Paarl on the R45, head off through Franschhoek, and then turn on to the N2 at Grabouw. If you're short on time, turn right and head straight back to Cape Town. If you have plenty of time, turn left and then turn off the N2 on to the R43 and return to Cape Town via Kleinmond, Betty's Bay, Pringle Bay, and Gordon's Bay. The view over False Bay from this coastal road is fantastic—especially toward sunset.

IF YOU HAVE 5 DAYS

Leaving Cape Town on the first day, take the N7 and head north to the 🏨 **Bushmans Kloof Private Nature Reserve,** in the Cedarberg. This drive will take you through the Swartland and Clanwilliam, the beginning of the wildflower route, which is best in spring. Try to reach the lodge by 3, giving you time to unpack, enjoy a sumptuous tea, and be ready for the late-afternoon game drive. Spend the second day here, taking in all that the lodge and its inspiring environment have to offer. Alternatively, spend these days at 🏨 **Karu Kareb,** which is a much less expensive option. On the third morning head west to the coast, and drive south through the fishing villages. Consider lunch at **Musibosskerm** or **Voorstrand** and then carry on to 🏨 **Langebaan** and the West Coast National Park, ending up at 🏨 **Noupoort** or 🏨 **Bartholomeus Klip,** where you could spend two days. It is a comfortable, 90-minute drive back to Cape Town on the fifth day. Alternately, do one of the above, and follow the itinerary above for three days.

IF YOU HAVE 7 DAYS

Spend the first two days as described in the itinerary for five days. Then choose between continuing as per the five-day itinerary or heading through Riebeek Kasteel and Wellington to **Paarl** ㉜ and spending the next two or three days as per the three-day itinerary. If you chose the former, choose between spending the next two days in Paarl, as per the three-day itinerary, or head farther east to the coast. Drive through **Franschhoek** ㉓ to the N2 and off on the R43 to **Hermanus,** either staying there or heading off to **Arniston.** Wherever you decide to spend the next two nights, spend the days exploring the coast. If it's winter, watch whales. Perhaps taste some of the Overberg wines if you're not all wined out. And then drive back to Cape Town via Betty's Bay and Gordon's Bay as described in the three-day itinerary.

When to Tour the Western Cape

The high season in the Western Cape is, of course, summer, and you will seldom visit major places of interest without the presence of busloads of fellow visitors. The weather is warm and dry, and although strong southeasterly winds can be a nuisance, they do keep the temperature bearable. If soaking up the sun is not of primary importance and you prefer to tour during quieter times, spring (September and October) and autumn–early winter (late March through May) are ideal. The weather is milder and the lines shorter. Spring also brings southern right whales close to the shores of the Western Cape to calve, and late August–October are the months to see the wildflowers explode across the West Coast. If the Winelands are high on your list of must-dos, remember that the busiest time in the vineyards and cellars is January–March.

THE WINELANDS

Frank Prial, wine critic for the *New York Times,* wrote that he harbored "a nagging suspicion that great wines must be made in spectacular surroundings." If that's true, the French may as well rip up their vines and brew beer, because the Cape Winelands are absolutely stunning.

All of this lies only 45 minutes east of Cape Town in three historic towns and valleys. Founded in 1685, Stellenbosch is a gem; it's also a vibrant university community. Franschhoek, enclosed by towering mountains, is the original home of the Cape's French Huguenots, whose descendants have made a conscious effort to reassert their French heritage. Paarl lies beneath huge granite domes, its main street running 11 km (7 mi) along the Berg River past some of the country's most elegant historical monuments. Throughout the region you will find some of South Africa's best restaurants and hotels.

It's no longer entirely accurate to describe these three valleys as *the* Winelands. Today they make up only 35% of all the land in the Cape under vine. This wine-growing region is now so vast you can trek to the fringes of the Karoo Desert, in the northeast, and still find a grape. There are altogether more than 10 wine routes, as well as an established brandy route, in the Western Cape, ranging from the Olifants River, in the north, to the coastal mountains of the Overberg.

Each of the wine-producing areas has its own wine route where member wineries throw open their estates to the public. They maintain tasting rooms where you can sample their vintages either gratis or for a nominal fee. Happily, no one expects you to be a connoisseur, or even to buy the wines. Just relax and enjoy yourself, and don't hesitate to ask tasting room staff which flavors to expect in what you're drinking. Some wineries have restaurants; at others you can call ahead to reserve a picnic basket to enjoy on the estate grounds.

The secret of touring the Winelands is not to hurry. Dally over lunch on a vine-shaded veranda at a 300-year-old estate; enjoy an afternoon nap under a spreading oak; or sip wine while savoring the impossible views. This may not be the Africa of *National Geographic,* but no one's complaining. Nowhere in South Africa is the living more civilized and the culture more self-assured.

The Winelands encompass scores of wineries and estates. The ones listed below are chosen for their great wine, their beauty, or their historic significance. It would be a mistake to try to cover them all in less than a week. You have nothing to gain from hightailing it around the Winelands other than a headache. The vineyards fan out around three major towns: Stellenbosch, Franschhoek, and Paarl. If your interest is more aesthetic and cultural than wine driven, you would do well to focus on the historic estates of Stellenbosch and Franschhoek, after which you might head south into the Overberg. Most Paarl wineries on this tour stand out more for the quality of their wine than for their beauty.

Helderberg

40 km (25 mi) southeast of Cape Town on the N2.

Helderberg is the official designation for this wine area on the edge of the Winelands that is referred to as Somerset West. Just before you reach the center of town you'll see the turnoff to Lourensford Road, which runs 3 km (2 mi) to Vergelegen and Morgenster.

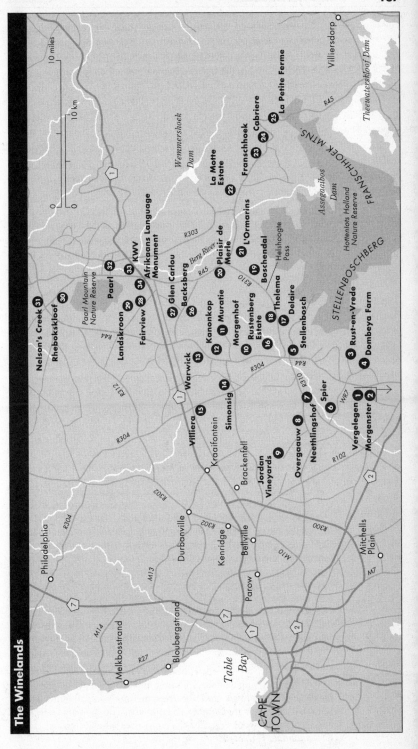

The Winelands

10 miles

10 km

Villiersdorp

La Petite Ferme 25

Cabriere 24

Franschhoek 23

La Motte Estate 22

L'Ormarins 21

Boschendal 19

Theewaterskloof Dam

R45

FRANSCHHOEK MTNS

Assegaaibos Dam

Hottentots Holland Nature Reserve

Helshoogte Pass

STELLENBOSCHBERG

Wemmershoek Dam

Afrikaans Language Monument

KWV

Paarl 32 33

Glen Carlou 34

Backsberg

R303

Berg River

R45

Plaisir de Merle 20

Kanonkop 11

Muratie

Morgenhof

Rustenberg Estate 18

Thelema 17

Delaire

Stellenbosch 5

Rust-en-Vrede 3

Dombeya Farm 4

Nelson's Creek 31

Rhebokskloof 30

Fairview 29 28

Landskroon 27 26

Paarl Mountain Nature Reserve

R44

R312

R304

R302

Philadelphia

R304

M14

M13

Melkbosstrand

Bloubergstrand

R27

Warwick 13

Simonsig 14

Villiera 15

Kraaifontein

Brackenfell

Jordan Vineyards

Overgaauw 8

9

Neethlingshof 7

Spier 6

Vergelegen 1

Morgenster 2

R304

R310

R44

R102

Durbanville

Kenridge

Bellville

Parow

R302

M10

Mitchells Plain

M7

R300

Table Bay

CAPE TOWN

1

2

7

★ ❶ **Vergelegen** was established in 1700 by Willem Adriaan van der Stel, who succeeded his father as governor of the Cape. His classic Cape Dutch homestead, with thatched roof and gables, looks like something out of a fairy tale. An octagonal walled garden aflame with flowers surrounds it, and huge camphor trees, planted almost 300 years ago, stand as gnarled sentinels. The estate was purchased for Lady Phillips by her husband, Sir Lionel, in 1917, and she spent vast sums on the restoration of the homestead, library, and gardens. The homestead is now a museum and is furnished in period style. Other historic buildings include a magnificent library and the old stables, now the reception area and interpretive center. Behind the house, Lady Phillips Tea Garden serves lunch and tea, and the Rose Terrace café looks onto a formal rose garden. Much of the fresh produce is supplied by the Margaret Roberts Herb and Vegetable Garden, which is next to the reception area.

Although Vergelegen still buys grapes from neighboring farms, the vineyards that were planted in 1989, during what is described as the renaissance of the farm, are beginning to give an inkling of some very good wines to come. You really should taste the flagship Vergelegen, a Bordeaux-style blend, or the merlot, with its ripe, plummy flavors. The chardonnay has touches of wood fermentation but is dominated by a fresh citrus nose. Guided tours are available by appointment and on Saturday and Tuesday at 8:30 AM. Cellar tours are offered from Monday to Saturday at 10:30, 11:30, and 2:30, and reservations are essential. There are no tours in the winter. ⊠ *Lourensford Rd., Somerset West,* ☎ *021/847–1334,* WEB *www.vergelegen.co.za.* ☞ *R7.50.* ☉ *Daily 9:30–4:30 (no tastings Sun. in winter).*

❷ Just before you reach Vergelegen, take the turnoff to **Morgenster.** This historic estate has been restored and is now producing wines. Look out for the Lourens River cabernet/merlot blend, which shows promise. They also bottle their own olives and make olive oil and olive pasta. ⊠ *Box 1616, Somerset West 7129,* ☎ *021/852–1738.* ☞ *Free.* ☉ *Tasting and sales by appointment only.*

❸ Nestled against the base of the Helderberg and shaded by giant oaks, the peaceful **Rust-en-Vrede** winery looks over steep slopes of vines and roses. Owned by former Springbok rugby great Jannie Engelbrecht, it's a comparatively small estate that specializes entirely in red wine—and produces some of the very best in South Africa. Rust-en-Vrede Estate is the flagship wine, a blend of predominantly cabernet sauvignon, shiraz, and just over 10% merlot grapes. It has already won several awards both locally and abroad, but it would do well to mature in the bottle for another 10 years or more. Another interesting wine is the shiraz, which has an inviting, spicy bouquet with a mellowness imparted by the American oak in which it is matured, but none of the characteristic cloying sweetness; it will age from five to eight years. ⊠ *R44, between Stellenbosch and Somerset West,* ☎ *021/881–3881,* WEB *www.rustenvrede.com.* ☞ *Free.* ☉ *Weekdays 9–5, Sat. 9–4 (Oct.–Apr.) and 9–3 (May–Sept.). Cellar tours on request.*

❹ Next door to Rust-en-Vrede is **Dombeya Farm,** one of the few places in the Western Cape to see spinning and hand weaving. The farm makes jerseys, blankets, and rugs from merino wool, all in the bright, floral patterns that are Dombeya's hallmark. The shop also sells knitting patterns and wool. A garden tearoom serves light lunches and snacks. ⊠ *Annandale Rd., Stellenbosch,* ☎ FAX *021/881–3746.* ☉ *Daily 9–5.*

Dining and Lodging

$$$$ ✕ **L'Auberge du Paysan.** Come to this little cottage near Somerset West for a formally presented mélange of southern and classic French cui-

sine that makes good use of South African game birds and venison. Tall upholstered chairs, small brass table lamps, and snowy linen create a Gallic setting for first courses like bouillabaisse or frogs' legs pan-fried in an herb and garlic butter. Fish entrées could include fresh *kabeljou* topped with sherried cream and grapes, while guinea fowl is given traditional cassoulet treatment. Seasonal berries—filling meringue baskets, pureed into sorbets, and teamed with spiked chantilly cream—make one of the irresistible desserts. Expect an unhurried and leisurely dinner here. ⊠ *Raithby Rd., off R45, between Somerset West and Stellenbosch,* ☎ *021/842–2008. AE, DC, MC, V. Closed Sun. and 1 month in winter. No lunch Mon.*

$$$–$$$$ ✕ **96 Winery Road.** This relaxed venue, with its rustic decor, is always buzzing with folk from the wine industry, regulars, and upcountry visitors. Inside, butternut-bright walls hold farm implements, while outside, terrace seating offers soothing mountain views. The menu tempts with fresh and flavorful items such as a first course of prawn tempura or salmon and line-fish sashimi on shredded cucumber with wasabi and pickled ginger. Steak lovers are treated well here, with dry-aged cuts of prime beef grilled and teamed with a variety of sauces. Butternut, sun-dried tomato, and feta parcels on creamed spinach with pine nuts are a meatless delight. A good cheese board makes a savory—and many think, superior—option to rich desserts. ⊠ *Zandberg Farm, Winery Rd., between Somerset West and Stellenbosch,* ☎ *021/842–2020. Reservations essential. AE, DC, MC, V. No dinner Sun.*

$$$ ✕ **Lady Phillips Restaurant.** In summer you need to reserve a table three weeks in advance at this idyllic country restaurant on the Vergelegen estate. Whether dining inside or alfresco on the terrace in the shade of three-century-old camphor trees, you will savor a luncheon of classy simplicity but presented with panache. Start with Portobello mushrooms filled with crabmeat, tomato, and feta and topped with tapenade, or baked Camembert on *ciabatta* with gooseberry chutney. Hearty appetites would relish the grilled beef fillet served with wild mushrooms and port-wine-marinated onions, but some diners always opt for one of the renowned savory pies. Make sure to keep space for dessert, both in winter and summer. If you can't get a reservation, head to the Rose Terrace during summer for light meals. ⊠ *Vergelegen Estate, Lourensford Rd., Somerset West,* ☎ *021/847–1334. Reservations essential. AE, DC, MC, V. No dinner.*

$$ ✕ **La Masseria.** Plum orchards rather than olive groves surround this former dairy farm, but the ambience is rustic Italian. Chef patron Miki Ciman presides over a casual eatery where large families arrive early for authentic meals served at long tables. Get there early and tuck into the delectable range of antipasti: marinated vegetables, cold meats, salads, and wonderful homemade cheeses and breads. This buffet meal costs R70, with additional items charged separately. Go on, if you wish, to one of the homemade pastas of the day: If gnocchi in burnt sage butter is available, don't hesitate. Make sure to call ahead and get good directions, and book for lunch rather than dinner. There's no corkage charged on brought-in wine, but sample the house grappa made from the plums right at hand and take home cheeses and dried pasta for another dose of peasant pleasure at home. ⊠ *Stellenrust Estate, Blaauwklippen Rd., Stellenbosch,* ☎ *021/880–0266. Reservations essential. AE, DC, MC, V. No lunch Mon. No dinner Sun.–Thurs.*

$$$$ ✕⊞ **Willowbrook Lodge.** This lodge, a member of the prestigious Relais & Châteaux group, makes a good base for exploring the entire southwestern Cape, including the peninsula, the Winelands, and the Overberg. The lodge lies hidden among beautiful gardens that extend down to the Lourens River; in the distance the peaks of the Helderberg are visible. It's a very peaceful place, with large, airy, comfortable rooms with pri-

vate bath and sliding doors opening onto the gardens. The cuisine is of an equally high standard, starring Provençal dishes, with a separate vegetarian menu. ⊠ *Morgenster Ave., Box 1892, Somerset West 7129,* ☎ *021/851–3759,* FAX *021/851–4152. 11 rooms. Restaurant, bar, pool. No children under 12. AE, DC, MC, V. BP.*

Golf

Somerset West Golf Club (⊠ Rue de Jacqueline, ☎ 021/852–2925, FAX 021/852–5879) is an easy course (⛳ R140 for 18 holes) with plenty of leeway for errant tee shots. **Erinvale Golf Club** (⊠ Lourensford Rd., Somerset West, ☎ 021/847–1144) is a Gary Player–designed course (⛳ R360 for 18 holes) nestled beneath the Hottentots Holland Mountains.

Stellenbosch

★ ⑤ *15 km (9½ mi) north of Somerset West.*

Stellenbosch may be the most delightful town in South Africa. It's small, sophisticated, and beautiful, and you could easily while away a week here. The second-oldest town after Cape Town, it actually *feels* old, unlike so many other historic towns in South Africa. Wandering the oak-shaded streets, which still have open irrigation furrows, you'll see some of the finest examples of Cape Dutch, Georgian, Victorian, and Regency architecture in the country. The town was founded in 1679 by Simon van der Stel, first governor of the Cape, who recognized the agricultural potential of this fertile valley. Wheat was the major crop grown by the early settlers, but vineyards now blanket the surrounding hills. The town is also home to the University of Stellenbosch, the country's first and most prestigious Afrikaner university.

A brief walking tour of the town starts at the corner of Dorp Street and the R44, where you first enter Stellenbosch. The **Rembrandt van Rijn Art Museum** occupies the historic Libertas Parva manor house, which displays the *H* shape so typical of Cape Dutch architecture. Built in 1780, the house has hosted some of the biggest names in South African history, including Jan Smuts (☞ Chapter 2), who was married in the house. The art museum displays the work of some major South African artists, including Irma Stern, Willie Bester, and sculptor Anton van Wouw. ⊠ *31 Dorp St.,* ☎ *021/886–4340.* ⛳ *Free.* ☉ *Weekdays 9–12:45 and 2–5, Sat. 10–1 and 2–5.*

Stroll up oak-lined Dorp Street, Stellenbosch's most historic avenue. Almost the entire street is a national monument, flanked by lovely, restored homes from every period of the town's history. Redolent with tobacco, dried fish, and spices, **Oom Samie Se Winkel** is a 19th-century-style general dealer and one of Stellenbosch's most popular landmarks. In addition to the usual Cape kitsch, Oom Samie's sells some genuine *boere* farmers' products, including *witblitz* and *mampoer,* the Afrikaner equivalent of moonshine. The shop operates a wine-export business and restaurant, too. ⊠ *82–84 Dorp St.,* ☎ *021/887–0797.* ☉ *Weekdays 8:30–6, weekends 9–5:30.*

As you continue up Dorp Street, keep an eye out for the historic **La Gratitude** home, built in the early 18th century in traditional Cape-Dutch town house style and still a private home (⊠ 95 Dorp St.); the all-seeing eye of God on its gable will be doing the same for you. **Voorgelegen** (⊠ 176 Dorp St.) and the houses on either side of it form one of the best-preserved Georgian ensembles in town.

When you reach Andringa Street, turn left and then right onto Kerk (Church) Street. On your left is **d'Ouwe Werf,** possibly the country's oldest boardinghouse, that first took in paying guests in 1802.

At the corner of Kerk and Ryneveld streets is the **Stellenbosch Village Museum,** which is well worth a visit. The museum comprises four dwellings scattered within a two-block radius. These houses date from different periods in Stellenbosch's history and have been furnished to reflect changing lifestyles and tastes. The oldest of them is the very basic Schreuderhuis, which dates from 1709. The others date from 1789, 1803, and 1850, respectively. ⊠ *18 Ryneveld St.,* ☎ *021/887–2902,* WEB *www.museums.org.za/stelmus.* 🖾 *R10.* ◴ *Mon.–Sat. 9:30–5, Sun. 2–5.*

Continue down Ryneveld to Plein Street. Turn left and walk to the **Braak,** the grassy town square. Some of Stellenbosch's most historic buildings face the square, which is a national monument. At the southern end is the **Rhenish Church** (⊠ Bloem St.), erected by the Missionary Society of Stellenbosch in 1823 as a training school for slaves and blacks.

St. Mary's Church stands at the far end of the Braak. Built in 1852, it was consecrated by Bishop Robert Gray in 1854 and reflects the growing influence of the English in Stellenbosch. Across Bloem Street from St. Mary's is the **Burgher House,** built in 1797. Today it houses the offices of Historical Homes in South Africa.

Next to the Burgher House, on a traffic island in Market Street, stands the **V.O.C. Arsenal.** It took 91 years for the political council to hammer out the decision that Stellenbosch needed its own magazine. With the hard part behind them, it took just six months in 1777 to complete the structure. ⊠ *Bloem St.,* ☎ *021/887–2937.* 🖾 *R5.* ◴ *Sept.– May, weekdays 9–2.*

Walk down Market Street past the Tourist Information Bureau. On your left, facing a large lawn, is the **Rhenish Complex,** one of the most impressive restoration projects ever undertaken in South Africa. The complex consists of the old Cape Dutch Rhenish parsonage (1815); the Leipoldt House, which melds elements of English and Cape architecture; and a two-story building that is typically English.

Continue down Market and turn left on **Herte Street.** The whitewashed cottages along this street were built for freed slaves after the Emancipation Act of 1834. Although they were originally thatched, the houses are still evocative of 19th-century Stellenbosch. From here follow Herte back to Dorp Street, where the walking tour began.

From Stellenbosch wine routes fan out like spokes of a wheel, making excellent day trips if you're staying in town. You could head west and south along the R310 and R306 toward Spier, Neethlingshof, Overgaauw, and Jordan toward Cape Town. (However, it's not a good route for returning to Cape Town as it gets a bit confusing.) If you head northwest along the R304 toward Simonsig and Villiera or north along the R44 to Morgenhof, Muratie, Delheim, Kanonkop, and Warwick, you'll hit the N1 and can continue to Paarl. Or you could head east on the R310, detouring to Rustenberg and then over the scenic Helshoogte Pass to Thelema Mountain Vineyard, Delaire, and Boschendal, after which you can decide to head right to Franschhoek or left to Paarl.

Stellenbosch is considered to be the center of the Winelands, and many of the older and more established wineries are here. Also based in the town is **Distell,** which is an amalgamation of Stellenbosch Farmers' Winery (SFW) and Distiller's Corporation—two of the biggest producers and distributors in South Africa. SFW was founded by a Kentuckian, William Charles Winshaw, and is responsible for almost 40% of the country's table wine. SFW also produces fortified wines, several brandies, and very good fruit juices. The SFW flagship is the Zonnebloem range of reds and whites, including among others a good shiraz (particularly those from the early 1980s). The Lanzerac pinotage was the first of the variety ever made in South Africa (back in 1961), and it's still a good wine.

6 Describing **Spier** as simply a wine estate is doing Spier Home Farms an enormous disservice. The vast complex comprises a manor house, wine cellars, wine and farm shop, rose garden, restaurants, conference center, open-air amphitheater, cheetah park, and equestrian facilities. It's all designed in Cape-country style, with whitewashed walls and thatched roofs, set along the verdant north bank of the Eerste River. You can even get to Spier's own little railway station by vintage train from Cape Town. So, yes, it's seriously touristy, but still delightful. In 2001 the original Spier label was resurrected, replacing the Three Spears label. Try the cabernet sauvignon or the consistently brilliant and well priced chardonnay—there's not a bottle to be found of the previous vintages, but see what the future brings. ✉ *R310, Stellenbosch,* ☎ *021/809–1143,* FAX *021/881–3634.* ☞ *Free, tastings R10, train ride R75.* ☉ *Daily 9–5.*

7 A long avenue of pines and oaks leads to the lovely estate of **Neethlingshof,** which traces its origins to 1692. The magnificent 1814 Cape Dutch manor house looks out across formal rose gardens to the Stellenbosch Valley and the Hottentots Holland Mountains. The wines produced on this estate and those from its sister farm, Stellenzicht, are highly regarded both locally and abroad, and so be prepared for a rush of tour buses during the high season. The gewürztraminer is an off-dry, very elegant wine with rose-petal and spice aromas, while the Weisser Riesling Noble Late Harvest is one of the best of its kind, having scooped almost every local award since 1990. However, an unfortunate accident has resulted in no 1999 or 2000 vintages, but the 2001 (due for release at time of writing) should be great. Another fantastic wine from this successful cellar is the almost iconic Stellenzicht Syrah. Buy a few bottles—in fact, buy three, which is the most they'll sell to any one person. And just take it on faith—it's not available for tasting. ✉ *R310,* ☎ *021/883–8988,* FAX *021/883–8941.* ☞ *Free, R20 for 6 tastings.* ☉ *Weekdays 9–5, weekends 10–4. Cellar tours by appointment (stays open 2 hrs later in summer).*

8 There are a number of established estates on Stellenbosch Kloof Road, one that definitely deserves a visit is **Overgaauw.** Admire the pretty Victorian tasting room while exploring the range of big proud red wines. Overgaauw was the first South African estate to make a merlot in 1982, and it's still up there with the leaders. It needs a few years to settle into itself, by when its delicious berry nose should be able to stand up to the mint/eucalyptus overtones. Or try the Tria Corda—it's a peppery, minty earthy wine with loads of fruit and oak. And also try the spicy, fruity Sylvaner—the only one in the Cape to date. ✉ *Box 3, Vlottenberg 7604,* ☎ *021/881–3815.* ☞ *Free.* ☉ *Weekdays 9–12:30 and 2–5, Sat. 10–12:30.*

9 At the end of the Stellenbosch Kloof Road is **Jordan Vineyards,** a newer winery. Flanked by the Bottelary hills and overlooking a vision of rolling vineyards and jagged mountains, it enjoys an enviable setting at the head of Stellenbosch Kloof. Gary and Cathy Jordan are a husband-and-wife team who studied at the University of California at Davis and worked at California's Iron Horse Winery. Although they produced their first vintage only in 1992, they have already established their reputation as producers of quality wines. The sauvignon blanc has refreshing hints of asparagus and a chalky undertone, and the multiawarded, dense but fruity chardonnay is quite popular. Also look for a combination of the two in the versatile Chameleon dry white, a flavorful, well-priced buy. Wine critics are keeping their eyes on the Jordans' spicy cabernet sauvignon, while the merlot shows great promise, too. ⊠ *Stellenbosch Kloof Rd.,* ☎ *021/881–3441.* 🖾 *Tastings R10.* ⊘ *Nov.–Apr., weekdays 10–4:30, Sat. 9:30–2:30; May–Oct., weekdays 10–4:30, Sat. 9:30–12:30. Cellar tours by appointment.*

Some of the Cape's most important wineries are on the stretch of the ❿ R44 that runs north from Stellenbosch. **Morgenhof** lies in the lee of a steep hill covered with vines and great pine trees. It's a beautiful Cape Dutch estate, with a history stretching back 300 years. In 1993 Morgenhof was acquired by the Cointreau-Huchons of Cognac, France. They have spared nothing to make this one of the jewels of the Winelands, and behind the glamour there is an extremely talented wine maker and distinguished wines. Jean Daneel, who made his mark with his award-winning 1992 merlot—it's a bold mouthful of a red wine—and his Morgenhof chenin blanc, which is currently making waves in the Cape, has moved on, but his student, Rianie Strydom, is carrying on the tradition. Apart from the above-mentioned celebrity wines, try the chardonnay with fresh coconut nose and hints of lime, or the smoky, somewhat Burgundian pinotage. A new release that should develop into something rather spectacular is the cabernet sauvignon reserve, a deep, complex wine with hints of tobacco, mint, and ripe plums. Morgenhof is an excellent place to stop for lunch. From October through April you can reserve picnic baskets and dine on the lawns under a huge tree. The rest of the year there are light lunches of homemade soup, freshly baked bread, cheese, and quiche. Reservations are advisable in summer. ⊠ *R44, between Paarl and Stellenbosch,* ☎ *021/ 889–5510,* WEB *www.morgenhof.com.* 🖾 *Tastings R10.* ⊘ *May–Oct., weekdays 9–4:30, weekends 10–3; Nov.–Apr., Mon.–Thurs. 9–5:30, Fri. 9–5, weekends 10–5. Cellar tours by appointment.*

After a mile or so turn right onto the well-signposted Knorhoek Road, ⓫ which will take you to Delheim, nice but not as nice as **Muratie,** which you'll pass en route. Ancient oaks and a cellar that truly seems to be more concerned with the business of making wine than in decor make this a refreshing change from the "prettier" wineries. It's a small estate, specializing in rich, earthy reds and full-bodied dessert wines. Muratie's port is an old favorite in the Cape, and the well-balanced amber is a fortified dessert wine of note, with pleasing citrus overtones to ameliorate the sweetness. The cellar produces two red wines, both of which deserve attention: a pinot noir, from some of the oldest vines of this cultivar in the Cape, and Ansela van der Caab, a dry red blend of cabernet and merlot, named after the freed slave who married the first owner of the farm and helped set up the vineyards. ⊠ *Box 133, Koelenhof,* ☎ *021/882–2330.* 🖾 *Free.* ⊘ *Apr.–Oct., weekdays 10–5, Sat. 10–3; Nov.–Mar., weekdays 10–5, Sat. 10–3, Sun. 11–3. Cellar tours by appointment only.*

Once back on the R44, you can continue to Kanonkop and Warwick, or you can turn left onto the Kromme Rhee Road and head off to Simonsig and Villiera.

In the days when ships of the Dutch East India Company used Cape Town as a revictualing station on the way to the East, a ship would fire a cannon as it entered the harbor to let farmers know provisions were needed, and a set of relay cannons, all set on hilltops, would carry the message far inland. One such cannon was on this farm, which was then called Kanonkop, which is Afrikaans for Cannon Hill. The beauty ⓬ of **Kanonkop** is not in its history or its buildings but in its wine. Since the early 1980s wine making has been in the hands of legendary Beyers Truter. In 1991 he won the Winemaker of the Year award and the

Robert Mondavi Trophy at the International Wine & Spirit Competition in London. Few would argue that Kanonkop's pinotage is the best new-style pinotage produced in South Africa. It's more wooded than most and shows excellent complexity and fruit; it will age from 8 to 15 years. Paul Sauer is a very good blend of about 80% cabernet sauvignon with the balance made up of equal parts merlot and cabernet franc. The 1995 vintage won a gold medal at the 1998 International Wine & Spirit Competition. No cellar tours are offered. ✉ *R44, between Paarl and Stellenbosch,* ☎ *021/884–4656.* 🗐 *Tastings free.* ⌚ *Weekdays 8:30–5:30, Sat. 8:30–12:30.*

⑬ Warwick is not a member of the Stellenbosch Wine Route, and you should visit this estate only if you're very keen to taste and buy wine; the tasting area is in a tiny cellar room cluttered with wine-making equipment (if possible, make an appointment first). The previous wine maker, Norma Ratcliffe, spent a couple of vintages in France perfecting her rather traditional techniques, which have left their mark on Warwick's reds. Trilogy is one of the finest blended reds in the Cape, a stylish and complex wine made predominantly from cabernet sauvignon, with about 40% merlot and 7% cabernet franc. The cabernet franc is undoubtedly one of the best wines made from this varietal in the Winelands. The new wine maker, Anna-Marie Mostert, has a hard act to follow, but she has proved her worth at Mont Rochelle in Franschhoek. ✉ *R44, between Paarl and Stellenbosch,* ☎ *021/884–4020,* ℻ *021/ 884–4025.* 🗐 *Tastings R5.* ⌚ *Weekdays 8:30–4:30, Sat. by appointment. Cellar tours by appointment.*

👆 ⑭ Simonsig sits in a sea of vines with tremendous views back toward Stellenbosch and the mountains. Its range of 15 white and red wines covers the whole taste and price spectrum. Kaapse Vonkel was South Africa's first Méthode Cap Classique sparkling wine and, 30 years on, is still among the best with 15% pinotage, 50% chardonnay, and 35% pinot. Tiara is among the best cabernet blends in the Winelands, and the pinotage is an excellent example of how well this varietal fares with no wood aging—but the Pinotage Red Hill, from old bush vines, shows just how much good oaking can improve it. You can bring your own picnic to enjoy at tables by the small playground. ✉ *Kromme Rhee Rd.,* ☎ *021/882–2044,* ℻ *021/882–2545,* ⬛ *www.simonsig.co.za.* 🗐 *Tastings R5.* ⌚ *Weekdays 8:30–5, Sat. 8:30–4. Cellar tours weekdays at 10 and 3, Sat. at 10.*

★ ⑮ Villiera is actually part of the Paarl Wine Route, but its location in the open flats near the N1 motorway makes it just as close to Stellenbosch as to Paarl. In a little more than 15 years of wine making, the Grier family has notched numerous successes. As John Platter, one of South Africa's foremost wine writers, says: "Other wine makers might jog or work out in the gym; Jeff Grier gets all the exercise he needs stepping up to the podium for wine industry awards." Try the Bush Vine Sauvignon Blanc, for which Grier was voted Winemaker of the Year, and you'll start to understand why it's become almost a cult wine. And then check out the range of Cap Classique sparkling wines—take a bottle of Tradition rosé brut home with you and relive the smells, textures, and special quality of sun-filled Cape days and balmy Cape nights. Made from pinot, chardonnay, and 10% pinotage, it's a delicate pink bubbly with soft, creamy overtones. This is one of the wineries that is, as far as possible, producing chemical-free wines. ✉ *R101 and R304 (Old Paarl and Stellenbosch Rds.), Koelenhof,* ☎ *021/882–2002.* 🗐 *Tastings free.* ⌚ *Weekdays 8:30–5, Sat. 8:30–1. Guided tours by appointment only.*

If you head east on the R310, take a detour up the Idasvallei Road and then follow a narrow lane, which runs through cattle pastures and groves

⑯ of oak to **Rustenberg Estate,** that dates to 1682. It's undergone a major refurbishment, and has a state-of-the art winery and underground vaulted maturation rooms. The estate is known for red wine, particularly its 100% cabernet Peter Barlow (named after the present owner's father). It's made from grapes from one lovely, well-tended vineyard that unfortunately suffered extensive damage in the fires of 2000. So the deep red 1999 vintage will be the last for a while. It's a lovely unblended wine that will age for a decade or two. Snap up a few bottles if there are any left. ☒ *Off R310 (Rustenberg Rd.), Ida's Valley,* ☎ *021/809–1200,* 𝖶𝖤𝖡 *www.rustenberg.co.za.* ☒ *Tastings free.* ☉ *Weekdays 9–4:30, Sat. 9–12:30 Cellar tours by appointment.*

⑰ Return to the R310 and head off across the Helshoogte where **Delaire** enjoys one of the most spectacular settings of any winery in the country. Sit on the terrace of the tasting room or restaurant and look past a screen of oaks to the valley below and the majestic crags of the Groot Drakenstein and Simonsberg mountains. It's an ideal place to stop for lunch or even a short breather. The restaurant (open from Tuesday to Saturday noon–2) serves light lunches and will provide picnic baskets if you want to follow one of the scenic trails through the estate (open from September 15 to April 15). The tasting room is unpretentious and casual. The winery produces under two labels; Botmaskop (try the cabernet sauvignon or the flagship merlot) and the alternative Green Door range, named after the winery restaurant. There are no cellars tours. ☒ *R310, between Stellenbosch and Franschhoek (Helshoogte Rd.),* ☎ *021/885–1756,* 𝖶𝖤𝖡 *www.delaire.co.za.* ☒ *Tastings R10, R12 glass deposit.* ☉ *Mon.–Sat. 10–5.*

⑱ On the slopes of the Simonsberg, **Thelema Mountain Vineyards** is an excellent example of the exciting developments in the Cape Winelands since the early 1980s. When Gyles and Barbara Webb bought the farm in 1983, there was nothing here but very good soil and old fruit trees. It's a testament to their efforts that the winery has had regular prizewinners ever since. The 1992 cabernet sauvignon–merlot blend won Gyles Webb the Diner's Club Winemaker of the Year title in 1994. Two years later he took the award again with the '94 cabernet. Not to say that his white wines do not win accolades—Thelema's sauvignon blanc and chardonnay are certainly among the Cape's best. To cap it all off, the view of the Groot Drakenstein Mountains from the tasting room is unforgettable. This vineyard also suffered quite severe damage in the fires of 2000 and will have a decreased output for a few years. ☒ *R310, between Stellenbosch and Franschhoek (Helshoogte Pass),* ☎ *021/ 885–1924.* ☒ *Tastings free.* ☉ *Weekdays 9–5, Sat. 9–1.*

Dining and Lodging

$$$$ ✕ **Jonkershuis at Spier.** The culinary influences that have contributed to traditional Cape cuisine—Cape Malay, Dutch, French, and German—are all celebrated here with a gargantuan R120-a-head buffet feast that you can savor under venerable oaks or inside the well-restored 18th-century homestead. Start with the soup of the day and farm breads or head for the cold table laden with local seafood dishes such as *snoek* pâté, smoked salmon trout, fish cakes, and excellent pickled fish. Salads complement hearty entrées of Cape chicken pie, *bobotie* (a light Malay curry of minced meat and dried fruit topped with a thin baked savory egg custard), *bredie* (lamb casserole in a tomato sauce), and Malay curries. Look for the time-honored desserts *melktert* (a sweet custard tart sprinkled with cinnamon and sugar), *koeksister* (a braided doughnut served with a gingery syrup), and brandy pudding. ✉ *Spier Estate, Lyne-doch Rd.,* ☎ *021/809–1172. AE, DC, MC, V. No dinner Sun. and Mon.*

$$$$ ✕⊡ **Lanzerac Manor.** The sense of history is almost tangible on this large working wine estate dating to 1692. The sheer beauty of the setting has been left untouched: a classic Cape Dutch manor house flanked by the rolling vineyards and mountains of the Jonkershoek Valley. The luxurious hotel and winery both boast state-of-the-art facilities; however, although service is always willing, it does not always live up to opulence of the surroundings. Guest rooms are tastefully decorated, and diners can choose from casual alfresco meals at the Terrace or more formal fare in the Governor's Restaurant. The latter presents a Cape Malay and cheese buffet at lunchtime, upholding a popular tradition dating back decades. Dinner entrées include loin of lamb filled with avocado and accompanied by oyster mushrooms, herbed mashed potatoes, and yellow tomato sauce or wild boar on gazpacho with potato gnocchi. ✉ *Jonkershoek Rd., 1 km (½ mi) from Stellenbosch (mailing address: Box 4, Stellenbosch 7599),* ☎ *021/887–1132,* 🖷 *021/887–2310. 43 rooms, 5 suites. 2 restaurants, bar, room service, pool. AE, DC, MC, V. BP.*

$$$$ ⊡ **d'Ouwe Werf Country Inn.** A national monument, this attractive 1802 inn is thought to be the oldest in South Africa. From the street guests enter the original living room, a beautiful space enlivened by wood floors, a lofty beamed ceiling, and elegant antiques. The hotel is divided into two parts: the old inn with luxury rooms on its Georgian second story and a new wing with more standard rooms. All luxury rooms are furnished with antiques, including four-poster beds, draped sash windows, and bronze bathroom fittings. The standard rooms have reproductions only. A lovely coffee garden in a brick courtyard shaded by trellised vines is open for meals and drinks throughout the day. Adequate free parking for guests is a bonus in this university town. ✉ *30 Church St., Stellenbosch 7600,* ☎ *021/887–1608 or 021/887–4608,* 🖷 *021/887–4626. 25 rooms. Restaurant, room service, pool. AE, DC, MC, V. BP.*

$$$$ ⊡ **The Village at Spier.** The innovative design of these two-story buildings grouped around six courtyards, each with its own pool and leisure area, achieves its goal of the feel of a Mediterranean village, albeit a very luxurious one. Rooms and suites are elegantly appointed, with Indonesian furniture, gas fireplaces, and stylish detail evident in the cotton throws and wide choice of pillows. Once the surrounding orchards and shade trees have matured, the complex and walkways will be both verdant and private. The restaurants at the village are quite popular. In addition to the large meals you can enjoy at Jonkershuis, you'll find lighter fare at Taphuis restaurant, or head to the Spier Cafe for Italian treats. Contemporary cuisine is on the menu at Figaro's. ✉ *Spier Estate, Lynedoch Rd., Stellenbosch 7600,* ☎ *021/809–1100,* 🖷 *021/809–1134,* ᴡᴇʙ *www.spier.co.za. 155 rooms. 4 restaurants, bar, room service, pool. AE, DC, MC, V.*

Nightlife

There's always much going on in Stellenbosch, especially in summer. The **Spier Festival** (☎ 021/809–1158) runs from mid-November to mid-March and usually has opera, classical music, and a host of other performances. Each summer concerts ranging from African jazz to opera and ballet are staged at the **Oude Libertas Amphitheatre,** a delightful open-air venue run and owned by Distell, previously Stellenbosch Farmers Winery (SFW). For bookings contact **Computicket** (☎ 083/909–0909).

Outdoor Activities

GOLF

Stellenbosch Golf Club (✉ Strand Rd., ☎ 021/880–0103) has long tree-lined fairways that will pose a problem if you don't hit the ball straight. Green fees are R200 for 18 holes.

HORSEBACK RIDING

Spier Equestrian Centre (☎ 083/627–2282) offers a gentle amble or a quick canter through the vineyards (R80 per hour), and you can do a tasting with your trusty mount standing by. (Some of the horses have developed a taste for Spier's wonderful chardonnay, so you have to look over your shoulder.) If you don't fancy getting into a saddle, you can do a horse-drawn wagon ride, R40 per person for half an hour, and R80 for an hour.

Franschhoek and the Franschhoek Valley

22 km (14 mi) northeast of Stellenbosch.

From Thelema the road runs down Helshoogte Pass into the fruit orchards and vines that mark the beginning of the Franschhoek Valley. This is the most isolated and spectacular of the three wine routes, a long valley encircled by towering mountain ranges and fed by a single road. Franschhoek (French Quarter) takes its name from its first white settlers, French Huguenots who fled to the Cape to escape Catholic persecution in France. By the early 18th century 270 Huguenots had settled in the Cape; their descendants—with names like de Villiers, Malan, and Joubert—now number in the tens of thousands. With their experience in French vineyards, the early Huguenots were instrumental in nurturing a wine-making culture in South Africa. As spectacular as the valley is today, it must have been even more so in the late 17th century, when it teemed with game. In calving season herds of elephants would migrate to the valley via the precipitous Franschhoek Mountains. The last wild elephant in the valley died in the 1930s. Some leopards still survive, but you won't see them.

⑲ **Boschendal** lies at the base of Helshoogte Pass. With a history dating back three centuries, this lovely estate competes with Groot Constantia as one of the Cape's major attractions; you could easily spend half a day here. Cradled between the Simonsberg and Groot Drakenstein mountains, the farm then called Bossendaal was originally granted to Jean le Long, one of the first French Huguenot settlers in the late 17th century.

Boschendal runs one of the most pleasant wine tastings in the region: You can sit inside at the Taphuis, a Cape Dutch longhouse and the oldest building on the estate, or outside at wrought-iron tables under a spreading oak. In 1980 Boschendal was the first to pioneer a Cape blanc de noir, a pink wine made in a white-wine style from black grapes. The Boschendal Blanc de Noir remains the best-selling wine of this style. If you prefer sparkling wines, try the extremely popular Boschendal Brut, a blend of pinot noir and chardonnay made by the Méthode Cap Classique. From the Taphuis it's a two-minute drive through vines and fruit trees to the main estate complex. The excellent Boschendal Restaurant serves a buffet of Cape specialties. Le Café serves light meals at tables under the oaks leading to the manor house. And Le Pique Nique (open November–April) provides picnic baskets that you can enjoy on the lawns. Calling ahead for the restaurant and the picnic is essential. A gift shop sells wine, locally made rugs, preserves, and other Cape kitsch. The estate is wheelchair-friendly. ⊠ *R310, between Franschhoek and Stellenbosch (Pniel Rd., Groot Drakenstein),* ☎ *021/870–4274,* WEB *www.boschendalwines.co.za.* ⊡ *Tastings R5.* ⊙ *Dec.–Jan., Mon.–Sat. 8:30–4:30, Sun. 9:30–12:30; May–Oct., weekdays 8:30–4:30, Sat. 8:30–12:30; Nov. and Feb.–Apr., Mon.–Sat. 8:30–4:30. Combined cellar and vineyard tours Nov.–Apr., daily 10:30 and 11:30.*

After leaving Boschendal, you will hit the R45, where you can go right to Franschhoek or left to Paarl. If you're heading to Franschhoek and are not planning to return via this route to Paarl, take a small detour ⑳ by turning left on the R45, and then left again to **Plaisir de Merle.** If you're planning to visit Franschhoek and then return to Paarl, leave it for the return trip. This huge estate (2,500 acres) is Distell's showpiece. With its innovative architecture and conservation area, this estate truly feels different from the rather run-of-the-mill, ubiquitous "oak and gable" wineries that you see all over the Cape. But forget all the frills—it really is about the wine. Don't miss the cabernet sauvignon, probably the smoothest, lowest-acid, lowest-tannin local example of this cultivar. ⊠ *Box 121, Simondium, 7670,* ☏ *021/874–171 or 021/874–1072,* WEB *www.plaisirdemerle.co.za.* ☉ *Weekdays 9–5, Sat. 10–1.*

Turn right off the R45 and continue through a tunnel of oaks to ㉑ **L'Ormarins,** which dates to 1811 and is spellbinding: a classic Cape Dutch building festooned with flowers and framed by majestic peaks. The huge tasting room is modern and slick, in great contrast to the manor house, indicating the modern wine-making style here. Using classic grape varieties, the wine makers produce big, complex red wines ready for early drinking but with excellent maturation potential. Optima is such a wine. A blend of predominantly cabernet sauvignon and merlot, it has great complexity that will improve in the bottle for 10–15 years. The straight cabernet is just as pleasing; among whites, try the pinot gris. ⊠ *R45 (Franschhoek Rd.), Groot Drakenstein,* ☏ *021/874–1026.* ☉ *Tasting by appointment only. Cellar tours weekdays at 10, 11:30, and 3.*

After L'Ormarins carry on toward Franschhoek or, if you have limited time, turn left onto the R301 and head toward Paarl.

The R45 shares a narrow bridge over the Berg River with the railway ㉒ line. Less than 2 km (1 mi) beyond the bridge is the **La Motte Estate,** owned by a branch of the same Rupert family that owns L'Ormarins. The elegant and rather formal tasting room looks into the cellars through a wall of smoked glass. You sit at a long marble-top table and sample from five to seven wines. The shiraz is one of the biggest and boldest you'll taste of this variety, full of rich flavors; it needs from four to eight years to reach its peak. The Millennium is a very good blend of just over 50% cabernet sauvignon with the balance consisting of merlot and a little cabernet franc. This wine needs time to develop, coming into its own in 5–10 years. There are no cellar tours. ⊠ *R45 (Huguenot Rd.),* ☏ *021/876–3119,* WEB *www.la-motte.co.za.* ☒ *Tastings R5.* ☉ *Weekdays 9–4:30, Sat. 9–noon.*

㉓ Continue along the R45 till you reach the village of **Franschhoek,** which lies at the base of the Franschhoek Mountains, which seal off the eastern end of the valley. It's a delightful village, with a pleasant, slow pace that belies the extraordinary number of restaurants, cafés, and small inns in town. It's makes a great stop for lunch or overnight.

The **Huguenot Memorial** (⊠ Lambrecht and Huguenot Sts.) stands at the end of the main road through Franschhoek. It was built in 1948 to commemorate the contribution of the Huguenots to South Africa's development. The three arches symbolize the Holy Trinity, the sun and cross form the Huguenots' emblem, and the female figure in front represents Freedom of Conscience. ☏ *No phone, contact Huguenot Memorial Museum.* ☉ *Daily 9–5.* ☒ *R3.*

Next to the memorial is the **Huguenot Memorial Museum.** Its main building is modeled after Thibault's 1791 Saasveld in Cape Town. The museum traces the causes of the Huguenots' flight from France and the life they carved out for themselves in the Cape. Wall displays profile some of the early Huguenot families. Exhibits also focus on other aspects of the region's history, such as the development of Cape Dutch architecture and the relationship of the Huguenots with the Dutch East India Company. Displays in the annex cover the culture and life of the Khoikhoi, also known as Hottentots, as well as the role of slaves and local laborers in the development of the Franschhoek Valley. ✉ *Lambrecht St.,* ☎ *021/876–2532.* ☞ *R4.* ◷ *Mon.–Sat. 9–5, Sun. 2–5.*

㉔ Built in 1994 on the lower slopes of the Franschhoek Mountains, **Cabrière** is the brainchild of Achim von Arnim, one of the Cape's most colorful wine makers. To avoid scarring the mountain, the complex hunkers into the hillside. There are five Cap Classique sparkling wines under the Pierre Jordan label, while the fruity, mouth-filling Haute Cabrière pinot noir is consistently one of the best. Also delicious is the chardonnay–pinot noir blend, an ideal, extremely quaffable wine to enjoy at lunchtime. Take a Saturday-morning cellar tour with von Arnim, and watch him perform his trademark display of *sabrage*—the dramatic decapitation of a bottle of bubbly with a saber. ✉ *R45,* ☎ *021/876–2630,* WEB *www.cabriere.co.za.* ☞ *Tastings R5, cellar tours and tastings R20.* ◷ *Sales, weekdays 9–1 and 2–4:30, Sat. 11–1; tours Sat. 11 or by appointment.*

㉕ Continue out of town along the R45 until you see **La Petite Ferme** on your right-hand side. You'll have to phone ahead to arrange a tasting, but it's worth it because then you'll know what to have with your lunch if you decide to dine here. True to its name, this is a small, family-run estate producing just enough wine for the restaurant and to keep its faithful regular customers happy. Try the chardonnay. ✉ *Box 55, Franschhoek 7690,* ☎ *021/876–3016.* ◷ *Sales daily noon–4, tasting and tours by appointment only.*

㉖ Head back toward the Helshoogte on the R45 from Franschhoek and turn left onto Simondium Road and then left into the **Backsberg** winery. Framed by the mountains of the Simonsberg, this lovely estate is run by the Back family, well known for producing great wines of good value. An unusual feature of the winery is the self-conducted cellar tour. You'll follow painted lines around the cellars, pausing to watch video monitors that explain the wine-making process. It's a low-pressure introduction to wine making and an ideal starting point for novices. Backsberg produces a comprehensive range of red and white wines, a Méthode Cap Classique sparkling wine, and a very fine brandy made from chenin blanc. The chardonnay is consistently one of the best made, a rounded, fruity wine that develops well in the bottle for five or more years. Backsberg is one of only a handful of estates that produce a malbec—and then only in very small quantities. The new Freedom Road range is made by a worker–management project—so far it has produced only a sauvignon blanc. ✉ *WR1, between R44 and R45 (Simondium Rd.),* ☎ *021/875–5141,* WEB *www.backsberg.co.za.* ☞ *Tastings R5, cellar tours free.* ◷ *Weekdays 8:30–5, Sat. 8:30–1.*

㉗ After leaving Backsberg, continue in the same direction on Simondium Road and take the first road to the right, which is signposted **Glen Carlou.** The cellar is not particularly pretty, but what comes out of it is rather special. As well as fine wines—especially the chardonnay reserve—the winery also produces a range of farm cheeses and olives. Add a loaf of bread, and you've got everything you could possibly want for an impromptu picnic. ✉ *Box 23, Klapmuts 7625,* ☎ *021/875–5528,* WEB *www.glencarlou.co.za.* ☞ *Tastings R5.* ◷ *Weekdays 8:45–4:45, Sat. 9–12:30.*

Continue along in the same direction and turn right into the R101 at the T junction and then immediately left, crossing over the highway, following the signs to **Fairview.** This is one of the few wineries where visitors might feel comfortable taking their families. Children will get a kick out of seeing peacocks roaming the grounds and goats clambering up a spiral staircase into a goat tower. Every afternoon at four the goats are milked. Fairview produces a superb line of goat cheeses, all of which you can taste gratis. If you want to put together a picnic for the lawn, a deli counter sells sausages and cold meats to complement the estate's wines and cheeses.

Don't let Fairview's sideshows color your judgment about the wines. Charles Back, a member of the family that runs Backsberg, is one of the most successful and innovative wine makers in the Cape, and the estate's wines are excellent and often surprising. Certainly, Back does not stick to the tried-and-tested Cape varietals. The zinfandel–cinsaut blend is quite unusual, and they make creative use of the many Rhône varieties planted on the farm. Perhaps it's just because the pun was irresistible, but (as claimed by the label) they send the milk-producing goats into the vineyard to personally select the best grapes, from which they make their very personal Goats-do-Roam. Yes, it is rather like a young Côtes du Rhône. ✉ WR3, off R101 (Suid-Agter-Paarl Rd.), ☎ 021/863–2450, WEB www.fairview.co.za. ☞ Tastings free. ☉ Weekdays 8:30–5, Sat. 8:30–1. Cellar tours by appointment.

Almost next door to Fairview is **Landskroon,** a venerable estate now run by the ninth generation of the de Villiers family. They produce a lovely cabernet franc, and their cabernet sauvignon—with hints of vanilla and oak—is up there with the best. For a little something to sip after a long, leisurely dinner, try the Murio Muscat Jerepico—a rich, velvety fortified wine with a fresh finish. There is a playground for children and a coffee shop on the terrace. ✉ Box 519, Suider Paarl, 7624, ☎ 021/863–1039, WEB www.landskroon.co.za. ☞ Free. ☉ Weekdays 8:30–5, Sat. 9–1.

Continue and then turn right into the R44 and, after about 10 km (6 mi), turn right onto a dirt road and right again to **Rhebokskloof.** The winery sits at the head of a shallow valley, backed by hillsides covered with vines and fynbos. It's a lovely place for lunch on a sunny day. The Victorian Restaurant serves à la carte meals and teas on an oak-shaded terrace overlooking the gardens and mountains; in inclement weather meals are served in the Cape Dutch Restaurant, as is a Sunday buffet lunch. The Chardonnay Sur Lie is the pick of the bunch, with a lovely balance and fruity, toasty overtones. You can also take horse rides through the vineyards. No cellars tours are offered. ✉ WR8, ☎ 021/863–8386, WEB www.rhebokskloof.co.za. ☞ Tastings R7. ☉ Daily 9–5.

Continue toward Paarl, stopping at Nelson's Creek and New Beginnings en route. **Nelson's Creek** is a wonderful place with so much that is different. A huge geological fault runs through the estate, and is partly responsible for the multiple soil types here that result in a profusion of microclimates. But that's just the physical background. In 1997 Alan Nelson, the owner of Nelson's Creek, decided that land redistribution was a good idea, so he gave 11 hectares(24 acres) of prime vineyard to the farmworkers to inaugurate the New Beginnings program. From the proceeds of their first vintage they bought another 9 hectares (20 acres). Mathewis Thabo, who started off as a part-time gardener on the estate, is now producing three pretty respectable wines—a red, a white, and a rosé. It would be unfair to not mention that Nelson's Creek, too, produces some fantastic reds. The cabernet sauvignon is a big, ripe blackberry-flavored wine with a hint of spice; the pinotage is unwooded and, although a bit unusual, has been well received. However, the best buy is probably the inexpensive, very drinkable Albenet, a cinsaut/shiraz blend. It's also a great place for a picnic or a walk. Cellar tours are by appointment only. ☒ *R44, Paarl,* ☎ *021/863–8453.* ☉ *Weekdays 8–5, Sat. 9–2.*

Dining and Lodging

$$$$ ✕ **Boschendal Restaurant.** Reserve well in advance for the buffet lunch here at one of the Cape's most beautiful and historic wineries. A wide selection of soups, quiches, and pâtés prefaces a bewildering array of cold and hot main dishes, including pickled fish, roasts, and imaginative salads; traditional Cape dishes are well prepared. End with an excellent sampling of South African cheeses and preserves or a classic Cape dessert like malva pudding. Unobtrusive, professional, but friendly service well complements the bounty, priced at R125 a head. ☒ *R310, between Franschhoek and Stellenbosch,* ☎ *021/870–4274. Reservations essential. AE, DC, MC, V. No dinner.*

$$$$ ✕ **Monneaux.** Rueben Riffel is one of a small band of talented homegrown chefs who are breaking culinary rules with passion and, mostly, delectable results. Asian and Western flavors and techniques merge in dishes starring local ingredients, best illustrated in the five-course gastronomic menu. From the à la carte menu, adventurous diners could start with raw beef marinated in lemongrass and dried shrimp, teamed with ruby grapefruit and dried mango, and dressed with a chili-mint chutney. Essence of spiced red bell pepper flavors the prawn risotto, while vegetarians score with farfalle paired with roast vegetables, basil pesto, and shaved Parmesan. Lunchtime diners can savor their meal on the shady terrace of this inviting 19th-century former *parfumerie* and guest house, where you can still stay the night in one of the 14 charming rooms if you reserve in advance. ☒ *Main Rd., Box 328, Franschhoek 7690,* ☎ *021/876–3386. Reservations essential. AE, DC, MC, V.*

$$$–$$$$ ✕ **Haute Cabrière.** Dine here atop a working winery built into the mountainside. Try to reserve a window table for views across the vine-clad valley as you select from a mix-and-match menu created to complement the estate wines maturing in the cellar beneath you. Half or full portions are available of renowned chef Matthew Gordon's mouthwatering fare that changes with the seasons. Titillate the palate with a basil risotto jeweled with oyster mushrooms, red bell pepper, and black olives and follow with fresh Scottish salmon teamed with spinach, potato galette, and horseradish cream. Those who would rather stay with indigenous ingredients can choose from local salmon trout, black mussels with cream and garlic, and roast rack of Karoo lamb. Belgian-trained chocolatiers contribute to the luscious selection of desserts. ☒ *R45, Franschhoek Pass, Franschhoek,* ☎ *021/876–3688. Reservations essential. AE, DC, MC, V. No dinner Tues.*

$$–$$$$ ✕ **Le Quartier Français.** This restaurant in a 19th-century home continues to garner impressive local and international awards. On summer nights glass doors open onto a spotlighted garden; in winter a log fire burns in the hearth. Proceedings could start with a colorful butternut risotto cake with smoked mozzarella, roasted vegetables, and sage butter, while in autumn you can indulge in mixed wild mushrooms on toasted brioche with Kalahari truffles and wild arugula. Roasted chicken with sweet-corn pancakes and fillet of veal are popular main courses. Cheese dishes—such as local Camembert with roasted pear and red-wine syrup—make innovative finales. ☒ *16 Huguenot Rd., Franschhoek,* ☎ *021/876–2151. Reservations essential. AE, DC, MC, V. No dinner Sun.*

$$$ ✕ **Topsi & Company.** Chef Topsi Venter, doyenne of the Cape culinary scene, is as renowned as a raconteur as she is for her innovative country fare. The decor is simple and rustic, and local art lines the white walls. The menus, written on a blackboard, change daily, and only local and fresh ingredients are used. Unexpected flavors meet in her horseradish-and-apple mousse with smoked butterfish, dressed with an apple-and-fennel vinaigrette. Entrées vary from a hearty dish of roast pork loin on colcannon, lent piquancy by a dried peach and yellow bell pepper salsa to panfried sirloin of gemsbok (venison) with and braised endive. More unconventional combinations are found in a dessert tart filled with Smyrna dried figs, hazelnuts, and chili, topped with a dollop of bay-leaf-infused cream. In this valley of wonderful wines it's great to be able to BYOB. ⊠ *7 Reservoir St., Franschhoek,* ☎ *021/ 876–2952. Reservations essential. DC, MC, V.*

\$\$–\$\$\$ ✕⌂ **Le Ballon Rouge.** Small but prettily decorated rooms all open onto the wraparound veranda of this early village homestead. Priced to please, this guest house is popular throughout the year with city visitors. The menu has been expanded to attract nonresidents for lunch and dinner, presenting a straightforward but substantial choice of well-cooked fare. Black mussels, local smoked salmon trout in pastry, and spring rolls filled with bobotie are among the first courses. Most entrées are priced at R42, including chicken breast in white wine, rainbow trout stuffed with spinach and almond butter, and line fish of the day. The small dessert list presents no surprises. ⊠ *7 Reservoir St., Box 344, Franschhoek 7690,* ☎ *021/876–2651,* ℻ *021/876–3743. 8 rooms. Restaurant, room service, pool. AE, DC, MC, V. BP.*

\$\$\$\$ ⌂ **Le Quartier Français.** In the center of town, this classy guest house is a Winelands favorite. Separated from the village's main drag by a courtyard bistro and a superb restaurant above, the guest house exudes privacy and peace. Rooms in two-story whitewashed cottages face a pool deck and central garden exploding with flowers. Decor is vibrant, with rustic furniture, sponge-painted walls, colorful drapes, and small fireplaces. Upstairs rooms have timber beams and mountain views, and suites have private pools. ⊠ *Huguenot Rd. (mailing address: Box 237, Franschhoek 7690),* ☎ *021/876–2248 or 021/876–2151,* ℻ *021/876–3105,* ⓦⒺⒷ *www.lequartier.co.za. 15 rooms, 2 suites. Restaurant, bar, pool. AE, DC, MC, V.*

Paarl

❸❷ *21 km (13 mi) northwest of Franschhoek.*

Paarl takes its name from the granite domes of Paarl Mountain, which looms above the town—*paarl* is Dutch for pearl. The first farmers settled here in 1687, two years after the founding of Stellenbosch. The town has its fair share of historic homes and estates, but it lacks the charm of its distinguished neighbor simply because it's so spread out. Main Street, the town's oak-lined thoroughfare, extends some 11 km (7 mi) along the western bank of the Berg River. You can gain a good sense of the town's history on a drive along this lovely street.

Main Street North doglegs to the right at Lady Grey Street before continuing as Main Street South. On your left, the **Paarl Museum** (formerly Oude Pastorie) occupies a gorgeous Cape Dutch home built as a parsonage in 1787. In fact, the building itself is of more interest than the collection, which includes odds and ends donated by local families, including silver, glass, and kitchen utensils. A pleasant café at the side of the museum serves tea and snacks at tables on the museum lawns. ⊠ *303 Main St.,* ☎ *021/872–2651.* 🎫 *R5.* ◷ *Weekdays 10–5.*

From the Paarl Museum walk about 200 yards along Pastorie Street to the **Afrikaans Language Museum** (Afrikaanse Taalmuseum), in the Gideon Malherbe House. It was from here in 1875 that the Society of

True Afrikaners launched their campaign to gain widespread acceptance for Afrikaans, hitherto considered a sort of inferior kitchen Dutch. However, the museum will be of only limited interest to many visitors because the displays are entirely in Afrikaans. ✉ *11 Pastorie St.,* ☎ *021/872–3441.* ▨ *R5.* ☺ *Weekdays 8–5.*

Continue along Main Street past the Paarl Publicity Office to **Zeederberg Square,** a grassy park bordered by some excellent examples of Cape Dutch, Georgian, and Victorian homes.

A little farther down Main Street on the left is the old **Dutch Reformed Church,** a thatched building dating to 1805. The cemetery contains the tombstones of the Malherbe family, which was instrumental in the campaign to gain official recognition for Afrikaans.

Continue down Main Street until you see signs leading to KWV Cellars. ❸❸ **KWV** is short for Ko-operatieve Wijnbouwers Vereniging (Cooperative Winegrowers' Association), which for nearly 80 years has regulated and controlled the Cape wine industry. KWV sells wine and spirits in more than 40 countries and more than 30 U.S. states, and its brandies, sherries, and fortified dessert wines regularly garner gold medals at the International Wine & Spirit Competition in London. It also offers one of the most popular and most crowded cellar tours in the Winelands. KWV's cellars are the largest in the world, covering some 55 acres. Among the highlights is the famous Cathedral Cellar, with a barrel-vaulted ceiling and giant vats carved with scenes from the history of Cape wine making. In an adjoining cellar you can see under one roof the five largest vats in the world. The tour begins with a short audiovisual presentation and ends with a tasting of some of KWV's products. ✉ *André du Toit Bldg., Kohler St.,* ☎ *021/807–3007,* WEB *www.kwv.co.za.* ▨ *Cellar tours and tastings R10.* ☺ *Tours by appointment only; English tours at 11 and 2:15; tastings weekdays 8–4:30, Sat. 8:30–4.*

Return to Main Street and turn left. After the N1 bridge a sign on your ❸❹ right points the way to the **Afrikaans Language Monument** (Afrikaanse Taalmonument), set high on a hill overlooking Paarl. Like the Voortrekker Monument in Pretoria, this concrete structure holds a special place in the hearts of Afrikaners, who struggled for years to gain acceptance for their language alongside English. The rising curve of the main pillar is supposed to represent the growth and potential of Afrikaans. When it was erected in 1973, the monument was as much a gesture of political victory as a paean to the Afrikaans language. Ironically, it may become the language's memorial. Under the new South Africa Afrikaans has become just one of 11 official languages and is gradually losing its dominance. The view from the top of the hill is incredible, taking in Table Mountain, False Bay, Paarl Valley, and the various mountain ranges of the Winelands. A short, paved walking trail leads around the hillside past impressive fynbos specimens, particularly proteas. ✉ *Afrikaanse Taalmonument Rd.,* ☎ *021/863–4809.* ▨ *R5.* ☺ *Daily 9–5.*

Halfway down the hill from the Afrikaans Language Monument is a turnoff onto a dirt road and a sign for the Paarl Mountain Nature Reserve. The dirt road is **Jan Philips Drive,** which runs 11 km (7 mi) along the mountainside, offering tremendous views over the valley. Along the way it passes the **Mill Water Wildflower Garden** and the starting points for myriad trails, including hikes up to the great granite domes of Paarl Mountain. The dirt road rejoins Main Street at the far end of Paarl.

Dining and Lodging

$$$$ ✕ **Bosman's.** Set amid the heady opulence of the Grande Roche hotel, ★ this elegant restaurant and Relais & Châteaux member ranks as one of the country's finest. The level of service is extraordinary, commensurate with that of the finest European restaurants, although some diners may find the attention a little suffocating. Having overcome the hurdle of which menu to choose—seafood, gourmet, Cape flavored, vegetarian, low-fat gourmet, or à la carte, all of which change daily—diners will start with a complimentary *amuse-bouche* (literally, something to entertain your mouth.) An à la carte first course of breast of pigeon with creamy leeks and a duo of truffle sauces could precede an entrée of roasted tuna with wild mushrooms and bacon foam or a combination of kingklip and crayfish teamed with tagliatelle and asparagus sauce. Gratinéed pineapple with coconut ice cream wraps up the meal in sophisticated style. ✉ *Grand Roche hotel, Plantasie St.,* ☎ *021/ 863–2727. AE, DC, MC, V. Closed June–Aug.*

$$$$ ✕ **Roggeland.** For an unforgettable Cape experience, make a beeline for this glorious Cape Dutch manor house on a farm outside Paarl. Meals are long, languid rituals, whether it's an alfresco lunch in the garden or a four-course dinner in the 18th-century dining room. An evening might start with sweet-corn soup with cilantro cream followed by trout fillet on handmade tagliolini with a basil sabayon. A main course of lamb loin comes teamed with roasted butternut and shallots in muscadel with an indigenous dessert of malva pudding with a rooibos tea mousse as the finale. This feast is priced at R130 and includes a different wine with each course. ✉ *Roggeland Rd., North Paarl,* ☎ *021/868–2501. Reservations essential. AE, DC, MC, V.*

$$–$$$$ ✕ **Pontac Manor.** Having established a popular small hotel in a striking Cape Victorian former farmstead, the owners added a restaurant that is fast becoming a Winelands favorite. The deep veranda is the place for lunch except on very hot days, when the elegant dining room makes a cooler option. All savory items can be ordered in starter or full portions. A distinct Cape accent is discernible in dishes like duck breast teamed with citrus segments, mango, and bell pepper and venison with polenta accompanied by burnt banana quenelles. Finish with country cheeses or try the cheesecake mille-feuille on an amaretto syrup garnished with chocolate cigars. ✉ *Pontac Manor, 16 Zion St., Box 6206, Paarl 7622,* ☎ *021/872–0445,* 𝖥𝖠𝖷 *021/872–0460. AE, DC, MC, V.*

$$$$ ▥ **Bartholomeus Klip Farmhouse.** For a break from a long bout of wine tasting, head to this Victorian guest house near Wellington on a nature reserve and working farm. Its luxurious accommodations and excellent food come in the middle of 9,900 acres of rare *renosterveld* scrubland that is home to the endangered geometric tortoise. There are also plenty of eland, zebra, wildebeest, springbok, rhebok, bontebok, bat-eared fox, Cape buffalo, and bird life in and around the mountains, streams, and plains. A wander around the farm, amid the barking of sheepdogs, is also amusing, and you can hike, mountain bike, or swim, as well. Rates include all meals, teas, and game drives. ✉ *Box 36, Hermon, 7308,* ☎ *022/448–1820,* 𝖥𝖠𝖷 *022/448–1829,* 𝖶𝖤𝖡 *www.parksgroup.co.za. 5 rooms, 1 suite. AE, DC, MC, V.*

$$$$ ▥ **Grande Roche.** A member of the prestigious Relais & Châteaux group,
★ this establishment can stake a claim as the best hotel in South Africa. In a gorgeous Cape Dutch manor house that dates from the mid-18th century, the hotel sits amid acres of vines beneath Paarl Mountain, overlooking the valley and the Drakenstein Mountains. Suites are either in the historic buildings—slave quarters, stables, and wine cellar—or in attractive terrace buildings constructed in traditional Cape Dutch style. Rooms are a tasteful mix of the modern and the old: Reed ceilings and thatch comfortably coexist with heated towel racks and air-conditioning. The staff, many of whom trained in Europe, outnumber the guests two to one and offer a level of service extremely rare in South Africa. ✉ *Plantasie St., Box 6038, Paarl 7622,* ☎ *021/863–2727,* 𝖥𝖠𝖷 *021/863–2220,* 𝖶𝖤𝖡 *www.granderoche.co.za. 5 rooms, 30 suites. Restau-*

rant, bar, room service, 2 pools, 2 tennis courts, gym. AE, DC, MC,
V. BP. Closed June–Aug.

$$$$ ⊡ **Roggeland Country House.** Dating to 1693, this historic farm is one
★ of the most delightful lodgings in the Winelands. The setting in Dal Jos-
aphat Valley is breathtaking, with stunning views of the craggy Drakenstein Mountains. Guest rooms in restored farm buildings have reed
ceilings, country dressers, and mosquito nets (not just for effect). The
1779 manor house, which contains the dining room and lounge, is a masterpiece of Cape Dutch architecture. Dinner and breakfast in the fine restaurant are included in the rates. ⊠ *Roggeland Rd., Box 7210, Northern*
Paarl 7623, ☎ *021/868–2501,* FAX *021/868–2113,* WEB *www.explore-*
africa.com/roggeland. 10 rooms. Restaurant. AE, DC, MC, V. MAP.

$$$ ⊡ **Lemoenkloof Guesthouse.** In the heart of Paarl and a national mon-
ument, this house is decorated in sophisticated country style. Although
the modern accoutrements such as television, air-conditioning, and tea-
and coffee-making facilities in each of the guest rooms make your stay
comfortable, the swimming pool and art gallery add an element of fun.
A full South African breakfast is included in the rate. ⊠ *396A Main*
St., Box 2726, Paarl 7620, ☎ *021/872–7520 or 021/872–3782,* FAX *021/*
872–753. 20 rooms. Pool. AE, DC, MC, V. BP.

Outdoor Activities

BALLOONING

Wineland Ballooning (☎ 021/863–3192), in Paarl, makes one-hour
flights over the Winelands every morning from about November until
March or April, weather permitting. The balloon holds a maximum
of six people, and the trip costs about R1,200 per person. After the
flight there's a champagne breakfast at the Grand Roche Hotel.

GOLF

Paarl Golf Club (⊠ Wemmershoek Rd., ☎ 021/863–1140) is sur-
rounded by mountains, covered with trees, and dotted with water
hazards. The greens fee is R170 for 18 holes.

HORSEBACK RIDING

Wine Valley Horse Trails (☎ 083/226–8735 or 021/863–8687) are based
at Rheboksloof and offer scenic rides around the vineyards or up into
the surrounding Paarl Nature Reserve. A longish ride of about four
hours gets you to the far side of the hill, from where you have a dis-
tant view of Table Mountain. Prices range from R80 for a one-hour
ride to R350 for a full day, including lunch.

Wellington and Bain's Kloof

16 km (10 mi) north–northeast of Paarl.

The **Bain's Kloof Pass,** built by engineer Andrew Geddes Bain, was opened
in 1853, linking Wellington to Ceres and Worcester. The road winds
northward from Wellington, through the Hawekwa Mountains, re-
vealing breathtaking views across the valley below. On a clear day you
can see as far as the coast. The road has a good tar surface, but unlike
many Western Cape passes, Bain's Kloof has not been widened much
since it was built, so take your time and enjoy the views. From Paarl
take the R301 toward Wellington, about 16 km (10 mi) distant. Fol-
low R301, which becomes the main road through Wellington, and this
will soon pan out into a eucalyptus-lined avenue, which becomes Bain's
Kloof Pass. There are places where you can park and walk down to lovely,
refreshing mountain pools—great on a hot summer's day.

En Route As you approach the initial slopes of Bain's Kloof, look out for the **Bovlei**
Winery, on the left. Built in 1987 in traditional style, the building it-
self is not particularly noteworthy, but it has a vast picture window

offering a stupendous view of the undulating vineyards beyond. Be sure
to try their light new-world-style reds and the fortified Red Hanepoot
or the Muscat d'Alexandrie (White Hanepoot) dessert wines. ✉ *Box
82, Wellington, 7655,* ☎ *021/873–1567.* 🖭 *Free.* ☉ *Weekdays 8–12:30
and 1:30–5, Sat. 8:30–12:30.*

THE BREEDE RIVER VALLEY

The upper and central part of the catchment of the Breede River extends over quite a large area and has been consolidated into a cohe-
sive, if slightly artificial, marketing region. It's a beautiful area with a
combination of fantastic mountain scenery, fabulous fynbos, pretty bucolic farmlands and small towns. A short drive over any one of the scenic
mountain passes is sure to bring you into a secluded valley, resplen-
dent with the greens of spring, the grape-laden vines of summer, the
myriad colors of autumn, or the snowcapped peaks and crisp misty
mornings of winter.

A natural climatic combination of comparatively mild but wet winters followed by long, warm summers makes this area perfectly suited
for the cultivation of deciduous fruit, especially viticulture. In the summer the intense sunshine allows the wine and table grapes to develop
rich ruby colors. Virtually deprived of rain in summer, the fungus-prone
vines nurture their precious crop, irrigated from the meandering Breede
River and its many tributaries.

Towns and sights are marked on the Western Cape map.

Tulbagh

50 km (32 mi) north of Paarl.

As the Bain's Kloof Pass ends, turn left onto the R46, which will lead
you through Wolsely (where it's not worth stopping) and then directly
to Tulbagh after about 15 minutes. Founded in 1743, the town of Tulbagh is nestled in a secluded valley bounded by the Witzenberg and
Groot Winterhoek mountains. A devastating earthquake in September 1969 shook the city and destroyed many of the original facades of
the historic town.

Much of the town is unlovely, having simply been rebuilt, often pre-
fab style, on old foundations, but the real attraction of Tulbagh is **Church
Street,** parallel to the main Van Der Stel Street, where each of the 32
buildings was restored to its original form and subsequently declared
a national monument.

The **Oude Kerk** (Old Church) museum stands at the entrance to Church
Street and is the logical departure point for a self-guided tour of the
area, which is well signposted. The church has been extensively restored
and has an interesting collection of artifacts from the area including
carvings made by Boer prisoners of war. A ticket includes admission
to another two buildings on Church Street, which operate as annexes
of the main museum. These show a practical history of events before,
during, and after the quake. The buildings have been authentically reconstructed and show painstakingly accurate period interiors. ☎ *023/
230–1041.* 🖭 *R5.* ☉ *Weekdays 9–5, Sat. 10–4, Sun. 11–4 (opens earlier on Sat. in summer).*

Just 3 km (2 mi) out of town, built on high ground commensurate with
its status, is the majestic **Oude Drostdy Museum.** Built by renowned
Cape architect Louis Thibault in 1804, the building was badly damaged by fire in 1934 and later by the 1969 quake, but it has been care-

fully restored to its original glory and is a fine example of neoclassic architecture. The building now houses an impressive collection of antique furniture and artifacts. As the original magistrate's house, the Drostdy had a cellar, which served as the local jail, and now hosts occasional wine tastings. ☎ 023/230–0203. 🎫 Free. 🕑 Mon.–Sat. 10–12:50 and 2–4:50, Sun. 2:30–4:50.

🍴 **Vera's Miniature Houses** museum is well worth a visit. Owner-curator Vera Humphris has created some 30 or more miniature houses, each furnished with authentic working replicas, so ask her to open the roll-top desk or the drawers of the armoire. At the time of writing, the museum was deciding whether to close for one afternoon or day during the week—phone ahead to find out. ✉ 4 Witzenberg St., Tulbagh, ☎ 023/230–0651. 🎫 R10. 🕑 Daily 9:30–12:30 and 2:30–4:30.

If you stand in front of the church on Van der Stel Street, you will see a wine barrel indicating the road to **Twee Jonge Gezellen,** which is about 8 km (5 mi) from town. One of the finest and oldest wineries in the area, it's a family-run estate best known for its fantastic Cap Classique—Krone Borealis Brut. But many Capetonians are more familiar with the old, tried, and trusted TJ39, an easily drinkable, well-priced blend of weisser (white) Riesling, chardonnay, chenin blanc, and sauvignon blanc that has been making a regular appearance on local tables for years. And, for the health conscious, the TJ light (at 8.5%) has good substance and bouquet for a low-alcohol wine. ✉ Box 16, Tulbagh 6820, ☎ 023/230–0680. 🎫 Free. 🕑 Weekdays 9–4, Sat. 10–2.

Dining and Lodging

$$–$$$ ✕ **Paddagang.** Though originally built as a private residence in 1809, by 1821 Paddagang was already serving as one of South Africa's first tap houses (like a pub with wine on tap). Immaculately restored after a 1969 earthquake, it was turned into a wine-house restaurant, where you can enjoy a good selection of traditional Cape fare. Try a starter of smoorsnoek, local smoked fish braised with potato and onion with grape jam on the side, and then go on to main courses of South Africa's national dish, bobotie. All the decor is traditional, including riempie (thong-upholstered) chairs. In good weather you can opt to dine under an immense vine-covered pergola. ✉ 23 Church St., ☎ 023/230–0242. AE, DC, MC, V. No dinner Mon., Tues., Thurs., and weekends.

$$ ✕ **Readers.** Housed in what was once the residence of the church reader (hence the name) diagonally opposite the old church, the restaurant is run by Carol Collins, a graduate of one of South Africa's most respected culinary schools—and it shows in the superb cuisine. The decor mirrors Carol's love for felines, with cat pictures and statuettes as well as a veteran well-fed tomcat guarding the door. The menu changes daily, depending on available fresh ingredients, but dinner could start with grilled haloumi (a Greek cheese), bacon, and watermelon salad or, more conventionally, with chicken on potato pancakes and a raspberry dressing. Entrées such as teriyaki stir-fry of beef with Thai spices contrast with slow-roasted lamb shanks with honey, balsamic, and garlic. Don't miss out on one of the simple but delectable desserts. ✉ 12 Church St., Tulbagh 6820, ☎ 023/230–0087. AE, DC, MC, V. Closed Tues.

$$$$ 🏠 **Rijk's Ridge Country House.** This spot is on the outskirts of the village, on a ridge overlooking a lake where you can enjoy sweeping views of the surrounding mountains. Each suite, decorated in a plush Cape cottage style, has a private terrace leading to the poolside garden. A full breakfast, wine tasting, and a tour of the wine cellar is included in the rate. ✉ Main Rd., Box 340, 6820, ☎ 023/230–1006, FAX 023/230–1125. 12 suites, 3 cottages. Restaurant, pool, billiards. AE, DC, MC, V. BP.

Worcester

About 50 km (30 mi) north of Paarl on the N1, on the other side of the du Toits Kloof Pass or tunnel.

Worcester is by far the largest town in the Breede River valley, often termed the region's capital by locals and with good cause. Much of the town's burgeoning commerce and industry are connected to agriculture—viticulture, in particular—and its brandy cellars produce the highest volume of the spirit in the country.

The **Karoo National Botanical Garden** lies on the opposite side of the N1 highway to the town of Worcester but is easy to find if you follow the signs eastward from the last set of traffic lights on High Street. Billed as one of the most important botanical gardens in the world, the collection here includes several hundred species of indigenous flora, succulents, aloes, and trees. Follow the road from the entrance to the main parking area, from where you can take one of three clearly marked walks. A special Braille Garden allows the visually impaired to touch, feel, and smell. ☎ 023/347–0785. ✉ R8. ☉ Nov.–July, weekdays 8–1 and 2–4:30; Aug.–Oct., weekends 9–4.

The **Kleinplasie Living Open-Air Museum** is a welcome change from dusty artifacts in glass cases. The fascinating museum is actually a collection of original buildings from the area that have been reerected around a working farmyard. Following a narrated slide show, venture into the farmyard and watch the museum staff, intent on keeping traditional skills alive, as they bake bread, twist tobacco, make horseshoes in a smithy, and distill *witblitz* (moonshine). The museum also has a shop where you can buy produce from the farmyard. ✉ *Kleinplasie Agricultural Showgrounds*, ☎ 023/342–2225 or 023/342–0430. ✉ R12. ☉ Mon.–Sat. 9–4:30, Sun. 10:30–4:30.

The **KWV Brandy Cellar** is the largest distillery of its kind in the world, with 120 pot stills under one roof. Informative guided tours, followed by a brandy tasting, will take you through the process of brandy making. The well-informed guide will give a layman's rundown of the various methods used, the pros and cons of pot-still distillation as compared to the continuous-still method, as well as a description of the maturation process. ✉ *Worcester Wine Route*, ☎ 023/342–0255. ☉ *Tours by arrangement only.*

Dining and Lodging

$$–$$$ ✕ **St. Geran.** Despite the town's appeal to visitors, locals still form the bulk of the clientele here, so don't expect a chichi presentation. That said, the steak house–style decor in this converted house belies a cuisine with touches of unexpected subtlety, coupled with good value for the money. Although the menu is suspiciously large for the one chef-patron to manage, it's the well-cooked red meat most diners order. Beef—ranging from small rump steaks to huge peppered fillets, panfried in cream and sherry—are followed in popularity by the lamb chops. Starters and desserts are run of the mill. ✉ *48 Church St., 6850*, ☎ 023/342–2800. AE, DC, MC, V. Closed Sun. No lunch Sat.

$$–$$$ ☷ **Cumberland Hotel.** In a town that is, for its size, surprisingly short on hotels, this centrally situated hostelry is large, convenient, and has a good range of facilities despite its old-fashioned and timeworn feel. The reception area spreads out into a courtyard, and the dining area and spa and gym facilities have been placed around a central landscaped swimming pool. Rooms—all air-conditioned against the hot Boland summer and scrupulously clean—are reasonably priced. ✉ *2 Stockenstrom St., 6850*, ☎ 023/347–2641, ✉ 023/347–3613. *54 rooms, 1 suite. Pool, sauna, tennis court, health club, squash. AE, DC, MC, V.*

Outdoor Activities

CANOEING

The Breede River has only tiny rapids near Worcester, where it twists and turns between clumps of *palmiet* (river reeds) and the overgrown banks. **Wildthing Adventures** (☎ 021/423–5804) offers a one- or two-day trip on the river. The one-day Wine Route trip (R265) is the most popular and is more about food and drink than paddling. The highlight is the tasting of local wines during the extensive picnic lunch. **Felix Unite River Adventures** (☎ 021/683–6433) also runs canoe trips, which include a light breakfast, not-so-light picnic lunch, and tasting of a selection of local wines (R265). **River Rafters** (☎ 021/712–5094) runs trips in two-person inflatables and offer a one-day trip with wine tasting for R265 and a two-day, two-night trip for R695.

Robertson

45 km (28 mi) southeast of Worcester.

Robertson was founded primarily to service the surrounding farms, and it retains its agricultural and industrial character. Some effort has been made to beautify the town with tree-lined roads, but there is little for visitors here, except as a stop-off for lunch on the way to McGregor or Montagu.

Take the R64 from the northern end of Worcester's High Street, and the road, lined with vineyards and farms, will take you straight into Robertson, but not before you have passed the **Rooiberg Winery** on the left. Try the red muscadel—reputedly one of the best in the world. Capetonians in the know have long considered this one of the best value-for-money wineries in the area, producing excellent wines at a good price—the shiraz is a particularly good buy. Check out the sand sculpture. ⊠ *Box 358, Robertson 6705,* ☎ *023/626–1663,* WEB *www.rooiberg.co.za.* 🖾 *Free.* ☉ *Weekdays 8–5:30, Sat. 9–3.*

If you have time, take a detour to **Van Loveren Winery,** just 9 km (5½ mi) along the R317 from Robertson in the direction of Bonnievale. Apart from sampling the unusual Fernão Pires, and a very delicate shiraz *blanc de noir*—all of which are very inexpensive—make sure to visit the unique grounds. The owner's mother has planted a garden of indigenous and exotic plants and trees, surrounding a water fountain that supplies the entire farm. Instead of visiting the usual tasting room, you sit out under the trees and the various wines are brought to you—and if you are lucky, you will be offered a snack from the farm kitchen. ⊠ *Off R317, Robertson,* ☎ *023/615–1505.* 🖾 *Free.* ☉ *Weekdays 8:30–5, Sat. 9:30–1.*

Graham Beck, Robertson Cellar. Sibling to another cellar of the same name in Franschhoek, this country cousin produces some notable wines. The Rhona Muscadel, a New Age muscat, fruity but not cloying, and the excellent Cuvée 2000 Cap Classique are two favorites, but the reds are not to be ignored. Try the Ridge Shiraz, which is garnering rave reviews. ⊠ *About 10 km (6 mi) from Robertson on the R60 toward Worcester, Robertson,* ☎ *023/626–1214,* WEB *www.gahambeckwines.co.za.* 🖾 *Free.* ☉ *Weekdays 9–5, Sat. 10–3; cellar tours by appointment.*

Springfield Estate. Although the cabernet has its fond following, this innovative winery is best known for its unusual approach to white wines, especially chardonnays. The Méthode Anciénne Chardonnay is made in the original Burgundy style and is only bottled if it's perfect—which happens about two years in five. The creamy Wild Yeast Chardonnay, with its all-natural fermentation, is an unwooded version of the above and comes highly recommended. Also try the two unusual sauvignon blancs. There is a children's playground, but you'll have to stay pretty close as there is an unfenced dam. ⊠ *Just north of Robertson on the R317, Robertson,* ☎ *023/626–3661,* ℻ *023/626–3664.* 🎫 *Free.* ☉ *Weekdays 8–5, Sat. 9–4; cellar tours by appointment only.*

Dining

$$–$$$ ✕ **Branewynsdraai.** You will see the sign to this restaurant as you enter Robertson; it's a superb place to have lunch under ancient pepper trees on the lawns or in the air-conditioned interior in midsummer. The menu is straightforward but includes traditional South African fare and top-quality steaks. Portions are generous, whether you opt for deep-fried calamari or sink your teeth into a giant sirloin topped with herb butter. As official stocker of Robertson Valley wines, this is the place to shop if lack of time limits your visits to the estates. ⊠ *1 Kromhout St.,* ☎ *023/626–3202. AE, DC, MC, V. Closed Sun.*

McGregor

20 km (12 mi) south of Robertson.

Saved from development as a result of a planned mountain pass that never materialized, McGregor is the epitome of the sleepy country hollow, tucked away between the mountains, and is one of the best examples of a preserved 19th-century Cape town.

From the R64, which runs through Robertson, take the turnoff to McGregor, which is clearly marked on the right, just after the entrance to the town. The road snakes between vineyards and farms—a picture of bucolic charm. Slowly, the farmsteads become less frequent, and you will see small cottages with distinctive red-painted doors and window frames. The McGregor Winery, on the left, heralds your entry into the town with its thatched cottages in vernacular architecture.

McGregor has gained popularity in recent years with artists who have settled here permanently and with busy executives from Cape Town intent on getting away from it all. Frankly, this is an ideal place to do absolutely nothing, but you can take a leisurely stroll through the fynbos, watch birds from one of several hides on the Heron Walk, or follow one of the hiking or mountain-bike trails if you are feeling more energetic. There is a great hiking trail across the Riviersonderend Mountains to Greyton.

The **McGregor Winery** is a popular attraction, with surprisingly inexpensive wines considering their quality. Try the unwooded chardonnay and the exceptional port. ⊠ *Main Rd.,* ☎ *023/625–1741.* 🎫 *Free.* ☉ *Mon.–Thurs. 8–12:30 and 1:30–5, Fri. 8–5, Sat. 9–12:30.*

Dining and Lodging

$$ ✕🏠 **The Old Mill Lodge.** This simple thatched lodge, its adjacent 19th-century waterwheel still intact, dreams on among tall trees at the far end of the village. Accommodations are in thatched cottages whose interior is decorated with antique-style beds and wood beams and thatch. Before dinner take a walk through the olive grove or a dip in the swimming pool. The lodge prides itself on a good table, and the menu changes daily, depending on what's in season. Rates are set at R185 per person for bed and breakfast and at R255 per person if dinner is included. This does not include wine and drinks. À la carte lunches were recently introduced, making a welcome addition to the limited number of village eateries. ⊠ *Box 25, McGregor 6708,* ☎ *023/625–1841,* ℻ *023/625–1941. 8 rooms. Pool. AE, DC, MC, V. MAP.*

Montagu

36 km (22 mi) northeast of Robertson.

Montagu bills itself as "the Gateway to the Little Karoo," and its picturesque streets lined with Cape Victorian architecture lend this some credence. Today the town's main attraction is the natural hot springs, and many of the Victorian houses have been transformed into bed-and-breakfast guest houses. Take the R64 from Robertson (you will have to return there from McGregor), and after 29 km (18 mi) you'll pass through the unlovely agricultural town of Ashton; keep left (don't turn off to Swellendam) and enter the short but spectacular Cogmans Kloof Pass. On either side of the pass, which runs in a river gorge, you can see the magnificent fold mountains, which are ultimately the source for the hot springs.

A three-hour ride on the popular **Langeberg Tractor Ride** will take you to the summit of the Langeberg (Long Mountain) and back. The tractor winds up some tortuously twisted paths revealing magnificent views of the area's peaks and valleys. After a short stop at the summit, a similarly harrowing descent follows, but you won't be disappointed by the views. Following your trip, you can enjoy a delicious lunch of *potjiekos* (traditional stew cooked over a fire in a single cast-iron pot). Reservations are essential. ⊠ *R318, Protea Farm, Montagu,* ☎ *023/614–2471.* 🎫 *R30, R40 for lunch.* ⊗ *Wed. at 10, Sat. at 10 and 2.*

Dining and Lodging

$$–$$$ ✕ **Jessica's Restaurant.** Pet Staffordshire bull terrier Jessica not only lends her name to this Victorian house that has been converted into a restaurant, but also features in blown-up photographs on the walls, interspersed with delightful doggy prints from previous eras. The superb cuisine is beautifully yet simply plated. If you cannot make up your mind after perusing the menu, stay with the recommended daily specials, and you will relish a feast that may start with an Asian chicken *satay* and follow with panfried springbok (venison) steak and ostrich fillet with balsamic butter, teamed with onion marmalade and polenta wedges. The butternut gnocchi on nut-studded wilted spinach, topped with fresh tomato sauce and feta, is a vegetarian delight. Other highlights are the crispy duck and satiny crème brûlée. ⊠ *47 Bath St.,* ☎ *032/614–1805. Reservations essential. AE, DC, MC, V. No lunch Mon.–Sat. No dinner Sun.*

$$$ ✕🏨 **Montagu Country Hotel.** This salmon-color hotel was built in Victorian times but was extensively remodeled in the early 1930s. Present owner Gert Lubbe highlights its many art deco features and collects furniture and artifacts from this era to complement the interior. A well-trained staff ensures efficient and personal service, inspired by the owner, a consummate professional. Centrally situated, this makes a good base for historical, scenic, and Wineland expeditions. The hotel's Wild Apricot restaurant serves an excellent breakfast, while the dinner menu is straightforward, with the addition of traditional country favorites like Karoo lamb pie. Entrées include fettuccine Alfredo and beef fillet. ⊠ *27 Bath St., Box 338, Montagu 6720,* ☎ *023/614–3125,* 📠 *023/614–1905.* 🌐 *www.montagucountryhotel.co.za. 23 rooms. Bar, air-conditioning, room service, pool. AE, DC, MC, V.*

THE OVERBERG

Overberg is Afrikaans for "over the mountains, an apt name for this remote region at the bottom of the continent, separated from the rest of the Cape by mountains. Before 19th-century engineers blasted a route through the Hottentots Holland R, the Overberg developed in comparative isolation. To this day it possesses a wild emptiness far removed from the settled valleys of the Winelands.

It's a land of immense contrasts, and if you're planning a trip along the Garden Route, you would be well advised to add the Overberg to your itinerary. The coastal drive from Gordon's Bay to Hermanus is as beautiful as anything in the Cape—an unfolding panorama of deserted beaches, pounding surf, and fractured granite mountains. Once you pass Hermanus and head out onto the windswept plains leading to Cape Agulhas, you have to search harder for the Overberg's riches. Towns are few and far between, the countryside comprising an expanse of wheat fields and sheep pastures. The occasional reward of the drive is a coastline of sublime beauty. Enormous stretches of dunes and unspoiled beaches extend for miles. Unfortunately, no roads parallel the ocean, and you must constantly divert inland before heading to another part of the coast.

Hermanus is one of the best places in South Africa for land-based whale-watching during the annual migration of southern right whales between July and November. Spring is also the best time to see the Overberg's wildflowers, although the region's profusion of coastal and montane fynbos is beautiful year-round.

The upper part of the Overberg, north of the N2 highway, is more like the Winelands, with 18th- and 19th-century towns sheltered in the lee of rocky mountains. Here the draws are apple orchards, inns, and hiking trails that wind through the mountains. The historic towns of Swellendam and Greyton make the most logical touring bases.

To tour the whole area would take three to four days. For a shorter trip focus on the splendors of the coastal route from Gordon's Bay to Hermanus, and then head north toward the Winelands.

Towns and sights are marked on the Western Cape map.

Gordon's Bay

70 km (44 mi) southeast of Cape Town.

Gordon's Bay is an attractive resort built on a steep mountain slope overlooking the vast expanse of False Bay. You can often see whales and their calves in False Bay in October and November.

From Gordon's Bay the road hugs the mountainside, slipping between the craggy peaks of the Hottentots Holland Mountains and the sea far below. The coastal drive between Gordon's Bay and Hermanus is one of the country's best, particularly if you take the time to follow some of the dirt roads leading down to the sea from the highway. There are numerous paths down to the seashore from the road between Gordon's Bay and Rooiels. It's worth taking a walk down to watch the waves pounding the rocky coast, but take care. If there are no other people around and the waves are quite big, stay a few yards back from the water, as this section of coast is notorious for freak waves in certain swell and wind conditions. Note the many crosses on the side of the road—each one denotes an angler who has been swept off the rocks.

The road passes the tiny settlement of **Rooiels** (pronounced *roy*-els) then cuts inland for a couple of miles. A turnoff leads to **Pringle Bay,** a collection of holiday homes sprinkled across the fynbos. The village has little to offer other than a beautiful wide beach (check out the sign warning of quicksand). If you continue through Pringle Bay, the tar road soon gives way to gravel. This road, badly corrugated in patches, runs around the looming pinnacle of **Hangklip** and along a deserted stretch of magnificent beach and dunes to Betty's Bay.

If you don't fancy the gravel road, return to the R44 and continue 1½ km (1 mi) to the turnoff to Stony Point, on the edge of Betty's Bay. Follow Porter Drive for 3 km (2 mi) until you reach a sign marked MOOI HAWENS and a smaller sign picturing a penguin. Follow the penguin signs to a **colony of African penguins,** one of only two mainland colonies in southern Africa (the other is at Boulders Beach in Cape Town, where it is much easier to see these endangered seabirds). The colony lies about 600 yards from the parking area along a rocky coastal path. Along the way you pass the concrete remains of tank stands, reminders of the days when Betty's Bay was a big whaling station. The African penguin is endangered, so the colony has been fenced off as protection against people, dogs, and other predators. This particular colony was once savaged by a leopard.

Return to Porter Drive and turn right to rejoin the R44. Back on the main road, go another 2 km (1 mi) to the **Harold Porter National Botanical Garden,** a 440-acre nature reserve in the heart of the coastal fynbos, where the Cape Floral Kingdom is at its richest. The profusion of plants supports 78 species of birds and a wide range of small mammals, including large troops of baboons. You couldn't ask for a more fantastic setting, cradled between the Atlantic and the towering peaks of the 3,000-ft Kogelberg Range. Walking trails wind through the reserve and into the mountains via Disa and Leopard's kloofs, which echo with the sound of waterfalls and running streams. Back at the main buildings, a pleasant restaurant serves light meals and teas, and there are a gift shop and a nursery selling indigenous plants. ⊠ *Box 35, Betty's Bay 7141,* ☎ *028/272–9311.* ✉ *R5.* ⊙ *Daily 8–6 (last entry 4:30 on weekdays, 5 on weekends. Exit gates stay open till 7 in summer.).*

Kleinmond

25 km (15½ mi) southeast of Gordon's Bay.

The small town of Kleinmond (small mouth) is nothing special—it has a couple of restaurants and guest houses—but it presides over a magnificent stretch of shoreline, backed by the mountains of the Palmietberg.Close to the town, on the Cape Town side and clearly marked with signs from the main street, is the **Kogelberg Nature Reserve,** a 66,000-acre area of fynbos that extends from the mountains almost to the sea and includes most of the course of the Palmiet River. The beach and small lagoon that front the reserve are also accessible from the Palmiet Caravan Park. Take one of the well-marked nature walks through the reserve, and you are sure to see some of the area's magnificent flora and bird life. The prices given below were correct at time of writing, but the reserve administration has been experimenting with charge structures, so it will probably change—in either direction. ⊠ *Kogelberg Nature Reserve,* ☎ *028/271–5138,* FAX *028/272–9425.* ✉ *R12 entrance, R20 for hiking.* ⊙ *Daily 7:30–7 (closes about 2 hrs earlier in winter).*

Almost as impressive are the 10 km (6 mi) of sandy beach that fringes Sandown Bay, at the eastern edge of town. Much of the beach is nothing more than a sandbar, separating the Atlantic from the huge lagoon formed by the Bot River. Swift currents make bathing risky.

The R44 cuts inland around the Bot River lagoon. Ten kilometers (6 miles) past Kleinmond, the road comes to a junction where you'd turn right to go to Hermanus on the R43, but take a quick detour by turning left and heading off to **Beaumont Wines,** which you'll see on your right before you reach the N2. This is a fabulous family-run winery.

It's just sufficiently scruffy to create an ambience of age and country charm without actually being untidy. But, charm aside, it's the wine you'd come here for, and it really is worth the small detour. It produces a range of dependable, notable wines, like the new-wave pinotage and the first mourvèdre to be bottled in South Africa. ✉ *R44, Bot River,* ☎ *028/284–9450.* ⛴ *Free.* ☉ *Weekdays 9:30–12:30 and 1:30–4:30, Sat. morning by appointment.*

Head back toward Kleinmond, continuing on the R43 toward Hermanus and across the Bot River. The R43 swings eastward around the mountains, past the not-particularly-attractive fishing village of Hawston and the small artists' colony of Onrus.

Less than 2 km (1 mi) farther is the turnoff to the R320, which leads through the vineyards and orchards of the scenic Hemel-en-Aarde (Heaven and Earth) Valley and over Shaw's Pass to Caledon. At the junction you'll find the **Wine Village Shop,** so you don't have to brave the rather dodgy dirt road. As well as a good selection of local wines, such as Hamilton Russel, the Hermanus Heritage Collection, and Southern Right, there is a small arts-and-crafts outlet. ✉ *Junction of R43 and R320,* ☎ *028/316–3988,* WEB *www.wine-village.co.za.* ☉ *Weekdays 9–6, Sat. 9–5, Sun. 10–5.*

A short way down this rutted road, **Hamilton Russell Vineyards** is in an attractive thatched building overlooking a small dam. This winery produces some of the best wine in South Africa. The pinot noir won loud acclaim from Frank Prial of the *New York Times* and is one of the two best produced in the country. The chardonnay comes closer to the French style of chardonnay than any other Cape wine, with lovely fruit and a touch of lemon rind and butterscotch. Unfortunately, the 2000 vintage is going to be a bit light, as many of the grapes were destroyed in a single, rather disastrous hailstorm. ✉ *Off R320, Walker Bay,* ☎ *028/312–3595.* ⛴ *Free.* ☉ *Weekdays 9–5, Sat. 9–1.*

A short distance farther on the Hemel en Aarde Valley Road is **Bouchard-Finlayson.** This Franco-Cape partnership of local lad Peter Finlayson and Burgundy-bred Paul Bouchard has cashed in on the best of both partners to create some fantastic deep-south wines. Try the French-style Galpin Peak pinot noir, of which the '97 vintage is particularly impressive. And lay down a few bottles each of the limited release Tête de Cuvée Galpin Peak Pinot Noir and the rather different pinot blanc–chardonnay blend. ✉ *Off R320, Hemel en Aarde Valley,* ☎ *028/312–3515,* WEB *www.bouchardfinlayson.co.za.* ⛴ *Free.* ☉ *Weekdays 9:30–5, Sat. 9:30–12:30.*

Return to the R43 and drive 3 km (2 mi) to Hermanus. On the outskirts of town, keep watch on your left side for a pair of white gateposts set well back from the road painted with the words ROTARY WAY—if ★ you pass the turnoff to the New Harbour, you've gone too far. The **Rotary Way** is a scenic drive that climbs along the spine of the mountains above Hermanus, with incredible views of the town, Walker Bay, and Hemel-en-Aarde Valley, as well as some of the area's beautiful fynbos. It's a highlight of a trip to the Overberg, and you shouldn't miss it. The Rotary Way turns to dirt after a few kilometers and becomes impassable to all but four-wheel-drive vehicles about 2 km (1 mi) after that. The entire mountainside is laced with wonderful walking trails, and many of the scenic lookouts have benches.

Dining and Lodging

$$$$ ✕🏠 **Beach House on Sandown Bay.** In quiet, seaside Kleinmond, this comfortable hotel overlooks a 10-km (6-mi) crescent of beach and a beautiful lagoon. It's a good base for whale-watching in October and

November, as well as for walks in the surrounding nature reserves. The hotel itself is attractive, the rooms simply decorated with wicker furniture and floral draperies and bedspreads; in sea-facing rooms sliding doors open onto small balconies with tremendous views of Sandown Bay. The restaurant specializes in seafood fresh in the local harbor. ⊠ *Beach Rd., Kleinmond 7195,* ☎ *028/271–3130,* FAX *028/271–4022. 22 rooms, 1 suite. Restaurant, bar, pool. AE, DC, MC, V. BP.*

Outdoor Activities

RIVER RAFTING

The Palmiet River is a low-volume, technical white-water river of about Grade 3. In high water **Gravity River Tours** (☎ 021/683–3698, WEB www.gravity.co.za) offers rafting trips in four-place or two-place inflatable rafts. In low water they do the same trip but on specially designed one-person inflatable crafts called "geckos." A half-day trip costs R240, including snacks, and a full day, R295, including breakfast and lunch. At time of writing, they were planning to start overnight trails.

Hermanus

24 km (15 mi) southeast of Kleinmond on the R43.

Hermanus is a popular holiday resort and the major coastal town in the Overberg. Restaurants and shops line the streets, and the town has lost much of its original charm, but it is still most definitely worth a visit. It's packed during the Whale Festival in September and October and over the Christmas school holidays.

Just a couple of miles away, pristine beaches extend as far as the eye can see, and the Kleinriviersberg provides a breathtaking backdrop to the town. Hermanus sits atop a long line of cliffs, which makes it one of the best places in South Africa to watch the annual whale migra-
★ tion from shore. An 11-km (7-mi) **cliff walk** allows watchers to follow the whales, which often come within 100 ft of the cliffs as they move along the coastline.

Originally, Hermanus was a whaling center. The **Old Harbour Museum,** in a small building at the old stone fishing basin, displays some of the horrific harpoons used to lance the giants. There are also exhibits on fishing techniques, local marine life, and angling records. The white building next to the harbor parking lot houses the PFV Old Harbour Museum Photographic Exhibition. There are photos of old Hermanus and many of the town's fishermen proudly displaying their catches of fish, sharks, and dolphins. Yes, dolphins. At time of writing, the museum was busy building a new whale museum, near the photographic exhibition. All the whale stuff will move from the Old Harbour Museum, which will then concentrate on fishing and other marine exhibits. The change is expected to be completed by the end of 2002, when the entrance fees will also increase. ⊠ *Old Harbour, Marine Dr.,* ☎ *028/ 312–1475.* R2. ☉ *Dec.–Feb., Mon.–Sat. 9–5, Sun. noon–4; Mar.– Nov., Mon.–Sat. 9–4:30, Sun. noon–4.*

From Hermanus the R43 continues eastward, hugging the strip of land between the mountains and the **Klein River Lagoon.** The lagoon is popular with water-skiers, boaters, and anglers. You can hire a variety of boats down at Prawn Flats, including small motor dinghies, canoes, and sailboards. Expect to pay R20–R50 for the first hour, depending on the type of boat, and then half that amount per hour thereafter. You can also join a sunset cruise up the Klein River for R70, which includes wine and snacks, or for R130 with a braai (barbecue) afterward, with **Walker Bay Adventures** (⊠ Prawn Flats, off R43, ☎ 028/314–0925).

Dining and Lodging

\$\$–\$\$\$\$ ✕ **Burgundy.** This restaurant occupies a fisherman's cottage overlooking the old fishing harbor. Ask for a table on the veranda or the lawn, from where you can savor views of Walker Bay. In winter stay cozy within the ocher-washed walls near the fireplace. Chef Deon Joubert brings French flair and consistency to South African ingredients, with an emphasis on seafood. The fresh line fish is always a good choice, either grilled or given Moroccan treatment with a *harissa* crust. There is always at least one traditional Cape dish, along with ostrich that comes on polenta with a port-and-currant jus. Desserts are mostly ice cream–based, or you could indulge in the chocolate mousse cake. ✉ *Market Sq.,* ☎ *028/312–2800. AE, DC, MC, V. No dinner Sun.*

\$\$ ✕ **The Greeks.** An authentic family-run Greek taverna usually means excellent fare, friendly service, and pleasing prices—exactly what you'll find at this little white-walled restaurant with its shiny red metal tables dressed with checked oilcloths. Start your meal with a complimentary pita, redolent with garlic and hot from the oven. Be prepared to wait for your choices, which could be a meze of *spanakopita* (spinach pie) or *soutzouakia* (meatballs with tomato and cumin), both served with Greek salad on the side. Among good entrées are Yianni's *schwarmas*—pita enveloping salad, *tatziki* (cucumber salad), and a choice of grilled chicken, beef, or vegetables. Although grilled steak is available, more typical is the slow-roasted lamb with herbs, accompanied by Greek-style potatoes and vegetables. As a change from the ubiquitous baklava, try the *galaktobourekoa* for dessert, a kind of milk tart. ✉ *16 Dirkie Uys St.,* ☎ *028/312–3707. AE, MC, V. Closed Sun.–Mon. No dinner Tues.–Thurs.*

\$\$\$\$ ✕🏨 **Marine.** In an incomparable cliff-top setting, this venerable hotel has sumptuously decorated rooms and suites, under-floor heating, and luxurious facilities. The sea-facing rooms, some with private balcony, provide whale-watchers with grandstand views over Walker Bay. The revamped orangery invites guests to linger over tea or drinks, while the two restaurants tempt with sophisticated menus. The Pavilion restaurant, with wonderful views of Walker Bay, offers up-to-the-minute fare that's both fresh and flavorful. Tandoori crocodile, served with a *poppadum* crouton and arugula-and-mango salad, makes an innovative first course. Spiced loin of lamb is accompanied by spinach, cardamom creamed potatoes, roasted tomatoes, and a mint jus, while visually stunning desserts include a raspberry soufflé with nectarine sorbet and shortbread. ✉ *Marine Dr., Box 9, Hermanus 7200,* ☎ *028/313–1000,* 🖷 *028/313–0160. 47 rooms. 2 restaurants, bar, room service, 2 pools, billiards. AE, DC, MC, V. BP.*

\$\$\$ 🏨 **Windsor.** If you come to Hermanus in October or November, stay at this hotel in the heart of town. It's a family-run hostelry that offers comfort but little pretense of luxury; however, the hotel's position atop the cliffs makes it a great place to view the annual whale migration. Request one of the second-floor, sea-facing rooms, with huge sliding-glass doors and unbeatable views. ✉ *Marine Dr., Box 3, Hermanus 7200,* ☎ *028/312–3727,* 🖷 *028/312–2181. 60 rooms. Restaurant, 2 bars. AE, DC, MC, V. BP.*

\$\$ 🏨 **Whale Cottage, Hermanus.** If you don't like whales, avoid this place—you'll find their image in your bathroom, on the walls, perched on furniture, and, almost literally, popping out of the woodwork. But the decor is not as busy as this sounds. Decorated in restful shades of blue with a fish motif, this is a great choice as a base from which to do long whale-watching walks. It doesn't have a sea view, but it's close to everything and about half a mile from the whale-watching cliffs. It has a homey feel, with an honesty bar and central tea and coffee station near the breakfast room. ✉ *20 Main Rd., 7200,* ☎ *028/313–0929,*

FAX *028/313–0912,* WEB *www.whalecottage.com. 5 rooms. Breakfast room, pool. AE, DC, MC, V. BP.*

Outdoor Activities

KAYAKING

For a really fun outing, join a gentle paddling excursion from the Old Harbour. You paddle in safe, stable double sea kayaks and are accompanied by a guide all the way. You'll pay R150 for a two-hour morning trip including breakfast or R70 for a quick one-hour paddle. A full-day trip on the lagoon, including lunch, is R250. Contact **Walker Bay Adventures** (⊠ Prawn Flats, off R43, ☎ 028/314–0925).

Bredasdorp

60 km (37½ mi) east of Stanford.

Bredasdorp is a sleepy agricultural town that has a certain charm, as long as you don't catch it on a Sunday afternoon, when everything's closed and an air of ennui pervades the brassy, windswept streets.

Once a year, however, the usual lethargic atmosphere is abandoned, and a radical sense of purpose takes its place when Bredasdorp hosts the Foot of Africa Marathon each spring. Don't be lulled by the small-town, country setting into thinking that this race is a breeze and that you might give it a go. Word has it that the undulating landscape has the fittest athletes doubting their perseverance.

Housed in a converted church and rectory, the **Bredasdorp Museum** has an extensive collection of items salvaged from the hundreds of ships that have gone down in the stormy waters off the Cape. In addition to the usual cannons and figureheads, the museum displays a surprising array of undamaged household items rescued from the sea, including entire dining room sets, sideboards, china, and phonographs. ⊠ *Independent St.,* ☎ FAX *028/424–1240.* ☜ *R5.* ☉ *Weekdays 9–4:45, weekends 11–4.*

OFF THE BEATEN PATH	**ELIM –** About 45 km (32 mi) west of Bredasdorp and accessible only by dirt road, Elim is a Moravian mission village founded in 1824. Little has changed in the last hundred years: simple whitewashed cottages line the few streets, and the settlement's colored residents all belong to the Moravian Church. The whole village has been declared a national monument. The easiest access is via the R317, off the R319 between Cape Agulhas and Bredasdorp.

De Hoop Nature Reserve is a huge conservation area covering 88,900 acres of isolated coastal terrain as well as a marine reserve extending 5 km (3 mi) out to sea. Massive white-sand dunes, mountains, and rare lowland fynbos are home to eland, bontebok, and Cape mountain zebra, as well as more than 250 bird species. You can rent cottages with cooking facilities. Access is via the dirt road between Bredasdorp and Malgas. It's worth planning ahead and renting a mountain bike before going here, as there are a number of wonderfully laid-out trails. This is also a fantastic place to watch whales from the shore—not quite as easy as Hermanus but much less crowded. ⊠ *Private Bag X16, Bredasdorp, 7280,* ☎ *028/542–1126.* ☜ *R13.* ☉ *Daily 7–6.*

Past De Hoop Nature Reserve on the dirt road from Bredasdorp is the small hamlet of **Malgas,** a major port in the 19th century before the mouth of the Breede River silted up. As well as a picturesque village, you will find the last hand-drawn car ferry in the country. It's fascinating to watch the technique, as the ferry operator, seemingly effortlessly, "walks" the ferry across the river on a huge cable, leaning into his "harness." The setting is beautiful, and the ride is unusual. ⊠ *50 km (30 mi) from the N2 on dirt road, signposted from the N2 about 5 km (3 mi) on Cape Town side of Swellendam. ☏ R20 per vehicle.*

En Route   From Bredasdorp it's just 37 km (23 mi) through rolling farmland to **Cape Agulhas.** Although it's not nearly as spectacular as Cape Point, it's a wild and lonely place—rather fitting for the end of a wild and wonderful continent.

Arniston, or Waenhuiskrans

★ *24 km (15 mi) northeast of Struisbaai.*

Although its official name is Waenhuiskrans, and that's what you'll see on maps, this lovely, isolated holiday village, is almost always called Arniston—after a British ship of that name that was wrecked on the nearby reef in 1815. Beautiful beaches, water that assumes Caribbean shades of blue, and mile after mile of towering white dunes attract anglers and holiday makers alike. Only the frequent southeasters that blow off the sea and the chilly water are likely to put a damper on your enjoyment. For 200 years a community of local fisherfolk has eked out a living here, setting sail each day in small fishing boats. Today their village has been named a national monument, and it's a pleasure to wander around the thatched cottages of this still-vibrant community. The village has expanded enormously in the last 15 years, thanks to the construction of a host of holiday homes. Fortunately, much of the new architecture blends effectively with the whitewashed simplicity of the original cottages.

Waenhuiskrans is Afrikaans for "wagon-house cliff," and the village takes its name from a vast cave 2 km (1 mi) south of town that is theoretically large enough to house several wagons and their spans of oxen. Signs point the way over the dunes to the cave, which is accessible only at low tide. You need shoes to protect your feet from the sharp rocks, and wear something you don't mind getting wet. It's definitely worth the trouble, however, to see this stunning spot.

Again, retrace your way to Bredasdorp. This time take the R319 toward Swellendam. The road runs through mile after mile of rolling farmland, populated by sheep, cattle, and an occasional ostrich. In the far distance looms the Langeberg. After 64 km (40 mi) turn right onto the N2 highway. Continue for another 15 km (9 mi) before turning right to the **Bontebok National Park.** Covering just 6,880 acres of coastal fynbos, this is one of the smallest of South Africa's national parks. Don't expect to see big game here—the park contains no elephant, lion, or rhino. What you will see are bontebok, graceful white-face antelope nearly exterminated by hunters earlier in the last century, as well as red hartebeest, Cape grysbok, steenbok, duiker, and the endangered Cape mountain zebra. Two short walking trails start at the campsite, next to the Breede River. ⊠ *Box 149, Swellendam 6740, ☎ 028/514–2735,* WEB *www.parks-sa.co.za. ☏ R12 per person. ☉ Oct.–Apr., daily 7–7; May–Sept., daily 7–6.*

Dining and Lodging

$$$–$$$$ ✕🏨 **Arniston Hotel.** You could easily spend a week here and still need
★   to be dragged away. The setting, in a tiny fishing village on a crescent of white dunes, has a lot to do with its appeal, but the hotel has also struck a fine balance between elegance and beach-holiday comfort. Request a sea-facing room, where you can enjoy the ever-changing colors of the horizon and have a grandstand view of the large concentration of cow and calf pairs found here during the whaling season, between May and October. The à la carte menu offers a substantial range of

fare, with few surprises, but the grilled catch of the day is as fresh as you can get. A salad of smoked chicken and sweet melon could precede a pasta topped with tomato, caper, and olive sauce. Lunch is served on the patio in fine weather, and wine lovers will rejoice at the quality of the deservedly renowned wine list. ⊠ *Beach Rd., Waenhuiskrans (mailing address: Box 126, Bredasdorp 7280),* ☎ *028/445–9000,* FAX *028/445–9633,* WEB *www.arnistonhotel.com. 34 rooms. Restaurant, bar, room service, pool. No children under 12. AE, DC, MC, V. BP.*

Swellendam

★ *72 km (45 mi) north of Waenhuiskrans.*

Return to the junction with the N2 and cross the highway into beautiful Swellendam, lying in the shadow of the imposing Langeberg. Founded in 1745, it is the third-oldest town in South Africa, and many of its historic buildings have been elegantly restored. Even on a casual drive along the main street, you'll see a number of lovely Cape Dutch homes, with their traditional whitewashed walls, gables, and thatched roofs.

The centerpiece of the town's historical past is the **Drostdy Museum,** a collection of buildings dating to the town's earliest days. The Drostdy was built in 1747 by the Dutch East India Company to serve as the residence of the *landdrost,* the magistrate who presided over the district. The building is furnished in a style that was common in the mid-19th century. A path leads through the Drostdy herb gardens to Mayville, an 1855 middle-class home that blends elements of Cape Dutch and Cape Georgian architecture. Across Swellengrebel Street stand the old jail and the Ambagswerf, an outdoor exhibit of tools used by the town's blacksmiths, wainwrights, coopers, and tanners. ⊠ *18 Swellengrebel St.,* ☎ *028/514–1138.* 🏛 *R10.* ⊙ *Weekdays 9–4:45, weekends 10–3:45.*

Swellendam's **Dutch Reformed Church** is an imposing white edifice, built in 1911 in an eclectic style. The gables are baroque, the windows Gothic, the cupola vaguely Eastern, and the steeple copied from Belgium. Surprisingly, all the elements work together wonderfully. Inside is an interesting tiered amphitheater, with banks of curving wood pews facing the pulpit and organ. ⊠ *7 Voortrek St.,* ☎ *028/514–1225.* ⊙ *Services (in Afrikaans) Feb.–Nov. at 10 and 6; Dec.–Jan. at 9 and 6.*

If you'd like to get your feet on the ground and breathe some clean local air, take a hike in the **Marloth Nature Reserve,** in the Langeberg above town. Five easy walks, ranging from one to four hours, explore some of the mountain gorges. An office at the entrance to the reserve has trail maps and hiking information. There is a five-day trail, which costs R45 per person, per day, in addition to the park entrance fee. If you're doing a day walk, park outside the entrance boom. Although you can stay in the reserve till sunset, the gates close at the time advertised. ⊠ *Box 28, Swellendam 6740,* ☎ *028/514–1410,* WEB *www.cnc.org.za.* 🏛 *R13.* ⊙ *Weekdays 7:30–4, weekends 7–6.*

Dining and Lodging

$$$$ ✕🏛 **Klippe Rivier Homestead.** Amid rolling farmland 3 km (2 mi) outside Swellendam, this guest house occupies one of the Overberg's most gracious and historic country homes. It was built around 1825 in traditional Cape style, with thick white walls, a thatched roof, and a distinctive gable. Guests stay in enormous rooms in the converted stables. The three downstairs rooms are furnished with antiques in Cape Dutch, colonial, and Victorian styles. Upstairs, raw wood beams, cane ceilings, and bold prints set the tone for less expensive Provençal-style rooms, with air-conditioning and small balconies. Some public rooms cannot support the sheer volume of antique collectibles, taking on a museum-

like quality. Delectable five-course dinners are table d'hôte, cost R120, and are prepared with fresh herbs, vegetables, fruit, and cream from surrounding farms. No children under eight are allowed. ⊠ *On dirt road off R60 to Ashton (mailing address: Box 483, Swellendam 6740),* ☏ *028/514–3341,* FAX *028/514–3337. 7 rooms. Restaurant, saltwater pool. AE, DC, MC, V. BP.*

$$$ ✕⌂ **Adin's and Sharon's Hideaway.** The Victorian homestead and its three luxury cottages are set in a peaceful garden that displays some 400 rosebushes and is home to varied bird life. Although the setting and beautifully appointed, cottages are excellent reasons to stay at this establishment, the level of hospitality sets this place above the rest. Adin and Sharon Greaves continue to win every award going for best South African bed-and-breakfast establishment. Their service dedication extends to providing lifts, planning routes, and presenting the best breakfast for many miles around. Not only is it the perfect base from which to explore historic Swellendam and environs, but it would still be recommended if it cost far more than its reasonable rate. ⊠ *10 Hermanus Steyn Rd.,* ☏ FAX *028/51–43316,* WEB *www.adinbb.co.za. 3 cottages, 1 room. Air-conditioning, pool. DC, MC, V. BP.*

Outdoor Activities

HORSE RIDING

You can take just a little trot or a longer excursion through the Marloth Nature Reserve on horseback with **Two Feathers Horse Trails** (☏ 082/494–8279, WEB www.twofeathers.co.za). Expect to pay between R85 for an hour and R400 for a full-day ride, including a packed lunch.

En Route   From Swellendam return to the N2 and turn right toward Cape Town. The road sweeps through rich, rolling cropland that extends to the base of the Langeberg. A few kilometers after the town of Riviersonderend (pronounced "riff-*ear*-sonder-ent"), turn right onto the R406, a good gravel road that leads to the village of Greyton in the lee of the Riviersonderend Mountains.

Greyton

32 km (20 mi) west of Swellendam.

The charming village of Greyton, filled with white thatched cottages and quiet lanes, is a popular weekend retreat for Capetonians as well as a permanent home for many retirees. The village offers almost nothing in the way of traditional sights, but it's a great base for walks into the surrounding mountains and a pleasant place to pause for lunch or tea.

After Greyton the R406 becomes paved. Drive 5 km (3 mi) to the turnoff to **Genadendal** (Valley of Mercy), a Moravian mission station founded in 1737 to educate the Khoikhoi and convert them to Christianity. Seeing this impoverished hamlet today, it's difficult to comprehend the major role this mission played in the early history of South Africa. In the late 18th century it was the second-largest settlement after Cape Town, and its Khoikhoi craftsmen produced the finest silver cutlery, and woodwork in the country. Some of the first written works in Afrikaans were printed here, and the colored community greatly influenced the development of Afrikaans as it is heard today. None of this went over well with the white population. By 1909 new legislation prohibited colored ownership of land, and in 1926 the Department of Public Education closed the settlement's teachers' training college, arguing that coloreds were better employed on neighboring farms. Genadendal began a long slide into obscurity until 1994, when then-president Nelson Mandela renamed his official residence Genadendal.

In town you can walk the streets of the settlement and tour the historic buildings facing Church Square. Genadendal is still a mission station, and the German missionaries may show interested visitors around. Of particular note is the **Genadendal Mission Museum,** spread through 15 rooms in three buildings. The museum collection, the only one in South Africa to be named a National Cultural Treasure, includes unique household implements, books, tools, musical instruments, among them the country's oldest pipe organ. Wall displays examine mission life in the Cape in the 18th and 19th centuries, focusing on the early missionaries' work with the Khoikhoi. Unfortunately, many of the displays are in Afrikaans. ⊠ *Off R406,* ☎ ꜰᴀX *028/251–8582.* ▣ *R7.* ☉ *Mon.–Thurs. 9–1 and 2–5, Fri. 9–1 and 2–3:30, Sat. 9–1.*

Outdoor Activities

There are so many exciting things you can do here, you'll be stuck for choice. Your best bet is to contact **IntrApid Adventures** (☎ 021/461–4918 or 082/536–8842, ᴡᴇʙ www.raftsa.co.za), which offers half- or full-day adventure trips that include anything from a gentle rafting trip on the Sonderend River (Riviersonderend), to a short mountain bike trail, a scenic rappel, horseback riding, or a fun quad-bike ride. Trips cost about R250–R350 for a half-day trip and R350–R450 for a full-day trip, which includes a packed lunch and a light Continental breakfast. Prices are based on a minimum of four people, but you can organize a trip for one or two people at a higher cost, if you like.

HIKING

Walking is one of the major attractions of the Overberg, and almost every town and nature reserve offers a host of trails ranging in length from a few minutes to an entire day. For detailed information about these trails, contact the local visitor information offices.

There are two wonderful two-day hikes through the **Vrolijkheid Nature Reserve** (☎ 023/625–1621). For each you need to get a permit from the reserve and pay R49 per person for the two days. You'll also need to book accommodations.

The **Boesmanskloof Trail,** 32 km (20 mi), wanders through the Riviersonderend Mountains from Greyton to the exquisite hamlet of McGregor. Book accommodations, in hiking huts on a private farm, through **Barry Oosthuizen** (☎ 023/625–1735). Accommodations cost R150 from one to four people, or R35 per person for groups of five or more. Oosthuizen will also do grocery shopping for you and leave food at the hut, charging you only what he pays.

The **Genadendal Hiking Trail** is booked through the **Vrolijkheid Nature Reserve** (☎ 023/625–1621) and costs R49 per person for a permit for two days. Accommodations are in huts on the farm **De Hoek** (☎ 023/626–2176 or 082/666–0230). There are a gas stove, hot showers, flush toilets, a braai, and wood. Accommodations cost R30 per person. If you like, you may spend a night at the **Moravian Mission Church** (☎ 028/251–8346), which is where the hike starts and ends.

En Route To head back toward Cape Town, follow the R406 to the N2. After the town of Bot River, the road leaves the wheat fields and climbs into the mountains. It's lovely country, full of rock and pine forest interspersed with orchards. **Sir Lowry's Pass** serves as the gateway to Cape Town and the Winelands, a magnificent breach in the mountains that opens to reveal the curving expanse of False Bay, the long ridge of the peninsula, and, in the distance, Table Mountain.

WEST COAST

The West Coast is an acquired taste. It's dry and bleak, and other than the ubiquitous exotic gum trees, nothing grows higher than your knees. It's a wild and wonderful place. An icy sea pounds long deserted beaches, or rocky headlands and the sky stretches for miles.

Historically, this area has been populated by hardy fisherfolk and tough, grizzled farmers. And over the years they have worked out a balance with the extreme elements—responding with a stoic minimalism that is obvious in the building styles, the cuisine, and the language.

Unfortunately, minimalism became fashionable, and urban refugees started settling on the West Coast. The first lot weren't bad—they bought tattered old houses and renovated them just sufficiently to make them livable. Then came those who insisted on building a replica of their suburban homes at the coast. And then—the worst of all—came the developers. They bought up huge tracts of land and cut them up into tiny little plots, popping horrid little houses onto them. Or perhaps they'd turn a whole bay into a pseudo–Greek village. As a result, the austere aesthetic that makes the West Coast so special is fast disappearing. But it's not gone—at least not yet.

Just inland from the West Coast is the Swartland ("black ground," a reference to the fertile soil that supports a flourishing wheat and wine industry). To the north, the Cedarberg is an absolutely beautiful and rugged range of mountains, most of which are designated wilderness area. In South Africa that means you may hike there with a permit, but there are no laid-out trails and no accommodations or facilities of any kind. Fantastic rock formations, myriad flowering plants, delicate rock art, and crystal-clear streams with tinkling waterfalls and deep pools make this a veritable hiker's paradise.

Towns and sights in West Coast, Swartland, and Cedarberg are marked on the Western Cape map.

West Coast, Swartland, and Cedarberg

A loop around the West Coast, Swartland, and Cedarberg, starting from Cape Town, will take a minimum of three days. Allow more time if you plan to walk extensively, do any water sports, or frolic in fields of flowers.

Darling

From Cape Town take the N1 toward Paarl. After just under 2 km (1 mi), exit left onto the R27 (the sign reads PAARDEN EILAND AND MIL-NERTON*), drive 80 km (50 mi) to the junction with the R315, and turn right.*

Before you reach the town of Darling, you'll pass the **Darling Cellars,** on your left. This large cellar produces wines under a number of labels. In the Onyx range look out for the pinotage/shiraz blend of which local wine experts predict the '99 will be quite spectacular. Also try the pinotage. Other labels include the Groenekloof range—the chardonnay was great in '98 and '99, and the shiraz is a dense, mineral, olivey wine. The DC range has some stalwart old reds, including a nice, plummy merlot, and the newer Flamingo Bay range still needs to prove that it can produce more than pleasant quaffables. ⊠ *R315, Groenekloof,* ☎ *022/492–2276.* ☜ *Tasting R5.* ☉ *Mon.–Thurs. 8–5, Fri. 8–4, Sat. 8–noon; cellar tours by appointment only.*

Darling is best known for its spectacular wildflowers and its annual **Wildflower and Orchid Show** (☎ 022/492–3361), but there is much more to this charming country town. Ignore the rather unattractive new houses on the Cape Town side of the village and head straight through to the Victorian section of town. Pretty period houses are set in spacious gardens. The Darling Museum is the only one in the country concentrating on the history of butter.

During the flower season the **Tienie Versfeld Wildflower Reserve** is just fantastic: a wonderful, unpretentious, uncommercialized little gem. Follow the signs through town to find the reserve. Admission is free.

For a formal flower experience, **Rondeberg Farm** (☎ 022/492–3099) has guided tours of its grounds. It's open during flower season, and admission is R20.

NEED A BREAK?
Through the Looking Glass (19 Main Rd., Darling 7345, ☎ 022/492–2858) is a lovely coffee shop that serves great lunches and teatime goodies, as well as selling a range of local produce, preserves, books, and artwork. The walls are adorned with a constantly changing exhibition of works by local artists, and there is always some interesting cultural happening.

From Darling stay on the R315, and then turn right onto the R27 and head north 11 km (7 mi) to **West Coast National Park.** Even if you don't spend time here, the road that runs through the park to Langebaan is far more scenic than the R27 and well worth taking. The park is a fabulous mix of lagoon wetlands, pounding surf, and coastal fynbos. On a sunny day the lagoon assumes a magical color, made all the more impressive by blinding white beaches and the sheer emptiness of the place. Birders will have a field day identifying waterbirds, and the sandveld flowers are among the best along the West Coast. Postberg, at the tip of the reserve, is only open in August and September, when the flowers are at their very best. It's easy to run out of superlatives when describing West Coast flowers, but imagine acres of land carpeted in multicolor blooms—as far as the eye can see. If you're lucky, you may catch glimpses of zebra, wildebeest, or bat-eared fox. ⌧ *Off R27,* ☎ *022/772–2144.* ⌧ *R16 in high season (Easter, Christmas, and flower season); ½ price at other times.* ☉ *Park, daily 7–7; Postberg Aug.–Sept, daily 9–5.*

OFF THE BEATEN PATH
GROOTE POST VINEYARDS – Head down the R307 toward Mamre, a good option for returning to Cape Town, as you can rejoin the R27 farther south. A few miles down the road on your right you'll see this vineyard. This is a large, well-run, environmentally sensitive wine and dairy farm with only a small grape production. They got off to a fantastic start when their maiden '99 sauvignon blanc was judged one of the best in the Cape. A good chocolaty, berryish merlot is set to follow, but it needs a few years to find its feet. Generally, the prediction is that this young estate will grow from strength to strength. ⌧ *Off R307 Darling,* ☎ *021/557–0606 for office; 022/492–2825 for winery.* ☉ *Weekdays 8–noon and 2–5, Sat. 8–noon.*

Dining and Lodging

$$ 🏨 **Trinity Guest Lodge and Restaurant.** This attractive old Victorian house has been elegantly transformed into a stylish and comfortable guest lodge. White linen and subtle furnishings create a restful atmosphere. Some bathrooms have Victorian claw-foot baths. ⌧ *19 Long St., Darling 7345,* ☎ *022/492–3430. 4 rooms. Restaurant, pool. MC, V. BP.*

$ 🏠 **Darling Guest House.** This is a pretty Victorian house in a peaceful garden. Some of the quiet rooms have claw-foot baths. At time of writing, an art studio was under construction, and the owners plan to run residential courses in many different art forms. ⊠ *22 Pastorie St., Darling 7345,* ☎ *022/492–3062,* 𝔽𝔸𝕏 *022/492–3916. 5 rooms. Pool. No credit cards. BP.*

Nightlife and the Arts

One of Darling's main attractions is **Evita se Perron** (☎ 022/492–2831, 𝕎𝔼𝔹 www.evita.co.za), the theater and restaurant started by satirist and drag artist Pieter-Dirk Uys. This really is worth a visit, particularly if Evita "herself" is performing. Pieter-Dirk Uys has made his alter ego, Evita Bezuidenhout, a household name in South Africa. The theater is on the platform of the Darling station (*perron* is the Afrikaans word for "railway platform"). Performances are on Friday evening, Saturday afternoon and evening, and Sunday afternoon. Come early and bring a picnic for lunch or early supper in the gardens. Performances are R55. For a really fun day out, take the **Spier Train** (☎ 021/419–5222) from Cape Town. The whole package, including a picnic lunch and the performance, costs R240, or R175 without lunch (bring your own picnic). **Evita's A en C** is an arts-and-crafts collective where you can see and buy works from all over the West Coast. It's open daily 10–5.

Langebaan

50 km (30 mi) northwest of Darling.

Langebaan is a great base from which to explore the region, and the sheltered lagoon makes for fantastic water sports, especially boardsailing, kite surfing, and paddling. This is probably the most popular destination on the coast, and it has a truly laid-back beach destination feel. To quote a local: "There is nowhere in Langebaan you can't go barefoot." Langebaan is internationally recognized as one of the best windsurfing and kite-surfing venues in the world.

Dining and Lodging

$$$ ✕ **Froggy's.** The food at this attractive and unpretentious establish-
★   ment would be impressive even in a smart city restaurant; but in a town where most people consider steak, egg, and chips to be the height of culinary achievement, it really does stand out. Froggy doesn't put on airs and graces. The menu is eclectic—basically it's what Froggy likes to cook and eat. The caramelized onion-and-brie tart is a masterpiece, and the Mediterranean salad with grilled vegetables is a Langebaan institution. Many people keep coming back for more of the Moroccan lamb shank, slow-baked with cinnamon, coriander, cumin, ginger, and garlic, as well as the Thai curries. ⊠ *29 Main Rd.,* ☎ *022/772–1869. No credit cards. Closed Mon. No lunch.*

$$$ ✕🏠 **Farmhouse Hotel.** The hotel centers around a restored farmstead built in the 1860s with thick white walls, tile floors, and timber beams. All rooms are decorated with rustic pine furniture and bright floral fabrics; some have fireplaces and views of the lagoon. The hotel's à la carte menu features a good selection of Cape cuisine, prepared fresh and served in the attractive dining room, notable for its Oregon-pine furniture, fireplace, and high ceiling. The breakfast is said to be the best in town. ⊠ *5 Egret St., Box 160, Langebaan 7357,* ☎ *022/772–2062,* 𝔽𝔸𝕏 *022/ 772–1980,* 𝕎𝔼𝔹 *www.thefarmhouselangebaan.co.za. 18 rooms. Restaurant, bar, pool. AE, DC, MC, V. BP.*

$$ 🏠 **Langebaan Beach House.** On the beach with uninterrupted views of the lagoon and close to the nightlife of Langebaan (such as it is), this comfortable, friendly place even has dogs you can take for walks on the beach. The suites are sea facing. ⊠ *44 Beach Rd., Langebaan 7357,* ☎

022/772–2625, FAX *022/772–1432,* WEB *www.langebaaninfo.com/beach.*
2 rooms, 2 suites. Pool. No children under 12. MC, V. BP.

$$ 🖼 **Puza Moya and Rex's Beach House.** If you're into water sports or
★ cycling or are generally pretty active, then this set of guest houses is a
great choice. Rex's is light and bright and airy and right on the beach.
Rooms have an outside shower for wet suits, boards, and such. The
sea-facing rooms at Rex's are ideal for families, with two beds down-
stairs and two in a loft. Puza Moya is one block from the beach and
has a central self-catering kitchen and lounge and six rooms arranged
around a grassed courtyard and barbecue area. The rooms are stylishly
minimalist, with white-painted brick walls and white and gray soft fur-
nishings. Both properties are connected to the Cape Sport Centre
(CSC) complex, where you can book boardsailing or kite-surfing
lessons as well as weekly packages. They also rent mountain bikes and
canoes. There's a lovely beachfront bar and restaurant at CSC as well.
✉ *Langebaan Lagoon, Box 280, Langebaan 7357,* ☎ *022/772–1114,*
FAX *022/772–1115,* WEB *www.capesport.co.za. 16 rooms. MC, V. BP.*

Paternoster

50 km (30 mi) northwest of Vredenburg.

Paternoster is a mostly unspoiled village of whitewashed, thatched cot-
tages perched on a deserted stretch of coastline. The population here
consists mainly of fisherfolk, who for generations have eked out a liv-
ing harvesting crayfish and other seafood. Despite the overt poverty,
the village has a character and sense of identity often lacking in larger
towns. It helps if you turn a blind eye to the rather opulent houses on
the northern side of the village.

Along the coast just south of Paternoster is the **Columbine Nature Re-
serve,** a great spot for spring wildflowers, coastal fynbos, and succu-
lents. Seagulls, cormorants, and sacred ibis are common here. ☎ *022/
752–2718.* 🎟 *R9.* ◷ *Daily 7–7.*

Dining

$$ ✕ **Voorstrand.** A little West Coast gem, this old corrugated-iron shack
★ on the beach stood empty for years and then suddenly metamorphosed
into a really innovative seafood restaurant. Literally set on the sand,
you can almost hear the ones that got away. They serve all the expected
seafood and fish, but the Malay-style and Thai fish curries are favorites.
✉ *On the beach,* ☎ *022/752–2038. MC, V.*

Elands Bay

75 km (46 mi) north of Paternoster.

A lovely destination, this long, lonely beach with excellent surf is a favorite haunt for Cape Town surfers. It's at the mouth of the beautiful
Verlorenvlei Lagoon—a birder's paradise. Also close by are some fantastic walks to interesting caves with well-preserved rock art.

Dining and Lodging

$$ ✕ **Muisbosskerm.** For the true flavor of West Coast life, come to this
★ open-air seafood restaurant on the beach south of town. It consists of
nothing more than a circular *boma* (enclosure) of packed *muisbos* (a
local shrub), with benches and tables haphazardly arranged in the
sandy enclosure. Cooking fires blaze, and you watch food being pre-
pared before your eyes: snoek is smoked in an old drum covered with
burlap, bread bakes in a clay oven, and everywhere fish sizzles on grills
and in giant pots. Bring your own drink and prepare to eat as much
as you can, using your hands or mussel shells as spoons. Be sure to try

some of the local specialties like *bokkems* (dried fish) and *waterblommetjie* (water lily) stew. Unless you have an enormous appetite, don't order the half crayfish (it costs extra). The only drawback is high-season crowding: As many as 150 diners can overwhelm the experience. ⊠ *Elands Bay Rd., 5 km (3 mi) south of Lambert's Bay,* ☎ *027/432–1017. Reservations essential. V.*

Clanwilliam

27 km (16 mi) north of Elands Bay

Then take the paved R364 to **Clanwilliam.** This attractive town is also the center of the rooibos tea industry. And in spring, not surprisingly, it's inundated with flower watchers.

The **Ramskop Wildflower Garden** is at its best in August. This is also when the **Clanwilliam Flower Show** takes place, and almost every available space in the town is filled with flowers. It's a wonderful opportunity to see many of the regions flowers all growing in one place. Even in other seasons the gardens are still quite attractive, but spring is orders of magnitude prettier. ⊠ *Ou Kaapseweg, Clanwilliam,* ☎ *027/482–2133.* 🎫 *R8.50.* ☉ *Daily 7:30–5.*

If you continue east on the R364, it becomes a spectacularly scenic gravel road called **Pakhuis Pass.** Fantastic rock formations glow in the early morning or late afternoon. A steep, narrow road to the right leads to the mission town of **Wuppertal** with its characteristic white-thatched houses. You can drive this road in an ordinary rental car, but be very careful in wet weather. There are no guided tours, but there is a factory where you can see and buy sturdy, handmade leather shoes and boots.

Clanwilliam is close to the northern edge of the **Cedarberg,** a mountain range known for its San paintings, its bizarre rock formations, and, once upon a time, its cedars. Most of the ancient cedars have been cut down, but a few specimens still survive in the more remote regions. The Cedarberg is a hiking paradise—a wild, largely unspoiled area where you can disappear from civilization for days at a time. About 172,900 acres of this mountain range constitute what has been declared the Cedarberg Wilderness Area, and entry permits are required if you wish to hike.

A scenic dirt road winds into the Cedarberg to **Algeria,** a Cape Nature Conservation campsite set in an idyllic valley. Algeria is the starting point for several excellent hikes into the Cedarberg. No permit is needed for the short, one-hour hike to a waterfall, but it's worth going into the mountains for a day or two, for which you will need to book and obtain a permit through **Cape Nature Conservation** (☎ 022/482–2812).

Dining and Lodging

$$$–$$$$ ✕🏨 **Karu Kareb.** At time of writing, this lodge had just opened. Previously, Frans and Beneta Bester ran a wonderful guest house called K'taaibos, near Elands Bay, and this new property should be just as good. Rooms are in a 100-year-old farmhouse surrounded by high mountains, a crystal-clear stream, and fantastic rock art. The Besters will almost certainly continue the tradition of excellent local cuisine for which they were renowned at their previous spot. Frans does incredible things with a braai or a potjie, and Beneta is surprisingly creative with special menus, cooking for vegetarians, diabetics, and lactose-intolerant people without batting an eyelid—a rarity in this part of the world. ⊠ *13 km (8 mi) from Clanwilliam on Boskloof Rd., Box 273, Clanwilliam 8135,* ☎ *027/482–1675. 5 rooms. Dining room, pond, hiking, horseback riding. MC, V. MAP.*

$$$ ✕▥ **Strassberger's Hotel Clanwilliam.** On the main street, this friendly family-run hotel makes an excellent base for exploring the area. Rooms are large, decorated with rustic cane furniture and plaid country fabrics. Dinner in the hotel restaurant is a traditional four-course affair that is satisfactory but lacks inspiration. ⊠ *Main Rd., Box 4, Clanwilliam 8135,* ☏ *027/482–1101,* ℻ *027/482–2678. 17 rooms. 2 restaurants, bar, pool, squash. AE, DC, MC, V. BP.*

$$$$ ▥ **Bushmans Kloof Wilderness Reserve.** This fantastic game lodge is
★ in an area of rich cultural significance: there are more than 125 San rock art sites that can be seen on an escorted tour with the resident archaeologist. The stark beauty of the mountains, the fantastic rock formations, and the waterfalls, pools, and potholes were as attractive to the San of long ago as they are to visitors today. The flowers are fantastic all year-round but are rather special in spring. The game here includes wildebeest, Cape mountain zebra, eland, mountain leopard, genet, mongoose, and blesbok. The freestanding thatch double cottages have every possible modern convenience; the food is of a high standard and in abundance; the hospitality is sincere and sophisticated; and the game rangers are experts in their field. ⊠ *Off Pakhuis Pass, Box 53405 Kenilworth 7945,* ☏ *021/797–0990,* ℻ *021/761–5551,* ⅦⅢ *www.bushmanskloof.co.za. 7 rooms, 9 suites. Bar, dining room, 3 pools, sauna, hiking, fishing, mountain bikes, private airstrip. No children under 12. AE, DC, MC, V. FAP. Closed June.*

$ ▥ **Travellers Rest.** If you're on a tight budget, this is the place to stay. Very simple and basic, but its comfortable cottages are dotted about the farm. There are no frills, but the surrounding mountains scenery is just as spectacular as at the expensive lodge next door. There are no escorted trips, but there is an inexpensive booklet (R50) that describes all the rock art on the farm. You can take a different hike every day for at least two or three days and not get bored. There is also a scenic drive for which you really need a four-wheel drive, although it's not an off-road challenge. ⊠ *Off Pakhuis Pass,* ☏ ℻ *027/482–1824. 11 cottages. Pool, tennis court, hiking. No credit cards.*

Citrusdal

50 km (31 mi) south of Clanwilliam.

From Clanwilliam, continue down the N7 to **Citrusdal,** a fruit-growing town in the Olifants River valley surrounded by the peaks of the Cedarberg. Just outside town is **Skydive Citrusdal** where you can do a first-jump course or, if you want someone to hold your hand, a tandem. The scenery from the air is fantastic. As you float down under the canopy, you can see the orange groves stretching out forever, and the surrounding mountains are particularly pretty in the late afternoon. A static-line first-jump course costs R595. The tandem costs R1,200, including a video of the whole proceedings. ☏ *021/462–5666,* ⅦⅢ *www.skydive.co.za.*

From here it's just 90 minutes back to Cape Town through the **Swartland.** As you turn back on to the N7 after leaving Citrusdal, look out for the turnoff to **Craig Royston Wines.** This lovely building has been a retail store continually since 1860 and has never been renovated or prettified. First it was the main trading store on the road north, and then, when the highway moved away, it sold groceries to farm laborers. It still maintains that basic farm-store feel but now also stocks a selection of all the wines grown in the Cedarberg region as well as a few touristy gimmicks. There is a coffee shop that serves all-day breakfasts and light lunches. ⊠ *Off N7,* ☏ *022/921–2963.* ☉ *Daily 8–5.*

Piketberg

45 km (27 mi) south of Citrusdal.

Once over the Piekenierskloof Pass, you enter the Swartland proper. Rolling wheat fields extend to the mountains on either side. On your left are the Groot Winterhoek Mountains and a road leading to the small town of Porterville. On your right is the village of Piketberg, where you would turn off to go to Noupoort or Excelsior.

Dining and Lodging

$$$ 🏠 **Noupoort Guest Farm.** Views that go on forever and many fantastic walks make this stylish, minimalist guest farm just the place to get away from it all. In spring the flowers are truly spectacular, and there are loads of birds at any time of the year—it's a good place to see the rather uncommon black eagle. Accommodations are in freestanding cottages, and meals are taken in a converted fruit-packing shed. In winter a roaring log fire warms things up, and the food is always good and innovative. They occasionally have soirees and theme evenings or weekends. Loft rooms have a queen-size bed downstairs and a three-quarter bed in the loft. There are also self-catering cottages—a two-sleeper is R280 per night, and a four-sleeper is R456. They regularly organize horse rides at the nearby Excelsior Farm. ⊠ *At end of Piketberg Mountain road,* ☎ *022/914–5754,* FAX *022/914–5834,* WEB *www.noupoort.com. 19 cottages. Bar, dining room, pool, sauna, spa, hiking, billiards, library. AE, DC, MC, V. MAP.*

Malmesbury

55 km (34 mi) south of Piketberg.

Continue on the N7 toward Cape Town and turn left at Malmesbury onto the R46 and travel 21 km (12 mi) to the **Swartland Wine Cellar.** Because of its location in the less fashionable part of the Winelands, this large cellar has had to work hard for its place in the sun. Previously a well-kept secret among local cost- and quality-conscious wine experts, it's slowly garnering an international reputation. Try the fantastic cabernet sauvignon–merlot, which can hold its own in any company, or if you're just looking for something pleasant to knock back with lunch, check out the low-alcohol (9%) Fernão Pires Light. There are no cellar tours. ⊠ *R46, Malmesbury,* ☎ *022/482–1134, 022/482–1135, or 022/482–1136.* ☺ *Weekdays 8–5, Sat. 9–noon.*

Continue along the R46 to the twin towns of **Riebeek Kasteel** and **Riebeek West,** famous as the birthplace of Jan Christian Smuts.

Outdoor Activities

Excelsior Farm (☎ 022/914–5853) is an organic peach and nectarine farm on top of the Piketberg Mountains. As well as offering day and overnight rides through the orchards and fynbos-clad mountains, they have two simple, inexpensive, self-catering cottages. Most people choose a two-hour ride for R100. A full-day excursion with lunch costs R200. There are overnight trails on request, starting at R300 per day.

WESTERN CAPE A TO Z

AIR TRAVEL

The closest airport in the area is Cape Town International.

➤ AIRPORT INFORMATION: **Cape Town International Airport** (☎ 021/934–0407).

BUS TRAVEL

Intercape Mainliner, Greyhound, and Translux have daily service throughout most of the Western Cape. The Baz Bus operates a hop-on/hop-off service among backpackers' hostels between Cape Town and the Garden Route.

➤ BUS INFORMATION: **Baz Bus** (☎ 021/439–2323, WEB www. bazbus.co.za). **Greyhound** (✉ 1 Adderley St., ☎ 021/418–4310; 083/909–0909 for Computicket, WEB www.greyhound.co.za). **Intercape Mainliner** (✉ 1 Adderley St., ☎ 021/386–4400 or 083/909–0909 for Computicket, WEB www.intercape.co.za). **Translux Express Bus** (✉ 1 Adderley St., ☎ 021/449–3333).

CAR TRAVEL

Driving yourself is undoubtedly the best way to appreciate this lovely and diverse area. The roads in the Western Cape are generally good, although some dirt roads—for example on the West Coast, Cedarberg, or the Overberg—may be a bit rutted and bumpy. The major car-rental agencies have offices in the smaller towns, but it's best to deal with the Cape Town offices, and you'll probably want to pick up a car at the airport anyhow. If you're already in the Winelands and would like a car for the day, try Wine Route Rent-a-Car, based in Paarl, which will drop off a car at your hotel. The wine route is easy to drive around, but of course driving limits the amount of wine you can taste, so unless you have a designated driver, it's best to take a tour, take a taxi, or—do it in style—rent a limo.

➤ MAJOR AGENCIES: **Avis** (✉ 123 Strand St., ☎ 021/424–1177; 021/934–0808 for airport; 0800/002–1111 toll-free, WEB www.avis.co.za). **Budget** (✉ 120 Strand St., ☎ 021/418–5232; 021/934–0216 for airport, WEB www.budget.co.za). **Europcar** (☎ 021/418–0670, WEB www.europcar.co.za). **Hertz** (✉ 40 Loop St., ☎ 021/425–8251, WEB www.hertz.co.za). **Wine Route Rent-a-Car** (☎ 021/872–8513 or 083/225–7089, WEB www.encounter.co.za/rentacar).

EMERGENCIES

➤ CONTACTS: **Ambulance** (☎ 10177). **Fire** (☎ 10111). **Police** (☎ 10111).

LIMOUSINES

The best, least stressful, and most stylish way to tour the Winelands is by limo. It's particularly cost effective (about R350–R400 per hour per limo) if you have a group of four or five.

➤ CONTACTS: **Cape Limo Services** (☎ 021/785–3100).

TAXIS

Paarl Radio Taxis will transport up to three people at about R6 per kilometer (R9 per mile) and R30 per hour waiting time. Larger groups can arrange transportation by minibus.

➤ TAXI COMPANY: **Paarl Radio Taxis** (☎ 021/872–5671).

TOURS

Generally, most tours are confined to the Winelands and/or the Overberg and are operated by companies based in Cape Town. Ferdinand's Tours offers an escorted hiking tour to the Cedarberg for decidedly young-at-heart travelers as well as fun and funky Wineland tours. More conservative tour companies include the dependable, reliable standbys Springbok Atlas, Welcome Tours & Safaris, and Hylton Ross.

If you're serious about wine, Vineyard Ventures is the best of several companies offering tours of the Winelands. Sisters Gillian Stoltzman and Glen Christie are knowledgeable and passionate about wine and will tailor tours to your interests. The cost ranges from R600 per person for four people to R1,500 for one person and includes all tastings, museum entries, and a fabulous lunch (with wine, of course).

➤ CONTACTS: **Ferdinand's Tours** (☎ 021/465–8550 or 083/462–0425, WEB www.ferdinandstours.co.za). **Hylton Ross Tours** (☎ 021/511–1784, WEB www.hyltonross.co.za). **Springbok Atlas** (☎ 021/460–4700, WEB www.springbokatlas.com). **Vineyard Ventures** (✉ 5 Hanover Rd., Fresnaye, Cape Town 8001, ☎ 021/434–8888 or 082/920–2825, WEB www.vineyardventures.co.za). **Welcome Tours & Safaris** (☎ 021/510–6001, WEB www.welcome.co.za).

TRAIN TRAVEL

Cape Metro trains run from Cape Town to Stellenbosch and Paarl, but with the increase in violent muggings and robberies in the area, the trains should be avoided. A far safer, more stylish, and more fun alternative would be to hop on the Spier Train when it is running. Regular trips run from Spier Monument Station out to Spier, in the Winelands, at R75 for a round-trip, and also to Darling, where they stop at Evita se Perron for a Pieter-Dirk Uys performance. The Darling trip costs from R175 to R240.

➤ CONTACTS: **Spier Train** (☎ 021/419–5222, WEB www.spier.co.za).

VISITOR INFORMATION

You can get almost all the information you need about the Western Cape from the very organized Cape Town Tourism offices in Cape Town, that are open weekdays 9–6, Saturday 8:30–2, and Sunday 9–1. The Flowerline is a central hot line that offers details about where the flowers are best seen each day. It is open June–October, daily 8–4:30. The Whale Hotline gives up-to-the-minute information about the movement of the southern right whales in season (about June–October).

There are tourist information offices in most small towns in the Western Cape. The Breede River Valley Tourism office is open weekdays 9–4:30. Citrusdal Information Center is open daily 8–5 in August and September, and 9–5 the rest of the year. The Clanwilliam Tourism Association is open daily in the flower season 8:30–6. During the rest of the year it is open weekdays 8:30–5 and Saturday 8:30–12:30. Darling Information is based at the museum and is open daily 9–1 and 2–4. Franschhoek Vallée Tourismé is open Monday–Saturday 10–5 and Sunday 10–1. The Hermanus Tourism Bureau is open Monday–Saturday 9–5. The Montagu Tourism Bureau is open weekdays 9–4:30 and Saturday 9–1. Paarl Tourism Bureau is open weekdays 8:30–5, Saturday 9–1, and Sunday 10–1. Somerset West Tourist Information Bureau is open weekdays 8:30–1 and 2–4:30, Saturday 9–noon. Stellenbosch Tourist Bureau is open weekdays 8–6, Saturday 9–5, and Sunday 9:30–4:30. The Suidpunt Publicity Association has information for Bredasdorp, Elim, Cape Agulhas, Struisbaai, and Arniston. It is open weekdays 8–5 and Saturday 9–12:30. The Swellendam Publicity Association is open weekdays 8–1 and 2–5, Saturday 9–12:30. Worcester Tourism is open weekdays 8–4:30 and Saturday 8:30–12:30.

➤ TOURIST INFORMATION: **Breede River Valley Tourism** (✉ Box 91, Worcester 6850, ☎ 023/347–6411). **Cape Town Tourism** (✉ The Pinnacle at Burg and Castle Sts. [Box 1403], Cape Town 8000, ☎ 021/426–4260, WEB www.cape-town.org). **Citrusdal Information Centre** (✉ 39 Voortrekker St., Citrusdal, ☎ 022/921–3210). **Clanwilliam Tourism Association** (✉ Main Rd., Clanwilliam, ☎ 027/482–2024). **Darling Information** (✉ Corner Pastorie and Hill Sts., Darling, ☎ 022/492–3361). **Flowerline** (☎ 083/910–1028). **Franschhoek Vallée Tourismé** (✉ Huguenot Rd., Franschhoek, ☎ 021/876–3603). **Hermanus Tourism Bureau** (✉ Main Rd., Hermanus 7200, ☎ 028/312–2629). **Montagu Tourism Bureau** (✉ 24 Bath St., Montagu 6720, ☎ 023/614–1116,

WEB www.montagu.org.za). **Paarl Tourism Bureau** (⊠ 216 Main St., Paarl, ☎ 021/872–3829 or 021/872–4842, WEB www.paarlonline.com). **Somerset West Tourist Information Bureau** (⊠ 11 Victoria St., Somerset West, ☎ 021/851–4022). **Stellenbosch Tourist Bureau** (⊠ 36 Market St., Stellenbosch, ☎ 021/883–3584, FAX 021/883–8017). **Suidpunt Publicity Association** (⊠ Dirkie Uys St., Bredasdorp, ☎ FAX 028/424–2584). **Swellendam Publicity Association** (⊠ Oefeningshuis, Voortrek St., ☎ FAX 028/514–2770). **Whale Hotline** (☎ 083/910–1028). **Worcester Tourism** (⊠ 25 Baring St., Worcester, ☎ 023/348–2795).

6 THE NORTHERN CAPE

In this land of sand dunes and spectacular vistas, you'll find the rugged desert panoramas of the Kalahari, the old diamond mines of Kimberley, the miraculous carpets of Namaqualand wildflowers spread out in spring—all lasting images of the Northern Cape, South Africa's least-known, yet in many ways most beautiful province.

By Tara
Turkington

S OUTH AFRICA'S LARGEST AND LEAST-POPULATED PROVINCE, the Northern Cape covers almost a third of the country, yet most South Africans know very little about it. Its deserts and semideserts—the Karoo, the Kalahari, Namaqualand, and the Richtersveld—stretch from the Orange River down vistas of space to the Western Cape border and from the small towns of Springbok and Port Nolloth, in the west 1,000 km (630 mi) across via places with names like Pofadder and Hotazhel, to its diamond capital, Kimberley, in the east. It is a province of grand and rugged beauty—a far cry from the verdant greenness of Mpumalanga and the Western Cape. The Northern Cape's appeal is in its sense of loneliness and its lunar landscapes, which would make an episode of *Star Trek* look tame. All told, it covers an area of 363,389 square km (225,665 square mi), roughly a third bigger than the entire United Kingdom, but it has a population of less than a million people (only about 2 per square km), and most are concentrated in a handful of towns. With its alien landscapes and endless horizons, it's the perfect place to reconnect with your soul. For the few travelers who do venture into the Northern Cape, its hidden treasures are all the richer for their isolation.

Many of the Northern Cape's attractions are linked to mining, which has been the province's economic backbone for more than a century. First, there was the copper mania of the 1840s in Namaqualand; the deepest copper mines in the world are still operating here, although they are now nearing the end of their productive lives. But the history of copper mining was eclipsed 30 years later by the frenzied scrabbling for diamonds on the other side of what is now the Northern Cape. Kimberley, known as the City of Diamonds, is the provincial capital and in the 1870s was the site of one of the world's greatest diamond rushes. Thousands of hopeful diggers trekked to the hot, dusty diamond fields sitting in what is more or less the geographical center of South Africa. In Kimberley five diamond-bearing volcanic pipes were eventually discovered within a few miles of one another—a phenomenon unknown anywhere else in the world. Apart from diamonds, the province's mineral deposits range from manganese to copper, zinc, lime, granite, gypsum, gemstones, and there are even oil and gas fields off the Namaqualand coast.

Although only a fraction of the province is regarded as arable because of low rainfall, the Orange River (known as the !ariep—the exclamation mark indicates a click of the tongue against the roof of the mouth—or "mighty river by the Nama") flows the breadth of the province, emptying into the Atlantic Ocean at Alexander Bay, on the Namibian border. South Africa's largest and longest river, the Orange supplies water to numerous irrigation schemes that sustain various farming activities, most noticeably in the "Green Kalahari." Agriculture employs the most people in the province, and you'll find varied agricultural production, from the second-largest date plantation in the world, at Klein Pella near Pofadder, to thousands of acres of grapes under irrigation in the Orange River Basin around Upington. The province boasts the country's second-largest national park, the newly named Kgalagadi Transfrontier Park (formerly the Kalahari Gemsbok National Park). Together with an adjoining national park in Botswana, this park forms one of the largest conservation areas in the world. Ecotourism also includes the annual pilgrimage of thousands of visitors to see the spectacular Namaqualand flowers.

The Northern Cape is not for the fainthearted. It's a harsh province, not yet really catering to travelers, but therein lies its beauty. There's plenty to see if you're the type who's not afraid to ask questions and to go where your nose leads you. Don't expect luxurious accommodations, fine cuisine, or well-stocked gift shops. What you can expect, given a little time and patience, are sleepy villages still much like they were a century ago, charming locals who appreciate visitors tremendously, though in some places they may only be able to communicate in very broken English, and an unusual and unique getaway that could well turn out to be the highlight of your trip to South Africa.

Pleasures and Pastimes

Arts and Crafts

Technology lags behind in the Northern Cape—much of the province has no cell-phone reception, and the full range of TV channels you would get elsewhere is a rarity anywhere in the province outside Kimberley. Perhaps because of technology's tenuous reach, many old traditions and ways are still in place. All around the province it is possible to buy original and interesting crafts, from ostrich shells painted by San (Bushmen) to Nama reed matting and curios made out of tigereye—one of the many semiprecious stones abundant in the province.

Dining

The Northern Cape cannot be described as gastronomically exciting. In the larger towns of Kimberley, Upington, and Springbok there are one or two good restaurants, but they are the exceptions rather than the rule. Where you are likely to taste something memorable is out on a farm in the midst of the Karoo, where Karoo lamb—often roasted on a *braai*—is a delicacy. Fresh fruits, especially grapes, are delicious and abundant in the summer months in the Orange River valley, from Upington to Kakamas. In winter look out for homemade preserves like peach chutney and apricot jam.

Lodging

Like good food, good hotels are hard to find in the Northern Cape. There are, however, guest houses in just about every little town, and the bigger centers like Kimberley and Upington are brimming with them—from basic units with cooking facilities to luxurious bed-and-breakfasts. Many farms also offer overnight accommodations that can be a saving grace late at night on the province's long and lonely roads.

Exploring the Northern Cape

The Northern Cape's vastness makes it a difficult place to travel, and you will probably decide to see only part of it on your first trip, such as Namaqualand in flower season, the Kalahari, or Kimberley. Namaqualand is most easily visited from Cape Town and the Western Cape, while Kimberley and the Kalahari are far more accessible from Johannesburg. If you are planning to drive from Johannesburg to Cape Town or vice versa, Kimberley makes an ideal stopover. The Kimberley route (along the N12) is less than 100 km (63 mi) longer than the sterile N1 route with its huge garages and stereotypical fast-food places. It's also more scenic and not as busy. Although Upington and the Kgalagadi Transfrontier Park are about the same distance from Cape Town as they are from Johannesburg, the roads from Johannesburg are far better.

Great Itineraries

IF YOU HAVE 3 DAYS

If you have three days, spend them in ⓜ **Kimberley,** soaking up its history and culture. Spend your first morning with one of the reasonably priced registered guides, seeing the town and its landmarks. Ask to see

The Northern Cape and Namaqualand

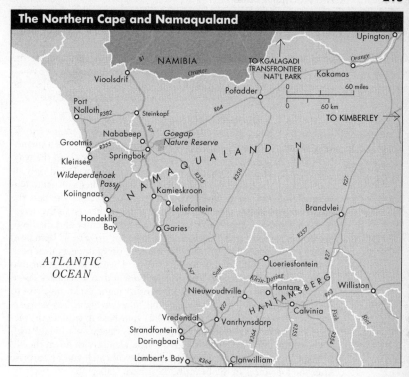

the **Honoured Dead Memorial,** built to commemorate those who died defending Kimberley during the siege, and the imposing and strange-looking Henry Oppenheimer House, where diamonds from all over South Africa are sorted for export (public access is prohibited for security reasons, but you can view it from the outside). The building was custom-built for diamond sorting under the correct light conditions—one side is concrete, while the other side is almost completely glass. Spend the afternoon at the **McGregor Museum,** or take a stroll through the **William Humphreys Art Gallery.** Finish off the day with dinner at 15 on Dalham and try out a traditional South African dish, such as *bobotie* (ground, curry-spiced meat topped with béchamel). On your second morning book an underground tour offered by **De Beers** down a working diamond mine—-Kimberley is the only place in the world where you can take such a trip. To get a fuller picture of what life in Kimberley was like during the diamond rush, make your way to the **Kimberley Mine Museum,** but first stop at Star of the West for a pub lunch. Spend a good three hours at this unusual museum, then rest your weary feet with a ride on a historic restored tram to the 100-year-old town hall and back. Devote most of your third day either to seeing the alluvial diggings with a guide, taking in the **Platfontein San Craft Centre** and the **Nooitgedacht rock engravings** on the way, or going out to the evocative Anglo–Boer War battlefield, **Magersfontein,** where the Boers beat the British marching to relieve Kimberley in December 1899. Take a picnic and have it under one of the ubiquitous thorn trees scattered across the battlefield.

IF YOU HAVE 5 DAYS

If it's spring (August–September), ☐ **Namaqualand** is worth a five-day visit, but if it's the middle of the year (from mid-May to late July, wintertime in South Africa), head for the huge spaces of the **Kalahari** via ☐ **Upington** (by air or road), perhaps even squeezing in the Augrabies

Falls National Park as an extra. Spend three nights roughing it in the ruggedly beautiful **Kgalagadi Transfrontier Park,** cooking your own meals and driving your own vehicle in search of the black-maned Kalahari lions and the beautifully symmetrical gemsbok. Then head for the decadent luxury of two nights at 🔟 **Tswalu Desert Reserve,** where you'll appreciate the game drives, bush walks, and attention to detail all the more for having roughed it on your own for the past few days.

IF YOU HAVE 7 OR MORE DAYS

If you enjoy huge, empty spaces, the drive from 🔟 **Kimberley** to 🔟 **Springbok**—perhaps taking in the **Kalahari** on the way—is a memorable one, with some excellent places to stop and stay along the way. But beware: This is a long and lonely trip and really should only be considered if the flowers are going to be in bloom when you get to **Namaqualand** (August–September). This route showcases the best the province has to offer, from the diamond fields in the east to the desert in the north, the Green Kalahari in the northern center and the flowers along the western seaboard. From Kimberley drive to 🔟 **Upington,** where you can spend a night in a guest house after taking a quick peek in the museum and a paddle in the Orange. Then head north for two nights in the vast **Kgalagadi Transfrontier Park** and continue back down to **Augrabies Falls National Park** for another night. Next day drive to 🔟 **Springbok,** the heart of Namaqualand. Stay two nights here and perhaps another in **Okiep,** using this area as your base to explore the picturesque towns of **Leliefontein** (with nearby Namaqua National Park), in the south, and **Port Nolloth,** in the north. Head south down the N7 to Cape Town, where the madding crowds will catch you by surprise after the loneliness of the beautiful Northern Cape.

When to Tour the Northern Cape

Between late November and the end of February it's exceptionally hot in Kimberley and just about intolerable in Upington and the Kalahari. Any other time is fine, although it can get very cold in the winter months—between the middle of May and early August. The best time to see the flowers in Namaqualand is usually between the middle of August and the end of September, depending on when and how much rain has fallen. The weather is generally milder in Namaqualand than the rest of the province. By South African standards the Northern Cape's climate is exceptionally hot in summer, often rising to above 35°C (95°F), and quite cold in winter, commonly dropping below 0°C (32°F) at night, so come prepared to sweat or shiver. Coincidentally, the province has the dubious honor of being home to the hottest town in South Africa in summer (Upington) and the coldest in winter (Sutherland, in the Karoo).

KIMBERLEY

Kimberley was born in the dust, dreams, and disappointments of a rudimentary mining camp that grew into a city of grace and sophistication in some quarters, still evident in many of its early buildings. Today Kimberley is a city of about 200,000 people spread out around its diamond mines—giant holes in the earth, like inverted *koppies* (hills). Kimberley has a host of comfortable guest houses, a few good restaurants, and many historical attractions, making it a wonderful place to spend a few days. It's an easy trip of about 500 km (313 mi) from Johannesburg and is about 970 km (606 mi) from Cape Town.

Kimberley's beginnings date to 1869, when diamonds were first discovered in the area. Through the late 1860s alluvial diamonds were mined on the banks of the Vaal River near Barkly West, about 30 km

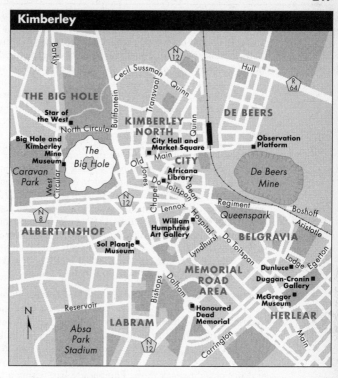

Kimberley

(19 mi) away. These were all but forgotten after the finds in Kimberley of five pipes bearing the diamondiferous Kimberlite, or "blue ground," so called because of its color. In 1871 the richest pipe of all, the Kimberley Mine (now known as the Big Hole), was discovered. Diggers from around the world flocked to stake claims in the mine, which produced more than 14.5 million carats before its closure in 1914, making it one of the richest diamond mines in history. At times there were as many as 30,000 people working in the hole, burrowing like a giant colony of termites. The history of the diamond fields is dominated by eccentric personalities, like Barney Barnato, who came to South Africa with so little he had to walk to the diamond fields yet died a magnificently wealthy man after mysteriously disappearing overboard on a trip to England. Then there was Cecil John Rhodes, the diamond magnate and colonizer who aspired to paint the map of Africa red for Britain and to build a railroad from Cape Town to Cairo.

Both Rhodes and Barnato were shrewd businessmen who watched the diggers toiling in Kimberley's five holes excavating their individual claims. As the miners met what they perceived to be bedrock, they would often give up and stop digging, but what they were actually hitting was the unweathered and hard blue ground that was fabulously rich in diamonds. The two men then snapped up claims at bargain prices, all the time increasing their shares in the mines. Eventually Barnato and Rhodes merged their companies into the De Beers Consolidated Mines Ltd. Today De Beers is the world's most powerful diamond-mining company. Its historic headquarters is still on Stockdale Street in Kimberley.

In addition to the allure of diamonds, another central part of Kimberley's history was its attack by the Boers during the Anglo–Boer War (1899–1902). Kimberley's close proximity to the border of the then-Boer Republic of the Orange Free State and its international fame as a diamond town occupied by prominent British citizens (including Rhodes) made it an ideal siege target. For four months in the summer of 1899 the town's citizens suffered dwindling rations, disease, Boer shell fire, and other hardships. British efforts to relieve the town were thwarted by the Boers at the famous Battle of Magersfontein, but eventually a sustained cavalry charge led by Major-General John French broke through to the beleaguered town. Kimberley's part in the Anglo–Boer War is brought to life everywhere through monuments, buildings, and statues.

Sights to See

Africana Library. This is one of the country's premier reference libraries. Housed in the old Kimberley Public Library built in 1887, books are shelved from floor to ceiling, and an ornate wrought-iron staircase connects the floors. You can choose from among the 20,000 books in the Africana collection, including such rarities as the Setswana Bible, printed by Robert Moffat in the 1850s—the first-ever printing of the Bible in an African language. The library also has four books dating to the 1400s and a good selection of locally published limited-edition books for sale. ⊠ *Dutoitspan Rd.,* ☏ *053/830–6247.* ☑ *By donation.* ⊘ *Weekdays 8–12:45 and 1:30–4:30.*

Canteen Kopje Archaeological Site and Barkly West Museum. Canteen Kopje is the site of some of the earliest alluvial diamond diggings in South Africa and home to a wealth of Stone Age artifacts over a million years old. Walk the 1-km (½-mi) trail and have a look at the open-air display there, then move on to the Barkly West Museum (500 meters away) for a more in-depth explanation. Finish off your tour with a drink or light snack in the Pumphouse Bar, within a stone's throw of the museum, for a spectacular view of the Vaal River. For more information on the site you can contact Troedie du Toit weekdays 8–5:30 at the municipality on the main road (☏ *053/531–0671* or *053/531–0672*). ⊠ *Barkly West (From Kimberley follow the R31 32 km [20 mi] north; you will see signs to the museum and Canteen Kopje before entering the town).* ☑ *R5.* ⊘ *Daily 9–4.*

De Beers Tours. You can take an underground tour in Kimberley of a working diamond mine, the only place in the world you can take such a trip. The tour starts with a short video on the history of Kimberley and diamond mining, then you are outfitted out with boots, hard hat, and gear. The underground experience itself is not at all claustrophobic—visitors are escorted through fairly spacious underground passages which are kept constantly cool. The tour entails quite a lot of walking and takes about 3½ hours. It is offered on Monday at 9:15 AM and Tuesday–Friday at 8 AM; book about two weeks in advance, although you could be lucky and get a place the day before or on the morning of the tour. No children under 16 are allowed, and you're advised not to wear contact lenses because of the dust. If you can't get on an underground tour, the 1½-hour surface tour is the next best thing (it's not necessary to do both). Surface tours are offered weekdays at 9 and 11. ⊠ *Visitors' Reception Centre, Bultfontein Mine Gate, Molyneux Rd.,* ☏ *053/842–1321.* ☑ *R75 for mine tour, R10 for surface tour.*

Duggan Cronin Gallery. The gallery houses early photographs of Africa and its inhabitants taken by A. M. Duggan Cronin, an Irishman who arrived in 1897 to work as a night watchman for De Beers. A keen photographer, he traveled widely through southern Africa, capturing his impressions—mostly of African peoples—on film. ⊠ *Egerton Rd., adjacent to McGregor Museum,* ☏ *053/842–0099.* ☑ *By donation.* ⊘ *Weekdays 9–5, Sat. 9–1 and 2–5, Sun. 2–5, public holidays 10–5.*

Dunluce. In the same tour to Rudd House, take in John Orr's Dunluce, a well-known Kimberley landmark, with its colonial wraparound veranda painted a distinctive green and white. On a tour you will hear about such details as the swimming pool (the first in Kimberley) and the memorable red dining room, which received a shell through its ceiling during the siege. The personalized tour of Dunluce and Rudd House, for R20 per person, is the best-value-for-the-money tour in Kimberley. ⊠ *Lodge Rd., Belgravia,* ☎ *053/842–0099.* ☞ *R10.* ⊙ *By appointment only, with a guide from McGregor Museum.*

★ **Kimberley Mine Museum and the Big Hole.** If there's one thing you do in Kimberley, visit the Big Hole, the largest hand-dug hole in the world. It is 820 meters deep, and although water and debris now fill the majority of its depth, it's still an impressive sight. On the lip of the Big Hole is the extensive, open-air **Kimberley Mine Museum,** comprising a host of authentic old buildings, many of which were moved here from the city center rather than be torn down. They include the first house erected in Kimberley in 1877 (which was brought piece by piece to the diamond fields from Britain by ship and ox wagon), Barney Barnato's boxing academy, and a bar reminiscent of a Wild West saloon. Replicas of the world's most famous diamonds, including the Eureka, a 21-carat yellow diamond that was the first recorded diamond discovered in South Africa, in 1866, are also on view. Allow a few hours here, and wear comfortable shoes. While at the Big Hole, take a ride on a restored **1914 tram** through Kimberley to City Hall (built in 1899) and back. Admission is R6 round-trip or R3 one-way; departures are from the Big Hole on the hour daily from 9 to 4 and from city hall at quarter past the hour daily 9:15 to 4:15. ⊠ *Tucker St.,* ☎ *053/839–4901 or 053/839–4902.* ☞ *R15.* ⊙ *Daily 8–6.*

Magersfontein Battlefield. This evocative, barren national monument is where the Boers resoundingly defeated British forces marching to relieve besieged Kimberley in December 1899. There is an excellent site museum with an 11-minute multimedia display that recalls the battle in pictures and sound so well that it will give you goose bumps. There are also several monuments dotted around the battlefield to visit and a pleasant tearoom. The battlefield is well signposted from Kimberley. ⊠ *31.5 km (20 mi) outside Kimberley on Magersfontein Rd.,* ☎ *053/ 842–0099.* ☞ *R10.* ⊙ *Daily 8–5.*

McGregor Museum. This museum is housed in a graceful Kimberley landmark that was built at Rhodes's instigation. It was used first as a sanatorium, then an upscale hotel, and later as a girls' convent school. Rhodes stayed here himself during the siege. The museum houses quite a good, recently updated display on the Anglo–Boer War. More impressive is the new Hall of Ancestors, the most up-to-date and extensive exhibition in South Africa on the history of humanity. It traces the evolution of prehistoric life up to the early 20th century, all with a focus on the Northern Cape but within a global context. The museum also runs tours of Dunluce (☞ *above*) and Rudd House (☞ *below*). ⊠ *Atlas St.,* ☎ *053/842–0099,* FAX *053/842–1433.* ☞ *R8.* ⊙ *Mon.–Sat. 9–5, Sun. 2–5, holidays 10–5.*

Pioneers of Aviation Memorial. On the road to Magersfontein, stop here, about 11 km (7 mi) from Kimberley. This was the site of South Africa's first flying school. There is a small museum, the centerpiece of which is a replica of a Compton Paterson biplane. ⊠ *Jan Smuts Blvd., Civic Centre,* ☎ *053/842–0099.* ☞ *Donation requested.* ⊙ *Weekdays 9–5.*

Rudd House. In the leafy suburb of Belgravia, Rudd House is the rambling home of Cecil John Rhodes's first business partner, the early diamond magnate Charles Dunnell Rudd. The house has been restored in the art deco style of the 1920s, when the Bungalow, as the house was known, was in its heyday. Look out for the croquet ground made out of Blue Ground and the massive snooker table surrounded by a multitude of animal heads from Rudd's trips north to Matabeleland. ⊠ *Loch Rd., Belgravia,* ☎ *053/842–0099.* ▱ *R10.* ☉ *By appointment only, with a guide from the McGregor Museum.*

Sol Plaatje's House. Worth a quick stop is this house where the multitalented Sol Plaatje (1876–1932) lived much of his life. In addition to being the first general secretary of the African National Congress, he was the first black South African to publish a novel in English. Plaatje was also an influential early black newspaper editor and was an energetic campaigner for human rights. As a young man he was besieged in the town of Mafeking during the Anglo-Boer War and wrote the only known war diary by a black South African. His house is now a small reference library and museum, with displays on his life and extracts from his diary. Call ahead for opening times; they tend to change daily. ⊠ *32 Angel St., Kimberley,* ☎ *082/804–3266.* ▱ *R2.*

Wildebeest Kuil Rock Art Tourism Center. This new attraction, 10 minutes from Kimberley, comprises a crafts shop and memorable rock art experience. The center offers a display and a 20-minute film as an introduction to a walk back in time to engravings by the ancestors of the Khoisan made between 1,000 and 2,000 years ago. Visitors follow an audio tour and take the boardwalk to the best of more than 400 images on the hill. Eland, elephant, rhino, wildebeest, hartebeest, ostrich, and dancing human figures are to be seen. The property is owned today by the !Xun and Khwe, San (Bushmen) refugees from the Angolan and Namibian wars who have settled here. The shop sells San crafts such as prints, ceramics, bags, necklaces, postcards, and T-shirts. The engravings are on a low ridge of ancient andesite rock. ⊠ *On the R31 to Barkly West, about 15 km (9 mi) from Kimberley,* ☎ *053/833–7045.* ▱ *R20.* ☉ *Daily 9–6.*

William Humphreys Art Gallery. In Kimberley's Civic Centre, this is considered one of the finest art museums in the country and is an air-conditioned haven of tranquillity on a hot summer's day. The gallery has impressive collections of South African works as well as Dutch, Flemish, British, and French masters. One area is devoted to local work. One of the most popular exhibits is the permanent display on rock art of the Northern Cape. Free guided tours (preferably booked two weeks in advance) will cater to specific interests on request. Light meals are available in the gallery's downstairs tearoom, the Palette. ⊠ *Jan Smuts Blvd., Civic Centre,* ☎ *053/831–1724 or 053/831–1725.* ▱ *R2.* ☉ *Mon.–Sat. 10–5, Sun. 2–5.*

Dining and Lodging

$$$ ✕ **Barnato's.** Set in a picturesque old colonial home dating to around the turn of the 19th century, Barnato's offers plenty of atmosphere and well-presented, tasty food—although both come at a price, comparatively speaking in Kimberley. The meat dishes here are especially good; try the spareribs or, if you're really hungry, perhaps the Barnato's Challenge—a 1-kilo (more than 2-pound) fillet or rump steak (R99)— which will earn you a plaque on the wall. Fish is also a good choice, in particular the sole, which is prepared in a variety of ways. ⊠ *6 Dalham Rd.,* ☎ *053/833–4110. Reservations essential. AE, DC, MC, V. Closed Sun. No lunch Sat.*

$$ ✕ **15 on Dalham.** This relatively new restaurant in an old house has a particularly Northern Cape flavor, from the tasteful decor that includes San (Bushman) paintings and digging sticks on the walls and bowls of ostrich eggshells, to the dishes on offer. Try the biltong (jerky) and butternut salad for starters, and pick from local delicacies like tomato *bredie* (slow-cooked stew), bobotie, or venison stir-fry for your main course. Finish up with *melktert* (custard tart) for an all-round South African meal. ✉ *15 Dalham Rd.,* ☎ *053/832–0608. Reservations essential. DC, MC, V. Closed Mon. No dinner Sun.*

$$ ✕ **Mario's.** The relaxed atmosphere in this historic Kimberley house and its cool outdoor seating in summer make this one of the town's most popular restaurants. The extensive menu includes excellent pizza and pasta. Steaks, especially the panfried fillet, the Karoo lamb chops, and fresh seafood flown up from Cape Town are recommended. ✉ *159 Dutoitspan Rd.,* ☎ *053/831–1738. Reservations essential. AE, DC, MC, V. Closed Sun. No lunch Sat.*

$ ✕ **Spill the Beans.** This coffee shop is an excellent place to grab a bargain breakfast (R20), scones with biltong and cottage cheese, or a light lunch. Try a *tramezzini*—an unusual toasted sandwich with a variety of fillings—and a Heavenly Coffee Shake. ✉ *Checkers Centre, Sydney St.,* ☎ *082/824–4019. No credit cards. Closed Sun. No dinner.*

$ ✕ **Star of the West.** The oldest continuously operating bar in Kimberley, the Star is a national monument and worth a visit even if just for a drink. Typical pub fare such as steaks, salads, toasted sandwiches, and burgers makes it a good lunch option. Its sleepy, nostalgic atmosphere during the day is traded at night (it's open quite late) for noise and smoke, when it's well frequented by locals. No meals are offered on Sunday except in the Carvery, for which you must reserve in advance (R30 per person). ✉ *Corner of N. Circular and Barkly Rds.,* ☎ *053/832–6463. AE, DC, MC, V.*

$$$ ⌂ **Edgerton House.** Each room in this gracious guest house is dedicated to a different personality who had some relationship with early Kimberley, including prominent architect D. W. Greatbach and Princess Radziwill. There is much attention to detail, from ball-and-claw baths in almost every bathroom to the reading material on the Anglo-Boer War laid out in the sitting room. Nelson Mandela and President Thabo Mbeki stay here when they come to Kimberley. There's also a pleasant tea garden in the courtyard, where you can have a light lunch or a luscious piece of cheesecake. Room prices include breakfast, and a three-course dinner can be booked for R120. ✉ *5 Edgerton Rd., Kimberley 8300,* ☎ *053/831–1150. 11 rooms, 10 with bath. Pool. AE, DC, MC, V. BP.*

$$ ⌂ **Langberg Guest Farm.** On the west side of the Magersfontein Bat-
★ tlefield, Langberg is far removed from the buzz of city life. Rooms here are all part of restored thick-walled, whitewashed farm buildings that date back to the days of the diamond rush. Since it's still an operating game and cattle farm, hunting for kudu, gemsbok, and other antelope can be arranged. The atmosphere is relaxed, and the food is excellent: A three-course set meal is served every night except Sunday and typically includes hearty dishes such as homemade chicken pie. Meals aren't included in the lodging price—breakfast will cost you R35 extra and dinner another R65 per person. Langberg is inexpensive considering the luxurious service and is highly recommended. ✉ *21 km (13 mi) from Kimberley on the N12 (main road to Cape Town), and another 2.6 km (1.6 mi) on a farm road, Box 10400, Beaconsfield 8315,* ☎ *053/832–1001. 5 rooms. Bar, pool, tennis court. MC, V.*

$ ⌂ **Belgravia Bed and Breakfast.** Set in a 100-year-old house on leafy Elsemere Road in the heart of historic Belgravia, this charming bed-

and-breakfast is within easy walking distance of many of Kimberley's historic attractions, including the McGregor Museum, Dunluce, and the Rudd House. The furnishings are tasteful yet homely and include antique wooden furniture, Persian carpets, and prints of Dutch masters and South African landscapes. The room rate includes a lavish breakfast. ⊠ *10 Elsemere Rd., 8300,* ☎ *053/832–5007, 082/224–3605, or 053/833–1600. 3 rooms, 2 with bath. No credit cards. BP.*

Shopping

Big Hole Gift Shop. Here you'll find the best range of Kimberley postcards, slides, books, videos, and knickknacks in town, as well as a wide range of ethnic souvenirs such as T-shirts and cushion covers. You can also buy diamonds and diamond jewelry here; it may be useful to compare pieces and prices with the Jewel Box, down the road. Buy your postcards of the Big Hole here and mail them outside the shop in the pre-1902 Victorian mailbox, and they will receive a Kimberley Mine Museum postmark. ⊠ *Big Hole, W. Circular Rd.,* ☎ *053/833–1557.*

Granny's Antiques. Head to this shop, near the Diamantveld Information Centre, if you're looking for an odd piece of authentic memorabilia like a 100-year-old ginger beer bottle manufactured in Kimberley or a pair of binoculars used in the Anglo-Boer War. The shop is closed Sunday and also Monday morning and does not accept credit cards. ⊠ *25 Angel St., Newpark,* ☎ *053/831–6886.*

Jewel Box & Big Hole Diamond Cutting Factory. The Jewel Box specializes in diamond jewelry and can custom-make a piece if you will be in town for a day or two. Although it doesn't boast about its prices, they are among the most reasonable in the country, which draws customers for things like engagement rings from as far afield as Johannesburg. There is also a factory on the premises where visitors can watch goldsmiths at work on weekdays. The shop is closed Sunday. ⊠ *18 W. Circular Rd. (directly opposite Big Hole),* ☎ *053/832–1731.*

Kimberley A to Z

To research prices, get advice from other travelers, and book travel arrangements, visit www.fodors.com.

AIR TRAVEL

South African Express flies between Kimberley and Johannesburg. At press time the fare was about R2,000 round-trip (R1,000 one-way). SA Airlink flies between Kimberley and Cape Town; the fare is R2,800 round-trip (R1,400 one-way). Various discounts—up to 50%—are often available if you book more than three weeks in advance; you should also be able to receive some sort of discount if you book more than two weeks in advance. To book tickets, you can also contact Rennies Travel in Kimberley.

➤ AIRPORT INFORMATION: **Kimberley Airport** (⊠ 12 km [7 ½ mi] from Kimberley on the N12 to Cape Town, ☎ 053/838–3337).

➤ AIRLINES: **SA Airlink** (☎ 011/978–1111). **South African Express** (☎ 011/978–1111).

➤ BOOKING AGENT: **Rennies Travel** (⊠ Box 512, Kimberley 8300, ☎ 053/831–1825 or 053/831–1826, FAX 053/833–5081).

BUS TRAVEL

The local company Tickets for Africa at the Diamantveld Visitors' Centre will be able to give you the latest schedules and prices for all bus transportation in and out of Kimberley. Greyhound and Translux operate a daily service from Kimberley to Johannesburg for R160 each way. Greyhound operates twice-daily service to and from Cape Town for R280, while Translux operates daily service on the same route for R285.

➤ CONTACT: **Tickets for Africa** (✉ Diamantveld Visitors' Centre, 121 Bultfontein Rd., ☎ 055/832–6040).

CAR TRAVEL

Having a car in Kimberley is a good idea as it gives you more freedom, but it's not mandatory if you're only staying a day or two and you hire a good tour guide (☞ Guide Services, *below*).

➤ RENTAL AGENCIES: **Avis** (✉ Kimberley Airport, Box 222, 8300, ☎ 053/851–1082, FAX 053/851–1062). **Budget** (✉ Kimberley Airport, Box 1409, 8300, ☎ 053/851–1182 or 053/851–1183, FAX 053/851–1154). **Imperial Car Rentals** (✉ Kimberley Airport, Box 187, 8300, ☎ 053/851–1131 or 053/851–1132, FAX 053/851–1108).

EMERGENCIES

➤ CONTACTS: **Ambulance** (☎ 10177). **Police** (☎ 10111). **Curomed Medi-Clinic** (✉ 177 Dutoitspan Rd., ☎ 053/838–1111 or 053/831–4730).

TOURS

GROUP TOURS

Consider a tour by chartered township taxi (minibus), which will pick you up from wherever you wish. These tours focus on the history and culture of Galeshewe, Kimberley's largest township, and will take you to the homes of legendary human-rights activists Sol Plaatje and Robert Sobukwe. The tours also take in a traditional *shebeen* (drinking place) and a restaurant. Tour lengths and prices vary; book through the Diamantveld Visitors' Centre.

Something different is the Kimberley Ghost Route, a trail taken at night that starts with sherry inside the Honoured Dead Memorial and then proceeds to several of Kimberley's (purportedly) haunted places such as the Kimberley Club and Rhodes' Boardroom. The tour ends with a visit to the historic Gladstone Cemetery, where a certain Mr. Frankenstein and his wife are buried. Price varies according to size of group. Book at least two days in advance through the Diamantveld Visitors' Centre, and make sure you specify that you want to go inside the haunted buildings, or the tour can be disappointing.

GUIDE SERVICES

Guide fees are not regulated, and guides therefore charge different rates. A half-day guide fee should not cost more than R300 per group and a full day not more than R600 per group. This excludes transport, entrance fees, and refreshments.

A variety of one-day tours tramping the battlefields where Boers and Brits clashed in the Northern Cape is offered by well-known local historian Steve Lunderstedt, of Steve's Tours. Steve is one of the more expensive guides in town, but he's also one of the best. He's a font of knowledge on Cecil John Rhodes and has an encyclopedic knowledge of early Kimberley.

First-class Anglo-Boer War registered guide Scotty Ross concentrates on the Kimberley Battlefield Route or will hone in on particular battles, such as Magersfontein or Paardeberg.

Janet Welsh offers specialized tours to sites relating to early nursing sister Henrietta Stockdale and another on human-rights activist Sol Plaatje and is also registered to do Kimberley and battlefield tours.

Jean Bothomley is an excellent person to show you around the Kimberley Mine Museum, especially if you've got limited time.

Yvonne Dreyer is very knowledgeable about Kimberley history and the history of diamond mining.

Dirk Potgieter of Diamond Tours Unlimited offers a good day tour to the alluvial diggings about 40 km (25 mi) from Kimberley, as well as bird-watching, canoeing on the Vaal River, the Kimberley Ghost Route, fly-fishing, and visits to the Kalahari.

Local archaeologist David Morris will show you a fascinating selection of rock art sites and local Stone Age sites; book early because he's busy.
➤ LOCAL GUIDES: **Jean Bothomley** (✉ Box 451, 8300, ☎ 053/833–5213 or 053/832–4712, FAX 053/831–2640). **Yvonne Dreyer** (✉ 13 Nicole St., Lindene, 8301, ☎ 053/861–4765 or 082/469–0275). **David Morris** (✉ Box 316, McGregor Museum, 8300, ☎ 053/842–0099 or 053/832–8355, FAX 053/842–1433). **Dirk Potgieter** (✉ Box 2775, 8300, ☎ 083/265–4795, ☎ FAX 053/843–0017). **Scotty Ross** (✉ 115 Main Rd., 8301, ☎ FAX 053/832–4083 or 082/320–4380). **Steve's Tours** (✉ Box 3017, 8300, ☎ 083/732–3189, ☎ FAX 053/831–4006). **Janet Welsh** (✉ 4 Camelot, Francey St., 8301, ☎ 053/832–8343 or 082/856–2280).

TRAIN TRAVEL
Trains between Kimberley and Johannesburg and Cape Town depart from all three cities once or twice daily. Travel first-class only, and preferably with a companion (make sure you book in tickets together so that they are issued for the same compartment). One-way fare between Kimberley and Johannesburg is currently R150, between Kimberley and Cape Town R295. Information on these routes can be obtained from Spoornet.
➤ CONTACT: **Spoornet** (☎ 053/838–2731, 053/838–2631, or 053/838–2060; 053/838–2092 in Kimberley; 011/773–2944 or 011/773 2131 in Johannesburg; 021/218–3871 or 021/218–3018 in Cape Town).

VISITOR INFORMATION
The Diamantveld Visitors' Centre has maps and brochures on the Northern Cape and the Kimberley region in particular and can make tour and travel bookings. The center is also the starting point for extremely popular Kimberley ghost tours.

At the Northern Cape Tourism Authority you can pick up information on the province.
➤ TOURIST INFORMATION: **Diamantveld Visitors' Centre** (✉ 121 Bultfontein Rd., Box 1976, 8301, ☎ 053/832–7298, FAX 053/832–7211, WEB www.kimberley-africa.com). **Northern Cape Tourism Authority** (✉ 187 Dutoitspan Rd., Private Bag x5017, 8300, ☎ 053/832–2657, FAX 053/831–2937, WEB www.northerncape.org.za).

UPINGTON, THE KALAHARI, AND THE ORANGE RIVER BASIN

Upington

411 km (257 mi) northwest of Kimberley.

Home to about 100,000 residents, Upington is a thriving agricultural center on the north bank of the Orange River. In the 1870s a Koranna captain named Klaas Lucas invited missionary Christiaan Schroder to come to *Olyvenhoudtsdrift* (ford at the olive wood trees), as Upington was first known. Construction on the first mission buildings, now part of the Upington museum complex, was started in 1873. The town was renamed after Sir Thomas Upington, an attorney general of the Cape who was responsible for ridding the area of its notorious bandits in the 1880s. Although convention has it that the first person to irrigate crops from the Orange was Christiaan Schroder himself, recent historical research has revealed that this honor should go to Abraham September, a *baster* (person of mixed race) and a freed slave, who first led water from the Orange in about 1882. Upington, which is known for its heat, is the start of what is called paradoxically the Green Kalahari—a basin of irrigated lands, mostly vineyards, that stretches about 80 km (50 mi) to the west, to the town of Kakamas. Also to the west and 40 km (25 mi) north of Kakamas is the Augrabies Falls National Park, which is well worth a visit. Upington is also the gateway to the Kalahari proper, the arid dunelands that are home to the oryx and black-maned lion.

En Route   If you are driving between Kimberley and Upington, stop for half an hour or so in Griquatown (144 km [90 mi] from Kimberley; 252 km [158 mi] from Upington). The town is locally known as Griekwastad and in the 1800s was the center of a state called Griqualand West that had its own flag, coinage, and even language. The Griquas are a social group that came into being in the late 18th century and were at first a mixture of indigenous Khoisan and black peoples, runaway slaves, freebooters, adventurers, and criminals escaping the Cape Colony to the south. Some people still identify themselves as Griquas today. In 1803 the London Missionary Society established a mission here. Mary Moffat, wife of explorer David Livingstone, was born here. The old mission house is now home to the **Mary Moffat Museum,** which has interesting displays and literature for sale on the history of the Griquas, the missionaries, and the area. ⊠ *Main St., Griquatown,* ☎ *053/ 343–0180.* ☜ *Donation requested.* ⊙ *Weekdays 8–1 and 2–5.*

The **Kalahari-Oranje Museum Complex** comprises simple whitewashed buildings that were erected by missionary Christiaan Schroder in the 1870s. There are displays on agriculture and local history, and collections of minerals and items used by the San (Bushmen) of the area. Just outside the complex is the unusual **Donkey Monument,** a bronze sculpture by Hennie Potgieter that is a testimony to the role played by the animal in developing the Lower Orange River valley. ⊠ *Schroder St.,* ☎ *054/331–2640.* ☜ *Free.* ⊙ *Weekdays 9–12:30 and 2–5, Sat. 9–noon.*

The **SA Dried Fruit Cooperative,** just outside Upington on the road from Kimberley, shows a video on the processing and drying of fruit, and special tours of this vast factory can be arranged in advance. A shop sells dried fruit at good prices. ⊠ *5 km (3 mi) outside Upington, on Groblershoop Rd.,* ☎ *054/334–0006.* ☜ *Free.* ⊙ *Video weekdays 9:45 and 1:45, tours by appointment.*

In Upington's industrial area is **Oranjerivier Cooperative Wine Cellars,** the second-largest wine cooperative in the world (the largest is in South America). Tastings of a variety of white wines—from the sweet and rich dessert wine Hanepoort to the lighter steens and chenin blancs—as well as grape juice are offered. Between January and March you can also take a tour of the cellars. ⊠ *Industrial Rd., Upington,* ☎ *054/337–8800,* ℻ *054/332–4408.* ☜ *Free.* ⊙ *Weekdays 7:30–5, Sat. 8:30–noon.*

The unusual **Camel Statue,** about 2 km (1 mi) down Schroder St. away from the museum, is a bronze monument in front of the Upington police station. It commemorates the police who used camels as mounts when they patrolled the Kalahari in frontier days.

At the center of the small **Spitskop Nature Reserve** is an outlook of granite boulders. An easy climb to the top offers a good view of the reserve. There is a telescope to help you spot the ostrich, gemsbok, eland, Burchell's zebra, and odd camel that inhabit the park. There are three walking trails, ranging from a morning to a full-day hike, as well as braai and picnic facilities and rather basic overnight accommodations. ✉ *15 km (9 mi) north of Upington on R360]*, ☎ *054/332–1336.* ✉ *R12.* ☉ *Daily sunrise–sunset.*

Dining and Lodging

$$$ ✕ **Le Must.** This is easily the best restaurant in town and one of the
★   top in the province as well. Candlelight and starched linens set off the interior, and the atmosphere is intimate and welcoming. Meat dishes are especially good; try the rump with a Kalahari biltong and Gariep port sauce or a T-bone with a banana, sweet mustard, and bacon sauce. For dessert, finish off with a piece of delicious brandy-and-date tart. There is a good wine list of mostly Cape wines, but there are also one or two of the local vintages. Both Mandela and President Mbeki have eaten here; it would be hard to find a higher recommendation. ✉ *11 Schroder St.,* ☎ *054/332–3971. AE, DC, MC, V. No lunch Sat.*

$ ✕ **Die Dros.** You can drop in for a meal or just a drink at the bar in this large and rowdy restaurant, which its owner has dubbed a "grill and wine cellar." Bottles are packed into the walls from ceiling to floor, and the numerous archways give the place a Mediterranean feel. There is seating outside and inside, and it's open daily from 9 AM until late. ✉ *Pick 'n Pay Centre, Le Roux St., Upington,* ☎ *054/331–3331. AE, DC, MC, V.*

$$ ⌂ **Le Must Guesthouse.** This Cape Dutch house is elegant without being pretentious; original artwork hangs in every room, and the beds are covered in French linens. There is a great view of the Orange River from the guest house, and the garden—where you can sit and have a cup of tea or a gin and tonic—sweeps right down to the waterside. Guests can take a dip in the river or a lazy paddle in a canoe. There is also access to the neighboring pool. ✉ *12 Murray Ave., 8801,* ☎ *054/332–3971,* FAX *054/332–7830. 7 rooms, 5 with bath. Air-conditioning. AE, DC, MC, V.*

$$ ⌂ **Riviera Garden Lodge.** In the middle of a row of guest houses, the Riviera is an oasis of personal attention, charm, and tasteful interiors. Hostess Anneke Malan loves to chat and tell people all there is to know about Upington and its environs, but she's sensitive enough to leave you alone if you want quiet. Breakfast, of scrambled ostrich eggs if you like, is included and is served on the veranda in summer. ✉ *16 Budler St., Upington 8801,* ☎ *054/332–6554. 2 rooms. Air-conditioning. No credit cards. BP.*

$$ ⌂ **Witsand Nature Reserve.** This beautiful site in the southern Kalahari, off the road between Griquatown and Upington, is well worth a couple of nights' stay. Owned by the provincial government, the thatch-and-stone accommodations are luxurious and blend well with the unique nature of the place. You can walk or mountain-bike in the reserve, which covers vast, very unusual white dunes, up to 60 meters (66 yards) high, stretching across an area 9 km (6 mi) long and 4 km (2½ mi) wide. There are also the "roaring sands," which mysteriously make a deep, roaring noise when walked on. Each lodge is privately placed in thick bush under large camelthorn trees and sleeps six, although you'll pay a per-person rate for a smaller group. ✉ *Drive 80 km (50 mi) west of Griquatown toward Upington; then follow signposts another 45 km (28 mi) to Witsand. Reservations: Witsand Nature Reserve, Box 1474, Postmasburg 8420,* ☎ *053/313–1061,* WEB *www.northerncape.org.za. 10 six-person lodges, 10 campsites, 7 four-person bungalows. Air-conditioning, pool, bicycles, shop. DC, MC, V.*

$ ⛰ **Nirvana Guesthouse.** A little out of town (5 km [3 mi]) and favored by businesspeople, this guest house is built around and above large koi ponds, and the constant sound of running water is soothing in sweltering Upington. Don't expect much personal attention or originality in the interior decoration, but it's a pleasant enough place to spend the night. There is an extra R30 charge per person for breakfast. ⊠ *Olifantshoek Rd., Box 193, Upington 8800,* ☎ *054/338–0384 or 082/ 820–2303,* ℻ *054/332–402. 8 rooms. Air-conditioning. DC, MC, V.*

The Kalahari

In an odd little finger of South Africa, jutting north and surrounded by Botswana in the east and Namibia in the west, lies the giant **Kgalagadi Transfrontier Park,** South Africa's second-largest park after Kruger National Park. Kgalagadi was officially launched in 2000 as the first transfrontier, or "Peace Park," in southern Africa by merging South Africa's vast Kalahari Gemsbok National Park with the even larger Gemsbok National Park in Botswana. The Kgalagadi is now one of the largest protected wilderness areas in the world—an area of more than 38,000 square km (23,750 square mi). Of this awesome area 9,600 square km (6,000 square mi) falls in South Africa, and the rest falls in Botswana. The Twee Rivieren Gate lies about 250 km (156 mi) to the north of Upington on the R360. Passing through the gate, you will encounter a vast desert under enormous, usually cloudless skies and a sense of space and openness that few other places can offer.

The Kgalagadi Transfrontier is less commercialized and developed than Kruger. The roads aren't paved, and you will come across far fewer people and cars. There is less game on the whole than in Kruger, but because there is less vegetation, the animals are much more visible. Also, as the game and large carnivores are concentrated in two riverbeds (the route that two roads follow), the park offers unsurpassed viewing and photographic opportunities. Perhaps the key to really appreciating this barren place is understanding how its creatures have adapted to their harsh surroundings to survive. Take the gemsbok, for example, which can tolerate extreme changes in body temperature. The white area around the animal's nose is home to a sophisticated cooling system that lowers the blood temperature before it circulates to the head. There are insects in the park that only inhale every half hour or so to save the moisture that breathing expends.

The landscape—endless dunes punctuated with blond grass and the odd thorn tree—is dominated by two dry riverbeds: the Nossob (which forms the border between South Africa and Botswana), and its tributary, the Auob. The Nossob only flows a few times a century, while the Auob flows only once every couple of decades or so. A single road runs beside each riverbed, along which windmills pump water into man-made water holes that help the animals to survive and provide good viewing stations for visitors. A third road traverses the park's interior to join the other two. The scenery and vegetation on this road changes dramatically from the two river valleys, that are dominated by sandy banks, to a more grassy escarpment. Two more dune roads have recently been added, and several four-by-four routes are being developed. From Nossob camp a road leads to Union's End, the country's northernmost tip, where South Africa, Namibia, and Botswana join. Allow a full day for the long and dusty drive, which is 124 km (77 mi) one-way.

The park is famous for its gemsbok and its large, black-maned lions. It also boasts leopard, cheetah, eland, and blue wildebeest and has recently introduced giraffe. A host of specialized desert species rarely seen elsewhere also make it their home, such as the desert-adapted springbok, the elusive aardvark, and the tiny Cape fox. The busy antics of meerkats and mongooses are an added attraction. For birders, the park is known as one of Africa's raptor meccas, with highlights being bateleurs, lappet-faced vultures, pygmy falcons, and the cooperatively hunting red-necked falcons and gabar goshawks.

The park can be stinking hot in summer and freezing at night in winter. Autumn—from late February to mid-April—is perhaps the best time to visit. It's cool after the rains, and many of the migratory birds are still around. The winter months of June and July are also a good time. It's best to make reservations as far in advance as possible, even up to a year or more if you want to visit at Easter or in June or July, when there are school holidays.

★ The park's legendary **night drives** depart every evening at about 5:30 in summer, earlier in winter (check when you get to the camp), from Twee Rivieren Camp. Reservations are essential and can made when you book your accommodations. The drives go out just as the gate closes to everyone else, in an open truck high off the ground that seats about 30 people. A ranger gives a brief background on the history, animals, plants, and insects of the Kalahari before setting off. You'll have a chance to see rare nocturnal animals like the brown hyena and the bat-eared fox by spotlight. The highly recommended drive lasts a few hours and costs R60 per person.

At present there are no roads within the park that join the South African and Botswana sides, although plans are afoot to change this by the end of 2003. Visitors who wish to go to both sides must therefore cross into Botswana at the Bokspits border post 60 km (38 mi) south of Twee Rivieren and reenter the park on the Botswana side. The park infrastructure in Botswana is very basic, with just three campsites. (This is the ultimate four-by-four terrain, however; a new 250-km [156-m] route has just been opened). Bookings for the Botswana side must be done through its **Parks and Reserves Reservation Office** (✉ Department of Wildlife and National Parks, Box 131, Gaborone, Botswana, ☎ 0926/758–0774 or 0926/758–0775).

Rest Camps

There are shops selling food, curios, and some basic equipment at all three camps, but Twee Rivieren has the best variety of fresh fruit, vegetables, milk, and meat and is the only camp with a restaurant. Gas is also available at all three camps. Electricity only runs for part of the day and at different times in each camp, so inquire on arrival about this. For reservations contact the **National Parks Board,** or you can reserve directly through the park (☎ 054/561–0021) if you happen to be there and would like to stay a night or add another night onto your stay. The price categories given below reflect the cost of standard accommodations for two persons; however, because the camps offer bungalows or cottages that sleep up to six, you'll find them an even better value if you're traveling as a family or larger party. All accommodations offer offer a fully equipped kitchen, a braai, and bathroom facilities unless otherwise noted. Visitors are advised to take a malaria prophylactic and use a mosquito repellent, especially during the summer months. Rental cars can be picked up from the Twee Rivieren Camp if reserved through a rental agency in Upington in advance. ✉ *Box 787, Pretoria 0001,* ☎ *012/343–1991,* FAX *012/343–0905; in Cape Town:* ✉ *Box 7400, Roggebaai 8012,* ☎ *021/222–810 or 021/222–816,* FAX *021/246–211;* WEB *www.parks-sa.co.za. AE, DC, MC, V.*

$$ 🏠 **Twee Rivieren.** On the Kagalagadi's southern boundary, this camp is home to the park's headquarters. It is the biggest of the camps and has the most modern facilities; all units have fully equipped kitchens, and the camp shop here is the best around, with a wide range of groceries and other necessities. Guests can choose between three types of bungalows, from a two-bedroom, six-bed family cottage to a bungalow with two single beds and a sleeper couch. There are educational exhibits on the Kalahari's animal and plant life. The recommended route from Upington to Twee Rivieren is 260 km (163 mi) on a relatively good road (only the last 52 km [32 mi] is gravel). *1 six-person cottage, 2 three-person bungalows, 28 four-person bungalows. Restaurant, bar, air-conditioning, pool.*

$–$$ 🏠 **Nossob.** This is the northernmost camp, on the Botswana border, 166 km (104 mi) from Twee Rivieren. Its facilities are basic, but for real bush atmosphere it can't be beat. There is no electricity in the camp, and the generators are turned off at 10 PM. *4 six-person cottages, 2 three-person bungalows, 4 three-person huts with shared bath.*

$ 🏠 **Mata Mata.** This camp is 120 km (75 mi) from Twee Rivieren on the Namibian border with South Africa—it's a straight vertical line down the 20th meridian. The camp's facilities are not as modern as those at Twee Rivieren. Note that there is no access to Namibia through Mata Mata. *2 six-person cottages, 3 three-person huts with shared bath.*

Tswalu Kalahari Reserve

★ Near the Kgalagadi Transfrontier Park is Tswalu, which at 900 square km (563 square mi) is the biggest privately owned game reserve in Africa; it's the perfect place to photograph a gemsbok against a red dune and an azure sky. Initially founded as a conservation project by the late multimillionaire Stephen Boler primarily to protect and breed the endangered desert black rhino, it is now owned by the Oppenheimer family. Today it spreads over endless Kalahari dunes covered with tufts of blonde veld and over much of the Northern Cape's Korannaberg Mountain range. It is the best place in Africa to see rhino—the reserve boasts 42 white and 11 black rhinos, which have adapted to living in the desert. Other rare species include roan and sable antelope, black wildebeest, and mountain zebra. There is not as much game as in some of the private reserves of the Lowveld because the land has a lower carrying capacity (the annual rainfall is only about 250 millimeters [9¾ inches]). But when you do see animals, the lack of vegetation makes sightings spectacular. And because only three or so Land Rovers are traversing an area two-thirds the size of the entire Sabi Sands makes your escape from the rat race all the more complete.

Nothing is left wanting at Tswalu, which is one of only a dozen Relais & Châteaux properties in South Africa. Children are welcome and well catered to (children under 12 accompanied by an adult are free), and unlike most southern African bush lodges, Tswalu is malaria free. Road transfers from Kimberley or Upington can be arranged, and there is a chartered flight from Johannesburg three times a week. ✉ *Reservations: Box 1081, Kuruman 8460, ☎ 053/781–9311 or 053/781–9211, 📠 053/781–9238. Bar, pool, air-conditioning, horseback riding, private airstrip. AE, DC, MC, V. FAP.*

$$$$ **Motse.** Tswalu's main lodge is made up of freestanding thatch-and-stone suites clustered around a large main building, with a heated, natural-color pool and a floodlighted water hole. The decor—in keeping with the unusual and unique Tswalu experience—is minimalist and modern, with an emphasis on echoing the landscape in colors and textures, "bringing the outside in." *9 huts.*

$$$$ **Tarkuni.** In its own private part of Tswalu is an exclusive, self-contained house decorated similarly to Motse and offering a comparable level of luxury. Perfect for small groups and families, Tarkuni sleeps eight and comes with its own chef, Land Rover, and tracker. The food almost matches the scenery in memorability, and every meal is served in a different location—from a lantern-lighted dune to alongside a crackling fire in the lodge's boma. Apart from guided walks and drives, horseback trails (riding is not included in the rate) that you traverse with a qualified guide offer close encounters with the wildlife. *1 house.*

Kuruman

250 km (156 mi) northwest from Upington.

If you have a car while in the Kalahari region, it's worth stopping at Kuruman, the hub of a dairy, cattle, and game farming area. Follow the signposts to THE EYE or DIE OOG, an amazing natural spring that bubbles out of the earth and is the source of the Kuruman River. (Kuruman can also be accessed easily from Kimberley; a Kimberley-to-Kuruman tour can take in the McGregor Museum Ancestors' Gallery, rock art, !Xun and Khwe arts and crafts, glacial pavements, Canteen Kopje, Wonderwerk Cave, and the mission, all en route. David Morris, a guide with the McGregor Museum in Kimberley, can arrange such tours; contact him at ☎ 053/842–0099 or 053/832–8355.)

Established in 1816, the **Kuruman Moffat Mission** is most famous mission station in Africa. It was headed by Robert Moffat from 1820 until his retirement in 1870. The site, with stone-and-thatch buildings dating from the 1820s and 1830s and surrounded by huge trees, represents an interface between precolonial history and the present. A complete Setswana Bible was printed here in 1857—the first time the Bible was printed in its entirety in a previously unwritten African language. The mission served as a springboard for many early adventures into the interior, including David Livingstone's expeditions. It's a lovely and gentle place, full of memories. It still functions as a mission and community center and has an excellent curio shop. ⊠ *Moffat La., 5 km (3 mi) outside Kuruman on the Hotazel Rd.,* ☎ *053/712–2645.* 🎟 *R5 adults.* ☉ *Mon.–Sat. 8–5, Sun. 3–5.*

Another fascinating heritage site is the **Wonderwerk Cave,** a spectacular cave 140 meters (460 ft) long that shows signs of 800,000 years of Stone Age occupation and early use of fire. Some 10,000-year-old engravings were found in the deposit, and the cave has unusual rock paintings on its walls. A good site museum adjacent to the cave gives detailed interpretation, and a resident guide will show you around. For more information contact McGregor Museum (☎ 053/842–0099). The cave is about 45 km (28 mi) from Daniëlskuil on R31 between Kuruman and Kimberley (200 km [125 mi] from Kimberley, about 50 km [31 mi] from Kuruman; the turn off is signposted). It is best to phone in advance, as opening times tend to vary. Accommodations and refreshments can be arranged; bookings are through Mrs. Nieuwoudt at ☎ 053/384–0680.

The Green Kalahari

Although the Kalahari rightfully conjures up mental images of dunes and desolation, the southern Kalahari—stretching west along the R64 from Upington to Kakamas and beyond—turns that stereotype on its head. All along the roadsides there is water in the form of irrigation canals from the Orange. Look out along the way for the waterwheels, an old-fashioned irrigation technique that involves elevating the water to make use of gravity for directing it into the vineyards. In winter the fields and vineyards are brown and bare, but in spring they turn from the neon green of new growth into a deep, lush summer green that makes the area look like the Winelands of Paarl and Stellenbosch. Grapes are one of the province's major industries: 80% of South African sultanas are grown in the Northern Cape, and there are thousands of acres of vineyards in the Green Kalahari.

Augrabies Falls National Park

120 km (75 mi) west of Upington on the N14.

The falls were called *Aukoerabis* (Place of Great Noise) by the Khoi, who lived in the area for thousands of years before the arrival of Europeans. Augrabies is truly impressive—it is South Africa's largest falls in volume of water, which plunges into the ravine below. Relatively speaking, this is a small national park (696,850 acres), mostly comprising smooth granite, which is strangely otherworldly and is unique to the area. The falls plunge 199 meters (653 ft) over terraces and into a gorge 18 km (11 mi) long that was carved into the granite over millions of years. Reports of sightings of a river monster in the gorge have been made frequently but are probably fanciful accounts of shoals of giant barbels, which reach about 2 meters (7 ft) in length. Legend has it that an unplumbed hole beneath the main falls is filled with diamonds washed down river over millennia and trapped there. Inside the park you can hike for an hour or several days, depending on what you're looking for. It's also worth a drive around the park to some of the lookout points, which offer spectacular views of the gorge below the falls. For the energetic there's the Gariep 3-in-1 Adventure, which includes rowing for 4 km (2½ mi) down the Orange, a 4-km walk (2½ mi), and a 12-km (7½-mi) mountain-bike ride. Inquiries and reservations can be made at the park. During peak times night drives are also offered by the park. The drives cost around R70 per person—it's money well spent. Book drives directly through the park. ☎ 054/451–0050, 054/451–0051, or 054/451–0052. ✉ R12; no extra vehicle charge.

White-water rafting and canoeing in the gorge are offered by a private company, the **Kalahari Adventure Centre** (✉ Box 20, Augrabies Falls 8874, ☎ 054/451–0177, FAX 054/451–0218).

Lodging

$$ 🏨 The accommodations at **Augrabies** are the nicest in the area, and there is a variety of modern, clean units near the main visitor center and close to the actual falls. All the units are air-conditioned and have braai areas and fully equipped kitchens. A 20% discount is offered from November 1 to the end of June, excluding the March/April school holidays. (Although leaving bookings to the last minute is risky, especially in holiday times, the park does take same-day walk-in bookings or bookings made a few days in advance. For these bookings contact the park directly at 054/451–0050, 054/451–0051, or 054/451–0052.) There are also 40 camping sites here, available for R44 for 1 or 2 people, R11 extra per person. *Reservations:* ✉ *National Parks Board, Box 787, Pretoria 0001,* ☎ *012/343–1991,* FAX *012/343–0905. 9 four-person cottages, 10 three-person bungalows, 40 four-person chalets, 40 camping sites. Restaurant, bar, 3 pools, shop. AE, DC, MC, V.*

Upington, the Kalahari, and the Orange River Basin A to Z

To research prices, get advice from other travelers, and book travel arrangements, visit www.fodors.com.

AIR TRAVEL

SA Airlink operates daily service between Upington and Johannesburg and Upington and Cape Town. The fare from Upington to Johannesburg is R1,368 one-way, from Upington to Cape Town R1,356 one-way. T-class tickets, discounted close to 50%, can be obtained if you book two weeks in advance.

➤ AIRLINE: **SA Airlink** (☎ 054/332–2161 or 011/978–1111, FAX 054/332–1884).

BUS TRAVEL

Inter Cape Ferreira Coaches has service several days a week between Upington and Johannesburg/Pretoria, Cape Town, and Windhoek. Fares are R200–R275 each way.

➤ CONTACT: **Inter Cape Ferreira Coaches** (✉ Box 202, Upington 8800, ☎ 054/332–6091, FAX 054/332–4450).

CAR TRAVEL

Upington and the Kalahari are usually approached from Kimberley, along the R64—a distance of 411 km (257 mi), although there is a slightly longer alternative route, of 501 km (313 mi), along the N14 on the northern side of the Orange River. Upington is 410 km (256 mi) from Springbok along an excellent paved road.

You can rent a car or a four-by-four in Upington, but if you choose this option, make sure to reserve well in advance.

➤ RENTAL AGENCIES: **Avis Car Rental** (✉ Box 1101, Upington 8800, ☎ 054/332–4746, FAX 054/332–4372). **Budget & Upington 4x4** (✉ Box 335, Upington 8800, ☎ 054/337–5222 or 082/773–1050, FAX 054/337–5222). **Venture 4x4 Hire** (✉ Box 1981, Upington 8800, ☎ 054/337–8400, FAX 054/337–8599).

EMERGENCIES

➤ CONTACTS: **Ambulance** (☎ 10177). **Police** (☎ 10111 or 054/337–3400). **Upington Private Hospital** (☎ 054/338–8900).

TOURS

Christiaan Klindt knows Upington and the Kalahari backward and forward. He'll organize tours for you to the nearby Augrabies Falls for an afternoon, or he'll plan an adventure into the Kalahari lasting a week, as well as exotic expeditions such as camel safaris or white-water rafting on the Orange River.

Kalahari Tours and Travel has tailor-made trips lasting from an afternoon to two weeks to Kgalagadi Transfrontier National Park, Augrabies Falls National Park, and Upington and to Namibia. Guides Dantes and Elize Liebenberg specialize in leading small, relatively luxurious tours.

Thuens and Truia Botha operate Spitskop Safaris and Tours from their home at Spitskop Reserve outside Upington. They offer tailor-made tours in the region according to clients' wishes.

➤ TOUR COMPANIES: **Christiaan Klindt** (✉ Box 383, Upington, ☎ 082/435–7744 or 054/332–3467, FAX 054/332–3467). **Kalahari Tours and Travel** (✉ Box 113, Upington 8800, ☎ 082/493–5041 or 054/338–0375). **Spitskop Safaris and Tours** (✉ Box 282, Upington 8800, ☎ 054/332–1336).

TRAVEL AGENT

Le Must Travel can organize anything from your plane reservations or car rental to a package taking in the area's top attractions.

➤ CONTACT: **Le Must Travel** (✉ Box 2929, Upington 8800, ☎ 054/332–3971, FAX 054/332–7830).

VISITOR INFORMATION

The Green Kalahari/Upington Information Centre is a great resource whether you're looking for a guest house or a Kalahari safari. For information on the region's national parks, you can contact the National Parks Board in Pretoria or Cape Town.

➤ TOURIST INFORMATION: **Green Kalahari/Upington Information Centre** (✉ Kalahari Oranje Museum Complex, 4 Schroder St., Upington, ☎ FAX 054/331–2640). **National Parks Board** (in Pretoria, ✉ Box 787, Pretoria 0001, ☎ 012/343–1991, FAX 012/343–0905; in Cape Town, ✉ Box 7400, Roggebaai 8012, ☎ 021/222–810 or 021/222–816, FAX 021/246–211, WEB www.parks-sa/co.za).

NAMAQUALAND

This huge, semidesert region extends north from the West Coast to Namibia, hundreds of miles north of Cape Town and west of Kimberley. It's a remote, unpopulated area, with few facilities and comforts. In spring, however, it puts on a spectacle that must be the greatest flower show on earth. Vast fields that seemed barren only a month before blush with blossoms. *Vygies* (a type of fynbos) and Namaqualand daisies brightly splash the hillsides and valleys with color.

Unless it's flower season think twice about trekking to Namaqualand. As in parts of the American West, distances are vast, and the landscape looks harsh, mostly hills dotted with giant boulders and *kokerbooms* (quiver trees, so named because Bushmen cut arrow quivers from them). Namaqualand's history is fascinating. Khoisan people have lived in the area for thousands of years. The first Europeans to venture into the area were Dutch settlers from the Cape, who came in search of the copper they knew existed here because the Khoi had used it to trade with them. While Simon van der Stel, a governor of the Cape Colony, sunk test shafts in 1685 and realized there were rich quantities of copper in the hills around Okiep and Carolusberg, it was almost two centuries before copper was first mined on a large scale. The commercial center of Namaqualand today is clustered in the dorps (villages) of Okiep, Concordia, and Nababeep and in the region's most prominent town, Springbok. All these towns' roots lie in copper, which has been extracted on a large scale in the area since the 1840s, when the Okiep Copper Mining Company first came to Namaqualand. Today the area is littered with heritage sites harking back to the early copper days, from the smokestack in Okiep to the Messelpad Pass, south of Springbok.

The life of the mines is now almost at an end, and most of Namaqualand is a poverty-stricken but still intriguing place. Tourism is the region's great hope as the copper mines finally reach the end of their lives, and slowly a tourism infrastructure is being put into place. That said, hotels and restaurants are still basic, and Namaqualand isn't the easiest place to get to. It's 909 km (568 mi) from Kimberley and 501 km (313 mi) from Upington. Although Namaqualand is part of the Northern Cape Province, it's actually more accessible from Cape Town, and many travelers choose this approach. It's 544 km (340 mi) from Cape Town to Springbok, and a four- to five-hour drive from Cape Town just to reach Kamieskroon, the closest Namaqualand hamlet with a decent hotel. To do the area justice, you need to budget four days or more. The tours below map out the best flower routes, assuming you are driving from Cape Town up to Namaqualand. If you have driven in to Springbok from Upington, you should read the recommended routes in reverse.

Garies

58 km (36 mi) northeast of Vanrhynsdorp.

Garies is a one-horse town cradled amid sun-baked hills, and one of the best flower routes runs just north of it for 100 km (60 mi) to Hondeklipbaai, on the coast. The road winds through rocky hills before descending onto the flat coastal sandveld. Flowers in this region usually bloom at the end of July and early August. If you're lucky, fields along this route will be carpeted with purple vygies, but also look for Namaqualand daisies, aloes, and orchids. Quiver trees are also common along this route.

Hondeklipbaai

100 km (60 mi) northwest of Garies.

Hondeklipbaai itself is a depressing, windblown settlement perched on desolate flats by the sea. It's a diamond-mining area, and huge holes gouged out of the earth mar the terrain. From Hondeklipbaai, take the road toward Kooiingnaas, another diamond-mining settlement, and then go northeast to Springbok. The road climbs steeply into the granite mountains to Wildeperdehoek (Wild Horses Pass), offering tremendous views back over the coastal plain and the sea. From here the road winds back and forth through the hills, cresting Messelpad Pass (Mason's Road) before rejoining the N7 highway. Have a close look at the Messelpad as you go over it. It was hand-built by convict labor in the 1860s to transport copper-bearing ore to the harbor at Hondeklip Bay, from where it was shipped to Britain for processing. You will see a sign to the prison (now in ruins), where the prisoners who built the pass lived. It's a short but steep walk from the road. The pass was eventually finished in 1869 but was only used for a couple of years because the Okiep Copper Company obtained permission to lay a railway from Okiep to Port Nolloth in the same year the pass was completed.

Kamieskroon

72 km (45 mi) south of Springbok on the N7.

Kamieskroon is another base for exploring Namaqualand in spring and is the closest decent place to stay to Namaqua National Park. The Kamieskroon Hotel, although no great shakes in accommodations, is probably the best source of information on wildflowers in Namaqualand.

The **Namaqua National Park** (formerly the Skilpad Wildflower Reserve), 18 km (11 mi) west of Kamieskroon on Wolwepoort Road, can usually be counted on for superb flower displays, even when there are no flowers anywhere else. The park has been upgraded significantly in the last couple of years and now covers an area of 550 square km (343 square mi), with the majority of the property owned by the World Wildlife Fund. ✉ *Wolwepoort Rd.,* ☎ *027/672–1948.* 🎫 *R10.* ⊙ *Daily 8–5.*

An interesting detour from Kamieskroon is 29 km (18 mi) to **Leliefontein,** an old Methodist mission station at the top of the Kamiesberg with spectacular views across the desert to the sea. The church, a national monument, was finished in 1855, but the adjacent parsonage is much older. The wildflowers in Leliefontein bloom much later than those on the coast, often lasting as late as the end of October. Even if there are no flowers, it's a beautiful drive back down the Kamiesberg to Garies, 72 km (45 mi) away.

Lodging

$$ **☲ Kamieskroon Hotel.** At first glance this hotel offers little to distinguish it from every other in Namaqualand. The newly renovated rooms are clean and comfortable, but certainly nothing to write home about. The reason to come is the hotel's world-renowned series of Namaqualand photographic workshops, which are conducted several times a year by the owners, Helmut and Maryna Kohrs, with professional photographers including Kolla Swart, a well-known local Namaqualander. Every day instruction is given in the field, and film is processed on site. Criticism sessions are held each morning. A six-day, seven-night workshop including accommodations, meals, and tuition but excluding film and processing is about R3,500 per person in a shared room. Even if you don't participate in a workshop, you can still benefit from their tremendous knowledge of the area; the Kohrs provide daily updates on where flowers are blooming. ⊠ *Off N7, Old National Rd., Box 19, Kamieskroon 8241,* ☎ *027/672–1614,* ⅢⅩ *027/672–1675,* ⅢⅢ *www.agape.co.za. 20 rooms. Restaurant, bar. MC, V.*

Springbok

85 km (53 mi) northeast of Hondeklipbaai.

Springbok is set in a bowl of rocky hills that form part of the Klipkoppe, a rocky escarpment that stretches from Steinkopf, in the north, to Bitterfontein, in the south. The town owes its existence to the discovery of copper. It's a buzzing little town compared to most of the dorps in the Northern Cape, and there are a fair number of things to see in the area if you need to take a break from flower gazing.

En Route Another excellent flower drive is a 320-km (200-mi) rectangular route that heads north on the N7 from Springbok to Steinkopf and then west on the paved R382 to Port Nolloth. From there a dirt road leads south through the sandveld to Grootmis, then east along the Buffels River before climbing the Spektakel Pass back to Springbok. If the rains have been good, the route offers some of the best flower viewing in the region. Try to time your return to Springbok to coincide with the sunset, when the entire Spektakel Mountain glows a deep orange-red.

Sixteen kilometers (10 miles) outside town is the **Goegap Nature Reserve,** which is transformed each spring into a wildflower mosaic. There are two short walking trails from the information center as well as several longer ones. In season the reserve conducts daily flower safaris (R25 per person, reservations essential). Bicycles are available for hire (R27 per day). Goegap is also home to the **Hester Malan Wildflower Garden,** which displays an interesting collection of succulents, including the bizarre *halfmens,* or "half person" (*Pachypodium namaquanum*), consisting of a long, slender trunk topped by a passel of leaves that makes it resemble an armless person, hence the name. ⊠ *R355 from Springbok (take airport road and follow signs),* ☎ *027/712–1880.* ⅢⅢ *R5.* ⊙ *Daily 8–6 (last admission at 4:15).*

Housed in an old synagogue, the **Namaqualand Museum** has displays on the history of Namaqualand and the town of Springbok. ⊠ *Monument St.,* ☎ *027/712–2011.* ⅢⅢ *Free.* ⊙ *During flower season, weekdays 9–4, shorter weekend hrs.*

The **Smelter chimney** was erected in 1866 by the Cape of Good Hope Copper Company to process low-grade copper ore from the nearby Springbokfontein mine, known as the Blue Mine. When the railroad between Springbok and Port Nolloth was opened in 1871, the smelter lost its value, but the chimney remained. ⊠ *At bottom of King St., on road to Okiep.*

The **Blue Mine** (behind and above the Springbok Visitors' Center) deserves a peek, just for how large and bright blue it is. This copper mine was first mined in 1852 by Phillips and King, a local trading company based in Cape Town. It was closed in 1868. The smokestack was built in 1880 and the Cornish Pumphouse in 1882 to house the steam-driven pump that "dewatered" the copper mines until the mid-1930s. One-hour guided tours are led daily (by request) into the building from the Okiep Country Hotel, next door. ⊠ *100 yards off Main Rd.,* ☎ *027/744–1114.* ▦ *R10.*

The **Simon van der Stel Mine** is the most impressive of six shafts sunk by Simon van der Stel, governor of the Cape from 1679 to 1699, during his visit to the area in 1685 to prospect for copper. There is a steep climb up to the shaft, around which the rocks are blue with copper. Graffiti from Van der Stel's trip is still visible at the mine's entrance. For guided tours contact Norman Featherstone (☞ Contacts and Resources *in* Namaqualand A to Z, *below*), or inquire at the Namaqualand Tourism Center in Springbok (☞ Visitor Information *in* Namaqualand A to Z, *below*). ⊠ *8 km (5 mi) from Springbok and 3 km (2 mi) south of Carolusberg on the R64.* ▦ *Free.*

Dining and Lodging

$$$ ✕▦ **Naries Guest Farm.** Twenty-seven kilometers (17 miles) west of Springbok along a dirt road, this Cape Dutch–style guest house looks out over the mountains of the Spektakelberg. Gracious host Allan du Preez makes guests feel comfortable and welcome and will take you out to a lovely overlook for evening cocktails. Guest rooms are large, and each is decorated differently. Dinner, included in the room rate (as is breakfast), is a three-course feast of robust Afrikaans home cooking, including such dishes as venison stew, pumpkin fritters, and cabbage and beans. In the morning work it off with a walk through the flowers. Reserve well in advance. ⊠ *Kleinzee Rd.,* ☎ *027/712–2462. 5 rooms, 1 five-person self-catering cottage. MC, V. MAP.*

$$$ ✕▦ **Okiep Country Hotel.** About 8 km (5 mi) from Springbok, this hotel is one of the nicest places to stay in Namaqualand, not only for the above-average accommodations and dining, but also simply because owner Norman Featherstone will provide answers to the most detailed questions about the area, from its history to its future. The hotel is right next door to the Cornish Pumphouse, a landmark on Okiep's main road. More basic accommodations under the same management are available over the road. ⊠ *Box 17, Okiep 8270,* ☎ *027/744–1000,* ℻ *027/744–1170,* ⓦⒺⒷ *www.okiep.co.za. 19 rooms. Restaurant, air-conditioning. AE, DC, MC, V.*

Port Nolloth

110 km (69 mi) northwest of Springbok.

Port Nolloth—a lovely drive from Springbok, particularly during flower time—started life as a copper port, but today is better known as a fishing and diamond center. Port Nolloth is also the springboard to the Richtersveld, the vast region of mountains and desert to the north, which is well known for its exquisite succulents and other flora but which should only be visited on an organized tour or once you have armed yourself with a considerable amount of information about the area. Port Nolloth's bay is safe for swimming, although the water's freezing. Head over to the harbor to check out the diamond-vacuuming boats, with their distinctive hoses trailing astern. Divers use the hoses to vacuum under boulders on the seabed in search of the diamonds that have washed into the sea from the Orange River over many millennia. It's a highly lucrative endeavor but not without its dangers; at least one diver has been sucked up the vacuum hose to his death. There's a museum in the main street with a huge basket outside that was used to winch people up from boats in times gone by. There's also an interesting old graveyard behind the police station, with graves dating to the Anglo-Boer War.

Lodging

$ 🏨 **Bed Rock Accommodation.** Across the street from the sea, these weathered old guest houses look from the outside as though they've seen better days. The interiors, however, are delightful, decorated with an eclectic collection of Africana and antiques. Each room has its own bathroom, not always in the room, however. ⊠ *Coast Rd., Port Nolloth,* ☎ *027/851–8865. 5 cottages. DC, MC, V.*

Namaqualand A to Z

To research prices, get advice from other travelers, and book travel arrangements, visit www.fodors.com.

AIR TRAVEL

National Airlines has round-trip flights between Cape Town and Springbok weekdays (R3,340 round-trip, R1,687 one-way). They also do charter flights to the Richtersveld and all over South Africa.
➤ AIRLINE: **National Airlines** (⊠ Box 64, Cape Town International Airport, 7525, ☎ 021/934–0350, FAX 021/934–3373).

BUS TRAVEL

Intercape Mainliner operates service up the West Coast to Springbok (R240) on Sunday, Tuesday, Thursday, and Friday stopping en route at Citrusdal, Clanwilliam, and Vanrhynsdorp, in the Western Cape, and Garies and Kamieskroon, in the Northern Cape. A service from Springbok to Cape Town runs Monday, Tuesday, Thursday, and Friday.
➤ CONTACT: **Intercape Mainliner** (⊠ Captour Office, Adderley St., Cape Town, ☎ 021/386–4400, FAX 021/386–2488).

CAR TRAVEL

Namaqualand is more than 320 km (200 mi) north of Cape Town and 900 km (563 mi) west of Kimberley.

With the great distances involved and the absence of any real public transportation, the only way to get around is by car. If you arrive by bus or air, you can rent a car through Tempest Car Hire. It's the only rental agency in town, so make your reservations early.
➤ RENTAL AGENCY: **Tempest Car Hire** (⊠ 75 Voortrekker St., Springbok, ☎ 027/718–1600, FAX 027/712–1769).

TOURS

Koperberg Tours' owner-operator Norman Featherstone is a well-known personality in the area—he also owns the Okiep Country Hotel and has done a lot for local tourism promotion. He is a charming, knowledgeable guide who specializes in Namaqualand and the Richtersveld and will tailor something for you lasting an afternoon or a few days. He's busy, so book well in advance.

Rey van Rensburg is noted for his excursions into the Richtersveld and the Namib in Namibia. Trips last upwards of five days, and the distances traveled are vast.
➤ TOUR OPERATORS: **Koperberg Tours** (⊠ Okiep Country Hotel, Box 17, Okiep, ☎ 027/744–1000, FAX 027/744–1170). **Rey van Rensburg** (⊠ Box 142, Springbok 8240, ☎ 027/712–1905, FAX 027/718–1460).

VISITOR INFORMATION

A delightful little Old Anglican Church in Springbok houses the excellent Namaqualand Tourism Center. It's open weekdays 7:30–4:15, later on weekends in season. You can also call for the latest updates on flowers.

➤ Tourist Information: **Namaqualand Tourism Center** (✉ Old Anglican Church, Namaqua St., Springbok, ☎ 027/712–2011, FAX 027/712–1421).

7 THE GARDEN ROUTE, THE LITTLE KAROO, AND THE EASTERN CAPE

The Garden Route takes its name from the region's riot of vegetation. Here you'll find some of South Africa's most inspiring scenery: forest-cloaked mountains, myriad crystal rivers, and golden beaches backed by thick bush. You'll also find Plettenberg Bay, South Africa's finest beach resort, and Knysna, a town built around an oyster-rich lagoon. The Little Karoo (pronounced cah-*rew*), separated from the coast by a range of mountains, is characterized by wide-open spaces and seemingly endless mountain ranges. The Eastern Cape is South Africa's most diverse province and has some of its best holiday destinations, including hundreds of miles of beautiful coastline.

Updated by
Jennifer Stern

THE 208-KM (130-MI) STRETCH of coastline from Mossel Bay to
Storms River encompasses some of South Africa's most spectacular and diverse scenery, ranging from gentle lakes and rivers to
long beaches and tangled forests to impressive mountains and rugged
coastal scenery with steep cliffs plunging down to a wild and stormy
sea. It's the kind of place where you'll have trouble deciding whether
to lie on the beach, lounge in a pretty pastry shop, or go on an invig-
orating hike.

The Garden Route owes its verdant mien to the Outeniqua and Tsitsikamma mountains, forested ranges that shadow the coastline, trapping the moist ocean breezes, which then fall as rain. These same
mountains are also responsible for robbing the interior of water, creating the arid semideserts of the Little and Great Karoo. A trip into
this sere world of rock and scrub offers a glimpse of what much of South
Africa's vast hinterland looks like. The Little Karoo, the narrow strip
of land wedged between the Swartberg and Outeniqua ranges, stretches
from Barrydale, in the west, to Willowmore, in the east. Although the
area is most famous for its ostrich farms, as well as the subterranean
splendors of the Cango Caves, there is much more for the discerning
visitor to see. However, unlike those found on the classic safari destinations, these treasures are not handed to you on a plate. You have to
really look. Scour the apparently dry ground to spot the many tiny and
beautiful plants. Or spend time walking in the sun to discover some
of the many bird species. A fairly energetic hike into the hills will reward you with fascinating geological formations, numerous fossils, and
extensive rock art. You can also just stand still and enjoy the space and
the silence. Even if all this leaves you cold, it is still worth the effort
to explore some of the spectacular passes that claw through the mountains into the desert interior.

Until recently anyone with limited time would have to choose between
seeing the Garden Route or visiting a classic African game lodge. This
is no longer the case. Gorah, in Greater Addo National Park, and
Shamwari Private Nature Reserve, both near Port Elizabeth and Grahamstown, offer excellent game viewing and the luxurious accommodations usually associated with top game lodges. They're both
malaria free and both offer fly-in packages from Plettenberg Bay.

GARDEN ROUTE

Pleasures and Pastimes

Cultural Attractions
There are some interesting museums, the odd lovely old building, and
even a ghost town hidden in the forest. The Garden Route has attracted
more than its fair share of creative types, so there is a flourishing arts-
and-crafts industry, and there are some interesting dance and theater groups.

Dining
Oysters, oysters, oysters—these are a major industry in Knysna, so
they figure strongly on most restaurant menus. The farms of the Little
Karoo provide fresh ostrich meat and organic mutton or lamb, which
will stand up to South African red wines. You should also try ostrich
biltong (jerky), widely considered the best variety of this national treat.

Lodging
The Garden Route wouldn't have such allure if it weren't for its exclusive seaside getaways and colonial manor houses or its more rustic

inland farms and national-park log cabins. Many of the better estab-lishments are set on little islands of well-tended gardens within wild forests. Breakfast is included in many lodges' rates, and if your guest house serves dinner, eating the evening meal in situ often has a wel-come intimacy after a day of exploring. The flip side of that is self-catering cottages where you can prepare your own meals—pick up some local delicacies and make yourself a feast.

Important Note: The prices listed are for high season, which in some cases are significantly higher than low season. If you're traveling dur-ing winter, don't let an excessively high tariff put you off before in-quiring about seasonal specials.

Outdoor Activities and Sports

The Garden Route is an outdoor enthusiast's paradise. Fantastic golf courses are sprinkled throughout the area, and the long coastline of-fers loads of marine diversions. The diving is excellent, especially off Knysna and Plettenberg Bay, as is the surfing off Mossel Bay, Victoria Bay, and Buffalo Bay (near Knysna). Plettenberg Bay is probably the best place in the world for watching marine mammals—on most days you will see three or four species, occasionally as many as seven on one day. Some of the best overnight hikes in the country are here, in-cluding the Otter and Outeniqua trails, and the forests and beaches are crisscrossed with good day walks, dedicated mountain-bike trails, and horseback-riding paths. There are also numerous paragliding and hang-gliding launch sites as well as a small but wonderful gliding op-eration. And keep Shamwari Game Reserve in mind if you want to get some malaria-free wildlife viewing in on this leg of your trip. You could even fly in there just for a day from Plettenberg Bay.

Wine

It was thought for many years that the only things that grew in the Karoo were ostriches and that the Boland was the only South African region producing quality wine. Well, the die-hard conservatives have been proved wrong. Ostriches flourish near Cape Town, and the wines grown in the Little Karoo are starting to muscle their way into the medals. Although the area is still justly renowned for its sweet varieties and fortified wines such as port, Karoo wine farmers have started producing a full range of wines. The reds, in particular, are more full bodied and tropical than those from the cooler and moister Boland, and they're worth a tasting trip.

Exploring the Garden Route

For most travelers the Garden Route remains very much a "route," a drive of several days from Cape Town to Port Elizabeth, or vice versa. Increasingly, though, people are eschewing the standard driving tour in favor of a longer holiday, basing themselves in a central town like Knysna (pronounced *nize*-nuh) and exploring from there. This certainly has its advantages, not least because almost the entire Garden Route lies less than an hour from this busy town.

In addition, resorts like Plettenberg Bay offer the kind of classic beach vacation you fantasize about during interminable office meetings. The beaches are among the world's best, and you can take your pick of water sports. The ocean may not be as warm as in KwaZulu-Natal, but the quality of the accommodations tends to be far superior.

Great Itineraries

Because of the compactness of the Garden Route, you can see much of it even in three days, but there's plenty to occupy you for a week or more. The essential places to see are Wilderness, Knysna, Plettenberg Bay, and Tsitsikamma—try to fit them into whichever itinerary you choose. They run in a line along the coast from Cape Town to Port Elizabeth, which makes them ever so easy to string together.

Numbers in the text correspond to numbers in the margin and on the Garden Route, Little Karoo, and Eastern Cape map.

IF YOU HAVE 3 DAYS

Choose one place as your home base, either 🔲 **Wilderness** ⑩, 🔲 **Knysna** ⑫, or 🔲 **Plettenberg Bay** ⑬, also called Plett. Do a day walk, either at Robberg Nature Reserve; a shorter, wheelchair-friendly one at the Garden of Eden; at the Featherbed Nature Reserve; or through the deep forest, where you may see abandoned gold mines. In the afternoon take a boat trip to see the dolphins, seals, and whales at Plett. On day two do a low-level scenic flight along the coast to **Tsitsikamma National Park** ⑮ from Plett, then do the Tree Top Canopy Tour or, for the less adventurous, a tractor tour of the forest, and then fly back. Dedicate day three to your chosen activity—just lounge on the beach, visit the museums, or spend the day paddling, horseback riding, abseiling (rappelling), or scuba diving (unless you're flying out, in which case dive on day one or two). You'll encounter wonderful crafts shops and studios in all these towns, so keep your credit card handy. Try to make the time to visit Monkeyland.

IF YOU HAVE 5 DAYS

Spend the first one or two days in Plett, Knysna, or Wilderness, doing walks and museums as described above, and then head over to **Oudtshoorn** ③, via the **Montagu Pass** ⑧ or **Outeniqua Pass** ⑦, arriving in the evening. Spend one day exploring Oudtshoorn, taking in the **Cango Caves** ④ and the **Swartberg Pass** ⑤. Have dinner at Jemima's. The next day head back to the coast via one of the above passes or take the **Robinson Pass** ② to **Mossel Bay** ① where you can visit the Bartolomeu Dias Museum Complex. If you miss Mossel Bay, continue eastward to Tsitsikamma National Park via the steep and twisty but fantastically scenic pass. Explore the Tsitsikamma area, either by taking the gentle strolls through the forest and the boat trip to see the gorge or by kloofing (canyoning) or mountain biking. If you have not been able to fit any game watching into your itinerary, do a one-day trip to Shamwari by air with African Ramble. You'll see lovely coastal scenery, dolphins, whales (in season), some wonderful game, and a cultural village, and you'll enjoy a traditional African lunch.

IF YOU HAVE 8 DAYS

Bliss—you have eight days and plenty to keep you busy. After spending several days in some combination of Plett, Knysna, and Wilderness, head toward the East Cape. Spend your first night in 🔲 **Port Elizabeth** ⑯, perhaps doing a cultural history tour in the morning, and then drive along the coast to Port Alfred. Have lunch overlooking the marina, and then continue through the historic villages of Bathurst and Salem to 🔲 **Grahamstown,** where you can spend the night at Assegai Lodge. Head back to Port Elizabeth via the N2, stopping at Shamwari for a game drive and tour of the Kaya Lendaba Cultural Village and the Born Free Centre en route. Remember, though, that these distances are long. You may just want to relax in one place. If so, choose Gorah or Shamwari for an indulgent game experience. You could also happily spend two days in Port Elizabeth, doing taking tours, lying on the beach, visiting the museum, and perhaps doing a day trip to Shamwari or **Addo Elephant Park** ⑰.

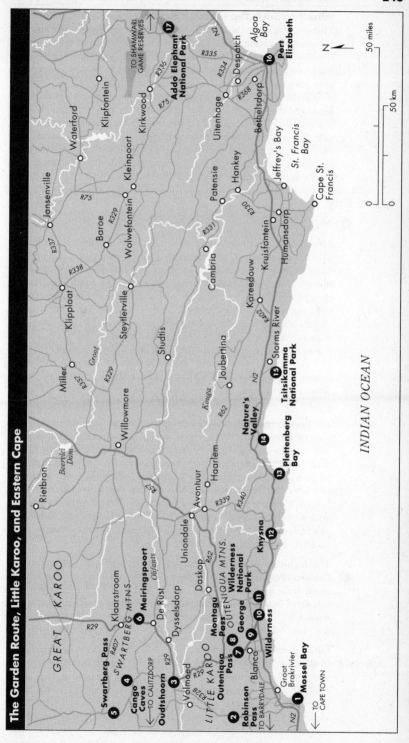

The Garden Route, Little Karoo, and Eastern Cape

When to Tour the Garden Route

There's no best time to visit the Garden Route, although the water and weather are warmest from December through March. If saving money is an issue, stay away during this peak season, when hotel prices soar. Even more important to know, the entire Garden Route is unbelievably crowded from mid-December to mid-January—try to avoid visiting at this time. Between May and September winter gets wet and cold. But—and it's a big but—it makes all the more cozy the huge, blazing log fires and large bowls of steaming soup that local hostelries provide. And, of course, there are fewer tourists. Even in these colder months you often get glorious sunny weather. Wildflowers bloom along the Garden Route from July to October, the same time as the annual southern right-whale migration along the coast.

Mossel Bay

❶ *384 km (240 mi) from Cape Town via the N2.*

Mossel Bay can't compete with Knysna or Plett as a resort town, but it's pleasant nevertheless, with some lovely old buildings. Its main attractions are an excellent museum complex, some of the best oysters along the coast, and good beaches with safe, secluded bathing. Be warned, though: it is also very popular with local families, and in summer it is a writhing, seething mass of juvenile humanity. The diving is pretty good, and the surfing is excellent. Dolphins—as many as 100 at a time—frequently move through the bay in search of food, and whales swim past during their annual migration (July–October). If you're not going to Plett, you may want to take a cruise out to Seal Island, home to a breeding colony of more than 2,000 Cape fur seals, and a slightly dubious operation offers the opportunity to crawl into a cage to view the numerous great white sharks (blue pointers) that hang around the seal colony.

The **Bartolomeu Dias Museum Complex** concentrates on the early history of Mossel Bay when it was a regular stopover for Portuguese mariners en route to India from Europe. Also here is the Post Office Tree. In the 15th century this was a lone tree on a deserted beach on an unexplored coast, but a few sailors decided it stood out sufficiently and left some letters there in the hope they would be found and delivered. They were. Unfortunately, the South African postal system has gone steadily downhill from that high point of efficiency. ⊠ *Church and Market Sts.,* ☎ *044/691-1067,* WEB *www.diazmuseum.museum.com.* ⛶ *R10.* ☉ *Weekdays 9–5, weekends 9–4.*

The highlight of the trip between Mossel Bay and Oudtshoorn is **❷** **Robinson Pass** (route R328), which cuts through the Outeniqua Mountains. Built in 1886 by Sir Thomas Bain, the road climbs through forests of exotic pine and hillsides covered with *fynbos* (pronounced *feign*-boss), the abundant native Cape flora. From May through July the proteas bloom.

Dining and Lodging

$$$–$$$$ ✕ **Gannet.** Tour-bus crowds occasionally descend on this popular spot, but don't let that put you off. Justly renowned for its seafood—the oysters are superfresh and wild, not cultivated—it also has good general and vegetarian menus. Try a pizza from the wood-fire oven or something a bit more exotic, such as the Brie and bacon baked in phyllo parcels or baked avocado with olives, feta, and garlic, topped with mozzarella and served on a fresh mango coulis. In summer sit outside on the shaded terrace overlooking the bay or inside with the eclectic collection of fish-themed African artifacts. ⊠ *Market and Church Sts.,* ☎ *044/691–1885. AE, DC, MC, V.*

$$$ ✕🖾 **Eight Bells Mountain Inn.** On the R328, 35 km (28 mi) from Mossel Bay and 50 km (31 mi) from Oudtshoorn, this lovely country hotel is a winner, set in a colorful garden that fades into cow-filled pastures before disappearing into 400 acres of forest and mountain. A number of day walks and horse rides are available, or you can just enjoy the ambience from the terrace restaurant. The decor is quite eclectic and rooms are loosely done in themes—floral, African, and even two that look vaguely like Swiss wooden chalets. Food is good country fare—they pride themselves on their plump country chickens, which are raised on the farm next door. ⊠ *Box 436, Mossel Bay 6500,* ☎ *044/631–0000,* FAX *044/631–0004,* WEB *www.eightbells.co.za. 18 rooms, 7 suites. Restaurant, bar, room service, pool, 2 tennis courts, horseback riding, squash. AE, DC, MC, V. BP.*

$$$ 🖾 **Old Post Office Tree Manor.** This pleasant guest house—the third-oldest building in Mossel Bay—has the best location of any hotel in town, just yards from the town's museum complex and overlooking the beach and sea. You can take that in while relaxing at the Blue Oyster Cocktail Bar, a delightfully colorful pub and terrace with panoramic views of Munro's Bay. The bright rooms are simply furnished but comfortable and have excellent bay views. Breakfast is served at the attached Gannet restaurant. ⊠ *Market St., Box 349, Mossel Bay 6500,* ☎ *044/691–3738,* FAX *044/691–3104,* WEB *www.oldposttree.co.za. 30 rooms. Restaurant, bar, room service, pool, meeting room. AE, DC, MC, V. BP.*

Outdoor Activities

BUNGEE JUMPING AND BRIDGE SWINGING

The Gouritz Bridge is about 35 km (20 mi) from Mossel Bay. It is only 65 m (220 ft) high, but it offers a range of wacky adrenaline opportunities. **Face Adrenalin** (☎ 044/697–7001, WEB www.faceadrenalin.com) offers three kinds of bungee jumps and also has a small climbing wall. Bungee jumps cost R150; the bungee swing costs R100 for a single and R120 for a tandem. **Wildthing Adventures** (☎ 021/423–5804, WEB www.wildthing.co.za) operates a bridge swinging operation. You jump from one bridge with climbing ropes and swing from the adjacent bridge. The first jump costs R120, after which you get a "wild card," which entitles you to half-price jumps for the next two years.

HIKING AND WALKING

The **St. Blaize Trail** is a 13-km (8-mi) hike that starts at the cave below the St. Blaize Lighthouse and runs along the coast to Dana Bay. The walk takes about five hours and has great views of cliffs, ocean, and numerous rocky bays and coves.

George

🟡 *45 km (28 mi) northeast of Mossel Bay, 50 km (31 mi) southeast of Oudtshoorn.*

George is the largest town and de facto capital of the Garden Route. It's about 11 km (7 mi) from the sea and not particularly appealing. It does have the best shopping in the area, but you won't find much to keep you here unless you are a keen golfer. But if you are, don't miss this town.

Halfway down York Street is **St. Mark's Cathedral** (⊠ York and Cathedral Sts., ☎ no phone), a tiny Anglican church that gives George its city status. Consecrated in 1850, the stone cathedral is notable for its interesting memorials and large number of stained-glass windows.

Dining and Lodging

$$–$$$$ ✕ **Copper Pot.** Cream walls and candlelighted tables set the tone for this elegant restaurant. There is a selection of typical South African dishes such as Cape Malay mutton curry and Karoo roast neck of lamb. Excellent starters are grilled calamari served on an avocado coulis or *snoek* tartare (snoek is a very popular local fish that's similar to a barracuda). Vegetarians might opt for a vegetable paella or homemade pasta with creamed spinach. Desserts include hazelnut gâteau, homemade ice cream, and a notable crème brûlée. ✉ *12 Montagu St., Blanco, George 6530,* ☎ *044/870–7378. Reservations essential. AE, DC, MC, V. Closed Sun. May–Sept. No lunch weekends.*

$$$$ ✕🏠 **Fancourt Hotel and Country Club Estate.** If you're someone who
★ believes that we were created with opposable thumbs solely to hold a golf club, you'll *love* Fancourt. In the shadows of the Outeniqua Mountains, this luxury resort has a country club feel and four golf courses, all designed by Gary Player. Bramble Hill is open to the public, but all the others are for members and guests of the hotel only. Each course has its own clubhouse and pro shop. At the heart of the hotel is an 1860 manor house. Elegant rooms are either in the old manor house itself or in white villas scattered around the huge complex. Some suites have kitchenettes. Of the five restaurants Bramble Hill is the most popular, with an innovative daily-changing menu featuring whatever is fresh. ✉ *Montagu St., Box 2266, George 6530,* ☎ *044/804–0000,* FAX *044/804–0700,* WEB *www.fancourt.com. 32 rooms, 63 suites. 5 restaurants, 2 bars, 1 indoor and 2 outdoor pools, hair salon, hot tub, spa, steam room, driving range, 4 18-hole golf courses, putting green, 4 tennis courts, bowling, croquet, gym, jogging, squash, volleyball, pro shop, billiards, cinema, baby-sitting, nursery, business services, convention center, meeting rooms, travel services. AE, DC, MC, V. BP.*

$$$ ✕🏠 **Hoogekraal.** About 16 km (10 mi) outside George, this historic
★ farm sits on a grassy hill with panoramic views of the Outeniqua Mountains and the Indian Ocean. The farm is about 650 acres and has been in the same family since the early 18th century. The public rooms are beautiful—filled with antiques and heirlooms—and just being in them makes a stay here worthwhile. Accommodations are in two sections, a building dating to 1760 or a newer one built in 1820. Although the buildings are characterful and there are many lovely old pieces of furniture, the rooms suffer from problems often encountered in historic buildings: the bathrooms are somewhat cramped and many rooms have unusual proportions. Suites have two bathrooms. Most guests choose to stay for the five-course dinner, served on fine porcelain at a communal table in the magnificent dining room. Almost all the vegetables come straight from the garden and the fish from the distantly glimpsed ocean; the milk and beef come from the cows in the field. ✉ *Glentana Rd., off N2 between George and Mossel Bay, Box 34, George 6530,* ☎ *044/879–1277 or 044/877–1009,* FAX *044/879–1300,* WEB *www.hoogekraal.co.za. 3 rooms, 2 suites. Restaurant. DC, MC, V. BP. No children under 13.*

$$$ 🏠 **King George Protea Hotel.** A more affordable option than others in the area, this pleasant Victorian-style hotel overlooks the George Golf Course. Most rooms have two double beds and are decorated in gentle pastels. Large tile balconies have elegant cast-iron garden furniture and overlook the pool or the golf course. ✉ *King George Dr., King George Park, Box 9292, George 6530,* ☎ *044/874–7659,* FAX *044/874–7664. 60 rooms, 64 suites. Restaurant, bar, 2 pools, golf privileges, tennis court, baby-sitting, playground, meeting room. AE, DC, MC, V. BP.*

Outdoor Activities

GOLF

You have to stay at **Fancourt Hotel and Country Club Estate** (✉ Montagu St., Box 2266, George 6530, ☎ 044/804–0000) to play on three of its Gary Player–designed championship courses, but the fourth course, Bramble Hill, also designed by Player, is public. Greens fees fluctuate with the seasons—high-season rates are about R450 for 18 holes; R175–R200 for club rental, and the same for cart rental (compulsory). There is an on-site golf academy.

The **George Golf Course** (✉ Langenhoven St., ☎ 044/873–6116) is a public course. Expect to pay about R200 in greens fees and R100 for a golf cart or R55 for a caddy. You can rent clubs (R100 for 18 holes) and pull trolleys (R20) from **George Golf Shop** (✉ George Golf Club, ☎ 044/873–4254).

Steam Train Trip

The *Outeniqua Choo-Tjoe* is an authentic narrow-gauge steam train that travels the scenic route between George and Knysna. Two trains do the round-trip in opposite directions daily except Sunday. In the off-season the train is also used to haul freight, but tourists are its main cargo. Unfortunately, when weather and vegetation conditions are very dry, the steam engine poses a real fire threat, so at these times the train is pulled by a diesel locomotive. Trains run several times daily from mid-August to mid-May. Reservations are essential and should be made at least a day in advance. ✉ *Station St., George 6530, ☎ 044/ 801–8288, 044/801–8289, or 044/801–8202, FAX 044/801–8286.* ✉ *R50 one-way, R60 round-trip.*

Oudtshoorn

❸ *85 km (51 mi) north of Mossel Bay.*

Oudtshoorn is the largest town in the Little Karoo. In summer it resembles a blast furnace, while winter nights are bitterly cold. Little Karoo refers to the narrow plain between the Outeniqua and Swartberg mountains and should not be confused with the Great Karoo, a vast scrub semidesert that starts on the other side of the Swartberg. The word *karoo* derives from the San (Bushman) word for "thirst."

Oudtshoorn has been famous for its ostriches since farmers began raising them around 1870 to satisfy the European demand for feathers to adorn women's hats and dresses. In the years leading up to World War I, ostrich feathers were almost worth their weight in gold, and Oudtshoorn experienced an incredible boom. Many of the beautiful sandstone buildings in town date to that period, as do the "feather palaces," huge homes built by prosperous feather merchants and buyers. Although feathers are no longer a major fashion item, these huge birds are now bred for their tough and distinctive leather and almost completely fat- and cholesterol-free red meat. Almost as much of a moneymaker, though, is the tourist potential of these weird and wonderful birds. As well as visiting an ostrich farm, you can buy ostrich products ranging from the sublime—feather boas—to the ridiculous—taxidermic stuffed baby ostriches emerging from cracked eggs. Several farms compete for the tourist buck, offering almost identical tours and a chance to eat an ostrich-based meal—among them are Highgate Ostrich Farm, Safari Ostrich Show Farm, and Cango Ostrich Farm. Be warned—these can be real tourist traps: glitzy, superficial, and, in summer, filled with horrendous crowds. As well as watching local "jockeys" racing on ostriches, you'll be offered the opportunity to ride one. Accept if you like, but this is pretty cruel; although the birds are incredibly strong, their legs are very thin, and many birds suffer broken legs when ridden. If this concerns you, instead visit the Cape Town ostrich farms, which do not allow this practice.

Most feather palaces are still private, but you can visit the sandstone **Le Roux's Town House,** built in 1909 and furnished in period style. ⊠ *High and Loop Sts.,* ☎ *044/272–3676.* ☒ *Free.* ☉ *Weekdays 9–4.*

The Town House is administered by the **C. P. Nel Museum,** one of the finest country museums in South Africa. Not surprisingly, it focuses on the ostrich and Oudtshoorn's boom period at the beginning of the 20th century. ⊠ *Baron van Reede St.,* ☎ *044/272–7306.* ☒ *R8.* ☉ *Mon.–Sat. 9–5.*

Cango Ostrich Farm is probably the least commercialized of the ostrich show farms. Guides take you through every step in the production of feathers, leather, and meat and explain the bird's extraordinary social and physical characteristics. It's conveniently located, en route to the Cango Caves from town, for those exploring the area by car. ⊠ *14 km (9 mi) from Oudtshoorn en route to the caves on the R328,* ☎ *044/ 272–4623,* ℻ *044/272–8241.* ☒ *R27.* ☉ *Daily 9–4:15.*

★ ❹ From Oudtshoorn follow the R328 for 32 km (20 mi) to reach the **Cango Caves,** deservedly one of the most popular attractions in the area. The caves are huge and stunningly beautiful, stretching for several miles through the mountains. Unfortunately, some of the grandeur is lost when you have to share the experience with as many as 200 people. The passage of so many people over the years has turned the cave formations from milky white to red and brown because of a buildup of iron oxide and acid damage from human breath. You can choose to do a short, standard, or adventure tour. The short tour is half an hour and only goes into the cathedral-like main chambers. The standard tour takes an hour, going a bit farther into the cave, and the adventure tour is aptly named. Think long and hard before taking this option if you're overweight, very tall, claustrophobic, or have knee or heart problems because you end up shimmying up narrow chimneys on your belly and wriggling your way through tiny tunnels. It's exhilarating, but the temperature and humidity levels are high, and there's not much oxygen. If you plan to do this option, wear shoes with a good tread and old clothes—you'll do a lot of sliding on your bottom. Adventure and half-hour tours leave hourly on the half hour, 9:30–3:30; one-hour tours leave every hour on the hour, 9–4. ⊠ *Off R328 between Oudtshoorn and Prince Albert,* ☎ *044/272–7410,* 🕸 *www.cangocaves.co.za.* ☒ *½-hr tour R17, 1-hr tour R33, adventure tour R45.* ☉ *Daily 9–4.*

NEED A BREAK?

Just at the turnoff to the Cango Caves is **Wilgewandel Coffee Shop and Country Farmstall** (⊠ on the R328, 2 km [1 mi] from the caves, ☎ 044/ 272–0878). They serve well-cooked simple food such as hamburgers, toasted sandwiches, and, of course, ostrich steaks, and a variety of sweet treats. The lemon meringue pie is naughty but nice. Shady outdoor tables overlook a big lawn and duck-filled dam, and camel and pony rides are on offer for children.

OFF THE BEATEN PATH

❺ **SWARTBERG PASS –** From the R328 head toward this pass, one of the most scenic highlights of any trip to South Africa. This pass was built between 1881 and 1886 by the legendary engineer Sir Thomas Bain, who warned that the road would have to be steep. He wasn't exaggerating. Soon after it begins to climb, the tar gives way to gravel and becomes very narrow. At times the road barely clings to the mountainside, held in place only by Bain's stone retaining walls. Cresting the pass at

5,230 ft, you look out toward the hot plains of the Great Karoo Desert and the distant mountains of the Nuweveldberg. Of more immediate note is the huge gorge that cuts through the mountains below, revealing sheer walls of deep red rock. Descending, the road snakes back and forth across the mountain. At every bend the views seem to get better until you're zigzagging through narrow cuts in the vertical rock walls. This is only one of the many fantastic passes in the area, and the best way to see all of them is to join an escorted tour. The Swartberg Experience (☎ 044/272-2143) is a tour run by Kobus Lategan, a large, jovial man who grew up in these mountains and knows them better than almost anybody. He'll keep you enthralled with myths, legends and many tall, tall tales. The Circle Tour (R600 per person) takes in the Swartberg Pass, Prince Albert, Meiringspoort, and De Rust. Breakfast or lunch at Kobus se Gat is included. Ostrich farms, the Cango Caves, or other attractions are optional additions. For the same price you could head over the Swartberg Pass and down into Die Hel, a little valley time forgot. When a road (of sorts) was finally built there in the 1960s, the inhabitants, who had been isolated for generations, left for the big city—well, for places like Oudtshoorn, which qualifies as a big city if you've lived in Die Hel. The now almost completely abandoned settlement is part of a nature reserve. You can go here on your own, but you'll need a four-wheel-drive vehicle and some off-road skill.

Dining and Lodging

$$–$$$ ✕ **Jemima's Restaurant.** Named after the mythical guardian angel of love,
★ good taste, and good cooking, this restaurant would not disappoint its muse. Run by sisters Annette and Celia le Roux, it's a family and community affair. Back on the farm, Dad makes wine and olive oil, while their brother raises chickens, ostriches, cows, and sheep. Most of the fresh veggies also are grown by him, and Mom grows and dries herbs and preserves fruit. What they can't get from the family, they source locally from small farmers. Meat lovers should opt for the "Three Tenors"—medallions of beef, ostrich, and springbok fillet. Herbivores will love the mushroom risotto. There is an extensive list of local wines, and in season, they offer picnic baskets. ✉ 94 Baron von Rheede St., ☎ 044/272-0808. Reservations essential. AE, DC, MC, V. Closed Sun. No lunch Mon.

$$ ✕ **Kobus se Gat.** This unusual "restaurant" offers a unique dining experience. There is no electricity, and all cooking is done on an open fire, including the baking of bread. Obviously, braaied (barbecued) meat features strongly, and Kobus is renowned in the region for his biltong potjie (stew), which has won local cooking competitions. A farmhouse breakfast is R25, and a three-course meal costs R60 per person or R80 for a spitbraai (a whole animal roast; busy season only). Seating is in an open boma. ✉ At foot of Swartberg Pass, ☎ 044/272-2143. Reservations essential. No credit cards.

$$$$ ✕▣ **Rosenhof Country Lodge.** In a restored Victorian farmhouse looking out at the Swartberg Mountains, the lodge has antiques and works by South African artists that complement the house's yellowwood beams and Spanish-tile floor. Rooms, in white cottages arranged around a central lawn and fountain, are bright and elegant. The restaurant serves an excellent five-course dinner, with an emphasis on regional cuisine given a cordon bleu twist. Look for such dishes as butternut soup enlivened with cream and nutmeg, phyllo parcels of mackerel, and ostrich paupiettes with port sauce. Nonguests can reserve a table if space allows. No children under 10. ✉ 264 Baron van Reede St., Box 1190, Oudtshoorn 6620, ☎ 044/272-2232, FAX 044/272-3021. 12 rooms. Restaurant, bar, room service, pool. AE, DC, MC, V. BP.

$ ▣ **Kleinplaas.** The name means "small farm," and although it isn't really a farm, there are sheep, goats, ostriches, ducks, and other animals in small pens where children can pet or feed them. Comfortable, well-pointed cottages with fully equipped cooking facilities are neatly arranged in a huge shady lawn area. There's also a pretty campsite with laundromat. Prices are per chalet for a max of four or six people (depending on the chalet). Extra people can be accommodated on sleeper-sofas at R50 per person. ⊠ *171 Baron von Reede St., Oudtshoorn, 6620,* ☎ *044/272–5811,* FAX *044/279–2019,* WEB *www.oudtshoorn.co. za/kleinplaas. 54 chalets. Pool, coin laundry. AE, DC, MC, V.*

Meiringspoort

6 *40 km (25 mi) NW of Oudtshoorn.*

A good route to or from Oudtshoorn is through Meiringspoort via De Rust. The road runs along the bottom of a deep gorge created by the Groot River. It doesn't have the panoramic views of Swartberg Pass, but it's still incredibly scenic. The road leapfrogs the river 26 times as it cuts through the red cliffs of the gorge. Halfway through the pass is a rest area from which a path leads to a 200-ft waterfall. The town of De Rust is a small, sleepy little Karoo village with a number of crafts shops and a fun coffee shop. Everything is on the main road, so you can't get lost if you stop for a break.

While in the area, pop in to **Domein Doornkraal** for a wine tasting. Although they do make some serious wines, such as a full-bodied cabernet, they are best known for their lighthearted, somewhat frivolous off-dry pink sparkling wine, Tickled Pink—sold with a shocking pink ostrich feather caressing the bottle. It's not a great wine, but it's fun. You may be lucky and find a few jars of their homemade olives, but the small stock is usually sold out pretty quickly. ⊠ *7 km [3 mi] on Oudtshoorn side of de Rust,* ☎ *044/251–6715.* ☺ *Mon.–Thurs. 9–5, Fri. 9–5:30, Sat. 8–1.*

Dining and Lodging

$$$$ ✕🏨 **Oulap Country House.** Oulap is an eclectic mix of textures and col-
★ ors: stone floors, winding staircases, and little book-filled nooks are furnished with antiques, and there is an impressive collection of contemporary South African art. The rooms are all individually decorated with original artworks. The owners grow their own olives and fruit, which they preserve. But the show is stolen by the almost unbelievable star-studded Karoo sky; you haven't seen stars till you've spent a night in the Karoo. The food is wonderful, and the conversation around the huge dining table possibly even better. Four-course farmhouse suppers that include Karoo lamb, hearty soups, and regional produce carry on until late in the evening. ⊠ *Box 77, De Rust 6650,* ☎ *044/241–2250,* FAX *044/241–2298. 5 rooms. Dining room, bar, pool. AE, DC, MC, V. MAP.*

OFF THE **7** From Oudtshoorn take the R29 to George by way of **Outeniqua Pass,**
BEATEN yet another of the stunning passes that cut through the region's moun-
PATH **8** tains. A more historic route leads you over **Montagu Pass,** a narrow gravel road that has excellent views and some great picnic sites. The road was built in 1843 by Henry Fancourt White, and the old tollhouse still sits at the bottom of the pass. To get to the head of the pass, turn left onto the R62 at its junction with the R29.

Wilderness

10 *12 km (7 mi) southeast of George.*

If you're coming from George, the road here descends steeply to the sea through a heavily forested gorge formed by the Kaaiman's River.

Look to your right to see a curved railway bridge spanning the river's mouth. This is one of the most photographed scenes on the Garden Route, especially when the *Choo-Tjoe* steam train is puffing over it. As the road rounds the point, a breathtaking view of mile on mile of pounding surf and snow-white beaches unfolds before you. There is a viewing point from which you often see dolphins and whales frolicking in the surf, and if you look up, you may see a colorful paraglider floating overhead.

Wilderness is a popular holiday resort for good reason. Backed by thickly forested hills and cliffs, the tiny town presides over a magical stretch of beach between the Kaaiman's and Touw rivers. These rivers constitute the western end of a whole system of beautiful waterways, lakes, and lagoons strung out along the coast, separated from the sea by towering vegetated dunes.

⑪ Much of the area now falls under the control of **Wilderness National Park,** a 6,500-acre reserve that stretches east along the coast for 31 km (19 mi). It's a wetlands paradise and draws birders from all over the country to its two hides. Walking trails wend through the park, including the circular 10-km (6-mi) Pied Kingfisher Trail, which covers the best of what Wilderness has to offer: beach, lagoon, marshes, and river. You can rent canoes for R12 per half hour for a double canoe to explore the lagoon and channels. ⊠ *Off N2, Wilderness,* ☎ *044/877–1197.* 🖾 *R12.* ☉ *Daily 8–5.*

Dining and Lodging

$$$$ ✕🖭 **Lake Pleasant Hotel.** Built around an old hunting lodge, this hotel has long been a favorite Garden Route destination. It's decorated in a quietly classical style that doesn't detract from the view over the beautiful lake which laps at the front lawns. The corridors are lined with old pictures of the Knysna Forest and local settlements. You can take an open Land Rover excursion into the adjacent Goukamma Nature Reserve, or a silent electric motorboat sundowner excursion to watch birds. The hotel has a large, well-equipped wellness center with a wide range of sophisticated beauty and health therapies. ⊠ *Off N2, Box 3530, Knysna 6570,* ☎ *044/343–1313,* 𝔽𝔸𝕏 *044/343–2040,* 𝚆𝙴𝙱 *www.lakepleasanthotel.com. 30 rooms, 6 suites. Restaurant, bar, lake, 1 indoor and 1 outdoor pool, hot tub, sauna, spa, steam room, golf privileges, tennis court, volleyball, boating, fishing, mountain bikes, shop, library, convention center, meeting rooms, travel services, airport shuttle, helipad. AE, DC, MC, V. BP.*

$$$ 🖭 **Dolphin Dunes.** This modern brick B&B is light and bright inside. But the main attraction is the view. Perched high on the dunes, it overlooks the sea, and a semiprivate boardwalk leads down to the beach. Public rooms are spacious, with clay-tile floors, and the rooms are white and cream, light and airy. ⊠ *Buxton Close, Box 158, Wilderness 6560,* ☎ *044/877–0204. 3 rooms, 1 apartment. Minibars. AE, DC, MC, V. BP.*

$–$$ 🖭 **The Ebb and Flow Restcamp, Wilderness National Park.** The rest camp is divided into two sections, North and South. The South section is larger and consists of brick family cottages, which sleep up to six; log cabins, which sleep up to four; and forest huts, which also sleep up to four. The houses and log cabins have bedrooms, kitchens, and bathrooms with balconies. The log cabins are prettier, but both are bright and pleasant, furnished in a plain but adequate manner with floral or geometric curtains and upholstery. The forest huts are smaller and come with or without an en-suite bathroom. The campsites are set out on a wide lawn under trees, some directly overlooking the river. Ebb and Flow North is much smaller, with a few grassy campsites and 15 rather unattractive *rondawels*. As with all National Park accommodations, the communal bathroom areas are well maintained, clean, and adequate. ✉ *Off N2, Wilderness,* ☎ *044/877–1197,* ℻ *044/877–0111. Reservations:* ✉ *Box 787, Pretoria 0001,* ☎ *012/343–1991,* ℻ *012/ 343–0905. 8 log cabins; 5 cottages; 20 huts, 10 with bath; 15 rondawels, 10 with bath; 100 campsites. AE, DC, MC, V.*

Outdoor Activities

There are lovely walks in the national park, and you can rent canoes from the park offices.

Eden Adventures (☎ 044/877–0179, WEB www.eden.co.za) offers a fun abseiling (rappelling) trip on the Kaaiman's River for R160. A canoeing and mountain bike trip costs R120, and an escorted kloofing (canyoning) trip costs R160. These are all half-day trips, and prices include lunch. They can be combined to form a full-day trip (R240–R260). Eden also rents two-seater canoes (R80 per day) and mountain bikes (R60 per day or R40 for two hours).

The **Wilderness National Park** offers a three-day escorted walking and hiking trail for which you do your own cooking that costs R300 per person. Booking is through the **National Parks Board** head office in Pretoria (☎ 012/343–1991, WEB www.parks-sa.co.za). However, the person sitting in the booking office in Pretoria may not be clued in to what's happening hundreds of miles away in Wilderness, so it may be hard to get information such as departure dates. Your best bet is to contact Eden Adventures for inquiries.

Wilderness is one of the best paragliding spots in the country, with loads of launch sites. You can ridge-soar for miles along the dune front, watching whales and dolphins in the sea. And if you've never done it before, don't worry—you can go tandem with an experienced instructor (R350). All you have to do is hang in there. Contact **Cloudbase Paragliding** (☎ 044/877–1414).

Knysna

⓬ *40 km (25 mi) east of Wilderness.*

Knysna is one of the most popular destinations on the Garden Route. The focus of the town is the beautiful Knysna Lagoon, ringed by forested hills dotted with vacation homes. Towering buttresses of rock, known as the Heads, guard the entrance to the lagoon, funneling the ocean through a narrow channel. The sea approach is so hazardous that Knysna never developed into a major port. Today, however, Knysna is very much a resort town, with the attendant hype, commercialism, and crowds, especially in summer. About the only aspect of the town that hasn't been modernized is the narrow, single-lane main road, so the traffic can be a nightmare—the N2 goes straight through the middle of town. Walking is the best way to get around the town center, which is filled with shops, galleries, restaurants, and coffeehouses.

Several walking and mountain-bike trails wind through Knysna's forests, many offering tremendous views back over the ocean. With luck, you may spot the Knysna *lourie*, a brilliantly plumed and elusive forest bird, or the even more outrageously colored and even more elusive Narina trogon.

You can get a feel for the growth of the town and its industries by visiting one or more of the small museums. **Millwood House Museum** was one of the few houses remaining in the Millwood area of the Knysna Forest. It was built in the 1880s and dismantled and rebuilt in its present spot between 1915 and 1920. It gives a pretty good idea of life in the short-lived but heady Knysna gold rush. ⊠ *Queen St.,* ☎ *044/382-5066 ext. 220.* ⊡ *Free.* ⏱ *Weekdays 9:30–4:30, Sat. 9:30–12:30.*

One of the most interesting buildings in the area stands across the lagoon from Knysna, in the exclusive community of Belvidere. The Anglican **Holy Trinity Church,** built in 1855 of local stone, is a lovely replica of a Norman church of the 11th century. Holy Trinity was erected by Thomas Duthie, a young ensign of the 72nd Highland Regiment who settled in Knysna in 1834. The interior is notable for its beautiful stinkwood and yellowwood timber and stained-glass windows. ⊠ *N2 west out of Knysna to Belvidere turnoff just after bridge, then follow signs.* ⊡ *Free.* ⏱ *Daily 8:30–5, except during services.*

NEED A BREAK?	If you visit Belvidere, be sure to stop at **Crabs Creek** (⊠ Belvidere Rd., ☎ 044/386–0011), a fun tavern that sits on the bank of the Knysna Lagoon. On a sunny day you may have to wait for an outside table, but it's worth it—the view across the water to Knysna is better than the food. Fried seafood is the focus—the pint of prawns is very popular—or you can order the usual pub fare.

You can't come to Knysna without making a trip out to the **Heads** at the mouth of the lagoon. These rock sentinels guard the narrow approach to the town and provide great views of both the sea and the lagoon. Only the developed, eastern side of the Heads is accessible by car, via George Rex Drive off the N2. You have two options: to park at the base of the head and follow the walking trails that snake around the rocky cliffs, just feet above the crashing surf, or to drive to the summit, with its panoramic views and easy parking.

Unlike its eastern counterpart, the western side of the Heads is relatively unspoiled and part of **Featherbed Nature Reserve** (☎ 044/382–1693), a private park that has been declared a National Heritage Site. In addition to a bizarre rock arch and a cave once inhabited by the indigenous Khoikhoi, the reserve is home to various small mammals, more than 100 species of birds, and 1,000 plant species. A trip here consists of a ride on one of the three ferries operated by the reserve, an escorted tractor-trailer ride to the highest point, and then an escorted walk back. Afterward, you can opt to have lunch in the attractive restaurant that serves basic but well-cooked meals. In season or when a tour bus is in town, both the tour and the restaurant can be pretty crowded. The trip costs R60 not including lunch. You can also take a ferry trip into the Heads.

It's a well-kept secret that there are no beaches in Knysna. The nearest is Brenton-on-Sea, which you reach by continuing past Belvidere. It is a beautiful, long, white-sand beach on which you can walk the whole 3½ km (2 mi) to Buffalo Bay. It's about a 10-minute drive—the turnoff from the N2 is about 12 km (7 mi) west of Knysna. The only other option is Noetzie, 7 km (4 mi) east of town. It's a steep walk up and down from the parking lot, but it's worth it, as it's a lovely beach. While there, take a look at the fanciful vacation homes built in the shape of European castles.

Dining and Lodging

Of course, there are restaurants that don't serve seafood, but very few of them are in Knysna. It's what the town's all about. There are more B&Bs than you can possibly imagine in Knysna, as well as some fantastic guest houses, self-catering resorts, and hotels, so you will not be short of choices.

$$–$$$ ✕ **The Drydock Food Company.** Since you're in Knysna, it's no surprise that you'll find oysters here. There's a choice between cultivated and coastal—six of the cultivated or coastal variety cost R32 and R55, respectively. The seafood theme continues with tiger prawns, fusion fish curry, or the Drydock seafood pan—mussels, prawns, calamari, shrimp, octopus, and game fish dressed in a beurre blanc, cooked and served in a paella pan. There's more than seafood, though. The Caribbean blue cheese salad with roasted butternut and *peppadews* (a cross between a sweet pepper and a chili, usually served pickled) is a big favorite, and meat eaters won't be disappointed with the Manchurian beef stir-fry and good old rump steak. ⊠ *Knysna Quays,* ☎ *044/382–7310. AE, DC, MC, V.*

$$–$$$ ✕ **Knysna Oyster Company.** If you love oysters, make a beeline for this
★ tasting tavern, attached to one of the world's largest oyster-farming operations. Diners sit at picnic tables next to the lagoon, with great views of the Heads. Each tasting consists of between six and eight fresh oysters and a basket of brown bread. Also worth ordering is a plate of mussels in garlic-lemon butter, into which you can dunk your bread. Chase the oysters with excellent local Mitchells beer—then do it all again. You'll pay about R30 for six medium oysters, R40 for six large ones. It's a good idea to order some coastal oysters, too, just to see what the fuss is about. They'll set you back R36 for six small ones and R65 for six large. ⊠ *Long St., Thesen Island,* ☎ *044/382–6942, ask for restaurant. DC, MC, V. No dinner.*

$–$$$ ✕ **34° South.** Not a fishmonger, a bar, or a bistro; not a deli, a coffee
★ shop, or a seafood restaurant—yet it's somehow all of these. Right on the water's edge in what appears to be a dolled-up warehouse, this place gives off a sense of abundance, with shelves, baskets, and display stands overflowing with all kinds of delicious goodies. Choose from the huge array of seafood or fresh fish; or nibble on the mezes while sitting on the jetty looking at the boats. Try a delicious sandwich laden with avocados and peppadews. Or just fill a basket with delicious breads, pickles, cheeses, meats, and other delights. It's worth traveling halfway round the world just for the cilantro pesto. ⊠ *Knysna Quays,* ☎ *044/382–7331. AE, DC, MC, V. No dinner.*

$$$$ ✕🏠 **Belvidere Manor.** This is an attractive establishment with lovely
★ views across the lagoon to Knysna, some 6½ km (4 mi) away. White cottages face each other across a lawn that slopes down to a boat jetty. Cottages are airy and bright, with a country feel. Choose from one- and two-bedroom units, all with dining areas, sitting rooms with fireplaces, and fully equipped kitchens. The manor house, a lovely 1834 farmstead, has been converted into a restaurant and guest lounge. In summer breakfast is served on a wooden deck looking over the lagoon. Sizable discounts are offered for long stays. ⊠ *Lower Duthie Dr., Belvidere Estate, Box 1195, Knysna 6570,* ☎ *044/387–1055,* 𝖥𝖠𝖷 *044/387–1059,* 𝖶𝖤𝖡 *www.belvidere.co.za. 33 cottages. Restaurant, room service, pool. AE, DC, MC, V. BP.*

$$$$ ✕🏠 **Phantom Forest Lodge.** Set in the midst of a privately owned 300-
★ acre nature reserve, this stunning lodge is built from sustainable natural materials—wood, thatch, coir, cotton. Accommodations are in luxury tree houses, and all living areas are joined by wooden walkways to protect the undergrowth. Rooms look straight out into the forest canopy. Even the swimming pool is kept clean with an ozone filter—proof of its chemical-free status is the papyrus growing in it. The cuisine is pan-African. This is a place to be quiet and restore your soul. A wellness center called the Body Boma offers massage, reflexology, and other treatments. ⊠ *On Phantom Pass, Box 3051, Knysna*

6570, ☎ 044/386–0046, FAX 044/387–1944, WEB *www.phantomforest. com. 9 suites. Restaurant, bar, pool, spa. AE, DC, MC, V. MAP.*

$$$$ 🏠 **Lightleys Holiday Houseboats.** For a real sense of freedom and adventure, take one of these fully equipped houseboats and cruise the lagoon. Interiors are standard and very much like a camper van, but the exteriors are an ever-changing vista of lagoon, forest, and mountain. This is self-catering at its very best. The minimum rental period is two days on weekends, five days in peak season. A four-berth boat costs R900 per day, a six-berth one about R1,500 per day. ⊠ *Box 863, Knysna 6570,* ☎ *044/386–0007,* FAX *044/386–0018,* WEB *www.knysna.co.za/lightleys. 7 four-berth boats, 5 six-berth boats. MC, V.*

$$$–$$$$ 🏠 **St. James of Knysna.** This elegant getaway is right on the edge of ★ Knysna Lagoon. There's a garden with tranquil koi pools, and a magnificent aviary shows off the plentiful bird life of the area. Indoors, the decor is light and bright, with some lovely antiques. Most rooms face the water with uninterrupted views and are individually decorated. Bathrooms range from a brick-tone retreat with a glass wall leading to a private leafy garden with an outside shower to Victorian fantasies. Activities include boating, picnicking, sunset cruising, canoeing, and waterskiing. ⊠ *The Point, Main Rd., Box 1242, Knysna 6570,* ☎ *044/ 382–6750,* FAX *044/382–6756,* WEB *www.stjames.co.za. 6 rooms, 10 suites. Restaurant, bar, 3 pools, tennis court, boating, waterskiing, croquet, fishing. MC, V.*

$$–$$$ 🏠 **Tonquani Lodge.** Pretty log cabins with full cooking facilities are set in neat lawns ringed by flower beds. All cabins have fans and heaters, and the superior cottage has air-conditioning and a private plunge pool. ⊠ *Welbedacht La., Knysna 6570,* ☎ *044/382–4355,* FAX *044/384–1269,* WEB *www.tonquani.co.za. 10 cottages. Breakfast room, pool. AE, DC, MC, V. BP.*

$$ 🏠 **Brenton-on-Sea.** What a fantastic position this hotel has, right on Brenton Beach. The views from the dining room are superb, and you can walk from the hotel all the way to Buffalo Bay on a long, white, sandy beach. Accommodations are in cute log cabins, some of which offer full self-catering facilities. ⊠ *CR Swart Dr., Brenton-on-Sea, Knysna 6570,* ☎ *044/381–0081,* FAX *044/381–0026,* WEB *www.brentononsea.com. 54 rooms, 16 chalets. Restaurant, bar, pool, beach. AE, DC, MC, V. BP.*

Outdoor Activities

Knysna offers a huge variety of outdoor activities, from the pretty extreme to the totally serene.

ABSEILING (RAPPELLING)

Seal Adventures (☎ 044/382–6329 or 083/654–8755) offers a fun and scenic paddleboating, walking, and abseiling trip. You paddle across the lagoon to Featherbed Nature Reserve, on the Western Head, and then take a scenic walk to the abseiling (rappelling) sites. The cost is R170.

BOATING

Boating on the lagoon is a lovely scenic experience and going through the heads is quite dramatic. It makes you think about how dangerous such anchorages were in the days of sailing, when big ships had to maneuver through wild narrow passages such as these on sails alone with no auxiliary engines. You'll get a pretty good view on the ferry ride across to Featherbed, or you can choose a dedicated trip.

Knysna Ferries (⊠ Thesen's Jetty, ☎ 044/382–5520), offers general scenic cruises of the lagoon. **Springtide Charters** (⊠ Knysna Quays, ☎ 082/470–6022, WEB www.springtide.co.za) operates a luxury 50-ft sailing yacht, the site of its scenic cruises in the lagoon and through the Heads (weather permitting). You can also choose to have breakfast, lunch, or a romantic dinner on board. They also offer fully catered overnight accommodation. The boat takes a maximum of 12 passengers, and dinner and overnight trips are limited to one party. Expect to pay R290 per person for a three-hour sail with snacks, R390 for a sunset cruise with snacks including oysters and sparkling wine, R380 for a breakfast cruise that includes a Continental breakfast and bubbly, R750 for a sail that includes dinner, and R1,650 per person to stay on the boat overnight, which includes dinner and breakfast.

CANOEING

Dolphin Adventures (✉ Box 3594, Knysna 6570, ☎ 083/590–3405, WEB www.dolphinkayak.com) offers a gentle half-day bird-watching trip in easy-to-paddle double canoes. The trip costs R100 and includes a leisurely tea break on the bank. Or you can paddle around the oyster beds, followed by an oyster feast with sparkling wine, all for R150.

GOLF

Sparrebosch Clifftop Estate and Country Club (✉ East Head, Knysna, ☎ 044/384–1222, WEB www.sparrebosch.co.za) is one of the most scenic golf courses in South Africa. It's a challenging 18-hole course designed by Ronald Fream and David Dale and is perched on the cliff top of the Eastern Head, and it has spectacular sea views. There's a comfortable clubhouse with a great restaurant. The greens fee is R230 for 9 holes, R340 for 18, which includes a golf cart; there are no caddies. Renting golf clubs costs R75 for 9 holes, R125 for 18. Resident pros are available for lessons.

HIKING AND WALKING

The two-day **Harkerville Trail** starts at the **Garden of Eden,** about 15 km (9 mi) from both Plett and Knysna. As well as the expected indigenous forests, pine plantations, and "islands" of fynbos, you will also pass through a small stand of huge redwoods (*Sequoia sempervirens*), so homesick Californians can hug a big tree. They were an experiment by the forestry officials years ago. Be careful on this trail, as you share sections of it with mountain bikers who usually shout a warning as they are hurtling downhill toward you. The kiosk at the Garden of Eden is open daily 7:30–5 (☎ no phone). For more information contact **Department of Water Affairs and Forestry** (☎ 044/382–5466).

MOUNTAIN BIKING

Knysna is mountain-biking heaven. There are four circular trails of varying length and difficulty at Harkerville, all starting and ending at the Garden of Eden. You can rent bikes from **Outeniqua Biking Trails** (✉ Harkerville, ☎ 044/532–7644), which also leads escorted trips and has a great place to relax afterward at its small tea garden. If you're cycling without a guide, booking is not necessary; just pay the nominal fee (usually about R5 per person) and register at the start.

Plettenberg Bay

❸ *32 km (20 mi) east of Knysna.*

Plettenberg Bay is South Africa's premier beach resort, as the empty houses on Beachy Head Road (known as Millionaires' Mile) during the 11 months when it's not beach season will attest. But in December the hordes with all their teenage offspring arrive en masse. Even then you can find yourself a stretch of lonely beach—if you're prepared to walk to the end of Keurboomstrand. Plett, as it is commonly known, presides over a stretch of coastline that has inspired rave reviews since the Portuguese first set eyes on it in 1497. Snow-white beaches beckon as far as the eye can see, curving around to form what the Portuguese dubbed Bahia Formosa (Beautiful Bay). Three rivers debouch into the sea here, the most spectacular of which—the Keurbooms—backs up to form a large lagoon. For swimming, surfing, sailing, hiking, and fishing, you can't do much better than Plett, although the water is still colder than it is around Durban and in northern KwaZulu–Natal.

Plett is one of the best places in the world to watch whales and dolphins. There are a number of ways of observing these wonderful animals. Boat-based trips are run from Central Beach, as are sea-kayaking trips, which, although loads of fun, are not quite as efficient as the big motorboats. Aerial viewing is available from standard planes, gliders, or motor gliders.

⟲ In a perfect world **Monkeyland** would not exist. However, we live in a decidedly imperfect world—and Monkeyland attempts to make it a little better for some. Throughout the world people buy cute baby monkeys and lemurs as pets, which become unmanageable as they grow up. These animals are then passed on to the local bar, where they're fed beer and peanuts, or to a laboratory for testing, or to substandard zoos, where they live in tiny cages. Most of these abused animals cannot be released into the wild, so Monkeyland was started to give them a chance at a reasonably happy life. They roam in a huge enclosed area of natural forest and are free to play, socialize, and do whatever it is that keeps primates happy. There are lemurs, gibbons, spider monkeys, indigenous vervet monkeys, howler monkeys, and many more. Escorted walks are run throughout the day, and the tamer "inmates" often play with guests. ⊠ *16 km (10 mi) east of Plettenberg Bay along the N2 just before Nature's Valley turnoff,* ☎ *044/534–8906,* WEB *www.monkeyland.co.za.* ☒ *R66.* ☉ *Daily 8:30–5.*

Dining

Plettenberg Bay is one of the most sophisticated destinations on the Garden Route, and there is a large selection of fabulous lodging establishments as well as some very fine restaurants.

$$–$$$ ✗ **Cornuti Al Mare.** Sibling to Cornuti the Cradle, in the Cradle of Humankind, outside of Johannesburg, this is Cornuti on holiday by the sea. Everything is far more casual and relaxed. Try the thin wood-fired pizzas or a nice solid pasta. In summer get there early to get a seat on the veranda. ⊠ *Corner Strand and Perestrello Sts.,* ☎ *044/533–1277. AE, DC, MC, V.*

$$–$$$ ✗ **Rafiki's.** If you like your food with a view, this one's for you. On the beach at the end of Keurboomstrand, it's a place where you can watch whales from your table. On sunny days the terrace is a pleasure. Try the bouillabaisse du Arch Rock, with line fish, mussels, squid, prawns, and saffron-and-tomato stock, or the inevitable ostrich fillet, here served with cranberry sauce. Less meaty dishes include a spinach-and-mushroom risotto and, a favorite standby, eggplant parmigiana. ⊠ *On beach at Keurboomstrand,* ☎ *044/535–9813. MC, V.*

Lodging

There are excellent accommodation options in Plett, but if you'd prefer to rent a home for an extended stay, **Rafiki's** (☎ 044/535–9552 or 072/251–9552, WEB www.rafikis.co.za) has a large selection—priced from R800 to R1,600 per day.

$$$$ ✗🏠 **Hunter's Country House.** Just 10 minutes from town, Hunter's is ★ one of those places you can't bear to leave. Perhaps it's the sense of tranquillity—of pure country silence that can often be so difficult to find—or perhaps it's the setting, amid gardens that fall away into a forested valley. The heart of the lodge is an old farmstead, a lovely thatch building with low beams and large fireplaces. Guest rooms are in individual white thatch cottages, each with its own fireplace and veranda. Three suites have private plunge pools. Antiques grace the rooms, and

claw-foot tubs are the centerpiece of many of the gigantic bathrooms. Service is outstanding. Most guests eat at the hotel's excellent table d'hôte restaurant, which brings a French touch to local South African produce. Reservations are essential for nonguests. The lodge is in the process of building a children's center and adding special children's programs that will make this one of the few places where you don't have to sacrifice sophistication for family accommodations. Hunters is a member of the exclusive Relais & Chateaux group. ⊠ *Off N2, between Plettenberg and Knysna, Box 454, Plettenberg Bay 6600,* ☎ *044/532–7818,* FAX *044/532–7878,* WEB *www.hunterhotels.co.za. 23 suites. 2 restaurants, 3 bars, pool, library. AE, DC, MC, V. BP.*

$$$$ ✕⊡ **Kurlands Hotel.** On the road out of Plett toward Tsitsikamma, this
★   magnificent estate is centered on a lovely historic Cape Dutch homestead. Spacious guest suites are in separate buildings. Huge bathrooms, antique furniture, book-filled shelves, fireplaces, and private balconies give you the feeling you're staying in your own country home. The view of the extensive paddocks filled with polo ponies just makes it seem that much more opulent an experience. Six of the rooms have staircases into charming children's attic rooms. The food is exactly what you would expect to find in such a refined atmosphere: well cooked, beautifully presented, and made from whatever's fresh. Rates include all drinks, except wine and champagne, and there is a complimentary minibar. ⊠ *On the N2, about 20 km (12 mi) from Plett,* ☎ *044/534–8082,* FAX *044/534–8699,* WEB *www.kurlands.co.za. 8 rooms. Bar, dining room, pool, massage, sauna, spa, steam room, tennis court, gym, baby-sitting, nursery, playground. AE, DC, MC, V. MAP.*

$$$$ ✕⊡ **Plettenberg.** High on a rocky point in Plettenberg Bay, this lux-
★   ury hotel has unbelievable views of the bay, the Tsitsikamma Mountains, Keurbooms Lagoon, miles of magnificent beach, and whales and dolphins during the right season. Built around an 1860 manor house, the hotel has two distinct parts: a summery beachside (blue) wing and a more formal winter (yellow) wing in the old house. Rooms borrow elements from both aspects of the hotel, and the result is bright and refreshing: sponge-painted yellow walls, bold butterfly-motif fabrics, and original paintings by South African artists. Service is wonderfully attentive, with a front-desk staff that tries to anticipate your every need. Even if you don't stay here, treat yourself to lunch on the hotel terrace. Diners sit under large fabric umbrellas looking out over a pool that seems to extend right into the incredible views. The lunch menu is small, with a selection of salads and sandwiches, as well as a pasta dish and catch of the day. Dinner is a fancier affair, focusing on local meat and seafood. The hotel is a member of the exclusive Relais & Chateaux group. Nonguests must make reservations for dinner. ⊠ *Lookout Rocks, Box 719, Plettenberg Bay 6600,* ☎ *044/533–2030,* FAX *044/533–2074,* WEB *www.plettenberg.com. 40 rooms. Restaurant, bar, 2 pools. AE, DC, MC, V. BP. No children under 12.*

$$$ ✕⊡ **Weldon Kaya.** This is a special place to spend the night. The whole place has been cunningly built on what was an old farm, and each of the cottages is decorated in a unique contemporary African style. Just one indication of the creativity in the renovations here was the transformation of a boring circular reservoir into an attractive swimming pool by the clever use of wooden decking, plants, and water features. The view from the upper deck is fantastic—overlooking the whole bay in the distance. A vibrant bar and a restaurant specializing in African food attract locals and visitors alike, with the one drawback of being rather noisy in season or on weekend nights. ⊠ *Corner N2 and Piesang Valley Rd., Plettenberg Bay 6600,* ☎ *044/533–2437,* FAX *044/533–4364,* WEB *www.weldonkaya.co.za. 10 rooms. Restaurant, bar, pool. AE, DC, MC, V. BP.*

$$ **★** ✕⊞ **Hog Hollow Country Lodge.** This lovely, friendly lodge is set in a small island of gardens on the edge of a forested gorge with vistas that stretch into the green misty distance. Rooms are decorated in a modern African motif, with cast-iron furniture, white linen, ocher finishes, and African artwork. In summer the private verandas with hammocks are as popular as the many fireplaces are in winter. The food is great, and meals are sociable affairs, taken around a huge table in the main house. Local seafood and dishes such as ostrich are well represented on the menu, but vegetarian food is handled with flair. Especially good is the homemade pasta with butternut squash filling. Breakfasts are taken on the patio to the accompaniment of varied birdsong. ⊠ *The Craggs, 18 km (11 mi) east of Plettenberg Bay, Box 1047, Plettenberg Bay 6600,* ☎ FAX *044/534–8879,* WEB *www.hog-hollow.com. 12 suites. Restaurant, bar, pool. AE, DC, MC, V. BP.*

$$$$ **★** ⊞ **Plettenberg Park.** The setting of this stylish, minimalist lodge—in splendid isolation on a cliff top in a private nature reserve on the western (wild side) of Robberg Peninsula—is one of the best anywhere, and the view of the open ocean across fynbos-clad hills is spectacular. Rooms are decorated in an understated African-colonial style in shades of white and cream; those that face the sea have dramatic views. A steep path leads to a private beach and natural tidal pool. On arrival guests are invited to confer with the two resident chefs and decide on a menu for their stay. ⊠ *Box 167, Plettenberg Bay 6600,* ☎ *044/533–9067,* FAX *044/533–9092,* WEB *www.plettenbergpark.co.za. 9 rooms. Restaurant, bar, 2 pools. AE, DC, MC, V. FAP.*

$$$$ ⊞ **Tsala Treetop Lodge.** At the time of writing, this fantastic guest house was nearing completion. Built on the same property as Hunters, it is also run by the Hunter family. Fabulous glass, stone, metal, and wood chalets are built on stilts overlooking a steep forested gorge and, in some cases, extending into the forest canopy. Suites have plunge pools with fantastic views, verandas, and fireplaces. The decor is quite spectacular with specially manufactured oval baths, hand-beaten brass plumbing fittings, and loads of glass. Suites are connected by raised timber walkways. This promises to be a wonderfully romantic destination. ⊠ *Off N2, between Plettenberg and Knysna, Box 454, Plettenberg Bay 6600,* ☎ *044/532–7818,* FAX *044/532–7878. 10 suites. Restaurant, bar. AE, DC, MC, V. BP.*

$$$ **★** ⊞ **Bitou River Lodge.** Some places just seem to get everything right. This lovely, quiet, restful B&B has a wonderful location on the banks of the Bitou River about about 3 km (2 mi) upstream from the lagoon. The rooms overlook a pretty garden and a quiet bird-rich and lily-filled pond. The decor is understated and soothing, with neutral pastels dominating. Breakfasts are delicious affairs with freshly baked bread, muffins, and other goodies in addition to the fruit, cereal, and eggs. Bitou feels like it's in the middle of nowhere, but it's only a 10-minute drive from the center of town. Don't pass up the opportunity to explore the river in one of the available canoes. ⊠ *About 3 km (2 mi) on the R340 to Wittedrif (off the N2) Box 491, Plettenberg Bay 6600,* ☎ *082/978–6164,* ☎ FAX *044/535–9577,* WEB *www.bitou.co.za. 5 rooms. Breakfast room, boating. MC, V. BP.*

Nightlife

Out of season nightlife consists of heading out for a pizza or popping in to one of the local bars. In season it gets pretty hectic, and every place is stuffed to capacity with vacationing teenagers displaying breeding plumage while their parents aren't watching. Probably one of the most interesting options is to attend a performance by the **Qolweni Theatre Company,** which operates in the local township. As well as having dance and quite innovative contemporary theater performances at night, it gives tours during the day. A theater performance and township tour costs R80. Book through Ocean Blue Adventures (☎ 044/533–5083 or 083/701–3583).

Outdoor Activities

HIKING AND WALKING

If you're not planning a multiday hike anywhere along the Garden Route, consider a stop at the **Garden of Eden** in Knysna.

At the **Robberg Nature Reserve** you can take either a short circular walk or spend the whole day getting to the end of the peninsula and back. There is a fascinating archaeological excavation at Nelson's Bay Cave here, where there is a display outlining the occupation of the cave over thousands of years. ⊠ *Robberg Rd., Plettenberg Bay,* ☎ *044/533–2125.* ⊠ *R14.* ☼ *Feb.–Nov., daily 7–5; Dec.–Jan., daily 7–8.*

SCENIC FLIGHTS

One of the best ways to see whales and dolphins is from the air. You can see the vast scope of the whale's mammoth body, and you also get an impressive view of the huge schools of up to 1,000 dolphins as they frolic in the surf.

African Ramble Air Charter (⊠ Plettenberg Bay Airport, ☎ 044/533–9006) does half-hour flights over the bay for R300 per person. They also offer charter flights to Shamwari game reserve in the Eastern Cape. It's a particularly scenic flight. You start off by flying over Robberg and out over the bay, where you may see whales or dolphins, before hugging the coast up to Nature's Valley, where you change course and head inland.

Bob Plane Motor Gliders (⊠ Plettenberg Bay Airport, ☎ 072/170–7533) offers scenic motor glider flights from Plettenberg Bay Airport over the bay. A half-hour trip costs R200.

SEA KAYAKING

A great way to see the sights and possibly enjoy a visit from a whale or dolphin is in a kayak. You aren't likely to see as many animals in a day as the people on the big boats, but it's a far more intimate and exciting experience if you do. You also get to paddle past the Cape fur seal colony on Robberg. **Dolphin Adventures** (☎ 083/590–3405, WEB www.dolphinkayak.com) offers regular trips in sleek double sit-upon kayaks at R150 for a half-day trip.

WHALE-WATCHING

Plettenberg Bay is truly one of the very best locations worldwide for boat-based whale- and dolphin-watching. Most days visitors see at least two cetacean species and Cape fur seals, as well as a variety of seabirds, including Cape gannets and African penguins. And on some days people have seen up to six cetacean species in the course of a few hours. Bottlenose dolphins frolic in the surf, Brydes whales are permanent residents, southern right whales come here to calve from about June to November, and humpback whales, which migrate between Antarctica and northern Mozambique, pass through and hang around a while from May to June and then again from November to February. Killer whales (orcas) are around all year, although they are not common. There are two similar operators. In both cases you board an open vehicle right outside the shop and then step directly onto the boat on the beach. The boats are fast, safe, and dry. Both operators offer a standard trip, in which the boat must stay 300 m (325 yards) from the animals, and a close encounter trip on a boat that is licensed to approach within 50 m (54 yards) of the whales. These trips are limited in order to minimize disturbance to the animals.

Ocean Blue Adventures (✉ Hopwood St., Central Beach, ☎ 044/533–5083 or 083/701–3583, WEB www.oceanadventures.co.za) runs trips from its shop on the beach, where it also sells some fantastic original African artworks with fishy motifs. Trips cost R240 for a standard two-hour trip and R300 for a close-encounter trip.

Ocean Safaris (✉ Hopwood St., Central Beach, ☎ 044/533–4963 or 082/784–5729, WEB www.oceansafaris.co.za) is based near the beach, where it shares a shop with a dive school and sells a wide range of dolphin- and whale-motif goodies, ranging from some beautiful crafts to fun, kitschy gifts. Trips cost R240 for a standard two-hour trip.

Shopping

Beware, you could end up spending a fortune at the various crafts shops near Plett. There is much to choose from and the quality is excellent.

Langa Lapu Fabrics creates beautiful fabrics by hand-dying pure cotton or silk with a range of subtle colors and using natural shapes, such as leaves and ferns, as design templates. The end result is often like looking into a deep forest. You can see and buy products made by Women on the Move, also at the same venue, a nonprofit, self-help antipoverty project that encourages and trains unemployed women to make functional and decorative articles from waste, natural, or free materials. ✉ On the N2, Craggs, ☎ 044/534–8612.

Old Nick was originally just a pottery and weaving studio but has grown to include a host of other crafts studios. You can spend a whole day here. There is a weaving museum, a shop selling lovely woven goods, a jeweler, and a small number of art galleries. Whatever you do, don't miss Earth-Sea Batiks, which produces unbelievably delicate artworks using this ancient technique usually associated with rather crude images. A handmade soap factory beckons with the scent of essential oils and fruits, while the Pansy Shell Country Kitchen competes for your olfactory attention with the heady aroma of freshly brewed espresso. Browse through antiques or a collection of Skycapes Aviation Art— limited-edition prints of World War II fighter planes, personally signed by the aviators themselves. ✉ On the N2, just east of town, ☎ 044/533–1395.

Porcupine is on a lovely farm in the Craggs, about 10 km (6 mi) east of Plett on the road to Hog Hollow Country Lodge. Here you can watch the molding, hand-painting, and firing of *raku* pottery, a wonderful blend of Asian technique, first-world design, and African motif. And, of course, there's a shop where you can purchase the fantastic finished products. There's also an outlet at Old Nick. ✉ Askop Rd., The Crags, ☎ 044/534–8910 or 082/553–8726.

Tsitsikamma National Park and Storms River

★ ⑮ *56 km (35 mi) east of Plettenberg Bay.*

From Nature's Valley the R102 climbs back into the mountains, ascending the Groot River and Bloukrans passes before finally rejoining the N2. It's another 24 km (15 mi) to the turnoff to Tsitsikamma National Park and the mouth of Storms River. About 1 km (½ mi) farther is the turnoff to the remote village of Storms River. Astonishingly, considering it is so close to the N2 and the hub of Plett, this is the place time forgot. For confirmation step into the general store on the main road—you'll feel like you've walked into a time warp. Tsitsikamma National Park is a narrow belt of coastline extending for 80 km (50 mi) from Oubosstrand to Nature's Valley and beyond. It encompasses some of the most spectacular coastal scenery in the country, including deep gorges, evergreen forests, tidal pools, and beautiful empty beaches. The best way to see the park is on the five-day Otter Trail, South Africa's most popular hike, or the easier Dolphin Trail. A less strenuous highlight is the Storms River mouth, at the midpoint of the park. The river enters the sea through a narrow channel carved between sheer cliffs. Storms River was aptly named: When gale winds blow, as they often do, the sea flies into a pounding fury, hurling spray onto the rocks and whipping spume high up the cliffs. From the visitor center a trail descends through the forest (different tree species are all labeled) and over a narrow suspension bridge strung across the river mouth. It's a spectacular walk, a highlight of any trip to the Garden Route. On the other side of the bridge, a steep trail climbs to the top of a bluff overlooking the river and the sea—the turning point of the Storms River MTB Trail. Other trails, ranging from 1 to 3.2 km (½ to 2 mi), lead either to a cave once inhabited by hunter-gatherers or through the coastal forest. A basic restaurant with great views of the river and the ocean serves breakfast, lunch, and dinner. Storms River Adventures operates a dive facility in the park and also offer boat trips on the *Spirit of Tsitsikamma* (R35), which is the easiest way to see the impressive gorge. ⊠ *Off N2,* ☎ *042/541–1836.* 🖼 *R5 per vehicle.* ⊙ *Daily 5:30 AM–9:30 PM.*

En Route   From Plett take the N2 east. The road runs across a flat coastal plain of fynbos, with the forested Tsitsikamma Mountains on your left. Just after the Crags, turn off the N2 onto the R102, a far more interesting and scenic route—the alternative to the toll road. The R102 passes through farmland before dropping suddenly to sea level through a steep gorge. It's a great descent, with the road worming back and forth through a tunnel of greenery, impenetrable bush pressing in on either side. At ⑭ the bottom of the pass, turn right into the small settlement of **Nature's Valley,** a magnificent lagoon hemmed in by bush-cloaked cliffs and hills. Part of the Groot River, the lagoon empties into the sea past a wide, idyllic beach—a popular spot for canoeing and sailboarding. There are toilet and picnic facilities, and a shop and restaurant.

Dining and Lodging

$$$ ✕🍽 **The Old Village Inn.** The rooms here are in pretty, colorful buildings that are neatly arranged around a village green. The inn is well known for its restaurant—De Oude Martha—which was named after the first cook of the hotel, who still presides over the kitchen with an iron hand and an eye for detail. Food is mostly dependable standbys, such as chateaubriand, grilled line fish, and chicken with some traditional Cape classics, such as Malay-style pickled fish. The inevitable ostrich steak is served with a creamy *amarula* (native fruit) and gooseberry sauce, and a new twist on an old favorite is grilled *kingklip* with *chakalaka*—a traditional African spicy relish. ⊠ *Box 53, Storms River 6308,* ☎ *042/281–1711,* 📠 *042/281–1669,* 🕸 *www.village-inn.co.za.* 49 rooms. Restaurant, bar, pool. AE, DC, MC, V. BP.

$$–$$$ 🍽 **Tsitsikamma Lodge.** Pretty wooden chalets are clustered around neat lawns on the edge of the forest at this lodge that's conveniently set on the N2. It's a friendly, casual place, and the staff goes out of its way to make your stay a worthwhile one. There are a number of forest walks from the lodge, ranging from 40 minutes to three hours. ⊠ *On the N2, Box 10, Storms River 6308,* ☎ *042/280–3802,* 📠 *042/ 280–3702,* 🕸 *www.tsitsikamma.com.* 32 chalets. Restaurant, bar, pool. MC, V. BP.

$–$$ 🍽 **Tsitsikamma National Park–Storms River Mouth.** Parks Board lodging is pretty basic, but it's clean and comfortable, and the setting, almost within soaking distance of the pounding surf at the mouth of the Storms River, is utterly spectacular. There is a range of log cabins, which sleep either two or four people. Forest huts are the cheapest but are very basic; the "oceanettes" are pretty much seaside apartments. ✉ *Off N2, near Storms River,* ☎ *042/281–1607. Reservations: Box 787, Pretoria 0001,* ☎ *012/343–1991,* FAX *012/343–0905 (*✉ *National Parks Board, Box 7400, Roggebai 8012,* ☎ *021/242–2810),* WEB *www. parks-sa.co.za. Restaurant. AE, DC, MC, V.*

Outdoor Activities

BLACKWATER TUBING

Storms River Adventures (✉ Main Rd., Storms River, ☎ 042/281–1836, WEB www.stormsriver.com) offers a fun experience in which you take a specially designed tube and flip and flop your way down the river. The scenery is impressive—300-ft-high cliffs tower overhead as you negotiate narrow canyons in deep, black water. It's an all-day trip, the cost of R325, includes lunch, snacks, and transportation.

BUNGEE JUMPING

If you only do one bungee jump in your life, make it this one with **Face Adrenalin** (✉ Bloukrans River Bridge, N2, ☎ 042/281–1458). It's 216 m (700 ft), the highest commercial bungee jump in the world. The Bloukrans River Bridge, where you jump off, is the third-highest bridge in the world and the highest in the southern hemisphere. The jump costs R500, and the video to show your friends back home is an extra R50.

HIKING AND WALKING

Storms River Mouth is hiking heaven. **Storms River Adventures** (✉ Main Rd., Storms River, ☎ 042/281–1836, WEB www.stormsriver.com) has guided tours of the area.

For the not-so-energetic, the **Dolphin Trail** is the perfect marriage between exercise and relaxation, rugged scenery and comfort. You meet at Storms River Mouth, from where you are transported to your first night's accommodation, to the east. You then hike the next day, with only a day pack, while all your luggage is transported by vehicle to the next spot. And on it goes. Accommodations are in comfortable cabins with private baths. The food is good and well prepared. And—the best part—it's only about 20 km (12 mi) over three days. It is hardly strenuous, but the scenery is quite special. This trail ends where the Otter Trail starts. It costs R2,400 per person, which includes a guide, all meals, transport, and a ride on the *Spirit of Tsitsikamma* at the end. Book through **Storms River Adventures** (✉ Main Rd., Storms River, ☎ 042/281–1836, WEB www.stormsriver.com).

The **Otter Trail** is the most popular of South Africa's hiking trails. It runs along the coast from the mouth of Storms River to Nature's Valley, passing rocky cliffs, beaches, fynbos, rivers, and towering indigenous forest. The trail is only 42 km (25 mi) long, but it's billed as a five-day hike to give you time to swim and just hang out. Accommodations are in overnight huts equipped with sleeping bunks, braais (barbecues), and chemical toilets. You must carry in all food and carry out all trash. Only 12 people are allowed on the trail per day, making it vital to book at least a year in advance. However, there are often cancellations, and often people book all 12 places and then arrive with only four or five people. If you really want to do this trail and have a bit of time, you could hang around for a few days and see if a spot opens up. The trail costs R350 per person. *Reserve through National Parks Board,* ✉ *Box 787, Pretoria 0001,* ☎ *012/426–5111,* WEB *www.parks.co.za.*

The **Tsitsikamma Trail** runs in the opposite direction of the Otter Trail, through the fynbos-clad mountains. It can be quite strenuous, as the distances between huts are longer than the Otter, and there is very little shade in some places. It's a great hike, though, and energetic hikers may want to do them back to back. The trail costs R47 per person per night. Book through SAFCOL (South African Forestry Company Ltd.; ✉ Box 1771, Silverton 0127, ☎ 012/481–3615).

MOUNTAIN BIKING

The **Storms River Mountain Bike Trail** is a scenic 22-km (13-mi) circular trail. It's administered by the Department of Water Affairs and Forestry, but there's no need to make reservations, and it's free. The starting point is near the police station at Storms River, and you fill in a form in a box at the gate to obtain a self-issue permit.If you want to rent bicycles (R75 for three hours), contact **Storms River Adventures** (☎ 042/281–1836). It also offers guided trails at R150 for the guide, plus the cost of the bike rental.

TREE TOP CANOPY TOUR

Deep in the forest you don a harness, climb up to a platform, clip in and "fly" to the next platform—on a long cable. You can control your speed so you can get a lourie's-eye view of the forest. The cost is R395. Book through **Storms River Adventures** (☎ 042/281–1836).

Garden Route A to Z

To research prices, get advice from other travelers, and book travel arrangements, visit www.fodors.com.

AIRPORTS

Two airports serve the Garden Route: Plettenberg Bay Airport, 6 km (4 mi) west of town, and George Airport, 10 km (6 mi) southwest of town, are served by S.A. Airlink.
➤ AIRPORT INFORMATION: **George Airport** (☎ 044/876–9310). **Plettenberg Bay Airport** (☎ 044/533–9026). **S.A. Airlink** (☎ 044/533–9041).

BUS TRAVEL

Both Intercape Mainliner and Translux Express offer regular service along the Garden Route between Cape Town and Port Elizabeth, stopping at all major destinations; Translux buses also call at Oudtshoorn, in the Little Karoo. The Baz Bus stops at all backpacker hostels along the Garden Route but will also drop you off at a B&B if you prefer.
➤ BUS INFORMATION: **Baz Bus** (☎ 021/439–2323, FAX 021/439–2343, WEB www.bazbus.com). **Intercape Mainliner** (☎ 021/386–4400 in Cape Town; 041/586–0055 in Port Elizabeth). **Translux Express** (☎ 021/449–3333 in Cape Town; 044/382–1971 in Knysna; 041/392–1333 in Port Elizabeth).

CAR TRAVEL

Mossel Bay, at the western end of the Garden Route, lies 384 km (240 mi) from Cape Town along the N2 highway. A trip up the Garden Route is a logical extension of a driving tour of the Overberg. Consider the less traveled and more interesting inland route. From Worcester, you travel on the R60 and R62 to Oudtshoorn, giving you a much better view of the Little Karoo.

Avis, Budget, and Imperial all have car-rental offices at George Airport. Budget also has an office in Plettenberg Bay. Europcar rentals include a cell phone. Its office is at Plettenberg Bay Airport.
➤ CAR TRAVEL INFORMATION: **Avis** (✉ George Airport, ☎ 044/876–9314). **Budget** (✉ George Airport, ☎ 044/876–9204; ✉ 9 Hill House, Main St., Plettenberg Bay, ☎ 044/533–2197). **Europcar** (✉ Plett Airport, ☎ 044/533–9006). **Imperial** (✉ George Airport, ☎ 044/876–9017).

EMERGENCIES

➤ CONTACTS: **Ambulance** (☎ 10177). **Police** (☎ 10111).

TRAIN TRAVEL

The luxurious *Blue Train* (☞ Train Travel *in* Smart Travel Tips A to Z) travels between Port Elizabeth and Cape Town once a month, stopping at George for a day trip to Oudtshoorn.

VISITOR INFORMATION

Most information bureaus in the area are very helpful. In high season you may find them open longer than the hours listed, and in very quiet periods the staff may close up shop early. The Oudtshoorn Tourism Bureau is open weekdays 8–5 and Saturday 9–1. George Tourism Information is open weekdays 8:30–5 and Saturday 9–noon. The Knysna Publicity Association is open weekdays 8–5 and Saturday 8:30–1. Plettenberg Bay/Tsitsikamma Tourist Information is open weekdays 8:30–5 and Saturday 9–1. The Wilderness Eco-tourism Association is open weekdays 8–5 and Saturday 9–5.

➤ TOURIST INFORMATION: **George Tourism Information** (⊠ 124 York St., George, ☎ 044/801–9295). **Knysna Publicity Association** (⊠ 40 Main St., Knysna, ☎ 044/382–5510). **Oudtshoorn Tourism Bureau** (⊠ Baron von Rheede St., Oudtshoorn, ☎ 044/279–2532). **Plettenberg Bay/Tsitsikamma Tourist Information** (⊠ Victoria Cottage, Kloof St., Plettenberg Bay, ☎ 044/533–4065). **Wilderness Eco-tourism Association** (⊠ Leila's La., Wilderness, ☎ 044/877–0045).

EASTERN CAPE

By David Bristow

Updated by Jennifer Stern

The Eastern Cape is South Africa's most diverse province and has some of its best holiday destinations, yet it is perhaps the most glossed over by overseas visitors. To the southwest it starts where the Garden Route stops. It includes much of the Great Karoo, abuts KwaZulu-Natal in the northeast, and touches Lesotho's mountain lands in the north. Look at a map, and you'll see that its coastline is its main attraction, largely undeveloped and running for some 640 km (400 mi) from temperate to subtropical waters.

The climate is mild right across the region and throughout the year with temperatures at the coast ranging between winter lows of 5°C (41°F) and summer highs of 30°C–32°C (85°F–90°F). It has many of the country's finest and least crowded beaches, African montane forests and heathlands, a rich biodiversity, intimate holiday resorts, a variety of water sports, and a wealth of cultural experiences. There are unsullied Xhosa villages where women still paint their faces with ocher clay and boys undergo circumcision ceremonies to become men.

Although there has been more fanfare and more written about the Zulu wars of a later century, it was here that black and white first met face to face on equal terms: with expanding black pastoralists against white settlers and the British military. Since the late 17th century up till the present, the Eastern Cape has been a frontier and the focus of black resistance. It was here the black trade union movement gained its first political footholds in the early 1970s and here where apartheid martyr Steven Bantu Biko came to prominence as the founder-leader of the Black Consciousness Movement.

The towns and even the cities of the province are relatively small, often quaint, and the distances between them are fairly large. There are proper airports only in Port Elizabeth and East London, so travel through the region is predominantly by car.

Pleasures and Pastimes

Touring, plain and simple, is the area's greatest attraction, without the hubbub of big cities or the seductiveness of theme parks, casinos, or any other artificial lures. The locals are always friendly, destinations are warm and simple, and it's a place where earth and sky underpin and overarch everything. A self-drive tour will be the most rewarding; it's a big place, and there are many tiny gems to discover. And no matter where you go, you'll feel like you're the only visitor in the region. Everything is affordable (often a downright steal). It's a place where, to misquote Eastern Cape bard Athol Fugard, real people still live.

Arts and Crafts

You will find many examples of the usual craft forms such as weaving, pottery, beadwork, baskets, and wire sculpture, as well as many newer, innovative ones if you look. And, as they do everywhere else in Africa, people celebrate the arts here with music and dance. The cultural highlight of South Africa is the annual Standard Bank National Festival of the Arts. It runs for 10 action-packed days every July in Grahamstown and is claimed to be second only to the one in Edinburgh, Scotland.

Outdoor Activities

South Africa has more than 300 hiking, biking, horseback-riding, canoeing, rafting, and other trails, and a fair share of these are found in the Eastern Cape. There are some really tough ones and some really easy ones like the Wild Coast Meander, where you can hotel-hop along the fantastically scenic coast. And, of course, the Eastern Cape has some of the best surfing in the world—some that is easily accessible at places like Jeffeys Bay, and some that is hidden in little-known coves along the Wild Coast.

Wildlife

The Eastern Cape has a rich and varied topography and floral assemblage. Consequently, it supports a wide range of game—much of which was once hunted to the brink of extinction by farmers and settlers trying in vain to tame this recalcitrant land. The first initiative to reclaim this area was Addo Elephant Park, proclaimed in the 1930s to protect the 11 remaining elephants in the area. In the 1980s Shamwari was carved out of some unprofitable farms. Not only has this ambitious project proved a success, it has inspired further development in conservation in the area. Addo Elephant Park has been (and is still being) expanded to include the sea, offshore islands, and the mountainous Zuurberg. And highly successful CCAfrica, which runs many lodges in southern Africa, opened Kwandwe in 2001. And the game is here. This is real bush—a place where black rhinos lurk in thick scrub, leopards hide out, never seen, and bushbuck wander at ease in the thick undergrowth. There are open areas, too, where herds of elephants wander, white rhinos graze peacefully, and buffalo roam. Shamwari now has free-roaming lions, Addo is in the process of releasing lions, and the area is becoming a real Big Five destination. And best of all—it's malaria free.

Port Elizabeth

16 Port Elizabeth—known as PE—is probably South Africa's best-kept secret. Along with its almost perfect weather, it has some fascinating cultural attractions and some beautifully preserved historic buildings, such as the 19th-century Feather Market, where ostrich feather auctions were once held. And there's a beach for every reason—from overdeveloped urban playgrounds to miles of deserted snow-white sands. Try Noordhoek for surfing; Hobie Beach for surfing, boogie boarding, sailing, and windsurfing and for checking out the surfers. If you like more resort-style beaches, opt for Kings Beach. The superb Humewood Golf Club is one of the top five courses in the country and the only true links course in South Africa. The town is also close to a number of fantastic destinations, both wild and cultural—including some great adventure activities, such as the fantastic Addo Elephant National Park and world-class surfing at Jeffrey's Bay and Cape St. Frances (immortalized in the surfing classic *Endless Summer*).

Sights to See

Donkin Reserve, Pyramid and Lighthouse. The Donkin Reserve is a large piece of open ground on which two unusual edifices form a very distinctive profile, used in graphic form all over the city. The lighthouse was built in 1861 and, because it was visible from the harbor, had a time ball dropped from it at 1 every afternoon. The building now houses the information office of **Tourism PE** (☎ 041/585–8884), which is open around the clock. The **Elizabeth Donkin Memorial** is the pyramid. Many people assume that Port Elizabeth was named after Elizabeth I of England—just because British royalty had a habit of spreading their names around. But it wasn't. Elizabeth Donkin, who died in India in 1818, was the wife of Sir Rufane Donkin, who named the city after her and had this memorial built. Two plaques proclaim his undying affection.

The Edward Hotel. This delightful building was completed in 1904, when it opened its doors as the King Edward's Mansions—a combination club, apartment building, and hotel. There were 120 bedrooms and 14 bathrooms. It has undergone a few changes since those days, like the conversion of the balconies into bathrooms. Fortunately, the staircase and elevator (the oldest in the city) have not changed. It is still run as a hotel—it's not bad but is far from the best accommodation option in town. ⊠ *Belmont Terr.,* ☎ *041/586–2056.*

The Library. Completed in 1902, this is an excellent example of Victorian Gothic architecture and is one of the most beautiful buildings in PE. The terra-cotta facade was manufactured in England and shipped out in numbered pieces. Go inside and look up to see the ornate galleries groaning with loads of books. In front of the library is a somewhat stern Sicilian marble statue of Queen Victoria, who looks decidedly unamused. ⊠ *Govan Mbeki Ave., Central,* ☎ *041/585–8133.* ☉ *Mon. 1–6, Tues.–Fri. 9–6, Sat. 8:30–1.*

Number 7 Castle Hill is one of a number of lovely settler cottages. It is furnished in a late Victorian fashion and shows how a middle-class family of English origin would have lived in Port Elizabeth in the mid-19th century. Note the lovely yellowwood floors. ⊠ *7 Castle Hill Rd.,* ☎ *041/ 582–2515.* 🖾 *R5.* ☉ *Mon. 2–5, Tues.–Fri. 10–1 and 2–5, Sat. 10–1.*

Prester John Monument. It is believed that this is the only monument to Prester John, the mythical figure reputed to have set up a Christian kingdom somewhere in Africa. His supposed presence gave courage to the early explorers, as they were convinced he would assist fellow Christians in their quest to find a sea route to Asia. Without him, Columbus may have stayed home. Any student of semiotics could spend hours here. The Prester John Monument is a large Coptic cross with, among other things, representations of the Portuguese coat-of-arms, the Lion of Judah, an elephant, a rhino and, of course, a representation of Prester John himself.

South End Museum. South End was the most vibrant part of Port Elizabeth until it was flattened by the apartheid-era government to "tidy up" the city and put everything and everyone in their places. A floor plan, photographs, and paintings give you an idea of what the old South End was like in its heyday. ⊠ *Corner Humewood Rd. and Walmer Blvd.,* ☎ *041/582–3325.* ☞ *Free.* ☉ *Weekdays 9–4, weekends on request.*

Dining and Lodging

$$$–$$$$ ✕ **34° South.** Sibling to the fabulous deli-cum-restaurant-cum-fishmonger in Knysna, this is the most popular restaurant at the well-frequented Boardwalk. The line fish is always fresh, and the best way to try it is as a kingklip *espatada*—skewered chunks of fish grilled with roasted peppers and onions and drizzled with lemon butter. For an equally fishy experience fill a huge platter from the seafood meze. Even the snack-type options, like sandwiches, are big enough to qualify as a meal. ⊠ *The Boardwalk, Marine Dr., Summerstrand,* ☎ *041/583–1085. AE, DC, MC, V.*

$$–$$$ ✕ **Crazy Zebra.** For something unique and local, nothing beats this funky restaurant, just 300 yards from the airport. You may want to try the namesake zebra steak, but there is much more interesting fare on offer such as the venison chili, tripe-and-potato clay-pot stew, or a chicken and guinea fowl potjie. The excellent fresh seafood dishes are also worth sampling. It can turn into a bit of a party here on weekends. ⊠ *3 3rd Ave., Walmer,* ☎ FAX *041/581–1523. Reservations essential. AE, DC, MC, V. Closed Sun.*

$$–$$$ ✕ **Ristorante di Mauro.** With constantly changing daily specials there's always something new to try here. If they're available, order the prawns in a white wine and onion sauce topped with mozzarella and oven baked or the grilled sweet-and-sour ostrich steak. A more traditional choice would be the linguine with a creamy chicken sauce. ⊠ *38 Newton St., Newton Park,* ☎ *041/365–1747. Reservations essential. AE, DC, MC, V. Closed Sun.*

$$$$ 🛏 **Hacklewood Hill Country House.** For superbly comfortable and gracious lodgings, try this inn set in English-style gardens in the leafy suburb of Walmer. Rooms are spacious and furnished with beautiful antiques, such as four-poster beds. Some of the bathrooms are absolutely enormous, with a sofa and huge wardrobe, as are the Victorian baths, with separate shower and marble-top vanity. All rooms have balconies except one. ⊠ *Box 319, Port Elizabeth 6000,* ☎ *041/581–1300,* FAX *041/581–4155,* WEB *www.pehotels.co.za/hacklewood. 8 rooms. Restaurant, bar, room service, pool, tennis court. AE, DC, MC, V. BP.*

$$$–$$$$ 🛏 **The Beach Hotel.** This light and airy hotel has fantastic views of the sea and is right next to the Boardwalk and across the road from Hobie Beach. Pastel colors predominate in the rooms. ⊠ *Marine Drive, Humewood,* ☎ *041/583–2161,* FAX *041/583–6220,* WEB *www.pehotels. co.za/beach. 57 rooms, 1 suite. 3 restaurants, bar, room service, pool, free parking. AE, DC, MC, V. EP.*

$$–$$$$ 🛏 **King's Tide Boutique Hotel.** In a quiet part of Summerstrand this hotel
★ feels cocooned, but it's close to the beach, the Boardwalk, and Humewood Golf Course. An enormous entrance lobby with wood-and-marble-detailed floor and a gurgling water fountain doubles as a stylish dining room. The rooms are richly furnished with heavy fabrics in deep, glowing blues or reds offset by pale yellow walls. The bathrooms are great—enormous tubs and triple-head showers in huge, roomy stalls. Four rooms have only a shower. There's a self-service espresso machine in the breakfast room that you can access at all hours and an honor bar. ⊠ *16 10th Ave., Summerstrand 6013,* ☎ *041/583–6023,* FAX *041/ 583–3910,* WEB *www.crowncollection.co.za. 10 rooms. Breakfast room, dining room, free parking. AE, DC, MC, V. BP.*

$–$$ 🛏 **Summerstrand Inn.** A great value for the price, this comfortable, well-run hotel is close to the beach and virtually on top of the excellent Humewood Golf Course. The Summerstrand does one of the best breakfasts in PE—a huge buffet for R45. ✉ *Box 204, Port Elizabeth 6000,* ☎ *041/583–3131,* FAX *041/583–2505. 218 rooms, 5 suites. Restaurant, bar, no-smoking room, pool, room service, meeting rooms. AE, DC, MC, V. EP.*

Shopping

Port Elizabeth is a decent-size city where you can get almost anything you want, but if you're looking for fun shopping, it has to be the **Boardwalk.** It's not your average mall, and even though it's attached to a casino, it's not your average gambling hangout, either. But, of course, it is both—and also a conference center. Perhaps it's just the space, the view of the sea, and the winding artificial lake that make it feel more open. There's the usual collection of shops, restaurants, and coffee bars as well as a five-screen cinema, adventure golf, and fun rides. ✉ *Marine Drive, Private Bag 777, Humewood,* ☎ *041/507–7777.*

Frontier Country

Formerly known as Settler Country, this area stretches from the outskirts of Port Elizabeth to Port Alfred, in the east, Grahamstown, in the northeast, and the Zuurberg Mountains, in the north. It was here that the early 19th-century immigrants (colloquially called the 1820 Settlers) tried to set up farms, some successfully, some not. This area encompasses Shamwari, Grahamstown, and Addo Elephant National Park, which has been extended to include the Zuurberg.

Shamwari

★ Shamwari is, in every sense of the word, a conservation triumph. Unusable land has been turned into a successful tourist attraction, wild animals have been reintroduced, and alien vegetation has been and is still being eradicated. The reserve is constantly being expanded and now stands at about 40,000 acres.

It's important to know what it is you're going to see when you visit here. This is not Kenya or Mpumalanga. The terrain is hilly with thick bush, so you won't see vast herds of animals wandering across open plains. Shamwari's mandate is to conserve, not only the big impressive animals but also the small things: the plants, buildings, history, and culture of the area. Shamwari has been awarded the Global Nature Fund Award for Best Conservation Practice, and wildlife manager Dr. Johan Joubert was voted one of South Africa's top 10 conservationists by the Endangered Wildlife Trust.

Part of the reserve has been set aside as the **Born Free Centre,** where African animals rescued from around the world are allowed to roam in reasonably large enclosures until they can be rehabilitated. If they can't be rehabilitated, they either stay and form part of the educational program or are moved to another protected environment. There is also a cultural center, called Khayalendaba, where you can see different aspects of African life. ✉ *Box 32017, Summerstrand 6019,* ☎ *042/203–1111,* FAX *042/235–1224,* WEB *www.shamwari.com. Private airstrip. AE, MC, V. FAP.*

$$$$ 🏨 **Bushmans River Lodge.** Until he moved back to Johannesburg, this was the home of seer Credo Mutwa. It has been extensively renovated and is decorated with beautiful antiques and some nice African touches. The rooms are spacious, and the bathrooms have both showers and baths. In good weather meals are served in a gazebo overlooking the Bushmans River. *4 rooms. Dining room, pool.*

$$$$ ⊞ **Lobengula Lodge.** This camp comes closest to the timber-and-thatch bush lodge most visitors tend to think of as the "real" Africa. The rooms are decorated in a somewhat understated ocher theme with beautiful East African artifacts. A huge wooden pool deck has pleasant views of the surrounding bush. Meals are served around a central fireplace and guests may choose wines from the extensive cellar. Three of the suites have private plunge pools. *6 suites. Bar, pool, spa, steam room, gym.*

$$$$ ⊞ **Long Lee Manor.** Long Lee will appeal to those looking for an *Out of Africa* romance, complete with four-poster beds, teak staircases, antique furniture, and manicured lawns. This renovated pink Edwardian mansion was the home of the original owner of the farm and is an authentic part of Eastern Cape history. Ask for one of the designer-decorated suites in the main house. Every other night supper is an opulent African feast—corn on the cob, game stews, *mielie pap* (a gritslike maize porridge)—served in a period courtyard. *17 rooms, 3 suites. Dining room, bar, 2 pools, tennis court.*

$$$$ ⊞ **Riverdene Lodge.** This is the newest of the lodges at Shamwari and has been built in a renovated barn. It's a long, white building, with rooms opening up onto private balconies. A large open-air dining area is used whenever the weather allows. The walls are adorned with interesting paintings and a collection of black-and-white photographs, all taken at Shamwari. *9 rooms. Pool.*

Kwandwe

Bankrolled by philanthropist and visionary conservationist Carl DeSantis of Rexall-Sundown and set in the malaria-free Eastern Cape, Kwandwe not only offers the Big Eight game experience (the Big Five plus dolphins, sharks, and whales), but also a fascinating glimpse of unusual ecosystems such as succulent thicket—a landscape alive with giant flowering aloes and their attendant sunbirds. Kwandwe has been rescued and restored from 40,000 acres of degraded farmland to its former pristine state. Today the starkly beautiful succulent thicket, forests, valleys, mountains, and hills are alive with game of all kinds, including the rare and endangered black rhino, white rhino, lion, cheetah, elephant, hippo, Cape buffalo, and antelope of numerous kinds. You'll also be able to see some of the Eastern Cape's smaller, endearing little animals such as the bat-eared fox, Cape fox, aardwolf, several varieties of mongoose, and more than 200 species of birds. Kwandwe is close to Addo Elephant Park and the Great Fish River Nature Reserve as well as the seaside towns of Port Elizabeth and East London, so it's the natural extension of a Garden Route itinerary.

$$$$ ✕⊞ **Kwandwe.** You'll be welcomed on arrival at Kwandwe at Heatherton Towers, a turreted, fortressed old farmhouse built as a home for the world's first ostrich farmer in 1834. Then a four-by-four will take you through the surrounding bush to the lodge, which is on a steep cliff edge overlooking Great Fish River. The luxurious glass-fronted thatch-roofed villas have wraparound decks, plunge pools, deep leather armchairs, handmade wooden furniture, indoor and outdoor showers, and every possible creature comfort. All have great river views and are surrounded by landscaped indigenous gardens. The food and the delightful young staff are charming and attentive. ⊠ *CC Africa, Private Bag X27, Benmore, Johannesburg 2010,* ☎ *011/809–4300,* FAX *011/809–4400,* WEB *www.ccafrica.com. 9 villas. Air-conditioning. AE, MC, V. FAP.*

The Greater Addo Area

⑰   Undoubtedly, the greatest attraction in this area is **Addo Elephant National Park.** Originally an expanse of 36,000 acres, it is being expanded to form the country's third-largest and biotically most diverse reserve, encompassing an area of 864,600 acres and stretching from 50 km (38 mi) northeast of Port Elizabeth to the sea at Woody Cape. Much of the additional land has already been fenced, and new animals are being introduced (it is hoped the fencing will be completed by 2003). Although its current attractions are 200 elephants and small herds of buffalo, white rhino, kudu, and other lesser creatures, it is being stocked with game to rival any Big Five reserve. Attractions range from lions to penguins, forests to deserts, and mountains to beaches. As well as some excellent accommodations in the surrounding areas, there are two options in the camp—one pretty budget, and one decidedly luxurious. You can explore the park in your own vehicle, or take a night or day game drive with a park ranger in an open vehicle from the main camp. A more adventurous option would be to ride a horse among the elephants. Less experienced riders may ride along the fence line. ⊠ *National Parks Board, Box 787, Pretoria 0001,* ☎ *012/343–1991,* FAX *012/ 343–0905.* ☞ *R12.* ☉ *Daily 7–7 (may vary with seasons).*

$$$$ ✕🏠 **Elephant House.** Not far from the park, this stylish guest house is on a small horse-breeding farm near the town of Addo. Most rooms are arranged around a central lawn. Decor is understated neocolonial. Rooms are individually decorated with neutral colors of cream and white, bare cement, rough painted brick, and reed ceilings. This is an excellent place to base yourself for Addo, which you may tour independently or on an escorted tour arranged by the lodge. It will also organize day tours of Shamwari. ⊠ *Box 82, Addo 6105,* ☎ *042/233–2462,* FAX *042/ 233–0393,* WEB *www.elephanthouse.co.za. 8 rooms. Restaurant, bar, in-room data ports, 24-hr room service, pool, croquet. AE, MC, V. BP.*

$$$$ 🐘 **Gorah Elephant Camp.** In a private concession within Addo Ele-
★ phant National Park, the lodge centers around an old farmhouse, which has been restored and filled with antiques. Roaring log fires warm chilly winter nights, and the wide veranda offers cool shade in the heat of the day. The lodge overlooks a water hole where a variety of animals come for water, the stars of which are the elephants. Accommodations are in huge tents with private baths, shaded under thick thatch. Mosquito nets are more for effect than necessity, as this is a malaria-free area. Meals are taken alfresco on the veranda or at smallish tables in the dining room. Cuisine and service are equal to the best in Africa. The lodge operates the usual two game drives per day. You can do an escorted walk, mountain-bike ride, or horse ride, all at an extra fee. ⊠ *In Addo Elephant National Park (Box 454, Plettenberg Bay 6600),* ☎ *044/532–7818 for reservations,* FAX *044/532–7878,* WEB *www. gorah.com. 10 tents. Dining room, bar, pool. AE, DC, MC, V. FAP.*

$$$ 🏠 **Zuurberg Mountain Inn.** This is one of the oldest hotels in the Eastern Cape. It's at the top of the Zuurberg Pass, which was once the main route from Port Elizabeth to the diamond fields at Kimberley. The hotel has the look and feel of a 1950s or '60s family country hotel. Children gambol in the gardens and run giggling through the lounge. There are thatch chalets of varying configurations sleeping from two to six people. The hotel is on the border of the northern, mountainous part of Addo Elephant National Park, which has an auxiliary stable here (in addition to the one near Main Camp) and offers hourly, daily, and overnight rides. Another major attraction is a full-day escorted tour in a four-wheel-drive vehicle following the old Kimberley road. ⊠ *Box 12, Addo 6105,* ☎ *042/233–0583,* FAX *042/233–0070,* WEB *www.addo. co.za. 5 rooms, 1 suite, 18 cottages. Restaurant, bar, pool, 2 tennis courts, bowling, hiking, horseback riding. AE, MC, V. BP.*

$ 🏠 **Addo Elephant National Park Rest Camp.** This is a typical National Parks Board rest camp, with comfortable self-catering chalets and a shop that sells basic supplies as well as souvenirs. There is an à la carte restaurant open for all meals and a floodlighted water hole nearby. Prices are worked out according to a complicated National Parks formula, and it works out to anything from R75 to R150 per person sharing. Camping ranges from R15 to R25 per person. Warning: No citrus fruit may be brought into the park, as elephants find it irresistible and can smell it for miles. Addo is malaria free. Reservations are through the National Parks Board. ✉ *National Parks Board Box 787, Pretoria 0001,* ☎ *012/343–1991,* FAX *012/343–0905. 39 chalets, 20 campsites. Restaurant, pool, shop. AE, DC, MC, V. EP.*

Grahamstown
120 km (75 mi) east of Port Elizabeth.

Although billed as a city, Grahamstown is much more of a sleepy hollow. In fact, the pretty town looks more like an English village than anything else—except, of course, for that alter ego of most South African towns, those desperately poor contiguous shanty townships. They're a big part of Grahamstown and contribute to the city's wealth of cultural history.

Home to Rhodes University and some of the country's top schools (St. Andrews, Kingswood College, Diocesan School for Girls), Grahamstown is considered by many to be the seat of culture and learning in South Africa. This claim is lent credibility by its stature as the venue forSouth Africa's premier cultural event—the **Standard Bank National Festival of the Arts** (☎ 046/622–4341), which takes place in July. The program includes local and international music, theater, ballet and modern dance, fine art, combinations of all of these, and then some. There's the formal program, an official fringe festival, and even a fringe of the fringe that gets seriously alternative. The events are staged throughout the town but mainly at the **1820 Settlers National Monument,** a concrete edifice on Gunfire Hill, next to the old garrison Fort Selwyn.

DINING AND LODGING
Grahamstown is an elastic city. Most of the year it's pretty small, but then around festival time in July it expands to fit the tens of thousands of festivalgoers. And in December it shrinks to a mere ghost of itself as the students and scholars go home. Your best bet for help with lodging is the **Grahamstown Accommodation Bureau** (✉ Box 758, Grahamstown 6140, ☎ 046/622–5777 or 082/758–4740, FAX 046/622–8949, WEB www.grahamstownaccom.co.za).

$$$ ✕ **La Galleria.** Italian is South Africa's alternate gastronomic culture, and there's a good family *ristorante* in almost every town. Choose from a selection of starters presented on a trolley, then perhaps try the pan-fried fillet of beef in a red wine and herb sauce or with blue cheese and brandy flambé. Naturally, all pastas are homemade. ✉ *13 New St.,* ☎ *046/622–2345. AE, DC, MC, V.*

$$$ ✕▥ **Assegai Lodge.** This is where historical figure Dick King's cavalry was stationed, and it was in these fields that his horse, Somerset, grazed. The original buildings still stand, and the garden shelters ancient rosebushes and azaleas. Old wells, water troughs, and the remains of the cavalry stables lie scattered around. There are three rooms in the house, two of which share a bathroom, and six rooms in a low-ceilinged outbuilding. The decor is quite eclectic, with comfortable contemporary furnishings rubbing shoulders with fantastic antiques. Dinners are fantastic affairs—homemade bread and pasta and whatever the garden can produce are highlights. The main dining room is an old wagon house, with rough stone walls a yard thick, broken only by gun slots—contrasting markedly with the draped red-velvet ceiling. Savvas, the owner, presides over medieval five-course dinners (R110)

at the long table, ably assisted by the ever-present butler, who seems to appear from nowhere to ensure you are well treated. ✉ *30 km (20 mi) on PE side of Grahamstown, signposted from the N2, Box 6084, Grahamstown 6140,* ☎ ℻ *046/636–2945,* WEB *www.assegai.co.za. 9 rooms, 7 with bath. 2 dining rooms, pool. MC, V. BP.*

$$ ✕ ⌂ **The Cock House.** A charming small hotel, this has been the home of distinguished citizens over the years, most notably academic and novelist André Brink. All rooms are individually decorated and named after previous owners of the house. Owners Peter and Belinda Tudge also serve the finest food in town, but space is limited, and you have to book in advance if you want to try their delicious lamb shank, served in a thyme-and-rosemary sauce, or feta cheese soufflé with peppadews. Dinner is usually a set menu (R85), and lunch is à la carte. ✉ *10 Market St., at George St., Box 6092, Grahamstown 6140,* ☎ *046/636– 1295,* ℻ *046/636–1287,* WEB *www.cockhouse.co.za. 7 rooms, 1 apartment. Restaurant, bar. AE, DC, MC, V. BP.*

$$ ⌂ **St. Aidans Guest Lodge.** This lovely old stone building with lots of nooks and crannies was built late in the 19th century as a Jesuit school. After several incarnations the building was taken over by the Department of Education in 1996, and a course in hotel management is now taught here, with students running the lodge. Service may be slightly erratic, but, on the other hand, the students do have to pass the course, so they'll be trying hard, and it's an excellent value for the money. Make sure to have a look at the beautiful old (deconsecrated) chapel. ✉ *Constitution St., corner of Milner St., Grahamstown 6140,* ☎ *046/622– 7135,* ☎ ℻ *046/622–4419. 8 rooms, 2 family suites. Meeting rooms. AE, DC, MC, V. BP.*

East London and the Wild Coast

150 km (90 mi) east of Grahamstown.

The Wild Coast is aptly but perhaps a little unfairly named. Sure, it does get some monumental storms, when huge waves crash into the beach and cliffs, but it also has a gentler face. Lovely long beaches stretch as far as the eye can see, with only a few cows and a small herd boy to break the isolation. Strictly speaking, the Wild Coast originally stretched from the Kei River mouth to Port Edward. As these things do, though, it has slowly extended itself, and now, for all intents and purposes, it starts in East London.

The people who live here are subsistence farmers, but they also harvest the spectacularly abundant seafood. It's not uncommon for a family that can't scrape together the price of a loaf of bread to dine on oysters and lobster.

It truly is still virtually unspoiled, and generations of South Africans have fond memories of fantastic family holidays here. Unfortunately, during the political uncertainty of the 1980s, this area lost a lot of its allure—more due to the perceived threat of violence than anything else. Hotels went out of business, the overnight huts on the fantastic Wild Coast Hiking Trail fell into disrepair, and the Transkei sank further into economic depression. For many years it was only die-hard locals with strong emotional ties and hordes of backpackers who frequented these still-lovely and little-known places. It was a well-kept secret.

However, it is once again becoming a fantastic, if limited, destination. The coastal hotels are being renovated one by one, and community projects are being put into place to ensure that the tourist dollar goes where it is intended. Although many coastal hotels are still a bit drab, dingy, and damp, many fantastic resorts are opening their doors, making the Wild Coast an attractive proposition once again.

Outdoor Activities

An escorted trek with **Amadiba Trails** is a fantastic, not-to-be missed experience. Trips are usually six days, with four on horseback, one spent paddling, and one spent hiking in the Nkambati Nature Reserve—a botanical and scenic paradise. The highlight of the trip, however, is the interaction with the community as well as the chance to sample local cuisine, such as wild spinach and maize meal or freshly caught seafood. Guides are all from the local community and include subsistence farmers, fisherfolk, and even one *sangoma* (traditional healer). This is the closest you can get in South Africa to genuinely spending time with ordinary folk. Although the accommodations are very comfortable, there are few frills. It will cost you R1,380 for a six-day all-inclusive trip. ⊠ *Box 50978, Musgrave 4062,* ☎ *039/305–6455,* ℻ *039/305–6456.*

Four- to six-day off-the-beaten-track trips through the area in a four-by-four are led by skilled guides from **African Coastal Adventures.** Roger and Tony talk the language and have lived, hiked, fished, and traveled this area for years. They'll take you to scenic waterfalls, fantastic beaches, and remote villages and keep you amused with anecdotes, myths, and perhaps just a few tall tales. Accommodations are usually in the more remote coastal hotels, ranging from OK to pretty darn good. A four-day all-inclusive trip costs about R3,100 per person, a comparable six-day excursion about R5,000. If you like, you can walk much of this trail—one guide will accompany you, and the other drives the gear around. ⊠ ☎ *082/650–1427 for Roger's cell phone; 083/654–7173 for Tony's cell phone,* ☎ ℻ *043/748–4550,* 🕸 *www.africoast.co.za.*

The Wild Coast has been a favorite hiking destination for years, but the huts have practically disintegrated. Perhaps they will be repaired, but until then there are still some good options. The five-day **Wild Coast Meander** is a lovely trail along the coast from hotel to hotel. If you really don't want to strain yourself, you can choose to have your luggage carried to the overnight spot by vehicle. The meander costs R1,850–R2,600 per person sharing, and the shorter **Wild Coast Amble,** which is closer to East London, costs R1,650–R2,200. Book through **Wild Coast Reservations** (☎ 043/743–6181).

East London

Even smaller and sleepier than Port Elizabeth, East London is a nice town, but you'd really only want to spend a day or two here on either side of a Wild Coast visit.

DINING AND LODGING

$$–$$$ ✗ **Michaela's.** A half hour's drive from East London, Michaela's is perched at the top of a high vegetated dune and has fantastic views. The emphasis here is on seafood, with prawns, mussels, and oysters appearing in almost every guise. Springbok carpaccio is an unusual twist on a familiar starter; fish and steak are napped with gringo sauce—garlic, chili, and cream. Breakfast and light lunches are served on the deck. ⊠ *Steenbras Dr., Cintsa East,* ☎ *043/738–5139. MC, V. Closed Tues.*

$$–$$$ 🏨 **Stratfords Guest House.** This stylish guest house is worth staying
★ in just to see the building. A masterpiece of design, it uses unusual materials like corrugated iron, bare concrete, wood, and glass in incredibly innovative ways to create a comfortable, restful environment. All rooms have tea and coffee stations, and loft suites have self-catering facilities. It's close to town. Children under 12 are accepted by prior arrangement only. ⊠ *31 Frere Rd., Vincent,* ☎ *043/726–9765,* ℻ *043/*

726–9233. 12 rooms, 4 suites. Bar, dining room, pool, meeting room, free parking. MC, V. BP.

Coffee Bay
295 km (180 mi) north of East London.

All the Wild Coast resorts have beautiful beaches, fantastic scenery, and friendly locals, so neither that nor even its fantastic surf make Coffee Bay special. Rather, it is exceptional because of its proximity, only 9 km (about 5 mi), to the spectacular Hole-in-the-Wall, a natural sea arch through a solid rock island. An added bonus is being able to get all the way there on paved roads. The village is a bit run down, but there are some lovely cottages and a couple of backpackers' hostels, ensuring there is always something fun going on. The surf is fantastic.

DINING AND LODGING

$$$ ★ ✕⊞ **Ocean View Hotel.** This is an old Wild Coast hotel that has been well renovated. It's clean and bright, with white walls and blue soft furnishings with fish and dolphin motifs. There's a resident tour operator, who will organize anything from day walks and gentle cruises to abseiling (rappelling), mountain biking, or canoeing. Activity prices range from R50 for a half day of mountain biking to R80 for a full day of hiking or abseiling (including lunch). Like all Wild Coast resorts, it's child-friendly. The food is good, well cooked, and unpretentious. However, bear in mind that here huge platters of seafood are considered unpretentious, and you may well find wild coastal oysters on offer as bar snacks. ⊠ *Main Beach, Coffee Bay (Box 566), Umtata 5100,* ☎ FAX *047/575–2005 or 047/575–2006,* WEB *www.oceanview.co.za. 30 rooms. Bar, dining room, pool, hiking, beach, baby-sitting, children's programs (3–12). AE, DC, MC, V. MAP.*

$$$$ ⊞ **Umngazi River Bungalows.** One of the most popular destination on the Wild Coast, this lovely resort is about 16 km (10 mi) from Port St. John's. Set in its own nature reserve, it has lots of water sports, outdoor activities, and children's and family programs. The bungalows are rather basic but provide all the necessities for a relaxed vacation. Request a water-facing location to be able to watch the dolphins right from your doorstep. Umngazi has fly-in packages from Durban—a great idea, as the resort is 11 km (7 mi) from the Umtata–Port St. John's road on a somewhat bumpy and rutted unpaved road. ⊠ *Box 75, Port St Johns 5120,* ☎ *047/564–1115,* FAX *031/701–7006,* WEB *www.epages. net/umngazi. 68 bungalows. Restaurant, bar, pool, tennis court, Ping-Pong, billiards, baby-sitting, nursery, playground. AE, DC, MC, V. FAP.*

Eastern Cape A to Z

To research prices, get advice from other travelers, and book travel arrangements, visit www.fodors.com.

AIR TRAVEL
Both Port Elizabeth and East London are served daily by South African Airways and SA Airlink. SA Airlink also flies between Umtata and Johannesburg.
➤ AIRLINES AND CONTACTS: **East London Airport** (☎ 043/706–0306). **Port Elizabeth Airport** (☎ 041/507–7319). **South African Airways** (☎ 043/706–0211 or 043/218, FAX 043/736–2790).

CAR RENTAL
It's easiest and best to tour by car. Avis is the most widely represented car-rental agent in the region and has offices at all the local airports.
➤ MAJOR AGENCIES: **Avis** (☎ 041/51–1306 in Port Elizabeth; 043/736–1344 in East London; 046/622–2235 in Grahamstown).

TOURS

One of South Africa's most seminal historical incidents is the 1819 Battle of Grahamstown, when the Xhosa chief Makana tried to rid his area of British colonizers. Makana was arrested and sent to Robben Island, where he died trying to escape. You can relive this battle from the point of view of young Xhosa historians with Egazini Tours. The cost varies according to the number of people on the tour but will be about R200 if you use their transport. If you have a rental car and are prepared to drive the guide around, it will be significantly cheaper.

Calabash Real City Tour examines Port Elizabeth's settler roots and the history of the freedom struggle and offers an intimate insight into the contemporary life of the city. Tours are R160. A separate shebeen tour, to see the vibrant modern side of black township life, is also available (R180).

Mbuleli Mpokela is a Grahamstown resident who offers insightful tours of Rhini Township and the Masithandane craft cooperative (R70).
➤ TOUR INFORMATION: **Calabash Real City Tour** (✉ 8 Dollery St., Central, Port Elizabeth 6001, ☎ FAX 041/585–6162, WEB www.axxess.web.za/calabash). **Egazini Tours** (☎ 083/545–0842 or 083/556–1268). **Mbuleli Mpokela** (☎ 082/979–5906).

TRAIN TRAVEL

An option well worth trying is the superbly luxurious *Blue Train* (☞ Train Travel *in* Smart Travel Tips A to Z), which runs between Cape Town and Port Elizabeth once a month, taking two days, with optional tours of the Garden Route.

Spoornet runs daily trips from Johannesburg (departing 2:30 PM) to Port Elizabeth (arriving 9 AM). A first-class one-way ticket costs R315. Train trips from Cape Town are run only in the December high season.

For a real trip down memory lane, the Union Limited Steam Rail Tours will transport you straight back to the great days of rail—from the 1920s to the 1940s. The Transnet Heritage Foundation is dedicated to keeping old railway stock rolling in as close to original condition as possible. So be warned—these are pretty authentic, and that means communal ablutions, though there are six suites with en-suite showers. Dinners are formal silver-service affairs, with stewards in period uniform, and the menus are the old, traditional Spoornet fare—soup, fish, main course with lots of meat, and dessert. The trip leaves Cape Town on Tuesday, spending five nights and six days meandering around the Garden Route and doing the odd day tour. The standard fare is R2,600 per person, sharing or single, or R22,400 per suite, which sleeps two people in luxury. The fare includes all meals and side trips, but does not include drinks.
➤ TRAIN INFORMATION: **Blue Train** (✉ Box 2671, Joubert Park 2044, ☎ 011/773–7631, FAX 011/773–7643 within South Africa; 0800/11–7715). **Spoornet** (☎ 041/507–1400). **Union Limited Steam Rail Tours** (☎ 021/449–4391, WEB www.steamsa.co.za, closed mid-Dec.—mid-Jan. and May–Sept.).

VISITOR INFORMATION

➤ TOURIST INFORMATION: **Eastern Cape Tourism Board** (✉ Box 186, Bisho 5608, ☎ 040/635–2115, WEB www.ectourism.co.za). **Tourism East London** (✉ 35 Argyle St., East London 5201, ☎ 043/722–6015, WEB www.eastlondontourism.co.za). **Tourism Port Elizabeth** (✉ Donkin Reserve, Belmont Terr., Central, Port Elizabeth; Box 357, Port Elizabeth 6000, ☎ 041/585–8884, WEB www.ibhayi.com).

8 DURBAN AND KWAZULU-NATAL

Steamy heat, the heady aroma of spices, and a polyglot of English, Indian, and Zulu give bustling Durban a tropical feel. Some of the country's most popular bathing beaches extend north and south of the city; inland you can tour the battlefields where Boer, Briton, and Zulu struggled for control of the country. The Drakensberg Mountains, a World Heritage Site, are a breathtaking sanctuary of soaring beauty, crisp air, and phenomenal hiking. In the far north, Hluhluwe-Umfolozi and several private reserves offer a big-game experience rivaling that of Kruger National Park.

By Bronwyn
Howard and
Peta Lee

Updated by
Sue Derwent
and Kate
Turkington

F OR SOUTH AFRICANS the comparatively small province of KwaZulu-Natal is one of the country's premier holiday areas. Here lie the highest and most beautiful mountains in southern Africa, some of the finest game reserves, and a landscape studded with memorials commemorating the great battles between Briton, Boer, and Zulu. The main draws, though, are the subtropical climate and the warm waters of the Indian Ocean. In fact, the entire 480-km (300-mi) coastline, from the Wild Coast in the south to the border with Mozambique in the north, is essentially one long beach, attracting hordes of bathers, surfers, and anglers.

Durban, South Africa's third-largest city, is the busiest port in Africa. Its chief appeal to tourists is its long strip of high-rise hotels and its popular promenade—known as the Golden Mile—fronting its beaches. To find beaches unmarred by commercial development, you need to travel northeast to Zululand. Much of the coastline here is protected, and until fairly recently this meant there were few decent places to rest your head. That is starting to change, however, as adjoining areas open up for tourism. If you really want to get away from the tourist routes, however, try Rocktail Bay Lodge, an idyllic getaway in Maputaland, in the far north of the province. With no other buildings for miles, the lodge presides over deserted beaches, towering dunes, and virgin bush, making it a highlight of any visit to South Africa.

But you don't have to go all the way to Maputaland to experience the true African wilderness. Just a couple of hours west of Durban are the Drakensberg Mountains, offering tremendous hiking amid some of the country's most spectacular, unspoiled scenery. Three hours northeast of Durban, in Zululand, lies a collection of game parks and nature reserves easily rivaling Kruger National Park. One of these, Hluhluwe-Umfolozi Game Reserve, is the jewel in the crown of the KwaZulu-Natal Nature Conservation Service and is responsible for bringing the white rhino back from the brink of extinction. It is also one of the best places to see the even rarer black rhino. It would be a mistake to visit Hluhluwe (pronounced shloo-*shloo*-ee) without also exploring the nearby St. Lucia Greater Wetland Park, an enormous estuary where crocodiles, hippos, and sharks all share the same waters.

Zululand, the region north of the Tugela River, is the traditional home of the Zulu people. In the early 19th century the Zulus established themselves under King Shaka as one of the preeminent military powers in the region. At the Battle of Isandlwana, Zulu *impis* (regiments) inflicted one of the most famous defeats on the British army in history, before being ultimately crushed in 1879 at Ulundi. A visit to Zululand would be incomplete without learning something of the Zulus' fascinating culture, and a tour of the old battlefields will enthrall history and battle buffs.

KwaZulu-Natal's two-part moniker is just one of the many changes introduced since the 1994 democratic elections. Previously, the province was known simply as Natal, a name bestowed by explorer Vasco da Gama, who sighted the coastline on Christmas Day 1497. KwaZulu, "the place of the Zulu," was one of the nominally independent homelands created by the Nationalists (1948–94) to deprive blacks of their South African citizenship. The two are now one.

During the years of white rule, parts of Natal were seen as a bastion of English-speaking South Africans, and to some extent they still are. Natal's first white settlers—a party of British officers seeking trade with the Zulu in ivory—established themselves in Port Natal (now Durban) in 1824. The colony of Natal was formally annexed by the British in 1843. Cities like Durban and Pietermaritzburg present strong reminders of the colonial past with Victorian architecture and public monuments. The province's huge Indian population is another reminder of Britain's imperial legacy. In the 1860s the British brought thousands of Indians to South Africa to work as indentured laborers cutting sugarcane, which grows abundantly on the coastal hills. Today the Indian population of Durban alone numbers 1 million, and it plays a major part in the economic, political, and cultural life of the province.

Warning: It is essential that visitors to the northern parts of the province, including Zululand, take antimalarial drugs, particularly during the wet summer months.

Pleasures and Pastimes

Dining

Durban's dining public is fickle by nature, and restaurants tend to change hands fairly often. This means that what is popular today may often be totally out tomorrow. However, there are a couple of old favorites whose food is consistent. Durban does have some superb dining, provided you eat to its strengths. Thanks to a huge Indian population, it has some of the best curry restaurants in the country. Durban's other great gastronomic delight is fresh seafood, especially prawns and langoustines, brought down the coast from Mozambique. LM prawns (LM stands for Lourenço Marques, the former Portuguese name for Maputo) are a revered delicacy in South Africa. Served with *peri-peri* (a spicy Portuguese marinade of chilies, olive oil, garlic, and sometimes tomatoes), they are a real taste sensation.

The growing international interest in Zululand, the battlefields, and the wilderness of the Drakensberg have encouraged the establishment of a number of outstanding restaurants in these areas. Most resorts include dinner and breakfast—a good option if you don't feel like going out after a day of hiking or sightseeing. At the same time, it's well worth the effort to take a short scenic drive to one of the many excellent, tucked-away restaurants, often run by the type of interesting and unusual people drawn to settle in beautiful rural places. Some of these dining spots have extras, such as champagne breakfasts as you watch the sun rise from the top of a mountain or sunset picnic baskets of local cheeses and wines.

For a description of South African culinary terms, *see* Pleasures and Pastimes *in* Chapter 1. For price ranges *see* Dining *in* Smart Travel Tips A to Z.

Fishing

The Drakensberg and its low-lying areas are not only famous for spectacular scenery; they are also popular with fly-fishermen. The crystal-clear Drakensberg streams are good for rainbow and brown trout, and many farmers have stocked their dammed ponds to cater to fly-fishermen. With its long stretch of coastline, saltwater fly-fishing is growing as a sport, and an early morning or an evening on the long, empty beaches of the north coast can provide some wonderfully rewarding fishing. Bear in mind, however, that most resorts require anglers to bring their own tackle. In winter, when huge shoals of sardines pass along the KwaZulu-Natal coast, rock and surf anglers are out following flocks of seabirds and hoping to catch some of the accompanying game fish. Obtain permits from the KwaZulu-Natal Nature Conservation Service or at post offices in larger cities and towns.

TO JOHANNESBURG

Vaal Dam
Nature
Reserve

N3

Piet Retief

3

11

FREE STATE

Charlestown

Paulpietersburg

Utrecht

Re

Ntshon-
Ce

Newcastle   Madadeni
Osizweni

Vryheid

N11

Mondlo

R34

R34

Bohlakong

Harrismith

N3

Talana
Museum
Dundee

Battle of
Blood River

Battle of
Isandlwana

Phuthaditjhaba

Glencoe

Wasbank

Rorke's Drift

Babanango

R68

Mel

Royal Natal
National Park

Ladysmith

KWAZULU-

R33

Bergville
Winterton

R74

Colenso

Weenen

NATAL

Kranskop

Zu
His
M

R600

Estcourt

R74

Greytown

R74

Wembesi
Mooi River

3

Howick

R33

LESOTHO

Pietermaritzburg

Tongaat
Verulam

Underberg

Edendale

N3

Valley of a
Thousand Hills

Kwamashu

Umh
Rock

R56

Pinetown
Westville
Queensburgh
Umlazi

Durban

Donnybrook

Isipingo
Amanzimtoti

Ixopo

Umzinto

Franklin

Kokstad

N2

Harding

2

Port Shepstone
Gamalakhe

EASTERN CAPE

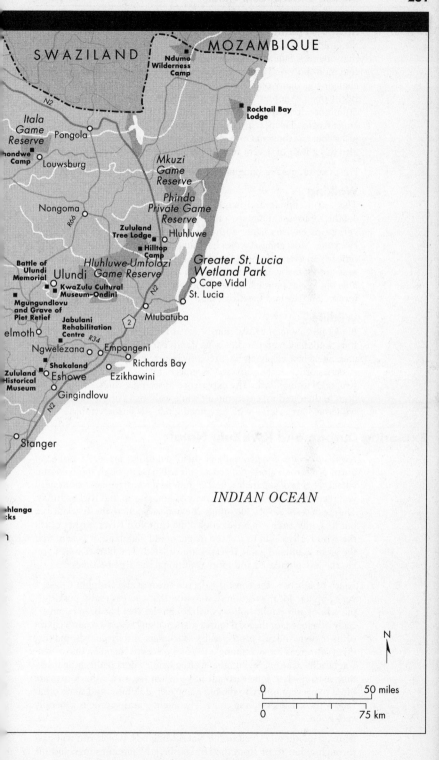

SWAZILAND

MOZAMBIQUE

Ndumo
Wilderness
Camp

Rocktail Bay
Lodge

N2

Itala
Game
Reserve

Pongola

hondwe
Camp

Louwsburg

Mkuzi
Game
Reserve

Phinda
Private Game
Reserve

Nongoma

R66

Zululand
Tree Lodge

Hluhluwe

Hilltop
Camp

Battle of
Ulundi
Memorial

Hluhluwe-Umfolozi
Game Reserve

Ulundi

KwaZulu Cultural
Museum-Ondini

Greater St. Lucia
Wetland Park

Cape Vidal

St. Lucia

N2

Mgungundlovu
and Grave of
Piet Retief

Jabulani
Rehabilitation
Centre

elmoth

2

Mtubatuba

R34

Ngwelezana

Empangeni

Zululand
Historical
Museum

Shakaland

Eshowe

Richards Bay

Ezikhawini

Gingindlovu

N2

Stanger

INDIAN OCEAN

hlanga
ks

N

0   50 miles

0   75 km

Lodging

Apart from the Royal Hotel, many of Durban's main hotels lie along the Golden Mile, Durban's beachfront. Southern Sun, the giant chain that operates Sun and Holiday Inn hotels in South Africa, has a virtual monopoly on Durban accommodations. However, this is rapidly changing as many outstanding, smaller boutique hotels and excellent B&Bs open. Another area to enjoy the surf, sand, and sun is about a 20-minute drive up the coast from Durban to the resort town of Umhlanga Rocks. The beaches there are excellent but in holiday season are just as busy as those in Durban. Umhlanga (pronounced M-*shlang*-gah) also has a host of decent restaurants, movie theaters, and shops.

For price ranges *see* Lodging *in* Smart Travel Tips A to Z.

Walking

The warm climate and magnificent scenery of KwaZulu-Natal are conducive to just about any outdoor activity you can imagine, and the variety of environments allows for hikes and walks to suit nearly everyone. Most game reserves have guided day walks, if you don't have time for an overnight hike. The landscapes of the Drakensberg wilderness are fantastic. The province also has hundreds of equally enjoyable but less dramatic hikes and walks along beaches, through coastal forests, and around the area's many nature reserves.

Wildlife

Big-game viewing in KwaZulu-Natal at Hluhluwe-Umfolozi, Phinda, Itala, and the Greater St. Lucia Wetlands Park—a Natural World Heritage Site where elephants have recently been reintroduced—in the northeastern corner of the province, is superb if not on the scale of that in Kruger National Park. The experience of seeing a rhino or a pride of lions in their natural environment while walking in one of the few true wilderness areas left—with an armed guide—is unforgettable.

Exploring Durban and KwaZulu-Natal

KwaZulu-Natal can generally be divided into five areas. As you head north of Durban along the coast, you will pass through small coastal villages, fields of sugarcane, and commercial forestry plantations until you reach the more industrial towns of Empangeni and Richards Bay. The greatest sphere of Zulu influence extended south to the Tugela River, but it is only after you have crossed the Umfolozi River farther north that you really begin to feel the magic of old Zululand; it is here that the great Zululand game reserves are situated. The farther north you go, the less populated and more traditional the area becomes.

South of Durban, the coastal strip is known as the Dolphin Coast, a very popular local vacation destination that can get really busy during school and public holidays. Although the area has been commercially developed for the local tourist market, many beaches retain a charm of their own and are protected by shark nets and lifeguards, making them safe areas for swimming and good places to spend an out-of-season beach vacation. Swimming is often banned during the annual sardine season—late June through July—when the area's shark nets are lifted to prevent injury to the big-game fish, dolphins, and sharks that follow the sardines up the coast. The angling at this time is generally very good.

Moving inland takes you to the Natal Midlands, which you will pass through either to or from the Drakensberg Mountain range and the coast. The rolling green hills and lush pastures have given rise to a local joke that the region is not really part of Africa at all but rather a small piece of England. Racehorse stud farms and large dairy farms are here;

the area has also attracted numerous artists, bohemians, and those who make their living from leather working, farming herbs, weaving and knitting, making cheeses, and practicing ceramics and fine art. A wonderful way to experience this part of the province is to follow the Midlands Meander (a route set up by the local tourism board), which starts outside Pietermaritzburg and takes you around farms and farm stands. You can stop for coffee and cakes or lunch at some of the quaint hotels or restaurants along the way.

Travel 20 minutes north of bustling downtown Durban, and you'll be in rural Africa watching small Zulu boys herding cattle in the Valley of Thousand Hills, so called because of the steep valleys that cut into the rolling countryside. This region is home to not only traditional Zulu people but also to many artists who have shops and studios here. On weekends many Durbanites drive out into the country to enjoy the quaint restaurants, hotels, and rural activities of the Thousand Hills region.

In the northwestern part of the province is the dramatic Drakensberg Mountain range, a spectacular wilderness national park. Spread along the base of the range are small hotels, restaurants, B&Bs, guest houses, and lodges catering to all tastes. Sharing the lowlands areas on the approach to the Drakensberg are white farmers, some of whose families settled in the area more than a hundred years ago, and a number of sprawling villages and subsistence farms populated by Zulus, many of whom were displaced by the system of forced removals during the apartheid years.

The farther north you go in the province, the more conservative the population, whether traditional Zulu, obstinate Afrikaner, or staunch English-speaking folk. The local towns, dotted among the Zululand battlefields, tend to be a little ugly and dusty during the dry winter months, but this is an area to visit more for its historic than its scenic value and for its opportunities to meet the salt-of-the-earth rural people who have made the country what it is.

Great Itineraries

IF YOU HAVE 2 DAYS

Two days doesn't give you much time for an in-depth experience of all this province has to offer, but you can get a good idea of it by basing yourself on the 🔢 **Durban** beachfront on arrival. Take an early morning walk along the Golden Mile to watch the surfers and later wander around the Indian District. You should leave jewelry and valuables in your hotel safe before venturing into this area. Spend the afternoon on a township tour. A 50-minute drive on the N3 the next morning will get you to **Pietermaritzburg** with its Victorian architecture and maze of small shopping lanes. On your way back to Durban from Pietermaritzburg take a detour into the beautiful rolling countryside of the **Valley of a Thousand Hills,** where, just minutes from the city, you can still experience rural Africa.

IF YOU HAVE 5 DAYS

With five days at hand, you can do a round-trip of many of the main places of interest in KwaZulu-Natal. Pick one of two combinations: the 🔢 **Drakensberg** and **Zululand,** or Zululand and the more northern section, which takes in the coastal strip and some of the northern game parks, such as 🔢 **Hluhluwe-Umfolozi Game Reserve** and the private lodges around it. If you opt for the mountains, plan a day or two hiking and walking, overnighting in one of the reserves or one of the small establishments in the area; then head toward the battlefield sites of **Isandlwana, Rorke's Drift,** and the **Talana Museum** at Dundee. If battlefields aren't your scene, try the **Southern Drakensberg,** where you can tour up the spectacular Sani Pass to the very roof of Africa. Afterward, travel north and take the alternative route off the N3 (the R103) to pick up on the **Midlands Meander,** which stretches north all the way to Mooi River, through the tranquil Natal Midlands. Within three hours of the battlefields or the Berg (the Drakensberg), you can be in **Durban** and at the coast. Spend at least one day in Durban, wandering around the Indian market and the African Traditional Healers Market or going on a township tour. It will give you a good perspective on urban living, as opposed to the rural areas from which you have just come.

If you decide to head up the north coast, after a day or two in Durban, stop off at **Shakaland** or **Simunye** for a night to get the total Zulu cultural experience. Then continue to **Hluhluwe-Umfolozi Game Reserve, Greater St. Lucia Wetlands Park,** and ⚀ **Phinda Private Game Reserve,** scheduling at least two days in the area to see some of the big game for which these reserves are well known. A trip in **Greater St. Lucia Wetlands Park** to see hippos and crocodiles in the wild is another great experience. There is a crocodile farm and education center nearby. Again, allow a day for Durban, either at the beginning or the end of this part of your trip.

IF YOU HAVE 7–10 DAYS
Don't pass **Durban** by altogether, but once you have spent a day or two exploring the area, shake off the city and head up to **Hluhluwe-Umfolozi Game Reserve** for the incredible wildlife. A three-day trail in the wilderness of Umfolozi or a two- or three-day hike or horseback ride in the **Drakensberg Mountains** could be a high point in your trip. Although these hikes are not terribly strenuous, you may still prefer something more sedate, in which case the long drive to spend three days at **Rocktail Bay Lodge,** close to the Mozambique border, is every bit worth the effort, particularly during the turtle breeding season, from September to March. If you are in the region of Rocktail Bay, it will be well worth your while to drive a little farther, to **Kosi Bay** with its pristine system of lakes and ancient fish traps, still in use by the Tsonga descendents. Diving around the reefs off of **Greater St. Lucia Wetland Park**'s Sodwana Bay is some of the best in the country; inshore snorkeling to see the abundance of colorful little tropical fish is also sensational. Another distant park near the edge of the province is the delightfully less-visited ⚀ **Itala Game Reserve.** You could incorporate it on a grand loop: head from Durban to Zululand, through Greater St. Lucia Wetland Park and Hluhluwe-Umfolozi Game Reserve or Phinda Private Game Reserve, then continue up to Rocktail Bay and Kosi Bay, and on to Itala, finally turning back toward Durban and driving through the battlefields.

When to Tour Durban and KwaZulu-Natal
The best time to tour KwaZulu-Natal is definitely early autumn through winter and into spring. Summer can be terribly hot and humid, and some facilities in the Zululand game reserves close because of the extreme and unpleasantly high temperatures in that area. The coast is particularly pleasant during winter, and it is at this time that the Ocean Action festival is held on Durban's Golden Mile. Centering on the world-famous surfing championships (once known as the Gunston 500, but now named for the year's competition sponsor), Ocean Action includes 10 days of exciting outdoor water-sport-related activities, including night surfing. An abundance of market stalls on the promenade are open until late.

Game viewing is better during winter (late June, July, and August), when the grass is shorter, many trees have lost their leaves, and the animals tend to congregate around water holes. Northern parts of the province are dry and dusty during winter, but the frosty mornings and crisp late afternoons make up for it. The cold weather does not deter the thousands of folk-music lovers of all ages who congregate in May every year for the folk-music festival held at Splashy-Fen Farm, in the Drakensberg; during this four-day celebration both local and international folk musicians perform.

DURBAN

No city in South Africa feels more African than Durban. Cape Town could be in the Mediterranean, and Johannesburg's endless suburbs could be anywhere in America. Durban alone has the pulse, the look, the complex face of Africa. It may have something to do with the summer heat, a clinging sauna that soaks you with sweat in minutes. You don't need to take a township tour here to see the emerging new South Africa. Hang out in Farewell Square in the city center and rub shoulders with Zulus, Indians, and whites. Wander into the Indian District or drive through the Warwick triangle area, and the *real* Africa rises up to meet you in myriad ways: traditional healers touting animal organs, vegetable and spice vendors crowding the sidewalks, and minibus taxis hooting incessantly as they trawl for business. It is by turns colorful, stimulating, and hypnotic.

By no means should you plan an entire vacation around Durban because there is so much more to see beyond the city. Nevertheless, it's definitely worth a stopover, perhaps between trips to the Drakensberg Mountains or the game reserves in the north. To get the most from a stay in the city, explore the areas where Durban's residents live and work. Be sure to take a drive through the lovely neighborhoods of the Berea or a walk through the vibrant markets of the Indian District.

Durban is a large port city with all the negative baggage that this implies. Don't wander around the Central Business District (CBD) alone at night, and in general be sure to hold onto that expensive camera that you might have slung over your shoulder. Another type of hazard altogether is the school holidays. It's best to avoid Durban and the KwaZulu-Natal coast during summer vacation (from mid-December to mid-January), when thousands of vacationers from the inland provinces descend on the beaches to cavort and carouse en masse.

The city breaks down easily into four parts: the city center around Farewell Square; the Indian District; the Durban beachfront; and outlying attractions. Apart from getting to the outlying districts, all four can be followed on foot, but you may need a taxi or car to get between them.

Numbers in the text correspond to numbers in the margin and on the Durban map.

City Center

A Good Walk

This walk takes you past several of Durban's historic buildings. Start at the **Tourist Junction** ①, the city's main tourist information center, on Pine Street. Cross the street to the early 20th-century **St. Paul's Church** ② and follow the pedestrian thoroughfare to West Street. Cross the street to **Farewell Square** ③ in front of the imposing **City Hall** ④, also built in the early 20th century. Walk down the Smith Street side of City Hall to get to the steps that lead up to the **Durban Natural Science Museum** ⑤, inside, and, above it, the **Durban Art Gallery** ⑥. Directly opposite is the entrance to the Playhouse Theatre, Durban's major cultural center. If you continue the short distance to the end of the Smith Street block, you will reach the **Local History Museum** ⑦. From outside the museum's front entrance on Aliwal Street, turn right and walk toward the bay. Cross the Esplanade and pass through the walkway under the railway line, and you'll reach the **Bartle Arts Trust (BAT) Centre** ⑧, on the quayside. Wander around the center's small shops and through the working studios, where all sorts of visual and performing artists are at work; you can also get a light bite to eat here while tugs and ships move in and out of the harbor. If you end up here in the late afternoon, you may catch local jazz musicians playing out on the deck.

TIMING

The center of the city can get horribly humid from December through February, so avoid town and avoid walking too much during the mid-day heat. This walk would be better to do a little later in the afternoon, having spent the morning on the beach or in shops. Remember to set aside enough time for browsing in the museums and galleries, most of which close at 4:30.

Sights to See

★ ⑧ **Bartle Arts Trust (BAT) Centre.** To some, the Bartle Arts Trust Centre seen from across the bay resembles a giant flying bat. The vibrant arts center is always abuzz with Durban's trendy set—artists, musicians, and other hipsters. Most days—and some nights—you can watch sculptors, dancers, musicians, and painters at work, and at night the BAT theater comes alive with plays, music, and African film or video festivals. A coffee bar overlooks the bay, Zansi Bar has live music, and shops sell bric-a-brac and artwork, including an excellent selection of high-quality African crafts, fabrics, and ceramics. ✉ *45 Maritime Pl., Small Craft Harbor,* ☎ *031/332–0468,* WEB *www.batcentre.co.za.* ◷ *Daily 8:30–4:30.*

④ **City Hall.** Built in 1910 in Edwardian neo-Baroque style, the hall looks as if it has been shipped straight from London column by column. The main pediment carries sculptures representing Britannia, Unity, and Patriotism, and allegorical sculptures of the Arts, Music, and Literature adorn the exterior. Ask the guard to allow you inside to see the huge theater's ornate molding and grand parterre boxes, or join an official tour run by Tourism Durban. ✉ *West and Church Sts.,* ☎ *031/311–1111,* WEB *www.cityofdurban.co.za.* ◷ *Daily 8:30–3:30.*

NEED A BREAK?

The **Royal Coffee Shoppe,** in the Royal Hotel, is a popular meeting place for Durban society and pre- and post-theater crowds. Crystal chandeliers, etched glass, and live piano music—in the nearby lounge at lunchtime—create a rich atmosphere of old-time Durban. The café serves a light breakfast as well as a selection of coffees, teas, and cakes, quiches, salads, and sandwiches. ✉ *267 Smith St.,* ☎ *031/304–0331.* ◷ *Daily 7 AM–1 AM.*

⑥ **Durban Art Gallery.** The museum presents the work of local and international artists. Exhibits have included the FNB Vita Craft Now show, staged to highlight the cultural diversity of handicrafts in South Africa. Exhibits change every few months, so call ahead to find out what's being shown. The first Friday of every month is set aside for Red Eye, a showcase of Durban performing and visual arts with bands, African drummers, musicians, and dancers performing among the exhibitions. For this special event hours are extended until 10 PM and a small entrance fee is charged. ✉ *City Hall, Smith St. at Church St., 2nd floor,* ☎ *031/311–2264.* ▨ *Free.* ◷ *Mon.–Sat. 8:30–4, Sun. 11–4.*

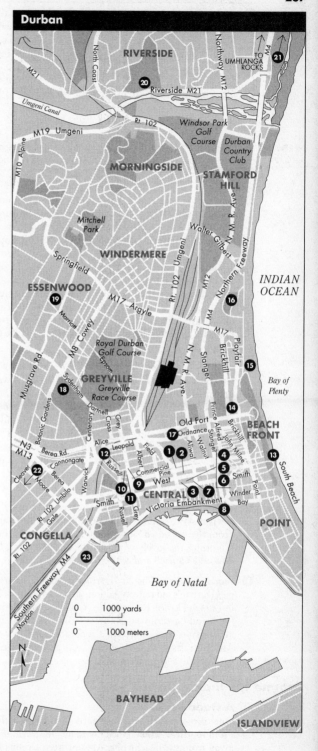

Durban

🖐 **❺ Durban Natural Science Museum.** Despite its small size, this museum provides an excellent introduction to Africa's numerous wild mammals, plants, birds, reptiles, and insects. It's a great place to bring the kids or to familiarize yourself with the local wildlife before heading up to the game parks in northern KwaZulu-Natal. A popular gallery is the KwaNunu Insect Arcade, where giant insect replicas adorn the wall, but what grabs the attention is the live display of Durban's infamous cockroaches. ☒ *City Hall, Smith St. at Church St.,* ☎ *031/311–2256.* 🎟 *Free.* ☉ *Mon.–Sat. 8:30–4, Sun. 11–4.*

NEED A BREAK?   In the Durban Natural Science Museum is the **Waterhole** coffee shop, where you can sip your cappuccino and have a snack sitting in the middle of a re-created mangrove swamp.

❸ Farewell Square. In the heart of Durban, the square is a lovely, shady plaza, bordered by some of the city's most historic buildings. Walkways lined with stately palms and flower beds crisscross the square and lead to monuments honoring some of Natal's important historic figures. The square stands on the site of the first European encampment in Natal, established by Francis Farewell and Henry Fynn in 1824 as a trading station to purchase ivory from the Zulus. A statue representing Peace honors the Durban volunteers who died during the South African War (formerly known as the Boer War; 1899–1902); the Cenotaph commemorates the South African dead from the two world wars. ☒ *Bounded by Smith, West, and Gardiner Sts., and the Church Street pedestrian mall.*

❼ Local History Museum. Exhibits focus on Natal's colonial past, including a reconstruction of Henry Fynn's original 1824 wattle-and-daub hut, as well as simulated shop fronts of a turn-of-the-20th-century apothecary and department store. Upstairs is a display of miniature dolls, replicas of important people in Durban's history and development. The museum is in the old courthouse, built in 1866. During the Zulu War of 1879, when Durban was in danger of attack, the exterior of the building was temporarily provided with loopholes so defenders could fire their rifles from inside. ☒ *Smith and Aliwal Sts.,* ☎ *031/311–2256.* 🎟 *Free.* ☉ *Mon.–Sat. 8:30–4, Sun. 11–4.*

❷ St. Paul's Church. The current Anglican church, built in 1909 in Gothic Revival style, stands on the site of a previous church dating to 1847. From the outside it's not much to look at, but the interior is beautiful: notice the lovely wood ceiling and the stained-glass chancel windows. ☒ *Church and Smith Sts.,* ☎ *031/305–4666.*

❶ Tourist Junction. The city's principal tourist information outlet occupies Durban's old railway station, an attractive brick building constructed in 1894 in Flemish Revival style. The NGR above the main entrance stands for Natal Government Railways. Tourism Durban, the city's tourist authority, is here, as well as a reputable jewelry store and an excellent African crafts shop. ☒ *160 Pine St., at Soldier's Way,* ☎ *031/304–4934.* ☉ *Weekdays 8–5, weekends 9–2.*

Around the Indian District

A Good Walk

One of the most fascinating parts of Durban is the **Indian District** ⑨. From **Tourist Junction** ① walk west up Pine Street or Commercial Road, away from the beachfront. About three or four blocks up, turn right on Grey Street, generally considered the heart of the district. A little farther along, near the junction of Queen and Grey streets, is the **Jumah Mosque** ⑩; right next door is the **Madressa Arcade** ⑪. At the corner of Queen and Russell streets, you'll reach the most-hyped part of the Indian District, the bustling **Victoria Street Market** ⑫. At the end of Victoria Street turn right onto Russell Street past the busy minibus and taxi stand. Under the bridges and along the road's shoulders, you will find the largest and most extensive *muthi* (traditional medicine) market in southern Africa.

TIMING

The best time of day to do this is in the morning. Set off just before nine, when it's still relatively cool. This also gives the street sellers time to set up their stalls. Their part of town can be quite grubby, and in the midday summer heat it can get unpleasantly humid. The walk should take between two and three hours.

Sights to See

★ ⑨ **Indian District.** The streets here are thronged with Zulus and Indians, producing an intoxicating mix of Africa and Asia. Narrow doorways lead into fascinating spice shops, and traders touting saris are squeezed in next to traditional herbalists, whose dark stores are hung with wizened claws, animal organs, and roots. Outside on the narrow sidewalks, vendors sell vegetables, hair weaves, and fake Rolexes. Head for Russell Street Extension to see hundreds of Zulu women selling *muthi*, traditional medicines concocted from crushed roots, bark, and other natural products. Many of the muthi sellers have moved into covered shelters, and although security here has improved considerably, it is still not wise to have your valuables too visible.

⑩ **Jumah Mosque.** Built in 1927 in a style that combines Islamic and colonial features, this is the largest mosque in the southern hemisphere. Its colonnaded verandas, gold-domed minaret, and turrets give the surrounding streets much of their character. Tours (the only way to visit) can be arranged through Durban Africa. No tours are offered during Islamic holidays. If you plan on going inside, make sure to wear modest clothes. ⊠ *Grey and Queen Sts.*

⑪ **Madressa Arcade.** The thoroughfare has a Kiplingesque quality, recalling the bazaars of the East. Built in 1927, it's little more than a narrow, winding alley perfumed by spices and thronged with traders. You can buy everything from plastic trinkets to household utensils and recordings of Indian music here. ⊠ *Entrances on both Queen and Cathedral Sts.*

NEED A BREAK? While you're in the Indian District, you should try one of Durban's specialties, bunny chow—a hollowed-out loaf of bread traditionally filled with bean curry, although meat is also used. Good bunny chow can be found at **Patel Vegetarian Refreshment** (⊠ Rama House, 202 Grey St., ☎ 031/306–1774) or the **Victory Lounge** (⊠ corner of Grey and Victoria Sts., ☎ 031/306–1906).

★ ⑫ **Victoria Street Market.** Masses of enormous fish and prawns lie tightly packed on beds of ice, and vendors competing for your attention shout their respective prices. In the meat section goat and sheep heads are stacked into neat piles, while butchers slice and dice every cut of meat imaginable. The noise is deafening. The place pulsates with life, and even if you have no kitchen in which to cook, it's tough to resist joining the fray. In an adjacent building—where all the tour buses pull up—you'll discover a number of curio shops whose proprietors are willing to bargain over wood and stone carvings, beadwork, and basketry. You'll also find shops selling spices, recordings of African music, and Indian fabrics. The current structures stand on the site of an original, much-loved market, a ramshackle collection of wooden shacks that burned down during the years of Nationalist rule. ⊠ *Queen and Russell Sts.,* ☎ *031/306–4021.* ⊙ *Weekdays 8–4:30, Sat. 7:30–3, Sun. 8–3.*

Durban Beachfront

A Good Walk and Drive

Either you will hate the **Durban beachfront** for its commercial glitz, or you will love it for its endless activity; it stretches for around four blocks, from South Beach to Snake Park Beach. Since it was turned into a pedestrians-only walkway, Durbanites have taken to this promenade in droves—strolling, jogging, rollerblading, cycling, or just sitting in the sun to watch the surfers and body-boarders. The beachfront is a bit of a hike from the city center; it's best to take a taxi or drive to the end of West Street or Commercial Road. A good place to start your tour is at South Beach's main attraction, **Sea World Durban** ⑬. Walk north along Marine Parade to reach the **Natal Museum of Military History** ⑭. A little farther along, almost on the beach itself, is the **Fitzsimons Snake Park** ⑮. If it's a weekend, finish your day on the lawns of **Water World** ⑯, right at the end of the Snell Parade.

TIMING

Depending on the weather, parts of the beachfront can be quite busy, especially during weekends. There is always something to see, even in the early mornings, when people come to surf or jog before going to work. Head off early, but try to time your walk so that you visit the snake park during feeding times or when there is a demonstration. At a leisurely pace this walk should take two or three hours.

Sights to See

Durban Beachfront. The Golden Mile, as it is known, extends from South Beach, at the base of Durban Point, all the way past North Beach and the Bay of Plenty. Once past the snake park, the shoreline is largely undeveloped and is used mostly by joggers and fishermen.

⑮ **Fitzsimons Snake Park.** The zoo houses a slithery collection of snakes, crocodiles, and other reptiles from around the world. Live snake demonstrations are held in a small amphitheater; on weekends these shows are followed by a feeding. There is also a snake breeding center and rehabilitation lab. Reserve in advance to book an interesting behind-the-scenes tour of what the snake park curators' job entails. ⊠ *Snell Parade,* ☎ *073/156–9606.* 🖾 *R12.* ⊙ *Daily 9–4:30. Snake demonstrations daily at 10, 11:30, 1, 2:30, and 3:30. Crocodile feedings daily at 2.*

⑭ **Natal Museum of Military History.** Housed in a huge warehouse on the beachfront, the museum displays a large collection of weapons and military equipment, much of it dating to World War II. Exhibits from different periods tend to be jumbled together, but military buffs will get a kick out of climbing about on a U.S. Sherman tank, a French Mirage jet fighter, and an enormous helicopter. ⊠ *Snell Parade and Old Fort Rd.,* ☎ *031/332–5305.* 🖾 *R6.* ⊙ *Daily 9–5.*

⑬ **Sea World Durban.** Attached to the Oceanographic Research Institute, Sea World has a wonderful collection of tropical fish, sea turtles, rays, and other sea creatures including a massive shark tank. There are daily dolphin and seal shows and shark feedings three times a week. ⊠ *South Beach,* ☎ *031/337–3536,* WEB *www.seaworld.org.za.* 🖾 *R40.* ⊙ *Daily 9–9. Dolphin and seal shows daily at 10, 11:30, 2:30, weekends also at 1. Fish feeding daily at 11 and 3:30. Shark feeding Tues., Thurs., and Sun. at 12:30.*

⑯ **Water World.** Just north of Battery Beach, this water park is a fun alternative to a day on the beach. There are enormous water slides, pools, and a variety of gentle, pulsating, or looping water-propelled rides. The ample grassy lawns surrounding the pools are a great place to cool off and relax. ⊠ *Battery Beach Rd., Snell Parade.*, ☎ *031/337–6336.* ☞ *R30.* ☉ *Dec.–Jan., Tues.–Sun. 9–5; Feb.–Nov., weekends 9–5.*

Around Durban

★ ⑲ **Campbell Collections.** Administered by the University of Natal, the collections here include the Killie Campbell Africana Library, the William Campbell Furniture Museum, and the Mashu Museum of Ethnology. The museum is housed in Muckleneuk, a lovely Cape Dutch–inspired home built in 1914 for Sir Marshall Campbell, a wealthy sugar baron, and his family. The house is furnished much as it was when the Campbells lived here and contains some excellent pieces of Cape Dutch furniture, an extensive collection of oil paintings by early settlers, as well as paintings by prominent black South African artists. The highlight, however, is the Mashu Museum of Ethnology, which displays perhaps the best collection of traditional beadwork in the country, in addition to African utensils, weapons, carvings, masks, pottery, and musical instruments. Paintings of African tribesmen by artist Barbara Tyrrell add vitality to the collection. ⊠ *220 Marriott Rd., at Essenwood Rd. (take Field St. to Epsom Rd., which turns into Marriott),* ☎ *031/207–3432,* 🌐 *khozi2.nu.ac.za.* ☞ *R15.* ☉ *Guided tours by appointment only.*

⑱ **Durban Botanic Gardens.** Opposite the Greyville Racecourse, the gardens are a delightful oasis of greenery in a rather drab city, interlaced with walking paths, fountains, and ponds. The site is renowned for its orchid house and collection of rare cycads. There is also a garden for the blind and a herb garden with many of the medicinal plants used by traditional African healers. The Tea Garden enjoys a sylvan setting far from the city's hustle and bustle. It's a great place to take the weight off your feet and settle back with a cup of hot tea and cakes. ⊠ *Sydenham Rd. (take Ordnance west to the M4, then the M13; turn right on the M8 to the gardens),* ☎ *031/201–1303,* 🌐 *www.durbanbotgardens. org.za.* ☞ *Free.* ☉ *Apr. 16–Sept. 15, daily 7:30–5:15; Sept. 16–Apr. 15, daily 7:30–5:45.*

⑰ **Kwa Muhle Museum.** It is ironic that a museum that tells the story of the city's apartheid past is housed in what used to be Durban's notorious Department of Native Affairs. During apartheid the department was responsible for administering the movement of black people into and out of the city, dealing with the dreaded passbooks that all blacks had to carry with them at all times, and generally overseeing the oppressive laws that plagued the black population during apartheid. Exhibits provides an often heartbreaking background to this period in Durban's history. Other exhibits change regularly but cover topics such as the race riots and forced removals. Also on display are many Zulu artifacts that have survived the area's turbulent past. ⊠ *150 Ordnance Rd.,* ☎ *031/311–2223,* 🌐 *www.durban.gov.za≠museumsplocalhistory.* ☞ *Free.* ☉ *Mon.–Sat. 8:30–4, Sun. 11–4.*

☺ **Mitchell Park.** The magnificent rose garden, year-round colorful floral displays, and leafy lawns are real treats on a hot summer day. Attached to the park is a beautiful, small zoo. The zoo was opened at the turn of the last century, and the massive Aldabra tortoises that were donated to the park in the early 1900s are still in residence today. There are also a number of small animals, reptiles, tropical fish, and birds in large aviaries. A great place to have breakfast or a light lunch is on the leafy terrace under bright umbrellas at the park's Blue Zoo Restaurant. ⊠

6 Nimmo Rd., Morningside, ☎ *031/303–3568.* ⊠ *Gardens free, zoo R3.* ☼ *Gardens, daily 7:30–5:30; zoo, daily 7:30–5:15.*

★ ㉑ **Natal Sharks Board.** Durban's shark-research institute is probably the foremost one in the world. Most of the popular bathing beaches in KwaZulu-Natal are protected by shark nets maintained by the institute. Each day crews in ski boats check the nets, releasing healthy sharks back into the ocean and bringing deceased ones back to the institute, where they are dissected and studied. The Natal Sharks Board offers regular one-hour tours that include a shark dissection and a fascinating audiovisual presentation on sharks and shark nets. You can also take an early morning trip out to sea through the harbor mouth on a Sharks Board ski boat to observe firsthand how the staff goes about its daily servicing of the shark nets off Durban's Golden Mile. At the same time, depending on the season, you will more than likely be able to see wild dolphins and whales close at hand. ⊠ *M12, Umhlanga Rocks (take the M4 [Northern Fwy.] out of Durban for 16 km [10 mi] to reach Natal),* ☎ *031/566–0400,* 🕸 *www.shark.co.za.* ⊠ *R12.* ☼ *Tours Tues., Wed., and Thurs. at 9 and 2, Sun. at 2.*

㉒ **NSA Gallery.** The National Society of the Arts' gallery complex houses not only three exhibition areas, a crafts shop, and the Durban Centre for Photography, but also a sophisticated open-air restaurant. The center's clean architectural lines and leafy setting make this a popular venue with Durban's trendy set. It's a wonderful place to cool off after a hot morning in town. The gallery and crafts shop support and promote local art, so it's worth wandering around the crafts shop for tasteful souvenirs. ⊠ *166 Bulwer Rd., Glenwood (follow Ordnance Rd. to the M4, then the M13; turn south on the M8, which is first Cleaver Rd. then Bulwer Rd.),* ☎ *031/202–3686,* 🕸 *www.nsagallery.co.za.* ☼ *Tues.–Fri. 9–5, Sat. 9–4, Sun. 10–4.*

㉓ **S. A. Sugar Terminal.** Much of Durban's early economy was built on the sugar industry, and even today the hills and fields around the city and along the north and south coasts are covered in sugarcane. It is not surprising then that Durban's Sugar Terminal is the largest in southern Africa and one of the most advanced in the world. A short video presentation gives you background about the sugar industry, and then you'll be taken on a walking tour of the sugar terminal. The entire tour and video presentation take 45 minutes. It is extraordinary to see the terminal's three enormous silos piled high to the domed ceiling with tons of raw sugar. The architectural design of the silos has been patented and used in other parts of the world. ⊠ *51 Maydon Rd., Maydon Wharf,* ☎ *031/365–8100 or 031/365–8153.* ⊠ *R10.* ☼ Tours at 8:30, 10, 11:30, and 2.

Shree Ambalavaanar Alayam Temple. One of Durban's most spectacular Hindu shrines is in Cato Manor, on the outskirts of town. The temple's facade is adorned with brightly painted representations of the Hindu gods, notably Ganesha, Shiva, and Vishnu. The magnificent doors leading to the cellar were salvaged from a temple built in 1875 on the banks of the Umbilo River and subsequently destroyed by floods. During an important Hindu festival held annually in March, unshod fire walkers cross beds of burning, glowing coals. There are no set visiting hours; however, if the temple is open, you'll be welcome to go inside. If not, the exterior of the building is still worth seeing. ⊠ *890 Bellair Rd., Cato Manor (take M13 [from Leopold St.] out of the city; at major fork in road after Westridge Park and high school, veer left onto Bellair Rd.),* ☎ *031/261–8114.*

㉚ **Umgeni River Bird Park.** Ranked among the top three in the world, this bird park has an extensive collection of indigenous as well as exotic birds. It's built under high cliffs next to the Umgeni River and has three huge walk-through aviaries, as well as a host of smaller, specialized ones. The variety of birds, both exotic and indigenous, is astonishing; the collection of extravagantly plumaged macaws is particularly outstanding. Try to time your visit to take in the bird show, which is a delight for both children and adults. ⊠ *Riverside Rd. (head north out of Durban on Umgeni Rd. and cross river to reach park),* ☎ *031/579–4600,* ⓌⒺⒷ *www.umgeniriverbirdpark.co.za.* ⊠ *R25.* ☉ *Daily 9–4:30; bird shows at 11 and 2.*

Dining

$$$$ ✕ **Royal Grill.** This restaurant in the Royal Hotel has one of Durban's most grand culinary settings. The dining room—all that remains of the original Royal Hotel—has the grace and opulence of an earlier age: silver and crystal reflect the light from chandeliers, burnished wood glows from decades of polishing, and a pianist or harpist plays unobtrusively in the background. The haute cuisine menu changes every six months or so and, for the most part, remains quite good. There are usually at least one or two game dishes on the menu, and the seafood platter is recommended. The dessert trolley displays a selection of gâteaux and puddings; most are heavy on the whipped cream, but try the delicious fresh fruit pavlova (meringue topped with cream and fresh fruit). ⊠ *Royal Hotel, 267 Smith St.,* ☎ *031/304–0331. Jacket and tie. AE, DC, MC, V. Closed Sun.*

$$$–$$$$ ✕ **Baanthai.** On the second floor of a converted town house, this Thai restaurant brings a refreshing flavor to Durban's dining scene. Thai chefs working in an open kitchen whip up authentic dishes that make heady use of lemongrass, coriander, and *galangal* (a type of ginger). Among the starters, the beef waterfall salad (thinly sliced grilled beef tossed with onions and coriander) is excellent, as are pad Thai noodles. Other winners are the whiskey prawns, Thai crab, and the Baanthai duck—deboned fillets basted in an almost-sweet sauce—are the most popular dishes. *Brinjal* (eggplant) with chilies is a delicious vegetarian option. ⊠ *138 Florida Rd.,* ☎ *031/303–4270. AE, DC, MC, V. BYOB. Closed Sun. No lunch. Sat.*

$$$–$$$$ ✕ **Cafe 1999.** This restaurant prides itself on its celebration of tastes. Small portions are served, and the way to eat here is to order a range of items, which are all brought to the table to share. The salads are delicious, and all the meals combine unusual ingredients such as strawberry-and-leek risotto with mascarpone cheese or prawns roasted with *harissa* (spicy pepper sauce) and served on mashed leeks. ⊠ *Shop 2, Silvervause Centre, 117 Vause Rd., Musgrave,* ☎ *031/202–3406. Reservations essential. AE, DC, MC, V. No lunch weekends.*

$$$–$$$$ ✕ **Harveys.** This sophisticated restaurant has won a number of awards, including one from the prestigious International Wine and Food Society, one of only five in the country. The decor is minimalist and chic, and the food is ambrosial. The menu changes fairly frequently, but there are always excellent game dishes such as the smoked warthog starter or the venison shank. Another favorite starter is the *rotolo di fungi,* assorted wild mushrooms, spinach, and ricotta smothered in sage butter sauce. Other standout dishes include duck confit with honey and hoisin sauce and rack of lamb with a Parmesan crust served with a Provençal bean casserole. Desserts are decadent, especially the chocolate trilogy—a teardrop chocolate shell filled with bittersweet chocolate mousse and chocolate ice cream. ⊠ *77 Goble Rd., Morningside*

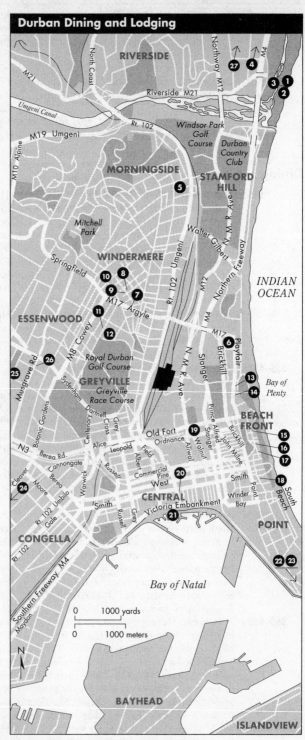

Durban Dining and Lodging

4001, ☎ *031/312–9064,* ℻ *031/312–6994. AE, DC, MC, V. Closed Sun. No lunch Mon.*

$$$ ✕ **Joop's Place.** No trip to South Africa would be complete without a good traditional steak, and without a doubt, Joop's is the best and most popular steak house in Durban. Joop's specialty is panfried steak, but the pepper steak and the Hollandse (Dutch/Afrikaans style) *biefstuk* are also great. For the exceptionally hungry, try the 800-gram T-bone. At about 21 ounces, it could easily feed more than one. ✉ *Avonmore Centre, Morningside,* ☎ *031/312–9135. Reservations essential. AE, DC, MC, V. Closed Sun.*

$$$ ✕ **Roma Revolving.** In business for nearly 30 years, this slowly revolving restaurant continues to be one of the most venerable establishments in Durban. It is still run by the original Italian owners and staff, and its breathtaking views over the entire city are complemented by the Italian charm and service. The menu focuses on Italian specialties with pasta handmade on the premises. Many ingredients are imported, but where possible local products are used, such as fresh north-coast oysters and fish purchased straight off the boats. The seafood dishes are excellent, and the mussel starters are some of the best in town. The way to order, though, is to ask Gino for the specialties of the day. ✉ *John Ross House, 32nd floor, Victoria Embankment,* ☎ *031/337–6707,* ℻ *031/337–2991. Reservations essential. AE, DC, MC, V. Closed Sun.*

$$–$$$ ✕ **Bean Bag Bohemia.** This is one of the few restaurants in Durban where you can get a good meal late at night after movies or the theater. The food served in this converted Victorian house is a wonderful mix of cosmopolitan/Mediterranean, with a decor reminiscent of Morocco. There is a vibey bar downstairs where lighter meals are served, often accompanied by a pianist or other live performers. Up rickety wooden stairs is the main restaurant. The food, clientele, and atmosphere tend to be on the trendy side. The most popular starter is the *meze* platter, which consists of Mediterranean snacks such as hummus, baba ghanouj, olives, and pita. Bohemia is well known for its vegetarian meals, but dishes such as lamb shank and duck are also good. The baked pecan praline is the best dessert. The wide, old upstairs Victorian veranda is a popular spot for brunch. ✉ *18 Windermere Rd., Morningside,* ☎ *031/309–6019. AE, DC, MC, V.*

$$–$$$ ✕ **Famous Fish Company.** The setting of this busy restaurant right at the mouth of the harbor makes up for the mostly ordinary menu and mediocre service. Sitting out on the deck, you can watch the yachts and massive tankers move in and out of the harbor, and at night the spotlights draw dolphins, which come to feed in the harbor's narrow mouth. Downstairs is a lively, sometimes noisy, but friendly pub. A comprehensive selection of shellfish and fresh line fish is served. ✉ *King George VI Battery, North Pier, Point Rd.,* ☎ *031/368–1060. AE, DC, MC, V.*

$$–$$$ ✕ **Razzmatazz.** With an ocean view to kill for, it's the perfect dining venue to while away an afternoon. Weather permitting, opt for the deck and tuck into an order of fresh oysters or the mouthwatering langoustines steamed in a Chinese bamboo basket. The chef is well known for his game dishes, so those with more adventurous palates might want to try the springbok carpaccio or fillet or the kudu gently simmered in red wine. ✉ *Cabana Beach, 10 Lagoon Dr., Umhlanga,* ☎ *031/561–5847,* ℻ *031/561–5672. Reservations essential. AE, DC, MC, V.*

$$–$$$ ✕ **Villa d'Este.** The consistently excellent Italian food here is highlighted by a fabulous seafood pasta packed with fish, prawns, langoustines, mussels, and calamari. Also good are the roast lamb or pork shank. As with many of the city's Italian restaurants, a description of the specialty dishes by the owner or chef is almost as enjoyable as the food.

⊠ *Davenport and Bulwer Rds., Glenwood,* ☎ *031/202–7920,* FAX
031/202–7921. Reservations essential. AE, DC, MC, V. Closed Mon.

$$ ✕ **Amaravath Palki.** If its authentic Indian curry you're after, look no
farther than the Palki. Chefs come from all regions of India, and the
restaurant serves both northern and southern Indian food such as tan-
doori, kebabs, and curries. There is an extensive vegetarian menu, and
it is the only restaurant in Durban that serves *dosas,* enormous crepes
made with rice flour and stuffed with a variety of fillings. The vege-
tarian dosa masala is good to share as a starter. Prawn Malai curry is
outstanding, as is the northern Indian favorite *gosht kashmiri rogan*—
a lamb curry with Kashmiri chilies. ⊠ *225 Musgrave Rd., Berea,* ☎
031/201–0019. AE, DC, MC, V. No lunch Mon.

$$ ✕ **Mo Noodles.** Don't let the name or the outside location of this Thai
★   restaurant dissuade you from coming here. This is no ordinary noo-
dle bar, but it is probably one of the best restaurants in Durban. The
decor is chic and minimalist, but not in a way that makes you feel uncomfortable and alienated. The prawn-coconut soup is a starter you'll
still be thinking about days later, and the prawn skewers in peanut dipping sauce are also stunning. Seared, marinated sesame fillet of beef
or any of the Thai-style curries are excellent. Because they don't take
reservations, go early, especially on weekend nights. ⊠ *Shop 5 Florida
Centre, 275 Florida Rd., Berea,* ☎ *031/312–4193. Reservations not
accepted. AE, DC, MC, V. Closed Sun.*

$$ ✕ **Passage to India.** At Durban's harbor mouth you can pass a long
lunch hour here watching the ships pass close by as you enjoy a se-
lection of Indian dishes such as onion *bhajiyas* (fritters) and *rogan gosht*
(lamb with yogurt). The chicken or fish *tikka* prepared in the tandoor
is also good. ⊠ *Shop No. 3, Point Waterfront,* ☎ *031/332–9106. AE,
DC, MC, V.*

$$ ✕ **Victoria Bar & Restaurant.** Adjoining the city's most charismatic and
earthy bar, this unpretentious Portuguese restaurant on the docks
serves good no-frills seafood. Red tablecloths and tightly packed tables give it a cozy appeal. If you decide on a bar lunch or supper, the
same food is slightly cheaper than in the restaurant, and you're likely
to meet some fairly colorful characters. Depending on the mood of the
chefs, your meal could be excellent or merely mediocre. Prawn curry
is a solid favorite, as is the chicken-calamari mix. Excellent main
courses are grilled or baked sole, line fish topped with a tomato-and-
onion sauce, peri-peri chicken, and grilled langoustines. A less expensive alternative to langoustines is prawns à la Victoria, done with
garlic and peri-peri. ⊠ *Point and Bell Sts.,* ☎ *031/337–4645. DC, MC,
V. Closed Sun.*

Lodging

Durban

$$$$ ☷ **Durban Hilton.** This is a massive luxury hotel adjacent to the International Convention Centre, somewhat sterile but within relatively
close walking distance to the CBD and the beachfront. There are
sprawling views of either the beachfront or city from the rooms, which
are a mixture of nouvelle safari crossed with ethnic chic. The Rainbow Room restaurant serves an excellent buffet and an unusual à la
carte menu. Executive floors have a small club room where breakfast
is served. Public areas are vast and impressive with marble pillars and
a pianist tinkling away on a baby grand. The Hilton also boasts impeccable service. ⊠ *12–14 Walnut Rd., Durban (mailing address: Box
11288, Marine Parade 4056),* ☎ *031/336–8100,* FAX *031/336–8200.
327 rooms, 19 suites. 2 restaurants, bar, in-room data ports, pool, hair
salon, health club, business services. AE, DC, MC, V.*

$$$$ ☆ **Royal Hotel.** The city's best hotel and a cherished Durban institution, the Royal stands in the heart of the CBD. The hotel caters mainly to businesspeople, but it's also an excellent option for tourists who don't insist on a beachfront location. It dates to 1842—the city's infancy—and has frequently hosted visits by British royals. The original Royal was replaced in 1978 by a high-rise, and all that remains of the old building is the grand Royal Grill. Nevertheless, the hotel maintains some luxurious and classic touches. The elegant rooms are a subtle blend of colonial and African furnishings: crystal, woven cloth, red wine, and carved wood, with antique bird prints on the walls. Request a room on the upper floor for a spectacular view of Durban Harbor. ⊠ 267 *Smith St. (Box 1041), Durban 4000,* ☎ *031/333–6000,* FAX *031/333–6002,* WEB *www.theroyal.co.za. 272 rooms, 17 suites. 4 restaurants, 3 bars, room service, pool, health club, squash. AE, DC, MC, V.*

$$$ ⛳ **The Edward.** One of Durban's oldest hotels, originally built in 1939 in a classic colonial style, the Edward has changed hands a few times, and although it's almost been restored to its former elegance, it seems to have lost a little of its soul. However, the service is excellent, and the stylish cut-glass chandeliers, molded ceilings, and subtle art deco details bring to mind echoes of Durban's older, more refined past. Rooms are tastefully furnished; 10 have balconies overlooking the sea, and the others have bay windows with sea views. The hotel faces South Beach, just a 10-minute walk from the CBD. ⊠ *Marine Parade (Box 105), Durban 4000,* ☎ *031/337–3681,* FAX *031/332–1692,* WEB *www.proteahotels. com. 100 rooms, 11 suites. 3 restaurants, 2 bars, room service, pool, hair salon, business services. AE, DC, MC, V.*

$$$ ⛳ **Holiday Inn Durban Elangeni.** Formerly known as the Elangeni, this is one of the best hotels on the Durban beachfront. The 21-story high-rise overlooks North Beach, a two-minute drive from the CBD, and attracts a mix of business, conference, and holiday guests. All rooms have views of the water, but request a room on an upper floor for a full-on ocean view. Rooms are small and narrow, with a beachlike seaside feel at odds with the formality of the marbled lobby and public rooms. The hotel has one of the few Japanese restaurants in the city as well as a first-class Indian restaurant. ⊠ *63 Snell Parade (Box 4094), Durban 4000,* ☎ *031/362–1300,* FAX *031/332–5527,* WEB *www.southernsun.com. 446 rooms, 10 suites. 3 restaurants, 2 bars, room service, 2 pools, hair salon, health club, business services. AE, DC, MC, V.*

$$$ ☆ **The Quarters.** Four converted Victorian homes comprise the city's most intimate boutique hotel, a contemporary European-style property with a colonial African feel. Rooms have mahogany furniture, cream damask-covered beds, and sunken tubs in the luxurious bathrooms. Many of the rooms have small verandas facing onto Florida Road with its swaying palm trees and sometimes rather busy traffic; but the rooms themselves all have double-glazed windows and are quiet. ⊠ *101 Florida Rd., 4001,* ☎ *031/303–5246,* FAX *031/303–5269,* WEB *www.quarters.co.za. 25 rooms. Restaurant. AE, DC, MC, V. BP.*

$$–$$$ ⛳ **The Palace Protea.** Facing right onto North Beach, this self-catering hotel is a good option for families; couples can probably do better at one of the nearby Holiday Inns. For groups of up to six, the large deluxe suites are ideal and incredibly cheap. Suites feature fully equipped kitchens, living rooms, two bedrooms, and outstanding sea views. Standard rooms, on the other hand, are small and basic. ⊠ *Marine Parade and Foster Pl. (Box 10539), Durban 4056,* ☎ *031/701–9999,* FAX *031/701–9966. 76 rooms. Restaurant, bar, 2 pools, steam room. AE, DC, MC, V.*

$$ ⛳ **Holiday Inn Garden Court—Marine Parade.** If you don't need room service, porters, or a concierge, choose this hotel over the more expensive Crowne Plaza, for the rooms are just as pleasant. You can't beat the location either, midway between South and North beaches, and the CBD is just a 10-minute walk. Rooms are attractive and modern, with textured wallpaper, bold floral bedspreads, and a small sitting area. All face the sea, but request one on an upper floor. Views from the pool deck on the 30th floor are superb. ⊠ *167 Marine Parade (Box 10809), Durban 4056,* ☎ FAX *031/337–3341,* WEB *www.southernsun.com. 340 rooms, 6 suites. Restaurant, bar, indoor pool. AE, DC, MC, V.*

$ 🖬 **The Benjamin.** Perched on trendy Florida Road with its excellent restaurants and nightlife, this small hotel is an excellent value for the money. In one of Durban's transformed historic buildings, it is ideally located on the major transport routes to both the beaches and the CBD—both approximately five minutes away. The residents' lounge is quiet and elegant but still warm and comfortable, as are the stylish rooms. The breakfast room has big glass doors opening out onto a small pool. ⊠ *141 Florida Rd., Morningside, 4001,* ☎ *031/303–4233,* FAX *031/303–4288,* WEB *www.benjamin.co.za. 45 rooms. Breakfast room, in-room data ports, pool. AE, DC, MC, V. BP.*

$ 🖬 **Blue Waters.** A Durban landmark, the family-owned Blue Waters stands right at the end of the Golden Mile. This means it's quieter than most of the other beachfront hotels. The circular resident's lounge, with its floor-to-ceiling windows, is a wonderful place to enjoy the stunning sea views and elegant tea and scones. The '60s-style mosaic indoor pool is also delightful. The rooms are comfortable, and all have balconies—which few of the other beachfront hotels can boast. ⊠ *175 Snell Parade, 4056,* ☎ *031/332–4272,* FAX *031/332–5817,* WEB *www.bluewatershotel.co.za. 250 rooms, 14 suites. Breakfast room, dining room, lounge, room service, pool, hair salon, sauna, squash. AE, DC, MC, V.*

$ 🖬 **Parade Hotel.** Popular among visiting surfers and other beach-lovers, this inexpensive hotel is a good value, if a little noisy at times. All rooms, including the family suites, have sea views and private balconies. The sundeck and pool room are usually full of young people. ⊠ *191 Marine Parade, 4001,* ☎ *031/337–4565,* FAX *031/332–0251,* WEB *www.paradehotel.co.za. 70 rooms, 9 family suites. 2 bars, breakfast room, billiards. AE, DC, MC, V. BP.*

Umhlanga Rocks

$$$$ 🖬 **Beverly Hills Sun.** In a high-rise building right on the beach, this upmarket hotel is popular with both vacationers and businesspeople. The service is excellent and the facilities superb. However, if you're the sort of beachgoer who likes to loll about in a bathing suit, you may find this hotel too formal. The public lounge, festooned with huge floral arrangements and yards of gathered drapes, serves a full silver-service tea in the afternoon, and a pianist plays in the evening. Guest rooms are fairly small, but all have terrific sea views, particularly those on the upper floors. The decor makes extensive use of bleached-wood furniture and bold floral fabrics. For a more open, beachlike feel, take one of the cabanas, large duplex rooms that open onto a lovely pool deck. ⊠ *Lighthouse Rd. (Box 71), Umhlanga Rocks 4320,* ☎ *031/561–2211,* FAX *031/561–3711,* WEB *www.interconti.com. 90 rooms, 5 suites, 10 cabanas. 2 restaurants, 2 bars, room service, pool, hair salon. AE, DC, MC, V. CP.*

$$$$ 🖬 **Zimbali Lodge.** One of only two luxury lodges in the province with direct access to the beach, this luxurious lodge's setting is in one of only three remaining coastal forests in the province. The decor is a stylish mix of colonial Malaysian/African, with lots of glass, dark wood, and rough woven fabrics. The rooms have crisp white linen and wooden carvings and balconies that look out onto the forest and the lake beyond. Its a wonderful place to laze around the pool, play a round of golf, or take a swim in the private Mauritian-style pool on the beach.

The service is warm and friendly. ✉ *Box 404, Umhlali 4390, 20 km (12 mi) north along the M4 from Umhlanga,* ☎ *032/538–1007,* FAX *032/ 538–1019,* WEB *www.sunint.co.za. 8 lodges, 76 rooms. Breakfast room, room service, 2 pools, hair salon, steam room, 18-hole golf course, 2 tennis courts, health club, beach, horseback riding, playgrounds. AE, DC, MC, V.*

$$$ 🏨 **Breakers Resort.** This resort enjoys an enviable position at the northern tip of Umhlanga, surrounded by the wilds of the Hawaiian Forest and overlooking the unspoiled wetlands of Umhlanga Lagoon. Of all the resorts in Umhlanga, this one suffers the least from crowds— amble north along the beach, and you will scarcely see another soul and no buildings. The disadvantage is that you probably need a car to get into town, and you can't swim directly in front of the resort be- cause the surf's too dangerous. The building is unattractive, with long, depressing corridors, but the rooms themselves are fine, with fully equipped kitchens and great views of the beach and lagoon. ✉ *88 La- goon Dr. (Box 75), Umhlanga Rocks 4320,* ☎ *031/561–2271,* FAX *031/561–2722,* WEB *www.southernsun.com. 80 rooms. 2 restaurants, bar, pool, tennis court, playground. AE, DC, MC, V. CP.*

$$$ 🏨 **Cabana Beach.** For families that want a traditional beach holiday, you
★ can't do better than this large resort in Umhlanga. Children under 18 stay free, the bathing beach lies directly in front of the hotel, and there are tons of activities to keep kids happy. Considering its huge size, the Cabana is one of the most attractive hotels on the beach: a Spanish-style whitewashed structure that steps down to the sea in a series of terraces. The room decor is simple, comfortable, and absolutely appropriate for a beach holiday. Each cabana comes with a fully equipped kitchen, a din- ing-living area, and a veranda with great sea views. Request a tower or beachfront apartment for the most attractive and practical space con- figuration. ✉ *10 Lagoon Dr. (Box 10), Umhlanga Rocks 4320,* ☎ *031/ 561–2371,* FAX *031/561–3522,* WEB *www.cabanabeach.southernsun.co.za. 217 rooms. 3 restaurants, bar, 2 pools, tennis court, health club, squash. AE, DC, MC, V. CP.*

Nightlife and the Arts

What's on in Durban, a free monthly publication put out by the tourism office, lists a diary of upcoming events. The "Entertainment" section of the *Sunday Tribune,* Durban's principal newspaper, and the *Mail & Guardian,* a weekly tabloid, are good information sources. Tick- ets for shows, movies, concerts, and other events can be obtained through **Computicket** (☎ 031/304–2753) or **Ticketweb** (☎ 0861/400– 500), which have outlets throughout the city.

The Arts

The **Playhouse** (✉ Smith St., across from City Hall, ☎ 031/369– 9555) stands at the heart of Durban's cultural life. The complex en- compasses five performing arts venues, and the Playhouse Company stages productions of music, ballet, drama, opera, and cabaret. The Playhouse is also home to the Natal Philharmonic Orchestra.

NIGHTCLUBS AND LIVE MUSIC

Famed for its foam parties and mind-bending shooters, **Bourbon St.** (✉ Argyle Rd., Greyville, ☎ 031/309–6939) is strictly for those under 25. **Rivets,** at the Hilton Hotel (✉ 12 Walnut Rd., ☎ 031/336–8110), offers some of the best jazz in Durban and lets you rub shoulders with the city's rich and wanna-be famous. One of the oldest and best- known downtown clubs, **Zoom** (✉ 19 Dick King St., City Center, ☎ 031/337–6916) attracts a mixed-race crowd that keeps coming back for the red-hot DJs and occasional live music. **Zansi Bar** (✉ BAT Centre, ☎ 031/368–2029) promotes local bands and shows off a breath-taking harbor view. On Durban's Point, **330** (✉ 330 Point Rd., ☎ 031/337–7172) attracts a hip crowd of models and glitterati with loud techno music. In Morningside, **Bonkers** (✉ Hotel California, 17 Florida Rd., ☎ 031/303–1146) is a club that caters to the over-30 crowd and has regular karaoke evenings.

Outdoor Activities and Sports

Beaches

The sea near Durban, unlike that around the Cape, is comfortably warm year-round: in summer the water temperature can top 27°C (80°F), whereas in winter 19°C (65°F) is considered cold. All of KwaZulu-Natal's main beaches are protected by shark nets and staffed with lifeguards, and there are usually boards stating the wind direction, water temperature, and the existence of any dangerous swimming conditions. The **Golden Mile,** stretching from South Beach all the way to Snake Park Beach, is packed with people, who enjoy the water slides, singles bars, and fast-food joints. A little farther north are the **Umhlanga Rocks beaches,** and on the opposite side of the bay are the less commercialized beaches on Durban's Bluff. A visit to the Wildlife Society of South Africa's coastal reserve and environmental education center, at **Treasure Beach on the Bluff,** will give you an idea of what this section of the coast looked like before it was commercially developed. Another pretty beach and coastal walk, just north of the **Umhlanga Lagoon,** leads to miles of near-empty beaches backed by virgin bush. Please note: You should not walk alone on deserted beaches or carry any valuables or jewelry.

Participant Sports

FISHING

Lynski Charters (☎ 031/561–2031) offers deep-sea fishing for barracuda, sailfish, marlin, shark, and reef fish. Trips, in a 35-ft game-fish boat, cost R2,500 for up to six people fishing, although the boat can take nine people altogether. The price includes equipment, tackle, bait, and cold drinks. **Mike Plotz** (☎ 031/561–3259), of Umhlanga Fishing Charters, will take you deep-sea fishing or dolphin viewing. He launches his small ski boat right off the beach and through the waves. Fishing trips cost about R250 per person, including equipment, tackle, bait, and refreshments; dolphin trips are R100.

GOLF

As long as you tee off between 7 and 8:30 on weekdays, you can play on two of the country's best courses while in town. **Durban Country Club** (✉ Walter Gilbert Rd., ☎ 031/312–8282) has hosted more South African Opens than any other course and is regularly rated the best in South Africa. Tees and greens sit atop large sand dunes, and trees add an additional hazard. Fees for the 18-hole, 72-par course are R250 per person; rental clubs are available. **Zimbali Country Club** (✉ M4 Fwy. between Umdloti and Ballito, ☎ 032/538–1041) incorporates one of the three remaining coastal forests in the province. The 18-hole world-class course was designed by American Tom Weiskopf and lies amid the sand dunes above a secluded beach, natural springs, and a lake. There is a fully stocked pro shop. The greens fee for 18 holes is R60 Monday and Thursday; other times it's R120. Compulsory cart rental is R100; rental clubs are available for R100. **Roger Manning Golf Shop** (✉ Windsor Park Golf Course, N.M.R. Ave., ☎ 031/303–1728) also rents out clubs for R50–R150 per day. **Royal Durban Golf Club** (✉ 16 Mitchell Crescent, Greyville, ☎ 031/309–1373), inside the Greyville Racecourse, offers no protection from the wind and makes hitting the narrow fairways very difficult. The fee for the 18-hole, par-72 course is R120 per person; rental clubs are available.

Spectator Sports

CRICKET

Kingsmead Cricket Ground (✉ 2 Kingsmead Close, ☎ 031/335–4200) is home to the Natal provincial team and a frequent venue for international test matches between South Africa and touring teams from abroad.

HORSE RACING

The main horse-racing season extends from May to August. Meets are usually held Wednesday and Saturday and tend to consist of 9 or 10 races. The area's three racecourses take turns holding meets. **Greyville** (✉ Avondale Rd., ☎ 031/309–4545) is almost in the city center and is the only course in the province to hold night meets, usually midweek. **Clairwood Park** is out near the airport, Exit 7 or 8 off Southern Freeway (☎ 031/42–5332), 11 km (7 mi) out of town. **Scottsville** (✉ New England Rd., exit off N3, ☎ 0331/45–3405), in Pietermaritzburg, is a pretty track in pleasant surroundings. The **Durban July**, at Greyville—probably the country's most famous horse-racing event—is a day when the outrageous fashions worn by racing fans attract almost as much attention as the horses themselves.

OFF THE BEATEN PATH

GREYVILLE RACECOURSE – Those with a passion for horse racing may enjoy Greyville Racecourse's **Stud Farm Tours** (☎ 031/561–4151). These one-day trips run from mid-May to the end of August and give you a wonderful opportunity to spend a relaxing day in the beautiful Midlands. Kick off the day with a Continental breakfast at Greyville Racecourse before you amble up to three of the top stud farms in the country. The R90 tour also includes a fabulous buffet lunch at the exquisite Rawdon's Hotel.

RUGBY

KwaZulu-Natal's Sharks play at **Kings Park Rugby Ground** (✉ Jacko Jackson Dr., ☎ 031/312–6368). The Sharks are strong contenders in the annual round-robin Bankfin Currie Cup competition.

SURFING

Surfing has a fanatical following in Durban, and several international tournaments are staged on the city's beaches, at nearby Umhlanga Rocks, or on the bluff. Crowds of more than 10,000 are not unusual for night surfing competitions or the annual Mr. Price Pro surfing championship event. This event became famous as the Gunston 500 and is the longest-running event of its kind in the world. The most popular surfing beach is probably the Bay of Plenty, on Durban's Golden Mile; for more experienced surfers there's Cave Rock on the Bluff.

Shopping

African Art Centre. This nonprofit center acts as a sales outlet for the work of rural artisans. It carries an excellent selection of original African arts and crafts, including Zulu beadwork, ceramics, wood sculptures, and beautifully crafted wire baskets. The store will ship purchases overseas. ✉ *Old Station Bldg., 1st floor, Pine St., City Center,* ☎ *031/304–7915.* ☺ *Weekdays 8:30–5, Sat. 9–2.*

Elizabeth Gordon Gallery. In a lovely Victorian home close to the trendy and vibrant Florida Road, the small gallery carries a wide selection of local and international artists and photographers. There are often opportunities to meet local artists at collaborative exhibitions.

Prints are also on sale. ⊠ *68 Windermere Rd., Morningside,* ☎ *031/ 309–4370.* ⊙ *Weekdays 9–4:30, Sat. 8:30–12:30.*

NSA Gallery. This small, trendy complex supports and promotes both local and international artists and craftsmen, whose creations are sold in the crafts shop. ⊠ *166 Bulwer Rd., Glenwood,* ☎ *031/22–3686.* ⊙ *Tues.–Fri. 9–5, Sat. 9–4, Sun. 10–4.*

The most exciting market in the city is the **Victoria Street Market,** where you can buy everything from recordings of African music to curios and curry spices. Bargaining is expected. If you don't want to go all the way to the Indian District for your spices, stop in at the **Haribhai & Sons Spice Emporium** (⊠ 31 Pine St., ☎ 031/332–6662), near the beachfront. You can select from a tantalizing array of fresh spices, as well as hand-mixed curry powders. The shop also sells mixes for creating your own vegetable *atchars* (Indian relishes), tea masala, and chili bites.

A busy shopping mall a nice short walk from the International Convention Centre and Durban Hilton is the **Workshop** (⊠ 99 Aliwal St., ☎ 031/304–9894), a slick renovation of the city's cavernous old railway workshops, where you'll find everything from expensive clothing stores to curio shops, cinemas, and fast-food restaurants. **Musgrave Centre** (⊠ Musgrave Rd., Berea, ☎ 031/21–5129) has everything from pharmacies to banks, travel agents, restaurants, and movie theaters. A giant mall in the suburbs north of the city is the **Pavilion** (⊠ Jack Martens Dr., Westville, ☎ 031/265–0558), which until Gateway opened was by far the biggest and best in the metropolitan area. **La Lucia Mall** (⊠ 90 William Campbell Dr., ☎ 031/562–8420), on the way between the city and Umhlanga Rocks, is fairly expensive. One of the biggest malls in the southern hemisphere, **Gateway** (⊠ corner Gateway Rd. and Sugar Close, Umhlanga Ridge, ☎ 031/566–2332) includes a rooftop drive-in movie theater, indoor basketball court, the world's biggest indoor rock-climbing wall, an IMAX and live theater, 23 movie theaters, and an adventure golf course. Apart from shopping, the main attraction is the wave pool, which has the world's first constantly rolling wave.

Flea Markets

KwaZulu-Natal has some of the best flea markets around. One of the most popular is the **Essenwood Flea Market** (⊠ Essenwood Rd., Berea, ☎ 031/208–9916), held every Saturday until 2, with a variety of classy stalls selling leather work, stained glass, and restored wooden furniture in a beautiful park setting. Also not to be missed is the **Stables** (⊠ Newmarket horse stables, Jacko Jackson Dr., next to King's Park Rugby Stadium, ☎ 031/301–9900), an upscale moonlight market open Wednesday and Friday evenings 6 PM–10 PM and Sunday 11–5, except for June and July. **South Plaza Market** (⊠ Durban Exhibition Centre, ☎ 031/301–9900) has more than 500 indoor and outdoor stalls and is open every Sunday 10–4:30. The **Point Flea Market** (⊠ harbor entrance, outside Thirstys/Famous Fish Company, ☎ 031/368–5436) has dozens of open-air stalls selling cheap but good leather works, clothes, and ethnic jewelry and is open on weekends and public holidays 9–5. **Farepark Market** (⊠ West and Farewell Sts., ☎ 031/368–2190) has permanent stalls in rustic cabins and is open daily 8–5. The **Open Air Amphitheatre Market** (⊠ Amphitheatre Gardens, North Beach) is open Sunday from 8:30 to 4 and sells traditional African crafts, cotton candy, samosas, and cheap plastic goods made in the Far East.

Side Trips from Durban

Pietermaritzburg

Pietermaritzburg lies in a bowl of hills in the Natal Midlands, 80 km (50 mi) inland from Durban. The city is the current co-capital of KwaZulu-Natal, along with Ulundi in Zululand. It's a pleasant town, with wide tree-lined streets and a temperate climate that escapes the worst of the coastal heat and humidity. Its redbrick colonial architecture offers tangible reminders of Natal's and South Africa's British past; dozens of late-19th-century buildings line the streets in the center of town. It's worth visiting just to see this slice of Victorian England.

The town is often referred to as the "Last British Outpost," even though it was first settled in 1838 by Voortrekkers escaping British rule in the Cape. The city takes its name from Pieter Maritz Retief, commonly known as Piet Retief, the famous Voortrekker leader who was murdered by the Zulu king Dingane.

Numbers in the text correspond to numbers in the margin and on the Pietermaritzburg map.

A GOOD WALK

Pietermaritzburg's city center is small, and most of the places worth visiting are within easy access of each other. Start your tour of Pietermaritzburg at the **Pietermaritzburg Publicity Association** ㉔, on Commercial Road, before crossing the street to the **Tatham Art Gallery** ㉕, that was the old Supreme Court building. The **Supreme Court Gardens** ㉖ are right next to the gallery. Across Commercial Road from the gardens stands the imposing **City Hall** ㉗. From here head down Church Street to reach the **Voortrekker Museum** ㉘. Walk back up Church Street, cross Commercial Road, and stroll along the Maritzburg Mall, a quasi–pedestrian thoroughfare lined with some superb examples of Victorian architecture. Fronting the Colonial Building is a **statue of Gandhi** ㉙. Next, turn left down Greys Inn Lane and then take another left toward Change Lane, continuing on to the **Old Natal Parliament** ㉚, on Longmarket Street. Back on Commercial Road, turn right and then right again onto Loop Street to reach the eclectic **Natal Museum** ㉛. To visit the **Macrorie House Museum** ㉜, a little more than 1 km (½ mi) southwest of Commercial Road on Loop Street (at the corner of Pine Street), you probably need a car. For a good view of Pietermaritzburg, drive back down Loop Street and turn left on Commercial Road, which after a while becomes Old Howick Road. Follow the signs to **World's View** ㉝.

TIMING

Even though many of the sidewalks are shaded and the mall is quite leafy, it is wise to get any serious walking done with either in the cooler earlier morning hours or in late afternoon, particularly in summer. Set aside a few hours in the morning to do this walk, and when the heat begins to settle in, take a drive out to World's View for a panoramic view of the town.

SIGHTS TO SEE

㉗ **City Hall.** Built in 1900, this grand building is the largest all-brick structure in the southern hemisphere. It's a classic Victorian edifice, notable for its stained-glass windows, soaring clock tower, and ornate gables and domes. You can take a self-guided tour with brochures available at the reception desk. ⊠ *Church St. and Commercial Rd.,* ☏ *no phone.* ⌨ *Free.* ☉ *Weekdays 8:30–4:30.*

㉜ **Macrorie House Museum.** This lovely residence with a corrugated-iron roof and ornate ironwork is typical of old Pietermaritzburg. Bishop

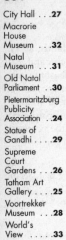

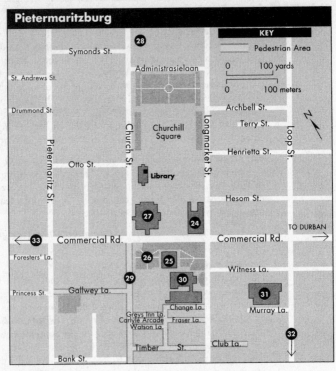

Macrorie lived in the house from 1870 to 1892, and it's been furnished to reflect that period. ⊠ *Loop and Pine Sts.,* ☎ *033/394–2161.* ▨ *R5.* ☉ *Mon. 11–4, Tues.–Fri. 9–1.*

③① Natal Museum. One of five national museums in the country, this contains a little of everything: a natural science hall displays dinosaurs, African animals, sea life, and Natal birds; a history section re-creates an 1880s Pietermaritzburg street, complete with a settler's cottage, shops, a pharmacy, and a blacksmith. The display on sub-Saharan cultures is by far the most interesting, highlighting religious, ceremonial, military, and household artifacts from across the continent. Several San (Bushman) rock paintings are on display, too. ⊠ *237 Loop St.,* ☎ *033/345–1404,* WEB *www.nmsa.org.za.* ▨ *R4.* ☉ *Weekdays 9–4:30, Sat. 10–4, Sun. 11–3.*

③⓪ Old Natal Parliament. The building once housed the twin-chamber colonial parliament. A statue of Queen Victoria stands in front of the red-brick building, which was erected in 1889. ⊠ *Longmarket St. and Commercial Rd.,* ☎ *033/345–3175.* ☉ *Tours by appointment only.*

②④ Pietermaritzburg Publicity Association. The office distributes detailed pamphlets and maps of the town. It's in a classic redbrick building erected in 1884 to house the Borough Police. In those days the bell tower signaled a curfew for blacks at 9 each night. ⊠ *177 Commercial Rd.,* ☎ *033/345–1348,* WEB *www.pmbtourism.co.za.* ☉ *Weekdays 8–5, Sat. 8–3, Sun. 9–3.*

②⑨ Statue of Gandhi. The statue marks the centenary of the day in 1893 when Gandhi, an Indian who had come to South Africa as a lawyer, was thrown off a train at Pietermaritzburg station because he was riding in a whites-only carriage. He later stated: "My active nonviolence began from that date." ⊠ *Church Street Mall.*

㉖ **Supreme Court Gardens.** The gardens are the city's memorial park. Several monuments commemorate those who died in wars that raged in this country and abroad: the Zulu War of 1879, the South African War (1899–1902), and World War I. The monuments all have a very English feel, emphasized by the legends on the commemorative stones extolling Queen, Country, and Empire. ⊠ *Commercial Rd. at Church St.*

㉕ **Tatham Art Gallery.** Completed in 1871 and housed in the old Supreme Court, the gallery is yet another of Pietermaritzburg's fine redbrick colonial structures. The museum is first-rate, with a solid collection of 19th-century English and French paintings. Of keenest interest, though, is the South African Collection, which displays works by contemporary black and white artists, including linocuts and such traditional crafts as beadwork, baskets, and tribal earplugs. The museum also presents changing exhibits. ⊠ *Commercial Rd. at Church St., across from Publicity Association,* ☎ *033/342–1804.* ☞ *Free.* ☉ *Tues.–Sun. 10–6.*

㉘ **Voortrekker Museum.** The museum occupies the Church of the Vow, an immensely important monument in the eyes of many Afrikaners. After the murder of Voortrekker leader Piet Retief in 1838, the Voortrekkers sought revenge on the Zulus and their king Dingane. A Boer commando under the leadership of Andries Pretorius vowed to build a church if God granted them victory. The result was the Battle of Blood River, in which 3,000 Zulus died and the Boers managed to emerge without a single casualty. Constructed in 1841 in typical Cape Dutch style, the church now houses a variety of Voortrekker artifacts, including an old wagon, flintlock rifles, and Piet Retief's prayer book. Next door, the thatched home of Andries Pretorius is also open to the public. ⊠ *Longmarket St.,* ☎ *033/394–6834.* ☞ *R3.* ☉ *Weekdays 9–4, Sat. 9–1.*

㉝ **World's View.** The spectacular outlook has panoramic views of the city and miles of surrounding countryside. The viewpoint lies on the route used by the Voortrekkers on their long migration from the Cape in the 19th century. A large diagram traces their route and labels the major landscape features. ⊠ *From town follow Commercial Rd. northwest until it turns into Howick Rd.; then follow signs to overlook.*

DINING

$–$$ ✕ **Tatham Coffee Shop.** On the second floor of the Tatham Art Gallery, this pleasant café serves a wonderful selection of teas and coffees, as well as light meals and desserts. Among the heartier dishes are chicken curry, quiche, and lasagna. If the weather's fine, sit outside on the narrow veranda overlooking Commercial Road. ⊠ *Commercial Rd. at Church St.,* ☎ *033/342–8327. No credit cards. Closed Mon.*

$ ✕ **Botanic Gardens Tea Shop.** One of the more pleasant places to spend an hour in town is the tea shop in the Botanic Gardens. You can relax over breakfast or a light lunch on a shady patio overlooking the enormous old trees and gardens. The shop has a great selection of teatime cakes. ⊠ *Botanic Gardens, Mayors Walk, Prestbury,* ☎ *033/342–207. MC, V. Closed Tues. No dinner.*

Valley of a Thousand Hills

The Valley of a Thousand Hills takes its name from the plunging gorges, hills, and valleys just 45 km (27 mi) inland from Durban. In the early part of the 19th century, before cars were introduced, transport wagons would travel from the port of Durban up along the ridge of the Valley of a Thousand Hills into the hinterland, where the mining industry was burgeoning. Today the Old Main Road (M103) still runs between Durban and Pietermaritzburg winding through a number of villages, offering stunning views out over the hills and valleys.

It is along this route that the Comrades Marathon—South Africa's most famous road race—is run. For purposes of exploring, the area has been organized into six routes by the **Thousand Hills Tourism Association** (⊠ Old Main Rd., Botha's Hill, 3660, ☎ 031/777–1874, WEB www.tourism.1000hills.com). A favorite with Durbanites, the routes wind through villages, past coffee shops, art galleries, restaurants, quaint pubs, small inns, farms, and nature reserves. There are a number of excellent B&Bs, small inns, and lodges in the area, often with fantastic views of the gorges.

The main route through the Valley of a Thousand hills is called the T1. It follows the M13 out of Durban, up Field's Hill, through the village of Kloof, past Everton, Gillits, and Winston Park, and joins the Old Main Road (M103) at Hillcrest. A number of small shopping centers along the M103 sell a variety of goods, from crafts to old furniture, and there are some excellent coffee shops, restaurants, and small hotels as well as cultural attractions. At the end of the M103 is Monteseel. Drive along the dirt roads to the viewing point for one of the best uninterrupted views of the Thousand Hills. There are four other routes in the Thousand Hills area. They are the Kranzkloof Route, the Assagay Averston Route, the Isithumba Route, and the Shongweni Shuffle.

SIGHTS TO SEE

Most shopping centers do not post hours, as individual stores set their own opening and closing times. For the most part, shop hours are daily from 9 to 4:30.

Assagay Coffee. The turnoff to Assagay Coffee is just before Heidi's Farm Stall. This homegrown coffee can be bought at most shops in the area and is very popular with locals. You can take a tour of the farm to see how beans are grown, roasted, and packaged. ⊠ *Just off Old Main Rd., Bothas Hill,* ☎ *031/765–2941.* ⊡ *Tours R10.* ☺ *Weekdays 8–4, Sat. 10–4.*

The Fainting Goat. A fairly ordinary looking shopping center, it has a very good secondhand furniture shop, a coffee roaster, and lively restaurant selling German specialties. Stop in at the fiber design shop for quality woven rugs and tapestries. ⊠ *Old Main Rd., Bothas Hill,* ☎ *031/765–5731.*

Heidi's Farm Stall. A long windy road up to Heidi's Farms Stall, on your left, gets you to your first real siting of the Thousand Hills. Along with fruit and vegetables, Heidi's sells everything from homemade cheese and farm milk to preserves and honey. ⊠ *Old Main Rd., Bothas Hill,* ☎ *031/765–3024.* ☺ *Daily 7–5.*

The Heritage Market. This pseudo-Victorian market is rather quaint and colorful, if a little contrived. It has more than 100 specialty stores dotted around a wonderful little central bandstand with rose gardens and twirling vines. There are a number of good coffee shops and restaurants, as well as secondhand book shops and numerous crafts shops. ⊠ *Old Main Rd., Hillcrest,* ☎ *031/765–2500.*

PheZulu Safari Park. Popular with big tour buses, PheZulu is the equivalent of a tourist fast-food venue where you can get your quick-fix African experience. A tour of the cultural village with its traditional beehive huts gives some insight into African traditions, and there are performances of traditional Zulu dancing, but the operation is not as vibrant or professional as the cultural villages up north in Zululand. An old-fashioned crocodile farm and snake park is fairly interesting, if a little tacky. The curio shop is enormous, and it is possible to get just about any type of African memento or booklet imaginable. ✉ *Old Main Rd., Drummond,* ☎ *031/777–1000,* WEB *www.phezulusafaripark. co.za.* ✉ *R40.* ☉ *Daily 8–4:30, shows at 10, 11:30, 1:30, and 3:30.*

☺ **Rob Roy Hotel.** This is probably one of the best lookout points for a view of the Valley of a Thousand Hills. On the lawns you'll find a tea garden where you can enjoy tea and scones. The service is not always that great, but the view makes up for it. There is a children's animal farmyard and the Izintaba Cultural Village, where there are fairly lackluster performances of traditional Zulu dancing and cultural celebrations. ✉ *Old Main Road, Bothas Hill,* ☎ *031/777–1305,* WEB *www. robroyhotel.co.za.* ✉ *Cultural village R25.* ☉ *Performances daily at 10, 11:30, 1:30, and 3:30.*

The Sugar Loaf Centre. Just before you start the steep ascent to Bothas Hill from Hillcrest and Assagay is a fairly scrappy-looking little center on the left-hand side of the road. Despite its appearance, there are some interesting shops selling handwoven rugs, fresh farm produce, all from the district, and some woodwork and furniture shops. ✉ *Old Main Rd., Assagay,* ☎ *no phone.*

DINING

$$–$$$ ✕ **The Tree House.** On the banks of the Sterkspruit River, this small wooden restaurant is built on stilts so that you have a unique view of birds flitting among the tree leaves. Summer and fall are the best times to come and sample the small menu—only two starters, two entrées, and two desserts—which changes weekly. Choices might include roast vegetables with polenta or roast lamb with rosemary and farm vegetables. ✉ *Follow signs through Hillcrest to Assagay and then on to Shongweni; or take Shongweni/Summerveld/Assagay off-ramp off the N3, then 7 km (4½ mi) into valley,* ☎ *031/769–1406 or 082/655–5931. AE, MC, V. Closed Mon.–Sat.*

$$ ✕ **Chantecler Hotel.** Eating outside in the garden of this quaint old brick, stone, and thatch hotel is Sunday tradition for Durbanites. In the winter there's a roaring fire to gather around. Breakfast is served until 11, and there's a buffet along with the regular menu. Try the soup of the day and the foot-long garlic roll for starters. The peri-peri chicken and the curries are also good. ✉ *27 Clement Stott Rd., Bothas Hill,* ☎ *031/ 765–2613,* FAX *031/765–6101. AE, DC, MC, V.*

$$ ✕ **Sprigs.** This buffet-style lunch has become something of a favorite for locals, and Durbanites will take the 20-minute drive to come here for lunch or breakfast. Breakfast is à la carte, and the lunch buffet changes daily but always includes two hot dishes, one of which is usually vegetarian, two hot quiches or savory tortes, and a variety of delicious salads. ✉ *Shop 34, Fields Shopping Centre, Kloof,* ☎ *031/764–6031. AE, DC, MC, V. Closed Sun. No dinner.*

OUTDOOR ACTIVITIES

One of the best ways to see the Valley of a Thousand Hills is a kayaking trip on the Umgeni River through the actual valleys of the hills, and there's no better outfitter to take you than **Chalupsky Paddling and Adventure School** (☎ 031/303–7336, WEB www.chalupsky.com). Oscar Chalupsky is a bit of a national celebrity, having won South Africa's version of an Iron Man–style kayaking competition almost every year it's been held. Chalupsky's professional and attentive staff, including many local Zulu guides whom Chalupsky has trained, can help even the most novice paddler feel at ease. Rates start at R400 for a half-day trip.

Durban A to Z

To research prices, get advice from other travelers, and book travel arrangements, visit www.fodors.com.

AIR TRAVEL

Durban International Airport, formerly known as Louis Botha Airport, is 16 km (10 mi) south of town along the Southern Freeway. South African Airways flies to Durban via Johannesburg. Domestic airlines serving Durban include SAA, BA/Comair, and Airlink.

The airport company operates a shuttle bus from outside the domestic terminal to the City Air Terminal in the center of town. Buses run about every hour, and the trip takes 20 minutes; the fare is R20 per person. The Magic Bus offers 24-hour minibus service between the airport and any address in Durban. Fares to the city center and beachfront are about R110 for two people. The more passengers, the cheaper it gets. Fares are slightly more expensive if you're heading in the direction of Umhlanga or if it's after 6 PM. Taxis to downtown and the beachfront from the airport should cost between R80 and R100.

➤ AIRLINES AND CONTACTS: **Durban International Airport** (☎ 031/408–1155). **Airlink** (☎ 031/408–1029). **BA/Comair** (☎ 031/450–7000). **South African Airways** (SAA; ☎ 031/450–2336). **Magic Bus** (☎ 031/561–1096). **Shuttle Bus** (⌧ Smith and Aliwal Sts., ☎ 031/21–1133).

BUS TRAVEL

Greyhound and Translux Express offer long-distance bus service to cities all over South Africa. A cheaper company, Golden Wheels, offers daily service to Johannesburg only. All intercity buses leave from New Durban Station.

Durban Transport operates two types of bus service, but you need concern yourself only with the Mynah buses. These small buses operate frequently on set routes through the city and along the beachfront and cost R2 a ride. Bus stops are marked by a sign with a mynah bird on it. The main bus depot is on Pine Street between Aliwal and Gardiner streets. You pay as you board; exact change is not required. Route information is also available at an information office at the corner of Aliwal and Pine streets.

Cheetah runs a minibus service twice daily between Durban and Pietermaritzburg and is probably the most convenient way to travel between the two cities.

➤ BUS INFORMATION: **Golden Wheels** (☎ 031/307–3363). **Greyhound** (☎ 031/309–7830). **Mynah Buses** (☎ 031/307–3503). **New Durban Station** (⌧ Off N.M.R. Ave. between Old Fort Ave. and Argyle Rd.). **Translux Express** (☎ 031/308–8111). **Cheetah** (☎ 033/342–2673).

CAR RENTAL

Avis, Budget, EuropCar, Imperial, and Tempest are rental companies with offices at the airport. The cheapest rental car costs about R130, including insurance per day, plus 85¢ per kilometer (per half mile). Prices fall dramatically if you rent for three days or more and plan to drive long distances. Another major car-rental agency is Berea Car & Bakkie Hire.

CAR TRAVEL

The easiest way to reach Pietermaritzburg from Durban is along the N3, a direct 80-km (50-mi) run. Far more interesting and scenic, however, is the route that follows Old Main Road (R103) through the Valley of a Thousand Hills and rejoins the N3 east of Pietermaritzburg.

➤ MAJOR AGENCIES: **Avis** (⌧ Ulundi Pl., City Center, ☎ 031/304–1741).

Berea Car & Bakkie Hire (⊠ 331 Berea Rd., ☎ 031/202–8410). Budget (☎ 031/408–1809). EuropCar Hire (⊠ Durban International Airport, ☎ 031/469–0667). Imperial Car Rental (⊠ 52 Stanger St., ☎ 031/337–3731). Tempest Car Hire (⊠ 47 Victoria Embankment, Esplanade, ☎ 031/368–5231).

EMBASSIES
➤ UNITED KINGDOM: **U.K. Embassy** (⊠ The Marine, Gardiner St., City Center, ☎ 031/305–2929).
➤ UNITED STATES: **U.S. Embassy** (⊠ Durban Bay House, 333 Smith St., City Center, ☎ 031/304–4737).

EMERGENCIES
Addington Hospital operates a 24-hour emergency ward.

Daynite Pharmacy is open daily until 10:30.

➤ EMERGENCY SERVICES: **Ambulance** (☎ 10177). **Fire Brigade** (☎ 031/361–0000). **Police** (☎ 10111).
➤ HOSPITALS: **Addington Hospital** (⊠ Erskine Terr., South Beach, ☎ 031/327–2000). **Entabeni Hospital** (⊠ 148 S. Ridge Rd., ☎ 031/204–1300).

➤ PHARMACIES: **Daynite Pharmacy** (⊠ West St. and Point Rd., ☎ 031/368–3666).

TAXIS
Taxis are metered and start at R2.50 with an additional R5 per kilometer (per half mile). Expect to pay about R20 from City Hall to North Beach, R80 to the airport. The most convenient taxi stands are around City Hall and in front of the beach hotels. Major taxi companies include Aussie's Radio Taxis, Bunny Cabs, Checker Radio Taxis, Deluxe Radio Taxis, and Morris Radio Taxis. Eagle Radio Taxis charges about R1 more per kilometer (per half mile) than other companies. If you're headed to the Indian Market on a weekend, consider having your taxi wait for you, as it can be difficult to flag a taxi in this neighborhood.
➤ TAXI COMPANIES: **Aussie's Radio Taxis** (☎ 031/309–7888). **Bunny Cabs** (☎ 031/332–2914). **Checker Radio Taxis** (☎ 031/465–1660). **Deluxe Radio Taxis** (☎ 031/337–1661). **Eagle Radio Taxis** (☎ 031/337–8333). **Morris Radio Taxis** (☎ 031/337–2711).

TOURS
Sarie Marais Pleasure Cruises and Isle of Capri offer pleasure cruises around Durban Bay or out to sea. Tours, which last about 90 minutes and cost between R23 and R28 per person, depart from the jetties next to the Natal Maritime Museum.

Strelitzia Tours offers daily minibus tours of Durban for about R80. The three-hour tours touch on all the major historic and scenic points in the city, including the beachfront and harbor, exclusive residential areas like Morningside, the Botanic Gardens, and the Indian District. Its specialty is the township tour, which is a must for anyone who has an interest in contemporary South African history.

Trips 'n Transport has standard sightseeing tours of Durban, including the Botanic Gardens, as well as tours to the Thousand Hills area. They can tailor-make trips for any interest.

Zulwini Safaris provides standard tours (including Drakensberg, the battlefields, game parks, and adventure travel) and designs custom tours to anywhere in the province; it also does tours for small groups. Its specialties are unusual, adventure, and off-the-beaten-path trips.

Tourism Durban has a series of city walking tours during the week for R25 per person. Tours depart from the Tourist Junction weekdays at 9:45 and return at 12:30. The Oriental Walkabout explores the Indian District, including Victoria Market and several mosques. The Historical Walkabout covers the major historic monuments in the city, while the Feel of Durban Walkabout explores some of the city's military past, including the Old Fort, Warrior's Gate, and the original armory.

➤ TOUR-OPERATOR RECOMMENDATIONS: **Isle of Capri** (☎ 031/337–7751). **Natal Maritime Museum** (⊠ Victoria Embankment at Aliwal Stand, the Point, ☎ 031/300–6324). **Sarie Marais Pleasure Cruises** (☎ 031/305–2844). **Strelitzia Tours** (☎ 031/266–9480). **Tourism Durban** (⊠ Tourist Junction, 160 Pine St., ☎ 031/304–4934). **Trips 'n Transport** (☎ 031/337–0230). **Zulwini Safaris** (☎ 033/347–1579).

TRAIN TRAVEL

New Durban Station is a huge, ghastly place that is difficult to find your way around. Spoornet's Trans-Natal train runs daily between Durban and Johannesburg, stopping at Pietermaritzburg, Estcourt, and Ladysmith. The trip takes 13 hours and costs about R180 one-way.

➤ TRAIN INFORMATION: **New Durban Station** (⊠ N.M.R. Ave., ☎ 031/308–8118). (☎ 031/308–8118).

TRAVEL AGENCIES

Rennies is the South African representative of Thomas Cook and also operates a foreign-exchange desk. It is open weekdays 8:30–4:30 and Saturday 8:30–noon. American Express is open weekdays 8–5 and Saturday 8:30–11 and has a full range of client services (no client mail pickup on Saturday). The AmEx foreign-exchange bureau is in a separate office, just 200 yards away.

➤ LOCAL AGENT REFERRALS: **American Express** (⊠ 2 Durban Club Pl., off Smith St., ☎ 031/301–5541). **AmEx foreign-exchange bureau** (⊠ 350 Smith St., ☎ 031/301–5562). **Rennies** (⊠ Durban Bay House, 333 Smith St., ☎ 031/304–1511).

VISITOR INFORMATION

The Tourist Junction, in the restored old station building, houses a number of tourist-oriented companies and services where you can find information on almost everything that's happening in Durban and KwaZulu-Natal. Among the companies represented are Tourism Durban, the city's tourism authority; an accommodations service; an intercity train reservations office; a KwaZulu-Natal Nature Conservation Service booking desk; regional KwaZulu-Natal tourist offices; and various bus and transport companies. It is open weekdays 8–5 and weekends 9–2. Sugar Coast Tourism is open weekdays 8–4:30 and Saturday 9–noon.

➤ TOURIST INFORMATION: **Sugar Coast Tourism** (⊠ Chartwell Dr. off Lighthouse Rd., Umhlanga Rocks, ☎ 031/561–4257). **Tourist Junction** (⊠ 160 Pine St., ☎ 031/304–4934).

THE DRAKENSBERG

Afrikaners call them the Drakensberg: the Dragon Mountains. To Zulus, they are uKhahlamba: the Barrier of Spears. Both are apt descriptions for this wall of rock that rises from the Natal grasslands, forming a natural fortress protecting the mountain kingdom of Lesotho. The Drakensberg is the highest range in southern Africa and possesses some of the most spectacular scenery in the country. It's a hiker's dream, and you could easily pass several days here just soaking up the awesome views. UKhahlamba/Drakensberg Park, a World Heritage Site, is the first site in South Africa to be recognized for its combination of natural and cultural attractions.

The blue-tinted mountains seem to stain the landscape, cooling the "champagne air"—as the locals refer to the heady, sparkling breezes that blow around the precipices and pinnacles. The mountains, with names like Giant's Castle, Cathedral Peak, and the Sentinel, seem to have a special atmosphere, as well as a unique topography. It's no surprise that South African–born J. R. R. Tolkien—legendary author of the cult classic *Lord of the Rings*—was inspired by the fantastic shapes of the Drakensberg massif when he created the phantasmagorical settings of his Middle Earth.

The Drakensberg is not a typical mountain range—it's actually an escarpment separating a high interior plateau from the coastal lowlands of Natal. It's a continuation of the same escarpment that divides the Transvaal highveld from the hot malarial zones of the lowveld in Mpumalanga. However, the Natal Drakensberg, or Berg, as it is commonly known, is far wilder and more spectacular than its Transvaal counterpart. Many of the peaks—some of which top 10,000 ft—are the source of crystalline streams and mighty rivers that have carved out myriad valleys and dramatic gorges. The Berg is a natural watershed, with two of South Africa's major rivers, the Tugela and the Orange, rising from these mountains. In this untamed wilderness you can hike for days and not meet a soul, and the mountains retain a wild majesty missing in the commercially forested peaks of Mpumalanga.

There are a range of places to stay in the Berg, including expensive hotels, lodges, and guest houses; campgrounds, self-catering cottages, and B&Bs. The older Berg resorts tend to be more family-oriented establishments that encourage guests to participate in outdoor activities and sports, including daily guided hikes, horseback rides, tennis, lawn bowling, even golf. However, not to be left out, many farmers in the area have opened B&Bs, which range from the quaint and the cute to the warm and the welcoming to the just plain mediocre.

Besides the hiking opportunities and the sheer beauty of the mountains, the other great attraction of the Berg is the San (Bushman) paintings. The San are a hunter-gatherer people who once roamed the entire country. More than 5,000 of their paintings are sprinkled in scores of caves and on rock overhangs throughout the Berg—probably the finest collection of rock paintings in the country. They tell the stories of bygone hunts, dances, and battles and touch on the almost mystical relationship of the San with the animals they hunted. With the arrival of the Nguni peoples from the north and white settlers from the southwest, the San were driven out of their traditional hunting lands and retreated into the remote fastnesses of the Drakensberg and the Kalahari Desert. San cattle raiding in Natal in the late 19th century occasioned harsh punitive expeditions by white settlers and local Bantu tribes, and by 1880 the last San had disappeared from the Berg. Today only a few clans remain in the very heart of the Kalahari Desert.

The best times to visit the Berg are spring (September–October) and late autumn (late April–June). Summer sees the Berg at its greenest and the weather at its warmest—and wettest, so don't forget to pack your rain gear. Vicious afternoon thunderstorms and hailstorms, which can put a severe damper on long hikes, are an almost daily occurrence. In winter the mountains lose their lush overcoat and turn brown and sere. Winter days in the valleys, site of most resorts, are usually sunny and pleasant, although there can be cold snaps, usually accompanied by overcast, windy conditions, depending on the severity of the winter.

Nights are chilly, however, and you should pack plenty of warm clothing if you plan to hike high up into the mountains or camp overnight. Snow is common at higher elevations. Hikers heading above the 10,000-ft level are obliged to sign the mountain register at the nearest Natal Parks Board/KwaZulu-Natal Nature Conservation Service office in case of emergency. Don't forget to sign out again on your return. It's also a good idea to check the weather forecast beforehand, particularly during winter (June–September), as extreme cold conditions may be experienced, many roads are closed, and hiking is dangerous and prohibited.

The Natal Drakensberg is not conducive to traditional touring. The nature of the attractions and the limited road system make a connect-the-dots tour impractical and unrewarding. Check into a resort for two or three days instead and use it as a base for hiking and exploring the immediate area.

Numbers in the margin correspond to points of interest on the Drakensberg map.

❶ A good place to start your Berg exploration is the small but fascinating **Winterton Museum.** It will give you a nice overview of the area. Most exhibits in this delightful and informative museum were donated, made, or built by people from the Winterton and other nearby communities. If you are planning to hike to see any of the San (Bushman) paintings in the Berg later in the day, first take a look at the museum's San Art Gallery, the most extensive photographic record of Berg San paintings, consisting of 10 panels of 180 photographs. The last San were seen by honeymooners in the area at the end of the 19th century. On a more contemporary note, a small but poignant display depicts Winterton residents casting their votes during the historic 1994 democratic elections. If you are planning a tour of the battlefields, pop into the reading room, where an outstanding private collection of books on the South African War is available for perusal. These volumes are used as reference sources by many of the professional battlefields tour guides. ✉ *Winterton Village,* ☎ *036/488–1885.* 🎫 *Free.* ☉ *Weekdays 9–3, Sat. 9–noon.*

The R600, accessible from the N3 via Winterton, leads to many of the resorts and attractions in the Central Berg. Seventeen kilometers (8 miles) **❷** down the R600 from Winterton is the turnoff to the **Ardmore Guest House, Ceramic Art Studio, and Tea Garden.** Started on a farm by artist Fée Berning in 1985, the studio is now home to nearly 40 Zulu and Sotho artists, each pursuing his or her own artistic visions in clay. Their ceramics have won national and international awards and are displayed in galleries around the world. The work is colorful and very African, with zebras and giraffes serving as handles on teapots, bowls, and platters. You can watch artists at work or just browse through the collection, which is housed in a converted farm shed. The studio ships purchases overseas. Have tea and scones in the tea garden or stay a night in the old farmhouse, now a unique guest house. ✉ *D275, off R600, Central Berg,* ☎ *036/468–1314.* ☉ *Weekdays 9–4:30.*

★ ❸ A couple of miles farther down the R600 is the turnoff to the **Drakensberg Boys' Choir School.** Mentioned in the same breath as the Vienna and Harlem boys' choirs, this is one of the most famous choral groups in the world. It performs in the school's auditorium on Wednesday at 3:30 and sometimes on Saturday. Performances run the musical gamut from the classics to ethnic songs. Reservations are essential. There are no performances during school holidays. ✉ *Off R600,* ☎ *036/468–1012,* 📠 *036/468–1709.*

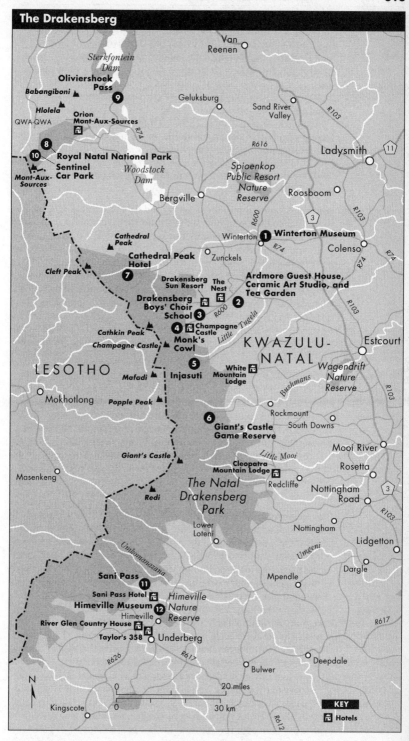

The Drakensberg

❹ The R600 runs directly into the mountains, ending at **Monk's Cowl,** a Natal Parks Board/KwaZulu-Natal Nature Conservation Service station. This is the gateway to several day and overnight hikes into the high Drakensberg. Among the highlights are a one-hour walk to Sterkspruit Falls, the largest waterfall in the area, and a 3½-hour walk to the top of the Little Berg. On this walk you pass the Sphinx—a formation that looks like the famous Egyptian monument—and Breakfast Falls before joining the Contour Trail for panoramic views of Champagne Castle, Cathkin Peak, Dragon's Back, and Sterkhorn. Hikers who wish to camp out in the mountains must sign the mountain register and pay R25 per person for the first night and R16 per person for each night thereafter. ✉ *Private Bag X2, Winterton 3340,* ☎ *036/468–1103.* 🎫 *R9.* ◷ *Oct.–Mar., daily 5 AM–7 PM; Apr.–Sept., daily 6–6.*

❺ **Injasuti,** 32 km (20 mi) down a dirt road off the Central Berg/Loskop Road, is a collection of huts set in the northern section of the Giant's Castle Game Reserve. A number of spectacular hikes start from here, including a guided 5-km (3-mi) walk (R30) up the Injasuti Valley to Battle Cave, which holds one of the most fascinating collections of San paintings in the country. Some 750 paintings cover the rock walls of the cave, but it's the subject matter that is most enthralling: one vignette clearly depicts two Bushman clans at war with one another. Tours of Battle Cave leave daily from the camp office at 8:30, and reservations are essential. ✉ *Private Bag X7010, Estcourt 3310,* ☎ *036/488–1050.* 🎫 *R9.* ◷ *Oct.–Mar., daily 5 AM–7 PM; Apr.–Sept., daily 6–6.*

❻ South of Monk's Cowl is **Giant's Castle Game Reserve,** an 85,500-acre reserve in the Central Berg region, encompassing rolling grasslands as well as some of the highest peaks in the Drakensberg. A host of trails, ranging in length from two hours to overnight, start at the main visitor center. The most popular tourist attraction is the Main Caves, which have the finest collection of San paintings in the Drakensberg. More than 500 paintings, some now barely discernible, adorn the faces of two huge rock overhangs just a 30-minute walk from the camp. Many paintings depict eland hunts, for the huge antelope holds a special religious significance for the San. 🎫 *R16.* ◷ *Guided tours daily on the hr 9–3.*

Lammergeyer Hide, set high on a cliff, is where bird-watchers can observe the endangered lammergeyer, or bearded vulture, and other birds of prey. On weekend mornings between May and September, rangers put out meat and bones for these birds below the hide (blind). In addition to giving birders a close-up view of the vultures, the feeding program is intended to draw the birds away from nearby farmland, where they might feed on poisoned carcasses. Afrikaner farmers erroneously believe that the birds kill their young livestock, hence the name *lammergeyer,* or "lamb killer." The hide accommodates a maximum of six people. If you don't have a four-by-four, take one of the hide tours, offered May through September, which are extremely popular and are sometimes fully booked six months in advance. Make sure you reserve a spot before leaving home, or call to see if there is availability the minute you arrive in the country. The fee is R100 per person. (✉ Hide Bookings, Giant's Castle Game Reserve, Private Bag X7055, Estcourt 3310, ☎ 036/32–4616). A ranger drives you up to the blind at 7:30 AM, and you're on your own for the walk back. ✉ *Mooi River toll plaza exit off N3 or Central Berg/Giant's Castle exit near Estcourt,* ☎ *036/353–3616.* 🎫 *R9.* ◷ *Oct.–Mar., daily 5 AM–7 PM; Apr.–Sept., daily 6–6.*

Another tremendous base for hikes—and drives—into the mountains ❼ is the **Cathedral Peak Hotel,** accessible from Winterton or via dirt roads off the R600. Although the Natal Parks Board/KwaZulu-Natal Nature Conservation Service levies a fee of R10 per person to enter the area, the hotel acts as the de facto center for hikers heading into the surrounding mountains. It publishes an excellent hiking booklet that describes all the trails, indicating their length and level of difficulty. A scale model of the area in the hotel lobby gives you the lay of the land before you set off. Cathedral Peak (9,900 ft) is the easiest of the major peaks to scale. Anyone who is fit and accustomed to long hikes can make the 19-km (12-mi) round-trip journey from the hotel to the summit and back; only the last portion to the summit is difficult. Budget 9–10 hours to get up and down, allowing plenty of time to drink in the view from the top—surely one of the highlights of the region. Another recommended route is the hike to Rainbow Gorge, about a six-hour trip, encompassing indigenous forest, pools, streams, and panoramic views. If you're traveling by car, drive up Mike's Pass (the road there is a little rough, so take it slowly) to experience a magnificent vista of the entire Champagne Range. This is also the start of a popular wilderness backpacking route to Ndedema Gorge, where some of the region's most superb examples of San paintings can be found. ✉ *Cathedral Peak Rd. (mailing address: P.O., Winterton, KwaZulu-Natal 3340)*, ☎ *036/488–1000*, ℻ *036/488–1889.*

⑧ Access to **Royal Natal National Park** is via the R74, north of Bergville. The park contains some of the most stunning mountain scenery in the Drakensberg. The highlight is the amphitheater, a sheer rock wall measuring an unbelievable 5 km (3 mi) across and more than 1,500 ft high. Another showstopper is the Tugela River, which flows off Mont-aux-Sources (10,836 ft) and plunges nearly 3,000 ft over the plateau in a series of five spectacular falls, making it the longest waterfall in South Africa. The park's most popular and scenic walk winds up the Tugela Gorge, a six-hour hike that crosses the river several times and passes through a tunnel before emerging into the amphitheater. Hikers often turn back at the first fording of the river; but persevere, for the scenery gets better and better. ✉ *N. Berg Rd., 19 km (8 mi) off R74*, ☎ *036/438–6303.* ☞ *R10.* ◔ *Oct.–Mar., daily 5 AM–7 PM; Apr.–Sept., daily 6–6.*

Just past the turnoff to Royal Natal National Park, the northbound ⑨ R74 begins a twisty ascent up the **Oliviershoek Pass** (6,912 ft), offering tremendous views over the plains and hills. If these views don't satiate you, continue on the R74 past the Sterkfontein Dam until the road ends at a T Junction. Turn left onto the R712 and head into Qwa Qwa, also known as Phuthaditjhaba. Follow signs to the Witsieshoek Mountain Resort. Just before the resort, the road splits and continues for ⑩ about 13 km (8 mi) to the **Sentinel Car Park** (8,580 ft), where you can follow a path some 450 ft to the very edge of the Drakensberg escarpment. The views from here are breathtaking—the entire Royal Natal National Park lies below you, and you can see all the way to Estcourt. You will need to purchase a permit from the guard at the parking lot before venturing onto the path. Visitors to the summit are restricted, so go early to avoid disappointment, particularly during popular vacation periods. The parking lot is also the starting point for a strenuous hike to the top of Mont-aux-Sources. From the parking lot it's an easy drive back down the R712 to Harrismith and the N3 to Johannesburg and Durban.

Dining and Lodging

$$ ✕ **St. Anton's Restaurant & Bar in the Mountains.** Close to the Drakensberg Boys' Choir School and with outstanding views of Champagne Castle and Cathedral Peak, St. Anton's has superfriendly service, a

wonderfully warm mountain atmosphere, and alfresco dining beside a tranquil lake. Start your meal with Thai pumpkin soup with lemongrass or the popular mushrooms St. Anton—button mushrooms in a creamy garlic cheese sauce with flaked almonds. Seafood creole and the Drakensberg trout are excellent main courses, and the chicken and prawn curry, oxtail, and pub lunches are also highly recommended. ⊠ *Off R600, Winterton,* ☎ *036/468–1218. Reservations essential. MC, V.*

$$$$ ✕🏠 **Cleopatra Mountain Farmhouse.** It would be difficult to find bet-
★ ter lodging or dining anywhere in southern Africa than at this en-
chanting hideaway tucked away at the foot of the Drakensberg Range. The lodge overlooks a trout-filled lake and is encircled by mountains and old trees. Richard and Mouse Poynton, legendary South African chefs and hosts, have renovated the 1936 family fishing farm and created a perfect combination of comfort, tranquillity, style, and excep-
tional food. Homemade biscuits, hand-painted and stenciled walls, lovingly embroidered cushions and samplers, fluffy mohair blankets, and heated towel racks are just a few of the details you'll find here. For meals you'll eat with ceremony but no pretension in an intimate din-
ing room warmed on cold days by a blazing log fire. Each meal is an occasion. Try Mozambique prawns served with Chinese rice noodles in a soy beurre blanc or loin of Midlands lamb. Then finish with a wicked, rich chocolate tart served with fresh orange sauce and a glass of Jerepigo (a port-style wine). Day trips to the surrounding area can be arranged on request. ⊠ *Box 17, Balgowan 3275,* ☎ 𝖥𝖠𝖷 *033/263–7243,* 𝖶𝖤𝖡 *www.cleomountain.com. 6 rooms, 3 suites. AE, DC, MC, V. FAP.*

$$$$ ✕🏠 **Orion Mont-Aux-Sources.** Although this hotel is more than 8 km (5 mi) from the hiking trails of Royal Natal National Park, it more than compensates with its views—stunning panoramas of the Drak-
ensberg that take in the amphitheater, the Eastern Buttress, and miles of the escarpment. These views are the hotel's greatest asset, so be sure to request a front-facing room. The rooms themselves are nondescript, reminiscent of chain hotels around the world. Likewise, the public rooms lack warmth, seeming more suited to the hotel's midweek conference business. Breakfast and dinner are served buffet style, with extensive selections ranging from roasts to vegetarian curries. ⊠ *N. Berg Rd., off R74 (mailing address: Private Bag X1670, Bergville 3350),* ☎ 𝖥𝖠𝖷 *036/438–6230,* 𝖶𝖤𝖡 *www.orion-hotels.co.za. 75 rooms. Restaurant, bar, room service, 2 pools, miniature golf, tennis court, horseback riding, squash, volleyball. AE, DC, MC, V. MAP.*

$$ ✕🏠 **Cathedral Peak Hotel.** Few hotels in South Africa can rival the
★ exquisite setting of this large resort, high above the Ulamboza River and ringed by towering peaks. Hiking trails start right from the hotel and wend their way through a dozen mountains and valleys. Choose from luxury or standard rooms or thatch bungalows. French doors open onto private verandas overlooking the gardens or the mountains, and pine furnishings give the rooms a pleasant, rustic feel. The hotel has a 9-hole golf course and daily helicopter sightseeing trips. Food is served buffet style and is fairly standard Drakensberg hotel fare, with an em-
phasis on roasts and and carved meats, fresh salads, and desserts such as trifle and cream cakes. ⊠ *Cathedral Peak Rd., 43 km (18 mi) from Winterton, mailing address: P.O., Winterton, KwaZulu-Natal 3340,* ☎ 𝖥𝖠𝖷 *488–1888 or 488–1889,* 𝖶𝖤𝖡 *www.cathedralpeak.co.za. 94 rooms. Restaurant, 2 bars, room service, pool, sauna, 9-hole golf course, tennis court, gym, horseback riding, squash, playground. AE, DC, MC, V. MAP.*

$$ ✕🏠 **The Nest.** Most guests at this well-run resort seem content to park themselves on the sun-drenched lawns, soak in the dazzling mountain views, and await the next round of tea, drinks, or meals. Few man-
age to muster the energy to drive the 8 km (5 mi) to the trailheads at

Monk's Cowl. The hotel, built by Italian prisoners of war, is one of the most attractive and appealing of the Berg resorts. Rooms are very pleasant, some with pine ceilings, heated towel racks, and under-floor heating (there are no TVs). Be sure to request a mountain-facing room. All meals are table d'hôte, with an emphasis on traditional South African cuisine, including home-cooked specialties like roasts, oxtail, and cottage pie. The quality of the food is much higher than that at most other Berg resorts. ⊠ *R600, Central Berg (mailing address: Private Bag X14, Winterton 3340),* ☎ *036/468–1068,* FAX *036/468–1390. 52 rooms. Restaurant, bar, pool, tennis court, croquet, horseback riding, mountain bikes, playground. AE, DC, MC, V. FAP.*

$$$$ ⊡ **The Drakensberg Sun Resort.** This hotel and resort is part of the Southern Sun Hotel Group but retains the ambience of a country hotel. The grounds are spectacularly set in a valley at the foot of the Champagne Range, with wonderful views of Champagne Castle and Cathkin Peak from most rooms and public areas. There are huge log fires everywhere, and the deck off the main dining area is very popular, even when the sun isn't shining. Decor is reminiscent of a country lodge, with brass lamps, pastel colors, and lots of wood. Activities focus on a range of sporting options and excursions, including horseback riding and helicopter flips. The resort is extremely family oriented, something to keep in mind during school holidays and other peak periods. ⊠ *On R600, Champagne Valley, Central Drakensberg (mailing address: Box 335, Winterton 3340),* ☎ *036/468–1000,* FAX *036/468–1224,* WEB *www.southernsun.com. 71 rooms. Restaurant, 2 bars, pool, 9-hole golf course, tennis court, gym, hiking, horseback riding, squash, volleyball, fishing. AE, DC, MC, V. MAP.*

$$ ⊡ **Champagne Castle.** Along with Cathedral Peak, this old family-style hotel enjoys one of the best settings of any of the Berg resorts. It lies right in the mountains, with magnificent views down Champagne Valley to the towering massifs of Champagne Castle and Cathkin Peak. A host of hiking trails begin practically on the hotel's doorstep, and the trailheads at Monk's Cowl lie just minutes away. There's nothing remotely fancy about the hotel itself, but it's a peaceful haven where genteel traditions linger—gentlemen are still required to wear ties to dinner. It also has a family-oriented bent, so expect to encounter South African families en masse during school vacations. Rooms, in thatch *rondawels* (traditional round huts) and bungalows scattered through the gardens, are pleasantly furnished and comfortable. Meals are served buffet style, with an emphasis on traditional South African roasts and vegetables. ⊠ *R600, Central Berg (mailing address: Private Bag X8, Winterton 3340),* ☎ *036/468–1063,* FAX *036/468–1306,* WEB *www.champagnecastle.co.za. 56 rooms. Restaurant, 2 bars, pool, putting green, tennis court, horseback riding, volleyball. AE, DC, MC, V. FAP.*

Self-Catering Lodging

You probably won't find all your self-catering requirements at resort or camp shops, which tend to be a little basic. Shop in one of the bigger towns, such as Winterton or Harrismith for Tendele and Bergville or Estcourt for Giant's Castle and Injasuti.

$ ⊡ **Giant's Castle.** This camp offers comfortable but basic accommodations in Giant's Castle Game Reserve. Hidden away in a beautiful valley close to the sheer face of the High Drakensberg, it is an ideal base for viewing the San paintings in the main caves and bearded vultures from the Lammergeyer Hide. Accommodations are either in chalets, which share communal kitchens, or in self-contained cottages. There is also a lodge accommodating seven people. If you choose this option, you must provide your own food, which is then cooked by camp staff. A store in the main office sells staples like milk, bread, charcoal, and packs of meat. ✉ *Reservations: Natal Parks Board/KwaZulu-Natal Nature Conservation, Box 13053, Cascades 3202,* ☎ *0331/845–1000,* 🖷 *0331/845–1002. 1 lodge, 1 cottage, 44 chalets. AE, DC, MC, V.*

$ 🏠 **Injasuti.** In the northern section of the Giant's Castle Game Reserve, this camp lies at the head of Injasuti Valley and has great views of Cathkin Peak, Monk's Cowl, and Champagne Castle. Cabins sleep up to six people, and all have kitchens and dining-living rooms. Electricity is available only from 5:30 until 10 each night. ✉ *Reservations: KwaZulu-Natal Nature Conservation Service, Box 1750, Pietermaritzburg 3200,* ☎ *0331/471–981,* 🖷 *0331/471–980. 18 cabins. AE, DC, MC, V.*

$ 🏠 **Tendele Hutted Camp.** Smack in the middle of Royal Natal National Park, this camp makes a great base for long hikes into the mountains. Accommodations are in a variety of bungalows, cottages, and chalets, each with excellent views of the sheer rock face of the amphitheater. You must bring all your own food, although you can purchase staples and frozen meat at the main visitor center. In the bungalows and cottages all food is prepared by camp staff, but you can do your own cooking in the chalets. There is one lodge, which accommodates six people. ✉ *Reservations: KwaZulu-Natal Nature Conservation Service, Box 13069, Cascades 3202,* ☎ *0331/845–1000,* 🖷 *0331/845–1002. 26 chalets, 2 cottages, 1 lodge. AE, DC, MC, V.*

The Southern Drakensberg

This attractive region is a ways south of the main Drakensberg Range, about a two-hour drive from Pietermaritzburg along pretty country roads. Its slightly remote location keeps it far from the madding tourist crowds.

⓫ **Sani Pass** attracts local four-by-four enthusiasts who test man and machine all the way into Lesotho. The pass, one of the traditional routes over the Drakensberg into the Lesotho highlands, ascends an incredible 5,730 ft through the upper valley of the Mkomazana River. The view from the top of row upon row of tall peaks is truly stupendous. Just inside the Lesotho border is a mountaineer's chalet known as Sani Top, the highest pub in Africa. The pass is only accessible by four-by-four vehicle, and most accommodations in the nearby country towns of Himeville and Underberg can arrange tours to the top with qualified guides. Remember to take your passport with you, as you will enter Lesotho on these excursions. The cost is approximately R160 per person for a full day, which usually includes lunch and teas.

Keen backpackers can walk the beautiful **Giants Cup Hiking Trail,** which begins halfway up the pass.

Underberg

This tiny town is accessed via a long but very pretty road from the town of Howick on the N3 (drive through Howick and take the R617 to Bulwer and then on to Underberg). Underberg comes as a surprise, set in a fertile green valley with views of the Drakensberg on the horizon. Stop first at the **Tourist Information Centre** (✉ on your left as you enter town, ☎ 033/701–1419) to find out all you need to know about the area. Most restaurants, accommodations, and attractions are on a tourist route known as the Sani Saunter, which doesn't necessarily mean they are all recommended.

Much of the area is accessed via a network of rough dirt roads. Although most are suitable for regular cars, drive carefully and slowly. If you should get a flat, stop and fix it immediately; you could severely damage your tire rims on pebbles if you don't.

$ ✕🏠 **River Glen Country House.** At this delightful and intimate inn set on a hill and surrounded by endless country views, each attractively furnished room has country and floral prints, deep pile carpets, and antique wood furniture. The warm and friendly communal lounge has the inn's only television, along with a wide array of books on various aspects of South African country life. The good country cooking here includes butternut-and-apple soup, trout with almonds, and fresh cream pavlovas. As at most other establishments, your hosts can arrange excursions farther afield; but don't forget to visit the dairy and cheese factory on the farm to sample the cheese made from an old Dutch recipe. ✉ *Box 604, 3257,* ☎ *033/701–1926,* WEB *www.riverglen.co.za. 4 rooms. In-room safes. No credit cards. BP.*

$ 🏠 **Taylor's B&B.** A delightful respite is just off the R617, 2 km (1 mi) from Underberg on the Swartberg road (look for the sign to the Banks, on the left). All rooms are attractively and individually decorated; upstairs units have lovely views across the surrounding countryside. Each room has snack-making facilities including a toaster and a *skottel-braai* (gas wok). A huge farm breakfast is included, and dinners can be arranged beforehand on request. Hosts Edith and John Taylor are extremely friendly and helpful and can arrange trips to Sani Pass as well as tennis, fishing, canoeing, and horseback-riding excursions. ✉ *Box 33, 3257,* ☎ FAX *033/701–2011. 6 rooms without bath. No-smoking rooms, refrigerator. No credit cards. BP.*

Himeville

This tiny hamlet lies just 5 km (3 mi) from Underberg, on the road to Sani Pass. The town's major claim to fame is its proximity to the fantastic Sani Pass, gateway to Lesotho and the summit of the Drakensberg. There's not much to choose from here, although you might want to stop for a pint at the Himeville Arms Hotel or visit the interesting Himeville Museum, on its main street.

⓬ If you have some time in town on the way to the pass, stop at the **Himeville Museum,** opposite the Himeville Arms Hotel. Originally built as a fort on lands belonging to the Natal Crown Colony in 1899 to protect the region's pioneer farmers, the building was later converted to a prison and used as such until the early 1970s, becoming a museum in 1976. The premises were subsequently declared a national monument. It's one of the best rural museums in the region, commemorating not only the way of life of the early European inhabitants of Himeville, Underberg, and Bulwer but also containing relics from the San and African tribes. There are also displays on the area's fauna and flora, geography, and topography. ✉ *Main St. (mailing address: Box 207, Himeville 3256),* ☎ *033/702–1184.* 🎫 *Free.* ⊙ *Tues.–Sun. 8:30–12:30.*

$$–$$$ 🏠 **Sani Pass Hotel.** Just 11 km (57 mi) from Himeville at the base of the spectacular Sani Pass lies this attractive country hotel. With its close proximity to the Roof of Africa, it's a favorite with international guests. Nestled in a tranquil valley, there are spectacular mountain views. Accommodations are either in attractive garden cottages or larger, more luxurious rooms and suites in the main building. The latter rooms all have mountain views. The food is delicious country fare, and candlelighted dinners are a hotel specialty. Activities are legion, including scenic walks and drives, various sporting activities, a choice of horseback rides (including plateau and sunset rides), and, of course, regular trips up that fabulous pass. ✉ *Box 44, Himeville 3256,* ☎ *033/ 702–1320,* FAX *033/702–0220,* WEB *www.sanipasshotel.co.za. 97 rooms. Restaurant, 2 bars, 2 pools, 9-hole golf course, tennis, badminton, horseback riding, squash, volleyball. AE, DC, MC, V. MAP.*

HIKING AND BACKPACKING

If you're into backpacking and want to see this beautiful region on foot, don't miss the **Giant's Cup Hiking Trail.** Although actually a five-day hike, the trail is never so far from civilization that you can't shorten it by a day or two. Giant's Cup winds through the Little Berg, with incredible views of the escarpment at every turn, and passes by a petrified forest, San paintings, rock shelters, streams, and deep blue pools. If you like swimming, definitely come in summer. Accommodations are in old forester's houses. The supply of firewood is plentiful, and roaring log fires will warm you. There aren't any comforts, though—water is usually heated by a donkey boiler, bunks have mattresses but no bedding, and only one hut has electricity, so don't forget your flashlight. You'll need to carry your own food, sleeping bag, hiking stove and fuel, eating utensils, and clothing. If you're equipped for backpacking and are reasonably fit, this one's a real treat, beginning halfway up Sani Pass and ending near the Lesotho border post at Bushman's Neck. The trail costs approximately R55 per person per night. ⊠ *Reservations: KZN Wildlife, Box 13069, Cascades 3202,* ☎ *033/845–1000,* FAX *0331/845–1001,* WEB *www.kznwildlife.com.*

Drakensberg A to Z

To research prices, get advice from other travelers, and book travel arrangements, visit www.fodors.com.

BUS TRAVEL
On request, most resorts will pick up guests at the Greyhound or Translux terminal in Estcourt, Ladysmith (Ted's Service Station), or Swinburne (Montrose Service Area). Buses from both lines stop at these towns at least once a day on their runs between Durban and Johannesburg.
➤ BUS INFORMATION: **Estcourt Terminal** (⊠ Municipal Library, Victoria St.). **Greyhound** (☎ 011/830–1400 or 031/309–7838). **Translux** (☎ 031/361–7461).

CAR TRAVEL
The main resort area of the Drakensberg lies 380 km (250 mi) from Johannesburg and 240 km (150 mi) from Durban—an almost direct shot along the N3. A car is not strictly necessary for a trip to the Berg, although it is certainly a convenience.

TRANSPORTATION AROUND DRAKENSBERG
Once at the resort—particularly those right in the mountains—most guests are content to hike or enjoy the hotel facilities. If you do want to see some of the surrounding area, you can usually arrange for guided tours and transport.

VISITOR INFORMATION
Drakensberg Publicity Association is open weekdays 9–4. Underberg Tourist Information is open Monday–Saturday 8:30–4:30.
➤ TOURIST INFORMATION: **Drakensberg Publicity Association** (⊠ Tatham St., Bergville, ☎ 036/448–1557, WEB www.drakensberg.org.za). **Underberg Tourist Information** (⊠ Main St., Underberg [mailing address: Box 230, Underberg 3257], ☎ 033/701–1419).

ZULULAND AND THE BATTLEFIELDS

Zululand stretches north from the Tugela River all the way to the border of Mozambique. It's a region of rolling grasslands, gorgeous beaches, and classic African bush. It has also seen more than its share of bloodshed and death. Modern South Africa was forged in the fiery crucible of Zululand and northern Natal. Here, Boers battled Zulus, Zulus battled Britons, and Britons battled Boers. The most interesting historic sites, however, involve the battles against the Zulus. Names like Isandlwana, Rorke's Drift, and Blood River have taken their place in the roll of legendary military encounters.

Indeed, no African tribe has captured the Western imagination quite like the Zulus. A host of books and movies have explored their warrior culture and extolled their martial valor. Until the early 19th century the Zulus were a small, unheralded group, part of the Nguni peoples who migrated to southern Africa from the north. King Shaka (1787–1828), the illegitimate son of a Zulu chief, changed all that. Before Shaka, warfare among the Nguni had been a desultory affair in which small bands of warriors would hurl spears at one another from a distance and then retire. Shaka introduced the assegai, a short stabbing spear, teaching his warriors to get close to the enemy in hand-to-hand combat. He also developed the famous chest-and-horns formation, a cattle analogy for a classic maneuver in which you outflank and encircle your enemy. In less than a decade Shaka created a military machine unrivaled in black Africa. By the time of his assassination in 1828, Shaka had destroyed 300 tribes and extended Zulu power for 800 km (500 mi) through the north, south, and west.

Fifty years after Shaka's death, the British still considered the Zulus a major threat to their planned federation of white states in South Africa. The British solution, in 1879, was to instigate a war to destroy the Zulu kingdom. They employed a similar tactic 20 years later to bring the Boer republics to heel and the rich goldfields of the Witwatersrand into their own hands.

Recently, interest in the battlefields has been growing, particularly in light of the Boer and Zulu War centenary celebrations, which started in January 2000. The best way to tour the battlefields is with an expert guide, who can bring the history to life. However, unless you've done extensive research or have a vivid imagination, you may find it difficult to conjure up the furious events of a century ago. Many of the battle sites are little more than open grassland, graced with the occasional memorial stone. If you're not a history buff, it's better to head straight to the game reserves and natural wonders of northern Zululand.

Towns and sights on this tour appear on the KwaZulu-Natal map.

Dukuza

75 km (47 mi) north of Durban on the N2.

Today Zululand starts on the other side of the Tugela River. In Shaka's day the Zulu empire was much larger, encompassing much of present-day KwaZulu-Natal. Shaka himself had his military kraal at Dukuza, the site of present-day Dukuza (formerly known as Stanger), on the north coast. Amafa AkwaZulu Natali (formerly the KwaZulu Monuments Council) has opened the **KwaDukuza Interpretive Center,** in Dukuza, which houses displays and information on the Shaka period, including a video on the Shaka. There's also a crafts shop and a bookshop. ⊠ *Main St.,* ☎ *032/552–7210.* ☉ *Daily 9–4.* ▭ *Free.*

Eshowe

45 km (28 mi) northwest of Stanger; leave the N2 at Gingindlovu and follow the R66.

Eshowe, the oldest town in Zululand and birthplace of King Cetshwayo, is a pleasant town high up in the hills with great views of the Dhlinza

BOERS, BRITS, AND BATTLEFIELDS

THE BOER WAR (1899–1902), now referred to as the South African War, was the longest, bloodiest, and most costly war fought by Britain for nearly 100 years. The Brits and the Boers, Afrikaner descendants of 17th-century Dutch settlers fighting for independence from Britain, engaged in numerous battles in which the little guys (the Boers) often made mincemeat of the great British colonial army sent out to defeat them. Britain marched into South Africa in the spring of 1899, confident that it would all be over by Christmas. However, the comparatively small bands of volunteers from the republics of the Transvaal and the Orange Free State were to give Queen Victoria's proud British army, as Kipling wrote, "no end of a lesson." Today history has also revealed the part played by hundreds of thousands of black South Africans in the war as messengers, scouts, interpreters, and laborers—hence the renaming of the war.

The most famous—or infamous—of the battles was fought on top of Spion Kop, in KwaZulu-Natal, where the mass grave of hundreds of British soldiers stretches from one side of the hill to the other. Of interest is that three men who were to change the course of world history were there on that fateful day: Winston Churchill, Mahatma Gandhi (who was a stretcher bearer), and Louis Botha, the first prime minister of the Union of South Africa.

— Kate Turkington

Forest and fields of sugarcane. It is the site of **Fort Nongqayi,** which houses the **Zululand Historical Museum.** The fort was built in 1883 and served as the headquarters of the Nongqai Police, a black police contingent under British command. Museum displays trace the role of the fort in the Bambata Rebellion of 1906, when Chief Bambata took up arms to protest a £1 poll tax on every African male. A particularly interesting exhibit deals with John Dunn (1834–95), the son of settler parents, who was fluent in Zulu, Afrikaans, and English. He became Chief Cetshwayo's political adviser in 1856 and was given the status of a Zulu chief. Dunn observed Zulu customs and laws, going so far as to marry 49 Zulu wives, by whom he had 117 children. Periodically, the descendants of John Dunn stage reunions. ⊠ *Nongqayi Rd., Eshowe,* ☎ *0354/74–1141,* FAX *0354/74–4976.* ⊡ *R10.* ⊙ *Weekdays 7:30–4, weekends 9–4.*

Thirteen kilometers (8 miles) north of Eshowe on the R66, you'll see the turnoff to **Shakaland,** a living museum of Zulu culture and one of the most popular tourist stops in the region. Originally the movie set for *Shaka Zulu,* Shakaland consists of a traditional Zulu kraal, with thatched beehive huts arranged in a circle around a central cattle enclosure. The emphasis here is on Zulu culture as it existed under King Shaka in the 19th century. You can watch Zulus dressed in animal skins or beaded aprons engaged in everyday tasks: making beer, forging spears, and crafting beadwork. Opt for a three-hour day tour or spend the night. A Zulu cultural adviser leads you through the kraal, explaining the significance of the layout and the roles played by men and women in traditional Zulu society. A highlight of the visit is a half-hour dance performance, featuring a variety of Zulu and other traditional dances.

The whole setup is touristy, and some critics have labeled it a Zulu Disneyland, but you learn a great deal about Zulu culture nevertheless. A buffet lunch is included in the tour. ⊠ *Off R66, 13 km (8 mi) north of Eshowe,* ☎ *03546/00912,* FAX *03546/00824,* WEB *www.shakaland. com.* ✉ *R137 (including lunch).* ☉ *Daily tours at 11 and 12:30.*

Dining and Lodging

$$$ ✕⌂ **Shakaland.** Shakaland is best known as a living museum of traditional Zulu culture, but it's also possible to stay overnight at the complex, an experience that is far more rewarding than the three-hour daytime tour. Overnight guests see a more extensive program of cultural events than day visitors (the program begins at 4 PM and concludes at 11 AM the next day) and get to experience a night in a quasi-traditional Zulu dwelling. The rooms here are among the most attractive and luxurious of all the African-inspired accommodations in the country: enormous thatch beehive huts supported by rope-wrapped struts are decorated with African bedspreads, reed matting, and interesting African art, creating an appealing ethnic elegance. Modern bathrooms are attached to all but three huts. All meals are included in the price and feature a selection of Western-style dishes as well as some Zulu specialties. ⊠ *Off R66, 13 km (8 mi) north of Eshowe (mailing address: Box 103, Eshowe 3815),* ☎ *035/46–912,* FAX *03546/00824. 48 rooms, 45 with bath. Restaurant, bar, pool. AE, DC, MC, V. FAP.*

Melmoth

30 km (19 mi) north of Eshowe.

Return to the R66 and turn left. After a couple of miles you come to the tiny settlement of Nkwalini. Turn right onto the R34 toward Empangeni to reach the **Jabulani Rehabilitation Centre.** Run by the Association for the Physically Challenged, the center is home to more than 100 Zulus with disabilities, many of whom are victims of polio. The residents learn a variety of crafts, from beadwork to spear- and shield making, and much of their work is used and sold at tourist centers such as Shakaland. The center has its own crafts outlet; prices here are often much lower than at curio shops, and you can watch the artisans at work. ⊠ *R34, between Nkwalini and Empangeni,* ☎ *0351/92–8144.* ✉ *Free.* ☉ *Daily 8–5.*

Return to the R66 and turn right. The road snakes up and over the beautiful **Nkwalini Pass,** where you'll have knockout views of valleys and hills dotted with Zulu kraals. Stay on the R34 through the town of Melmoth and then continue for another 32 km (20 mi) to the turnoff and bear right to **Ulundi.** Ulundi is currently the joint capital—with Pietermaritzburg—of KwaZulu-Natal. Except for a huge legislative complex, however, it's an empty, ghastly place, full of blowing trash and ramshackle buildings.

Lodging

$$$ ⌂ **Simunye Pioneer Settlement.** If Shakaland is too commercial for your
★   tastes, consider this small settlement tucked away in a remote valley of Zululand. Like Shakaland, Simunye attempts to introduce you to traditional Zulu culture, but the emphasis here extends to contemporary Zulu lifestyles, too. You'll reach the camp on horseback or ox wagon, and the one-hour ride into the valley is one of the highlights of a visit. During a stay you'll watch Zulu dancing and visit a working kraal, complete with traditional beehive huts, where you'll learn about Zulu culture and meet the kraal's residents. You can opt to sleep overnight in one of the beehive huts; otherwise, stay in the more lux-

urious main camp, built into the side of a hill overlooking the Mfule River. The rooms, built of stone and thatch, are a classy mix of Zulu and pioneer cultures. You'll sleep in a wooden bed handmade by local villagers in a room decorated with Zulu cooking pots, cow-skin rugs, and handmade wooden African chairs. Only the lodges have electricity; in the rooms light is provided by candles and hurricane lanterns. Unfortunately, the stone bathrooms were designed more for their aesthetic value than any practical purpose: awkward steps lead to a hand-filled stone bath, and just getting in and out requires balance and agility. Most people stay only one night, but try to book for two days over a weekend and arrange to attend a wedding or coming-of-age ceremony in a neighboring village. These ceremonies are purely local affairs, and you won't experience a more authentic celebration of rural Zulu culture. ⊠ *D256, off the R34, 6 km (4 mi) south of Melmoth (mailing address: Box 248, Melmoth 3835),* ☎ *03545/03111,* ℻ *03545/02534. 6 rooms, 5 rondawels, 2 beehive huts, 5 lodges. AE, DC, MC, V. FAP.*

Ulundi

35 km (22 mi) north of Melmoth.

Two kilometers (1 mile) before you reach Ulundi, you'll see the turnoff to the **Battle of Ulundi Memorial.** A stone temple with a silver dome marks the site of the battle on the sunbaked uplands surrounding Ulundi. The Battle of Ulundi marked the culmination of the Zulu War of 1879. Lord Chelmsford, smarting from his defeat at Isandlwana, personally led the march on Ulundi and King Cetshwayo's royal kraal, Ondini. Cetshwayo, already disheartened by heavy losses at Kambula and Gingindlovu, sent messengers to the British seeking peace. In reply, Chelmsford demanded the disbandment of the Zulu regiment system and the surrender of the royal cattle herd. To the Zulu, for whom cattle are the very thread of the social fabric, such terms were unacceptable.

On July 4, 1879, a British force of 5,317 crossed the White Mfolozi River, marched onto the open plain near Ondini, and formed an infantry square. Mounted troops then harassed the 15,000-strong Zulu force into making an undisciplined attack. None of the Zulu warriors got within 100 ft of the British square before being cut down by rifle and artillery fire. Within 45 minutes the Zulus were in flight, and the British 17th Lancers and a flying column were giving pursuit, spearing the fleeing Zulus from horseback. The Zulu dead numbered 1,500. British losses amounted to a mere 13.

The British burned Ondini to the ground, and King Cetshwayo fled into the Ngome Forest. He was captured two months later and exiled to Cape Town and, finally, to England. Although he was restored to the throne as a puppet in 1883, the Zulu empire had been shattered. ⊠ *Cetshwayo Hwy.,* ☎ *no phone.*

Continue down the dirt road to the **KwaZulu Cultural Museum—Ondini,** the original site of King Cetshwayo's royal kraal. Ondini was modeled after Dingane's kraal at Mgungundlovu. At the time of its destruction in 1879, the kraal consisted of 1,500 huts and was home to some 5,000 people. Today only the royal enclosure has been restored, but a stroll among the deserted beehive huts gives you a feel for the kraal's size and scope. An interesting site museum at the entrance traces the history of the Zulu kings and displays the silver mug and Bible presented to King Cetshwayo by Queen Victoria in 1882. The Cultural Museum, in a separate building, is excellent and well worth a visit. It houses a superb collection of beadwork from various tribes, plus detailed exhibits on Zulu life, including some of the changes in Zulu customs in modern times. ⊠ *Cetshwayo Hwy.,* ☎ *0358/70–2051.* 🎫 *R8.* ☉ *Daily 9–4.*

En Route From Ulundi retrace your route back down the R66 and turn right onto the R34 toward Vryheid. The turnoff to **Mgungundlovu** and the **Grave of Piet Retief** lies just a couple of miles farther on. Mgungundlovu was the site of Dingane's royal kraal and home to his 500 wives. Dingane (ruled 1828–40) was Shaka's younger brother; he killed Shaka in 1828 to seize power for himself. During Dingane's rule the Zulu came under increasing pressure from white settlers moving into the area. In 1837 Piet Retief and a party of Voortrekkers petitioned Dingane for land. The king agreed on condition that Retief retrieve some Zulu cattle stolen by a rival chief. Retief duly recovered the cattle and returned to Mgungundlovu with nearly 100 men. Dingane welcomed the Voortrekkers into the royal kraal, instructing them to leave their guns and horses outside. Once they were inside, Dingane shouted, "Kill the wizards!" and 8–10 warriors seized each of the unarmed men. The Voortrekkers were dragged to Execution Hill and murdered. A monument now stands on the hill where Piet Retief and his men are buried. Retaliation from the Voortrekkers was slow in coming but ultimately terrible. At the Battle of Blood River, in December 1838, Dingane's army was completely destroyed. Dingane burned Mgungundlovu to the ground and fled to the north. He met his end in 1840 at the hands of another brother, Mpande, who succeeded him as king. Today the beehive huts of the royal enclosure have been reconstructed on their original foundations, and a guide leads short tours of the kraal. There's also a small site museum. ⊠ *R34,* ☎ *no phone.* 🎫 *R8.* ☉ *Daily 8–4.*

Babanango

6½ km (4 mi) from the Grave of Piet Retief, turnoff on the R34, turn left (west) onto a good-quality dirt road for the 32-km (20-mi) run to Babanango.

A dirt road connecting the R34 to Babanango passes through some of the most beautiful countryside in Zululand, with seemingly endless views over rolling grasslands. The road ends at the tarred R68. Turn right and drive less than 2 km (1 mi) into the pleasant hamlet of Babanango.

From Babanango follow the R68 for 48 km (30 mi) to the turnoff to Isandlwana. The **Battle of Isandlwana,** on January 22, 1879, was a major defeat for the British army. Coming as it did at the very beginning of the Zulu War, the defeat sent shudders of apprehension through the corridors of Whitehall and ultimately cost Lord Chelmsford his command. Chelmsford was in charge of one of three invasion columns that were supposed to sweep into Zululand and converge on Cetshwayo's capital at Ulundi. On January 20 Chelmsford crossed the Buffalo River into Zululand, leaving behind a small force at Rorke's Drift to guard the column's supplies. He encamped at Isandlwana. Two days later, believing there was no danger of attack, he led a large portion of his troops on a mission in support of another commander, leaving the camp woefully unprepared to defend itself. Unknown to Chelmsford, the heart of the Zulu army—20,000 men—had taken up a position just 5 km (3 mi) away. Despite their obvious advantage, the Zulus stayed their attack, persuaded by a *sangoma* (diviner) that the moment was not propitious. When a British patrol stumbled on the hidden army, however, it rose up and charged. Using Shaka's classic chest-and-horns formation, the Zulus swept toward the British positions arrayed beneath the distinctive peak of Isandlwana. The battle hung in the balance until the Zulus' left horn outflanked the British. The fighting continued for two hours before the British fled the field, with the Zulus in triumphant pursuit. About 1,000 Zulus perished in the attack, as did 1,329 British troops. A further 300–400 British soldiers fled by various routes back toward Rorke's Drift and Natal. Today the battlefield is dotted with whitewashed stone cairns and memorials marking the resting places of fallen soldiers. The visitor center houses a small but excellent museum of mementos and artifacts, following the course of the battle in marvelous detail—a good place to start if you're here without a guide. Allow at least two or three hours for a visit here. ⊠ *Off R68,* ☎ *no phone.* 🔲 *R8.* ☉ *Daily 8–4.*

Dining and Lodging

$$ ✕🔲 **Babanango Hotel.** In the small Babanango Hotel you can relax in one of the country's most famous watering holes. It's a tiny place decorated in country style, with lots of wood and earthy colors. The pub serves a variety of inexpensive meals including grilled rump steak and french fries. ⊠ *16 Justice St.,* ☎ *0358/35–0029. 5 rooms. No credit cards.*

$$$ 🔲 **Babanango Valley Lodge.** This tiny guest lodge lies at the end of a rutted 15-km (9-mi) dirt road on an 8,000-acre cattle farm. Obviously, it's not the sort of place where you constantly pop in and out, but that's okay—you probably won't want to leave anyway. The lodge sits at the head of a steep valley, far from any other buildings and with tremendous views of acacia-studded grasslands and hills. John and Meryn Turner, the charming young hosts, and their very hospitable team, go out of their way to make guests feel at home. John is a registered guide, and many people stay at the lodge as part of his battlefields tour. Rooms are decorated with rustic armoires and dressers, white fluffy duvets, and frilly lamp shades—simple, comfortable country stuff. The four-course table d'hôte dinner focuses on traditional South African fare, including fresh farm produce. ⊠ *15 km (9 mi) off R68, near Babanango (mailing address: Box 10, Babanango 3850),* ☎ *082/321–7141,* 🄵🄰🄷 *082/320–4134. 6 rooms. Pool. DC, MC, V. MAP.*

Rorke's Drift

★   *35 km (22 mi) east of Isandlwana; turn left when you get back to the R68, and continue to the turnoff to Rorke's Drift.*

Rorke's Drift is by far the best of the Zulu War battlefields to see without a guide. An excellent museum and orientation center retells the story of the battle, with electronic diagrams, battle sounds, and dioramas. From the British perspective this was the most glorious battle of the Zulu War, the more so because it took place just hours after the disaster at Isandlwana. The British force at Rorke's Drift consisted of just 141 men, of whom 35 were ailing. They occupied a Swedish mission church and house, which had been converted into a storehouse and hospital. The Zulu forces numbered some 3,000–4,000 men, composed of the reserve regiments from Isandlwana. When a survivor from Isandlwana sounded the warning at 3:15 PM, the tiny British force hastily erected a stockade of flour bags and biscuit boxes around the mission. The Zulus attacked 75 minutes later, and the fighting raged for 12 hours before the Zulus faltered. When the smoke cleared, 500 Zulus and 17 Britons lay dead. ⊠ *Rorke's Drift Rd., off R68,* ☎ *034/642–1687.* 🔲 *R8.* ☉ *Daily 8–4.*

Rorke's Drift is still a mission station, run by the Evangelical Lutheran Church. The **Rorke's Drift ELC Art and Craft Centre,** at the mission, sells wonderful pottery, handwoven rugs, and linocuts, all created by mission artists. ⊠ *Rorke's Drift Rd., off R68,* ☎ *034/642–1627.* ☉ *Weekdays 8–4:30, weekends 10–3.*

Retrace your steps to the R68 and turn left. After 24 km (15 mi), the road intersects with the R33. Turn right and drive 21 km (13 mi) to the turnoff to the site of the **Battle of Blood River,** one of the most important events in the history of South Africa. This battle, fought between the Boers and the Zulus in 1838, predates the Anglo-Zulu War by more than 40 years. After the murder of Piet Retief and his men at Mgungundlovu in February 1838, Dingane dispatched Zulu impis to kill all the white settlers in Natal. The Voortrekkers bore the brunt of the Zulu assault. For the next 10 months their future hung in the balance: entire settlements were wiped out, and a Boer commando was smashed at the Battle of Italeni. By November a new commando of 464 men and 64 wagons under Andries Pretorius had moved out to challenge the Zulus. On Sunday, November 9, the Boers took a vow that should God grant them victory, they would forever remember that day as a Sabbath and build a church in commemoration. They repeated the vow every night for the next five weeks. On December 16 an enormous Zulu force attacked the Boers, who had circled their wagons in a strategic position backed by the Blood River and a deep *donga,* or gully. Armed with only spears, the Zulus were no match for the Boer riflemen. At the end of the battle 3,000 Zulus lay dead, but not a single Boer had fallen. The immediate effect of the victory was to open Natal to white settlement, but the long-term effects were far more dramatic. The intensely religious Voortrekkers saw their great victory as a confirmation of their role as God's chosen people. This deeply held conviction lay at the spiritual heart of the apartheid system that surfaced more than a century later, in 1948. Indeed, when you see the monument, there's no mistaking the gravity and importance that the Nationalist government ascribed to its erection. The laager of 64 wagons has been reconstructed in exacting detail, made from a mix of cast steel and bronze. It's a truly haunting monument, made even more so by its position on empty grasslands that seem to stretch for eternity. ✉ *Off R33, between Dundee and Vryheid,* ☎ *03424/695.* ⌕ *R8.* ☉ *Daily 8–4.*

Lodging

$$$$ 🏨 **Fugitives' Drift Lodge.** Set on a 4,000-acre game farm, this attractive lodge lies just a couple of miles from the site of the famous engagement at Rorke's Drift and overlooks the drift where survivors of the British defeat at Isandlwana fled across the Buffalo River. Even more important, the owner is Dave Rattray, the best battlefield guide in the country. Rooms, in individual cottages that open onto gardens, have fireplaces and wood furniture. The focal point of the lodge is the lounge and dining room, decorated with old rifles, British regimental flags, Zulu spears, and antique military prints. The lodge has no electricity, although a generator is switched on in the morning and evening. Unfortunately, it's switched on late in the morning, and if you're visiting the region during winter, this could mean fumbling around in the dark while you find matches for the paraffin lamps. Battlefield tours cost R395 per person. ✉ *On Rorke's Drift Rd. (mailing address: P.O. Rorke's Drift, KwaZulu-Natal 3016),* ☎ FAX *034/6421–843,* WEB *www.fugitives-drift-lodge.com. 8 chalets. Bar, dining room. DC, MC, V. FAP.*

$$$$ 🏨 **Isandlwana Lodge.** This American-owned lodge is built on Nyoni Rock and has sweeping views of the entire Isandlwana battlefield. The building is shaped like a Zulu shield and commemorates Isandlwana with rooms named for Zulus who were significant in the war and shield-shape basin pedestals in bathrooms. Decor is modern yet Afrocentric; rooms are comfortable, with African prints and wooden furniture. Picture windows in public areas make the most of the incredible battlefield views. Trips to the local battlefields (R200)

are the main activity at this lodge. ✉ *Box 30, Isandlwana 3005,* ☎ *034/ 271–8301,* FAX *034/271–8306,* WEB *www.isandlwana.co.za. 13 rooms. Bar, pool. AE, DC, MC, V. MAP.*

$$$$ ⊡ **iSibindi Lodge.** A mere 9 km (4 mi) from Fugitive's Drift, iSibindi lies within the iSibindi Eco Reserve and combines game viewing and an optional Zulu cultural experience with battlefield tours. A Zulu prince who speaks English, French, and Zulu fluently is the resident historian and will take you on your battlefield tour. Rooms are in elevated Zulu-style huts facing glorious vistas across hills and valleys and have private decks. An attractive lounge-bar area shows off African prints and Zulu artifacts, and an outdoor bar and sunken pool look out over the view. In addition to battlefield tours and game drives to view antelopes, giraffes, zebras, and wildebeests, the highlight of the lodge is its cultural evenings, when Zulu dancers from a local school perform for guests. You can also have the bones read by a traditional sangoma to reveal your past, present, and future. In summer river rafting is possible on the Buffalo River. ✉ *Box 275, Umhlali 4390,* ☎ *032/947– 0538,* FAX *032/947–0659,* WEB *www.zulunet.co.za. 6 huts. Bar, pool. AE, DC, MC, V. MAP.*

Dundee

35 km (22 mi) north of Rorke's Drift.

The first-rate **Talana Museum,** on the outskirts of Dundee, encompasses 10 buildings and is well worth a visit. Fascinating exhibits trace the history of the area, from the early San hunter-gatherers to the rise of the Zulu nation, the extermination of the cannibal tribes of the Biggarsberg, and, finally, the vicious battles of the South African War (1899–1902). The museum itself stands on the site of the Battle of Talana (October 20, 1899), the opening skirmish in the South African War. Two of the museum buildings were used by the British as medical stations during the battle. There are also superb glass and coal exhibits relating to the history of Dundee itself. The Miners Rest Tea Shop, in a delightfully restored miner's cottage, serves refreshments as well as more substantial dishes like peri-peri chicken livers or spinach, feta, and chicken pie in phyllo pastry. The food is good, the atmosphere most welcoming. Or you can take advantage of the braai facilities here, and have a do-it-yourself barbecue. ✉ *2 km (1 mi) east Dundee on R33 to Vryheid,* ☎ *034/ 212–2654.* ▣ *R10.* ☉ *Weekdays 8–4:30, weekends 10–4:30.*

Ladysmith

60 km (37 mi) southwest of Dundee.

Ladysmith became famous around the world during the South African War, when it outlasted a Boer siege of 118 days. Nearly 20,000 people were caught in the town when the Boers attacked on November 2, 1899. During the next four months there was little fighting around Ladysmith itself—the Boers seemed content to shell the town with their Long Tom siege guns—but the town's food supply steadily dwindled. By the end of the siege the desperate residents were slaughtering half-starved horses to supplement their diets, and each day 28 people died from sickness and malnutrition.

Much of the early part of the war revolved around British attempts to raise the siege. The incompetence of British general Sir Redvers Buller became apparent during repeated attempts to smash the Boer lines, resulting in heavy British losses at Spionkop, Vaalkrans, and Colenso. Finally, the sheer weight of numbers made possible the British defeat of the Boers in the epic 10-day Battle of Tugela Heights and raise the siege of Ladysmith on February 28, 1900.

The **Ladysmith Siege Museum** brings the period of the siege skillfully to life, with the use of electronic mapping, artifacts from the period, and black-and-white photos. The museum can arrange guided tours, but it also sells two pamphlets that outline self-guided tours: the "Siege Town Walkabout" and the "Siege Town Drive-About." ✉ *Murchison St., next to Town Hall,* ☎ *036/637–2992.* 🖅 *R2.* ☉ *Weekdays 9–4, Sat. 9–1.*

Next to the Siege Museum, directly in front of Town Hall, stands a replica of a **Long Tom,** the 6-inch Creusot gun used by the Boers during the siege. Also in front of Town Hall are two howitzers used by the British and christened Castor and Pollux.

Dining and Lodging

$$ ✕🏨 **Royal Hotel.** The Royal will suffice if you find yourself in Ladysmith at the end of the day. It's a typical South African country hotel that has seen more glorious days. The hotel was built in 1880, just 19 years before the town was attacked by the Boers during the war. During the siege a shell from a Long Tom gun exploded on the hotel veranda, killing a doctor. Expect small rooms, although TVs and air-conditioning are standard features. The hotel offers several dining options, from a family-style restaurant to expensive Continental cuisine at Swainsons. ✉ *140 Murchison St., Ladysmith 3370,* ☎ 🅵🅰🆇 *036/637–2176. 71 rooms. 3 restaurants, 3 bars, room service. AE, DC, MC, V. CP.*

Zululand and the Battlefields A to Z

To research prices, get advice from other travelers, and book travel arrangements, visit www.fodors.com.

CAR TRAVEL

Unless you're on a tour, it's almost impossible to see this part of the country without your own car. Your best bet is to rent a car in Durban and perhaps combine a trip to the battlefields with a self-drive tour of KwaZulu-Natal's game reserves. Roads are in good condition, although some of the access roads to the battlefields require more careful and slower driving.

TOURS

The visitor information offices at the Talana Museum in Dundee and Ladysmith have lists of registered battlefield guides. At the Talana Museum in Dundee you can also rent or buy cassette tapes describing the events at Rorke's Drift and Isandlwana. Of all the battlefields guides in the region, David Rattray is widely considered to be the finest. His accounts of the action at Rorke's Drift, Isandlwana, and Fugitives' Drift sometimes move listeners to tears. Many combine one of David's tours with a stay at his lodge, just a couple of miles from Rorke's Drift. David is slowly losing his voice, so part of the tour now consists of his taped narrative. Other reputable guides to the Zulu battlefields are John Turner of the Babanango Valley Lodge and Raymond Heron of Spionkop Lodge. For information about battlefields guides, contact any of the information centers. For those more interested in exploring authentic Zulu culture, there are two excellent SATOUR registered guides: Henry Bird, a regional Zululand guide with particular experience in Zulu sites, and Graham Chennels, who specializes in authentic rural Zulu experiences. You can contact them through the tourism offices.

➤ TOUR-OPERATOR RECOMMENDATIONS: **Henry Bird** (☎ FAX 0354/74–2348). **Graham Chennels** (☎ 082/492–6918). **David Rattray** (☎ FAX 0341/23319). **John Turner** (☎ FAX 0358/35–0062).

VISITOR INFORMATION
The Information Regional Tourism Office is open weekdays 7:30–4. The Ladysmith Information Bureau is open weekdays 9–4, Saturday 9–1, and Sunday by request. Talana Museum is open weekdays 8–4:30 and weekends 10-4:30.

➤ INFORMATION: **Information Regional Tourism Office** (✉ Main St. and Osborn Rd., ☎ 0354/74–1141). **Ladysmith Information Bureau** (✉ Town Hall, Murchison St. [in Siege Museum], ☎ 036/637–2992). **Talana Museum** (✉ R33, 3 km [2 mi] east of Dundee, ☎ 0341/22654, FAX 0341/22376).

HLUHLUWE-UMFOLOZI GAME RESERVE

Hluhluwe-Umfolozi (pronounced Shloo-*shloo*-ee Uhm-fuh-*low*-zee) lies in Zululand, 264 km (165 mi) up the north coast from Durban. In an area of just 906 square km (325 square mi), Hluhluwe delivers the Big Five plus all the plains game, as well as species like nyala and red duiker that are rare in other parts of the country. Equally important, it boasts one of the most biologically diverse habitats on the planet, a unique mix of forest, woodland, savanna, and grassland. You will find about 1,250 species of plants and trees here—more than in some entire countries.

The park was previously administered by the highly regarded Natal Parks Board, the wildlife arm of KwaZulu-Natal Province. It has now combined with the KwaZulu-Natal Nature Conservation Service. Thanks to its conservation efforts, the park can take credit for saving the white rhino from extinction. So successful was the park at increasing white rhino numbers that in 1960 it established its now famous Rhino Capture Unit to relocate rhinos to other reserves in Africa. The park is currently trying to do for the black rhino what it did for its white cousins. Poaching has decimated Africa's black rhino population from 14,000 a decade ago to a saddening 2,250. Twenty percent of Africa's remaining black rhinos live in this reserve, and you won't get a better chance than this of seeing them in the wild.

Until 1989 the reserve consisted of two separate parks, Hluhluwe in the north and Umfolozi in the south, separated by a fenced corridor. Although a road (R618) still runs through this corridor, the fences have been removed, and the parks now operate as a single entity. Hluhluwe and the corridor are the most scenic areas of the park, notable for their bush-covered hills and knockout views, whereas Umfolozi is better known for its broad plains.

Compared with Kruger, Hluhluwe-Umfolozi is tiny—less than 6% of Kruger's size—but such comparisons can be misleading. You can spend days driving around this park and still not see everything, or feel like you're going in circles. Probably the biggest advantage Hluhluwe has over Kruger is that game viewing is good year-round, whereas Kruger has seasonal peaks and valleys. Another bonus is its proximity to Mkuze Game Reserve and the spectacular coastal reserves of Greater St. Lucia Wetland Park. The park is also close enough to Durban to make it a worthwhile one- or two-day excursion.

Parks and lodges in this section appear on the KwaZulu-Natal map.

Bush Walks

Armed rangers lead groups of eight on two- to three-hour bush walks departing from Hilltop Camp. You rarely see much game on these walks, but you do learn a great deal about the area's ecology and tips on how to recognize the signs of the bush, including animal spoor. Walks leave daily at 5:30 AM and 3:30 PM (6 and 3 in winter) and cost about R50; reserve a few days in advance at Hilltop Camp reception.

Game Drives

A great way to see the park is on game drives led by rangers. These drives (about R80 per person) hold several advantages over driving through the park yourself: you sit high up in an open-air vehicle, with a good view and the wind in your face; a ranger explains the finer points of animal behavior and ecology; and your guide has a good idea where to find animals like leopards, cheetahs, and lions. Game drives leave daily (except Sunday) at 5:30 in summer, 6:30 in winter. The park also offers three-hour night drives, during which you search for nocturnal animals with powerful spotlights. These three-hour drives depart at 7, and you should make advance reservations at Hilltop Camp reception.

Wilderness Trails

The park's wilderness trails are every bit as popular as Kruger's, but they tend to be tougher and more rustic. Led by an armed ranger, you must be able to walk 16 km (10 mi) a day for a period of three days and four nights. All equipment, food, and baggage are carried by donkeys. The first and last nights are spent at Mndindini, a permanent tented camp. The other two are spent under canvas in the bush. While in the bush, hikers bathe in the Mfolozi River or have a hot bucket shower; toilet facilities consist of a spade and toilet-paper roll. Trails, open March–November, are limited to eight people and should be reserved a year in advance. Expect to pay about R1,600 per person.

If that sounds too easy, you can always opt for the **Umfolozi Primitive Trail.** On this trek hikers carry their own kits and sleep out under the stars. A campfire burns all night to scare off animals, and each participant is expected to sit a 90-minute watch. A ranger acts as guide. The cost is R1,600 per person.

A more genteel wilderness experience is **Weekend Trails,** based out of the tented Dengezi Wilderness Camp, where you're guaranteed a bed and some creature comforts. The idea behind these trails is to instill in the participants an appreciation for the beauty of the untamed bush. The weekend begins on Friday at 2:30 and ends on Sunday at 3. Participation is limited to eight people and costs about R800 per person.

Lodging

Hluhluwe-Umfolozi offers a range of accommodations in government-run rest camps, with an emphasis on self-catering (only Hilltop has a restaurant). Unfortunately, most foreign visitors can't avail themselves of the park's secluded bush lodges and camps, as each of them must be reserved in a block, and the smallest accommodates at least eight people. At Hilltop you can expect to pay R145 per person for a rondawel and R410 for a chalet with private bath and cooking facilities.

$–$$ ⚄ **Hilltop Camp.** It may be a government-run camp, but this delightful lodge in the Hluhluwe half of the park beats anything you'll find in Kruger. Perched on the crest of a hill, it has panoramic views over the park, the Hlaza and Nkwakwa hills, and Zululand. Thatch and ocher-color walls give it an African feel. Scattered across the crown of the hill, self-contained chalets have high thatch ceilings, rattan furniture, and small verandas. If you plan to eat all your meals in the restaurant, forgo the more expensive chalets with fully equipped kitchens. If you're on a tight budget, opt for a basic rondawel with two beds, a basin, and a refrigerator; toilet facilities are communal. The shop at the camp won't supply all your needs for this purpose: rather, shop in Hluhluwe town itself or at one of the main centers such as Empangeni, Eshowe, or Piet Retief that you pass en route to the park. There is a gas station on the premises. ⊠ *Reservations: KwaZulu-Natal Nature Conservation Service, Box 13053, Cascades 3202,* ☎ *035/562–0255,* FAX *035/562–0113,* WEB *www.rhino.org.za. 20 rondawels, 49 chalets Restaurant, bar. AE, DC, MC, V.*

Near Hluhluwe-Umfolozi

$$$$ 🏨 **Hluhluwe River Lodge.** Overlooking the False Bay Lake and the Hluhluwe River flood plain, this luxurious, spacious family-owned lodge set in indigenous gardens is the ideal base for visiting the game reserves and the Greater St Lucia Wetland Park. After your day spent game-viewing, canoeing, bird-watching, boating, fishing, or walking in the pristine sand forest, you can relax in a terra-cotta-color A-frame chalet with cool stone floors, wood and wicker furniture, and cream-and-brown decor and furnishings, or sit out on your wooden deck overlooking the bush, the floodplain, and the lake. This lodge is the only one with direct access to the lake, and as you chug along through bird-filled papyrus channels decorated with water lilies en route to the broad expanses of the main body of water, you might easily feel as though you were in Botswana's Okavango Delta. The food is excellent—wholesome country cooking with lots of fresh vegetables and good roasts. ⊠ *Box 105, Hluhluwe 3960,* ☎ *035/562–0246,* FAX *035/562–0248,* WEB *www.hluhluwe.co.za. 12 chalets. Restaurant, bar, pool. AE, DC, MC, V. MAP.*

$$$$ 🏨 **Zululand Tree Lodge.** Sixteen kilometers (8 miles) from the park,
★ this classy lodge lies in a forest of fever trees on the 3,700-acre Ubizane Game Reserve, a small park stocked with white rhino and plains game, and makes a great base from which to explore Hluhluwe, Mkuze, and St. Lucia. Built of thatch and wood, the open-sided lodge sits on stilts overlooking the Mzinene River. Rooms are in separate cottages, also on stilts, along the riverbank. The rooms themselves are small, but among the most tastefully decorated you will find mosquito nets covering old-fashioned iron bedsteads made up with fluffy white duvets, African-print cushions, wicker, and reed matting. If you want the experience of sleeping alfresco, fold back the huge wooden shutters dividing the bedroom from the open deck. Game rangers lead bush walks and game drives through the small reserve. ⊠ *Hluhluwe Rd. (mailing address: Box 116, Hluhluwe 3960),* ☎ *035/562–1020,* FAX *035/562–1032. 24 rooms. Restaurant, bar, pool. AE, DC, MC, V. MAP.*

Excursions from Hluhluwe-Umfolozi

Mkuze Game Reserve. Forty-eight kilometers (30 miles) north of Hluhluwe-Umfolozi, this 88,900-acre reserve lies in the shadow of the Ubombo Mountains, between the Mkuze and Msunduze rivers. The park is famous for birds and rhinos. More than 400 bird species have been spotted here, including myriad waterfowl drawn to the park's shallow pans in summer. Several blinds, particularly those overlooking Nsumo Pan, offer superb views. Along with Hluhluwe, Mkuze is probably the best place in Africa to see rhinos in the wild. With an area only a fraction of the size of Kruger, the park supports a population of some 70 black and 120 white rhinos. You won't find any lions, buffalo, or elephants, but the low-lying thornveld supports healthy populations of general game, including zebras, giraffes, kudus, and nyalas. The park also features a spectacular forest of towering sycamore figs.

✉ *Follow N2 north from Hluhluwe for 37 km (23 mi) and follow signs,* ☎ *035/573–9004.* ✆ *R35 per vehicle, R10 per person.* ☉ *Daily 6–6.*

Greater St. Lucia Wetland Park. This huge park, a Natural World Heritage Site, is one of the most important coastal and wetland areas in the world. The focal point is Lake St. Lucia, a broad 95,545-acre lake dotted with islands and populated by crocodiles and hippos. Bird-watchers rave about the avian life, too—at times the lake is pink with flamingos. The KwaZulu-Natal Nature Conservation Service offers guided trips up the estuary aboard the *Santa Lucia*, an 80-seat motor launch that makes the 90-minute voyage three times daily (reservations are essential). The KwaZulu-Natal Nature Conservation Service maintains an office and self-catering camp in the small but rapidly expanding fishing resort of St. Lucia, near the mouth of the estuary. The village is also the access point to the thin strip of land that runs up the coast between Lake St. Lucia and the Indian Ocean, with some of the country's best beaches as well as the highest vegetated dunes in the world. The small KwaZulu-Natal Conservation Service camp of Cape Vidal, 20 km (12 mi) north of St. Lucia, has whale-watching towers and is one of the world's best places for shore-based sightings of southern right whales and humpbacks, which drift south on the warm Aghulas current around October each year. The area is also a magnet for beer-swilling fishermen with more horsepower than sense and real cowboy mentalities. ✉ *24 km (15 mi) east of Mtubatuba exit off the N2 (mailing address: Officer-in–Charge, Cape Vidal, Private Bag X04, St. Lucia Estuary 3936),* ☎ *035/590–1340,* ℻ *035/590–1300.* ✆ *Boat tours R56.* ☉ *Tours daily at 8, 10:30, and 2:30 with an additional trip Fri. and Sat. at 4.*

Lodging

$$ 🏠 **Ghost Mountain Inn.** This family-owned country inn near Mkuze is the gateway to the cultural, historical, and ecological wonders of Maputaland and is an excellent stopover en route to Mozambique, Swaziland, or Kruger National Park. If you're not interested in spotting the strange lights and flickering fires that give the mountains here their moniker, you can relax in the bougainvillea-filled gardens, take a walk over the sweeping lawns, take a leisurely boat ride, or watch the waterbirds from a tall hide. The huge public areas in the lodge are decorated with terra-cotta tiles and comfortable cane furniture. An intimate lounge has prints of old Africa, and a huge veranda is where you can have an alfresco breakfast. The bedrooms are also big but unmemorable. The Zulu dancing is some of the best you'll see, and afterward you can tuck into a succulent barbecue under the stars. An enthusiastic and knowledgeable young ranger will take you on a cultural tour, a game drive, fishing, or bird-watching. ✉ *Box 18, Mkuze 3965,* ☎ *035/573–1025,* ℻ *035/573–1025,* 🌐 *www.ghostmountaininn.co.za.* *33 rooms. Restaurant, bar, air-conditioning, pool, shop, meeting rooms. AE, DC, MC, V. BP.*

Hluhluwe-Umfolozi A to Z

To research prices, get advice from other travelers, and book travel arrangements, visit www.fodors.com.

AIR TRAVEL

The closest airport to the park is at Richards Bay, about 100 km (60 mi) south of Hluhluwe-Umfolozi. The airport is served by SA Express Airways, which has daily flights from Johannesburg.

➤ AIRLINES AND CONTACTS: **SA Express Airways** (☎ 035/786–0301).

CAR RENTAL

Avis and Imperial have car-rental offices at the Richards Bay airport.
➤ CAR RENTAL INFORMATION: **Avis** (☎ 035/789–6555). **Imperial** (☎ 035/786–0309).

CAR TRAVEL

From Durban drive north on the N2 highway to Mtubatuba; then cut west on the R618 to Mambeni Gate. Otherwise, continue up the N2 to the Hluhluwe exit and follow the signs to the park and Memorial Gate. The whole trip takes about three hours, but watch out for pot-holes.

SIGHTSEEING TOURS

Umhluhluwe Safaris is by far the largest tour operator in Zululand and offers a full range of half- and full-day game drives in Hluhluwe-Um-folozi, as well as night drives and bush walks. The company also leads game drives into the nearby Mkuze Game Reserve and guided tours to the bird-rich wetlands and beaches of St. Lucia.
➤ TOUR-OPERATOR RECOMMENDATIONS: **Umhluhluwe Safaris** (✉ Box 273, Hluhluwe 3960, ☎ ℻ 035/562–0414).

ITALA GAME RESERVE

Itala is in the north of KwaZulu-Natal, 221 km (138 mi) from Hluh-luwe-Umfolozi, close to the southern Swaziland border. At 296 square km (107 square mi), it is small even compared with the relatively com-pact Hluhluwe-Umfolozi. Its size and its dearth of lions are probably why this delightful park is usually bypassed, even by South Africans—although they clearly don't know what they're missing. The other four of the Big Five are here—it's excellent for black and white rhinos—and the park is stocked with cheetahs, hyenas, giraffes, and an array of antelopes among its 80 mammal species. It's also an excellent spot for birders. The stunning landscapes and the relaxed game viewing make this area a breath of fresh air after the Big Five melee of Mpumalanga.

Founded in 1972, the reserve, run by KZN Wildlife, is a rugged re-gion that drops 3,290 ft in just 15 km (9 mi) through sandstone cliffs, multicolor rocks, granite hills, ironstone outcrops, and quartz forma-tions. Watered by nine small rivers rising in its vicinity and covered with rich soils, Itala supports a varied cross section of vegetation, en-compassing riverine thicket, wetland, open savanna, and acacia wood-land. Arrival at its Ntshondwe Camp is nothing short of dramatic. The meandering road climbs from open plains to the top of a plateau dot-ted with granite formations, which at the last minute magically yield the rest camp at the foot of pink and russet cliffs.

Self-Guided Trails

An unusual feature of Itala is its self-guided walking trails, in the mountainside above Ntshondwe camp. It gives you a chance to stretch your limbs if you've just spent hours cooped up in a car. It also has the advantage of giving you the chance to get really close to the euphor-bias, acacias, and other fascinating indigenous vegetation that festoon the hills. Ask at the camp reception for further information.

Lodging

Although Itala has several exclusive bush camps, these are booked up months in advance by South Africans, making the chalets at its main camp the only practical accommodations for foreign visitors. Two people sharing a two-bed unit at Ntshondwe will pay about R260 per person per night.

$$ ⊡ **Ntshondwe Camp.** In architecture, landscaping, and style, this beau-
★ tiful government-run rest camp comes closer than any other in the country to matching the expensive private lodges. Built around granite boulders and vegetation lush with acacias, wild figs, and giant cactuslike euphorbias, the airy chalets with steep thatch roofs blend perfectly with the surroundings. Its two-, four-, and six-bed units can accommodate a total of 200 guests. Each chalet has a spacious lounge simply furnished with cane chairs, a fully equipped kitchen, and a large veranda surrounded by indigenous bush. If you're cooking yourself, buy supplies in Durban or one of the larger towns, such as Vryheid, before you come because the camp shop is poorly stocked and Louwsburg is a one-horse town. A magnificent game-viewing deck juts out over a steep decline to provide views of the water hole and extensive panoramas of the surrounding valleys. There's a gas station on the premises. ⊠ *Reservations: KZN Wildlife, Box 13069, Cascades 3202, ☎ 033/845–1000, ᶠᴬˣ 034/907–5190. 39 chalets. Restaurant, bar, pool, private airstrip. AE, DC, MC, V.*

Itala Game Reserve A to Z

To research prices, get advice from other travelers, and book travel arrangements, visit www.fodors.com.

AIR TRAVEL

The closest airport to the park is at Richards Bay, about 224 km (140 mi) south of Itala. The airport is served by SA Express Airways, which has daily flights from Johannesburg.

➤ AIRLINES AND CONTACTS: **SA Express Airways** (☎ 035/786–0301).

CAR RENTAL

Avis and Imperial have car-rental offices at the Richards Bay airport.
➤ CAR RENTAL INFORMATION: **Avis** (☎ 035/789–6555). **Imperial** (☎ 035/786–0309).

CAR TRAVEL

From Durban drive north on the N2 to Empangeni, and then head west on the R34 to Vryheid. From here cut east on the R69 to Louwsburg. The reserve is immediately northwest of the village, from which there are clear signposts. The journey from Durban takes around five hours and from Hluhluwe-Umfolozi about 2½ hours.

PRIVATE GAME RESERVES AND LODGES

KwaZulu-Natal's best private lodges lie in northern Zululand and Maputaland, a remote region close to Mozambique. With one exception, the lodges reviewed here do not offer the Big Five. However, they are sufficiently close to one another and Hluhluwe-Umfolozi Game Reserve to allow you to put together a bush experience that delivers the Big Five and a great deal more, including superb bird-watching opportunities and an unrivaled beach paradise. Malaria does pose a problem, however, and antimalarial drugs are essential. Summers are hot, hot, hot.

CATEGORY	COST*
$$$$	over R2,500
$$$	R1,750–R2,500
$$	R1,000–R1,750
$	under R1,000

All prices are per person sharing a double room, including all meals, bush walks, and game drives.

Ndumo Wilderness Camp

This bush camp lies in Ndumo Game Reserve in Maputaland, a remote northern region of KwaZulu-Natal, near the Mozambique border. The 24,700-acre park does not have the Big Five, and visitors wanting to see big game should head elsewhere. What makes Ndumo famous are its birds. Along with Mkuze, the park is probably the premier bird-watching locale in the country. More than 400 species of birds—60% of all the birds in South Africa—have been spotted here, including the gorgeous purple-crested lourie, the green coucal, and the elusive narina trogon. Myriad waterfowl also flock to the reserve's Nyamiti and Banzi pans, and summer migrants take up residence from October until April.

Ndumo has no lions or elephants, but it supports a healthy population of black and white rhinos, rare Suni antelopes, and red duikers, as well as the usual plains animals. And even though it may not have the Big Five, it is one of the most beautiful reserves in the country. Forests of yellow fever trees are mirrored in glassy lakes, and giant sycamore figs provide shelter for crowned eagles and rare fishing owls. Crocodiles numbering in the hundreds bask on the grassy banks, while hippos honk and blow in deep pools. In addition to leading the usual game drives, rangers often take guests on extended bush walks. The best time to visit is October, when migrant birds return and antelope start bearing their young.

$$ \quad \triangle \quad$$ **Ndumo Wilderness Camp.** This is a small tented lodge raised on stilts in a fig forest abutting Banzi Pan. Wooden walkways connect the camp's luxurious East African safari-style tents, each with its own bathroom and veranda overlooking the pan, which is home to scores of crocodiles. The main lodge is an open-sided thatch shelter with broad decks extending over the water. Armed with a pair of binoculars, you could sit here for hours and never get bored. $$\boxtimes$$ *Box 78573, Sandton 2146,* $$\textcircled{2}$$ *011/883–0747,* FAX *011/883–0911. 8 tents. Bar, pool. AE, DC, MC, V.*

Phinda Private Game Reserve

Established in 1991, this flagship CC Africa reserve is a heartening example of tourism serving the environment with panache. Phinda (*pin-duh*) is Zulu for "return," referring to the restoration of 42,000 acres of overgrazed ranchland in northern Zululand to bushveld. After 10 years it's a triumph—you'll find it impossible to believe the area wasn't always the thick bush you see all around you. The Big Five have established themselves firmly, and Phinda still boasts a first in South African game lodges: a stunning variety of ecosystems to rival any in Africa. You'll see the unique sand forest (which grows on the fossil dunes of an earlier coastline), savanna, bushveld, open woodland, and verdant wetlands.

Phinda can deliver the Big Five, although not as consistently or in such numbers as its sister lodge, Londolozi, in Mpumalanga. Buffalo, leopard, lion, cheetah, spotted hyena, elephant, white rhino, hippo, giraffe, impala, and the rare, elusive tiny Suni antelope are all here, and the rangers work hard to find them for guests. The birdlife is prolific and extraordinary, with some Zululand specials: the pink-throated twin spot, the crested guinea fowl, the African broadbill, and the crowned eagle. Where Phinda also excels is in the superb quality of its rangers, who can provide a fascinating commentary on everything from local birds to frogs. There are also adventure trips (optional extras) down the Mzinene River for a close-up look at crocodiles, hippos and birds; big-game fishing or scuba diving off the deserted, wildly beautiful Maputaland coast; and sightseeing flights over Phinda and the highest vegetated dunes in the world. ✉ *Private Bag X27, Benmore 2010,* ☎ *011/809–4300,* FAX *011/809–4400,* WEB *www.ccafrica.com. AE, DC, MC, V.*

$$$$ ✕▣ **Forest Lodge.** Hidden in one of the last remaining sand forests in
★ the world, this fabulous lodge overlooks a small water hole where nyalas, warthogs, and baboons frequently come to drink. The lodge is a real departure from the traditional thatch structures so common in South Africa. It's very modern, with a vaguely Japanese feel thanks to glass-panel walls, light woods, and a deliberately spare, clean look. The effect is stylish and very elegant, softened by modern African art and sculpture. Guest suites use the same architectural concepts as the lodge, where walls have become windows, and rely on the dense forest (or curtains) for their privacy. As a result, guests feel very close to their surroundings, and it's possible to lie in bed or take a shower while watching delicate nyalas grazing just feet away. This lodge is a winner. *16 suites. Bar, pool, private airstrip.*

$$$$ ✕▣ **Mountain Lodge.** This attractive thatch lodge sits on a rocky hill overlooking miles of bushveld plains and the Ubombo Mountains. Wide verandas lead into the lounge and bar, graced with high ceilings, dark beams, and cool tile floors. In winter guests can snuggle into cushioned wicker chairs next to a blazing log fire. Brick pathways wind down the hillside from the lodge to elegant split-level suites with mosquito nets, thatch roofs, and large decks overlooking the reserve. African baskets, beadwork, and grass matting beautifully complement the bush atmosphere. *15 suites, 7 chalets. Bar, pool, private airstrip.*

$$$$ ✕▣ **Vlei Lodge.** The smallest and most intimate of the lodges at Phinda, the elegant guest lodging here is nestled in the shade of the rare sand forest and is so private it's hard to believe there are other guests. Suites—made of thatch, teak, and glass—have a distinct Asian feel and overlook a wet marshland on the edge of an inviting woodland. The bedrooms and bathrooms are huge, and guests have private plunge pools (a recent visitor had a lion drinking from his) and outdoor decks. The lounge/living area of the lodge has two fireplaces on opposite glass walls, a dining area, and a large terrace under a canopy of trees, where breakfast is served. The bush braai, with its splendid food and fairy-tale setting, is a memorable occasion after an evening game drive. *6 suites. Bar, pool, private airstrip.*

Pongola Game Reserve

One of the largest inland bodies of water in Zululand is the Jozini Dam, covering an area of some 39,520 acres along the Pongola River, close to the southern Swaziland border. Some 200 km (120 mi) of its pristine shoreline is bounded by the Pongola Game Reserve, today only a part of the original area declared a reserve in 1894 by President Paul Kruger. The dam, built in the 1960s to provide irrigation to sugarcane farmers and hydroelectric power to the region, was never used for those purposes and, for many years, was something of a white elephant. Today it has found its niche, becoming a magnet for tourists to northern KwaZulu-Natal. Surrounded by pristine bushveld and scrub, the dam provides sanctuary to a large number of crocodiles and hippos. Tiger fish that had nowhere to swim to after the river was dammed stayed put, and now fish of up to 24 pounds have been caught in the dam's waters. The region hosts an annual tiger-fishing competition in late September, drawing fishing enthusiasts from around the country. The dam has also ensured that the area is a birding hot spot, with more than 300 species of bushveld and waterbirds being recorded. The purple-blue Lebombo Mountains looming behind the lake add majesty to the picturesque scenery.

Game here includes four of the Big Five (except lions), all of which have been reintroduced. The most interesting are the elephants, to the south of the reserve: it is the first time in more than 100 years that the great beasts have populated the region, and their effect on bushveld ecology is being monitored by a dedicated team. In addition, you may see warthogs, wildebeests, giraffes, zebras, and a variety of antelopes, including nyalas.

Pongola Game Reserve is definitely not for the armchair wildlife enthusiast. Activities include traditional game drives in open safari vehicles, as well as guided bush walks, fishing, big-game tracking, and boat trips on the Pongola River and Jozini Dam.

To access the northern part of the reserve, travel north on the N2, past Umfolozi and Hluhluwe, toward the town of Pongola. Approximately 30 km (19 mi) south of Pongola, look out for the sign to Golela and take this road to the right. After about 4 km (2 mi), you will see a sign to Pongola Game Reserve. The gate is on the right-hand side. *Note: Do not take the first right-hand turn, also signposted* PONGOLA GAME RESERVE, *off the N2. This accesses the southern part of the reserve only.*

$ ✕🏠 **Pongola Game Reserve.** This beautiful and affordable lodge is high on the banks of the Pongola River and has endless, unspoiled views of silver river, blue sky, and rolling green hills. You'll stay in attractive thatch-and-wood chalets that face the magnificent panorama; however, bathrooms are rather small, containing only a sink and shower. A stone-walled communal lounge-bar area, attractively furnished with huge basket chairs, has sliding doors that open onto a wooden deck. Breakfasts are usually served on a thatch deck, and a traditional boma is the place for dinner, where, if you're adventurous, you can try such meats as kudu rumps or impala schnitzel. There's also a swimming pool—a must during summer, when temperatures soar beyond 38°C (100°F).

Self-catering accommodations across the N2 at **Mhlozi Camp** are also available. The camp can hold up to 12 people in thatch rondawels. There is a fully equipped communal kitchen where you can do your own cooking; dining and lounge-bar facilities; and a swimming pool. You can purchase food and drinks in Pongola. ✉ *On Golela Rd., off the N2 (mailing address: Box 767, Pongola 3170),* ☎ *034/435–1123,* 🆐 *034/435–1104,* 🌐 *www.pongolagamereserve.co.za. 8 rooms, 6 rondawels. Bar, lounge, pool. AE, DC, MC, V. MAP.*

To access the southern part of the reserve, travel north on the N2, past Umfolozi and Hluhluwe, toward the town of Pongola. Fifty kilometers (28 miles) from Pongola, look for the brown signboard to Pongola Game Reserve and turn right off the N2.

$$ 🐘 **White Elephant Lodge.** Once you are in the Pongola Reserve, follow the Pongolwane signs (painted on rocks) and white arrows (*do not turn off to Mpelane*) and the logos of white elephants. White Elephant is a lovely lodge that captures the elegance of colonial Africa, with white furniture, African prints, sepia photographs of local historical scenes, and antiques. The lounge and dining room are in a historic farmhouse, with wide verandas providing sweeping views of the bushveld and Lebombo Mountains. Behind the house, sheltered from the prevailing winds, a traditional Zulu boma is the venue for dinners and Zulu dancing. Accommodations are in luxury East African safari tents—airy, cool, and perfect for hot subtropical nights. Each tent has a private bathroom with a claw-foot tub, an outdoor shower surrounded by canvas screens, and a private veranda. Paths link the tents and the main house. You can choose from among taking part in the lodge's elephant monitoring program, viewing game from an open vehicle, or fishing for a whopping tiger fish or two. ⊠ *Off the N2, south of Pongola (mailing address: Box 792, Pongola 3170),* ☎ FAX *034/413–2489,* WEB *www.whiteelephantlodge.co.za. 8 tents. Minibars, pool. AE, DC, MC, V. FAP.*

Mkuze Falls Lodge

Thirty-seven kilometers (19 miles) west of Pongola lies Mkuze Falls Lodge, in a private game reserve covering some 15,000 acres of pristine wilderness on the Mkuze River. The focal point of this very luxurious lodge is the fabulous Mkuze Falls, which stretch 90 ft across the entire Mkuze River at this point and plunge 36 ft in a wild cataract of foam and spray. Set in a valley between high hills, the entire lodge faces the falls and river, making the most of this eye-catching display in the wet summer. If you go during the dry winter season, you'll probably see an azure pool at the base of a spectacular cliff but not the raging waters of the falls.

Mkuze Falls has all of the Big Five, in addition to wildebeests, zebras, giraffes, and a variety of antelopes, including the shy nyala. Most animals have been reintroduced, with the exception of leopards, which remain secretive and very difficult to spot. In addition, a wide variety of bird species will delight birders.

$$ ✕⌸ **Mkuze Falls Lodge.** Accommodations here are in thatch-and-brick units. You may find the decor a little over the top, with huge mock elephant tusks framing the bed's headboard and a particularly voluminous mosquito net; however, this is made up for by the bathroom, which leads onto a private patio with a sunken pool and outdoor shower. Public areas are sumptuously decorated with curios, African prints, and paintings of the Big Five. The staff is not as friendly at first as at other lodges but is still competent and informed. ⊠ *Follow signs off the N2, just south of Pongola (mailing address: Box 248, Pongola 3170),* ☎ *034/414–1018,* FAX *034/414–1142,* WEB *www.mkuzefalls.com. 16 units. Bar, minibars, in-room safes, pool. AE, DC, MC, V. FAP.*

Rocktail Bay Lodge

If Robinson Crusoe had washed ashore on the pristine coastline of Maputaland, he wouldn't have found anybody to call Friday—and he certainly wouldn't have cared what day of the week it was. It's that empty and that magnificent. No other buildings lie within 16 km (10 mi) of Rocktail Bay Lodge, tucked away in Maputaland Coastal Reserve, a narrow strip of wilderness that stretches from St. Lucia all the way to Mozambique. If you love exploring along untouched beaches, fishing, diving, snorkeling, and walking, coming here will be one of the highlights of a visit to South Africa. Rocktail Bay is not a game lodge—the only animals you're likely to see are loggerhead and leatherback turtles. It is included in this section because it lies far from any other major tourist destination and operates much like a game lodge. In fact, unless you have a four-wheel-drive vehicle, the lodge must collect you for the final 11-km (7-mi) journey along deep sand tracks carved through coastal dune forest.

Rocktail Bay *does not offer traditional game viewing,* although you can combine a visit here with a trip to Phinda, about 95 km (60 mi) to the south. Besides glorious beaches, its major attraction is the annual arrival of giant loggerhead and leatherback turtles to lay their eggs. The beaches here are one of the few known egg-laying areas of these endangered animals, and the season extends from the end of October through February. During these months rangers lead after-dinner walks down the beach to look for turtles, and you can expect to cover as much as 16 km (10 mi) in a night. From a weather standpoint the best times to visit the lodge are probably spring (September–October) and autumn (March–May). In summer the temperature regularly soars past 38°C (100°F), and swimming during winter is a brisk proposition. August is the windiest month, and it's in November that the turtles come ashore to dig their nests and lay their eggs—an awesome spectacle.

$$$ ✕🖭 **Rocktail Bay Lodge.** The lodge lies in a swale formed by enormous
★ dunes fronting the ocean. Walkways tunnel through the dune forest to a golden beach that sweeps in a gentle arc to Black Rock, several miles to the north. There are no lifeguards or shark nets, but the swimming and snorkeling are fabulous. The lodge consists of simple A-frame chalets raised on wooden platforms above the forest floor. Wood and thatch create a rustic ambience, complemented by solar lighting and basic furnishings. A large veranda and adjoining thatch bar provide the backdrop for alfresco meals under a giant Natal mahogany tree. Activities include great surf fishing (tackle provided), snorkeling, and walking along the beach. Rangers lead excursions to see hippo pools, the rich bird life of Lake Sibaya, and Kosi Bay, where the local Tembe people catch fish, using the age-old method of basket netting. For many people, though, a trip to Rocktail Bay is a chance to kick back and just soak in the atmosphere of an unspoiled coastal wilderness. ✉ *Box 78573, Sandton 2146,* ☎ *011/883–0747,* 𝔽𝔸𝕏 *011/883–0911. 10 chalets. Bar, pool. AE, DC, MC, V. FAP.*

9 SWAZILAND

From the rolling hills in the northwest to the purple Lubombo Mountains in the east, Swaziland has the look of an African paradise, where you can explore crafts markets, ride horses through Ezulwini Valley, and raft the mighty Usutu River.

Updated by
Kate Turkington

COVERING A MERE 17,000 SQUARE KM (6,570 square mi), Swaziland is one of the smallest African countries. Surrounded by the giants of South Africa and Mozambique, this tiny, landlocked kingdom has somehow retained its ancient Swazi culture.

The same prehistoric upheaval that created the Drakensberg Mountains in South Africa also formed the Swazi Highveld, a spectacular escarpment cut by deep gorges, lush valleys, and fast-flowing rivers and waterfalls. The Highveld is also home to Swaziland's main game areas, where you can watch crocodiles and hippos at a water hole, surprise antelope on foot, see Goliath herons take flight, and raft the country's fastest river. The Middleveld, a densely populated grassland plateau, links the west with the Lowveld, where sugarcane plantations briefly tame the African bush, and "fever trees," acacias with greenish bark, mark this as a malarial area. Against the Lowveld sky are the spectacular, inaccessible Lubombo Mountains, a lofty, blue divide.

The picturesque Swaziland region has been inhabited since the Stone Age, first by nomadic bushmen, then by the Sotho and Nguni tribes, as part of a vast human migration from east and central Africa. In 1750 King Ngwane III led a band of Nguni to settle among the hills overlooking the Pongola River, where he became a fierce custodian of his domain. Perhaps as tribute, the members of the tribe came to call themselves the Ngwane.

Despite fierce opposition from the Zulus, the next king, Sobhuza, gained control of southern Swaziland. But the Zulus continued to cause trouble until the king requested assistance from traders at Lorenço Marques (Maputo). From this encounter with Westerners the Ngwane first discovered maize, a food that was to become the staple of southern African peoples. Swaziland acquired its name from Sobhuza's son, Mswati II.

During the mid-1800s, white adventurers began arriving in large numbers, attracted by rumors of gold. In 1880 King Mbandzeni began selling land concessions, and by the time King Sobhuza II had inherited the throne in 1899, most of the country belonged to the concessionaires. Sobhuza II embarked on an extensive campaign to return land to his people. Even today, no Swazi owns land outright; it remains the property of the nation.

After World War II a sizable cash injection from the British fostered economic development. In 1967 Swaziland became independent of Britain, with Sobhuza as the new nation's official leader. In April 1986 his successor, and the current king, King Mswati III, was crowned.

Today's Swazis mix age-old traditions with modern Western influences. Although many have converted to Christianity and wear Western dress, you will still find locals in colorful traditional costume. Rites, rituals, and customs passed down through generations still govern every aspect of a person's life. Ancestors are respected, and their spirits play a part in family affairs; chastity is valued, as are strict courtship rituals; marriage requires the payment of *lobola*—a dowry, usually in the form of cattle, a sign of wealth in Africa; and a young bride adopts the youngest child from her husband's family until she has children of her own. Even the king is not exempt from tradition: his eldest son is not necessarily the one who inherits the crown; the Royal Council chooses a new king, who must be unmarried.

Pleasures and Pastimes

Arts and Crafts

Swaziland never really had an industrial revolution, and many people still obtain their livelihood from cottage industries, making everything from pottery and leather ware to candles and batiks. You shouldn't miss Swaziland's unique arts-and-crafts routes in the Ezulwini and Malkerns valleys, where you'll be welcomed into many workshops to see the master craftspeople perform their tasks. As you examine the lines of curios at roadside stalls, keep your eyes open for wooden bowls (usually unadorned), baskets woven from banana leaves, dolls dressed in traditional Swazi garb, and hand-dyed bolts of cloth.

Dining and Lodging

Since the South African rand is widely accepted throughout Swaziland, and is tied to the local currency, Dining and Lodging prices are given in rand throughout this chapter.

For dining:

CATEGORY	COST*
$$$$	more than R65
$$$	R45–R65
$$	R25–R45
$	less than R25

*Rates are for a main course.

For lodging:

CATEGORY	COST*
$$$$	more than R750
$$$	R500–R750
$$	R250–R500
$	less than R250

*Rates are for a standard, high-season double room, including VAT.

Festivals

Despite Westernization, Swazi traditions are still strongly upheld. The main ceremony is the Ncwala (Festival of First Fruits), in December or January, a six-day event celebrating the dawn of a new year. The colorful festival involves singing, dancing, and sacred rituals performed by the king. Another important ceremony is the Umhlanga (Reed Dance), in late August and early September. Marriageable Swazi maidens gather at the queen mother's residence and are sent to gather reeds to repair a windbreak. After spending the fifth day preparing their elaborate dresses, the girls sing and dance on the sixth and seventh days. The Incwala (Ncwala) is the most sacred ceremony of the Swazi people. Held near Lobamba, in the Ezulwini Valley, between late December and early January at a time determined by the royal astrologers, it's a "first fruits" ceremony, when the king gives permission for his peoples to eat the first crops of the new year. At full moon young Swazi men carrying the branches of *lusekwane*, a small tree, begin the long trek to the Royal Kraal. The ceremony lasts for several days, until the king dances before his people and eats a symbolic pumpkin that is then followed by a ritual burning of the items used in the ceremony. Unlike the Reed Dance ceremony, photographs are forbidden at Incwala, but a free admittance permit is available from the Government Information Service in Mbabane.

Hiking

Although the weather can be extremely rainy at times, Swaziland is great hiking country, particularly in the Highveld toward Piggs Peak.

Reserves such as Malolotja, which have a wide network of stunningly scenic routes, are favorites with backpackers and day walkers. Almost every country hotel has nature trails, and you can go on guided or self-guided walks at many game reserves.

Horseback Riding

Most Swazis are keen riders, and there are stables everywhere. You can make arrangements to ride wherever you stay: if the establishment doesn't have its own horses, it's sure to be able to refer you to a stable in the vicinity. You don't have to be an accomplished horseperson either; novices are always welcome. It's a wonderful way to see the countryside—the Mlilwane Wildlife Sanctuary even features horseback riding as a way of getting up close to wildlife.

Wildlife

Although it's not often thought of in conjunction with big game, Swaziland has its fair share. Poaching activities were a major problem in Swaziland's reserves during the early 1990s, but vigilant antipoaching measures and strict wildlife laws have effectively controlled the problem. Swaziland's four game areas offer different wildlife experiences. You can see antelope and smaller game at Malolotja while on a hiking trail. Mlilwane was the first area to be declared a reserve, but the largest animals you're likely to see there are hippos basking in a water hole. There are also unique accommodations in Swazi beehive huts. Mkhaya *is* big-game country, where you can see everything except lions. The reserve is set in pristine bushveld, and you traverse the area in Land Rovers, accompanied by knowledgeable Swazi game rangers. Hlane Game Reserve is similar to Mkhaya but has all the Big Five (the lions are in an enclosure, however) and two marvelous water holes.

Exploring Swaziland

The main geographic units of Swaziland are the very distinct Highveld, Middleveld, and Lowveld. The four main game reserves are Malolotja, Mlilwane, Mkhaya, and Hlane.

Great Itineraries

Swaziland makes a good side trip from South Africa. You will need a minimum of two days to see the highlights, but there's easily enough to do for five days. Wildlife experiences are more hands-on than in many places in South Africa: Most rest camps are unfenced and you could conceivably be chased by a warthog or surprise antelope outside the door of your cottage.

If you've got a little longer, spend more time in the tranquil mountain areas before taking in the major tourist route in Ezulwini and Malkerns.

Numbers in the text correspond to numbers in the margin and on the Swaziland map.

IF YOU HAVE 2 DAYS

If you enter Swaziland at Jeppes Reef/Matsamo, travel down the scenic route through the beautiful Ngwenya Hills to ⊡ **Mbabane** ①. If you enter at Oshoek/Ngwenya, pause en route to Mbabane to see the Ngwenya Glass Factory and Endlotane Studios. In Mbabane have something to eat at the Swazi Mall or Omni Center before seeing the Mbabane Craft Market. Take the route toward Manzini through the ⊡ **Ezulwini Valley** ⑤, exploring crafts markets along the road to Malkerns. At Malkerns see the cottage industries, specializing in batiks and candle making, before returning to the Ezulwini Valley. Stay overnight

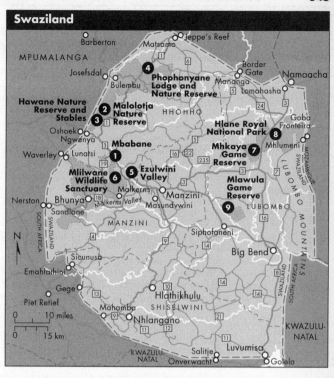

Swaziland

at one of the hotels or ⊡ **Mlilwane Wildlife Sanctuary** ⑥. Travel to Manzini and take the road to Siphofaneni and Big Bend. Approximately 7 km (4½ mi) from Siphofaneni, you will see signs to ⊡ **Mkhaya Game Reserve** ⑦. A ranger will meet you at this point. Spend the day at Mkhaya, going on game drives and having lunch (don't forget to book this one in advance). Depart Swaziland via Big Bend and the Lavumisa-Golela border post to explore the KwaZulu-Natal (☞ Chapter 8) game reserves.

IF YOU HAVE 5 DAYS

Enter Swaziland at Oshoek/Ngwenya and drive through picturesque scenery to Piggs Peak; stay overnight at ⊡ **Phophonyane Lodge** ④. Move on to the ⊡ **Malolotja Nature Reserve** ②, where there are self-guided auto trails, bird-watching, and hiking. Spend the night at the reserve, self-catering (there is a shop at the entrance gate where you can purchase most provisions). The following day drive to Mbabane and spend a few hours viewing the city. Spend the night outside town en route to the Ezulwini Valley or stay in the valley itself. If you wish, take a morning horseback ride at your accommodations before spending the rest of the day exploring crafts markets and cottage industries in Ezulwini and Malkerns. As an alternative, spend the night at ⊡ **Mlilwane Wildlife Sanctuary** ⑥ and in the morning enjoy one of the many activities at Mlilwane. Afterward, drive to Manzini, where you can obtain provisions if you're self-catering. Move on to ⊡ **Mkhaya Game Reserve** ⑦ for an afternoon game drive. Spend the day at the game reserve, enjoying bush walks and game drives. Leave the reserve and drive back to Siphofaneni (or drive past the reserve entrance to Simunye) to stock up with provisions before continuing on to ⊡ **Hlane Royal National Park** ⑧, where you'll spend the night.

When to Tour Swaziland

As in South Africa, the hottest time of year is November–February. Visit in autumn (March–May) and spring (September–October) for the best weather. The Swazi Highveld has a climate similar to that of Johannesburg: hot, rainy summers and cool, frosty winters. Chill winds blow during late winter and early spring. Heavy fog may occur in the hill country near Piggs Peak when it rains. In winter smoke from grass fires can blur those magnificent scenic panoramas. To the east the climate becomes considerably hotter and more humid, becoming almost subtropical close to the Lubombo Mountains. This can make life very unpleasant during summer. Winter is definitely the time to tour eastern Swaziland; malaria is also less prevalent then.

Mbabane

❶ Mbabane is the capital and largest city of Swaziland. By South African standards it's dusty, small, and laid back. Traffic tends to be confusing; once you leave the main routes, you're likely to find yourself in a warren of small streets.

En route to Mbabane you'll pass the **Ngwenya Glass Factory,** where recycled glass is used to create beautiful African animals as well as tableware and glasses. The factory lies at the base of a mountain that looks like a basking crocodile (Ngwenya is the Swazi name for crocodile). Ngwenya Glass has a workshop where you can watch the glassblowers at work and an inviting shop full of glass treasures. Be sure to visit the coffee shop upstairs, which has glorious views, and take a look around the indigenous gardens, which have an array of other interesting crafts. ⊠ *Box 45, Motshane, H104, Kingdom of Swaziland,, 5 km (3 mi) southeast from Oshoek-Ngwenya border post, follow yellow signposts,* ☎ FAX *268/442–4142 or 268/442–4151,* WEB *www.ngwenyaglass.co.sz.* 🖾 *Free.* ☉ *Weekdays 8–4:30, weekends 9–4.*

Fabulous **Endlotane Studio** is the home of Phumalanga Tapestries. The German owners emigrated from Europe in the 1970s, having previously developed a love for all things African. The couple combine their artistic talents—graphic design, weaving, sculpting, and painting—to produce unique tapestries. African themes inspire their designs, which are based on rock paintings, African animals, and rural villages. Wool is hand-dyed, and Swazi weavers work the enormous looms. *1 km (½ mi) from Ngwenya Glass—follow the signs on the road,* ☎ *268/442–4326,* FAX *268/404–4327.* 🖾 *Free.* ☉ *Daily 9–4.*

In a house in town the **Indingilizi Gallery** contains treasures from all over Africa. Walls are lined with colorful artwork, beadwork, and wall hangings. The rooms are a potpourri of pottery, masks, cloth, batiks, and candlesticks. Behind the house is an informal restaurant serving light lunches with an African flavor. ⊠ *112 Johnson St., Mbabane,* ☎ *268/404–6213,* WEB *www.indingilizi.com.* 🖾 *Free.* ☉ *Weekdays 8–4:30, Sat. 8–1.*

Dining and Lodging

$$–$$$ ✕ **La Casserole.** Light wooden paneling and pale green and apricot decor
★   create a relaxed atmosphere at Mbabane's best restaurant. Enormous picture windows make the place light and airy, and on warm days and evenings you may venture out onto the patio—corrugated iron roofs, alas, mar the view, but the cool air is welcome. Starters include soups and crepes; main courses include steaks, fish dishes, schnitzels, and other German specialties. The restaurant has a full liquor license, and all wine comes from South Africa. On a practical note, there's plenty of safe

underground parking. ⊠ *Omni Centre, Allister Miller St.,* ☎ *268/404–6426,* ⅄ *268/404–6715. AE, DC, MC, V.*

$$$ 🏨 **Mountain Inn.** This airy, Mediterranean-style hotel has stunning views of the Ezulwini Valley from its prime location 4 km (2½ mi) from Mbabane. The outer decor is a little shabby, but it's still one of the most popular hotels in Mbabane. There are glorious vistas from every attractively furnished room, where wooden furniture and pastel shades predominate. The pastel theme continues throughout the public areas, creating a fresh, breezy atmosphere. The pool area takes full advantage of the view but is not very private. The bar downstairs is a disappointment: it has a neglected air of faded grandeur. ⊠ *Box 223,* ☎ *268/404–2781 or 268/404–2773,* ⅄ *268/404–5393,* WEB *www.mountaininn.sz. 60 rooms. Restaurant, bar, room service, pool. AE, DC, MC, V.*

$$ 🏨 **Foresters Arms Hotel.** This delightful family-run establishment is high in the mountains near Mhlambanyatsi, 27 km (17 mi) from Mbabane. Rooms are furnished in bright floral prints, and beds have thick feather duvets—a must on cool mountain nights. Some rooms have fireplaces. Verandas equipped with chairs command sweeping views across pine forests. Relax in the comfortable lounge, library, and bar reminiscent of old England, with armchairs, old-fashioned wallpaper, and enormous log fires. You can also dine by candlelight and savor delicious country cuisine, or have a hot toddy at the bar. Golf clubs, rackets, and fishing rods are available for use in the extensive facilities. Nearby you can tour a genuine Swazi homestead or see a practicing *inyanga* (traditional doctor) throwing the bones. ⊠ *Box 14, Mhlambanyatsi,* ☎ *268/467–4177 or 268/467–4377,* ⅄ *268/467–4051,* WEB *www.forestersarms.co.za. 30 rooms. Restaurant, bar, in-room VCRs, pool, hot tub, sauna, 18-hole golf course, tennis court, gym, squash, fishing, recreation room. AE, DC, MC, V. MAP.*

Shopping

The pleasant **Mbabane Craft Market** is worth seeing, and the local women selling the crafts are very friendly. You'll find row upon row of the ubiquitous African masks, malachite bracelets, and wildlife carvings. But among the rows you'll also find quality Swazi drums, locally woven cloth, basket ware, and wooden bowls. Prices are reasonable. Don't despair if there's not much activity outside: go behind the scenes, where indoor stalls abound. If you're self-catering after Mbabane, go next door to the informal fruit-and-vegetable market for quality, reasonably priced fresh produce. ⊠ *Bypass Rd. and main road to Manzini,* ☎ *no phone.*

Omni Centre, a business center with a shopping concourse, deserves a mention as it has one of the city's few Internet cafés, which offers e-mail service. It also has Mbabane's best restaurant (☞ *above*). ⊠ *Allister Miller St.,* ☎ *no phone.*

Swazi Mall has the most upmarket South African shops, such as Woolworth's (the African equivalent of Britain's Marks and Spencer) and Spar, and numerous smaller establishments. Enjoy an ice cream or coffee and cake out on the terrace. Swaziland Big Game Parks has its offices here. ⊠ *Bypass Rd. (opposite Swazi Plaza),* ☎ *no phone.*

Malolotja Nature Reserve

2 *32 km (20 mi) northeast from Mbabane.*

Set in the Ngwenya Hills, this pristine nature reserve is well worth visiting, either en route from Piggs Peak or as a side trip from Mbabane. Malolotja is a hiker's paradise, and the best way to experience its natural wonders is on your own two feet. At the gate ask for the comprehensive hiking map (R5) and the backpacking and walking guide (R4). Walks are graded according to degree of difficulty—and they're not to be taken lightly. Walks graded easy are generally shorter and easier, but allow more time if you're unfit, since walking at Malalotja tends to be rough and can be heavy going. Cairns mark the route, but trails often cross each other and this tends to be confusing, so its important to purchase the hiking map, not the general reserve maps, which do not go into enough detail. Even with maps in hand, make a note about where you start and the general direction in which you are heading. It might also be a good idea to set a time for turning back, as some routes are longer than they look. Self-drive dirt roads lead to the start of walks or to picturesque points for viewing. Some of the more interesting walks are the Gold Mine Walk, the Malolotja Falls Walk—these falls are the highest in Swaziland, accessible only on foot—and walks along the Majolomba River.

Most routes descend, and the return journey entails a lot of uphill effort. On longer routes allow sufficient time by starting as early as possible. Wear sturdy footwear and carry a minimum of 2 liters of water, as it can be very hot and dry. Some roads may be fairly rough in places. Look out for routes marked 4x4 and avoid them. The roads are not all weather and may be closed in wet conditions. Take note of any ROAD CLOSED signs you encounter.

Walk quietly in single file, and you'll probably see a variety of animals. It's worth asking at the gate which areas have been burned recently, as blue wildebeests, blesboks, zebras, and red hartebeests will concentrate there. Also look out for black wildebeests, a variety of antelope, warthogs, bush pigs, baboons, vervet monkeys, and black-backed jackals. The Cape clawless otter lives near streams and rivers. The bird life is also magnificent, with more than 280 recorded species. Finally, you'll find an incredible diversity of plants and flowers.

Malalotja has worthwhile game drives, so try a scenic drive in the morning (departing at around 7 in summer and 8 in winter), which will allow you time to visit Ngwenya Mountain and other parts of the reserve rarely accessible to most visitors. An evening game drive (departing at about 6 in winter and 6:30 in summer) is a good way to see the nocturnal animals in the reserves. Morning drives cost around R60 per person, with a minimum of two people (maximum four people) and R30 for the accompanying ranger, while evening drives cost around R40 per person, with a minimum of two people (maximum four people) and R20 for the accompanying ranger.

Worth visiting, and also falling under Malalotja, is the incredible **Ngwenya Mine** (accessed from the Ngwenya Glass road). A ranger-guide will take you to Lion Cavern, an ancient mine dating back some 45,000 years where steep ladders descend into the cavern itself. Here hematite and specularite were mined and rubbed together to form the red ocher powder used in tribal rituals. With its steep sides and aura of the ancients, the mine has an eerie atmosphere in misty conditions. From above, the site has extensive views of the Ngwenya Hills. You need to be accompanied by a ranger-guide for the mine tour, so it is essential you arrange this trip in advance, particularly if you will be there on a weekday. ✉ *On the road to Piggs Peak; take Piggs Peak–Matsamo turnoff from the main Ngwenya–Mbabane road (mailing address: Box 1797, Mbabane),* ☎ *268/24–1442 or 268/24–4241.* 🎫 *R15 per person, R6 per car; R5 for mine.* ☉ *Reserve, daily 6–6; mine, daily 8–3.*

Lodging

$$ 🏠 **Log Cabin Camp.** Close to the main gate, this beautiful camp has fully furnished and equipped log cabins (self-catering only) that sleep six and face sweeping views across the reserve's hills. Picture windows in the main living areas take full advantage of the scenery. It's not unusual to see antelope grazing on the plains below or to be woken by the echoing calls of red-winged starlings. Each cabin has a fireplace—a blessing on cool evenings. A small but well-equipped shop at the reserve gate should be able to supply most of your needs for a one-night stay; or you can shop in Mbabane at Swazi Mall. ✉ *Box 1797, Mbabane,* ☎ *268/442–4241. 13 log cabins. Hiking. No credit cards.*

Hawane Nature Reserve and Stables

❸ *22 km (14½ mi) northwest from Mbabane.*

If you're keen on horseback riding, consider a ride through these hills bordering the Malalotja Nature Reserve. Hawane Stables is on the road between Oshoek and Piggs Peak, not far from Hawane Dam. You can do a short one- or two-hour trip, or go on a two- or three-day overnight trail. Sights to see on longer trips include Mantenga Falls and the towering Rock of Execution with its uninterrupted views into Mozambique. Overnight accommodations on the longer trips tend to be rather basic, however. Other outdoor activities such as hiking, fishing, bird-watching, and white-water rafting are also arranged by Hawane Stables. Comfortable, casual outdoor clothing is recommended. Horseback-riding tuition is also offered. ☎ *268/442–4109.*

Lodging

$$$ 🏠 **Hawane Village.** The village comprises traditional Swazi beehive huts, which are pleasantly cool in summer and warm in winter. Each hut can accommodate up to four people. Rooms are decorated with fairly basic decor; each has three twin wooden beds, a heater, a fan, and small dressing table that fills the space. The huts tend to be dark inside, as access is through a low door and there are no windows. The well-lighted shared bathroom area with showers and toilets is in close proximity to the huts and is clean and attractive. There is a communal lounge–dining area under a thatched roof with a round, central fireplace where dinner and breakfast (included in the price) are served. ✉ *Box 597, Mbabane,* ☎ *268/404–0060,* 🅵🅰🆇 *268/404–0069. 6 huts. Hiking, horseback riding. AC, DC, MC, V. MAP.*

Phophonyane Lodge and Nature Reserve

❹ *42 km (26 mi) northeast from Malolotja Nature Reserve.*

This picturesque lodge and reserve is high in the hills among the pine forests 17 km (9 mi) north of Piggs Peak. The grounds resemble a green tropical paradise, with the **Phophonyane Falls** as a focal point, tumbling down a series of steep drops.

Nature trails wind through the cool, green forest to spectacular view sites. Small game abound at Phophonyane: look out in particular for bushbuck, the Cape clawless otter, and the rare red duiker. The reserve is a bird-watcher's paradise, and the prize sighting here is the colorful narina trogon. Day visitors are welcome on the grounds for an R7 fee.

Dining and Lodging

$$$ ✕🏠 **Phophonyane Lodge.** The reference to a lodge is a misnomer: self-catering accommodations are in romantic self-contained cottages, each set in its own private garden. Cottages are open plan, with spacious bathrooms, African prints, wooden furniture, and fully equipped kitchens. At the edge of the Phophonyane River is a tented camp where comfortably furnished safari tents face the river. Meals and drinks are delivered to most cottages, tents share a communal kitchen and washing facilities, and you can also eat in an open-air dining hut or the attractive Leadwood Bar. If you're looking for peace and medicine for the soul, Phophonyane is definitely a get-away-from-it-all type of place. If you're a keen landscape photographer or artist, or just love stunning scenery, then treat yourself to the Gobolondlo Mountain Drive (R85 per person), where a ranger will drive you on a gorgeous scenic trip. ✉ *Box 199, Piggs Peak, 20 km (12½ mi) north from Piggs Peak, on the road to Matsamo,* ☎ *268/437–1319 or 268/437–1429,* FAX *268/437–1319. 3 cottages, 1 suite, 5 safari tents. Restaurant, bar, pool, hiking. AE, DC, MC, V.*

Ezulwini Valley and Malkerns

⑤ *Ezulwini is 9 km (6 mi) south of Mbabane; Malkerns is 19 km (12 mi) south beyond Ezulwini.*

The Ezulwini Valley is a delightful enclave on the way to Manzini. It's home to some of Swaziland's most exclusive hotels, a casino, an 18-hole golf course, horse-riding stables, and numerous cottage industries. It's also known for some of the country's finest restaurants.

To find the **Malkerns craft route,** follow the sign to Malkerns Sentra from the highway—this road will take you straight to town.

At the **Swazi Candle Factory** you'll find the famed regional candles in every shape and size. You can purchase candles shaped like mushrooms, birds, wildebeests, and so on, and you also get the chance to observe its unique candle-making process. ✉ *Box 172, Malkerns,* ☎ *268/ 528–3219,* FAX *268/528–3135.* ◷ *Weekdays 8–5.*

On leaving Swazi Candle Factory, turn right onto the road and travel a short distance to **Baobab Batik,** on your left. Batik lovers will be in their element with this vast collection of wax imprinted fabrics ranging from wall hangings to clothing. You can go behind the scenes in the workshop and see how it's done. ✉ *Box 35, Malkerns,* ☎ *268/ 528–3439.* ◷ *Weekdays 9–5.*

Go back toward Swazi Candle Factory and turn right into Malkerns. **Gone Rural** is the first crafts place you'll find on the Malkerns road. Upstairs, the shop sells a selection of place mats, coasters, baskets, and rugs, all created from grass. Gone Rural employs a score of local women to collect grass and make items for the shop. The grass is dyed in enormous vats, weighed, and tied into bundles; go behind the house to see it all happening. ✉ *Box 446, Malkerns,* ☎ *268/528–3439,* FAX *268/528–3078,* WEB *www.gone-rural.com.* ◷ *Daily 8–4:45.*

NEED A   Near Gone Rural, and adjoining Malandela's Farm House Restaurant, is
BREAK?   the **Sigubhu Internet Cafe** (☎ 268/528–3423, ◷ Mon.–Sat. 8–5) which serves tea, coffee, scones, and toasted sandwiches.

Mantenga Cultural Village. Named Ligugu Lemaswati (pride of the Swazi people) by King Mswati III, this living museum representing the Swazi lifestyle of the 1850s and is well worth a visit. There are 16 beehive huts, all built in traditional style from leather strips, cow dung, and earth from termite mounds. Keep an eye out for demonstrations of traditional crafts, such as weaving and basket making, and also for the ubiquitous goats and cattle. There are morning and afternoon tours of the village that include traditional dancing, tasting traditional food, and a consultation with the traditional doctor (inyanga). You can also stay overnight in either a luxury safari-style tent or in a traditional hut. ✉ *Follow signs for Mantenga Nature Reserve and Swazi Cultural Village, Box 100, Lobamba,* ☎ *268/416–1013.* 🎫 *Free.* ☉ *Sun.–Mon. 6–6, Tues.–Sat. 6 AM–10 PM; cultural tours Wed.–Sun. 9 and 2.*

Dining and Lodging

\$\$–\$\$\$\$ ✕ **Calabash International Restaurant.** Plush maroon decor, fresh flowers, and bird prints combine to make this restaurant one of the more stylish in the Ezulwini Valley. Airy luncheon rooms are perfect for groups, and the attractive bar area tempts you to have that predinner drink. A Swiss chef ensures a very Continental menu: choose from dishes originating in Austria, France, Germany, Italy, Portugal, and Switzerland. *Eisbein* (pork knuckle) is very popular, as are seafood dishes. ✉ *Box 85, Ezulwini,* ☎ *268/416–1187. AE, DC, MC, V.*

\$\$–\$\$\$ ✕ **Malandela's Farm House Restaurant.** If you're on the Ezulwini–Malkerns crafts route, this spot, next to Gone Rural, is a great lunch stop. The design is based on a Dutch barn, combining burnt-umber walls, a thatched roof, and heavy timber ceiling beams. Dine indoors or alfresco on the wide, shady porch and admire the wonderful view across the farms. The food is excellent, with a varied, changing menu chalked up daily on a blackboard. Only fresh, homegrown produce is used, together with farm cream and milk produced in the area. Mozambique prawns are a Thursday-night specialty. South African wines are served. ✉ *Box 39, Malkerns,* ☎ *268/528–3115. AE, DC, MC, V. No dinner Sun., no lunch Mon.*

\$\$\$\$ 🏨 **Ezulwini Sun Hotel.** Part of the Sun International group, this open, airy hotel has a Caribbean feel, with a pastel decor and pineapple motifs on the doors and tiles. Rooms are simply furnished and have spectacular views across the pool terrace, the flower-filled gardens, and into the valley. The hotel restaurant serves buffet breakfasts and à la carte lunches and dinners. Casino vouchers for the Royal Swazi Sun Casino and a shuttle-bus service to other Sun International hotels in the valley are available. Guests can use the facilities at the Royal Swazi Sun Hotel. ✉ *Private Bag, Ezulwini,* ☎ *268/416–6000,* 📠 *268/416–1782,* 🌐 *www.suninternational.co.za. 60 rooms. Restaurant, bar, lounge, pool, tennis court, horseback riding, volleyball. AE, DC, MC, V. BP.*

\$\$\$\$ 🏨 **Royal Swazi Sun Hotel & Casino.** This Sun International hotel is perhaps the most exclusive and gracious in Swaziland. Luxury surrounds you from the moment you enter the cavernous reception area. Comfortable, tastefully furnished rooms face the pool area or golf course, both set against the magnificent backdrop of the surrounding hills. All public areas are immaculate, and you'll notice fresh flowers everywhere. There is traditional Swazi dancing on the pool terrace most evenings. At the spa pamper yourself with beauty treatments ranging from massage to pedicures. ✉ *Private Bag, Ezulwini,* ☎ *268/416–5000,* 📠 *268/416–1859,* 🌐 *www.suninternational.co.za. 202 rooms. 3 restaurants, bar, lounge, room service, pool, hot tub, 18-hole golf course, 2 tennis courts, health club, squash, casino. AE, DC, MC, V. BP.*

\$\$ 🏨 **Mantenga Lodge.** If you've no desire to stay in a chain hotel, try this quaint place close to the Ezulwini–Malkerns arts-and-crafts route in the heart of a beautiful riverine forest. Rooms are furnished with white-cane furniture and have an apricot-and-green color scheme. The bathrooms are a little on the small side, with either showers or baths. Chalet verandas overlook the forest. Meals are taken in a separate dining area where a Mauritian chef imbues the menu with a French flavor. Ask for your meal to be served under the Toon tree with its spectacular view of Nyoni (Executioner's Rock) Mountain. There's not much to do on the premises, but the lodge borders the Mlilwane Wildlife Sanctuary. ✉ *Box 68, Ezulwini,* ☎ *268/416–1049 or 268/416–*

2168, FAX *268/416–1049,* WEB *www.iafarica.sz/biz/mantenga. 8 chalets, 18 rooms. Restaurant, bar, pool, hiking. AE, DC, MC, V. BP.*

Shopping

Mantenga Craft Centre. A group of shops in a rustic "shopping center" off the main road, Mantenga specializes in crafts made by rural groups. **Country Leather** has handmade leather ware of all kinds. If angora's your pleasure, you'll love **Carol of Swaziland's** selection of woolens. The **Little Silver Shop** is a fine jewelry shop stocked with beautifully crafted items. Handwoven cotton rugs and tapestries are the province of **Shiba Rugs.** Color is everything at **Vivwak,** which sports colorful baskets, model catamarans, tie-dye T-shirts, and brightly painted galvanized iron buckets among its wares. **King Craft** is an archetypal African curio shop (one of the best in the region), with wooden walking sticks, baskets, masks, drums, and wooden animals. Nearby is **Rosecraft,** selling a selection of chunky wool jerseys and rugs, together with more delicate shawls and wraps. ⊠ *Box A5, Swazi Plaza,* ☎ *268/416–1136.* ⊙ *Daily 8:30–5.*

Mlilwane Wildlife Sanctuary

❻ *20 km (12 mi) west from Ezulwini Valley and Malkerns.*

Mlilwane (Little Fire) Wildlife Sanctuary was the first region set aside for conservation in Swaziland by renowned Swazi conservationist, Ted Reilly. It's a beautiful, secluded area where rolling grassland sweeps to the foot of craggy mountains.

Enjoy a morning, sunset, or evening game drive (R100 for two hours), take a guided walk through the reserve (R15 per hour), or go horseback riding (R75 per hour), a unique way of getting really close to game. Mlilwane also offers a four-hour horseback-riding trip up Nyonyane Mountain (R300) and an overnight ride up the Nyagato Horse Trail (R600). You can also take a guided mountain bike trail (R50 per hour). Alternatively, choose from five self-guided walking trails, winding through forest and grassland, rivers and mountains. Don't walk too close to the water, however, as crocodiles frequent many of the dams and rivers you will encounter. *Note:* A minimum of two people are required for most activities.

The only big game you'll see here are the hippos in the water hole at the main camp (don't miss feeding time daily at 3 PM). View giraffes, zebras, wildebeests, bonteboks, impalas, nyalas, and warthogs. The main camp is unfenced, so you can surprise impalas early in the morning. And watch out for ostriches that wander through the camp.

Dining and Lodging

Book all lodgings listed below through the **Big Game Parks Central Reservations** (⊠ Box 234, Mbabane, ☎ 268/404–4541, FAX 268/404–0957, WEB www.biggame.co.sz. AE, DC, MC, V).

$$$$ ✕🏠 **Reilly's Rock.** This 1900s stone-and-thatch homestead has been painstakingly restored by owners Ted and Liz Reilly, and it really epitomizes the old colonial style that we've now come to associate with the book and movie *Out of Africa.* More a luxurious country house than a lodge, it's set on the Nyonyane Mountain and has endless views of Mlilwane and the surrounding area. Constructed in exchange for an ox wagon at the end of World War I, the lodge is built of hand-hewn rock, and today there's a lot of Swaziland's early pioneer history locked within these solid stone walls. Accommodations are in two stone houses with pine floorboards and pressed-tin ceilings complemented by colonial-style decor including deep, cream-color settees; African-print cushions; country prints; wood finishes; and ball-and-claw-foot tubs. The attention to detail, from old-fashioned light fittings to African artifacts, is incredible. In the rooms you'll find brass bedsteads and the sort of antique wood furniture your grandmother used to have. In fact, in the main suite, Gogo's Room, you'll sleep in the original bed used by Ted's mother early in the 20th century. Lush, beautiful gardens include secluded hideaways dotted with wrought-iron tables and chairs. Guests have use of Main Camp facilities. *6 rooms. MAP.*

$ ✕🏠 **Main Camp.** Accommodations here consist of basic log cabins and beehive huts, accommodating two to five people. Each cabin has a private bathroom; a communal kitchen, dining room, and lounge are housed in a separate building. The lounge has a vast picture window suspended over the water hole, so you can watch game and birds in comfort. A large, roofed wooden deck and bar area with lounge chairs and light wood furniture is a lovely, airy facility for watching game and birds at the water hole. The restaurant offers a limited menu specializing in game-based dishes. Main Camp also has an open-air dining area. A summerhouse and bathroom area are available for day visitors, and there is a viewing area beside the water hole. A small shop sells wine, beer, soft drinks, and some canned goods and toiletries. *6 cabins, 8 cottages, 2 beehive huts. Bar, dining room, lounge, pool.*

$ 🏠 **Beehive Village.** Each beehive hut accommodates two or three people and contains only beds. Communal bathroom facilities are shared with campers. Guests have use of Main Camp facilities. *8 huts.*

$ 🏠 **Shonalanga.** This is a self-contained, fully equipped cottage accommodating six. The cottage comprises a lounge, dining room, kitchen with refrigerator, bathroom, and two bedrooms. An open-air barbecue area affords attractive views over the reserve. Guests have use of Main Camp facilities. *1 cottage.*

Mkhaya Game Reserve

❼ *95 km (59 mi) east from Mlilwane Wildlife Sanctuary.*

Mkhaya Game Reserve is a small private game reserve, established in 1979 to save the pure Nguni cattle breed from extinction, and is a proclaimed nature reserve, designated as a refuge for endangered species. Covering more than 12,500 acres, the reserve lies off the Big Bend–Lavumisa road. Strict antipoaching measures have been adopted, and Mkhaya boasts what is arguably Africa's most effective antipoaching unit staffed and patrolled entirely by Swazis. Entry to the reserve is carefully controlled—you cannot enter the park on your own—and a ranger will meet you at the turnoff and escort you from there to a central point with secure parking. Arrival and departure times are 10 AM and 4 PM, respectively. You will be taken the rest of the way by Land Rover. Mkhaya is totally self-financing through visitor revenues, which means your visit here helps to sustain this unique international conservation effort.

The chief activity at Mkhaya is game drives, of which there are two: a morning drive at 6 and a sunset drive at 4. In addition, you can arrange for a three-hour guided walking safari with your ranger.

At Mkhaya it's possible to get really close to big game. It's not unusual to experience elephants patting the Land Rover with their trunks or to have rhinos staring at you from a few yards away. Animals you might see include elephants, black and white rhinos, buffalo, giraffes, and hippos. Usually seldom seen, the majestic male nyala is plentiful in the reserve. Expect to also see impalas, kudus, waterbucks, elands, roan and sable antelopes, zebras, and wildebeests. After good rains it's possible to see several animals with their young. The birding is fabulous, too, so don't forget your binoculars. To visit, you must book your visit in advance with Royal Swazi Big Game Parks in Mbabane (268/528–3944 or e-mail reservations@biggame.co.sz). The price for a day visit is E185, including lunch, but the best way to see the park is to spend the night. There are cottages and safari tents here for R730 per night. The cost includes dinner, breakfast, game drives in open vehicles, and guided bush walks.

Hlane Royal National Park

8 *105 km (66 mi) east from Mbabane.*

On the eastern side of Swaziland in the heart of sugarcane country, Hlane, meaning "wilderness," so named by King Sobhuza II, offers a relaxed wildlife experience. To get here, follow signs to Lomahasha on the MR3; approximately 12 km (7½ mi) from the Lonhlupheko junction you will see a signboard to the reserve. The access road is dirt but in good condition. You will need to call here and pay your entrance fee before proceeding to Bubesi Camp. Rangers at the gate will direct you to Bubesi, as the road through the park is not always accessible during the rainy season.

Take your own vehicle and enjoy a self-driving tour along the vast network of roads through the park. (Get directions from the staff, however, as the standard-issue reserve map is not terribly accurate, and you could conceivably drive around in circles.) While here, visit the enormous **Mahlindza water hole,** where hippos yawn in the water, waterbirds feed along the shore, and countless other wildlife come to drink in the mornings. Alternatively, plan to spend dusk here, where the sunsets are spectacular. You can also take a guided walk with a Swazi ranger (R15 per hour). Visitors can arrange to see the lion- or cheetah-breeding enclosure (R20 per person), a unique opportunity to get fairly close to these wonderful creatures.

Hlane has all of the Big Five—lions, elephants, rhinos, buffalo, and leopards. The lions and cheetahs are in a separate enclosure, however. Besides these, you may see a wide range of antelopes, zebras, wildebeests, warthogs, giraffes, crocodiles, ostriches, baboons, and vervet monkeys. In the late afternoon look out for hyenas. Hlane has one of the densest bird populations in any of Swaziland's game areas, including several birds of prey.

Hlane has a wooden deck facing the main water hole at Ndlovu Camp. It's quite likely that you'll see white rhinos, ostriches, and other animals wandering down to drink on any given evening. Afterward, the staff may get all togged up in traditional outfits and treat you to a display of traditional Swazi dancing and singing. This happens most days, but you can also request it specifically.

Lodging

Accommodations at Hlane Game Reserve are self-catering. There are two camps, both of which provide fully equipped accommodations, including refrigerator and stoves. There is no shop in the reserve, so stock up with provisions at Manzini, where the shops at Manzini Mall should satisfy all your requirements. Or as an alternative, if you're going on to Hlane from Mkhaya, return to Siphofaneni, which has an excellent general dealer who has most of what you'll need.

$ 🏠 **Bubesi Camp.** Three delightful two-bedroom stone cottages come fully equipped as at Ndlovu and sleep four people each. They are modern and spacious and there is electricity. The staff will cook for you on request. The cottages face the river, and there is a great view from their back porches. A short trail along the river starts here as well. ⊠ *Reservations: Big Game Parks Central Reservations, Box 234, Mbabane,* ☎ *268/404–4541,* 🖷 *268/404–0957. 2 cottages. AE, DC, MC, V.*

$ 🏠 **Ndlovu Rest Camp.** Accommodations here at the main camp are in small thatched huts, each of which has a living room, upstairs bedroom, kitchen, and bathroom (with shower), which are rather cluttered with heavy wooden furniture. Each comes fully equipped with cutlery, crockery, pots and pans, basic kitchen utensils, bedding and towels, dish-washing liquid, and dishcloths. Other facilities at the camp include three bomas where firewood is provided and a communal bathroom area. There is also a water hole, but no electricity: lighting is by candles and paraffin lamps, which are brought to your cottage at dusk. The water heater, refrigerator, and stove are all run by gas. ⊠ *Reservations: Big Game Parks Central Reservations, Box 234, Mbabane,* ☎ *268/404–4541,* 🖷 *268/404–0957. 2 eight-bed cottages, 5 four-bed huts. AE, DC, MC, V.*

Mlawula Game Reserve

❾ *15 mi (22 km) northeast from Hlane Game Reserve.*

Owned and run by the Swaziland National Trust Commission, Mlawula is at the foot of the Lubombo Mountains and is both beautiful and unspoiled. The reserve protects more than 1,000 plant species, including rare Lubombo ironwoods. Look out for Umbuluzi cycads, found nowhere else in the world. Vegetation is dense: you will need to work to find the animals, which include leopards, pangolins, and rare Samango monkeys. All in all, there are 57 mammal species present, together with a variety of tortoises, lizards, and terrapins. Nile crocodiles frequent the rivers and dams, so don't go too close to the shore. There are three self-guided walking trails, affording beautiful views across the reserve and taking walkers to pools or rock shelters once inhabited by early man. Secluded and quiet, it's far from the madding crowds. The bird life is spectacular, with more than 350 different species including the African finfoot, pink-throated twinspot, and African broadbill. Stop by for a day or half-day visit if you've entered Swaziland via the Mananga–Border Gate border post. Inquire about basic, self-catering accommodations, which are available but quite spartan. ⊠ *Reservations: Box 312, Simunye,* ☎ *268/416–1481.* 🖪 *R25 per person and R5 per car.* ☉ *Daily 7–5:30.*

SWAZILAND A TO Z

To research prices, get advice from other travelers, and book travel arrangements, visit www.fodors.com.

AIR TRAVEL

Swaziland has only one airport, Matsapha, 8 km (5 mi) from Manzini. An airport departure tax of R20 is levied. Although the airport has sophisticated equipment, there are times when it is not functioning properly, and certain airlines may refuse to fly to Swaziland on occasion, particularly during inclement weather. Bear this in mind and make allowances for delays. There is also some controversy about whether the planes of the national airline, Royal Swazi National Airways, are airworthy, although there have been no unfortunate incidents. S.A. Airlink also has daily flights.

➤ AIRLINES AND CONTACTS: **Matsapha** (⊠ Box 487, Manzini, ☎ 268/ 518–4372). **Royal Swazi National Airways** (☎ 268/518–6155 or 268/ 518–6192 in Swaziland; 011/395–3333 in Johannesburg, 🖷 268/518–

6148 in Swaziland; 011/395–1319 in Johannesburg). **S.A. Airlink** (☎ 011/961–1700, ℻ 011/395–1440).

BUSINESS HOURS

BANKS

Banks all open at 8:30, but many close at as early as 2:30, or at 1 on Wednesday. All banks are open until 11 AM Saturday.

SHOPS

Offices and shops are open 8:30–5 on weekdays and 8:30–1 on Saturday. Most establishments are closed on Sunday. Lunch hour is 1–2.

BUS TRAVEL

Courtesy buses are offered by Sun International Hotels.

CAR RENTAL

➤ MAJOR AGENCIES: **Avis Rent-A-Car** (✉ Box 31, Manzini, ☎ 268/ 518–6226). **Imperial Car Hire** (✉ Box 1825, Manzini, ☎ 268/518–4396 or 268/518–4862, ℻ 268/518–4396).

CAR TRAVEL

The major border post between Swaziland and South Africa is Oshoek–Ngwenya, open daily from 7 AM to 8 PM. On weekends or public holidays expect to wait in long lines behind busloads of Swazi nationals coming in from South Africa to visit their families. If you can, it's recommended that you use one of the other border posts at such times.

If you're traveling to Swaziland from Mpumalanga, enter at Jeppe's Reef–Matsamo or Mananga–Border Gate, both open daily from 7 AM to 6 PM. If you're entering from the KwaZulu–Natal side, the nearest border posts are either Golela–Lavumisa (near Jozini) or Mahlamba (near Piet Retief), both open daily from 7 AM to 10 PM.

A road toll levy (R10) is payable at the border, and a receipt is issued. Keep the receipt with you. As in South Africa, drive on the left. Unlike in South Africa, distances are much shorter, particularly if you're doing most of your traveling on the western side of the country. There are no highways: the major through routes tend to be the tarred roads. There's a two-lane road between Mbabane and Manzini. To access sights in the Ezulwini and Malkerns valleys, you will need to exit this highway (follow the Ezulwini signs).

Logistically, the easiest way to get around Swaziland is by car, even though it's not without its pitfalls. Roads are extremely narrow (one lane each way) and invariably have solid white barrier lines, allowing no passing for long stretches. Road shoulders are often nonexistent or unpaved. Although tarred roads are in reasonable condition, you won't find the superhighways of the sort you experience in South Africa. Official speed limits are 60 kph in town and 80 kph on the open road, but you'll quickly find you need to travel at slower speeds. Off the beaten track, you'll more than likely need four-wheel drive. Check when making bookings as to whether places are accessible, particularly during the rainy season.

Swazi drivers have little regard for other road users. Be careful on blind rises in particular: it's not unusual to reach the crest of a hill or round a series of bends to find yourself facing an oncoming vehicle on your side of the road. Logging trucks negotiating winding mountain roads are particularly bad at staying on their side (watch out for logs slipping off, too). You will need to be patient, as many people drive slowly or suddenly turn off the road without signaling. It is recommended that you do not drive at night, because even major routes are not lighted, and with the unpredictability of most of Swaziland's driving population, it's simply not worth the trouble.

International driving permits are recommended. If you intend to take a hired car from South Africa into Swaziland, ensure that the car-rental company provides you with a letter authorizing you to take the vehicle across the border.

Avis Rent-A-Car and Imperial Car Hire can arrange for cars to be delivered or collected at your hotel.

GASOLINE

Gas (or petrol as it is known in southern Africa) is easily available in main centers, such as Mbabane, Manzini, Piggs Peak, and the Ezulwini Valley, where garages are numerous and many offer 24-hour service. Gas is cheaper in Swaziland than in South Africa, so plan to fill up when you arrive and before you leave. Unleaded gas is not always available. When traveling to outlying areas, bear in mind that the gasoline supply can be erratic: there may be garages, but the fuel reservoirs will not necessarily be full.

EMBASSIES

➤ UNITED KINGDOM: **British High Commission** (✉ Private Bag, Allister Miller St., Mbabane, ☎ 268/404–2581, FAX 268/404–2585).
➤ UNITED STATES: **U.S. Embassy** (✉ Central Bank Bldg., Warner St., Mbabane [mailing address: Box 199, Mbabane], ☎ 268/404–6441 or 268/404–6445, FAX 268/404–5959).

EMERGENCIES

It is not recommended that you go to any of the public hospitals in Swaziland. Clinics in outlying areas are usually not a good bet either. Ask your hotel to refer you to a reliable private practitioner.

LANGUAGE

English and Seswati are the official languages. Most Swazi people speak and understand English very well.

MAIL AND SHIPPING

Post offices in Swaziland are open 8:30–4 on weekdays and 8:30–11 Saturday morning. All the usual postal services are available. Postage stamps may also be purchased at the larger hotels.

MONEY MATTERS

ATMS

Some ATMs in the big casinos take international cards, but most ATMs in Swaziland are usually for Swazi bank account holders only. Ask at your hotel if any others have been upgraded to take international cards.

CREDIT CARDS

Credit cards—American Express, MasterCard, and Visa—are accepted in most places, although not in markets or informal trading areas. The national parks don't always accept them, so put aside enough cash to be able to pay for these excursions.

CURRENCY

The Swazi currency is the lilangeni (plural: emalangenii), which is tied to the South African rand: one rand equals one lilangeni. The currency is denoted by the letter E. The rand is accepted almost everywhere in Swaziland, and you're better off using it, as you won't be able to change emalangenii outside Swaziland. However, South African coins are not always accepted. Most banks and hotels will change traveler's checks but usually at a poorer exchange rate. Don't ever change money on the street or from an unauthorized dealer—it's illegal and highly risky.

PASSPORTS AND VISAS
ENTERING SWAZILAND
Ask your tour operator about visa requirements, or phone your local embassy. If you will be reentering South Africa from Swaziland, make sure that you obtain a multiple-entry visa before leaving South Africa.

TAXIS
Taxis operate from the airport to hotels and main towns. Be very careful of the condition of the taxi: make sure it's road worthy. Approximate costs are as follows: airport to Ezulwini, E60; to Mbabane, E80; to Manzini, E60.

TELEPHONES
The country code for Swaziland is 268 followed by the destination number. There are no area codes in Swaziland. If you want to make an international call, dial 00 followed by the country and area codes and finally the destination number. Country codes are the same as those dialed from South Africa. For inquiries phone 919490, or ask your hotel switchboard.

TOURS
Swazi Trails offers full- and half-day tours including history and culture tours, Swazi arts-and-crafts trails, wildlife trails (at Mlilwane, Hlane, and Mkhaya game reserves), and adventure trails taking in hiking, horseback riding, river rafting, rappelling, paragliding, and four-by-four excursions. Specialist, incentive, and conference group tours are also arranged. The group offers airport-to-hotel transfers and accommodation booking services.

➤ Tour-Operator Recommendations: **Swazi Trails** (✉ Box 2197, Mbabane, ☎ 268/416–2180, FAX 268/416–1040, WEB www.swazitrails.co.sz).

TRAVEL AGENCIES
The main travel agency in Swaziland is Swazi Trails. Big Game Parks offers packages and information for the active and adventurous traveler. Activities center on the game reserves at Mlilwane, Mkhaya, and Hlane. Enjoy game viewing, bird-watching, game driving, horseback riding, mountain biking, river rafting, and rappelling. Big Game Parks will also arrange and take bookings for accommodations in the parks.

➤ Local Agent Referrals: **Big Game Parks** (✉ Box 234, Mbabane, ☎ 268/404–4541, FAX 268/404–0957, WEB www.biggame.co.sz).

VISITOR INFORMATION
The Department of Tourism is open weekdays 8–4, Sat 8–1.

➤ Tourist Information: **Department of Tourism** (✉ Ministry of Tourism, Environment, and Communications, Swazi Plaza, Mbabane [mailing address: Box 2652, Mbabane], ☎ 268/404–4556 or 268/404–2531, FAX 268/404–6438).

10 ZIMBABWE

From hippos snorting in the Zambezi River to elfin klipspringer antelopes bounding around the granite hills of Matobo National Park, the landscape and wildlife of Zimbabwe are some of the most amazing in all of Africa. In between are a swathe of national parks and one of the world's seven wonders, dramatic Victoria Falls.

T HE FANTASTIC ARRAY OF WILDLIFE is the reason most people visit Zimbabwe: from the lions, elephants, and wild dogs of Hwange National Park to the hippos and stealthy crocodiles of Mana Pools—and all kinds of birds and beasts in between. The professional guides who will guide you safely to them must pass rigorous proficiency tests—so rigorous in fact, that Zimbabwe has become the standard by which neighboring countries measure their own guides.

By Michael McKeown and June Muchemenyi

Updated by Jennifer Stern

The country also prides itself on its largely successful game management policies and on the fact that a good 13% of Zimbabwe is dedicated wildlife country or protected nature reserves (although in the past two decades they have become sadly neglected). Although a lack of strong management—or possibly official corruption—allowed rhinos to be poached to the brink of extinction here in the early 1990s, the park's authority has recently been responsible for the successful reintroduction of these and other endangered species into some national parks. There's more to the country than wildlife parks and safaris, though. Victoria Falls and a host of smaller places, like Mana Pools, are also intriguing destinations.

At the time of writing, a number of developments, such as political violence and economic disruption, were causing problems for the people of Zimbabwe and its visitors. The tourist industry has been surprisingly resilient, and there appears to no threat to visitors in the main tourist areas. The healthy air charter industry allows for continued and easy access from one destination to another. Driving from place to place in your own rental car, however, is not recommended—more because of the irregular supply of gasoline than any real threat to personal safety.

Warnings: Most areas of Zimbabwe (with the exception of Harare and the central plateau) are malarial, so be sure to take the proper precautions.

Due to the unstable nature of the current political system in Zimbabwe, you may want to check with the **U.S. Department of State** for the latest travel advisories and warnings at travel.state.gov/zimbabwe.html.

At time of writing, the Zimbabwean dollar was rapidly devaluing due to the country's political situation. Try to pay as much as you can with cash, either U.S. dollars, pounds sterling, or South African rand. Most prices in this chapter are quoted in U.S. dollars.

Pleasures and Pastimes

Arts and Crafts

You'll discover plenty of roadside vendors selling curios and other local crafts, such as crocheted bedcovers and tablecloths or large printed cotton cloths that could be also be used as tablecloths and bed coverings, even curtains. There is also a vibrant, trendy Afro-style clothing industry, and you will find well-made, well-designed, excellently priced safari clothing in most of the local stores.

Be prepared for the typical selling style of Zimbabwe's vendors: many insistently accost or pursue you, trying to take you to the finest of their items, whether you show interest or not. If you decide to buy, feel free to bargain away.

Dining

If you're a carnivore, then you've arrived in a land where you can eat great beef and game meat to your heart's content. However, if you're

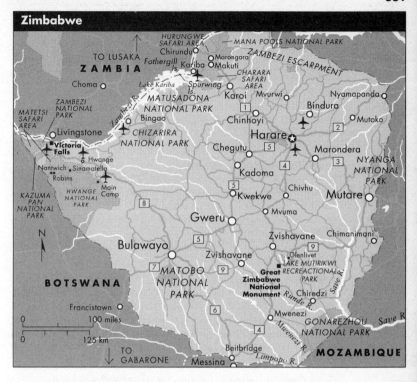

looking for more of a epicurean challenge, don't come to Zimbabwe for the food: the most interesting fare you'll encounter is at the trend-setting larger hotels that have started experimenting with traditional Zimbabwean foods such as *sadza,* the staple thick porridge, usually made of maize flour and often accompanied by *nyama* (a meat stew) and green vegetables. They also serve such delicacies as *madora* and *macimbi*—sun-dried caterpillars harvested from mopane trees and cooked with peanut butter or seasoned and served as a snack.

CATEGORY	COST*
$$$$	over Z$500
$$$	Z$350–Z$500
$$	Z$200–Z$350
$	under Z$200

per person, for a main course at dinner.

Lodging

Although conventional hotels are found in the major resort areas, lodges are often a friendlier and more attractive option. They come in both the safari-camp variety—in the midst of the bush, in everything from a zip-up tent with a shower to the currently fashionable stone-and-thatch, African-inspired dream hut. Typically, lodges take no more than 20 guests at a time.

At private game lodges, all meals are included in the rate. Usually drinks are as well. Professional guides are on staff to take you on game drives and walks. These guides and the camp managers look after your needs throughout the day and dine with you at meals. You can also book a camp site in a national park, which are significantly cheaper albeit self-catered and far less cushy.

Because of the instability of the Zimbabwean dollar, most lodges quote prices in U.S. dollars and, in many cases, you will have to pay in foreign currency. Confirm your payment plan when making reservations.

CATEGORY	COST*
$$$$	over US$400
$$$	US$200–US$400
$$	US$100–US$200
$	under US$100

All prices refer to a standard double room in hotels or a per-person rate in all-inclusive resorts, including tax.

Wildlife and National Parks

Apart from the thundering Victoria Falls, Zimbabwe is justifiably well known for its excellent national parks. Here you will get plenty opportunity to see lions, elephants, buffalo, zebras, giraffes, and many species of antelope. Hippos and crocodiles inhabit almost every body of water larger than a bathtub.

Exploring Zimbabwe

Until the political situation settles down, driving yourself is not really a good idea. It's best to choose one or two prime destinations, such as Victoria Falls, Mana Pools, Hwange, Kariba and/or Matobo and fly in to them. Another good option is a package to a number of lodges in different areas, spending a few days in each. Classic Safari Camps of Africa and Wilderness Safaris offer these, all of which include both air charters and all meals and activities.

Great Zimbabwe is one of the most interesting archaeological destinations in Africa, but it is quite difficult to get to in the present political climate. If this is something you just have to see, you can charter a plane from Bulawayo or Harare. If there is sufficient demand, Classic Safari Camps will include a stop there in one of its fly-lodge packages.

The entry points to Zimbabwe by plane are Victoria Falls, Harare, and Bulawayo.

Great Itineraries

IF YOU HAVE 3 DAYS

If your itinerary begins with ⚁ **Victoria Falls,** take the first day to visit the falls, the rain forest, and **Big Tree**—no need to contain your curiosity once you've arrived. This could take the better part of an afternoon or morning. Then visit the Soper Road boutiques and **Falls Craft Village** for some bargaining for curios and falls memorabilia if the spirit moves you. If you're adventurous, give day two over to activities in or around the river, which could include white-water rafting, body boarding, canoeing, bungee jumping, horseback riding, or doing an aerial flip over the falls. On day three (or day two if you skip the river activities), head for ⚁ **Hwange National Park,** a nearby opportunity for great game viewing.

IF YOU HAVE 6 DAYS

With six days you need to decide whether to add time in ⚁ **Harare** and ⚁ **Bulawayo,** for a taste of Zimbabwean city life, or go all-wilderness. In the first category, you could spend the first day in ⚁ **Victoria Falls,** leaving town first thing in the morning for **Kariba,** the connection on the way to or ⚁ **Mana Pools National Park.** After two or three days, transit back to civilization for a day or two in Harare. The wilderness option would be to combine Victoria Falls with Hwange National Park and then Mana Pools or the haunting ⚁ **Matobo National Park.**

When to Tour Zimbabwe

Zimbabwe has two distinct seasons—the wet summer (November–March) and the dry winter (April–October). Generally June and July are the coolest months, with night temperatures dipping toward 0°C (32°F). Summer highs can reach 40°C (104°F) in the low-lying Zambezi Valley. During the rainy season, the vegetation is thick and tall, which reduces wildlife visibility. Water is abundant, and animals are scattered over large areas because there is no need to gather at watering holes, where they are easier to spot by predators. Summer, too, is when malaria-carrying mosquitoes are most active. Winter is a good time for everything. Victoria Falls are at their highest level because waters from the Zambezi's catchment areas north in Angola are flowing into the river. Drier, shorter vegetation makes game viewing easier all over the country. And cooler temperatures allow for more comfortable walking, riding, canoeing, and hiking.

Time your city stays so that you're not in town on Sundays, when just about everything worth seeing is closed.

HARARE

Harare is a clean, fairly well-managed city with some nice open spaces and parks. Many of its 1.5 million residents live in a belt of informal housing around the city. The most interesting sights—Chapungu Sculpture Park and the Mbare Musika—market are actually outside the city. If you're traveling in September, Harare has far more jacaranda trees than Pretoria and offers a spectacular display of purple blossoms. It's a vibrant, interesting place, but unless you are really interested in African urban life, it's not worth more than a day or two.

Dining and Lodging

$$$ ✕ **Amanzi.** By far the best choice in Harare, this fantastic restaurant is set in a huge, treed, water-filled garden. Julia and Andrew have lived all over the world, and the menu reflects the recipes they have collected in their travels. A definite Asian influence is evident in the Japanese noodle broth and Thai fish curry. Good Zimbabwean beef is showcased in a fillet with blue cheese, and their stint in Nigeria is celebrated with a traditional West African chicken groundnut stew. Lunch is à la carte, while dinner is a set menu, and priced at US$10. ✉ *158 Enterprise Rd., Highlands, Harare,* ☎ *04/49–7768 or 091/33–6224. DC, MC, V. Closed Sun.*

$$$$ ✕🏠 **Meikles Hotel.** With its landmark bronze lions guarding the entrance, marble lobby, and efficient air, Harare's oldest and best-known hotel has a pleasant dignity about it. Rooms in the north wing are tastefully decorated in pastels and Canadian maple wood with English country prints on walls, while the south wing is done in a smart colonial *Out of Africa* style. Front-facing rooms in both wings have views of Africa Unity Square and the Anglican Cathedral. A member of the Leading Hotels of the World, the hotel can supply almost all your needs while in Harare. Rooms have multi-adapter plug points, minibars, cable TV and direct-dial phones. There is a 24-hour business center, an on-site bureau de change, an Avis desk, and a concierge who can organize city tours, shopping expeditions, and ongoing travel arrangements. Bagatelle restaurant (reservations essential) is one of the city's classiest restaurants, with fine service and a Continental steak and seafood menu. ✉ *Jason Moyo Ave. at 3rd St., (Box 594),* ☎ *04/70–7721,* 🆕 *04/70–7753 or 04/70–7754,* 🌐 *www.meikles.com. 318 rooms. 3 restaurants, bar, lounge, pool, hair salon, sauna, gym, concierge. AE, DC, MC, V. BP.*

$$$$ ⊞ **Wild Geese Lodge.** English country gardens meld into *miombo* woodland at this lodge–cum–guest house named after the novel and film starring Richard Burton and Roger Moore. Rooms are decorated with floral prints, pastel-tinted walls, and white carpeting and have private bougainvillea-covered pergolas with Victorian-style wrought-iron tables and chairs. There are quiet glades to walk, game-rich surroundings to explore on horseback, and several good golf courses in close proximity. ⊠ *Box BW 198, Borrowdale,* ☎ *04/86–0466* ℻ *04/86–0276,* 🕸 *www.wildgeese.co.zw. 8 rooms, 3 suites. Restaurant, bar, pool, hiking, horseback riding. AE, MC, V. BP.*

Harare A to Z

To research prices, get advice from other travelers, and book travel arrangements, visit www.fodors.com.

AIR TRAVEL
Harare International Airport lies about 15 km (9 mi) south of the city center. The taxi fare between the airport and the city is about Z$150.
➤ AIR TRAVEL INFORMATION: **Harare International Airport** (☎ 04/57–5188).

EMERGENCIES
The Avenues Clinic is a large, well-equipped private hospital.
➤ EMERGENCY INFORMATION: **General emergencies** (☎ 999). **Ambulance** (☎ 994). **Fire station** (☎ 993). **Police** (☎ 995). **Avenues Clinic** (⊠ Baines Ave. and Mazowe St., ☎ 04/73–2055 or 04/73–2075).

GREAT ZIMBABWE NATIONAL MONUMENT

The granite ruins of Great Zimbabwe, the largest ancient stone building south of the Sahara, sprawl across 4 square km (2½ square mi) of a wide, grassy valley surrounded by *koppies* (rounded granite hills). Developing from a small settlement in the 8th century, it evolved into a wealthy and powerful city state that flourished between AD 1250 and 1450 and at its zenith contained nearly 20,000 people. Most colonial historians believed it to be the site of the biblical Ophir, known to Solomon and Sheba and built by some unknown Mediterranean race. Now a World Heritage site, the ruins stand some 20 km (12½ mi) from the provincial capital of Masvingo in southeastern Zimbabwe.

Unfortunately, at the time of writing, it was almost impossible to visit this site on your own because you need to drive to its remote location—an extremely difficult task with Zimbabwe's current gas shortage. Check with tour operators to see if they include Great Zimbabwe in their itineraries. ⊠ *270 km (170 mi) west of Bulawayo, and 27 km (17 mi) south of Masvingo.* 🖼 *US$5, museum US$2.* ⊙ *Daily 8–5:30.*

BULAWAYO AND MATOBO NATIONAL PARK

Matobo National Park is characterized by massive granite boulders and wind-sculpted koppies that climb chaotically one upon the other like the discarded playthings of some capricious god. As well as fantastic rock art, there are some more modern historical attractions. The brooding splendor of the hills made a lasting impact on three key figures of the last 19th century whose destinies were interwoven in the making of modern Zimbabwe. King Mzilikazi, a former commander in the army of the legendary Zulu general Shaka (1787–1828), led his people northward from South Africa across the Limpopo River into the towering granite outcrops and grassy valleys of the Matobo hills and founded the Matabele (now Ndebele) nation. Arch-colonialist Cecil Rhodes regarded the Matobo with considerable awe. It was here that he held his peace *indaba* with the Ndebele chiefs a little more than a 100 years ago and, about the same time, came across the great granite dome of Malindidzuma—Place of Benevolent Spirits. Impressed by the grandeur of the setting, he named it **World's View**, which is now a favorite excursion because of its marvelous views—sunsets here are a must—and as the site of Rhodes's grave.

Nearby **Bulawayo** evolved from the kraal of King Lobengula (1836–94), Mzilikazi's son, who lost the desperate fight to save his lands from Rhodes's colonizing zeal. It's a pleasant city but it's not worth spending more than a day here en route to Matobo.

★ **Khami Ruins and Leopard Koppie.** An important archaeological site, 22 km (13.6 mi) north of Bulawayo, Khami Ruins preserves both the Stone Age and Iron Age heritage of Zimbabwe. The stone ruins here—one of about 150 similar mazimbabwe stone cities—are second only to the hard-to-reach Great Zimbabwe ruins, but the dry-stone walling is more ornate and the *daga* (clay mixed with crushed termite mounds) hut floors still clearly visible. Stop by the Museum of National History for an interpretive pamphlet (fee). ⊠ *US$3.* ☉ *Daily 8–5.* ☎ *Museum of Natural History, 09/6–0045 or 09/6–0046*

★ **Museum of National History.** If you see nothing else, visit the Museum of National History. The dioramas of Zimbabwean mammals are superb, and the collection includes the second largest mounted elephant in the world, its ivories weighing 88 and 90 pounds respectively. As a quick guide to everything you ever wanted to know about the bush before heading off into it, this is ideal preparation. ⊠ *Centenary Park, Leopold Takawira Ave. at Park Rd.,* ☎ *09/6–0045 or 09/6–0046.* ⊠ *US$2.* ☉ *Daily 9–5.*

Lodging

There is a campsite with chalets in the park, but no catered lodging of any kind. There are, however, a number of stylish lodges on the borders of Matobo.

$$$$ 🏚 **Camp Amalinda.** If hobbits had an aristocracy, they'd live someplace like this. Exquisitely stylish rooms are tucked away under the trees on the steep slopes of a wooded kopje. Each has a cavelike quality with at least one wall of natural granite. All the rooms huddle beneath the tree canopy, but some have wonderful private viewing platforms that overlook the valley. There is a mini-gym where you can cycle to nowhere with a great view, a sauna and beautiful pool—also with a great view. There are trained African elephants at the lodge that you may ride (US$50 per hour). ⊠ *Londa Mela Safaris, Box 130, Queen's Park, Bulawayo,* ☎ *083/8268 camp; 09/4–3954 reservations,* FAX *09/4–6436,* WEB *www.amalinda.co.zw. 10 rooms. Bar, pool, sauna, gym, hiking. AE, DC, MC, V. FAP.*

$$$ 🏚 **Big Cave Camp.** Built right into the rock high up on a granite whale-
★ back, the setting gives a sense of light, freedom, and—almost—reverence. It's a lovely lodge with great food, fantastic views, rock art on site, and a host of wonderful activities, including game drives, rhino tracking, and fascinating interpretive nature, culture, rock art, and history walks. The stone-and-thatch rooms are stylishly decorated in an almost minimalist style. Each has a small private balcony with a fantastic view.

Iridescent sunbirds and glossy starlings flit around, while blue-headed lizards and squirrels scuttle for shelter at the sound of footsteps. In the afternoon whole families of dassies (rock hyraxes) sun themselves meters from your room. ☎ FAX *09/7–7176 or 09/7–6843,* WEB *www. bigcave.co.za. 7 chalets. Bar, pool, hiking, horseback riding. MC, V. FAP.*

$$$ 🏰 **Nesbitt Castle.** Set in 14 acres of woodland and gardens, Nesbitt Castle is the real thing, a castle with turrets, yard-thick walls, high-ceiling rooms, antique furnishings, and narrow, twisty corridors reminiscent of Camelot. Most of the rooms are furnished with red velvet and satin—a suitably over-the-top style to match the improbable architecture. It's worth staying here just to see it. The Coach House Restaurant is popular with locals. Nesbitt Castle is 6 km (4 mi) from the center of town. ⊠ *6 Percy Ave., Hillside, Bulawayo,* ☎ *09/28–2735 or 09/ 28–2726,* FAX *09/28–1864. 9 rooms. Bar, pool. AE, DC, MC, V. BP.*

Bulawayo A to Z

To research prices, get advice from other travelers, and book travel arrangements, visit www.fodors.com.

AIR TRAVEL AND TRANSFERS

Bulawayo Airport is 22 km (14 mi) north of the city. It is served by Air Zimbabwe, South African Airways, and Migration Air (charter). Expect to pay from US$25 to US$40 for taxi fare into town.
➤ AIRPORT INFORMATION: **Bulawayo Airport** (☎ 09/22–6575, 09/22–6491, or 09/22–6492, FAX 09/22–6232). **Air Zimbabwe** (☎ 04/57–5111, FAX 04/57–5069, WEB www.airzim.co.zw). **South African Airways** (⊠ Takura House, 2nd floor, 69–71 Union Ave., ☎ 04/73–8922). **Migration Air** (☎ 09/28–4394).

BUS TRAVEL

Blue Arrow Luxury Coach Services runs air-conditioned buses to Harare (6 hrs) and to Victoria Falls via Hwange (6 hrs).
➤ BUS CONTACT: **Blue Arrow Luxury Coach Services** (⊠ Fife St., opposite police station, ☎ 09/6–5548, FAX 09/6–5549).

EMERGENCIES

Day–Nite Pharmacy is open 365 days a year.
➤ EMERGENCY INFORMATION: **Police** (☎ 09/7–2515 or 09/7–2516). **Central Hospital** (☎ 09/7–2111). **Day–Nite Pharmacy** (⊠ 8th Ave. at Robert Mugabe Way, ☎ 09/6–6241 or 09/6–6242). **Medical Air Rescue Services** (MARS; ⊠ 42 Robert Mugabe Way, ☎ 09/6–0351).

TRAIN TRAVEL

National Railways of Zimbabwe has passenger service from Bulawayo to Victoria Falls, Harare, and Johannesburg aboard a luxury steam train. Its lavish 1920s-style coaches evokes memories of a more elegant and leisurely age.

The central railway station is on Anthony Taylor Avenue, off the south end of Lobengula Street in Bulawayo.
➤ TRAIN CONTACT: **National Railways of Zimbabwe** (☎ 09/32–2294 ticket office; 09/32–2210 reservations; 09/32–2718 inquiries).

HWANGE NATIONAL PARK

Almost the size of Belgium, covering an area of more than 14,600 square km (5,800 square mi) in northeast Zimbabwe, Hwange is the country's premier wildlife park and one of the continent's last remaining great elephant sanctuaries. The park is particularly well known for its large herds—at last count almost 40,000. Once there were plenty of black and white rhinos, too, but they were poached out; those now being reintroduced are jealously guarded. About 400 species of birds can be spotted here, which is nearly half the total for southern Africa. Large raptors, such as tawny and martial eagles, are also regularly seen.

Spotting a dozen species in the space of a 10-minute drive through the park isn't unusual. Besides the better-known species—elephants, giraffes, zebras, wildebeests, baboons, kudus, impalas, and the occasional pride of lions or a cheetah—there is a good chance of seeing such rare animals as gemsboks, tsessebes, pangolins (primitive, scaly anteaters), aardvarks, and rare wild dogs, for which Hwange is becoming well known.

Lodging

The National Parks accommodations include chalets, campsites, and caravan sites, all of which offer only self-catering. Although quite basic, these are comfortable and cost a fraction of what you would pay at a private lodge. The National Parks Department does not accept credit cards, so be prepared to pay cash for lodgings, game walks, and drives. You can make arrangements for game walks and drives with guides when you arrive at the park. There are no walking trails offered in the rainy season. ⊠ *National Parks, Box CY 140, Harare,* ☎ *04/70–6077 or 04/70–6078, 04/70–7624 through 04/70–7629, 04/70–3376,* FAX *04/72–6089.*

$$$$ ⚠ **Makalolo Lodge.** Luxury tents and walkways on raised teak platforms, as well as the outdoor—yet private—bathrooms, give virtually 360-degree views of the game that visit the Samavundhla Pan grounds. The luxe tents have enormous four-poster beds crafted from local timber and iron, Persian carpets, white linens, claw-foot baths, and hand-carved teak furnishings. The dining room is Bedouin-style with ballooning drapes and candlelight. Animals are never far away and elephants constantly browse the trees around the grounds, hence the raised walkways—and rangers on call. Two smaller satellite camps nearby, Little Makalolo and Linkwasha, have 14 additional tents. ⊠ *Mailing address: Wilderness Safaris, 1st floor, Elephants Walk, Adam Standers Ave., Victoria Falls,* ☎ *013/43371 or 013/43372,* FAX *013/4–4424. 10 tents. Bar, private airstrip. MC, V. FAP.*

$$$$ ⚠ **Hide Safari Camp.** On the eastern boundary of the national park, this friendly lodge is on the grassy banks of a large water hole. You can view animals in privacy from the veranda of simple tented rooms, from the huge, thatch A-frame main lodge, or from the namesake hide, a modest (if claustrophobic) underground bunker at water's edge with a narrow window for a dramatic front-row, hoof-level viewing experience. Meals are sociable affairs served at one enormous teak dinner table. ⊠ *27–29 James Martin Dr.,Box ST274, Southerton,* ☎ *04/66–0554, 04/66–0555, 04/55–0556, or 091/22–0641,* FAX *04/62–1216. 8 tents. Bar, dining room, airport shuttle. MC, V. FAP.*

Hwange A to Z

To research prices, get advice from other travelers, and book travel arrangements, visit www.fodors.com.

AIR TRAVEL

Air Zimbabwe does the only scheduled flights to Hwange. Both Sefofane and Migration Air fly regular charters, mostly to the Wilderness camps and the Hide, respectively.

➤ AIRPORT: **Hwange Airport** (☎ 018/435 or 018/338). **Air Zimbabwe** (☎ 04/57–5111, FAX 04/57–5069, WEB www.airzim.co.zw). **Migration Air** (☎ 09/28–4394). **Sefofane** (☎ 04/70–8622, ☎ FAX 04/73–5570, WEB www.sefofane.co.zw).

BUS TRAVEL

Blue Arrow Luxury Coaches stops at Hwange on its run between Bulawayo and Victoria Falls.

All private lodges and camps arrange transfers from and to the airport. UTc does transfers from Victoria Falls, Hwange Airport, or the Blue Arrow drop-off to the National Parks camps.

➤ BUS INFORMATION: **Blue Arrow Luxury Coaches** (☎ 04/72–9514, FAX 04/72–9572 in Harare). **UTc** (☎ 118/217, 118/287, or 018/393).

CAR TRAVEL

The park is only 160 km (100 mi) from Vic Falls, which is an easy drive, so this is an exception to the "don't drive" advice above. Hertz has a rental desk at Hwange Safari Lodge.

➤ MAJOR AGENCIES: **Hertz** (☎ 118/393 or 118/217).

VICTORIA FALLS

Victoria Falls, which plunges into a gorge seasonally hidden by a veil of roaring spray, spans the entire 1½-km (1-mi) width of the Zambezi River, is locally known as Mosi-Oa-Tunya—the "Smoke That Thunders." On a clear day the falls' white spray is visible from 32 km (20 mi) away, a writhing mist rising above the woodland savanna like the smoke from a bush fire. That the falls is one of the seven natural wonders of the world may offer a forewarning of the blockbuster drama, the majesty, and the exquisite beauty of this archetypal African sight.

Over 300 ft high and over a mile wide, it almost defies description. If you divided it up into 10 separate falls, each one would be absolutely spectacular on its own.

The river serves as the border between Zambia and Zimbabwe, with each country competing for tourist dollars. Most first-time visitors opt to stay on the bustling Zimbabwean side, in the town of Victoria Falls, although the Zambian side has as much, if not more, to offer.

Some of southern Africa's greatest game parks lie within easy driving distance of Victoria Falls, and the area is renowned for a huge variety of adventure activities.

Most visit during the April–June high-water peak, when more than 2 million gallons of water hurtle down every second. At this time of year, the spray is so intense, you can hardly see the falls. However, the weather tends to be sunny and pleasant. In September and October, when it gets progressively hotter and more humid, the water level is at its lowest and some of the falls may dry up, but it's easier to see the actual falls. November through March is the rainy season, when malaria-carrying mosquitoes pose their greatest threat.

Sights to See

❹ Big Tree. This giant baobab is said to be 1,500 years old—the tree measures 80 ft in circumference and about the same in height. Early pioneers on their way north into Zambia used to camp under its massive branches. This is a favorite place for elephants to cross the river—so take care. This section of the river is also good for spotting some unusual birds, such as the shy African finfoot or the endemic black-cheeked lovebird. ✉ *Zambezi Dr.*

❶ Falls Craft Village. The "village" consists of life-size model homes typical of five Zimbabwean tribes, as well as a San (Bushman) dwelling. A pamphlet and on-site guides explain the living arrangements, various crafts, and the uses of different tools. If you've an hour to spare,

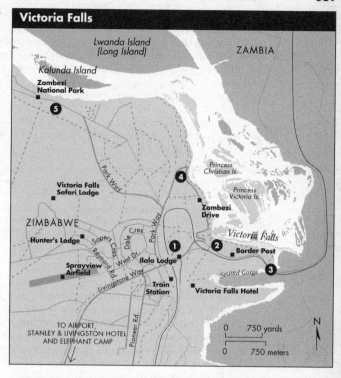

it's probably worthwhile. At the back of the village you can watch artisans carving the stone and wood sculptures that are sold in the adjoining shop. For a small fee you can have a *n'anga*, or witch doctor, "throw the bones" to tell your fortune. There is traditional dancing every night (about US$20). ✉ *Stand 206, Soper's Crescent, off Livingstone Dr., behind banks,* ☎ *013/4–4309.* ✇ *US$8.* ☉ *Daily 8:30–5.*

❸ **Victoria Falls Bridge.** This graceful structure spans the gorge formed by the Zambezi River, 360 ft below. Built in 1905, it's a monument to Cecil Rhodes's dream of completing a Cape-to-Cairo rail line. It would have been far easier and less expensive to build the bridge upstream from the falls, but Rhodes was captivated by the romance of a railway bridge passing over this natural wonder. Miraculously, only two people were killed during construction. Steam-powered trains still chug over the bridge, re-creating a spectacle seen here for almost 100 years. To get onto the bridge, you first have to pass through Zimbabwean immigration and customs controls. Depending on crowds, the simple procedure can take from five minutes to a half hour. The border posts are open daily from 6 to 6. From the bridge you get a knockout view of the river raging through **Batoka Gorge**—as well as a section of the falls. An added bonus is watching adrenaline junkies hurling themselves off the bridge in the second-highest and one of the most scenic bungee jumps in the world.

★ ❷ **Victoria Falls National Park.** Plan to spend at least two hours soaking in the splendors of this park. If you visit the falls during the high-water peak, between April and June, you'll do well to carry a raincoat or umbrella (you can rent them at the entrance) and to protect your camera in a waterproof bag because you will, literally, be soaking—in the spray from the falls, which creates a permanent downpour, while you soak in the splendors of the park. The constant drizzle has created a unique rain forest that extends in a narrow band along the edge of the falls.

A trail running through this dripping green world is overgrown with African ebony, Cape fig, Natal mahogany, wild date palms, ferns, and flame lilies. Side trails lead to viewpoints overlooking the falls. The most spectacular is **Danger Point**, a slippery rock outcropping that overlooks the narrow gorge through which the Zambezi River funnels out of the **Boiling Pot**. In low-water months (September–November), most of the water goes over the falls through the **Devil's Cataract**, a narrow and mesmerizingly powerful section of the falls. During the full moon the park stays open late so you can see the lunar rainbow formed by the spray—one of the most beautiful sights in Africa. ⌑ *US$20.* ☉ *Daily 6–6, later during full moon.*

☝ ❺ **Zambezi Wildlife Sanctuary.** Originally a crocodile farm, the addition of several wildcats in cages and some ostriches makes this an interesting stop—but hardly the highlight of the area. What could be fun, though, is watching baby crocodiles hatch—an almost continuous process in the latter half of December. There is a tea garden. ✉ *Park Way,* ☎ *013/ 4–3576 or 013/4–4604,* ⍟ *www.ilalalodge.com.* ⌑ *US$3 (US$10 including transfers from Vic Falls).* ☉ *Daily 8–5.*

Dining and Lodging

If you want good food, you'll have to go to hotel restaurants, but in town you'll find a couple of nondescript pizza joints and fast-food outlets, all of which offer perfectly edible food. Smarter restaurants spring up, perform wonderfully for a while, and then fade into the mediocre background again. If you're looking for something a little different, try the **Boma** at the Victoria Falls Safari Lodge, where you sit in a traditional African enclosure around a fire and sample various game meats; traditional dancers perform twice nightly. **Kabika-Place of Eating,** at Ilala Lodge, is a casual, fun Mongolian stir-fry restaurant where you can pick ingredients from a range of meat, fish, and vegetables and watch while the chef stir-fries it for you on a huge central grill that resembles a large wok. For elegant dining and dancing there is only one option—the **Livingstone Room** at the Victoria Falls Hotel, where you will need to dress up. There are two other excellent eating options at this hotel, both with fantastic views.

$$$$ ✕⌂ **Elephant Camp.** Miz Elly, named after the soap-opera matriarch, is
★ one of four African elephants that will be your transport—and friends— at this bush camp near the falls. The camp takes only eight guests, which is how many can ride at a time. But you'll do more than just ride here— you'll also be encouraged to bond with your beast by helping to feed and wash it. Game walking in the bush with the largest guide you'll ever have is quite a memorable experience; just remember that these animals remain semiwild and are immensely powerful. Rooms here are spacious brick, canvas, and thatch structures, with wood furniture and muted colors. The central lounge area has a vaulted thatch roof and beautiful views of the sweeping green lawn and the nearby water hole where many animals, including wild elephants, come to drink. Transfers to Victoria Falls are extra. ✉ *Mailing address: Wild Horizons, Box 159, Victoria Falls,* ☎ *013/4–4219, 013/4–2004, or 013/4–2029,* ℻ *013/4–4349,* ⍟ *www.wildhorizons.co.zw. 4 tents. Bar, pool. MC, V. FAP.*

$$$$ ✕⌂ **Victoria Falls Safari Lodge.** About 6 km (4 mi) outside town, the hotel sits on a hilltop overlooking the Zambezi National Park. A water hole below the lodge attracts herds of game, including buffalo and elephants. The lodge itself draws its inspiration from the colorful Ndebele culture. Soaring thatch roofs, huge wooden beams, and reed ceilings envelop you in a luxurious African atmosphere. The sides of the lodge are completely open to admit cooling breezes. All rooms have

scenic views, and you can fold back the glass-and-wood screens leading to your private veranda. There is a courtesy shuttle to and from town and Victoria Falls. The lodge has five-hour night drives in open vehicles with spotlights. ⊠ *Off Park Way, 6 km (4 mi) from Victoria Falls (mailing address: Box 29, Victoria Falls),* ☎ *013/4–3208 or 013/4–3220,* FAX *013/4–3205 or 013/4–3207. 72 rooms, 5 suites. 2 restaurants, 2 bars, room service, 2 pools, travel services. AE, MC, V. BP.*

$$$ ✕🖬 **Ilala Lodge.** This small hotel is a gem. Near the center of town,
★ it's just 10 minutes from the falls on foot. Thatch roofs give the lodge a pleasant, African look. The dining room, with its curving thatched shelter, raw beams, and outdoor seating, is particularly attractive. Rooms are hung with African paintings and tapestries and filled with delicately caned chairs and tables and with dressers made from old railway sleepers. French doors open onto a narrow strip of lawn backed by thick bush. Unlike most hotels in town, Ilala Lodge has no fence around it, so at night it's not uncommon to find elephants browsing outside your window or buffalo grazing on the lawn. ⊠ *411 Livingstone Way (Box 18), Victoria Falls,* ☎ *013/4–4737,* FAX *013/4–4417,* WEB *www.ilalalodge.com. 32 rooms. 2 restaurants, 2 bars, air-conditioning, room service, pool. DC, MC, V. BP.*

$$$ ✕🖬 **Victoria Falls Hotel.** Hotels come and go, but this landmark, built
★ in 1904, has retained its history and former glory as a distant, stylish outpost in the empire days, while pandering to today's modern tastes, needs, and wants. Such grandeur can be shock, especially if you've just been on safari. After checking your e-mail in the E-Lounge, visiting the salon, and dragging your fancy clothes from your bag, you can dine and dance at the elegant Livingstone Room restaurant. Two far less formal restaurants include The Terrace, with an à la carte menu and daily high tea, and Jungle Junction, with a huge barbecue buffet and traditional dancers. The hotel's manicured lawns are perched on the falls' edge with a view of the bridge; and the soothing sounds permeate the gardens (and the rooms if you leave the windows open). ⊠ *Mallet Dr. (Box 10), Victoria Falls,* ☎ *013/4–4751 through 013/4–4759,* FAX *013/4–4586. 180 rooms. 3 restaurants, bar, room service, pool, hair salon, tennis, playground, business center, travel services. AE, DC, MC, V. BP.*

$$$$ 🖬 **The Stanley and Livingstone at Victoria Falls.** This restrained, clas-
★ sical small hotel is set on its own 6,000 acres of game reserve 10 minutes out of town. Public rooms are furnished with some spectacular antiques and have verandas overlooking a water hole where elephants and other animals come to drink. Spacious suites are decorated with dark wood and green marble—and all share that view over the water hole. The accommodation rate includes game drives, all on-site activities except elephant rides, and transfers to the airport or to town. ⊠ *Box 160, Victoria Falls,* ☎ *013/4–4421 or 013/4–4557 for hotel; 011/465–8764 for reservations (through the Mantis Collection in Johannesburg),* FAX *011/465–6904,* WEB *www.ipresumeonline.com. 10 suites. Restaurant, bar, pool, gym, fishing, boating. AE, MC, V. FAP.*

$ 🖬 **Hunters Lodge.** This friendly, basic B&B in the suburbs is a good choice if you want to escape the glitz and noise of Vic Falls—and more importantly—to save your money for rafting, elephant riding, and such. Rooms are clean, spacious, and pleasantly furnished, with fridge and tea and coffee stations. Sensitive viewers may find the decor in the public areas a bit disturbing—the walls are adorned with stuffed animals ranging from fish and fowl to buffalo (in keeping with the name). ⊠ *598 Nguhwuma Crescent, Victoria Falls,* ☎ *013/4–4614 or 011/20–8367. 6 rooms, 1 three-bedroom cottage with kitchen. Pool. MC, V. BP.*

Outdoor Activities and Sports

There is so much to do in Victoria Falls and Livingstone, across the river in Zambia that you will be spoiled for choice and you'll be excused for being confused. You can book all the adventures listed below (and any new ones) through your hotel or through one of the major booking offices.

Shearwater (☎ 013/4–4471 through 013/4–4473, or 013/4–3392, FAX 013/4–4321, WEB www.shearwateradventures.com) operates many adventure services in Vic Falls as well as acting as a booking agent for most of the other operators in the area. **Safari Par Excellence** (⊠ Shop 4, Pumula Centre, ☎ 013/4–4424, FAX 013/4–4510, WEB www.safpar.com) operates a number of adventure activities on both the Zimbabwean and Zambian side of the river.

Aviation Adventures

There are a number of flights on offer to fly over the falls. Generally speaking, though, this is a better option from the Zambian side as Vic Falls Airport is a long way from the Zimbabwean side of the falls.

Shearwater Helicopter Tours (☎ 013/4–4471 through 013/4–4473, or 013/4–3392, FAX 013/4–4321, WEB www.shearwateradventures.com) take off from the Elephant Hills Hotel. From the hotel you're over the falls in a couple of minutes. It costs US$75 for 15 minutes, US$150 for a half hour.

Victoria Falls Balloon Company (☎ 013/4–4471 through 013/4–4473, or 013/4–3392, FAX 013/4–4321, WEB www.shearwateradventures.com) offers not so much a flight as a viewing platform. This state-of-the-art tethered helium balloon is winched up to a height of 250 m (400 ft) on a site a few hundred yards from the falls. You get to see the spray, the falls, the gorges below the falls, the river, the game reserve, and the town. There are a sunrise trip, a sunset trip, and a nighttime one when there's a full moon. In the afternoon you get a better view of the rainbow. The standard 15-minute trip costs US$25, and the 30-minute sunrise trip costs US$40, which includes transfers, coffee, and pastries.

Bungee Jumping

As the second-highest bungee jump in the world, the 111-m (340-ft) high Victoria Falls Bridge (Shop 14, Soper's Arcade, Park Way Victoria Falls, ☎ 013/4471 through 013/4473 or 013/3392, FAX 013/4321, WEB www.shearwateradventures.com) is a major magnet for adrenaline junkies. The view, if you can stomach it, is pretty spectacular, too. It costs US$90, and you must produce your passport to get a bridge pass.

Canoeing

Kandahar Safaris (⊠ Adrift, The Train Carriage, Parkway Dr., Victoria Falls, ☎ 013/3589 or 013/2279, ☎ FAX 013/2014, WEB www.adrift.co.nz) leads canoe trips on the Zambezi River above the Falls. The river here is mostly wide and flat, winding through islands and splitting into myriad channels. Occasionally, tiny rapids—nothing to worry about—propel you through narrows. Along the way, you are likely to spot crocodiles, hippos, and elephants. The one-hour game drive through Zambezi National Park to reach the launch point is an added bonus. Most trips provide a bush breakfast before you start, a brief coffee or tea break, and a casual lunch on an island in the river. You can select either a half- or full-day trip, or two- to three-night expeditions. No experience or physical prowess is required. Expect to pay about US$65 for a half day, US$90 for a full day.

Shearwater Adventures (Shop 14, Soper's Arcade, Park Way, Victoria Falls, ☎ 013/4471 through 013/4473 or 013/3392, FAX 013/4321, WEB www.shearwateradventures.com) offers half- or full-day canoe trips and a very gentle "wine route" trip, on which you don't even paddle, you just watch the view while your guide does the work and hands you drinks and snacks (US$45).

Elephant-back Riding

The Shearwater Elephant Company (☎ 013/4471 through 013/4473 or 013/3392, FAX 013/4321, WEB www.shearwateradventures.com), at the Stanley & Livingstone hotel, has morning and evening rides accompanied by breakfast or snacks and sunset drinks (US$90). You can also book a table for lunch at **Jumbo Junction**, Shearwater's on-site restaurant. The menu includes light lunch options (salad, chicken, and quiche, for example), but the main attraction is the elephants. You get to touch them, talk to them (they don't reply) and ask the guide (who replies quite knowledgeably) all kinds of questions about their history, biology, and personal quirks (US$60).

Wild Horizons (✉ Elephant Camp, ☎ 013/2004 or 013/2029, FAX 013/4349, WEB www.wildhorizons.co.zw) has elephant rides (US$90); the rate includes transfers and either a full breakfast or drinks and snacks.

Horseback Riding

Riding a horse through the game-rich Zambezi National Park is an unforgettable experience. You get to sneak up on unsuspecting antelope and even buffalo and elephants. **Safari Par Excellence** (✉ Shop 4, Pumula Centre, ☎ 013/4–4424, FAX 013/4–4510) is the booking agent for **Zambezi Horseback Safaris**, which is run by Alison Baker—a Vic Falls legend in her own time. She knows the bush like the back of her hand, rides hard, and can shoot straight. Even more important, though, she knows how to avoid having to. Experienced riders may do game-viewing rides that range anywhere from 2½ hours to one, two, or three days. Novice riders can go for 1½ hours but will not be allowed close to animals such as elephants and lions. Costs range from US$35 for 1½ hours to US$80 for a full-day ride including lunch and drinks. Multiday trails are done on request only.

Senanga Safaris (☎ 013/4–5989, 011/20–8367, or 011/21–3534) offers game-viewing rides in the park. Choose between a two-hour (US$40), three-hour (US$50), half-day (US$80), or full-day ride (US$100). Half- and full-day rides include lunch and drinks.

River Boarding

For something completely different, try river boarding with **Shearwater Adventures** (☎ 013/4–4471 through 013/4–4473, or 013/4–3392, FAX 013/4–4321, WEB www.shearwateradventures.com). You stop at suitable rapids on the rafting trip and (still clad in helmet and life jacket) hop on a body board and surf the standing waves. It costs US$115.

River Cruises

A cruise on the Upper Zambezi is a great way to see game and the scenery and to relax in general. **Zambezi Wildlife Safaris** (☎ 013/4–4737, WEB www.ilalalodge.com) offers a range of options, including a 1½-hour sunrise cruise with coffee and pastries (US$18), a two-hour breakfast or lunch cruise (US$30 each), and a two-hour sundowner cruise with drinks and snacks (US$22). This is on a big, safe boat that you can just walk on to—no paddling, and you stay dry. **Shearwater Adventures** (☎ 013/4–4471 through 013/4–4473, or 013/4–3392, FAX 013/4–4321, WEB www.shearwateradventures.com) has sunset or dinner cruises at prices ranging from about US$18 to US$30.

White-Water Rafting

The Batoka Gorge is reputed to be the world's best one-day white-water rafting trip. If you want to be a passenger, choose an oar boat, in which you'll need to hang on tight and throw your weight around to keep the raft upright. If you have some experience or you're pretty strong and fit, you can join a paddleboat, in which you paddle, of course. The walk in and out of the gorge is quite strenuous.

Adrift (⊠ The Train Carriage on Parkway Dr., Victoria Falls, ☎ 013/4–3589 or 013/4–2279, ☎ FAX 013/4–2014, WEB www.adrift.co.nz) offers full- or half-day rafting trips, as well as a 2½-day trip. **Shearwater Rafting** (☎ 013/4–4471 through 013/4–4473, or 013/4–3392, FAX 013/4–4321, WEB www.shearwateradventures.com) has half-day, one-day, and 2½-day rafting trips. The full–day rafting trip costs US$85, regardless of which company you use, and the 2½-day trip is between US$280 and US$300. Lunch, drinks, and transfers are included.

Shopping

Several curio and crafts shops lie just beyond the Falls Craft Village, on Sopers Crescent, including the stylish new Elephant Walk Mall. Here you can buy a variety of crafts, from an 8-ft-tall wooden giraffe to soapstone carvings and brightly colored Zimbabwean batiks. If you're concerned about how to get your acquisitions back home, there's an international shipping agent sandwiched between the curio shops.

Victoria Falls A to Z

To research prices, get advice from other travelers, and book travel arrangements, visit www.fodors.com.

AIR TRAVEL

Victoria Falls Airport lies 22 km (14 mi) south of town. Both South African Airways and Air Zimbabwe fly direct between Johannesburg and Victoria Falls, usually on alternating days. There are direct flights from Maun. There are domestic flights from Harare, Bulawayo, Kariba, and Hwange.

Most hotels send free shuttle buses to meet incoming flights and provide free airport transfers for departing guests: arrange this in advance with your hotel. Taxis, at time of writing, could get to or from the airport for about US$20, payable in local or foreign currency, but taxi fares fluctuate drastically. Also be prepared to have any number of local drivers accosting you with with offers of rides into town.

➤ AIRLINES AND CONTACTS: **Victoria Falls Airport** (☎ 013/4–4250). **South African Airways** (⊠ Takura House, 2nd floor, 69–71 Union Ave., ☎ 04/73–8922). **Air Zimbabwe** (☎ 013/4–4316 in Victoria Falls).

BUS TRAVEL

Blue Arrow runs between Vic Falls and Bulawayo four times a week.

Most of the outlying hotels operate shuttle buses that run hourly into town. Inquire at your hotel in advance.
➤ BUS INFORMATION: **Blue Arrow** (☎ 04/72–9514 or 04/72–9518 in Harare) or book through **Shearwater** (☎ 013/4–4471 through 013/4–4473, or 013/4–3392, FAX 013/4–4321, WEB www.shearwateradventures.com).

MONEY MATTERS

If you limit your Zimbabwe visit to Vic Falls, it's not absolutely necessary to change money into Zimbabwean dollars because everyone from taxi drivers to curio vendors accepts foreign currency (the same applies on the Zambian side of the falls), but you will be given change in Zimbabwean dollars—probably at a pretty bad exchange rate. It's expected that tour operators will soon accept only U.S. currency; check before you go. If the trip is run by a Zambian operator just across the river—even if you book it in Zimbabwe and they pick you up at your Zimbabwean hotel—you *must* pay in foreign currency.

PASSPORTS AND VISAS

If you cross the river to do a one-day trip with a recognized Zambian-registered tour operator, you don't need to buy a Zambian visa if you book 24 hours in advance. If you cross into Zambia on your own, you will need a day visa, which costs US$10. Americans, but not Canadians or Brits, need to have a reentry pass to cross back to the Zimbabwean side.

TAXIS

Taxis are a cheap and convenient way to get around town. Hotels can summon them quickly, or you can find them at the falls.

TOURS

Victoria Falls is practically sinking under the weight of all the safari operators that have sprung up in the last few years. Most offer a few special tours of their own design but survive by selling the same trips as everyone else. You can book your rafting trips, bungee-jumping excursions, scenic flights, and game drives at a number of safari companies, including Safari Par Excellence, Shearwater Adventures, United Touring Company (UTc), and Zambezi Wildlife Safaris.

➤ TOUR-OPERATOR RECOMMENDATIONS: **Safari Par Excellence** (✉ Shop 4, Pumula Centre, Park Way, ☎ 013/4–4424, ℻ 013/4–4510). **Shearwater Adventures** (☎ 013/4–4471 through 013/4–4473, or 013/4–3392, ℻ 013/4–4321, 🖥 www.shearwateradventures.com). **United Touring Company (UTc;** ✉ Zimbank Bldg., Livingstone Way, ☎ 013/4–4267). **Zambezi Wildlife Safaris** (✉ Ilala Lodge, Livingstone Way, ☎ 013/4–4637, ℻ 013/4–4417, 🖥 www.ilalalodge.com).

TRAIN TRAVEL

South Africa's *Blue Train* (☞ Train Travel *in* Smart Travel Tips A to Z) runs a monthly two-night trip north from Pretoria to Zimbabwe, calling at Bulawayo and Victoria Falls. The vintage Rovos Rail (☞ Train Travel *in* Smart Travel Tips A to Z) offers a twice-monthly trip from Pretoria to Pietersburg, where you disembark and board a vintage Convair 440 plane to fly the last leg to Vic Falls, flying back to Pietersburg and then on the train to Pretoria. The Rovos Rail train passes through Vic Falls on its annual run from Cape Town to Dar es Salaam.

VISITOR INFORMATION

The Victoria Falls Publicity Association is fairly well stocked with brochures. It's open weekdays from 8 to 1 and 2 to 5 and on Saturday from 8 to 1. It's also a good idea to seek advice from the many safari companies in town.

➤ VISITOR INFORMATION: **Victoria Falls Publicity Association** (✉ 412 Park Way, ☎ 013/4202).

LAKE KARIBA AND THE LOWER ZAMBEZI RIVER

Much of the Zambezi, which forms Zimbabwe's northern border with Zambia, passes through Zimbabwe's wildest and least populated region. The area from Kariba downstream is known as the Lower Zambezi, and it is mostly broad and placid and offers fabulous game viewing.

Lake Kariba

Lake Kariba was formed in 1958 when the Zambezi was dammed at a narrow, almost vertical gorge 620 km (390 mi) downstream from Victoria Falls to provide hydroelectric power for Zimbabwe and Zambia. When constructed, the dam was the largest in the world, its slender arching wall more than ½ km (⅓ mi) long and 420 ft high.

After the valley was flooded, the tops of *mopane* and other trees remained above the water, where they stand today like fossilized relics from an earlier age, providing perches for cormorants, kingfishers, and fish eagles. More than anything else, perhaps, it is these ghostly trees and their black skeletal branches framed against one of Kariba's molten sunsets that form the lake's most enduring image. Matusadona National Park, on the shores of the dam, offers sightings of elephants frolicking in the water, black rhinos, lots of birds, and much more.

Lodging

$$$$ ⊡ **Matusadona Water Wilderness.** Voted one of the world's 10 most
★   fantastic getaways by *Condé Nast Traveler* magazine, this floating wonderland combines top lodge facilities with a unique location among the mopane skeletons of Matusadona National Park. Crickets chirp, frogs chirrup, hippos grunt, male lions roar out their territories—and you're right in the thick of it. Rooms are spacious and comfortably furnished. You travel between your floating chalet and the double-decker dining barge by motorized pontoon or, if you like, canoe. ✉ *On Lake Kariba, 20-min flight from Kariba Town, Mailing address: Wilderness Safaris, Box 288, Victoria Falls* ☎ *013/4–3371 through 013/4–3373 or book through Johannesburg* ☎ *011/807–1800. Bar, pool, fishing, boating. AE, DC, MC, V. FAP.*

Outdoor Activities

CANOE SAFARIS

River Horse Safaris (☎ 061/2944, 061/2447, or 061/2286, ℻ 061/2422, WEB www.riverhorse.co.zw) is based at Kariba Breezes Hotel and has three-day, four-day, or seven-day trips on the Lower Zambezi and a one-day trip in the spectacularly scenic Kariba Gorge, just below the dam (US$75). Both trips are on the Zambian side, but you don't have to pay for a visa if you book at least 24 hours in advance. **Canoeing Safaris** (☎ ℻ 06/2459 or 06/2265, or book through Johannesburg ☎ 00/27/11/609–3185, ℻ 00/27/11/609–0007, WEB www.cansaf.com) operates camping trips on three sections of the river. Kariba to Chirundu is a three-day trip with pretty scenery on the first day. Chirundu to Mana takes four days with excellent game-watching, generally improving as you move toward the park. Mana to Kanyemba, on the Mozambique border, includes the very scenic Mupata Gorge. There are no walking safaris on this trip. Cost is about US$100–US$150 per day (depending on the section done), all inclusive.

FISHING

Angling is taken seriously at Kariba, where the tiger fishing is regarded as the best in the world. An annual international tournament is held in October for this saber-toothed game fish, which can strike with such a lightning combination of strength and speed that many an unwary angler has lost a rod. It's worth trying to get one on fly, but you'll have to bring your own equipment. **Kariba Breezes Marina** (☎ 061/2475) is one of the best options for renting a boat and fishing gear (but not fly rods).

HOUSEBOATS

Floating around on a houseboat is one of the most popular Kariba activities. There are, literally, hundreds of boats to choose from ranging from very comfortable but unpretentious four-sleepers to veritable floating gin palaces with Jacuzzis, chefs, and a whole platoon of crew members. You can view the whole range of boats on the Web site of **River Horse Safaris** (☎ 061/2944, 061/2447, or 061/2286, FAX 061/2422, WEB www.riverhorse.co.zw).

SAILING

🖐 **Sail Safaris** (☎ 04/33–9123, FAX 04/33–9045, WEB www.sailsafaris.com) offers four- and seven-day safaris in easy-to-sail Wharram Tiki 30 catamarans, which are built more for comfort than performance. In the evening you moor at creek mouths and in bays. Game sightings are frequent. The fleet is made up of a number of boats, each crewed by a couple, family, or party, and the main meals are taken on a mother craft. This is suitable for families with sensible children. The season runs from April to August. If you just want to sail for a day, contact **Rex Taylor** (☎ 06/2983), who is about as close as you can get to an old salt on freshwater. He's sailed Kariba for years and probably knows the lake better than you know your own bathtub. He charges US$120–US$150 for a day's sailing on a quite sleek monohull, including drinks and meals.

Mana Pools National Park

Mana Pools National Park is arguably the wildest and most beautiful part of Zimbabwe. Heat-hazed escarpments and the timeless river—its lush green banks crowded with game during the dry season—are the enduring images of this immensely beautiful area. Buffalo and elephants are prolific, and there is every prospect of encountering lions. Raucous, grunting hippos warm themselves on the sandbanks, sharing them with those last remaining links from the time of the dinosaur, the Nile crocodile.

Bird life at Mana is also sensational, with more than 380 species recorded. Among them are the brilliant carmine bee-eaters, Lilian's lovebirds, hornbills, leggy saddle-billed storks, ibis, jacanas, orioles, herons, and Bateleur eagles.

Mana Pools National Park, but not the private lodges, closes during the rainy season, from the end of October to the end of April.

Lodging

The main camp, **Nyamepi,** offers campsites and clean ablutions, or you can stay in one of the numerous smaller camps. Booking is through **National Parks,** which also have a few riverside "houses" for rent. But your best bet is to stay in a private lodge or take a canoe trip.

$$$$ 🔊 **Chikwenya Lodge.** This luxury wilderness camp is just beyond the eastern extreme of the park and is built entirely on raised wooden platforms connected through a series of walkways. Accommodations are in canvas cottages with thatch roofs, and most meals are taken beneath a giant mahogany tree that is the center of camp activities. From the pool deck or the shady dining area you can watch hippos cavorting, waterbuck going down to the river for a drink, or lots of different birds flitting past. ⊠ *Mailing address: Wilderness Safaris, Box 288, Victoria Falls,* ☎ *013/4–3371 through 013/4–3373,* FAX *013/4–4224. 8 tents. Pool. MC, V.*

$$$$ 🔲 **Ruckomechi Camp.** In a corner where the Ruckomechi meets the Zam-
★ bezi, under enormous stands of mahogany and winterthorn trees, the camp has been voted the best safari lodge in the country three years in a row by the local association of travel agents. Accommodations are in thatch cottages, and the camp has views over a broad swathe of the river and the Zambian escarpment beyond. An open thatch bar above the river allows you to sit mesmerized by the flow of the water and

the birds flying past: kingfishers, ibis, and carmine bee-eaters, among others. There is also a marvelous open-air bath on the riverbank, with one side completely open to the water. The camp has game drives, bush walks, and canoe trips on the Zambezi, with cocktails served midway if the crocs and hippos permit. ✉ *Mailing address: Wilderness Safaris, Box 288, Victoria Falls,* ☎ *013/4–3371 through 013/4–3373,* FAX *013/ 4–4224. 10 lodges. Restaurant, bar.*

Outdoor Activities and Sports

Canoeing and Walking Tours

The very best way to experience Mana Pools is by canoe—you can arrange to do a short paddle from your lodge or, far more comfortably, via a luxury, vehicle-supported expedition.

Chipembere Safaris (☎ 061/2946, 011/61–0010, or 011/71–1355) operates overnight camping trips, from Chirundu to Mana Pools. You'll canoe by day and spend the night on islands—you set up your own tent, but you don't have to cook. You may do guided wildlife walks on this route, although most of it's not within the park boundaries (but the game doesn't always know that). It costs about US$120 per day, all inclusive. Guide Steve Pope also gives walking tours to the Chitake Springs area near Mana Pools. He appears to know the local lions personally—he certainly gets you closer to them than almost anyone else would dare—and can take you to some fascinating archaeological remains.

Natureways (☎ FAX 04/86–1766, WEB www.natureways.co.zw) offers a four-day, three-night canoeing safari. All the gear is carried by vehicle, the camp is set up by the time you paddle in, and staff members are on hand to offer you ice-cold or piping-hot drinks and snacks. Each day, for a few hours, you paddle past basking hippos and crocs and countless birds—then stop on the bank for a walk. You can get surprisingly close to elephants, buffalo, or lions. The trips cost between US$210 and US$300 per day, depending on length of trip and activity.

Kariba and Lower Zambezi River A to Z

To research prices, get advice from other travelers, and book travel arrangements, visit www.fodors.com.

AIR TRAVEL

Air Zimbabwe flies four times a week between Harare, Victoria Falls, Hwange, and Kariba. Sefofane Air Charters also have fairly regular flights between these destinations—particularly between the Wilderness Safari lodges—usually landing at Kiplings (a small dirt strip on an island in Matusadona). UTc does airport transfers for about US$8.
➤ AIRLINES AND CONTACTS: **Kariba Airport** (☎ 061/2913 or 061/ 2914). **Air Zimbabwe** (☎ 061/2913). **Sefofane** (☎ 04/70–8622, ☎ FAX 04/73–5570, WEB www.sefofane.co.zw). UTc (☎ 061/2262, 061/2312, or 061/2376, FAX 061/3313).

ZIMBABWE A TO Z

To research prices, get advice from other travelers, and book travel arrangements, visit www.fodors.com.

AIR TRAVEL

Air Zimbabwe and Zimbabwe Express Airlines have daily flights from Harare, Victoria Falls, and Hwange to Kariba Airport.

Air Zambezi flies regularly to connect Kariba, Bumi Hills adjacent to Matusadona, Hwange, and Victoria Falls.

There are small airstrips at Mana Pools National Park, Chikwenya, Chewore, and Mavuradona.

➤ AIRLINES AND CONTACTS: **Air Zimbabwe/Zimbabwe Express** (☎ 04/57–5111, FAX 04/57–5069, WEB www.airzim.co.zw). **Kariba Airport** (☎ 061/2913 or 061/2914). **Bulawayo Airport** (☎ 09/22–6575, 09/22–6491, or 09/22–6492, FAX 09/22–6232). **Harare International Airport** (☎ 04/57–5188). **Migration Air** (☎ 09/28–4394). **Sefofane** (☎ 04/70–8622, ☎ FAX 04/73–5570, WEB www.sefofane.co.zw).**South African Airways** (✉ Takura House, 2nd floor, 69–71 Union Ave., ☎ 04/73–8922).

BUS TRAVEL

Blue Arrow Luxury Coach Service runs between Bulawayo and Harare daily, between Harare and Mutare three times a week, and between Vic Falls and Bulawayo three times a week. They have comfortable, safe, air-conditioned Greyhound-style buses with videos and sound systems (which don't always work). At time of writing the cost of a longer trip was about US$30, payable in local currency. As the fuel supply and prices are constantly fluctuating (mostly upward), this price will almost certainly increase—by how much is anyone's guess.

➤ BUS INFORMATION: **Blue Arrow Luxury Coaches** (☎ 04/72–9514 in Harare; 09/65548 in Bulawayo, FAX 04/72–9572 in Harare; 09/65549 in Bulawayo, www.bluearrow.co.zw). In Vic Falls book through Shearwater (☎ 013/4–4471 through 013/4–4473, or 013/4–3392, FAX 013/4–4321, WEB www.shearwateradventures.com).

EMBASSIES

➤ CANADA: **Canadian High Commission** (✉ 45 Baines Ave., Box 1430, Harare, ☎ 04/25–2181 through 04/25–2185, FAX 04/25–2186 or 04/25–2187).

➤ UNITED KINGDOM: **British High Commission** (✉ Corner House, Samora Machel Ave. and Leopold Takawira St., 7th floor, Harare, ☎ 04/77–2990 or 04/77–4700, FAX 04/77–4617).

➤ UNITED STATES: **U.S. Embassy** (✉ 172 Herbert Chitepo Ave., Box 3340, Harare, ☎ 04/79–4521, FAX 04/79–6488).

EMERGENCIES

➤ EMERGENCY SERVICES: **General Emergencies** (☎ 999). **MARS** (**Medical Air Rescue Services**; ☎ 04/72–7540 or 04/73–4512 in Harare; 013/4–4646 or 091/23–5620 in Victoria Falls).

MONEY MATTERS

Zimbabwe's currency is the Zimbabwe dollar. There are Z$2, Z$5, Z$10, Z$20, and Z$50 bills; coins come in 1¢, 5¢, 10¢, 20¢, 50¢, and Z$1 denominations. At time of writing, this currency was particularly volatile and changing money with the banks was a bad idea because the rate of exchange was artificially high to prop up Mugabe's failing economy. Bureaux de change, which are not tied directly to the government, were giving a better rate (by almost double) and are perfectly legal. Also, you will be offered the opportunity to do a little informal trading by freelance street financiers; but don't, because you *will* be ripped off. Also be aware that there are often high charges associated with using a credit card in most establishments.

NATIONAL PARKS

All bookings for national parks are through the head office in Harare.

➤ NATIONAL PARKS: **National Parks** (National Parks, Box CY 140, Harare, ☎ 04/70–6077 or 04/70–6078, 04/70–7624 through 04/70–7629; 04/70–3376 in Harare, FAX 04/72–6089).

PASSPORTS AND VISAS

Citizens of Canada and the United Kingdom do not need visas. Americans can buy visas at point of entry for US$30 for a single entry or US$45 for a double entry. If you leave Zimbabwe for more than 24 hours, you will need to buy another (unless you splurged on a multiple entry), so think before you save that US$15. There are fun things just over the border. If you cross the border into Zambia for a day, Britons, Canadians, and Americans will need to purchase a Zambian day visa for US$10.

SHIPPING

If you're tempted to buy a 40-pound hippo, a 6-ft giraffe, or even a massive stone sculpture, you can get it shipped back home.

➤ SHIPPING AGENTS: **Cargo Marketing International** (✉ The Trading Post, Livingstone Way, Victoria Falls, ☎ 011/40–7402 or 011/40–7403, 𝐅𝐀𝐗 091/55–5066; ✉ 114 Borgward Rd., Msasa, Harare, ☎ 04/48–7881 through 04/48–7883, 𝐅𝐀𝐗 04/49–7021; ✉ First Mutual Life Bldg., 9th Ave., Bulawayo, ☎ 09/7–6753, 𝐅𝐀𝐗 09/7–6251).

TAXES

DEPARTURE TAX

All foreigners leaving the country by air must pay a US$20 departure tax.

TELEPHONES

Zimbabwean phone numbers in this chapter are printed as they should be dialed within Zimbabwe. When dialing from outside the country, add your country's international exit code as a prefix to the 263 country code, and drop the initial 0 of the city code. Non-Zimbabwean numbers are mostly South African and are listed as they would be dialed from Zimbabwe. To dial internationally from Zimbabwe, add 00 to the number. You can rent cell phones at the airport. Public phones operate on cards that you can purchase in small stores, at hotel reception desks, and similar places.

TOURS AND PACKAGES

This is probably one of the best ways to see a good selection of the country's sights. **Wilderness Safaris** will put together a fly-accommodations package linking any or all of their lodges in Mana Pools, Hwange, and Water Wilderness in Matusadona, usually starting and ending in Vic Falls. **Classic Safari Camps of Africa** takes bookings for a number of camps but also offers a fantastic package—the best of Zimbabwe in a short time. Its standard package starts in Vic Falls, transferring by air to the Hide at Hwange for two nights, then a flight to Musango Safari Camp in Matusadona. After two days at Musango, you fly to Nduna Safari Lodge in the southeast lowveld for two nights, then to Big Cave Camp near Matobo for two nights, and then transfer to Bulawayo Airport. The package costs US$3,520 per person, including all internal flights, all meals, and activities. Obviously, you can choose to do only part of the whole package, arrange to stay longer in one place, or even mix and match with other destinations. **UTc** can book lodges, and organize transfers, airfares, tours and more.

➤ TOUR-OPERATOR RECOMMENDATIONS: **Classic Safari Camps of Africa** (☎ 091/60–7305; 00/27/11/465–6427 in Johannesburg, 𝐅𝐀𝐗 04/87–0265; 00/27/11/465–9309 in Johannesburg, 𝐖𝐄𝐁 www.classicafricacamps.com). **UTc** (✉ 4 Park St., at Jason Moyo Ave., Harare, ☎ 04/77–0623, 𝐖𝐄𝐁 www.utc.co.zw; ✉ Johannesburg Office, ☎ 00/27/11/789–1681, 𝐅𝐀𝐗 00/27/11/789–8603). **Wilderness Safaris** (✉ Mailing address: Wilderness Safaris, Elephants Walk, Adam Standers Ave., 1st floor, Victoria Falls, ☎ 013/4–4527 or 013/4–3371 through 013/4–3373, 𝐅𝐀𝐗 013/4–

4424; ✉ Johannesburg Office, ☎ 011/807–1800, FAX 011/807–2110, WEB www.wilderness/safaris.com).

VISITOR INFORMATION

Often you will get the best (if somewhat biased) info from tour operators, but you can also try Zimbabwean Tourism Authority (which is not necessarily unbiased, either).

➤ TOURIST INFORMATION: **Zimbabwe Tourism Authority** (✉ 3 Anchor House, 4th St. and Jason Moyo Ave., 7th floor, [Box CY286 Causeway], Harare, ☎ 04/75–8712, 04/75–8714, or 04/75–8730, FAX 04/75–8826 through 04/75–8828).

11 BOTSWANA

Botswana itself is a natural wonder. Its variety of terrains, from vast salt pans to the waterways of the Okavango Delta to the Kalahari Desert, have diversity seldom found in such a small area. And because there is so little industry, you may have never seen stars as bright as this. The Kalahari Bushmen say that you can hear the stars sing—listen.

By Kate
Turkington

NCE UPON A TIME—a mere 20 or so years ago—Botswana was a Cinderella among nations, one of the world's poorest countries. Then the Fairy Godmother visited and bestowed her gift: diamonds. The resulting economic boom transformed Botswana into one of Africa's richest countries as measured by per capita income.

The 1960s were a decade of self-determination all over Africa, led by Uganda, Ghana, and Nigeria. The British Protectorate of Bechuanaland was granted independence in 1966 and renamed Botswana. Where other nations' celebrations quickly turned sour, Botswana's independence brought an enduring tide of optimism. The country sidestepped the scourge of tribalism and faction fighting that cursed much of the continent—including bordering South Africa and Zimbabwe—and is considered one of Africa's most stable democracies. The Batswana (singular: Motswana) are renowned for their courteousness and dignity.

Roughly the size of France or Texas, Botswana, once relatively unknown on the tourist map, is now becoming a popular safari destination. Although cities such as Gaborone (pronounced "*ha*-bo-rone"), the capital, have been modernized, Botswana has little in the way of urban excitement. Outside the cities, though, it's a land of amazing variety: the Kalahari Desert is in stark contrast to the lush beauty of the Okavango Delta, one of Botswana's most magnificent and best-known regions. A vast area of tangled waterways and aquatic, bird, and animal life, it's sometimes referred to as the Swamps, but this gives a false impression. There are no murky mangroves here, no sinister everglades, just open tranquil waters of breathtaking beauty leading into narrow, papyrus-fringed channels.

Nearly 18% of this very flat country's total land area is proclaimed for conservation and tourism. The Moremi Wildlife Reserve, the first such reserve in southern Africa to have been created by an African community (the Tawana people) on its own tribal lands, is a major draw. Here, as in other parts of northern and southeastern Botswana, you'll see elephants, lions, buffalo, wild dogs, cheetahs, leopards, giraffes, kudus, wildebeests, hippos, and hundreds of awesome birds.

Pleasures and Pastimes

Boating and Bird-watching

In the Okavango you can glide in a *mokoro* (indigenous canoe) through papyrus channels among reeds and water lilies and past palm-fringed islands on some of the purest water in the world, as your guide and poler avoids bumping crocs and hippos. Bird-watching from these boats is a special thrill: the annual return of thousands of gorgeous carmine bee-eaters to the Swamps in August and September is a dazzling sight, as is a glimpse of the huge ginger-color Pel's fishing owl, the world's only fish-eating owl and one of its rarest birds.

Dining

Don't come to Botswana expecting a profound gastronomic experience. There is little or no local cuisine, so the food in the camps and lodges is basically designed to appeal to a wide variety of international visitors—soups, roasts, pies, quiches, curries, vegetables, and fruits. Most camps bake their own excellent bread, muffins, and cakes and often make desserts such as meringues, eclairs, and homemade ice cream. And you'll find plenty of tasty South African wine and beer.

CATEGORY	COST*
$$$$	more than P90
$$$	P60–P90
$$	P30–P60
$	less than P30

prices are for a main course at dinner.

Fishing

If you're an experienced angler, you can pit your skills, wits, and rod against the savage fighting tiger fish (three out of five hooked get away). If you're a novice, or have always wanted to try fishing, then go for it now—the delta in season, from May to September, is full of fish, particularly bream. Cast a spinner or trawl your line behind a small chugging boat and get both dinner and a picture to amaze your friends.

Lodging

There are first-class private camps or game lodges all over Botswana, most in spectacular settings with stunning views, comfortable accommodations, and superb personal service. "Land camps" are in one of the game reserves or contiguous concessions, with two daily game drives, morning and evening. If you're not in a national park, you'll be able to go out for night drives off-road with a powerful spotlight to pick out many nocturnal animals. "Water camps" are deep in the Okavango and often only accessible by air or water. But many of the newer camps now offer both a land and a true water experience, so you get the best of both worlds. The average price per person per night at private lodges is US$400, which includes accommodations, all meals, soft drinks, and good South African wine. And each camp will arrange transfers for you from the nearest airport.

Hotels in Maun and Gaborone are reasonably priced, but quality varies, and it's better to check them out first unless they're reviewed here or they belong to a well-known chain.

CATEGORY	COST*
$$$$	over US$400
$$$	US$200–US$400
$$	US$100–US$200
$	under US$100

All prices refer to a standard double room in hotels or a per-person rate in all-inclusive resorts, including tax.

Wilderness and Wildlife

In Botswana superlatives are unavoidable—and never quite adequate. Some of the last great wilderness areas left in the world are here, all remarkable in their diversity. A short plane ride can whisk you from scorching desert to water wonderlands, from great salt pans to fertile floodplains. There are limitless horizons, deafening silence, spectacular beauty, and few people—including tourists. Northern Botswana and the Moremi Wildlife Reserve are teeming with game. For photographers Chobe sunsets are life altering. The dry and rugged Tuli Block in the southeast has huge elephant herds, spectacular 10,000-year-old ruins, and a multitude of leopards. The unique Okavango Delta really will show you that there is a peace that passeth all understanding. Go back to hunting-gathering mode with a San (Bushman) in the Makgadikgadi Pans and share his myths and magic as you starbathe, or take a trip to Botswana's largest game reserve, the harsh, remote Central Kalahari. And that's just a start.

Exploring Botswana

The country is basically a flat, sand-filled basin. The Kalahari Desert covers the center and south of the country and extends into Angola, South Africa, and Namibia. The northwest of the country is the unique watershed produced by the Okavango River (southern Africa's third-largest watercourse), which rises in the highlands of Angola and then flows south, west, and south again into Botswana's interior. Here, as it fans out over the Kalahari sandveld, it creates an immense inland delta, a fragile and perfectly balanced ecosystem that is one of the wonders of the natural world.

Great Itineraries

You'll have to decide which is first on your list of priorities—the certainty of seeing wall-to-wall wildlife in Chobe, Moremi, or Kwando; the peace of the Okavango Delta; the salt-pan moonscapes of the Makgadikgadi Pans; or the Kalahari Desert.

IF YOU HAVE 3 DAYS

Arrive in 🔅 **Maun** and catch an air charter to one of the camps in the 🔅 **Moremi Game Reserve.** Take your first thrilling game drive in an open vehicle with a knowledgeable local guide. After your early morning game drive, hop another plane to one of the true water camps deep in the 🔅 **Okavango Delta.** Next day marvel at its beauty from a mokoro and watch the sun set on the tranquil waters. Or stay for two nights at a camp that offers both a land and water experience. On the third day fly reluctantly back to Maun and the real world.

IF YOU HAVE 8 DAYS

Spend your first three days as outlined above. On the fourth day fly to Jack's Camp, in the **Makgadikgadi Pans.** After a good rest get up the next morning and roam the vast expanses of the largest salt pans in the world. On your sixth day head to **Moremi, Chobe,** or **Kwando** and the best wild game in the country. Next day head to the capital, ⊞ **Gaborone,** to take in a small African city in action. Leave from Gaborone on your last day.

When to Tour Botswana

The best time is in the southern hemisphere's autumn and winter months, April through September. In the delta the water has come in from the Angolan highlands, and elsewhere, as it's the dry season, the grass and vegetation are sparse, and it's much easier to see game, which often have no choice but to drink at available water holes or rivers. But be warned: it can be bitterly cold, particularly early in the morning and at night. Dress in layers (including a thigh-length thick jacket, hat, scarf, and gloves), which you can discard or add on to as the sun goes up or down. From October onward it gets very hot; so unless you're a tropical blossom or a keen bird-watcher—for it's then the migrants return—stick with winter.

THE OKAVANGO DELTA

The Okavango Delta is in Ngamiland, the tribal land of the BaTawana tribe. It's the legendary hunting area that fueled the 19th-century European imagination with Dr. David Livingstone's accounts of his explorations. The delta is formed by the Okavango River, which descends from the Angolan highlands and flows south and then fans out over northwestern Botswana. It's made up of an intricate network of channels and crystal-pure quiet lagoons, papyrus- and reed-lined backwaters, and myriad animal, bird, plant, and aquatic life. The mokoro boat, synonymous with the Okavango, was introduced to the area in the mid-18th century, when the Bayei tribe moved down from the Zambezi. Today, because of the need to protect the great jackalberry, morula, and sausage trees from which the crafts are fashioned, you may find yourself in the modern equivalent: a fiberglass canoe. Your skilled poler—who would put any tightrope walker to shame—is always on the alert for the ubiquitous hippos but is quite laid-back about the mighty crocs lying smiling in the sun. This is a water wilderness experience above all others, so don't miss the chance to go on a guided walk on one of the many islands.

There is big game, but it's more elusive and difficult to approach than in the game reserves. You'll almost certainly see elephants, hippos, crocs, and red lechwes (a beautiful antelope endemic to the Swamps) and may catch a glimpse of the rare, aquatic Sitatunga antelope. You'll probably hear lions but may not always see them. On the other hand, you might see lots of game. But you're not in the delta for the big game—you'll see plenty of that elsewhere in Botswana. You're here for the unforgettable beauty of the world's greatest wilderness areas.

Camp Okavango

An electric fence around the camp keeps the elephants out of Okavango, but hippos and whatever is in the area at the time stroll around at night; you're quite safe within your canvas walls. The major experience here is the water. In season fishing is good; and because the camp is so well established, the bird life is prolific. There's no dawn chorus quite like it.

Dining and Lodging

\$\$\$\$ ⚠ **Camp Okavango.** Most people involuntarily draw a breath when
★   they walk from the airstrip into the sprawling campsite. On remote Nxaragha Island in the heart of the permanent Delta, it's only accessible by plane or water. Built by an eccentric American millionaire many years ago (she used to jet off to L.A. to get her hair done), it combines

style, comfort, and a year-round water-wilderness experience. Huge old trees arch over an outdoor lounge area with sweeping lawns leading down to the water where hippos snort all night. Your super luxury tent with private bathroom, built on a raised wooden platform overlooking the delta, is set among groves of ancient trees and is so well separated from the others that you might believe yours is the only one in camp. Cool pastel linens, handcrafted wooden furniture, and colorful handwoven rugs make up the spacious interior. Common areas have comfortable colonial-style furniture among worn flagstones, carved elephant stools, where you can watch hundreds of birds feed, bathe, and drink aided and abetted by a few cheeky squirrels. Dinners are served in the high-thatched dining area, where an original sycamore fig mokoro is suspended over the long wooden dining table. Don't miss out on a spectacular sunset view from your fiberglass mokoro as you sip chilled drinks from a bar set up in the middle of a water-lily-studded lagoon tended by a wading barman. If you're going to the sister camp, Camp Moremi, go by water transfer, a three-hour trip with an island coffee stop on the way. ⊠ *Desert & Delta Safaris, Box 130555, Bryanston, South Africa,* ☎ *27/11/706–0861,* 🆙 *27/11/706–0863,* 🆆🅴🅱 *www.desertanddelta.com. 11 double tents. Bar, pool. MC, V. FAP.*

Xugana Island

On a big, permanent waterway, Xugana (pronounced "*koo*-gana") lets you do all the things the Okavango Delta does best: lap up tranquillity as you glide in a mokoro through the papyrus; get the adrenaline going as you fight a tiger fish; listen to an elephant midnight snacking next to your *mesasa* (the Setswana word for "dwelling"), walk on a lovely island searching for a Pel's fishing owl, and watch tiny jewel-like sunbirds sip nectar from flowering trees. The island also has the Mokoro Trail, a three-night accompanied camping excursion by canoe that slowly follows the river and goes on to the next camping site (not offered in January, February, and March).

Dining and Lodging

$$$ ✕🅼 **Xugana Island Lodge.** The lodge consists of stylish reed-and-thatch mosasa perched high on stilts, under massive ebony and jack-alberry trees overlooking the wide Xugana lagoon. In fact, in this camp everything is on the very edge of the lagoon. Each mesasa has a private bathroom. They're spacious, with wooden floors, high roofs, colorful blinds, sturdy wooden furniture, and a ceiling fan. Huge mosquito-proof windows provide one of the best views in the delta. Early morning tea and coffee are brought to your own wooden deck where you can sit and watch a wading elephant or listen to the tumultuous birdsong. Enjoy a drink at the cozy thatched bar that overlooks the lagoon, then dine on excellent food alfresco under the stars. This is a classy, well-established, gracious camp with a wonderfully intimate atmosphere, the result of years of experience and professionalism. ⊠ *Desert & Delta Safaris, Box 130555, Bryanston, South Africa,* ☎ *27/11/706–0861,* 🆙 *27/11/706–0863,* 🆆🅴🅱 *www.desertanddelta.com. 18 mosasa. Bar, pool. MC, V. FAP.*

Delta Camp

Activities from the camp include guided mokoro trails into the maze of waterways and game walks on adjacent islands with a professional licensed guide. Your walks will teach you about the African environment ranging from the habits of dung beetles and warthogs to superb bird-spotting to how to dodge a charging elephant. A major conservation plus for Delta Camp is that motorboats are not used, as the emphasis is on preserving the pristine purity of the environment, which adds immeasurably to the relaxed, peaceful atmosphere that pervades this lovely camp. The Sitatunga Trail can be arranged for select groups of at least four who wish to further explore this wondrous place for six nights or more. You may meet big or little game; in the delta there's no way of knowing.

Dining and Lodging

$$$$ ✕⊡ **Delta Camp.** This is an enchanting traditional camp set deep in the Okavango. Reed chalets, each with private bathroom, are furnished with wooden furniture and upturned mokoros; they look like something straight out of *The Swiss Family Robinson*. Each chalet faces northeast to catch the first rays of the sun as it rises above the palm trees, and below your windows are shallow, bird-filled pools, with deeper waterways only paces from your front door. Family owned for many years, the camp has an intimate, relaxed atmosphere, and the emphasis is on offering you the opportunity to experience the tranquillity of the environment. Sit under the stars at mealtimes, chill out on the extended deck with its spectacular views of the surrounding waterways, and at night sip tea or coffee round a blazing log fire. ⊠ *Lodges of Botswana, Box 39, Maun, Botswana,* ☎ *267/661–154,* ℻ *267/660–589,* WEB *www.okavango.bw. 9 chalets. MC, V. FAP.*

Duba Plains

This tiny, intimate camp, deep, deep in the delta, is built on an island shaded by large ebony, fig, and garcinia trees and surrounded by horizon-touching plains that are seasonally flooded, usually from late April to early October. It's one of the best-kept secrets in the Okavango, tucked into the delta's farthest reaches. When the water is high in winter, the game competes with the camp for dry ground, and lions and hyenas become regular dusk-to-dawn visitors. You'll hear the roar of lions pervading the camp as night falls. There's wall-to-wall game including herds of hundreds of buffalo, leopards, lions, cheetahs, elephants, hippos, lechwes, and the most beautiful of all the antelopes—the sdable—all of which you can watch from one of only two four-by-four open game vehicles in the reserve. Duba Plains is also a birder's paradise, with an abundance of waterfowl.

Dining and Lodging

$$$$ ✕⊡ **Duba Plains.** Your big, cool, tented room is built on a raised
★   deck, with an overhead fan and gleaming furniture of Rhodesian teak inside that perfectly complement the subtle grays and greens of the soft furnishings. A lattice-wood screen divides your bedroom/sitting area from your private bathroom with its ceramic washbasin, glass shower, and plenty of storage space. The lounge and dining area of the lodge is small and inviting, with comfortable chairs and couches, a bar, and a stupendous view. There's a poolside gazebo where you can relax and watch the plains after a refreshing dip, as well as a bird hide tucked away behind the camp. If it's exclusivity and solitude you're after, then this camp hits the spot. ⊠ *Wilderness Safaris, Box 5219, Rivonia 2128, South Africa,* ☎ *11/807–1800,* ℻ *11/807–2110,* WEB *www. dubaplains.com. 6 rooms. Bar, pool. MC, V. FAP.*

Chitabe Camp

Chitabe is in an exclusive photographic reserve bordered by the Moremi Game Reserve, to the north, the Gomoti Channel, to the east, and the Santantadibe River, in the west. It's a lovely and popular camp whose big, comfortable tents on stilts are connected by environmentally friendly raised wooden walkways that put you safely above the ground and give you a Tarzan's-eye view of the surrounding bush—you might come eye-ball to eyeball with a wandering elephant. Not only elephants, but also buffalo, lions, leopards, and cheetahs are among the main attractions of this area, as well as a host of small nocturnal game such as porcupines, civets, and bush babies. Chitabe lies within a study area of the Botswana Wild Dog Research Project, which has up to 160 dogs in packs of 10–12, so you're almost certain to see these fascinating "painted wolves." Night drives are particularly rewarding. The area has a good variety of habitats, from marshlands and riverine areas to open grasslands and seasonally flooded plains, but although it's on one of the most beautiful islands in the delta and has classic Okavango scenery, it's not a water camp as such and doesn't offer water activities.

Dining and Lodging

$$$$ 🦌 **Chitabe Camp.** This very attractive and popular camp has luxurious, twin-bedded, East African–style tents with wooden floors, woven lala palm furniture, wrought-iron washstands, and private bath. Tents are reached by walking along raised wooden walkways that wind their way through palms and mopane trees—it's a bit like being in the middle of a Tarzan movie set. A separate thatched dining room, bar, and lounge area, also linked by wooden walkways, looks out over a floodplain. However, the shallow water that surrounds the camp is hidden by the long grass, so it's difficult to believe that you're actually in the Okavango Delta; there are no vistas of water. For groups that would like a camp to themselves, Chitabe Trails Camp, often used by overland safaris, accommodates eight guests in similar tents built on the ground with private bathrooms, private dining room, bar, and lounge area. ✉ *Wilderness Safaris, Box 5219, Rivonia 2128, South Africa,* ☎ *11/807–1800,* FAX *11/807–2110,* WEB *www.wilderness-safaris.com. 8 tents at Main Camp, 4 tents at Trails Camp. Bar, pool. MC, V. FAP.*

Nxabega Camp

This gorgeous camp (pronounced "*na*–becka"; a sister camp to Okavango and Moremi) is in the very heart of the delta. Renowned for its scenic beauty, this 17,000-acre private concession encompasses all the vegetation types of the Okavango—mopane, riverine, mixed, palm and acacia woodland, terminalia sandveld, perennial swamp, and seasonally flooded grassland. This means you can have both a water and a land experience—viewing from a mokoro or an open four-by-four. You could well see most of Botswana's 550 species of birds, or follow the lions or wild dogs as they hunt at dusk. Because this is a private concession, you can thrill to a night drive in an open Land Rover and by spotlight pick out not only the big predators but also some of the smaller ones: civets, bush babies, genets, or—if you get really lucky—a pale prehistoric aardvark or scaly pangolin. A special bonus is the resident naturalist on hand to complement the team of knowledgeable and friendly guides.

Dining and Lodging

$$$$ 🦌 **Nxabega Camp.** One of only two camps in the delta run by CCA (of South Africa's Londolozi and Phinda fame), this beautiful camp offers both a land and a water experience. Safari tents are on raised teak platforms, each with a private veranda overlooking idyllic water and bush views. The main lodge is of thatch and wood with dark wooden paneling inside. Skin rugs, fine woven cane furniture, cushions in various ethnic designs, hand-carved wooden tables, wooden bowls full of ostrich eggs, and lamps fashioned out of guinea fowl feathers and porcupine quills give the lounge an exotic African ambience, while the high-roofed paneled dining room has an almost medieval banqueting-hall

feel. Be sure to zip up your tent at night (there's lots of game around)
before you retire to your comfortable bed with its leather headboard
and fresh white linen. Zip your way through to the dressing room and
bathroom area with its big wooden wardrobe, glass-enclosed shower,
and reed walls. Tea or coffee is brought to your tent so that you can
watch the early morning delta world go by in splendid seclusion. The
food is excellent, so make sure you lose some of those calories by taking a guided walk on one of the nearby islands to track game and marvel at the different varieties of bird life. ⊠ CC *Africa, Private Bag X27,
Benmore, Johannesburg 2010, South Africa,* ☎ *011/809–4300,* FAX *011/
809–4400,* WEB *www.ccafrica.com. 10 tents. Bar, pool. MC, V.*

Sandibe Camp

Sandibe, the sister camp to Nxabega Camp, is also run by CC Africa
of Londolozi and Phinda fame. It's absolutely gorgeous. Both a land
and a water camp, Sandibe clings to the edge of one of the delta's beautiful pristine channels. You can step into your mokoro at the campsite
and switch off stress and modern-day living as you cocoon yourself in
another, gentler world. Sandibe's guides are superb, thrilling you with
campfire tales at night, fishing with you in the open water spaces, pol-
ing your mokoro through tunnels of interlacing feathery papyrus,
walking with you on one of the many palm-studded islands, tracking
big game—hippos, lions, cheetahs, buffalo, wild dogs, leopards, elephants, and some Okavango specials: the aquatic tsessebe antelope,
fastest of all antelope, and the rare, secretive Sitatunga antelope—in
an open Land Rover or on foot, depending on which you prefer.

Dining and Lodging

$$$$ ✕🏨 **Sandibe Camp.** The camp has a fairy-tale feel, as if a giant had
fashioned an idyllic tiny village out of adobe and thatch and set it down
amid an enchanted forest full of birds nestled beside a papyrus-fringed
secret lagoon. Honey-color cottages with stepped and fringed thatched
roofs add to the unique visual effect of this spectacular camp. The cottages are open and airy and decorated with a lavish use of wood; each
contains a huge carved bed covered with a woven leather bedspread,
colorful kilims, skillfully chosen African artifacts, and lamps fabricated
of woven metal and ostrich eggs. Sit on your stone veranda or tiny personal deck that overlooks the waterways, shaded by huge old African
ebony trees, or walk along the elephant dung paths to the main lodge
area, where sheets of tattered russet bark waft in the breeze. This is a
wonderful place to sit and relax or swap big-game stories with your
fellow guests. Climb up to the secluded wooden decks with their comfortable sitting areas, above the main sitting and dining area, and
catch up on your reading or game and bird lists, or just sit and relax
in the outdoor *boma* (hut) around a crackling fire and stargaze as you
sip your after-dinner coffee or liqueur. ⊠ CC *Africa, Private Bag X27,
Benmore, Johannesburg 2010, South Africa,* ☎ *011/809–4300,* FAX *011/
809–4400,* WEB *www.ccafrica.com. 8 cottages. Bar, pool. MC, V. FAP.*

Jao Camp

This spectacular and stunning camp, a pure Hollywood-meets-Africa
fantasy, is in a private concession bordering the Moremi Game Reserve,
west of Mombo, on a densely wooded island overlooking vast plains.
The landscape includes a great variety of habitats, including permanent waterways and lagoons, open floodplains, and thick Kalahari soils.
The place is teeming with creatures of all kinds—fish, fowl, and game.
Jao can offer both land and water activities, depending on the seasonal
water levels, so you can take a day or night game drive in an open four-

by-four, glide in a mokoro through rippling meadows of water lilies in possibly the most beautiful setting in the whole of the delta, chug along hippo highways in a motorboat, or go on a guided walk. You'll see lots of predators, especially lions, who live here in the highest concentration in the country, according to a recent wildlife census.

Dining and Lodging

$$$$ X⊡ **Jao Camp.** If you love the fanciful, enjoy fairy tales and fantasy, and have an exotic imagination, then Jao will delight you. You'll be one of only 16 pampered guests when you sleep in your own spacious tree house with superb views over the vast floodplains. You can lie in your canopy bed and watch the sun rise, or recline on megacushions, pasha style, and watch the translucent waters beyond the lush palms below. Private bath facilities include an indoor shower, flush toilet and basin, a Victorian claw-foot bath, as well as an outdoor shower. Rare and fascinating African artifacts decorate the wooden multitier interior of the main building. The food is delicious, and the superb standard of service can best be appreciated as you dine in the cool thatched dining area under a canopy of trees alive with birdsong. After a night drive eat under the night sky in the outdoor boma and watch the sparks from the roaring fire compete with the dazzling stars. ⊠ *Mailing address: Wilderness Safaris, Box 5219, Rivonia 2128, South Africa,* ☎ *11/807–1800,* FAX *11/807–2110. 8 chalets. Bar, pool. MC, V. FAP.*

Moremi Game Reserve

In the northeastern sector of the Okavango lies the spectacular Moremi Game Reserve. In 1963 Chief Moremi III and the local BaTawana people proclaimed 1,800 square km (1,116 square mi) of pristine wilderness—ancient mopane forests, lagoons, islands, seasonal floodplains, and open grassland—as a game sanctuary, a first in southern African conservation history. Here, where the life-giving waters of the Okavango meet the vast Kalahari, lies one of Africa's greatest parks, teeming with game and birds and, unlike the Masai Mara or Kruger Park, with hardly any people. You'll love the Garden of Eden atmosphere even if you do encounter the odd snake or two.

As there are no fences, the big game—and there's lots of it—can migrate to and from the Chobe park in the north. Sometimes it seems as if a large proportion of Botswana's 70,000 elephants have made their way here, particularly in the dry season. Check off on your game list lions, cheetahs, leopards, hyenas, wild dogs, buffalo, hippos, dozens of different antelopes, zebras, giraffes, monkeys, baboons, and more than 400 kinds of birds. Although during the South African school holidays (around July) there are more vehicles than normal, traffic is mostly light, and unlike many of Africa's other great reserves you'll often be the only ones watching the game.

There are three main camp areas in the reserve. At Camp Moremi you get the best of both water and land. The early morning and evening game drives with excellent rangers (one is aptly named "Relax") will pretty much ensure that you see lions galore, elephants, giraffe, zebras, all kinds of antelope, and often the elusive leopard, cheetah, and wild dog. The rare Pel's fishing owl regularly plummets down to the shallow pool below Tree Lodge to snag a fish and carry it away to the only spotlighted tree. Bird-watching is excellent throughout the year; marabou and yellow-billed storks, pelicans, and cormorants nest here in the summer months. You can take a powerboat to the heronries on Gadikwe and Xakanaxa lagoons. You'll see similar game at Xigera, which overlooks the floodplain and has access to water year-round. The camp offers mokoro and boat trips, ranger-lead walking safaris, and driving safaris if conditions aren't too wet (summer is your best bet for this). Mombo Camp is strictly a land activity camp. Although there is plenty of surface water in the area (marshes and floodplains), it's not deep enough for water activities. Mombo is set deep within the Moremi and has exclusive use of a large area of the reserve, so privacy is assured. Because of its great wildlife, including all of the large predators, several well-known documentaries have been filmed here.

Dining and Lodging

$$$$ ⚠ **Camp Moremi.** This is the luxurious sister camp to the delta's Camp Okavango, so expect the same high level of service, food, and accommodations. Huge old African ebony trees, home to two-legged, four-legged, winged, and earthbound creatures, dominate the campsite, on the edge of a lovely lagoon. From the high viewing platform in the trees you can look out on a limitless horizon as the sun sets orange and gold over the smooth, calm waters. Tastefully decorated, comfortable tents are well spaced to ensure privacy. Camp Moremi's attractive timber-and-thatch tree lodge has a dining area, bar, main lounge, small library, and sundeck with great views of Xakanaxa Lagoon. ⊠ *Desert & Delta Safaris, Box 130555, Bryanston, South Africa,* ☎ *27/11/706–0861,* FAX *27/11/706–0863,* WEB *www.desertanddelta.com. 11 tents. Bar, pool. MC, V. FAP.*

$$$$ ✕🛏 **Mombo Camp.** On Mombo Island, off the northwest tip of Chief's
★ Island, this legendary camp surrounded by wall-to-wall game is sometimes linked to land depending on the ebb and fall of the delta. The excellent game at Mombo has made this area Botswana's top wildlife documentary location—*National Geographic* and the BBC are among those who have filmed here. Rebuilt in 1999, the stunning camp has identical guest rooms divided into two distinct and independent camps. These camps are among the best known, most expensive, and most sought after in Botswana, so be sure to book months in advance if you hope to stay here. Mombo has nine rooms, and Little Mombo only three. Each spacious room is built on a raised wooden platform with wonderful views over the open plains, and although the rooms have a tented feel, they are very luxurious, with padded chaise longues, comfortable sofas, interesting lamps, woven rugs, and polished wooden floors. You can wash off the day's dust in your private bathroom or cool off in your outdoor shower. The dining room, lounge, and bar are also built on big wooden decks overlooking the magnificent savanna landscape dotted with animals and birds. The atmosphere is friendly, the attention to personal service great, the food excellent, and the guides top class. The camp isn't fenced, so make sure you are escorted back to your room after dinner, and then just lie back in your comfortable bed and listen to the sounds of the African night: lions roaring, hyenas yipping, a solitary leopard coughing, and owls and nightjars calling. ⊠ *Wilderness Safaris, Box 5219, Rivonia 2128, South Africa,* ☎ *11/807–1800,* FAX *11/807–2110,* WEB *www.mombo.co.za. 12 rooms. Bar, pool. MC, V. FAP.*

$$$$ ✕🛏 **Xigera Camp.** The cry of the fish eagle permeates this exception-
★ ally lovely camp (pronounced *Kee*'jer-a) set on aptly named Paradise Island amid thickets of old trees in one of the most beautiful parts of the delta deep in the Moremi Game Reserve. Huge airy suites of timber and canvas are built on a high wooden platform overlooking a floodplain. Reed walls separate the sleeping area from the spacious dressing room, which in turn, leads into a reed-floored shower and separate toilet. Or you can choose to shower under the stars as hippos and frogs compete in the loudest-noises-of-the-night competition. Raised wooden walkways connect the rooms to the main lodge, which sprawls beside a lagoon where a small wooden bridge joins the island to the main-

land. At night this bridge becomes a thoroughfare for lions and hyenas, and it's not uncommon to see one of these nocturnal visitors walk by as you sip your postprandial coffee or liqueur by the blazing fire. This camp does not concern itself with designer ethnic chic but concentrates on old-fashioned comfort and elegance. The food is varied and excellent, and the staff all seem to be chosen not only for their superb sense of service but also their great sense of humor. ✉ *Wilderness Safaris, Box 5219, Rivonia 2128, South Africa,* ☎ *11/807–1800,* FAX *11/807–2110,* WEB *www.xigera.com. Bar, pool. 5 rooms. MC, V. FAP.*

Vumbura Camp

Deep in the delta, this spacious yet delightfully intimate tented camp nestled among stands of ancient African ebony trees offers both land and water activities. Go drifting through watery carpets of day and night water lilies in a mokoro; catch your fish supper from a motorboat; or look for lions, elephants, and wild dogs on your early morning or spotlighted night drive in an open four-by-four vehicle. The privacy of the area, about 25 km (15 mi) north of Mombo, is one of its greatest attractions. The surrounding Botswana communities work in concert with the camp, deriving direct benefits from the wildlife through significant concession fees, jobs, and training and contributing with their detailed local knowledge and exceptional friendliness and helpfulness. Sit on your private wooden deck and watch a spectacular sunset over the floodplain, or after dark listen to the lions roaring or the elephants and hippos noisily trudging through the shallow water in front of your tent.

Dining and Lodging

$$$$ 🏕 **Little Vumbura.** You hardly notice this tiny charming camp as you walk along a wooden jetty after your boat transfer through a winding waterway. That's because it's hidden among, and part of, a fairy-tale forest of African ebony, marula, knobthorn, and fig trees. The sitting and dining area is built of canvas and reeds, and living trees form part of the structure. Cool blues predominate, and this color scheme is carried right through to the beaded salt cellars, indigo pottery, and blue cushions. Blue dominates your tented and timber bedroom with terracotta-tile veranda and floor, rush mats, and blue tie-dye bedspreads. White-linen curtains and blinds and a comfortable wicker armchair complete your forest hideaway. Outside one room, wooden steps lead up to an enchanting open-air shower built round two huge jackalberry trees—you can exfoliate your back on the rough bark in true rhino style. The public areas also include a reed-enclosed deck for alfresco dining by firelight and a reed-shaded sundeck where you can lie by the inviting small pool and look out over the never-ending waterways. Although Little Vumbura offers all the activities of it bigger neighbor, Vumbura, it's a delightful small world that seems to grow organically out of the surrounding trees and gently lapping water—a cross between a Hans Christian Andersen fairy tale and the Swiss Family Robinson. ✉ *Wilderness Safaris, Box 5219, Rivonia 2128, South Africa,* ☎ *11/807–1800,* FAX *11/807–2110,* WEB *www.littlevumbura.com. 5 tents. Bar, pool. MC, V. FAP.*

$$$$ 🏕 **Vumbura Camp.** There's nothing quite like sleeping in a tent, however luxurious and comfortable, for getting the real feel of Africa. The large tents here are so privately situated you might feel as if you're alone in the camp. Remember, however, that even though elephants may be making the ground tremble right outside the wooden door of your tent, you are perfectly safe between your canvas walls. Sit tight and enjoy the experience. Wooden wicker screens and a sturdy wooden-top low wall separate your comfortable bedroom area from the private bathroom. Laze in a deck chair on your small tiled deck and listen to the

cries of the brightly colored parrots and green pigeons chattering in the huge trees encircling your tent. Tasty meals are served in an open-sided dining area tucked beneath a canopy of indigenous trees with a superb view across the floodplain. ✉ *Wilderness Safaris, Box 5219, Rivonia 2128, South Africa,* ☎ *11/807–1800,* FAX *11/807–2110,* WEB *www.vumbura.com. 8 tents. Bar, pool. MC, V. FAP.*

The Okavango Delta A to Z

To research prices, get advice from other travelers, and book travel arrangements, visit www.fodors.com.

AIR TRAVEL
Gaborone and Kasane International airports and the northern safari capital of Maun are the gateways to the Okavango. There are regular flights to Kasane from Zimbabwe and Namibia. *See* Botswana A to Z, *below,* for airline contact information.

CAR TRAVEL
Only the western and eastern sides of the delta panhandle and the Moremi Game Reserve are accessible by car; but it's wisest to always take a four-by-four vehicle. Maun, the starting point for the panhandle, is easy to reach from all sides, including South Africa, Namibia, and Zimbabwe, but the distances are long and not very scenic. The road from Maun to Moremi North Gate is tarred for the first 47 km (29 mi) up to Sherobe, when it becomes gravel for 11 km (7 mi) and then a dirt road.

GETTING AROUND
Once you get into camp, staff will take you where you need to go. The age-old way to get around the delta is by mokoro boat, made from the trunks of the great jackalberry, morula, and sausage trees. A skilled poler will guide the craft at some speed through the narrow channels. In deeper waters powerboats are an option.

Much of the delta, especially its game, can only be enjoyed on foot. A good guide and a good pair of boots are required at all times.

TOUR OPERATORS
Most operators charge a per diem rate of around US$400, per person, double occupancy.

Afro Ventures has 30 years of experience as a tour operator and has ready-made trips and tours, or can tailor one to your personal choice, ranging from the budget-conscious to the lavish.

Desert & Delta Safaris has inclusive fly-in safari packages to Camp Moremi, Camp Okavango, and Nxabega Okavango Safari Camp, with daily departures from Maun, Kasane, and Victoria Falls.

Hartley's Safaris has planned safaris to their Xugana (Okavango) and Tsaro (Moremi) Camps.

Wilderness Safaris offers planned, detailed tours between their many camps, both fly-in safaris and overland. Itineraries include a four-night, five-day safari combining the Okavango and Moremi Game reserves, or a longer trip continuing on to Savuti/Linyanti and the central Kalahari.

➤ Tour Operator Information: **Afro Ventures** (✉ CC Africa, Private Bag X27, Benmore 2010, Johannesburg, South Africa, ☎ 011/809–4300, FAX 011/809–4514, WEB www.afroventures.com). **Desert & Delta Safaris** (✉ Box 130555, Bryanston, South Africa, ☎ 27/11/706–0861, FAX 27/11/706–0863, WEB www.desertanddelta.com). **Hart-**

ley's Safaris (✉ Hartley's Safaris, Box 69859, Bryanston 2021, South Africa, ☎ 11/465–5075, ☎ FAX 11/467–3099, WEB www.hartleysafaris. co.za). **Wilderness Safaris** (✉ Box 5219, Rivonia 2128, South Africa, ☎ 11/807–1800, FAX 11/807–2110, WEB www.wilderness-safaris.com).

MAUN

Maun is the gateway to the delta for everyone from well-heeled retirees to young broke backpackers. It's grown from being a tiny pioneering outpost 100 years ago to having a population of 60,000 today. The government has poured in millions of pula over the last few years, and the infrastructure is developing fast. It's also the tribal capital of the BaTawana people, who live in large traditional villages within the town's boundaries. African mud-and-grass huts, unchanged for centuries, happily rub shoulders with modern brick structures. There's a great spirit in Maun and always has been. It's also a place of exceptional, hard-living, hardworking, warm, and generous people who are bound in a spirit of sharing and friendship that is less common elsewhere in Africa. From the city it's possible to organize all your trips to the delta.

Exploring Maun

A Good Drive

A block from Maun Airport is the **Nhabe Museum**—you can even catch it between planes if you're not staying. Just south of the delta, only a 90-minute drive from Maun via Toteng, is **Lake Ngami.**

Sights to See

Lake Ngami. When flooded (December–March), Ngami is one of the greatest bird-viewing areas of Africa. You'll see thousands of flamingos, huge flocks of pelicans, herons, storks, ducks, and geese, and many other migrants. Traditional Herero and Yei villages cluster round the lake. There are no accommodations, so rent a car or hire a local tour operator, take a picnic, and make it a day trip.

Nhabe Museum. The museum exhibits the work of local Batswana painters, printmakers, sculptors, woodworkers, and weavers. If you're in Maun for a couple of days, try to catch a show at the outdoor performance annex behind the main building. ✉ *Airport Rd., opposite Safari South, Private Bag 268, Maun,* ☎ *267/661–346.* ☎ *Free.* ☉ *Weekdays 8–5, Sat. 9–4:30.*

Dining and Lodging

For cheap fast food there's a **Steers,** two blocks from the airport (✉ New Mall, ☎ 267/660–122); it's open 7:30 AM–8 PM. Or try the **Sports Bar and Restaurant,** which not only offers good Italian or steak-house cuisine but is where the action is in Maun (✉ Airport Rd, Maun, ☎ 267/662–676. MC, V. ☉ Tues.–Sun. 5 PM–midnight).

$ ✕🖼 **Island Safari Lodge.** On the way to the Moremi Game Reserve and only 12 km (7½ mi) outside Maun, this lodge will give you your first taste of the delta. You'll sleep in simple but comfortable chalets all with private bathrooms, three of which nestle on the banks of the Thamalakane River under the shade of big trees. You can make your own barbecue, have a bar snack, or eat in the decent restaurant. The atmosphere is very friendly and informal, with lots of partying at the weekends. The lodge will also arrange Okavango trips by boat or mokoro, houseboat trips on the river, and vehicle trips with licensed

guides throughout northern Botswana. ⊠ *Box 116,* ☎ *267/660–300.*
12 chalets, campsite. Restaurant, bar. MC, V.

$ ✕🖬 **Riley's Hotel.** A Maun institution, the comfortable modern hotel
(a member of the Cresta Hotels chain) you see today is a far cry from
the seven dusty rooms built by the legendary Harry Riley in the mid-
'30s. In those days government officers, traders, hunters, and the rest
of Harry's crew took board and lodging at Riley's for months at a
time. It's still one of the main gathering places in Maun, although planes
no longer taxi straight up to the bar as in the good old days. With
luxurious rooms and good eating at Riley's Grill (P25–P60), it's a top
choice for discerning travelers. In the popular Harry's Bar, if you
listen carefully enough, you might just hear the raucous merriment
of the original Riley's crew. ⊠ *Box 1, Maun,* ☎ *267/375–376,* 🆆🅴🅱 *www.*
cresta-hospitality.com. 51 rooms. Restaurant, bar. MC, V. BP.

$ ⚠ **Audi Camp and Bar.** Audi means fish eagle in Setswana, and this
lively tented camp offers the budget option for the Okavango Delta.
The camp, which has extensive experience with educational groups and
safaris for school or university groups, offers a wide range of activities
from vehicle safaris and mokoro trips to walking safaris and cultural
trips. There's a great bar that is very popular with the locals and a restaurant with a wooden deck for sunset viewing. Grab a toasted sandwich
or burger or try a fillet steak or a chicken dish. ⊠ *Private Bag 28, Maun,*
☎ *267/660–599,* 🅵🅰🆇 *267/660–581,* 🆆🅴🅱 *www.audi-delta.com. Restau-*
rant, bar, pool, 9-hole golf course, shuttle.

Maun A to Z

To research prices, get advice from other travelers, and book travel ar-
rangements, visit www.fodors.com.

AIR TRAVEL
Air Botswana flies once daily to Maun from Johannesburg and
Gaborone. Air charter companies serve the Kasane–Maun connec-
tion. You can leave your bags at the airport and walk into town (about
a 30-minute walk), which is very hot in summer, or try to hitch a ride.
There are no taxis at the airport. The hotels will provide transporta-
tion on request.
➤ AIRLINE INFORMATION: **Air Botswana** (☎ 267/351–921).

BUS TRAVEL
A Windhoek shuttle bus departs from Audi Camp on Wednesday and
returns from Windhoek on Monday, US$50 round-trip. A Victoria Falls
shuttle departs from Audi Camp on Sunday and returns from Victoria Falls on Monday, US$60 one-way.

CAR TRAVEL
Gaborone to Maun is 915 km (572 mi) on a good tar road. To get to
Maun from Victoria Falls, you would first have to drive to Chobe and
then to Maun from there, not really a practical option.

You'll probably need a car to get around Maun. Roads are mostly tarred
or good sand roads and driving is safe and easy. Avis Safari Hire and
Holiday Safaris 4x4 Hire are both good options for rentals.
➤ CAR TRAVEL INFORMATION: **Avis Safari Hire** (☎ 267/660–039). **Hol-**
iday Safaris 4x4 Hire (☎ 067/662–429).

WALKING
You'll share the streets with lots of colorfully dressed locals and
kamikaze goats. Find out in advance how long each walk will be; heat
exhaustion can be a problem.

CHOBE NATIONAL PARK AND THE LINYANTI AND KWANDO RESERVES

Chobe National Park

A hundred kilometers (62 miles) west of Victoria Falls in Botswana's northeast corner is Chobe National Park, another of Africa's finest game sanctuaries. The 12,000-square-km (7,440-square-mi) reserve is home to some 35,000 elephants. The wide and tranquil Chobe River is surrounded by a natural wilderness of floodplain, dead lake bed, sand ridges, and forest. Upstream it is known as the Linyanti and forms the border between Botswana and Namibia, downstream it joins the mighty Zambezi on its journey through Zimbabwe and Mozambique to the Indian Ocean. The north of the park comprises riverine bush, so devastated by the hordes of elephants coming down to the perennial Chobe to drink that in winter it looks like a World War I battlefield. Fortunately, the wide sweep of the Caprivi floodplains, where hundreds of buffalo and elephant graze silhouetted against almost psychedelic sunsets, softens this harsh, featureless landscape where it faces neighboring Namibia. Unlike the rest of Botswana, Chobe can be crowded by visitors; there are too many vehicles on too few roads, particularly in season. However, the Ngwezumba River area of forests and pans in the more remote middle of the park is quieter, though the game is harder to find. In the southwest the wide grassy sweep of the Savuti channel, dry now for more than 15 years, is renowned for its abundant game, particularly the legendary carnivores.

As well as spotting Chobe's great elephant herds, you should see lions, leopards, hyenas, possibly wild dogs, and impalas, waterbucks, kudus, zebras, wildebeests (gnus), giraffes, warthogs, and much more. Watch closely at the water holes when prey species come down to drink and are most vulnerable—they are so palpably nervous that you'll feel jumpy, too. Lions in this area are often specialized killers with one pride targeting giraffes, another zebras, another buffalo, or even young elephants. But lions are opportunistic killers, and you could see them pounce on anything from a porcupine to a lowly scrub hare. Bird life along the river is awesome: Rarely seen birds will get the twitchers frenetic, including slaty egrets, rock pratincoles, pink-throated longclaws, and lesser gallinules.

Dining and Lodging

$$$ ✕🏠 **Chobe Savanna Lodge.** On the banks of the Chobe River, overlooking the Chobe National Park, nestles this luxury lodge. You'll stay in a North African–inspired stone and thatch cottage with a private deck, air-conditioning, and private bathroom. Cream textured linen, vases of dried grasses, ethnic-design cushions, polished wooden floors, handcrafted furniture, and handwoven cream-and-brown rugs provide a comfortable and elegant haven. You can cruise the wide river game spotting, bird-watching, or just soaking up an awesome sunset, go for a guided game walk through the unspoiled bush, or just sit out on the viewing deck with its magnificent views of the Chobe floodplains and river and watch scores of elephants pass by. ✉ *Desert & Delta Safaris, Box 130555, Bryanston, South Africa,* ☎ *27/11/706–0861,* 🔲 *27/11/706–0863,* 🌐 *www.desertanddelta.com. 12 cottages. Bar, pool. DC, MC, V. FAP.*

$$$ 🏠 **Chobe Game Lodge.** The only permanent lodge set in Chobe National Park, this grand old dame—Liz Taylor and Richard Burton got married for the second time here in the '70s—still offers one of Botswana's most sophisticated stays. Terra-cotta tiles, Rhodesian teak

furniture, African artifacts, and the ubiquitous beautiful handwoven Botswana baskets give the feel of the dark continent. The solid Moorish-style buildings—with their graceful high arches and barrel-vaulted ceilings—insulate the not-so-intrepid traveler from too-close encounters of the animal kind: baboon mothers have been known to teach their young how to turn a doorknob! The gorgeous gardens are a riot of color and attract lots of small fauna. There's a well-stocked curio shop with great clothes and wildlife books. Don't miss out on the well-run daily activities from game drives to river cruises. An early morning canoe ride is also a must. ✉ *Mailing address: Desert & Delta Safaris, Box 130555, Bryanston, South Africa,* ☎ *27/11/706–0861,* 𝖥𝖠𝖷 *27/11/706–0863,* 𝖶𝖤𝖡 *www.desertanddelta.com. 46 rooms, 4 suites. Bar, pool, billiards. DC, MC, V. FAP.*

Savuti

The fabled Savuti area—world famous for its predators—offers a sweeping expanse of savanna brooded over by seven rocky outcrops that guard a relic marsh and the Savuti Channel, Africa's Stolen River of myth and legend. Once the lifeline of the area, this wide channel has now been dry for more than 16 years. Savuti is dramatically different from elsewhere in Botswana; there are open spaces, limitless horizons, wide skies, and unending miles of waving tall grass punctuated by starkly beautiful dead trees—the legacy of the relentless drought. You may see wild dogs hunting where only two decades ago crocodiles swam and basked on the channel banks. And while you're in the Gubatsa Hills looking for leopards and the tiny acrobatic klipspringer antelopes, be sure to pay a visit to the striking rock paintings, early man's attempts to represent the wildlife all around. Savuti is also famed for its elephants, but the female of the species is rarely seen here, for the area is the domain of the male. Bull elephants abound: old grandfathers, middle-aged males, and feisty young teenagers. The old ones gaze at you with imperturbable dignity, but it's the youngsters who'll make your adrenaline run riot as they kick up the dust and bellow belligerently as they make a mock charge in your direction. In summertime thousands of migrating zebras and wildebeests provide the equivalent of fast-food for the lion prides, hungry hyenas, and cheetahs who follow the herds. The Cape buffalo herds also arrive in summer along with thousands of returning bird migrants. The raptors—birds of prey—are spectacular. You'll also see falcons, eagles, kestrels, goshawks, ospreys, and sparrow hawks.

Dining and Lodging

$$$$　🏨 **Savute Safari Lodge.** As your small plane arrives at this attractive lodge, you can see the wide swathe the dry riverbed makes through the surrounding countryside. The exterior of the main building and the safari suites are traditional thatch and timber; however, when you enter your spacious suite, it's a bit like walking out of Africa into a Scandinavian design center—blond wood, dazzling white bed linens, comfortable furniture in bright primary colors, gaily colored handwoven rugs, and lots of glass set this lodge apart from the more usual African style of other lodges. Outside on your spacious wooden deck it's back to Africa: by full moon watch the gray, ghostly shapes of elephants drinking from the water hole in front of the camp, or if the moon is not yet full, marvel at the myriad stars in the African night sky. Excellent safari guides can reveal the secrets of the African bush to you on game drives; you may see hundreds of elephants drinking from pools at sunset, hippos and hyenas nonchalantly strolling past a pride of lions preparing to hunt, or thousands of water and land birds in flight. When you're not watching the abundant game, there's a large elegant dining room

where you can enjoy scrumptious late-morning brunches and candle-lighted silver-service dinners, a lounge with a huge fireplace, and an upstairs viewing deck. ✉ *Desert & Delta Safaris, Box 130555, Bryanston, South Africa,* ☎ *27/11/706–0861,* FAX *27/11/706–0863,* WEB *www.desertanddelta.com. 12 suites. Bar, pool, library. MC, V. FAP.*

Linyanti Reserve

This reserve, which borders Chobe National Park, is one of the huge concession areas leased to different companies for up to 15 years by the Department of Wildlife and National Parks and the Tawana Land Board. It's a spectacular wildlife area comprising the Linyanti marshes, open floodplains, rolling savanna, and the famed Savuti Channel. Because it's a private concession, open vehicles can drive where and when they like, which means superb game viewing and thrilling night drives with spotlights.

At Linyanti your basic choices for viewing wildlife are on a game drive (including night drives), on a boat, or going for a walk with a friendly and knowledgeable Motswana guide. Even in peak season there are only a maximum of six game vehicles driving around at one time, allowing you to see Africa as the early hunters and explorers might have. The Savuti Channel has starred in several *National Geographic* documentaries, and it's not hard to see why—stock up on film, and for once you won't bore your friends with the results: hundreds of elephants drinking from pools at sunset, hippos and hyenas nonchalantly strolling past a pride of lions preparing to hunt under moonlight, and thousands of water and land birds everywhere.

Lodging

$$$$ 🏠 **Duma Tau.** This classy camp, with imaginatively decorated and furnished raised tent chalets under thatch and overlooking the water, lies at the very heart of the concession. The spacious chalets have African fabrics; clever cane furniture decorated with plaited reeds, brass, and local beadwork; wooden floors with handwoven rugs; an indoor shower and another one on your outside deck so you can wash as you view; and personal touches such as a guinea fowl feather or dried seed pod placed artistically among your towels. The lounge and dining area of the main lodge are open on all sides (a bit cold in winter); the toilet at the end of the deck must have the best view of any in the world. The food is simple but superb. Before you set out on your early morning game drive, try a plate of piping hot porridge, a Danish straight from the oven, or a freshly cooked muffin. ✉ *Wilderness Safaris, Box 5219, Rivonia 2128, South Africa,* ☎ *11/807–1800,* FAX *11/807–2110,* WEB *www.dumatau.com. 8 chalets. Bar, pool, library. MC, V. FAP.*

Kwando Reserve

★ Like the Okavango, the Kwando River, lifeblood of the Linyanti, Savuti, and Chobe systems, comes down from the wet Angola highlands, then meanders through a few hundred kilometers of wilderness. The 2,300-square-km (900-square-mi) private Kwando concession, newly opened to tourists, has more than 80 km (50 mi) of river frontage. It stretches south from the banks of the river, through huge open plains and mopane forests to the Okavango Delta. It's an area crisscrossed by thousands of ancient game trails—migratory trails of elephants, buffalo, zebras, and wildebeests that move freely between the Okavango Delta, Chobe, and the open Namibian wilderness, to the north.

As you fly in, you'll see a web of thousands of interlacing natural game trails—from hippo highways to the tiny paths of smaller animals. This should clue you to the area's wildlife diversity; wall-to-wall elephants, crowds of buffalo, antelope of all kinds including roan and sable, wild dogs, and lions. The experienced rangers—who learned their animal ethics at South Africa's Londolozi and Phinda camps—and their Bushman trackers have already managed to habituate what is truly wild game to vehicles and cameras. Those on one famed night drive came upon a running battle between a pack of 14 wild dogs and two hyenas who had stolen the dogs' freshly made kill. The noisy battle ended when a loudly trumpeting elephant, fed up with the commotion, charged the wild dogs and drove them off. There's a sheer joy in knowing you are one of only four vehicles in a half million acres of wilderness.

If you want to bring your kids to Botswana and enjoy a life-changing experience with your whole family, then there's no better place than Kwando, where, under the special care of top ranger Mark Tennant, you'll not only have a truly memorable time but also learn lots about the bush. You'll start this safari with a safety briefing; your kids will be given their own tents next to Mom and Dad, or they can share yours. Your kids will learn to track and take plaster casts of spoor (to show their friends at home), sit up in the tracker's seat on the vehicle and follow game, cook marshmallows over the boma fire, tell stories, catch and release butterflies, make bush jewelry, find out about ecology, and lots more. The kids can eat on their own or with you, and if you want an afternoon snooze, they'll be supervised in the pool or on some other fun activity. This program is available at both Kwando camps; the price is the same per night as for an adult. ⊠ *Kwando Wildlife Experience, Box 550, Maun,* ☎ *067/661–449,* FAX *067/661–457,* WEB *www.kwando.co.za. DC, MC, V. FAP.*

Lodging

$$$$ ⚠ **Kwando Lagoon Camp.** The camp perches on the banks of the fast-flowing Kwando River, quite literally in the middle of nowhere. Comfortable walk-through tents with private bathrooms and verandas nestle on grassy slopes under the shade of giant jackalberry trees that are hundreds of years old. After a night spent next to one of these mighty trees, a major source of natural energy, people say you wake up rejuvenated, your body buzzing with new life. From the thatched dining and bar area you can watch herds of elephants only meters away as they come to drink and bathe or hippos snoozing in the sun. You might also spot a malachite kingfisher darting like a bejeweled minijet over the water. Go for a morning or evening game drive, drift along the river in a small boat, or go spinner- or fly-fishing for tiger fish and bream. The emphasis in the camp is on informality, simplicity, and soaking up the unique wilderness experience. The lodging price here includes air transfers from Maun, Kasane, or other camps. *6 tents.*

$$$$ ⚠ **Kwando Lebala Camp.** Lebala Camp is 30 km (18 mi) to the south of Lagoon Camp and looks out over the Linyanti wetlands. The secluded tents, built on raised teak decks, are magnificent. All have private bathrooms with Victorian claw-foot bathtubs. If you want to get even closer to nature, bathe in your own outdoor shower or just sit on your sundeck and look out at the endless vistas. On morning or evening game drives you'll see loads of game, and if you fancy a freshly caught fish supper, try your hand at spinner fishing. The lodging price here includes air transfers from Maun, Kasane, or other camps. *8 tents.*

Chobe, Linyanti, and Kwando A to Z

To research prices, get advice from other travelers, and book travel arrangements, visit www.fodors.com.

AIR TRAVEL

Kasane International Airport is 3 km (2 mi) from the entrance to Chobe National Park. *See* Botswana A to Z, *below,* for airline contact information.

CAR TRAVEL

This is not a practical way to travel unless you have plenty of time and don't mind driving very long distances. The drive from Victoria Falls to Chobe takes about an hour and a half on a good tarred road.

A four-by-four vehicle is essential in the park itself. The roads are sandy and/or very muddy, depending on the season.

THE MAKGADIKGADI PANS

These immense salt pans in the eastern Kalahari—once the bed of an African superlake—provide some of Botswana's most dramatic scenery. Two of these pans, Ntetwe and Sowa, the largest of their kind in the world, have a flaky, pastrylike surface that might be the nearest thing on earth to the surface of the moon. In winter these huge bone-dry surfaces, punctuated by islands of grass and lines of fantastic palm trees, dazzle and shimmer into hundreds of mirages under the beating sun. In the summer months the last great migration in southern Africa takes place here: more than 50,000 zebras and wildebeests with predators in their wake come seeking the fresh young grass of the flooded pans. Waterbirds also flock here from all over the continent; the flamingos are particularly spectacular.

You can see game elsewhere in Botswana (although not in these numbers), so you should visit May through September to find out just why this place is unique. You can see stars as never before, maybe, as the Bushmen say, even hear them sing. You might also ride four-by-four quad bikes into an always-vanishing horizon; close your eyes and listen as an ancient Bushmen hunter tells stories of how the world began in his language, whose clicks will sound strange to your ears, and just wander over the pristine piecrust surface of the pans.

Lodging

$$$$ ⚠ **Jack's Camp.** If you're bold-spirited, reasonably fit, and have kept
★   your childlike sense of wonder, then Jack's should definitely be a stop on your itinerary. In the Kalahari Desert on the edge of the great salt pans, it's a cross between a Fellini movie, a Salvador Dalí painting, and *Alice in Wonderland.* Although it doesn't offer the cocooned luxury of some of the Okavango camps, it has East African safari tents, ancient Persian rugs, brass-hinged boxes to store your things in, teak and canvas furniture, unending views over endless plains, copper jugs full of water for washing, a flush toilet of your own, and a hot or cold bucket shower on demand. You'll eat your meals under a spreading acacia tree and drink tea and coffee in a large, open-sided pagoda-like tent, sprawled on more antique rugs and propped against venerable embroidered cushions. The rangers—zoologists and biologists every one— are known throughout Botswana and beyond for their love and knowledge of this unforgettable area. Remember, though, this is the Kalahari Desert, very hot in summer and very cold in winter. ✉ *Un-*

charted Africa Safari Co., Box 173, Francistown, Botswana, ☎ *267/
212–277,* FAX *267/213–458. 8 tents. MC, V. FAP.*

Makgadikgadi A to Z

To research prices, get advice from other travelers, and book travel arrangements, visit www.fodors.com.

AIR TRAVEL

Synergy Seating (☎ 267/660–044, FAX 267/661–703) has air transfers from Maun.

CAR TRAVEL

There's a tar road to Gweta from Gaborone via Francistown and Nata, but the trip is 1,162 km (726 mi).

THE TULI BLOCK

This ruggedly beautiful corner of northeastern Botswana is very easily accessible from South Africa and well worth a visit. Huge, striking red-rock formations, unlike anywhere else in Botswana, mingle with acacia woodlands, riverine bush, hills, wooded valleys, and open grassy plains. Be sure to visit the Motloutse ruins where ancient baobabs stand sentinel over Stone-Age ruins that have existed here for more than 30,000 years, as majestic black eagles soar overhead.

Still relatively unknown to foreign travelers, the Tuli Block is home to huge elephant herds, the eland—Africa's largest and highest-jumping antelope—zebras, wildebeests, leopards, and prolific bird life. Try to catch a glimpse of the elusive and diminutive klipspringer antelope perching on top of a rock zealously guarding his mountain home. Gareth Patterson, southern Africa's "Lion Man," lived here alone with three young lions over a period of years, successfully reintroducing them to the wild after having brought them down from Kenya after George *"Born Free"* Adamson was brutally murdered there by poachers.

Mashatu Game Reserve

Mashatu offers a genuine wilderness experience on 90,000 acres that seem to stretch to infinity on all sides. There are wall-to-wall elephants—breeding herds often with tiny babies in tow—as well as aardvarks, aardwolves (a type of hyena), lots of leopards, wandering lions, and hundreds of birds. All the superb rangers are Batswana—most were born in the area and some have been here for more than 10 years. Their fund of local knowledge seems bottomless.

Dining and Lodging

$$ ✕▥ **Mashatu Main Camp.** A sister camp to South Africa's world-famous Mala Mala Camp, the professionalism of the staff here is so unobtrusive you only realize later how superbly and sincerely welcomed, entertained, and informed you have been during your stay. Accommodations range from attractive old-style rondawels (round huts) to tasteful suites where Jacobean-patterned fabrics pick up and enhance the terra-cotta floor tiles. Furniture of natural basket weave, russet-and-cream handwoven wool rugs, and pine-paneled ceilings promote the overall atmosphere of quiet good taste. Comfort is assured by heaters in the cold winter months and air-conditioning in the hot summer ones. The thatched outdoor dining area overlooks a large water hole where elephants, zebras, wildebeests, and other Mashatu regulars drink. ✉ *Rattray Reserves, Suite 4, Tulbagh, 360 Oak Ave., Fer-*

ndale, Randburg 2125, South Africa, ☎ *11/789–2677,* FAX *11/886–4382. 17 rondawels. Bar, pool, shop, meeting rooms. AE, DC, MC, V. FAP.*

$$ 🔊 **Mashatu Tent Camp.** This small and intimate camp offers the same excellent service as Main Camp but with a firsthand bush experience. The camp is deep in the wilderness, and as you lie in your tent and listen to a lion's roar, a hyena's whoop, or a leopard's cough, you'll feel part of the heartbeat of Africa. Seven spacious tents with carpeted floors, each with a tiny veranda overlooking the surrounding bush, provide an unparalleled back-to-nature feeling. A fenced walkway leads to an en-suite bathroom where the stars are your roof. Knowledgeable, long-standing local rangers will open your ears and your eyes to the environment: on one night game drive guests saw a male leopard up a tree jealously guarding his impala kill from a female leopard who was hoping for a slice of the action, while a hopeful hyena lurked nearby. There's plenty of water in the vicinity, so the game is particularly plentiful—once two guests were trapped in their tent when a pride of lions killed a zebra outside it. This camp may not be for everyone; but for something truly different, real, and very special, a stay here won't soon be forgotten. ✉ *Rattray Reserves, Suite 4, Tulbagh, 360 Oak Ave., Ferndale, Randburg 2125, South Africa,* ☎ *11/789–2677,* FAX *11/886–4382. 7 tents. Bar, pool. AE, DC, MC, V. FAP.*

Tuli Block A to Z

To research prices, get advice from other travelers, and book travel arrangements, visit www.fodors.com.

AIR TRAVEL

South African Airlink flies daily from Johannesburg International Airport to Pietersburg, where you can pick up a self-drive or chauffeur-driven car from Budget Rent a Car for the just under two-hour drive to Pont Drift, the South African/Botswana border post. Mashatu also has direct flights from Johannesburg directly to the camp. Check with Mashatu itself for the latest fly-in details. There are also scheduled charter flights every Wednesday, Friday, and Sunday from Lanseria Airport, just outside Johannesburg, direct to Mashatu.

➤ AIR TRAVEL INFORMATION: **South African Airlink** (☎ 11/973–2941, FAX 11/973–2501).

CAR TRAVEL

Mashatu is an easy five-hour drive from Johannesburg. You'll be met at Pont Drift, the South African/Botswana border post, where you leave your car under huge jackalberry trees at the South African police station before crossing the Limpopo river by four-by-four vehicle or cable car—depending on whether the river is flooded. Mashatu is a five-hour drive from Gaborone.

➤ CAR TRAVEL INFORMATION: **Budget Rent a Car** (☎ 11/392–3929; 0800/01–66222 toll-free number in South Africa; 0800/11–7722 toll-free international).

THE CENTRAL KALAHARI AND KHUTSE GAME RESERVES

In the very heart of Botswana lies the 52,000-square-km (32,292-square-mi) Central Kalahari Game Reserve—the second largest in the world. Crisscrossed by fossil rivers and covered with myriad dead lake beds, this legendary area straddles the Tropic of Capricorn. Harsh, inhospitable, undeveloped, and largely inaccessible to humans, there's little or no water available and no fuel for vehicles for up to 400 km

(240 mi) at a stretch. It's not a desert such as the Namib or Sahara, but a savanna-type environment with scrub, thornveld, and tall grasses of greens, yellows, and browns. The true beauty of the Kalahari is in its vastness and the feeling that people have not left this area the poorer for their presence. The Basarwa or Bushmen still live in the Kalahari. Now called RADS (remote area dwellers), they can go to school, herd cattle, or opt for the traditional way of life—one that is fast disappearing. The game and wilderness experience in the Central Kalahari is dramatic—as befits this stark, desolate place. In the rainy season large herds of gemsbok (oryx), zebras, springboks, and other Kalahari game such as kudus, and hartebeests are abundant, as are the huge black-maned Kalahari lions. Even in the drier months there is still much to be seen including the brown hyena, bat-eared fox, caracal, cheetah, honey badger, jackal, and many birds of prey. Deception Valley was the site for the research and experience of Mark and Delia Owens, so vividly captured in their best-seller *Cry of the Kalahari*.

Khutse Game Reserve lies immediately to the south of the Central Kalahari Game Reserve, and the scenery is dramatically different. There are rolling grasslands, savanna woodlands, well-vegetated fossil dunes, and dry riverbeds. Artificial watering points attract animals throughout the year, and you are almost certain to see lions and other predators.

Lodging

$$$ 🏠 **Deception Valley Lodge.** Until a few year ago the only inhabitants of the Central Kalahari region were the San (Bushmen) and a few farmers. There were no lodges, and the nearest accommodation was in Maun or Ghanzi, more than 200 km (120 mi) away. Now there's a fine lodge with a gravel airstrip on the property, which means this previously almost inaccessible destination is now a choice for travelers who wish to see an almost unknown and unvisited part of the world. Marvel at the stark beauty of the Kalahari, where you may be lucky enough to see lions, honey badgers, porcupines, hyenas, and jackals, as well as herds of springbok antelopes, on daily game drives. Overlooking a small pan—filled with water only after the rains—the thatch-and-timber lodge blends into its background beautifully. Chalets have twin beds, bathrooms with elegant Victorian claw-foot baths, outdoor showers, and private lounges that face the open wilderness. Meals are taken in the Persian-carpeted dining room under an ostrich-egg chandelier or are served outside on the wide veranda, which runs the length of the main building. There's a sparkling pool for hot desert days. This is a true oasis in the midst of the desert. ✉ *Deception Valley Lodge, TSM Destinations, Box 1315, Pretoria, South Africa,* ☎ *012/665–8554, 012/665–8555, or 012/665–8556,* 🖷 *012/665–8597. 5 chalets. Bar, pool. MC, V. FAP.*

The Central Kalahari A to Z

To research prices, get advice from other travelers, and book travel arrangements, visit www.fodors.com.

CAR TRAVEL
Don't consider a trip on your own unless you have spent months researching the whole project, and then you would need to travel with a convoy of other vehicles.

TOUR OPERATORS
The office of the Department of Tourism will supply you with a list of reputable tour operators, though one of the most distinguished is Penduka Safaris, which runs ethnic and specialized safaris. Afro Ventures

include trips to the Central Kalahari in its organized safaris.

➤ TOUR OPERATOR INFORMATION: **Afro Ventures** (✉ CC Africa, Private Bag X27, Benmore, Johannesburg 2010, South Africa, ☎ 11/809–4300, ℻ 011/809–4400). **Department of Tourism** (✉ Private Bag 0047, Main Mall, Gaborone, Botswana, ☎ 267/353–024). **Penduka Safaris** (✉ Box 7242, Pretoria 0001, South Africa, ☎ 012/329–6799, ℻ 012/329–6429, 🕸 www.penduka.co.za).

GABORONE

Gaborone is not one of the world's tourist meccas: there are no beaches, quaint inns, or nightlife to speak of (other than a couple of casinos), no performing arts, only one rather featureless golf course, no nearby scenic wonders, no public transport, and little in the way of craft works. At best, Gaborone is a staging post for tourists traveling posthaste to and from the Okavango Delta, Moremi Game Reserve, Chobe, and the Kalahari Desert. The city does have quite an interesting history, though. Gaborone was declared the capital of the new, independent Botswana in 1966, although it was little more than a village with a population of a few thousand. Even after more than 30 years of urbanization, Gaborone's population is still well under 200,000. It's big enough to have a decent infrastructure, embassies and consulates, a small stock exchange, travel agents, an international airport only 15 km (9 mi) from the city center, good roads, and hospitals and medical services. But Gaborone has retained its small-town personality, a place where time moves at a different pace than that of more dynamic cities and you can observe southern African people going about the routines of their daily lives.

Exploring Gaborone

The best time in Gaborone is late afternoon, when the sun has lost its fierceness and citizens and office workers stroll round the broad square of the Mall—the main business and commercial area—pausing to pass the time of day with friends. It's a colorful scene, too, with its mixture of traditional and European dress and splashes of primary colors on the sidewalk stalls.

A Good Tour

Begin at the Mall and take a short walk to the **National Museum and Art Gallery.** Then hop in your rental car and take the Lobatse road for 14 km (9 mi) to the **Mokolodi Nature Reserve,** or go the 40 km (25 mi) north of the city to scenic **Mochudi** village. Twenty-two kilometers (14 miles) along the Kanye road, past Kumakwane village and over the Kolobeng River, you'll come to the **Livingstone Memorial.**

Sights to See

Livingstone Memorial. The name of Scots missionary Dr. David Livingstone is synonymous with the early exploration of this part of Africa. Located here are Livingstone's house and two graves, one of which is said to belong to his son. *22 km (14 mi) along the Kanye road, past Kumakwane village and over the Kolobeng River.*

Mochudi. This large, scenic Batswana village (a real one, not a tourist trap) will give you a good idea of how traditional life still goes on. Beautifully painted courtyards front buildings with huge thatched roofs where people go about their daily lives. Mochudi has its own museum and arts-and-crafts center—the **Phuthadikobo Museum.** It's open weekdays 8–5 and weekends 2–5, and admission is free.

Mokolodi Nature Reserve. You'll see game here, including lions, but the reserve is small and fenced and therefore won't be of great interest to you if you've recently seen game in the true wilderness or plan on doing so. Still, the park is worth visiting for a taste of the bush and its great bird-spotting opportunities. There are very sparsely furnished rustic stone huts available for overnight stays, priced from P320 to P460 and sleeping up to six people. ⊠ *Mokolodi Nature Reserve, Plot 183 Queen's Rd., Box 170, Gaborone,* ☎ *067/311–414,* ℻ *067/565–488.* ☜ *P15 per person, P20 per vehicle.* ☉ *Daily 7–6.*

National Museum and Art Gallery. It isn't a big museum and your visit won't take long, but you'll get a fascinating glimpse of a culture that is quickly disappearing. There are displays of Botswana's early history, its wildlife, and traditional and modern arts and crafts. The museum booklet, "A Guide to Places of Historic and Natural Interest in and around Gaborone," will give you plenty of suggestions if you do have more time. ⊠ *Independence Avenue, Gaborone,* ☎ *267/374–616.* ☜ *Free.* ☉ *Tues.–Fri. 9–6, weekends 9–5.*

Dining

The following restaurants will average about P85 (US$30) for a three-course meal excluding drinks.

$$–$$$$ ✕ **Mokolodi Restaurant.** For a truly African feel, try this excellent restaurant on the edge of the Mokolodi Nature Reserve where the buildings and ambience reflect the bush setting. You can eat in the open-sided dining area—a large, high-ceilinged, thatched rondawel—or alfresco under the stars. The menu emphasizes southern African food with venison a specialty, although there's plenty more to choose from. ⊠ *Mokolodi Nature Reserve, Plot 183 Queen's Rd., Box 170,* ☎ *067/ 561–547,* ℻ *067/328–692. Reservations essential. DC, MC, V.*

$$–$$$ ✕ **The Swiss Inn.** Once a farm owned by Botswana's founding president, the late Sir Seretse Khama, and his English wife, Ruth, the restaurant serves pastas and pork, veal, chicken, superb Botswana beef, and delicate fish dishes, all complemented by the finest of South African wines. On a fine day stroll out on the rolling lawns; on a winter's one enjoy the blazing open fire. Lunch reservations are essential. ⊠ *24 km (14 mi) from Gaborone at Ruretse, Plot 69, Ruretse,* ☎ *067/3939– 488. DC, MC, V. No dinner Sun.*

Lodging

$ 🏨 **Cresta Lodge.** This lodge is centrally located, and rooms are straightforward but comfortable. The landscaped gardens offer a shady retreat; you can even go on a short nature trail. ⊠ *Private Bag 00126, Gaborone,* ☎ *267/375–375,* ℻ *267/375–376. 80 rooms. Restaurant, bar, air-conditioning, pool, airport shuttle. D, DC, MC, V. BP.*

$ 🏨 **The Gaborone Sun.** Attractively situated by a golf course 2 km (1 mi) from the city center, this is a first-class, modern hotel with extensive conference facilities. There are two excellent restaurants, Savuti, for buffet, and Giovanni's, for à la carte, both with live entertainment. ⊠ *Private Bag 0016, Gaborone,* ☎ *267/351–111,* ℻ *267/322–727 ext. 2522. 192 rooms, 4 suites. 2 restaurants, pool, 2 tennis courts, squash, casino. D, DC, MC, V.*

$ 🏨 **Grand Palm.** Four kilometers (2½ miles) outside Gaborone, this luxurious complex is surrounded by lush gardens, walking trails, and a much-frequented bird pond. The rooms are nothing special, but they're clean and functional. ⊠ *Private Bag BR 105, Gaborone,* ☎ *267/312– 999,* ℻ *267/312–989. 199 rooms, 10 suites. 2 restaurants, 3 bars, sauna, tennis court, squash, casino. D, DC, MC, V.*

Shopping

The few smart shops are in the **Mall,** and at **Broadhurst,** a few kilometers north of the city center. These informal trading sectors, a collection of shops and stalls, are also home to street vendors offering beads, leather work, basketry, and carvings. Some of the carvings—often Zambian or Zimbabwean because Botswana doesn't have a strong tradition of this kind of handicrafts—are beautifully fashioned and merit some of your precious baggage space. The best local craft work is basketry—a skilled tradition handed down from mother to daughter—and woven wall hangings. Curio shops around town are a good source of traditional Bushman crafts and artifacts, which range from bracelets made from tiny ostrich-egg beads to bows and arrows, pipes, and handmade traditional women's aprons. Curio shops in larger hotels often have interesting items but are more expensive.

A variety of handwoven articles, from rugs and tapestries to bedspreads and table mats, are for sale at the well-signposted **Oodi Weavers** (✉ 20 km [12½ mi] north of Gaborone on Francistown Rd., ☎ 267/ 392–268), where you can watch the weavers at work. It's open weekdays 8–4:30, weekends 10–4:30.

Gaborone A to Z

To research prices, get advice from other travelers, and book travel arrangements, visit www.fodors.com.

AIR TRAVEL
Sir Seretse Khama Airport ☎ (267/314–518), 15 km (9½ mi) from the city center, has flights to and from Maun, Kasane, Francistown, and Selibi-Phikwe, and international flights to Johannesburg, Victoria Falls, and Harare in Zimbabwe, and Windhoek in Namibia. *See* Botswana A to Z, *below,* for airline information.

Most hotels provide courtesy transport between the airport and the city center. Taxis are available at the airport for about 40 pula. This, however, is strictly negotiable, so make sure the driver agrees to a price before you get into the taxi.

CAR TRAVEL
Gaborone is 915 km (571 mi) from Maun on a good (though very boring) tar road.

Generally speaking, drivers are careful and courteous in Gaborone, but keep a sharp lookout for the ubiquitous African taxis (minivans), that often may be overloaded and unsafe. Avoid rush-hour traffic. Drive on the left. The speed limit is 120 kph (75 mph) on major routes, 60 km (40 mph) in built-up areas. It's not a good idea to venture out of the town at night as the roads are unlighted and strewn with domestic animals (and the occasional antelope), and you could well get lost.

The main car rental firms in Botswana are Avis, Imperial, and Europcar, all of which have offices at the airport.
➤ CAR RENTAL INFORMATION: **Avis** (☎ 067/313–093). **Europcar** (☎ 267/307–233). **Imperial** (☎ 267/307–233).

EMBASSIES AND CONSULATES
British High Commission (✉ 1079 Queen's Rd., Private Bag 0023, Gaborone, ☎ 267/352–841, FAX 267/356–105).

U.S. Embassy (✉ Government Enclave, Embassy Dr., Gaborone, ☎ 267/357–326, FAX 267/324–404).

EMERGENCIES

If you need to see a doctor, consult your hotel, look in the pink pages of the telephone directory, or go to the local hospital as an outpatient. Avoid government hospitals unless you have hours and hours to spend waiting. Gaborone Private Hospital is a good one to use. Medical Rescue International offers 24-hour emergency help.

➤ EMERGENCY INFORMATION: **Ambulance** (☎ 997). **Fire Brigade** (☎ 998), **Police** (☎ 999). **Gaborone Private Hospital** (☎ 267/301–999). **Medical Rescue International** (☎ 267/301–60).

TAXIS

Since public transportation is nonexistent, taxis are a good choice for getting around. Your hotel concierge will help you call a cab, or you can look for a blue-numbered plate, which indicates the vehicle is a licensed taxi. Always negotiate your fare before taking off and expect to share with others; taxis stop and start at will to pick up passengers.

BOTSWANA A TO Z

To research prices, get advice from other travelers, and book travel arrangements, visit www.fodors.com.

AIR TRAVEL

In this huge, often inaccessible country, air travel is the easiest way to get around. Your starting points will be Gaborone, the capital, or Maun, gateway to the delta. Air charter companies operate small planes from Kasane and Maun to all the camps. Flown by some of the youngest-looking pilots in the world, these flights, which your travel agent will arrange, are reliable, reasonably cheap, and average between 25 and 50 minutes. Maximum baggage allowance is 12 kilograms in a soft, squashy sports/duffel bag (no hard cases allowed), excluding the weight of camera equipment (within reason). Because of the thermal air currents over Botswana, flights can sometimes be very bumpy—take air-sickness pills if you're motion-sickness susceptible; then sit back and enjoy the fabulous bird's-eye views.

Air Botswana has scheduled flights from Johannesburg to Gaborone and Maun on a daily basis. SA Express Airways also has daily flights to and from Johannesburg to Gaborone. There are also regular scheduled flights from Harare and Victoria Falls, in Zimbabwe, and Windhoek, in Namibia.

Chobe Air flies into Kasane. Mac Air, Northern Air, Sefofane Air, Swamp Air, and Synergy Seating fly directly between Johannesburg's Grand Central Airport and Maun on private charter.

➤ AIRLINE INFORMATION: **Air Botswana** (☎ 267/351–921). **Chobe Air** (✉ Box 349, Kasane, ☎ 267/650–133, ℻ 267/650–174). **Mac Air** (✉ Private Bag 329, Maun, ☎ 267/660–675, ℻ 267/660–036). **Northern Air** (✉ Box 27, Maun, ☎ 267/660–385, ℻ 267/661–559, or 267/661–282). **SA Express Airways** (✉ Central Reservations, Johannesburg, ☎ 11/978–1111). **Sefofane Air** (✉ Private Bag 159, Maun, ☎ ℻ 267/66–0778, ℻ 267/661–649). **Swamp Air** (✉ Private Bag 33, Maun, ☎ 267/660–569, ℻ 267/660–040). **Synergy Seating** (✉ Box 39, Maun, ☎ 267/660–044, ℻ 267/661–703).

AIRPORTS

Sir Seretse Khama Airport, 15 km (9½ mi) from Gaborone's city center, is Botswana's main point of entry. Kasane International Airport, near the entrance to Chobe National Park, has flights to Namibia and Zimbabwe.

➤ AIRPORT INFORMATION: **Kasane International Airport** (☎ 267/650–598). **Sir Seretse Khama Airport** (☎ 267/314–518).

CAR TRAVEL

All the main access roads from neighboring countries are tarred, and cross-border formalities are user-friendly. Maun is easy to reach from South Africa, Namibia, and Zimbabwe, but the distances are long and not very scenic. Gaborone is 360 km (225 mi) from Johannesburg via Rustenburg, Zeerust, and the Tlokweng Border Post. Driving is on the left-hand side of the road.

Forget about a car in the delta unless it's amphibious. In the game parks a four-by-four vehicle is essential. The roads within the parks tend to be sandy and/or very muddy, depending on the season. You'll need a car in Maun and Gaborone, as public transport doesn't exist. The "Shell Tourist Map of Botswana" is the best available map.

EMERGENCIES

In case of mechanical breakdown, contact your car-rental company in Botswana. Most safari companies include medical insurance in their tariffs. Medical Rescue International has 24-hour emergency help.
➤ EMERGENCY INFORMATION: **Medical Rescue International** (☎ 267/301–601, FAX 267/302–117).

GUIDED TOURS

There are many smaller specialist safari companies including Bird Safaris, Des Pretorius Photographic Safaris, Elephant Back Safaris, Mike Watson Fishing Safaris, and African Horseback Safaris.

Afro Ventures offers guided tours, special safaris, and lodge bookings throughout Botswana. Wilderness Dawning Safaris specializes in camping safaris where you'll get a high degree of comfort and service and be accompanied by very experienced guides.
➤ TOUR OPERATOR INFORMATION: **African Horseback Safaris,** (✉ Box 20538, Maun, ☎ FAX 267/663–154). **Afro Ventures** (✉ Afro Ventures, CC Africa, Private Bag X27, Benmore 2010, Johannesburg, South Africa, ☎ 011/809–4300, FAX 011/809–4514, WEB www.afroventures. com). **Bird Safaris** (✉ Box 15, ☎ 267/660–614, FAX 267/660–925). **Des Pretorius Photographic Safaris** (✉ Box 236, ☎ FAX 267/660–493). **Elephant Back Safaris** (✉ Private Bag 332, Maun, ☎ 267/166, FAX 267/66–1005). **Mike Watson Fishing Safaris** (✉ Private Bag 41, Maun, ☎ FAX 267/660–364). **Wilderness Dawning Safaris** (✉ Private Bag B017, Maun, ☎ FAX 267/662–962).

LANGUAGE

Although the national language is Setswana, English is the official one, and it is spoken nearly everywhere.

MONEY MATTERS

The pula (the Setswana word for rain) and the thebe comprise the Botswana currency; one pula equals 100 thebe. You will need to change your money or traveler's checks into pula, as this is the only legally accepted currency. However, you can use use U.S. dollars as tips at the lodges and camps, and most camp prices will be quoted in in U.S. dollars.

There are no restrictions on foreign currency notes brought into the country as long as they are declared. Travelers can carry up to P10,000, or the equivalent in foreign currency, out of the country without declaring it. Banking hours are weekdays 9–3:30, Saturday 8:30–11. Hours at Barclays Bank at Sir Seretse Khama International Airport are Monday–Saturday 6 AM–10 PM. In Gaborone and the other larger towns you will be able to use an ATM—check with your hotel or tour operator first.

TELEPHONE NUMBERS
Both Botswana and South African telephone numbers appear in this chapter. Botswana numbers begin with the 267 country code, which you shouldn't dial within the country (there are no internal area codes in Botswana). South African numbers begin with that country's code (27) and are usually followed by the Johannesburg area code (11).

TRAVEL AGENCIES
Harvey World Travel (✉ Box 1950, Gaborone, ☎ 267/304–360, FAX 267/305–840). **Kudu Travel** (✉ Private Bag 00130, Gaborone, ☎ 267/372–224, FAX 267/374–224). **Manica Travel Services** (✉ Box 1188, Gaborone, ☎ 267/352–021, FAX 267/305–552). **Travelwise** (✉ Box 2482, Gaborone, ☎ 267/303–244, FAX 267/303–245).

VISITOR INFORMATION
Department of Tourism (✉ Private Bag 0047, Main Mall, Gaborone, ☎ 267/353–024). **Tourist Information Centers** (✉ Maun, ☎ 267/660–492, FAX 267/661–676; ✉ Kasane, ☎ 267/650–357, FAX 267/650–841.

12 NAMIBIA

From the oldest, most beautiful desert on earth, the Namib, where the highest sand dunes in the world rumble, roar, smoke, and wander, to the fog-enshrouded Skeleton Coast with its evocative shipwrecks; from the seemingly limitless expanses of Etosha, one of the world's great game parks, to the stark beauty of Damaraland and its amazing desert elephants; from the sand-choked, windswept ghost towns of the south and the awesome Fish River canyon to bustling small cities with their fascinating mix of colonial and modern, you've never visited anywhere quite like Namibia.

NAMIBIA IS UNIQUE. Many other countries in Africa also boast teeming wildlife and gorgeous scenery, but few, if any, can claim such limitless horizons; such huge, untamed wilderness areas; such a pleasant sunny climate; so few people (less than two per square mi); the oldest desert in the world; a wildly beautiful coastline; one of Africa's greatest game parks; plus—and this is a big bonus—a First World infrastructure and tourist facilities that are among the best in Africa.

By Kate
Turkington

A former German colony, South West Africa, as it was then known, was a pawn in the power games of European politics. Although the Portuguese navigators were the first Europeans to arrive in 1485, they quickly abandoned the desolate and dangerous Atlantic shores of the "Coast of Death," as they called it. By the late 1700s British, French, and American whalers were using the deepwater ports of Lüderitz and Walvis (Whalefish) Bay, which the Dutch, now settled in the Cape, then claimed as their own. A few years later, after France invaded Holland, England seized the opportunity to claim the territory together with the Cape Colony. Then it became Germany's turn to throw its hat into the ring. In the wake of its early missionaries and traders, it claimed the entire country as a German colony in 1884, only to surrender it to South African forces, who were fighting on the Allied side during World War I. South Africa was given a League of Nations mandate to administer the territory after the war; and despite a 1978 UN resolution to revoke the mandate, South Africa held on to Namibia for a further stormy 10 years. A bitter and bloody bush war with SWAPO (South West African People's Organization) freedom fighters raged until Namibia finally won its independence on March 21, 1990, after 106 years of foreign rule. Although most of the earlier colonial influences have now vanished, everywhere you go in Namibia today you'll find traces of the German past—forts and castles, place-names, cuisine, and German efficiency.

Bounded by the icy Atlantic on the west, the Kalahari Desert on the east, the Kunene River on the north, and the Orange River on the south, this land, harsh and often inhospitable yet full of rare beauty, has been carved out by the forces of nature. The same savage, continuous geological movements produced not only spectacular beauty but also great mineral wealth: alluvial diamonds, uranium, platinum, lead, zinc, silver, copper, tungsten, and tin—still the cornerstone of Namibia's economy. Humankind has lived here for thousands of years; the San (Bushmen) are the earliest known people, although their hunting-gathering way of life is now almost extinct. Today most Namibians are employed in the agricultural sector, from subsistence farms to huge cattle ranches and game farms. It's a big country, four times as large as the United Kingdom and bigger than Texas, but its excellent road network means you can get around very easily. As you travel through the changing landscapes of mountains and plains, lush riverine forests, and high sand dunes, marvel at the amazing diversity of light and shade, color and contrast, and soak up the emptiness and isolation, the silence and the solitude. Far from crowded polluted cities, you could easily imagine yourself on another planet or in a land where time has stood still—a land you will never forget.

Pleasures and Pastimes

Arts and Crafts

You'll find beautifully made, and relatively inexpensive, arts and crafts in Namibia. The street markets are crammed with wooden carvings,

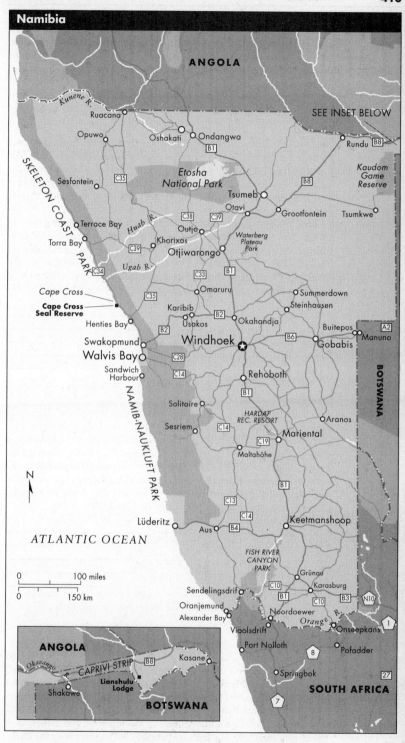

Namibia

ANGOLA

Kunene R.

Ruacana

SEE INSET BELOW

Opuwo

Oshakati

Ondangwa

Rundu

B8

B1

Sesfontein

C35

Etosha
National Park

Kaudom
Game
Reserve

SKELETON COAST

Tsumeb

Terrace Bay

Huab R.

C38

C39

Otavi

Grootfontein

Tsumkwe

B8

Torra Bay

Khorixas

Outjo

C39

C34

Ugab R.

Otjiwarongo

Waterberg
Plateau
Park

PARK

Cape Cross

C35

C33

B1

Omaruru

Summerdown

Cape Cross
Seal Reserve

Karibib

Steinhausen

Henties Bay

B2

Usakos

B2

Okahandja

Buitepos

Manuno

A2

Swakopmund

Windhoek

B6

Gobabis

Walvis Bay

C28

Sandwich
Harbour

C14

Rehoboth

BOTSWANA

NAMIB-NAUKLUFT PARK

B1

Solitaire

HARDAP
REC. RESORT

Aranos

N

Sesriem

C14

Mariental

C19

Maltahöhe

ATLANTIC OCEAN

B1

0 — 100 miles
0 — 150 km

C13

C14

Lüderitz

Aus

B4

Keetmanshoop

FISH RIVER
CANYON
PARK

Grünau

C10

Sendelingsdrif

Karasburg

Oranjemund

B1

C10

B3

N10

Alexander Bay

Noordoewer

Orange R.

Onseepkans

1

Vioolsdrift

8

Pofadder

Port Nolloth

Springbok

27

SOUTH AFRICA

7

ANGOLA

Okavango R.

CAPRIVI STRIP

B8

Kasane

Lianshulu
Lodge

Shakawe

BOTSWANA

finely woven baskets (the Caprivian ones are the best), and local hand-made pottery. In the curio shops and boutiques you'll see African clothing, jewelry made from ostrich eggs, and exquisite embroidery work. In Windhoek you can buy handmade dolls from the crinolined Herero women in front of the Kalahari Sands Hotel. The farther you go from Windhoek, the cheaper and often more unusual the crafts you see will become. It's well worth stopping your car and having a look when you pass a roadside stand.

Dining

You won't find much truly Namibian food except in the good restaurants in the bigger cities. Cuisine is mainly European, but if you like German food, you'll enjoy some excellent meals at reasonable prices. Seafood is deliciously fresh, and Namibian oysters are among the best and healthiest in the world. At lodges, pensions, and guest farms, you'll also enjoy good home-style cooking—pies, pastries, fresh vegetables, lots of red meat, venison, mouthwatering desserts, and the traditional *braai* (barbecue). Because of its German past, Namibia is known for its superb lagers, and it's well worth trying a Hansa or a Windhoek Export. South African wine, which is excellent, is readily available. On average, a sandwich, appetizer, or dessert will cost you under N$25, a pizza N$25, and a main course between N$25 and N$45.

CATEGORY	COST*
$$$$	over N$45
$$$	N$35–N$45
$$	N$25–N$35
$	under N$25

*for a main course at dinner.

Lodging

You'll find good accommodations at all levels throughout Namibia, including excellent hotels, private camps, game lodges and game reserves, national park facilities, backpackers' accommodations, comfortable pensions, and guest farms renowned for a particularly warm brand of Namibian hospitality. They are set in contrasting landscapes, each with its own distinctive appeal. Specialized safari operators offer exciting wilderness experiences, or if you feel like doing it yourself, campers and camping equipment can be rented.

CATEGORY	COST*
$$$$	over N$800
$$$	N$600–N$800
$$	N$400–N$600
$	under N$400

*Rates are for a standard, double room at high season including tax. The cost usually includes breakfast. At bush lodges prices usually include all meals and activities.

People

People-watching is a fascinating pastime here, as Namibia is home to more than 10 ethnic groups: Basters, San (Bushmen), Caprivians, Damara, Herero, Himba, Kavango, Nama/Hottentot, Owambo, and White Namibians, or "Southwesters." The San are generally regarded as the oldest inhabitants of southern Africa, here for at least 25,000 years, although their traditional way of life—hunting and gathering—has largely vanished. The Damara people, who together with the Bushmen and Nama are the original inhabitants of Namibia, speak a similar language pronounced with click sounds, and the women wear the same adapted Victorian dress as the Herero and Nama women. In the north are the Himba, with their distinctive red ocher body coverings and elaborately plaited hair, who live the way they have for centuries, as do the Owambo—the largest ethnic group in Namibia—who farm traditional crops as well as tend huge cattle herds. White Namibians are mainly descendants of the former German colonists, although there are many Afrikaners who moved here when South Africa took over the administration of the country from the Germans after World War I.

Photography

Namibia is a photographer's paradise. Picture-worthy locales include landscapes, deserts, mountains, and the cruel coastlines; gorgeous colonial German buildings; the biggest outdoor art gallery of rock paintings and engravings in the world, some 3,000–5,000 years old; Dali-esque ghost towns half-filled with sand; wildlife, birds, seals, shipwrecks, and uniquely adapted plants; and the stupendous Fish River canyon. Early morning and late afternoon will give you the best photographic opportunities.

Scenery

Namibia is a vast, mostly untamed, uniquely beautiful land of staggeringly diverse landscapes. Visit the water wonderlands of the far north: the hippo heaven of the Caprivi region, with its waterfalls, fecund rivers, and elephant herds; the breathtaking beauty of the Namib Desert, where the rare quality of light infuses the pristine landscape with a kaleidoscope of shifting colors; the surrealist sandscapes of the once-prosperous diamond towns of the south; the stark, rugged beauty of Damaraland; or the fog-enshrouded Atlantic coast. Wherever you go, you'll be amazed, delighted, enthralled—and will find yourself constantly wondering where all the people are. If you drive yourself, relax, appreciate the truly Namibian feeling of unconfined space, slow down, and enjoy the views. Don't forget that Namibia is one of the best locations in the world for stargazing, so take time out to marvel at the clarity and brightness of the night skies.

Wildlife

The best place to see wildlife is in Etosha (the Great White Place), which takes its name from the vast, flat, white salty depression that 12 million years ago was a deep inland lake. Game-watching here is unlike that in many other of Africa's game parks. Because of the lack of surface water, particularly in winter, Etosha's plentiful game accumulates at water holes on a continuous basis, so you'll see it close up. Each water hole has its own character and appearance, and if you stay in your vehicle for an hour or so at any one of them, the passing show will astound you. In Madumu, Mahango, and Mamili parks, in the north, you'll see big elephant herds and heaps of hippos. Many of the small lodges and private game reserves also have good game. You're almost certain to see cheetahs on your travels, as Namibia has the largest wild population in the world.

Exploring Namibia

Namibia, a huge country twice the size of California, is bisected from north to south by a fertile, hilly central plateau, which is where most of the country's farming activities take place. To the east the land slopes down gently to the great Kalahari Desert and merges into Botswana. To the west it falls away dramatically down a steep escarpment to the spectacular Namib Desert, the shipwreck-littered wild Atlantic coast, and some of Namibia's most spectacular scenery. If you have time, driving is challenging and rewarding, but the distances are vast—there are more than 38,000 km (23,600 mi) of road. You can, however, fly in to most of the top tourist attractions, or your travel company will get you there safely and comfortably by rail or road.

Great Itineraries

Visitors come to Namibia for its spectacular scenery: the Namib Desert and its famous dunes at Sossusvlei; the harsh beauty of Damaraland and its amazing desert elephants; the eerily beautiful Skeleton Coast; Lüderitz and the nearby ghost town of Kolmanskop; or the magnificent, little-visited Fish River canyon.

IF YOU HAVE 3 DAYS

Arrive in ⊞ **Windhoek** and either drive yourself, take a bus shuttle, or fly to the ⊞ **Namib Naukluft National Park** and its star attractions—**Sesriem** and **Sossusvlei.** Make your way through the shifting sands and multicolor towering dunes to the starkly beautiful **Dead Vlei,** with its 500-year-old dead trees. Overnight at one of the comfortable lodges or guest farms just outside the park. Back in Windhoek, travel by train to ⊞ **Swakopmund** on the luxurious *Desert Express,* visiting game farms, the **Valley of the Moon,** some of the world's oldest plants, and Namibia's Matterhorn, the **Spitzkoppe,** en route.

IF YOU HAVE 7 DAYS

From **Windhoek** fly to ⊞ **Etosha National Park** and spend two nights at one of the rest camps on the grounds or at one of the luxurious private lodges just outside. Don't miss the **Okuakuejo** water hole—one of the most famous in the world—where you can sit on benches all day or night and eyeball rhinos, elephants, and lions at very close quarters. Head back to Windhoek and either take the *Desert Express* train, which includes wonderful side trips en route, or other transport to the delightful little seaside town of **Swakopmund,** or make your way to **Sesriem** and **Sossusvlei,** staying overnight in the gorgeous **Namib Desert.** Then choose between flying or driving the eerily beautiful **Skeleton Coast** with a stopover in Swakopmund; alternatively, go south to ⊞ **Lüderitz,** visiting the ghost town of **Kolmanskop,** or the awesome, tourist-free **Fish River Canyon,** second in size only to Arizona's Grand Canyon.

When to Tour Namibia

Any time is a good time to visit Namibia. The country has a subtropical desert climate with nonstop sunshine throughout the year. The air is sparkling and pollution practically unheard of, and although nights always come early with dramatic suddenness, your days will be crystal clear and perfect for traveling. The hottest season (top temperature 104°F), the rainy season, is from December to March, but unless you're in the north, you're unlikely to see much rain or experience much humidity. Sometimes there's no rain at all in the southern Kalahari and the Namib Desert, where it can get very hot indeed. From April to September the weather is clear, dry, crisp, and nearly perfect, averaging 77°F during the day, but in the desert areas it can drop to freezing at night. If it's game you're after, then winter and early spring, from June to September, are the best because the lack of surface water ensures the animals congregate around the water holes. If you're driving, whatever time of year, make sure your vehicle has air-conditioning.

Warning: The northern area of Namibia, especially on the border of Angola, may be dangerous because of active fighting by Angolan military forces that is spilling into Namibia. Exercise extreme caution if you plan on visiting this part of the country, including the Caprivi Strip and the Trans-Caprivi Highway. Note also that you are advised to take antimalarial drugs when traveling in this region.

WINDHOEK

Namibia's parliamentary and administrative capital is in the middle of the country at the head of a valley 5,400 ft up in the Central Highlands. The 42-km (26-mi) drive from Hosea Kutako International Airport through rugged red mountains and shale-covered valleys gives you your first taste of Namibia's wide-open spaces and spectacular scenery, so it's quite a quantum leap when you suddenly find yourself driving through small leafy suburbs, down a steep hill, and straight into the bustling, modern city of Windhoek. It's famous not only for its hospitality but also for its rich historical and cultural heritage. It's a delightful little town where old, historic German colonial buildings nudge up against taller modern ones, and Namibians of contrasting cultures mingle in cafés and colorful shopping malls. Independence Avenue, the main street, seems like a microcosm of Namibia's First and Third World status. Air-conditioned stores offering luxury goods compete with busy street markets where local traders display curios and handmade wares on blankets or in rickety stalls while international tourists and businesspeople rub shoulders with traditional Herero women in full Victorian dress. Although, since Namibia's independence in 1990, there is no longer legal and political discrimination against certain racial groups, the old demographics of the pre-independence city remain much the same. The center of town, where most of the action and sights are, spreads out into the affluent, formerly whites-only suburbs, then into the newer middle-income suburbs, then north and northwest to the black townships of Katutura and Khomasdal. You'll find lots to do in Windhoek, from great shopping opportunities to loads of sporting activities (including sensational gliding and skydiving). Take a twilight tour, a birding trip to a nature reserve, or a game drive into the mountains.

It's easy to explore this mountain-encircled little town on foot because there are several places of interest in close proximity to one another. There are a few hills to climb but none formidable. A good place to start is the Lutheran **Christuskirche** (Church of Christ), inaugurated in 1910, which is German colonial architecture at its best—a mixture of art nouveau and neo-Gothic. You'll notice its graceful spire, Windhoek's most imposing landmark, as you drive into town. The stained-glass windows were donated by German emperor Kaiser Wilhelm II, the altar Bible by his wife, Augusta. ⊠ *Robert Mugabe Ave.,* ☎ *061/23–6002.* ⊙ *Daily, guided tours Wed. and Sat. 11 AM–11:30 AM.*

Walk along the tree-lined avenue behind the Christuskirche to the beautifully proportioned building that houses the National Assembly of the Republic of Namibia. It's known locally as the **Tintenpalast** (Palace of Ink) and was built in 1914—a time when civil servants still used pen and ink to perform their labors. ⊠ *Robert Mugabe Ave.,* ☎ *061/ 288–2627.* ⊙ *Weekdays 8–5.*

Next to the Tintenpalast is the **Office of the Prime Minister,** attractively decorated in indigenous woods, marble, and copper. Security personnel can take you on a guided tour during office hours. ⊠ *Robert Mugabe Ave.,* ☎ *061/287–9111.* ☞ *Free.* ⊙ *Weekdays 8–1 and 2–5.*

While strolling round the Parliament Gardens, look for a sign that says YEBO GALLERY. It's part of the **John Muafangeyo Art Centre,** where young artists gather to work, and is well worth a visit. ⊠ *Parliament Gardens,* ☎ *061/23–1391.* ☞ *Free.* ⊙ *Tues.–Fri. 8–5, Sat. 9–2.*

To the right of the Christuskirche, it's just a short walk to the **Equestrian Memorial,** which commemorates the German soldiers who lost their lives in colonial wars.

The **Alte Feste Museum** (1894), with its Beau Geste–like charm, is the oldest building in the city. Although it is now a historical museum, it once garrisoned the first contingent of colonial troops sent to Windhoek from Germany. The Independence Collection, which reflects events leading up to Namibian independence on March 21, 1990, is the pride of the museum. ⊠ *Robert Mugabe Ave.,* ☎ *061/293–4362.* 🎫 *Free.* ⊙ *Weekdays 9–5, Sat. 10–12:30, Sun. 10–12:30 and 3–5.*

Namibia's biggest permanent art collection is in the **National Art Gallery of Namibia.** There is an enormous number of animal paintings of all kinds, exhibits ranging from 1864 to the present, as well as temporary displays. ⊠ *Robert Mugabe Ave. and John Meinert St.,* ☎ *061/23–1160.* 🎫 *Free.* ⊙ *Tues.–Fri. 8–5, Sat. 9–2.*

The tiny **Bushman Art Museum,** tucked away behind a curio-gift shop, is well worth a visit. You'll find Bushmen apparel, tools, and other items on display, often for sale. ⊠ *187 Independence Ave.,* ☎ *061/22–8828.* 🎫 *Free.* ⊙ *Weekdays 8:30–5:30, Sat. 8:30–1, Sun. 9–1.*

In the **Owela Museum** there are exhibits of Namibia's various cultural groups, as well as flora and fauna, with special emphasis on the birds of Namibia. ⊠ *Upper Robert Mugabe Ave.,* ☎ *061/293–4358.* 🎫 *Free.* ⊙ *Daily 9–5.*

In the **Post Street Mall** in the heart of the city, just off Independence Avenue, stop to admire the Meteorite Fountain, which has 33 meteorites mounted on slender steel columns. Their origin is the Gibeon meteorite shower, which rained down some 600 million years ago, the heaviest such shower known on earth.

If you're a transportation buff, especially fond of trains, then don't miss the **TransNamib Museum,** on the first floor of the historic Railway Station building, which depicts the history of Namibia's railways over the past 100 years. Relive the heyday of steam locomotives and the pioneering of a railway system in this vast and rugged country. ⊠ *Bahn St.,* ☎ *061/298–2186.* 🎫 *N$5.* ⊙ *Weekdays 8–1 and 2–5.*

The whole time you're in Namibia, keep looking upward because Namibia is one of the best places in the world for stargazing and astronomical observations. At the **Cuno Hoffmeister Memorial Observatory,** Sonja Itting-Enke unravels the mysteries of Namibia's night skies. For the best sightings contact her more than three days after a full moon or not more than four days after the new moon. Reservations are essential, and the fee (usually a donation) should be negotiated. ⊠ *B1 (15 km [9 mi] south of Windhoek, turn left at sign for Harmony Centre),* ☎ *061/23–8982,* 𝖥𝖠𝖷 *061/23–8982.*

Dining and Lodging

In this cosmopolitan little city you'll find Namibian chefs combining European flair with a range of unique local ingredients. For a casual and inexpensive bite of the light, Continental kind, try the **Cauldron** (⊠ Gustav Voigts Centre, Independence Ave., ☎ 061/23–1040). Or tuck into generous portions of excellent Namibian and German pub food alfresco at the popular and convivial **Joe's Beerhouse** (⊠ 440 Independence Ave., ☎ 061/23–2457.)

$$$$ ✕ **Fürstenhof Restaurant.** For many years head chef Jurgen Raith has provided some of the best food in the city. His unique cuisine combines German and French nouvelle techniques with local ingredients. Try Namibian saddle of springbok with grapes, bacon, and mushrooms accompanied by homemade noodles and red cabbage. For dessert treat yourself to warm homemade cheesecake on a forest-berry sauce garnished with whipped cream. Jacket and tie are appropriate for dinner but not de rigueur. Light lunches and breakfast are served in the casually elegant bistro, Chez Max. ⊠ *Bulow St.,* ☎ *061/23–7380. Reservations essential. AE, DC, MC, V.*

$$$–$$$$ ✕ **Gathemann Restaurant.** For many years owner-chef Urs Gamma has maintained a consistently high standard in his classy restaurant, which boasts the best location in the city. You can dine in a turn-of-the-20th-century building with antique furniture and historic photographs or sit out on the balcony, which has a splendid view of Zoo Park and Independence Avenue. A memorable meal may start with a delicately aromatic truffle soup, followed by marinated springbok fillet complemented by a fine Meerlust 1992. Urs Gamma has now opened the **Zoo Cafe**, in the park opposite the restaurant; it serves light meals and great coffee. ⊠ *175 Independence Ave.,* ☎ *061/22–3853. Reservations essential. AE, DC, MC, V. Closed Sun. No lunch Sat.*

$$–$$$$ ✕ **Gourmet's Inn.** Thomas and Carol-Jean Rechter, serious foodies, have been dispensing good food and service for years and have created one of the most convivial atmospheres in town. Try specialties such as oysters Rockefeller, Cajun-flavored prawn ragout in a coconut sauce, or an ostrich fillet prepared in a bacon-apricot sauce and served in a three-leg cast-iron pot. Terrace seating is lovely during the day. ⊠ *Opposite Municipal Swimming Pool on Jan Jonker Rd.,* ☎ *061/23–2360. Reservations essential. AE, DC, MC, V. Closed Sun.*

$$$–$$$$ ✕▥ **Heinitzburg Castle Hotel.** This is your chance to stay in a turn-of-the-20th-century castle, a white fort with battlements set high on a hill—commissioned by a German count for his fiancée in 1914. The spacious interiors, handmade furniture, and antiques will transport you to a stylish bygone age. The unique bedrooms are decorated in luxurious fabrics and have four-poster beds and luxe wood furnishings. Adding to its allure, the Castle is cheaper than some of the big modern hotels, and from its vantage point has amazing views over the city. You'll need a reservation for the romantic restaurant where you can sample Continental cuisine accompanied by one of 1,500 bottles of top-class South African wine. ⊠ *22 Heinitzburg St.,* ☎ *061/24–9597,* ℻ *061/24–9598. 16 rooms, 1 suite. Restaurant, bar, pool. AE, DC, MC, V. BP.*

$$$$ ▥ **Kalahari Sands & Casino.** Known locally as the Sands, it was here that England's Queen Elizabeth II and Prince Philip stayed in 1990, the year Namibia gained independence. The central location of this elegant luxury hotel—regarded by some as Windhoek's best—is ideal for exploring the city on foot or shopping. Guest rooms are pleasant if somewhat bland, and you could be anywhere in the world once inside. Most rooms have good views of the city. ⊠ *Independence Ave.,* ☎ *061/22–2300,* ℻ *061/22–260. 167 rooms, 5 suites. Restaurant, bar, pool, health club, casino, business services. AE, DC, MC, V.*

$$$$ ▥ **Windhoek Country Club Resort & Casino.** On the southern outskirts of Windhoek, the resort is surrounded by strangely shaped desert plants and mountain. Although it's not uniquely Namibian, other than its setting, it's perfect if you want to unwind in a peaceful atmosphere, play golf or tennis, have a swim, or just soak up the first-rate service amid elegant grounds. There's a free shuttle to the city center. ⊠ *Box 30777, Windhoek,* ☎ *061/20–55911,* ℻ *061/25–2797. 152 rooms. 2 restaurants, bar, pool, 18-hole golf course, 2 tennis courts, casino. AE, DC, MC, V. BP.*

$$$ ▥ **The House on the Hill.** Perched on a hill up a quiet winding road with splendid views in the pleasant suburb of Klein Windhoek, this 40-year-old home, run by experienced and knowledgeable hosts Lumley Hulley and Nikki Waterhouse, has been lovingly restored and decorated in colonial style. The spacious rooms are stylishly furnished with handcrafted Knysna blackwood furniture, cream fabrics, genuine

African artifacts, and original wildlife paintings. Choose between a "health" breakfast or a full English one served in the comfort of your own room or on the pool patio, and try one of their delicious "light" meals such as an onion, bacon, and spinach frittata with a fresh green salad; stir-fried Cajun chicken; or a crepe with cream cheese, leek, and black-mushroom filling. ⊠ *12 Lessing St., Klein Windhoek,* ☎ *061/ 24–9116,* FAX *061/24–7818. 6 rooms. Pool. AE, DC, MC, V. BP.*

$$–$$$ 🏨 **Safari Court Hotel.** Although this is Namibia's largest hotel, it's privately owned and still manages to retain some of the feeling of a family business with a long tradition of hospitality. It's a comfortable, modern hotel with pleasant, if rather unmemorable, rooms—you could be anywhere in the world. There's a daily bus service to and from Hosea Kutako International Airport and a free shuttle to the city center every 30 minutes. ⊠ *Box 3900, Windhoek,* ☎ *061/24–0240,* FAX *061/24– 9300. 252 rooms. Restaurant, bar, pool. AE, DC, MC, V. BP.*

$–$$$ 🏨 **Hotel Fürstenhof.** Voted in the past as the best hotel in the country by the Hotel Association of Namibia, this small, characterful hotel has spacious rooms done in a traditional German style. It's just a five-minute walk from the city center, but you could also stay on the grounds and dine at the locally renowned restaurant. ⊠ *Box 316, Windhoek,* ☎ *061/23–7380,* FAX *061/22–8751. 33 rooms. Restaurant, bar, pool. AE, DC, MC, V.*

$ 🏨 **Hotel-Pension Kleines Heim.** This is a good choice if you're looking for an alternative to the big hotels. This friendly and attractive establishment, which used to house the colonial governors' VIP guests, is a five-minute drive from the city center and an excellent value for the money. Comfortable, spacious, well-appointed rooms look out onto gracious old palm trees. Rooms have ceiling fans for summer and under-floor heating for winter. ⊠ *10 Volans St., Box 22605, Windhoek West,* ☎ *061/24–8200,* FAX *061/24–8203. 14 rooms. Pool. AE, DC, MC, V. BP.*

Pensions and Guest Houses
You'll find plenty of friendly and inexpensive pensions, guest houses, and guest farms in and around Windhoek that will give you a taste of Namibian life. Most offer really good value for the money. Find out more from **Namibia Tourism** (⊠ Private Bag 13346, Windhoek, ☎ 61/ 284–2111, FAX 061/284–2364).

Nightlife and the Arts

Windhoek has quite a vibrant nightlife, with good music and entertainment, but clubs—like in any other city—tend to go in and out of fashion very quickly. Ask for the most up-to-date information in your hotel or look in the local papers. As taxi drivers may have a vested interest in where they take you, it's not a good idea to ask them for advice. For good live music don't miss out on the trendy **Warehouse Theatre** (⊠ 48 Tal St., ☎ 061/22–5059), which is safe, lively, and lots of fun. Depending on who's playing, you could listen to local music, rock and roll, funk, or jazz. The University of Namibia's **Space Theatre** (☎ 061/ 206–3111) often has interesting experimental local productions. There's a small studio theater at the **John Muafangeyo Art Centre** (⊠ Parliament Gardens, ☎ 061/23–1160), where you can also see the work of contemporary young Namibian artists.

Shopping

There's great shopping in Windhoek, mostly in and around the city center, ranging from expensive but beautifully made jewelry with uniquely African designs to high-fashion leather goods. If you're in town on the first or third Saturday of the month, there's a colorful market on Independence Avenue that sells local produce and homemade goodies. Most shops take credit cards, but you'll need cash for the street traders. All luxury items are duty free to visitors.

Arts and Crafts

The **Namibia Crafts Centre** (⊠ Old Breweries Bldg., 40 Tal St., ☎ 061/24–2222) sublets 29 stalls and supports in excess of 1,600 rural and urban crafters. Here you'll be able to pick up striking and original handmade African outfits, beautifully woven baskets, distinct Caprivian pots, wood carvings, exquisite embroidery work, jewelry, Marula oils and soaps, pottery, and much more. The center is open weekdays 9–5:30 and Saturday 9–1:30 in summer, weekdays 8:30–5 and Saturday 9–1:30 in winter.

The **Omba Gallery,** in the center, hosts both fine-art and crafts exhibitions from Namibia and abroad. At the **Craft Cafe** you can grab a soda, tea, coffee, and snacks.

Namos & Tameka (⊠ Gustav Voigts Shopping Center, ☎ 061/24–2036) markets the incredible work of disadvantaged communities from all over Namibia. You'll be amazed at the workmanship and sophistication of these rural crafts, ranging from gorgeous, hand-embroidered cotton duvet covers to ostrich-egg jewelry and from carved pots and walking sticks to brightly colored handmade cushions and clothing. You can also buy handmade dolls from the Herero women in their colorful and graceful Victorian-style dresses in front of the shopping center.

The **Post Street Mall** (⊠ Independence Ave., ☎ no phone), with its bustling street market of crafts and curio displays, houses artists from rural areas who display wall masks, salad bowls and servers, drums, carved walking sticks, and wooden African animals galore.

The **Oshiwa Gallery** (⊠ Sinclair St., ☎ 061/22–9891) produces stunning, easily transportable hand-carved picture frames.

If you're looking for a wide variety of arts and crafts, including collectors' items from all over Africa, then look no farther than the gallery **Rogi Souvenirs** (⊠ 77 Independence Ave., ☎ 061/22–5481).

The **Penduka Project Centre** (⊠ Goreangab Dam, off Brakwater Rd., ☎ 061/25–7210), 20 km (12½ mi) north of Windhoek, has a workshop, tearoom, and crafts outlet. Specialties are embroidered and quilted bedroom furnishings, table linens, rucksacks, bags, wall hangings, handwoven baskets, wood carvings, and dishes and trays. It's open Monday–Saturday 8–5.

Clothing

If you fancy some gorgeous and classy clothing, then check out the reversible lightweight coats and jackets of Namibian Persian lamb (*swakara*), printed goatskin and suede clothing, buffalo and ostrich leather accessories, and beautiful and durable kudu shoes in the stores and boutiques on **Independence Avenue.**

Jewelry

Buy your genuine Namibian gemstones—or watch them being sorted, cut, faceted, and polished—at **House of Gems** (⊠ 131 Stübel St., near John Meinert St., ☎ 061/22–5202), run by one of the country's top gemologists. Tourmalines are a local specialty.

Miscellaneous

Namibian stamps are among the most beautiful and sought-after in the world, so if you're a philatelist visit the **Namibian Post Office Stamp and Gift Shop** (⊠ Main Post Office, Independence Ave., ☎ 061/

201–3107, WEB www. nampost.com.na); there's also a Nampost counter at Hosea Kutako Airport.

For a gift with a difference, take home some canned impala, kudu, or crocodile; shark liver pâté; kudu salami; smoked oryx; or ostrich from **Raith's Meat Delicatessen** (⊠ Wecke & Voigts Complex, Independence Ave., ☎ 061/23–4061). They are open weekdays 8–6, Saturday 8:30–noon, and Sunday 9–1.

For camping and other outdoor equipment, visit **Greensport** (⊠ 60 Mandume Ndemufayo Ave., ☎ 061/23–4131, WEB www.cymot.com.na, open weekdays 8–1 and Saturday 8–noon.

Worth a visit if you're driving to Swakopmund is **Henkert Tourist Centre** (⊠ 38 Main St., Karibib, ☎ 064/55–0028), on the main Windhoek/Swakopmund road. For more than 30 years it's been a mecca for traders, collectors, enthusiasts, and browsers. Choose from gemstones and minerals, antiques, leather products, gold and silver, stone and wood carvings, carpets and rugs, and toys. The center has rest rooms and a coffee shop.

Windhoek A to Z

To research prices, get advice from other travelers, and book travel arrangements, visit www.fodors.com.

AIR TRAVEL

Hosea Kutako International Airport, 42 km (26 mi) from Windhoek, has international flights to and from Europe (check airlines with your travel operator). Namibia's national carrier, Air Namibia, operates regular and reliable flights around the country. Eros Airport, near the B1, the main road on the way south to Reheboth, handles local flights and charters.

There's a frequent bus service (N$50 one-way) from Hosea Kutako International Airport to Windhoek city center. Pickup and drop-off are opposite the Kalahari Sands & Casino on Independence Avenue. Most hotels provide courtesy transport. Taxis are available at the airport, but ask at the airport information desk for the current rate and always negotiate the price before you catch the cab.

➤ AIRLINES AND CONTACTS: **Hosea Kutako International Airport** (☎ 061/299–6606). **Air Namibia** (☎ 061/298–2605). **Eros Airport** (☎ 061/299–6500).

CAR RENTAL

➤ MAJOR AGENCIES: **Avis** (⊠ Box 2057, Eros Airport, Windhoek, ☎ 061/23–3166, FAX 061/22–3072). **Budget** (⊠ Box 71, Hosea Kutako International Airport, Windhoek, ☎ 061/22–8720, FAX 061/22–7665). **Imperial** (⊠ Box 1387, Eros Airport, Windhoek, ☎ 061/22–7103, FAX 061/22–2721).

CAR TRAVEL

Windhoek is 1,558 km (967 mi) from Cape Town via the Noordoewer border post (open 24 hours). You can also drive from Johannesburg to Windhoek (1,791 km/1,112 mi) via the Narochas (Nakop) border post (open 24 hours). This is a good route if you want to visit the Augrabies Falls and Kalahari Gemsbok National Park in South Africa first.

Generally speaking, the driving is not too bad, but keep a sharp eye out for the ubiquitous, overladen, and often unsafe African taxis (minivans). Their drivers speed like there's no tomorrow, with little regard for themselves, other drivers, or their passengers. In Windhoek, as in the rest of Namibia, drive on the left. The speed limit is 120 kph (75 mph) on major routes, 60 kph (40 mph) in built-up areas.

TAXIS
In central Windhoek most sights and shops are close together, so it's easiest to walk. However, taxis are available; your hotel concierge can help you flag one down, or you can look for the TAXI sign on the roof of cars. Always negotiate your fare before taking off and expect to share with others: Taxis stop and start at will to pick up other passengers. Windhoek Radio Taxis is safe and reliable, as is White Rhino Radio Taxi.
➤ TAXI COMPANIES: **White Rhino Radio Taxi** (☎ 061/22–1029). **Windhoek Radio Taxis** (☎ 061/23–7070).

VISITOR INFORMATION
➤ TOURIST INFORMATION: **Hospitality Association of Namibia** (**HAN;** ✉ Box 11942, Windhoek, ☎ 061/22–2904, FAX 061/22–8461). **Namibia Tourism** (✉ Continental Bldg., ground floor, 272 Independence Ave., Private Bag 13346, Windhoek, ☎ 061/284–2111, FAX 061/284–2364, WEB www.tourism.com.na). **Tour & Safari Association of Namibia** (**TASA;** ✉ Box 11534, Windhoek, ☎ 061/23–2748, FAX 061/22–8461).

SWAKOPMUND AND WALVIS BAY AREA

Swakopmund clings to the Atlantic shores as if the scorching desert beyond were trying to push it into the sea; it's a trendy, bustling little town and the focus of this delightful region. Namibia's only true seaside resort, Swakops, as it's known by the locals, is Namibia's adventure center, where you can test your daring and skills in all kinds of outdoor activities. If you're not an adrenaline junkie, then just relax on the beaches, or take day excursions to unique places such as ghost towns, forbidden diamond areas, and one of the biggest seal reserves in the world. Or try your skill at some of the best sea fishing in the world. Walvis Bay, because of its deepwater harbor, has always been of vital political and strategic importance in this part of southern Africa and has been busy reinventing itself as a center of thriving commerce and industry since it was returned to Namibia by South Africa in 1994. If you're a bird-watcher, a visit to Walvis Bay and Sandwich Harbour is nonnegotiable.

Swakopmund

368 km (228 mi) northwest of Windhoek on the B1.

More than 500 years ago, a group of daring Portuguese navigators dropped anchor on a desolate beach on the southwest African coastline and erected a cross in honor of their king, John I, who had inspired their perilous, unknown journey. Fast-forward to the present, where a couple of miles south of Cape Cross, Swakopmund clings to the edge of the continent, much as it has done since the first 40 German settlers, complete with household goods and breeding cattle, landed with 120 German colonial troops more than 400 years after those first maritime adventurers. You'll find it hard to believe that this little town with its old German buildings, palm-lined streets, well-kept flower beds, inviting sidewalk cafés, and shore-side European-style promenade is in one of the wildest and most untamed parts of the African continent. It's packed at Christmas and New Year's, so make your hotel reservations well in advance. Then choose between a leisurely seaside holiday, soaking up sun and the sparkling, unpolluted air, or an endorphin-packed adventure that will cool your adrenaline fever in any number of thrilling ways—from skydiving and sand boarding to jet skiing and horseback riding in the desert.

You can explore life in the Namib Desert and South Atlantic and the culture of Namibia's indigenous peoples at the **Swakopmund Museum.** View an original ox wagon that operated between Grootfontein and Angola some 100 years ago, marvel at the huge collections of birds' eggs and insects, and take in some colonial German history, too. ✉ *Next to municipal swimming pool on the Strand,* ☎ *064/402–046.* 💳 *N$14.* ◷ *Daily 10–1 and 2–5.*

The **Sam Cohen Library** includes the famous 2,000-title Africana Collection. It's a treasure for scholars, students, scientists, and all book lovers. Particularly fascinating are the local newspapers from 1898 to the present day. There's also a collection of evocative old photographs and maps. ✉ *Kaiser Wilhelm and Windhoeker Sts.,* ☎ *064/40–2695.* 💳 *Free.* ◷ *Weekdays 9–1 and 3–5, Sat. 10–12:30.*

The small but impressive **National Marine Aquarium** has great displays of marine life in its 20 tanks, including a huge main tank that is crossed by an underground walkway. Catch the action when the big fish are hand-fed by divers at 3 on Tuesday, Saturday, and Sunday. ✉ *Opposite the Strand,* ☎ *064/40–5744.* 💳 *N$8.* ◷ *Tues.–Sun. 10–4.*

Take a walk around the town and enjoy the numerous **historic old German buildings,** many dating back to the turn of the 20th century and most in perfect condition. The railway station, the prison, the Woermann House, the Kaserne (barracks), the Lutheran church, and the **District Court** look more like illustrations from some Brothers Grimm fairy tale than the working buildings they once were and are. The Sam Cohen Library (☞ *above*) can arrange guided walking tours, and informative pamphlets are available at the museum.

Swakopmund Information Bureau has plenty of details about local attractions. ✉ *28 Kaiser Wilhelm St., Box 829,* ☎ *064/40–4827,* FAX *064/40–4827.*

Dining and Lodging

$$$$ ✕ **Hansa Hotel Restaurant.** This well-reviewed European restaurant serves rich, good food such as venison and steak and Namibian delicacies such as fresh oysters and locally caught fish and seafood, all accompanied by fine South African wines. ✉ *3 Roon St.,* ☎ *064/40–0311,* FAX *064/40–2732. Reservations essential. AE, DC, MC, V.*

$$$–$$$$ ✕ **The Tug.** As its name suggests, this restaurant is actually an old tugboat that has been moored next to the jetty. Have a drink out on deck, or sit inside at a colorfully decorated table. The seafood is highly recommended, particularly the tasty seafood platter, or try venison or ostrich stir-fry. Try to reserve the corner table, where you can watch the crashing ocean just a few yards away. ✉ *The Strand,* ☎ *064/40–2356. Reservations essential. AE, DC, MC, V. No lunch weekdays.*

$–$$ ✕ **Café Anton.** At one of the town's visitor institutions, you can sit on the palm-shaded terrace overlooking the lighthouse and the sea and watch the world go by as you eat breakfast or enjoy a home-baked, mouthwatering cake or pastry—the chocolate-drenched Florentiners are divine, and the Black Forest cake is made exactly as in Germany. Scrumptious lunch packs are available on request. After 5:30 the menu changes to dinner, which might include a fresh seafood platter, line fish of the day, or grilled prawns. ✉ *Schweizerhaus Hotel, 1 Bismarck St., overlooking the Mole,* ☎ *064/40–0331, 064/40–0332, or 064/40–0333. AE, DC, MC, V.*

$$$ 🏨 **Swakopmund Hotel and Entertainments Centre.** Turn back the clock and stay at Swakops's most notable landmark, the historic Old Station Building, built in 1901. Declared a national monument in 1972, this magnificent example of German colonial architecture came to life again in the early 1990s, when it was restored and renovated in a style evoking the charm and nostalgia of the old railway days. There is a huge lobby—a remnant of the building's former life as a railway station—and rooms decorated in Victorian style that look out over a central grass courtyard and pool area, shaded by palms and surmounted by tinkling fountains. It's a very popular place, so be prepared for lots of tour groups milling around. ⊠ *Bahnhof St., Box 616,* ☎ *064/40–0800,* FAX *064/40–0801. 90 rooms, 2 suites. Restaurant, bar, pool, casino, cinema. AE, DC, MC, V.*

$$ 🏨 **Burning Shore Beach Lodge.** If you fancy sweeping views of the Atlantic coastline, then try this ocean-side lodge at Long Beach, halfway between Swakopmund and Walvis Bay. Treat yourself to the colonial-style Peninsula Suite with its unobstructed view of the Atlantic and a private Jacuzzi, or relax in an ocean-view room or intimate courtyard room. Go dolphin spotting or quad biking on the dunes, marvel at the moon landscape or go to Sandwich Harbour on a bird safari. Your friendly hosts, Rian and Liesl Liebenberg, will arrange all your activities. The price includes breakfast and dinner. Cocktails are offered. ⊠ *152 4th St., Long Beach,* ☎ *061/24–8741,* FAX *061/209–836. 3 rooms, 4 suites. AE, DC, MC, V. MAP.*

$ 🏨 **Europa Hof Hotel.** For a taste of Europe in the middle of Africa, try the Europa, which looks like a combination of Bavarian Gothic, Swiss chalet, and gingerbread house. It's so charming, in fact, that once inside you'll find it hard to believe you're not in Germany. The accommodations are comfortable, the location very central, and the restaurant serves both traditional German food and local delicacies such as crocodile and springbok. ⊠ *39 Bismarck St., Box 1333,* ☎ *064/40–5898,* FAX *064/40–2391. 35 rooms. Restaurant, bar. AE, DC, MC, V. BP.*

$ 🏨 **Schweizerhaus Hotel.** This small family hotel is full of character and ideally set beside the sea yet only minutes from the city center. Two times the winner of a Namibian award for small hotels, it has quaint, comfortable rooms, most with a balcony and sea view. Don't forget to greet the parrots and other colorful birds in the hotel courtyard. ⊠ *1 Bismarck St.,* ☎ *064/40–0331, 064/40–0332, or 064/40–0333,* FAX *064/40–5850. 24 rooms. Restaurant. AE, DC, MC, V. BP.*

Outdoor Activities and Sports

Namibia Adventure Centre (⊠ Shopping precinct between Moltke and Roon Sts., ☎ 064/40–273) offers adrenaline junkies skydiving, sand boarding, jet skiing, kayaking, paragliding, horseback riding, and camel trips. **Okakambe Trails** (⊠ Box 1688, Swakopmund, 11 km [7 mi] from Swakopmund on the B2 to Windhoek, next to the Camel Farm, ☎ 064/40–2799) has day, moonlight, or sunrise/sunset horseback rides through the Swakop riverbeds and up into the moonlike landscape. You can book most outdoor activities at the **Swakopmund Adventure Centre** (⊠ Atlanta Hotel, Roon St., ☎ 064/40–6096, FAX 064/40–5038, WEB www.swakop.com/adv).

Walvis Bay

30 km (18½ mi) south of Swakopmund.

It's unlikely you've ever driven along such a spectacularly different road as the one from Swakopmund to Walvis Bay. The tarred coast road is dwarfed by magnificent towering sand dunes on one side and the wild Atlantic on the other. Don't miss Dune 7, just outside Walvis Bay, one of Namibia's highest dunes. Those big structures you'll notice among the waves are guano platforms, the source of so-called white gold. Self-confident and bright, although lacking Swakops's vibe, Walvis Bay, the main center of Namibia's fishing industry, is a pleasant little town and a handy base for excursions into the Namib Naukluft Park and to Sandwich Harbour. Formerly a South African enclave, strategically important because it's the coast's only deepwater port, it was handed over to Namibia in 1994, the year of South Africa's transition to democracy. There's a lot of new industrial and commercial development, as the town is now linked to South Africa by the Trans-Kalahari Highway. It's great for angling, and if you're a bird-watcher, it's one of the most exciting places on earth. The salt pans and lagoon are home to thousands of flamingos, pelicans, cormorants, terns, and other seabirds, as well as migrant waders of every shape and size.

Dining and Lodging

$$$$ ✕ **The Raft Restaurant.** Perched on a large platform in the middle of the lagoon, the restaurant was built as an environmentally friendly structure on stilts so as not to disturb the bird and marine life. Judging by the impressive array of waders, flamingos, gulls, terns, and ponderous pelicans all round the restaurant, the builder succeeded admirably. If you want to watch the birds while you eat, try to be there at low tide when the mudflats are exposed. Then tuck into one of the excellent seafood dishes—try the seafood curry or the seafood platter of crab, langoustines, prawns, and local fish—or the generous helpings of red meat for which Namibia is famous. Dinner reservations are essential if you want a table with a view. ⊠ *The Lagoon,* ☎ *064/20–4877. AE, DC, MC, V. Closed Sun.*

$$ 🏨 **Walvis Bay Protea Lodge.** Although it basically attracts a business crowd, this small hotel is a relaxing and serene place, well designed and furnished, with enough oceanic touches to remind you that you're by the sea. The helpful and friendly staff can organize all kinds of local activities and trips for you, from deep-sea angling to desert excursions. ⊠ *7th and 10th Rds., Box 30,* ☎ *064/20–9560,* 🅵🅰🆇 *064/20–9565. 26 rooms. Restaurant. AE, DC, MC, V.*

$ 🏨 **The Courtyard.** This delightful hotel, not too far from the harbor, is centered on a grassy, palm-studded courtyard. Each room has a microwave, coffeemaker, and small refrigerator. There are a sauna and a small, heated indoor pool. The Courtyard offers a really good value for the money. ⊠ *16 3rd Rd., Box 2416,* ☎ *064/20–6252,* 🅵🅰🆇 *064/20–7271. 17 rooms. Pool, refrigerators, sauna. AE, DC, MC, V. BP.*

$ 🏨 **Lagoon Lodge.** This delightfully funky guest house has six luxurious, uniquely decorated rooms, each with a private balcony or terrace overlooking the Walvis Bay lagoon. Your charming French hosts are Hélène and Wilfried Meiller, who also speak English and Spanish. Dinner is available on request. ⊠ *2 Nangolo Mbumba Dr., Box 3964,* ☎ *064/20–0850,* 🅵🅰🆇 *064/20–0851,* 🆆🅴🅱 *www.namibweb.net/lagoonlodge. 6 rooms. Pool. AE, DC, MC, V. BP.*

$ 🏨 **Langholm Hotel.** The Langholm is a stone's throw from the lagoon and the municipal golf course and swimming pool, and the hotel can arrange lagoon or desert tours. After a good night's sleep in your comfortable bedroom, tuck into a lavish breakfast. Go for a bike ride, or order a picnic basket and set off for some sightseeing in the beautiful surroundings. A *teller essen* (dinner of the day) can also be ordered. ⊠ *Box 2631,* ☎ *064/20–9230,* 🅵🅰🆇 *064/20–9430. 12 rooms. Bar. AE, DC, MC, V. BP.*

OUTDOOR ACTIVITIES

Mola Mola (⊠ Box 980, Walvis Bay, ☎ 064/20–5511, 🅵🅰🆇 064/20–7593, 🆆🅴🅱 www.mola-mola.com.na) organizes birding and angling cruises and will also take you to watch dolphins. If you're feeling energetic, go kayaking among seals and dolphins with **Ecomarine Kayak Tours** (⊠ Box 225, Walvis Bay, ☎ FAX 064/20–3144).

Sandwich Harbour

40 km (25 mi) south of Walvis Bay.

The old whaling station of Sandwich Harbour is one of Africa's most important wetlands, comprising mudflats, a huge salt lagoon, and freshwater pools. Not only a twitcher's (bird-watcher's) paradise, it also has spectacularly beautiful desert dunes stretching down to the bird-covered beaches. If you're reasonably fit and energetic, hike up Dune 7, where you'll be rewarded with spectacular views. Camping and overnight stays are not allowed, but permits for day visits can be obtained from **Namibia Wildlife Resorts** (⊠ Woermann Arcade, Swakopmund, ☎ 064/405–513; N$10 per person, N$10 per car). But don't try to drive yourself unless you have a four-wheel-drive vehicle and are extremely experienced, and even then you'll need a permit and may still run the risk of getting stuck. Instead, see the area guided by someone from **Turnstone Tours** (⊠ Box 307, Swakopmund, ☎ FAX 064/40–3123, FAX 064/40–3290), which has very knowledgeable and friendly guides. Tours are also offered by the reputable and long-standing **See Africa Safari Shop** (⊠ Roon St., Swakopmund, ☎ 064/40–4037, FAX 064/40–4203). A wonderful way to see the coastline with its rusting shipwrecks, salt pans, deserted mining camps, flocks of flamingos, scavenging seashore jackals, and seals is by small plane. Contact **Pleasure Flights & Safaris** (⊠ Box 537, Swakopmund, ☎ FAX 064/40–4500, ☎ 081/129–4500 mobile phone).

NAMIB NAUKLUFT PARK

Namib Naukluft Park, south of Walvis Bay, is the fourth-largest national park in the world and is renowned for its unique beauty, isolation, tranquillity, romantic desert landscapes, and rare desert-adapted plants and creatures. Covering an area of 12.1 million acres, stretching 400 km (250 mi) long from Swakopmund in the north to Lüderitz in the south and 150 km (93 mi) wide, it accounts for a tenth of Namibia's surface area. To examine the park properly, it's best to think of it as five distinct areas: the Northern Section—between the Kuiseb and Swakops rivers—synonymous with rocky stone surfaces and granite islands (*inselbergs*) and dry riverbeds; the Middle Section, the 80-million-year-old heart of the desert and home of Sesriem Canyon and Sossusvlei, the highest sand dunes in the world; Naukluft (meaning "narrow gorge"), some 120 km (74½ mi) northwest of Sesriem, that has wall-to-wall game and birds and is the home of the Kuiseb Canyon; the Western Section, with its lichen-covered plains, prehistoric plants, and birding sanctuaries of Walvis Bay and Sandwich Harbour; and the Southern Section, where, if you're traveling up from South Africa by road, it's worth having a look at Duwisib Castle, 72 km (46 mi) southwest of Maltahöhe beside the D286—an anachronistic stone castle built in 1909 by a German army officer who was later killed at the Somme. The park's southern border ends at the charming little town of Lüderitz. If you're the adventurous type, then you can drive yourself from Windhoek or Swakopmund, but it's easier and quicker to take scheduled trips, which a tour operator will arrange for you.

Wildlife

The kind of wildlife you'll encounter will depend on which area of the park you visit. In the north look out for the staggeringly beautiful gemsbok (oryx), locally believed to be the animal behind the unicorn myth. Also visible are springbok, spotted hyenas, black-backed jackals, and the awesome lappet-face vultures, the biggest in Africa. In Naukluft you'll see the most game, more than 50 species of mammals, including leopards, caracals, Cape and bat-eared foxes, aardwolves, and klipspringers. There are almost 200 species of birds, from the startlingly beautiful crimson-breasted boubou shrike to soaring falcons and buzzards. You'll notice huge haystacks weighing down tall trees and telephone poles, the condominiums of the sociable weavers, so called because they nest communally, sometimes with thousands of occupants, yet each tiny bird has its own exit and entrance.

Where there are sand dunes, you'll be able to observe some of the earth's strangest creatures: the dune beetle, which collects condensed fog on its back into a single droplet that it then rolls down its back into its mouth; a beetle that digs a trench to collect moisture; the golden mole (thought until recently to be extinct), which spends its whole life "swimming" beneath the sand, ambushing beetles and grubs on the surface; the sidewinding adder, a sand-diving lizard that raises one foot at a time above the hot sand in a strange stationary dance to nonexistent music.

Don't overlook the amazing desert-adapted plants. Ask your guide to point out a dollar bush (so called because its leaves are dollar size) or an ink bush, both of which can survive without rain for years; the gold, frankincense, and myrrh of the *Commiphora* species of plants; or the Namib's magic plant, the *nara* melon, still harvested and eaten by the locals. Watch for one of the withered-looking desert lichens—if you pour a tiny drop of water onto one, you will see it seemingly rise from the dead. And last, but by no means least, there is the mind-boggling *Welwitschia mirabilis,* the Namib's most famous, and the world's oldest, living plant.

Sesriem and Sossusvlei

Even if you're not a romantic, the Sossusvlei's huge, star-shape desert dunes rising dramatically 1,000 ft above the surrounding plains and sprawled like massive pieces of abstract sculpture are guaranteed to stir your soul and imagination—you might even dash off a sonnet or two. And then there's the landscape of continuously shifting colors, from yellow-gold and ocher to rose, purple, and deep red, growing paler or becoming darker according to the time of day. The dunes have their own distinctive features, ranging from the crescent-shape *barcan* dunes—which migrate up to 2 or 3 yards a year, covering and uncovering whatever crosses their path—to the spectacular, stationary starshape dunes, formed by the multidirectional winds that tease and tumble the sands back and forth. The park gates open an hour before sunrise, so if you can, try to be among the dunes as the sun comes up—it's a spectacular sight. If you're in good shape, you can hike to the top of Big Daddy, the highest sand dune in the world. If you haven't been eating all your Wheaties, you can climb halfway up and sit and admire the stupendous views. And if you just don't feel up to any physical exertion, simply walk up to see the stark beauty of Dead Vlei and then leisurely make your way down to sit in the shade of camel-thorn trees and watch the bird life. A stupendous, not-to-be-missed view of the desert can be had in a hot-air balloon piloted by the legendary Eric. You ascend at dawn and watch the sun come up over the breathtaking, silent landscape, followed by a champagne breakfast amid the dunes. Contact **Namib Sky Adventures** (✉ Box 5197, Windhoek, ☎ 063/29–3233, ℻ 063/29–3241).

About 4 km (2½ mi) from Sesriem Gate, your entry point to Sossusvlei, is **Sesriem Canyon,** named after the six *rieme* (thongs) that were tied to the buckets of the early Dutch settlers when they drew up water from the canyon. If you have time, cool off in the cold water and climb the towering **Elim Dune,** about 5 km (3 mi) away; it will take you well over an hour, but the superb views of the surrounding desert and gravel plains are worth the effort. Be warned: Dune climbing is exhausting, so make discretion the better part of valor. If you're driving yourself, check with your car-rental company for distances and times, which can vary according to the state of the roads. It's more than an hour's very hot walk (4 km [2½ mi]) to Sossusvlei from the parking area. With a four-wheel-drive vehicle you can park just below Dead Vlei.

African Extravaganza offers a three-day Windhoek/Sossusvlei shuttle for N$2,500 per person, which includes minibus transport via the scenic, serpentine Spreetshoogte Pass, accommodations at the Namib Naukluft Lodge, your own guide, all meals, and an excursion to Sesriem and Sossusvlei. ✉ *Box 22028, Windhoek,* ☎ *061/26–3082, 061/26–3083, 061/26–3086, 061/26–3087, or 061/26–3088,* 𝔽𝔸𝕏 *061/21–5356,* 𝕎𝔼𝔹 *www.natron.net/afex.*

If you're pressed for time, **Dune Hopper Air Taxis** is the way to go. Operated by NatureFriend Safaris, several fly-in packages are offered from Windhoek or Swakopmund to the Sossusvlei area ranging from two to five nights and catering to every taste and price range. You'll stay at one of the beautiful lodges in the area and choose your own activities. ✉ *Box 5048, Windhoek,* ☎ *061/23–4793,* 𝔽𝔸𝕏 *061/25–9316,* 𝕎𝔼𝔹 *www.dunehopper.com.*

Dining and Lodging

$$$$ ✕🏠 **Camp Mwisho.** This rustic, intimate camp is built at the foot of the red dunes beside a water hole where springbok and oryx come to drink. In the NamibRand Nature Reserve, 50 km (31 mi) south of the park entrance on the D826, it can be reached by sedan-size cars. It's owned and operated by the inimitable Eric of Namib Sky ballooning. You'll sleep in simply furnished, comfortable tents built on a raised wooden platform. Each has a small veranda with commanding desert views. There's an attractive open-sided lounge area and good French cooking; full board and an afternoon nature drive are included in the price. ✉ *Box 5197, Windhoek,* ☎ *063/29–3233,* 𝔽𝔸𝕏 *063/29–3241. 4 rooms. AE, DC, MC, V. FAP.*

$$$$ ✕🏠 **Kulala Desert Lodge.** In the heart of the Namib and bordering the Namib Naukluft Park, this lodge offers magnificent views of the famous red dunes of Sossusvlei, superb mountain scenery, and vast open plains. You'll sleep in a tented chalet with a thatch roof (*kulala*) on a wooden platform overlooking the dry riverbed. In summer you can move your mattress on to your rooftop to sleep under the stars. The veranda at the main lodge overlooks a water hole and is the perfect place to watch or photograph the magnificent desert sunset. Excursions, game drives, trips to Sossusvlei, hot-air ballooning, and spotlighted night drives can be arranged. ✉ *Box 40584, Windhoek,* ☎ *063/29–3234,* 𝔽𝔸𝕏 *063/29–3235,* 𝕎𝔼𝔹 *www.kulalalodge.com. 12 chalets. Bar, pool. AE, DC, MC, V. FAP.*

$$$$ ✕🏠 **Sossusvlei Lodge.** If you want to be on the spot when the park gates open at first light, then this hotel, right at the Sesriem entrance, is the right choice for you. Recently refurbished, its decor in shades of terra-cotta, burnt sienna, and apricot blends perfectly with the desert surroundings. You'll feel like an upmarket bedouin in your spacious and luxurious tented room, imaginatively constructed of concrete, ironwork, canvas, and leather. After a hot, dusty day in the desert, wallow in the swimming pool, which faces the dunes, and later gaze at the dazzling brilliance of the night skies. There's a good restaurant serving light meals. ⊠ *Box 6900, Windhoek,* ☎ *063/69–3223,* ℻ *063/69–3231. 45 rooms. Restaurant, bar, pool. AE, DC, MC, V. MAP.*

$$$$ ✕🛏 **Sossusvlei Mountain Lodge.** In the heart of the Namib Desert in
★   the NamibRand Nature Reserve is this gorgeous lodge, one of the best in Africa. Its desert villas, at the foot of ancient mountains, are built of natural rock and look out over a plain ringed by peaks. It would be difficult to match their luxury anywhere else in Namibia. Huge desert-facing suites have private patios and sundecks and big open fireplaces to keep you warm on chilly desert nights. Shower in your megasize bathroom (even your toilet has an incomparable view) or outside in your own little walled garden. You can lie in bed and watch the stars through the skylight overhead or climb up to the observatory behind the lodge, that has its own state-of-the-art telescope through which an astronomer/ranger will guide you through the heavens. The food is as creative as the lodge itself—try tandoori-baked *kingklip* (a delicious southern African fish) served with mango salsa—and there's a super wine cellar. You can explore the area on an ecofriendly quad bike, go for guided nature walks or drives, spot some endemic desert birds and animals, or just sit and gaze at the incredible views. ⊠ *Afroventures, Box 1772, Swakopmund,* ☎ *064/46–3812 or 064/46–3813,* ℻ *064/40–0216,* 🌐 *www.afroventures.com. 10 villas. Pool. AE, DC, MC, V. FAP.*

$$$$ ✕🛏 **Sossusvlei Wilderness Camp.** In one of the most dramatic settings in Africa, each exquisitely appointed rock, timber, and thatched bungalow here clings to the side of a mountain with spectacular views of the desert as it stretches away to the horizon. You'll enjoy breakfast under the spreading camel-thorn trees at the foot of Sossusvlei after the bumpy 20-km (12½-mi) drive to the dunes before returning to camp at midday via the Sesriem Canyon. Then cool off in your private plunge pool as you watch the sun set over awesome desert scenery to the calls of barking geckos. ⊠ *Mailing address: Wilderness Safaris, Box 5219, Rivonia 2128, South Africa,* ☎ *011/807–1800,* ℻ *011/807–2110,* 🌐 *www.sossusvleicamp.com. 9 bungalows. Restaurant, bar, pool. AE, DC, MC, V. FAP.*

$$ ✕🛏 **Namib Naukluft Lodge.** On a vast plain and surrounded by mountainous boulders, this new lodge has comfortable accommodations with awesome views. Sit on your private veranda and watch the fiery desert sunset, sip a sundowner by the pool, or enjoy a meal in the open-air restaurant. The lodge will arrange outings and activities for you—don't miss out on an easy walk in the world's oldest desert. ⊠ *Box 22028, Windhoek,* ☎ *061/26–3082, 061/26–3083, or 061/26–3086,* ℻ *061/21–5356. 14 rooms. Restaurant, bar, pool. AE, DC, MC, V. MAP.*

$$ ✕🛏 **Zebra River Lodge.** From this delightful lodge you can drive yourself to Sesriem and Sossusvlei (90 km [56 mi] to the gate) or to Naukluft, or take a full-day excursion with Rob Field, the friendly and knowledgeable owner (book this when you reserve your room). The comfortable and unpretentious lodge has its own canyon, hiking trails, and superb cooking. The seven guest rooms all have views of the plunge pool and green garden. ⊠ *Box 11742, Windhoek,* ☎ *063/29–3265,* ℻ *063/29–3266. 7 rooms, 1 cottage. Bar, pool. MC, V. FAP.*

Outdoor Activities and Sports

Going on a desert walk, even if it's only a short one, is a unique experience. If you're going on your own, always keep the road in sight and go armed with a hat, water bottle, and camera.

SOUTHERN NAMIBIA

Southern Namibia boasts the awesome and almost tourist-free Fish River canyon (second only in size to Arizona's Grand Canyon); the evocative, picturesque little town of Lüderitz; the eerie ghost towns of Pomona and Kolmanskop, once prosperous diamond-mining towns; and the Sperrgebiet—Diamond Area 1, the Forbidden Territory—where diamonds still abound and plants and animals survive in a pristine state because of the lack of human intrusion and interference.

Lüderitz

A small, atmospheric town on the southwest coast, with the Namib Desert on one side and the wild, icy Atlantic on the other, Lüderitz is chockablock with the exciting history of prospectors and diamonds, of fortunes made and lost, of the adventures of the early whalers, sealers, fishermen, and guano collectors who originally settled this area. When Bartholomew Dias arrived here in 1488, he left behind a commemorative cross and a solitary black woman—one of four whom he had kidnapped from Guinea. She was supposed to spread the fame of Portugal to the locals, but she obviously failed in her mission, as the little port remained happily in the hands of its indigenous rulers and inhabitants until it was finally ceded by the local chief to the German trading firm of Adolf Lüderitz in 1883 for 200 rifles and became Germany's first colony. The diamond boom followed in the early 1900s, and today you'll see some of the beautifully preserved German colonial buildings from that era.

Be prepared for weather that can contain four seasons in one day, from thick fog that rolls in from the surging sea over the rocky cliffs and casts a dark pall over the town to the strong winds that disperse the fog and let in brilliant sunshine. Try to get to Lüderitz before the afternoon, as sandstorms can blow up later in the day. If you arrive on the road from Aus, keep an eye out for Namibia's legendary wild horses, perhaps the only desert-dwelling wild horses in the world. If you turn off the highway at Mariental and drive on gravel roads via Maltahöhe and Helmeringhausen, you'll see some of Namibia's most spectacular scenery.

Goerke Haus (Blue House) is Lüderitz's most famous landmark, visible from all over town. Built in 1910 at the height of the diamond boom, it is one of the legendary "diamond palaces." Architectural highlights include Roman arches, Egyptian lotus columns, and Gothic spires; in addition, the interior has art nouveau light fittings, wall friezes, and original stained-glass windows. From the balcony of the top-floor bedroom there's a marvelous view over the town and harbor. ⊠ Zeppelin St., Diamantberg, ☎ no phone. 🖅 N$5. ⊙ Weekdays 2–3, weekends 4–5.

The **Lüderitz Museum** has interesting photographs and records of the diamond-rush days, a good section on the San (Bushmen), and displays on the natural history of the area. ⊠ Diaz St., ☎ 063/20–2532. 🖅 N$5. ⊙ Weekdays 3–5.

Driving through the desert fog is an eerie experience, especially if you are on the way to the ghost town of **Kolmanskop** (⊠ 10 km [6 mi] east of Lüderitz), where at one time handfuls of diamonds could be collected by moonlight. If you're driving yourself, be sure to get a visitor's permit from the **Kolmanskop Tour Company** (⊠ Box 357, Lüderitz, ☎ 🖷 063/20–2445) before you go, or take one of their organized tours at 9:30 AM or 10:45 AM (Sunday at 10 AM); the cost is

N\$285. You can also take an organized trip set up in advance through your travel operator or with one of the tour companies in town. The buildings, once part of a thriving and prosperous town, now lie half-covered by the shifting sands. Today it's a paradise for photographers and artists, but stories and legends of its colorful past abound: flowing champagne, elegant imported dresses from Paris, and the tame ostriches that used to pull Father Christmas's sleigh over the sand dunes.

Sperrgebiet Diamond Area No 1 (Sperrgebiet means "forbidden territory") harbors some of the richest sedimentary diamond deposits on earth. Apart from its mining history, this fragile, parched paradise—locked away for nearly 90 years—is a perfect microcosm of the unique local ecology, with what appear to be sandy beaches, red dune fields, and magnificent mountain ranges, plains, and inselbergs. Fossil deposits of rhinos, giant dassies (rock hyraxes), bear dogs, and ancient elephants share space with plants, animals, and an environment that remains in pristine condition—because of the unique atmosphere, some plant species occur nowhere else on the planet. If possible, ask your guide to show you one of the *Lithops* species, the famous "stone" plants, or a desert orchid if in bloom. Wander around the ghost town of **Pomona,** whose windswept graveyard must be one of the loneliest and most desolate in the world, on the way to the spectacular rock arch of **Bogenfels,** which rears up 180 ft out of the storm-tossed Atlantic. To visit Sperrgebiet, you must book at least three working days in advance. Guided tours cost N\$350–N\$400 per person. Book your trips and tours through the **Kolmanskop Tour Company** (⌧ Box 357, Lüderitz, ☎ FAX 063/20–2445) or **Lüderitz Safaris and Tours** (⌧ Bismarck St., Box 76, Lüderitz, ☎ 063/20–2719, FAX 063/20–2863). For a self-guided adventure in a four-wheel-drive vehicle, talk to **Coastways Tours** (☎ 063/20–2467).

Dining and Lodging

\$\$–\$\$\$ ✕🏨 **The Nest Hotel.** Given top honors by the Hospitality Association of Namibia, this hotel has a great beachfront location, literally on the rocks. Grit your teeth (the Atlantic can be freezing!) and swim off the private beach, go windsurfing, or just soak up the sun in the solarium. The rooms are modern and comfortable, if rather bland, but perfectly adequate for a holiday where you'll be spending most of your time outdoors. In the restaurant tuck into superb local rock lobsters or delicious fresh oysters as you gaze out to sea from the sundeck. Accompanied by a glass of champagne, there's no better way to enjoy seafood. ⌧ *820 Ostend St., Box 690, Lüderitz,* ☎ *063/20–4000,* FAX *063/20–4001. 70 rooms, 3 suites. Restaurant, bar, pool, sauna, solarium. AE, DC, MC, V. BP.*

\$\$\$ 🏨 **Seaview Hotel zum Sperrgebiet.** Most rooms in this small, modern hotel in a quiet residential area have sea views. Rooms are decorated in shades of dark green and blue—echoing a sea theme—and each has a balcony as well as thoughtful amenities such as a hair dryer and a tea/coffeemaker. The restaurant is a great place to sample excellent seafood and enjoy the magnificent view. ⌧ *Woermann St., Box 373,* ☎ *063/20–3411,* FAX *063/20–3414. 22 rooms. Restaurant, bar, pool, sauna. AE, DC, MC, V. BP.*

Fish River Canyon

400 km (248 mi) south of Windhoek, via Mariental and Keetmanshoop.

This is one of Africa's most spectacular and least-visited wonders, speculated to be second in size only to the Grand Canyon. You can either hike into its depths or take in the view from the rim—either way it's a breathtaking experience. If the rains are good, you'll see the river engorged, but even when it's dry, there are always a few pools dotted here and there on the riverbed. The canyon, part of the **Fish River Conservation Area,** has been home to humankind for more than 50,000 years; both Stone Age and Iron Age sites exist in the canyon. It's a geologist's paradise, too, where layers of rocks and geological formations (that date from 1,800 million years ago to a mere 50 million years ago) unfold like a textbook diagram. The main viewing area is near Hobas, where you'll get a stunning view of Hell's Bend, one of the canyon's notorious and dangerous hairpin bends. Get another great view of the switchback bends at Palm Springs Viewpoint (Sulphur Springs). If you keep your eyes open you'll see Hartmann's mountain zebras, baboons, klipspringer, and a number of the ubiquitous rock dassies. There's not a lot of vegetation on the sides and top—the odd quiver tree and big euphorbias—but at **Ai-Ais** and Palm Springs at the bottom of the canyon, where there's water, the vegetation is lush with ebony trees, acacia, and wild tamarisk. Several hot mineral springs, which are claimed to be highly therapeutic, occur on the canyon floor, including the well-known resort of Ai-Ais (Nama for "firewater").

Don't even think about hiking the **Fish River Hiking Trail** unless you are superfit and an experienced hiker (a letter from a doctor pronouncing your medical fitness is compulsory). But if you do meet all the criteria, it's an unforgettable experience: a four- to five-day 90-km (56-mi) hike in total wilderness along the course of the river from Ai-Ais to Hiker's Point. Because of the scorching heat in summer and the danger of flash floods, it's only operational from mid-April to mid-September. It costs N$90 per person—you take all your own food and equipment and are responsible for your own transportation and safety. Your lodge will arrange to get you to the starting point; otherwise, you make your own arrangements. As it's a very popular trail, book as far in advance as possible. Children under 12 are not permitted. ✉ *Ministry of Wildlife, Conservation and Tourism (MET), Private Bag 13306, Windhoek 9000,* ☎ *061/23–6975,* 🖷 *061/22–4900.* ☉ *Weekdays 8–3.*

If it's gain and no pain you're after, then forget the serious hiking and just enjoy the hot mineral-rich springs at **Ai-Ais Hot Springs Resort** (☎ 063/26–2045), open in season only, from the second Friday in March to October 31. Day visitors are admitted between sunrise and sunset only. If you've booked accommodations, then entry is unrestricted, but you can't leave the resort between 11 PM and 6 AM. You can take a dip in the large, naturally hot outdoor pool or in a private hot tub, or use the resort as a jumping-off point for a leisurely walk in the canyon. Accommodations range from economy huts to luxury apartments (N$190–N$320 per night); bedding and towels are available for an extra fee, but no cutlery or crockery is provided.

Lodging

There are no campsites within the canyon itself, but you can rest your head or climb into your sleeping bag under the brilliant stars, wherever your fancy takes you.

$$–$$$ 🏨 **Canyon Hotel.** If you're exploring southern Namibia or driving between Namibia and South Africa, this hotel just south of Keetmanshoop is a great base. The architecture is straight Foreign Legion, with stunning wood carvings. The rooms, although clean and comfortable, are pretty undistinguished. The buffet breakfasts are decadent. ✉ *Box 950, Keetmanshoop, Namibia,* ☎ *063/22–3361, 063/22–3362, or 063/22–3363,* 🖷 *063/22–3714. 70 rooms. Restaurant, bar, pool, gym. AE, DC, MC, V. BP.*

$$ 🏨 **Cañon Lodge.** In the heart of the privately owned Gondwana Cañon Park, 20 km (13½ mi) from the main viewing point of the canyon, this

gorgeous lodge has stone-and-thatch chalets built around the natural
rock formations, some with huge chunks of rock forming part of the
interior design. If you're feeling energetic, choose from horseback
rides, daily hikes, or scenic drives, or go for a gentle stroll on your own
and soak up the unique landscape. Or treat yourself to an early morning or sunset flight across the awesome splendor of the canyon. Scrumptious Namibian, Continental, and German dishes are on the menu in
the restaurant—a restored German colonial–style farmhouse with part
of a wrought-iron bedstead on its roof. ⊠ *Box 80205, Windhoek,* ☎
061/23–0066, 𝖥𝖠𝖷 *061/25–1863. 26 rooms. Restaurant, bar, pool. AE,
DC, MC, V. BP.*

Outdoor Activities and Sports

Hiking, both strenuous and gentle, is very popular here. From Ai-Ais
you can take a walk up the canyon or tackle a day hike, or drive to
Hiker's Point and take a short walk from there. You can get the information on what's available at the rest camps or your lodge. At Ai-
Ais you can enjoy a game of tennis, go horseback riding, take a stroll
into the surrounding countryside, or just chill out in a hot pool. Some
tour operators offer guided canoe or rafting tours down the river from
three to five days, available only when the river is high—check with
MET in Windhoek (☎ 061/23–6975) or your local travel operator before you get here.

Intu Afrika Kalahari Game Reserve

*289 km (180 mi) northeast of Fish River Canyon National Park; 11
km (7 mi) north of Mariental.*

Set among the red dunes of the Kalahari, this is both a private game
reserve and home of a small San (Bushman) community project. You
can take your pick from a range of accommodations, from upmarket
chalets to a self-catering campsites (campsites with cooking facilities),
any of which will serve as a launch pad for desert and game experiences. A special trip here is going for an early morning walk with a
San tracker, visiting his traditional village, and purchasing traditional
crafts at the crafts center. All meals and activities are included in basic
price of the lodgings listed below.

Lodging

$$$$ 🏨 **Camelthorn Lodge.** A bit more rustic, although still luxurious and
comfortable, this camp has roomy thatch bungalows set among indigenous camel-thorn trees. ⊠ *Box 40047, Windhoek,* ☎ *061/24–8741,
061/24–8742, 061/24–8744, or 061/24–8745,* 𝖥𝖠𝖷 *061/22–6535, 061/
22–6536, or 061/22–6537. 10 bungalows. Bar, pool. DC, V. FAP.*

$$$$ 🏨 **Dune Lodge.** This is the best and most luxurious of the camps—and
the most expensive—and privacy and personal service are the keys here.
You'll stay in stylish chalets and have your own personal vehicle and
ranger. ⊠ *Box 40047, Windhoek,* ☎ *061/24–8741, 061/24–8742,
061/24–8744, or 061/24–8745,* 𝖥𝖠𝖷 *061/22–6535, 061/22–6536, or 061/
22–6537. 5 chalets. Bar, pool. DC, V. FAP.*

$$$$ 🏕 **Suricate Tented Camp.** You'll stay in a luxury tent, with a small lounge
area, electricity, and your own open-air private bathroom. All your meals
are served under a giant camel-thorn tree in the outdoor boma. Accommodation is available at a bed-and-breakfast rate or fully inclusive rate, which includes three meals and all activities with an Intu Africa
ranger. ⊠ *Box 40047, Windhoek,* ☎ *061/24–8741, 061/24–8742,
061/24–8744, or 061/24–8745,* 𝖥𝖠𝖷 *061/22–6535, 061/22–6536, or 061/
22–6537. 10 tents. DC, V. FAP.*

$$$$ 🏨 **Zebra Lodge.** Set among huge old acacia trees and fronted by a stylish
swimming pool, accommodations here are in one of four twin rooms

with cool tile floors and private bathrooms on either side of the substantial main-lodge building (look out for the enormous tree-trunk carvings in reception) or in one of five split-level small bungalows each with a sitting room. ✉ *Box 40047, Windhoek,* ☎ *061/24–8741, 061/24–8742, 061/24–8744, or 061/24–8745,* FAX *061/22–6535, 061/22–6536 or 061/ 22–6537. 4 rooms, 5 bungalows. Restaurant, bar, pool. DC, V. FAP.*

$ △ **!XOO Campsite.** This is a very basic campsite with cooking facilities and shower blocks. If you wish, you can book activities with the lodge subject to availability. ✉ *Box 40047, Windhoek,* ☎ *061/24–8741, 061/24–8742, 061/24–8744, or 061/24–8745,* FAX *061/22–6535, 061/ 22–6536, or 061/22–6537. DC, V. FAP.*

NORTHWEST NAMIBIA

This is the home of the notorious Skeleton Coast—one of the most spectacular and desolate wilderness areas in the world. Still comparatively unknown to tourists, it's well worth including in your itinerary. There's no place on earth quite like it.

The Skeleton Coast Park and Conservation Area

205 km (127 mi) north of Swakopmund to the Ugab Gate.

This wildly beautiful but dangerous coastline, one-third of Namibia's western coastline, stretches from the Ugab River in the south to the Kunene River in the north, right up to the border with Angola. The Portuguese, facing the coast in tiny, frail caravels, called this treacherous coast with its cold Benguela Current and deadly crosscurrents the Coast of Death. Its newer, no-less-sinister name, the Skeleton Coast, still testifies to innumerable shipwrecks, to lives lost, to bleached whale bones, and to the insignificant, transient nature of puny man in the face of the raw power of nature. Expect stark beauty and an awesomely diverse landscape—gray gravel plains, rugged wilderness, rusting shipwrecks, desert wastes, meandering barcan dunes, distant mountains, towering walls of sand and granite, and crashing seas. You won't see an abundance of game, but look out for brown hyenas, springbok, oryx, jackals, and, if you're really lucky, a coastal lion. However, the best activity here is to concentrate on the freedom, beauty, and strange solitude of the area. You can drive (a four-by-four gives you more flexibility) from Swakopmund north through Henties Bay via the Ugab Gate with its eerie painted skulls and crossbones on the gates or from the more northerly Springbokwater Gate. You must reach your gate of entry before 3 PM. Always stick to the demarcated roads and avoid driving on treacherous salt pans. Look out for one of the most unusual wrecks lying next to the road between the Ugab River and Terrace Bay—an abandoned oil rig, now home to a huge colony of cormorants. If you are only passing through, you can buy a permit (N$30 per adult, N$20 per car) at the gate. For a longer trip you must obtain a permit in advance from MET in Windhoek (☎ 061/23–6975).

Lodging

NB: Expect prices for upscale safari lodges to be in US$ when you make your reservation. Prices average about $2,500 per person for a five-day safari.

$$$$ △ **Skeleton Coast Camp.** If you long for one of the most remote wilder-
★   ness areas on earth, consider a four- or five-day fly-in safari into this desolate camp in 660,000 acres of the Skeleton Coast National Park. You'll sleep under canvas in an elegantly furnished tent with your own small deck and awesome desert view and eat in the open-air dining room under an ancient leadwood tree. You'll visit an authentic Himba set-

tlement, picnic beside the crashing Atlantic, visit the loneliest grave in the world, and drive through oryx-studded plains and shifting sand dunes with their endemic desert birds. The days are long—you leave camp after breakfast as the morning mists drift from the coastline into the interior and don't return till after sunset—but they are packed so full of excitement and beauty that your head will still be spinning as you fall into your comfortable bed after a splendid dinner. Departures are from Windhoek every Wednesday and Saturday. ✉ *Wilderness Safaris, Box 5219, Rivonia 2128, South Africa,* ☎ *011/807–1800,* 🖷 *011/807–2110,* 🖳 *www.skeleton-coast.com. 5 tents. AE, DC, MC, V.*

$$$$ △ **Skeleton Coast Fly-In Safaris.** One of Namibia's most highly respected family businesses offers superb four- and six-day trips to this starkly beautiful, hardly visited wilderness. Included is a visit to the remarkable Himba people who, with their red ocher body coverings, elaborate plaited hair, and intricate bead necklaces and leather aprons, live much as they have for centuries. You'll fly to the park from Windhoek over the impressive Kuiseb Canyon and its surrounding spectacular sea of red dunes, staying at tented camps throughout, experiencing the desert from open Land Rovers. These safaris provide an unforgettable and unique experience. ✉ *Box 2195, Windhoek,* ☎ *061/22–4248,* 🖷 *061/22–5713,* 🖳 *www.orusovo.com/sksafari.*

$$ ☷ **Terrace Bay.** This isolated outpost is the farthest point north you can drive to in the park. Surrounded by gravel plains, it's a popular spot for fishermen or people who want to get to know the desert; don't miss the surprising Uniab River delta—a lush green oasis in a miniature canyon a couple of miles from Terrace Bay. It's also a good stop if you're going on into Damaraland. The accommodations, once part of a diamond-mining operation, are simple and basic, though each bungalow has a refrigerator, shower, and toilet. All meals are provided, and there's a small shop that stocks basics. Book at MET in Windhoek: ✉ *Private Bag 13306, Windhoek 9000,* ☎ *061/23–6975,* 🖷 *061/22–4900. Restaurant, bar. MC, V. MAP.*

Damaraland

Stretching 600 km (370 mi) from north to south and 200 km (127 mi) from east to west, this stark, mountainous area borders the Skeleton Coast Park. You can drive into Damaraland from the park via the Springbokwater Gate, or drive from Swakopmund to Uis, where you can visit the Daureb Craft Centre and watch the craftspeople at work, or make it part of your tailor-made safari. A good base for touring southern Damaraland is the little town of Khorixas. From here you can visit the **Organ Pipes,** where there are hundreds of angular rock formations, or watch the rising or setting sun bathe the slopes of **Burnt Mountain** in fiery splendor. You'll find yourself surrounded by a dramatic landscape of steep valleys, rugged cliffs of red, gray, black, and brown, and towering mountains including **Spitzkoppe** (Namibia's Matterhorn), where Damara guides will show you the Golden Snake and the Bridge—an interesting rock formation—and the Bushman paintings at Bushman's Paradise. There are more spectacular Bushman rock paintings at the **Brandberg,** especially the famous **White Lady of Brandberg,** at Tsisab Gorge, whose depiction and origin have teased the minds of scholars for decades. Other stops of interest are the **Petrified Forest,** 42 km (25 mi) west of Khorixas, and **Twyfelfontein,** 90 km (56 mi) west from Khorixas, the biggest outdoor art gallery in the world, where thousands of rock paintings and ancient rock engravings are open to the sky. It's extremely rare for this many paintings and engravings to be found at the same site. Give yourself a full day here, start early (it's hard to pick out some of the art in full sun), take binoculars, wear sturdy shoes, and take water (at least 2 liters) and a hat.

Northern Damaraland consists of concession areas that have been set aside for tourism, with many tourist operators working hand in hand with the local communities. It's a mountainous landscape dotted with umbrella-shape camel-thorn trees; candelabra euphorbias raising their prickly, fleshy arms to the cloudless sky; salt bushes; and the ubiquitous Shepherd's tree. Look out for black rhinos and the first traces of the amazing desert elephants, their huge footprints trodden over by the herds of goat and sheep belonging to the local farmers. Ask your guide to point out the *welwitschia* (fossil plant) and the "enchanted" *moringa* tree. The **Kaokoveld,** north of Damaraland, although enticing because it is pristine and rarely visited, is also inhospitably rugged. If you're driving yourself, it's only for the intrepid, do-it-yourself explorer.

Guided rock-art safaris, including a fully inclusive six-day hike in the Brandberg (you need a doctor's certificate of fitness), are conducted by Joe Walter of **Damaraland Trails and Tours** (✉ Box 3073, Windhoek, ☎ 061/23–4610, WEB www.natron.net/tour/dtat/dtte.htm). Few people know the Brandberg as intimately as Joe, who also has a wealth of knowledge on the rock art and flora of the mountain range.

Dining and Lodging

$$$$ ⚶ **Epupa Camp.** For a memorable visit and a close encounter with the Himba people of the area, plan to stay at this shaded, tented luxury camp whose modern amenities belie that the surroundings haven't changed for more than 400 years—emissaries of the local Himba chief may well pop into camp while you're here looking for fuel or food. You'll be taken to one of the temporary villages of the Himba, where you'll learn about the sacred fire, the twin that stayed behind, the holy oxen, and how a day is spent in Africa by people who don't have calendars. A trip to the Epupa Falls—a 10-minute walk or three-minute drive—for sunset cocktails is one of the camp's most popular activities. You can also eat warm, wild honey—scented by the flowers of the baobab tree—bartered for a few cigarettes from the Himba hunters, or bathe among the cool rocks. This is a place where time stands still. ✉ *Namibia Travel Connection, Box 90466, Windhoek,* ☎ *061/23–2740,* FAX *061/24–9876, 9 tents without bath. AE, DC, MC, V. FAP.*

$$$$ ⚶ **Wilderness Damaraland Camp.** A joint community venture with ★ the local *riemvasmakers* (thong makers), the camp is on the Huab River in central Damaraland, midway between Khorixas and the coast. From your large, comfortable walk-in tent, you can look out over a landscape of craggy beauty formed by millions of years of unending geological movement: Brick-red sediments complement gray-lava slopes punctuated by black fingers of basaltic rock creeping down from the rocky horizons. You'll drive with an experienced ranger in an open four-by-four to see Namibia's famous fossil plant—the welwitschia—and go tracking desert elephants. After a day in the desert, cool off in the natural rock pool and watch the desert birds. ✉ *Mailing address: Wilderness Safaris, Box 5219, Rivonia 2128, South Africa,* ☎ *011/807–1800,* FAX *011/807–2110,* WEB *www.damaraland.com. 8 tents. Bar, pool. AE, DC, MC, V. FAP.*

$$ ⌂ **Brandberg Minerals and Rest Camp.** Run by Patrik and Evelyne de Villet with the help of the local Damara people, the camp is an old mining complex, now a great base for exploring the Brandberg. While here you can take a guided tour of the mountains, track black rhinos, or collect gemstones on a mineral exploration tour. You'll stay in extremely comfortable bungalows; enjoy good, wholesome food (meals are extra) and learn lots about the area. There is one group guest house that sleeps

14. ⊠ *Box 35, Uis* ☎ *064/50–4038,* ℻ *064/50–4037. 5 bungalows, 1 guest house. Restaurant, bar, pool. AE, DC, MC, V.*

$$ ☷ **Khorixas Restcamp.** This spot is not the last word in luxury, but it is clean, budget priced, unpretentious, and very handy for exploring the major attractions of the area. ⊠ *Box 2, Khorixas, Namibia,* ☎ *067/ 33–1111,* ℻ *067/33–1388. 38 bungalows and campsite. Restaurant, bar, pool. AE, DC, MC, V. BP.*

$$ ☷ **Vingerklip Lodge.** In a dramatic locale in Damaraland's Valley of the Ugab Terraces, the lodge is set against the backdrop of a mighty stone finger pointing toward the sky. Take time while you're here to listen to the silence. The 360-degree views from the Sundowner Terrace are magnificent. The friendly and knowledgeable staff will organize tours for you to the well-known sights in the vicinity. Bungalows cling to the side of a rocky hill and are clean and comfortable, but it's the remarkable views that you'll always remember. ⊠ *Box 443, Outjo,* ☎ *061/25–5344,* ℻ *061/22–1432. 11 bungalows. Restaurant, bar, pool. AE, DC, MC, V. MAP.*

ETOSHA NATIONAL PARK

★ Translated as the "Great White Place," this incredibly photogenic and startlingly beautiful park takes its name from the vast, flat depression that 12 million years ago was a deep inland lake. Although the park is never crowded with visitors like some of the East African game parks, the scenery here is no less spectacular: huge herds of animals that dot the plains and accumulate at the many and varied water holes, the dust devils and mirages, terrain that changes from densely wooded thickets to wide-open spaces and from white salt-encrusted pans to blond grasslands. It's best to come in winter (May–September), when the weather is cooler, the grass shorter, and the game easier to see. But if you can stand the heat, summer sees the return of thousands of waterbirds to the flooded pan, as well as the great annual migration of tens of thousands of zebras, wildebeests, giraffes, and springbok and other antelope from their winter feeding grounds on the Andoni Plains to the new, lush feeding grounds around Okuakuejo. Although many tour companies offer safaris, it really is best to drive yourself: a two-wheel-drive car is fine, and you can stop and start at your leisure; however, remember that you have to stick to marked roads. As well as patience, you'll need drinks, snacks, and loads of film. There are more than 40 water holes, with Rietfontein, Okuakuejo, Goas, Halali, Klein Namutoni, and Chudob regarded as the best for game-watching and taking pictures, but nothing is certain in the bush. Keep your eyes and ears open all the time, and you may come across game at any time, in any place.

The park gates are open from sunrise to sunset, and the daily entrance fee is N$20.

Game Experience. They're all here—the Big Five—large and small, fierce and gentle, beautiful and ugly. On the road from the Von Lindequist Gate to the well-restored white-wall German colonial fort that is now Namutoni rest camp, look out for the smallest of all African antelopes, the Damara dik-dik. If you see a diminutive Bambi sheltering under a roadside bush, that's it. The Namutoni area and the two Okevi water holes are probably your best chances of seeing leopards, particularly Klein Namutoni and Kalkheuwel. And don't miss the blackface impala, endemic to Etosha. But the real secret of game-watching in the park is to settle in at one of the many water holes, most of which are on the southern edges of the pan and each with its own unique personality and characteristics, and wait. Repeat, wait. Even if the hole is small and deep, like Ombika on the western side, you'll be amazed at what may arrive. Old Africa hands maintain you should be up at dawn for the best sightings, but you can see marvelous game at all times of day; one visitor was lucky enough to see a leopard and her cubs come to drink at high noon. The plains, where you should spot cheetahs, are also home to huge herds of zebra, wildebeest, and springbok, and you may see the silhouettes of giraffes as they cross the skyline in stately procession. Salvadora, a constant spring on the fringe of Etosha Pan near Halali, is a favorite watering point for some of these big herds. And where there's water, there's always game. Predators, especially lions, lurk around most of the water holes looking for a meal. Don't overlook the more than 340 dazzling varieties of birds—the crimson-breasted shrike is particularly gorgeous—and watch for ostriches running over the plains or the raptors hunting silently overhead.

Lodging

A minimum of two nights at any camp is essential if you want to get the most out of your visit—as everywhere in Namibia, distances are huge, and you don't want to hurry.

Private Lodges

$$$$ 🏨 **Mokuti Lodge.** Since it's in its own park a stone's throw from the Von Lindequist Gate, the eastern entrance to Etosha, you may well wake up and find an antelope or warthog munching the grass outside your room. It was Namibia's first lodge and is also its largest, and the experience is obvious in the impeccable service and good food. The rooms are rather sparsely furnished, but you'll be out most of the day game spotting. It's a great place to take a walk, either guided or on your own, and be quite safe. Follow the paths, and you may come face to face with a giraffe or any number of gorgeous birds. Don't miss the amazing reptile park, where you can meet pythons, scorpions, tortoises, and the odd crocodile. To catch sight of the bigger game, take an early-morning or afternoon tour into Etosha from the lodge. Air Namibia flies regularly to and from Mokuti five days a week. ✉ *Reservations through Namib Sun Hotels Head Office, Box 2862, Windhoek,* ☎ *061/23–3145,* FAX *061/23–4512. 8 suites, 8 family units, 92 rooms. Restaurant, bar, pool, tennis court, horseback riding. AE, DC, MC, V. BP.*

$$$$ 🏨 **Ongava Lodge.** Set on the southern boundary of Etosha close to the Andersson Gate, the lodge has its own surrounding game reserve as well as its own entrance into the park. It's one of Namibia's most luxurious lodges, with accommodations in private, spacious thatched chalets with handmade wooden furniture—and gold taps in the bathrooms. Chalets also have wooden decks, which cling to the side of a steep, rocky outcrop overlooking a couple of busy water holes. The stunning main area has stone floors and sweeping thatched roofs, as well as myriad spots to gaze at the never-ending plains beyond. Take a guided walk and sneak up on some zebras and wildebeests, or sit in the bird hide just before sunset and listen to the soft twittering calls of hundreds of sandgrouses as they come to drink. Lions sometimes stray in from Etosha and join the evening party. If you want to be more on the wild side, you can stay at Ongava's Tented Camp, a small, intimate site nestled deep in the bush. You'll sleep in a walk-in tent set on a slate base under a thatched awning with a private bathroom. After a day spent game-watching (tracking rhino on foot is a highlight), it's great to cool off in the outside shower or in the plunge pool. ✉ *Wilderness Safaris, Box 519, Rivonia 2128, South Africa,* ☎ *011/807–1800,* FAX *011/807–2110,* WEB *www.ongavalodge.com. 10 chalets, 6 tents. Restaurant, bar, pool. AE, DC, MC, V. FAP.*

$$ 🏨 **Etosha Aoba Lodge.** Family owned, this small, delightful lodge is 10 km (6 mi) east of the Von Lindequist Gate—about a 30-minute drive from the park. You'll enjoy slipping into crisp, white bed linens in your cool, thatch bungalow after a hot, dusty day in the park. Or sip a cocktail on your mini veranda and listen to the noises of the night. The owners put a lot of emphasis on excellent cuisine, which you'll enjoy under the thatched roof of the main building. Most visitors have their own vehicles, but the lodge can arrange trips into the park for you. Only kids at least 13 years are old allowed. ⊠ *Box 21783, Windhoek,* ☎ *061/22–6979,* 𝔽𝔸𝕏 *061/22–6999. 10 chalets. Restaurant, bar, pool. AE, DC, MC, V. BP.*

National Park Camps

Accommodations at national-park camps are basic but clean and comfortable, and it's much cheaper than in the private lodges outside the park. It's often more fun, too—after all, you're in the very midst of the big-game action. Each camp has a restaurant with adequate, if not memorable, food; a shop selling basic foodstuffs and curios; a post office; filling station; and swimming pool. Most rooms have private toilets, baths or showers, air-conditioning, a refrigerator, and a *braai* (barbecue). Linen and towels are provided. Some of the bigger bungalows have a full kitchen with cutlery and crockery. On the whole, the accommodations are clean and functional. The current **MET Accommodation Guide for Tourists** can give you more details of the different camps. Book as far in advance as possible. ⊠ *Ministry of Wildlife, Conservation and Tourism (MET), Private Bag 13306, Windhoek 9000,* ☎ *061/23–6975,* 𝔽𝔸𝕏 *061/22–4900.* ☉ *Weekdays 8–3. MC, V.*

$–$$$ 🏨 **Okuakuejo.** On the western side, this is the biggest and noisiest camp (the noise comes from the staff quarters), and the staff could certainly do with a few workshops on how to deal with the public in a pleasant way. But its floodlighted water hole—regarded as one of the finest in Africa—more than makes up for any inconvenience. Climb the spiral staircase to the top of the round tower for a good view of the surrounding countryside, and then settle down to an all-night game-watching vigil. ☎ *067/22–9800. 97 cottages.*

$ 🏨 **Halali.** Etosha's smallest camp, roughly halfway between Okuakuejo and Namutoni, is rather barracklike and dusty, but if you're a birdwatcher, it merits a giant tick on your list. Rare violet woodhoopoes and bare-cheeked babblers frequent the camp, and if you walk up the rocky path to the pleasant floodlighted water hole and are prepared to sit and wait, there's a good chance you'll spot lions, elephants, and black rhinos. ☎ *067/22–9400. 60 huts, 2 cottages. Closed Nov.–mid-Mar.*

$ 🏨 **Namutoni.** On the eastern edge of the park, this is the most picturesque of the camps, a restored colonial camp where you can hear the bugle call at sunrise and sunset from the watchtower—you almost expect to see the French Foreign Legion come galloping over the horizon. The historic rooms are tiny—the troops didn't live all that well—so if it's comfort rather than history you're after, you should choose one of the new, fully equipped bungalows, built at a respectful distance from the fort so as not to destroy the ambience. Directly behind the fort is a floodlighted water hole for game viewing. ☎ *067/22–9800. 18 bungalows, 10 rooms, 1 apartment, 4 cottages, 4 hostel quarters sleeping 30 people each.*

Nearby Dining and Lodging

$ ✕🏨 **Namatubis Guest Farm.** Fifteen kilometers (9 miles) from Outjo on the Okuakuejo road to Etosha Namatubis is this oasis in the surrounding dry countryside. You'll find pastel-color chalets with tile floors and Namibian rugs surrounded by green lawns and multicolor carpets of flowers and shrubs. The food is good farm-style cooking; choose from among the superb steak, venison, chicken pie, or a decadent brandy pancake. You can also take day excursions from the lodge to the Vingerklip, Twyfelfontein, or the Petrified Forest and still be back in time for dinner. ⊠ *Box 467, Outjo,* ☎ FAX *065/43–061. 23 chalets. Restaurant, bar, minibars, refrigerator, pool. AE, DC, MC, V.*

$$$$ 🖫 **Okonjima Guestfarm.** Located 130 km (80 mi) north of Okahandja, this is an excellent stopover point on your way to Etosha. Nestled among the Omboroko Mountains, this lovely lodge is also home to the environmental-award-winning Africat-Foundation (www.africat.org), which has rehabilitated and cared for leopards and cheetahs for many years. You can get a close look at these magnificent cats feeding, and if you feel like stretching your legs, there are guided San or Bantu walking trails. A bonus is the spacious hide, within walking distance of your thatched room, where you can sit and watch some of the smaller animals and hundreds of birds. There's also a bush camp comprising eight thatched African-style chalets with a canvas "front wall" that can be lifted during the day so you can enjoy the view. No children under 12 are permitted. ⊠ *Box 793, Otjiwarongo,* ☎ *0651/30–4563, 0651/30–4564, or 0651/30–4566,* FAX *0651/30–4565,* WEB *www.okonjima.com. 10 rooms. Restaurant, bar, pool. AE, DC, MC, V.*

Etosha National Park A to Z

To research prices, get advice from other travelers, and book travel arrangements, visit www.fodors.com.

AIR TRAVEL

All Etosha's camps have their own landing strip. Have your tour operator arrange charters or fly-in safaris for you. Air Namibia flies directly to Mokuti daily on the regularly scheduled flight between Windhoek and Victoria Falls. Chartered flights and fly-in safaris also use the Ongava airstrip.

➤ AIRLINE: **Air Namibia** (☎ 061/29–6174).

CAR TRAVEL

You can drive from Windhoek, via Otjiwarongo and Tsumeb, and arrive at the park on its eastern side by the Von Lindequist Gate (near Namutoni rest camp), 106 km (65 mi) from Tsumeb and 550 km (330 mi) north of Windhoek. Alternatively, you can drive from Windhoek via Otjiwarongo and Outjo and come in the Andersson Gate, south of Okuakuejo, 120 km (74½ mi) from Outjo, 450 km (280 mi) north of Windhoek, which is the most popular route. Both drives are long, hot, and dusty, so you might want to fly if you're short on time. Travel time will depend on your driving and choice of vehicle, so check with your car-rental company. Etosha's gates open at sunrise and close just before sunset. You pay for your vehicle entry permit at the gate, N$20 for most small vehicles, and for any balance remaining on your prebooked accommodations (which include personal entry fees) at the reception area.

WATERBURG PLATEAU PARK

91 km (56 mi) east of Otjiwarongo.

Proclaimed a game reserve in 1972 when several rare and endangered species were introduced from other areas of Namibia and South Africa, this is one of the most peaceful and relatively unknown wilderness areas in Namibia. It's also an ideal stopover on the way from Windhoek to Etosha. The plateau is a huge, flat-top massif rising abruptly from the surrounding plain and offering superb views of the park, the outstanding rock formations, and the magnitude of the plateau. Edged with steep-sided, rugged reddish-brown cliffs, the plateau is covered with red Kalahari sand, which supports a whole range of dry woodland vegetation from the red syringa trees and Kalahari apple leaf to the kudu bush. You're not allowed to drive yourself, but game-viewing tours operate every morning and evening from the beautifully landscaped Bernabé de la Bat rest camp, which is surrounded by one of the largest varieties of plant species in southern Africa. The park's a wonderful place to hike, whether on one of the many walks around the camp (the longest is 3 km [2 mi]), to the much-sought-after Waterburg Wilderness Trail, an accompanied trail that takes three days and must be booked well in advance. Day visitors must make advance arrangements with the resort management (☎ 067/30–5901, 067/30–5902, or 067/30–5903) and leave the park by 6 PM.

Although you won't see the big numbers of game that you'll find in Etosha because the isolation and inaccessibility of the plateau guarantee the animals' protection, on your game drive you could spot the rare roan and sable antelope, Cape buffalo, white and black rhino, giraffe, hyena, leopard, cheetah, and lots more. Always be aware, though, that game spotting is not an exact science, it's often the luck of the draw. If you hike the 3-km (2-mi) Kambazembi walking route to Mountain View (well worth the climb), you'll probably see baboons, kudus, gemsboks, and magnificent black eagles. On the Anthill Way walk look out for the diminutive Damara dik-dik, the smallest antelope. You'll certainly notice the banded and dwarf mongooses that play among the rocks close to your bungalow—they're enchanting, highly intelligent animals. Visit the Vulture Restaurant and observe some of these mobile trash cans in action, and ask about Namibia's only breeding colony of Cape vultures.

The park offers morning and late-afternoon game drives—it's best to book them in advance by phoning the **rest camp** (☎ 067/30–5901, 067/30–5902, or 067/30–5903) before you arrive, or you may find them fully booked. Drives cost N$50 per person. There are unguided short walks that meander through the lush vegetation; an unguided 50-km (30-mi), four-day trail open from April to November for 3–10 people; and a three-day (Thursday–Sunday) guided Waterburg Wilderness Trail on the second, third, and fourth weekend of each month from April to November that's limited to eight people (the cost is N$200 per person, and you must provide your own food and sleeping bag). Book well in advance at MET in Windhoek (☎ 061/23–6975).

Rest Camp

$ 🏨 **Bernabé de la Bat Rest Camp.** At this beautifully sited camp on the escarpment's wooded slopes, you can take a dip in the swimming pool fed by a natural spring at the foot of the towering sandstone cliffs, then relax in front of your bungalow and watch the sun set over the plateau. It's best to book accommodations in advance at MET in Windhoek, although you can take a chance and book when you arrive at the park office if it's between 8 AM and sunset. ✉ *Ministry of Wildlife, Conservation and Tourism (MET), Private Bag 13306, Windhoek 9000,* ☎ *061/23–6975,* 📠 *061/22–4900. 35 bungalows. Restaurant, pool. AE, DC, MC, V.*

Waterburg Plateau Park A to Z

To research prices, get advice from other travelers, and book travel arrangements, visit www.fodors.com.

CAR TRAVEL

The turnoff to Waterburg is on the B1, 22 km (13½ mi) south of Otjiwarongo. Turn on to the C22 and travel 40 km (25 mi) before taking the D2512, a gravel road that covers the last 20 km (12½ mi) to the rest camp. As you approach along the C22, you'll see the plateau rising majestically from the flat savanna. Treat all gravel roads with caution and never speed.

THE CAPRIVI STRIP

248 km (154 mi) northeast of Grootfontein.

The water wonderland of northeastern Namibia is one of the country's best-kept secrets and abounds with spectacular scenery—woodlands, floodplains, swamps, and channels carpeted by water lilies. It's difficult to believe that this lush land could be in the same country as the arid desertscapes of the south. The Caprivi Strip is wedged like an arthritic index finger between Botswana and Zambia and points authoritatively toward Victoria Falls, in Zimbabwe. Its strange shape is the result of European power politics and petty jealousies among the royal families of England and Germany in the colonial past, with Germany wanting the Strip for access to central Africa. The Strip officially begins at Bagani and the Okavango River, in the west, and ends at the Botswana border near Kasane, in the east, which is the transit point into Zimbabwe. The only town of any note is Katimo Mulilo, which is a good departure point for fishing and angling expeditions on the Kwando and Zambezi rivers—the far-eastern tip of the Caprivi Strip is a fly-fisherman's paradise, and fighting and landing a razor-toothed tiger fish is an experience not soon to be forgotten. While here you can also visit the Caprivi Art Centre near the African market. It's a community project selling beautifully crafted baskets, carvings, and handmade pottery. In addition, there are several national parks in the Strip—the Caprivi Game Park covers nearly half of the Caprivi, and the Mahango and Mudumu National parks adjoin it to the west and east, respectively. The Mamili National Park borders on the Linyanti River and its swamps at the border with Botswana to the southwest.

The **Mahango Game Reserve,** 20 km (12½ mi) south of the Caprivi Game Park, is well worth a visit. Look out for the magnificent baobab trees and large herds of elephant, and red lechwe (the antelope of the floodplains). You may also see croc, hippo, buffalo, sable and roan antelope, and, if you're very lucky, the Sitatunga, a rare aquatic antelope. Bird-watchers can try to identify the more than 400 species that call the park home.

In **Mudumu National Park** on the western border of the Kwando River, you'll be in hippo heaven and should see elephant, buffalo, roan and sable antelope, kudu, zebra, and possibly the painted wolves—wild dogs.

You'll see much the same animals and birds in **Mamili National Park,** the largest wetland area in Namibia with conservation status, which lies in the southwest corner of the eastern Caprivi Strip. It's a complex network of channels, reed beds, oxbow lakes, and tree-covered islands. You're almost certain to see buffalo because Mamili is home to the largest concentration of these animals in Namibia.

Game Experience. Watch hippos lined up like so many parked cars on the riverbanks as they snooze in the sun, often with crocodiles basking alongside. Uprooted trees and broken branches will alert you to elephants in the vicinity, and there's always the chance of seeing the predators—lions, leopards, and wild dogs. If you're in the papyrus swamps, watch out for the elusive Sitatunga and the tiny oribi antelope. The best time to visit is between late April and early August. The summer months (October–March) are the best for bird-watching, but large areas of Mudumu and Mamili become virtually inaccessible between December and February.

Private Lodges

$$$$ 🏠 **Impalila Island Lodge.** At the crossroads of four countries—Namibia, Botswana, Zambia, and Zimbabwe—this all-inclusive lodge is famous for its hospitality, accommodations, food, and range of activities. Raised wood-and-thatch chalets, furnished with polished local mukwa wood, open onto wide wooden verandas overlooking the Mambova Rapids at the confluence of the Zambezi and Chobe rivers. The main thatched dining and bar area is built around two huge baobab trees. After your day's activities, relax on the wooden deck and chat about the tiger fish that did or didn't get away, the herd of elephants that passed by, or that special bird. Don't miss a guided trip to the edge of Botswana's Chobe National Park for some superb game viewing or a tranquil *mokoro* (traditional canoe) trip in the fringed papyrus channels. ✉ *Box 70378, Bryanston 2021, South Africa,* ☎ *011/7066–7207,* FAX *011/463–8251,* ☎ FAX *011/706–7207,* WEB *www.islandsinafrica.com. 8 chalets. Restaurant, bar, pool. AE, DC, MC, V. FAP.*

$$$$ 🏠 **Lianshulu Lodge.** Nestled on the banks of the Kwando River among lush riverine forest on a private concession in the Mudumu National Park, the gorgeous lodge is renowned for its relaxed atmosphere, tranquillity, excellent service, and outstanding cuisine. This is the place for a true African wilderness experience. You'll sleep in an A-frame reed-and-thatch hut (with private bathroom) overlooking the river and its floodplains. You can go on a game-and-nature drive or walk, chug along the Kwando River in a boat and eyeball hippos, go bird-watching, visit the Lizauli Traditional Village (a community development project), or just chill out. ✉ *Box 90392, Windhoek,* ☎ *061/21–4744 or 061/21–4745,* FAX *061/21–4746,* WEB *www.namibiaweb.com/lianshulu. 8 rooms, 1 suite. Restaurant, bar, pool, car rental. AE, DC, MC, V. FAP.*

The Caprivi Strip A to Z

To research prices, get advice from other travelers, and book travel arrangements, visit www.fodors.com.

AIR TRAVEL

There are regular Air Namibia flights into Katimo Mulilo from Windhoek—check with the airline, as they change on a seasonal basis. Your travel operator can also arrange private flights.

➤ AIR TRAVEL INFORMATION: **Air Namibia** (☎ 061/298–2605, FAX 061/22–1382).

CAR TRAVEL

The main road from Rundu to Katimo Mulilo, the Golden Highway, is a tarred road that goes through the middle of the Caprivi National Park. Keep a close watch out for animals crossing the road. Distances are huge—just over 500 km (310 mi) from Rundu to Katimo Mulilo—so never underestimate the time it will take you to travel between one point and another. The Ngoma Namibia–Botswana border post is 69 km (43 mi) from Katimo. Two-wheel-drive is fine for the main B8 road, but if you want to visit the game parks, then four-wheel-drive is essential.

NAMIBIA A TO Z

To research prices, get advice from other travelers, and book travel arrangements, visit www.fodors.com.

AIR TRAVEL

Namibia's main point of entry is Hosea Kutako International Airport. It's a small, bustling, modern airport with a splendidly scenic 42-km (26-mi) drive into Windhoek. The smaller Eros Airport handles local flights and charters. Once in the country you can make use of scheduled flights or charter. The national carrier is Air Namibia, which operates international flights from London and Frankfurt to and from Windhoek, flights to and from Johannesburg and Cape Town to Windhoek, and internal flights to most of Namibia's major tourist destinations. South African Airways (SAA) operates links to Johannesburg and Cape Town. Air Botswana links Maun with Windhoek, and SA Express Airways flies between Johannesburg and Walvis Bay.

There's frequent bus service from Hosea Kutako International Airport to Windhoek's city center; the pickup and drop-off point is opposite the Kalahari Sands Hotel, on Independence Avenue. Expect to pay N$40 each way. Many larger hotels run a courtesy shuttle service to and from the airport. Taxis are available, but negotiate the price before you get in. Check on current fares at the airport information counter.

➤ AIRLINES AND CONTACTS: **Air Botswana** (Johannesburg, ☎ 011/447–6078). **Air Namibia** (☎ 061/298–2605, ☎ 061/22–1382). **Eros Airport** (☎ 061/23–8220). **Hosea Kutako International Airport** (☎ 062/540–315 or 062/540–229). **SA Express Airways** (Johannesburg, 011/978–5577). **South African Airways (SAA**; Johannesburg, ☎ 011/778–1111).

BUS TRAVEL

Intercape Mainliner offers luxury regular bus service between Cape Town and Johannesburg, between Windhoek and Victoria Falls, and between Windhoek and most major cities in Namibia. Reservations must be made at least 72 hours in advance.

➤ BUS INFORMATION: **Intercape Mainliner** (☎ 061/22–7847, ☎ 061/22–8285).

CAR RENTAL

If you have the time, the best way to see Namibia is to drive yourself. There's an excellent road network to all the major tourist attractions, virtually no traffic, and the scenery is stupendous. It's easier (and usually cheaper) to arrange your car rental from your home base and then to pick up your vehicle on arrival at the airport. Alternatively, you can fly to the main centers (Windhoek, Sossusvlei, Lüderitz, or Mokuti, on the edge of Etosha), pick up a car, and then do your own thing. You can always make use of the resident guides and specialized local excursions at your particular destinations. A two-wheel-drive vehicle is fine because all the main roads are tarred. Make sure to get a car with air-conditioning. Four-wheel-drive vehicles guzzle gas and are more expensive and more difficult to drive, especially over some of Namibia's rocky, sandy, or muddy terrain. In some parks, especially parts of the Namib Naukluft, Damaraland, Caprivi, and Kaokoveld, a four-wheel-drive is essential; but otherwise, most of the main tourist attractions are accessible by regular car. Always check the state of the roads with the nearest tourist office before you set off anywhere. Never underestimate the long distances involved, and never drive at night unless you absolutely have to. Roads are unlighted, and animals like to bed down on the warm surfaces. If you hit an animal, even a small one, it could be the end of you and your vehicle. Never speed on gravel roads (80 kph [50 mph] is a reasonable speed), which can often be very slippery. It's very easy to skid or roll your vehicle—at least one tourist per year is killed this way.

When renting a car, if possible opt for a "Group B" car with air-conditioning, a radio/tape player, and more luggage space. Expect to pay around US$140 per day for less than seven days, around US$110 per day for 14–20 days. Recommended local companies are East End 4X4 & Car Hire, Kessler, and Odyssey.

➤ MAJOR AGENCIES: **Avis** (⌧ Box 2057, Eros Airport, Windhoek, ☎ 061/23–3166, ℻ 061/22–3072). **Budget** (⌧ Box 1754, Hosea Kutako International Airport, Windhoek, ☎ 061/22–8720, ℻ 061/22–7665). **East End 4X4 & Car Hire** (⌧ Box 11438, Windhoek, ☎ 061/23–3869, ℻ 061/22–8855). **Eyandi** (⌧ Box 264, Otjiwarongo, ☎ 0651/30–3898, ℻ 0651/30–3892). **Imperial** (⌧ Box 1387, Eros Airport, Windhoek, ☎ 061/22–7103, ℻ 061/77–7721). **Kessler** (⌧ Box 20274, Windhoek, ☎ 061/23–3451, ℻ 061/22–4551). **Odyssey** (⌧ Box 20938, Windhoek, ☎ 061/22–3269, ℻ 061/22–8911).

CAR TRAVEL

You will need a current international driver's license. Be warned: Driving to and from Namibia, as well as driving inside the country, is tiring and time-consuming because of the huge distances involved. There are two major highways—the Trans-Caprivi Highway, which links Namibia to Botswana, Zimbabwe, and Zambia; and the Trans-Kalahari Highway, which links Windhoek, Gaborone, and Johannesburg. From Johannesburg to Windhoek on the Trans-Kalahari is 1,426 km (885 mi). There are no fences in the Kalahari to allow free access to game, so don't speed, and look out for antelope as well as donkeys and cows on the road. You can also drive from Johannesburg to Windhoek (1,791 km [1,237 mi]) via Upington going through the Narochas (Nakop) border post (open 24 hours). This is a good route if you want to visit the Augrabies Falls and Kalahari Gemsbok Park in South Africa first. You can also drive from Cape Town to Namibia along the N7, an excellent road that becomes the B1 as you go into Namibia at the Noordoewer border post (open 24 hours). It's 763 km (474 mi) from Cape Town to Noordoewer, 795 km (493 mi) from Noordoewer to Windhoek. Border posts are efficient and friendly—make sure you have all your paperwork to hand over.

EMBASSIES

➤ CANADA: **Canadian Consulate** (⌧ Box 239, Windhoek, ☎ 061/22–7417, ℻ 061/22–2859).
➤ UNITED KINGDOM: **British High Commission** (⌧ 116 Robert Mugabe Ave., Box 22202, Windhoek, ☎ 061/22–3022, ℻ 061/22–8895).
➤ UNITED STATES: **U.S. Embassy** (⌧ 14 Lossen St., Box 12029, Windhoek, ☎ 061/22–1601, ℻ 061/22–9792).

EMERGENCIES

Ambulance, fire department, and police (☎ 21–1111 in Windhoek). There are no standardized emergency numbers in the rest of the country.

There's a high standard of medical care in Namibia. Consult your hotel about particular doctors or consult the white pages of the telephone directory under *M* for medical practitioners. If you get sick, go to a private clinic rather than a government one. Windhoek and Otjiwarongo both have excellent private clinics. In Windhoek there is the Medi Clinic and the Catholic Mission Hospital. In Otjiwarongo there is a Medi-Clinic. Be sure you have comprehensive medical insurance before you leave home.

➤ CONTACTS: **Catholic Mission Hospital** (✉ 92 Stubel St., Windhoek, ☎ 061/23–7237). **Medi-Clinic** (✉ Son St., Otjiwarongo, ☎ 067/30–3734 or 067/30–3735). **Medi Clinic** (✉ Heliodoor St., Eros Park, Windhoek, ☎ 061/22–2687).

TOURS

African Extravaganza specializes in shuttle services, scheduled safaris, charter tours and fly-ins, self-drive options, day excursions, and transfers. African Kirikara Safaris, whose base of operations is the family-owned farm Kiripotib, 160 km (100 mi) southeast of Windhoek in the Kalahari Desert, offers small, exclusive, tailor-made safaris throughout Namibia—even for as few as two people. Dune Hopper Air Taxis, operated by NatureFriend Safaris, offers flexible fly-in packages from Windhoek or Swakopmund to the Sossusvlei area. Pasjona Safaris offers tented safaris, guided tours, accommodations in lodges or hotels, and self-drive tours. Wilderness Safaris has a seven-day fly-in safari from Windhoek, which covers most of the main tourist destinations.

NACOBTA (Namibia Community Based Tourism Association) promotes community-based tourism projects throughout Namibia benefiting both the indigenous people and the tourist. There are 45 established community-based tourism enterprises, which include campsites, crafts centers, traditional villages, indigenous tour guides, tourism information centers, and museums.

Sunvil Discovery, based in the United Kingdom, has some of the best and most interesting tours and trips in Namibia.

➤ TOUR-OPERATOR RECOMMENDATIONS: **African Extravaganza** (✉ Box 22028, Windhoek, ☎ 061/26–3082, 061/26–3087, or 061/26–3088, FAX 061/21–5356). **African Kirikara Safaris** (✉ Private Bag 13036, Windhoek, ☎ 062/57–3319, FAX 061/22–3617, ☎ FAX 061/22–3617). **Dune Hopper Air Taxis** (NatureFriend Safaris, ✉ Box 5048, Windhoek, ☎ 061/23–4793, FAX 061/25–9316, WEB www.dunehopper.com). **NACOBTA** (✉ Box 86099, 18 Liliencron St., Windhoek, ☎ 061/25–0558, FAX 061/22–2647, WEB www.nacobta.com.na). **Pasjona Safaris** (✉ Box 90485, Windhoek, ☎ FAX 061/22–3421). **Sunvil Discovery** (✉ Upper Square, Old Isleworth, Middlesex TW7 7BJ, United Kingdom, ☎ 0181/232–9777, FAX 0181/568–8330). **Wilderness Safaris** (✉ Box 5219, Rivonia 2128, South Africa, ☎ 011/807–1800, FAX 011/807–2110).

TRAVEL AGENCIES

➤ LOCAL AGENT REFERRALS: **Namib Travel Shop** (✉ Box 6850, Windhoek, ☎ 061/22–6174, FAX 061/23–9455). **Namibia-Direkt** (✉ Box 2766, Windhoek, ☎ 061/23–3691, FAX 061/24–8718). **Sand Rose** (✉ Box 40263, Windhoek, ☎ 061/24–5455, FAX 061/24–5454).

VISITOR INFORMATION

The Ministry of Wildlife, Conservation and Tourism (MET) has information on the national parks. It's open weekdays 8–5. Namibia Tourism, open weekdays 8–1 and 2–5, will provide you with a free map, a "Welcome to Namibia" booklet that covers all the major tourist attractions, and an accommodations guide that covers all levels of lodging from rest camps to first-class luxury establishments.

➤ TOURIST INFORMATION: **Ministry of Wildlife, Conservation and Tourism (MET;** ✉ John Meinert and Moltke Sts., Private Bag 13306, Windhoek 9000, ☎ 061/23–6975, FAX 061/22–4900). **Namibia Tourism** (✉ Independence Ave., Private Bag 13346, Windhoek [next to the kudu statue], ☎ 061/284–2111, FAX 061/22–1930).

13 ZAMBIA

Bound to southern Africa by geography yet long separated from it by politics, Zambia occupies a socioeconomic limbo somewhere between southern, Central, and East Africa. Since stabilization in the region, however, it has been emerging as very special destination for people who are looking for something off the beaten track.

By David
Bristow

Updated by
Jennifer Stern

A LARGE, SADDLE-SHAPE COUNTRY, Zambia, at 752,614 square km (467,373 square mi), is nearly twice the size of Zimbabwe. For the most part it comprises small villages with mud-and-grass huts surrounded by hand-tilled fields, beyond which is the seemingly endless *miombo* savanna and game reserves that are as wild as Africa ever was.

Modern Zambia was born as a country and unified nation in 1911 as the colonial territory of Northern Rhodesia, which, with present-day Zimbabwe and Malawi, made up the Federation of Rhodesia and Nyasaland. In 1964 it gained independence from the crumbling British Empire, with Kenneth Kaunda as its first president and major exponent of African socialism.

Although the interior is composed mostly of arid savanna, Zambia's borders are defined by water: the mighty Zambezi, in the southwest, with Victoria Falls, known as Mosi-oa-Tunya in Zambia, at its center; Lakes Mweru and Bangweulu and the Laupula River, in the northwest; the east, cut by the Luangwa River, the southern extremity of the Great Rift Valley; and the north, where Lake Tanganyika lies, the world's longest and second-deepest freshwater reservoir. These waterways are in themselves major attractions, and Mosi-oa-Tunya, especially, is the region's adventure-sport capital. Here you can canoe while placidly watching the game-filled banks; raft the world's most extreme, commercially run white-water river; take a helicopter trip over the falls; bungee-jump off a historic spray-washed bridge; go game viewing or horseback riding; or simply enjoy the spectacle of one of nature's great wonders.

The heart of Zambia is its people, as warm as the African sun. A visit to a traditional village such as Mukuni or Maramba, near Livingstone, offers you the opportunity to partake of everyday life as it's been lived out here for centuries. You can see traditional dancing, consult a *sangoma* (soothsayer) and have the bones read, hear the oral tradition of the people around a boma, and even seek an audience with a chief. However, it is the wild bush that is the country's soul. In the game parks there is little interference by humans—although in recent decades poaching for ivory and rhino horn has left an ignominious legacy for the country's conservation record.

Still, rhinos aside, wildlife remains Zambia's biggest attraction, and game is otherwise abundant—the leopards of South Luangwa are legendary and plentiful, as are buffaloes in North Luangwa, and rare aquatic Sitatungas antelope, roan, and sable antelopes are commonly seen. Vast herds of black lechwe dominate the fauna of Bangweulu, where you have a great chance of seeing the preposterous shoebill stork.

Zambia should be considered the southern entry point into untouristed Africa. Some credit cards will be accepted by hotels and restaurants in main cities, as well as at most upscale lodges. However, in most other cases, you will need to have U.S. dollars in cash (be sure to include small denominations)—this is the part of Africa where local money devalues so quickly that some people don't even accept their own currency. Also be aware that getting around Zambia, where paved roads are often worse than unpaved ones, scheduled flights few, and small planes and dirt airstrips the norm, can be tricky. But that can be half the fun. The less intrepid visitor can rely on operators and agents who can handle all logistics: transportation, safaris, sports, and even visas if you need them.

Note: All of Zambia should be considered a malaria endemic area, except around Lusaka, with the low-lying waterways carrying the great-

Zambia

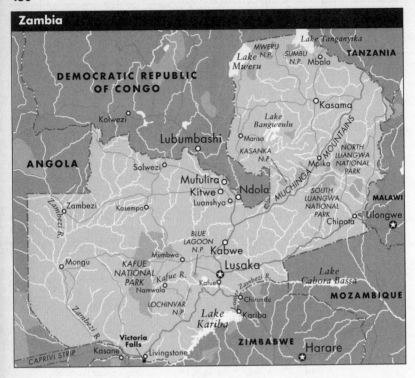

est risk. The best way to avoid this disease is not to get bitten by mosquitoes—make liberal use of insect repellent, wear long sleeves and trousers at dawn and dusk, and always sleep under a mosquito net. Consult a knowledgeable health practitioner about malaria prophylaxis before you leave home.

Pleasures and Pastimes

Arts and Crafts

There are some fantastic artists in Zambia—ranging from roadside wood-carvers and fabric printers to distinctive fine artists. Look out for works by Stephen Kapata; this Zambian native depicts the life, history, and culture of his country in evocative oil paintings. You'll also find fantastic handmade furniture and many artifacts from West Africa.

Dining

The staple diet of the native people consists of a stiff gritslike porridge called *nsima,* made from either maize or cassava and eaten with wild spinach and relish or meat. Around Kariba and the lakes, fish is a major source of protein. Tiny, sardinelike *kapenta* are dried and then fried up as relish, and bigger fish are preserved by smoking or sun-drying. Then there's mopane worms, fried flying ants, and other bush food, which, to paraphrase Crocodile Dundee, is edible but tastes pretty awful.

Luckily for travelers, the lodges all have rather spectacular food—both in quality and quantity—but otherwise the fare is limited. There are good restaurants in Lusaka, but elsewhere you'll be limited to pizza, steak, salad, french fries, and the odd pasta. The wines served are invariably medium-quality South African table wines. Even if you're not a beer fan, the hot weather might encourage you to sample the locally brewed Mosi-oa-Tunya beer, usually just called Mosi.

CATEGORY	COST*
$$$$	more than US$15
$$$	US$10–US$15
$$	US$5–US$10
$	less than US$5

*Rates are for a main course.

Lodging

Lusaka has hotels of international standard, but you won't want to spend more than one night when arriving or departing, because the capital has little of genuine interest to recommend it.

Game lodges and camps range from luxe *Out of Africa* style to very modest safari tents or reed-and-pole shelters. However, no matter what the style, basic creature comforts necessary to *mzungus* (foreigners) are always provided: a comfortable bed romantically draped by mosquito netting, hot water, and hot food and cold drinks. Deep in the bush, though, you may have to get used to the idea of a "thunder box": a long-drop toilet topped by a wooden box and (if you're lucky) crowned by a toilet seat.

CATEGORY	COST*
$$$$	over US$400
$$$	US$200–US$400
$$	US$100–US$200
$	under US$100

*All prices refer to a standard double room in hotels or a per-person rate in all-inclusive resorts, including tax.

People

The national motto is "One Zambia, One Nation," which is appropriate for a country that was created by colonialism and that brought together some 10 million people from more than 70 disparate tribes, each with its own language (or dialect) and customs. One thing that all these cultures share is a love of music, dance, and ceremony, which still exists at the center of social life.

The most widely spoken indigenous languages are Nyanja, in the east, Bemba, in the north, Tonga, in the south, and Lozi, in the west (roughly), but English is the official language and is widely spoken. Zambians of all cultures are—mostly—warm, friendly people.

Wildlife and National Parks

There are 17 national parks throughout Zambia, large and small. Kafue is the biggest, at 22,400 square km (8,600 square mi), while tiny Kasanka, in the Congo Basin, is so small it was all but forgotten until a few years ago. The country's vast size, compounded by its poor infrastructure, has left wildlife management greatly wanting, and poaching is a constant problem. But this is slowly changing for the better under the government of President Frederick Chiluba.

Although parks such as Sumbu, on Lake Tanganyika, and Liuwa Plains, near Angola, remain beleaguered by poaching, South and North Luangwa, Kafue, and the Lower Zambezi have strong private investment or aid programs that have helped them emerge as good examples of modern conservation. Also, the national wildlife department is in the process of being privatized, which should ensure better management and less corruption.

Definitely the star of Zambia's national parks is South Luangwa, which lies to the southeast, close to Malawi, between the Rift escarpment and the sinuous Luangwa River, with its serpentine course, myriad oxbow lakes, and attendant channels and seasonal pans. The result of poaching has been the loss of the entire 10,000 rhino population and the reduction of elephants from around 100,000 to some 10,000, but that's still quite a lot of pachyderms and probably about as much as the park can support. Most visible are the large herds of buffalo and antelope including puku, impala, and waterbuck. The uniquely patterned Thornicroft's giraffes are plentiful, as are their main predators—lions, leopards, hyenas, and wild dogs. Birds occur in great variety and number, from large raptors to the clouds of tiny queleas that congregate in early winter.

Exploring Zambia

Although there are road and rail links between major centers and neighboring countries, they are mostly of the Third World variety. These subpar roads and rails, together with what are often great distances between places, are why most itineraries will be dictated by air schedules or charter flights. Some tour operators combine fly-drive safaris that ensure that you get to see more of the country. However, driving yourself is also an option, as the people are friendly and the country about as safe as anywhere—it's just slow and a bit uncomfortable.

Great Itineraries

IF YOU HAVE 3 DAYS

With so little time, it's best to stick to one destination, and your best bet would be ⊞ **Livingstone.** Livingstone offers a range of accommodations, from the fun and friendly action-packed Waterfront to exquisite lodges set in tranquil, magnificent surroundings. Either option will give you easy access to all the activities of the falls and the river. Adrenaline-pumping adventures include bungee jumping, white-water rafting, and river boarding. Not quite as heart pounding are canoeing and horseback riding; game viewing and visiting the falls and crafts villages are more sedate. There is more than enough to keep you busy.

IF YOU HAVE 6 DAYS

The simplest and best itinerary for up to a week would be to visit **Livingstone** and ⊞ **South Luangwa.** Or you could combine either one of these with a canoe trip on the Zambezi through the ⊞ **Lower Zambezi National Park.** For a relaxing and unstressed vacation, you could also choose just *one* of these fantastic options, or even a long, leisurely walking safari in **North Luangwa National Park.**

IF YOU HAVE 10 OR MORE DAYS

Spend five days in **Livingstone** rafting, canoeing, taking a flightseeing trip over the falls, and leaving at least one full day for lying in a lounge chair next to the Zambezi River. For the second half of your trip, choose between a canoe safari on the river through **Lower Zambezi National Park** and some serious game viewing. Either do an escorted trip to **Kafue National Park** with Chundukwa Safaris or head off to **North Luangwa National Park** or **South Luangwa National Park** for some dedicated animal watching.

When to Tour Zambia

The best time for birding is summer—November to April—when it is wet everywhere and summer migrants are in abundance. This is also the time of torrential rains, heat, and mosquitoes and when some of the best game-viewing areas are inaccessible. The winter months—June to September—are best for game viewing, when the seasonal water sources dry up and game teems around the main waterways. However, at this time of year it is dry and dusty and nights can be bitterly cold, so pack appropriately. October offers even better game viewing, but the weather is pretty horrid—very, very hot (over 100°F [38°C]) and very, very humid (over 90%). If you can handle it, though, you'll see more animals than you'd ever have believed possible.

Lusaka

The capital is a city of 2 million souls, most of whom are unemployed. It is a shambles of a town, where urban planning is virtually unknown and where poverty, petty crime, and civil corruption prevail. But to embrace the African spirit, you have to come to terms with these realities, just as you would in Mumbai or Calcutta if you visited India. It is one of Africa's fastest-growing centers, and sidewalks in the central business district (CBD) have been entirely taken over by street traders and loiterers.

Although many visitors choose not to stay in Lusaka, it is wise to overnight there after an international flight before you immerse yourself in the bush. Lying at an altitude of 4,265 ft, Lusaka has a pleasant climate year-round, and it's malaria free.

Chaotic as it is, Lusaka is a fascinating city, and you may enjoy exploring it—just try not to look too obviously like a tourist, and leave your jewelry at home. The main road through the central business district (CBD), a double-lane boulevard named Cairo Road, was one link in empire builder Cecil John Rhodes's plan to build a road from the Cape to Cairo.

Dining and Lodging

$$–$$$ ✕⊡ **Lilayi Lodge.** Only 20 minutes' drive from the city, you'll feel like you're way out in the bush. With 1,300 acres of pretty woodland, this lovely lodge is a great place to relax and fit in a spot of game watching. Accommodations are in attractive thatched *rondawels* (round huts). The food is great—especially the generous Sunday-lunch buffets, which feature a variety of roasted meats, loads of imaginative vegetable dishes, and a deadly dessert trolley. ⊠ *Chirundu Rd., about 19 km (12 mi) south of the city, Lusaka,* ☎ *01/27–9022,* 🕿 *01/27–9026,* 🌐 *www.zambiatourism.com/lilay. 18 rooms. Restaurant, bar, pool, horseback riding, mountain bikes, meeting room. AE, MC, V. BP.*

$$$ ⊡ **Hotel Inter-Continental Lusaka.** The Inter-Continental, totally refurbished in 2001, is one of the best choices in town for dependable, world-class accommodations. There are a few subtle African touches in decor and cuisine, but as with most members of this chain, once you're inside the hotel, you could be in almost any city in the world. ⊠ *Haile Selassie Ave., Box 32201,* ☎ *01/25–0000 or 01/25–0600,* 🕿 *01/25–1880. 221 rooms. 2 restaurants, bar, coffee shop, room service, pool, spa, gym, shops, meeting rooms, airport shuttle, free parking. AE, DC, MC, V. BP.*

Livingstone

Livingstone is a fantastic destination with a wealth of attractions, natural beauty, and sports and game-viewing opportunities, most centered around the river and the falls. It was the old colonial capital and, after a few decades of neglect, is now reviving. It's a pleasant, sleepy little town with a low-key tourist industry starting to bring a bit of renovation to some tired old buildings, as well as a spark to the social scene.

Many visitors to this side of the falls opt to stay in one of the several secluded safari-style lodges on the Zambezi River. The Zambian experience offers a tranquil respite from the noisy jostling and crowding of hotels you'll find across the border in Zimbabwe. However, Livingston and Victoria Falls really should be regarded as one destination, as many activities are run from either side with a juggling skill you will find astonishing.

Sights to See

The main place of interest in town—apart from the mighty falls, that is—is the **Livingstone Museum,** the country's oldest and largest museum. It has a historical and archaeological section, some David Livingstone memorabilia, and a natural history display. ⊠ *Mosi-oa-Tunya Rd., between the civic center and post office,* ☎ *03/32–4428.* ☞ *US$3 or ZK9,000.* ☽ *Daily 9–4:30.*

Another picayune pleasure is **Mosi-oa-Tunya National Park,** a pocket-size reserve where the main attraction is what might well be the country's only surviving white rhinos, which are guarded 'round the clock. Although there are no predators, in a game drive of an hour or two you'll get to see most of the animals you would in the other, bigger parks. If you're not staying at a lodge, Mokora Quest (☎ 03/32–1679, ⅁ 03/32–0732) conducts day trips. ☞ *US$3 or ZK9,000.* ☽ *Daily 6–6.*

★ Then, of course, there's **Mosi-oa-Tunya,** the "Smoke that Thunders," which more than lives up to its reputation as one of the world's greatest natural wonders. No words can do these incredible falls justice, and it's a difficult place to appreciate in just a short visit, as it has many moods and aspects. The Zimbabwean side—Victoria Falls—may offer more panoramic views, but the Zambian side—especially the Knife Edge (a sharp headland with fantastic views)—allows you to stand virtually suspended over the Boiling Pot, with the deafening water crashing round you. From around May to August you'll get absolutely drenched if you do venture onto the Knife Edge, and at this time the falls are a multisensory experience, although there may be too much spray to see the bottom of the gorge. If you get the sun behind you, you'll see that magic rainbow. From the air you'll be able to appreciate the geological makeup of the falls and how, over time, the Zambezi has cut seven zigzagging fall lines. The eighth is currently being chiseled away at the Devil's Cataract, between Livingstone Island and Livingstone's statue on the Zimbabwe bank. A network of paths leads to the main viewing points; some are not well protected, so watch your step, especially at high water, when you are likely to get drenched. The bridge to the Knife Edge can also be very slippery, so take care. When it's drier, this vantage point gives you dramatic views of the full 1½ km (1 mi) of the ironstone face of the falls, the Boiling Pot directly below, the railway bridge, and Batoka Gorge. At times of low water it is possible to walk to Livingstone Island, right on the lip of the abyss. ☞ *US$3 or ZK9,000.* ☽ *Daily 6 AM–7 PM.*

Dining and Lodging

Livingstone town is a bit of a culinary wasteland, and the suggestions that follow are the best of a mediocre bunch. You will, however, be very well fed at your hotel or lodge. The Falls Entertainment Center at the Zambezi Sun has a reasonable fast-food joint and an excellent coffee shop, in addition to the hotel restaurants. When it comes to lodging, though, you will be spoiled by choices. There are a series of fantastic lodges strung out like a rosary on the riverbank upstream from the falls. Each has its own character and special attraction, but they are all pretty great.

$$$$ ✕ **Livingstone Island Picnic.** Only available in the dry season, at low
★   water (usually June through October), this is a spectacular, romantic dining option. Livingstone Island is perched right on the edge of the abyss, and here you'll sit on chairs around a linen-decked table while being plied with delicious food and drink by liveried waiters. There is a maximum of 10 guests, and you get there by boat (two engines, just in case). Brunch and afternoon tea are US$70; lunch is US$80, including transfers. The trips are run by Tongabezi Lodge. ⊠ *Box 31, Living-*

stone, ☎ *03/32–4450, 097/77–0917, or 097/77–0918,* Ⅸ *097/84–0920. MC, V. Closed Nov.–May, depending on water level. No dinner.*

$ ✕ **Pilgrim's Tearoom.** If you find yourself in town and in need of sustenance, have lunch at this bright and airy British-style respite. Try a ploughman's platter if you've got a big appetite, or one of the fresh venison pies. For dessert the lemon meringue pie is a treat. ✉ *Mosi-oa-Tunya Rd., just south of town,* ☎ *03/32–2692. No credit cards. No dinner.*

$ ✕ **Zig Zag Coffee House.** This young, funky place has tables on the sidewalk in a roped-off area. They serve the best coffee in town, including espresso and cappuccino. Meals are simple and good—soups, pastries, pancakes, and all-day breakfasts. ✉ *Mosi-oa-Tunya Rd.,* ☎ *03/32–4081. No credit cards. Closed Sun. No dinner.*

$$$$ 🔝 **The River Club.** Where Tongabezi has lawn tennis and African élan, ★ here it is croquet and colonial splendor. Most accommodations are duplex units, with bathrooms downstairs opening onto the river and the bedrooms upstairs partially open to the sky (two rooms have only a few stairs to negotiate, an obvious choice for the less agile). Colors are muted and the tone elegant and almost formal. The main complex is stark white set in green lawns, with sculling oars, hunting bugles, and *Punch* cartoons setting a British tone. Dinner is memorable, with waiters in Indian cotton dress and red fezzes to make it a proper colonial affair. The lodge is approached from the river—purely for effect, as this shows its spectacular location to perfection—but it necessitates negotiating a rather steep set of stairs. If you think you'll struggle, ask to be transferred by vehicle. ✉ *Box 60469, Livingstone,* ☎ *03/32–3672,* Ⅸ *03/32–3659. 10 rooms. Pool, croquet. MC, V. FAP.*

$$$$ 🔝 **The Royal Livingstone.** Part of a multimillion-dollar resort complex opened in April 2001, this upmarket hotel is on possibly the best spot on the river, just upstream from the falls. The attractive colonial-style buildings are set amid lawns and trees and have fantastic views. There's a riverside sundowner deck, and guests can use all the facilities at the Zambezi Sun. The decor of both the guest rooms and public rooms is lovely, but unfortunately the service doesn't match up. Within the first few months of operation, although the staff was friendly and tried to be helpful, it was clear that management systems were still under development—resulting in numerous communication problems, omissions, and errors. Perhaps these are just teething pains. ✉ *Mosi-Oa-Tunya Rd., Livingstone.* ☎ *03/32–1122,* Ⅸ *03/32–1128,* 🌐 *www.suninternational.co.za. 173 rooms. Restaurant, bar, pool, room service, hair salon, gift shop. AE, DC, MC, V. CP.*

$$$$ 🔝 **Thorntree Camp.** A swimming pool with sunken bar and underwater seats and a water hole where elephants, waterbucks, and other game come to drink are the highlights of this friendly lodge. Rooms are in separate thatch-and-stone or wood chalets overlooking the river. Reservations are made through Safari Par Excellence in Johannesburg. ✉ *Nakatindi Rd.,* ☎ *03/32–3349; 011/781–3851 for reservations. 8 chalets. 2 bars, pool. MC, V. FAP.*

$$$$ 🔝 **Tongabezi.** The standard rooms here are soothing and spacious ★ cream-and-ocher rondavels (round, thatched huts) featuring magnificent verandas that can be enclosed in a billowing mosquito net. For real luxury, though, little can beat the three suites built into a low cliff and protruding into the riverine forest canopy. Each one is private, extensive, and open to the elements, with king-size beds set in tree trunks and covered by curtains of linen netting. But the bathrooms are the pièces de résistance—virtually on the level of the river and open to it on three sides. If you want to be an African queen or king, this is the place. On arrival you'll be assigned a smiling personal valet who will handle all your room service, escort you to your room at night, and generally look after you. The lodge has a satellite camp downriver, on

exclusive Sindabezi Island, that's a tad more primitive but beautifully remote. ⊠ *Box 31, Livingstone,* ☏ *03/32–4450, 097/77–0917, or 097/77–0918,* FAX *097/84–0920. 5 suites, 5 cottages. Pool, tennis court, boating. MC, V. FAP.*

$$$ 🖻 **Chundukwa Tree Lodge.** The four chalets at Chundukwa, standing on tall stilts right in the river, have catwalks leading you into a canopy of waterberry trees. The wooden A-frame bedrooms are quite small and very simply furnished and open onto the river for a rustic experience. The ambience here is created by people who live and walk in the bush, and, indeed, Chundukwa is used largely as a base for walking safaris into the Kafue National Park and for horseback-riding excursions led by lodge guides through the woodland and along the river. ⊠ *Box 61160, Livingston,* ☏ *03/32–4452 in Livingstone; 011/794–1446 in Johannesburg,* FAX *03/32–4006. 4 chalets. Bar, pool, horseback riding. MC, V. FAP.*

$$$ 🖻 **Zambezi Sun.** Part of the same complex as the Royal Livingstone, this hotel is less expensive, less pretentious, and a whole lot more welcoming than its pricier cousin. The design borrows freely from a variety of (mostly African) cultures and is vibrant and fun. The buildings are earth red and round cornered, blending in with the surroundings, and the decor is wildly colorful. Rooms are decorated in bright primary-color murals, and the spacious bathrooms have colorful tiles and handmade basins. The hotel is cheerful and child-friendly, with family rooms and a play center. Although the Zambezi Sun doesn't share the Livingstone's fantastic view, it's even closer to the falls (which is walking distance from both hotels). ⊠ *Mosi Oa Tunya Rd., Livingstone,* ☏ *03/32–1122; 27/11/780–7444 for reservations,* FAX *27/11/780–7449 or 27/11/780–7061,* WEB *www.suninternational.co.za. 212 rooms. 2 restaurants, bar, pool, wading pool, cabaret, baby-sitting, children's programs, nursery, playground, meeting rooms. AE, DC, MC, V. CP.*

$$–$$$ 🖻 ⚠ **Kubu Cabins.** This lovely lodge, about 43 km (27 mi) above the falls and 26 km (16 mi) from Livingstone, is a winner, especially if you'd like to keep an eye on expenses. Although not as opulent as many of the other riverside lodges, it's not lacking in style and has a refreshing informality. The bar and dining room are on a huge, thatched wooden platform suspended over the river. Accommodations are in small teak cabins with private bath or in gorgeous tents right on the river's edge. The tents have a much better view, are basically furnished, and have open-air bathrooms with chemical toilets and bucket showers with loads of hot water. Meals are simple, well cooked, and well presented. There is also a campsite. Some tents lack a little privacy (auditory more than visual), so if you want to hear only the birds and the hippos, ask for one farther from the campsite. A sundowner cruise is offered. ☏ FAX *03/32–4091,* WEB *www.zambiatourism.com/kubu. 5 cabins, 6 tents, campsite. Restaurant, bar, pool. MC, V. MAP.*

$–$$ 🖻 **Jungle Junction.** If you miss the vibe of California and Marrakesh in the 1960s and '70s, you'll love Jungle Junction. Set on its own tropical island in the Zambezi 56 km (35 mi) upstream from the falls, this is the place to chill out. Take a good book or an excellent companion. Accommodations are in snazzy but basic huts, and there are hot showers and flush toilets, good food, and better coffee than most of the upmarket lodges serve. Swimming pools are sections of the river blocked off with rustic poles, and there are hammocks scattered all over in beautiful spots. Warning: "island time" operates here, and this place is totally unsuitable for the staid or conservative. The longer you stay, the cheaper your nightly rates gets, and the fifth night is free. The rates include all meals, guided walks, village visits, and dugout excursions but do not include drinks. ⊠ *P.O. Box 61122, Livingstone,* ☏ *03/32–4127 or 03/32–3708. 15 huts. Restaurant, bar, 2 pools. MC, V. FAP.*

$ 🏠 ⚠ **Waterfront.** Owned and run by Safari Par Excellence, this is a vibrant place with a young crowd where the emphasis is on rafting, bungee jumping, microlighting (flying in superlight aircraft), and other sports. Accommodations range from inexpensive camping (US$5) to comfortable chalets with private bath. ✉ *Sichanga Rd. just off Mosi-oa-Tunya Rd.; reservations through Safari Par Excellence in Johannesburg,* ☎ *011/781–3851. 21 chalets, 30 tents, 20 campsites. Restaurant, 2 bars, 2 pools, travel services. MC, V. EP.*

Shopping

Kubu Crafts. If you fall in love with the furniture in your lodge, visit this stylish home decor shop. Locally made furniture in hardwood and wrought iron is complemented by a selection of West African masks and weavings and the work of numerous local artists, including the fantastic oil paintings of Stephen Kapata. There are two outlets in town and a smaller one planned at the airport. Shipping can be arranged anywhere in the world—even for items as large as an eight-seat dining table. ✉ *Stanley House, 67B Mosi-oa-Tunya Rd.; 133 Mosi-oa-Tunya Rd.;* ☎ *03/32–4093,* WEB *www.kubucrafts.com.*

Mukuni Craft Market. At the entrance to the falls view sites, this market has substantial stalls where you can find stone and wood carvings and simple bead and semiprecious stone jewelry at better prices than across the river in Zimbabwe. This is a place to bargain; you'll be quoted top dollar, but shop around and watch the prices drop. ☉ *Daily 6 AM–7 PM.*

Outdoor Activities and Adventures

Livingstone is one of the best places in the world for adrenaline junkies and outdoor enthusiast to indulge their wildest fantasies. Most Victoria Falls activities are better from this side of the river, but the Zimbabwean bank does offer some unique attractions, too, so don't overlook those. You can book all these trips directly with the operators, let your hotel or lodge handle all activities, or book through **Safari Par Excellence** (☎ 03/32–1629). If your time is limited, or you just want to go wild, you might consider one of this company's trip combinations. The "Big Day Out" (US$325), for instance, consists of rafting, river boarding, jet boating, and a helicopter trip up the gorge, finishing with a bungee jump. You can mix and match these to your own design. One of the most popular is the "Raft-Heli" (US$190), which saves you a bit of a walk and offers a spectacular view of the gorge; it's also an excellent value, working out to be cheaper than booking a rafting trip and helicopter ride separately. "Heli-Jet" (US$170) involves no strenuous walking. You helicopter in, jet-boat, and then helicopter out. You can substitute tandem kayaking for rafting (at a greater cost) in all the combos, unless you want to do river boarding.

ABSEILING (RAPPELLING) AND GORGE SWINGING

For something completely different, **Abseil Zambia** (☎ 03/32–3454) offers abseiling (it's the local term for rappelling) into one of the dry gorges. It's 90 meters (300 ft) to the bottom, and you can do it as often as you like (remembering that you have to walk out each time). This is a full- or half-day activity that includes lunch, snacks, and two other rather unusual activities. One is the gorge swing—a high-level Superman flying-type thing on a cable across the gorge, and the other is a giant swing on climbing ropes into the gorge. (The rope is attached to the center of another cable stretched across the gorge.) It's similar to a bridge jump. It's US$95 for a full day and US$80 for a half day.

AVIATION

Batoka Sky (☎ 03/32–0058, FAX 03/32–4071) offers microlighting trips and fixed-wing flights over the falls and/or the game reserve, and helicopter flights over the falls and through the gorges. Prices range from about US$50 to US$200, depending on length of flight and aircraft.

BUNGEE JUMPING

Bungee jumping off the 111-meter-high (340-ft-high) Victoria Falls Bridge with **Africa Extreme** (☎ 03/32–4156) is a major adrenaline rush. The view is pretty spectacular, too. It costs US$90.

CANOEING

A gentle canoeing trip on the upper Zambezi is a great opportunity to see birds and a variety of game. It costs between US$70 and US$85 for a half day and US$80 and US$95 for a full day. Multiday trips are also available. **Bundu Adventures** (☎ 03/32–4407) offers half- and full-day trips. **Makoro Quest** (☎ 03/32–1679) is one of the oldest upper Zambezi canoe operators on the Zambian side. They offer half-, full-, and multiday trips. If you're staying at **Tongabezi,** you can canoe straight from your lodge. **Chundukwa Adventure Trails** (☎ 03/32–4156) offers multiday trips (US$180 per person, per night, all inclusive). You can also book through its Johannesburg agents (☎ 011/794–1446).

GAME VIEWING

The game viewing around Livingstone is not bad, and you may see white rhino in the Mosi-oa-Tunya Park, although the Zambezi National Park, across the river in Zimbabwe, is better. An even better option is to join a one-day excursion to Chobe National Park in Botswana with **Makoro Quest** (☎ 03/32–1679). The trip includes transfers from Livingstone, a game drive, a boat cruise, and all meals. Trips cost about US$130. You need to buy a reentry visa in Livingstone before you leave on this trip, but the cost is negligible—it's paid in kwacha and amounts to a couple of dollars, and the tour operator will probably organize it.

HORSEBACK RIDING

You can take a gentle horseback ride through the bush along the banks of the Zambezi with **Chundukwa Adventure Trails** (☎ 03/32–4156). If you know what you're doing, you may watch game from horseback or do a multiday trail trip (US$180 per person, per night).

JET BOATING

If you want some thrills and speed but rafting seems a bit daunting, or you can't face the walk in and out, you'll probably enjoy jet boating with **Jet Extreme** (☎ 03/32–1375)—you can be driven to the start and flown out from the end by helicopter, or helicopter in both ways. It costs US$60 for 45 minutes. This trip can be combined with a rafting excursion.

KAYAKING

If you're feeling brave, try tandem kayaking. You do the same rapids as the rafting trips but in a two-seat kayak with a guide. This is not for the faint of heart or, strangely, the big and macho—there's a weight limit of 80–90 kilos (175–200 pounds), although the limit may change depending on which guides are available. This trip costs US$140 and is offered by **Safari Par Excellence** (☎ 03/32–1629).

RAFTING

The Batoka Gorge, below the falls, has the best one-day white-water rafting in the world. It's big and wet and scary but very well run. **Safari Par Excellence** (☎ 03/32–1629), operating from the Waterfront lodge, is the biggest operator. They offer an "elite" rafting trip for US$115—the transport is more comfortable, the refreshments are nicer, there is a maximum of six passengers per raft, and you are guaranteed veteran guides (they have a minimum of five years' experience). Most operators offer rafting excursions that cost US$85 for either a full- or half-day trip, that includes a one-day visa if you're crossing the border to do it. This involves a steep walk in and out—if you want to avoid walking out, you can do a helicopter-and-rafting combination trip. Similar, equally well run trips are offered from the Zimbabwean side of the river, with minor differences.

RIVER BOARDING

For something completely different, try river boarding with **Serious Fun** (☎ 03/32–3912). It's a weird and wacky experience. You stop at suitable rapids on the rafting trip and (still clad in helmet and life jacket), hop on a body board, and surf the standing waves. It costs about US$115.

Side Trip from Livingstone: Kafue National Park

Kafue is Zambia's oldest and largest game reserve, lying midway between the capital, Lusaka, and the copper belt, and yet it is largely undeveloped, with only a handful of lodges and camps. It was also fairly neglected until a few years ago, allowing poachers to have a field day hitting mostly the elephants, which are now bad tempered and largely tuskless. Huge herds can, however, be seen around the massive Itezhi Tezhi Dam on the Kafue River. Just about all of Africa's savanna species can be viewed here, including some special ones such as stately sable and the even more regal and rare roan (second in size only to the eland), the elsewhere uncommon Defassa waterbuck, and the endemic Kafue lechwe.

Kafue becomes virtually inaccessible in the wet summer season (from late October to late April), but if you go from late June to late October, you are in for a treat.

LODGING

$$$–$$$$ ⚠ **Chundukwa Adventure Trails.** There are a number of lodges in the park, but the easiest, and possibly the best, way to see this immense reserve is on a walking safari with Doug Evans's Chundukwa Adventure. You base yourself at either Zebra Camp or the slightly more expensive Nanzhila Camp. Both are tented camps with private bush showers and flush toilets. Every now and then in Africa you get to meet true sons of the bush, and Doug is one. He might serve you lunch out of plastic containers, but once he's in the bush, his composure and knowledge are awe inspiring. If walking doesn't excite you, you can opt to stay in one place and do only vehicle safaris. ⊠ *P.O. Box 61160, Livingstone,* ☎ *03/32–4452 in Livingstone; 011/794–1446 in Johannesburg,* 𝖥𝖠𝖷 *03/32– 4006,* 𝖶𝖤𝖡 *www.zambiatourism.com/chundukwa. MC, V.*

Livingstone A to Z

To research prices, get advice from other travelers, and book travel arrangements, visit www.fodors.com.

AIR TRAVEL

Nationwide and SA Airlink fly regularly from Johannesburg. Depending on your routing, it may be more convenient to fly into Victoria Falls in Zimbabwe, as most of the lodges regularly do transfers across the border. But be aware that this may result in extra visa expenses, unless you're planning to spend some time in Vic Falls, anyhow.

➤ AIRLINES & CONTACTS: **Nationwide** (☎ 03/32–4575). **SA Airlink** (☎ 03/32–4266).

CAR RENTAL

The roads are appalling—with more potholes than tar in some places. You don't need a four-wheel drive but it's not a bad idea, especially if you want to travel farther afield. Imperial Car Rental operates from the offices of Voyagers at the Falls Entertainment Center near the Zambezi Sun. Foley's 4x4 Hire rents out Land Rovers, fully equipped with tents and other camping equipment.

➤ LOCAL AGENCIES: **Foley's 4x4 Hire** (☎ 03/32–0888 or 011/20–8228, FAX 03/32–0887, WEB www.4x4hireafrica.com). **Imperial Car Rental** (☎ 03/32–2753, FAX 03/32–0277).

CAR TRAVEL

From Kazangula in Botswana you can drive on tarred roads to Victoria Falls; from there it's a short drive across the bridge into Livingstone. Or you can drive direct from the Zambian side of Kazangula, on a dreadful road, but it saves you visa costs. If you are driving this route, buy as much fuel as you can in Botswana, where it's pretty cheap—it's hard to come by in Zimbabwe and expensive in Zambia. From Lusaka or Chirundu, on the Zimbabwean border downstream, you can drive via the small farming town of Mazabuka, which is about halfway.

EMERGENCIES

Your best chance of receiving proper medical care for minor injuries, a test for suspected malaria, or treatment for non-life-threatening ailments is at surgeon Dr. Shafik's clinic. For more serious problems you'll need to be transported to Johannesburg; contact MARS (Medical Air Rescue Services).

➤ MEDICAL CLINIC: **Shafik Clinic** (⊠ JJ Lowe Flats, 49 Akapelwa St., ☎ 03/32–1130).
➤ OTHER EMERGENCIES: **General Emergency** (☎ 999). **Police** (☎ 03/32–0116). **Fire** (☎ 03/32–4043). **MARS** (**Medical Air Rescue Services;** ☎ 263/91/23–5620 or 263/91/21–9477 [Zimbabwean mobile phone lines], or 263/13–4646 [Victoria Falls landline], or radio Channel 3). If you phone these numbers from a Zimbabwean mobile phone, you don't need the international code (263), but you must add a 0—you just dial 091 or 013 and then the number.

TELEPHONES

Livingstone, just across the border from Victoria Falls in Zimbabwe, has much cheaper telephone rates. So check the listed numbers very carefully as some are Zimbabwean mobile phones. They usually have the code 011, which is the same as Johannesburg in South Africa, where many Zambian operators have booking offices. Fortunately, Zimbabwean mobiles have six-digit numbers, and Johannesburg landlines have seven-digit numbers. You must dial Zambia's exit code, 00, to access these numbers if you are calling from within Zambia. If you are phoning these numbers from the country they're in, drop the country code (263 for Zimbabwe and 27 for South Africa) and add an initial 0 to the area (or mobile) code. Also note that if you are phoning these numbers from inside Zambia from a landline or Zambian mobile, you need to add the Zimbabwean code, but not if you're phoning from a Zimbabwean mobile (which will work in Livingstone, as if it were in Zimbabwe). Most Livingstone residents and businesses use a Zimbabwean mobile phone for calls to Zimbabwe and for all their other international calls.

VISITOR INFORMATION

➤ TOURIST OFFICE: **Zambia National Tourist Board** (⊠ Mosi-oa-Tunya Rd., ☎ 03/32–1404 or 03/32–1405, FAX 03/32–1487, WEB www.zambiatourism.com).

South and North Luangwa

The Luangwa River flows, turns, and curls back on itself, sometimes with great certainty, at others with reticence, as it loses itself in oxbow lakes, backwaters, and weed-covered ponds. As it evaporates in the withering winter sun, the surfaces of the wide pans crack. The cold wind that sweeps down from the distant escarpment blows dust, a fish eagle's feather, and dried mopane leaves over the bleached bones of a buffalo that went to feed other drought-hungry mouths. Thousands of hippos and crocodiles have to crowd into the main channel or remain entombed in the cracked, gray mud of the rapidly desiccating floodplain. This wide floor is the southernmost extension of the Great Rift Valley, terminating where the river finally loses itself in the greater force of the Zambezi.

For centuries, even millennia, game teemed around the river, while humans were a tentative presence kept at bay by mosquitoes, tsetse flies, and the extremes of flood and drought—plus the untamable savagery of this wilderness. In 1938, when young Norman Carr was sent here from the colonial office in Lusaka as the new reserve's first ranger, he found a wildlife paradise hardly changed from the past, and today it remains much the same. It has had its problems, like the total demise of its black rhino population in the 1980s through poaching. Still it abounds with herds of elephants, buffalo, pukus, zebras, and Thornicroft's giraffes. The park was created primarily to protect this endemic subspecies of giraffe. And after them came the predators—the lions, hyenas, wild dogs, and leopards for which the park has become famous.

South and North Luangwa national parks are administered separately and have very different characters. Although South Luangwa is rather wild and really very unspoiled, North Luangwa is just wild—really wild. This is the Africa that Hemingway and Ruark wrote about. You are unlikely to see any other tourists in the park while you're there, but buffalo are ubiquitous, and so are lions, who love buffalo meat. There are leopards and hyenas, too, and tsetse flies, so take a can (or three) of insect repellent. It's so wild here, you might see leopards on a kill while you're on foot—it's a thrilling place all 'round.

Although some of the lodges will accept credit cards, they are rather remote and will almost certainly add a service charge. They all prefer cash.

As strange as it sounds, one of the easiest ways of getting to Luangwa is from Lilongwe in Malawi, so you might consider that as an approach.

Lodging

$$$$ 🏠 **Buffalo Camp.** On the banks of the Mwaleshi River, Buffalo Camp has fantastic views of the floodplain where game come to drink in the dry season. The camp is simply built from reeds and thatch, with twin beds, mosquito nets, and private bathrooms. The emphasis here is on being out in the bush, not on decor. The nearby Base Camp is used in conjunction with Buffalo Camp to accommodate larger groups. The food, in tune with the accommodations, is more honest subsistence than cuisine. The daily routine is usually a long walk in the morning, with two armed guides, and a drive in the afternoon. You can opt to stay at Base Camp on a self-catering basis (US$50 per person), but you'll still have guides to look after you in the bush. If you are doing a fly-in safari with Shiwa Safaris, you will spend a night or two at Kapishya Hot Springs, on the Harveys' Shiwa Ngandu estate with its impressive English-style manor house. ⊠ *Zambian Safari Co., Box 30093, Lusaka,* ☎ *01/22–8682; 01/22–8683 in Lusaka. 10 huts. AE, DC, MC, V. FAP.*

$$$$ 🏠 **Kaingo.** Kaingo means "leopard," which immediately puts pressure
★ on owner-manager-guide Dereck Shenton to produce; luckily, he very often does, as he is the son of a park warden and grew up in the bush. The lodge is in a beautiful ebony grove, and the main *chitenge* (outdoor dining area) is supported by a stout lead-wood trunk. Unlike most other camps and lodges in Luangwa, that have either tents or pole-and-reed structures, this lodge has solid, earth-tone thatched bungalows with

private bathrooms. Just upriver of camp is a hide on a meander where you can spend hours watching the hippos (often hundreds), crocodiles, birds, and other game that come to drink on the sandbanks. The atmosphere at Kaingo reflects the host; it's superbly laid back but highly professional. And, of course, it's all about game, of which there is in profusion. Eight kilometers (five miles) from Kaingo is Mwamba, a small walking camp. Three reed-and-thatch chalets there have hot water, flush toilets, and solar lights. ⊠ *Box 57, Mfuwe,* ☎ *062/4–5064 June–Nov.; 053/6–2188 Nov.– May,* 𝖥𝖠𝖷 *01/29–5546. 5 chalets. Bar. V. FAP. Closed Nov.–May.*

$$$$ 🏠 **Kapani.** Lush lawns lead to Kapani's main buildings, done in a style that might best be described as African-lodge-meets-Spanish-American-hacienda; the terra-cotta walls vividly complement the bright green gardens. Bedroom units are set far apart in semiformal gardens and contain large double beds draped with mosquito net, and each has a white-tile bathroom. Because this is partially a family home, guests may get the feeling they are being treated as outsiders at a family gathering rather than being fawned over as at most other lodges. However, there is no faulting the food or service. The real business of Kapani, as with most other lodges, is the three bush camps that they run in the north of the park; you can walk through the bush with expert guides and get to know it intimately. Another highlight is brunch served on the deck hanging above a perennial pan—perfect after an early morning drive. There is a service charge for noncash payments. ⊠ *Box 100, Mfuwe,* ☎ *062/4–5015,* 𝖥𝖠𝖷 *062/4–5025,* 𝖶𝖤𝖡 *www.normancarrsafaris.com. 8 suites. V. FAP.*

$$$$ 🏠 **Mwaleshi Camp.** Remote Africa Safaris, who operate Tafika, run this a grass-and-pole bush camp in North Luangwa. Electricity is all solar, and although each hut does have its own flush toilet and hand basin, showers are communal (but they do have good views). The rate does not include transfers—US$150 per person by air or US$50 per person by vehicle. Vehicle transfer is long, hard, uncomfortable, and not recommended. ⊠ *P.O. Box 5, Mfuwe,* ☎ *062/4–5018 or 870/76127–5398 (satellite phone, operational GMT 4:30 to 17:00),* 𝖥𝖠𝖷 *062/4–5059 or 871/76127–5399 (satellite fax, operational GMT 4:30 AM–5 PM),* 𝖶𝖤𝖡 *www.tecc.co.uk/bbs/remote/remote.htm. 5 chalets. V. FAP. Closed Nov.–mid-June.*

$$$$ 🏠 **Tafika.** Tafika is nestled in the shade of huge lead-wood trees on the banks of the Luangwa River. The wood-and thatch chalets have private toilets and open-air showers. Tafika offers a few out-of-the-ordinary options. In the rainy season, usually February and March, you can canoe among the crocodiles and hippos on the Luangwa River when there are few other people about. In the dry season go mountain biking among the leopards and wild dogs (seriously, these options are available and are escorted by experienced, armed rangers). Microlight flights are also offered, as are the usual walking and driving safaris. At press time the satellite Chikoko Bush Camp was near completion. It will have three chalets, each raised approximately 3 meters on stilts and with private flush toilets and hand basins. There will be two communal showers. It will be a slightly more rustic, less expensive option. ⊠ *P.O. Box 5, Mfuwe,* ☎ *062/4–5018 or 870/76127–5398 (satellite phone, operational GMT 4:30 AM–5 PM),* 𝖥𝖠𝖷 *062/4–5059 or 871/76127–5399 (satellite fax, operational GMT 4:30 AM–5 PM),* 𝖶𝖤𝖡 *www.tecc.co.uk/bbs/remote/remote.htm. 5 chalets. V. FAP. Closed Dec.–Feb. 9 and Apr. 11–May 14.*

$$$$ 🏠 **Tena Tena.** This is the main base of Robin Pope Safaris, one of the
  ★   most respected walking guides in South Luangwa. Safari tents with reed walls and private bathrooms are set beneath large riverine trees. When the weather's good—which is most of the time—meals are laid out on a long table under the trees with a view of the big river. Although RP Safaris operates three very fine and intimate lodges in the park (including

the park's original safari camp at Nsefu), the ultimate South Luangwa experience is a walking safari. Options range from 5 to 12 nights and use a combination of the lodges and smaller, primitive bush camps. Another option from Tena Tena is a day or overnight visit to nearby Kawaza village, where you can partake in village life, be entertained by tribal dances and folklore, and join in the day-to-day activities. ✉ *Box 80, Mfuwe,* ☎ *062/4–5090,* FAX *062/4–5051,* WEB *www.robinpopesafaris.net. 6 tents. No credit cards. FAP. Closed Nov.–Mar.*

$ ☆ **Flatdogs.** If you're driving yourself and counting your pennies, or
★ if socializing is more important to you than luxury and seclusion, this friendly camp just across the Luangwa River from the park is your best option. The bar is fun and is frequented by interesting locals, especially on Friday night, when it can get a bit loud. This isn't just a party venue, though. Game viewing is taken very seriously. You can take your own vehicle into the park (US$15 for 24 hours) or Flatdogs has day and night drives, game walks into the park, and a nature trail outside the park with experienced rangers (all US$25 each). An all-day drive into the park, including picnic, is US$60. Chalets have kitchens, or you can opt to have meals included in your lodging rates. A couple, with all meals, two game drives, and one escorted walk per day, would pay a total of US$260–US$295. This is the only really child-friendly option in Luangwa. Only e-mail reservations are accepted. ✉ *P.O. Box 100, Mfuwe,* ☎ *No phone,* WEB *www.campafrica.com. 3 two-room chalets, 1 three-room chalet, camping. Restaurant, bar, pool, shop, recreation room, baby-sitting. MC, V. EP.*

Lower Zambezi National Park

This is Zambia's newest park and is relatively undeveloped, having previously been part of a much larger game-management and hunting area. Its main attraction is the wide floodplain, where tall trees create a park-like setting. Focal points of the park are the mighty river, the towering *Faidherbia albida* (winterthorn trees or acacia), and the elephants that go ga-ga for their apple-ring seedpods. There are also healthy populations of lions and hyenas here, as well as creatures of the river: birds, hippos, and crocs. Sometimes elephant herds 100 strong move through the riverine forest and along the reed beds at the water's edge (and sometimes through the camps). Waterbucks are the most common antelope, and there are also plenty of impalas, zebras, kudus, and buffalo. There are no public facilities, so visitors invariably stay in one of the safari lodges.

This park is on the Zambian side of the Zambezi, right opposite Zimbabwe's Mana Pools National Park, and one of the best ways of seeing it is to canoe down the river on an escorted safari.

Lodging

$$$$ ☆ **Kayila.** About 45 km (27 mi) downstream from Chirundu, opposite Mana Pools National Park, Kayila has a central dining area on higher ground that affords fantastic views of the river and the escarpment. Accommodations are in twin-bedded stone-and-thatch chalets with private showers and toilets. The honeymoon suite has a large sunken bath, and there is a tree house. Make a point of visiting the unique toilet built in a huge, hollowed-out baobab tree. Short canoeing trips are available at extra cost for those not on a canoe safari. ✉ *Box 61009, Livingstone,* ☎ *03/32–3349,* FAX *03/32–3542. 4 chalets, 1 suite, 1 tree house. Bar, dining room, pool. AE, DC, MC, V. FAP. May be closed in Feb.*

$$$$ ☆ **Mwambashi.** This camp is used mainly for Safari Par Excellence's Great Zambezi Trail canoe trips. But even hydrophobics will have a good time if all they want to do is see animals from the safety of a game-

drive vehicle. There are eight large safari tents set under giant winterthorns, with private bathrooms (shower only) under canvas. The camp itself combines adventure with a slow-paced but close-to-nature experience. The food is pleasantly varied, with Thai green curries and tasty stir-fries. Short canoeing trips are available at extra cost for those not on a canoe safari. ⊠ *Box 61009, Livingstone,* ☎ *03/32–3349,* FAX *03/32–3542. 8 tents. Bar. AE, DC, MC, V. FAP.*

\$–\$\$ 🏠 **Lower Zambezi River Camp.** This is by far the most affordable option if you're driving yourself. Accommodations are in twin-bedded tented structures on raised platforms with private shower and toilet. A thatched bar and dining room overlook the river, and there is a campsite (US\$15 per person). Meals are available at US\$10 for breakfast, US\$15 for lunch, and US\$25 for a three-course dinner. All reservations are through the Durban office in South Africa. ⊠ *Box 35196, Northway, Durban 4065, South Africa,* ☎ *27/31/563–9774,* FAX *27/31/563–1957,* WEB *www.kiambi.co.za. 8 tents. Bar, dining room, pool. MC, V. EP.*

Outdoor Activities

CANOEING SAFARIS

In addition to the companies below, **Kiambi Safaris,** based at the Lower Zambezi River Camp, offers canoe trails ranging from a half-day paddle from the camp (US\$50 per person) to a five-night camping, three-day canoeing expedition (US\$448 per person, all inclusive).

River Horse Safaris. River Horse is based in Kariba, in Zimbabwe, but operates on the Zambian side. The trip is broken down into two modules, of which you may choose either one or both. From Kariba to Chirundu is a three-day trip, starting directly below the dam wall. The highlight is the spectacular Kariba Gorge on the first day. The section from Chirundu to Chongwe passes some traditional villages and affords the opportunity to see game from the river. Prices are about US\$100 per person, per day, including food and transfers from Kariba. Transfers can be arranged from Lusaka at about US\$120 per person round-trip. It is a participatory camping trip, which means you put up your own tent and help with cooking. Camping is on deserted islands in the river. ⊠ *Kariba Breezes Hotel, Kariba, Zimbabwe,* ☎ *061/2447 or 061/2422,* WEB *www.riverhorse.co.zw. MC, V.*

Safari Par Excellence. Based at the Mwambashi lodge, Safari Par Excellence offers a choice of two three-night/four-day trips, both of which start at the Kafue Confluence and end at Chongwe. The "Island Canoe Trail" (US\$450 per person all-inclusive) is a real expedition, in that you canoe from island to island and camp. Walking safaris are not included. The trip is not offered December 1–February 28. The "Great Zambezi Trail" (US\$950 per person all-inclusive), on the other hand, is a luxury soft option. You spend some time canoeing, and in between you are transported by motorboat or safari vehicle. Nights are spent at Kayila and Mwambashi lodges. This trip is not offered November 1–May 15. ⊠ *Box 61009, Livingstone,* ☎ *03/32–3349,* FAX *03/32–3542. 8 tents. Bar. AE, DC, MC, V. FAP.*

Zambia A to Z

To research prices, get advice from other travelers, and book travel arrangements, visit www.fodors.com.

AIR TRAVEL

Zambian Airways flies from all neighboring countries, and all the regional airlines fly from their countries of origin to Lusaka. The best way to get to Zambia is to fly to Johannesburg with South African Airways or some other international carrier and then to Livingstone or

Lusaka with SAA or Nationwide. International carriers include Air Botswana, Air Namibia, British Airways, Nationwide, and South African Airways.

There are a number of charter companies in Zambia, or if you're flying from a neighboring country, you could use a charter company in the country of origin. Airwaves does regular charters, particularly into the Lower Zambezi.

There is a US$5 (also payable in other currencies) departure tax for all internal flights and US$20 (payable only in U.S. dollars) for international flights.

➤ AIRLINES AND CONTACTS: **Air Botswana** (☎ 01/22–7739, FAX 01/22–3724). **Air Namibia** (☎ 061/298–2605, FAX 061/22–1382). **Air Zambia** (☎ 01/22–2350). **Air Zimbabwe** (☎ 01/22–1750, 01/22–5431, or 01/22–4683, FAX 01/22–5540). **British Airways (Comair;** ☎ 01/25–4444 or 01/25–5320). **Nationwide** (☎ 03/32–4575). **South African Airways** (☎ 01/25–4357 or 01/26–1810, FAX 01/26–2836).

CAR TRAVEL

You can enter Zambia by road from Botswana, Namibia, or Zimbabwe. In every case you will need the vehicle's registration papers, a temporary import permit (TIP), or a *Carnet de Passage,* and, if the driver is not the owner, a letter of authorization from the owner. You will need to purchase third-party insurance at the border. If you plan to drive into Zambia, check with your local AAA office before leaving home to find out if any of these conditions have changed. Otherwise, write to the controller of customs and excise. Most borders are open 6–6. Victoria Falls Bridge is open 6 AM–8 PM. The roads are pretty awful and the distances quite long, but Zambia is a friendly place, and reasonably adventurous travelers will enjoy stopping in small, little-visited towns and interacting with the residents.

➤ INFORMATION: **Controller of Customs and Excise** (✉ Box 60500, Livingstone).

EMBASSIES

➤ CANADA: **Canadian Embassy** (✉ 5119 United Nations Ave., Box 31910, Lusaka, ☎ 01/25–0833, FAX 01/25–3895).

➤ EUROPEAN UNION: **European Union Delegation** (✉ Plot 4899, Los Angeles Blvd., Lusaka, ☎ 01/25–0711, 01/25–1140, 01/25–5586, or 01/25–5587, FAX 01/25–0906 or 01/25–2336).

➤ UNITED KINGDOM: **British Embassy** (✉ Independence Ave., Box 50050, Lusaka, ☎ 01/25–1133, FAX 01/25–3798).

➤ UNITED STATES: **United States Embassy** (✉ Corner of United Nations Ave. and Independence Ave., Box 31617, Lusaka, ☎ 01/25–0955, FAX 01/25–2225).

EMERGENCIES

Specialty Emergency Services have offices in all the major centers and can put you in touch with the best-available local medical facilities. In case of a life-threatening emergency, contact MRI in South Africa or MARS in Zimbabwe. You could also try Health International Medical Air Rescue Services in Lusaka.

➤ EMERGENCY NUMBERS: **Health International Medical Air Rescue Services** (☎ 01/25–1163 or 01/25–1371). **MARS (Medical Air Rescue Services;** ☎ 263/91/23–5620, 263/91/21–9477 or 263/13/4646). **MRI (Medical Rescue International;** ☎ 27/11/242–0111). **Specialty Emergency Services** (☎ 097/77–0302 or 097/77–0303 Lusaka; 097/77–0306 or 097/77–0307 Kitwe, Luangwa, Bangweulu; or contact the emergency number in Johannesburg, 27/82/895–5402 [South African mobile]).

MONEY MATTERS

Most hotels accept credit cards, and you can get advances in local currency on your credit card from most banks in the main centers. Barclays and Standard have ATMs, but they give money in Zambian kwachas only.

TOURS

Zambia is a great destination for driving yourself if you have plenty of time, but can be frustrating if you're on a tight schedule. Zambian Safari Company offers standard safaris, which include most of the highlights of this lovely country, concentrating on the more remote game destinations, such as Bangweulu and Luangwa. Trips last from 7 to 21 days, but customized itineraries are available.

➤ SAFARI COMPANIES: **Zambian Safari Company** (⊠ Box 30093, Lusaka, ☎ 01/22–8682 or 01/22–8683).

VISAS

All U.S., Canadian, and British citizens must buy visas to enter Zambia. However, if you are on a prebooked package with a registered tour operator, the visa requirement is waived. Visas may be bought at the point of entry. A single entry or transit visa costs US$25 for Americans and Canadians and £35 for British citizens (£33 if you buy them in London). Canadians and Americans pay US$40 for a double entry visa and US$80 for a multiple entry, while Britons pay £45 for a double/multiple entry. Day-trip visas cost US$10—for example a trip across the river from Victoria Falls or Kariba (this is also waived if you're doing a prebooked trip like rafting or microlighting). If you leave Zambia for less than a day, for example, to do ballooning or elephant riding in Victoria Falls or to go to Chobe, you need a reentry visa (ZK5,000), or you'll have to buy a new visa—at the full price. You must get this before you leave for the trip or as you leave Zambia. If you're doing a organized tour, the operator should take care of it, but double-check anyway. At time of writing, it seemed that day visas would be done away with.

➤ ZAMBIAN MISSIONS ABROAD: **United Kingdom** (⊠ 2 Palace Gate, Kensington, London, ☎ 171/589–6655, FAX 171/581–1353. **United States** (⊠ 2419 Massachusetts Ave. NW, Washington, DC, ☎ 202/265–9717, FAX 202/332–0826).

VISITOR INFORMATION

Zambia National Tourist Board is friendly but not particularly organized. However, its Web site is one of the better travel sites, and they do have some excellent publications.

➤ TOURIST INFORMATION: **Zambia National Tourist Board** (⊠ Century House, Cairo Rd., Box 30017, Lusaka, ☎ 01/22–9087, 01/22–9088, 01/22–9089, or 01/22–9090, FAX 01/22–5174, WEB www.zambiatourism.com).

14 OTHER DESTINATIONS

From the snowy heights of Lesotho to the tropical beaches of Mozambique to the fantastic game in the reserves of Malawi, you'll experience more in these three underestimated destinations than in the rest of southern Africa combined. You can see *dugongs* (similar to manatees) and whale sharks in Mozambique, ice rats in Lesotho, and the Big Five in Malawi.

By Jennifer
Stern

T HE PEOPLE OF Lesotho, Mozambique, and Malawi are friendly and warm and readily welcome visitors, but that's all they have in common. Lesotho is an independent kingdom that has never been colonized, and its people, the Basotho, are the only African people who live in snow part of the year. Mozambicans speak Portuguese as their second language and harvest all manner of seafood from the abundant ocean. Malawians are typical central African people with a subsistence agrarian economy supplemented by lake fishing. Although these three countries are among the poorest in the world, they are rich in natural beauty.

Malawi and Lesotho are among the safest and most stable African countries in which to travel, but their relatively undeveloped infrastructure has discouraged all but adventurous travelers.

Mozambique, on the other hand, was Africa's most developed and popular holiday destination until the beginning of the devastating war of the 1970s and '80s. Since the early '90s this beautiful country has been rebuilding its infrastructure and, despite some dramatic natural setbacks, has some fantastic vacation destinations all along the lovely, long tropical coast.

Lodging

Price categories throughout the chapter are based on the following ranges:

CATEGORY	COST*
$$$$	over US$400
$$$	US$200–US$400
$$	US$100–US$200
$	under US$100

All prices are for a standard double room in hotels or are per-person rates in all-inclusive resorts, including tax.

LESOTHO

Called the Kingdom in the Sky, this tiny country is a constitutional monarchy. It has its origins in the dreadful Mfeqane—the 19th-century period of total destabilization caused, in part, by the empire-building rampages of King Shaka of the Zulus. In 1824, at the height of this chaos, a minor chief called Moeshoeshoe (Mo-*shwe*-shwe) retreated to a steep-sided hill called Thaba Bosiu—the Mountain of the Night—where he fought off all invaders. Moeshoeshoe's tribe, the Bakoena (pronounced Ba-*kwe*-na), and the many refugees he welcomed to his hilltop fortress formed the nucleus of the Basotho nation.

The country is divided into two distinct sections, the Highlands, in the west, and the Lowlands, in the east, the latter a bit of a misnomer as the lowest point of Lesotho is 1,500 m (about 5,000 ft) above sea level. All the towns and villages of any significance are in the Lowlands, and it is here that almost all of Lesotho's food is grown. The Highlands are spectacularly rugged and isolated, populated by hardy people living in isolated communities too small to be called villages.

Exploring Lesotho

The major attraction of Lesotho is the fantastic mountain scenery, and the major activity is horse treks. You can reach most of Lesotho on good tarred roads, but at present you'd need a four-wheel-drive to traverse the country on the rather adventurous back roads.

Lesotho

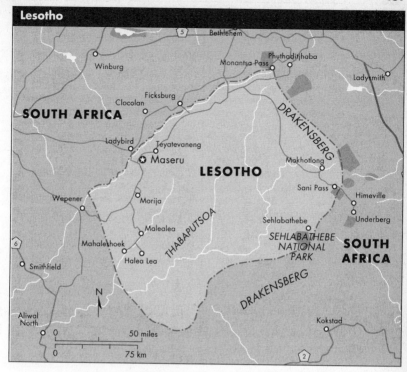

Great Itineraries

IF YOU HAVE 2 DAYS

Drive in through Peka Bridge, and visit the craft centers in Teyateya-neng, then continue to 🏨 **Malealea.** Spend the next day hiking or riding. There are beautiful waterfalls and rock art to see and isolated settlements to visit.

IF YOU HAVE 5 DAYS

Start off as described above, but after one night at Malealea, head off on a multiday horseback-riding trail, traversing the sparsely populated highlands and overnighting in remote villages.

When to Tour Lesotho

The best times to tour Lesotho are spring and autumn. Winter (from May to June) is bitterly cold, the landscape is sere and brown, the air dry and bone chilling, and it often snows. Summer is beautiful and green, but it is the rainy season, and this area is known for absolutely spectacular Technicolor, surround-sound thunderstorms. It *can* snow at any time of year, even midsummer.

Maseru and Teyateyaneng

The capital of Lesotho, Maseru, is a scruffy African town with little to recommend it. However, the nearby town of Teyateyaneng, which is even scruffier, is a crafts center of note.

Lodging

$ 🏨 **Maseru Sun.** Maseru is not really a place you want to spend the night; but, if you must, the Sun is a haven of familiarity and comfort. It could be a standard hotel anywhere in the world with neat, pastel-color rooms furnished with everything you'd expect—TV, tea and coffee stations, phone, and air-conditioning. Every room has two double beds and a balcony overlooking the garden. ⊠ *12 Orpen Rd.,* ☎ *31–2434,* ⨓ *31–0158. 109 rooms, 3 suites. 2 bars, restaurant, pool, sauna, 2 tennis courts, gym, volleyball, shops, casino, business services, meeting rooms, airport shuttle, free parking. AE, DC, MC, V.* ⬛ *www.sunint.co.za.*

Shopping

If you only buy one thing on your trip, make sure it's a Basotho blanket. The wool ones are extremely good quality, warm, and hard wearing. The colors are attractively muted, and designs include stylized maize plants, peanuts, and leopard prints. Cheaper blankets are made from acrylic and are inferior in quality to the wool ones. Note that most stores are closed on Sunday.

You will find blankets all over Lesotho in **Fraser's Trading Stores,** but the best selection will be in Maseru. **Ha Mafafa** (⊠ Kings Way, ☎ 31–2001) is the Maseru branch of Frasers. **Mofuthu oa Kobo** (⊠ Traderect Centre, next to Something Fishy, Kings Way) has a good selection of blankets.

About 19 km (12 mi) north of Maseru is the small settlement of Teyateyaneng, usually called TY, which has many crafts centers that specialize in spinning and weaving.

As you enter TY from the Maseru side, you'll see **Elleloang Basali** (pronounced El-el-*wung* Ba-*sud*-ee) on the left. It's scruffy on the outside, but the craftswomen inside hand-knit fantastic sweaters from hand-spun, hand-dyed mohair (average price about R300). They also weave wall hangings and carpets and will custom-make a weaving to your design. ⊠ *Box 449, Teyateyaneng 200,* ☎ *501–520.* ⊙ *Mon.–Sat. 8–5.*

Just past Elleloang Basali is the turnoff to **Helang Basali,** which is run by the St. Agnes Mission. Follow the road past the mission school and swing left at the church—it's only a few hundred yards off the road. This is the oldest weaving center in TY, and it still carries on the tradition of fine hangings and rugs with some quite innovative designs. They will also make a rug to your design. Prices range from R60 for a small hanging to R4,500 for a carpet about 5 ft by 7 ft in size. ⊠ *Private Bag X30, Teyateyaneng 200,* ☎ *50–1546.* ⊙ *Mon.–Sat. 8–5, Sun. 10–5.*

Malealea

★ *50 km (30 mi) from Maseru, turn left in the village of Motsokua (there is a small, battered sign reading* MALEALEA LODGE). *Follow the Malealea signs. The last 7 km (about 3 mi) are on dirt.*

Malealea is an old trading post that was turned into a low-key guest house in 1986 and is an important part of the local community. Malealea markets pony trails run by the villagers. Local children have formed a band and a choir and perform for lodge guests before supper (donation of minimum R15). The money raised in this way has already built two new classrooms in the village school. They have also cut two CDs, which are sold at the lodge.

There are numerous walks, drives, four-wheel-drive trails, and pony treks from the lodge, which take you to scenic waterfalls, lovely mountain streams with pools, cave paintings, and isolated villages. You could also choose to spend time with the local people, visiting the village and getting to know them and how they live. A visit to a traditional healer is a fascinating experience.

$ ⊞ **Malealea Lodge.** Rooms are scattered around a small plantation of conifers (cedars, cypresses, and pines). The *rondawels* (round houses) are the most comfortable and are decorated on the outside with traditional Sotho designs. Rooms are simple, and some have private bathrooms, but there are budget rooms that share bathrooms and a backpackers' room, which is definitely the least attractive option. The campsite is pretty, nestled under the trees. You can choose to do your own cooking in a communal kitchen if you like, but it's not worth the trouble as the dining here is great. Definitely more hearty home cooking than haute cuisine, it is tasty, well prepared, and plentiful. There are no phones at Malealea. If you bring clothes you're getting a bit tired of, you can give them to staff members as tips. ⊠ *Mailing address: Box 12118 Brandhof, Bloemfontein 9324, South Africa,* ☎ *27/51/447–3200 or 27/82/552–4215,* ☎ FAX *27/51/448–3001,* WEB *www.malealea.co.ls. 34 rooms, 27 with bath; 7 huts. Bar, restaurant, pool, tennis court, hiking, horseback riding, camping, shops, meeting rooms, airport shuttle. MC, V. FAP.*

Outdoor Activities

PONY TREKKING

You can choose to go out for a short day or half-day ride (about R150) or head off into the mountains for up to a week—staying in village huts, which are very simple and basic but clean(ish). You don't need to be a great rider, and if you are nervous, you can hire a child to lead your pony (at about R10 per day). Overnight trails cost about R180 per day plus about R40 per person for accommodations.

During the course of your trek, you'll get to see magnificent mountain scenery, high waterfalls, and ancient rock art. In hot weather you'll be able to stop and swim in cool mountain pools. All booking is through Malealea Lodge.

Morija

30 mi (50 km) south of Maseru.

Morija is considered to be the cultural center of Lesotho. Each October, there is a three or four-day **Morija Arts and Cultural Festival** (WEB www.morijafest.com), with traditional dance, theater, art, pony races, and *marabaraba* (a traditional board game) competitions. There is, quite literally, something for everyone.

The **Morija Museum** is the only museum in Lesotho. It is very small but contains some interesting exhibits. Dinosaur bones and casts of footprints are a small indication of what you might see if you take the trouble to hike up the hill to see the original giant reptile tracks. Interesting displays of traditional clothes and ornamentation are overshadowed by the traditional healer paraphernalia, consisting of all manner of bones, claws, and strange things strung together into somewhat macabre necklaces and bracelets. ⊠ *Main South Rd.,* ☎ FAX *36–0308.* ☒ *R5.* ☉ *Mon.–Sat. 8–5, Sun. noon–5.*

Sani Pass and Sani Top

200 miles (120 km) southeast of Maseru.

Sani Pass is the only southern entry to Lesotho from KwaZulu-Natal, and is a vitally important transportation route. Bearing this in mind, you'll be amazed at how primitive it is; it's little more than a steep mountain track. The attraction here is the view and the friendly people who live in Sani Top Village and Ntaba Ntlenyana—the highest point in southern Africa. The best place to take in the view is over a drink at the **Sani Top Chalet** (☎ 27/33/702–1158 or 27/82/574–5476) which bills itself as the highest pub in southern Africa. There are rustic accomodations here as well, but they're not recommended.

While in Sani Top, you can take a short pony ride, hike up Ntaba Ntlenyana, or just wander round the village taking in the sites and sounds. In winter, there may be snow and you can sometimes ski. There are antique skis for rent at the hotel.

Lesotho A to Z

To research prices, get advice from other travelers, and book travel arrangements, visit www.fodors.com.

AIR TRAVEL

SA Airlink flies between Johannesburg and Maseru three times daily, except Sunday, when there are two flights. Moeshoeshoe I International Airport is 20 km (about 12 mi) south of Maseru.

➤ AIR TRAVEL INFORMATION: **Moshoeshoe I International Airport** (☎ 35-0777). **SA Airlink** (☎ 35-0418 or 35-0419; 27/11/975-2241 in Johannesburg).

CAR TRAVEL

Although most of Lesotho can be reached by standard cars on good tarred roads, it is a great place for a four-wheel-drive safari. Maui Camper Hire, in Johannesburg and other locations in South Africa, is an international company specializing in the rental of off-road vehicles. There is no problem taking cars rented in South Africa into Lesotho. Avis, Budget, and Imperial all have offices at the airport and in Maseru.

➤ CAR TRAVEL INFORMATION: **Avis Car Rental** (☎ 31-4325 during office hrs; 85-7225 after hrs; 35-0328 at airport). **Budget** (☎ 31-6344 or 85-5082, FAX 31-0461). **Imperial Car Hire** (☎ 32-3641; 35-0292 at airport), FAX 35-0299). **Maui Camper Hire** (☎ 011/396-1445 in Johannesburg, FAX 011/396-1757).

GASOLINE

Gas stations in Lesotho are few and far between. You can fill up in Maseru and Buthe Buthe.

ROAD CONDITIONS

If you stick to the main routes, you'll be pleasantly surprised at the condition of the roads, but once off the beaten track, you'll be in rough territory.

EMERGENCIES

For serious emergencies contact MRI (Medical Rescue International) or leave Lesotho and head to South Africa: Johannesburg is about a four-hour drive from Maseru, and Bloemfontein can be reached in less than two hours.

➤ EMERGENCY INFORMATION: **MRI** (☎ 0027/11/242-0242—this is written exactly as it should be dialed from Lesotho).

HEALTH

Lesotho is malaria free.

LANGUAGE

The official language of Lesotho is Sesotho, but many people speak at least some English.

MONEY MATTERS

The currency of Lesotho is the Loti (plural Maloti), which is linked to the South African rand. You can use rands in Lesotho quite freely.

PASSPORTS AND VISAS

ENTERING LESOTHO

At time of writing, Lesotho did not require visas from any visitors. If you need a visa for South Africa, ensure that you obtain a multiple-entry visa before entering Lesotho.

TELEPHONES

The phone system in Lesotho is erratic, and you may have trouble placing calls from standard phones; however, cell phones work in the Lowlands. The country code for Lesotho is 266. There are no area codes.

TIPPING

Tipping is appreciated throughout Lesotho. At Malealea you can give clean used clothes in good condition as tips.

VISITOR INFORMATION

The Lesotho Tourist Board has been incorporated into the Ministry of Tourism. It has an excellent information bureau in Maseru, opposite the Basotho Hat, that is open weekdays from 8 to 5 and Saturday from 9 to 1. Di Jones, of Malealea, is a mine of information.

➤ INFORMATION: **Ministry of Tourism** (✉ Kings Way, ☎ 31–9485).

MOZAMBIQUE

If there were an awards ceremony for countries, Mozambique would win the vote for resilience and grace under extraordinary pressure. After 20 years of a terrible war, two cyclones, and devastating floods, this beautiful country is bouncing back. The scenery is breathtaking—long, tranquil tropical beaches backed by dense African bush. The people are warm and friendly, and the pace decidedly laid-back. The diving and fishing are fantastic, and the seafood is almost obscene in its quantity and quality.

Pleasures and Pastimes

Arts and Crafts

Try to be in Maputo on a Saturday, when the Praça 25 Junho (25th June Square) is covered wall to wall with curio sellers. Here you will find something a little different from the run-of-the-mill souvenirs you see everywhere else. Multicolor, tall, thin birds are almost Bali-like in their style, and boxes ranging from tiny trinket holders to enormous linen chests are well made and inexpensive. You'll find helicopters made from wood or wire with battery-operated propellers that actually go round. In fact, helicopters are a popular craft subject in southern Africa, and there is a amazing variety of them almost everywhere. Do look out for the poignant and well-executed Rosa tableaus: sculpted in the style of a nativity, these depict the girl who was born in a tree during the floods of 2000. Madonna-like, the mother clutches the child to her breast at the top of the tree, and in the background a helicopter and rescue worker.

Dining

If you come to Mozambique solely for the seafood, you won't be disappointed: enormous prawns, giant lobsters, rock oysters, freshwater prawns, langoustines, shrimp, calamari, and, of course, a huge range of fish are commonplace. In even relatively grubby little pubs, you may find prawns on the counter as bar snacks. But there is more to food here than just fish. Tropical fruits grow in profusion, and Mozambique produces a large proportion of the world's cashew nuts. You can buy them raw, roasted and salted, or—you have to try this—roasted with

Mozambique

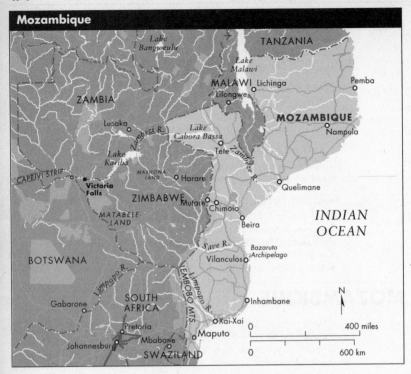

peri-peri. You'll also find peri-peri (a spicy garlic and chili concoction) on a range of other foods such as prawns, fish, and chicken.

Diving
Coral reefs dot the coast like a rosary, and there are some rocky reefs here, too. You're likely to see all the usual tropical fish plus some species, and even families, such as the beautiful Moorish idol, that are endemic to the Indian Ocean. Whale sharks are not uncommon; manta rays, eagle rays, and huge game fish are often seen here, too. If you are fly-ing back to Johannesburg, take your no-flying limit very seriously, as Johannesburg is 2,000 m (nearly 7,000 ft) above sea level. August and September are the worst months for diving anywhere along the coast as it is very windy.

Exploring Mozambique

Mozambique is a difficult country to travel in, but it is not unsafe, just a bit disorganized. The roads are shoddy and the service in all but the main tourist areas slow and unreliable. If you have a sense of adven-ture, you could hop on a bus and travel the length of the country, but you'll probably prefer to fly directly to your destination.

Great Itineraries
IF YOU HAVE 2 DAYS
Fly into 🏨 **Maputo,** and stay at either the Hotel Polana or the Rovuma Carlton. Take a tour of the city, visiting the municipal market, where you can stock up on cashew nuts, and the museum, and just soak up the atmosphere of this lovely but somewhat battered city. Fly across to 🏨 **Inhaca Island,** and do a boat trip to Portuguese Island, where you can walk for miles on absolutely deserted snow-white beaches, snorkel, swim in the lagoon, and explore the mangrove forests. The next day fly back to Maputo and catch a flight out.

Start out as described above, but after Inhaca Island fly to **Vilanculos** and transfer to the islands. Then divide your time between snorkeling, diving, fishing, suntanning, going on day trips, and eating seafood.

When to Tour Mozambique

The winter months, from May to July, are lovely—coolish by tropical standards, and there should be little to no rain and very little wind. The malaria risk is also much less at this time of the year. The diving is good, but the water not quite so warm, hovering around the 20°C (70°F) mark. In late February and March there is a small possibility of cyclones, but the weather is great and the diving good. The whale sharks are around in summer, and the humpback whales pass through between June and September.

Querimba Archipelago

The Querimba Archipelago, in the far north of the country, is a fantastic mix of ancient Arab trading centers, local villages, and crystal-clear waters with spectacular coral reefs. Walk through the centuries-old narrow streets of Ibo Island or the historic capital of Cabo Delgado (the northern part of Mozambique), or dive the wonderful reefs of the Matemo or Mejumbe islands.

LODGING

$$$$ 🏨 **M.Y. Fantastique.** The best way to visit the Querimba Archipelago is to take a cruise on this luxury motor yacht. Cruises are five or seven days long and visit the many islands of the archipelago, where you can dive, paddle off to explore small coves and inlets, or visit historic settlements. The stateroom and double cabin have private bathrooms, and the two twins rooms share a bathroom. The price includes everything except flights. ✉ *Reservations: Rani Africa, Box 2682, Witkoppen, Johannesburg 2068, South Africa,* ☎ *00/27/11/465–6904,* FAX *00/27/11/465–8764,* WEB *www.myfantastique.com. 1 stateroom, 3 cabins. Bar, air-conditioning, sauna, dive shop, waterskiing, fishing, airport shuttle. AE, DC, MC, V. FAP.*

Bazaruto Archipelago

As the tide changes, sandbanks appear or disappear, deep azure channels stand out in the pale turquoise water, and turtle-grass beds appear as dark indigo patches. In the evening it all turns a golden pink tinged with purple, as a huge, red sun sets over the African coast. Long, white beaches stretch as far as you can see; behind them, the occasional coconut palm sways in the breeze, and farther back, indigenous scrub gives way to lotus-filled wetlands, seas of rolling white dunes, and permanent freshwater lakes. And just as brilliant-hued birds flit past you on land, brilliant-hued fish flit around the reefs underwater. It's a magical place—a real tropical, African, paradise.

The two main activities in this warm-water playground are diving and fishing. All the hotels here offer both of these activities. Diving prices range from approximately US$35 for a single-tank close dive to US$75 for a double-tank far dive and between US$120 and US$150 for a Discover Scuba course. Escorted snorkeling trips are usually about US$5. Fishing prices range from US$35 for a half-day guided surf-fishing expedition up to US$800 per day (plus US$6 per gallon of fuel) for a marlin boat. Island tours range from US$35 per vehicle or US$30 per person for a one-hour tour to US$70 per person for a four-hour trip and picnic. The above prices are approximate and differ a bit between hotels.

All the hotels offer boat or vehicle excursions to deserted beaches and interesting islands.

Lodging

Note: Most establishments prefer U.S. dollars or S.A. rand, and although they accept credit cards, there is sometimes a delay in obtaining authorization because of erratic communications, so cash is best.

$$$$ ★ Benguerra Lodge. The most stylish of the lodges in the archipelago, the beautiful, open-sided, stilted rooms here nestle in the indigenous forest only yards from the beach. The decor can only be described as *Out of Africa* meets *Lawrence of Arabia*. Opulent soft furnishings and brass filigree work contrasts pleasingly with hand-plastered ocher walls and wooden floors. The bathrooms are a masterpiece in free-form ocher, ceramic basins, and brass fittings. The size of the rooms and the enormous billowing mosquito nets create a feeling of space and light. You could spend all day indoors here—although you'd be crazy to, as there is so much to do. Benguerra has the most established dive operation in the archipelago and has very easy access to Two-Mile Reef, as well as a few others. In addition to the usual fishing, it also has a permanent fly-fishing guide and rents fly-fishing gear. ⊠ *Northern end of Benguerra Island; Reservations: Box 87416, Houghton 2041, Johannesburg, South Africa,* ☎ *27/11/483–2734 or 27/11/483–2735,* FAX *27/11/728–3767,* WEB *www. benguerra.co.za. 13 rooms. Bar, dining room, hiking, beach, dive shop, snorkeling, boating, fishing, shop, airport shuttle, private airstrip. AE, MC, V. FAP.*

$$$$ Marlin Lodge. Simple, attractive wood-and-thatch chalets have lovely balconies with sea views and direct access to the beach. They are joined together by a raised timber walkway that has views of the indigenous scrub behind the lodge. There is a well-equipped dive and fishing operation, and the lodge is close to Two-Mile Reef and Margaruque. ⊠ *Southern end of Benguerra Island; Reservations: Box 15013, Sinoville, Pretoria 0129, South Africa,* ☎ *27/12/543–2134,* FAX *27/12/543–2135,* WEB *www.marlinlodge.co.za. 14 rooms, 3 suites. Bar, dining room, air-conditioning, pool, beach, dive shop, boating, waterskiing, fishing, airport shuttle. AE, DC, MC, V. FAP.*

$$$ Bazaruto Lodge. Ernest Hemingway would have loved this place. There are no frills, neither the staff nor the guests affect any airs and graces, the fishing and dive boats are constantly at work, the bar is lively, and the views are pure tropical paradise. The accommodations are in simple thatch A-frame huts clustered along a sinuous path that meanders through the coconut trees and ilala palms. ⊠ *Northwestern end of Bazaruto Island; Reservations: Box 4376, Maputo,* ☎ *01/30–5000,* FAX *01/30–5305. 25 huts. Bar, dining room, snack bar, fans, pool, hiking, beach, dive shop, snorkeling, boating, fishing, shop, billiards, airport shuttle, helipad. AE, DC, MC, V. FAP.*

$$$ ★ Indigo Bay. If you like the great outdoors and all the comfort of home indoors, this is the right place for you. The rooms have all the comforts of a city hotel; it's the only place on the islands with in-room TVs and hair dryers. This is the newest of the lodges in the archipelago, and no expense has been spared in its construction. An enormous, indigo, infinity-edge pool overlooks the sea and incorporates a large pool bar. The food, consisting mainly of seafood, of course, is wonderful. ⊠ *Southwestern end of Bazaruto Island,* ☎ FAX *023/8–2339, www. indigobayonline.com; Reservations: Rani Africa, Box 2682, Witkoppen, Johannesburg 2068, South Africa,* ☎ *0027/11/465–6904,* FAX *0027/11/465–8764 or Mantis Collection Box 10802 Steenberg Estate, Cape Town 7945, South Africa,* ☎ *0027/21/713–2222,* FAX *0027/21/713–2251,* WEB *www.mantiscollection.com. 50 rooms. Bar, dining room, air-conditioning, saltwater pool, hiking, horseback riding, beach,* *dive shop, snorkeling, boating, fishing, shop, meeting rooms, airport shuttle, private airstrip. AE, DC, MC, V. MAP.*

YACHTS

$$$$
★ 🗺 **Island Castaways.** This luxury yacht outfitter operates up to three sailing catamarans in the archipelago at any one time. Depending on what boat is in the area, it will have anywhere from three to five luxury cabins. All boats have dive gear and full galleys and are staffed by a skipper, a cook, and a dive master. ⊠ ☎ *0027/11/678–0831 or 0027/83/601–7331,* ℻ *0027/11/678–4306,* WEB *www.islandcastaways.co.za. No credit cards. FAP.*

Maputo

Maputo is to South Africans what Havana is to Americans. For many years it was an exotic tropical paradise where the nightlife went on till morning, the fishing was legendary, and the food was fantastic. And like Havana, a conflict—a product of the Cold War—put it out of reach to practically everyone except those who lived there and a few Russian and Cuban advisors. So near yet so far, many younger South Africans yearned to re-create the stories their parents told of carefree days and reckless, steamy, tropical nights.

Well, the war's over, and Maputo is bouncing back. Sure, it's quite obvious that building upkeep was the last thing many people bothered with over the last 30 years, but the city still has some beautiful buildings. Many late-19th- and early 20th-century buildings remain, and there are entire neighborhoods of art deco houses. You could spend days just wandering the streets—there is something fascinating around every corner.

Sights to See

The **Catholic Cathedral,** on Praça da Independência, is a city landmark. Have a look at the wonderful stained-glass windows. It is notable that even during the many years of socialism in Mozambique, churches, cathedrals, and mosques were not damaged.

The **Fortaleza da Nossa Senhora da Conceição,** built between 1851 and 1867, is a squat, stone fortress that formed the nucleus of the colonial town of Lorenço Marques. It is now a museum, mostly depicting Mozambique's colonial history. The impressive equestrian statue of Mouzinho de Albuquerque lords over the lawns that are scattered with ancient cannons lying around like discarded toys. This and other colonial statues have been moved here from positions of prominence in the city. And in state lie the remains of Ngungunhane, the last chief of Gaza Province, who fought to resist colonialism. Take note of the beautiful *Kigalia africana* (sausage tree) outside the door. ⊠ *At bottom of Av. Samora Machel, near the sea,* ☎ *01/30–7285.* 🎫 *Free.* ☉ *Daily 9–5.*

The **Mercado Municipal** (municipal market) is a beautiful old building with stalls selling all manner of consumer items and seafood so fresh it's practically still wriggling. Dewy vegetables glow in bright reds and greens, and stalls selling cashew nuts and spices compete against each other. ⊠ *Av. 25 de Setembro.* ☉ *Weekdays 6–6, Sat. 6–noon.*

The **National Museum of Art** houses fantastic works by local artists. Disturbingly bizarre Makonde sculptures rub their many shoulders with paintings, ranging from pretty to pretty weird, and both decorative and functional ceramics. Many pieces are for sale. ⊠ *1233 Av. Ho Chi Minh, 1 block north of Av. Karl Marx,* ☎ *01/42–0264.* 🎫 *Free.* ☉ *Sun.–Tues. 3–7.*

If you're feeling energetic, you can include the ornate, Portuguese Gothic-style **Natural History Museum** in your walking tour of Maputo, but it's a bit far. It houses comprehensive displays of animals and birds and the world's only complete collection of elephant fetuses (one for each month of its gestation). ⊠ *Corner Rua do Lusiados and Patrice Lumumba,* ☎ *01/49–1145.* 🎫 *50,000 mets.* ☉ *Tues.–Sun. 9–noon and 2–4.*

The beautiful copper-dome railway station on one side of the **Praça do Trabalhadores** was designed by Gustave Eiffel.

Lodging

$$ 🏨 **Hotel Polana.** Built in 1922, this hotel was for many years the epit-
★ ome of grace and style in Mozambique, and it remains a Maputo landmark. Its clientele dried up during the war, but it has been refurbished at considerable expense and now is once again one of southern Africa's foremost lodging establishments. Although everything is new and shiny (except the elevator, which is shiny but dates to 1927), the hotel exudes an air of old money and old-fashioned values. From the enormous signature arrangement of pink anthuriums to the silver-shrouded canapés brought to your room every afternoon, you get a sense of routine and tradition. ⊠ *Av. Julius Nyerere 1380, Maputo,* ☎ *01/49–1001,* FAX *01/49–1480,* WEB *www.polana-hotel.com. 167 rooms, 23 suites. Restaurant, bar, coffee shop, air-conditioning, in-room data ports, in-room safes, minibars, pool, hair salon, steam room, tennis court, gym, shop, casino, concierge, meeting rooms, airport shuttle, car rental, free parking. AE, DC, MC, V. EP.*

$$ 🏨 **Rovuma Carlton.** In downtown Maputo, this comfortable, modern hotel has loads of facilities. The rooms are decorated in a classical style but with subtle African touches. A useful feature is that the hotel has the best, most concentrated shopping in the city, with a veritable minimall in the lobby. The well-appointed business center makes this a popular choice for business travelers. ⊠ *Box 4376, Maputo,* ☎ *01/30–5000,* FAX *01/30–5305,* WEB *www.pestana.com. 175 rooms, 48 suites. 2 restaurants, 2 bars, coffee shop, air-conditioning, in-room data ports, kitchenettes (some), minibars, room service, pool, hair salon, steam room, gym, shops, concierge, business center, meeting rooms, travel services, airport shuttle, free parking. AE, DC, MC, V. CP.*

$ 🏨 **Terminus Hotel.** This comfortable, vibrant hotel is the best option if you're on a budget. It's light, bright, and leafy, with huge, colorful animal murals in the public areas. The rooms are comfortable and pleasantly, if unremarkably, furnished. For a relatively low budget option, this hotel has a surprising array of facilities. Each room has satellite TV and modem lines, and there's free Internet access in a corner of the lounge. ⊠ *Rua Francisco Orlando Magumbwé 587, Maputo,* ☎ *01/49–1333,* FAX *01/49–1284,* WEB *www.terminus-hotel.com. 43 rooms, 4 family suites. Restaurant, 2 bars, pool. AE, DC, MC, V. BP.*

Inhaca Island

In the middle of Maputo Bay, a 45-minute boat ride or a 10-minute flight from Maputo.

So close to a major city, Inhaca (pronounced in-*yah*-ke) is amazingly undeveloped, with a small population and only one hotel. Mangroves penetrate far inland, following the curve of the Sac de Inhaca, a huge bay that is almost, but not quite, a lagoon. Here juvenile fish hang out in safety until they're prepared to brave the Bay of Maputo and its many fishing folk in their *dhows.* Dugongs (manatees) idle the days away, occasionally diving down to the shallows to munch on turtle grass, and game fish swim by in huge shoals.

The hotel organizes day trips by boat or tractor-trailer to deserted beaches, the lighthouse, or the biological station run as part of ongoing research by Eduard Mondlane University, where there are shells, preserved fish, and all manner of things marine oriented. Although most of the captions are in Portuguese, the resident scientists do speak pretty good English and will talk about the flora and fauna of the island as long as you keep asking questions.

Lodging

$$$ 🏨 **Inhaca Island Lodge.** This fun hotel is set between the sea and the lagoon. Bright and breezy rooms are in separate buildings arranged around a bright green lawn scattered with tall coconut palms. On most Saturday nights a dance troupe from Maputo struts its stuff and will then teach you the local marabente dance (if you have the energy and courage). It's a wild mix of Latin and African rhythms, not entirely unlike the tango. ✉ *Box 4376, Maputo,* ☎ *01/30–5000,* WEB *www.pestana.com. 40 rooms. Bar, dining room, pool, beach, dive shop, snorkeling, boating, fishing, billiards, recreation room, baby-sitting, nursery, airport shuttle. AE, DC, MC, V. MAP.*

Mozambique A to Z

To research prices, get advice from other travelers, and book travel arrangements, visit www.fodors.com.

AIR TRAVEL

Maputo International Airport lies about 19 km (12 mi) north of the city. Vilanculos International Airport is about 6 km (4 mi) south of town. There is a flight every day between Johannesburg and Maputo, with either SA Airlink or LAM (Mozambican Airlines). LAM flies between Maputo and Vilanculos four times a week and also flies between Lisbon and Maputo once a week. TTA flies from Vilanculos to the islands daily in an amphibious Cessna Caravan and also flies from Johannesburg International to Vilanculos twice weekly with a connection to the islands. Transairways flies between Maputo and Inhaca daily and between Maputo and Vilanculos six times a week.

Some of the lodges organize charter flights, usually from Lanseria Airport near Johannesburg, or from Johannesburg International. Pestana can organize air transfers (including all airport transfers) between the Rovuma Carlton, in Maputo, and Bazaruto Lodge, via Vilanculos, with Transairways.

➤ AIR TRAVEL INFORMATION: **Maputo International Airport** (☎ 46–5133 or 46–5074). **Vilanculos International Airport** (☎ 023/8–2207 or 023/8–2208). **LAM (Mozambican Airlines;** ✉ Av. Karl Marx 220, Maputo, ☎ 01/42–600, 01/42–601, 01/42–604, 01/46–5874, or 01/46–5879; in Johannesburg: ✉ 43 Bradford Rd., 4th floor, Eastgate Office Tower, Bedfordview, ☎ 011/622–4889). **S.A. Airlink** (☎ 011/978–1111 in Johannesburg, WEB www.flysaa.com). **Transairways** (☎ 01/465–108). **TTA** (✉ Box 8461, Greenside 2034, South Africa, ☎ 083/375–2008 or 082/871–2727, FAX 011/726–8712; TTA Vilanculos, ☎ 023/8–2348; TTA Maputo, ☎ 01/49–1765, FAX 01/49–1763).

CAR TRAVEL

It is safe to travel to and around Mozambique in a car, but it is a bit of a hassle, and there is no need. All the hotels have excellent shuttles to everywhere you could possibly want to go.

If you do drive, whatever you do, **don't leave the paved, or well-used roads**—even to just go a few yards off the road for a rest stop. The whole country was land-mined and there may be mines left in unusual places. Also, there is a small chance you may be accosted by rather fierce-looking "officials," often uniformed and armed, who may try to ex-

tort bribes. Whatever you do, don't become arrogant and don't say
"I'm an American Citizen" in your best movie-actor voice. Your best
course is to refuse politely to give bribes, say you know it is illegal and,
if you can't get away without some "donation" give something small.
Usually you can get by with cigarettes, beer, or other small token. It is
a good idea to leave a pack of cigarettes on your dashboard for this
purpose, even if you don't smoke. Carry small denominations of U.S.
currency ($10 is good) for this purpose, but use this only as an abso-
lute last resort. It's not easy but if you can talk or joke your way through
this with a sincere smile, you'll win all the way around.

➤ CAR TRAVEL INFORMATION: **Avis** (✉ Maputo International Airport,
☎ 01/46–5140). **Europcar** (✉ Hotel Polana, ☎ 01/49–1001; ✉ Airport desk, ☎ 01/46–6172 or 01/46–6182). **Hertz** (✉ Hotel Polana,
☎ 01/491–001; ✉ Airport desk, ☎ 01/46–5534).

EMBASSIES AND CONSULATES

➤ EMBASSIES AND CONSULATES: **Canadian Consulate** (✉ Av. Julius Ny-
erere 1128, Maputo, Mozambique, ☎ 01/49–2624). **United Kingdom
High Commission** (✉ Caixa Postal 55, Maputo, Mozambique, ☎ 01/
42–0111 or 01/42–112, 🖷 01/42–1666). **United States Embassy** (✉
Av. Kenneth Kaunda, Maputo, Mozambique, ☎ 01/49–2797, 🖷 01/
49–0114).

EMERGENCIES

Medical service in Mozambique is underfunded, but your hotel can organize treatment for minor ailments. For serious emergencies contact
MRI in Johannesburg. For diving emergencies contact DAN (Divers
Alert Network) in Johannesburg. The nearest decompression facility
is in Durban.

➤ EMERGENCY INFORMATION: **DAN** (☎ 00/27/11/242–0112).**MRI** (☎
00/27/11/242–0242). These are written exactly as they would be dialed from anywhere in Mozambique.

HEALTH

All of Mozambique is a high-risk malarial area.

LANGUAGE

Almost all locals speak Portuguese, but most hotel employees speak some
English.

MONEY MATTERS

The official currency is the meticais. One thousand meticais is a mil.
So, instead of 250,000 meticais, you will be quoted 250 mil (which is
about US$10). Most hotel prices are U.S. dollar–based, although you
can pay in ZAR (South African rand) and even meticais in some cases.
In the islands communications are erratic, so credit-card authorization
can take a while. It's best to use cash or traveler's checks. Rand or dollars are accepted almost everywhere.

PASSPORTS AND VISAS

ENTERING MOZAMBIQUE

Visas are required by all visitors and must be bought in advance at a
Mozambican embassy. If you are in Johannesburg, contact Mozambican Visa Services, which specializes in this single, rather red-tape-
fraught function. A single-entry visa costs between R125 and R200.

➤ VISA INFORMATION: **Mozambique Embassy** (✉ 1990 M St. NW, No.
570, Washington, DC 20036-3404, ☎ 202/293–7146, 202/293–7147,
or 202/293–7148, 🖷 202/835–0245). **Mozambican Visa Services** (✉
27 Merriman Ave., Highlands, Johannesburg, ☎ 011/786–9714 or 082/
973–0454).

SAFETY

Generally, Mozambicans are friendly, nice people, but there have been a few incidents of hijacking in remote areas. It is safe to walk around Maputo in the daytime (and probably at night, too). But, like anywhere, don't flash expensive jewelry, cameras, and watches. You will be accosted by the odd beggar and by scores of people wanting to sell you all manner of things. Don't feel threatened—they are not violent, just desperately poor. If you are traveling in the remoter parts of the country, be aware of the possibility of land mines: never leave the beaten track, explore deserted areas or buildings, or venture off on your own.

TELEPHONES

The telephone system is erratic. It operates quite well in Maputo, but that's about it. The lodges on the Bazaruto Archipelago communicate with their head offices via radio telephone. Cell phones work near Maputo. They can be rented at the Maputo International Airport.

COUNTRY AND AREA CODES

The international code for Mozambique is 258; the area code for Maputo is 01 and for Vilanculos 023. If you are dialing from outside the country, drop the initial 0—so the code would be 258–1 for Maputo and 258–23 for Vilanculos.

Please note that many of the telephone numbers listed are in South Africa. The international exit code from Mozambique is 00.

➤ VISITOR INFORMATION: **Mozambique Tourist Information** (✉ Av. 25 de Setembro, No. 1203, Maputo, ☎ 01/30–7329, 01/30–7321, or 01/30–7322, ✉ 01/30–7324). **Public Information Bureau** (✉ Av. Eduard Mondlane, corner Mártires da Machava, Maputo, ☎ 01/49–1226).

MALAWI

Malawi markets itself as the Warm Heart of Africa—an incredibly well-chosen phrase, as it accurately describes its position in the continent (not quite center), its climate (very warm), and the character of its citizens, who are genuinely among the friendliest in Africa (if not the world). Malawi is a long, thin country that follows the shoreline of Lake Malawi, the ninth-largest freshwater lake in the world. At 365 mi by 52 mi and at a depth of more than 2,000 ft deep, Lake Malawi is virtually an inland sea. An interesting bit of trivia is that the first naval battle of World War I—between the British colony of Nyasaland (Malawi) and German East Africa (now Tanzania)—was fought on Lake Malawi.

Exploring Malawi

Malawi is easy to travel around, and it is a popular budget traveler's destination. The range of experiences is vast, but those listed are the absolute highlights—and involve the least effort.

Great Itineraries

IF YOU HAVE 3 DAYS

Fly in to 🔟 **Lilongwe** and take a connecting flight to Club Makakola, where you can relax on the beach, take a boat trip to Boadzulu Island, dive, snorkel, or sail. From here you can take day trips to Mvuu, the high-lying Zomba Plateau, a cashew nut farm, or the nearby town of Mangochi to see the pottery and museum.

IF YOU HAVE 5 DAYS

Fly in to Lilongwe, and transfer to 🔟 **Nyika National Park** via Mzuzu. Spend a few days watching game, fly-fishing and hiking, or walking. Return to Lilongwe and drive down to **Senga Bay,** spending your last day relaxing on the beach.

Malawi

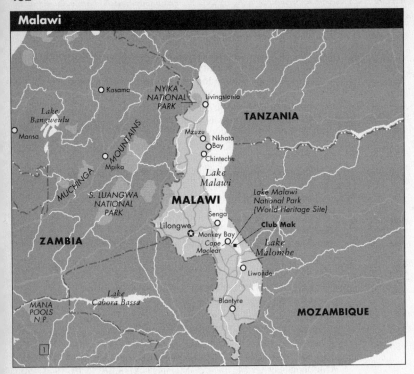

When to Tour Malawi

The best time to visit Malawi is in winter, from May to August, when it is cool and dry. By September the country starts to heat up a bit, but it's not unbearable. The rainy season—from mid-November to February—is hot, rainy, and muggy, and there is a high malaria risk. March and April are great—getting cooler and usually dry. You can't fly into Nyika in the rainy season, although you can drive in.

Lilongwe

Lilongwe is a somewhat schizophrenic city. Originally a small village, it was promoted to capital city status in 1975 for political rather than practical reasons. The old city centers around a bustling market and remains much as it has probably been for countless decades. The new part of the city, known as Capital City, consists of huge '70s-style government buildings. Quite honestly, there isn't much reason to stay here. Try to plan your flight so you don't need to spend the night.

If you have very limited time and want to see the lake, **Senga Bay** is the closest resort to the capital and is a drive of about two hours or less. Here you will find lovely, crystal-clear, warm water in which to frolic; snorkeling at pretty Namalenji Island; and a range of fun water sports.

Lodging

$$$ 🏨 **Lilongwe Hotel.** Conveniently located in the old part of town, the hotel is close to the market and the golf course. All rooms are light and airy, and the bar and restaurant are popular with Lilongwe residents. ✉ Box 44, Lilongwe, ☎ 265/75–6333, 🖷 265/77–1273. 78 rooms, 8 suites, 9 chalets. 3 bars, restaurant, pool, golf privileges, shop, airport shuttle, free parking. AE, DC, MC, V.

Liwonde National Park

200 km (125 mi) southeast of Lilongwe

Tall ilala palms stand sentinel, enormous baobabs are dotted about, and elephants, lions, and many species of antelope wander through the bush. Black rhinos have recently been reintroduced into the park but, at time of writing, they were still being held in a protected area.

Lodging

$$$$ ⚠ **Mvuu Lodge.** This very comfortable lodge is on the edge of a small lagoon. Large safari tents have two beds, private shower, a balcony, hammocks, and mosquito nets. The honeymoon suite has a romantic bathroom with an enormous bath. ⊠ *Central African Wilderness Safaris, Box 489, Lilongwe,* ☎ *265/77–1153 or 265/77–1393,* 𝐅𝐀𝐗 *265/ 77–1397,* 𝗪𝗘𝗕 *www.wilderness-safaris.com. 4 tents, 1 suite. Bar, dining room, pool, boating, library, airport shuttle. AE, MC, V. FAP.*

Club Makakola

352 km (220 mi) northeast from Lilongwe.

$$$ ⌗ **Club Makakola.** This resort hotel on the beach of the southern lakeshore is large and comfortable and has fantastic views of the distant Mozambique shore and Boadzulu Island. Rooms—decorated in an understated African theme—are scattered around a bright green lawn with huge flowering trees. There is a range of water sports including scuba diving and sailing. All nonmotorized water sports are included in the room price. ⊠ *Box 59, Mangochi,* ☎ *265/58–4244 or 265/58– 4445,* 𝐅𝐀𝐗 *265/58–4217. 35 rooms, 10 suites, 11 family suites. Restaurant, 2 bars, lake, pool, 9-hole golf course, 2 tennis courts, squash, beach, dive shop, snorkeling, boating, parasailing, fishing, baby-sitting, meeting rooms, private airstrip. DC, MC, V. BP.*

Nyika National Park

483 km (300 mi) north of Lilongwe.

In the northern part of the country, this high-lying plateau is totally different from the rest of Malawi, with rolling Afromontane grassland that contains huge stands of proteas, more than 100 species of orchids, and many more flowering plants. High-altitude game such as eland, reedbuck, bushbuck, zebras, and the rare roan antelope make this a special safari destination.

Lodging

$$$$ ⌗ **Chelinda Lodge.** Rooms here are in attractive double-story wooden chalets and are decorated with an African motif. They are joined together by raised timber walkways. The lodge has a wonderful indigenous garden and fantastic views over the rolling hills. ⊠ *Box 2338, Lilongwe, Malawi,* ☎ *265/75–2379,* 𝐅𝐀𝐗 *265/75–7316,* 𝗪𝗘𝗕 *www.nyika.com. 8 rooms. Bar, dining room, hiking, horseback riding, fishing, mountain bikes, airport shuttle, private airstrip (June–Oct.). No credit cards. FAP.*

Malawi A to Z

To research prices, get advice from other travelers, and book travel arrangements, visit www.fodors.com.

AIR TRAVEL

Air Malawi flies between Johannesburg and Lilongwe three times a week and between London and Lilongwe once a week (via Nairobi) and has regularly scheduled flights between Lilongwe, Blantyre, Club Mak, and Mzuzu.

British Airways flies between London and Lilongwe once a week. South African Airways flies between Johannesburg and Lilongwe three times a week and between Johannesburg and Blantyre twice a week. You can take a charter flight from Mzuzu to Chelinda Camp, in Nyika National Park, from June to October.

Lilongwe International Airport (LIA) is 28 km (about 17 mi) north of Lilongwe. Taxis do not have meters, so agree on a fee before setting off—about US$20 from the airport to town. Mzuzu Airport is 1 km (½ mi) north of Mzuzu town. Club Mak Airstrip is on the hotel grounds. An airport tax of US$20 is levied on all international flights, and a tax of MK100 is levied on all domestic flights.

➤ AIR TRAVEL INFORMATION: **Lilongwe International Airport (LIA;** ☎ 70–0311). **Air Malawi** (☎ 265/75–3181; 265/75–0757 for Lilongwe; 265/70–0811 for LIA; 265/62–0811 for Blantyre). **British Airways** (☎ 265/77–1747 for Lilongwe; 265/70–0649 for LIA; 265/62–4333 for Blantyre; 265/62–0811 for Chileka). **South African Airways** (☎ 265/77–2242 for Lilongwe; 265/70–0610 for LIA; 265/62–0629 for Blantyre; 265/62–0811 for Chileka).

CAR TRAVEL
Avis and Hertz both have kiosks at Lilongwe International Airport, but all lodges offer airport transfers. Hertz's head office is in Blantyre.
➤ CAR TRAVEL INFORMATION: **Avis** (✉ LIA, ☎ 265/75–6105, 265/75–6103, 265/75–0530, or 265/75–0141). **Hertz** (✉ LIA, ☎ 265/67–4516).

EMERGENCIES
The best contact in the case of an emergency is MRI in South Africa.
➤ EMERGENCY CONTACT: **MRI** (☎ 0027/11/242–0242). This is written exactly as it should be dialed from Malawi.

HEALTH
Malaria is a **serious** risk in Malawi. There is bilharzia in some parts of the lake, so you should have a checkup a few months after you get home. To try and protect yourself from bilharzia, swim in deep water only. Don't lounge around in the warm shallow water at the edge of the lake. When you've finished swimming, dry yourself vigorously with a towel, this helps to dislodge any flukes before they can burrow through your skin.

LANGUAGE
English is the official language of Malawi.

MONEY MATTERS
The unit of currency is the Malawian kwacha. At the time of writing, the exchange rate was approximately MK70 to the dollar.

PASSPORTS AND VISAS
American, British, and Canadian nationals do not need a visa to enter Malawi.

SAFETY
Malawi is one of the safest countries in Africa—but that doesn't mean there is absolutely no safety risk. As everywhere else, crime is on the increase, and there is always that element, even in a pretty nonviolent society. So, like everywhere else in the world, be careful and use common sense.

SIGHTSEEING TOURS

Land and Lake Safaris can organize tours ranging from a quick cycle to a 15-day Malawian safari, taking in the best of the country. Kayak Africa offers fantastic, luxury multiday kayaking tours of the Lake Malawi National Park.

➤ TOUR INFORMATION: **Kayak Africa** (✉ Box 48112, Kommetjie, Cape Town 7976, ☎ 27/21/689–8123, FAX 27/21/689–2149, WEB www.kayakafrica.co.za.) **Land and Lake Safaris** (☎ 265/75–7120 or 265/75–4303, FAX 265/75–4560, WEB www.landlakemalawi.com).

TELEPHONES

The country code for Malawi is 265; there are no area codes.

TIPPING

Tipping is expected in restaurants and on escorted trips. The usual tip is about 10%–20% of your bill. You can give guides their tips, but the rest of the tip should be given directly to the manager to distribute among other staff. Figure 50% to 60% for the guide and the rest for the staff. Porters and such should be tipped a minimum of about MK20 or MK30 (about U.S. 50¢), or a dollar.

VISITOR INFORMATION

You can get good official information from the Ministry of Tourism, Parks and Wildlife, the Malawi Consulate General in South Africa, or the Malawi Tourist Association. Also check out www.malawi.net/travel.

➤ INFORMATION: **Malawi Consulate General** (South Africa: ✉ Box 3881 Rivonia, Johannesburg 2128, ☎ 27/11/803–4919). **Malawi Tourist Association** (✉ Aquarius House, Lilongwe, ☎ 265/77–0010 or 265/77–4713, FAX 265/77–0131). **Ministry of Tourism, Parks and Wildlife** (✉ Private Bag 326, Lilongwe, ☎ 265/77–5499, FAX 265/77–4059 or 265/77–0650.)

15 PORTRAITS OF SOUTHERN AFRICA

Big-Game Adventures

Books and Videos

BIG-GAME ADVENTURES

MENTION AFRICA and most of us conjure up visions of wildlife—lions roaring in the gathering dusk, antelope skittering across the savanna, a leopard silhouetted by the setting sun. The images never fail to fascinate and draw us in, and once you experience them in the flesh, you're hooked. The look, the feel—the dusty smell—of the African bush seep into your soul, and long after you've gone, you find yourself missing it with an almost physical longing. The wildlife experience in South Africa rivals the very best on the continent, and a trip to the bush should be a major part of your vacation.

Do everyone a favor, though, and pass up the impulse to rush out and buy khakis and a pith helmet. The classic safari is dead. Hemingway and the great white hunters took it to their graves, along with thousands upon thousands of equally dead animals. The closest you'll come to a real safari today is if you spend an ungodly sum of money to trek into the wastes of Selous National Park, in Tanzania, to nail some unfortunate lion.

Indeed, too many wildlife documentaries have conditioned foreign visitors into thinking that Africa is overrun with animals, and they half expect to be greeted by a lion in the airport's arrivals terminal. The truth is far less romantic—and much safer—especially in South Africa, where fences or rivers enclose all major reserves. The rest of the country is farmland, towns, and suburbs.

South Africa has 17 national parks and a host of provincial reserves, but only a few contain all the indigenous species that once roamed the veld in vast herds. The crown jewel of South Africa's reserves is Kruger National Park, the second-largest game reserve in Africa. It's a magnificent tract of pristine wilderness that is home to an astonishing number of animals. Like all of South Africa's parks, it's completely open to the public, and you can tour and view game from the comfort of your own car. Good roads, plentiful and cheap accommodations, and excellent facilities are

what differentiate South African parks from their East African counterparts.

The other, much more expensive option is to stay in a lodge on a private game reserve. If you can afford it, don't miss out because these exclusive lodges offer a wildlife experience without parallel. You could spend a month bumping fenders with tourist minibuses in East Africa and never get as close to game as in these lodges. Bouncing over dirt tracks in an open Land Rover, you *know* you're in Africa. These luxury lodges give you a taste of the bush and the experience of living out in the wilds. Sure, you get comfortable beds, flush toilets, running water, hot showers—even air-conditioning—but the bush lies right outside your door, and nothing stops an elephant from joining you for dinner.

Talk to travel agents about private lodges and sooner or later they will start babbling about the "Big Five." This was originally a hunting term referring to those animals that posed the greatest risk to hunters on foot—elephant, black rhino, leopard, lion, and buffalo—yet it has now become the single most important criterion used in evaluating a lodge or reserve. Although the Big Five label may have helped engender tourist interest in African wildlife, it can also demean the entire bush experience, turning it into a treasure hunt. You will be amazed how many visitors ignore a gorgeous animal that doesn't "rank" in the Big Five or lose interest in a species once they've checked it off their list. After you've spent a few days in the bush, you will also recognize the idiocy of racing around in search of five animals when there are another 150 equally fascinating species all around you. It's up to you to tell your ranger exactly what kind of wildlife you want to see.

It's no coincidence that old game-watching hands find their thrills in the smaller, rarer animals—and in birds. South Africans are maniacal bird-watchers for very good reason: it's one of the best birding regions in the world. More than 500 species of birds have been recorded in Kruger alone, and their beauty and diversity are extraordinary. Don't overlook them just because they're small and harmless—your trip will be poorer for it.

Whether you're searching for elephants or the arrow-marked babbler, a sturdy pair of binoculars is essential, as is a camera. Use a point-and-shoot camera only if you want pictures of you and your companions out in the bush; forget about it if you want good wildlife shots. Ideally, you should use a 35mm camera with at least a 300mm lens and a sandbag to act as a rest because you can't set up a regular tripod on a vehicle. The best all-purpose film is ASA100, but ASA400 is great for action photography, like a cheetah hunt. Light readings in the African glare can be tricky, so be sure to bracket your shots. No matter what camera or film you use, you're bound to take an embarrassing number of bum shots—animals caught fleeing—so it pays to shoot bucket loads of film.

When you go on safari, take precautions against malaria. The disease is no joking matter, and it claims its share of victims in South Africa every year. Summer is the height of malaria season, when the annual rains provide plentiful breeding grounds for mosquitoes. With a couple of notable exceptions, every reserve and lodge in this chapter lies in a malarial zone, and it's imperative that you take prophylactics. At time of writing Malarone is the preferred drug, with almost none of the possible side effects of once popular Lariam (mefloquine). See your doctor at least a month before you depart—and don't put all your faith in pills. Even the most powerful medications don't always work, and the only absolute protection against the disease is to avoid getting bitten in the first place. Cover up between dusk and dawn (when the mosquitoes are active) and apply a repellent to exposed skin. In your room at night sleep under a net if possible and use an electric mosquito destroyer, which takes a vaporizing pad, or burn coils. Leave that mosquito "zapper" at home, as it's totally useless.

Game viewing can't be rushed. To make the most of your trip, plan on no fewer than two nights at any one place—be it a private lodge or a rest camp. Racing around from camp to camp on safari is a waste of time and money—give yourself the pleasure of slowing down, appreciating your surroundings, and taking in the sights and sounds of the bush, which are as much a part of the whole experience as the Big Five.

Timing

No two people can agree on the best time to visit the bush. Summer (December–March) is hellishly hot, with afternoon rain a good possibility, but the bush is green, the animals sleek and glossy, and the bird life prolific. Unfortunately, it's the worst time of year to spot game. All of the foliage makes finding game harder, and animals tend to disperse over a wide area because they are no longer reliant on water holes and rivers. Winter, on the other hand, is a superb time for game viewing because trees are bare and animals congregate around the few remaining water sources. Because the weather's cooler, you may also see lions and leopards hunting by day. Most lodges drop their rates dramatically during winter months, often lopping as much as 30%–40% off their peak-season prices. The drawbacks to a winter visit are the cold and that the bush looks dead and the animals thin and out of condition.

A happy compromise may be the shoulder seasons. In October and November the weather is pleasant, the trees have blossoms, and migrant birds are arriving—even better, the antelope herds begin to drop their young. In April the temperature is also fine, many of the migrant birds are still around, and the annual rutting season has begun, when males compete for the right to mate with females and are much more visible.

What to Pack

Just because you're going to Africa, don't think you can pack light cottons and nothing else. If you're heading to a private lodge, be sure to take a long, thigh-length padded jacket, even in midsummer (from December to March) because it can get mighty cold in an exposed, open four-by-four at 8 PM. All lodges provide blankets and rain ponchos in their vehicles, but that's often not enough. If you're traveling in winter, pack a scarf, hat, and gloves as well. Neutral colors like khaki are best, and a couple of pairs of pants with zip-off legs are versatile and useful, as is a photographer/safari vest with lots of pockets. Don't forget sunscreen, mosquito repellent, Band-Aids, and useful medications like painkillers, indigestion pills, and eyedrops. A small flashlight is always useful.

National Parks and Game Reserves

If you picture yourself bouncing across the golden plains of Africa in an old Land Rover in pursuit of big game, South Africa's national parks will disappoint you. They bear less resemblance to the Serengeti than to America's national parks: they are superbly managed, frequently overcrowded, and a little too civilized. You could tour Kruger National Park in a Porsche if you so desired. Many of the park roads are paved, and rangers even set up speed traps to nail overzealous game-watchers (take your car off-road, and the dung will really hit the fan). Signposts throughout the park direct visitors to everything from scenic viewpoints to picnic sites and rest areas selling soft drinks and snacks.

It's no wonder, then, that foreign visitors sometimes act like they're in a giant petting zoo. In recent years an Asian tourist was eaten when he left his car to hug some cuddly lions, and a European's rental car was turned into Swiss cheese when he drove too close to an elephant and her calf. South Africa's game reserves may impose a veneer of domesticity on the wilderness, but underneath it's the same raw, violent Africa you see on National Geographic specials.

The national parks look the way they do for good reason: They are the country's natural heritage, set up for the use and enjoyment of its citizens, which until recently meant whites only. For white South African families a trip to a game reserve is an annual rite, as certain as death and taxes. We're talking load up the station wagon, cram the kids into the back, and drive, baby, drive. On December weekends Kruger's rest camps look like they're on fire because of all the barbecue smoke. One reason for this popularity is their affordability: a couple probably won't pay more than R500 to stay in a rest camp.

Until recently, foreign travelers composed an insignificant minority of visitors to the national parks, and if they didn't like what they found, they could just lump it. That attitude is changing, but South Africa's game parks are still not geared to foreign travelers and their needs. Accommodations in the park rest camps are cheap, comfortable, and numbingly institutional. In Kruger the National Parks Board symbol—the head of a kudu bull—is plastered over everything from your towel to the sheets to the bathroom walls. All the camps are fenced against the animals, and some have better facilities than small towns: gas stations, mechanics, grocery stores, laundromat, cafeterias, restaurants—even a car wash. And the restaurants' food tends to be mediocre. Not surprisingly, many foreign visitors shy away from the rest camps in favor of luxury hotels on the park fringes.

It would be the biggest mistake of your trip, though, to write off the public parks. Few people can afford to stay in the exclusive private lodges more than a few days, and the game reserves offer visitors a chance to explore some of Africa's richest and most beautiful country at a fraction of the cost, especially if you drive yourself. Armed with a good field guide to wildlife, you can learn an enormous amount about African game from the driver's seat of a rental car. If possible rent a van or a four-by-four. The higher off the ground you are, the better your chances of spotting game.

It does take time to develop your ability to find motionless game in thick bush. On the first day you're less likely to spot an animal than to run it over. All those fancy stripes and tawny colors really do work. Slowly, though, you learn to recognize the small clues that give away an animal in the bush: the flick of a tail, the toss of a horn, even fresh dung. To see any of this, you have to drive *slowly,* 15–25 kph (10–15 mph). Fight the urge to pin back your ears and tear around a park at 50 kph (30 mph) hoping to find something big. The only way to spot game at that speed is if it's standing in the road or if you come upon a number of cars already at a sighting. But remember that being the 10th car at a game sighting is less exciting than finding the animal yourself. Not only do the other cars detract from the experience, but you feel like a scavenger—a sort of voyeuristic vulture.

The best time to find game is in the early morning and early evening, when the animals are most active, although old Africa hands will tell you that you can come across good game at any time of day. Stick to the philosophy "You never know what's around the next corner," and keep your eyes and ears wide open all the time. If your rest camp offers guided night drives on open vehicles with spotlights—go for it. You'll rarely be disappointed, seeing not only big game, but also a lot of fascinating little critters that only surface at night. Book your night drive in advance or as soon as you get to camp.

An indispensable aid is a good park map, showing not only the roads but also the location of watering holes, different eco-zones, and the types of animals you can expect to find in each. It's no good driving around open grassland searching for black rhino when the lumbering browsers are miles away in a woodland region. You can buy these maps when you enter a park or at rest-camp shops, and it would be a foolish economy to pass them up.

When planning your day's game drive, plot your route around as many water holes and rivers as possible. Except during the height of the summer rains, most game must come to permanent water sources to drink. In winter, when the land is at its most parched, a tour of water holes is bound to reap great rewards. Even better, take a picnic lunch along and park at the same watering hole for several hours. Not only will you see plenty of animals, but you'll find yourself slipping into the drama of the bush. Has that kudu seen the huge crocodile? What's making the impala nervous? What's that sitting on my car?

In South Africa, Kruger, Hluhluwe-Umfolozi, and Pilanesberg are the only national parks that have the Big Five. In Zimbabwe and Botswana, the national parks in which all five of these most threatening animals are most readily viewable are Hwange, Chobe, and Moremi. In Nambia you'll find them all at Etosha National Park.

Private Game Reserves and Lodges

You never forget your first kill. Mine was at night with three other tourists. We were trailing a pride of 13 lions padding single-file through thick bush. We battled to keep up in an open Land Rover, picking our way around rocks and flattening scrub that blocked our advance. Murderous thorns scraped the side of the vehicle, forcing us to duck again and again. Ahead, another Land Rover's spotlight caught the reflected glow of impala eyes and the rangers immediately doused their lights to avoid blinding the jittery antelope. We edged forward in the weak moonlight, tracing the outline of the lead lioness as she slunk closer and closer to the herd. When she charged, we all heard the thump of contact, the cry of a panicked impala, then silence. The arrival of the rest of the pride set off a free-for-all of slashing claws, snarling, and ripping flesh. The impala was devoured in seconds. It was cruel, it was thrilling—it was Africa. And it's the kind of experience that only a private lodge can offer.

No lodge can *guarantee* you a kill, but nowhere are your chances of seeing one better. And even if you don't witness this elemental spectacle, you will come within spitting distance of more animals than you imagined possible: hyenas in a den, an elephant herd, wild dogs on the prowl, even a leopard with her cubs. Most lodges will show you the Big Five in three days or less.

These game lodges are not zoos or a Disney Africa. Most reviewed here are either in a national park or abutting one with no fence in between. You can get close to the animals only because, after many years of exposure, they no longer see the game vehicles as a threat. That doesn't mean they don't sometimes object to your presence: an elephant charge will clear out more than your sinuses.

The quality of the game viewing is obviously the major attraction of a private game lodge, but the appeal goes far beyond that. These lodges also sell exclusivity, and many of them go out of their way to unite shameless luxury and bush living—the sense that you really are living in the African wilds. Many camps are unfenced, although after a guest was eaten by a lion a few years ago, the tendency now is for electric fencing all round. If your camp *is* unfenced, make sure you're escorted back to your room by a ranger or member of the camp staff, as animals can and do wander through the camp. Thatch roofs, mosquito nets, and mounted trophies add to the ambience, although more and more lodges are now opting for luxury East African safari tents to provide that extra bush touch. Dinners are served in an open-air *boma* (traditional thatch dining enclosure). On game drives the ranger will stop at a scenic viewpoint so you can enjoy a gin and tonic with the sunset. If you stay more than two days, most lodges will also serve a bush *braai,* a full barbecue spread out in the veld, with hurricane lanterns hanging in the thorn trees, a crackling fire, and the sounds of Africa all around you. Under a full moon it's incredibly romantic.

Make no mistake—you pay for all this pampering. Expect to spend anywhere from R2,000 to R8,000 (US$250 to US$1,000) per person per night. All meals and game drives are included (although for that kind of money they should probably throw in a buffalo as well). A visit to one of these lodges will be your single biggest expense on a trip to southern Africa. If you can afford it, a three-night stay is ideal, but two nights are usually sufficient to see the big game.

The time you spend at a private lodge is tightly structured. With some exceptions, the lodges offer almost identical programs of events. An early-morning game drive is followed by breakfast and a short bush walk. After lunch many people sleep or swim until tea before heading out for the evening or nighttime game drive. Dinner is usually served around 8. If you're tired after your drive, ask for something to be sent to your room, but don't miss the bush braai and at least one night in the boma.

During the four-hour game drives you'll sit on tiered benches in open four-wheel-drive vehicles. Depending on the lodge, the vehicle will seat anywhere from 6 to 10 guests. The rear bench has the best view, but it's tough to hear the ranger from the back, and you spend a lot of time ducking thorn branches. You're better off on the first bench, where you can talk easily with the ranger.

On game drives rangers at bigger camps stay in contact with one another via radio. If one finds a rhino, for example, he relays its location to the others so they can bring their guests to have a look. It's a double-edged sword. The more vehicles you have in the field, the more wildlife everyone is likely to see. At the same time, too many vehicles create a rush-hour effect that can destroy the whole atmosphere—and the environment. Most lodges are very well disciplined with their vehicles, rarely allowing more than three or four vehicles at a sighting. As your vehicle arrives, one already there will drive away. In choosing a game lodge remember to check how

much land a lodge can traverse and how many vehicles it uses. Try to go on a bush walk with an armed ranger—an unforgettable experience. Your ranger will introduce you to the sights and sounds of Africa that you may have missed: a medicinal shrub, a male dung beetle busily rolling its ball of dung to a suitable site, with wife clinging on for dear life, an ant lion trapping its prey, a flycatcher's nest in a dead tree, or the spoor of any number of animals. The low-traffic alternative to drives is bush walks with armed guides.

For better or worse, the quality of your bush experience depends most heavily on your guide or game ranger. He is your host for your entire stay: leading you on game drives, often eating meals with you, taking responsibility for both finding the animals and explaining their habits and behavior, and, if you're on foot, keeping you alive in the presence of excitable elephant, buffalo, hippopotamus, or lion. A good guide will have you lauding the glories of Africa; a bad one just makes the bill look bigger.

The vast majority of rangers used to be white and male, but this is changing rapidly. Very often now your ranger will be local and have come up through the ranks of trackers. Ask him about his people, their ways, and their bush lore—it's fascinating stuff. Most rangers are personable, knowledgeable, and devoted to conservation. The turnover rate is so high, however, that it's impossible in this book to recommend a particular ranger at a specific lodge. The best you can do is select a lodge that has a proven ranger-training program.

If you do get a black guide or ranger, you'll find that in addition to seeing and learning about animals and plants, you will hear about local native cultures and their traditional relationships with the land and its creatures—don't hesitate to ask about these things if this is your interest. This link with traditional cultures adds immeasurably to an experience of Africa. In some parks where local villages are nearby—Zimbabwe's Matobo, for example—guides can take you to settlements where people are living much as they have for centuries.

At the end of your stay you are expected to tip both the ranger and the tracker, who monitors the animal spoor from a seat mounted on the front of the vehicle. These trackers are invariably blacks who grew up in the area and know the bush intimately. Some of them become rangers, but few speak English well enough to communicate the extraordinary wealth of their knowledge. Tipping guidelines vary from lodge to lodge, but plan to give the local equivalents of about US$10 per person per day to the ranger and not much less to the tracker; an additional tip of US$25 for the general staff would be sufficient for a couple staying two days.

All lodges arrange transfers from nearby airports, train stations, or drop-off points, as the case may be. In more remote areas most have their own private airstrips carved out of the bush and fly guests in on chartered aircraft at extra cost. If you're driving yourself, the lodge will send you detailed instructions because many dirt back roads don't appear on maps and lack names.

— By Andrew Barbour

BOOKS AND VIDEOS

Books

History and Politics

For 45 years South Africa's political and historical writing focused on the issues of apartheid. With the democratic elections of 1994 and 1999, much of that writing has now lost a lot of its relevance and often seems dated and anachronistic. The best way to put the record straight is to hear the personal observations and histories of the people who have lived and worked through "the struggle"—as South Africa's stormy passage to democracy is known. Foremost among these is *Long Walk to Freedom*, by Nelson Mandela. An inspiring account of the triumph of idealism, the book looks back over Mandela's life and also takes a pragmatic view of the political road ahead—it should be required reading for South Africans and visitors alike. A more accessible read, illustrated with striking photographs, is the shortened version, *The Illustrated Long Walk to Freedom*.

Rainbow People of God tells the story of another of the heroes of the struggle, Archbishop Desmond Tutu, through his speeches, sermons, and letters from 1976 to 1994.

His recent and poignant personal account of the proceedings, stories, and people he presided over as chairman of the Truth and Reconciliation Commission (TRC) is remarkable for its sense of balance and lack of bitterness, in spite of the accounts of the horrors and trauma he heard on a daily basis for many months. His compassion and willingness to forgive mirror Nelson Mandela's own remarkable positive attitudes toward the past.

For a lyrical, impassioned, and disturbing account of the TRC hearings, try poet Antje Krog's *Country of My Skull*. *Mandela: The Authorized Biography,* by Anthony Sampson, is the definitive biography of the man who changed South African politics, assessing the years before, during, and after his imprisonment.

More required, and compulsive, reading for every visitor is *Indaba, My Children,* by Credo Mutwa, the most famous and best loved of all African *sangomas* (healers, prophets, and shamans). Described by the *London Sunday Times* as "a work of genius," it's an unputdownable compilation of African tribal history, legends, customs, and religious beliefs by a master storyteller.

A classic and very readable study of the San (Bushmen), Elizabeth Marshall Thomas's *The Harmless People* describes the traditional ways of this hunting-gathering culture, which has become endangered and made almost extinct by the intrusion of industrial civilization. Thomas Pakenham's reader-friendly, fascinating, and definitive study *The Boer War* explains an important and evocative part of South Africa's colonial history, when thousands of British soldiers died fighting for a cause they didn't understand in a country they barely knew. Their enemy? The brave independent Boers, the founders of fierce and innovative guerilla warfare, who were fighting for the fatherland they had carved out of the African wilderness.

Fiction

South African writers have drawn steadily from the well of racial injustice to produce some of the finest literature of the 20th century. One of the first such novels is one of the best: Alan Paton's *Cry, the Beloved Country* (1948). The story of the simple, dignified black pastor who heads from his rural Zululand parish to Egoli—Johannesburg, City of Gold—to save his son from execution for murder, the book contains writing of such breathtaking beauty and emotion that you find yourself reading passages again and again. Nobel Prize for literature nominee Professor Es'kial Mphahlele's classic *Down Second Avenue* is the story—moving, sad, funny, painful—of his upbringing in the black slums outside Pretoria and with his fearsome grandmother in the mountains of South Africa's Northern Province. Nadine Gordimer, who won the Nobel Prize for literature in 1991, is known both for her short stories and her novels. *The Conservationist* and *July's People* will give you insights into South Africa, its peoples, problems, and history. Other major writers include Booker Prize winner J. M. Coetzee (*Life and Times of Michael K, Waiting for the Barbarians, Disgrace,* and other books); Athol Fugard (*Master Harold and the Boys, Boesman and Lena*), South Africa's most famous playwright; and Andrè Brink, whose accessible novels make for compulsive reading: try his historical novel *A Chain of Voices* or the magical realism of *Devil's Valley* for a start. Alexandra Fuller's entertaining autobiography *Don't Let's Go to the Dogs Tonight* is a look at how a white farming family settled in Rhodesia (Zimbabwe).

Until the turn of the 19th century, South Africa was like America's Wild West (some say it still is today)—an untamed frontier of marauding animals, gold rushes, skirmishes with the locals, and desperadoes of all kinds. Sir Percy Fitzpatrick's classic *Jock of the Bushveld* captures this pioneer excitement perfectly. Set in the late 19th century, it follows the exploits of Jock, a fearless and lovable Staffordshire bull terrier, in the untamed bush around Kruger National Park and its environs.

A short-story writer who captured the slow, measured life of Afrikaner farmers and early settlers is Herman Charles Bosman. Laced with humor and irony, Bosman's stories recapture a time in South Africa when survival was a triumph and religion and peach brandy were necessary crutches.

Lost World of the Kalahari, by the late Laurens van der Post, mentor to Britain's Prince Charles, is a fascinating mix of fact and fantasy, recalling the author's expedition into the Kalahari Desert after World War II to study the San. The book has a mystical, spiritual quality befitting a people who lived in such complete harmony with nature and each other.

Videos

Most movies about South Africa have traditionally focused on the tragedy of apartheid. Well worth watching is the remake of *Cry, the Beloved Country* (1995), starring James Earl Jones. *Cry Freedom* (1987), starring Denzel Washington and Kevin Kline, follows the story of white South African journalist Donald Woods and Steve Biko, a prominent black activist who died in 1977 after being beaten in police custody in Port Elizabeth. *Breaker Morant* (1979), a superbly crafted and acted Australian movie about the Anglo–Boer War (1899–1902), looks at British military hypocrisy through the eyes of three Australian soldiers on trial for shooting Boer prisoners.

The South African movie industry, although in its relative infancy, has produced one major hit, *The Gods Must Be Crazy* (1980), the enchanting story of a San clan in the Kalahari Desert. Try to get your hands on the 1980s movie version of *Jock of the Bushveld,* starring Jonathan Rand, with music by Johnny Clegg and Savuka—it's delightful. Gavin Hood's fine movie *A Reasonable Man* (1999) tells the story of a simple Zulu cowherd on trial for killing a child whom he believed to be an evil spirit. With a superb performance by Sir Nigel Hawthorne as the trial judge, this groundbreaking and thought-provoking movie, based on an actual case in South African law, attempts to answer the questions: Who is a reasonable man? Which standards do we apply—those of Western law or traditional African belief? And which, if either, is right?

— Kate Turkington

INDEX